The Papers of Dwight David Eisenhower

THE PAPERS OF DWIGHT DAVID EISENHOWER

NATO AND THE CAMPAIGN OF 1952: XII

LOUIS GALAMBOS, *EDITOR*

DAUN VAN EE, *EXECUTIVE EDITOR*

ELIZABETH S. HUGHES, *SENIOR ASSOCIATE EDITOR*

ROBERT J. BRUGGER, *ASSOCIATE EDITOR*

KATHLEEN CRAIG, *PRODUCTION EDITOR*

GERALD J. CONTI, *ASSISTANT EDITOR*

JANET SERAPHINE, *RESEARCH ASSISTANT*

FAITH TOWNSEND, *EDITORIAL ASSISTANT*

THE JOHNS HOPKINS UNIVERSITY PRESS

BALTIMORE AND LONDON

This book has been brought to publication with the generous assistance of the National Endowment for the Humanities and the National Historical Publications and Records Commission.

The Johns Hopkins University Press, 701 West 40th Street, Baltimore, Maryland 21211
The Johns Hopkins Press Ltd., London

All illustrations in this volume are from the
Dwight D. Eisenhower Library, Abilene,
Kansas, unless indicated otherwise.

Frontispiece: U.S. Army

The paper used in this publication meets the minimum requirements of American National
Standard for Information Sciences—Permanence of Paper for Printed Library Materials,
ANSI Z39.48-1984.

Library of Congress Cataloging-in-Publication Data
(Revised for vols. 12-13)

Eisenhower, Dwight D. (Dwight David), 1890-1969.
The papers of Dwight David Eisenhower.

Vol. 6 edited by A. D. Chandler and L. Galambos;
v. 7-   , by L. Galambos.
Includes bibliographies and index.
Contents: v. 1-5. The war years.—[etc.]—
v. 10-11. Columbia University.—v. 12-13. NATO and the
Campaign of 1952.
1. World War, 1939-1945—United States.   2. World War,
1939-1945—Campaigns.   3. United States—Politics and
government—1953-1961.   4. Presidents—United States—
Election—1952.   5. Eisenhower, Dwight D. (Dwight David),
1890-1969.   6. Presidents—United States—Archives.
I. Chandler, Alfred Dupont, ed.   II. Galambos, Louis, ed.
III. United States. President (1953-1961 : Eisenhower)
IV. Title.
E742.5.E37   1970   973.921'092'4 [B]   65-27672
ISBN 0-8018-1078-7 (v. 1-5)
ISBN 0-8018-2061-8 (v. 6-9)
ISBN 0-8018-2720-5 (v. 10-11)
ISBN 0-8018-3726-x (v. 12-13)

Published in cooperation with
The Center for the Study of Recent American History
at The Johns Hopkins University

Contents

Part V: The Crusade; May 1952 to January 1953

Acknowledgments

Dwight David Eisenhower's long career was spent almost entirely in the type of large-scale, bureaucratic organization that has come to characterize our society in the past century. Although he frequently proclaimed and fervently believed in the small-town, nineteenth-century values of individualism, localism, and community, he was in fact an exemplar of the modern organizational system. He was also a patriot who spent much of his time involved in international endeavors. A master at working with and through others, he encouraged men and women with whom he cooperated to contribute their best efforts to a common enterprise.

Eisenhower would then have fully understood why even such a small undertaking as the project editing his papers must in this age depend upon the support and contributions of many individuals and organizations, both public and private. An experienced staff was headed by Executive Editor Daun van Ee, who did all of our research in Abilene, Kansas, and in Washington, D.C., ran the project on a day-to-day basis when the editor was away, and drafted many of the most difficult notes. His deep knowledge of the sources for and history of modern military developments was of great importance to our joint efforts. He was helped immensely by Senior Associate Editor Elizabeth S. Hughes. She trained and supervised our several research assistants, researched and wrote notes, and played the central role in guiding our manuscripts through publication. We were also fortunate to have an experienced editor and historian, Robert J. Brugger, join our staff as Associate Editor when we were completing these manuscripts. Brugger, Hughes, van Ee, and I were supported in numerous ways by Janet Seraphine, who has continued to run our office and manage all of our word processing while developing new skills in conducting research and in verifying our historical references. Assistant Editor Gerald J. Conti also helped to conduct research and draft notes, as did talented Production Editor Kathleen Craig and Editorial Assistant Faith Townsend. They were assisted by several energetic graduate and undergraduate students, including Andrea Bruce, Indra Caudle, Robert C. Davis, Jeffrey Horn, Josh Knights, Grant E. Mabie, Margaret Rung, Susan Shone, Mary Gwaltney Vaz, and James Wiley. While their undertakings may not always have seemed important to them—checking bibliographical references, for instance, is dreary work—they were all crucial to us and we appreciate their contributions.

The Johns Hopkins University, whose board of trustees launched and sustains this enterprise, has provided both moral and fiscal support. We are grateful to the board and its chairman George G. Radcliffe and to University President Steven Muller. President Muller has guided us over the years with a firm hand, assisted by provosts Richard P. Longaker and John V. Lombardi, vice-presidents Ross Jones, Robert C. Bowie, and Robert J. Haley, and deans George W. Fisher and Lloyd Armstrong. Jill E. McGovern, senior assistant to the president, has long helped steer us past the shoals of fiscal crisis. University counsel Estelle A. Fishbein has been very supportive on several significant occasions, as have Marcus M. Diamond and (in the Office of Homewood Research Administration) Director John Dearden, Milton T. Cole, and Dawn Finnerty.

Others at Hopkins have been similarly helpful. In the history department, chairman John Russell-Wood, administrative assistant Betty Whildin, and graduate secretary Sharon A. Widomski have aided us in numerous ways. The Milton S. Eisenhower Library, where we are housed, has been supportive throughout; we would like to thank Director Susan K. Martin, Charles A. Baughan III, James E. Gillispie, Edith Overstreet, Patricia R. Van Daniker, and Kevin P. Haney.

An undertaking of this sort would not be possible, moreover, without extensive assistance from the government. Some of that support has been financial. The National Endowment for the Humanities, headed by Lynne V. Cheney, has provided significant matching grants and other outright grants to sustain our work; we are especially indebted to Kathy Fuller, Charles Meyers, and David Nichols for guidance. At the National Historical Publications and Records Commission—also a granting agency—we are pleased to have been helped over the years by Frank G. Burke, Roger Bruns, Mary A. Giunta, Richard A. Jacobs, and Timothy Connelly. Others in the government helped in different but equally important ways. At SHAPE we are indebted to Command Historian Morris Honick and to former SACEUR General Bernard Rogers. At the Department of Defense our thanks go to Assistant Secretary of Defense D. O. Cooke, OSD Records Administrator E. E. Lowry, and Acting Administrator Brian V. Kinney. All helped us obtain the materials we needed for these volumes.

The National Archives are an important source of records in our research. We are indebted to Archivist Don W. Wilson, former Archivist Robert M. Warner, and former Acting Archivist Frank G. Burke. We also benefited from the assistance of Deputy Archivist Claudine J. Weiher, Assistant Archivist Trudy Huskamp Peterson, Records Declassification Division Chief Edwin Alan Thompson, and Special Archives Division Chief William H. Cunliffe. Others in this division who contributed were John A. Duffy, Thomas H. Graf, and JoAnn Williamson. At the Military Archives Division, Chief Garry Ryan was helpful, as was Chief Robert Wolfe in the Military Reference Branch. We are indebted as well to Wilbert B. Mahoney, Edward J. Reese, John E. Taylor, Leroy Jackson, Teri Hammett, and Edwin R. Coffee. Two staff members handling the Nixon Presidential Materials, James J. Hastings and B. A. Parham, were helpful, as was Benedict K. Zobrist, Director, Harry S. Truman Presidential Library.

Special thanks go to the staff of the Dwight D. Eisenhower Library, where Director John E. Wickman leads a well-trained and enthusiastic corps of archivists. Of special help were Martin M. Teasley, James W. Leyerzapf, David J. Haight, Rod Soubers, and Hazel O. Stroda.

As we completed our manuscripts and began the process leading to publication, we were fortunate to be working with an experienced, enthusiastic, and skillful staff at the Johns Hopkins University Press. Director Jack G. Goellner was extremely supportive, as were Barbara B. Lamb, James S. Johnston, Henry Y. K. Tom, George F. Thompson, Glenn L. Saltzman, Angeline Polites, and Mary Lou Kenney. Once again the talented Joanne Allen was our copyeditor. While we were preparing for this, our maiden voyage in word processing, Professor David R. Chesnutt was our helpful computer consultant.

There would have been no word processing to do had we not also received significant financial support from the private sector. We are deeply grateful to the John M. Olin Foundation, to Gordon Gray, and to the family of Ellis D. Slater for their timely help. The Eisenhower World Affairs Institute assisted in this regard, and we are especially indebted to its president, Susan E. Eisenhower, and to her staff, including Renee Kortum, Rick LaRue, Julie Wagner, and Sandra Dalal. Over the years John S. D. Eisenhower has repeatedly come to our aid in numerous ways, ably filling the gap left when the Johns Hopkins University and this project lost Milton S. Eisenhower in 1985. We dedicate these volumes to Milton S. Eisenhower because he did so much to launch this project and to sustain it in the years that followed. We hope these books are worthy of his support.

Introduction

When Dwight Eisenhower left New York for Europe shortly after New Year's Day in 1951, he expected to return and complete the work that he had begun as president of Columbia University. Instead of resigning that post, he took a leave of absence to organize the Allied command in Europe for the members of the North Atlantic Treaty Organization. As Supreme Allied Commander, Europe (SACEUR), during the following two years he would stay in touch with Columbia and especially with the American Assembly, a university innovation to which he had devoted substantial energy and time. While the General was in Europe, the university launched the Assembly—a forum at which scholars, businessmen, public officials, and other institutional leaders discussed major issues facing the nation—and the program's success was a source of satisfaction to him while he struggled to make the NATO forces operational.

America's problems in Europe, and indeed its national security problems around the world, were formidable. In early 1951 the global outlook was bleak. In Korea the Chinese routed the U.N. forces, which had appeared to be on the brink of total victory. The retreat that followed created a crisis atmosphere in Washington. In Europe the official mood was even more dangerously depressed. Confronted by overwhelming Soviet and Eastern European land forces, divided and discouraged by cold-war tensions, and preoccupied with the tasks of rebuilding their war-ravaged economies, America's European allies were badly divided on issues of defense.

Nor were all Americans certain that the United States should be directly and significantly engaged in the defense of Europe. Opposition to sending U.S. troops out of the Western Hemisphere had long been a dominant theme in U.S. foreign policy, and that opposition was still powerful in the early fifties. In Congress, spokesmen for these ideas and the so-called fortress America approach to national security fought a bitter rearguard action against the use of U.S. manpower and money in the defense of Europe.

During 1951 and 1952, Eisenhower wrestled with these problems at home and abroad, first as a military commander and then as a candidate for the presidency. Although his final plunge into politics appears to have been a decisive turning point in Eisenhower's career, the continuity was actually more substantial than the change. As SACEUR, Eisenhower's tasks were as much political as they were military. During his World War II duty, the General had carefully drawn the boundary between political and military decisions, insisting throughout that his responsibilities were entirely military. But in Europe in 1951 and 1952 he was in effect an American proconsul, spending much of his energy building an ideology of common defense and modifying national ambitions, concerns, and animosities. He also sustained the informal domestic political network that he had begun to build while he was at Columbia. The General's correspondence with Lucius Clay, Clifford Roberts, and William Robinson, among others, is particularly revealing of this aspect of his career. When he at last made his public debut as a candidate for the Republican nomination, he and his supporters were well prepared for the fight that followed.

By that time Eisenhower had sharpened his ideas about America's position in the world and about several aspects of domestic public policy. During the Columbia years, he had laid the foundation stones of a political philosophy that stressed "a path straight down the middle of the road." For Eisenhower that meant a moderately conservative course in domestic affairs and a frankly internationalist posture in global relations. The NATO experience strengthened his belief that the United States could no longer go it alone. It also convinced him that the economic rationale for U.S. involvement overseas was of overwhelming importance. As he explained in early 1952, "We have become accustomed to thinking of ourselves as a completely self-sufficient, self-supporting nation and of our relations . . . with others as of automatic benefit to foreign nations but of no special value to ourselves. . . . [But to the contrary,] our economy and our way of life depend upon great quantities of imports—some of them coming from the remote corners of the earth." "America's foreign policy," he said, "must include the purpose of maintaining access to, and trade with, all of the areas of the world from which we draw vital supplies." The United States could not afford to see the industry and skilled labor of Europe and Japan fall to the Soviets. Nor could the United States stand aside when commerce with Iran was endangered: "We cannot ignore the tremendous importance of 675,000 barrels of oil a day." If isolated economically, the United States would be weak and vulnerable.

To be strong, America would have to be involved in the defense of the entire free world, but the U.S. commitment had to be held within the limits imposed by the domestic economy. Eisenhower repeatedly stressed that *"the only way we can achieve military success . . . is through preserving the integrity of our economy and our financial structure."* There were, he knew, real limits to what the Unites States could afford to do. He never lost sight of "the importance of America's solvency to her own security." While in 1951 U.S. troops were needed in Asia and in Europe, Eisenhower looked forward to a day when European and Asian forces would take their places. "We cannot be a modern Rome guarding the far frontiers with our legions if for no other reason than because these are *not*, politically, *our* frontiers." In his approach to national security he found that "the truth, as usual, lies in the gray zone . . . ," in his favorite middle ground.

So it was as well with questions of domestic policy, but here Eisenhower's experience was thin, his ideas far less fully developed. Ever mindful of the importance of good staff work, he sought advice from experts, from those who knew the facts. As he noted in a humble vein, "When ordinary mortals like us undertake to form convictions about a controversial question, we are acutely dependent upon some knowledge of the truth in the matter." In some cases—agricultural policy, for instance—this approach was successful. With emotion-charged, polarized issues in which there were two well-defined sides and no tenable middle ground, Eisenhower had more difficulty working out in detail where he stood. This was true of racial questions and of the difficult challenge posed by Senator Joseph McCarthy's sensational and frequently slanderous efforts to protect the nation from an unseen army of enemy agents. Where, however, Eisenhower could apply the basic principles that he had spelled out before 1951—a desire for limited federal government involvement; an emphasis upon individual, private-sector solutions; a conviction that history could not be shifted into reverse in an effort to repeal the New Deal; and an insistence that the government live within its means—he was able to develop a set of policies and to hold together an effective team of political supporters dedicated to his philosophy and programs. He badly needed support as he juggled the demands of politics and the intense, overriding pressures to build the NATO military force.

No man could have been better suited for the NATO post than Eisenhower. He enjoyed the immense prestige of having been Supreme Commander of the victorious allies in World War II and the edge provided by his coherent, persuasive vision of foreign affairs. The lessons he had learned in the 1940s all served a useful purpose in the early 1950s. If NATO were to succeed, the common purpose had to override the particular concerns of nations, of services, and of individuals. Eisenhower preached that sermon and pumped some optimism into the Western European scene during a whirlwind tour of the alliance governments in early 1951. He knew that public and government attitudes were a vital "part of history," and he helped to create the climate of ideas that he needed in Europe and in the United States. After solidifying his support at home and abroad, he got down to the hard tasks of selecting his personnel and building an effective organization.

Both jobs were complicated by parochial concerns. The British insisted that either the Atlantic or the Mediterranean command had to go to one of their officers. The French were suspicious of the British and were also opposed, for understandable reasons, to German rearmament. Later, Turkey and Greece rejected British leadership of their forces. Eisenhower's own government contributed to his problems by developing war plans that were sharply at odds with the NATO strategy for dealing with a Soviet invasion. IRONBARK, the U.S. plan, assumed that NATO forces could delay but not prevent Communist land and air forces from sweeping across the Continent. Europeans perforce found that assumption unacceptable, particularly when they were struggling to provide NATO with the men and resources they thought were needed to mount a defense along the Rhine River. Eisenhower had to maneuver between these conflicting nationalisms, as he did when his NATO officers were denied access to certain U.S. intelligence reports and atomic information. The job was, he told one close friend, "the most delicate military task of my career."

As he gradually consolidated his support, Eisenhower also began to build up the institutions he needed to exercise effective command in Europe. He acquired able and prestigious subordinates in crucial positions. Foremost was General Alfred Maximilian Gruenther, a brilliant chief of staff, old personal friend, experienced military diplomat, and bridge expert. Eisenhower leaned heavily upon Gruenther personally and professionally for the type of assistance that all successful commanders need. His Deputy Supreme Allied Commander, the nettlesome Bernard Law Montgomery, played a different role, but this British officer's long experience and professional stature were important factors in getting the NATO force quickly under way. From France came the talented General Alphonse Pierre Juin, who commanded NATO's ground units in central Europe. The United States provided Admiral Robert Bostwick Carney, who led the forces protecting NATO's troublesome Mediterranean flank, and General Lauris Norstad, who headed NATO's major air command. This core of outstanding officers enabled Eisenhower to establish plans for the joint efforts indispensable to modern military operations.

To build the unified institutional framework that would enable these officers to operate effectively, Eisenhower had to contend with a variety of factors that tended to divide his commands. His own Joint Chiefs of Staff were loath to surrender all operational control of U.S. units; nor were they able to forgo service rivalries in order to make NATO a success. The two most difficult problems, however, were centered in Germany and the Mediterranean, where major French and British interests were at stake.

Although hampered by these pressures, Eisenhower was able to build an effective command structure and to preserve the unity of NATO. He developed a workable system of war plans and a realistic set of mobilization and rearmament goals. He provided for the establishment of the NATO Defense College and encouraged the reconciliation of national differences in tactical doctrines. At a time when the U.S. Asian proconsul, General Douglas MacArthur, was relieved from his post after a bitter struggle with civilian authority, Eisenhower was able to maintain a smooth working relationship with the White House, in part by frequently reporting to President Truman on an informal basis either directly or through W. Averell Harriman. With the U.S. legislature, too, he carefully nurtured favorable ties, devoting more time to briefing visiting congressmen than he would have preferred. Throughout, he encouraged his own country to increase its short- and middle-term support for Europe and urged the European nations themselves to move toward greater political, economic, and military integration. The capstone of these efforts came in Lisbon in February 1952, when the members of NATO solidified the alliance by agreeing on German rearmament, on a single schedule for their military buildup, on a strengthened supreme commander, and on solutions for a number of other divisive issues.

While Lisbon clearly marked the solidification of the alliance, Eisenhower's accomplishments as SACEUR were all qualified in greater or lesser degree. The national animosities and interests that he helped to moderate were still there, waiting to surface, as they did in later years. The European Army for which he campaigned so ardently would not become a reality. Nor would French support for NATO endure. While Eisenhower would adroitly juggle two sets of war plans—one European, one American—he would not be able to overcome U.S. reservations about sharing its atomic weapons or secrets. (The same forces were at work on the other side of the Iron Curtain, but Eisenhower would never acknowledge that when Yugoslavia broke away from Russia and drew closer to the Western alliance—a development that he carefully nurtured—it represented a significant break in the supposedly monolithic Red Empire.) On the NATO side of the Iron Curtain, Eisenhower steadily ground away at the job of building an effective international force to defend Western Europe. But neither he nor his successors were able to will away the national divisions that made his job difficult and essential in the first place.

All the while, NATO's supreme military leader was becoming more deeply engaged in partisan politics. A fascinating portrait emerges. Publicly, Eisenhower proclaimed himself to be a military leader determined to remain "aloof from domestic struggles," a man with "a violent antipathy for anything that might be called partisan politics." As he said to his brother Arthur, "To me the picture of a man seeking to satisfy personal ambition through the means of trumped up argument and by use of the devious routes and methods inherent in our current day politics is completely repulsive." Privately, however, Eisenhower was nurturing the informal political staff that would carry him to the nomination as the Republican candidate for the presidency. Initially he was determined that he would "never seek anything." But he could see from the first "bridges that are still a long way ahead." He knew all the time that there was likely to be "a heavier and more responsible burden" in his future, a duty that would be "imposed by a National Convention."

His ardent supporters wanted him to eliminate the tension by simply declaring that he was a candidate for the presidency. They were fearful that the conservative wing of the Republican party, led by Ohio Senator Robert A. Taft, would outmaneuver them and lock up the nomination for their man if Eisenhower continued to try to balance himself on the loose tightrope he was walking in 1951. But the General persisted. He refused to jump into "the great political pot in the United States."

The demands grew relentlessly, however, and soon the call of duty, ambition, and pride became irresistible. Eisenhower stepped off the rope: in January 1952 he announced that he was a Republican. He speeded up his efforts to broaden his grasp of domestic issues, to achieve an "education in the obvious." The following month he was overwhelmed by pictures of the enthusiastic gathering of Eisenhower supporters in Madison Square Garden. Then he won the primary in New Hampshire and came very close to winning (with only write-in votes) in Minnesota. He was now fully committed, ready to "start a crusade."

On June 1, 1952, Eisenhower returned to the United States to campaign actively, and he discovered shortly that party politics could indeed involve all of the unpleasantness that he had expected. His kickoff speech in his hometown was a political dud which the media compared unfavorably with his subsequent press conference. The Abilene speech prompted intense controversy inside his camp as to the proper style for the candidate to adopt. On one point there was unanimity: Eisenhower could not win by promising specific policies to particular interest groups. Indeed, Eisenhower the candidate received his first full introduction to interest-group politics and recognized at once that he could not build his political strategy out of the narrow, highly particular needs of these groups. The road to the White House was the middle way. He focused his "crusade" on the kinds of general principles that he had been working out during the last five years: opposition to further growth of the federal bureaucracy; emphasis upon sound fiscal programs; solid support for America's overseas allies. In his quest for the nomination he waged a positive campaign and challenged both Taft, who attacked Eisenhower directly, and the Washington establishment. As always, he maintained warm ties with the media.

After winning a tight victory at the Republican convention at Chicago, Eisenhower selected Richard Milhous Nixon as his running mate. The choice was reasonable given Nixon's record as an ardent anti-Communist, tireless campaigner, and astute politician. Nixon's party roots ran deep and reached from the far right to the liberal left of the GOP. He was a counterpoise to Eisenhower in several important regards. Where Eisenhower was expert in foreign affairs, Nixon was associated primarily with domestic concerns. Where Eisenhower had long scorned partisanship, Nixon was the embodiment of the party man. While Eisenhower sought to envelop, to absorb opposition, Nixon's style was to mount frontal attacks against opponents while skirmishing on the flanks with innuendo. The General was experienced and enormously popular in the United States and abroad; Nixon, young and vigorous, had only recently begun to attract widespread attention. If Ike presented himself as a reluctant candidate, Nixon was as eager as a man could be to move from Capitol Hill to the White House.

That trip was shortly imperiled when in September 1952 the Nixon fund crisis broke, threatening to derail the Eisenhower crusade. The General had earlier tidied up his own financial affairs, avoiding even the appearance of impropriety. He had to be, he told Texas oil tycoon Sid Richardson, as clean as a "hound's tooth." For whatever reason, Nixon was less circumspect. His special expense fund seemed to make a mockery of the Republican campaign effort to tar the Democrats with charges of corruption. What was Eisenhower to do? While he and his advisers debated, Nixon took the offensive in the famous "Checkers" speech of September 23, 1952 (so named because of Nixon's reference to his family's dog Checkers as one of the gifts he had received). This emotion-laden television address evoked a public response that took the initiative away from Eisenhower, sharply reducing his maneuvering room. While Eisenhower's first choice might have been the politically dangerous one of dropping Nixon, the Checkers speech encouraged him to keep the ticket and the party intact.

A somewhat different problem arose in Eisenhower's dealings with Senator Joseph McCarthy. Eisenhower wanted very badly to keep his party unified. Throughout his career he had always sought to achieve unity—during World War II, as Army Chief of Staff, and as SACEUR. He had tried to coopt the opposition, whether it was Field Marshal Montgomery, Charles de Gaulle, or, more recently, Senator Robert Taft. Frequently he had succeeded, but during the 1952 campaign, and in particular in dealing with the unsavory McCarthy, the Eisenhower approach probably lost more support than it gained, probably cost more in terms of the nation's ability to deal with the political crisis of McCarthyism than it earned in terms of ensuring a united Republican party in Congress. This was especially true insofar as Eisenhower's Wisconsin speech was concerned. His failure on that occasion to defend General Marshall from McCarthy's spurious charges served neither the nation nor the GOP well. Some observers, fearing that Eisenhower had capitulated to the far right wing of the Republican party, saw this episode as the low point of the campaign.

There were, however, many high points as Eisenhower developed his winning campaign style. His assets were many. He was a bona fide war hero. He was defining a course that had broad appeal to an American electorate less beguiled by liberal solutions to the nation's domestic problems than at any other time in the twenty years since 1932. But clearly what was most appealing about Eisenhower was the set of values—small-town, traditional values—that he embodied and made a central feature of his political persona. Never mind that he had traveled around the world and become a master administrator and renowned military diplomat. He still identified himself with Kansas. "Dickinson County is something deep within me," he wrote in 1952, and the American people sensed that truth and voted for it. They voted for a man who kept his friends, who was positive about the future, who dealt fairly with his subordinates and peers, who respected authority, democracy, and individual effort—a man who symbolized traditional heartland values while he struggled with the problems of the 1950s.

There were problems, and chief among them was the Korean War, which Eisenhower made a central feature of his campaign. "K^1C^2" was the formula—Korea, Communism, Corruption—and once the Nixon fund crisis had passed, Eisenhower put the Democratic candidate, Adlai E. Stevenson, on the defensive. Eisenhower pledged to go to Korea and to do all that he could to end the war. He would cut taxes and government spending. He would restore moral leadership. In November 33,936,234 voters gave Eisenhower and this program their support; he and Nixon carried all but nine states and overwhelmed Stevenson 442 to 89 in the electoral college. By a narrower margin, Eisenhower won a Republican Congress to implement the policies of the Middle Way.

In the months that followed this sweeping victory, Eisenhower put together his administration and redeemed one of his campaign pledges. The quick trip to Korea in December 1952 gave the President-elect a chance to gain firsthand impressions by speaking directly to the front-line troops, as he had during World War II in Europe. The slow voyage back on the cruiser *Helena* enabled him to confer at length with several of the men who would play central roles in his first administration. John Foster Dulles, corporate attorney and international affairs pundit, was slated to head the State Department; Herbert Brownell would be Attorney General; General Motors Chairman Charles Wilson would become Secretary of Defense; business leaders George Humphrey and Douglas McKay would take over at the Treasury and Interior departments. Together, they steered the new administration through a tense but relatively efficient transition with the Truman White House and to the eve of inauguration, where these two volumes of *The Papers of Dwight David Eisenhower* end.

SELECTION AND ANNOTATION

As we passed the halfway mark in this documentary edition, we were concerned to maintain as far as possible the same techniques of selection and annotation that we used in the preceding volumes. To a considerable extent we have succeeded in that task, focusing once more on the man, the organizational leader, rather than the institutions he headed. This was especially important in dealing with Eisenhower's NATO career because of the problems that still remain in conducting research on and obtaining records from that multinational organization. As a consequence, we could not produce a documentary record comparable to the one we provided for Eisenhower's service as Army Chief of Staff. We were nevertheless able to present the Supreme Commander's responses to the problems of launching SHAPE and could along the way present more NATO-related sources than have heretofore been available to scholars.

The political campaign presented a different set of problems. No longer did Eisenhower have a single, settled office with standard, formal procedures. His meaningful correspondence became slimmer, his recordkeeping more precarious. As a result, we were forced to put the superscript zero (^{0}), indicating that we were not certain who drafted the letter or memorandum in the first instance, on a relatively large number of entries. In each case, however, we did have substantial reasons for believing that Eisenhower was directly involved in producing the document—as always our major criterion for selection. We continued to screen out routine correspondence of the sort that all major political figures send in abundance but never actually see for more than the few seconds it takes to sign their name.

The papers we selected—the letters, cables, memorandums, and diary entries—provide a unique perspective on two major transitions in modern U.S. history. The first involved the use of U.S. troops in peacetime on a more or less permanent basis overseas. The debates over sending U.S. troops to Europe were particularly intense for this reason, as was the struggle between Robert Taft and Eisenhower for the Republican nomination. From this watershed on, the United States was committed to the defense of Europe in a new and significant manner. The second grand turning point involved the presidency. Eisenhower's election in 1952 marked a new era in U.S. political behavior. The Republican party would continue to be a minority party by a large measure, but it would thereafter win six of the next nine elections for the presidency. The United States had clearly changed, and we hope that these volumes help our readers understand how the nation was evolving and the role Dwight David Eisenhower played in that transition.

The Papers of Dwight David Eisenhower

NATO and the Campaign of 1952

Mustering NATO's Force

JANUARY 1951 TO MAY 1951

1

Landing on the "Floating Island"

Left N.Y. City at 4:00 PM for Washington, from which latter place I shall take off for a preliminary trip to Europe. The trip is "preliminary" in the sense that it is exploratory in preparation for my new assignment as Supreme Commander of Allied Forces in Europe.[1]

Yesterday (rather day before) I was visited by Sen. Duff, Gen. Ed Clark, Mr. Forgan, a Mr. Benton & Russell Davenport.[2] The purpose was to talk over our foreign problems & try to develop a "positive" approach to the obvious problems.

During the conversation I happened to speak in derogatory terms of "war profits"—and Mr. Benton followed this up persistently, saying that if such things were to be said, any mobilization plan would be killed.[3] While he had obviously misunderstood me (my conception of war profits is the making of money out of national disaster) yet the significant thing was that he kept talking about the "appeal" and the "reception" rather than the plan I laid out. Later, thinking this over it struck me that he was thinking of "political" effects, possibly in connection with a possible political future for me.

This irritated me—so much so that I felt it necessary to repeat again what I've so often said before. So my last chore in N.Y. was to telephone Ed Clark (I kept Schulz[4] in room, not because I don't trust E.C., but because I wanted a check on what *I* said. I told him that it was important that he (and all his associates) understand that I had *not* changed my mind about politics & I still say as I've always said— "I hope always to do my duty to my country; but I cannot even conceive of circumstances as of this moment that could convince me I had a *duty* to enter politics." [God knows I should not be compelled to reiterate my attitude toward "duty." My going to Europe should, I think, prove that I'm determined to meet every requirement of duty.]

Anyway, I told him that if Benton is *assuming* that I'm going to enter politics he'd better be disabused in a heck of a hurry or, someday, he'd get a rude shock.[5]

[1] On December 19, 1950, President Harry S. Truman had designated Eisenhower as the first Supreme Allied Commander, Europe (SACEUR) (for background see no. 1134 in *The Papers of Dwight David Eisenhower* [Baltimore, 1970-], vols. X-XI, *Columbia University*, ed. Louis Galambos [1983], hereafter cited as Galambos, *Columbia University*). Eisenhower was planning to visit the capital city of each of the North Atlantic Treaty Organization (NATO) member nations in order to learn about the problems that he would encounter as SACEUR and "to impress upon NATO authorities his confidence in their ability to meet [the] present challenge and of his readiness to swing into action promptly" (Gruenther to Bruce *et al.*, Dec. 22, 1950, EM, Subject File, Trips; see also U.S. Department of State, *Foreign Relations of the United States, 1951*, 7 vols. [Washington, D.C., 1977-83], vol. III,

European Security and the German Question, Part I [1981], pp. 392–95). In Washington Eisenhower would be briefed by military, diplomatic, and intelligence officials.

On January 2 he would attend the funeral of Lieutenant General Walton Harris Walker, who had been killed in a jeep accident (for background on Walker, who was commanding the American Eighth Army in Korea at the time of his death, see *Eisenhower Papers*, vols. I–XI; see also *New York Times*, Dec. 23, 1950, and Jan. 3, 1951).

[2] Eisenhower had met with Pennsylvania Senator-elect James Henderson Duff, Brigadier General Edwin Norman Clark (USA, ret.), James Russell Forgan, John Gordon Ben*nett*, and Russell Wheeler Davenport on Saturday afternoon, December 30, 1950. For background on Duff, Governor of Pennsylvania since 1947, see Galambos, *Columbia University*, no. 937, n. 1; for background on Clark, a business consultant and executive who had served with Eisenhower in Europe during World War II, see *The Papers of Dwight David Eisenhower* (Baltimore, 1970–), vols. VII–IX, *The Chief of Staff*, ed. Louis Galambos (1978), hereafter cited as Galambos, *Chief of Staff*, nos. 1456 and 1643. Forgan was a partner in the investment firm of Glore, Forgan & Co. (see Galambos, *Columbia University*, no. 581), and Bennett, a Republican from Rochester, New York, was a self-described "real estate man" (*New York Times*, Feb. 17, 1955). Davenport had been moderator of Life Round Tables since March 1948 (see Galambos, *Columbia University*, no. 871). All of these men had been promoting Eisenhower's participation in politics (see *ibid.*, nos. 638, 1105, and *passim*; see also Clark to Eisenhower, Feb. 9, [1950], EM).

[3] Eisenhower was deeply concerned about the recent reverses in the Korean War (see Galambos, *Columbia University*, nos. 1093, 1108, and 1112). For his thoughts on economic mobilization see *ibid.*, no. 914; and his memoir *At Ease: Stories I Tell to Friends* (Garden City, N.Y., 1967), pp. 210–13.

[4] For background on Eisenhower's aide Lieutenant Colonel Robert Ludwig Schulz see *Eisenhower Papers*, vols. VII–XI.

[5] Speculation on Eisenhower's political future would nevertheless continue (see nos. 63, 72, and 78).

2   *Eisenhower Mss., Diaries*

DIARY   *January 3, 1951*

So far as my new job is concerned—the "staff mind" is working in typical channels in Washington.[1] Instead of everybody concerning himself with the substance of the problem (Nat'l Attitudes; industrial capacities; military programs and present strength) the principal subject of discussion is the one so dear to the hearts of academic soldiers & sailors—"command systems." Principally this stems from the primary failure to see that command in Allied ventures implies & imposes a great national responsibility upon the nation assuming it. Since staff think of command in terms of kudos & glory (arising out of the erroneous thinking that such command is comparable to that exercised by the individual over his own service).[2]

Anyway there has already been discussed in some detail the various applicable "systems of command" within my over all organization & each country's "staffs" have been encouraged to give their attention to these matters & *fix* their own conclusions. The result will be *trouble*— and I warned Al Gruenther (who is to be my C/S)[3] to keep still about it. He probably thinks I'm a bit nuts—but I've been through it before. We are going to find (as always) that *our* system will make everyone a bit angry—but now we've given them the right to advise & suggest, so, we are going to make them believe we've violated their *considered* opinions instead of their casually expressed comments.

In 1944 the British & Monty situation was not unlike this one.[4]

[1] Eisenhower was in Washington, D.C., for a series of briefings (for background on this trip and on his mission to Europe see the preceding document). On January 2 he had met with NATO's Standing Group, the Washington-based executive body of the NATO Military Committee, composed of representatives of France, the United Kingdom, and the United States (see Galambos, *Columbia University*, no. 1113). On that same day he ate lunch with Lord Arthur William Tedder, Marshal of the Royal Air Force (RAF) and the United Kingdom's representative on the Standing Group (for background see *Eisenhower Papers*, vols. I–XI); he also attended briefings on planning, intelligence, public information, and the itinerary for his trip. On the following day Eisenhower received a briefing on the Mutual Defense Assistance Program (MDAP), which the United States had instituted in 1949 in order to rearm its allies (see Galambos, *Columbia University*, no. 303; and Lawrence S. Kaplan, *A Community of Interests: NATO and the Military Assistance Program, 1948-1951* [Washington, D.C., 1980]). He also completed a briefing from the Joint Chiefs of Staff (JCS) on planning and intelligence and met with Secretary of Defense George Catlett Marshall. On the following day, January 4, Eisenhower would meet with Major General Cortlandt van Rensselaer Schuyler, Chief of the Plans Group in the Office of the Assistant Chief of Staff of the Army, G-3, for a briefing on Army forces organization. Eisenhower would also receive an extensive briefing by Secretary of State Dean Acheson (an outline of Acheson's presentation is in State, *Foreign Relations, 1951*, vol. III, *European Security and the German Question, Part I*, pp. 396-400; portions of the briefing book the State Department prepared for Eisenhower are in ibid., pp. 1-6, 460-64. For background on Marshall, Schuyler, and Acheson, see *Eisenhower Papers*, vols. I–XI).

[2] Eisenhower's new international command would be fitted into a complicated organizational structure. The North Atlantic Council (NAC), NATO's governing body, comprised the foreign ministers of the treaty nations and met in various locations. When the NAC was not in session, its policies were to be carried out by the council deputies, who met in continuous session in London. Two of the NAC's most important subordinate bodies were its Defense Committee, composed of the defense ministers of the NATO countries, and the Military Committee, which had been established by the Defense Committee and comprised the military chiefs of staff of the NATO nations. The policies formulated by the Military Committee were to be executed by the Standing Group (see n. 1), to which Eisenhower was to report (see Hastings Lionel Ismay, *NATO: The First Five Years, 1949-1954* [Netherlands, 1954], pp. 14-15, 24-25, 174-76, 184; Robert Endicott Osgood, *NATO: The Entangling Alliance* [Chicago, 1962], p. 46; Jerauld Wright, "North Atlantic Treaty Organization," *Army Information Digest* 6, no. 7 [1951], 24-30; and DM 2-1-

51, Jan. 2, 1951, CCS 092 Western Europe [3-12-48], Sec. 66. See also U.S. Department of State, *Foreign Relations of the United States, 1950*, 7 vols. [Washington, D.C., 1976–80], vol. III, *Western Europe* [1977], pp. 548–64).

At this time a command structure for the Allied forces under the control of Eisenhower's Supreme Headquarters Allied Powers, Europe (SHAPE), had not been determined. Eisenhower, who was studying the problem, had three specific proposals under consideration. The first contemplated a commander in chief (C in C) for each of the three European regions under SHAPE (North, Central, and South). A second plan envisaged only a C in C North and a C in C South, with SHAPE's central forces falling directly under Eisenhower's command. Under a third scheme all major units would be directly commanded by SACEUR until major subordinate commands could be established. Eisenhower had not formed any tentative views on the subject, nor had he decided on the identity of the prospective subordinate NATO commanders (Gruenther to Perkins, Dec. 29, 1950, CCS 092 Western Europe [3-12-48], Sec. 66).

The formation of two other major NATO commands was also under consideration: a naval command for the Mediterranean (see Galambos, *Columbia University*, no. 1113) and a supreme allied command for the Atlantic (see nos. 45 and 52 in this volume). Neither of these commands would report to SHAPE (see JCS 2073/107 and JSPC 757/97, Dec. 28, 1950; and SM-23-51, Jan. 4, 1951, all in CCS 092 Western Europe [3-12-48], Sec. 66).

[3] Lieutenant General Alfred Maximilian Gruenther, the Army's Deputy Chief of Staff for Plans since March 1, 1950, would accompany Eisenhower on his exploratory trip to NATO capitals. He would also become Chief of Staff to SACEUR in February (for background on this close personal friend of Eisenhower's see *Eisenhower Papers*, vols. I–XI).

[4] Eisenhower was referring to Field Marshal Viscount Bernard Law Montgomery of Alamein, who in 1944 had pressed Eisenhower to appoint an overall ground force commander (presumably Montgomery himself or another British general) to conduct operations against the Germans in northwest Europe. Early in 1945 British Prime Minister Winston Spencer Churchill and the British Chiefs of Staff (BCOS) had also urged that such a course be followed. One of the major factors in that dispute over command structure had been the nationality of the proposed ground commander (see nos. 2210 and 2233 in *The Papers of Dwight David Eisenhower* [Baltimore, 1970–], vols. I–V, *The War Years*, ed. Alfred D. Chandler, Jr. [1970], hereafter cited as Chandler, *War Years*; see also Stephen E. Ambrose, *The Supreme Commander: The War Years of General Dwight D. Eisenhower* [Garden City, N.Y., 1970], pp. 574–75, 580–89).

Montgomery would become Deputy Supreme Allied Commander under Eisenhower (for developments see nos. 52, 53, 74, and 77).

3   *Eisenhower Mss.*

To MINNIE STEWART   *January 3, 1951*

Dear Miss Minnie:[0] Thank you very much for your nice note.[1] I assure you that I am just as sorrowful going to Europe as you could possibly be about my new assignment.[2] It is tragic that the poor world is in such a state and, of course, from a personal angle it is a terrible wrench to begin again to break up housekeeping—when we thought that at last we were on a sort of permanent family basis[3]—and finally it is a terrible wrench to give up, entirely, the many constructive jobs on which I was working to go back again into the military field.[4]

This note brings to you my every wish for a fine 1951. *Cordially*

[1] Stewart had been Eisenhower's mathematics teacher at Abilene High School (for background see Galambos, *Chief of Staff*, nos. 738 and 1587).

[2] In her undated letter (EM) Stewart had written that it had been "with mingled feelings of pride and sorrow" that she had read of Eisenhower's appointment as SACEUR. She was pleased that her former pupil had been chosen for such an important task but regretted that "the world crisis required such a dangerous and responsible position" (for background on Eisenhower's apppointment see no. 1 in this volume; and Galambos, *Columbia University*, no. 1134).

[3] The Eisenhowers had recently purchased a farm in Pennsylvania, on which they planned to establish their first truly permanent residence. For background on the farm see Eisenhower, *At Ease*, pp. 358–61; and nos. 48 and 179. For the General's personal concerns regarding the move to Europe see Galambos, *Columbia University*, no. 1045.

[4] In his three years as president of Columbia University, Eisenhower had initiated several new programs and reorganized certain university procedures (see *ibid.*, esp. nos. 54, 124, 979, 1039, and 1056).

4   *Eisenhower Mss.*

To Earl North   *January 3, 1951*

Dear Earl:[0] I thank you very much for your splendid letter.[1] I apologize for the necessary shortness of this reply but I am in the last throe of preparing for a hasty trip to Europe[2]—there is little of a personal nature that I can do.

I have no misconceptions about the toughness of the job and the bleakness of the outlook. Moreover, the assignment means for Mamie and me another, and this time particularly difficult, breaking up of our home. For me, it means also the turning back from a lot of constructive things that we had underway at Columbia and going again into the military field.[3] (Sometimes I get dangerously close to feeling sorry for myself.) In spite of the bleakness of the barren outlook I do *not* consider the situation hopeless. While I hope that my own direct connection with the affair will not be too prolonged I am certainly going to work at top speed while I am at it.[4] I hope my effort will be helpful to whatever successor may some day be appointed.

I hope that I may be successful in bringing about more effective cooperation among the several nations of the North Atlantic Union.

In any event, the very best to you both.[5] *Cordially*

[1] Colonel North (USA, ret.) had been a mathematics instructor at West Point during Eisenhower's days as a cadet and had later served with him in the Office of the Assistant Secretary of War. "I often think of the care free days of the 1930's," North had written to Eisenhower on December 13 (EM), "when you and I were a couple of unknown soldiers buried in the old State, War and Navy building . . ." (for background on North see Galambos, *Chief of Staff*, no. 1772; for Eisenhower's work with the Assistant to the Secretary of War see Eisenhower, *At Ease*, pp. 210–13).

[2] On Eisenhower's exploratory trip to Europe see nos. 1 and 9.

[3] For the unfinished projects being left behind and for Eisenhower's personal concerns see the preceding document.

[4] In his letter North had called the NATO assignment "the toughest job any man was ever handed" but said he was certain that Eisenhower's "ability and gift of diplomacy . . . will be able to get some quick and concerted action among the Atlantic Pact countries . . ." (for Eisenhower's views on the dangers faced by the West and on his role as NATO forces commander see Galambos, *Columbia University*, nos. 1113, 1129, and 1144).

[5] North's wife was Dorothy Gatewood North.

5   *Eisenhower Mss.*

To Hastings Lionel Ismay   *January 3, 1951*

Dear Pug:[0] Your note brought to me most heartwarming encouragement.[1] I agree with you as to the bleakness of the outlook but I refuse to consider the assignment an impossible one.[2] I believe that if all of us get in and do the kind of job that we should and can success will be ours. It is just not sensible to think that 190 million backward Eurasians can conquer the entire western civilization with its great history and its great economic, political and material resources, if we are merely ready to forget all lesser considerations and get together on an intensive and cooperative program.[3]

Please be sure to be on tap when I come to London. I must see you.[4] *As ever*

[1] During World War II Lieutenant General Lord Ismay had been Chief of Staff to Winston Churchill. In the spring of 1948 he became chairman of the Council for the Festival of Britain, a centenary celebration of the Hyde Park Great Exhibition of 1851 (for background on Ismay see Galambos, *Columbia University*, no. 259).

[2] In his note of December 21, 1950 (EM), Ismay had written that Eisenhower's assignment as Supreme Allied Commander for NATO "was far more intractable . . . than 'Torch' or 'Overlord'," but he was certain Eisenhower would "triumph once again" (for background on World War II operations TORCH, the invasion of North Africa, and OVERLORD, the invasion of Northwest Europe, see Chandler, *War Years*, vols. I–V; and Dwight D. Eisenhower, *Crusade in Europe* [Garden City, N.Y., 1948], pp. 74–114, 220–65).

[3] For Eisenhower's thoughts on the development and organization of the Allied defense see Galambos, *Columbia University*, nos. 1113 and 1129.

[4] Eisenhower apparently did not see Ismay during the exploratory trip to Europe of January 7–25, but the two generals met in Paris shortly after Eisenhower returned to Europe to establish permanent headquarters (on the exploratory trip see no. 9; on Ismay's visit to SHAPE headquarters see Hastings Lionel Ismay, *The Memoirs of General Lord Ismay* [New York, 1960], pp. 456–57).

---

6 *Eisenhower Mss.*

To Marcellus Hartley Dodge
January 3, 1951

Dear Marcy:[01] I regret that I do not have a final opportunity to chat with you but I am certainly planning on seeing you when I come back to the states toward the end of the month.[2] I have taken to heart the suggestion in your note of December 27th and have already talked to a number of men here in Washington about the problem. I share your feeling that we simply *must* get our production started speedily and at full blast.[3]

This note brings to you my very best wishes for 1951. *Affectionately*

[1] Chairman of the board of the Remington Arms Company, Dodge was also clerk of the Columbia University board of trustees (for background see Galambos, *Columbia University*, no. 41).
[2] Eisenhower would embark on a twenty-four-day European exploratory trip for NATO on January 7 (see nos. 1 and 9 in this volume).
[3] There is no copy of Dodge's December 27 letter in EM, but it apparently concerned matters of industrial mobilization, a subject of ongoing concern to Eisenhower. On America's lack of preparation for the Korean War see Galambos, *Columbia University*, nos. 944 and 957. For the need for military production to aid NATO see *ibid.*, nos. 1099 and 1108; no. 16 in this volume; and *New York Times*, December 22, 1950, and January 9, 1951.

---

7 *Eisenhower Mss.*

To Clifford Roberts
January 4, 1951

Dear Cliff:[01] Thanks for the note you wrote to me from the "Clipper."[2] I have no intention of answering Mr. Hoover's talk—it is not my business to do so. Moreover, there is much in his speech with which I fully agreed; it was only the ending which left us all in a state of "waiting"—in my opinion, waiting for our own starvation or destruction—that disturbed me so. I really believe that he stated his case a little bit more strongly than he actually intended.[3]

I know you realize that, by and large, I have a deep born antipathy to allowing cash to lie around doing nothing. Of course, I do not know when is the right time to buy or the right things to buy.[4] But if we should count as cash the money that is now invested in bonds, in the Morgan account, and add to it the amount in actual cash we would have, as I recall, something more than fifty per cent of the entire sum in cash.

I know that you will use your discretionary rights to put me into as good an investing position as your judgment dictates. I have no interest in buying and selling except when some extraordinary circumstance so demands. I really do not know why I should write these things to you because you are fully alive to them; maybe I just got to thinking about them because of the way the market has been acting the last few days.[5]

I hope to see you about January 26th or 27th.[6] In the meantime, the very best of wishes and, as always, warm personal regard. *Cordially*

P.S. My University office can always get in touch with me within a matter of hours.

---

[1] Roberts was a partner in the New York City investment firm of Reynolds & Company and chairman of the executive committee of the Augusta National Golf Club, to which Eisenhower belonged (for background see Galambos, *Columbia University*, nos. 69 and 520).

[2] Roberts, who was then on a trip to South America, Europe, and Africa (see Eisenhower to Roberts, Dec. 15, 1950, EM), had written to the General on December 24 using Pan American Airways stationery with the heading "en route by 'Clipper'" (EM; see also R. E. G. Davies, *Airlines of the United States Since 1914* [Washington, D.C., 1972], pp. 230–39).

[3] On December 20, 1950, the day following Eisenhower's appointment as supreme commander of the NATO forces (see Galambos, *Columbia University*, no. 1134), former President Herbert Hoover had delivered a twenty-minute radio and television address urging the United States to alter its foreign policies. Beginning with a survey of the world military situation, Hoover had gone on to say that the only center of aggression on earth was "the Communist-controlled Asian-European land mass," which, with "over 300 trained and equipped combat divisions," could turn Western Europe into the "graveyard of millions of American boys," engaging the United States in a "war without victory." To avert this disaster, he proposed seven principles for the nation to pursue: (1) preserve the Western Hemisphere as a "Gibraltar of Western Civilization"; (2) hold the Atlantic and Pacific oceans, with defensive frontiers established on the islands of Great Britain, Japan, Formosa, and the Philippines; (3) "[a]rm our air and naval forces to the teeth," so that they might be better able to defend the oceans; (4) after initial outlays for defense, reduce expenditures, balance the budget, and reduce inflation; (5) continue to feed the hungry of the world but offer military aid to foreign nations only after they have "displayed spirit and strength in defense against communism"; (6) renounce all attempts to appease the Communists (Hoover said the nation "can retrieve a battle but cannot retrieve an appeasement"); and (7) realize that "the prime obligation of defense of Western Continental Europe rests upon the nations of Europe." Hoover went on to state that free Europe had "more manpower and more productive capacity today" than it had had in either world war and that only

evidence of a strong sense of European unity and willingness to combat communism should warrant further U.S. aid. The former President contended that to send another American man or dollar to Europe before the free nations there had established "organized and equipped combat divisions" sufficient to "erect a sure dam against the red flood" would only invite another no-win situation like Korea (see *New York Times*, Dec. 21, 1950).

In his December 21 letter Roberts had written, "I have just read Hoover's speech and I hope you don't answer it—now that you are wearing your military hat" (EM). Eisenhower would issue no formal statement in reply to the Hoover address, but he would comment on it privately (see Galambos, *Columbia University*, no. 1138; and no. 57 in this volume. For Eisenhower's views on the course the United States should follow see Galambos, *Columbia University*, no. 1113).

[4] Roberts frequently handled investments for the General (see nos. 38, 416, and 780).

[5] The New York Stock Exchange had closed 1950 with the best averages and heaviest trading since 1933. The upward trend continued until the date of this document, when a drop took place—a result, no doubt, of the major setbacks suffered by the U.N. forces in Korea (see *New York Times*, Jan. 1, 2, 3, 4, 1950).

[6] According to Eisenhower's appointment calendar, he did not see Roberts until February 8.

8 Columbia University Files

To Clarence Francis January 4, 1951

Dear Mr. Francis:[01] The world situation that confronts us today and in the foreseeable future convinces me that we have even greater need for the American Assembly than we first envisioned.[2]

I intend to continue my personal supervision of the Assembly within the limits of time dictated by present duties and I plan to be on hand for conference participation. My current assignment, however, requires me to delegate part of the responsibility.[3]

When I left the campus earlier this week we were nearing the $400,000 mark toward our working capital goal of $500,000.[4] We were also getting our conference sponsorship program underway. You may recall that we wished to secure fifty sponsorships at $25,000 each. Although we have concentrated on the working capital fund we already have in hand or have commitments for nine sponsorships.[5]

I am writing to a few of my friends to ask them if in my absence they would be willing to serve as my personal representatives in securing conference sponsorships. If you feel that you can do so I would like very much to have you serve in this capacity.

Furthermore, in my absence I would appreciate your taking on the additional job of assisting and advising Philip Young in maintaining liaison with business as regards The American Assembly.[6]

Philip is in hearty accord with my dual request of you. In the interest of time, since I will be away from campus, would you kindly write to him direct if you are willing to undertake these tasks.[7]

With all good wishes.[8] *Sincerely*

[1] Francis (B.S. Amherst 1910) had been chairman of the board of the General Foods Corporation since 1943. He was one of many business and professional men from whom Eisenhower had sought funds for Columbia University's American Assembly project (for background on the General's fund-raising activities see Galambos, *Columbia University*, nos. 1061, 1068, and 1078; on Francis see *ibid.*, nos. 120 and 826).

[2] The American Assembly project was developed by Eisenhower to draw together, in a conference setting, leaders from business, government, labor, and education to examine problems of major concern to America (see Eisenhower, *At Ease*, p. 350).

[3] Although Eisenhower would maintain close contact with Columbia officials concerning the Assembly, his duties as SACEUR would prevent him from attending the first conference session (see nos. 184 and 202).

[4] See n. 1 above for Eisenhower's efforts to raise funds for the Assembly.

[5] See EM, American Assembly, for correspondence regarding conference sponsorship, esp. MacKenzie to Campbell, November 8, 1950.

[6] Philip Young was dean of the Columbia Graduate School of Business and the executive director of the American Assembly (for background see Galambos, *Columbia University*, nos. 54, 1062, and 1159).

[7] Francis agreed to serve as one of Eisenhower's personal representatives for the Assembly (see Eisenhower to Francis, Nov. 1, 1951, EM. For a similar request by Eisenhower see Galambos, *Columbia University*, no. 1119).

[8] This letter was drafted by Ossian R. MacKenzie, an assistant to Dean Young and acting secretary of the National Policy Board of the American Assembly (see Minutes, Luncheon Meeting of the National Policy Board, American Assembly, Aug. 30, 1951; and MacKenzie to Schulz, Apr. 3, 1952, both in EM).

9   *Eisenhower Mss., Family File*

To MILTON STOVER EISENHOWER   *January 5, 1951*

Dear Milton:[1] It was careless of me to fail to tell you that we were stopping with the George Allens in Washington.[2] The week has been a very difficult one for us because I have been in a whirlwind of conferences, briefings and discussions, the net results of which have been to leave me in a state of practical confusion—almost shock![3]

We, of course, are most profoundly gratified that Helen continues to show some improvement.[4] The other day I ran into Ruth Butcher[5] who thought that when Helen was here in Washington, a week or so ago, she looked fine.

As of this moment my impression is that I would not try to influence Buddy[6] *too drastically*. He is completing college at a very early age and if he feels that he would like to do his military service in such a way as to achieve a commissioned status you should not forget that there is a very definite likelihood that it might prove to be the most valuable four years of his entire training period. His leadership qualities would be matured and developed, and when he starts, say four years from now, to take his graduate work, it is possible that he would be much better qualified to absorb and profit from the advanced instruction. Moreover, there is the possibility that Buddy is subconsciously thinking of all the years ahead of him and expressing, without knowing it, an ambition to do just a little bit more than his *minimum* share in building up the defenses of this country.[7]

I do not mean to say that you should by any manner of means fail to let him see *every* side of the picture. I merely believe that if he has a definite desire, to which you may be sure he has given a very great deal of consideration, you should not oppose him too severely.

It is difficult for us to realize that our children grow up and gradually acquire a capacity for reasoned decision—a capacity that seems to come to them sometimes overnight.

All of the above is just a bit of thinking aloud; I shall most certainly be delighted to talk or write to Buddy at any time you should want me to do so.

On my first hurried trip to Paris Mamie will stay behind.[8] She will go back to New York about Monday and be at the house there. I will be delighted if you would keep in touch with her.

My devoted love to Helen and Ruthie[9] and warm regard to yourself.
Devotedly

---

[1] Milton, Eisenhower's youngest brother, was president of Pennsylvania State College (for background see *Eisenhower Papers*, vols. I–XI).

[2] George Edward Allen, a Washington, D.C., lawyer and business executive, and his wife, Mary Keane Allen, were old friends of the Eisenhowers' (for background see Eisenhower, *At Ease*, pp. 282–87, 360–61; and *Eisenhower Papers*, vols. I–XI).

[3] Eisenhower had flown to Washington on New Year's Day for five days of meetings with government and military officials before departing for a preliminary European trip to NATO capitals on January 6 (see n. 8 below. For background on the General's hectic Washington schedule see nos. 1 and 2 in this volume).

[4] Milton's wife, Helen Eakin Eisenhower, had recently been released from the hospital following surgery (see Groesbeck to Eisenhower, Oct. 21, 1950, and Dwight Eisenhower to Milton Eisenhower, Nov. 21, 1950, both in EM, Family File). In his letter of January 3, Milton had written that an "x-ray . . . several weeks ago . . . showed no additional trouble" (EM).

[5] Ruth Barton Butcher was the ex-wife of Eisenhower's World War II naval aide Harry Cecil Butcher (for background see Galambos, *Columbia University*, no. 444).

[6] Buddy was Milton Eisenhower, Jr., then a student at Kansas State College, where his father had been president from 1943 until October 1950.

[7] After receiving his bachelor's degree in journalism, Buddy would undertake graduate study in marketing, economics, and advanced ROTC at Pennsylvania

State College. He later served as a lieutenant with the 6th Infantry Regiment in Germany (see Bela Kornitzer, *The Great American Heritage: The Story of the Five Eisenhower Brothers* [New York, 1955], p. 130; Milton Eisenhower to Dwight Eisenhower, May 17, 1951, EM, Family File; and *New York Times*, Sept. 28, 1954).

[8] Eisenhower would leave Washington, D.C., the afternoon of January 6 and fly to Paris for the start of a twenty-day, eleven-nation exploratory trip for NATO. Mirroring his week in Washington, the days in Europe would be filled with meetings, briefings, conferences, and formal calls. For developments see nos. 11, 14, 15, 16, and 17.

[9] Milton's daughter, Ruth Eakin Eisenhower.

10   *Eisenhower Mss.*

To Fowler McCormick   *January 5, 1951*

Dear Mr. McCormick:[01] After talking to you in New York, Dean Young sent me a message that he is more than ever convinced you are the right man to head up the Current Manpower Studies.[2]

Your acceptance would mean much to me. On the personal side it would assure me, as I go off to Europe, that this one important subject, which has been one of those at the University to which I have devoted most of my effort and intent, is in competent hands. It would likewise be a satisfaction to know that our manpower situation, currently one of the vital factors in the country's preparedness program, is being examined by capable individuals under competent leadership.[3]

In any event I send you my most profound thanks for the sympathetic consideration you have given the problem—one for which the country must quickly find a sound answer.

I am just completing a final frantic round of conferences and briefings preparatory to taking off for Paris,[4] or I would telephone to thank you a bit more personally.

With best wishes. *Sincerely*

[1] McCormick was the grandson of inventor Cyrus McCormick and chairman of the board of the International Harvester Company. During World War II he had served on an ordnance advisory committee and on the War Department's Manpower Board. For background on another invitation from Eisenhower to McCormick see Galambos, *Columbia University*, no. 739.

[2] The current Manpower Studies Plan was an extension of the Columbia Conservation of Human Resources Project (see *ibid.*, no. 1121), which, under the directorship of Eli Ginzberg, would soon complete a year of preliminary study of the nation's manpower strength.

[3] McCormick would not accept Eisenhower's offer. The chairmanship of what would be called the National Manpower Council would be held instead by San Francisco business executive James David Zellerbach. The objectives of the commission were to examine areas in which major manpower wastage occurred and to

recommend workable methods of utilizing and developing human resources. Columbia Graduate School of Business dean Philip Young would serve as deputy chairman of the fifteen-man body, made up of leaders from business, labor, agriculture, education, and science (see *New York Times*, Apr. 5, 1951; and Young to Eisenhower, Mar. 9 and Apr. 2, 1951, EM, for background on the council). For developments see no. 139.

[4] See nos. 1 and 9.

11   *Eisenhower Mss.*

To Jules Moch   *January 8, 1951*
Personal and confidential

Dear Mr. Minister:[01] This note brings to you my expression of appreciation for the meetings with the French staffs which you so kindly arranged today.[2] It was additionally an honor to meet with you and have lunch with you and your charming wife.[3]

The clearest conviction that I carried with me from the staff meetings was that the task the North Atlantic Treaty Nations have set for themselves can be accomplished. The one basic requirement is that each of the nations involved must demonstrate to all the nations its sincerity of purpose and its determination to perform at maximum rate and efficiency at carrying out its mission in our great common effort to achieve security.[4]

At this moment, one of my own principal tasks is to form judgments as to the clarity of purpose of each of the European nations and, provided this judgment can support a real conviction that each of our European allies is determined to do its very best, to present this picture to the American Government so as to insure maximum rate of flow of needed assistance from the other side of the Atlantic.

I shall be passing through Paris again later in January, just prior to my departure for the United States.[5] In the preparation of any memoranda which you may deem useful to me in further developing these purposes, I especially request that you clearly set forth all those aspects of French physical and moral effort which you consider will show the intensity of French purpose. Because of the great importance of your country's part in this whole effort, I am vastly concerned about this particular presentation.[6]

Please accept, my dear Mr. Minister, my assurance of continued respect and esteem. *Sincerely*

[1] Moch, a socialist, was the French Minister of Defense. During World War II he had fought with the Free French in the Mediterranean. After the war he had served as Minister of National Economy and Reconstruction (in October and November

1947) and as Minister of the Interior (from 1947 until July 1950, when he had become Defense Minister).

[2] Eisenhower had arrived in Paris, the first stop in his visit to Western Europe, on January 7 (for background see nos. 1 and 2). On that day he met with Field Marshal Montgomery (see no. 2) and with a number of American military officers and civilian officials. On the following day he met with French Premier René Pleven (see Galambos, *Columbia University*, no. 1045, n. 9). Later the General also talked with French military leaders and defense officials, including Moch. At this latter meeting Eisenhower learned of the French plans to increase their military strength and of the difficulties that had to be overcome before this goal could be realized. For records of these conversations see EM, Subject File, Trips, SHAPE no. 1; and State, *Foreign Relations, 1951*, vol. III, *European Security and the German Question, Part I*, pp. 402–7.

[3] Eisenhower had attended a brief luncheon with Moch and other defense officials on January 8. Madame Moch, the former Germaine Picard, was in attendance (see *New York Times*, Jan. 9, 1951).

[4] Eisenhower expressed this idea in all his talks with French leaders on this day and on January 9, when he called upon Vincent Auriol, President of the French Republic since January 1947. Auriol, like the French military leaders, told Eisenhower that France was determined to rearm and promised to do all he could "to mobilize the French Government and people" in support of Eisenhower's mission. He also stressed the importance of the French effort to defeat the Communist-backed insurgency in Indochina (see no. 28; and State, *Foreign Relations, 1951*, vol. III, *European Security and the German Question, Part I*, pp. 405–6).

[5] Eisenhower would return to Paris on January 23 and would resume his conversations with Moch and French military leaders on the following day. Eisenhower would discuss his search for a SHAPE headquarters site and the desirability of having the French government prepare the French people for the stationing of Americans in France. Eisenhower and Moch would also discuss the place of France in the proposed command structure (see Memorandum of Conversation, Jan. 24, 1951, EM, Subject File, Trips, SHAPE no. 1; and State, *Foreign Relations, 1951*, vol. III, *European Security and the German Question, Part I*, pp. 405–6).

[6] Eisenhower would leave Paris for Brussels, Belgium, the afternoon of January 9. For developments see nos. 14 and 16.

12   *State*, Foreign Relations, 1951, *vol. III, p. 401*[1]

To Dean Gooderham Acheson   *January 8, 1951*
Cable DTG 082345Z

I am becoming increasingly doubtful of the advisability of visiting Germany at this time. My doubts are based on the adverse propaganda surrounding the question of German rearmament.[2] As alternative would plan on meeting the three Allied commanders at some designated point outside Germany, probably Paris.[3]

[1] We have been unable to locate a copy of this document in the files of the Department of State.

[2] For background on the controversial issue of the rearmament of West Germany see Galambos, *Columbia University*, no. 1113. Secretary of State Acheson, in his briefing prior to Eisenhower's departure (see no. 2), had deplored the public attention given to the question whether NATO should use German troops in the defense of Western Europe. Acheson believed that the excessive publicity had given the Germans an exaggerated sense of their own importance. Moreover, Communist propaganda within Germany had sought to establish the notion that the move to allow the Germans to participate in the defense of the West stemmed from a desire to sacrifice German manpower as cannon fodder.

When Eisenhower had called upon René Pleven on this day (see the preceding document, n. 2), the French Prime Minister had said that many people felt that "German rearmament might be considered a provocation." Eisenhower, who had been warned by U.S. High Commissioner for Germany John Jay McCloy to remain silent on this issue, declined to comment and said that "great harm had been done by too much talk on this subject" (State, *Foreign Relations, 1951*, vol. III, *European Security and the German Question, Part I*, pp. 399, 404; McCloy to Acheson, no. 437, Jan. 11, 1951, EM, Subject File, Trips; *New York Times*, Jan. 7, 1951. For background on McCloy see *Eisenhower Papers*, vols. I–XI).

[3] In their replies (Jan. 9) to this cable both McCloy and Acheson strongly urged Eisenhower to visit Germany. They said that canceling his visit would hurt morale in West Germany and would lend credence to the idea, currently being spread by Communist propagandists, that Eisenhower disdained the Germans and had refused to treat them as honorable enemies of World War II. On January 14 General Gruenther would inform Acheson that Eisenhower would visit Germany as planned. According to Gruenther, Eisenhower's response to the Acheson and McCloy cables had been "Okay, okay, okay" (State, *Foreign Relations, 1951*, vol. III, *European Security and the German Question, Part I*, pp. 401–2). Eisenhower would meet with the American, British, and French commanders of the occupation forces in Germany at Heidelberg on January 20. He would also meet with German leaders, including Konrad Adenauer, Prime Minister since September 1949 (for background see Galambos, *Columbia University*), and former German generals Hans Speidel and Alfred Heusinger. Eisenhower told Speidel and Heusinger that he now realized that the German Army had not been a Nazi organization and that he had never meant to impugn the honor of German soldiers during World War II (State, *Foreign Relations, 1951*, vol. III, *European Security and the German Question, Part I*, pp. 445–47).

13   *Eisenhower Mss.*

To ARTHUR WILLIAM SIDNEY HERRINGTON   *January 8, 1951*

Dear Art:[01] Thank you for your kind letter and good wishes on my new job. I have been in such a spin the last two weeks that I am only now getting around to a little correspondence in Paris.[2] I find myself in full agreement with your comments on the international situation and believe that once we have built up a respectable strength instead of the present vacuum, the chances for avoiding war will be vastly improved.[3]

Should you come to Europe at any time I shall be delighted to see you. *Sincerely*

[1] Herrington was chairman of the board of the Marmon-Herrington Company, Inc., of Indianapolis, manufacturers of buses, trucks, and military vehicles. He had been a member of the Army Motor Transportation Corps following World War I and had served with Eisenhower in a transcontinental motor vehicle convoy in 1919 (see Galambos, *Chief of Staff*, no. 1758; *New York Times*, Mar. 25, 1950; and Eisenhower, *At Ease*, pp. 156–66, for additional background).

[2] For the General's trip to Europe see nos. 1, 2, and 9.

[3] In his letter of January 2 (EM) Herrington had written that he was now "breathing somewhat easier" concerning the world situation and believed that "the longer we can stave off direct action, the better chance we have of . . . avoiding it entirely." He assured Eisenhower that Marmon-Herrington's plants in Western Europe had tremendous military potential and added that he was "in a position to hit things hard on the production. . . ." For Eisenhower's views on the necessity of defense production see Galambos, *Columbia University*, nos. 753, 870, and 914.

14   *Eisenhower Mss.*

To SELDEN CHAPIN   *January 13, 1951*

Dear Mr. Ambassador:[01] Herewith a letter that I have written with the thought that it may be useful to you in the furtherance of NATO objectives in Holland.[2] I have not tried to be particularly discreet, but, if you should so desire, I have no objections whatsoever to your showing this letter to anyone in the Government whenever you think such action would be desirable. I would not want to provide copies indiscriminately to anyone.[3] *Sincerely*

[1] Chapin (USNA 1919) had been Ambassador Extraordinary and Plenipotentiary to the Netherlands since 1949. During World War II he had been Counselor, American Diplomatic Mission, and Executive Officer, Civil Affairs Section, Allied Force Headquarters (AFHQ); he had also served as chargé d'affaires in Algiers and Paris and had been the American representative to the French Committee of National Liberation (FCNL) (see Chandler, *War Years*, no. 1996, n. 2). In 1947 he had been appointed Envoy Extraordinary and Minister Plenipotentiary to Hungary, whose Communist government had declared him *persona non grata* in 1949.

[2] Eisenhower had arrived in the Netherlands the afternoon of January 10, following a brief visit to Belgium (for background see no. 11; for the trip to Belgium see no. 16, n. 9). He was welcomed at Amsterdam's Schipol Airport by Ambassador Chapin, Dutch Defense Minister Hendrik L. s'Jacob, and the Dutch Chiefs of Staff. Eisenhower attended an informal dinner at Ambassador Chapin's residence at The Hague, and on the following day he met with s'Jacob, the Dutch Chiefs of Staff, Prime Minister Willem Drees, and Foreign Minister Dirk Uipko Stikker (see no. 16). Eisenhower was dissatisfied with the attitude displayed by some of the Dutch officials (for details and for his reaction see the following document). The General flew from the Netherlands to Copenhagen, Denmark, the afternoon of January 11 (see no. 16).

[3] Chapin gave the letter to a number of Dutch officials, including Stikker and s'Jacob. The letter was subsequently leaked to the press (see State, *Foreign Relations*,

1951, vol. III, *European Security and the German Question, Part I*, pp. 436–37). The letter itself is the following document.

15

To SELDEN CHAPIN

Eisenhower Mss.

January 13, 1951

Dear Mr. Ambassador:[1] On the personal side, our visit to The Hague was completely enjoyable. The members of my party were, without exception, impressed by the abilities, the friendly attitude, and the breadth of comprehension of the Governmental officials with whom we came in contact. It was instructive, of course, to learn about the disruptive effects and internal difficulties caused by the Indonesian War. This we fully understood.[2]

On the purely official side, our impression was one of disappointment. Strictly speaking the Dutch Government does not seem to have a clearly defined goal commensurate with obvious needs, to be rapidly attained. Consequently, no description of the current program would convince the American Government that The Hague was showing a sense of urgency, readiness to sacrifice, and determination to pull its full share of the load.[3]

General Gruenther and I did not, by any means, have the feeling that any Dutch official was being deliberately blind to the existing threat. But we did feel that the struggle for efficiency, both in training and production, was over-emphasized to the point that it seemed to become the predominating influence rather than secondary to the overriding importance of providing the maximum of security for the country at the earliest possible date. Frankly, we can see no reason for the rather restricted target that the Dutch set for themselves. We do not understand why a country of 10 million people should not plan on a regular training and organizational framework of something on the order of four or five divisions, a framework which would, over the years, produce an additional group of reserve divisions and necessary auxiliary troops.[4]

We believe that a 12-month period of service is not satisfactory, either from the standpoint of training or of ready strength unless it is accompanied by frequent and thorough periods of refresher training. We do not recognize that, as of this moment, the Dutch could not instantly undertake a two-year program.[5] But we feel that if this longer period of service became the accepted doctrine of the country, and that even if, for the moment, the full term had to be restricted to officers, noncommissioned officers and specialists, yet, under this kind of program, there would not only be speedier progress in the country, but there would most certainly be a great increase in the confidence that other nations feel with respect to the Dutch effort. There would also be greater readiness on their part to provide help where help is needed.[6]

You understand, of course, that it is not our function to attempt interference with the internal workings of any country nor to advise, directly, any North Atlantic Treaty nation on the methods to be used in its military program. However, the questions discussed in this letter are of tremendous importance, particularly at this time when the picture presented by each nation to all the others should, if possible, be one showing a "higher than average" performance. This applies to the speed with which the plan is executed and, within reason, to the ultimate size of the force. Consistent with these considerations, the utmost in efficiency and economy should prevail, but both General Gruenther and I sincerely hope that the Dutch Government will arrange these considerations in an order of priority that does not put efficiency at the top.[7] *Very sincerely*

[1] For background on Chapin and on Eisenhower's visit to the Netherlands see the preceding document.

[2] The Netherlands had recently lost their rich and populous colony of Indonesia after an unsuccessful attempt to retain it by force. The United States, working in part through the United Nations, had favored Indonesian independence during the conflict; as a consequence Dutch-American relations had been affected adversely. Furthermore, the Dutch armed forces were in disarray as a result of the Indonesian War (see State, *Foreign Relations, 1950*, vol. III, *Western Europe*, pp. 1523–29; *New York Times*, Jan. 21, 1951; John C. Campbell, *The United States in World Affairs, 1948–1949* [New York, 1949], pp. 312–22; Dirk U. Stikker, *Men of Responsibility: A Memoir* [New York, 1966], pp. 113–52, 244, 285; Evelyn Colbert, *Southeast Asia in International Politics, 1941–1956* [Ithaca, N.Y., 1977], pp. 54–92; and George McTurnan Kahin, *Nationalism and Revolution in Indonesia* [Ithaca, N.Y., 1952]. See also no. 16; and Memorandum of Conversation with Dutch defense officials in EM, Subject File, Trips, SHAPE no. 1).

[3] In their meetings with Eisenhower the Dutch civilian officials had not responded with as much enthusiasm as he had hoped for. Chapin noted in a report to Washington that "the Dutch invariably put [their] worst foot forward" (State, *Foreign Relations, 1951*, vol. III, *European Security and the German Question, Part I*, pp. 412–15). At this time (according to Foreign Minister Dirk Stikker's later recollection), the Dutch defense officials had not yet produced any satisfactory plans for providing adequate military forces (Stikker, *Men of Responsibility*, p. 244; see also Vernon A. Walters, *Silent Missions* [Garden City, N.Y., 1978], p. 213. Transcripts may be found in EM, Subject File, Trips, SHAPE no. 1). After the conversations with Eisenhower, the Dutch Chief of Naval Staff told a member of the General's party that the Dutch military leaders, unlike their civilian superiors, thought that their rearmament programs were inadequate. He urged Eisenhower to press his government toward greater efforts (Memorandum for Record, *ibid.*).

[4] Although we have been unable to locate a copy of DC 28, which listed force requirements for the Medium Term Defense Plan (MTDP) (see Galambos, *Columbia University*, no. 1113; and Joint Secretariat, *The History of the Joint Chiefs of Staff: The Joint Chiefs of Staff and National Policy*, 5 vols. to date [Wilmington, Del., 1979–], vol. IV, *1950–1952*, by Walter S. Poole [1980], p. 213, n. 69, hereafter

cited as Poole, *History of the Joint Chiefs of Staff*, vol. IV, *1950–1952*), the force levels that the NATO member nations had pledged to attain by July 1, 1951, may be derived from an earlier memorandum from the JCS to the U.S. representative to the Standing Group (see no. 2, n. 1). In the fall of 1950 the Netherlands possessed only the equivalent of two-thirds of a division; by mid–1951 the Dutch armed forces were supposed to comprise a readily available force of three divisions. JCS plans called for a Dutch ground force of six regular or readily available reserve divisions by mid–1954; this figure was probably derived from the MTDP (Memorandum, "United States Forces in Defense of Western Europe," approved June 27, 1951, OS/D, 1951, Clas. Decimal File, CD 091.7 Europe; SM 2597 50, Oct. 18, 1950, CCS 092 Western Europe [3-12-48], Sec. 60. See also Brookings Institution, *Current Developments in United States Foreign Policy* 4, no. 2 [1950], 43–44). The Dutch military leaders, however, told Eisenhower that they had no troops then ready to fight and that it would be a long time before they had any (Memorandum of Conversation with Dutch defense officials, Jan. 11, 1951, EM, Subject File, Trips, SHAPE no. 1).

[5] This sentence should probably read, "We do recognize that . . ." (see State, *Foreign Relations, 1951*, vol. III, *European Security and the German Question, Part I*, p. 417).

[6] The Dutch national military service term for conscripts was twelve months; officers and noncommissioned officers served longer terms. In 1950 NATO's Military Committee had recommended that the required military service be at least eighteen months, and preferably two years (*ibid.*, p. 104; D-D/182, Nov. 15, 1950, NATO Files, microfilm. See also C7-D/10, Sept. 15, 1951, *ibid.*, and U.S. Congress, Senate, Committee on Foreign Relations and Committee on Armed Services, *Assignment of Ground Forces of the United States to Duty in the European Area: Hearings on S. Con. Res. 8*, 82d Cong., 1st sess., 1951, p. 10). The current term of service for inducted Americans was twenty-one months, although American military leaders hoped to increase this to twenty-seven months (Omar N. Bradley, "Toward a Long-Range Manpower Policy," *Army Information Digest* 6, no. 3 [1951], 15; see also Eisenhower to Anderson, Jan. 15, 1951, EM).

On January 15 Eisenhower would send two similar letters, advocating longer terms of military service, to the Ambassador to Denmark for use in that country (Eisenhower to Anderson, Jan. 15, 1951, EM).

[7] Chapin would show Eisenhower's letter to Stikker on January 16. Stikker said that the letter was both blunt and fair, and he asked Chapin to tell Eisenhower that he would try to have the Dutch government increase its defense efforts. Eisenhower's visit and this letter engendered much controversy within the Netherlands and may have led to the Dutch government's decision, announced in March, to increase defense expenditures and to extend the term of service for conscripted soldiers from twelve to eighteen months (see Eisenhower to Drees, Mar. 19, 1951, and Drees to Eisenhower, Apr. 3, 1951, EM. See also State, *Foreign Relations, 1951*, vol. III, *European Security and the German Question, Part I*, pp. 103–4, 413, 425–26, 430–31; Brookings Institution, *Current Developments in United States Foreign Policy* 4, no. 8 [1951], 21; Blair Bolles and Francis O. Wilcox, "The Armed Road to Peace: An Analysis of NATO," *Headline Series, Foreign Policy Association*, no. 92 [March–April 1952], 27; *New York Times*, Jan. 21, Feb. 2, 1951; *International Herald Tribune*, Paris ed., Mar. 19, 1951; and Stikker, *Men of Responsibility*, pp. 244–48). When Eisenhower reported on his European tour to President Truman and other government leaders on January 31 (see no. 18, n. 2), he criticized both the Dutch reluctance to build up their army and their desire to emphasize their naval forces instead (see State, *Foreign Relations, 1951*, vol. III, *European Security and the German Question, Part I*, pp. 452–55; see also C7-D/10,

Sept. 15, 1951, NATO Files, microfilm). An informal report on his visit to the Netherlands is contained in the following document.

16   *Eisenhower Mss.*

To William Averell Harriman   *January 14, 1951*
Top secret. Personal

Dear Averell:[01] We are catching a Sunday breathing space in London after a whirlwind tour that afforded us two days in Paris and one day, each, in Brussels, The Hague, Copenhagen and Oslo.[2] Tomorrow we have day-long conversations with the British Staff and, the following day, a talk with the NATO Deputies before taking off for Lisbon in the afternoon.[3]

There is little of a tangible nature to report—indeed, I suppose that it would be unrealistic to expect to do more during these early days than to gain an impression of the professional and political thinking in the various countries and, as a result, to begin to plan for long term developments.

In Paris, we were frequently told that the Government was much more concerned about the growth of "Neutralist" thinking than by the strength of the Communists. Nevertheless, they take extraordinary security measures around the various public offices and certainly provided plenty of visible protection for me and my party.[4]

The clearest evidence of French determination to push ahead courageously is the provision in their military service law that permits no exemptions for any reason whatsoever. While their term of service is, for the moment, only 18-months, they tell me that they intend to push this up progressively to two years as they find themselves able to provide instructors and other overhead for the increased force. The French will attempt to attain their '54 goals at an accelerated pace.[5]

In Paris I talked to the President, Pleven, Schuman, Moch, the Chiefs of Staff, General Juin, and Field Marshal Montgomery.[6] I encountered no defeatism but, on the other hand, there has not yet been sufficient progress in rearmament to justify any feeling of special gratification. Conversations with the principal American officials in Paris were most informative. Mr. Katz,[7] who seems to me to be a very dynamic person, is confident that if about four million a year were spent, intelligently, in France, the present effectiveness of Communist propaganda could be at least 75 percent destroyed. It is a point that I should like to see pursued by experts in that line. They should consult him. Incidentally, I was most favorably impressed by the quality of the American individuals that I met at Ambassador Bruce's house.[8]

In Brussels, we found a sense of urgency at least equal to that sensed in Paris. I was informed that the Government is going before the Parliament this coming week with a bill for 24 months' conscription; with a reasonable certainty that the bill will pass. I not only talked with all the principal Ministers but also with Mr. Spaak of the powerful Socialist Party, and with Mr. Motz and Baron Kronacker, leaders of the small Liberal Party. All of these men announced their intention to support NATO vigorously, although I failed to ask Mr. Spaak specifically about his attitude on the two-year conscription program. Mr. Murphy is doing a splendid job as the Ambassador. He was invited by the Government to be present at all meetings while I was there.[9]

In Holland, I think that both General Gruenther and I felt we encountered an atmosphere and type of thinking completely new to us.[10] There seems to be a fetish for worshipping "perfection and efficiency." If, in developing a plan, the Dutch discover anything that appears to be a bottleneck, they instantly trim the whole program to the rate of flow imposed by the bottleneck rather than to push for immediate enlargement of the passageway. I told them that we, in America, were doing many things in the arms production program that violated theoretical efficiency—but our Government did so because of its feeling of urgency in the present situation.

The Dutch have a military program based upon one year's initial training. This might be satisfactory if there were frequent callbacks to refresher training, but in the hurried look we had at their plan it appeared that their target both in quality and quantity was much lower than that of the Belgians, although the Dutch population is some 12 per cent larger than the Belgian.

The Dutch point out that, not only were they occupied by the Germans for several years, but they subsequently waged a costly conflict in Indonesia, a struggle which absorbed all of their training and overhead personnel. Consequently, they say it is now necessary, as a first priority, to produce the junior officers and noncommissioned officers needed for instructional and organizational purposes. Actually, I believe that among the troops they withdrew from Indonesia and demobilized, there must be a considerable amount of good cadre material.

The Foreign Minister in Holland, Mr. Stikker,[11] seems to be of a little different type than some of the other officials. He is quick, forceful, and possessed of a feeling of urgency in the matter of rearmament; the others seem to prefer talking in terms of 1954 rather than of July 1952. This does not mean to say that the other Ministers are not both likable and intelligent. We were personally impressed by several of them. But we could not pierce through the wall which stolid and good natured adherence to their gods of efficiency and economy has erected around them.

In Copenhagen, spirits seemed better. But the country is small—four million—and they feel terribly exposed. They are avoiding belligerent gestures (which is proper in any event) and are trying to develop a very well-trained home guard and a small active Army that can be made the basis of mobilization of the entire manpower. They have a one-year program, and as yet are unclear as to the amount of refresher training they will give to their reserve units.[12]

With respect to the several systems of training armies, it must be understood that if refresher training is on a sufficiently large scale, it tends to make good two of the deficiencies that normally arise when the initial training period is as short as one year. First, refresher training carries on and improves the training given initially. Secondly, and equally important, it supplies additional force in being—if this refresher training is intelligently carried on, its reinforcing functions for the active units can be most important. Incidentally, both General Gruenther and I felt that Mrs. Anderson[13] is highly respected in Copenhagen as our Ambassador. She seemed to us to be working hard at her job.

In Oslo, we encountered what we felt to be the most clear-sighted perception of the current situation that we have had, thus far, on the trip.[14] The Norwegians have a very young Defense Minister named Mr. Hauge who seems to be quite influential in the Government and who is working hard at the business of establishing a national defense.[15] They have a vast territory and only three million people. Their entire national income last year was one and one-half billion dollars. While their national budget, for all purposes, was only one-seventh of the entire income, an economic situation such as theirs cannot accurately be compared to one like ours. Their standard of living is low and I was told that there are only a few wealthy families in the whole country. These are shipping men.

The basis of the present Norwegian military training is ten months' compulsory service, but on to this they plan to attach frequent calls to refresher training varying in length from 60 to 90 days. While they should lengthen the tour of their initial service, we have not the slightest doubt as to their earnestness, intentions and sturdiness. *They will not again be occupied if they can avoid it.* Our purpose should be to make Norway, Denmark and Holland defense hedgehogs—all supported by a large naval and air force commanding the North Sea and surrounding waters.

We have talked, of course, about many phases of the situation and related programs. Some of these referred to the possibilities of local manufacture of munitions—things that we will talk over with Spofford, Batt and others.[16]

The Northern countries are deeply concerned over the German question and we have, on this, preserved the attitude that I discussed with you before I left.[17] We urge avoidance of public statements. We believe also in holding off military advances until the political situation has been properly clarified.

Up to this moment, my talks in Britain have been completely informal. Already I have run into one thing, however, that may have considerable significance. Some British individuals are sure that a number of the smaller countries are deliberately "failing to undertake a number of manufacturing projects of which they are capable because of a belief that the United States will provide all." The United States must find some way of determining, *at once*, that a nation is going full out in developing its own human and material resources for defense, as a condition of receiving American aid. It is a complicated business and it will defeat our purpose to make a bad error on either side of the question. (Another thing that I will talk to Batt about but maybe you can do something too.)

One more thing. Some individuals are also puzzled by what they believe to be our reluctance to use, to the maximum, existing manufacturing facilities. For example, the Phillips Electronics factory in Holland![18] All these things must be straightened out quickly. There is no time to lose!!

On the personal side, the trip has not been too difficult except that it gets wearing because of the crowded schedules of each day and the need for filling every hour with appointments. We have had a couple of fairly bad flying days, but our crew is a capable one. Yesterday we took off in a real snow storm from Oslo but reached here ahead of time.[19]

Gruenther or I shall probably write to you again before we return. In the meantime, the best of everything and, of course, warm personal regard. *Cordially*

[1] For background on millionaire statesman William Averell Harriman see *Eisenhower Papers*, vols. I–XI. At this time Harriman was serving as the President's Special Assistant on Foreign Affairs (see Galambos, *Columbia University*, no. 852; and Dean Acheson, *Present at the Creation: My Years in the State Department* [New York, 1969], pp. 410–11).

[2] On Eisenhower's exploratory trip to Europe and the NATO capitals see nos. 1, 11, and 15. On January 12 he had flown from Copenhagan to Oslo, Norway, and on the following day he had flown to London, where he was to remain until January 16 (see Eisenhower's itinerary in EM, Subject File, Trips; see also Walters, *Silent Missions*, pp. 213–19).

[3] On Monday, January 15, Eisenhower would meet with the British Chiefs of Staff in both morning and afternoon sessions. There is no record of their discussions in EM. He also met with Emanuel Shinwell, the United Kingdom's Minister of Defence since 1950 (he had previously served as Secretary of State for War from 1947 to 1950). Eisenhower later praised the British defense program and expressed his admiration for Shinwell's energetic efforts to prod the British military staffs to send more troops to the Continent (State, *Foreign Relations, 1951*, vol. III, *European Security and the German Question, Part I*, pp. 428–29, 452). On the following day he

met with NATO's Council of Deputies (see no. 2, n. 2). Eisenhower told the deputies that although he was encouraged by the increasingly confident attitude he had encountered, he was disappointed with the rearmament plans. The Europeans, he said, were not working swiftly enough to build up their forces "to meet [the] needs of [the] present crisis." Eisenhower said that all nations should meet the force goals of the MTDP (see no. 15, n. 4) before 1954, when NATO was to have achieved an adequate defensive force, by "telescoping [the] fulfillment of existing plans into [the] shortest possible time irrespective of formal schedules" (State, *Foreign Relations, 1951*, vol. III, *European Security and the German Question, Part I*, pp. 426–28).

On the afternoon of January 16 Eisenhower would fly to Lisbon, Portugal, for more talks with civilian and military leaders. Summaries of these talks, held on January 17, are in EM, Subject File, Trips, SHAPE no. 1. Antonio de Oliveira Salazar, Portuguese Prime Minister since 1932, would agree with Eisenhower's contention that concerted action by all the NATO nations would help prevent another war; he said that "every effort should be made to avoid war[,] which if it occurred would leave neither victor nor vanquished, but would be [a] universal catastrophe in which there would be little difference between victory and defeat." Eisenhower replied that "there was only one thing worse than war and that would be to have a war and lose it" (State, *Foreign Relations, 1951*, vol. III, *European Security and the German Question, Part I*, pp. 432–33). The Portuguese Foreign Minister also urged NATO to work with fascist Spain (which had not been invited to join NATO) in order to provide for a common defense of the Iberian Peninsula. Eisenhower acknowledged that there was a problem in this regard, but he said that the problem was political in nature and should be pursued through diplomatic channels. Later, when asked about Spain and NATO during his report to President Truman (see the preceding document, n. 7), Eisenhower said, "I feel about the question of keeping Spain out [of NATO] the same as I feel about keeping a sinner out of church. . . . You can't convert the sinner unless you let him inside the front door" (State, *Foreign Relations, 1951*, vol. III, *European Security and the German Question, Part I*, pp. 424–25, 434–35, 452, 454–55. See also SM 2597 50, Oct. 18, 1950, CCS 092 Western Europe [3-12-48], Sec. 60; and *New York Times*, Jan. 21, 1951). For background on the question of integrating Spain into the defensive systems of Western Europe see Poole, *History of the Joint Chiefs of Staff*, vol. IV, *1950-1952*, pp. 318–21; for developments, see no. 240.

Eisenhower would leave Portugal and fly to Rome, Italy, the afternoon of January 17 (see no. 18).

[4] For background on Eisenhower's visit to France see no. 11. He had discussed the problem of French neutralism with Premier René Pleven and President Vincent Auriol on January 8 and 9. Eisenhower compared the neutralists to American isolationists and stated that neutralism could be overcome if the supporters of Western defense put their minds to it (State, *Foreign Relations, 1951*, vol. III, *European Security and the German Question, Part I*, pp. 403, 405). Eisenhower would later describe the impressive French efforts to isolate him from Communist demonstrations by saying that he personally never saw a demonstrator in Paris (U.S. Congress, House, Committee on Armed Services and Committee on Foreign Affairs, *General Dwight Eisenhower's Testimony on the Mutual Defense Assistance Program*, in U.S. Congress, House, Committee on International Relations, *Selected Executive Session Hearings on the Committee, 1943-50*, vol. VI, *Military Assistance Programs*, pt. 2 [Washington, D.C., 1976], pp. 277–78).

[5] The goals Eisenhower is referring to were those outlined in the MTDP (see no. 15, n. 4). By 1954, according to the plan, the French Army was supposed to comprise twenty-eight divisions ninety days after the outbreak of a general war (D + 90) (Memorandum, "United States Forces in Defense of Western Europe,"

approved June 27, 1951, OS/D, 1951, Clas. Decimal File, CD 091.7 Europe). In the fall of 1950, however, the French had only six and one-third divisions available for NATO (SM 2597 50, Oct. 18, 1950, CCS 092 Western Europe [3-12-48], Sec. 60). The United States, fearing that the massive Chinese intervention in Korea presaged a third world war (see Galambos, *Columbia University*, nos. 1089 and 1096), had recently decided to meet its own 1954 rearmament goals by mid-1952. On December 14, 1950, President Truman had approved a report stating that the Chinese intervention had created a "new crisis" worldwide and that "the period of greatest danger" was directly ahead. The same report also stated that the United States should try to encourage, persuade, and enable the NATO nations to increase their own contributions to the defense of Western Europe (*ibid.*, no. 1129; State, *Foreign Relations, 1950*, vol. I, *National Security Affairs; Foreign Economic Policy* [1977], pp. 467-77. See also Poole, *History of the Joint Chiefs of Staff*, vol. IV, *1950-1952*, pp. 68-71, 79-81; and Omar N. Bradley and Clay Blair, *A General's Life: An Autobiography by General of the Army Omar N. Bradley* [New York, 1983], pp. 609-19).

Eisenhower later praised the French for enacting "one of the strictest, most inclusive conscription laws that would be possible to devise." He would tell George Catlett Marshall, Secretary of Defense since September 1950 (see Galambos, *Columbia University*, no. 982; for further background see *Eisenhower Papers*, vols. I-XI), that in its conscription procedures the French government had "so cracked down on its people that even a widow with five sons, four of whom have been killed, gets no exemption for the fifth son" ([Marshall] to Rosenberg, Jan. 29, 1951, OS/D, 1951, Clas. Decimal File, CD 381 General; Senate Committee on Foreign Relations and Committee on Armed Services, *Assignment of Ground Forces of the United States to Duty in the European Area*, 1951, p. 4; State, *Foreign Relations, 1951*, vol. III, *European Security and the German Question, Part I*, p. 452).

[6] For background on French President Vincent Auriol, Premier René Pleven, and Defense Minister Jules Moch see no. 11. Robert Schuman, Foreign Minister since July 1948, had previously been Finance Minister (1946-47) and Prime Minister (1947-48). During World War II he had been imprisoned by the Germans, had subsequently escaped, and had worked in the French underground. For background on General Alphonse Pierre Juin see Chandler, *War Years*; and *The Papers of Dwight David Eisenhower* (Baltimore, 1970-), vol. VI, *Occupation, 1945*, ed. Alfred D. Chandler, Jr., and Louis Galambos (1978), hereafter cited as Chandler and Galambos, *Occupation, 1945*. Juin was currently serving as French Resident General of Morocco. In March Eisenhower would appoint him to command the ground forces of central Europe (see no. 77). For background on Montgomery see no. 2; and *Eisenhower Papers*, vols. I-XI.

[7] Milton Katz (LL.B. Harvard 1931) had been American Special Representative in Europe under the Foreign Assistance Act of 1948 since June 1950. He also served as chairman of NATO's Defense Financial Economic Committee, which had been established in 1949 to advise the NAC (see no. 2) on the economic and financial aspects of NATO's defense measures (Ismay, *NATO*, pp. 178-80). During World War II he had served with the War Production Board, the Combined Production and Resources Board, and the Office of Strategic Services (OSS).

[8] David Kirkpatrick Este Bruce, Ambassador to France since May 1949, had served in the OSS during World War II. In 1947 he had become Assistant Secretary of Commerce, and in May 1948 he had been appointed Chief of the Economic Cooperation Administration mission in France. Before entering government service he had practiced law in Baltimore, Maryland. Eisenhower had dined with Bruce the evening of January 7.

[9] Eisenhower had flown from Paris to Brussels the afternoon of January 9 (for background see no. 11). There he met with Robert Daniel Murphy, U.S. Ambassador to Belgium since September 1949 and a former wartime associate of Eisen-

hower's (for background see *Eisenhower Papers*, vols. I–XI). At Murphy's residence that evening Eisenhower met Paul-Henri Spaak (LL.D. Université Libre de Bruxelles 1921), a leader of the Belgian socialists who had served his country as Prime Minister and Minister of Foreign Affairs at various times from 1938 until 1950. In 1946 he had been President of the United Nations General Assembly, and in 1949 he had become President of the Consultative Assembly of the Council of Europe. An original signer of the North Atlantic Treaty, Spaak was a tireless supporter of European international organizations and Western solidarity. In his conversation with Eisenhower he told the General that Europe should strive toward a new concept of an integrated defense force. He pledged his support to Eisenhower, whom he thought could build European unity because he was uninfluenced by traditional European rivalries and prejudices (State, *Foreign Relations, 1951*, vol. III, *European Security and the German Question, Part I*, pp. 409–10).

On the following day Eisenhower conferred with a number of Belgian military and civilian officials, including Prime Minister Joseph Pholien, Minister of Foreign Affairs Paul van Zeeland, Minister of Defense Édouard De Greef, and the chiefs of staff of the Belgian armed forces. He also met with political leaders Roger Motz, President of the Liberal party since 1944 and member of the Belgian Senate since 1946; and Baron Paul Georges Kronacker, a former cabinet minister and member of the Belgian House of Representatives. Eisenhower told Motz and Kronacker, whose Liberal party had opposed the ruling Catholic party's effort to extend the conscription period, that while he understood the difficulties of local politics, a "proportionate and united" Belgian effort to increase their defense effort would lead to greater American support for European defense. Records of Eisenhower's talks with Belgian leaders are in *ibid.*, pp. 410–12, 415–16; and EM, Subject File, Trips, SHAPE no. 1.

Belgium would extend its conscription period to twenty-four months in March (see U.S. Congress, Senate, Subcommittee on Foreign Relations, *United States Foreign-Aid Programs in Europe: Hearings on United States Economic and Military Assistance to Free Europe*, 82d Cong., 1st sess., 1951, pp. 231–35. See also State, *Foreign Relations, 1951*, vol. III, *European Security and the German Question, Part I*, pp. 182–84; Eisenhower, *At Ease*, p. 373; and no. 56).

[10] Eisenhower's trip to the Netherlands is covered in nos. 14 and 15.

[11] Dirk Uipko Stikker (LL.D. University of Groningen 1922) had been Minister of Foreign Affairs of the Netherlands since August 1948. Before entering government service he had been managing director of the Heineken Lagerbeer Brewery Company. At this time he was also chairman of the Council of the Organization for European Economic Cooperation, created in 1948 to foster economic integration and growth (Paul-Henri Spaak [see n. 9 above] had been the first chairman of this organization) (see Stikker, *Men of Responsibility*, pp. 165–72). A record of Eisenhower's conversation with Stikker on January 10 is in State, *Foreign Relations, 1951*, vol. III, *European Security and the German Question, Part I*, pp. 413–14; see also no. 15, n. 7. At that time Stikker told Eisenhower that he favored German rearmament (see no. 12) and that if war came, the fighting should be as far to the east (in Germany) as possible.

[12] Eisenhower had flown from the Netherlands to Copenhagen, Denmark, the afternoon of January 11. On the following day he had called upon King Frederik IX (see Chandler and Galambos, *Occupation, 1945*, no. 463) and later met with Danish political leaders and military officials. In these meetings Eisenhower learned of Danish plans to place their forces under Eisenhower's command and of their thirty-thousand-man home guard force. The home guards were for the most part former resistance fighters who still kept their rifles, automatic weapons, and explosives in their homes. Eisenhower again urged his listeners to make greater efforts so that the amount of aid the United States was planning to give could be better

justified. He also stressed the need for an adequate period of instruction for conscripts, with two years as a desirable goal. At a luncheon that same day Danish military leaders told members of Eisenhower's party that the General's strong presentation would be influential in prodding the Danish government to increase the magnitude of its defense effort. Records of Eisenhower's conversations with the Danes may be found in EM, Subject File, Trips, SHAPE no. 1; and State, *Foreign Relations, 1951*, vol. III, *European Security and the German Question, Part I*, pp. 418–19. Eisenhower would leave Denmark for Oslo, Norway, the afternoon of January 12.

[13] Eugenie Moore Anderson had been U.S. Ambassador to Denmark since 1949. In 1948 she had been a member of the Democratic National Committee; she had also represented Minnesota at the Democratic National Convention that had renominated President Truman.

[14] Eisenhower's round of appointments with Norwegian leaders had taken place during the morning of January 13. He met with the King, the Crown Prince, the Prime Minister, the Foreign Minister, the Defense Minister (see n. 15 below), and the Norwegian military chiefs. The military leaders told him of their efforts to improve their combat readiness and listed their deficiencies. Among the latter were the lack of trained commissioned and noncommissioned army officers; the inefficiency of their navy (in part a result of the short conscription period); and the shortage of aircraft and aircraft parts. Eisenhower urged the Norwegians to make even greater efforts in the common defense and said that the NATO nations could choose either to "meander" or to "go forward, lift up our hearts and heads, and find we have arrived" (State, *Foreign Relations, 1951*, vol. III, *European Security and the German Question, Part I*, pp. 421–24; see also the account of these conferences in EM, Subject File, Trips, SHAPE no. 1). The Norwegians would soon take steps to increase the size and efficiency of their military forces (see Senate, Subcommittee on Foreign Relations, *United States Foreign-Aid Programs in Europe: Hearings*, 1951, p. 99).

[15] Jens Christian Hauge, Minister of Defense since November 1945, had previously been secretary to the Norwegian Prime Minister. During World War II he had served in the Norwegian resistance movement. In his conversation with Eisenhower on January 13 he outlined the history and current status of Norway's defense program, which he characterized as a "brave beginning but no more and no less." Hauge also advocated a fair method for apportioning the burdens of defense and promised that his country "would not shirk its duty and had a good conscience given its resources and capabilities" (State, *Foreign Relations, 1951*, vol. III, *European Security and the German Question, Part I*, pp. 422–23).

[16] For background on Charles Merville Spofford, U.S. representative to and chairman of NATO's Council of Deputies since July 1950, see Galambos, *Columbia University*, no. 303, n. 19. William Loren Batt (D.Eng. Purdue 1933), Chief of the Economic Cooperation Act mission to Great Britain since November 1950, had recently been appointed U.S. representative to NATO's Defense Production Board (see Galambos, *Columbia University*, no. 1095, n. 1). Before assuming these posts Batt had been president of S.K.F. Industries.

[17] Eisenhower had discussed the controversial issue of German rearmament with the Dutch, the Danes, and the Norwegians. (For Dutch Foreign Minister Stikker's views see n. 11 above.) Leaders of all three nations wanted to fight any future battles in Germany rather than in their own countries; they all realized that such a "forward strategy" necessitated the use of German troops (State, *Foreign Relations, 1951*, vol. III, *European Security and the German Question, Part I*, pp. 419, 423). Eisenhower believed that nothing should be done to exacerbate feelings on the issue (see no. 12).

[18] In March 1950 the Phillips Corporation at Eindhoven, the Netherlands, had complained that it had been discriminated against when contracts for producing

military supplies had been awarded. The restrictions at question stemmed from the fact that during World War II the North American branch of the company had been accused of breaches of security. Between March and July 1950 the State Department had lifted the restrictions placed upon Phillips's American and European branches, but by then most of the money for military aid programs had been committed elsewhere (see Marshall to Eisenhower, May 31, 1951, OS/D, 1951, Clas. Decimal File, CD 370.21 [SHAPE 1951]). Eisenhower would again tell Harriman of his belief that the industrial capacity of Europe was not being used to its fullest extent (see no. 81).

[19] For further developments concerning Eisenhower's trip to Europe see no. 18.

17   *Eisenhower Mss.*

To Bernard Law Montgomery   *January 15, 1951*

Dear Monty: As I expressed to you in our recent conference in Paris,[1] I have not yet determined when I shall be in the position actively to assume field command of the forces which the Pact nations are now prepared to assign to me. I am urgently studying the problem, and have set up in Paris a small advanced planning group, with representatives from the various NATO countries to go into all aspects to include staff and command organization, location of headquarters, and other allied matters.[2] It will, however, be some time yet before I can firm up in my own mind exactly what the proper solution to these important basic problems should be. Until I can reach these conclusions I shall have neither the facilities nor the staff available to permit me usefully to take over active command.

Meanwhile, I should like to have you continue under your present organization and responsibilities until I am in a position to advise you otherwise.[3] Particularly I should like for you and your staff to know that I deeply appreciate the work you have done and are doing, and that I shall hope to make full use of your combined knowledge, experience and demonstrated abilities in the future activities of NATO.[4] *As ever*

[1] Eisenhower had met with Montgomery on January 7, when he had arrived in France on the first stop of his trip to the NATO capitals (for background see no. 11). There is no record in EM of any of the General's conversations with Montgomery. On January 10 David Bruce, the U.S. Ambassador to France (see no. 16), had informed Eisenhower's party that the French were aware of Eisenhower's meetings and feared that he would offer Montgomery direct command of NATO's Western European troops in addition to the position of deputy supreme allied commander (State, *Foreign Relations, 1951*, vol. III, *European Security and the German Question, Part I*, pp. 406–7).

[2] A SHAPE planning group had been established at the Hotel Astoria in Paris. Under the command of Colonel Benjamin Easton Thurston (USMA 1926), it

studied problems of command, organization, and staffing. It soon included officers from nine NATO nations (see Gruenther to Bruce *et al.*, Dec. 20, 1950, EM; Ismay, *NATO*, pp. 37–38; and State, *Foreign Relations, 1951*, vol. III, *European Security and the German Question, Part I*, pp. 393–94). Eisenhower had met with this group when he arrived in Paris on January 7. He would choose Versailles as the site of his headquarters (see no. 60; and *New York Times*, Jan. 24, 1951).

[3] At this time Field Marshal Montgomery was chairman of the Commanders-in-Chief Committee of the Western Union (for background see Galambos, *Columbia University*, nos. 375, n. 4, and 1134). The Western Union Command Organization had been studying the problems of creating and controlling a multinational military force to defend the central European area, and its plans were to prove useful to Eisenhower and his staff in the establishment of SHAPE and its subordinate commands (Ismay, *NATO*, pp. 9, 37–38. See also Wright to Collins *et al.*, Nov. 29, 1950, CCS 092 Western Europe [3-12-48], Sec. 63; and Lindsay to Director, Joint Staff, Dec. 7, 1950, *ibid.*, Sec. 64).

[4] Eisenhower would meet with Montgomery on January 16 in London. He would appoint Montgomery as Deputy SACEUR in March (see no. 74).

18   *Eisenhower Mss., Family File*

To Mamie Doud Eisenhower   *January 17, 1951*
Cable

Arrived in Rome this evening in good shape.[1] I plan on calling you from Luxembourg Friday around noon New York time.[2] Staff is still looking at several houses and I hope to get a chance to pick one out when in Paris next week.[3] *Love*

[1] Eisenhower had arrived in Italy after flying from Portugal (for background see no. 16). On January 18 he met with a number of political and military leaders, including Italy's Prime Minister, Foreign Minister, Defense Minister, and military service chiefs. Eisenhower learned of Italy's armament program, which was to result in a total force of five divisions available to Eisenhower by mid-1951. Randolfo Pacciardi, Italian Defense Minister since 1948, told Eisenhower that Italy had received only a small amount of the total American military aid sent to Europe. He urged the General to make sure that his country received matériel in proportion to the efforts his countrymen were making. Eisenhower told Pacciardi that he would look into the matter and inquired about Italy's feelings toward its neighbor Yugoslavia (see no. 142; and State, *Foreign Relations, 1951*, vol. III, *European Security and the German Question, Part I*, pp. 438–44. See also SM 2597 50, Oct. 18, 1950, CCS 092 Western Europe [3-12-48], Sec. 60; and Memorandums of Conversations in EM, Trips, SHAPE no. 1).

[2] Eisenhower would leave Italy for Luxembourg the morning of January 19. After meetings with leaders there he reported to President Truman on January 31 that Luxembourg, while short of manpower, had presented an "optimistic picture" and had recently established a program of universal military service (State, *Foreign Relations, 1951*, vol. III, *European Security and the German Question, Part I*, p. 453). Eisenhower's next stop was Germany (Jan. 20–23), where he visited American, Allied, and German officials in Heidelberg, Darmstadt, and Frankfort. From

Germany he returned to Paris (see no. 11; and n. 3 below), where he remained until January 25, when he flew to Iceland for more discussions with local officials. On January 26 Eisenhower would fly to Ottawa, Canada, for additional talks, and on the following day he would return to the United States. From January 27 until January 31 (while staying at West Point, New York), he would prepare a series of reports to the President, the Congress, and NATO's Standing Group on his exploratory tour. Eisenhower would finally return to Washington on January 31 (see no. 23; Eisenhower, *At Ease*, pp. 366–68; Walters, *Silent Missions*, pp. 217–19; and State, *Foreign Relations, 1951*, vol. III, *European Security and the German Question, Part I*, pp. 445–58). Eisenhower's discussions with leaders in Italy, Luxembourg, and Iceland are in EM, Subject File, Trips, SHAPE no. 1).

[3] A suitable house for the Eisenhowers would prove difficult to find (see no. 83; and Alden Hatch, *Red Carpet for Mamie* [New York, 1954], pp. 229–30). After many delays and a long wait for necessary renovations and redecorating, the General and his wife would move into the Villa St. Pierre at Marnes-la-Coquette, ten miles west of Paris, in August 1951 (see *ibid.*, pp. 231–33; Dorothy Brandon, *Mamie Doud Eisenhower: A Portrait of a First Lady* [New York, 1954], pp. 267–68; and no. 393).

19   *Eisenhower Mss.*

To Herman Stok   *January 17, 1951*

Dear Mr. Stok:[0] It pleased me very much to hear about your organization[1] and to receive such an inspiring offer of assistance. As you know, I am on tour at the present time[2] and have not as yet been able to establish more than a small nucleus of my permanent staff.[3]

For these reasons, it is impossible for me to say, at the moment, just how your organization might assist us in the great task ahead. However, I am passing your letter to a member of my staff who will give the matter full consideration and ask the appropriate individual or agency to communicate with you directly.

With appreciation and every good wish to you and the members of the Youth Amateur Radio Organization.[4] *Sincerely*

[1] Stok was president of the Youth Amateur Radio Organization of the Netherlands.
[2] On this day Eisenhower was on a visit to Portugal, where he met with Prime Minister Antonio de Oliveira Salazar, President Antonio Oscar de Fragoso Carmona, and the chiefs of the Portuguese Army and Navy (see no. 16). In the afternoon the General flew to Rome.
[3] The process of selecting and organizing the NATO staff would prove to be long and complex (for further information see Peter Lyon, *Eisenhower: Portrait of the Hero* [Boston, 1974], pp. 421–22; and nos. 59, 106, and 149).
[4] There is no further correspondence with Stok in EM. For other offers of assistance to SHAPE see nos. 237 and 496.

To Louis Francis Albert Mountbatten   *January 18, 1951*

Dear Dickie:[1] I am so sorry that we did not see each other in London, but I understand completely that you were fully engaged during the weekend. My brief stay in England was extremely enjoyable, as it provided an opportunity to see a great number of friends.[2]

With regard to General Wildman-Lushington, it is impossible to make any commitment at the present time. However, I am glad to have your recommendation.[3] We intend to build up the staff slowly, hoping to keep it small but representative of all the nations in the Pact.[4]

With warm regards and the very best of wishes. *As ever*

[1] Earl Mountbatten of Burma had been appointed Fourth Sea Lord of the British Admiralty in 1950. During World War II he had been Supreme Allied Commander in Southeast Asia (SACSEA), and afterward he had served first as Viceroy and then as Governor General of India (for background see Galambos, *Columbia University*, no. 1087; and Chandler, *War Years*, vols. I–III).

[2] Eisenhower wrote this message from Italy. While in London (Jan. 13–16), he had met with British government officials and several of his World War II associates, among them James Gault, Jock Whiteley, Louis Greig, and Field Marshal Montgomery (see appointment calendar).

[3] In his letter of January 4 (EM) Mountbatten had recommended Major General Godfrey Edward Wildman-Lushington of the Royal Marines for a position on Eisenhower's staff. Wildman-Lushington had been Mountbatten's Chief of Staff of Combined Operations from 1942 to 1943 and his Assistant Chief of Staff in the Southeast Asia Command. "I doubt if there is anybody more experienced in inter-Service inter-Allied headquarters work . . . ," wrote Mountbatten.

[4] Wildman-Lushington would not join Eisenhower's staff; he would instead become chief executive of the Sulfur Exploration Syndicate.

21   *Eisenhower Mss.*

To Willis Dale Crittenberger   *January 18, 1951*

Dear Critt:[01] Your letter in regard to Captain Joseph Smolenski[2] has only just reached me but I do appreciate the interest which prompted you to write. We seem to have a good navigator as we haven't been lost as yet but we certainly will keep your recommendation in mind.[3]

Thanks very much to both you and Josephine[4] for your good wishes. *Sincerely*

[1] Lieutenant General Crittenberger (USMA 1913) was the commanding general of the First Army and chairman of the U.S. delegation to the United Nations Military Staff Committee (for background on the general see Galambos, *Chief of Staff*).

[2] In his letter of January 2, 1951 (EM), Crittenberger had recommended that Eisenhower consider Captain Joseph Smolenski (USAF) for the position of navigator on the plane the General would use as NATO commander. Crittenberger wrote that Smolenski had been his navigator while he served as Commander in Chief, Caribbean, and that he was, "consistently courteous, efficient . . . a man of outstanding ability," and "a reliable officer . . . of high moral ethics."

[3] Eisenhower would not use Smolenski but instead would keep the navigator he presently had, Captain Vincent Puglisi (USAF) (see Cannon to Schulz, Dec. 27, 1950; Eisenhower to Puglisi, Nov. 2, 1951; and trip itineraries, all in EM, Subject File, Aircraft.

[4] Crittenberger's wife, the former Josephine Frost Woodhull.

22   *Eisenhower Mss.*

To Forrest Percival Sherman   *February 4, 1951*

Dear Admiral Sherman:[1] I am writing this letter because of a conviction that I may have inadvertently been guilty of an injustice towards a distinguished naval officer, Admiral Alan G. Kirk, now retired and serving as the American Ambassador to the Soviet Union.

Admiral Kirk served under my command in two critical battle operations in World War II and, in a position of great responsibility, he performed his duties gallantly and brilliantly.[2] For these services he has never received the Distinguished Service Medal of the Navy.[3] In one amphibious landing, that in Sicily, he landed his troops under such conditions of weather that my Naval Commander in Chief, Admiral Cunningham, pronounced it the finest act of seamanship he had seen in his long Navy service.[4] Admiral Kirk's leadership at the critical landings in Normandy in 1944 was equally important to victory.[5] Later he served as my U.S. Naval Commander in Europe, in which capacity he measured up, in every respect, to the reputation he had already established.

At the end of hostilities, I apparently made the false assumption that Admiral Kirk would be duly recommended by U.S. Navy officers for the Distinguished Service Medal of his service. Consequently, I have obviously been guilty of a neglect that has worked to the disadvantage of Admiral Kirk, because it seems clear to me that, if the character of his service had been understood in the Navy Department, the Distinguished Service Medal would long since have been awarded him.[6]

In any event, I sincerely hope that such an award can now be made; approval of this recommendation would lift a real load from my mind.[7]
Sincerely

[1] Admiral Sherman had been Chief of Naval Operations (CNO) since November 1949 (for background see Galambos, *Chief of Staff* and *Columbia University*). This letter was drafted by a member of Eisenhower's staff.

[2] Admiral Alan Goodrich Kirk (USNA 1909) had commanded the U.S. naval task forces under Eisenhower during both the invasion of Sicily in 1943 and the D-day invasion of Normandy. He afterward served as Commander of U.S. Naval Forces, France, from September of 1944 to June 1945. In 1949 he was appointed U.S. Ambassador to the Soviet Union (for background on Kirk's career see Chandler, *War Years*; *New York Times*, Oct. 6, 1963; Lydia Kirk, *Postmarked Moscow* [New York, 1952]; and EM, Subject File, Alan Goodrich Kirk).

[3] Following the successful landing and invasion of Sicily, Eisenhower recommended Kirk for the Army's Distinguished Service Medal, which he received in 1944; but no similar action had yet been taken regarding the Navy's comparable decoration (see Chandler, *War Years*, no. 1191).

[4] For background on Kirk's role in the invasion of Sicily and on this remark by British Admiral of the Fleet Andrew Browne Cunningham see Eisenhower, *Crusade in Europe*, p. 173; and Samuel Eliot Morison, *Sicily-Salerno-Anzio, January 1943-June 1944*, History of United States Naval Operations in World War II, vol. IX (1954; reprint ed., Boston, 1964), pp. 126–47. For information on Cunningham's career see Chandler, *War Years*.

[5] On Kirk's service as Commander of the Western Naval Task Force, which landed American troops and materials on Omaha and Utah beaches see Chandler, *War Years*, nos. 1592, 1739, and 1782; and Samuel Eliot Morison, *The Invasion of France and Germany: 1944-1945*, History of United States Naval Operations in World War II, vol. XI (1957; reprint ed., Boston, 1964), pp. 29–30, 52–56, 152, 155, 162, 168.

[6] Sherman informed Eisenhower on February 6 (EM) that he had recommended to the Secretary of the Navy that Kirk be awarded the Navy's Distinguished Service Medal for his World War II accomplishments. On March 5 Eisenhower sent Kirk a copy of Sherman's letter, adding in his own hand, "Possibly this is secret information—but, I trust you to observe such requirements if they apply. I hope it works!"

[7] Kirk would be awarded the Navy's Distinguished Service Medal later this year. On March 13 (EM) Sherman wrote Eisenhower, "Pursuant to your recommendation . . . I am glad to report that on March 12, 1951, the Secretary [of the Navy] approved such an award for Admiral Kirk."

23   *Bermingham Papers*

To EDWARD JOHN BERMINGHAM   *February 8, 1951*

Dear Ed:[1] Probably you have read in press reports the general tenor of the convictions I have formed with respect to the current American problem of national security.[2] I assure you that I approach this whole matter from no other standpoint than that of the enlightened self-interest of our country—I sincerely wish that I knew of some way we could possibly sustain our economy, our prosperity and, indeed, our very existence in a world where all other countries that are important to us have fallen, one by one, under Soviet domination.[3] I wish I could believe that we could, over the long term, secure adequate supplies of manganese, uranium, and a number of other vital materials without the need for assisting in the defense of countries other than our own.[4] I wish I knew how to ignore the menace that would arise for us if the Western European industrial complex and its enormous pool of skilled labor would fall under the domination of a dictatorial government.[5]

On the other hand, although I recognize certain vital interdependencies between ourselves and foreign countries, I share most emphatically the average American's understanding that this country cannot carry the world on its own shoulders—that unless we have a cooperative effort, then we, as a nation, will be forced back into a constantly narrowing limit of influence and existence—a situation that, if ever faced, will be indeed a black and bleak one.[6] So, the only answer I see in this whole unfortunate business is to make certain that we are doing our own part in a cooperative enterprise and then to assert the full influence deriving from our financial, economic, political and military power to see that the other free nations of the world, particularly those of Western Europe, do likewise.[7] This middle ground solution is, of course, unacceptable, both to the "do-gooders" and to the strict isolationists.[8] For myself, it is a solution that holds me to a job that is crowded with nothing but personal inconvenience and sacrifice. Of course, I need not speak to you on this point, as you well know how deeply my heart has become involved in the effort to do something really constructive at Columbia and, through it, for our country.[9] The only reason for mentioning this personal angle is to reinforce my earlier observations that I most urgently *wish* I could find some other solution that would bear the test of what I conceive to be simple logic.

In any event, I wanted you to know that my participation in this particular problem carries no implication of my approval of governmental policies in other parts of the world, of any special political philosophy here at home, or of anything else that could stamp me as a partisan or a member of any political or any other group. I am no more now a member of any Administration than I have been a member of any Administration during the 40 years since I first entered the military service.[10]

Of course, I am quite sure that you understand all these things. But I am quite certain also that, because you have been such a good friend of mine, you will from time to time be asked by others as to the general implications of my convictions in this matter. I thought you might be interested, therefore, in having this reiteration of my views. I shall most certainly try my very best to do my duty as a soldier and, when called upon, will express my convictions concerning the security position of the United States and the requirements that those convictions place upon us. But, beyond this, I refuse to be identified or tagged as an agent for any particular political organization or group.

When you see again any of the friends that you collected at your luncheon in Chicago, an event that I always look back upon with the greatest pleasure, I hope that you will remember me warmly to each of them.[11]

Please convey my greetings to Mrs. Bermingham[12] and to the children and, of course, warmest regards to yourself.[13] *Cordially*

---

[1] Bermingham was a retired investment executive and Columbia University alumnus who was involved in university fund-raising and other activities. He frequently represented Columbia in discussions with western and midwestern businessmen, seeking support for university projects. He would also become active in Eisenhower's presidential campaign (for background see Galambos, *Columbia University*, nos. 381, 593, and 730).

[2] These press reports concerned Eisenhower's series of meetings and speeches in Washington from January 31 to February 2, following his tour of the NATO nations (for background on the trip see nos. 9, 14, and 16).

[3] In his speeches and discussions in Washington Eisenhower had strongly urged all-out American participation in NATO. He had as a result been severely criticized by certain Republican congressmen who were at odds with Truman over his decision to send U.S. troops to Korea without congressional consent. Senators Kenneth Spicer Wherry of Nebraska and Robert Alphonso Taft of Ohio, both of whom had voted against the NATO treaty, were opposed to the President's assignment of troops to Europe on his own authority, with Wherry offering a resolution to that effect. These senators accused Eisenhower of adhering too closely to Administration policies and of being an advocate of other Truman programs as well. It was with the thought of answering these allegations that Eisenhower wrote to Bermingham (see Robert J. Donovan, *Tumultuous Years: The Presidency of Harry S. Truman, 1949-1953* [New York, 1982], pp. 217-24; Lyon, *Portrait of the Hero*, p. 419; and *New York Times*, Feb. 2, 4, 1951).

[4] In his discussions of the NATO tour Eisenhower had stressed the manner in which the United States and the nations of Western Europe were interrelated. The General said that if America's European allies fell to the Communists, their colonies, which depended upon them for finished goods, would be forced to follow Europe into communism. Under these circumstances the resources then being imported by the United States from the colonial nations would be unattainable (see Report to the Nation by Radio and Television, Feb. 2, 1951, in EM, Subject File, Speeches; *New York Times*, Feb. 2, 3, 1951; House of Representatives, *Hearings before the Committee on Armed Services and Foreign Affairs*, Executive Session, in EM, Subject File, Hearings; and House Committee on International Relations, *Selected Executive Session Hearings, 1943-50*, vol. VI, *Military Assistance Programs*, pt. 2, pp. 294-97).

[5] During a meeting with the cabinet on January 31 Eisenhower had said that Western Europe contained approximately 350 million skilled and educated people whom America could not afford to lose to Russia. The military and industrial exploitation of these millions by the Communists would leave the United States "gravely imperiled, grossly imperiled" (see State, *Foreign Relations, 1951*, vol. III, *European Security and the German Question, Part I*, p. 450; and Senate Committee on Foreign Relations and Committee on Armed Services, *Assignment of Ground Forces of the United States to Duty in the European Area*, 1951, p. 3).

[6] In his testimony before congressional committees on February 1 and 2 Eisenhower had stressed that to be successful the NATO effort had to be a cooperative enterprise of the United States and Western Europe. Although America's contributions in manpower and the production of war materials would at first be greater than those of its allies, the European countries would assume growing responsibilities as the program progressed (see State, *Foreign Relations, 1951*, vol. III, *European Security and the German Question, Part I*, pp. 451-54; and House Committee on International Relations, *Selected Executive Session Hearings, 1943-50*, vol. VI, *Military Assistance Programs*, pt. 2, p. 287).

[7] According to Eisenhower, the assignment of U.S. troops and the exportation of military goods to the NATO nations would boost the morale of the countries of Western Europe. Even though Europe had been devastated by World War II, there was evidence of "a rejuvenation, a growth of determination, a spirit to . . . try to live the lives of freemen." The uplifting of European spirit and the nurturing of its morale were, as Eisenhower saw it, the primary goals of NATO and the most important role of the United States in its leadership position within the pact (see Senate Committee on Foreign Relations and Committee on Armed Services, *Assignment of Ground Forces of the United States to Duty in the European Area*, 1951, pp. 3-4).

[8] For background on recent American isolationist tendencies and Eisenhower's thoughts on this subject see no. 7.

[9] On Eisenhower's reaction to accepting the position of supreme commander of NATO and on the effect it would have on his personal life see Galambos, *Columbia University*, no. 1045; see the same source for Eisenhower's work at Columbia.

[10] See n. 3 above.

[11] Eisenhower was referring to a luncheon Bermingham had held for the General and some Chicago businessmen on November 13, 1950 (see Bermingham to McCann, Nov. 9, 1950, and guest lists in EM).

[12] Bermingham's wife, the former Katherine Carpenter (Galambos, *Columbia University*, no. 810).

[13] Eisenhower would write to Bermingham again on the twenty-eighth of this month, expanding upon the thoughts he expressed in this document (see no. 51).

24   *Eisenhower Mss., Family File*

To Edgar Newton Eisenhower   *February 8, 1951*

Dear Ed:[1] Thank you very much indeed for your nice letter of the fourteenth.[2] I wish that I had time to answer it, but I am pushed harder than the proverbial one-armed paper hanger.[3] Possibly after I return to Europe, I will have a chance to tell you the story as I see it. However, as a stop-gap and to explain one or two points that may be of some interest to you, I am sending you herewith a copy of a letter I recently wrote to Ed Bermingham who is one of our prominent alumni and my close associate and friend in much of the work I have tried to do at Columbia.[4]

With the best of everything. *As ever*

[1] The General's older brother Edgar was a corporation lawyer in Tacoma, Washington (for background see *Eisenhower Papers*, vols. I–XI; and Kornitzer, *The Great American Heritage*, pp. 73–83, 173–82).

[2] In his letter (EM, Family File) Edgar had expressed concern about the General's new post as supreme commander of NATO: "I think it is the most difficult job that has ever been given you or any other man in the history of the world."

[3] Eisenhower had been back in New York City since February 3, attending to Columbia University business. This evening the General and Mrs. Eisenhower would fly to Puerto Rico for a three-day vacation. Other members of the party included the General's son, John Sheldon Doud Eisenhower, his wife Barbara, and their two children, Dwight David II and Barbara Anne; Major General Howard McCrum Snyder, Sr., and Mrs. Snyder, the former Alice Elizabeth Concklin; Mamie's mother, Elivera Doud; Clifford Roberts; William Robinson; Philip Reed; and Colonel Paul Thomas Carroll (see trip itinerary in EM, Subject File, Aircraft).

[4] Eisenhower's letter to Bermingham is the preceding document.

25   *Eisenhower Mss.*

TO FRED D. FLETCHER   *February 8, 1951*

Dear Mr. Fletcher: Thank you very much for your thoughtful letter of the third and, particularly, for the generosity of your comments with respect to my recent efforts in Washington and in other capitols.[1] There are two thoughts in your letter to which I shall, of course, devote no comment. One of these is criticism of past policies and actions on the part of our Government. No soldier on active duty could possibly, with propriety, express an opinion on such matters.[2] The other is your feeling that my personal duty might finally lead me into the political field. On this point I have nothing to add to previous statements.[3]

With the rest of your letter I am in very substantial agreement. In fact, the kind of National Advisory Staff that you suggest has been quite frequently and eloquently urged by Mr. Baruch, while I have likewise supported the idea in more than one public statement.[4] I hope you keep hammering away at it because I personally believe that in some such development lies a tremendous advantage, perhaps a vital one, for the future of America.

Indeed, so certain am I that the brains of America—drawn from every walk of life—must devote themselves to the broad and fundamental phases of our interrelated foreign-domestic problems that, with the help of friends, I have been busy over the past few months in organizing the American Assembly.[5] This institution, to be sponsored by Columbia University and supported by business, labor, farm and professional groups throughout the country, will have the mission of conducting intensive research on each of these problems vital to our welfare and then, on the basis of this research, to hold a conference made up of a cross-section of America. The findings, opinions and convictions of this conference will be published to our people—thus making it possible for each of us to have a better understanding of the facts when called upon to discharge our own responsibilities in such functions as casting our votes, and so on.[6]

The Assembly will, therefore, inevitably develop into a type of advisory group or general staff and one which will certainly have the virtue of impartiality and thoroughness. (Incidentally, it will not be suffocated in the "academic" atmosphere—to the contrary, many of the most prominent leaders of finance, business and farm groups have promised me their active participation.)[7] In spite of all this, I still believe there is virtue in the establishment of the kind of group that you suggest.

It would be interesting to talk over these matters with you if reasonable opportunity should ever present itself. For example, should you by chance be in Europe during the next few months I hope you will give my office a ring to determine whether or not we could get together, at least for a brief conversation.[8]

Again my thanks for the thoughtfulness of your letter, and with kind personal regards. *Sincerely*

[1] Fletcher, a lawyer from Klamath Falls, Oregon, had written Eisenhower concerning the General's February 2 radio and television address on American participation in NATO (for background on Fletcher see Galambos, *Columbia University*, no. 882; on Eisenhower's speech see no. 23 in this volume). In his letter (EM) Fletcher had said that he was reminded of "Churchill's great war speeches" when he listened to the General and that it was obvious Eisenhower had a "clear understanding of a logical course to be followed. . . ."

[2] Fletcher had criticized recent American decisions, particularly involvement in Korea, writing that the intervention was not "well thought out in advance." Later, he said, the Washington leadership had panicked.

[3] In urging Eisenhower to become a candidate for the presidency, Fletcher had said that he believed the General was the only person "on the horizon" capable of saving the United States from disintegration. He went on to write that he felt Eisenhower could approach internal and external problems "with the reasoning of a man like Lincoln." According to Fletcher, Senator Taft and Governor Thomas Dewey of New York, two potential Republican nominees, were too isolationist in their perspectives and unable to "reason far enough" (for background on Dewey see Galambos, *Columbia University*, no. 33; on Eisenhower's earlier statements about the presidency see Galambos, *Chief of Staff*, no. 1998; and Galambos, *Columbia University*, no. 106). During the next year Eisenhower would be forced many times to repeat his convictions that a soldier on active duty should not become involved in politics (see, for example, nos. 195, 232, 351, and 538).

[4] Most of Fletcher's letter dealt with his suggestion that a nonpolitical committee of representatives from banking, labor, industry, science, and the military should be established to advise the President and aid in long-range planning for the nation. Fletcher wrote that Stalin "consults the best minds in Russia. . . ," and the President of the United States should be in a position to take advantage of the advice of American "Park Bench Statesmen," such as Bernard Mannes Baruch and Senator Arthur Hendrick Vandenberg (for background on these men see Galam-

bos, *Columbia University*, nos. 191 and 537, respectively). Baruch was a friend of Eisenhower's and a benefactor of Columbia University. For Baruch's own suggestion that a national advisory staff be established see *ibid.*, no. 764; on Eisenhower's support for the Baruch Plan see *ibid.*, nos. 113 and 555.

[5] For background on the American Assembly see *Eisenhower Papers*, vols. X–XI.

[6] The first American Assembly, devoted to the relationship of the United States to Western Europe, would be held in May 1951, and the final report would be issued in September (see *New York Times*, May 26, Sept. 26, 1951).

[7] The first conference, run under the auspices of Columbia University's Graduate School of Business, would include representatives from labor, agriculture, and various professional groups, as well as business (see *New York Times*, Sept. 26, 1951).

[8] Fletcher would write again on the twenty-third of this month urging the General to strengthen his personal security while serving in Europe (EM).

26

To EDWARD JOHN BERMINGHAM   *February 8, 1951*

Dear Ed:[0] This morning is, to all intents and purposes, the first opportunity I have had of catching up with the huge backlog of personal correspondence that built up while I was overseas and in Washington.[1] Before anything happens to cut short the free time available, I want to thank you once again for all you have done on behalf of Columbia, and particularly for your assurance in your last letter that the working capital for the American Assembly will be acquired.[2]

Of course, both Mrs. Eisenhower and I would thoroughly enjoy every minute of a stay at Enon Farm, and we are both grateful to Mrs. Bermingham and you for your invitation.[3] This year, however, we simply cannot even think of the things that we should like to do. Time and a relentless schedule harness us completely this season.[4] Nevertheless, we both hope that some day we may be with you in Alabama. Until then, we join in thanks and best wishes to you both. *Cordially*

[1] For Eisenhower's trip to Europe see nos. 9 and 18; for his stay in Washington, D.C., see no. 23.

[2] In his letter of January 18 (EM) Bermingham had written that progress was being made on raising the working capital for the Columbia University American Assembly and that he was certain they would receive the amount sought. For background on the Assembly, on Bermingham's involvement with this and other Columbia projects, and on Eisenhower's role in establishing the Assembly see Galambos, *Columbia University*; and Eisenhower, *At Ease*, p. 350.

[3] Enon Farm was Bermingham's summer home in Midway, Alabama, where Eisenhower had vacationed briefly during the previous year. Bermingham had written that he and his wife were hoping the Eisenhowers might come to stay with them during the week of February 4. For background on Eisenhower's earlier visit see Galambos, *Columbia University*, nos. 656, 682, and 690.

[4] Eisenhower would leave this evening for a short vacation in Puerto Rico, after which he would briefly return to Washington and New York before departing for Europe on February 16. On the trip to Puerto Rico see no. 24; on his return to Europe see no. 38.

27   *Eisenhower Mss.*

To Eric Allen Johnston   *February 8, 1951*

Dear Eric:[1] I had been hoping for a few minutes with you to talk to you, among other things, about an ex-OPA man, named Albert A. Kaplan, who has volunteered his services for duty with your organization. Time and a relentless schedule have robbed me of a chance to seek an engagement with you—hence this letter.

It is my understanding that Mr. Kaplan has a very considerable background in consumer goods, at manufacturing and retail levels.[2] The details of his experience, both in business and in governmental agencies, are on file in the office of Mr. DiSalle.[3]

Mr. Kaplan believes he is especially well qualified for Consumer Goods Price Division. He prefers an operating position in New York to a "policy" job in Washington.

My own acquaintanceship with Mr. Kaplan comes through the friendship of our wives; he married a niece of Cecil DeMille.[4] Through this connection I have known him for four or five years and have found him to be gentlemanly, frank and friendly.

While I know nothing whatsoever of the qualifications required in your assistants, I am moved, by reason of Mr. Kaplan's apparent success in this type of work in World War II, to request that you examine his record personally. While I believe that his present business is a profitable one, he assures me that his purpose is to serve, during this emergency, in some position that will result in advantage to our country.[5]

I do hope this request will not cause you needless bother; in any event, please do not send me any answer. My duty, both to Mr. Kaplan and to the country has been discharged, in this instance, by the mere bringing of his name to your attention.

With warm personal regard, *Cordially*

[1] Johnston (LL.B. University of Washington 1917) was Administrator of the Economic Stabilization Agency (ESA), an officer of several companies, and former president of the Chamber of Commerce of the United States. He had been an adviser to Presidents Roosevelt and Truman and would later serve Eisenhower in a similar capacity (see *New York Times*, Aug. 23, 1963). The ESA had been established by executive order in 1950 for the purpose of controlling inflation (see

Hugh Rockoff, *Drastic Measures: A History of Wage and Price Controls in the United States* [Cambridge, 1984], p. 179).

[2] Albert A. Kaplan was an economist and business consultant with an extensive background in retailing. During World War II he had served in three different positions with the Office of Price Administration (OPA): head of the Textile, Apparel and General Merchandise Branch of the Cleveland regional office; price executive of the Manufactured Articles Branch of the national office; and associate price executive of the New York regional office (see *New York Times*, Oct. 14, 1943, and July 20, 1944).

[3] Michael Vincent DiSalle (LL.B. Georgetown 1931) was the senior member of the Toledo law firm of DiSalle, Green & Haddad and Director of the Office of Price Stabilization (OPS). The OPS, established in 1951, administered price controls (as had the OPA in World War II); it reported to the ESA (see Rockoff, *Drastic Measures*, p. 179).

[4] Kaplan's wife and Mrs. Eisenhower's friend was businesswoman Margaret De Mille.

[5] Kaplan would not take a post with the ESA. Johnston himself would resign from his position as Administrator in November of this year, returning to his former position as president of the American Motion Picture Association (see *New York Times*, Jan. 20, Sept. 3, Nov. 16, 1951).

28   *Eisenhower Mss.*

To Jean de Lattre de Tassigny   *February 10, 1951*

Dear General de Lattre:[1] While in Europe and since returning to the United States, I have been hearing accounts of the excellent work you and your valiant troops have been performing under such difficult conditions in Tonkin.[2] I have been particularly impressed by the manner in which the troops have responded to your leadership, and also by the growing response you are apparently gaining from the Vietnamese.[3]

I congratulate you and the men of your command. I hope your successes will continue,[4] and that French arms, in their great tradition, will continue their fine contribution to the common cause.

Let me take this occasion to express my appreciation for the contribution you have made to the preparedness and defense of Western Europe. As I take up my duties, I am keenly aware of the accomplishments achieved up to this time, in which you have taken such a prominent part.[5] *Sincerely*

[1] General de Lattre had commanded the French First Army during the final year of World War II. He later served on the Allied Control Commission for Germany and as Chief of Staff of the French Ground Forces (for background see *Eisenhower Papers*, vols. I–IX; Eisenhower, *Crusade in Europe*, p. 313; and Jean de Lattre de Tassigny, *The History of the French First Army*, trans. Malcolm Barnes [New York, 1953]). This letter was drafted by a member of Eisenhower's staff.

[2] On December 10, 1950, de Lattre had been appointed Colonial High Commissioner and Commander in Chief of the French forces in Indochina. During the fall and winter of 1950 the French Expeditionary Force, which had been fighting Ho Chi Minh's guerrillas since the close of World War II, suffered a series of disastrous defeats at the hands of the newly organized, Chinese-trained Vietminh Regular Army. Forced to abandon its outposts near the Chinese border, the reduced and demoralized French Army was at the point of evacuating Hanoi when de Lattre was given command. The appointment of a popular hero was seen as one of the only ways the French government could restore the self-confidence and spirit of the shattered army (see Lucien Bodard, *The Quicksand War: Prelude to Vietnam*, trans. Patrick O'Brian [Boston, 1967], pp. 259–354; and Joseph Buttinger, *Vietnam: A Dragon Embattled*, vol. II, *Vietnam at War* [New York, 1967], pp. 733, 755–56).

[3] Upon his arrival in Saigon on December 17 de Lattre had at once begun to revive the morale of the French Expeditionary Force. He reorganized the army staff, canceled orders for a planned evacuation of French civilians, impressed nonmilitary personnel for guard and other duties, and began to build a non-Communist Vietnamese army to assume some of the burden from the French (see Bodard, *Quicksand War*, p. 325; and Bernard B. Fall, *The Two Viet-Nams: A Political and Military Analysis* [New York, 1967], pp. 114–16).

[4] On January 17 de Lattre had defeated a superior force of the Vietminh in a pitched battle at the town of Vinh Yen, forty miles northwest of Hanoi (see Edgar O'Ballance, *The Indo-China War, 1945–1954: A Study in Guerilla Warfare* [London, 1964], pp. 120–29).

[5] Before his assignment to Indochina, de Lattre had been directly involved in the planning and operations for the defense of Western Europe; he had served as Commander in Chief for the Army in the Western Union Defence Organization and as a member of the Supreme War Council (see Ismay, *NATO*, p. 9; and *New York Times*, Jan. 12, 1952). For further developments see nos. 88 and 197.

29   *Eisenhower Mss.*

To THOMAS JEFFERSON DAVIS   *February 10, 1951*

Dear T.J.:[1] I was deeply touched by your offer of service, and while I do not see anything as of this minute, I will certainly remember your letter as I would like to have you with me.[2]

We have started out with a very small nucleus of young US officers, and must build upon that an organization which will ultimately include members from the twelve NATO countries. As I insist that the Headquarters be kept small, there will consequently be only a limited number of US vacancies. With regard to your desire to be an aide, I now have more than I can support.[3] That is one category which I had to build up from the start because of our exploratory trip through Europe and other requirements.[4]

Mamie and I are having a week-end of sunshine and rest before going back to Washington and New York on the way to Europe.[5] I appreciate the chance to get a second wind.

Please give our very best to Nina.[6] It would be nice to have you with us, and things might turn out that we can.[7] *Sincerely*

[1] Brigadier General Davis (USA, ret.) had known Eisenhower since the 1930s, when they both had been stationed in the Philippines. During World War II he had served as Eisenhower's Adjutant General in ETOUSA (the European Theater of Operations, United States Army), AFHQ, and SHAEF (Supreme Headquarters, Allied Expeditionary Force), and had later become Assistant Chief of Staff (for background see *Eisenhower Papers*, vols. I–IX). Eisenhower dictated an outline of this letter, and Colonel Paul Thomas Carroll drafted it (see JJG to Carroll, EM).

[2] Davis, who owned a pheasant farm in South Carolina, had written to Eisenhower on January 20, 1950 (EM), offering again to serve his former commander. Enclosed with the letter Davis sent a report from a recent physical examination he had undergone at Greenville Air Base. As he noted, it was "very thorough and encouraging." In October 1946 Davis had been forced to retire as Assistant to The Adjutant General because of a heart ailment, but he wrote that he had now "been put into high gear again by the favorable report and the prospect of being able to return to duty . . . once more" (see Galambos, *Chief of Staff*, nos. 1991 and 2025).

[3] At this time Eisenhower's aides were Lieutenant Colonel Robert Ludwig Schulz, and Lieutenant Colonel Charles Craig Cannon, and Colonel Paul Thomas Carroll, all of whom had worked with the General in the Army and at Columbia University (see SHAPE staff lists in EM, Subject File, Personnel). For background on Schulz, Cannon, and Carroll see *Eisenhower Papers*, vols. VI–XI.

[4] For Eisenhower's exploratory trip to Europe see nos. 9, 15, and 18.

[5] The Eisenhowers were presently vacationing with friends and family in Puerto Rico (for background see no. 24). On the General's return to Europe see no. 38.

[6] Davis's wife, the former Nina Eristova-Shervashitze.

[7] Davis would not become a member of Eisenhower's SHAPE staff.

30   *Eisenhower Mss.*

To Robert Cutler   *February 12, 1951*

Dear Bobby:[1] Thomas Cabot tells me that he is very anxious to get you as his Deputy Director of ISA.[2] He has asked me to urge you to accept.[3] I believe that your presence in such a position would be extremely effective in stimulating support of the overall program and hope you may find it possible to accept. Yet I know how busy you are and I cannot find the effrontery to be too emphatic.[4]

Am in Washington after a few days rest and sunshine in Puerto Rico with the family.[5] It did me a world of good after a rather hectic month. Tomorrow I shall be off for New York, enroute to Europe.[6]

With warm personal regard,[7] *Sincerely*

[1] Cutler (LL.B. Harvard 1922), a World War II brigadier general, was president and director of the Old Colony Trust Company of Boston (for background see Galambos, *Columbia University*, nos. 973 and 1119).

[2] Thomas Dudley Cabot, formerly president of United Fruit Company and director of the First National Bank of Boston, had been Director of the International Security Affairs Office of the State Department (ISA) since its inception in December 1950. President Truman had established the office to coordinate America's military efforts with those of its allies and to empower one person, the director, to "represent and speak for the Department of State on matters of policy and program relating to the North Atlantic Treaty, other similar international programs, and military and economic assistance for mutual defense" (see *New York Times*, Dec. 22, 1950).

[3] Cabot had recently spoken with Eisenhower's aide Craig Cannon expressing fears that Cutler had previously turned down the ISA deputy directorship because he was interested in securing a post under Eisenhower in Europe. Cabot said Cutler's "exceptional talents would be extremely effective" in increasing support for NATO in the United States; he urged Cannon to persuade his boss to convince Cutler that he should accept the proffered position (see undated memorandum, Cabot to Eisenhower, EM, Cutler Corr.).

[4] After dispatching this document via air mail/special delivery on February 13, Eisenhower sent Cutler a telegram the following day (EM) requesting that he make no decision about the ISA post until he had received the General's letter. For developments see no. 212.

[5] Eisenhower had arrived in Washington this evening after a four-day vacation on the Caribbean island (for background on the trip see no. 24).

[6] Following meetings in Washington, New York City, and West Point with government, military, and Columbia University officials, the Eisenhowers would sail for Europe on February 16 (see no. 38).

[7] This letter was drafted by a member of the General's staff.

31   *Eisenhower Mss.*

To Grayson Louis Kirk   *February 14, 1951*
and John Allen Krout[1]

I am informed by Dean Young[2] that he is confident that we will obtain the full half million we need as working capital for the American Assembly[3] without having to use the $50,000 donated to us on a somewhat flexible basis by the New York Times. This circumstance makes it possible for us to count upon this particular $50,000 in helping to finance the Institute for War and Peace[4] if this should be necessary.

I learned from General Edwin Clark[5] this morning that he is counting upon obtaining pledges which will total some fifty or sixty thousand dollars a year for the War and Peace Institute. Dean Krout should keep in close touch with him constantly. If his predictions should prove correct, then it would seem best to hold the $50,000 in reserve since, by avoiding its immediate use, we would have a sum to be used in favor of either project if need should arise.[6]

In this connection, I call your attention to the very obvious relationship between the Institute for War and Peace and the American Assembly and the possibilities that will exist for their mutual support, both intellectual and financial, if the normal contribution for an Assembly conference includes a very considerable sum for research. With the Institute in full sway the money for research on important subjects (which would be typical problems for the Assembly) would be automatically provided, thus saving the Assembly a very considerable sum. At the same time, the Institute, instead of renting expensive facilities for a conference or seminar, would do this at Arden House under the best of auspices.[7] I need say no more in order for you to see clearly what I am getting at.

I am sending a copy of this memorandum to Dean Young.

[1] As vice-president and provost of Columbia, Kirk would serve as acting president during Eisenhower's absence (see Galambos, *Columbia University*, no. 1158). Krout, associate provost and dean of the faculties of political science, philosophy, and pure science, had been actively involved in many of the projects Eisenhower initiated at Columbia (for background on both men see Galambos, *Columbia University*).

[2] For background on Young see no. 8.

[3] For background on Columbia's American Assembly conference plan and Eisenhower's special interest in it see Galambos, *Columbia University*; and Eisenhower, *At Ease*, p. 350.

[4] The Institute of War and Peace Studies was one of several special projects Eisenhower had initiated at Columbia (see Galambos, *Columbia University*, no. 1056). Established solely as a research organization, with a small staff, the institute would examine problems of national security; international relations; preparedness; the coordination of military, domestic, and diplomatic policy; and the effects of technological advances on policy making (see *New York Times*, Dec. 10, Nov. 18, 1951). The institute's emphasis would be on "the analysis of [the] long-range security problems . . . facing American foreign policy makers" (see L. Gray Cowan, *A History of the School of International Affairs and Associated Area Institutes, Columbia University* [New York, 1954], pp. 90–92). For developments see no. 159.

[5] Eisenhower's old friend retired General Edwin Norman Clark was head of the fund-raising campaign for the Institute of War and Peace Studies (for background on Clark see Galambos, *Chief of Staff* and *Columbia University*).

[6] In the next few months there would be an extensive correspondence between the Columbia administration and the executives of the *New York Times* concerning the $50,000 gift, its potential uses, and the possible release of an announcement naming the newspaper as benefactor. The donation would eventually be utilized by the Institute of War and Peace Studies, but no mention of the specific sources of the funding would be made (see Anger to Norton, Mar. 5, 1951; Norton to Sulzberger, Mar. 6, 1951; MacKenzie to Norton, Mar. 10, 1951; Norton to Adler, Mar. 12, 1951; Norton to Anger, Apr. 6, 1951; and Gentzler to Lane, Apr. 9, 1951, all in Columbia University Files, hereafter cited as CUF. See also *New York Times*, Dec. 10, 12, 1951).

[7] For developments concerning the American Assembly see nos. 155 and 177; on the Institute of War and Peace Studies see no. 568. For background on Arden House see no. 184, n. 3.

To Arthur Krock   *February 14, 1951*

Dear Arthur:[1] Thank you very much indeed for your memorandum about Gordon Gray.[2] Frankly, I am astonished that I had not thought of him myself and, as of this moment, I am quite sure that if we determine we have a need for a senior Political Advisor, I shall ask the proper authorities to approach him.[3] My admiration for him is equal to yours, I assure you.

It was nice to see you at the luncheon yesterday.[4] Incidentally, if you should be traveling in Europe at any time that I am there, please accept my very cordial invitation to stop off with me for a visit.

Thank you again for the courtesy and the wisdom of your suggestion. *Cordially*

[1] Krock was the Washington correspondent of the *New York Times* and a member of the advisory board of the Columbia University School of Journalism (for background see Galambos, *Columbia University*, nos. 110 and 735).

[2] In a memorandum of February 13 (EM) Krock had suggested that Eisenhower investigate the possibility of obtaining Gordon Gray as a political adviser for SHAPE. Former Secretary of the Army Gray was then serving as president of the University of North Carolina (for background on Gray see Galambos, *Columbia University*).

[3] Instead of becoming the SHAPE political adviser, Gray would serve from July until December 1951 as director of the newly established Psychological Strategy Board (see Gray to Eisenhower, Aug. 23, 1951, EM). Douglas MacArthur II, nephew to General MacArthur, would become the SHAPE adviser on international affairs (for background on MacArthur II see Chandler, *War Years*, no. 443).

[4] On February 13, while in Washington for last-minute meetings before departing for Europe, Eisenhower had attended a luncheon given by Marquis Childs of the United Feature Syndicate for several American newspapermen (see guest list in EM, Childs Corr.).

33   *Eisenhower Mss.*

To George Edward Allen   *February 14, 1951*

Dear George:[1] I just had a telegram from Walter Kerschner[2] about the gift of the two young bulls and two young heifers. This, of course, is a gift to us as partners since that is the way we are running the Gettysburg farm.[3] I have a call in now to tell Art Nevins.[4]

It would seem to me that this gift will make it possible for us to start soon replacing part of the other herd with these fine cattle. The better stock we have the more income there should be. Moreover, Art will have an income producer in the two registered bulls. There must be other Guernsey herds in that region where they would want to use them.[5]

Since we are leaving for Europe tomorrow evening, it seems that I will not see you again since I have no word that you are coming back today.[6] Last night I was visited by a prominent individual who wanted to give me a lot of advice.[7] Part of it annoyed me a bit, especially as it referred to several of my friends and I shall talk to you about it when next I get to see you.

Walter Kerschner's telegram says that you and Mary are in love with your new homes. I did not know that you were going in for the purchase of residences on a multiple scale, but I am delighted that you are so pleased with your venture.[8]

I cannot even guess when I may be coming back to the States, but it will not be as often as it would be if Mamie really liked to fly. Nevertheless, I rather think that sometime in midsummer we will probably get back for a minimum of a few days.[9]

In the meantime, my very best love to Mary[10] and, of course, affectionate regards to yourself. *As ever*

[1] For background on Eisenhower's old friend see no. 9.

[2] Walter Kirschner was a friend of George Allen's and chairman of the board of the New York City clothing stores Grayson-Robinson, Inc., and S. Klein on the Square (see Kirschner to Eisenhower, Dec. 9, 1948, and undated note, MacKinnon to Eisenhower, both in EM).

[3] On the Gettysburg farms and the General's partnership with Allen see Galambos, *Columbia University*, no. 1003; and nos. 170, 297, and 770 in these volumes.

[4] Brigadier General Arthur Seymour Nevins (USA, ret.) had been Chief of the Operations Section of SHAEF (see *Eisenhower Papers*, vols. I-XI, for background). Before departing for Europe Eisenhower had hired Nevins and his wife, the former Ann Louise Stacy, to serve as the managers of both his and Allen's farms. On Nevins's management of the farms see Arthur S. Nevins, *Gettysburg's Five-Star Farmer* (New York, 1977); and nos. 179 and 376.

[5] Later this month Allen would send Eisenhower a list of the names of twenty-three cows then on the Gettysburg farm (see Allen to Eisenhower, Feb. 26, 1951, and Brown to Allen, Feb. 19, 1951, both in EM). On the business aspects of the joint farming venture see Lyon, *Portrait of the Hero*, p. 513.

[6] For the Eisenhowers' departure for Europe see no. 38.

[7] According to the General's appointment calendar, he had met with a "Mr. Lockwood" the evening of February 13. This was a code name that New York Governor Thomas E. Dewey used when he was holding political discussions with the General (see Richard Norton Smith, *Thomas E. Dewey and His Times* [New York, 1982], p. 556; and no. 196).

[8] In addition to a farm near Eisenhower's in Gettysburg, Allen had recently purchased a home in La Quinta, California (see no. 73).

[9] Eisenhower would be unable to return to the United States until November 1951.

[10] Allen's wife (for background see no. 9).

To Arthur B. Eisenhower   *February 14, 1951*

Dear Arthur:[1] Thank you very much for your promptness in sending the money on to Sid Richardson.[2] There is another investment that I have been working on for a couple of years, involving the purchase of some real estate in the Denver area. I am hoping that it will come to a head sometime this spring and, if it does, I will request you to send the remainder of my account ($40,000) to Aksel Nielsen, President, Title Guaranty Company, Denver, Colorado.[3]

Since I am leaving tomorrow for Europe and do not expect to return for a very considerable time, this request will probably come to you by cablegram.[4] I will, however, promptly thereafter confirm it by letter so that you will have on file my own signature confirming it.

Please give my love to Louise.[5] *As always*

[1] Arthur B. Eisenhower was the General's oldest brother and a director and executive vice-president of the Commerce Trust Company of Kansas City, Missouri (for background see *Eisenhower Papers*, vols. I–XI).

[2] Sid Williams Richardson was a wealthy oil man from Fort Worth, Texas, and an old friend of Eisenhower's (for background see Galambos, *Columbia University*). On Eisenhower's investments with Richardson see the following document.

[3] For background on Eisenhower's long-time friend see *Eisenhower Papers*, vols. I–XI. For background on their real estate investments in the Denver area see Galambos, *Columbia University*, nos. 998, 1003, and 1100; for developments in regard to this transaction see nos. 235 and 275 in these volumes.

[4] On Eisenhower's trip to Europe to assume command of the NATO forces see no. 38.

[5] Arthur's wife, Louise Sondra Grieb Eisenhower.

---

35   *Eisenhower Mss.*

To Sid Williams Richardson   *February 15, 1951*

Dear Sid:[1] Just a final note to say good-bye and to thank you again for your kindness in your offer to seek a few good investments for me. I assure you that not only do I approve of whatever you do, but I will be thankful for the fact that I get your expert advice and convictions as a present from you.[2]

I understand that our great purpose is to get a fairly long-term position so as to work on a capital gains basis wherever possible.[3] This, of course, I much prefer, but it is likewise true, if it means anything in the whole situation that, while I am back in uniform, my income basis becomes fairly meager.[4] This is just an additional piece of information that might mean something to you.

I had a talk with Amon[5] on the phone but, when you receive this, tell him it brings to him also another good-bye message.

Remember me kindly to Perry[6] and to our other mutual friends.[7] *Cordially*

P.S. Bob has just told me about the Standlion gift! Hooray—& thanks a lot!![8]

[1] For background on Richardson see no. 34.

[2] At Eisenhower's direction, a portion of his funds had recently been sent to Richardson for purposes of investment (see no. 34).

[3] In regard to the sorts of choices Richardson would make see no. 232.

[4] Excluding allowances for subsistence and quarters, the pay of a General of the Army at this time was $16,457 per year. This was a reduction of nearly $10,000 per year from the salary Eisenhower received as president of Columbia University (see Schulz to Department of the Army, Jan. 13, 1951, and Certificate for Increased Allowances, Jan. 18, 1951, both in EM, Family File; and Lyon, *Portrait of the Hero*, p. 374).

[5] Amon Giles Carter, Sr., was president and publisher of the *Fort Worth Star-Telegraph* (see *Eisenhower Papers*, vols. VI–XI).

[6] Richardson's nephew and "office top hand" was Perry Richardson Bass (see Richardson to Eisenhower, June 14, 1951, EM).

[7] For further developments concerning Eisenhower's investments see nos. 471 and 558; see also Eisenhower to Richardson, May 29 and August 30, 1951, EM.

[8] Eisenhower was probably referring to the Stan*olind* Oil and Gas Company gift to Columbia University's American Assembly (see American Assembly, *The American Assembly in Action*, [New York, 1951], p. 16). On the Assembly see nos. 8 and 25; on Eisenhower's aide Robert Schulz see no. 1.

36   *Eisenhower Mss.*

To HELEN ROGERS REID   *February 15, 1951*

Dear Helen:[1] Only an hour ago I talked to you on the phone, but I simply cannot leave the country without making a bit of a written record of my very great appreciation for the generous contribution from the Herald Tribune to the American Assembly.[2] Incidentally, from a personal standpoint, its timing was perfect. Not only does it insure our going over the top in securing the initial operating fund, but it comes on the very day that I am forced to give up active participation in the project.[3]

My gratitude to you and to all your associates.

(As of tomorrow morning, I shift to the Paris edition of the Herald Tribune.)[4]

With affectionate regard. *Cordially*

[1] Reid was president of the *New York Herald Tribune* (for background see *Eisenhower Papers*, vols. VI–XI).

[2] For information on the American Assembly conference plan which Eisenhower had initiated at Columbia see Galambos, *Columbia University*. Working capital totaling $500,000 had been raised from individuals and organizations largely through the personal efforts of the General. In a public statement this same day Eisenhower praised American business, labor, and professional groups for supporting these conferences, which would deal with "critical domestic and international problems" (see *New York Times*, Feb. 16, 1951).

[3] The General and Mrs. Eisenhower would sail for Europe the following morning (see no. 38).

[4] The first American Assembly conference, on the relationship between the United States and Western Europe, would take place during the week of May 21, 1951. Although Eisenhower would be unable to attend this conference, he would maintain close contact with the Assembly's staff, organizers, and participants (see nos. 154, 184, 220, 497, and 612). The *Herald Tribune* would make a second donation to the Assembly in September 1951 (see *New York Times*, Sept. 26, 1951).

37   *Eisenhower Mss.*

To Bernard Mannes Baruch   *February 15, 1951*

Dear Bernie:[1] I am personally delighted with your kind offer to speak with Dr. Kirk[2] about Columbia's Engineering Center plans which, in my own estimation, are of major significance to the nation in every sense of the word.[3] My overseas trip has convinced me of that more than ever.

Through the North Atlantic Treaty Organization, this country and our European allies are wisely undertaking to build a protective wall of military might between us and the aggressive imperialism of the Soviets.[4] But the basic ingredient of success in securing our way of life against Red aggression, in my opinion, will be our ability to counterbalance potential enemy superiority in numbers with continued superiority of our own in the fields of science, technology and production.[5] That, as I see it, is the compelling and urgent reason for carrying our Engineering Center Program to early realization.

Sometimes we tend to overlook the obvious, and I realize suddenly that one of the great assets in our Engineering Center Program is the fact that it will enjoy the dynamic leadership and vision of Dr. John Dunning, whose engineering genius contributed so much to our possession of the atom bomb. This young scientist-engineer now acts both as Director of Research for the University and as Dean of the School of Engineering.[6]

Should it be convenient for you some time in the coming weeks to

talk with Dr. Kirk, I would hope that Dean Dunning, whom I believe you know, might have the pleasure of joining in the discussion.[7]
Sincerely

[1] For background on Baruch and on Eisenhower's relationship with him see no. 25; and Galambos, *Columbia University.*
[2] See no. 31.
[3] In March 1951 the university would announce its plans for the creation of an Institute for Advanced Engineering Science. The $22,150,000 project would "advance a new concept of engineering education . . ." combining "teaching, research and practice in engineering with the fundamentals of science . . . 'to a degree never before achieved' " (see *New York Times*, Mar. 2, Nov. 5, 1951).
[4] For Eisenhower's thinking on the military organization of NATO see nos. 23, 84, and 153.
[5] For more on this see nos. 221 and 566.
[6] For background on Dunning, who had been a division director of Columbia's atomic research laboratories during World War II, see Galambos, *Columbia University.*
[7] For developments regarding the Engineering Center see nos. 266 and 328.

38   *Eisenhower Mss.*

To CLIFFORD ROBERTS   *February 16, 1951*

Dear Cliff:[1] Of course, it was wonderful to see you and Bill at luncheon yesterday.[2] For some reason, I made an unwarranted assumption that when we left the place, you and Bill and I were going to drive off together, and that I would get a chance to talk to you just a bit more. My chief reason was just to say a special good-by to you, one of the friends to whom I owe so very much indeed. Anglo-Saxon men do not spend much time telling each other, face to face, anything of their mutual affection and regard. Consequently, I must trust to your own intuition to give you an understanding of the real weight of the value I place upon the friendship you have so generously given me. I have, of course, been aware of the amount of devoted thought and study you have given to my material welfare. But this, valuable as it is, has been as nothing to Mamie and me compared to the unselfishness of your devotion to our whole family.[3]

At the moment, I am trying to get you on the phone to correct the mistake I made in not coming to see you to talk about the investment my nephew and Sergeant Dry want to make. If I do succeed in getting you on the phone, I will give you all the details—in the meantime, if either Richard Gill, Jr., or Sergeant Leonard Dry should come to you, by mail or in person, to help them out, I will be very deeply in your debt if you will buy for them whatever appears to be a conservative, but dividend paying stock.[4] And bill me for all charges, that is commissions, taxes, etc. I should like, just as a present to these two individuals, to pay the incidental expenses. A note to me at my headquarters in Europe (I suppose that you know the simplest address is APO 55, c/o Postmaster, New York) will bring a check from Bob[5] to cover these costs.

Mamie and I have been busy this morning opening presents and putting away flowers.[6] However, I am going to try to keep her in bed for three solid days. She was completely worn out with the drudgery of breaking up her household. She asks me to give her deep love to send along with my abiding affection.[7] *Cordially*

[1] For background on Roberts see no. 7.

[2] On the previous afternoon Eisenhower had attended a farewell luncheon given for him by William Edward Robinson and several of his close friends at the Union League Club (see appointment calendar). For background on Robinson see the following document.

[3] Aside from his many rounds of golf with Eisenhower, Roberts frequently handled investments for the General and his family and had been instrumental in raising the working capital for Columbia University's American Assembly (see Galambos, *Columbia University*, nos. 1062, 1079, and 1115; and EM, Roberts Corr.).

[4] For background on Eisenhower's long-time chauffeur and orderly, Master Sergeant Leonard D. Dry, and on Mrs. Eisenhower's nephew Richard Gill, Jr., see *Eisenhower Papers*, vols. VI–XI.

[5] Eisenhower's aide Robert Ludwig Schulz (see no. 29).

[6] Eisenhower was then at sea, bound for France and the full-time responsibilities of SHAPE command. The previous evening he had attended the annual dinner of the Association of the Alumni of Columbia College, at which Dr. Harry James Carman, dean emeritus of the college (see Galambos, *Columbia University*), had received the Alexander Hamilton Medal for distinguished public service. Following a few brief remarks on the purposes of NATO and his dedication to Columbia, the General and Mrs. Eisenhower departed for the Cunard liner HMS *Queen Elizabeth*. They set sail shortly after midnight for Cherbourg, France (see itinerary, Jan. 6–Feb. 21, 1951, in EM, Subject File, Trips; and *New York Times*, Feb. 15, 16, 1951).

[7] On the General's concern over Mrs. Eisenhower's health see Galambos, *Columbia University*, no. 1045. On his decision to bring her to Europe with him see no. 46 in this volume.

39   *Eisenhower Mss.*

TO WILLIAM EDWARD ROBINSON   *February 16, 1951*

Dear Bill:[1] Never has anyone received a letter that could be more highly prized than the one you handed me along with the beautiful brief case.[2] It means all the more to me for the sincerity it brings—this whole expedition to Europe may be nothing but a series of headaches and heartaches,[3] but it at least brings to me one memento I shall treasure always.

Yesterday after luncheon, I should have liked to take a bit of time to tell the assembled company something of what their friendship has meant to me. Actually, I was just a little fearful that, in trying to express my sentiments, I would have been guilty of a touch of sentimentality. In any event, I shall never cease to be grateful to you for your kindness in gathering them together.[4] While it is difficult to believe that there could have been any improvement on the occasion whatever, still it would have been nice if Hap Flannigan, Pete Jones, George Allen and Charlie McAdam could likewise have been present.[5]

At present, I do not see how you could occupy a more advantageous position than you already do for potential assistance to me and to the beliefs that you and I have in common. However, it is wonderful to know that you are ready at any moment to take on any new chore.[6] Incidentally, I hope that business with the paper may bring you to Europe some time this summer, if only for a brief stay. Mamie and I will expect you to stay with us, if we have even as much as a hall closet to serve as a bedroom.[7]

Mamie has already opened up her wonderful desk set, but probably will not attempt to write to you before she gets to Europe. I am doing my best to keep her in bed to recover from the strenuous activity of breaking up her household.[8] In any event, she asked me to tell you that the present will not only be of the greatest usefulness, but she is entranced with its attractiveness.

For myself, I am, of course, intrigued by the beautiful leather case, but when you gave me your friendship, you gave me the most wonderful present one man can give another.

With abiding affection, *Cordially*

P.S. Assuming that there is no embarrassment involved, won't you convey to Madge[9] my warm greetings? I am devoted to her and I truly regret that I had no chance to tell her good-by in person. Of course, the same goes for Wilma.[10]

---

[1] Robinson was executive vice-president and a director of the *New York Herald Tribune* (for background see *Eisenhower Papers*, vols. VI–XI).

[2] In his note, dated February 14, Robinson had expressed his gratitude at having been invited to vacation with the Eisenhowers in Puerto Rico earlier in the month (see no. 24). He had said as well, "To know you is great honor and a precious privilege. To have, in addition, your understanding friendship, is a treasure beyond any value I know" (EM).

[3] On Eisenhower's departure for Europe see the preceding document.

[4] For background on the farewell luncheon see the preceding document.

[5] In regard to Eisenhower's friends Horace C. Flanigan, William Alton Jones, George Edward Allen, and Charles Vincent McAdam see Galambos, *Columbia University* (see also Eisenhower to Flanigan; Eisenhower to Jones; and Eisenhower to McAdam, all Feb. 16, 1951, EM). Robinson would send a copy of this para-

graph of the General's letter to the four men mentioned and to each of the others who had attended the luncheon (see Robinson to Roberts *et al.*, Feb. 28, 1951, William E. Robinson Papers).

[6] In his note of the fourteenth Robinson had offered his services: "No hope of mine could transcend the fervent wish that somehow I can be of service to you . . . I am completely at your command" (EM). Over the following year Robinson would do some favors for Eisenhower and would keep him abreast of developments on the American scene, particularly those concerning press treatment of NATO and the General himself (see nos. 44, 447, and 750; and correspondence in EM).

[7] On the *Herald Tribune* and the Eisenhowers' difficulties in finding suitable housing see nos. 44 and 60.

[8] See Galambos, *Columbia University*, no. 1045; and no. 46 in this volume.

[9] Robinson's wife, the former Marguerite Luddy.

[10] Wil*l*ma was the Robinsons' daughter.

40   *Eisenhower Mss.*

To William H. Burnham   *February 16, 1951*

Dear Bill:[1] Not only was our room jammed with special and intriguing gifts from you, but it was quite clear that your efforts to promote a "subscription" were very successful. We had everything from rare orchids to chewing gum.[2]

It is difficult indeed for either of us to attempt to tell you how much your devoted friendship has meant to us, but we are quite sure that your own intuition will assure you on this point. Moreover, we have appointed you permanent aide to Min—this is not only with her consent, but at her insistent demand.[3]

I truly hope that by the time you come over at the end of March, we will be really settled, so that you can stay with us.[4] Under those circumstances, we can then make up for many of the conversations we have missed in the past.

Incidentally, when you write to our many mutual friends who have helped out on the American Assembly, I would appreciate a delicate hint that, as they now make up their yearly gift budgets or programs, they will remember to include Columbia, either for general purposes or specified support for the American Assembly. I would rather that your hint be on the delicate side, than be of the sledge hammer variety.[5]

In any event, don't fail to come over in March.[6] Mamie and I send our devoted affection and regard. *Cordially*

[1] Burnham was a New York City investment banker and an active participant in the Eisenhower-for-President movement (for background see Galambos, *Columbia University*).

[2] On the Eisenhowers' departure for Europe see no. 38. On their bon voyage gifts see Brandon, *A Portrait of a First Lady*, p. 266.

[3] For background on Mrs. Eisenhower's mother, Elivera Carlson Doud, see *Eisenhower Papers*, vols. I–XI. Burnham would keep in contact with Mrs. Doud, and during her struggle with pneumonia in the next month he would keep the Eisenhowers informed regarding her condition (see Burnham to Eisenhower, Mar. 19, 1951, and Burnham to Mrs. Eisenhower, Mar. 20, 1951, both in EM; and correspondence in EM, Family File). For developments see no. 118.

[4] In regard to the Eisenhowers' difficulties in their search for suitable Paris accommodations see nos. 44 and 122; and Hatch, *Red Carpet for Mamie*, pp. 229–33.

[5] Burnham had been active in raising the working capital for the American Assembly (see Galambos, *Columbia University*, nos. 987 and 1159). In his reply of February 23 (EM) Burnham wrote, "The sledge hammer attack on American Assembly friends will give way to the velvet but grasping glove." For developments see no. 182.

[6] Burnham, who would visit the General in March, would be employed at SHAPE headquarters from May until November 1951 as an economic analyst. While in the United States, he sent Eisenhower detailed letters on the national political climate and the actions of Eisenhower's friends and supporters (see EM, Burnham Corr., esp. Burnham to Eisenhower, Mar. 19, 1951, and Eisenhower to Burnham, Nov. 2, 1951; and Lyon, *Portrait of the Hero*, p. 426). For developments in Eisenhower's relationship with Burnham see nos. 626 and 640.

41   *Eisenhower Mss.*

To WILLIAM DOUGLAS PAWLEY   *February 16, 1951*
AND EDNA PAWLEY

Dear Edna and Bill:[1] Just how you figured out that Mamie and I would be on the Queen Elizabeth I don't know. But I do know that the orchids and roses you sent were among the most beautiful and entrancing I have ever seen. The orchids are now in the icebox, in the fervent hope that they will stay fresh until Mamie can debark at Cherbourg.[2] But the roses are quite the most attractive thing in our suite.

Their arrival reminds me of how often I have thought, with something akin to nostalgia, of your beautiful home there in the country. I cannot tell you what both of us wouldn't give this minute to be able to sit leisurely there a week or two, on the back porch of your home, with no thought of going farther astray than the bass lake to see if the big ones are rising to fly.[3]

You were most thoughtful to remember us, and we are truly appreciative. With our affectionate regards to you both, *Cordially*

P.S. For Bill: I did not fail to voice my sentiments around Washington that you would have made an ideal representative at Madrid. Obviously, it had no immediate effect, but the future is still a long time.[4] If either or both of you should come to Europe please, by all means, give us advance notice so we will be sure to get together.

[1] Former U.S. Ambassador to both Peru and Brazil, Pawley had known Eisenhower since 1947. For background see Galambos, *Chief of Staff.*

[2] At this time the Eisenhowers were aboard the ocean liner HMS *Queen Elizabeth*, sailing for France (see nos. 38, 40, and 43).

[3] The Eisenhowers had been guests at the Pawleys' Virginia farm (see EM, Pawley Corr.).

[4] At this same time the new American ambassador to Spain, Stanton Griffis, was also at sea bound for Europe. Allied displeasure with the regime of Generalissimo Francisco Franco, both during and after World War II, and a U.N. ban on member nations' appointing representatives to Madrid had kept the U.S. ambassador's post vacant since 1945. A strong desire for Spanish military support in NATO and a recent rescinding of the U.N. ban had prompted Truman to name Griffis, the former Ambassador to Argentina, to the Madrid post in December 1950 (see *New York Times*, Dec. 25, 28, 1950; Feb. 19, 20, 21, 1951).

42   *Eisenhower Mss.*

To Arthur Michael Godfrey   *February 16, 1951*

Dear Arthur:[1] Whenever you desire to undertake a temporary tour of Naval duty I shall be ready to take you, with Admiral Sherman's approval, of course, for duty in Europe. You'd always be welcome just as a casual visitor, but what we talked about was the tour of duty.[2]

As the calendar year begins, I hope you'll tell your business manager to keep Columbia on whatever gift budget he makes up for you for the year! While we're over the top in initial operating funds for the American Assembly, I'm determined that that program will really be a wonderful thing for our country.[3]

With best regard, *Cordially*

[1] For background on Eisenhower's friendship with radio personality Godfrey see Galambos, *Columbia University*, nos. 971 and 1078.

[2] Godfrey, who was a commander in the Naval Reserve, had recently discussed with Eisenhower the possibility of receiving an assignment with SHAPE (see *ibid.*, nos. 1027 and 1150. See also Collins to SHAPE, Jan. 19, 1951; Sherman to Gruenther, Mar. 14, 1951; and Gruenther to Sherman, Mar. 15, 1951, all in EM, Godfrey Corr.). Godfrey replied on March 2 (EM), "I am very proud and happy to be able to report that . . . I have received my certificate of proficiency as a Navy Jet Pilot . . . and I shall not rest until I have qualified as a Carrier Jet Pilot. I will write you immediately [once] I have received Admiral Sherman's approval and I hope I will be seeing you very soon." Godfrey would not be assigned to SHAPE, but he would visit the General in Paris during July (see no. 333; undated cable, Godfrey to Eisenhower; and Eisenhower to Godfrey, July 3, 1951, EM). On Admiral Sherman see no. 22.

[3] For background on the American Assembly conference plan see Galambos, *Columbia University*; in reference to Godfrey's contributions to the plan see *ibid.*, nos. 971, 1078, and 1103.

43   *Eisenhower Mss.*

To Leslie Clarke Stevens   *February 22, 1951*

Dear Admiral Stevens:[1] I have just finished reading your paper, "The National Strategy for the Soviet Union." Permit me to congratulate you on completion of a paper which, for its readability and for the splendid logic of its argument, has few if any equals in current military and political writings.[2]

I note that your paper is labeled TOP SECRET and, consequently, I am allowed to distribute it, here, only to those who have been cleared for this classification of document. Nevertheless, for all those, I am going to make it required reading at once.[3]

Incidentally, you may be slightly interested in the one point in the whole document where I find myself at some variance with your conclusions. It is that Communism is making a tool of Russian Nationalism, rather than the reverse. In this particular point, I personally doubt that either is the tool of the other; I think that we have here an unholy wedding between Russian Imperialism and personal greed for power with the ideological doctrine of Communism. While it possibly makes no great difference in the progeny of such a union as to which parent was the dominating one, I always find myself tending toward a state of intellectual confusion when I attempt to regard either of these influences as the master and the other nothing but a tool.[4]

In any event, with this one inconsequential remark, I repeat my expression of admiration for your document and my personal feeling of gratitude for your producing it.[5] *Very sincerely*

[1] Rear Admiral Stevens (USNA 1918) had been American naval and naval air attaché in Moscow from 1947 to 1949. He was presently in Washington on assignment as consultant to the Office of Policy Coordination of the Central Intelligence Agency (CIA) for the Joint Chiefs of Staff (see Leslie Clark Stevens, *Russian Assignment* [Boston, 1953]).

[2] On January 25, 1951, Stevens had delivered his paper on Soviet beliefs, aims, and capabilities to the National War College in Washington. The thirty-seven-page document was considered to be of such importance that Robert Prather Joyce, a member of the Policy Planning Staff of the Department of State, sent excerpts of it to Special Assistant to the President W. Averell Harriman (see State, *Foreign Relations 1951*, vol. 1, *National Security Affairs: Foreign Economic Policy* [1979], p. 42; for background on Harriman see no. 16). Harriman, in turn, had sent a complete transcript of Stevens's paper to Eisenhower, writing in the margin, "This is must reading. I am sure you will agree" (see copy in EM, Harriman Corr.).

[3] Eisenhower was referring to the members of the SHAPE staff. After setting sail from New York aboard the HMS *Queen Elizabeth* on February 16, he and Mrs. Eisenhower had been at sea for five days, arriving in Cherbourg, France, on the twenty-first. Following brief ceremonies in Normandy, where the World War II Allied liberation of Europe had begun, the General had traveled to Paris to begin his SHAPE duties (for background on the Eisenhowers' departure from New York see nos. 38 and 40. On their arrival in France see Carroll to Gruenther, Feb. 19, 1951, EM; *New York Times*, Feb. 22, 1951; *International Herald Tribune*, Paris ed., Feb. 22, 1951; and Eisenhower, *At Ease*, pp. 363–64).

[4] In his paper Stevens had written that he believed that in Russia "Marxist-Leninist-Stalinist doctrine is predominant, and that the position of the Soviet Union as a world power is more in the nature of a tool through which that doctrine may be effected." He went on to explain that Russian nationalism was used by the Communist regime to further its goal of worldwide revolution rather than as a means of attaining any strictly national ends. In comments in the margin of the paper Eisenhower wrote, "This is 180° different from what I've believed. If he is right I think the USSR is even more dangerous than we have normally assumed" (see copy in EM, Harriman Corr.).

[5] Eisenhower underscored several sentences and numbered forty-two paragraphs and sections of the paper that he believed were important. He wrote comments— some of agreement and others expressing disagreement—beside many of the paragraphs. While most of these comments were of a positive nature, the nationalism question was not the sole point with which he seems to have disagreed. Stevens felt the atomic bomb would be a far more decisive factor in any possible war between the Soviet Union and the United States than Eisenhower believed it would be. Beside a paragraph concerning the "great advantage" to a nation that struck first with atomic weapons Eisenhower wrote, "Air-men might believe this.—I do not" (see copy in *ibid.*).

44   *Eisenhower Mss.*

To WILLIAM EDWARD ROBINSON   *February 24, 1951*

Dear Bill: Little did I think that, this soon after leaving you, I would be sending you a wail for help.[1] It is a weird one.

On Friday morning, the European edition of the Herald Tribune published quite a sarcastic story about the Eisenhowers, with unusual and, I must say, unjustified emphasis on Mamie. It involved quite an unfavorable story at the Hotel Trianon on Friday, and I am very much afraid that Mamie, who is heartsick about it, is going to write you.[2] Of course, I assume that you will send her a sympathetic reply, but the purpose of this note is to ask you *to do nothing official about it*. I would not want you even to tell Helen Reid[3] about it, and certainly no instructions—at least none that would refer to this specific story— should be sent here. I am smart enough to know that any action that should be taken by a publisher could result in a most complicated and unfortunate situation. In fact, I am not even going to talk to your local editor about it, unless he should first bring it up to me.[4]

While the story has all the earmarks of a planted, slanted one, I cannot believe that there was any deliberate purpose on the part of the boss, and therefore have to assume that the whole thing was a fantastic tissue of misunderstanding. In any event, I repeat my request—*please do nothing about it* other than to write anything to Mamie that you choose. All this assumes that she is going to carry out her purpose and send you the clipping.[5]

We had a nice crossing, and if you see George Allen, to whom I have just written, remind him that I am losing weight rapidly enough to meet completely *my* commitment for the 1st of March.[6]

My very best to all our friends that you may encounter. *Cordially*

[1] For Eisenhower's farewell to Robinson see no. 39.

[2] After their arrival in France on February 22 the Eisenhowers had taken up temporary residence in a suite at the Trianon Palace Hotel in Versailles (for background on their trip see nos. 38 and 43). On the day following their move to the hotel a story appearing in the *International Herald Tribune* criticized Mrs. Eisenhower for not graciously accepting accommodations offered by the French government. The story depicted her as a fussy, spoiled American. According to the article, Mrs. Eisenhower had turned down a fourteen-room villa that had been purchased by France as a permanent house for the SHAPE commander and his wife because she "didn't like the combination of Louis XIV and XVI furniture." The story went on to relate that on three occasions Mrs. Eisenhower had blown out electrical fuses in the Trianon Hotel by plugging in electrical heaters because she found the seventy-degree temperature maintained by the management too cold (see *International Herald Tribune*, Paris ed., Feb. 17, 23, 1951; and Hatch, *Red Carpet for Mamie*, pp. 229–30).

[3] For background on Helen Rogers Reid, president of the *New York Herald Tribune*, see no. 36.

[4] After receiving this letter from Eisenhower, Robinson cabled Buel Fellows Weare, president of the paper's European edition, to take no action against the author of the article. Robinson explained to Eisenhower that the writer, Robert Yoakum, was "a bright, energetic, over-aggressive young reporter" who had had no training in New York before going to Paris. This, Robinson said, partly accounted for "the atrociously bad, gratuitous example of high school journalism" (see Robinson to Eisenhower, Feb. 26, 1951, EM; and no. 60).

[5] Mrs. Eisenhower would not send the article to Robinson (see no. 60). On the Eisenhowers' search for a suitable residence see nos. 18, 119, and 254.

[6] For Eisenhower's bet with his old friend George Allen see nos. 48, 73, and 93.

To WILLIAM AVERELL HARRIMAN   *February 24, 1951*
Secret

Dear Averell:[1] If ever there should occur in Washington a lull in the
pressures on you, I am sure it would be a fine thing for you to run
over here for a few days. There are numbers of points to discuss and,
while none of them is at the moment of critical importance, it would be
well, I think, to begin establishing a close liaison between you and me
so that, as the important phases of this work develop, we can communicate concerning them on the basis of a common understanding.

This statement is, of course, a bit vague, something to be expected
at this early date. But in more specific language, I shall give you some
idea of what I am getting at.

I engaged, when last I saw the President,[2] to submit to him occasional reports of progress, informal in character, either written or
verbal. This was in recognition of the fact that my work is not and
cannot be exclusively military; neither is it exclusively of a kind pertaining to the State Department, to the E.C.A.,[3] to Charley Wilson's
organization,[4] or to any other. So, while simple military matters will
be reported to the Standing Group or, if exclusively American, to the
Defense establishment, the normal subject with which it will be necessary for someone high up in the administration to have some familiarity, will be a composite one.

Because of these complications—which often involve details—it is
inappropriate to write directly to the President; but, on the other hand,
if I should write to any particular Department, the paper would have
to be processed around until it landed in the hands of someone who
would be interested in all phases of the subject. All this indicates to
me that you are the one to whom I shall submit my informal reports
(although I have just written one letter to the President which I hope
he will give to you).[5] It is for this reason that I think it desirable that
you and I have, at all times, a common understanding of the situation
then current, as well as of probable future developments.

As of now, we are encountering the frustrations normal to the early
days of any important effort of this kind. With us, the confusion and
the irritations are multiplied by the hazy, almost chimerical character
of the organization to which I am officially responsible. For example,
the job of obtaining a site for headquarters, of constructing the necessary buildings and temporary barracks, of obtaining quarters in which
officers can live together and in harmony (particularly when the scale
of pay of these officers varies from that of the American down to that
of the Norwegian), of devising an organization that satisfies the nationalistic aspirations of twelve different countries or the personal ambi-

tions of affected individuals, is a very laborious and irksome business but one that must be done before we can get very far along the road of real progress. Yet there is no budget, not even for housekeeping, and there is no clear line to follow in getting these things accomplished, because each government is $\frac{1}{12}$ responsible and to refer them to committees will condemn us to inaction.[6]

When we get into the more difficult chores of producing troops and training them, of bringing over munitions and new American units, we begin to realize just how necessary it is that a few key figures in the whole development have commonly understood purposes, based upon a common understanding of the entire affair. It is completely futile to try to draw into this effort more than few individuals—the moment that we should make the attempt, we would be right back where we are at this point.

For fear that all this sounds pessimistic, I want to make clear that what I am talking about is a practical means for getting ahead; the more complicated any organizational or administrative problem becomes, the more necessary it is that a simple scheme or plan be devised through which the whole can be guided intelligently and thus gain the ends for which the organization was set up.

Because it is quite clear to me that you must be one—in fact, one of the most important ones—of these key figures, I am quite keen to talk to you whenever it is convenient for you to pay us a visit.

One of the subjects I discussed in my letter to the President was the importance I attach to the need for making clear, at home and abroad, that the six division total proposed for American land forces in Europe applies to *this year* only.[7]

At the end of World War II, I thought that nations and services had learned well the rudiments of the principles applicable to unified military effort among Allies and would be prepared, in the future, to act accordingly. I was wrong! All the old questions of nationality of commanders and their identification as to service are with us again. Perhaps you noted Mr. Churchill's bitter comments on this point in the House of Commons and, more important, the enthusiasm with which his criticism was received.[8]

In view of the urgent character of the job we have, it seems a pity to be using up time on this kind of thing. But even experienced persons are not free of muddying up the water in order to obtain the kind of job and charter they consider suitable to their station and talents. I have had some of these men come to me, praise me highly on what they call my readiness to pay the personal cost of occupying this post, and end up by implying that unless their own assignments should provide an increase of prestige and authority over what I had planned for them, it would be unfair to themselves or to their respective services or countries for them to serve!!

Of course, after my World War II experiences, I suppose you wonder why I am astonished at such reactions! I think the answer is that I had falsely assumed we now were so aware of danger that we had no time for such considerations! But I'm tempted to believe that human nature is still slightly overrated!!

Well, you can see that we could talk a long time![9] *As ever*

P.S. On second thought, I'll ask you to transmit to the President the letter I wrote to him—D

[1] For background on Harriman, President Truman's Special Assistant on Foreign Affairs, see no. 16; and *Eisenhower Papers*, vols. I–XI. Eisenhower had recently arrived in France and had started to organize his European Allied command (see no. 43).

[2] Eisenhower had met with President Truman and the cabinet on January 31 (see State, *Foreign Relations, 1951*, vol. III, *European Security and the German Question, Part I*, pp. 449ff.; see also nos. 18 and 23). Prior to this meeting he had lunch with the President at Blair House (Harry S. Truman, *Memoirs by Harry S. Truman*, 2 vols. [New York, 1955–56], vol. II, *Years of Trial and Hope*, p. 258).

[3] For background on the Economic Cooperation Administration (ECA), which supervised U.S. aid to Europe, see Galambos, *Columbia University*, no. 343.

[4] Charles Edward Wilson was Director of the Office of Defense Mobilization (ODM), which had been established in December 1950 to oversee a program of wartime controls and rearmament (Donovan, *Tumultuous Years*, pp. 324–25; S. Michaelis, ed., *The American Year Book: A Record of Events and Progress, Year 1950* [New York, 1951], p. 6). For background on Wilson see Galambos, *Columbia University*, no. 684.

[5] The letter to President Truman is the following document.

[6] Officers and men assigned to SHAPE were paid by their respective governments, and as Eisenhower noted, the rates of pay varied considerably (see John Gunther, *Eisenhower: The Man and the Symbol* [London, 1951], pp. 112–13). Early in February Eisenhower's chief of staff, General Gruenther (see no. 2), had reported to the Standing Group that a headquarters site for SHAPE had been selected and that $1.8 million would be needed to construct the necessary facilities and provide for communications. On February 20 SHAPE announced plans to locate its headquarters in Marly Forest, fifteen miles west of Paris and near Versailles (Gruenther to Standing Group, SH 20096, Feb. 8, 1951, CCS 092 Western Europe [3-12-48], Sec. 69; *International Herald Tribune*, Paris ed., Feb. 20, 1951). At this time, however, no decision had been reached on the question who would pay for the establishment and operating costs of Eisenhower's headquarters. The American position was that all of NATO's member governments should pay equal amounts to support the administrative functions of SHAPE, while the costs for larger, operational projects should be apportioned according to each nation's economic resources and ability to pay. The British and the French disagreed with this proposal (D-D [51] 52, Feb. 20, 1951, NATO Files, microfilm). Neither a budget for SHAPE nor a formula for cost sharing would be worked out until much later (see no. 167).

[7] See the following document.

[8] On February 22 Winston Churchill had criticized the pending appointment of an American admiral as Supreme Allied Commander, Atlantic (SACLANT) (see no. 2). In December 1950 NATO's Defense Committee had directed that this position, one that was roughly equivalent to the post of SACEUR, be filled as soon as possible after Eisenhower's appointment, and on February 19 the Council of Dep-

uties had approved the appointment of Admiral William Morrow Fechteler (USNA 1916), Commander in Chief of the Atlantic Fleet, as SACLANT. After news of this prospective appointment appeared in the London newspapers, Churchill asked British Prime Minister Clement Attlee in the House of Commons whether there were no British admirals capable of filling this post. Churchill queried, "How is it that when our experience is longer and wider than that of any other country and when we have all agreed with so much pleasure that Gen. Eisenhower should command the armed forces on land, we should have resigned any claims we might be thought to have to the command of the Atlantic?" (*International Herald Tribune*, Paris ed., Feb. 23, 1951). Churchill's questions inspired a raucous debate and forced Attlee to promise that he would reconsider Great Britain's agreement to an American as SACLANT (State, *Foreign Relations, 1951*, vol. III, *European Security and the German Question, Part I*, pp. 473–79; Poole, *History of the Joint Chiefs of Staff*, vol. IV, *1950–1952*, pp. 230–31). For background on the appointment of SA-CLANT see JCS 2073/96, Dec. 1, 1950, CCS 092 Western Europe (3-12-48), Sec. 63, and other papers in this same file, Secs. 65–66; for developments see no. 111. A SACLANT would not be appointed until early in 1952.
[9] In his reply (Mar. 1, 1951, EM) Harriman said that he had passed along Eisenhower's letter to President Truman and that he would "have every intention of following as closely as I can the problems in Washington that relate to your affairs. . . ." Eisenhower would soon write Harriman again (see no. 56).

46   *Eisenhower Mss.*

To Harry S. Truman   *February 24, 1951*

Dear Mr. President: By way of submitting the first of the informal reports I engaged to send you, the following is a rather sketchy account in which you may find some interest. However, assuming your permission, because of reasons outlined in this letter, I propose to send future communications of this kind to Averell Harriman,[1] who will transmit to you such of them as he may consider worthy of your personal attention.

I returned to Europe by ship, bringing with me my wife because of widespread and insistent advice that to fail to do so would create unfortunate psychological reaction in Europe. We reached Paris on February 21, and I have since been engaged more in settling irritating problems involved in the business of getting down to work rather than in the more far-reaching—but less immediate—ones of organizing, training, and indoctrinating the forces of NATO. I shall not trouble you with these details, which involve such matters as housing, financing, individual assignments, and so on.

Because of the somewhat involved position I now occupy, it would appear that frequently my best point of American contact will be through Averell, unless the subject should either be of such importance as to justify direct message to you or should be so specifically American and military in description as to indicate the U.S. Defense Department as the proper destination of the communication. Most subjects are of such complicated character as to affect jointly State, Defense, E.C.A., Charley Wilson,[2] and others. So Averell would normally be your only assistant (at least of my acquaintance) who could take cognizance of all aspects of the problem.

As you know, I have a single *official* point of contact with 12 governments—namely a composite body called The Standing Group.[3] But that body is $\frac{1}{3}$ French and $\frac{1}{3}$ British, whereas a goodly portion of our most serious problems will be purely American. This is because of our country's position of power and leadership, to say nothing of its inescapable function as the principal arsenal of NATO.

When I was in Washington, I testified before Congress, after presenting the case to you and to the Cabinet, that there is no present possibility of estimating accurately what will be the eventual requirement in Europe for American units.[4] This statement I believe is completely accurate and I've made this conviction plain in capitals on both sides of the Atlantic. I'm delighted that the Administration has decided on six divisions as our target in American ground units in Europe for *this year*, but I think it highly important that no one at home or abroad assume that this figure necessarily represents a permanent solution. Future strength could vary within fairly wide limits; moreover, if we can by combined effort help produce quickly the strengths needed, it should be possible, within some 4–8 years, to reduce the American ground forces stationed here at the same rate that European systems develop the trained reserves to replace American units.

I mention this specific point because it is one that frequently comes up for discussion with foreign officials and it is important that whatever statements I make conform to the basic understanding of the President.

I suppose your attention was invited to Winston Churchill's critical remarks in the House of Commons.[5] This is typical criticism in ventures of this kind, and illustrates again how necessary it is, in NATO, to plan for details of command so as to gain public support in a number of nations—or at least to avoid inciting resentment. I've a number of these problems in my lap right now; the arguments will be intensified because of the re-awakening of interest in the matter and because of the fixed personal ambitions, or possibly it is fair to say, convictions, of some of the individuals involved.

Our biggest problem is production. I have no doubt that eventually we shall be all right as to quantity and quality; but the element of time may well be critical. How to solve this one without going hysterical I don't know—but I have tremendous faith in Charley Wilson and

Lucius Clay.[6] I suspect that priorities in production are going to be necessary so as to solve the problem of timing.

With best wishes. *Respectfully*

[1] See the preceding document.

[2] See the preceding document, nn. 3 and 4.

[3] See no. 2, n. 2.

[4] In his testimony before a joint session of the Senate Foreign Relations and Armed Services committees on February 1 Eisenhower had argued for "a certain flexibility in action," adding, "I think that in advance to specify that X number of divisions can go to France, or that such and such a thing must be done in mathematical or arithmetical ratio—in my opinion that decision would be an error." On February 15, however, Secretary of Defense Marshall told the same two committess that the United States would send only four more divisions to Europe and that no further shipments were contemplated (Senate Committee on Foreign Relations and Committee on Armed Services, *Assignment of Ground Forces of the United States to Duty in the European Area*, 1951, pp. 10, 40, 49. See also Schulz to Eisenhower, Feb. 15, 1951, EM, Persons Corr.; Acheson, *Present at the Creation*, pp. 494–95; and Donovan, *Tumultuous Years*, pp. 322–24).

[5] See the preceding document.

[6] For background on General Lucius Du Bignon Clay, Eisenhower's friend and currently a special assistant to Director of Defense Mobililzation Charles E. Wilson, see *Eisenhower Papers*, vols. I–XI. Clay was also chairman of the board and chief executive officer of the Continental Can Company. He would soon testify before a joint Senate committee on sending additional troops to Europe (see no. 54). For an assessment of shortages in military production see Kaplan, *Community of Interests*, pp. 120–26, 136–38, 156; see also nos. 173 and 174.

47   *Eisenhower Mss.*

To PHILIP YOUNG   *February 24, 1951*

Dear Philip: I hope that, from time to time, you will drop me a note to keep me up-to-date on your progress in securing conference sponsorship for the American Assembly.[1] I think that, just before I left, I sent you complete information on three gift promises, two for $10,000 each and one for $25,000.[2]

Did the statement that was released at Columbia on the day I left get any kind of play? It is possible that we watered it down too much to make it an interesting news story.[3] In any event, you should plan carefully for the statement you are going to make on the day you can announce Lew Douglas' acceptance of the chairmanship of the Policy Board.[4] His standing in the country is certain to be most effective in assuring the success of the Assembly program. I am anxious to know also the identity of the individual that you obtain to act as the permanent professional Director.[5]

In this job, there are more than the usual number of frustrations—it is really hard to see any noticeable progress from day to day. But we keep plugging, and we shall finally get there.[6]

Please give my love to Faith,[7] and my warm regards to all my associates working on the Assembly. *Cordially*

[1] For background on Young, dean of the Columbia University Graduate School of Business, and on the American Assembly see nos. 8 and 25, respectively.

[2] Eisenhower had written Young on November 18, 1950 (EM), concerning when and to whom pledged gifts to the Assembly should be sent. The three donations mentioned here were probably those of Arthur Godfrey, Thomas John Watson, Jr., and Hugh Roy Cullen (see Schulz to Eisenhower, Nov. 17, 1950, EM; for background on the three donors see Galambos, *Columbia University*).

[3] On the day of Eisenhower's departure for Europe (see no. 38) Columbia had released a press statement containing the General's assessment of the university's civic research projects. In the release Eisenhower had emphasized the American Assembly over the other programs begun during his administration of Columbia, saying that public support for the plan had been "most gratifying" (see *New York Times*, Feb. 16, 1951; and no. 36).

[4] On March 14, 1951, Columbia would announce that Lewis Williams Douglas, American Ambassador to Great Britain from 1947 to 1950, business executive, and former congressman from Arizona, had been appointed chairman of the National Policy Board of the American Assembly. Among other duties, it was the board's responsibility to select delegates for each assembly session, seeking "a fair cross-section of competent responsible citizens" (see *New York Times*, Mar. 14, 1951). Eisenhower had been urging Douglas to accept the chairman's post for several months, and he had agreed to do so shortly before the General sailed for Europe (see Galambos, *Columbia University*, nos. 1081 and 1117; and EM, Douglas Corr.).

[5] Philip Young would continue as Executive Director of the Assembly, but lawyer and businessman Edwin T. Gibson would become Associate Executive Director in 1952 (see Young to Eisenhower, Jan. 2, Feb. 8, 1952, both in EM). For announcements of other Assembly officers and participants see *New York Times*, Mar. 31, Apr. 24, 1951.

[6] On Eisenhower's early difficulties with the SHAPE organization see nos. 45, 46, and 53.

[7] Young's wife, the former Faith Adams.

48   *Eisenhower Mss.*

To George Edward Allen   *February 24, 1951*

Dear George:[1] It seems more than a month since I have had any direct word of you, although Mr. Kirchner informed me, just before we left New York, that you were with him in the desert.[2] Since I suspect that you were out there on a health and reducing program (including a lot of exercise), I must inform you that I should easily be inside my limit by the first of the month. I am now two pounds away, and still have 5 days to go. I used the time on the ship to exercise every day, and to start a truly rigid diet, from which I have not varied in over two weeks. I forget the details of our bet, but I am sure that you have them in your book. All I am doing about it is making sure that I get down to my allotted weight of 174. In fact, I am going a couple of pounds lighter than that.[3]

Before I left New York, I had a long talk with Art Nevins,[4] who told me that he had a date to go to Gettysburg on March 2nd, to look after our farming interests. This discussion brought out a number of problems, concerning which he will speak to you soon. Since his work will be largely managerial, rather than manual, he probably should have a somewhat bigger outlay of land in order to realize the maximum on our overhead. In other words, there ought to be a farm of yours that would be tillable or usable in an agricultural way and lying close enough to mine so that the same implements and, in some cases, even the same labor could be used on both. Certainly, the same manager could handle both. Such an arrangement would eliminate the $120.00 monthly rent that we, as partners, pay to me for the use of the land. Also, such an arrangement could provide some kind of a house where we could have a permanent farmer-tenant. Such a person we badly need and he, in turn, could probably board extra labor that we would have to hire from time to time, which would eliminate trips back and forth to town. All this would put us on a completely equal basis both as to equipment and to land, houses, etc. If yours should be a bigger one, of course we would have to make some arrangement with the monthly rent going to you for the differential in acreage.[5]

All this is just an idea that I discussed with Art—you can do about it whatever you please.

I hope that something will bring you over this way before long, particularly if you could get Mary[6] to fly with you for a transoceanic trip. Incidentally, we thoroughly enjoyed the journey on the Queen Elizabeth. And remember, even if you cannot come over, there is no reason why you should not spend a few cents to mail me a letter every now and then.

Love to Mary and my very best wishes to you.[7] *Cordially*

P.S. On this job, I need advice even more urgently than I did in June, 1942.[8]

[1] For background on Eisenhower's old friend Allen see no. 9; and *Eisenhower Papers*, vols. I–XI.

[2] On clothing store chairman Walter Kirschner see no. 33.

[3] The correspondence concerning Eisenhower's bet with Allen and the exact amount the loser would have to pay would continue for the next month (see EM; and nos. 73 and 93).

[4] For background on Brigadier General Arthur Nevins, Eisenhower's farm manager, see no. 33.

[5] Under the terms of their partnership, Allen was to provide all operating funds for both farms, including the upkeep costs of the General's buildings and acreage; Allen would also absorb all losses that were incurred. The profits made from the farms would be shared by Allen and Nevins, with Eisenhower benefiting through his partner and manager's efforts in general maintenance, increased soil fertility, and physical improvements to the property. Allen would not purchase additional land in the Gettysburg area, but parcels adjoining the Eisenhower farm would later be obtained by the General's friend oil executive William Alton Jones (see Nevins, *Five-Star Farmer*, pp. 84, 87, 100, 109, 126. For background on Jones see no. 38 in this volume; and Galambos, *Columbia University*, no. 388).

[6] On Allen's wife Mary see no. 9.

[7] For developments see nos. 73 and 93.

[8] Eisenhower had first met Allen in London in June 1942, shortly after the General had assumed his responsibilities as Commanding General, European Theater of Operations (see Chandler, *War Years*, nos. 329, 333, and 352; and Eisenhower, *At Ease*, pp. 282–87).

49   *Eisenhower Mss.*

To Robert Lowry Biggers   *February 26, 1951*

Dear Bob: Thank you for your thoughtful letter and your offer to keep an eye on our limousine which my brother Milton is keeping in storage for us.[1] We made these arrangements because of the great care you and your engineers took to see that that particular car carried with it the latest refinements and, to all intents and purposes, was a "handmade" vehicle. We could not just abandon it.[2] Of course, should the time come when you would counsel us to trade it for a newer model, we would rely entirely on your judgment.

Mrs. Eisenhower and I thought we would give the children the advantage of the somewhat newer Windsor and I hope we did not embarrass you in any way in making the switch and turning in John's car as ours for credit.[3] Schulz tells me that whatever will be realized on the sale of this car will be held as a credit in the Company's books at Detroit, as we are not certain just where we will purchase the replacement.[4] Through him, I am also advised that it will not be long before we see the latest in the line of Crown Imperials right here in Paris. It will indeed be a touch of home.

I hope it will not be too long before you find reasons for coming to Europe and that you will make my headquarters a stop on your itinerary. By that time I should have a "guest room" that will be yours.

With warm personal regard and best wishes, in which Mrs. Eisenhower joins. *Cordially*

[1] For background on Robert Lowry Biggers, president of the Fargo Motor Division of the Chrysler Corporation, and on the Eisenhower's seven-passenger Crown Imperial limousine see Galambos, *Columbia University*, no. 699; and Biggers to Eisenhower, February 16, 1951, EM.
[2] On the storage of the limousine see nos. 119 and 686.
[3] Eisenhower's son John had purchased a new Chrysler Windsor in 1950 (see Galambos, *Columbia University*, no. 565).
[4] In the spring of 1952, shortly before his return to the United States to campaign for the Republican presidential nomination, Eisenhower would have the stored vehicle traded in on the purchase of a new Chrysler limousine (see Biggers to Eisenhower, Apr. 3, 1952; and Eisenhower to Biggers, Apr. 9, 1952, both in EM; see also no. 686).

50   *Eisenhower Mss.*

To WILLIAM H. BURNHAM   *February 28, 1951*

Dear Bill: Your letter of the 23rd and the packet of clippings you forwarded on the 21st have reached my desk. Both were interesting, the letter even more than the booklet.[1]

Just in order to give one old friend a fairly clear exposition of my current views, I am writing to Ed Bermingham. I have always had confidence in his judgment and I should like him to know that in my mind the current security problem is not as simple black-and-white as the "Internationalist" versus the "Nationalist" debaters would like to make it appear. In order to avoid long duplication in re-stating my position, I enclose with this a copy of the letter I am sending him.[2]

I cannot tell you how deeply appreciative I am of the trouble you are taking to keep me informed. Also, tell Bob Whitney I am looking forward with real anticipation to the letter that his father is sending to me.[3]

Don't let anything interfere with your plans for coming to Europe in a month or so and, in the meantime—whenever you run into any of our common friends—give them warm greetings from me.[4] *As ever*

P.S. I brought with me on the QUEEN ELIZABETH the first part of the printers' proof on General Bradley's book, which I have now read. Sometime I'll talk to you about it.[5]

[1] Burnham frequently kept the General informed on political developments in the United States, sending him detailed letters concerning persons with whom he had spoken, clippings of newspaper articles, and political cartoons (see EM, Burnham Corr.; for background see no. 40).
[2] Eisenhower's letter to Bermingham is the following document. On an earlier draft of this letter (copy in EM) Eisenhower had crossed out the name of General Charles Gates Dawes and substituted Bermingham's name in the first sentence of this paragraph. Dawes, vice-president under Calvin Coolidge and a brigadier general

on Pershing's staff during World War I, was chairman of the board of the City National Bank and Trust Company of Chicago.

[3] Robert Bacon Whitney and his father George, assistant vice-president and chairman of the board, respectively, of J. P. Morgan & Company, Inc., had been supporters of Eisenhower's programs at Columbia University. George Whitney would soon begin to send the General letters on the American business scene (see nos. 55 and 221). For background on Robert Whitney see Galambos, *Columbia University*, no. 1005.

[4] Burnham would visit Eisenhower in Paris during March (see nos. 75 and 102).

[5] General Omar Nelson Bradley, chairman of the United States JCS since 1949, would publish his memoir of World War II, *A Soldier's Story*, later this year (see no. 199; on Bradley see *Eisenhower Papers*, vols. I–XI).

51   *Bermingham Papers*

To EDWARD JOHN BERMINGHAM   *February 28, 1951*
Personal and confidential

Dear Ed: Just before I left New York, I sent to you a very short letter in an attempt to lay before you the basis of my thinking with respect to our current international problems. While I have had no reply, I am now expanding somewhat on the same theme for a reason that I think to be valid.[1]

Firstly: I want, fundamentally, to test my own conclusions against such as you have formed. This is because of my respect for the clarity of your thinking. If there should be a difference between us, I would certainly be most appreciative if you would point out to me any point where you think that I have gone astray.[2]

Secondly: I have had rumors that a number of individuals look upon my acceptance of military duty as a "joining of the Administration" and that, as a result, I not only participate in its policy-making, but I support all its foreign programs, possibly even, its domestic ones.[3]

Of course, you personally understand that my performance of military duty bears no such implication whatsoever—you are quite well aware of the extreme degree in which I differ with some of our governmental foreign and domestic policies of the past years. So, I do not need to expound upon that phase of the question. But, on the other hand, I thought it might be a good thing to have in your hands some exposition of my convictions with regard to our national security problem so that, from time to time, you would be in a position—if you find any validity in my line of reasoning—*to help achieve that unity of basic purpose that we must have if this effort is ever to enjoy any success.*[4]

The nation's security problem is not as simple a black-and-white matter as the "Great Debators" would like to make it appear. There is only one angle from which to approach any international problems; from that of "America first." I realize that argument cannot be presented in terms of slogans and catch words but, because we have always attempted to classify people into conveniently labelled groups, I want to make clear that I am *not* one of these "Internationalists" in the sense that I am willing to trust America's welfare to an international Congress of any kind.[5]

We, as Americans, face a deadly danger for a very simple reason. Communism, both ruthless in purpose and insidious as to method, is using the traditional Imperialistic designs of Russia and the present physical strength of Asia and Eastern Europe to promote the Communistic objective of *world revolution and subsequent domination of all the earth* by the Communistic Party, centering in Moscow.

My own adult life has been given over to the study of questions involving America's security and of serving in uniformed capacities in our security forces. During the latter part of this service, this Communistic danger has been steadily rising and has now reached a peak where definite, prompt, and comprehensive measures are necessary if we are to survive. Our position as the chief exponent of the free system—of the dignity of the individual and of a capitalistic economy—not only makes us the chief target of Communistic destructive purpose, but makes it incumbent upon us to be a bit wiser and more determined in our defense of freedom than would be the case in a country where devotion to these free principles does not burn so brightly.[6] Up to this point, I think there is no loyal American today who would disagree; the sole point of difference seems to be as to *how* we should go about the task we understand must be performed.

First and foremost, it is almost trite to say that our own country must remain solvent; that bankruptcy for us would be a tremendous, if not a decisive, victory for the Kremlin. One of the things Communism tries to prove to the peoples of the earth is that our system is weak, inefficient, and unfair. I violently disagree with any plan or program that ignores this basic principle, either explicitly or implicitly. I am sure that one thing worse than bankruptcy would be military defeat, yet it is my contention that *the only way we can achieve military success either in preventing war or in winning a war is through preserving the integrity of our economy and our financial structure.* This means courage in facing up to sacrifice—both individual and national.[7]

Communism acts both through threat of aggression by means of armed force and by internal subversion, bribery, and corruption. This combined effort has been so long sustained against Western Europe that this region is by no means the healthy, strong, and virile portion of the world that we considered it back in the days of 1914 or indeed in 1934. *Yet the importance of Europe to America's security is not by any means to be minimized.*

On the purely military side, the transfer, by force or by subversion, to Communistic control of the great industrial complex of Western Europe, including its tremendous numbers in skilled labor, would be for us a major catastrophe. If the Eurasian Continent were one solid mass of Communist-dominated people and industry, there would be no possible military dispositions on our part that could protect the Continent of Africa except possibly its southern areas. Among other areas, the Belgian Congo, the Mid-East, and the Suez Canal would be gone!

The military strength of such a Communistic combination, organized and armed under Communist dictatorship, would be staggering; and the existence of such a vast organism, hostile to us, would pose a military problem that would defy solution. Aggravating the whole situation would be the fact that over and beyond this would be the economic problem. Where would we get the materials needed for our existence? For making steel, for making atomic bombs? It is this kind of possibility that keeps me awake nights, keeps me pondering as to applicable policy, and keeps me working in a position and in a region that I had fervently hoped and prayed would forever belong only to my past.[8] Nothing else could have moved me to the personal and family sacrifices entailed. So, as far as personal inclination is involved, this kind of thinking and concern for my country completely defeats my former hope of devoting the remainder of my years to constructive aims. I thoroughly believe that, at Columbia University, I was contributing something toward the future safety and health of the American form of democracy.[9]

If all the eventualities I have presented on the world situation are only reasonably accurate, it is clear that American efforts to rejuvenate in Europe a feeling of self-respect, of self-confidence, and of self-dependence—including the burning purpose and desire of self-defense—are not only worthwhile, they are mandatory because of the utter bleakness of the alternative. I have no means of knowing just how efficiently the Marshall Plan has been administered nor exactly how effective it has been in restoring economic capacity and in helping revive the spirit of Europe. The testimony here is to the effect that without the Marshall Plan, Europe would already be under the control of Moscow. In any event, the present question is how to inspire Europe *to produce for itself those armed forces that, in the long run, must provide the only means by which Europe can be defended.* Over the years, I agree that there is no defense for Western Europe that depends exclusively or even materially upon the existence, in Europe, of strong American units. The spirit must be here and the strength must be produced here.

We cannot be a modern Rome guarding the far frontiers with our legions if for no other reason than because these are *not*, politically, *our* frontiers. What we must do is to assist these people [to] regain their confidence and get on their own military feet.[10]

The American *material* effort, I think, could and should be limited as to *length of time*; I consider it an error to try to predict and fix its limits, as of this moment, in terms of exact degree of effort. While I do not know the length of time that some occupational troops may necessarily be in Germany, I would say this: If in ten years, all American troops stationed in Europe for national defense purposes have not been returned to the United States, then this whole project will have failed.[11]

There is no use exploring the various directions in which the international situation could have, in the meantime, been drifting, but it is quite certain that should Europe as a whole fail, in ten years and with our help, to rebuild the *economic, military, and internal* strength required to preserve itself inviolate against Communism and Communistic attack—then the United States will have no recourse but to seek some other solution to this desperate problem. But, in the meantime, the issues are so great, the contrast between what could be won and what would, through neglect, be lost is so all-embracing, that I do not believe we should place, in advance, announced size limitations upon our effort. These would tend to retard or discourage the rebuilding of European spirit, which must be the foundation for European strength.[12]

I repeat that there is no reason whatsoever for writing this letter except my respect for your ideas and convictions; and the thought that you may find occasional opportunity to help clarify thinking on these vital matters.

My warm greetings to your lovely bride,[13] and warm regards to yourself. *Cordially*

P.S. While my purpose is to give you, personally, a thumb-nail sketch of my thinking—I request that you do not give this letter to any other person (I except, of course, your own family).[14]

---

[1] Eisenhower had written Bermingham in early February after testifying before Congress on the development of the NATO military organization (see no. 23).

[2] Bermingham was influential with conservative groups in both business and politics in the United States. Without attracting public attention, he would serve as a conduit of information between Eisenhower and members of those groups through the 1952 presidential election. Bermingham would interpret the General's views on issues and report on conservative thought regarding Eisenhower's actions (see nos. 146, 386, and 754; other correspondence in EM, Bermingham Corr.; and Lyon, *Portrait of the Hero*, pp. 388, 413–14).

[3] Strong congressional opposition had arisen in regard to Truman's right to assign U.S. troops to duty in Europe. Eisenhower—a staunch advocate of the need for U.S. participation in the defense of Western Europe—had been accused by these

same congressmen of being an Administration man (see no. 23, esp. n. 3; and *New York Times,* Jan. 16, 1951).

[4] For some of Eisenhower's points of disagreement with the Truman Administration see Galambos, *Columbia University,* nos. 443, 981, and 1108.

[5] The international movement for the formation of a world federal government had recently gained a great deal of publicity in both Europe and the United States. In the past Eisenhower had been contacted by the United World Federalists in attempts to gain his support for their plans, but he had always refused (see *ibid.,* nos. 436 and 729; Cord Meyer, Jr., *Peace or Anarchy* (Boston, 1948); and *New York Times,* Jan. 6, Feb. 4, 10, 12, Sept. 28, 1951).

[6] Eisenhower had recently received a paper on Soviet national strategy prepared for the National War College (see no. 43).

[7] American expenditures in the NATO effort were a major issue of debate in Congress (see no. 23; and *Congressional Record,* 82d Cong., 1st sess., 1951, 97, pt. 1: 34, 54-69, 94). For Eisenhower's thoughts on American military spending in Europe see Senate Committee on Foreign Relations and Committee on Armed Services, *Assignment of Ground Forces of the United States to Duty in the European Area,* 1951, pp. 16, 22, 33.

[8] Eisenhower had expressed these same ideas concerning the importance of Western Europe and its colonies to the United States during his congressional testimony in early February (see *ibid.,* pp. 3-4, 31; no. 23; House Committee on International Relations, *Selected Executive Session Hearings,* vol. VI, *Military Assistance Programs,* pt. 2, pp. 294-95; *Newsweek,* Feb. 12, 1951, 16; and *Time,* Feb. 12, 1951, 15-20).

[9] On Eisenhower's efforts at Columbia see nos. 36 and 47; and Galambos, *Columbia University.* For the personal sacrifices made in accepting the NATO command see nos. 3, 4, and 38.

[10] In his address to both houses of Congress (Feb. 1) Eisenhower had said that the "effects of the Marshall plan have been marked and have been important to the partial rehabilitation of Europe . . . ," but pessimism and defeatism still existed in the nations devastated by World War II. The United States was the only free nation capable of providing the leadership necessary to "establish an upward-going spiral which meets this problem of strength and morale" (Senate Committee on Foreign Relations and Committee on Armed Services, *Assignment of Ground Forces of the United States to Duty in the European Area,* 1951, pp. 3, 6). For background on the European Recovery Program, known as the Marshall Plan, see Galambos, *Chief of Staff.* nos. 1938 and 2023, and *Columbia University,* nos. 303 and 343.

[11] Thirty years later the United States would have 490,000 troops stationed in different locations overseas (Trevor N. Dupuy, Grace P. Hayes, and John A. C. Adams, *The Almanac of World Military Power* [San Rafael, Calif., 1980], p. 348).

[12] Eisenhower had repeatedly stressed this point in answering the efforts of Senators Robert Alphonso Taft (Republican from Ohio), Kenneth Spicer Wherry (Republican from Nebraska), and others to limit the size of the U.S. forces sent to Europe. Before the Senate Foreign Relations Committee and the Committee on Armed Services on February 1 the General had said that the number of U.S. troops should be determined by the President, acting upon the recommendations of the Chiefs of Staff. Eisenhower believed that if common sense were violated and "an inordinate amount of strength" were to be transferred to Europe, Congress could then intervene (Senate Committee on Foreign Relations and Committee on Armed Services, *Assignment of Ground Forces of the United States to Duty in the European Area,* 1951, pp. 11-12).

[13] See no. 23, n. 12.

[14] Eisenhower would himself send copies of this letter to certain of his friends (see, for example, nos. 50 and 63).

To Joseph Lawton Collins   *February 28, 1951*

Dear Joe:[1] There are numerous and sometimes annoying details coming up in connection with our attempt to get started in NATO work that would make fine conversation for you and me over a highball; I doubt that they are of sufficient importance at the moment to constitute logical subjects for a letter. Nevertheless, I feel it very important that you and I stay pretty close together, at least as to what each of us is thinking, and so occasionally I will try one-sided implementation of this purpose with a letter.

There is no need, I presume, to tell you that the early task of organization here is cursed with all of the old conceptions of national and service prestige, as well as individual ideas of exactly how particular details of organization will mean success or failure.[2] The older I grow, the more weary I become of those people who find, in a particular detail of organization, something more important than the quality of the individuals manning it. Give me a sufficient number of real personalities and I wouldn't trade them for *perfection* in organization— even if this were guaranteed by Saint Peter himself. Nevertheless, each conversation with these various individuals brings us a little closer to a common understanding of the problem, and therefore that much nearer to its solution.

In a short time, I hope that we will be making certain announcements—some of which should go a long way towards quieting the bitter battle of words now going on in Britain.[3] Incidentally, it does seem odd to me that high governmental leaders have not learned something from past experiences. The terrific impact upon public opinion in Allied Countries of command assignments in World War II was full of specific lessons that apparently are now being ignored.[4] However, it is not the business of soldiers to get into these things too deeply. But we too often find ourselves in the position of having to work like dogs to smooth out situations that should never have been created.

Recently, I talked to a few persons who had been to Korea. It is just a bit amusing to find some of them taking the stand that everything learned *before* Korea should now be completely erased from our minds; nothing is valid in war unless drawn directly from particular experiences in that conflict.[5] However, some of these contentions would be far more convincing if there was any unanimity of opinion. Actually, I have found that one man draws one lesson from a certain experience, while another one draws an opposite one from the selfsame set of facts. This, of course, is as it has always been.

Of one thing I am quite certain. Ground and air alike must get busy and perfect the methods of actual battlefield cooperation and together must develop better and more *widely understood doctrines* affecting their combined use.[6] It does no good merely to say who should "command"; unless there are commonly understood doctrines, all the command authority in the world cannot assure effective cooperation and coordination. Moreover, there is a point in which the American ground officer is likely to make a serious error. It is in the differences in "commanding" a man of your own service and controlling one in another. Up to and including World War II, American officers of ground and air could actually *"command"* each other; now, any serious differences will invariably be sent to respective bureaus. What must be developed is complete confidence in some individual in the war zone—he can always settle these things.

In spite of the widely held belief on the part of the ground forces that the air has been very neglectful in this matter during the past few years, what we are concerned with now is the present and future—and not in looking back for scapegoats or for someone to criticize. The responsibilities of the air in this matter are never, under any organization, going to be properly carried out until every single man in the Air Force, from the newest recruit to the most senior general, understands that one important reason for their existence is to work effectively with and for the ground forces. This must be hammered home day after day, all of the time, without end. They must even understand that their so-called "strategic bombing," while directed at the enemy's will to resist, is going to reach maximum effectiveness only when it attacks something that is vitally necessary to the enemy in all of his defensiveness plans and efforts. Fuel and ammunition for the ground forces are good examples.

When it comes to the tactical phases of ground-air action, there must not only be common doctrine, but common study of procedures and techniques, until we are, in truth, *part of the same team.*

All this is trite, that I realize. But I do find, again and again, instances of thinking that is faulty because it directs itself only toward organization and command arrangements in an effort to cure all evil.

On the part of the ground, we must indoctrinate all with a clear understanding of the limitations of the Air Forces as well as its power and possibilities. For example, in war, the ground soldier in battle always yells for more and more air. Would it not be well to show, in our schools, how much of the national resources, measured in money or in man-hours, must go into a light bomber, as compared, let us say, to field guns? Now, if you were to say to a division commander on the battlefield, "What do you want, that one plane or X field guns?" I wonder what the answer would be when the going is tough. But, if there is to be a limit (and there always is), some decision must be applied to every item we have.

Our minimum purpose in ground-air preparations is to make sure that we have the kind and number of airplanes that will *prevent the enemy air from interfering* decisively with our ground operations. Since we will always be initially on the defensive, we will never have this much in the beginning of a war, except possibly at some chosen place of our own concentration. More than this will not be forthcoming for a long, long time. This means, of course, that the Army must learn to fight without the *ground* aid of airplanes, but we must depend upon our own air to keep the other fellows from blasting us with impunity.

There has been much talk of air and sea winning a war, etc.—I honestly believe that, if we view the future with naked eyes, and reject all wishful thinking, we will find that the training, indoctrination, conditioning, equipping, and readying of our ground forces is possibly going to be an even more important thing in any future war than in the past. This certainly does not minimize the effect and influences of sea and air power, both of which I believe in implicitly. Moreover, I believe that these two elements are particularly important in time of peace, because of the deterrent effect on those who might seek war as a solution to the world's ills. By all means, let us support both.

But let us also remember that men on the ground are *not* cannon fodder, except when they are committed to battle improperly led, trained, conditioned, or equipped. Where ground troops are necessary, at that point these particular qualities may be so vital as to influence the fate of the nation.

I am not quite certain how I got to wandering off on such a line, in this kind of a letter. Possibly, I just get tired of so much loose thinking in the business of producing armed forces efficiently. We like to think that we can *buy* out of our problems, or use some legerdemain to escape the bitter realities that common sense shows are facing us. And sometimes the individual thinks that if he is just given, on paper, an all-inclusive authority, the battle is won!

Actually, of course, it is my earnest conviction that, unless we can prevent a war, the only thought that we can cling to thereafter is that winning it will be better than losing it. But if I did not believe that our efforts today were directed toward the prevention of war—and, in fact, that they give, for the present, the only sensible way of carrying out a preventive purpose—I would most certainly not be here.

We are beset with a thousand obstacles in administrative details in our effort to get truly at our work. Some of these affect living conditions, national and international budgets, which, incidentally, do not exist,[7] and details of organizing and of naming staffs and commanders.[8] Others involve news from home that the public mind is still widely divided on the basic virtues of this effort with some evidence that authorities are already trying to compromise on the matter by saying that six divisions is our total objective, instead of this year's objective, as explained to me by General Bradley and, I think, by you.[9] All these and a thousand other influences and problems make it difficult to get into the stage of actual preparation. However, we have also an accumulation of small bits of evidence that are on the optimistic side. These we cling to and get on with the job.

Anytime that you can see a few days free during which you could visit us, send us a cable so that I will be certain to be at my headquarters; then come right ahead. We will find a lot of things to talk about that will prove of real interest, possibly of value. And, on the personal side, it will always be fun to see you.[10]

My love to Gladys[11] and, of course, warmest regard to you. *Cordially*

[1] For background on Collins, Chief of Staff of the Army since August 1949 and Eisenhower's close associate since World War II, see *Eisenhower Papers*, vols. I–XI. A notation on the file copy of this letter in EM reads, "I don't believe this was used—." This note was probably written by Eisenhower's aide Craig Cannon (see no. 29, n. 3). There is no reply in EM.

[2] For background see no. 2; and n. 3 below.

[3] See no. 45. Criticism of the proposed appointment of an American as SACLANT had continued in the British House of Commons after Winston Churchill raised the issue on February 22. Eisenhower would soon announce that three British officers would be appointed to positions on SACEUR's staff, but these appointments would not completely alleviate British ill-feeling (State, *Foreign Relations, 1951*, vol. III, *European Security and the German Question, Part I*, pp. 477–80, 98; see also Press Release, Mar. 5, 1951, EM, Subject File, Personnel, SHAPE). The General would also urge that increased emphasis be placed on British command positions in the Mediterranean (see no. 56).

[4] See no. 2; see also John S. D. Eisenhower, *The Bitter Woods* (New York, 1969), pp. 46–47, 267–71, 282.

[5] We have been unable to locate any record of these discussions in EM. On February 23 Eisenhower had met with Marshal of the Royal Air Force Sir John Slessor (see no. 62), who would send the General several memorandums concerning Korean operations (see Slessor to Eisenhower, Feb. 26, 1951, and other papers in EM, Slessor Corr.). For a list of Eisenhower's other visitors see the chronology, in vol. XIII.

[6] For background see Galambos, *Chief of Staff*, no. 1840; see also Galambos, *Columbia University*, no. 639. The Korean War had sparked renewed controversy over the proper employment of tactical air power in close support of ground troops. In a transcript of a lecture sent to Eisenhower by Air Marshal Slessor (see n. 5 above), a British airman had criticized the U.N. tactical air effort in Korea and had called for "more joint training and education between all echelons of Army and Air Force personnel" (see Russell Frank Weigley, *The American Way of War: A History of United States Military Strategy and Policy* [Bloomington, Ind., 1977], pp. 383–85; Malcolm W. Cagle and Frank A. Manson, *The Sea War in Korea* [Annapolis, Md., 1957], pp. 71–74; and Richard H. Kohn and Joseph P. Harahan, *Air Superiority in World War II and Korea* [Washington, D.C., 1983], pp. 66–83). The problem would arise in Eisenhower's own command (see no. 53).

[7] See nos. 45 and 167.

[8] See no. 53.

[9] See no. 46.

[10] Collins would visit Eisenhower in May (see no. 183).

[11] Collins's wife, the former Gladys Easterbrook.

I have now been in Paris for about ten days occupying a temporary headquarters in the Astoria Hotel.[1] The problems to date have centered far more on the annoying and frustrating details that impede the effort to get *ready* to work rather than any important subject connected with the arming and training of European forces.

Yesterday, I went to see the British Chiefs of Staff. We had lunch at Claridge's and I immediately returned to this City. The general talk was about plans and schemes for organizing for the defense of Western Europe, with one eye on the possibilities of doing something to alleviate the bitterness of British popular reaction to the recent announcement of Fechteler as the Supreme Commander in the North Atlantic.[2] I personally believe we can do something by emphasizing the importance of the Mediterranean area command and announcing some British Naval officer as the commander. (This command would not include control over the American Naval Forces given me for protection of my right flank, nor would it interfere in any way with my scheme of command for the protection of Western Europe.)[3]

Admiral Sherman is coming to see me tomorrow with Admiral Carney.[4] I hope that we shall reach such clear understandings of what we are trying to do, that I can push right ahead in forming up the various sub-sectors of this command, making announcements as to commanders, and thereafter getting on with the real job that we have. General Juin, who I want for command of ground forces in the center, will not return to Paris for some days.[5] I understand that I will have some difficulty with him because he will insist upon taking actual operational control of supporting air forces. But he does not see that such an organization will give both the American and British Air Forces the excuse to hold back on allocation of air units to this command. They will claim that the "ground" viewpoint is manifesting itself and that the air cannot afford to make sizeable allocations in an area where the air "will not be so used as to realize its maximum capabilities."[6]

Of course, all this kind of talk is largely balderdash, but each of the Services has its own little fetishes and prejudices and insists upon living by them. In our own way, we service people are not completely free of the kind of thing that motivates the ordinary or small-time politician— this is the inability to shake loose from considerations of a short-term self-aggrandizement or advancement in favor of the long-term, eventual good for all of us. (In spite of this statement, I still believe that the uniformed Services produce a higher average of concern for the public good and selfless devotion to sheer duty than do any other professions or industrial or labor organizations.)

Right now, France is without a Government. The one headed by Mr. Plevin has fallen and we do not know when one can be successfully organized to take its place.[7] Britain is torn apart by savage resentment against the Government for consenting to Fechteler's appointment in the Atlantic.[8] The source of this, of course, is England's traditional concern with the sea and the sea lanes that connect it to all other parts of its Empire. Moreover, national prestige and glory have been damaged. This is the type of thing that should be foreseen by so-called statesmen and political leaders but, instead, they just blunder along and leave the results of their errors for someone else to clean up. Too often, these poor victims are the men in uniform.

I am collecting a most able staff. I am particularly impressed with Schuyler and Anderson, two Americans.[9] In addition, a little personal group I have made up of Gault, McCann, and Carroll are most unusual.[10] De Havilland, a Britisher on the Council of National Representatives, seems likewise to be a very capable person.[11] Among the French officers, I have not formed any real conclusions; but among the Government officials who have just lost their places, I liked Plevin, Schumann, and Moch very much indeed.[12]

[1] The Hotel Astoria had been the site of the SHAPE advance planning group (see no. 17). Eisenhower would not move his headquarters to its permanent location in Marly forest until June (see Ismay, *NATO*, p. 38; see also no. 45, n. 6).

[2] See nos. 45 and 52. Eisenhower had flown to London from Paris the morning of March 1 and had met with British military leaders at Claridge's Hotel. He had returned to France after lunch (see papers in EM, Subject File, Trips, SHAPE no. 2).

[3] In January the JCS had proposed that NATO appoint a commander in chief of Allied Naval Forces in the Mediterranean, with operational control over all Mediterranean naval forces except those nationally commanded units engaged in defense of coastal waters. Although this commander was to be under the Standing Group, and not SACEUR (see no. 2), he was to be responsible for providing Eisenhower's command "such naval forces as may be required [by Eisenhower] for the accomplishment of his missions in Europe" (SM-23-51, Jan. 4, 1951, CCS 092 Western Europe [3-12-48], Sec. 66). For developments see no. 57.

[4] On March 3 Eisenhower would discuss European naval command problems with Chief of Naval Operations Forrest Percival Sherman (see no. 22) and with Admiral Robert Bostwick Carney, Commander in Chief, United States Naval Forces, Eastern Atlantic and Mediterranean (CINCNELM) since November 1950 (for background on Carney see Galambos, *Columbia University*, no. 313, n. 5).

[5] For background on French general Alphonse Pierre Juin see no. 16.

[6] Eisenhower had discussed this subject in a letter to U.S. Army Chief of Staff J. Lawton Collins (see no. 52).

[7] On February 28 the French cabinet, led by Premier René Pleven (see no. 11), had resigned after a prolonged political dispute over electoral reform. A new government, containing many of the same leaders as Pleven's, would not be formed until March 10 (Brookings Institution, *Current Developments in United States Foreign Policy* 4, no. 7 [1951], 14, and no. 8 [1951], 9; Philip Williams, *Politics in Post-War France: Parties and the Constitution in the Fourth Republic* [London, 1954], pp. 37–38, 223–24; *International Herald Tribune*, Paris ed., Mar. 1, 1951).

[8] See no. 45; and n. 2 above.

[9] For background on Brigadier General Cortlandt van Rensselaer Schuyler see no. 2. Captain George Whelan Anderson, Jr. (USNA 1927), an aviator, had served in the Navy Department and in the Pacific during World War II. After the war he became a member of the Joint War Plans Committee of the JCS and commanded an anti-submarine aircraft carrier. In July 1950 he was designated as Fleet Operations Officer on the staff of the U.S. Sixth Fleet. In December 1950 he was assigned to SHAPE, where he and Schuyler were members of the Plans and Operations staff.

[10] These three men were all Eisenhower's personal assistants. For background on British Brigadier General James Frederick Gault, who had served with Eisenhower during World War II, see *Eisenhower Papers*, vols. I–XI. Kevin Coyle McCann had been Eisenhower's assistant at Columbia (for background see Galambos, *Columbia University*). Lieutenant Colonel Paul Thomas Carroll had served with the General in the Pentagon when Eisenhower was Army Chief of Staff (see *ibid.*, nos. 25, n. 1, and 816, n. 4).

[11] British Brigadier General Peter Hugh de Havilland had served in France, the Middle East, North Africa, and northwest Europe during World War II. Before coming to SHAPE he had been Deputy Head of the United Kingdom's delegation to the Western Union's Five Power Military Committee (see *ibid.*, no. 375, n. 4). As a national military representative, de Havilland was currently providing liaison between SHAPE and the United Kingdom (see State, *Foreign Relations, 1950*, vol. III, *Western Europe*, p. 557; State, *Foreign Relations, 1951*, vol. III, *European Security and the German Question, Part I*, pp. 496–97; and Walters, *Silent Missions*, p. 221).

[12] For backgrond on Pleven see n. 7 above; on Foreign Minister Robert Schuman and Defense Minister Jules Moch see nos. 16 and 11, respectively. Schuman and Moch would retain their positions in the new French government, headed by Henri Queuille; Pleven would become Vice-Premier (Brookings Institution, *Current Developments in United States Foreign Policy* 4, no. 8 [1951], 9).

54   *Eisenhower Mss.*

To Lucius Du Bignon Clay   *March 2, 1951*

Dear Lucius:[1] I have just read such excerpts of your Wednesday's testimony as the international air edition of the New York Times carries. I hope you will keep up that line of talk.[2]

The simple political approach to all these problems is to make them black or white, depending upon the conclusion of the speaker as to the trend of thought then current in his own constituency. Actually, the truth normally lies somewhere in the gray zone—with respect to the European problem you have traced the line as clearly as is now possible. Particularly, I like your insistence upon the truth that this problem is going to be measured in terms of self-confidence and morale in Western Europe; as long as we direct our effort toward rapid and justifiable increase of that self-confidence and that morale we are on the right track. I am delighted that you and I see this problem in the same light, and I am even more delighted that someone of your eloquence is in Washington where he can bring home these truths constantly to the faint-hearted and the opportunist, as well as to those who are honestly seeking the facts.[3]

Moreover, I agree with you, and so informed the Congressional Committees, that we should constantly be reviewing and reexamining the situation so that if our efforts were failing we could either change their type and character or, if finally forced to the dismal conclusion that we had to depend solely upon ourselves—then we have to face probably the most desperate situation that any major government has been called upon to face in modern times.[4]

Give my regards to Charlie Wilson [5] and any other friends you may happen to meet, and, of course, my love to Marjorie.[6]

With all the best.[7] *As ever*

[1] For background on General Clay see no. 46.

[2] On February 28 Clay had testified before a joint session of the Senate Armed Services and Foreign Relations committees concerning the stationing of American forces in Western Europe (see *New York Times*, Mar. 1, 1951; and Senate Committee on Foreign Relations and Committee on Armed Services, *Assignment of Ground Forces of the United States to Duty in the European Area*, 1951). Following his return from his initial NATO inspection trip, Eisenhower had testified before this same body (see no. 23).

[3] Clay had echoed sentiments expressed by Eisenhower earlier in the month regarding the need for increased self-confidence and improved morale among the nations of Western Europe. He said that the United States was taking a risk in supplying men and materials for Western Europe but that "freedom and allies" could not be valued in terms of numbers of divisions and dollars. He believed that if the United States showed a solid commitment in aiding its allies, the European nations would "become more confident of the accomplishments of their real objective, more willing to raise more troops, more willing to risk the possible threat of Russian aggression . . ." (Senate Committee on Foreign Relations and Committee on Armed Services, *Assignment of Ground Forces of the United States to Duty in the European Area*, 1951, pp. 750, 776). For former President Herbert Hoover's testimony before the same committees see no. 58.

[4] Both Eisenhower and Clay had testified that they believed Congress played an important role in the American defense of Western Europe; if U.S. efforts proved draining, ineffective, or disproportionate to those of the NATO allies, Congress should check the program (see Senate Committee on Foreign Relations and Committee on Armed Services, *Assignment of Ground Forces of the United States to Duty in the European Area*, 1951, pp. 10, 11, 751, 754, 765, 767, 785; *New York Times*, Mar. 1, 1951; and no. 23).

[5] Charles Edward Wilson, president of the General Electric Company and Director of the ODM (see no. 45).

[6] Clay's wife, Marjorie McKeown Clay.

[7] For developments see nos. 196, 396, and 537.

Dear Mr. Whitney: I am tremendously appreciative of the trouble you took to write such an interesting and informative document for me. While I realize that this kind of thing imposes an unwarranted intrusion upon the time of a busy man, I am selfish enough to hope that you will continue.[1]

The reason for this is not entirely personal. In the execution of a task such as has been assigned me, there are many factors to watch. As of this moment, none of these factors can possibly be of greater importance than the thinking of America. Newspapers do not always give an accurate gauge of people's morale, and certainly they often fail to give any kind of picture of potential results of proposals, projects, and movements.[2]

Actually, I do not even have a suggestion as to the particular subject of any letter you might write; what I am interested in is a mere setting down in your own words of the trends you see developing within the United States and of the things that most occupy your attention and concern from day to day.[3]

Along with my thanks for your valuable letter, I send my warm greetings to young Bob[4] and to all the other members of your nice family. *Cordially*

[1] Through William Burnham, Whitney had offered to send Eisenhower periodic letters on the current state of the American economy and business community (see Burnham to Eisenhower, Feb. 23, 1951, EM; for background on Burnham and Whitney see no. 50).

[2] Whitney would become one of the General's several regular correspondents on specific aspects of the American scene. The others included Edward Bermingham, Clifford Roberts, William Burnham, and Lucius Clay. The information these friends provided would prove valuable over the next twelve months, as Eisenhower moved toward becoming a presidential candidate (see, for example, nos. 221, 386, 473, 605, and 667; and Lyon, *Portrait of the Hero*, pp. 418, 427).

[3] In his letter of February 23 (EM) Whitney had reported on developments since Eisenhower had sailed for Europe on the sixteenth. He included information on the effects of recent wage and price regulations on the cotton and woolen industries, labor dissatisfaction with the ODM, and congressional inactivity toward passing a military draft bill. For background on these issues see *New York Times*, February 1, 2, 4, 19, 21, 25, 1951; and Donovan, *Tumultuous Years*, pp. 324–31. For developments in the Federal Reserve situation see no. 64.

[4] On Whitney's son see no. 50.

TO WILLIAM AVERELL HARRIMAN   *March 2, 1951*

Dear Averell: This letter will be on the rambling side, for lack of time
to write it succinctly. Moreover, the kind of thing that has, this week,
occupied a great deal of my attention is not susceptible to clear explanation in writing. For example, the governmental crisis in France and
the passing from the scene of Mr. Plevin, who has been so helpful to
us, cannot be evaluated until we know the identity and the attitude of
his successor.[1]

In Belgium, a governmental fight is raging over defense affairs, but
my information is that the fight is really political and that the defense
feature is incidental.[2]

Another concern has been centered on the fight in the British Parliament over the announcement of Admiral Fechteler's command. I
have a very deep suspicion that none of us has really learned the lessons
from World War II that he should have learned. Among other things,
the super-sensitiveness of the British public to anything and everything
Naval is one of the factors that apparently we have not thought through
carefully, particularly as it may have an effect on the success of NATO,
in which we are investing so much. Yet we saw much of this a few
years ago.[3]

Yesterday, I went to London and had some of the British Chiefs to
lunch to discuss a number of problems with them.[4] So great is British
and, to some extent, Continental opinion centered on the single point
of Atlantic Naval command that nearly all the newspaper speculation
is to the effect that I must have gone over there to try to develop ways
and means for lessening the bitterness of the reaction. While it seems
to be generally recognized that my command has nothing to do with
the particular incident that has aroused this wrath, it is, of course,
also recognized that I am bound to be deeply interested in the morale
of Britain as a whole.

How it will all come out, I cannot predict with certainty, but of one
thing I am sure: It now becomes more necessary than ever that I be
particularly careful in developing my own command system and, in
addition to this, that I be particularly careful in the *way* that any news
is given out about it.

In the case of the Fechteler announcement, I understand that a leak
occurred in a European capital and that this leak forced the issuing of
an official statement.[5]

In the case of SHAPE, it appears advisable that we should discuss,
in advance, with the several military staffs of Europe the various
combinations and possibilities of command and organization that
might be acceptable, thus evolving a scheme that, at the very best, will

cause no more of these outbursts. If this headquarters should pursue the normal procedure and first develop, as an internal staff study, a detailed scheme, and, with the approval of the Standing Group, submit it to the military staffs of the several countries, then any leak could properly be regarded as a revelation of a decision already taken, at least by me. Thereafter, any violent objection by any government would, of course, be a very serious matter. On the other hand, any leak that could occur during staff discussions would be mere gossip.[6]

Another thing that I feel we must do is to push ahead as rapidly as possible in the naming of principal subordinates, both in staff and command, so that these announcements can act to some extent at least as an alleviating factor in the British argument. Since my own Naval and other problems will compel a very important degree of British participation in all command arrangements, we may be able to do something effective along this line.[7]

There is, of course, the possible feeling on the part of the Standing Group that these procedures would present to it (when my command organization is finally crystallized) only a fait accompli. In other words, the Standing Group would have no other recourse than to stand firmly by the details of my plan, or would presumably be flying in the face of a laboriously arrived at agreement with NATO capitals that could not now be undone. While I recognize this possibility, it is nevertheless clear that the preliminary conversations to which I refer must be carried out by someone; if the Standing Group should attempt to do this through national representatives or through its own staff members, I am sure that the results would not be so good, and would take months.[8]

In any event, you can see the kind of underbrush that must be cleared away quickly before we can get at the real business of chopping wood. Add to the kind of thing I have just been discussing all the minor problems in getting offices, quarters, signals, etc., etc., and you can see that there is plenty to do.

Come see me when you can. Please pay my respects to the Commander in Chief. *As ever*[9]

[1] For background on the French governmental crisis see no. 53. For Eisenhower's relationship with White House special assistant Harriman see nos. 16 and 45.

[2] On March 6 the Belgian Chamber of Deputies would vote to increase compulsory military service terms from one year to two (see no. 16, n. 9). Socialist and Liberal opposition to this measure stemmed from a belief that the same end—a strengthening of the Belgian defense effort—could be accomplished by other and more desirable means (Memorandums of Conversation with Belgian Prime Minister, Foreign Minister, and Defense Minister, Jan. 10, 1951, EM, Subject File, Trips, SHAPE no. 1; MacArthur to Eisenhower and Gruenther, Feb. 4, 1952, EM, MacArthur Corr.; Brookings Institution, *Current Developments in United States Foreign Policy* 4, no. 8 [1951], 18; *International Herald Tribune*, Paris ed., Mar. 7, 1951). On March 21 the Belgian Senate would also pass the bill (see no. 126).

[3] For background on the controversy over the appointment of a supreme allied commander for the Atlantic see nos. 45, n. 8, and 52.
[4] See no. 53.
[5] The Danish government had announced prematurely that Admiral Fechteler would be named to command NATO's Atlantic forces. No official statement had been issued by NATO or SHAPE (State, *Foreign Relations, 1951*, vol. III, *European Security and the German Question, Part I*, pp. 465–66, 473–76, 490).
[6] For Eisenhower's earlier thoughts on this subject see no. 2.
[7] On Eisenhower's SHAPE appointments see nos. 52 and 74.
[8] As SACEUR, Eisenhower reported to NATO's Standing Group (see no. 2, nn. 1, 2).
[9] For developments see no. 68.

57   *Eisenhower Mss., Diaries*

DIARY   *[March 3, 1951][1]*

On Wednesday (Feb. 28, 1951) Gen. Clay appeared before the Senate Joint Committee and ably and persuasively advocated the wisdom of placing no present limit on American military aid to Europe.[2] He was so much more effective and convincing in his approach than Marshall, Bradley or any of the others that I cannot escape the fervent wish that he were our Sec. Defense. So far as newspaper reports could convey the impressions he made upon the Senators; it was profound.

Adm Sherman came to see me today.[3] Mar. 3—Saturday.

Some days ago I read a remarkable paper on Soviets, by an Admiral Stevens.[4] I think I'll put it in back of this book *because*, with minor exceptions it represents my beliefs exactly. But he states the thing *clearly*!

[1] These three handwritten paragraphs appear to have been written on the same day. They follow the typewritten diary entry that appears as no. 53.
[2] General Lucius D. Clay's testimony is discussed in no. 54.
[3] Chief of Naval Operations Forrest P. Sherman, accompanied by Admiral Robert B. Carney, CINCNELM (see no. 53, n. 4), had met with Generals Eisenhower and Gruenther. Eisenhower, who was attempting to bolster European morale and to build support for NATO, told Sherman and Carney that the controversy in Great Britain over the proposed appointment of an American (Admiral Fechteler) to NATO's Atlantic command (see nos. 45 and 56) was a matter of serious concern to him. Fearing a loss of British support for NATO and the general collective security effort, Eisenhower said that it was "absolutely necessary" that a British officer be given an important position in the Mediterranean command structure in order to offset the perceived loss of prestige associated with the Atlantic appointment. Admiral Carney said that the Mediterranean command should not be divided and that Eisenhower needed to have control over the naval forces protecting his southern flank. Furthermore, said Carney, the United States would provide most of the Mediterranean forces, and besides, Italy, Greece, and Turkey would

prefer American commanders to British. Eisenhower replied that the United States should "be generous in the matter of titles and could afford to call the British commander 'Supreme' even though our contribution was greater." Carney disagreed. He said that "Americans might well object to the implication of actual supremacy, whereas British might well feel that we were welching on our agreement if all of our forces were not, in fact, under the Supreme Commander." Carney said that the British wanted to take "strategic control of the entire war effort from the North Cape to the Indian Ocean" and that "the British always had in mind the importance of cultural and economic prestige, to which military leadership was a heavy contributing factor." Sherman told Eisenhower that he would meet with the British in London and propose a three-part compromise to settle the Atlantic and Mediterranean command problems. He would (1) offer to consider downgrading Fechteler's title from Supreme Commander to Commander-in-Chief; (2) that Carney be appointed as C in C of a southern region under SHAPE; and (3) agree to the designation of a British admiral as Allied Naval C in C, Mediterranean, to be responsible to Carney. All U.S. naval forces in the Mediterranean would be at Eisenhower's disposal whenever he desired. Eisenhower agreed with this approach (Carney to Eisenhower and Sherman, Mar. 3, 1951, CCS 092 Western Europe [3-12-48], Sec. 72; see also Poole, *History of the Joint Chiefs of Staff*, vol. IV, *1950–1952*, pp. 231-32). For developments see no. 62.

[4] See no. 43.

58 *Eisenhower Mss., Diaries*

DIARY *March 5, 1951*

Don't think I'll write in this any more unless note is purely personal or involving some of this political drivel.[1]

And one good thing about this dismaying and unattractive assignment is that I should be finally & fully removed from the personal political ambition of others—which are reflected often, in their presentations to me.[2]

One of the men I've admired extravagantly is Herbert Hoover. I am forced to believe he's getting senile. God knows I'd personally like to get out of Europe and I'd like to see U.S. _able_ to sit at home & ignore the rest of the world! What a pleasing prospect—until you look at ultimate consequences—destruction.[3]

[1] Since Eisenhower's return from Europe in 1945, speculation concerning his political future had never truly ceased. With the approach of the party conventions for the 1952 presidential race, the possibility of his candidacy had again gained wide attention. Friends, acquaintances, and strangers frequently urged him to campaign for the nomination and offered him advice on potential issues to raise or policies to pursue (see, for example, nos. 232, 308, and 329; and *Eisenhower Papers*, vols. VII–XI). The uncertainties about Eisenhower's party affiliation and willingness to enter politics also provided the press with fertile material for conjecture (see, for example, *Newsweek*, Dec. 12, 1949, pp. 13-14; *U.S. News & World Report*,

Dec. 16, 1949, pp. 15–16; George Horace Gallup, *The Gallup Poll: Public Opinion, 1935–1971*, 3 vols. [New York, 1972], vol. II, *1949–1958*, pp. 779–1032; and no. 60).
[2] See, for example, Galambos, *Columbia University*, nos. 1041, 1050, and 1077; and nos. 195, 205, and 313 in these volumes.
[3] Former President Herbert Clark Hoover had recently stated his opposition to U.S. involvement in Western Europe. In two radio and television addresses—one in December on the day following Eisenhower's official designation as supreme commander of the NATO forces—and in testimony before the Senate Foreign Relations and Armed Services committees Hoover had called for a suspension of U.S. troop commitments and military aid to Western Europe. Hoover believed that by defending with naval and air power the Atlantic and Pacific oceans with outposts in England, Japan, Formosa, and the Philippines, the United States could be kept safe, making itself the "Gibraltar of Western civilization." Once the nations of Western Europe had evidenced a determination to combat communism, according to Hoover, the United States could resume military assistance. In his address of February 9 the former President had reenforced these sentiments, making particular reference to NATO and Eisenhower's role. Hoover had said that the General was "the potent symbol of the policy of at once sending American ground troops to Europe"; but he stressed that Eisenhower's appointment "does not commit the American people as to policy" (see *New York Times*, Dec. 21, 1950, Feb. 10, 11, 28, 1951; Galambos, *Columbia University*, no. 1138; Senate Committee on Foreign Relations and Committee on Armed Services, *Assignment of Ground Forces of the United States to Duty in the European Area*, 1951, pp. 720–44; and no. 60 in this volume).

59   *Eisenhower Mss.*

To Ellis Dwinnell Slater   *March 5, 1951*

Dear Slats:[1] Your letter of February 13th concerning Dr. Perrin Long has been around for some time, but at least we had some opportunity to give to the subject of my Medical staff more deliberate consideration than would have been possible had I attempted to write you earlier. I read Long's letter very carefully and was greatly gratified at his generous and patriotic reactions to our present emergency. His accomplishments in the Medical field are, of course, too well known to require any discussion.[2]

While I realize fully the implications which our present venture carries with it in the Medical and other technical and professional fields, and am taking steps to provide for those requirements in the formation of my staff, I believe it is too early for us to establish provision for consulting services or other highly specialized staff activities at the moment. As our command structure is developed, our staff requirements will be worked out in consonance with it and will, of course, require at a later date more specialized talent than I feel we need at this stage of our organization. The real reason for this haziness is the effort on my part to delegate to other headquarters all tasks other than those of an operational, policy and diplomatic character.[3]

I feel, therefore, that it would be demanding too many sacrifices on the part of some of our more eminent professional men such as Long, to ask them to give up their private activities to assist us at this time. Won't you please convey these ideas to Long. I would appreciate it if, in doing so, you would emphasize the gratification which his attitude gives me.[4]

Incidentally, no cracks about the pictures—I am in a new field, but getting a tremendous kick out of it![5]

With best wishes—and my best to "the gang."[6] *As ever*

[1] Slater, president of Frankfort Distillers Corporation, had been a friend of the General's since 1948 (for background see Galambos, *Columbia University*, no. 244).

[2] On February 7 Johns Hopkins University professor of preventative medicine Perrin Hamilton Long (M.D. University of Michigan 1924) had written to Slater offering his services for Eisenhower's SHAPE medical staff (copy in EM, Slater Corr.). Long, who had served in Europe with the Army Medical Corps during World War II, had written that he was already well known in most of the NATO countries, that he was familiar with Army medical department organization and functions, and that he firmly believed that "SHAPE must bring stability to this world. . . ."

[3] On the development of Eisenhower's staff and other offers of assistance see nos. 29, 53, 62, and 116.

[4] At the top of Slater's letter (EM) Eisenhower wrote to his chief of staff, Lieutenant General Alfred Maximilian Gruenther, "Al—Please study this well—we might have something here—you must remember Perry!" (for background on Gruenther see *Eisenhower Papers*, vols. I–XI). Long would not join the SHAPE staff, and Eisenhower's old friend Major General Howard McCrum Snyder, Sr., would serve as medical officer at NATO headquarters in Paris (on Snyder see Galambos, *Chief of Staff* and *Columbia University*).

[5] The Eisenhowers and Slater frequently exchanged photographs, and while in Europe, the General would sometimes send film to Slater for processing (see no. 82; undated draft letter, Eisenhower to Slater, EM; Ellis D. Slater, *The Ike I Knew* [Baltimore, 1980]; and Mamie Eisenhower, "A Collection of Letters and Related Ephemera from Mamie Eisenhower Received by Mr. and Mrs. Ellis D. Slater from Mamie Eisenhower during the Years 1950–1979," Special Collections, Milton S. Eisenhower Library, The Johns Hopkins University, Baltimore, Md.).

[6] Eisenhower was probably referring to fellow members of the Augusta National Golf Club, of Augusta, Georgia. The General had first met Slater while a guest at Augusta (for background on the club and Eisenhower's membership see Galambos, *Columbia University*).

To William Edward Robinson   *March 5, 1951*

Dear Bill:[1] Your long letter reached me just in time to remind me, before
going home this evening, that Mamie asked me to write to you. Fortunately, she has forgotten (practically) the Yoakum story.[2] Curiously
enough, I have found several people both in Paris and in London who
thought that was a splendid, *humanizing* story. In fact, only this morning,
Mamie received from a Sergeant's wife in London a long and glowing
letter saying that she, the writer, was delighted that some other American
woman agreed with her that much of the so-called swank of these
chateaus and historical houses was poor sales propaganda for unsus-
pecting Americans. Mamie, of course, felt that the story made her
appear to be a whining, dissatisfied, spoiled individual. This she resented very deeply because of her own feeling that she has sacrificed
much to come over here. In any event, I think the whole business all
belongs to the past, and I am truly grateful that you told Weare that he
was, under no circumstances, to attempt any disciplinary action.[3]

The subject of Mamie's current request is that I ask whether you
could arrange to send to us, weekly, the first two sections of your
Sunday paper. In further explanation of what she is after, she says that
one of her chief sports is to read the advertising columns in the Herald
Tribune. All the other parts she wants to forget, because, in this way,
she feels she can get what she wants by airmail.[4]

It goes without saying that I should like to send a check to pay for a
year's advance subscription on this basis, together with mailing costs.
My attempts to do likewise for anything connected with the Herald
Tribune in the past have always been repulsed, which creates an embarrassing situation when I want a favor like the present one. I must
say, however, that as long as Mamie wants the first two sections of the
Sunday Herald Tribune, by air, I am ready to pay the cost either in
embarrassment or in cash. While my choice is by far the latter, yours
is the decision.[5]

Give my love to Helen[6] and, of course, warm regards to all my
other friends on the paper. *As ever*

P.S. Recently, I wrote quite a lengthy letter to an old friend named
Ed Bermingham. This week sometime, I will arrange to have a few
extra copies made and I shall possibly send you one. The reason for
this is that it attempts, as briefly as possible, to outline again, and in
slightly different language than I have used in the past, my attitude
toward this job.[7]

My best to Cliff and all the gang.[8]

---

[1] For background on Robinson, executive vice-president and director of the *New
York Herald Tribune*, see no. 39.

[2] Mrs. Eisenhower's reaction to the February 23 *International Herald Tribune* story, concerning her dissatisfaction with housing accommodations offered to the Eisenhowers by the French government, is discussed in no. 44. The author of the story, reporter Robert Yoakum, had since published an equally critical piece on the establishment of SHAPE (see no. 45). Yoakum reported that the efforts of a local preservation group were being thwarted by the plans to erect one-story office buildings and a permanent barracks on sixty acres of Marly Forest donated to SHAPE by the French (see *International Herald Tribune*, Paris ed., Feb. 26, 1951).

[3] Weare was president of the *Herald Tribune*'s European edition (see no. 44).

[4] On March 13 (EM) Robinson replied that he was having the daily edition and the Sunday main and second news sections of the paper sent to the Eisenhowers. He commented, "All of us here would naturally want to be sure that you see the Herald Tribune regularly."

[5] There is no indication in EM that Eisenhower was billed for the subscription.

[6] Helen Rogers Reid, owner of the *Herald Tribune* (for background see no. 36).

[7] Eisenhower's letter to Bermingham is no. 51. The letter was sent to Robinson on the following day (see no. 63).

[8] On Clifford Roberts see no. 7.

61   *Eisenhower Mss.*

TO MARK WAYNE CLARK   *March 6, 1951*

Dear Wayne:[1] Al Gruenther told me he would write separately about the issue of staff representation raised by Mr. Pacciardi.[2]

I was glad to get your letter and to hear that you might be over to see us sometime this summer. I hope we will have something to show you. We are hard at work but there are so many governments involved and so many theories of command that things seem to move very slowly. I hope that U.S. troop shipments to Europe will be just as prompt as is humanly possible.[3] Nothing is more important from the psychological standpoint.

With warm personal regard, *Sincerely*

[1] For background on Clark, Chief of the Army Field Forces since August 1949, see *Eisenhower Papers*, vols. I–XI. In his letter of February 27 (EM) he had said, "If there is anything in the world we can do through training here [in the United States] to assist you in your tremendous job, please do not hesitate to call upon us." Carroll drafted this note.

[2] In January Eisenhower had met with Italian Defense Minister Randolfo Pacciardi (see no. 18, n. 1). Pacciardi, a lawyer, journalist, and former opponent of Fascist dictator Benito Mussolini, had spent part of World War II in the United States before returning to Italy in 1944. In 1947 he had become Vice-Premier of Italy, and the following year he had assumed his present position. According to Clark, Pacciardi had been "quite upset at the thought that Italy might not have a representative on your [Eisenhower's] General Staff" and had written Clark to that effect. In a letter to Clark (Mar. 5, 1951, EM, Clark Corr.) Eisenhower's C/S, Gruenther, explained that Pacciardi's concern had arisen out of a poorly translated

remark that Gruenther had made to an Italian liaison officer. Gruenther added that several Italians were already working at SHAPE and that an Italian (Rear Admiral Ferrante Capponi) had been designated as Chief of SHAPE's G-1 (Personnel) Section.

[3] Clark had mentioned a possible visit to Europe in the summer (see Clark to Gruenther, June 25, 1951, EM). He also had described plans to send two U.S. Army divisions to Europe and had promised Eisenhower that they would be well trained by the time they reached him. "Unfortunately," Clark said, "heavy levies to the tune of 3,500 infantrymen have been made on each division to send to General MacArthur. It is a shame that every time we get a unit's head above water, it must be knocked off due to the requirements for the Far East." For developments see no. 77.

62   *Eisenhower Mss.*

To John Cotesworth Slessor   *March 6, 1951*

Dear Slessor:[1] Thank you very much for remembering to send to me the documents in which I was interested.[2] I have read four of them, but it will take me some time before I get through the two manuals.

When Sherman and Carney were here, I found that their views did not wholly agree with mine in certain points of the broad NATO organization.[3] Although I am quite ready, as you know, to express my views at any time about such things, I realize that, in particular phases of this problem, my own position does not place upon me any responsibility whatsoever. Consequently, my interest is academic, except as the morale of whole peoples may be affected.

Regardless of specific convictions in this organizational point, there is one feature in which I think that all of our governments have been quite remiss—in some ways, just a bit awkward. This is in failing to stress the national *burdens* and *responsibilities* involved in the acceptance of command, rather than permitting the spread of the unwarranted assumption that these positions are awarded in recognition of the strength, prestige, or wisdom of some particular nation, service, or individual. Until we grow a bit more skillful in this matter, every appointment in any of the organizations maintained under NATO will always be regarded with some jealousy and concern by all nations and services, other than the one from which the individual came. It is silly to accept this handicap to successful operation when we could so easily do a lot to eliminate it.

In any event, I profoundly hope that all of the principal assignments can soon be made so that this kind of thing can be behind us.

Thank you again for sending me the documents. *Sincerely*
P.S. I am returning the Alsop document herewith.[4]

[1] Sir John Slessor, who had met with Eisenhower on February 23 (see no. 52, n. 5), had been Marshal of the Royal Air Force and Chief of the Air Staff since 1950 (for further background see Chandler, *War Years*).

[2] On February 26 Slessor had sent Eisenhower a number of items: a report on the defense debates in the British House of Lords on February 21–22; an article written by author and newspaperman Joseph Wright Alsop, Jr. (A.B. Harvard 1932); a transcription of a lecture on the use of air power to support ground operations in Korea (see no. 52); and selections from three British military publications dealing with land/air warfare (Slessor to Eisenhower, Feb. 26, 1951, EM).

[3] For background see no. 57. After meeting with Eisenhower on March 3, Admiral Sherman and Admiral Carney had met with British military leaders (including Marshal Slessor) in London two days later. Sherman reported that the naval command situation had "developed into a military problem having serious implications." Sherman said that British leaders had tried to placate the public by minimizing the authority that an American SACLANT would have over the Northeast Atlantic. Furthermore, said Sherman, the British people had been inspired to think in terms of an independent British supreme allied commander in the Mediterranean (see no. 57; and State, *Foreign Relations, 1951*, vol. III, *European Security and the German Question, Part I*, pp. 477–79, 488–92), but such a British-led command would deprive Eisenhower of some of the naval forces necessary for the accomplishment of his mission. Admiral Carney wrote Eisenhower that although he and Sherman had yet to reach an agreement with their British counterparts, the United States should not consider "relinquishing, or abdicating, the post–World War II American leadership which we have built up by vast economic and moral support." Sherman recommended that the Atlantic command appointment be deferred until these differences could be settled, and the JCS accepted this proposal on March 12 (Sherman to JCS [copy to Eisenhower], Mar. 6, 1951, CCS 092 Western Europe [3-12-48], Sec. 72; Carney to Eisenhower, Mar. 8, 1951, *ibid.*, Sec. 74; Poole, *History of the Joint Chiefs of Staff*, vol. IV, *1950-1952*, pp. 232–33). For developments see nos. 68 and 77.

[4] See n. 2 above. Slessor replied in a letter of March 9 (EM) that the Atlantic command announcement had been "badly handled politically." The reaction was, he said, "an inevitable psychological reaction of a maritime people, all of whom have a percentage of salt water in their veins." Slessor reminded Eisenhower that "Britannia did rule the waves for 3 or 4 hundred years before 1942—and did so, incidentally, to the great benefit of the United States." Slessor also hinted that the outcry over Fechteler's appointment was motivated at least in part by Winston Churchill's desire to overthrow Britain's Labour government. For developments see no. 107.

63   *Eisenhower Mss.*

To William Edward Robinson   *March 6, 1951*
Personal and confidential

Dear Bill: I told you the other day that I intended to send you a copy of a letter I wrote to Ed Bermingham. I enclose it for your personal and background information.[1]

Also attached you will find an excerpt from a column by a man named George Rothwell Brown. His piece was written as political speculation, and, from that viewpoint, I am not concerned at all. The only thing that makes the column worthy of a moment's notice is *the allegation that I have embraced without reservation almost all of the foreign, domestic, and political policies of the Administration.* All this, apparently, merely because I have responded to a simple call to military duty and have expressed the opinion that American security involves also the safety of Western Europe.[2]

There are certainly far greater areas of intellectual agreement between me and Mr. Hoover, for example, than there are between me and so-called New-Dealers. But I cannot accept the views of Mr. Hoover with respect to the wisdom of attempting to make America a military Gibraltar in which we could dwell peacefully and happily no matter what happened to the rest of the world.[3]

Most of us like to classify people on the basis of some particular, dramatic issue; so, forever, I suppose Mr. Hoover and I will be represented as very great intellectual antagonists when, as a matter of fact, except on this one issue, I do not recall anything in recent years in which I have found my own views in direct opposition to his. (Of course, there may be others.)[4]

In any event, what started me writing this particular letter is to ask you to recall—rather, to look up—a couple pages in the book I wrote, starting with the last paragraph on page 475 and reading to the middle of page 477. I cite this just to prove that far from "joining" a doctrinal group within the past few months, my own thinking, years ago, clearly included the maintenance of military strength (long before the Korean war broke out); the need for unity among free nations to combat the Soviet menace, and the understanding that no nation today could stand by itself alone.[5]

You and I have often talked about some of the policies of the current Administration to which we both are violently opposed. So, you can see why I get just a bit irritated when I find anyone interpreting my readiness to respond to military orders, or the coincidence that, in a particular case, my views happen to coincide with those of the Administration, as meaning that I am a member of any particular political or intellectual group. I certainly *try* to think for myself, and I suppose there is no one in the world who attempts to gauge, modify, and test his views more than I do through the method of conversing and discussing them with friends and personalities in whom he has confidence.[6]

Now I've blown off a bit of steam, I feel a little less irritated.[7]

As ever

[1] For background on Robinson and on Eisenhower's promise to send him the Bermingham letter see no. 60. Eisenhower's letter to Bermingham is no. 51. A copy of this letter and one of no. 23 are in the Robinson Papers.

[2] There is no copy in EM of the excerpt Eisenhower sent to Robinson, but it was probably from George Rothwell Brown's "The Political Parade" column. Brown, a former editor of the *Washington Herald*, had worked for the Hearst newspapers since 1929, writing on politics, labor, government, and the economy. In his column of February 19 Brown had speculated on Eisenhower's political future, warning that while the General was being supported as a potential Republican candidate by New York Governor Thomas E. Dewey and others, he might actually choose to run as a Democrat. Citing both the Republican party's weak showings in recent elections and Eisenhower's service to Democratic administrations since World War II, Brown had written that the NATO commander's chances of being elected might be far better if he were to run on a Democratic ticket. With Administration support, as Brown saw it, "Eisenhower could count on the Solid South [and] could carry the northern Roosevelt states which have gone along with Trumanism." This decision on the General's part, aided by the "big Republican build-up . . . by Dewey, Stassen, and others, might develop a support for him . . . that would go along with him, even if he were nominated for President by the Democrats." This would leave the Republicans divided, without a strong candidate (see *San Francisco Examiner*, Feb. 19, 1951). For Dewey's efforts on Eisenhower's behalf see Galambos, *Columbia University*, nos. 602 and 1041; for background on president of the University of Pennsylvania and former Governor of Minnesota Harold Edward Stassen see *ibid.*, nos. 116 and 483. Eisenhower had reacted to allegations similar to those made by Brown (see nos. 23, 58, and 383 in these volumes). For his declaration of party affiliation see nos. 582 and 587.

[3] For background on former President Herbert Clark Hoover's recent statements concerning America's national policies see Galambos, *Columbia University*, no. 1138; and no. 58 in this volume.

[4] On Eisenhower's earlier relationship with Hoover see *Eisenhower Papers*, vols. VI–XI.

[5] The section of *Crusade in Europe* to which Eisenhower refers concerns the roles of Russia and the United States following World War II. On the need for military readiness and cooperation among the nations of the free world he had written:

> The compelling necessities of the moment leave us no alternative to the maintenance of real and respectable strength—not only in our moral rectitude and our economic power, but in terms of adequate military preparedness. To neglect this, pending universal resurgence of a definite spirit of cooperation, is not only foolish, it is criminally stupid. . . .
>
> The democracies must learn that the world is now too small for the rigid concepts of national sovereignty that developed in a time when the nations were self-sufficient and self-dependent for their own well-being and safety. None of them today can stand alone (pp. 475–78).

In regard to Eisenhower's recent thoughts on these matters see no. 23; on *Crusade in Europe* see Galambos, *Columbia University*.

[6] See n. 3 above; and no. 83 on Eisenhower on the Truman Administration. On the sorts of friends who were giving the General advice see nos. 7, 23, 50, and 55.

[7] Robinson would pass the General's letters on to the editor and publisher of the *Herald Tribune* with the suggestion that the newspaper counter the anti-Eisenhower propaganda with a story of its own (see Robinson to Helen Rogers Reid and Whitelaw Reid, Mar. 13, 1951, Robinson Papers).

To Clifford Roberts   *March 6, 1951*

Dear Cliff:[1] Yesterday, your letter came and, of course, I am always interested to learn of the reasons that lead to your decisions in investment matters—even though anything you do is fully and unequivocably approved in advance.[2]

This morning's paper carried a little story to the effect that the Treasury Department and the Bankers of the United States had settled their differences over interest rates and the support of United States bonds. I hope that this is true, because, if it is, it must mean that the Treasury has abandoned the position that had so alarmed a number of my banking friends.[3] When next you write, won't you please tell me whether my interpretation is correct?[4]

I am grateful for your readiness to help out Dry and young Richard Gill.[5] I imagine that the reason that you have not heard from the youngster is that his whole family has been in the hospital with every kind of winter disease known to man. Possibly, they will have their heads up soon.

There is no great news with us at the moment, but I do hope that you will remember to say hello for me to any of our old friends of Blind Brook, Augusta, or New York.[6] *Cordially*

[1] For background on Eisenhowers's friend and adviser Roberts see nos. 7 and 38.

[2] Roberts sometimes handled investments for the General and his family (see no. 38).

[3] Eisenhower had probably dictated this letter on the preceding day; a report on the accord recently reached between the U.S. Treasury and the Federal Reserve System (Fed) appeared in the *International Herald Tribune* of March 5. The conflict between the Fed and the Treasury had grown intense in late 1950 following a price surge caused by the Korean War. During World War II the Fed had agreed to purchase government bonds at predetermined levels, enabling the Treasury to borrow cheaply at a low interest rate. This arrangement, which had been continued following the war at the insistence of the Treasury, made it difficult for the Fed to control credit expansion; Marriner Eccles, former chairman of the Federal Reserve Board, called it an "engine of inflation." Under the accord reached in late February, the Fed agreed temporarily to continue limited support of long-term government securities at the World War II level of 2.5 percent, while pursuing a flexible policy toward the Treasury's new bonds (see Donovan, *Tumultuous Years*, pp. 327–31; Milton Friedman and Anna Jacobson Schwartz, *A Monetary History of the United States: 1867-1960* [Princeton, 1963], pp. 12-13, 610-12; Herbert Stein, *The Fiscal Revolution in America* [Chicago, 1969], pp. 262-77; and no. 55).

[4] In his reply of March 13 (EM) Roberts assured Eisenhower that his view was correct and said that Truman had attempted to impose political control on the independent Federal Reserve System "purely for the purposes of saving interest on the public debt." He approved of the accord.

[5] For background on Roberts's investments for Eisenhower's nephew Richard Gill, Jr., and SHAPE driver Leonard Dry see no. 38.

[6] The Blind Brook Club, of Port Chester, New York, and the Augusta National

Golf Club (Georgia) were two of the General's favorite golf and recreation spots (see Galambos, *Columbia University*).

65   *Eisenhower Mss.*

To Lewis Williams Douglas   *March 6, 1951*

Dear Lew:[1] Thank you very much for your letter of the 23rd which reached me only today in Paris. I hope that by the time you reach here in June, we will have a house of our own. If we do, I further hope that you will do us the honor of staying with us.[2]

All the news I have had about the American Assembly, since I left the United States, has been on the favorable side. The few personal friends to whom I confided the secret of your acceptance of the Chairmanship have responded enthusiastically. I know that the general reaction will be the same as soon as you and Phil Young can release the news.[3]

With warm regard and, of course, lasting gratitude. *Cordially*

[1] Douglas, former U.S. Ambassador to Great Britain, would shortly be named chairman of Columbia University's American Assembly Policy Board (see no. 47; and Galambos, *Columbia University*).

[2] On the search for a house see nos. 18, n. 3, and 254, n. 4. Because in July renovations on the Eisenhowers' home remained incomplete, Douglas, then visiting Paris, would stay at the Maurice Hotel (see correspondence in EM). He would meet with the General and the dean of Columbia's Graduate School of Business, Philip Young, on July 9 (see no. 239, n. 6; and appointment calendar. On Young see no. 8, n. 6).

[3] The American Assembly conference plan is discussed in Galambos, *Columbia University*; and in nos. 8, 47, 184, and 202 in this volume. Douglas's appointment as chairman of the plan's policy board would be announced later this month (*New York Times*, Mar. 14, 1951).

66   *Eisenhower Mss.*

To Herbert Bayard Swope   *March 7, 1951*

Dear Herbert:[01] As always, I was very happy to hear from you. I didn't really know how attached I had become to New York until I got away from there. Your summation of the news is surely succinct; probably your training![2]

We are working hard and I like to feel that we are making some progress every day.[3] However, there is a great deal to be done. I do hope that, at home, the "Great Debate" soon is settled.[4]

With warm regard, *Cordially*

[1] Swope was a New York public relations and policy consultant. For background on his friendship with Eisenhower see *Eisenhower Papers*, vols. VI–XI.

[2] In his letter of March 1 (EM) Swope, the former executive editor of the *New York World*, had briefly surveyed developments at home. Foremost among the items he mentioned was the recent ratification of the Twenty-second Amendment to the United States Constitution, limiting the tenure of the President to two terms. Swope, who would later urge the General to seek the presidency (see documents in EM), had written that the amendment "has buried beyond disinterment the President's chances for reelection. If the country is asked to foreclose all chances of anyone ever serving more than two terms . . . then it is quite certain . . . that there is no chance of shifting from that position in favor of the present incumbent, even though a special exemption is made in his case. . . ." Truman, of course, would not seek a second nomination (see *New York Times*, Feb. 27, 1951; and Donovan, *Tumultuous Years*, pp. 171–72, 392–94).

[3] For Eisenhower's progress in organizing SHAPE see nos. 46, 53, and 61.

[4] The Great Debate over Truman's actions in Korea and his plans to commit U.S. troops to the defense of Western Europe under the terms of the NATO treaty had occupied Congress for several months. Eisenhower had become involved in the controversy in February, when he returned from his exploratory trip to Europe and urged strong support for NATO (see nos. 63 and 23, respectively).

67   *Eisenhower Mss.*

To Frank Alexander Willard   *March 7, 1951*

Dear Frank:[1] Thank you for sending me a copy of the article by Mr. Bernays.[2]

With much of what he says, I am in emphatic agreement, but I feel that he very greatly over-estimates the overseas effect of specific domestic laws in America.[3] He seems to feel that enactment of an F.E.P.C. law or a repeal of poll taxes in some of the States would be almost critical in their beneficial effect upon the value of our foreign propaganda.[4] I fear that he sadly over-estimates the knowledge that the ordinary citizen of another country has of our domestic laws. Of course, no one can possibly object to the basic purpose of assuring that our nation's laws reflect a profound regard for the concepts of justice and of freedom. Yet, completely disregarding the effect upon those concepts of centralizing the police power in our country,[5] I am quite sure that the ordinary, reasonably informed European would have great difficulty understanding the meaning of the kind of law of which he speaks—even if that European should ever hear about it.

The *real* fact that our propaganda should be able to emphasize is that there is no lynching in the United States, that no worthwhile citizen is really kept from voting because of any poll tax, and that no man is kept out of employment merely because of race or religion or other factor of this kind.[6] The enactment of national law is only his idea of the means to establish this fact—it is far from the fact itself. Witness the 18th Amendment![7] In any event, I have fun reading.

My regards to Grindel, Cliff, and any of your other partners that I know.[8] *Cordially*

[1] Willard had been a general partner in the New York investment firm of Reynolds & Company since 1934. For Eisenhower's friendship with another member of the firm, Clifford Roberts, see nos. 7 and 64.

[2] In his letter to Eisenhower of March 1 (EM) Willard had enclosed a copy of a February 17 *New York Herald Tribune* article entitled "Winning the War of Ideas" (see copy in EM). The author, Edward L. Bernays (B.S. Cornell 1912), was a public relations counsel and former member of both the Hoover Emergency Commission for Employment and the New York State Commission on Discrimination in Employment.

[3] Bernays had written that the efforts of the United States to spread information in Western Europe and behind the Iron Curtain needed to be greatly intensified. Writing specifically of the radio broadcasts of the Voice of America and referring to remarks made by Eisenhower in early February regarding the need for improved American propaganda, Bernays suggested that the Voice of America place its emphasis on actions rather than on ideas and intangibles. Writing that "domestic activity . . . affects our standing in foreign countries as much as foreign activity," he suggested the passage of certain laws that would make the United States "conform as closely as possible in deeds both at home and abroad to the words we use to enlist favorable interest for it" (on the Voice of America see Galambos, *Chief of Staff*, no. 1446, and *Columbia University*, nos. 55 and 785).

[4] Bernays had specifically mentioned the passage of a Fair Employment Practices Commission (FEPC) law, an anti-lynching law, and legislation banning poll taxes as actions that would have "potent and profound . . . effect" on foreign attitudes toward the United States. President Truman had endorsed these measures and had recently renewed efforts to bring them into law (see *New York Times*, Jan. 15, 19, 1951; *Public Papers of the Presidents of the United States: Harry S. Truman, January 1 to December 31, 1951* [Washington, D.C., 1965], p. 80; and Truman, *Memoirs*, vol. II, *Years of Trial and Hope*, pp. 179–83. On poll tax legislation in South Carolina, Tennessee, and Virginia see *New York Times*, Feb. 14, 17, 28, Mar. 11, May 29, June 2, 1951).

[5] Truman had been strongly criticized by Republicans and Southern Democrats in Congress for taking actions that exceeded the constitutional powers of the chief executive (for background on the Great Debate over the President's right to enter the Korean War and to commit U.S. troops to Europe for NATO see no. 23, n. 3, and the preceding document; and Donovan, *Tumultuous Years*, pp. 319–24. On the FEPC legislation see *New York Times*, Dec. 4, 5, 1951).

[6] The Tuskegee Institute of Alabama reported two lynchings and seven instances of racially motivated mob violence during 1950. For 1951 the institute would record one lynching of a black farmer in Florida and the mysterious deaths of two others in the same state (see *New York Times*, Jan. 1, Dec. 31, 1951). That there was discrimination in employment and voting at this time cannot be doubted; see, for instance, U.S. Congress, Senate, Subcommittee on Labor and Labor-Manage-

ment Relations of the Committee on Labor and Public Welfare, *Discrimination and Full Utilization of Manpower Resources: Hearings on S. 1732 and S. 551*, 82d Cong., 2d sess., 1952. In October 1951 the National Negro Labor Council would announce that the average black's household income was 55 percent below the national average (*New York Times*, Oct. 28, 29, 1951; see also *ibid.*, Jan. 23, June 8, 1951). Although two states eliminated the poll tax in early 1951, five Southern states still retained that racially motivated barrier to voting (see *ibid.*, Mar. 11, 1951).

[7] The Eighteenth Amendment to the Constitution, the Volstead Act, had prohibited the manufacture, sale, and importation of liquor. In force from January 17, 1920, until December 5, 1933, the amendment was never popular and was widely ignored and defied (see Herbert Asbury, *The Great Illusion: An Informal History of Prohibition* [Garden City, N.Y., 1950], pp. 141–330).

[8] On Clifford Roberts see n. 1 above. Eisenhower probably meant Herbert Weld Grinda, another partner in the Reynolds firm and a director of several corporations.

68   *Eisenhower Mss.*

To WILLIAM AVERELL HARRIMAN   *March 8, 1951*
Secret

Dear Averell: Thank you very much for your March 1st letter. It was full of interesting news.[1]

My newspaper brings repeated assertion that our Congress has now been informed that our final, over-all objective in American divisions in France will never exceed six.[2] Now, I do not mean to say that, as of this moment, such an assertion can be proved wrong. But I do most earnestly believe that *no one can prove it to be correct*, and certainly the psychological effect of stating this in unequivocal language might prove harmful.

When I was in Washington, no one even hinted at disagreement with my presentation to the President, Cabinet, and Congress that strength figures, even in terms of ratios, could not be foreseen at this time, so I do not see what could have occurred to change the position. Possibly, there is some mistake in the reports that I read in the papers.

There is one limitation that I think we should very carefully explore, and this is the limitation as to *time*. It seems clear to me that unless, with relatively strong American support, Europe can attain a satisfactory self-defense on the ground within a calculated number of years, then we could draw no other conclusion except that this effort has been a failure, and face the bitter consequences of such failure. But the *scope of the effort* during the particular period that we calculate as sufficient is something else again, and I do not see how we can find, in fearful limitations of this character, any real inspiration for the European populations.

Some of the NATO negotiators, or, possibly, the Public Relations people, have handled part of the over-all organizational and command problem quite poorly.[3] I believe that the trouble stems directly from a general failure to insist that these command assignments are great national burdens and responsibilities. Instead, we have allowed the populations of NATO to assume that command assignments are awards or kudos conferred upon various nationalities because of strength, wisdom, or prestige. With this latter feeling prevailing, each appointment becomes one to be struggled for jealously; therefore, its influence becomes divisive. It's like a number of political parties trying to elect a sheriff. On the other hand, if allied command were always treated, in every public utterance, as a great responsibility, then the influence should be somewhat the opposite. We must not ever forget for a single moment that we are engaged in a "morale" problem. If we do not solve this one, we will never, by any means, produce the material strength that is needed.

Right now, there are misunderstandings, or at least divisions of opinion, developing about over-all command in the Mediterranean and other places that, to my mind, are inconsequential as compared to the great issues that we face. It happens that the real quarrel lies outside my own sphere of responsibility. Nevertheless, the eventual effect will not only be noticed in the morale of populations, but it will be an included factor in my own problems because of the probable need of postponing the organization of this command pending the settlement of the broader command organization.

Among other things, it appears that the title "Supreme" has become an important feature in these discussions. Of course, all this kind of thing is particularly frustrating when one looks ahead to the enormous importance of such basic problems as those involving length of military service, the training and equipping of troops, their indoctrination, and their support by all services.

I think that, in spite of the lack of a Government in France, we are making some progress in our arrangements for quarters, both office and living. This is all to the good and, if ever we get it completed, will release some energy for application to the bigger job ahead.[4] The President was certain, when he talked to me, that the soft currencies that the United States had piled up in these countries would be available to us in meeting this kind of problem. It appears that there are restrictive laws applying to these funds, and so the matter has not been so easy of solution as it might otherwise have been. Right now, we're trying to get the city of Paris to go into a housing project near our planned headquarters, with SHAPE officers to have the privilege of becoming the first renters. We hope that E.C.A. can make the necessary loans to Paris.[5] I would very greatly appreciate your applying your own fertile mind to this particular problem; with your great experience in these matters, you might well be able to turn up the key to the difficulty. In any event, I'll be heartened by the knowledge that you're really working at the job.

Of course, I constantly meet individuals from various nations and go over with them phases of the task the free world has undertaken. I encounter all shades of conviction, ranging from deep despair and pessimism to, sometimes, unwarranted complacency. I continue to believe that the truth, as usual, lies in the gray zone; success is attainable, assuming energy, wisdom, and devotion.

Of course, I have no objection to your showing my letters to the President. That is understood! Nevertheless, I should like to ask you, and you to ask him, to keep them confidential. I want to give no one the slightest excuse for intimating that, in this kind of communication, I am doing anything other than I was requested to do by the Commander in Chief; namely, to keep him informed of the principal worries that we currently have.[6]

Now I enter a command argument with the French.[7]

Warm regard. *Cordially*

---

[1] Harriman's letter is in EM. He told Eisenhower that the Great Debate (see no. 66) was over and that the Truman Administration had won, adding cryptically that "the problem is now to seize defeat from the jaws of victory." He also discussed developments concerning Yugoslavia (see no. 142), Turkey (see no. 423), and the Organization for European Economic Cooperation (see no. 16, n. 11).

[2] See no. 46.

[3] On the controversies over the proposed Atlantic and Mediterranean commands see nos. 45, n. 8, 53, 57, and 62.

[4] Construction of buildings for SHAPE would soon begin (see *New York Times*, Mar. 10, 13, Apr. 11, 1951).

[5] Under the provisions of the Economic Cooperation Act of 1948 (see Galambos, *Columbia University*, nos. 101 and 343), countries receiving American Marshall Plan grants were required to deposit an equal sum in local currency in a "counterpart" account. Five percent of this account would be available to cover ECA administrative expenses or purchases of critical materials for stockpiling. The remaining 95 percent could be spent "for purposes of internal monetary and financial stabilization, for the stimulation of productive activity and the exploration for and development of new sources of wealth . . ." (U.S., *Statutes at Large*, vol. 62, pt. 1, pp. 151–52). The recipient country had to secure U.S. agreement before any of the so-called 95 percent counterpart funds could be spent (see Collins to Eisenhower, May 26, 1950, EM; Bissell to Small, Mar. 5, 1951, OS/D, 1951, Clas. Decimal File, CD 092.3 NATO; Hadley Arkes, *Bureaucracy, the Marshall Plan, and the National Interest* [Princeton, 1972], pp. 156–58; Joyce Kolko and Gabriel Kolko, *The Limits of Power: The World and United States Foreign Policy, 1945–1954* [New York, 1972], pp. 380–81; Harry Bayard Price, *The Marshall Plan and Its Meaning* [Ithaca, N.Y., 1955], pp. 67, 315–16; and Michael J. Hogan, *The Marshall Plan: America, Britain, and the Reconstruction of Western Europe, 1947–1952* [Cambridge, 1987], pp. 85–86, 152–54, 388).

In his reply (Mar. 23, 1951, EM) Harriman agreed that the "legal aspects" of using the 95 percent counterpart funds for SHAPE construction would "create some problems." Harriman added, however, that the ECA had made some of these funds available to help solve Eisenhower's housing problems. In October 1951 Congress would create a new agency—the Mutual Security Agency (MSA)—and provide for the use of the 95 percent counterpart funds for defense (see U.S., *Statutes at Large*, vol. 65, pt. 1, pp. 373, 385; Price, *Marshall Plan*, pp. 164–66; U.S. Mutual Security Agency, *First Report to Congress on the Mutual Security Program* [Washington, D.C., Dec. 31, 1951], pp. 16–17; U.S. Congress, Senate, Committee on Foreign Relations, *Executive Sessions of the Senate Foreign Relations Committee [Historical Series]*, 82d Cong., 1st sess., 1951, vol. 3, pt. 2, pp. 56–57; and State, *Foreign Relations, 1951*, vol. III, *European Security and the German Question, Part I*, pp. 166–68, 247, 282–84).

[6] In his letter of March 1 Harriman had told Eisenhower that he had shown the General's letter of February 24 (no. 45) to President Truman: "As you know, he reads a great deal, and likes to get general atmosphere."

[7] On this day Eisenhower would meet with French General Alphonse Pierre Juin (see nos. 16 and 53) and with Hervé Alphand, French Deputy Representative on the NAC. For a description of these conversations see no. 77.

69   *CCS 092 Western Europe (3-12-48), Sec. 73*

To JOINT CHIEFS OF STAFF   *March 9, 1951*
Cable SH 20174. Top secret [0]

In WAR 99078 dtd 16th Dec 1950,[1] I was authorized as necessary for the accomplishment of my mission, to exercise operational command over US Army and Air Force Forces, Europe, and US Naval Forces, Eastern Atlantic and Mediterranean. It is my understanding that this authority extends to US Forces in Austria and Trieste.[2] It is also my understanding that the Commanding Gen, US Forces in Austria is responsible for coordinating the planning and training of US Forces in Trieste. If above is correct request confirmation thereof.[3] If not correct request that necessary action be taken to establish these relationships. In view of Four-Power considerations in Austria and UN considerations in Trieste, recommend that my relations with US and other Allied Forces in Austria and Trieste be on a classified basis.[4]

[1] This cable (not in EM) was undoubtedly a formal version of President Truman's letter of December 19, 1950, designating Eisenhower as SACEUR and outlining the extent of his authority over U.S. military forces in Europe and in the Mediterranean (see no. 2; see also JCS 2073/105, Dec. 26, 1950, CCS 092 Western Europe [3-12-48], Sec. 65). This message appears as an enclosure to JSPC 876/265/D, of March 12, 1951.

[2] For background on the U.S. occupation troops in Austria and Trieste see Chandler and Galambos, *Occupation, 1945*; and Galambos, *Chief of Staff*. The United States had approximately ten thousand troops (one regimental combat team) in Austria and five thousand troops (one regiment) in Trieste (see Allison A. Conrad, "In *Trust*, We Guard," *Army Information Digest* 6, no. 3 [1951], 3–10; and Gavin to Marshall, Jan. 11, 1951, OS/D, 1951, Clas. Decimal File, CD 032.1). In consid-

ering Eisenhower's cable, the JCS noted that current war plans called "for the withdrawal of U.S. forces in Austria and Trieste either into or through northern Italy in the event of hostilities." The JCS admitted that SACEUR's control of these forces would be desirable "from a purely military point of view," but they feared a "possible unfavorable reaction on the part of the Soviets" to the allocation of U.S. troops to SHAPE (JCS 2073/137, Mar. 19, 1951, CCS 092 Western Europe [3-12-48], Sec. 74). In April the U.S. High Commissioner for Austria would tell Eisenhower that even though Austria could not join NATO, the Austrian government was covertly organizing resistance forces (State, *Foreign Relations, 1951*, vol. IV, *Europe: Political and Economic Developments, Part II* [1985], pp. 1031–35, 1045–47).

[3] Army Chief of Staff Collins would inform Eisenhower in April that the American commander in Austria was responsible for planning for the Trieste forces but not for training them (DA 88900, Apr. 19, 1951, CCS 092 Western Europe [3-12-48], Sec. 78).

[4] After deliberations, the JCS would tell Eisenhower that the Secretary of Defense and the Secretary of State had decided to authorize Eisenhower to assume command of the American units in Austria and Trieste "at the outbreak of war, or at such earlier period as the JCS may authorize." Eisenhower was to direct the appropriate American commanders in planning for that contingency. Eisenhower's authority in those circumstances would also cover the British and French forces in Austria and Trieste (DA 88900, Apr. 19, 1951, and JCS 90234, May 3, 1951, CCS 092 Western Europe [3-12-48], Secs. 78, 80). In 1952 a similar question would arise with respect to the American forces in Berlin (see papers in CCS 381 [8-20-43], Sec. 27).

70   *Eisenhower Mss.*

To WILLIAM FLETCHER RUSSELL   *March 9, 1951*

Dear Will:[1] Naturally, I am delighted to learn that the response to the initial tryouts of our Citizenship Education project for the Armed Services was enthusiastic. That result is perfectly understandable. The first package designed by your people was so dramatic and striking in its presentation and content, that no other reaction would be possible— given a reasonably alert audience.[2]

The demonstration illuminated the origin of individual advantage— and private property, too, for that matter—in such a way that none could miss the point. I cannot think of any more forceful technique for presenting—to soldiers, at least—the three most common means of getting on in life—the lucky chance of picking the right envelope or number, the arbitrary decision of powers that control distribution of rewards or tasks, and the intelligent sustained effort of the individual himself.[3]

I am sure that every soldier who participated, even though the subject was only theater tickets and knee-bends, now has a better appreciation and comprehension of our free, competitive system that aims at making merit the principal basis of success. I wish I could have sat in on one of the troop sessions. I would have gotten a lot of profit out of it.[4]

Now that the Army and Air Force interest in the project has been won, the big job is to develop a series of similar packages that are equally forceful in driving home to troops or students the other principles underlying the American system. I am looking forward to a report on how your staff develops dramatizations of such complicated, yet fundamental, problems as: the inescapable obligation that accompanies every right in our society, if any rights are to survive; the dividing lines between the responsibilities of the Federal Government, the State Government, the home community, and the individual citizen; and the maintenance of national unity despite the divisive pressures of group and factual interest.

We can talk hours on end about these things. But no matter how inspired and dedicated the speaker himself may be, or how brilliant his speech, the result may be nothing more than a flood of words. One concrete example can do far more good than a week of inspirational addresses.

I hope that you will tell all of your people who are concerned in the development of package presentations that, in my opinion, the impact of their work will be felt by millions who could not be stirred by any purely intellectual or rhetorical effort. Especially, if they hit hard at the element of self-interest, as they did so well in the first package, they will be doing a great job in arousing a realistic understanding of what the American system is all about.[5]

Now, as regards the extension of the Citizenship Education Program across the ocean, I am hesitant to make any decision at the moment. I have thought of it several times since we talked it over in my office just before my departure. I have read the memorandum you gave me then, and the second that you gave to Kevin McCann. Of course, I am completely in sympathy with the general idea. While I am no authority on education for citizenship in the European countries, I emphatically feel that there is a tremendous task confronting educators in all free countries—the development of a common faith, understanding, and loyalty among all the free peoples, based on a common attitude toward the individual human being, and a common purpose to maintain for him the maximum freedom possible. However, I am not sure that the initial step should be a conference of official representatives of NATO countries at SHAPE. Although my mission has economic, political, and especially morale facets, as well as military, SHAPE is primarily a military headquarters. And for months to come, all our efforts must be bent toward the establishment and maintenance of forces adequate for the armed defense of Europe and powerful enough to give pause to any possible aggressor. If every man I have could work round the clock, seven days a week, there would still be little time for matters other than those directly and immediately concerned with the military mission.

Nevertheless, I feel that so much good can come out of your idea that I hope you will examine the entire situation and suggest ways and means of accomplishing our purpose without intervention or action by SHAPE at this time. The convention of the World Organization of the Teaching Profession in Malta seems an ideal platform from which to launch your proposal.

Couldn't you, as President, immediately start exploratory operations through national groups; a presentation of what we are doing at Columbia, what we have accomplished so far, what you think can be done on an international scale, should produce an immediate and factual reaction. Undoubtedly, those objecting might exceed those welcoming the proposal. But at the outset, objections are what you want. If they are valid, corrections can be made to accommodate them and a comprehensive program drawn up for submission to the convention in Malta.[6]

In the meantime, the military aspects of SHAPE may have developed so successfully that we can, in some way, participate. Certainly, I myself would be delighted to help in any way compatible with my duties here. I hope that you will mull over this suggestion and let me know as soon as you reach a decision.[7]

I should add that it was good to hear from you again. Despite the crowded hours and the hurried pace of SHAPE, I still miss visits from my good friends at Columbia.[8]

Mamie joins me in best wishes to Mrs. Russell[9] and yourself.

Sincerely

[1] William Fletcher Russell was president of Columbia University's Teachers College and Director of the Citizenship Education Project, which was begun during Eisenhower's tenure as university president (for background on Russell see Galambos, *Columbia University*, nos. 67 and 772; on the Citizenship Education Project see *ibid.*, nos. 811 and 871).

[2] Russell had written to Eisenhower on February 26 (EM) about the success of recent trial citizenship education exercises in the Army and Air Force. The General had originally suggested to Secretary of Defense George Catlett Marshall that the military use the Columbia program to increase servicemen's awareness of American history and national concepts (see Galambos, *Columbia University*, no. 1073).

[3] Russell had explained that numbered envelopes, each containing specific instructions known only to the leader of each class, were distributed to the servicemen in the training classes. Two sets of five "special numbers" were called first, and the servicemen were requested to open the envelopes and read the instructions they had received. One group of five received orders to do a number of deep knee bends, and the other received free theater tickets. Then another number was called, and the trainee was asked to read the contents of his envelope, which contained the questions: "Is this a fair way to distribute advantages and disadvantages? Is this the American Way?" The trainees next formed a jury to hear both sides of the issue

from the original ten men called upon, with the winners receiving the tickets and the losers the deep knee bends.

[4] Russell had written that the "*success was electric,*" with discussions continuing after the classes and the officers present reporting that they had never before witnessed such a vital exercise.

[5] The Citizenship Education Project and the Army, Navy, and Air Force established the Armed Services Planning Project for testing the exercises in the military. Based on the experimental "situation exercise," ten one-hour teaching units called Hours on Freedom were developed to teach basic American values in participatory formats. The ten units were: The Worth of the Individual, Freedom of Expression, Responsibility to Serve, Rule of Law, The Threat to Freedom, Freedom of Religion, It Takes Courage, Community Relations, Citizen Control of Government I, and Citizen Control of Government II (see Columbia University, Teachers College, *Improving Citizenship Education: A Two-Year Progress Report of the Citizenship Education Project* [New York, 1952], pp. 24–28, copy in EM, Russell Corr.).

[6] In a memorandum to Eisenhower of February 6 (EM) Russell had proposed a citizenship education project for the NATO Allies. Russell had written that the military and industrial unity being developed in Western Europe needed to be "bolstered by unity arising from common ideals and a sense of the reasons why they should be defended." In his later memorandum to McCann (n.d., EM), who drafted this letter for Eisenhower, Russell had suggested specific steps to establish such a program in the NATO nations. He thought that after the special conference of SHAPE representatives, the nations should be encouraged to send special delegations of "influential school officials and teachers" to discuss the plan at the July meeting of the World Organization of the Teaching Profession (see also Russell to Eisenhower, Mar. 30, 1951, EM).

[7] On May 9, 1952, Russell would send Eisenhower a brief report (EM) on the project's work with the European Allies. By that time the forces of Britain, France, Italy, and Norway had been contacted and were either using or planning to adopt the Hours on Freedom exercises for the training of their military personnel. SHAPE would take no direct role in training these foreign soldiers, and since the Department of the Army had not approved the Hours on Freedom, the program was not in use with American NATO forces.

[8] Russell would visit the General in Paris during May to discuss the project (see Russell to Eisenhower, May 9, 1951, EM; and appointment calendar).

[9] The former Clotilde Desjardins.

71   *Eisenhower Mss.*

To HARRY JAMES CARMAN   *March 9, 1951*

Dear Harry:[1] Thanks for the letter and the photograph. Never in my life have I seen so impressive an air of philosophical detachment as appears on your face as you listen to my presentation![2]

I must say that, in dropping in on the Alexander Hamilton dinner, the privilege was mine. If it required me to leave with one trunk still unpacked, or to beg for a delay in the sailing of the QUEEN ELIZABETH, I would not have missed it. I cannot think of any better way in which I could have spent my time on the eve of departure.[3]

The news of Columbia, and particularly of George Pegram's recovery and the scholarship hopes, was welcome.[4] Here in my office in the Astoria Hotel, overlooking the Champs Elysées, it comes as a surprise sometimes to look out the window and see the Arc de Triomphe— instead of Butler Library. The Columbia ties are very strong and every word about the place is heartening.[5]

While I must admit that I am at times terrifically rushed here, I know that your pace is far faster and heavier than mine. If you should come to Paris this season, I hope I can find out from you how you do it.[6]

As soon as I get home this evening, I shall tell Mamie of your letter. I know that, in writing to you now, she will expect me to assure you of the affectionate regards and best wishes of us both.[7] *Sincerely*

[1] For background on Carman, dean emeritus of Columbia College, see no. 38.

[2] With his letter of March 1 (EM) Carman had enclosed a copy of a photograph taken at the February 15 Alexander Hamilton award dinner in New York City. As president of Columbia University, Eisenhower had been among the speakers who had presented Carman with the Alexander Hamilton Medal of the Association of Columbia College Alumni (for background on the dinner see no. 38; and *New York Times*, Feb. 16, 1951).

[3] For Eisenhower's departure for Europe see no. 38.

[4] Carman had written that retired Columbia University vice-president and special adviser George Braxton Pegram was recovering from the flu. He had also said that Columbia had recently submitted to the Ford Foundation a joint proposal with four other universities for fifty twelve-hundred-dollar scholarships per school. On Pegram see Galambos, *Columbia University*; on Columbia's dealings with the Ford Foundation see *ibid.*, nos. 419, 726, and 1007.

[5] For Eisenhower's continuing contacts with the university see nos. 8, 31, and 47.

[6] The General's activities in organizing the SHAPE command are discussed in nos. 46, 61, and 62, among others.

[7] This letter was drafted for the General by Kevin McCann (for background see no. 53, n. 10).

72   *Eisenhower Mss.*

To Edwin Norman Clark   *March 10, 1951*

Dear Ed:[1] I attach hereto an excerpt from a letter I have just received from home, because, as I recall, it was through you that I met Mr. Bennett.[2]

I know that you understand how delicate are some of the factors that will be important to the success or failure of this irksome but all-important job that I have undertaken. Among these factors is the need for retaining the maximum support that I can achieve in our homeland. Any effort to generate or further excite the political speculation about me is bound to react unfavorably on this job. If evidence comes to me that such developments are going to endanger the great objective of Western security, I will forget my current determination to keep my mouth shut about any political matter affecting me personally, and will issue a statement that, by comparison, will make all others I have ever made appear pale and insignificant.[3]

I know that you understand all this. I don't know that there is a single thing to be done at the present time, particularly because the attached reference to Mr. Bennett's activities may be unsupported rumor. What I am merely trying to say is that, in some instances, rumors could be just as damaging to my work here as could fact.[4]

I hope that you are still adhering to your plan to be over this way sometime in the spring.[5]

With warm personal regard. *Cordially*

[1] For background on Clark see no. 31, n. 5.

[2] Rochester, New York, real estate man and Republican political activist John Gordon Bennett had been present at two luncheon meetings with the General during December 1950 (see Galambos, *Columbia University*, no. 1105; no. 1 in this volume; and *New York Times*, Feb. 17, 1955). There is no copy of this excerpt in EM, and the correspondent was not identified.

[3] The topic of both December luncheons had been Eisenhower's political future, and it is likely that Bennett was then doing some unauthorized promotion of the General's nomination as a presidential candidate. For Eisenhower's heated reaction to a discussion with Bennett on December 30, 1950, see no. 1; on the General's earlier statements concerning his potential role in politics see no. 25, n. 3.

[4] For similar reactions see nos. 57, 135, and 205; in regard to Bennett see no. 610.

[5] Clark would meet with Eisenhower in Paris during late July and early August. Bennett would visit SHAPE in January of the following year, traveling there for newspaper correspondent Andrew Russell "Drew" Pearson (see no. 581).

73   *Eisenhower Mss.*

To George Edward Allen   *March 10, 1951*

Dear George:[1] Don't pull this business on me that you don't know what the size of the bet was. It's in your black book that you always carry around with you, and you well know it. We had a $200 "do and don't" bet, which I told you I was trying to make big enough so you would actually get down to work.[2]

Now I'll tell you what I'll do—you get busy on your diet and get down to 202 pounds by the 15th of May, and you can keep your check and merely deposit it to our joint account of good wishes.[3]

*   *   *   *   *

After all the above, I just learned from Mamie that she thinks she owes you $500. She asked me whether I had given you a $500 check and I told her, "No; I had depended upon you to pay to George all the money that he puts out for our joint enterprise out of the Riggs account." If she still owes you the $500, tell me in your next letter and she will send you a check immediately.[4]

I hear that you are terrifically intrigued with your California home and that you may even consider giving up your Gettysburg farm. This will be bad news for me, but, if you do decide to sell, I would consider it a favor if you would offer Art Nevins or General Snyder[5] a chance at its purchase. Assuming that you would just as soon hold a good big mortgage as a paying investment, either one of them ought to swing it. (Make no mistake, though; I *don't want* you to sell to anybody.)[6]

However, if you and Mary[7] and all her family are so delighted with the Western home, then, of course, that is what you should plan to occupy some day. *Cordially*

P.S. For goodness sake, get your weight down, or you won't be around to live anywhere.

[1] For background on Eisenhower's old friend Allen see nos. 33 and 48.

[2] Allen and the General had recently made a bet as to whether Eisenhower could trim down to 174 lbs. and Allen to 202 lbs. Aside from the $200 "do and don't" payment, the loser was to pay an additional $10 for each pound by which he exceeded his goal. On March 6 (EM) Allen had written that he was thirteen pounds over the agreed-upon 202 and owed Eisenhower $130 but that he could not remember what the "big bet" had been (see letters and cables in EM, Allen Corr.; and no. 48).

[3] Allen and Eisenhower were partners in operations on their two Gettysburg, Pennsylvania, farms and kept a joint bank account for expenses incident to the partnership. For background and developments on their venture and other matters see nos. 33, 48, and 170. On their continuing bet see nos. 93 and 192; and Schulz, Memorandum for Record, June 21, 1951, in EM, Allen Corr.

[4] There is no further mention of this $500 in EM. Allen had sent his check for $130 to Eisenhower's farm manager and friend, Arthur S. Nevins (see Allen to Eisenhower, Mar. 6, 1951, EM; on Nevins see nos. 33 and 48).

[5] Retired Major General Howard McCrum Snyder, Sr., was Eisenhower's doctor (see nos. 24 and 59).

[6] Allen would not sell his Gettysburg property in the immediate future (see no. 93).

[7] Allen's wife (see no. 9).

To Bernard Law Montgomery   *March 12, 1951*
Restricted

My dear Field Marshal:[1] I trust that you realize how delighted I am that
the British Government has agreed to make you available for duty in
SHAPE, in which you are hereby designated as the Deputy Supreme
Allied Commander. In this capacity, you will have a most important
role to play in the development of an integrated force for the defense
of Europe, which is our objective.

You will act, during any temporary incapacity of mine, as Supreme
Allied Commander, Europe, under the authority invested in me by the
North Atlantic Council.[2] Your principal normal duty will be to further
the organization, equipping, training, and readiness of National Forces
contemplated for later allocation to this command, and through and
in cooperation with subordinate commanders, to perform a similar
function for troops already allocated to SHAPE.

These duties will require your direct contact, in my name, with the
several governments, military staffs and agencies of NATO nations,
and with principal subordinate headquarters established by competent
orders of SHAPE. I suggest that you acquaint yourself with the terms
of the directive issued to me by the Standing Group, particularly those
provisions that authorize direct communication between this headquarters and the several governments of NATO.[3] For assisting you in this
work, the entire SHAPE staff, through its Chief of Staff,[4] will be at
your disposal. Any executive instructions to subordinate commanders
are, of course, to be issued through the staff.[5] *Cordially*

[1] For background on Montgomery and his appointment as Deputy SACEUR see
nos. 2 and 17.

[2] See no. 2, n. 2.

[3] *Ibid.*, n. 1. We have been unable to locate this document. Eisenhower's original
directive authorized him "to communicate with National Chiefs of Staff, and with
their respective Defense Ministers, and the heads of government, directly as necessary to facilitate the accomplishment of his mission" (State, *Foreign Relations,
1950*, vol. III, *Western Europe*, p. 559; see also Beebe to Gruenther, Apr. 5, 1951,
Gruenther Papers).

[4] General Alfred M. Gruenther (see no. 2, n. 3).

[5] SHAPE would announce Montgomery's appointment on March 20, ending speculation that other men were being considered for the post. Eisenhower would also
announce that General Alphonse Pierre Juin (see no. 53) would become commander of the Allied Land Forces in central Europe (*New York Times*, Mar. 7, 21,
1951).

To WILLIAM H. BURNHAM *March 12, 1951*

Dear Bill:[1] I am grateful for your letter of the 8th. It cleared up a lot of things for me and will make a very fine basis for our conversations when next we meet. I trust that I have left no doubt in your mind that I am anxious to see you again, as soon as possible.[2]

My former caution about military aircraft was merely to avoid some little thing that could be made to appear of unusual significance by any unfair critic.[3]

My morning's paper stated that the loans made by R.F.C. to the Negro Tabernacle in Washington are coming under fire. I used to be an Honorary Deacon in that Church—I most sincerely trust that the head of it has not been guilty of anything unethical.[4] *Cordially*

[1] For background on Eisenhower's friend and adviser Burnham see no. 40.

[2] There is no copy of a March 8 letter from Burnham in EM. In a letter of March 2 (EM) he had said that he intended to make a business trip to Holland and would visit the General in Paris on March 15 (see appointment calendar).

[3] The General was normally circumspect in matters of this sort. It is also likely that in this case the General feared that any use of military transportation would increase the speculation about him as a potential presidential candidate. Burnham had been one of the leading directors of the 1948 National Draft Eisenhower League and was still active in gaining support for an Eisenhower candidacy (see Galambos, *Chief of Staff*, no. 2015; nos. 450 and 626 in these volumes; and EM, Burnham Corr.).

[4] The head of the Negro Tabernacle was Washington evangelist and community leader Elder Lightfoot Solomon Michaux; on Eisenhower's appointment as honorary deacon in Michaux's Universal Church of God see Chandler and Galambos, *Occupation, 1945*, no. 326. The Senate investigation into the Reconstruction Finance Corporation (RFC) dealings had begun in 1950 by examining allegations that officers of the federal lending agency had reaped benefits for friends and family members from loans, accepted bribes from borrowers, and shown favoritism toward Democrats (see Donovan, *Tumultuous Years*, pp. 332–39; and *New York Times*, Jan. 13, Feb. 28, Mar. 6, 9, 1951).

On March 11 it was reported that in 1942 and 1943 Michaux had obtained RFC loans of $3.5 million for his Mayfair housing project; he was later granted an additional $325,000 for a shopping center extension, despite the fact that his original loans were in arrears. The article Eisenhower had read implied that because Michaux was a friend of Presidents Roosevelt and Truman and an "active Democratic politician," he had received the loans due to his political connections (see *International Herald Tribune*, Paris ed., Mar. 11, 1951). Another honorary deacon of Michaux's church and close Eisenhower friend, George Allen, had been a director of the RFC at the time the loan for the shopping center extension was granted. According to one report, Allen, who was also a director of the Mayfair project, had helped the evangelist obtain the loan. Michaux had, however, denied any special action on Allen's part (see *New York Times*, Mar. 12, 1951; for background on Allen see nos. 9 and 73). In a letter to Eisenhower of March 6 (EM) Allen had written that the political situation at home was "boiling but the only real news that is talked about is the RFC." He went on to quote a Washington newspaper that had printed an excerpt from his book *Presidents Who Have Known Me*: "What I forgot was that . . . an RFC directorship was regarded as a plum . . . that could be squeezed for the benefit of constituents seeking plum juice in the form of loans. . . ." The Senate committee would not investigate the loans to Michaux (see U.S. Congress, Senate, Subcommittee of the Committee on Banking and Currency, *Study of Reconstruction Finance Corporation: Hearings on Lending Policy, Part 3*, 82d Cong., 1st sess., 1951). For more on the RFC investigations see no. 95.

76   *Eisenhower Mss.*

To EUGENIO SICAGUSA   *March 12, 1951*

Dear Mr. Sicagusa:[1] Your recent letter reached Mrs. Eisenhower and both of us were deeply touched by the sentiments you expressed. Your concern for the future of your children is very natural and understandable.[2]

It is my hope—and my belief also—that an enduring peace will be secured by the common efforts of the Western nations. There is much to be done, involving hard work and sacrifice from the individual citizen, but the goal stands out as worthy of whatever it costs.[3]

With appreciation and good wishes to you and your family.[4] *Sincerely*

[1] Eugenio Sicagusa, who worked with the local government in Catania, Sicily, had written to Mrs. Eisenhower on February 27 expressing his admiration for the General and for his efforts on behalf of NATO (see original and SHAPE translation in EM).

[2] Sicagusa, the father of two children, had written that he was concerned for their futures. He said he placed his hope and "unconditional trust in the American people . . . particularly in . . . President Truman and in General Eisenhower. . . ."

[3] Sicagusa said he had been a noncommissioned officer in the Italian Navy during World War II, but he now wholeheartedly believed in the efforts the United States was making in Europe and was ready to "fight for the same cause that your Ike and the American people are fighting for." For background on Italian participation in NATO see nos. 153 and 158.

[4] This letter was drafted by a member of the General's staff.

77   *Eisenhower Mss.*

To GEORGE CATLETT MARSHALL   *March 12, 1951*
Top secret

Dear General: While I have no intention of making a practice of bothering you with my own problems, yet the habit I developed in World

War II of presenting to you occasional informal reports reasserts itself at least in some degree.[1] This missive is intended as background, and requires no answer.

Because NATO is more an idea or concept than it is a real organization, it lacks those offices and facilities that would be useful in performance of ministerial functions indicated as necessary in such efforts as this. The situation is more complicated than it was in World War II because of the increased number of nations, and is further confused because the economic and political factors enter into *everything* we do. Budgets and a dozen other administrative problems just sort of hang in the air for want of a definite and decisive authority to act on them![2]

NATO has no adequately developed Public Relations organization, and, therefore, announcement of such things as command and organization intentions has sometimes resulted in creation of schism and division rather than of unity and confidence.[3] The difficulties thus created plague us to some extent in trying to put together a command organization that seems to resemble a picture puzzle. The pieces are made up of individual ambitions and rigid conceptions of service functions, of prestige and tactical doctrine, and of nationalistic jealousies, suspicions, and economic interest. As a consequence of all these things, we proceed laboriously, slowly, and sometimes on practically a clandestine basis, in order that all of these conflicting considerations can be brought together and so articulated as to create reasonable satisfaction everywhere, even if no individual service or country can be completely overjoyed.

It has been my purpose to draw the British and French into prominent posts of command and of staff organization. In the staff itself, I have spread this theory somewhat to include Italy in an important post; but, with respect to smaller nations, I must avoid creating jealousies among them, and, therefore, I feel that, except in most unusual circumstances, a representative of one of these nations would not be assigned to a very high command or a staff post.

As of now, my conversations have been directed toward securing French, British, and Italian compliance to an organization somewhat as follows: Deputy Supreme Commander, Field Marshal Montgomery. He would have no portfolio but would be exactly what the name implies—my personal deputy.[4] My "Deputy for Air" will be a British officer.[5] Quite naturally, Jack Slessor[6] wanted to make this officer both a Deputy and a Commander, with all of the functions pertaining to both staff and command. This could not be—such complete control vested in one man would be unacceptable to the American Air Forces, and, indeed, to me. The Admiral in my headquarters will be strictly a staff man and probably carrying the title "Deputy for Naval Affairs." If appointed, he will probably be a Frenchman.[7]

None of these Deputies would have any command functions but

would have numerous tasks of an administrative, advisory, consultative, and preparatory nature, involving contacts both with my own staff and with the governments of NATO.

My G-1 is an Italian, and my G-2 is British.[8] Organization and Training is also in the hands of the British, while Plans and Operations goes to a Frenchman.[9] My Fiscal Officer is likewise French.[10] Two Deputies to my Chief of Staff are French and British, respectively.[11]

Incidentally, I think we are hurling the adjective "Supreme" around rather carelessly these days. It was invented, as I understand it, to designate an Allied Commander who would necessarily control troops of *all* services. Soon we'll have to use "Colossal Supreme."[12]

In World War II, we normally proceeded on the theory that the national identity of a Supreme Commander completely counter-balanced the nationalistic influence of subordinate Deputies or Commanders-in-Chief, even where these three or four subordinates were all of the same nation.

The over-all Mediterranean–Middle East command and the Atlantic Naval command lie, of course, outside my direct responsibility; yet the announcement of the latter has created such reactions throughout the United Kingdom that some way should be found to give to the British the type of command and command title that would help ameliorate their obvious resentment.[13]

I am *not* concerned with the *territorial* organization of the Mediterranean–Middle East except as it bears directly upon my responsibility for the defense of Europe.[14] I am concerned that: (1) there should be no possible interference with the employment of the United States naval fighting force which, I have been assured by Sherman and by the President, will be maintained strongly to operate under my command in support of our right flank; (2) there will be proper influence and emphasis in the development of morale and military power of all the European nations of the Northern Mediterranean littoral; (3) Northwest Africa will be available to support me as a base and staging area; and (4) my lines of communication in the Western Mediterranean are properly safeguarded.

I leave all other problems of organization in the Mediterranean to the governments concerned. Any assigned responsibility to a Commander-in-Chief, Mediterranean, should be so qualified as to safeguard the interests of this headquarters as outlined above. With respect to that particular phase of my own organization, Carney's headquarters will be ashore in Italy and he will be responsible for the control and coordination of effort between the allocated land, air, naval, and logistic forces. The British do not by any means approve of this organization and are quite anxious that I observe on that flank the triumvirate system, but I see no necessity as of this moment for accepting that clumsy arrangement.[15]

Land forces in the South at present are of two kinds—those assigned to occupational duties, and others making up the couverture forces of the Italians. I plan to give (American) General Irwin planning and operational charge of Allied ground forces now in Austria and Trieste until such time, in actual operations, as they may have to fall back upon and join up with the Italian couverture forces. The best Italian General I can find will be in over-all charge of the ground forces, but Irwin's command will continue to operate *as a unit and will not be broken up.*[16] Incidentally, I hope to get some moderately-sized reinforcements for Irwin's command which should have a very great effect in strengthening that flank. I do not yet need to bother my head about an Air Force Commander in that region, because there is virtually no air except United States naval aviation.

In the center, I plan to have Juin for a Ground Commander, and Norstad to command all the air.[17] It was difficult to get Juin to accept this post because of his conviction that all supporting air should be under his "command." I have promised to him that the primary mission of the central air forces would be the support of the land battle (which includes gaining air superiority), and that they could not be taken away, even temporarily, except upon my personal order. This persuaded him. I regard his membership in this command as of vital importance because of his standing in the French services and in the French popular mind. I convinced him that, if some feature of my organization should completely defy the basic doctrines of the British and American Air Forces, there would be developed by them every excuse in the world to avoid allocating additional air power to the Central Command.[18] Yet it is in this area that we must be strong, the earlier the better.

In the North, where the only disposable strength will, of necessity, be furnished by the British Navy and where the whole area lies directly to the front of the United Kingdom, I would prefer to establish a Commander-in-Chief who would be a British Admiral.[19] Under him would be Norwegian and Danish Commanders who would, in effect, be Task Force Commanders.[20] Moreover, I had hoped that under this arrangement, I could get the agreement of the British Admiralty to provide, in operational emergency, Naval strength to support Norway and Denmark, both of which I expect to develop as hedgehogs of defense. As of now, I shall have to accept, temporarily at least, the triumvirate system on this flank. This is because of my need for getting the Admiralty to accept some *responsibility* for me; and the Admiralty will not accept single command on that flank! All this will require some adjustment with the Eastern Atlantic Command and further modification of the command structure as larger forces are generated.

As of now, I have one request to make upon you and Bradley. It is that you try to make sure that no American official, military or other, may upset these delicate negotiations through lack of understanding or through over-simplification of this kind of a job. There will be elements throughout such a structure that violate specific personal convictions and beliefs, but we must never forget that we are putting together a mechanism that has a terrific morale job to accomplish. If we start off by doing things that damage or destroy morale at the outset, the later job could well prove impossible. American interest, prestige, and doctrine are amply represented in this layout, even though I've omitted these particular details in preparing this letter. But we have such people as Gruenther, Handy,[21] Carney, Norstad, and a batch of fine young men. We won't let the United States down!

No one will necessarily agree with every detail of my planned organization, but I sincerely hope all will recognize the fact that only an office situated such as is mine could possibly carry forward the laborious conversations, conferences, arguments, and struggles that must precede the formation of any organization that has the slightest chance of acceptance.

If the innumerable Committees of NATO once start trifling with these specific features of organization, we'll be helpless to proceed.

I have dozens of irritating, preliminary problems, involving places to live and work, financing of joint administrative functions, and so on. Life is never dull!

If you have no objection, would you pass this letter to Bradley for his background understanding? It would save me writing a special one.[22] *Cordially*

P.S. I just received your note of the 8th.[23] I fully understand your reasons—and I concur.

[1] During World War II Secretary of Defense Marshall had been Chief of Staff of the Army. For Eisenhower's extensive correspondence with him see Chandler, *War Years*; see also Joseph P. Hobbs, *Dear General: Eisenhower's Wartime Letters to Marshall* (Baltimore, 1971).

[2] For background on the dispute over the SHAPE budget see no. 45, n. 6; for developments see no. 167, n. 5. See also *New York Times*, April 9, 1951. On March 22 a special committee set up by the NAC deputies (see no. 2, n. 2) would report that the NATO member nations still had not agreed on a cost-sharing formula to pay for SHAPE and that the Standing Group considered the problem urgent (D-D [51] 81, Mar. 22, 1951, NATO Files, microfilm).

[3] On the controversies over the proposed Atlantic and Mediterranean commands see nos. 45, 53, 57, and 62. The NATO Information Service at this time consisted of a director and two assistants (D-D [51] 38, Feb. 8, 1951, NATO Files, microfilm). The NAC deputies were still in the process of defining the responsibilities of a proposed information staff for SHAPE (D-R [51] 20, Mar. 15, 1951, *ibid.*; see also State, *Foreign Relations, 1951*, vol. III, *European Security and the German Question, Part I*, p. 89).

[4] For background on Montgomery's appointment see no. 74.

[5] SHAPE would announce the appointment of Air Chief Marshal Sir Hugh Wil-

liam Lumsden Saunders as Deputy Supreme Commander for Air on March 20. During World War II Saunders, a native South African, had served with the British Fighter Command and in New Zealand and Burma. Before his appointment to SHAPE he had been Inspector General of the Royal Air Force.

[6] See no. 62.

[7] Eisenhower would not appoint Vice-Admiral André Georges Lemonnier as his naval deputy until April (see no. 149).

[8] Rear Admiral Ferrante Capponi had served in the Italian Navy during World War II and since 1949 had been commandant of the Italian Naval Academy. He was appointed Assistant Chief of Staff for Personnel and Administration on March 6 (see no. 61, n. 2). Major General Terence Sydney Airey was appointed SHAPE's Assistant Chief of Staff for Intelligence the same day (see no. 271).

[9] Major General Francis Wogan Festing was SHAPE's Assistant Chief of Staff for Organization and Training (see no. 219). Major General Pierre Louis Bodet, SHAPE's Assistant Chief of Staff for Plans, Policy and Operations (PPANDO) had commanded the French Air Forces against Germany during World War II. From 1947 until 1950 he had been in charge of the French air effort in the war in Indochina.

[10] Guillaume C. LeBigot had been named SHAPE's budget and fiscal officer on March 7. He had been head of the French Defense Ministry's Finance Section since 1947.

[11] The Deputy Chief of Staff for Administration was Lieutenant General Marcel-Maurice Carpentier, and the Deputy Chief of Staff for Plans was Air Vice-Marshal Edmund C. Hudleston. Carpentier had served as General Juin's chief of staff during World War II and had commanded French forces in Indochina in 1949. Hudleston had served in the Middle East, Africa, the Mediterranean, and Western Europe during World War II and had been head of the British delegation to the Western Union's Military Staff Committee from 1948 until 1950.

[12] See nos. 57, n. 3, and 68.

[13] See n. 3 above.

[14] For background on the proposed Mediterranean command see nos. 53 and 57.

[15] On the U.S.-British dispute during World War II over the doctrine of unity of command see Chandler, *War Years*, nos. 811 and 1256; for developments see nos. 85 and 107 in this volume. Admiral Carney (see no. 53) would become Eisenhower's Commander in Chief, Allied Forces, Southern Europe (for developments see nos. 148, 198, and 236).

[16] For background on Lieutenant General Stafford LeRoy Irwin, commanding general (CG) of the U.S. Forces in Austria since October 1950, see *Eisenhower Papers*, vols. I–XI; on the question of operational command of the forces in Austria and Trieste see no. 69. "Couverture forces" are those covering a mobilization (see no. 153). In May Eisenhower would designate Italian General Maurizio Lazzaro de Castiglioni as commander of the ground forces in Southern Europe (see nos. 153 and 158; see also D-D [51] 159, June 19, 1951, NATO Files, microfilm).

[17] For background on French general Alphonse Pierre Juin see no. 16; and n. 18 below. On Lieutenant General Lauris Norstad, Commander in Chief, United States Air Forces, Europe (CINCUSAFE), since October 1950, see *Eisenhower Papers*, vols. I–XI. Norstad would be named Commander of Allied Air Forces in central Europe on March 20.

[18] For background see no. 53. Eisenhower had met with Juin and with French Ambassador Hervé Alphand on March 8 (see no. 68, n. 7). At that time he had told Alphand that France would not be able to contribute to NATO's tactical air forces for several years to come and that it was in her own interests "to see a solution which would attract maximum air in defense of [the] central sector under [a] system which would provide [the] best possible air support for ground forces"

(State, *Foreign Relations, 1951*, vol. III, *European Security and the German Question, Part I*, pp. 485–86).

[19] This would be Admiral Eric James Patrick Brind (see no. 99). The British were opposed to Eisenhower's ideas, favoring instead a "tripartite organisation with a British Admiral as Chairman, not C-in-C of the Region" (Slim to Gruenther, Mar. 14, 1951, Gruenther Papers).

[20] On March 20 Eisenhower would name as Allied commanders Lieutenant General Wilhelm von Tangen-Hansteen, Chief of Staff of the Norwegian Army, and Lieutenant General Ebbe Gørtz of Denmark.

[21] For background on General Thomas Troy Handy, the American Commander in Chief, Europe (CINCEUR), since September 1949, see *Eisenhower Papers*, vols. I–XI.

[22] Marshall would give Eisenhower's letter to JCS Chairman Bradley, who in turn would read it to the JCS on March 16. The Joint Chiefs would instruct the U.S. representative on the Standing Group "to fully back" Eisenhower's plans (Marshall to Eisenhower, Mar. 21, 1951, OS/D, 1951, Clas. Decimal File, CD 370.21 [SHAPE 1951]; copy in EM).

[23] On March 8 Marshall had written to inform Eisenhower that the Truman Administration had delayed announcing the shipment of additional U.S. divisions to Europe because of fear that an adverse political reaction would jeopardize the outcome of the Great Debate then taking place in Congress (see nos. 23, 112, and 128). Marshall assured Eisenhower that he was "very anxious here not only to come out with a statement as indicated above, but to alert the divisions and get things well underway." Marshall added that he had already made the announcement that additional troops would be sent to Japan: "Strange to say, the announcement regarding the two divisions to Japan gave rise to very few comments—none adverse" (Marshall to Eisenhower, Mar. 8, 1951, EM; see also papers in OS/D, 1951, Clas. Decimal File, CD 371 Europe, and in CCS 381 [2-8-43], Sec. 20).

78   *Eisenhower Mss., Diaries*

DIARY   *March 13, 1951*

Each day we get a cabled summary of news from the U.S. In general *our* summary covers subjects connected only with SHAPE or some military subject—sometimes merely with me as an individual.[1]

One phase of the reports now coming in reminds me that I never seem to catch up with the true intensity of American interest in any and all men who may be considered even remotely, as Presidential possibilities. I thought my coming to Europe would tend to still the gossip about me. Not only am I out of the States—I'm on a uniformed duty! But the nagging, speculation and suspecting grows worse.[2]

Today I received a cartoon from Detroit Free Press—date Mar. 5.[3]

Drew Pearson reports Sen. McCarthy is digging up alleged dirt with which to *smear* me *if* I run for Pres.[4]

Pegler hints darkly that by character & ability I'm something of a scoundrel & moron.[5]

And so on.

Now—I realize that these curious people have a full right to their own convictions—and a right to talk about them. But it would seem to be the role of decency to avoid heaping poisonous criticism on the head of anyone who is doing only one thing—working like a dog just to *preserve their* right to say whatever they choose. At least they might wait until I by some word or token imply that I *want* a political career.[6]

Actually my name is more often mentioned in dispatches as a possible President than it is as a slave—with one of the most irksome jobs ever designed by man![7]

[1] These news summaries are not in EM.

[2] In newspaper and magazine articles concerning the 1952 presidential election Eisenhower's party affiliation, his stand on foreign and domestic issues, and his desire to become a presidential candidate were being widely discussed (see, for example, *New York Times*, Jan. 20, 28, 31, Feb. 11, Mar. 4, 11, 1951; *U.S. News & World Report*, Jan. 19, Feb. 16, 1951; *Newsweek*, Jan. 20, Feb. 12, 1951). Reports from the General's friends in the United States also frequently touched on the growing support for, and incidental opposition to, an Eisenhower candidacy (see nos. 1 and 72).

[3] Eisenhower was referring to Burt Thomas's cartoon "Poor Ike!" which had appeared in the March 5 *Detroit News* (for background see the following document).

[4] Syndicated columnist and radio commentator Drew Pearson had supposedly made this remark during his March 11 broadcast. Denying the allegation, Senator Joseph R. McCarthy would write to the General on March 22 (EM) calling Pearson a "degenerate . . . liar" and enclosing an anti-Pearson pamphlet (see documents in EM, McCarthy Corr.). For background on McCarthy's feud with Pearson and the lawsuit involving the anti-Pearson pamphlet see *New York Times*, March 3, 1951. On Pearson and McCarthy see also nos. 72 and 84, respectively.

[5] Ultraconservative King Features Syndicate columnist Westbrook Pegler had recently begun a series of articles attacking a potential Eisenhower candidacy and calling for a careful examination of the General's record. Linking him closely to the foreign and domestic policies of the Roosevelt Administration, the columnist wrote that Eisenhower was one of the persons primarily responsible for the present world political and military situation. According to Pegler, Eisenhower's acquiescence in Roosevelt's political decision not to invade the Balkans during World War II was an "awful mistake in military strategy which now has placed our country in the preliminary stages of another World War." Quoting extensively from the war memoir of Commander of Army Field Forces General Mark Clark (see no. 61), Pegler maintained that because of this failure to invade the Balkans, the war had been needlessly prolonged. Unless Eisenhower had had "serious doubts" regarding the consequences of the Soviet invasion of the Balkans, Pegler wrote, "he must have been a very stupid man" (see *New York Journal American*, Mar. 10, 13, 1951; and Mark W. Clark, *Calculated Risk* [New York, 1950], pp. 368–72, 408–9, and 420–22). On Eisenhower's adherence to stated government policy concerning the Balkans see his memoir *Crusade in Europe*, pp. 284, 474–75; and Chandler, *War Years*. For further developments see no. 101.

[6] In reference to Eisenhower's decision to seek the 1952 Republican presidential nomination see nos. 587, 592, and 678.

[7] Eisenhower's recent struggles in forming the NATO command are discussed in nos. 53 and 77.

79   *Eisenhower Mss.*

To William Steele Gilmore   *March 13, 1951*

Dear Mr. Gilmore:[1] Thank you very much for the original of Mr. Thomas' cartoon, "Poor Ike!" I think I shall instantly circulate it through this staff of mine; I think there is some failure around here to share the belief in my miraculous powers. Maybe this will do something to correct such an error.[2]

The Miss MacKinnon who suggested that you send me the cartoon must be *Mrs.* MacKinnon who used to be my very competent Secretary at Columbia. I know that she and her husband moved to Detroit— which is the basis for this assumption.[3]

When you next see some of our mutual friends at the American Press Institute at Columbia, remember me to them warmly.[4] In the meantime, thank you very much for your thoughtfulness and for the chuckle it gave to me. *Cordially*

[1] Gilmore had been editor in chief of the *Detroit News* since 1933.
[2] On March 6 Gilmore had written to Eisenhower (copy in EM) enclosing the original drawing of a cartoon by *Detroit News* staff artist Burt Randolph Thomas. The cartoon consisted of four panels, each depicting a different character making an outlandish claim about what Eisenhower would do once elected President. In the first panel a woman informed her butcher that he would not dare to charge such high prices when the General was in office; in the next a man said he would wait until Eisenhower built him a good house rather than live in a "Plywood Palace"; the third panel promised that the General would force Russia to disarm within twenty-four hours; and the fourth stated that under Eisenhower, racketeers would be jailed, and their money used to pay off the national debt and abolish taxes (see *Detroit News*, Mar. 5, 1951).
[3] In his letter Gilmore had said that a "Miss" MacKinnon had called to suggest that the cartoon be sent to Eisenhower, who might be "in need of a smile" (for background on Marilyn MacKinnon see Eisenhower, *At Ease*, p. 346).
[4] On the Press Institute see Galambos, *Columbia University*, no. 89.

80   *Eisenhower Mss.*

To Leon Harry Gavin   *March 13, 1951*
Personal and confidential

Dear Mr. Gavin:[1] I have carefully studied the report you rendered to the Military Affairs Committee upon completion of your European trip late last year.[2] The first purpose of this note is to express my appreciation of the public spirited attitude that prompted your trip and the preparation of such an interesting report. Much of it I agree with, emphatically. I refer especially to those parts that insist upon full-out support by European countries of the collective security we are hoping to construct.[3] I personally believe that we should evolve with these countries sensible and attainable—and mutually agreed upon—standards of accomplishment, to which we must give earnest attention as we go along.

Our own future policies could then be modified by the United States Government if necessary. Moreover, a special importance to me in this post, would be this kind of a guide for our efforts as we strive to produce a maximum performance by each European government in the purpose of building security.[4]

The one item not covered in your document should make an interesting subject of conversation:—What do we do if some or any of these governments refuse to see that the safety of the free world now demands full cooperation and readiness to sacrifice among us all? Great as is the danger while we are hanging together, even tenuously, it would appear to be magnified if we simply break apart into pieces, each of the others to be picked up by Communism, with the U.S. left alone as the single exponent of freedom.[5]

When you again come to Europe, I trust you will drop in at my office.[6]

With best wishes. *Sincerely*

[1] Congressman Gavin (who represented the Nineteenth District of Pennsylvania and was a member of the Armed Services Committee) had written to Eisenhower on February 26 (EM) enclosing (1) a transcript of remarks he had made on the floor of the House that day concerning NATO and (2) a newspaper clipping from the February 19 *Washington Times Herald* (EM). The clipping, on which Gavin had requested comment, alleged that the General had promised both New York Governor Thomas E. Dewey and University of Pennsylvania president Harold E. Stassen cabinet posts in return for their support of Eisenhower as a presidential candidate (for background on Dewey and Stassen see nos. 25 and 63, respectively). Eisenhower's aide Colonel Robert L. Schulz had replied on March 5 (EM) explaining that the General's schedule would make it impossible for him to read the transcript at that time and that he would be unable to comment on the clipping (for background on Schulz see no. 1).
[2] The General was referring to a report Gavin had prepared and sent to Secretary of Defense George C. Marshall and Congressman Carl Vinson, chairman of the House Armed Services Committee, on January 11, which Marshall had passed along to Eisenhower (see OS/D, 1951, Clas. Decimal File, CD 032.1). Following the November–December tour of six European nations, Gavin had become a strong advocate of American commitment to NATO. For background on Marshall see no. 2; on Vinson see Galambos, *Columbia University*, no. 294.
[3] Gavin's report consisted of his observations on conditions in Western Europe and specific suggestions for U.S. involvement in the NATO defense. Gavin had concluded that "the defense of Western European nations must be accomplished chiefly by those countries. We can only aid and assist." For Eisenhower's views on mutual defense see nos. 23 and 46.

In his remarks to the House of Representatives on February 26 Gavin had said that Eisenhower would not allow Western Europe to take advantage of the United States and "sit idly by while we pump in our money and equipment to help them. . . . [Eisenhower] is going to see to it that they get down to business" (see "Remarks of L. H. Gavin," Feb. 26, 1951, EM).

[4] During his testimony before the Senate Foreign Relations and Armed Services committees in February Eisenhower had been questioned concerning European contributions to NATO (see no. 23). On the efforts of each nation and the role of the United States he had said that it was necessary to "expect from all a comparable and good performance" and that officials of the American government should "keep their fingers on it and . . . satisfy themselves that that is being done" (see Senate Committee on Foreign Relations and Committee on Armed Services, *Assignment of Ground Forces of the United States to Duty in the European Area*, 1951, p. 27).

[5] For Eisenhower's fears concerning the fate of America if this should happen see no. 23, n. 4; for his difficulties with isolationists such as former President Herbert Hoover see nos. 58 and 63.

[6] Gavin would later send the General a copy of his June 18 remarks on the floor of the House urging closer ties with Spain in the European defense effort ("Remarks of Representative Leon H. Gavin," EM). On the debate over Spanish participation in NATO see nos. 16, n. 3 and 240.

81   *Eisenhower Mss.*

To WILLIAM AVERELL HARRIMAN   *March 14, 1951*
Secret

Dear Averell: Won't you please tell the President that I most deeply appreciate the letter he wrote to me from Key West.[1] I am especially glad that he so clearly understands some of the oddities of the position I now occupy. While I should, of course, much prefer to regard my role as strictly military, I am more and more impressed with the fact that you earlier called the turn when you said, "For a long time, your job will be far more civil than it is military, and will involve every conceivable kind of international interest."

One of the most noticeable characteristics of this headquarters is that it is sort of a "floating island," not firmly attached to anything by traditional chains of responsibility, authority, and interest. By becoming a servant of twelve governments, I am personally, of course, disassociated from the normal American channels that apply to duties of soldiers in the field. While it is true that I am still an American public servant, merely loaned to a rather nebulous organization which we call NATO, in a larger sense I have become a modern Ishmael.[2] At the same time, the prescribed NATO channels of direction and control, extending through the Standing Group, then the Military Committee, then the Council of Deputies, and then the Council of Ministers,[3] grow more and more nebulous when one realizes that it is well nigh useless to put up any critical problem before a joint international body until *after* that proposition has been thoroughly discussed and cleared with each of the national staffs that may be affected. This we have to do daily.

All this is confusing, but, fortunately for us, we are avoiding the development of a "squirrel in the cage" feeling because of the fact that every responsible American official in Europe, to say nothing of the several European staffs with which we deal, all seem anxious either to consult with us concerning their own particular problems or even to secure our help in channeling and pushing these questions to decisions.

In any event, the whole system, since it makes my direct connection with American staffs so nebulous, emphasizes our previous conclusion that I, purely as an American citizen, should keep you as well informed as I possibly can.

Naturally, as I told the President, all strictly military questions are channeled through the Standing Group, and, if any such type of question affects the United States alone, it will, of course, go to the Defense Department.

I notice recurring indications of a feeling in Europe that local manufacturing facilities and available labor pools are not being used to the maximum in helping to meet the needs of NATO. I hope soon to arrange for a meeting with Herrod, Katz, and one or two others in order to get a clear comprehension of what is behind this type of thing.[4] I suspect that it is directed toward a hope of having the United States step in and increase money or material allocations to the country concerned, in return for such production. It would appear that, if these nations are deadly serious about defending Europe, inter-governmental arrangements could be made for manufacture and exchange, if only on a basis resembling barter. I am going to try to run this thing down because possibly both Herrod and Katz may point out some direction in which I can be of some help.

A different type of thing occurred recently. In the last few days, there have been copies of cable messages shown to me that touch upon the unhappiness of the French because they were not included in the so-called Malta conferences between Naval representatives of the United States and Great Britain.[5] In this particular case, I have no doubt that the purposes of the meeting could have been defeated by inclusion of a third party; but, in handling this kind of thing, we have to show a very considerable amount of skill if we are, as a group of twelve nations, to build up among ourselves that feeling of confidence and union, without which such an effort as this cannot succeed.

To create, unnecessarily, a feeling on the part of any government that it has been callously excluded from participation in some discussion in which it believes it has a reasonable interest, is well nigh inexcusable. That kind of thing, far from supplementing and supporting the efforts that a headquarters like this makes to develop mutual confidence, will go a long way toward defeating it.

It is, of course, clear that occasionally there are subjects of bilateral interest that cannot be discussed with representatives of any third nation. Moreover, it seems logical that this type of thing will occur more often between the United States and Britain than between almost any other two countries in NATO. The point is, when need arises for this kind of conference, it should not normally be advertised. Such meetings should be conducted informally, as a matter of routine business, and should not appear to the public as decisive, conclusive affairs, particularly when accompanied by a suspicion that the agenda of such a conference will include subjects that are at least of some interest to third parties.

I request that you do not take any specific action in this particular case, or even admit that you know of its occurrence; but possibly you could, in future conversations with British and appropriate American officials, advance some of *your own* observations along this line. Certainly, this type of thing could eventually cause a great deal of embarrassment and could damage an effort on which the United States is spending a tremendous amount of money and effort. By being on the alert, a person is sometimes able to help prevent the occurrence of errors.

Such incidents illustrate again the wide range of subject in which this unique headquarters is forced to take an interest.

My best wishes and respects to the President. Warm regard to your good self. *Cordially*

---

[1] Truman's letter of March 9 is in EM (see no. 46). The President told Eisenhower that he appreciated "the sense of responsibility which is yours as you enter into the work of the herculean mission which I gave you." He added, "Some of your problems began with the Creation; others extend themselves into imponderables—those incalculable forces that project themselves into world affairs today, like pride of race and of blood, and always national jealousies."

[2] In the Old Testament, Ishmael was the son of Abraham and his wife's handmaid, Hagar. Through no fault of his own he had been disinherited and banished into the wilderness (Gen. 16:1–16, 21:9–21).

[3] Eisenhower was referring to the North Atlantic Council, NATO's governing body. For a description of the various NATO agencies see no. 2, n. 2.

[4] William Rogers Herod (Ph.B. Yale 1918) was at this time on leave from his position as president of the International General Electric Company and was serving as Coordinator of NATO's Defense Production Board. For background on Milton Katz, U.S. Special Representative for the ECA, and on Eisenhower's concern with European production see no. 16.

[5] In January Admiral Robert B. Carney (see no. 53, n. 4) had gone to Malta to discuss the defense of the Middle East with the commander of the British forces in

that region. On January 30 French Premier René Pleven (see no. 11, n. 2) had expressed to President Truman his concern about the meeting and had asked that French representatives be invited to participate in any future conferences. Truman had assured Pleven that there had been no intent to exclude the French from any conversations. On March 8, however, Admiral Carney's headquarters publicly announced that Carney would again meet with British leaders in Malta to discuss defense plans for the Mediterranean and Middle East areas. Two days later the French Ambassador to the United States requested that the French be invited to participate in the Malta talks, but the request was denied. On March 12 the United States Navy, citing press reports that the Malta conversations would include a discussion of a proposed Mediterranean naval command (see no. 77, n. 3), issued a statement claiming that the talks would be limited to military matters in the Middle East and outside the NATO area. In a State Department–JCS meeting held in Washington on March 14, Chief of Naval Operations Forrest Sherman claimed that "the French worries regarding the Malta Conference would never have arisen if the U[nited] K[ingdom] had not spilled the beans to the French." After a State Department representative explained that the "British always like to inflate their special relationship with the U.S.," Army Chief of Staff Collins agreed that the British "must have had some dirty reason for acquainting the French with this Conference" (State, *Foreign Relations, 1951*, vol. III, *European Security and the German Question, Part I*, pp. 494–95; vol. IV, *Europe: Political and Economic Developments, Part I* [1985], pp. 324–25; and vol. V, *The Near East and Africa* [1982], pp. 27–29. U.S. Department of State, "Background Memoranda on Visit to the United States of Vincent Auriol, President of the French Republic," Mar. 1951, in OS/D, 1951, Clas. Decimal File, CD 337 [Four Powers]. *International Herald Tribune*, Paris ed., Mar. 9, 1951. *New York Times*, Mar. 13, 1951). For developments see no. 126.

82   *Eisenhower Mss.*

To Ellis Dwinnell Slater   *March 14, 1951*

Dear Slats:[1] Last evening, Mamie received the colored prints you had prepared of her little cherubim and seraphim. When I got home, she had practically a convention of Army women in her house, showing off the excellence of the photography, the perfection of the color tints, and, above all, the unusual features and obvious intelligence of her grandchildren.[2] It would appear that the roll of film I took in Puerto Rico came out pretty well, and I am looking forward to seeing the mounted results.[3]

I assume that Mamie will be writing to you very quickly, but the chief purpose of this note is to urge that you and Priscilla[4] allot a good share of your planned European vacation to the Paris area. Possibly, by that time, we will even have a house of our own and then, of course, we would expect you to stay with us. But, in any event, we are certainly looking forward to your coming, and counting on having a lot of things to talk about with you.[5]

Mamie and I were distressed to learn of the death of Priscilla's mother. We realize that, even when a loved one has reached the ripe old age of 87, there is still an inescapable shock and lasting grief when the time of passing comes. Soon after the war, I lost my own mother, when she was 84; so far as I was concerned, she was still in her 40s.[6]

Don't forget that you will have a warm welcome in this region when you come this summer. It is almost useless for me to send to you my grateful acknowledgments every time a new series of pictures arrives— you keep me eternally in your debt.

With very best to you both, *Cordially*

[1] For background on Eisenhower's friend Slater see no. 59.

[2] The Eisenhowers' grandchildren were the two children of John Sheldon Doud Eisenhower and Barbara Jean Thompson Eisenhower, Dwight David II and Barbara Anne (see Galambos, *Columbia University*, nos. 27 and 524).

[3] The Eisenhowers had taken a three-day vacation in Puerto Rico in early February (for background see no. 24).

[4] Slater's wife, the former Priscilla Allen.

[5] The Slaters would visit the Eisenhowers in August 1951 in Paris. The Eisenhowers had finally found a home in Marnes-la-Coquette, a village outside of Paris, and they moved in during the Slaters' visit (for background on the housing question see nos. 44 and 393. See also Slater, *The Ike I Knew*, pp. 12–13; Brandon, *A Portrait of a First Lady*, pp. 267–70; and Hatch, *Red Carpet for Mamie*, pp. 228–34).

[6] Eisenhower's mother, Ida Elizabeth Stover Eisenhower, had died on September 11, 1946 (see Galambos, *Columbia University*, no. 792; and Eisenhower, *At Ease*, pp. 305–7).

83   *Eisenhower Mss.*

To WILLIAM EDWARD ROBINSON   *March 15, 1951*

Dear Bill: Just a hurried note to thank you for your fine letter brought to me by Bill Burnham.[1]

I was particularly intrigued with your exposition on the evolution that has taken place in our capitalistic economy. Perhaps I have used that term too loosely—meaning, of course, that it is a system that does yield profit to private ownership.[2] In any event, the reading of your little essay gives me a thought. Why do not we invent a new term and call it a "customer economy?" By this, we would mean that it is the best type of economy to give the greatest possible satisfaction to all the people who use its products. Since everybody in the United States is affected by the workings of this economy, this term would include the worker in the factory as well as all other groups.[3]

This may be a thought.[4] *Cordially*

¹ The March 13 letter from *New York Herald Tribune* director and executive vice-president Robinson (EM) had been delivered to the General on March 15 by his friend and adviser William H. Burnham. For background on Robinson see no. 39; on Burnham, who was then visiting Europe on business, see no. 75.

² On March 6 Eisenhower had sent Robinson a copy of a letter to Edward J. Bermingham (see no. 63; the letter is no. 23). For recent accusations that the General had become an "administration man" see nos. 58 and 63.

³ Robinson had written that the General's letter was "so literate, so wise, so scholarly" that he was reluctant to take exception with any part of it; nevertheless, he objected to Eisenhower's use of the term "capitalistic economy" to describe the system in existence in America. He went on to explain that true capitalism, in which the management of a business was in the hands of an individual owner who financed the operation, met the payroll, and reaped the profits, had not existed for thirty or more years. According to Robinson, heads of business were no longer the owners, and profit was no longer the sole motivating factor of management. The three major considerations of business heads were now the customer—seeing that he was well served at low prices; the worker—offering "good conditions of work" and high wages; and lastly, profits, which fluctuated with competition and were frequently sacrificed by management in order to meet the needs of both the customer and the worker. Robinson said that a business manager had become a "referee between . . . the customer, the worker, and the capitalist [stockholder]" (see no. 101).

⁴ For Eisenhower's continuing correspondence with Robinson on political and economic issues in the United States see nos. 101, 110, and 143.

84   *Eisenhower Mss.*

TO JOSEPH RAYMOND McCARTHY   *March 15, 1951*
Personal

*Dear Senator McCarthy:*¹ I thank you very much for sending me a copy of your speech.²

While it is, of course, true that a soldier in our form of government is merely an executor of policy and not its maker, yet I do assure you that I shall be most watchful of every conceivable angle as I attempt to perform the difficult national and international duties that have been assigned to me.³ Everyone realizes that, on the long-term basis, Europe cannot be defended except by its own heart and brains and strength. Within a measurable limit of time, the United States must see such unmistakable European progress in the development of defensive capacity as will assure its ultimate ability to stand largely alone, or we will have to take an entirely different approach to our own security problem.⁴

My personal views on such matters have been, of course, frequently expressed. As I see it, America can lead the world but cannot carry it; economically, militarily, or politically. The problem we have is to apply our efforts in the world in such fashion as to secure for our country the maximum measure of security, serenity, and economic opportunity. I do not consider my own views as anything sacrosanct as I seek methods for accomplishing this purpose; but I do believe that every loyal American would agree, in general, with the purpose itself.[5]

Thank you again for sending me a copy of your talk.[6] *Sincerely*

[1] McCarthy, a Republican senator from Wisconsin, had recently gained national attention for his assertions that Communists and Communist sympathizers had infiltrated the federal government (for background see Galambos, *Columbia University*, no. 733; and Michael O'Brien, *McCarthy and McCarthyism in Wisconsin* [Columbia, Mo., 1980], esp. pp. 90–98).

[2] On March 10 McCarthy had sent Eisenhower an advance copy of the remarks on U.S. foreign policy and national defense that he delivered to the Senate on March 14 (see McCarthy to Eisenhower, Mar. 10, 1951, and "Foreign Policy Speech of Senator Joe McCarthy," both in EM; and *Congressional Record*, 82d Cong., 1st sess., 1951, 97, pts. 1–2: 2388–98).

[3] In his March 14 speech on the Senate floor McCarthy had accused certain high officials in the Department of State of "treachery or incompetence" in pursuing a foreign policy designed to weaken national defense and bring about the downfall of non-Communist Allied governments. By offering only a "phony resistance to communism," they had tied the hands of Eisenhower and other military leaders. Speaking specifically of the military potentials of Formosa, West Germany, and Spain, McCarthy asserted that by not accepting their offers of manpower, State Department traitors were intentionally ensuring the ultimate failure of American efforts in both Korea and Europe. Speaking of Eisenhower he said, "It is difficult for a soldier of integrity . . . to believe that people in high positions . . . could be actually disloyal to the Nation." For background on the Great Debate see no. 63. On the situation in mainland China see Galambos, *Columbia University*, no. 112.

[4] Eisenhower had voiced these same sentiments in congressional testimony earlier this year (see nos. 23 and 80).

[5] In his speech of March 14 McCarthy had contended that the "traitors" in the Department of State were forcing America to carry on the fight against communism alone, despite the fact that foreign troops were available for the effort. He advocated an increase in military aid to non-Communist forces within China, on Formosa, and within the Russian satellite nations. According to McCarthy, only a defense utilizing troops from Japan, West Germany, and Spain would relieve America's burden and prevent U.S. troops from being "condemned either to death or to live out their lives in some Siberian slave-labor camp." For Eisenhower's views on America's role in leading the defense of the free world see nos. 23 and 51; for his thoughts on the admission of Spain into NATO and the use of West German troops see nos. 16, n. 3 and 12, respectively.

[6] Later this month McCarthy would write thanking the General for his letter and denying charges made by radio commentator and newspaper columnist Drew Pearson that the senator was digging up material with which to smear Eisenhower (EM; see no. 78).

To OMAR NELSON BRADLEY

Cable SH 20203. Top secret. Personal

Dear Bradley:[01] The Staff is dispatching to the Standing Group an initial and only partially complete plan of organization and command.[2] As it now stands, it is the result of weeks of hard and sometimes frustrating work, but it agrees generally with the rough ideas you and I have previously discussed. I hope you will try to assure the speediest possible acceptance because it is believed by all of us that these announcements will help alleviate the bitter criticism and correct adverse psychological reactions that have developed out of erroneous understandings. Some features of the plan were agreed only today and some of course are not yet settled.[3]

Congratulations on your talk.[4]

I shall write you a letter soon.[5]

[1] For background on Bradley, chairman of the Joint Chiefs of Staff, see no. 50.

[2] We have been unable to locate SH 20202, in which SHAPE outlined its initial plan of organization. The provisions of this message probably adhered closely to the ideas Eisenhower had expressed in no. 77. In that case the plan called for the establishment of Northern, Central, and Southern commands, with headquarters for these subordinate units to be located in Oslo, Norway; Fontainebleau, France; and Naples, Italy, respectively. Eisenhower retained operational control of the Central Command himself, with three subordinate commanders for the land, naval, and air forces (Poole, *History of the Joint Chiefs of Staff*, vol. IV, *1950–1952*, p. 225; and State, *Foreign Relations, 1951*, vol. III, *European Security and the German Question, Part I*, p. 497).

[3] As Eisenhower explained in a cable sent to the JCS on this same day (AL0 106, same file as document), an agreement on the structure of the proposed Northern Command had not been reached until the afternoon of March 15 (see nos. 90 and 99). Eisenhower told the JCS that the Norwegians and Danes had wanted an American to command the air forces in that region and that he believed "the advantages of that arrangement outweigh the disadvantages." Discussions concerning Eisenhower's proposed Southern Command would continue (see SM-712-51, Mar. 16, 1951, same file as document; and no. 107).

[4] Eisenhower may have been referring to an address Bradley had delivered on February 22 at Valley Forge, Pennsylvania. Speaking at a Freedoms Foundation award ceremony, Bradley had said that America would triumph in the struggle with its totalitarian foes because NATO was stronger than the "compulsory league of Soviet satellites" and because free societies individually were stronger than nations oppressed by tyranny (*New York Times*, Feb. 23, 1951). At this ceremony a speech made by Eisenhower in 1950 received first prize for public addresses.

[5] Eisenhower's letter to Bradley is no. 111. On the following day the JCS would tell Eisenhower that it had approved his proposed command structure. In a separate cable General Bradley would tell Eisenhower, "We realize that your solution was arrived at after many conferences and considerable compromise and while, as you say, it is not one which we consider perfect, we believe that you should be given full support in trying it out" (Bradley to Eisenhower, JCS 86048, and JCS to

Eisenhower, JCS 86039, Mar. 16, 1951, same file as document). After the Standing Group approved these arrangements, the commands and the names of their commanders would be announced on March 20 (*New York Times*, Mar. 21, 1951; see also no. 77).

86   *Eisenhower Mss.*

To Lucius Du Bignon Clay   *March 16, 1951*

Dear Lucius:[1] For so long, I've placed so much confidence in your judgment that I cannot possibly find it in my heart to say "No," when I receive such an earnest request as is contained in your letter of March 1st. Moreover, the present case involves something in which I've long believed, and I still believe as firmly in the aim of the Crusade for Freedom as earnestly as ever.[2]

You must, of course, realize that, when I accepted this Allied post, my position somewhat changed, and I must be careful that no connection of mine with any other organization can possibly react adversely on this responsibility. Moreover, my remoteness from America definitely prevents my participating in any active work of the organization.[3]

Because of these considerations, I must make my acceptance conditional upon assurance from you as to the following:

(a) That, in allowing my name to become one of the members of the corporation of the Crusade for Freedom, there is no possibility that this connection can work adversely against the mission to which I am assigned here. [For example, I am thinking of the possibility that any activity supported by the Crusade could be considered inimical to the policies of any of the twelve governments making up NATO.]

(b) That, by being named as one of the members of the corporation, I assume no responsibility either in matters of financial support or in any other phase of the activities of the corporation. Since I am completely unaware of applicable law, you will understand that I must have your assurance on this point.

A final condition of mine is that, assuming favorable answers to (a) and (b), I would remain a member as long as you, personally, were active in formulating the policies and activities of the corporation. I shall give you a final answer as soon as I have a reply to the questions posed.[4]

Give my love to Marjorie,[5] and with warm personal regard to yourself. *Cordially*

[1] Clay was national chairman of the Crusade for Freedom (for background see no. 46).

[2] On March 1 Clay had written to the General asking that he agree to become a corporate member of the Crusade, which was then raising funds for its Radio Free Europe broadcasts behind the Iron Curtain (EM; for background on the Crusade see Galambos, *Columbia University*).
[3] Eisenhower had been active in the Crusade for Freedom before accepting his appointment to NATO; he had worked closely with Clay in planning the group's first fund-raising drive and had opened the drive with a four-network speech on Labor Day 1950 (see Galambos, *Columbia University*, no. 962). In the six weeks following the General's broadcast the Crusade had gained 15.5 million members and received $1.3 million in donations (see Clay to Eisenhower, Mar. 1, 1951, EM).
[4] For developments see no. 112.
[5] Clay's wife, the former Marjorie McKeown.

87   *Eisenhower Mss.*

To PHILIP YOUNG   *March 16, 1951*

Dear Philip:[1] Thank you very much for your nice letter. Bill Burnham had already told me about your tonsil operation—which I trust is now nothing but a memory.[2]

Your news about the American Assembly makes good reading. You cannot imagine how much I would like to be back there with you working on the three or four projects that we considered so very much worthwhile.[3]

At this moment, I could not possibly predict with certainty that I can be at the opening of the Assembly on the 23rd of May. As of now, I have a June 6th fixed date in Europe, with another one about a week later. Other engagements are inescapably made from time to time, but I shall certainly try desperately to keep clear a space that would allow me to come home.[4]

In the meantime, I most sincerely trust that you will arrange for a moderate opportunity for recreation for those who attend your conferences. For example, someone ought to fix up a driving range, which would certainly be an inexpensive sort of thing. I do not know whether the fishing lake would come under a State restriction or not; but, if it would, I am quite certain that the State would be glad to cooperate by sending down a representative to sell fishing licenses the first day of each conference, and, in addition, would assist you in keeping the lake well stocked both with bass or trout and with the proper kind of feeder fish, like bluegills.

I think that a small softball outfit, and maybe even a skeet range, could all be inexpensively constructed, but still attractive in appearance and in appeal. For skeet shooting, a moderate charge could be made, but, in general, I think that things ought to be free if they would not be abused by such a crowd.

Of course, your program will be built around the working hours—men will come there to learn and to understand. But something to do during recreation hours, something that appeals to the average man, will do much to help build up in the country the reputation of the place as one to which everybody is anxious to go.[5]

All of these things I believe to be important, but, of course, you and I know that the value of the place will be measured by the thoroughness and skill in which the research is conducted and by the leadership and personalities of those put in charge of conducting the various discussions. I think that you should explore every possible source to get assistance in this matter. In some instances, some well-known businessman might be a remarkable discussional leader; again, you might get a man from the CED,[6] from the government, from the labor organizations, from other universities—in fact, the opportunities are limitless. (Suddenly, it strikes me as just a bit ridiculous that I should be talking to you about these things. You have thought over them so much that my comments must appear to you to be a bit trite.)[7]

In any event, my love to Faith,[8] and warm regard to yourself. *Cordially*

P.S. Remember me to any of my old friends around the campus whom you may encounter.

[1] For background on Dean Young, the executive director of the American Assembly, see no. 8, n. 6.

[2] In his letter of March 9 (EM) Young had told Eisenhower that he was in the Johns Hopkins Hospital in Baltimore, Maryland, for a tonsillectomy. There is no mention of Young's illness in William Burnham's correspondence with the General in EM (on Burnham see no. 40).

[3] Young had written Eisenhower about the progress of the American Assembly in selecting members of the policy board, in public relations, and in preparations for the first conference. Columbia's newly established National Manpower Council (see no. 139) and the Institute of War and Peace Studies (see no. 31) were probably the projects to which Eisenhower was referring. Young would be deputy chairman of the National Manpower Council (see no. 10).

[4] Eisenhower would not attend the first American Assembly conference on U.S.-West European relations the week of May 21: on May 24 and 25 he would be in Norway on an inspection tour (see no. 196, n. 2). The June 6 ceremony in Normandy commemorating D-day was probably the "fixed date" to which Eisenhower referred (see no. 208). For developments concerning the American Assembly see nos. 201 and 202.

[5] At this first American Assembly conference the recreational facilities would not be used (see no. 204).

[6] The Committee for Economic Development (CED), of which Eisenhower was a trustee, was a private group of educators and businessmen concerned primarily with business and public fiscal policy in the United States (see Galambos, *Columbia University*, no. 732; and no. 164 in this volume).

[7] One responsibility of the American Assembly policy board was the selection of delegates for the conferences (see no. 47).

[8] Young's wife, the former Faith Adams.

Gen. de Lattre is to be here in a few minutes (at 8:45 a.m) to see
me reference his request for reinforcement for Indo-China:[1] The French
have a knotty problem on that one—the campaign out there is a
draining sore in their side.[2] Yet if they quit & Indo China falls to
Commies, it is easily possible that the entire S.E. Asia & Indonesia
will go, soon to be followed by India.[3] That prospect makes the whole
problem one of interest to us all. I'd favor *heavy* reinforcement to get
the thing over at once; but I'm convinced that no military victory is
possible in that kind of theater, & Even if Indo China were completely
cleared of Communists, right across the border is China with inex-
haustible manpower!!![4] Well, we'll see what Gen. De Lattre has to
say—but I know he'll *want* me to make a recommendation to the
French govt; this I shall not do. (Unless, of course, asked by the govt
itself.)[5]

Day before yesterday we sent in a partially complete organizational
system, including selectees for principal command assignments. If
promptly approved it should do something to help European morale.[6]

---

[1] General Jean de Lattre de Tassigny, now commanding the French forces in the
Far East, had come to Paris to petition the French cabinet for reinforcement of the
160,000 troops then fighting the Communist Vietminh in northern Vietnam (see
International Herald Tribune, Paris ed., Mar. 15, 17, 1951). For background on de
Lattre see no. 28.

[2] De Lattre had evidently written to Eisenhower on February 24 explaining the
need for immediate reinforcement until such time as the non-Communist Vietnamese force he was then training could assume the duties of the Expeditionary Force
(see Donald R. Heath to Eisenhower, Mar. 3, 1951, EM; and State, *Foreign
Relations, 1951*, vol. VI, *Asia and the Pacific, Part I* [1977], pp. 408-9. On the
staggering costs of the war in men and money see Buttinger, *Vietnam*, vol. II,
Vietnam at War, pp. 761, 790, and 797-98; and *International Herald Tribune*, Paris
ed., Mar. 19, 1951). For Eisenhower's concern regarding the number of French
officers being lost see Senate Committee on Foreign Relations and Committee on
Armed Services, *Assignment of Ground Forces of the United States to Duty in the European
Area*, 1951, p. 7.

[3] This "domino theory" was of major influence in the Department of State's
programs in the region; the maintenance of a non-Communist Vietnam was regarded as "the keystone of our policy in the rest of Southeast Asia." Control of the
area's resources of rice, rubber, and tin was seen as essential in the event of world
conflict. To keep the region out of the hands of the Communists, the United States
had given over $214,341,000 in military and economic aid during 1950-51. Of this
figure, $164 million—over five times the combined defense assistance given to
Burma, Thailand, Malaya, Indonesia, and the Philippines—had been granted in
military assistance to Vietnam (see State, *Foreign Relations, 1951*, vol. VI, *Asia and
the Pacific, Part I*, pp. 18, 20-22). On French requests for increased military aid see
New York Times, January 30, 31, February 11, July 28, August 30, 1951.

[4] The threat of direct Chinese intervention in Vietnam would be a topic of discussion during de Lattre's visit to the United States in September 1951 (see nos. 360, 361, and 362). For background on the overwhelming effect of Chinese entry into the Korean War see Galambos, *Columbia University*, nos. 1046 and 1089. On Chinese aid to the Vietminh Army see no. 28 in this volume.

[5] On March 11 U.S. Minister to Cambodia, Laos, and Vietnam Donald R. Heath had cabled Eisenhower through State Department channels to inform him of de Lattre's impending trip to Paris. Heath said the French general would arrive on the fifteenth and desired to meet with Eisenhower "incognito" to explain the need for reinforcements. This type of visit was not encouraged by the State Department, and Eisenhower replied to Heath on March 12 through U.S. Ambassador to France David K. E. Bruce that he would gladly meet with de Lattre, but only after his official arrival in Paris and his meeting with the French cabinet. Eisenhower wrote that he would not see the French commander "on any kind of incognito or clandestine basis" (see State, *Foreign Relations, 1951*, vol. VI, *Asia and the Pacific, Part I*, pp. 391–95). For developments see the following document.

De Lattre would be granted twelve battalions plus additional auxiliary forces, to carry on the war (see *ibid.*, pp. 404–9; and *International Herald Tribune*, Paris ed., Mar. 29, 1951).

[6] For background see nos. 81 and 85.

89

*CCS 092 Western Europe
(3-12-48), Sec. 74*

To Omar Nelson Bradley
Cable ALO 110. Secret. Personal[0]

March 17, 1951

The French are in the midst of deciding what to do about Indo China. De Lattre is meeting today with French Government officials to request substantial reinforcements, the major portion of which consist of 12 Infantry Battalions.[1] He estimates total personnel augmentation at 20,000 men.

De Lattre feels that with these reinforcements, he stands an excellent chance of being able to insure the security of the Tonkin Area, and perhaps of actually settling the Indo China conflict favorably. Without them, he visualizes a distinct possibility of actually "losing the conflict."[2] He has pledged to return the Infantry Battalions to France in less than a year.

It is more than possible that I will be requested for views as to the relationship between the NATO effort and the Indo China campaign in the overall struggle against Communism. If additional French Forces requested by De Lattre go to that area for an estimated 10 months, there will be a noticeable and adverse effect on the speed of French buildup here, particularly because such a contingent, though relatively small in number, will contain the best source of trained cadre and instructor personnel which are so badly needed here. Moch told De Lattre yesterday that if the reinforcements are sent, French will not be able to organize the planned 10 divisions by the end of 1951.[3]

In March 9 issue of US News and World Report is an article which assumes that the Indo China campaign is part of the struggle against Communism.[4] However, it is also true that part of world press claims that this is merely another instance of "brutal imperialism beating down the aspiration of liberty-loving peoples."

I personally feel that, if French should serve notice on NATO that they are ready to call it quits and get out of Indo China, all of us would object strenuously. Moreover, US action in supplying munitions appears to recognize the overall importance of that campaign in protecting adjacent critical areas and in fighting Communism.[5] More than this I think that the outcome will have a definite bearing on general morale and effectiveness of NATO.

I badly need views of US civil and military officials. It would be most helpful if you could place the question urgently before either the JCS or the NSC as you and General Marshall might consider appropriate.[6]

Thanks.

[1] For background on de Lattre and the French struggle in Indochina see the preceding document.

[2] Tonkin was the northernmost portion of Vietnam, adjacent to China. At his meeting with Eisenhower on this day (see *ibid.*, n. 5) de Lattre had told Eisenhower that he expected two Vietminh attacks, the first to take place soon and an even greater effort, with Chinese support, coming in September; the additional troops were to meet the fall offensive. Eisenhower had questioned de Lattre on such matters as the extent and nature of the support for the Vietminh and what de Lattre thought was "the long-term position of the white man in the Far East." Eisenhower also told de Lattre that it was important that the American people be convinced that the struggle in Indochina was one against communism and not merely an imperialist effort to preserve the French empire (Memorandum of Conversation, Mar. 17, 1951, EM, Subject File, Conversations).

[3] For background on French Minister of Defense Jules Moch see nos. 11 and 53. France had promised to raise ten divisions for NATO by the end of 1951; the French said that if reinforcements were to be shipped from metropolitan France to de Lattre in Indochina, they would only be able to raise nine divisions by that date (State, *Foreign Relations, 1951*, vol. IV, *Europe: Political and Economic Developments, Part I*, pp. 364–65).

[4] Eisenhower had seen an article ("Indo-China: Another Korea," *U.S. News & World Report*, Mar. 9, 1951, pp. 22–23) that had not emphasized the colonial aspects of French efforts to regain control of their territories in Indochina. The article concluded, "The chances are that the Communists missed their chance to spread out in Asia and add Indo-China to their side. . . . Under present circumstances, there is no immediate prospect of a decisive victory for either side." Eisenhower's concern with this problem would continue (see Stephen E. Ambrose, *Eisenhower*, 2 vols. [New York, 1983–84], vol. II, *The President*, pp. 100–101).

[5] On American support for the French efforts in Indochina see the preceding document, n. 5.

[6] For background on the National Security Council (NSC), which advised the President on broad questions of national security policy, see Galambos, *Chief of Staff* and *Columbia University*. Army Chief of Staff Collins would reply for Bradley on March 20 (DA 86339, same file as document) that Eisenhower "should resist French tendency to share responsibility for Indo-China with SHAPE, US JCS and US Government." Collins also advised Eisenhower to "stress effect on SHAPE [of] plans of movement of additional troops to Indo-China." Collins added, "You are familiar with DeLattre[']s characteristic of always demanding additional forces. This may be legitimate in this case but indications are that Viet Minh attack may be launched before 12 battalions could reach Indo-China. Estimated here that 3 months would be required for movement." Collins concluded by suggesting that if Eisenhower felt "impelled" to recommend a course of action, he should advocate a "compromise solution to send some additional troops at once and [to make] preparations for possible dispatch of others depending on further developments." In any case, said Collins, a "definite commitment to return to France whatever reinforcements are sent" would be essential. The State Department would soon agree that Eisenhower should refrain from participating in the decision (State, *Foreign Relations, 1951*, vol. IV, *Europe: Political and Economic Developments, Part I*, pp. 348–49, 356).

90   *Eisenhower Mss.*

To Bruce Austin Fraser   *March 17, 1951*

Dear Fraser:[1] It would scarcely be possible for me to tell you how deeply I appreciate your fine note, to say nothing of the cooperative spirit that brought you to agree to acceptance of command in the north.[2] I know you did not particularly care for that one—but I assure you that you've cemented some firm friendships in Denmark and Norway by taking it on.[3]

Come over to see me when you can! In the meantime, I have a little present for the BC/S waiting upon the scheduling of some necessary flight to the U.K.[4] It's purpose is merely to remind you that "The man means well, even though he's too often a so and so and a this and that." *Cordially*

[1] Fraser, of North Cape, first baron of Molesey, had been First Sea Lord and Chief of the British Naval Staff since February 1948. During World War II he had served with the British Home, Eastern, and Pacific fleets. In December 1943 Fraser had led the British naval forces that sank the German battle cruiser *Scharnhorst* and opened the Arctic convoy route to the Soviet Union.
[2] In his letter of March 15 Fraser had wished Eisenhower "every success in a most difficult task." He observed that although Eisenhower "had almost a decade's experience" working with allies, it was "easier to deal with one or two than a dozen!" He also confirmed that the British had agreed to the designation of one of their admirals as Eisenhower's commander in northern Europe (for background see nos. 77 and 85; for developments see no. 99).

[3] See no. 85, n. 3.

[4] Eisenhower would send the British Chiefs of Staff a case of champagne. They would thank him on March 20: "British Chiefs of Staff received with pleasure General Eisenhower's present and will be delighted to drink his health at their next meeting" (Gault to Eisenhower, Mar. 20, 1951, EM; see also Fraser to Eisenhower, Mar. 22, 1951, EM).

91   *Eisenhower Mss.*

To FORREST PERCIVAL SHERMAN   *March 19, 1951*

Dear Forrest:[1] Your letter bringing to me the news about Kirk's Distinguished Service Medal gave me a big lift. As I told you before, I always felt that part of the fault for his earlier failure to obtain this deserved recognition rested right squarely on my shoulders.[2]

In a day or so, I will be writing you more of a business letter;[3] in the meantime, many, many thanks. *Cordially*

[1] For background on Chief of Naval Operations Sherman see no. 22.

[2] Sherman had written on March 13 (EM) that Eisenhower's recommendation of Admiral Alan Goodrich Kirk for the Navy's Distinguished Service Medal for his services under the General during World War II had been acted upon favorably. Secretary of the Navy Francis Patrick Matthews had approved the decoration on March 12. For background on Kirk, who was then serving as U.S. Ambassador to the Soviet Union, see Chandler, *War Years*; Kirk, *Postmarked Moscow*; and Morison, *Sicily–Salerno–Anzio*, pp. 126–47. On Matthews see Galambos, *Columbia University*, no. 464.

[3] Eisenhower's letter to Sherman concerning organization of the NATO naval command in the Mediterranean is no. 107.

92   *Eisenhower Mss.*

To THOMAS EDMUND DEWEY   *March 19, 1951*

Dear Governor:[1] Among the stream of papers going over my desk I found a little clipping containing a report that I had "coldly snubbed" you. How would one go about it to *snub* the Governor of a great state? That was not explained.[2]

My greetings to your family[3]—warm regard to you. *Sincerely*

[1] For background on Dewey, Governor of New York and a strong supporter of Eisenhower's candidacy for president, see Galambos, *Columbia University*, nos. 33, 602, and 1041; and nos. 25 and 63 in this volume.

[2] Eisenhower was probably referring to Drew Pearson's syndicated column "The Washington Merry-Go-Round," which reported that following Dewey's October 1950 announcement that he supported the General for the 1952 presidential nomination, Eisenhower had consistently snubbed Dewey (see Galambos, *Columbia University*, nos. 1040, 1041, and 1061; and *Washington Post*, Mar. 18, 1951). According to the article, Dewey was upset by Eisenhower's several declinations to meet for political discussions. It was alleged that Eisenhower's animosity toward Dewey had begun in 1948, when Dewey supporters created a file of information on Eisenhower to be used against him if he declared himself a candidate for the presidency (see Herbert S. Parmet, *Eisenhower and the American Crusades* [New York, 1972], p. 38; on Pearson see nos. 78 and 84).

In a letter of March 21, 1951 (EM), Dewey replied that after seeing the article he had "laughed because, over the years I have learned that if it's in a gossip column the opposite is automatically the truth."

[3] Dewey and his wife Frances Hutt Dewey had two children, Thomas Edmund, Jr., and John Martin (see Galambos, *Columbia University*, nos. 119 and 147). Eisenhower's handwritten copy of this letter was sent to Dewey; a typed copy is in EM.

93   *Eisenhower Mss.*

To George Edward Allen   *March 20, 1951*

Dear George: A couple of weeks ago, I had three letters from you, all in one day; the effort must have been exhausting because, since then, I have had no direct word from you whatsoever.[1] In the meantime, Mamie finally got a note from Mary[2] which indicated that you had completely retired from business and all your other activities in order to take full advantage of the California sun and your new palace. She did say, however, that you are *not* contemplating the sale of your Gettysburg farm. That is a relief to me, because I certainly will want someone in that region who will reminisce with me on World War II events rather than on those of the war between the States.[3]

When I left Washington, you talked very bravely about a probable trip to Europe, either with Mary or by yourself. I would much prefer the former, but I am afraid that the desert has become so attractive to Mary that she will not possibly consider a trans-oceanic journey. This does not excuse you, because even if you are as enamored as she is of the sunny sands, I doubt that they are a very good place in the summertime for a man of your girth and weight, and, besides—as proven by former experience—I shall probably be sadly in need of your strategic advice.[4]

Speaking of your girth reminds me of a question I should like to ask. Just exactly how much do I have to bet you in order to get you seriously interested in your weight? I have found that the mere matter of a couple hundred dollars is not nearly so important to you as your taste for cream pie and sweet potatoes, to say nothing of fried chicken. Now, will you just please name the amount that will really get you down to work? For my part, I will, on the next bet, even agree to take off two[5] more pounds than I did last time. I will go down to 172 and you to a flat 200. Since that will make you take off about 20 pounds, you ought to have 90 days (because of your inexcusable laziness).[6]

Tell Mary that I am sure Mamie will be writing her a note in a few days. I assure you that we do miss you tremendously. I couldn't imagine any more fun than to have you with us for a while, even though we are living in a suite in a hotel out at Versailles. I am at my old business of keeping everybody cheered up and working like dogs, and, when you consider the kind of job this is, I think you will agree that I occasionally deserve a chance to be cheered up myself.[7]

Love to Mary, to her Mother, and to young Michael.[8] And, of course, always warmest regards to yourself. *As ever*

[1] For background on Allen and his recent correspondence with the General see no. 73.

[2] Allen's wife.

[3] In regard to Allen's farm see no. 73; for background on the General's own farm and his partnership with Allen see nos. 48 and 73. On their association during World War II see Eisenhower, *At Ease*, pp. 282-87.

Despite this remark, Eisenhower was actually an avid student of American history, with a particular interest in the Civil War (see *ibid.*, pp. 39-50; and Richard L. Graves, "At Gettysburg: A Battlefield Tour with Eisenhower," *Civil War Times* 3, no. 7 [1961], pp. 6-8).

[4] Allen would travel to Europe in June of this year (see the Chronology, in vol. XIII).

[5] In the copy of this letter in EM the word *three* is crossed out, and *two* is written in by hand.

[6] The General and Allen made a series of bets regarding their diets (see no. 73; for developments see nos. 192, 297, and 493).

[7] For background on the Eisenhowers' difficulties in finding a suitable home in Paris see nos. 60 and 82.

[8] The Allens' six-year-old nephew, Michael Brewer (see Cannon to Mary Allen, Apr. 9, 1948, EM).

94   *Eisenhower Mss.*

To David Randolph Calhoun, Jr.   *March 20, 1951*

Dear Dave:[1] Thanks for your very newsy letter and clippings.[2] We keep up pretty well on the major events through various cable and news services but one does feel somewhat out of touch with friends at this distance. I got a kick out of the "best-dressed" list that "Stu" Symington composed, but I must say that I found it no funnier than the original list![3]

Your report on American Assembly support in St. Louis was very pleasant to read. You and your friends have done a first class job. With the backing we have had, I feel that the project should get off to a good start at the first session in May and, from that point on, should generate a good deal of steam on its own. Obviously, the Assembly will require continuing support but, once underway, its purpose and usefulness should be fully apparent.[4]

I note that you are making a trip to New York and will see mutual acquaintances. I trust you won't get too deeply involved.[5]

I told Mamie that you and your wife[6] might be over here in late July and she and I are delighted at the prospect of seeing you. It is impossible on this job, to predict what trips I might have to make at any given time, but I am reasonably certain that I can arrange to be in Paris sometime during your stay.[7]

With warm personal regard, *Sincerely*

[1] Calhoun had been president of the St. Louis Union Trust Company since 1946. After studying at the University of Virginia, Calhoun had become vice-president of the Ely and Walker Dry Goods Company in St. Louis. He was also a member of the Augusta National Golf Club (see Galambos, *Columbia University*, nos. 581 and 687).

[2] With his letter of March 12 (EM) Calhoun had enclosed several articles on the General from St. Louis newspapers. Two of the clippings were editorials discussing Eisenhower as a potential presidential candidate, and one was a copy of the *Whaley-Eaton Service* newsletter, which speculated on when his work with NATO would be concluded (see *St. Louis Post Dispatch*, Mar. 7, 1951; *St. Louis Globe Democrat*, Mar. 8, 1951; and *Whaley-Eaton Service* newsletter, Mar. 10, 1951, all in EM).

[3] In 1950 the Custom Tailors' Guild had voted Eisenhower one of the ten best-dressed men. According to Calhoun, William Stuart Symington had had another "America's Best-Dressed Men" list printed as a joke. Calhoun was now included in the list as a "close second" to Eisenhower. Calhoun commented on the article: "Symington reaches a long way for a laugh!" (see *Time*, Feb. 20, 1950; and correspondence in EM, Calhoun Corr.). Symington was currently the chairman of the National Security Resources Board (NSRB) (see Galambos, *Columbia University*, nos. 73 and 913).

[4] In his letter Calhoun reported that the American Assembly had reached the goal of $500,000 in working capital. In addition, three companies were donating $25,000 each as sponsors of the conferences (for background on the first American Assembly conference, which was to be held in May, see nos. 201, 202, 204, and 220).

[5] In his March 12 letter Calhoun had mentioned an invitation to meet in New York with some of Eisenhower's political supporters, including Senator James Duff (see nos. 1, n. 2, and 63). On September 26, 1951 (EM), Calhoun would pledge his support of Eisenhower if he became a presidential candidate: "I would do everything in my power . . . to promote your candidacy." To this letter, which was drafted by Lieutenant Colonel Paul T. Carroll (see no. 29), the General added in a handwritten note, "Just smile at the boys; remember, *I don't want anything.*"

[7] The Calhouns planned to sail for Europe on July 26 and would visit the Eisenhowers in Paris in August (see Calhoun to Eisenhower, July 6, Sept. 26, 1951, EM).

95   *Eisenhower Mss.*

To Ellis Dwinnell Slater   *March 21, 1951*

Dear Slats:[01] The slides arrived in perfect condition, though, as always, I feel that somehow I am imposing on your time in processing them through you.

Your newsy letter arrived the following day, one of several I received from our friends, each mentioning the Jamboree—all of which made me vow I would not miss the next one.[2]

While television has not progressed as rapidly over here, we are, nevertheless, fully posted on all the latest investigations. I must admit I could easily become discouraged at times if it were not for my faith in the American people.[3]

Be sure to let me know the details of your arrival. I may be called away on a short trip from time to time, and I want to be here to welcome you if at all possible.[4]

Mamie joins in sending love to you and Priscilla.[5] *Cordially*

P.S. We make progress so slowly on getting a home that you may have to live in hotel accommodations—but we'll have a lot of fun, anyway.[6]

[1] For background on Slater and on Slater's processing of Eisenhower's film see no. 59.

[2] In Slater's letter of March 16 (EM) he had mentioned the "Jamboree at Augusta." The jamboree was an annual golf tournament put on by the members of the Augusta National Golf Club, in Augusta, Georgia, to help raise funds. In 1951 the jamboree was held the week of March 19 (see Roberts to Eisenhower, Mar. 26, 1951, EM; and nos. 113, 750, and 751. See also letters in EM, Clubs and Associations, Augusta National Golf Club).

[3] Slater had discussed several news items, including Alger Hiss's appeal for review of the Senate investigations of organized crime and the RFC (on Hiss see *New York Times*, Mar. 13, 1951; and Galambos, *Columbia University*, nos. 167 and 925. In regard to the probe into organized crime see *ibid.*, no. 795; and William Howard Moore, *The Kefauver Committee and the Politics of Crime, 1950-1952* [Columbia, Mo., 1974]. For background on the RFC investigation see no. 75; and *New York Times*, Mar. 2, 4, 14, 15, 1951, Feb. 26, 1952).

[4] In August 1951 the Slaters would visit the Eisenhowers in Paris (see no. 82, n. 5).

[5] Slater's wife.

[6] See no. 82, n. 5.

Dear Andrew:[1] I must write to tell you how much I appreciate your kind invitation for Mrs. Eisenhower and myself which you have extended in such a thoughtful and considerate manner through Jimmy Gault. It would be an honor and a great pleasure if it was possible for us to be your guests when you are in residence at Holyrood.[2]

My program for the coming months is a heavy one; consequently, I feel hesitant to make any further commitments at this time. I well know, however, that you will be the very first to understand my position.[3]

I have a long standing engagement to attend the celebration of the Fifth Centenary of the University of Glasgow towards the end of June. As you know, I shall be in London for the Ceremony at St. Paul's on 4th July. These are my present commitments in the United Kingdom.[4]

You have been particularly kind in suggesting that I may settle at a later date if it is possible to accept your cordial invitation. I will let you know at the first opportunity. If events should make this impossible, you will know how sincere our disappointment will be.[5]

It was a great pleasure to see you at Julius Holmes' dinner.[6] I hope we shall meet again soon.

Please pay my respects to Lady Cunningham.[7]

With warm personal regards, *As ever*

[1] Admiral of the Fleet, retired First Sea Lord and Chief of the British Naval Staff, Viscount Cunningham of Hyndhope had served under Eisenhower during World War II (for background see *Eisenhower Papers*, vols. I–XI).

[2] Cunningham had written to Brigadier General (U.K.) James F. Gault extending an invitation for the Eisenhowers to visit him in Edinburgh, Scotland, later that year (see Cunningham to Gault, Mar. 16, 1951, EM; for background on Gault see no. 53).

[3] In extending the invitation to visit Holyrood (one-time home of Mary, Queen of Scots, and burial place of the Scottish kings), Cunningham had written, "My wife & I would dearly love to have him & Mrs Eisenhower . . . but at the same time I don't want him pressed at this time when he has so much on his hands & to think about" (see Cunningham to Gault, Mar. 16, 1951, EM).

[4] For background on Eisenhower's invitation to attend the 500th anniversary of the founding of the University of Glasgow see Galambos, *Columbia University*, nos. 706, 841, and 959. On July 4, 1951, the General would participate in the dedication ceremony at London's St. Paul's Cathedral of the American Roll of Honour, which commemorated the American dead of World War II (for background see *ibid.*, no. 745; and no. 252 in this volume).

[5] Eisenhower's busy schedule during May would prevent him from accepting Cunningham's invitation (see Eisenhower to Cunningham, Apr. 26, 1951, EM).

[6] On January 15, during his exploratory trip to the NATO member nations, Eisenhower had attended a dinner for former SHAPE and AFHQ officers at the London home of American Minister Counselor to Great Britain Julius Cecil Holmes

(see the Chronology, in vol. XIII. For background on Holmes see *Eisenhower Papers*, vols. I–XI; on the General's trip to Europe see nos. 1 and 23 in this volume).
[7] Nona Christine Byatt Cunningham, viscountess of Hyndhope.

97   *Eisenhower Mss.*

To NORMAN COUSINS   *March 22, 1951*

Dear Mr. Cousins:[01] There has just come to my desk a copy of an article that you wrote upon completion of your globe encircling trip. I hope that you will permit me to congratulate you sincerely upon the excellence of your presentation.[2]

While you did not discuss the particular need and functions of armed forces in the critical situation of today, you did state, far more clearly than I could, my own conception of the broad basis on which we must fight out the battle of freedom versus Communism in the world.[3] My appreciation of your technique is all the greater because, in a groping and far less convincing way, I tried to express something of this idea in the final two pages of a book I wrote in 1947.[4]

I most earnestly hope that you will keep pounding away to present the picture to more and more people, everywhere.[5]

With personal regards, *Sincerely*

[1] Norman Cousins had been the editor of the *Saturday Review of Literature* since 1942. He had studied at Columbia University before working as an educational writer for the *New York Post* and was later editor for *Current History* magazine.
[2] Cousins had just returned from a trip around the world that had taken him to Japan, Korea, Hong Kong, Ceylon, India, Pakistan, the Near East, and Europe. His article "A Policy to Counter Soviet Strategy" appeared on the editorial page of the *International Herald Tribune* on March 22, 1951.
[3] Cousins had addressed the problems of Soviet military strategy and the threat of atomic war. He used the Berlin blockade and the Korean War as examples of a successful Russian strategy that created situations in which "our military success is not enough to give us victory but in which military defeat for us may be conclusive." Cousins recommended a widespread dissemination of democratic ideals: "America has to start talking not only political freedom but economic freedom and human freedom." He also proposed that America mobilize world public opinion in support of the United Nations as a powerful law-enforcement agency (*ibid.*).
[4] Eisenhower was referring to his wartime memoir, *Crusade in Europe*, in which he had emphasized the importance of adequate military preparedness and unity among the democratic nations. He also had recognized the need for an international agency with the power to enforce justice (pp. 475–78). Earlier in the month Eisenhower had discussed these pages of his book in a letter to William Edward Robinson (see no. 63). In his reply (Mar. 30, 1951, EM) Cousins complimented Eisenhower on *Crusade in Europe*, describing the book as "a vital contribution to the historic record."
[5] In 1952 Cousins would become honorary president of the United World Federal-

ists; later he would be international president of the World Association of World Federalists, groups dedicated to bringing about peace and nuclear control through world government (for background see Cousins's books *Modern Man Is Obsolete* [New York, 1945], *Who Speaks for Man?* [New York, 1953], and *In Place of Folly* [New York, 1961]; for Eisenhower's opinion on world federalism see Galambos, *Columbia University*, nos. 436, 729, and 908).

98   *Eisenhower Mss.*

To ALFRED MAXIMILIAN GRUENTHER   *March 23, 1951*
Top secret

Memorandum for Chief of Staff: Herewith a memorandum from the British Chiefs of Staff that I would like to see studied very carefully by our Planning Groups.[1]

I cannot forbear making some observations. The point is made two or three times in this memorandum that, if we want air forces for intervention in the land battle, we should not be wasting our money on carriers but using it to produce land-based aviation. This, of course, is such an obvious statement of fact—when considered in the realm of theory—that it would scarcely seem necessary to repeat it. However, here are some facts that the paper does not take into consideration:

(a) We are not proposing the building of aircraft carriers; the reports we saw were that the United States was taking out of its Reserve Fleet and putting into active operation a minimum of 26 carriers larger than the escort type. We have understood from Carney that a fair proportion of this strength will constantly be in the Mediterranean, and, in case of emergency, sizeable reinforcements will quickly arrive.[2]

(b) Land aviation is useless unless we have fields. The job of getting proper fields is already causing trouble; in time of peace, no nation wants to give up the ground and accept the irritations that come from stationing foreign air units in its national territory. Yet the nations of Continental Europe, themselves incapable of producing large air forces at this time, are not keen on providing the fields that might give us sufficient D-day air.[3]

(c) The only thing that is certain about the beginning of the next war, (if ever we have to face that bitter day) is that it will come in a spot and under conditions that are entirely unexpected. Consequently, carriers may, in the early months of any war, provide us the only air strength that we can bring to bear in a critical area. I am quite ready to admit that, if we are going to carry out sustained operations in any particular region, we cannot do so except by establishing fields and land-based aviation. But I consider it nothing short of criminal to avoid planning for the use of whatever assets we may have upon the outbreak of such an emergency, especially of assets that have cost us as much to build as have the carriers.

(d) The American Navy is far more optimistic about the capabilities of carrier-based aviation than is the British Navy. It is, of course, quite possible that the British are completely correct in this estimate, but, again I say, if we have the resource, we have to make the best possible use of it, and I cannot see why we should keep large carriers roaming the Atlantic looking for submarines—for such a job, we certainly have more economical types.[4]

(e) In every category of unit, the free countries are going to be out-manned and out-gunned if ever a war should start. This is because the dictators will choose the moment and place of attack. We will have to use everything we have; let us not belittle any of our assets and write them off before put to the test.

[1] We have been unable to locate the memorandum mentioned by Eisenhower. For background on the regional planning groups see the following document.

[2] On Eisenhower's interest in the wartime role of naval aviation and aircraft carriers see Galambos, *Columbia University*, esp. nos. 413, 506, and 598. Following the outbreak of war in Korea, the United States had begun an extensive program of rearmament. In June 1950 the Navy had eleven aircraft carriers larger than escort size (see *ibid.*, no. 358). By June 1951 the Navy would be operating seventeen of these ships; a year later it would add two more large carriers to the fleet. Navy plans called for a total of eight fleet carriers to be available to NATO commanders six months after mobilization began. During the first six months of 1951 only one new aircraft carrier was built, and none were under construction; ten existing aircraft carriers were, however, undergoing conversion and modernization (Lovett to Eisenhower, May 17, 1951, OS/D, 1951, Clas. Decimal File, CD 091.7 Europe; U.S. Department of Defense, *Semiannual Report of the Secretary of Defense, and the Semiannual Reports of the Secretary of the Army, Secretary of the Navy, Secretary of the Air Force, January 1 to June 30, 1951* [Washington, D.C., 1951], pp. 160–61). Eisenhower would later posit a SHAPE requirement for sixteen aircraft carriers in the event of war (see no. 532).

[3] The United States had been negotiating on a bilateral basis with a number of NATO nations for the provision of operating facilities in Greenland, Morocco, Iceland, Norway, Italy, France, and the Azores. Some of the nations involved, however, had been reluctant to build air bases for American forces. The Norwegians were opposed to the presence of foreign troops on their soil and feared a strong Russian reaction. Negotiations had stalled over Iceland's insistence that it be allowed to terminate any base agreements unilaterally. The French government was reluctant to pay for building the airfields and feared that Communist propagandists would charge French leaders with submitting to a U.S. occupation (State, *Foreign Relations, 1951*, vol. IV, *Europe: Political and Economic Developments, Part I*, pp. 480–98, 505–6, 757–60, 765–70; *New York Times*, May 29, June 8, July 2, 1951; Beebe to Marshall, May 1951, and Patrick to Marshall, May 7, 1951, OS/D, 1951, Clas. Decimal File, CD 092.3 NATO). For developments see no. 223.

[4] See Galambos, *Columbia University*, no. 358. Although the British Navy had six aircraft carriers under construction at this time (see Raymond V. B. Blackman, ed., *Jane's Fighting Ships: 1951–52* [London, n.d.], pp. iv, 14–21), there had been some criticism of their role in the Korean War. In a report forwarded to Eisen-

hower by Chief of the Royal Air Force Staff Sir John Slessor (see no. 62), one British observer had noted that aircraft carriers had difficulty providing a steady flow of aircraft to targets of opportunity and that the reluctance of carriers to divulge their locations at sea had impeded communication ("Report from Korea," attached to Slessor to Eisenhower, Feb. 26, 1951, EM). There is no reply to this note in EM.

99   *Eisenhower Mss.*

To Eric James Patrick Brind   *March 29, 1951*
Restricted

My dear Admiral Brind:[1] I am delighted that the British Government has agreed to make you available for duty within the command structure of SHAPE, in which you are hereby designated Allied Commander-in-Chief, Northern Europe.[2] In this capacity, you will have a most important role to play in the defense of NATO Europe.

Your primary mission will be the integrated defense of the Northern European area. In accomplishing this mission, you will maintain close relationship with Commanders-in-Chief of adjacent forces not under your command, particularly the allied Commander-in-Chief of the Eastern Atlantic area.[3]

Your command area will comprise initially the area for which the Northern European Planning Group is responsible.[4] You will be notified shortly of your relationship with national authorities in this area.

The forces to be allocated to you will be designated by me. In war, you will exercise operational command over these forces, under my strategic direction. In peace, your primary task is to ensure that the forces allocated or to be allocated to you are organized, equipped, trained, and ready to perform their war missions. You will establish your headquarters with an integrated combined staff.

I have appointed Major General Robert K. Taylor, United States Air Force, as Commander Air Forces, Northern Europe;[5] Lieutenant General Wilhelm von Tangen Hansteen, Norwegian Army, as Commander Allied Army Forces, Norway; and Lieutenant General Ebbe Gørtz, Danish Army, as Commander Allied Army Forces, Denmark.[6] Under letter of appointment issued by me, these Commanders will be directly responsible to you and will be charged with such missions as you prescribe. Initially, you will act also as the Commander, Allied Naval Forces, Northern Europe, in addition to your duties as Allied Commander-in-Chief.

It is my intention formally to assume command of the Central and Northern European Areas at 0001Z hours on 2 April 1951.[7]

151

Will you notify me when you are ready formally to assume command? *Cordially*

[1] Brind, the British Commander in Chief, Far Eastern Stations, since 1948, had served with the Home and Pacific fleets during World War II. He had also been Assistant Chief of Naval Staff from 1942 until 1944 and president of the Royal Naval College, Greenwich, from 1946 until 1948. In a letter to Eisenhower written on March 15 (EM) First Sea Lord Bruce Fraser (see no. 90) had recommended Brind for the command of Eisenhower's forces in northern Europe. Fraser had said that Brind had "worked well" with the American admirals in the Far East.

[2] For background on this command see nos. 77, n. 19, and 90. Eisenhower would send other letters of appointment on this same day (see, for example, Eisenhower to Juin, Mar. 29, 1951, EM).

[3] The Allied command structure for the eastern Atlantic was still a controversial subject (see no. 62).

[4] At its first session in 1949 the North Atlantic Council established five regional planning groups, which were instructed to "develop and recommend to the Military Committee, through the Standing Group," plans for the defense of their regions. The Northern European Planning Group comprised Denmark, Norway, and the United Kingdom. This agency was to form the basis of Eisenhower's proposed Northern Command, and the Planning Group was to continue to function until the new command was fully operational (Ismay, *NATO*, pp. 24-25, 72, 102, 175-76; JAMAG 621 P, Mar. 24, 1951, and SH 20243, Mar. 28, 1951, both in CCS 092 Western Europe [3-12-48], Sec. 75).

[5] Robert Kinder Taylor (USMA 1928) had been Chief of Staff (C/S) of the Fifteenth Air Force in Italy during World War II. He had been CG of Brookley Field, Alabama, since 1947.

[6] For background on von Tangen-Hansteen and Gørtz see no. 77, n. 20.

[7] Eisenhower would assume command at 11:59 P.M., April 1, 1951 (D-D [51] 87, Apr. 2, 1951, NATO Files, microfilm). For developments in the establishment of the northern European area see no. 287.

100   *Eisenhower Mss.*

To Herbert Bayard Swope   *March 29, 1951*

Dear Herbert:[1] Thanks very much for your fine letter of the 15th. To get rid at once of an acute embarrassment, I make my humble apology for not earlier acknowledging receipt of the bound volume of The World Almanac. Actually, I keep it on my desk, a circumstance which I quote to assure you of the sincerity of my belated thanks.[2]

I, of course, completely share your good opinion of David Sarnoff. For a long time, I have admired both his abilities and his qualities. With respect to the particular kind of individual that Bernie and I talked about, I think he would fill the bill admirably; I am grateful for the suggestion.[3]

I shall be on the lookout for the volume you are sending me, and shall make a point of reading the chapter that you suggest. While the book was in my library at home, I had found it necessary to adopt a non-reading policy on war books, so you may be sure the subject matter will be new to me.[4] Please remember me kindly to our good friend Bernie when you see him. Assure him, also, that I have never ceased to follow up on his suggestion to me, and the reason for the current delay is the arrival here in Europe of a man named Herrod who, as head of the NATO "Productions Board," seems to be tearing into things in a good way, and I want to give him a chance for real self-briefing before I take the matter up with him.[5]

With warm personal regards, *Cordially*

[1] For background on Swope see no. 66.

[2] On December 15, 1950 (EM), Swope had written to tell the General that a 1951 world almanac would shortly be sent to him as a "token of an old affection."

[3] David Sarnoff, chairman of the board of the Radio Corporation of America (RCA), had served as communications consultant to Eisenhower during the Normandy invasion in 1944. In his March 15 letter (EM) Swope had mentioned that Bernard Baruch had suggested Sarnoff as someone who could possibly be of assistance to Eisenhower in Europe (for background on Sarnoff see Galambos, *Columbia University*, nos. 334 and 1135; on Baruch see nos. 25, n. 4, and 37 in this volume). Sarnoff would not assume any official post with SHAPE, but he would travel to Europe on behalf of the Voice of America during the summer of 1951 (see correspondence in EM, Sarnoff Corr. For developments in Sarnoff's activities see no. 1020; on the Voice of America broadcasts see Galambos, *Columbia University*, no. 55).

[4] In his letter of the fifteenth Swope had told Eisenhower that he would be sending him a copy of Basil Henry Liddell Hart's book *The German Generals Talk* (New York, 1948). Swope felt that the best portion of the book was the second chapter, which discussed the organization and training of the German Army under General Hans von Seeckt following World War I (for background on Liddell Hart and a dispute concerning the book see Galambos, *Columbia University*, no. 500).

[5] Baruch, an expert on industrial mobilization, had met with Eisenhower in January to discuss these areas of the NATO effort. The "suggestion" referred to probably concerned European defense production (see letters and telegrams for January 1951 in EM, Baruch Corr.). William Rogers Herod was then on leave of absence from his post as president of the International General Electric Company and was serving as Coordinator of the NATO Defense Production Board. Eisenhower would arrange a meeting with him on June 8 to discuss the work of the board (see Herod to Eisenhower, May 7, 1951, and Eisenhower to Herod, n.d., both in EM).

To WILLIAM EDWARD ROBINSON

Dear Bill:[1] I haven't had much of a chance to answer your fine letter of a few days ago because I have had an attack of a local intestinal infection that has kept me in bed.[2]

I doubt that there is much use trying to explain again the necessary differences between military and political decisions, and the reasons why any movement into the Balkans in World War II *had* to be a political decision. All of those things are clear enough if anyone wants to look facts in the face—to hold otherwise seems to me to be clear evidence that any explanation would be useless.[3]

At this moment, we have many newspapers of the world bitterly criticizing MacArthur[4] because he has proposed a cease-fire action in Central Korea—so there you are on the other side of the same corner.[5]

Thank you for your suggestions respecting my letter. If I ever decide to send a similar explanation to any other friend, I shall make the type of modification you suggested.[6]

Right now, I am in a terrific hurry, but possibly in a few days I will have a chance to write you a decent letter. In the meantime, please don't forget that your observations, suggestions, opinions, and just plain reporting, are terrifically valuable to me.[7]

My very best to all the members of the Blind Brook and Deepdale crowd.[8] *Cordially*

[1] For background on Robinson see no. 83.

[2] Mrs. Eisenhower was also ill at this time, having contracted influenza (see the following document). For background on the General's intermittent but persistent intestinal disorders see Galambos, *Columbia University*, nos. 401 and 407; and Lyon, *Portrait of the Hero*, pp. 394, 532, 676.

[3] With his letter of March 19 (EM) Robinson had enclosed the latest in a series of articles on the General by syndicated columnist Westbrook Pegler. Pegler heavily criticized Eisenhower for not capturing the Balkans for the West during World War II and cited both this and Eisenhower's apparent support for the presidency by the *New York Herald Tribune* (of which Robinson was executive vice-president) as proof that the General was unfit for election and perhaps soft on communism. According to Pegler, the General's election could give America "a President who might be so bad that we might never have a chance to elect another." The columnist suggested that Commander of the Army Field Forces General Mark Wayne Clark be considered for the presidency. Using Clark's memoir, *Calculated Risk*, as proof, Pegler wrote that Clark recognized that America had erred by failing to invade the Balkans, while "Eisenhower apparently never has seen the error" (see *New York Journal American*, Mar. 16, 1951, copy in EM, Robinson Corr.). On Eisenhower's policy in regard to the Balkans see his war memoir, *Crusade in Europe*, pp. 284, 474-75; on the Pegler series see no. 78. For developments see nos. 162 and 163.

[4] General of the Army Douglas MacArthur, Commander in Chief, Far East (CINCFE), was then heading the U.N. military operations in Korea (for background see Galambos, *Columbia University*, nos. 33 and 870).

[5] On March 24 MacArthur had precipitated an uproar among U.N. member nations by issuing a communiqué offering a cease-fire to the Chinese Communist forces in North Korea. MacArthur was accused of having exceeded his military authority. Truman later wrote that the communiqué was the "most extraordinary statement for a military commander of the United Nations to issue on his own responsibility" and that "further statements like this could only do untold harm." MacArthur was instructed to refrain from making further political statements without first consulting the U.S. government (see Truman, *Memoirs*, vol. II, *Years of Trial and Hope*, pp. 441-43; State, *Foreign Relations, 1951*, vol. VII, *Korea and China, Part I* [1983], pp. 264-68; Joint Secretariat, *The History of the Joint Chiefs of Staff: The Joint Chiefs of Staff and National Policy*, 5 vols. to date [Wilmington, Del., 1979-], vol. III, *The Joint Chiefs of Staff and the Korean War*, by James F. Schnabel and Robert J. Watson [1979], pt. 1, pp. 526-29, hereafter cited as Schnabel and Watson, *History of the Joint Chiefs of Staff*, vol. III, *The Joint Chiefs of Staff and the Korean War*, pt. 1; D. Clayton James, *The Years of MacArthur*, 3 vols. [Boston, 1970-85], vol. III, *Triumph and Disaster, 1945-1964*, pp. 584-89; Bradley and Blair, *A General's Life*, pp. 627-28; Douglas MacArthur, *Reminiscences* [New York, 1964], pp. 386-89; William Manchester, *American Caesar: Douglas MacArthur, 1880-1964* [Boston, 1978], pp. 633-38; and Joseph C. Goulden, *Korea: The Untold Story of the War* [New York, 1982], pp. 478-83). For developments see nos. 116, 128, n. 3, 136, and 143, n. 3.

[6] For Robinson's suggestions see no. 83, n. 3.

[7] Robinson would continue to send Eisenhower information on events in the United States and the General's treatment by the press (see, for example, nos. 110, 307, and 447, n. 3).

[8] For background on the Blind Brook and Deepdale clubs, two of the General's favorite golf courses, see Galambos, *Columbia University*, nos. 834 and 891, respectively.

102   *Eisenhower Mss.*

To William H. Burnham   *March 29, 1951*

Dear Bill:[1] Your latest bunch of clippings, together with the letters to Mamie and me, all arrived while the both of us were in bed. I had one of these local attacks of an internal variety, and she is not yet completely over her flu, or, at least, the effects of the medicines the doctors gave her to keep it from turning into pneumonia.[2]

Your letters are always full of news, to say nothing of valuable information—we enjoy them tremendously.

Already, we are looking forward to your return trip, and if, by that time, we have succeeded in getting into a house, we will really have a lot more fun than when you were here before.[3]

I took a look at your picture this morning. It is as good as I can do. I shall not touch it again except possibly to put a light coat of varnish on it after it has really dried out.[4]

I am trying to get off a short note to George Whitney, but, in the meantime, if you see young Bob, tell him that I find his Dad's communications not only thoroughly enjoyable, but most instructive.[5]

When next you write to our "Minneapolis Priscilla,"[6] tell her that I actually painted the photograph as a new John Alden technique, but that the Captain himself will be the possessor and have to deliver it according to her instructions.[7] *As ever*

[1] On Eisenhower's friend and political adviser Burnham see no. 40.

[2] Burnham sent Eisenhower newspaper clippings on a variety of subjects, and on March 20 (EM) he wrote Robert Schulz, Eisenhower's aide, that he was sending six binders to hold them (EM, Burnham Corr.). In a letter of March 19 (EM) Burnham had suggested that people needed to be informed of the importance of SHAPE's success. Burnham was very interested in Eisenhower's future in politics, and he advised him that in response to questions about his possible candidacy: " 'No comment' will kill off the news value." In Burnham's letter of March 22 (EM) he had written that he hoped Eisenhower would not return for the first American Assembly conference (see no. 87) in May, because he would be plagued with such questions. Burnham supported Eisenhower's "present attitude of being above political thoughts." The following week Burnham would be in Texas, and he told Eisenhower, "You can well imagine what your Texas friends are going to discuss. I will probably lose five pounds from dodging." For background on the Eisenhowers' illnesses see the previous document, n. 2.

[3] Burnham had visited Eisenhower in mid-March (see Burnham to Eisenhower, Mar. 2, 19, 1951, EM) and would do so again in April (see Burnham to Carroll, Apr. 2, 1951, EM). The Eisenhowers would not move into a home before Burnham's next visit (see no. 82, n. 5).

[4] Eisenhower was apparently painting a picture for Burnham (see Burnham to Eisenhower, Jan. 6, 1952, EM; for background on the General's painting see Galambos, *Columbia University*, nos. 51 and 171).

[5] George Whitney was another friend of Eisenhower's who was keeping him informed of current developments in the American political arena. "Young Bob" was Robert Bacon Whitney, George's son (see nos. 50, n. 3, and 105; and Burnham to Eisenhower, Mar. 22, 1951, EM).

[6] Mrs. Gaylord Dillingham, of St. Paul, Minnesota.

[7] This was a joke shared by Burnham (who described himself as a "cantankerous old bachelor"), Mrs. Dillingham, and Eisenhower (see Burnham to Eisenhower, Feb. 23, 1951, and Mar. 18, 1952, EM). The reference is to the story Henry Wadsworth Longfellow popularized in his poem "The Courtship of Miles Standish" (see *The Poems of Henry Wadsworth Longfellow*, ed. Louis Untermeyer [New York, 1943]). Captain Standish courted Priscilla through John Alden, but Alden became Priscilla's husband. The "captain" is probably Burnham, as Eisenhower referred to himself as a member of the "John Alden Club for William H. Burnham" (Nov. 13–20, 1950, EM, Burnham Corr.).

103

Eisenhower Mss.

To Amon Giles Carter, Sr.   *March 29, 1951*

Dear Amon:[1] Yesterday, I got your letter telling about the beef and other things arriving at the Waldorf-Astoria.[2] At the same time, I got a message from the Waldorf-Astoria saying that everything had arrived in good shape and had been properly stored in the deep freeze.[3] All this makes me more than anxious to get ourselves settled in a house, but we have had a God-awful time trying to do it. As you well know, things don't seem to move over here like they do in Texas, and, at times, I get terrifically impatient. However, both Mamie and I are tremendously appreciative, and now, for goodness sake, don't send any more beef there until we get on our feet and can get this largely used up, and then I shall tell you how things are going.[4]

All the clippings were most interesting. I am glad you remembered to send them.[5]

I must dash off a quick note to Sid.[6] Don't forget to give my very best to young Amon, and, of course, my love to Minnie.[7]

Again, my grateful thanks and warm personal regard. *Cordially*

[1] For background on Carter, president and publisher of the *Fort Worth Star-Telegraph*, see no. 35.

[2] In his letter of March 20 (EM) Carter had written that three hind and two front quarters of beef, "together with various and other sundry things," had been sent to New York's Waldorf-Astoria Hotel for delivery to Eisenhower and aide Robert Schulz. The beef and other items were gifts from Carter and his fellow Texan Sid Richardson. For background on Richardson see no. 34 and the following document; on Schulz see no. 1.

[3] There is no copy of this message in EM; however, in an April 16 letter (EM) to the hotel's resident manager, Edwin K. Hastings, Eisenhower would mention that the beef had arrived safely.

[4] For background see nos. 60 and 82, n. 5. Until they could move, Eisenhower would store the beef in freezer facilities borrowed from the American Embassy (see Schulz to Richardson, Apr. 11, 1951, EM).

[5] With his letter Carter had enclosed a number of "clippings, editorials and stories" from the *Star-Telegram*, including a piece on the new Amon Carter Stadium at Texas Christian University in Fort Worth (copies not in EM).

[6] See the following document.

[7] Carter's wife, the former Minnie Meacham Smith.

104

Eisenhower Mss.

To Sid Williams Richardson   *March 29, 1951*

Dear Sid:[1] Word from the Waldorf-Astoria says that the beef has arrived there.[2] The only tragedy in the whole affair is that Mamie and I have not yet succeeded in getting into a house—a condition that we are hopeful of correcting, but, at times, we get fairly well discouraged. At the moment, we are living in a nice hotel in the suburbs, and, even if you should get over here before we can have our own home, we will still have a good time.[3]

Of course, you know how deeply grateful Mamie and I are for your splendid gift. If you had to eat some of this Paris beef, you would understand exactly how grateful we are.

Progress on my main job is not too speedy, but, of course, it is the kind of job in which revolutionary action cannot be expected. The task itself is confining, onerous, and devoid of the excitement that prevails in a command headquarters in time of an emergency. If I knew of any logical sane alternative to what we are trying to do in Europe, I would most certainly be for it; but I believe that the only alternative implies for the U.S. a steadily deteriorating situation which would finally result in disastrous consequences.[4]

I do not recall that I ever sent to you, personally, my actual thinking on this line, and it just occurs to me that, within a day or so, I shall write you, for your *personal and confidential* information, an outline of my approach to this serious task. Of course, I have no objection to your showing such a letter to Amon, but it would be under the same conditions of personal, confidential information.[5]

Anyway, don't forget that I would like to have an occasional letter from you, and, in the meantime, thanks again for the Texas beef.

As always, warm personal regard. *Cordially*

P.S. My very best to Perry and his family.[6]

[1] For background on Texas millionaire and Eisenhower political supporter Richardson see no. 34.

[2] On Richardson's frequent gifts to the Eisenhowers see correspondence in EM, same file as document; and in EM, Philippe Corr. See also the preceding document.

[3] For background on the search for a house see the preceding document, n. 4, and nos. 18, n. 3, and 44. Eisenhower would see Richardson in London during February 1952 (see no. 678, n. 4).

[4] Eisenhower discusses some of his difficulties in establishing an Allied command for NATO in his memoir *At Ease*, pp. 364–66, 372–77. For the General's views on the U.S. efforts in the alliance see no. 23.

[5] There is in EM no letter to Richardson written during this time that deals with these issues. For a later letter from the General concerning U.S. politics see no. 558. On Amon Carter see the preceding document.

[6] For background on Richardson's nephew and business assistant Perry Bass see no. 35, n. 6.

105   *Eisenhower Mss.*

To George Whitney   *March 29, 1951*

Dear Mr. Whitney:[1] Thank you so much for your second letter. You
explained a number of things that have been puzzling me from the
information I could glean from the newspapers. I am beginning to
think that the luckiest thing I did before leaving the United States was
to persuade you to undertake this chore. As of this moment, I have no
chance to comment on any of these things, but I do want you to know
that I thoroughly appreciate the generous donation of your time to my
enlightenment.[2]

With warm regard, *Sincerely*

[1] For background on Whitney see no. 50, n. 3.

[2] Whitney had been corresponding with Eisenhower concerning the U.S. economy
(see no. 55). In his letter of March 20 (EM), his second to Eisenhower, Whitney
had said that he felt the economy was improving in several areas: in the capacity
for producing defense articles, in monetary controls to fight inflation, and in labor
leaders' cooperation with the government's "war effort." Whitney also mentioned
the debate between the Treasury Department and the Federal Reserve Board over
monetary policy and Charles E. Wilson's disputes with labor organizations (see
New York Times, Feb. 19, 1951; and no. 64. For background on Wilson see no. 45,
n. 4). At the end of his letter Whitney described the situation in Korea as "not too
bad" and said that the Senate crime investigations were popular. He mentioned the
trip to Paris he would take in May (see nos. 101, 95, and 221, n. 6, respectively).
Eisenhower would comment on this report in greater detail in later letters to
Whitney (see nos. 221 and 306).

106   *Eisenhower Mss.*

To Henry Spiese Aurand   *March 29, 1951*

Dear Henry:[1] The reading of your letter was a pleasant interlude in an
otherwise fairly drab day. Like everyone else, I am always complimented when some friend believed me equal to an onerous task—I
assure you that this one can be classified as nothing else. What the
outcome will be, of course, none of us can foretell. My own feeling is
that the alternative to making a full-out effort along the general lines
that we have started is complete hopelessness and eventual disaster. So
I shall give it everything I have.[2]

For some time, we have been desperately trying to whittle down,
rather than build up, the American side of the staff here. Most foreign
nations (except Britain and Canada) have, for a variety of reasons,
been very short in qualified staff officers, so, whenever any joint

venture of this kind is begun, we always find ourselves furnishing far more than our share. This, in itself, is bad enough, but then there is always the added sting of public criticism in other countries where it is asserted, "America is trying to take over control."[3]

All this does not mean that I am not deeply grateful for your giving me the name of Colonel Palfrey. I shall instantly have recorded in our files his full name, number, address, and such qualifications as you gave me. It is always possible that we will have a very critical need for such individual.[4]

I thoroughly enjoyed the '35 Year Book. I had a wonderful chance to read it in the last couple days during which the doctors kept me home because of some kind of an upset. It was about the only fun I had out of that particular experience.[5]

Of course, there have been songs written about Paris in the spring-time, but though I have spent, during my lifetime, at least five springs in this general section of the world, I can't recall any during which the weather was as pleasant as it is every day of the year in Hawaii— all of which is a backhanded inquiry as to your desire to changing stations.[6]

Give our love to Betty,[7] and thanks again for your fine letter.
Cordially

[1] Lieutenant General Aurand, a classmate of Eisenhower's at West Point, had been CG, Pacific, since 1949. He was presently stationed at Schofield Barracks, Honolulu, Hawaii (for background on his association with Eisenhower during and after World War II see *Eisenhower Papers*, vols. I–XI).

[2] In his letter of March 21 (EM) Aurand had extended his own and his wife's best wishes for the success of Eisenhower's efforts at SHAPE: "Like many, many others, we feel that you, Ike, are the only one who can . . . undertake this union of military force under a single command."

The General's appointment calendar indicates that he had two meetings on this day, an early lunch with Admiral of the Fleet, First Sea Lord, and Chief of the (British) Naval Staff first baron Bruce Austin Fraser of North Cape and an afternoon appointment with Congressman Harold Dunbar Cooley (a Democrat from the Fourth District of North Carolina), the chairman of the House Committee on Agriculture.

[3] Aurand had written that he had waited until after the announcement of all SHAPE staff appointments to send his letter because he did not wish to give Eisenhower the impression that he was writing "in connection with [obtaining] an assignment with you." For background on the recent staff selections see nos. 56 and 77; and *New York Times*, March 2, 7, 8, 20, 21, 1951.

[4] Aurand had suggested Thomas Rossman Palfrey (Docteur de l'Université de Paris 1927) as a possible staff assistant for SHAPE. Palfrey, then a professor of Romance languages at Northwestern University, had served in the Army of the United States (AUS) during the Punitive Expedition against Pancho Villa and World Wars I and II; at this time he was a colonel in the infantry reserve. Aurand wrote that Palfrey, who had been his G-5 (assistant chief of staff for civil operations) from 1942 to 1946, could be of "very great assistance to someone in your staff, as he was to me." Palfry would not, however, receive an assignment with SHAPE.

[5] On Eisenhower's contribution to a "'35 Year Book" published by the West Point class of 1915 see Galambos, *Columbia University*, no. 983; on the General's recent illness see no. 101 in this volume.
[6] Aurand would remain in his present post until his retirement in 1952.
[7] Aurand's wife, the former Elizabeth Steele.

107   *Eisenhower Mss.*

To Forrest Percival Sherman   *March 30, 1951*
Secret

Dear Admiral: I greatly appreciate your message of March 16th in which you assured me of your active support for my command arrangements here in Europe.[1] I only wish that it were possible to achieve such objectivity and sincerity on the part of every responsible officer and official throughout the Nations of NATO. If so, the seas which I have to sail would be much smoother.

In your message you raised two questions relative to decisions on naval matters which will eventually have to be made when the command problems for my southern flank and for the Mediterranean as a whole are resolved.[2] As I view the situation these are matters for your decision, and whatever arrangements you adopt will be acceptable to me provided Carney will not be so burdened as to detract from his primary responsibility to me.

Were I to be placed in Carney's position, I am inclined to believe that I would greatly prefer to retain the authority which attends the added responsibility of administrative command of the U.S. Naval Forces in the Mediterranean. As such, I would plan to use my integrated combined staff for my primary duty, and have a well qualified deputy for my U.S. Naval administrative tasks. Operational command at sea would be exercised by my fleet or striking force commander. That is a similar arrangement to my own command during the war. Some people may offer objections based on theoretical considerations but it has many transcending practical advantages.[3]

With respect to the rank of your London representative, I have no unalterable opinion. From the information available to me I see no need for a full admiral in London after Carney moves to the South. The presence of another 4 star U.S. Admiral in Europe would seem to diminish Carney's prestige—it could even cause a few sardonic chuckles among those who always claim that the U.S. Services are very "rank conscious." However, I shall cheerfully accept the conclusions of yourself and the U.S. Chiefs of Staff.[4]

Admiral Lord Fraser came over to have luncheon with me yesterday.

During our conversations, I learned from him of the progress of negotiations with respect to the solution of command arrangements in the Mediterranean. I am firmly convinced that Lord Fraser is genuinely anxious to obtain a mutually satisfactory solution to this problem. I am sure that you will find him most cooperative. I understand that a proposal has been made for the U.S. and British Chiefs of Staff to meet at some time in the near future in a further effort to reach agreement. I hope it is soon.[5]

Incidentally, I suggested to Fraser that he or you or both should develop some sound reason to meet soon with the French Admiralty and to advertise the meeting *in advance*.[6]

It was a great pleasure to see you on the occasion of your recent visit and I trust that you will find it possible to return soon again. Next time I hope that you will find my headquarters and subordinate commanders all well organized and functioning efficiently in meeting the tremendous tasks before us.[7] *Sincerely*

[1] We have been unable to locate Admiral Sherman's message, which apparently was in response to Eisenhower's letter of March 12 to Secretary of Defense Marshall (no. 77). Captain George Anderson (see no. 53, n. 9) drafted this letter.

[2] For background on the controversy over command arrangements for southern Europe and the Mediterranean see nos. 57, n. 3, 62, and 77. On March 21 the JCS had sent Eisenhower its views on command arrangements in the Mediterranean–Middle East area (JCS 86466, in CCS 092 Western Europe [3-12-48], Sec. 75). Eisenhower would respond to these proposals in no. 148.

[3] During World War II Eisenhower had been both Supreme Commander of the Allied Expeditionary Force (a multinational organization) and Commander of the wholly American ETOUSA. Eisenhower's deputy theater commander had actually taken the major role in administering the U.S. Army forces in the theater (Hobbs, *Dear General*, p. 148, n. 5). Admiral Carney (see n. 4 below) was the prospective commander of the NATO forces on Eisenhower's southern flank.

[4] At this time Admiral Carney, as CINCNELM (see no. 53, n. 4), still had his headquarters in London. Carney would shift his headquarters to Naples when he became C in C of Eisenhower's Southern Command (see Carney to Eisenhower, Nov. 8, 1951, EM, Fechteler Corr.; see also no. 236). In September a new chief of naval operations would propose the creation of a separate and purely American naval command in London (see no. 429, n. 1).

[5] For background on Bruce Fraser, Chief of the British Naval Staff, see no. 90. On April 4 Fraser would propose that NATO establish a supreme command (under British leadership) for the Mediterranean, with subarea commanders for the western and eastern halves. Under this plan the western Mediterranean commander was to be French, and Eisenhower's Southern Command would include both Italian and Yugoslav forces (supported by aircraft carriers) but would not include the Mediterranean itself. At that time Field Marshal Sir William Joseph Slim, Chief of the Imperial General Staff since October 1948 (see Galambos, *Columbia University*, no. 276), stated that these proposals were predicated upon British political considerations and that the dispute over the Mediterranean commands could be cleared up if only the United States would make the single concession of consenting to the appointment of a British supreme commander (Wright to Bradley, 041327Z, Apr. 5, 1951, CCS 092 Western Europe [3-12-48], Sec. 76). For developments see no. 148.

[6] Eisenhower's suggestion was in response to the controversy over the exclusion of the French from the British-American conference held at Malta (see no. 81, n. 5). On this same day Secretary of State Dean Acheson and French Foreign Minister Robert Schuman (see nos. 2, n. 1, and 16, n. 6) would discuss the possibility of having French, British, and American representatives meet to discuss matters covered during the Malta conferences (State, *Foreign Relations, 1951*, vol. IV, *Europe: Political and Economic Developments, Part I*, pp. 369–72).
[7] In a handwritten postscript Eisenhower said, "Dear For[r]est: This letter is written on the formal side—but I didn't have the heart to make someone type it again. D.E." There is no reply in EM.

108   *Eisenhower Mss.*

To Jules Moch   *March 30, 1951*
Restricted

My dear Mr. President:[1] For such circulation[2] as you see fit, I am sending you copies of my directives to the Commanders-in-Chief of Allied Army and Air Forces and to the Flag Officer, Central Europe.[3]

You will see from these directives that I shall rely on my subordinate Commanders to develop and maintain very close cooperation with the appropriate military authorities in each of the countries which lie within or adjoin their areas of responsibility.[4] I shall be most grateful if you will do all you can to facilitate this cooperation at all appropriate military levels, as the strength of our whole military organization will depend largely on the spirit in which this is done.

May I also express to you personally, and to your Chiefs of Staff, my very sincere appreciation for agreeing to make available to me the services of General Juin and Admiral Jaujard. I am sure we have now established a team of Commanders who will not only cooperate very closely with each other, but who have the full confidence of all our nations.[5] *Cordially yours*

[1] For background on Moch see no. 11.
[2] A note at the bottom of Eisenhower's copy of this message indicated that General Gruenther was "to personally advise Mr. Moch that the word 'official' should preceed 'circulation' in [the] first para[graph]."
[3] The C in C, Allied Army Forces, Central Europe, was General Alphonse Pierre Juin; the C in C, Allied Air Forces, for the same region was General Lauris Norstad (see nos. 16 and 77). On March 20 Eisenhower had designated Vice-Admiral Robert Jaujard as Flag Officer, Central Europe. His responsibilities would include the Allied naval patrol on the Rhine (*New York Times*, Mar. 21, 1951). Jaujard, who had commanded French warships in both world wars, had been commander of the French Home Fleet in 1947 and 1948. He was Flag Officer of the Western Union Defense Council from 1948 until he received his NATO command.

[4] In his directive to General Juin (Mar. 29, 1951, EM) Eisenhower had authorized him to "direct and control the land operations within the Central European area, in close and continuous cooperation . . . with combat commanders of land forces and National Commanders of land forces in areas adjacent to your combat zone." Eisenhower's directive to Admiral Jaujard (Mar. 29) is also in EM.

[5] Eisenhower would send the same letter to other defense ministers (see, for example, Eisenhower to Shinwill, Mar. 30, 1951, EM). On April 4 (EM) Eisenhower would tell Moch that he appreciated having Vice-Admiral André Georges Lemonnier available as his naval deputy (see nos. 77 and 149).

109   *Eisenhower Mss.*

To James William Fulbright   *March 30, 1951*

Dear Senator Fulbright:[1] It would be difficult for me to express the fullness of my agreement with your sentiments in the speech reported in the NEW YORK TIMES on Wednesday, March 28th.[2] Incidentally, I wonder whether you noticed that, on the same page of the NEW YORK TIMES, there was the story by Gladwin Hill[3] from which I quote the first paragraph:

"The rise in illegal border-crossing by Mexican 'wetbacks' to a current rate of more than 1,000,000 cases a year has been accompanied by a curious relaxation in ethical standards extending all the way from the farmer-exploiters of this contraband labor to the highest levels of the Federal Government."[4]

There are so many specific points in your talk to which I am moved to say, "Amen," that the only thing I can say is that, as a citizen, I am truly grateful you made your talk. As to the suspicion that you may be called naive,[5] I have so often had this adjective applied to myself and for such odd reasons, that I have come to look upon it as a very distinct compliment; at the very least, it would seem to imply the opposite of deliberate racketeering.[6]

With warm personal regard,[7] *Cordially*

[1] Senator Fulbright (a Democrat from Arkansas) was chairman of a Senate subcommittee then investigating the lending practices of the RFC (for background on the investigation see nos. 75 and 95).
[2] On March 27 Fulbright had urged Congress to establish a commission on ethics in government. According to the senator, the RFC investigations had uncovered many instances of unethical conduct by government officials who had accepted gifts and favors from private individuals for special consideration in the granting of federal loans. The senator had asked, "How do we deal with those who, under the guise of friendship, accept favors which offend the spirit of the law, but do not violate its letter?" He suggested that a commission of nonpoliticians be created to examine the practices of the government, make recommendations concerning ethi-

cal standards, serve as "a catalytic agent . . . to draw forth meaning from the mass of data revealed . . . [and] strengthen the faith of all decent men in our democratic society" (see *New York Times*, Mar. 28, 1951).

[3] Hill had headed the Los Angeles bureau of the *New York Times* since 1946. During World War II he had been the first reporter to fly into Germany on an American bombing raid and had filed the first eye-witness story of the 1944 Normandy invasion. Hill's piece on illegal Mexican aliens appeared in the same issue but not on the same page as the article concerning Fulbright's suggestions (see *ibid.*).

[4] This quotation is from the third in a five-part series of articles by Hill on the effects of illegal Mexican immigration into the United States. This installment concerned the laxity with which the laws were being enforced (see *ibid.*, Mar. 27, 1951).

[5] In his address to Congress Fulbright had said that he was prepared to be dubbed naive because of his proposal and was certain that "to expect . . . improvement in the moral climate at Washington" would be looked upon as "thoroughly Utopian" (see *ibid.*, Mar. 28, 1951).

[6] The majority of this letter, including all of this paragraph, would be quoted in Drew Pearson's *Washington Post* column of June 6, 1951. Pearson introduced the long excerpts with "It has never been made public, but General Eisenhower has written 'amen' to Senator Fulbright's plan for drawing up a moral code for Government conduct" (see clipping in EM, same file as document. On Pearson see no. 84).

[7] Following Fulbright's introduction on March 27 of a resolution for the establishment of a commission on ethics, the Senate would form a subcommittee to investigate the proposal. This subcommittee of the Committee on Labor and Public Welfare would in turn recommend the formation of a fifteen-member commission on ethics in government to be established by a joint resolution of Congress (see *New York Times*, Mar. 29, Apr. 3, June 4, 20, July 1, 3, 23, Oct. 6, 8, 10, 18, 1951; U.S. Congress, Senate, Subcommittee of the Committee on Labor and Public Welfare, *Establishment of a Commission on Ethics in Government: Hearings on Resolution 21*, 82d Cong., 1st sess., 1951, pp. 1–6; and *ibid.*, *Ethical Standards in Government: Report*, 82d Cong., 1st sess., 1951, pp. 1–2). In a reply of April 4 (EM) Fulbright said that both he and Senator Paul Howard Douglas (Ph.D. Columbia 1921), a Democrat from Illinois who would chair the subcommittee on ethics, hoped soon to discuss with the General the lack of inspired leadership in either party.

110   *Eisenhower Mss.*

To WILLIAM EDWARD ROBINSON   *March 30, 1951*

Dear Bill:[1] When you have the opportunity please tell Walter Lippman[2] that in his N.Y. Tribune column of 22 March I found more sense and wise observation than I've seen for a long time. I particularly like his insistence upon good sense and the long view in determination of policy as opposed to the futile attempt to ride the popularity wave. Also give him my warm greetings.[3]

All the best—[4]

[1] For background on Robinson see nos. 83 and 101.
[2] Walter Lippman*n* (B.A. Harvard 1910) was a columnist for the *New York Herald Tribune* (for background see Galambos, *Chief of Staff*, no. 699).
[3] The article, entitled "The Big Spotlight," which had appeared in the March 24 Paris edition of the *International Herald Tribune*, concerned public reaction to national events. Lippmann had written, "The business of a democracy cannot be conducted successfully if public men come to depend on spasms of passionate popular feeling. The spasms do not last long enough." The Korean War and the recent Senate investigations into racketeering and the RFC were three matters requiring sustained efforts, according to Lippmann. Policy had to be formulated with long-range considerations in mind. It was, as well, the responsibility of individuals in high places to set a standard of "honor and honesty and decorum," and if that standard were high, the public would provide sustained support for their efforts. For background on the Kefauver crime investigation see no. 95; on the RFC investigation see no. 75.
[4] A notation on the copy of this document in EM indicates that Eisenhower wrote the original by hand.

111   *Eisenhower Mss.*

To Omar Nelson Bradley   *March 30, 1951*
Personal

Dear Brad: For some time, I have had it in mind to write you a record of developments in the SHAPE project. One difficulty has been a woeful lack of visible progress, and another has been personal preoccupation with problems that, at times, seem so petty and unnecessary as to be completely irritating. Then, of course, I knew that you saw the letter I wrote to General Marshall, which gave our story for the first two or three weeks that I was here.[1]

This letter will contain references to a few of our difficulties. Some of them are small caliber, but it seems very important that the principal figures in NATO guard against the destruction of the whole program through the piling up of a record of inconsequential and useless items of *negative* evidence.

I found, when I came here and got down to work, that there were a number of things still unsolved or not touched upon that I had supposed had already been accomplished. For example, the ratios of national contributions to meet the relatively inconsequential costs of establishing several sets of operating headquarters in Europe is not agreed upon.[2] Some may feel that this is not a serious matter when, as yet, there are few forces to command, and even the most effective control, in time of emergency, would add little to the efficiency of defense. However, I have learned through the press that, within a couple of weeks, bills and proposals of the greatest importance to NATO will be before the United States Congress.[3] If Committees should then ask *you*—as a key figure in this whole affair—for a recital of accomplishments *since* last January that would tend to confirm the belief that the NATO nations were pushing ahead, abreast and aggressively, for the meeting of their obligations under the Treaty, you would probably have an embarrassingly small number to exhibit. When they asked for evidence to the contrary, you'd have to say that some of them seemed very fearful of helping out even in little things.

So far as SHAPE is concerned, a broad system of organization has been agreed upon, and generally capable officers have been supplied us for most positions.[4] But none of these can do really effective work until the necessary machinery is set up, and each headquarters has an official and personal home that is something more than hotel rooms in a big city.

I do not need to recite to you how much popular resentment was created in Britain by the Fechteler announcement.[5] While I think that, through a number of circumstances, that storm has temporarily, and at least partially, abated, it is another indication of how little has been done by national leadership to sell a full-out, healthy support for the NATO conception. In this field, moreover, my own headquarters and all attached to us have to move with the greatest circumspection because another item for governmental and non-governmental concern has been the fear that SHAPE might get into the field of political statement and propaganda. I'm pinning some hopes on the Information Service of the Committee of Deputies—but it's only a hope at the best![6]

In this country, where the French Central Government has been extremely helpful and sympathetic, we had an instance the other day that is indicative of the lack of popular understanding of what we are about. The City of Paris owns a piece of ground on which the French Government hoped to start a housing development, the dwellings on which would be first rented by the members of this Allied Staff. The piece of ground is out in the country, across the road from where our headquarters has begun to go up. While there were technical difficulties involved, these, the Government assured, could be worked out; yet, the City Council voted 45 to 15 against allowing the Government to have the ground. And the principal speech made against the project was that the ground should not be allocated to this use by "American" officers![7]

The failure of the Deputies to agree on the proportion of overhead expenses that should be assumed by each country is, to my mind, a circumstance that could certainly be used by opponents to make it appear as reflective of a determination to "soak Uncle Sam."[8] The expenses of headquarters, communications, transportation, clerks, secretaries, rentals, buildings, and everything else, will come during the next two years to a fairly sizeable amount. Yet this sum, *compared to what the United States has already engaged to spend in this gigantic effort, is so inconsequential as almost to create a resentment that it should ever be allowed to become a problem.* We hear rumors that certain representatives are expressing fears that they "will not have an opportunity to review SHAPE's budget," and others are expressing some criticism of "large headquarters." Actually, we have not only invited American and other budget officials to look over our estimates, but, in the matter of numbers, I have fixed an arbitrary limit for the first year of 200 officers for SHAPE itself; this, in spite of the fact that already the senior foreign officers I have put in key positions are complaining that it is impossible to do the work with the numbers allotted. The smallest preorganizational estimate of our minimum need was 561.

Obviously, in an organization which is far more of a mere conception than it is of a real organism, it is necessary to trust somebody, or no action will be taken. Realization of this truth was apparently the reason for deciding to set up a Supreme Command before there was much to command.

Of course, I would not have you think that the record to date is exclusively one of frustration and inaction. Entirely aside from the increased defense structures already voted in the United Kingdom, Belgium, Holland, and Norway,[9] we have pleasant and profitable connections with the French Government; we have been intelligently supported by the British Chiefs of Staff as well as other military people with whom we have come in contact. We have collected a very good staff composed, with few exceptions, of capable officers. (It will take a little bit of diplomacy to get rid of the others.) Construction of our headquarters has been started by the French Government[10] and though, as I understand it, we are now completely out of cash, we are hopeful that additional amounts will be provided before the contractor goes broke.

Britain has sent the Eleventh Armored Division to Germany, where it will close[11] early in April; I shall go to see it soon thereafter.

While it is true that both you and I have testified that the real reason for this effort is the lack of an acceptable alternative, I think it is clear that, without the needed spirit of devotion and urgency on this side of the water, it would be silly for America to pour billions of equipment money into the region.

Actually, a thousand small indications tend to show that understanding and morale are going up. But we need dynamic, steady, and *visible* progress; nothing less will do. Leadership in all nations is needed—and I personally believe that, though men in uniform may have to maintain public silence on some of these matters, they are the only ones who can educate and inspire our civil leaders.

The NAT Organization must learn to put real trust and authority in its organized bodies. From my viewpoint, most important of these is the Standing Group. A reasonable sum to cover field overhead and organizational costs for a year or so should be set up under the Standing Group, and its approval should be all that is necessary for expenditure. Otherwise, we will certainly pile up a useless and silly record of frustration that will have a tremendous effect on the great issues involved. Maybe you can start something rolling.

Our contacts with all the mass of American officials in Europe are the best. This includes also the people who have come over to see us. Webb and Cabot were here only the other day, while Sherman was particularly understanding and helpful.[12] Incidentally, I think more of him every time I see him, and I have known him for quite a number of years.[13] *Cordially*

---

[1] The letter to Secretary of Defense George C. Marshall is no. 77.

[2] For background see no. 77, n. 2. The NAC deputies had not yet agreed upon a method for apportioning the construction and operating costs of the various NATO headquarters. On March 31 SHAPE would submit an interim budget to the Standing Group for its approval, and on April 4 representatives of the Standing Group and SHAPE would meet with the NAC deputies in an unsuccessful attempt to resolve the problem. The deputies would refuse to authorize any interim advances to SHAPE until the cost-sharing principles had been agreed upon (D-R [51] 25, Apr. 6, 1951, and D-D [51] 91, Apr. 6, 1951, NATO Files, microfilm). The disagreement would continue (see no. 167).

[3] On April 4 the Senate would vote on a resolution concerning the proposed shipment of four American Army divisions to Europe (see no. 128). On April 26 President Truman would recommend that Congress extend and broaden the Defense Production Act of 1950, a Korean War measure. On May 24 Truman would also send to Congress his proposed Mutual Security Program (*Public Papers of the Presidents: Truman, 1951*, pp. 244–53, 302–13). Most of the assistance requested by Truman under the Mutual Security Program would be for military equipment destined for the NATO nations (*ibid.*, p. 303; see also nos. 2, 68, 286, and 290).

[4] See nos. 77 and 85.

[5] For background see no. 45, n. 8.

[6] On March 7 British Prime Minister Clement Attlee (see no. 45, n. 8) had complained about the "very large information staff" reported to be planned for SHAPE. Attlee told the U.S. Ambassador to the United Kingdom that "he felt there was real question as to [the] desirability of SHAPE engaging in psychological warfare activities; that conduct of psychological warfare by army officers might cause resentment among civilian populations in continental countries and might be construed as having [a] too pronounced American flavor" (State, *Foreign Relations, 1951*, vol. III, *European Security and the German Question, Part I*, pp. 88–89). On March 13 the NAC deputies had clarified the role of the SHAPE public information staff: it was to provide only a standard public relations campaign and troop information and education. SHAPE was not to engage in psychological warfare (D-R [51] 20, Mar. 13, 1951, NATO Files, microfilm).

For background on the NATO Information Service see no. 77, n. 3; see also D-D/187, Nov. 20, 1950, NATO Files, microfilm; Robert S. Jordan, *The NATO International Staff/Secretariat, 1952–1957: A Study in International Administration* (London, 1967), pp. 175–76; and Ismay, *NATO*, pp. 154–56, 184. Although NATO's

Information Service was charged with the task of promoting and coordinating the release of information about NATO activities, the responsibility for public information programs remained with the NATO member governments.

[7] For background on SHAPE's plans to have a housing project built on property owned by the city of Paris see no. 68, n. 5. A housing project for SHAPE officers ("SHAPE Village") would open in October. It would be built on land obtained from the French government and located eight miles from SHAPE (*New York Times*, Oct. 31, 1951; see also no. 395).

[8] See n. 2 above.

[9] Aspects of the British rearmament program are covered in nos. 16 and 98. In February Britain's Labour government had proposed a 23 percent increase in defense expenditures for 1951-52. The government had survived a vote of confidence on the issue in Parliament on February 15 (*New York Times*, Feb. 16, 17, 1951; see also State, *Foreign Relations, 1951*, vol. IV, *Europe: Political and Economic Developments, Part I*, pp. 911-14).

The Belgians had recently increased their term of military service (see nos. 56 and 126; see also *New York Times*, Mar. 7, 22, 1951). On April 16, however, Robert D. Murphy, the U.S. Ambassador to Belgium (see no. 16, n. 9), would publicly criticize the Belgian defense effort (State, *Foreign Relations, 1951*, vol. IV, *Europe: Political and Economic Developments, Part I*, pp. 273-74. See also *ibid.*, vol. III, *European Security and the German Question, Part I*, pp. 183-84; and Cabot to Burns, Feb. 23, 1951, OS/D, 1951, Clas. Decimal File, CD 091.7 Europe).

For background on the Dutch defense effort see nos. 14, 15, and 16. Soon after Eisenhower's visit to the Netherlands in January the Dutch cabinet had agreed upon a 76 percent increase in the defense budget and a corresponding increase in the size of the army (*New York Times*, Feb. 21, Mar. 18, 1951).

In February Norwegian Defense Minister Jens Christian Hauge (see no. 16, n. 15) had presented a new and more vigorous defense program to the Storting, the Norwegian parliament. These measures, which the Norwegian cabinet had approved, envisioned a budget increase of 112 percent and a 30 percent increase in the number of men under arms. The Storting would enact these proposals, together with an increase in the term of military service, in May and June (Senate Subcommittee on Foreign Relations, *United States Foreign Aid Programs in Europe: Hearings*, 1951, p. 99; *New York Times*, Feb. 22, May 22, 1951).

[10] For background see nos. 45 and 68, n. 4. Construction of the headquarters buildings would be completed in the summer, and Eisenhower would move there in July (see no. 281, n. 4).

[11] To "close" is to bring the tail of a military column into an area.

[12] For background on James Edwin Webb, Under Secretary of State since 1949, see Galambos, *Columbia University*, nos. 296 and 443. On Thomas D. Cabot, Director of the State Department's International Security Affairs Office since December 1950, see no. 30, n. 2, in this volume. Webb and Cabot had recently spent two days in Paris and had met informally with General Eisenhower (see State, *Foreign Relations, 1951*, vol. III, *European Security and the German Question, Part I*, pp. 103-5). On Chief of Naval Operations Forrest P. Sherman's meeting with Eisenhower see nos. 53, n. 4, and 57, n. 3.

[13] Bradley's reply of April 12 is in EM. He would assure Eisenhower that efforts were being made in his behalf, and he would sympathize with Eisenhower's difficulties: "I know of no one who is as well qualified to get things going or who would command the respect of the European people as much as you do. I must confess that at times during the war some of our allies sorely taxed my patience, but you always seem to be able to straighten them out" (see also Bradley and Blair, *A General's Life*, p. 646).

To Lucius Du Bignon Clay   *March 30, 1951*

Dear Lucius: On the basis of the understanding outlined in your letter
of March 26th, I have no objection to being named, for the next year,
as one of the members of the corporation of the Crusade for Freedom.
Since it appears, from your letter, that you are to belong to it for one
year only, I would not want to engage myself for a longer term.[1]

Thanks for sending along to me the note from Jack Franklin. I shall
write to him this morning.[2]

In thinking over this whole program of collective security, and the
plan on which the United States has embarked, I am frequently puzzled by the fact that so few people seem to do any real thinking about
the matter. This even includes, I think, the need for stating the proposition in such terms that the ordinary man can understand our purpose, the obstacles to be encountered, and the broad plan we have for
overcoming those obstacles.[3]

For example, in a current argument, we have finally come to fighting merely about "arms for Europe" and we are for or against the
proposition according to some preconceived notion or because of our
faith in someone who does a lot of talking on one side or the other.
Actually, we get down to the point where we talk about this thing in
forms of 4 divisions, or of 10 divisions, or of some other figure, just as
if anyone in the world, including the most brilliant tactician, could
now make this kind of decision with any semblance of wisdom or of
common sense.[4]

Certainly, the basic assumption of our whole program is that the
retention of the European complex in the free world is vital to America's prosperity and safety—even her very existence as a free nation.
The next assumption is that, if Europe is helped sufficiently to regain
her own confidence and morale and build her initial forces, she can
permanently defend *herself*. (It is clear that no principal portion of the
world can be constantly defended by forces furnished from another
portion of the world.)

In this particular situation, the question becomes as to how to fix
or to state our assistance plan so that every person can struggle toward
a definite objective and yet *not* state the problem in such terms as to
ignore our basic purpose which is to re-create the morale that will
insure the *self*-defense of Europe.[5]

I am not going to run on at great length to explain my ideas to you
because, from what I have read of your statements, we are in accord.
But I have very definitely pondered the wisdom of working out for
ourselves a rough limitation measured in *time*. The fixing of a goal in
terms of time, rather than of *scope* of effort, would seem to me to serve

simultaneously the purpose of building morale and of assuring the earliest possible physical defense of this region. Moreover, this particular equation should be capable of at least approximate solution. We know what the needs are in Europe in the way of developing training cadres, training camps, and equipment, of organizing active units, and in producing reserve units that, in this situation, must be a very critical part of the whole defense structure.

Such an approach would possibly make sense to me; but the effort to fix an *exact limit on the scope of assistance* quite palpably ignores the over-riding importance of the morale factor and, moreover, tends to ignore whatever danger the immediate future has for all of us.[6]

There is no use saying any more. You see what I mean.

Give my love to Marjorie and tell her that I am quite sure Mamie is going to be most envious when I tell her about the twins. If her complacency is sufficiently jarred, I imagine that I will hear some dark and far from subtle observations and comments about the peculiar quality of her own grandchildren, which goes a long ways to make up for the lack of quantity. (Don't pass this particular one on to Marjorie, else we will start a trans-Atlantic essay contest on the virtues of our respective prodigies!!!)[7]

With all the best, *Cordially*

---

[1] For background on Clay and his request that Eisenhower serve as a corporate member of the Crusade for Freedom see no. 86. In his letter of March 26 (EM) Clay had assured the General that he would not be required to participate actively on the Crusade's board of directors and that he would be expected to withdraw from the post if it in any way adversely affected his SHAPE duties. Clay had written, "You are so identified with the Crusade that if you left it I am afraid it would cast doubt on our program." See also Galambos, *Columbia University*, nos. 739 and 994. For developments see *New York Times*, May 3, September 4, 1951.

[2] John Merryman Franklin, president of the New York-based passenger ship company United States Lines, had been a brigadier general and Assistant Chief of Transportation, War Department, during World War II (see Chandler, *War Years*, no. 2101). His letter of February 7, 1951, offering the Eisenhowers passage to Europe aboard the *America* and Eisenhower's reply of March 31, 1951, are both in EM. Clay, who had been given Franklin's letter to convey to Eisenhower in February, had not seen the General before his departure for Europe (Clay to Eisenhower, Mar. 26, 1951, EM).

[3] For background on Eisenhower's testimony before Congress on the importance of collective security see no. 23.

[4] For background on the Great Debate in Europe over assignment of U.S. troops to Europe see nos. 23, 63, and 84; and n. 6 below. For Eisenhower's testimony in opposition to strict numerical limits for the U.S. divisions to be sent to Europe see Senate Committee on Foreign Relations and Committee on Armed Services, *Assignment of Ground Forces of the United States to Duty in the European Area*, 1951, pp. 34–35, 475–77.

[5] See no. 23.

[6] Following an Easter recess, Congress would once again resume debate on the troops issue, with Republican senators seeking to obtain veto power in the matter.

Led by Senators Robert Taft and Homer Ferguson (a Republican from Michigan), the anti-Administration group sought a joint resolution vesting control of the force assignments in Congress, not in the presidency (see *New York Times*, Mar. 26, 31, 1951). For developments see no. 111.

[7] In his letter of the twenty-sixth Clay had written that he and his wife Marjorie had recently been made grandparents for the fourth and fifth times by the birth of twin girls to their son and daughter-in-law. On the Eisenhowers' grandchildren, Barbara Anne and Dwight David Eisenhower II, see nos. 24 and 82, n. 2.

113   *Eisenhower Mss.*

To Clifford Roberts   *March 30, 1951*

Dear Cliff:[1] Thanks very much for your note about the Jamboree. It made me homesick—I just cannot tell you how much I miss my spring visit to Augusta—a visit that I have now made three years running, and which has really become the highlight of my year.[2]

As I remember, our Greek syndicate didn't do too well last year, and we ended up with a small net loss. Nevertheless, I am delighted to have a 5% interest in it and only trust that I will have enough in the way of assets to meet any obligations that this rash commitment involves.[3]

I think I shall send this letter directly on to Augusta in the hope that it will reach you there, and you can give my greetings to those of my old friends that you will see. Among the members, I do not need to name anyone, because all of my good friends are likewise close to you. But I would be glad if you would particularly remember the local ones, including Bobby Jones, Dick Garlington, Jerry Franklin, Gummy Harrison, Howard Creel, and, of course, Bob Woodruff if he drops in.[4] Among the professionals, I don't know any of them too well outside our old friend Ed Dudley, but I was impressed by Ben Hogan, Gene Sarazen, and, by all means, our good friend Nelson.[5] I know that all of you will have a wonderful time, and I hope that the Greek syndicate has about five of the top money winners.[6]

With all the best, *Cordially*

[1] For background on Roberts see no. 7.

[2] The jamboree golf tournament at Augusta National Golf Club, Augusta, Georgia, had been held earlier in March. In a letter of March 26 (EM) Roberts had written Eisenhower about the results of the tournament. "The old guard," he said, "came through in splendid shape" (see no. 95; and correspondence in EM, Subject File, Clubs and Associations. For background on Eisenhower and Augusta National see Galambos, *Columbia University*).

[3] The "Greek syndicate," a group of Eisenhower's friends at Augusta National, speculated on who would be the top players in the annual Masters Tournament.

This event, which included both professional and amateur players, would be held April 5-8.

[4] Robert Tyre Jones, Jr., was president of Augusta National and one of golf's all-time greats. Thomas Richard Garlington, Jerome A. Franklin, William Montgomery Harison, and Robert Winship Woodruff were all members of the club (see Galambos, *Columbia University*, nos. 829, 1107, 423, 416, and 656, respectively). Howard W. Creel, of Houston, Texas, was also a member of Augusta National.

[5] All four were professional golfers. For background on Edward Bishop Dudley, Jr., and Gene Sarazen see Galambos, *Columbia University*, nos. 416 and 838. Ben Hogan had won both the American Open and the British and had placed second in the Masters Tournament several times (see *New York Times*, Aug. 9, 1953). Byron Nelson, another top professional, had achieved a record of eleven consecutive wins in 1945 (see *ibid.*, Sept. 21, 1952; Feb. 18, 1973).

[6] Ben Hogan would win the Masters Tournament (see telegram, Roberts to Eisenhower, Apr. 8, 1951, EM). On April 9 (EM) Eisenhower would wire his congratulations to the "Greeks" and "hurrahs for Champion Ben." For the choices of the "Greek syndicate" see EM, Roberts Corr. Eisenhower would receive a check for eighty-two dollars, his 5 percent share of the profits (see no. 147).

In a handwritten note at the bottom of this letter the General wrote: "A special 'How' to 'Bud.' " Bud was Lewis Bergman Maytag, a past president of the Maytag Company, who had retired in 1926. He was also a vice-president and member of the executive committee at Augusta National (see Galambos, *Columbia University*, no. 724).

114   *Eisenhower Mss.*

To ARTHUR HAYS SULZBERGER   *March 31, 1951*

Dear Arthur:[1] It is, of course, evident that the Chairman's attitude toward acceptance of an honorary degree is founded in deep conviction. He, more than most of us, is concerned with matters of precedent and tradition. Consequently, he may feel that the contemplated action in this case could break down a wall that would thereafter continue to crumble until finally some future action could be so extreme as to be ridiculous.

Now, you and I, of course, believe that Columbia chooses as its Trustees men who would never give way to this kind of thing, but I certainly feel that, if one of the proposed recipients has such a deep feeling about this matter as has been expressed to you by Mr. Coykendall—then the only thing to do is to drop the whole affair. I remember that, when it was first suggested, it seemed to me like a most thoughtful and courteous thing to do—but we must respect the Chairman's feelings.[2]

Some days ago, I saw a bit of a squib in one of my papers saying that Harold Stassen has asked Winston Churchill to come to the United States. I have forgotten whether it was a date anywhere near the one for which we asked him to come to the United States, but I am quite helpless to venture any reason for his accepting such an invitation as that, after declining one that came from you, with your intimate association in the publication of his books; and from me, with my background of long association with him during the war. So, in answer to your question, I would be "nonplussed," and possibly that is not a strong enough word.[3]

Before he left for Yugoslavia and Greece, I had a couple of very interesting talks with young Cy. I have found him a very well informed fellow, and certainly lots of fun.[4] *Cordially*

[1] Sulzberger was the publisher of the *New York Times*, a trustee of Columbia University, and chairman of the university Honors Committee (for background see Galambos, *Columbia University*).

[2] In a letter of March 27 (EM) Sulzberger had informed the General that a move to award honorary degrees to Columbia's five senior trustees had met with the disapproval of the proposed recipients. Chairman of the trustees Frederick Coykendall had threatened either to refuse the honor or to resign his position with the university if the plan were not canceled. For background on Coykendall and the other senior trustees, Marcellus Hartley Dodge, Willard Vinton King, Frederic René Coudert, and Albert William Putnam, see Galambos, *Columbia University*.

On April 3 (EM), the day following the next trustees' meeting, Sulzberger wrote to Eisenhower, "Napoleon had an army of a hundred thousand men. He marched them up the hill and then he marched them down again! . . . We voted to rescind the action that was taken at the previous meeting." See also Sulzberger to Eisenhower, February 27, 1951, and Sulzberger to Eisenhower, March 20, 1951, both in EM.

[3] In his letter of the twenty-seventh Sulzberger had asked Eisenhower how he felt about Winston Churchill's apparent acceptance of an invitation from Harold Stassen to visit the United States. For background on the earlier invitations from Eisenhower and the publisher see no. 120; and *New York Times*, March 22, 1951. On Stassen see no. 63. The *New York Times* had published excerpts of Churchill's multivolume history of World War II (see Galambos, *Columbia University*, nos. 114, 366, 996, and 1109. For Eisenhower's association with Churchill during World War II see Chandler, *War Years*).

[4] Sulzberger's nephew Cyrus Leo Sulzberger II (B.S. Harvard 1934) was the chief foreign correspondent of the *New York Times*. During January 1951 the younger Sulzberger had contacted Eisenhower to arrange an interview and had visited the General in Paris during early March (see appointment calendar; and correspondence in EM, same file as document). He subsequently published two articles, the first on Eisenhower's positive influence on the morale of Western Europe since his assumption of the NATO command, the second a character study of the General and an account of the development of SHAPE (see *New York Times*, Mar. 12, 1951, and *New York Times Magazine*, Mar. 25, 1951, respectively).

2

Assuming Command

Eisenhower Mss.

To William Averell Harriman   *April 2, 1951*
Secret

Dear Averell: This particular letter will be directed more toward some
of our frustrating experiences than it will toward the brighter things.[1]
The reason for this is to illustrate the necessity for unremitting work
in the twelve NATO countries to insure the only kind of unity that can
make the organization a success—the unity based on a common comprehension of our purposes, our problems, and the most effective ways
of solving them.

So far as the American groups and officials in Europe are concerned, my relations have been, from my viewpoint, perfect. I like
them all and think they are doing good jobs. Chiefs of Staffs in all
countries have been the same, as has the French Government. Moreover, I still believe that, among *most* European people, there is a
growing determination to do something effective in their own defense.
But I do have some concern about a record of frustration and inaction,
often in mean, petty, and inconsequential problems, of which the
accumulated effect can be next to disastrous.

I came to Europe laboring under a misunderstanding, in that I
thought much had already been accomplished in the way of over-all
agreement concerning numerous details of collective administration
that, in fact, had never been touched upon at all. As I go along and
find cropping up, here and there, evidence of a quick readiness to be
critical, or to hold back needed confidence, or to be watchful in the
matter of comparative sacrifices no matter how tiny these may be, I
have a keen realization that the key figures in this whole movement
had better seek a common understanding of the factors involved or,
frankly, collective security will not have a chance in the world.

Of course, there is a specific record of accomplishment over the past
two months, particularly in the form of legislative action in Britain,
Holland, Belgium, and Norway.[2] Moreover, there are other material
signs of progress, some of it on the significant side. Included in this
category is the arrival in Germany of a new British Division.[3] But
there is, on the other hand, accumulating a list of negative items—
some of which, I believe, grows out of a lack of day by day effort and
sense of urgency on the part of political leaders in European nations.

As a soldier in uniform, I observe strict limitations upon the kind
of activity in which I personally engage, especially in public. I can
take up non-military things with friends in each of the governments as
I visit them, but this is not good enough. We must have a dynamic
and forceful campaign of enlightenment of all NATO populations, and
this means that the inspiration must come largely from civilian sources.

An important case of the kind I refer to was the reaction to Fechteler's appointment.[4] And, in the ensuing conversations with some principal officials in this region, I found that there existed a feeling of resentment because of the charge that the United States was concerned in seizing positions of authority and influence. This was shocking to me for the simple reason that it does not appear to be in keeping with our feeling as to the seriousness of the world threat, or a desire to get ahead with the establishing of a common security, ignoring national jealousies, and such things as details of command and staff arrangements.

Some of these things are irritating *because* they are useless. The idea of urgency seems to be completely refuted. The Council of Deputies cannot even agree on a ratio of cost sharing for the relatively insignificant amount that will be required for the establishment of headquarters and communication lines in this region.[5] (I know that the American representative has worked hard on this matter, but has gotten nowhere.)[6] My point is that this item is so small as compared to the tremendous amounts that America (and Britain) are putting into the affair that the very worst kind of interpretation can be made of the refusal to agree.

In spite of my decision to organize this headquarters on such an austerity basis that every experienced staff officer and associate has thrown up his hands in horror, we hear rumors that some of the national representatives on the London Council of Deputies are quite worried about the great size of the staff we are building up and of our intention, therefore, to get into things that cannot possibly concern us—to wit, propaganda or political doctrine!!!

As to size, what do amateurs know about it? As to the function that seems to cause such concern, if we are so stupid as to fail to understand that an American in Europe, where the practice of socialism daily increases, cannot publicly uphold the social and political principles that he has been taught to respect and revere, then why was SHAPE established? But, on the other hand, if there is to be any esprit de corps within the forces of this command, it is certain that we cannot escape our responsibility of exploiting every means by which the understanding and fervor of those forces can be heightened. This includes the stressing to our soldiers of *basic* political and social objectives of free countries. Such a picayunish criticism (important only because it was repeated, in one case at least, by the Prime Minister of Britain) cannot fail to imply that there is no real understanding of the vital issues at stake.[7]

The French Government itself has been very cooperative, but the obstacles we have found in trying to get irritating housekeeping problems out of the way have been indicative of an indifference in quarters where it would be least expected. For example, an owner of a race horse establishment refused to rent to us a small, vacant field on which to build our headquarters because he thought that the future racing of horses would be more important. We particularly wanted his place because it lent itself to the building of both a peacetime and operational headquarters. The Paris Council voted 45 to 15 against allowing the Federal Government to use a piece of ground it owned in the country (and of which no use is being made) because "there was no need to allocate ground for the use of *American* officers."[8] This is the kind of thing that you and I must brush aside, and say to ourselves that we must not allow it to bother us, but some will exaggerate this meaning.

We hear that we are soon to get a blast from De Gaulle because there are not more French officers in positions of high command and control.[9] To everybody, I've urged the need for publicly insisting upon regarding command positions as national *responsibilities*, not kudos!

The setting up of SHAPE seemed to be an acknowledgment by NATO nations that committees cannot handle critical questions when time is important, so it seemed implied that any executive solution developed by a commander (so long as it was reasonably fair and violated no established policy) would be approved by the multiplicity of agencies that have been established under the name of NATO. Moreover, I thought there was, in each country, an enthusiastic national leadership that would *constantly be working at the chore of enlightening all people of the issues at stake, the obstacles to success, the concept in which this organization was devised, and the need for unity.*

I understand that soon major bills will be before our Congress and that these bills will determine the fate, at least so far as United States support is concerned, of this whole venture.[10] When Congress begins to ask for evidence of the increasing and growing morale that all of us have agreed is the sole guarantee of future success, we must be sure that a public record of shortsightedness in details will not rise up to obscure either broad purpose or a solid but unspectacular record of accomplishment.

I repeat again that I see no *acceptable* alternative for the free nations to developing real, collective security. So, there must be some way of getting over to our associated populations a realization that we need a constantly applied leadership in the business of informing our own peoples concerning NATO. You will know the appropriate means of putting this over to all governments far better than I. But I am sure there is no time to waste.

Success in the NATO purpose is attainable—the only thing we need is hard enough work by enough people in the right places!

My continuing respects to the President, and warm regard to yourself.[11] *Cordially*

[1] Eisenhower had sent a similar letter to Chairman of the Joint Chiefs of Staff Omar Bradley (see no. 111). This was Eisenhower's first day at work after assuming command (see no. 99, n. 7).

[2] See no. 111, n. 9.

[3] This was the British 11th Armoured Division (see no. 111, n. 11).

[4] For background on the controversy over the nationality of the Supreme Allied Commander, Atlantic, see nos. 45, n. 8, and 52, n. 3.

[5] For background on the NAC deputies' deadlock over the question of a cost-sharing formula for SHAPE expenditures see no. 111, n. 2.

[6] The American representative and chairman of the NAC deputies was Charles M. Spofford (see no. 16, n. 16).

[7] See no. 111, n. 6.

[8] SHAPE had originally planned to construct its headquarters buildings on a part of a breeding farm near Versailles owned by a wealthy French industrialist. These plans had been abandoned after Eisenhower's exploratory trip to Europe in January (*International Herald Tribune*, Paris ed., Feb. 22, 1951; see also no. 45, n. 6). For details on Eisenhower's unsuccessful attempt to obtain land from the Paris municipal government see no. 111.

[9] On Eisenhower's stormy relationship with French wartime leader Charles André Joseph Marie de Gaulle see Chandler, *War Years*; and Chandler and Galambos, *Occupation, 1945*. After World War II de Gaulle had briefly led the French people as president of the government, minister of national defense, and head of the armies. In 1946 he had gone into political opposition as head of the Rassemblement du Peuple Français (Rally of the People of France, or RPF) (see no. 318). In March an RPF deputy in the French National Assembly had criticized Eisenhower's command arrangements because they did not give General Juin (Eisenhower's C in C, Allied Army Forces, Central Europe) as much power as Eisenhower had given the Northern European C in C, Admiral Brind (State, *Foreign Relations, 1951*, vol. III, *European Security and the German Question, Part I*, p. 500; see also nos. 77, 99, and 108). On April 2 Douglas MacArthur II, SHAPE's political adviser (see no. 32, n. 3), warned General Gruenther that "De Gaulle will continue to beat the drums over the fact that France is not playing the great role that it should as the leader of European defense. . . . He will endeavor to impress on the electorate that if he comes to power France will be restored to her rightful great historic role etc." (MacArthur to Gruenther, Apr. 2, 1951, Gruenther Papers). On May 1 de Gaulle would call for changes in Eisenhower's command structure before any air bases were built upon French soil (see no. 98). Under de Gaulle's scheme "a French leader" would "command the land, air and naval forces for the whole—the Rhine, the Alps and French North Africa" (*New York Times*, May 2, 1951). Shortly afterward de Gaulle told journalist Cyrus Sulzberger (see no. 114, n. 4) that General Juin should have had naval and air forces included in his command because Juin's central command (which Eisenhower controlled directly) "includes France's special interests and France is the biggest factor in it" (C. L. Sulzberger, *A Long Row of Candles: Memoirs and Diaries [1934-1954]* [New York, 1969], p. 631; see also *New York Times*, May 14, 1951).

[10] See no. 111, n. 3.

[11] In his reply (Apr. 9, 1951, EM) Harriman wrote, "I am sorry you are having so many minor troubles with all the big things you have to do. I hope it's not getting under your skin."

To Joseph Lawton Collins   *April 2, 1951*

Dear Joe:[1] This attempt at personal typing will undoubtedly be characterized by X's and mis-spelling than by any other quality but at
least I have the advantage of privacy while you will not have to undergo the agony of trying to decipher my handwriting (so-called).[2]

My own irritation was no more excusable than was yours—and I
ask your pardon for going temperamental in an affair where even a
moment's reflection would have convinced me that you, of all people,
never intended to be anything but objective and direct.[3]

When I first had word that I might come over here I picked (only
in a mental list) Michaelis as one of the men I would want.[4] This was
partially the result of coincidence, as just at that time I received a
letter from Mary Michaelis; I may even have told her of my intention
of eventually asking for him.[5] In any event, I soon discovered that in
our accumulation of American and foreign staff officers and commanders we did not have a single man who had any experience in
Korea! I have a clear conviction that all of us have too much neglected
guerrilla warfare as well as its hand-maiden, psychological warfare.[6] I
knew that the people in Korea had learned a healthy respect for these
things and Michaelis came instantly to my mind as one to fill a crying
need. Since I wanted someone who, among other things would have to
convince doubters and ritualists I obviously needed someone who had
a fine combat record in conventional war as well as in Asia. Mike
seemed a natural; while of course it was easy for me to think in such
terms because he and I are old friends. (He was once my ADC)[7]

When I told my C/S[8] to start the ball rolling he expressed great
skepticism; saying that MacArthur[9] would release no one from his
theater upon request—insisting that only routine rotation could take
one of his officers away. Al[10] felt that it was hopeless to send in the
request, believing that I would merely embarrass the WD[11] officials,
who, Al knew, would do their best to help me out. So—because of my
long association with MacA (and a real friendship that has persisted
in spite of flareups of various kinds)[12] I said that if anyone was to be
rebuffed it would be I—that I would put my case before MacA and if
he turned me down I'd drop the matter; if he should agree, I'd put
the request before the WD. Frankly, I've never pursued or known any
other to pursue a different practice than that of first determining the
availability of an officer in terms of his own desire and his commander's before asking the WD to start any official proceedings.[13]

In any event, your message through Brooks[14] and Al reached me
during an exhaustive period of argument here about matters so petty,
so inconsequential as compared to the things to which we *should* be

devoting our efforts, that I had the sudden feeling that everybody in the world, including those to whom I'd always given my complete trust and confidence were joining the ranks of those trying to wear us all out with *little* things. I just told Al to say that I was through with the Michaelis case—and I went on home.[15]

Now—with all that out of the way (because I certainly owed to you as an old and valued friend as complete an explanation as you so kindly gave me)[16] the next question is; what now?

I personally think that we should wait until Michaelis comes home in his proper turn because MacA has already been informed of the withdrawal of my request. Beyond this I think the man (Michaelis) has earned the right to express some preference as to assignment and if he would rather stay in the States a while you should tell your personnel office to find me someone else. Beyond this, if you believe that some arrangement that would put Michaelis on the Benning or other job and send me someone who carries enough guns to put over for me the things I alluded to above, why you work it out. Much as I admire Michaelis, and much as I like him personally, I'm not so dumb as to see that it could be better for all of us to accept a second choice on my own job.[17]

As to Lanahan.[18] He was with me during the war and I understand has established a fine record at Monmouth, both as a technician and as an administrator. For that reason I asked him to come over here briefly to advise me on signal matters. This I did after those already here gave me an estimate on the cost of hqrs[19] signal communications that practically floored me—and Al. When Lanahan got all done he gave us a picture that came to about one third of the first estimates. Since one of our fetishes here is austerity organization, I was greatly impressed. That is why I sent him to you with the message he brought,[20] but suspecting that he could easily be designated as the new signal chief . . . I told him that I did not want to get in the Army's way on such a matter and would not put in a formal request until that choice had been announced. In view of what I *think* your letter says I'd like for you to go ahead and process the matter so that he can come over to supervise this costly signal business. (This sentence sounds funny but what I mean to say is that I'm assuming that there is no real chance of his being selected for the job of CSO.)[21]

I should like to have you come over for a visit when you can. We have found that an individual C/S can come here without arousing any great anxiety—but when I meet with any official *group*, then look out for your hat; anything can happen. But I consider it of the utmost importance that the key figures in the several capitals of NATO have a common understanding of some of our problems. We are in a complex business and quite frequently the people who have most at stake seem to be the most complacent. I have searched diligently for any acceptable alternative for the United States to that of taking leadership (and a regrettable burden of cost and effort) in the purpose of insuring the collective security of the North Atlantic community. I can see none, but that does not mean that for that reason alone success will be assured. This we will not have except with effective European cooperation; and our nation will not exert the skillful and determined leadership necessary to bring these separate and sometimes antagonistic countries into a real team except as the mass of our people (and theirs) get a clear understanding of the problem. The mainspring for all this educational process must be provided by service men; even though their responsibility must be exercised only in an advisory capacity to their civilian superiors. They cannot go directly to populations . . . any effort on their part to do so would not be in keeping either with their own desires or with our basic concepts of government—but they will nevertheless have to keep everlastingly after their civilian superiors to work on this or I much fear that the threats and dangers that the poor old world now faces will develop into something so terrifying and tragic as to make decent peace an unattainable goal in our time. This is the reason I attach so much importance to intermittent visits; so that all of us may continue to search our minds and souls together, and make our presentations to civilian governments on the basis of a common understanding and in the spirit of devotion to decency and justice.

It appears that I've almost mounted the pulpit; but Joe, no one could long be on this job without realizing keenly how badly the world needs understanding and leadership that can be trusted; a leadership that will be exerted all the time, every day to get us all to do our jobs in furthering the purpose of common security—today half the world looks upon this venture either as a hopeless and lost cause, a clumsy and ineffectual plan or as some deliberate move on the part of the U.S. to extend her influence and commercial interests in the world. (ALL these are easy prey to the Soviet propaganda.)[22]

Well, this has been something—I've not tackled a typewriter for many years. But if I've made you understand my appreciation of your letter and my own purpose of not allowing fool misunderstandings to occur in the future, it's been worth the time and labor.[23]

Good luck and all the best

---

[1] For background on Army Chief of Staff Collins see no. 52.

[2] For Eisenhower's earlier attempts at typing see Galambos, *Columbia University*, nos. 638 and 741. In accordance with our editorial policy we have corrected the typographical errors that appear in this letter (see Joseph P. Hobbs, "Notes to the Reader," in Chandler, *War Years*, vol. V, p. 2).

[3] In a handwritten letter of March 26, 1951 (EM), Collins had apologized for his

reaction to Eisenhower's request for the transfer of Brigadier General John Hersey Michaelis from the Far East Command (FECOM) to SHAPE.

[4] Since July 1950 Michaelis, then a lieutenant colonel, had led the 27th (Wolfhound) Regiment, 25th Infantry Division, through heavy fighting in Korea. In February 1951 he had become assistant commander of the 25th Infantry Division (see Roy E. Appleman, *South to the Naktong, North to the Yalu [June–November 1950]*, U.S. Army in the Korean War, ed. Stetson Conn [Washington, D.C., 1961], pp. 108, 200–203, 235–39, 243–45, 360–61; J. Lawton Collins, *War in Peacetime: The History and Lessons of Korea* [Boston, 1969], pp. 91, 96, 109; and John H. Michaelis with Bill Davidson, "This We Learned in Korea," *Collier's*, Aug. 18, 1951, 13).

[5] Mary Wadsworth Michaelis, wife of General Michaelis, had written to Eisenhower on December 10, 1950, and in a reply of December 15 Eisenhower had told her of his wish to have Michaelis assigned to SHAPE (see Galambos, *Columbia University*, no. 1128).

[6] For Eisenhower's interest in guerrilla and psychological warfare see *ibid.*, nos. 897 and 898.

[7] *Aide-de-camp*. See *Eisenhower Papers*, vols. VI–XI.

[8] Lieutenant General Alfred M. Gruenther was Eisenhower's chief of staff (C/S) at SHAPE (on Gruenther see no. 2).

[9] General of the Army Douglas MacArthur, CINCFE (on MacArthur see no. 101).

[10] General Gruenther (see n. 8 above).

[11] War Department.

[12] From February 1933 until September 1935 Eisenhower had been special assistant to MacArthur, the Army's Chief of Staff. In September 1935 Eisenhower accompanied MacArthur to the Philippine Islands, where he served as the General's Assistant Military Adviser, later senior U.S. military assistant to the Commonwealth government on defense affairs. Their working relationship ended in December 1939, when Eisenhower returned to the United States.   Both generals discuss the long association in their memoirs (see Eisenhower, *At Ease*, pp. 212–32; and MacArthur, *Reminiscences*, p. 315). For another view of the Eisenhower-MacArthur relationship see Manchester, *American Caeser*, pp. 166, 173, 478, 530, 578, 688–89. See also Galambos, *Columbia University*, n. 1046; and for developments see no. 181.

[13] In his message to MacArthur dated March 7, 1951 (SH 20171, EM, Michaelis Corr.), Eisenhower had said that he had a "critical need for an American Brigadier General of outstanding qualifications and with Korean battle experience" to assist in the "training, organization, and indoctrination of a heterogeneous ground and air force." Eisenhower specifically requested Michaelis, citing his reputation and their long friendship. "He would," Eisenhower said, "ideally and almost uniquely fill my need." Eisenhower further asked that Michaelis's willingness to accept the assignment be determined. On March 9 MacArthur cabled Eisenhower that Michaelis was agreeable to the assignment and would be made available on call (C 57305, EM, MacArthur Corr.).

[14] Lieutenant General Edward Hale Brooks, Assistant Chief of Staff, G-1 (Personnel), since January 1949. Prior to this appointment Brooks had been CG, Antilles Department, San Juan, Puerto Rico, and CG, U.S. Army, Caribbean. For further background on Brooks see *Eisenhower Papers*, vols. I–IX.

[15] The message to which Eisenhower refers was dated March 13, marked "Personal" for Gruenther, and signed by Brooks (DA 85623, EM, Michaelis Corr.). "The Chief of Staff," it said, "is frankly disturbed that SHAPE should correspond directly with another Army Commander and present a fait accompli to him . . . this points up the wisdom of the Army's traditional policy of sticking to normal channels." In a reply of March 14 (SH 20191) Gruenther told Brooks that "General Eisenhower . . . has instructed me to advise you that he will take no further action in the Michaelis matter" (EM, Michaelis Corr.).

[16] Collins had told Eisenhower that he felt "guilty" about the message sent to SHAPE on March 13 (DA 85623 [see n. 15 above]). He explained that General MacArthur had recently rejected his own request for the transfer of Michaelis from FECOM to Fort Benning, Georgia, for a special assignment in the techniques of guerrilla warfare. "You can imagine my feelings," Collins said, "when I learned that your headquarters, presumably Al, had been in communication with FECOM and had received ready acceptance of Michaelis' transfer to SHAPE." Collins admitted that he was "exasperated" and asked Eisenhower to "please forget it—I guess I am just human like the rest of us."

[17] On April 24 Eisenhower would be informed that Michaelis had been assigned to SHAPE (Brooks to Gruenther, DA 89277, EM, Michaelis Corr. See also Collins to Eisenhower, Apr. 5, 1951, DA 87672; Michaelis to Eisenhower, Apr. 16, 1951; Eisenhower to Michaelis, Apr. 28, 1951, AP 80453; Eisenhower to Collins, Apr. 30, 1951, AP 80465; and Collins to Eisenhower, May 1, 1951, DA 90021, all in *ibid*.

[18] Major General Francis Henry ("Duke") Lanahan, Jr. (USMA 1920), had been assigned to the European Theater of Operations (ETO) in 1943. He became Chief Signal Officer (CSO) for SHAEF in March 1945; later he held the same post for the United States Forces, European Theater (USFET). In 1947 Lanahan became CG of the Signal Corps Center at Fort Monmouth, New Jersey.

[19] Headquarters.

[20] Lanahan had met with Collins on March 26, 1951 (see Lanahan to Eisenhower, Mar. 29, 1951, EM).

[21] Collins had said that Frank C. Pace, Jr., Secretary of the Army since 1950, and President Truman would soon meet to discuss the selection of a successor to retiring Major General Spencer Ball Akin, the Army's Chief Signal Officer since April 1947 (for background see Galambos, *Columbia University*, no. 380). "Unless the President is not satisfied with the names recommended by the selection board," Collins said, "Lanahan can be made available to you." Eisenhower had correctly interpreted Collins's meaning—that Lanahan was not being considered for the post. The appointment went to Major General George Irving Back, and Lanahan would become Eisenhower's CSO on May 8, 1951 (see General Orders No. 10, Staff Assignment, EM, Lanahan Corr.).

[22] Collins had commented on the difficulties Eisenhower was experiencing in "reconciling conflicting personal ambitions and national aspirations." Collins concluded, "Our problems here seem trifling and simple in comparison to the importance and complexity of your many tasks." Eisenhower's concern for effective European cooperation and leadership in the NATO experiment is the subject of a number of his letters (see, for example, nos. 45, 115, and 142).

[23] In a cable of April 5 Collins told Eisenhower that he appreciated this letter (DA 87672, EM).

117

Eisenhower Mss.

To Leonard D. Dry

April 2, 1951

Dear Sergeant Dry:[1] My failure to write to you does not reflect any lack of thinking about you or wanting you with me. The fact is that we have had such a terrible time trying to get living arrangements for all of us that it seemed silly to have you and Geraldine and your two babies all upset before it was necessary.[2] Actually, I am now using a rented car with a French driver.[3] I shall hope to keep him as a second driver after you arrive, but we will no longer need the private car. I understand that the Chrysler is already here.[4]

Tell Geraldine that my little picture of Mary Alice is about as good as I can do. It is certainly no work of art, but something I have had fun doing.[5]

My very best to all of you, in which Mrs. Eisenhower and all of your other friends join. *Cordially*

P.S. Of course, Colonel Schulz[6] will keep you advised as to the exact time of coming, and other necessary details. I assume you will make the trip by air because my plane frequently has to go back to the U.S.[7]

---

[1] Master Sergeant Dry had been Eisenhower's driver during World War II and his chauffeur-courier when the General was Army Chief of Staff and later when he was president of Columbia University. Since September 1, 1950, Dry had been assigned to Headquarters, First Army, at Governors Island, New York (see Galambos, *Columbia University*, esp. nos. 934, 935, and 936; see also no. 38 in this volume).

[2] Dry and his wife Geraldine had two children, Mary Alice and Leonard, Jr. On Eisenhower's problems with living arrangements see nos. 18 and 60.

[3] Maurice Lefebvre. Regarding his employment see correspondence in EM, Subject File, Personnel.

[4] Eisenhower would have a new Chrysler sedan at his disposal in Paris (see Biggers to Eisenhower, May 4, 1951; Callaghan to Dry, Apr. 9, 1951; Dry to Schulz, May 7, 1951; and Wall to Dry, June 26, 1951, all in *ibid.*).

[5] Eisenhower had painted a portrait of Dry's daughter. Dry wrote to Eisenhower on April 21, 1951: "Geraldine says that she will appreciate having the picture you painted of Mary Alice much more than you enjoyed painting it" (*ibid.*). On Eisenhower's painting see Galambos, *Columbia University*.

[6] Lieutenant Colonel Robert L. Schulz, A.D.C.

[7] Dry would be assigned to Eisenhower's Headquarters Command effective April 2, 1951.

118   *Eisenhower Mss., Family File*

To Elivera Carlson Doud   *April 3, 1951*

Dear Min:[1] Our latest news of you is that you are safely back in Denver after a long siege of illness in Washington. The other day, Mamie kept track of your scheduled flight from Washington on to Denver, and I recall that, when she got in bed, she said, "Well, Mother is now a half-hour out of Denver."[2] My guess is that Aksel,[3] and probably Cy,[4] met you at the plane and took you home.

Before I forget it, should you see either one, remember me to them kindly. You know how much I think of them, particularly of Aksel's great consideration for the family, of watching after business affairs, and so on.[5]

We are not yet in a house and, at the very best, cannot be in one for the next month or six weeks. It is rather discouraging and, at times, I think Mamie practically takes her Rosie[6] and heads for the port to get on a ship to come home. The house that we are supposed to get is a quite nice one situated in the center of a little park.[7] The trouble is that, every day, there seems to be some new delay.

I had a spell of illness brought about by some kind of an internal upset, but, after a few days in bed, am out and around again feeling fine. Mamie has recently had a bad cold and had to take a few doses of aureomycin but she, also, seems to me to be in pretty good shape.[8]

Of course, we hope that, when you got home, you found things in good condition, and that Dad[9] and Mrs. Cannon[10] were holding down the fort in good style.

It was too bad that you had to take sick during your vacation, but we are certainly delighted with our latest reports which are to the effect that you are really nearing full recovery. Next time you start out on a jaunt, you must plan to come all the way to France.[11]

Give my warm greetings to all our old friends, including the Culvers and the people next door—also, all the household personnel. My special [love?] to Dad and to you. *As ever*

[1] Mrs. Eisenhower's mother, affectionately known as "Min" (see no. 40).

[2] Mrs. Doud had contracted pneumonia during a vacation trip and had convalesced in Washington, D.C., at the home of her daughter Mabel ("Mike") Frances Doud Moore (for background on Mrs. Moore see *Eisenhower Papers*, vols. I–XI). Mrs. Doud was now well enough to travel by plane to her home in Denver, Colorado, and had arrived there the morning of April 2 (CSSCO SVC 491 and CSSCO SVC 492, both dated Apr. 2, 1951, EM, Family File, Mamie Eisenhower Corr.).

[3] Aksel Nielsen (for background see no. 34).

[4] Cyril C. Croke, of Denver, Colorado, a close friend of the Doud family (for background see *Eisenhower Papers*, vols. I–XI).

[5] See no. 235.

[6] Rose Wood, Mrs. Eisenhower's personal maid (see Galambos, *Columbia University*, no. 582).

[7] The Eisenhowers would live in a country house, Villa St. Pierre, located at Marnes-la-Coquette, ten miles west of Paris.

[8] On the Eisenhowers' illnesses see nos. 101, n. 2, and 102.

[9] John Sheldon Doud, Mamie Eisenhower's father (for background see *Eisenhower Papers*, vols. I–XI).

[10] Probably a nurse-companion to Mr. Doud.

[11] In June 1951 Mrs. Doud would visit the Eisenhowers in France (see no. 224).

To Milton Stover Eisenhower   *April 3, 1951*

Dear Milton:[1] I hope that, before I left the United States, I urged upon you the great desirability of making a visit over this way this summer if you find such possible. However, for fear that I didn't make my invitation as urgent as I intended, I am writing this note to say that, from every standpoint, I think that you should try to make such a trip.

During the months to come, there is no question that will be before the American people that will demand more earnest study and analysis than our over-all relationships with this particular region. The more of our people who come and see what they can for themselves, the more these questions are taken out of the realm of preconception and prejudice, the more certain we are to achieve something in the way of decent and proper answers. Consequently, I cannot see how someone in your position could better use a period of two to three, or even more, weeks than by making a trip through Europe.[2]

Of course, I do not know under what circumstances Mamie and I will then be living—we have not yet been able to get a house of our own, but I think that you should additionally consider the possibility of bringing Helen[3] with you. It has been a very long time since she came to Europe, and she might like to see some of the changes. Let me know if there is the slightest chance of your doing this.

I trust that the keeping of our car is causing you no great trouble. I hate to let it go because we like it so much, and I am fearful that there may be no good cars for sale at whatever time Mamie and I might be coming back to the United States. Of course, if our tour here stretches out indefinitely, then it will be up to me to get rid of the car and take a credit slip for it. That is what I did with the smaller one.[4]

Give my love to Helen and to the children,[5] and, of course, all the best to you. *As ever*

[1] For background on Eisenhower's youngest brother see no. 9.

[2] In a reply of April 12 (EM, Family File) Milton said that although he realized the value of a visit to Western Europe, he saw no possibility of making such a trip. Eisenhower had another reason for wanting his brother to plan a visit (see no. 195, n. 5).

[3] For background on Milton's wife Helen see no. 9. On the problems Eisenhower had with housing see no. 18.

[4] Milton had stored Eisenhower's Crown Imperial Chrysler at Pennsylvania State College while his brother was living in France. For background on Eisenhower's cars see no. 49.

[5] Ruth Eakin Eisenhower and Milton Stover Eisenhower, Jr. (see no. 9).

To Arthur Hays Sulzberger   April 3, 1951

Dear Arthur:[1] The papers this morning say that Mr. Churchill accepted
the invitation to the University of Pennsylvania.[2] Frankly, unless some
financial inducement was involved, I am at a complete loss to understand why he should have found it impossible to accept the invitation
from the Associated Press and from Columbia University—regardless
of any lack of influence in the strong urging by you and me—and still
could have accepted one to go to Philadelphia only two weeks after the
date on which you wanted him.[3] The next time I go to London, I will
try to do a little nosing around among a few friends to find out whether
the reasons actually included the adverse personal implications that,
on first glance, they seem to do.[4]

In any event, I regret that I failed you in a pinch. *Cordially*

[1] Sulzberger was the publisher of the *New York Times* and a trustee of Columbia
University (see no. 114).
[2] Winston Churchill had been invited by University of Pennsylvania president
Harold Stassen to speak in May at the bicentennial celebration commemorating
the founding of the university by Benjamin Franklin (see *New York Times*, Mar. 22,
1951).
[3] Sulzberger and Eisenhower together had urged Churchill's acceptance of invitations to address the annual luncheon meeting of the Associated Press in New York
City (Apr. 23) and to receive as well an honorary Doctor of Literature degree at a
special Columbia University convocation (see Sulzberger to Eisenhower, Jan. 17,
20, 1951; Eisenhower to Sulzberger, Jan. 18, 1951; and Eisenhower to Churchill,
Jan. 21, 23, 1951, all in EM).
    Churchill would decline all of these invitations, and as it turned out, he would
cancel his visit to the United States. In a letter to Eisenhower of May 1, 1951
(EM), Sulzberger said, "As you know, Mr. Churchill has decided not to come over
at this time. He was decent enough to send me a cable saying in part, 'Alas I have
had to put off my visit just now.' He certainly owed us that!" (see Sulzberger to
Eisenhower, Jan. 21, 23, 1951, EM, Churchill Corr.; Jan. 29, 1951, EM, Sulzberger Corr.).
[4] Eisenhower and Churchill would meet in London in July 1951 (see no. 252).

121   *Eisenhower Mss.*

To Ralph James Furey   April 3, 1951

Dear Ralph:[1] There just arrived at my desk your letter acknowledging
receipt of my little gift to the support of Columbia athletics. I had one
reason for particular pleasure in the ability to make the gift. This was
the fact that, when I first came to Columbia, it was gently hinted to

me that a University present [president?] in the IVY League never—
by any remote chance—evinced too great an interest in athletics. So,
in this case, while I did not even know that my own name would be
attached to the gift, I am delighted that those on the inside realize that
my interest in Columbia athletics is a sincere one.[2]

Of course, I was pleased with the generally favorable news about
our athletic situation. I had been able to follow the record of the
basketball team through the papers, but all the other items were brand
new to me. I congratulate you and all the coaches, players, and managers that have had a part in this fine development.[3] I hope that you
will especially remember me to Lou Little[4] when you see him. Please
do the same for all my other friends you may encounter. *Cordially*

[1] Furey was Director of Athletics at Columbia University (for background see
Galambos, *Columbia University*).
[2] In his letter of March 28 (EM) Furey had told Eisenhower that the first use of
his gift would be the purchase of "the Eisenhower Watch," to be presented to the
outstanding scholar among the varsity "C" winners. "Our undergraduate letter
winners," he said, "have always been thrilled by your very evident interest in and
support of the intercollegiate athletic program." In his memoir Eisenhower wrote
of his participation in sports—as an athlete, a cheerleader, and a coach (see
Eisenhower, *At Ease*, esp. p. 16).
[3] Furey had summarized Columbia's current athletic year, noting successes in
football, basketball, baseball, and crew. "In my humble opinion," he concluded,
"your leadership in this field has been one of the important factors in our continued
improvement."
[4] Louis L. Little was Columbia University's football coach (for background see
Galambos, *Columbia University*).

122   *Eisenhower Mss.*

To FRED G. GURLEY   *April 4, 1951*

Dear Fred:[1] I was delighted to receive your letter, and promptly advised
Mamie of the possibility of your friends visiting with us.[2]

It is possible that I shall not be in Paris the day they arrive,[3] but
there will be someone in my office should they call, and schedule some
kind of a visit upon my return to the city.

Your mention of bridge reminds me that I have had no opportunity
to play since my arrival in Paris, a matter which I hope to correct
within a short time.[4]

We have had a few disappointments with respect to our final residence. We hope now to be able to be "at home" in about 30 or 40
days. The house the French Government has secured is in the suburbs
of Paris and is near the selected site of the new headquarters. In the

meanwhile, we are living in a hotel in Versailles, admittedly a bit cramped. Mamie, being a good soldier, manages to keep things rolling.[5]

Some of our experts are trying to determine a way of creating sufficient Santa Fe traffic here in Paris in order that you and Ruth can find adequate reason for paying us a visit.[6]

Please be sure to remember us kindly to any of our friends that you happen to meet in your travels.

Mamie joins in sending our very best to Ruth and your family, and, of course, the warmest regard to yourself. *Cordially*

[1] Gurley, of Chicago, was president of the Atchison, Topeka and Santa Fe Railway System (for background see *Eisenhower Papers*, vols. VI–XI).

[2] Gurley had written to tell Eisenhower that his friends John and Elsa Whipple and Aubrey and Bunny Mellinger hoped to visit the Eisenhowers in Paris in mid-April (Mar. 27, 1951, EM). Both Whipple and Mellinger were members of the board of directors of the Atchison, Topeka and Santa Fe.

[3] Eisenhower would be in Luxembourg and Heidelberg at the time of their expected arrival; there is no further correspondence in EM to indicate that the Whipples and the Mellingers called on the Eisenhowers in Paris.

[4] Gurley had said that the Whipples and the Mellingers were good bridge players. For Eisenhower's interest in bridge see Galambos, *Columbia University*.

[5] On the housing problems see no. 18.

[6] In July 1951 Gurley and his wife Ruth would plan a fall trip to Europe but would find it necessary to cancel arrangements at the last minute. On the proposed trip see Gurley's correspondence with Eisenhower in EM.

123   *Eisenhower Mss.*

To Orlando Ward   *April 5, 1951*

Dear Pink:[1] In accordance with your request I have read, although very hurriedly, the text of the document, "Strategic Planning for Coalition Warfare;" Chapters 1 to 12 inclusive. If my memory is to be trusted, those parts of this history that touch upon events in which I had any part or knowledge are accurately done. The thoroughness and exhaustiveness of the work appear obvious, almost terrifying.[2]

With respect to the matter of "atmosphere or climate," which I assume is to be regarded as much a part of history as the actual record of deed and word, I feel that, in certain instances, matters are presented in such a way as to accentuate the tensions, if not antagonisms, in those instances where prominent officials did not instantly agree. I do not mean that I detect any deliberate effort in this direction, but the reaction I obtain from the reading of the document is that the great areas of agreement among members of the American High Command are rather ignored or, at least, treated very casually, while all points of differing opinion seem to be emphasized. This same observation applies with respect to differences between American staffs on the one hand, and British on the other. It must be remembered that many of the documents that recorded these differences were prepared in greatest good will and merely in an effort to be fully explanatory in the presentation of a viewpoint or plan.

It is perfectly true that everyone in official life was then living under tension; consequently, opinions or convictions were often expressed far more emphatically than prior study may have justified. There was a tremendous premium on speed, in both decision and action.

Individuals were normally over-worked to the point of acute fatigue so that recorded language must be read with sensible interpretation.[3]

There is only one point of fact in which I find myself somewhat puzzled. The document states, both in Chapters 11 and 12, that when General Marshall returned from London in midsummer of 1942, he did *not* consider that the decision as to TORCH had been irrevocably taken—the impression is given that he felt that the matter was still in the discussional stage.[4] (This, in spite of the fact there is recorded a cable from the President to the Prime Minister somewhere about July 25th of that year, in some such words as, "Hurrah! Full speed ahead.")[5]

My personal testimony on this point is as follows:

> The series of conferences in London between General Marshall and Admiral King on the one hand, and the British Chiefs of Staff on the other, were concluded on (I think) July 26th.[6] That afternoon, about 3 or 4 o'clock, I got a hurried call from General Marshall, who was staying at the Claridge Hotel. I walked into his room and, although he was in an adjoining bathroom cleaning up, we talked through the door, and he started telling me at once about the decisions reached. The gist of these decisions was that the Allies would conduct joint British-American effort against North Africa, and that I would be in command of the expedition. In this connection, he stated that the Chiefs of Staff had agreed that the assaulting troops should be as nearly exclusively American as possible, and, because of this, the British Chiefs of Staff had asked for an American Commander. Admiral King had suggested that I was already present on the ground and should be named, and that, to this, the British Chiefs of Staff quickly agreed. General Marshall added that my appointment was, of course, not yet official, but that written orders would come through at an early date. In the meantime, he said that I should get promptly started on the planning. He said that he personally would immediately return to the United States.

I do not, of course, question the accuracy of the statements made concerning General Marshall's attitude after returning to the States, but certainly, on the afternoon in question, in London, he left no possibility of doubt in my mind as to the finality of the decision and of my duty with respect to it.[7]

As you requested, I am returning, under separate cover, the document which you sent me.

With personal regard, *Cordially*

[1] For background on Major General Ward, the Army's Chief of Military History, see *Eisenhower Papers*, vols. I–XI.

[2] In a letter dated March 9 (EM) Ward had asked Eisenhower to review a manuscript titled "Strategic Planning for Coalition Warfare, 1939–42," to be published in the United States Army in World War II series. Ward invited Eisenhower's comments on the facts and interpretation, as well as his overall impression of this history of American strategy in the early phases of World War II.

Authors Maurice Matloff and Edwin M. Snell had thoroughly studied the problems facing War Department planners as the United States was drawn into the war. The manuscript addressed the resolution of conflicts in strategy between the military services—specifically the Army and the Navy—and in military policy among the Allied Powers (see Maurice Matloff and Edwin M. Snell, *Strategic Planning for Coalition Warfare, 1941-1942*, U.S. Army in World War II, ed. Kent Roberts Greenfield [Washington, D.C., 1953]).

[3] In his foreword to the volume, Ward echoed Eisenhower's views on this point (p. vii):

> It may seem to the reader that controversy and differences of opinion are stressed and that agreement and co-operative endeavor are slighted. Since planners are occupied with unsettled problems, their work necessarily involves differences of opinion. It is only when all sides of an issue are forcefully presented and the various solutions thereof closely scrutinized that the final plan has any validity. The reader must bear in mind that the differences related herein are those among comrades in arms who in the end always made the adjustments required of the members of a team engaged in a common enterprise.

[4] Eisenhower is referring to a decision made in London in July 1942: President Roosevelt had asked Army Chief of Staff George C. Marshall, Fleet Admiral Ernest Joseph King, and presidential adviser Harry Lloyd Hopkins to meet with the British Chiefs of Staff to work out joint operational war plans for 1942–43 (for background on Marshall see no. 2; on King and Hopkins see *Eisenhower Papers*, vols. I–XI). Matloff and Snell discuss Marshall's disappointment at the decision for an Allied invasion of Africa in 1942 (TORCH, originally GYMNAST) instead of a cross-channel attack (SLEDGEHAMMER and ROUNDUP) (pp. 233–93). According to these authors, Marshall did not consider the decision to be final (pp. 282–84).

Marshall's biographer, Forrest C. Pogue, also concludes that following the London conference, Marshall was not convinced that the decision to go forward with TORCH was definite (see Forrest C. Pogue, *George C. Marshall*, 3 vols. [New York, 1963–73], vol. II, *Ordeal and Hope, 1939-1942* [1966], pp. 348–49).

[5] On July 25, 1942, Roosevelt had cabled Hopkins asking him to tell Churchill that "we will go ahead full speed" in the launching of TORCH (COS, 1941–43, 381 TS). This message is discussed in Chandler, *War Years*, no. 393, as well as in a number of other accounts of the decisions made at the London meeting (see Robert

E. Sherwood, *Roosevelt and Hopkins: An Intimate History* [New York, 1948], pp. 611–12; Winston S. Churchill, *The Second World War*, 6 vols. [Boston, 1948–53], vol. IV, *The Hinge of Fate* [1950], pp. 447–48; and Ernest J. King and Walter Muir Whitehill, *Fleet Admiral King: A Naval Record* [New York, 1952], p. 407).

[6] The London conference ended on July 25, 1942 (see Chandler, *War Years*, vol. V, Chronology).

[7] In a letter dated April 12 (EM) Ward would request Eisenhower's permission to quote from his "personal testimony . . . in order to complete the record on a vital point. . . ." Matloff and Snell included Eisenhower's recollection of these events in the annotations to their book, pp. 286–87. For further background see Chandler, *War Years*, nos. 371, 379, 381, 386, 387, 389, 393, and 404; and Galambos, *Columbia University*, no. 583. See also Ambrose, *Supreme Commander*, pp. 64–78; Eisenhower, *At Ease*, p. 252; and Harry C. Butcher, *My Three Years with Eisenhower: The Personal Diary of Captain Harry C. Butcher, USNR* (New York, 1946), pp. 23–34.

124   *Eisenhower Mss.*

To Bernard Law Montgomery   *April 6, 1951*
Cable SH 20299. Top secret

Pass to Field Marshal The Viscount Montgomery of Alamein KG, GCB, DSO. Dear Monty: Very many thanks for your Memorandum FM/38, which I have had reproduced and given to the Staff for active consideration.[1]

For the immediate future, I agree wholeheartedly with your suggestion that the Short Term Plan, worked out at Fontainebleau, should be used as a basis for operations. A signal to this effect is being dispatched to all concerned.[2] I feel, however, now that our forces are at last beginning to build up, that SHAPE should produce as soon as possible an emergency war plan of its own.[3] The Fontainebleau Plan will form the basis for the emergency plan, our capabilities being reexamined against the forces now allocated and those earmarked for us. The excellent and exhaustive work which has been done at Fontainebleau will be of inestimable value to my planners in this task.

I'll discuss these matters with you on your return and hope you have a pleasant and useful tour.[4] *As ever*

[1] A copy of FM 38, a memorandum written by Deputy SACEUR Montgomery dated March 27, is in EM; Montgomery's covering note of March 29 is in the same file. This message was sent to Montgomery through the U.S. Army's military attaché in Denmark. Eisenhower had suggested that Montgomery visit the various NATO capitals, and Montgomery had begun his tour with a visit to Norway on April 2. This same message had been drafted in the form of a letter (Apr. 2, EM) by Air Vice-Marshal Edmund C. Hudleston, SHAPE's Deputy Chief of Staff for Plans (see no. 77; see also Schulz to Eisenhower, Mar. 13, 1951, and Eisenhower to Montgomery, Apr. 2, 1951, same file as document).

[2] Montgomery had formerly chaired the Western Union's Commanders-in-Chief

Committee, whose headquarters was located at Fontainebleau (see no. 17, n. 3). The "Short Term Plan" (designated CPS [1949] T. 15) was probably the plan adopted by the Western European Regional Planning Group (see no. 99), which comprised the same nations (Belgium, France, Luxembourg, the Netherlands, and the United Kingdom) as the Western Union (Ismay, *NATO*, pp. 8, 176). This plan was based on the forces available in September 1950 to stop a Russian drive into Western Europe. The plan had been considered inadequate by the American JCS because it called for a "rigid defense" along the Rhine-Ijssel line. Montgomery had proposed a more realistic strategy envisioning successive delaying actions west of the Rhine, but French opposition, based on political and psychological factors, had defeated his efforts. On April 3 Eisenhower had announced that the Western Union's plan would be placed in effect pending completion of a SHAPE emergency war plan (State, *Foreign Relations, 1951*, vol. III, *European Security and the German Question, Part I*, pp. 460–61; JCS 2073/106, Dec. 28, 1950, CCS 092 Western Europe [3-12-48], Sec. 66; JSPC 877/203, Nov. 2, 1951, *ibid.*, Sec. 102). The emergency war plan that the Joint Chiefs had adopted for their own forces (OFFTACKLE) envisioned conceding most of continental Europe to the Russian onslaught (Poole, *History of the Joint Chiefs of Staff*, vol. IV, *1950-1952*, pp. 161–63; see also Galambos, *Columbia University*, no. 380).

[3] Eisenhower had already started to develop an emergency war plan as "an operational matter of outstanding urgency" (JCS 2073/139, Mar. 25, 1951, CCS 092 Western Europe [3-12-48], Sec. 75).

[4] Montgomery would end his tour on the following day (*New York Times*, Apr. 6, 8, 1951). For further developments concerning war plans see nos. 364 and 553.

125   *CCS 092 Western Europe*
                                              (3-12-48), Sec. 77

To Omar Nelson Bradley   *April 7, 1951*
Cable SH 20306. Top secret. Personal

I have directed General Gruenther to send at once to the United States Chiefs of Staff a description of our Intelligence situation together with suggestions for some corrective measures.[1] As of this moment we are helpless in the field and our situation has grown to be intolerable. While the general problem has been placed before the Standing Group it cannot be expected that a satisfactory solution can be immediately developed by them. The whole problem was discussed at length with Admiral Wright[2] and he was requested to make an exhaustive presentation to you. I request an all-out effort to get something satisfactory developed at the earliest possible moment. I personally shall be spending the next week in inspection of troops in Germany.[3] Many thanks.[4]

[1] Eisenhower was concerned about the inability of his intelligence section, headed by British Major General Terence Sydney Airey (see nos. 77, n. 8, and 271, n. 3), to obtain information generated by U.S. intelligence authorities. On April 2 Airey

had requested that the U.S. Army Assistant Chief of Staff, G–2, provide him with "all available US intelligence estimates obtainable for disclosure on a need to know basis." Airey also had requested "any recent estimates of US or US–U[nited] K[ingdom] origin of concern to SACEUR and which are obtainable for disclosure only to US and UK officers on a need to know basis" (JAMAG 665 P, Apr. 2, 1951, CCS 092 Western Europe [3–12–48], Sec. 76). On April 14 Eisenhower's headquarters would request U.S. Air Force photographic intelligence, and an Air Force officer in Europe would be directed to discuss the matter with SHAPE (JCS 88698, Apr. 17, 1951, and JCS 88860, Apr. 18, 1951, *ibid.*, Sec. 78).

[2] For background on Vice-Admiral Jerauld Wright, who had served under Eisenhower during World War II, see Chandler, *War Years*. After the war he had served in the Office of the Chief of Naval Operations, as head of the Operational Readiness Section, and as commander of the Atlantic Fleet's Amphibious Forces. In November 1950 he was appointed U.S. deputy representative to NATO's Standing Group.

[3] On Eisenhower's trip to Germany see no. 128.

[4] In a cable dated April 10 (JCS 88126, same file as document) Bradley would tell Eisenhower that he shared his concern and was working on the matter. In a letter to Eisenhower of April 12 (EM) Bradley would add that he also had spoken to Admiral Wright and that he (Bradley) hoped the problem could be "straightened out very promptly." He said, "I should think that except for Special Intelligence, 70 or 80% of it could be released to your integrated staff, maybe more." The term "special intelligence" probably refers to information based on decrypted communications intercepts (see Galambos, *Chief of Staff*, no. 966, n. 5; and Ronald Lewin, *Ultra Goes to War: The First Account of World War II's Greatest Secret Based on Official Documents* [New York, 1978], p. 244). Despite these efforts, SHAPE continued to experience difficulties in obtaining access to U.S. intelligence information (see nos. 144 and 449).

126   *Eisenhower Mss.*

To HARRY S. TRUMAN   *April 7, 1951*

Dear Mr. President: Thank you very much for your understanding letter, commenting on the Malta affair.[1] In expressing to Averell my own feelings about that particular incident, I did not mean to exaggerate its importance—I merely was citing it as one type of difficulty that is always irritating because it is normally unnecessary.[2]

Only recently, Belgium enacted a two-year military service law.[3] On the continent itself, this makes Belgium the first nation to take this forward-looking step. It is very pleasing to us in this headquarters where we follow with greatest concern every new piece of evidence that Europe will act vigorously in its own defense. While, in certain cases, I think it is politically impossible for some of the individual nations *immediately* to follow Belgium's example, I do hope that, in order to encourage emulation, there can be some expression in Washington of general satisfaction concerning this event.

As you can well imagine, we keep busy. This coming week I shall spend inspecting Allied troops in Germany.[4]

With best wishes to you and yours, *Respectfully*

[1] For background see no. 81, n. 5. Truman's letter (Mar. 26, 1951, EM) had described the "Malta affair" as "entirely unnecessary." The President blamed Admiral Carney for stirring up the adverse publicity and said that the meeting could have been held quietly. Truman added, "I do everything I possibly can to prevent things of that sort from happening but when a fellow gets three stars on his shoulder he has to let people know that he wears them."

[2] On March 16 the French government, citing its longstanding interests in the Near East, had strongly protested the exclusion of France from the Malta talks. In a note delivered to David K. E. Bruce, the American Ambassador in Paris (see no. 16, n. 8), French Foreign Minister Robert Schuman (*ibid.*, n. 6) expressed his hope that there would be no recurrence of such closed U.S.-U.K. meetings and asked that the United States "define with full clarity its position regarding the association of France with the organization of the defense of the Near East" (U.S. Department of State, "Background Memoranda on Visit to the United States of Vincent Auriol, President of the French Republic," Mar. 1951, in OS/D, 1951, Clas. Decimal File, CD 337 [Four Powers]). On March 23 French Vice-Premier René Pleven (see no. 11, n. 2) publicly expressed his dissatisfaction to the French National Assembly and declared that his government would not agree to any defense arrangement unless France had participated in the early planning stages (*New York Times*, Mar. 24, 1951). Schuman again expressed his displeasure in Washington to Averell Harriman and Secretary of State Acheson on March 30. At that time Schuman admitted that French distrust of British policy was a factor in the French reaction to the meeting, and he urged that NATO's Standing Group, which included France, "play a preponderant role in the common strategy" for the Middle East and the Mediterranean. In response, Acheson suggested that the Washington members of the Standing Group meet informally to discuss these matters (State, *Foreign Relations, 1951*, vol. IV, *Europe: Political and Economic Developments, Part I*, pp. 369–71; see also Davis to Marshall, Mar. 21, 1951, OS/D, 1951, Clas. Decimal File, CD 337 [Malta]).

[3] On Belgium's action see no. 56, n. 2; see also Eisenhower, *At Ease*, p. 373.

[4] For Eisenhower's trip to Germany see no. 128, n. 1.

127   *Eisenhower Mss.*

TO KENNETH CLAIBORNE ROYALL   *April 7, 1951*

Dear Kenneth:[1] I am grateful for your heart-warming letter, and I most truly appreciate your quick analysis of the situation, including reasons for our difficulty at home. As you know, I came back to this kind of duty with many deep regrets, but I am so convinced that the safety of the free world depends upon the development of sound, practical, and effective cooperation among us all, based on clear appreciation of the important facts, that I do not see how any man now can fail to respond to anything that even has the appearance of a call to duty. Feeling as I do, you can understand how much a letter like yours means to me.[2]

If you and Margaret[3] ever find any reason for coming over this way, give me as much advance notice as you can. I should like to be here at the time, and, if ever we succeed in getting a home of our own, it would be wonderful to have you with us.[4]

Give our love to Margaret, and, of course, all the best to yourself. *Cordially*

[1] Former Secretary of the Army Royall was presently a partner in the law firm of Dwight, Royall, Harris, Koegel and Caskey of New York City and Washington, D.C. (for background see *Eisenhower Papers*, vols. I–XI).

[2] In a letter of April 2 (EM) Royall had told Eisenhower that "it is heartening—and, in view of the present wave of general criticism, noteworthy—that the public generally has supreme confidence in your important work. . . . As was never before the case in my memory, the country needs someone whom they look up to and believe in." Royall was referring to press coverage of the worldwide tensions over the possibility of another war in Europe and of President Truman's problems with General MacArthur over the fighting in Korea. Royall had undoubtedly also seen two of C. L. Sulzberger's recent articles on Eisenhower's role as commander of the NATO forces (see *New York Times*, Mar. 12, 25, 1951; and no. 114, n. 4).

[3] Mrs. Royall, the former Margaret Best.

[4] On the Eisenhowers' problems in regard to a home see no. 122.

128

DIARY

Today I go to Germany to inspect some troops in each of the occupational (western) zones. I shall be gone until a week from today.[1]

The Senate voted to send 4 divisions to Europe—if more are needed, it is the "sense of the Senate" that Congress should be consulted.[2]

Curiously enough—in spite of the fact that I believe this particular action to be awkward, if not damaging to the cause for which we are spending so much—I agree with the basic thought expressed by the Senate. *If* American public opinion does _not_ support adequate reinforcement of Europe pending the development of adequate _European_ force, and to inspire such development, then it is absurd for the President to send here a single soldier. I've tried to get everybody to see that a union of minds & hearts is the indispensable formula for success—if this union is not established then we must seek some alternative to collective security for the free world. Any alternative promises little more than tragic failure; this, it seems to me is the basic truth that we at home—and Europe especially—must understand, _now_!!

Yet with all the free world in an uproar because people believe that MacA is trespassing on purely civilian functions—it becomes difficult for anyone in uniform (and especially me as the Commander in Europe) to preach this truth unendingly. Every personal enemy and every communist would find some way of making capital out of the circumstances. So far as the personal part is concerned, I don't care one whit, but such people would not hesitate at damaging the NATO concept in order to attain their ends.[3]

Had a nice note from Harold Stassen.[4] Recently I exchanged notes with Gov. Dewey (on basis of a columnist's report that he & I were deadly enemies.)[5] Bill Burnham is coming to see me soon?[6]

Jim Wise came to see me today. Reminded me to write a note to Bill Donovan re Columbia University. This I'll do as soon as possible—maybe I have time before my next engagement.[7]

---

[1] On this day Eisenhower would begin a visit to West Germany where he would inspect troops in the British, French, and U.S. zones. His itinerary included stops at Gütersloh, Senne Lager, and Wiesbaden in the British zone; and Heidelberg, Neubiberg Air Force Base, and Augsburg in the U.S. zone. The General and Mrs. Eisenhower would leave Germany on April 13 to spend several days in Luxembourg as guests of Perle Mesta, American Minister there (for background on Mesta see Galambos, *Columbia University*, no. 545. For Eisenhower's trip schedules and itinerary see the Chronology, in vol. XIII; EM, Subject File, Trips; and *New York Times*, Apr. 15, 16, 17, 1951). For developments see no. 136.

[2] On April 4 the U.S. Senate had adopted a resolution approving the dispatch of four U.S. divisions to Europe. The 69–21 vote on Senate Resolution 99 brought to an end the long and bitter Great Debate over the issue of sending troops to Europe (for background see nos. 23 and 112; see also Acheson, *Present at the Creation*, pp. 491–96).

Among the main provisions of the Senate resolution were: approval of Eisenhower's appointment as SACEUR; acknowledgment of the need to station armed forces abroad as a fair contribution by the United States to the joint defense of Europe; and approval of the understanding that Europeans would make up the major contribution to the NATO ground forces under Eisenhower's command. It was the "sense of the Senate" that President Truman should consult top military, foreign relations, and congressional advisers before taking any action to send ground troops to Europe and that he should report regularly to Congress on the implementation of the North Atlantic Treaty. Reaction to the resolution, which was advisory and not statutory, was mixed. Some took the view that it was a setback for the Administration—in fact, a vote of no confidence in Truman's policies. Truman himself hailed it as a confirmation of the nation's support for the North Atlantic Treaty (see *Congressional Record*, 82d Cong., 1st sess., 1951, 97, pt. 3: 3254–94; *New York Times*, Apr. 3–5, 1951; and *International Herald Tribune*, Paris ed., Apr. 2–6, 1951).

[3] General Douglas MacArthur's problems in the Far East were on Eisenhower's mind at this time. For months MacArthur had been at odds with President Truman and the JCS over the conduct of the Korean War. MacArthur had come under heavy fire both in the United States and abroad for what his critics termed meddling in the foreign policy of the United States (and thus frustrating U.N. efforts to gain a peace settlement in Korea). Truman, in concert with his military and diplomatic advisers, would decide to relieve MacArthur of all of his com-

mands. For background on this important and well-documented controversy see no. 101, nn. 4–5; and the following volumes: James, *Years of MacArthur*, vol. III, *Triumph and Disaster*, pp. 584–604; Truman, *Memoirs*, vol. II, *Years of Trial and Hope*, pp. 432–50; State, *Foreign Relations, 1951*, vol. VII, *Korea and China, Part I*, pp. 298–301; Collins, *War in Peacetime*, pp. 269–93; Russell Frank Weigley, *History of the United States Army* (New York, 1967), pp. 512–19; MacArthur, *Reminiscences*, pp. 382–96; Donovan, *Tumultuous Years*, pp. 340–62; Acheson, *Present at the Creation*, pp. 517–24; Manchester, *American Caeser*, pp. 629–43; Richard H. Rovere and Arthur M. Schlesinger, Jr., *The MacArthur Controversy and American Foreign Policy* (New York, 1965), pp. 168–73; Courtney Whitney, *MacArthur: His Rendezvous with History* (New York, 1955), pp. 481–90; and Joseph William Martin, Jr., *My First Fifty Years in Politics*, as told to Robert J. Donovan (New York, 1960), pp. 198–211. For developments see nos. 131 and 136.

[4] Harold E. Stassen was president of the University of Pennvania (for background see no. 63). In his note of April 3 (EM) Stassen had commented on the Senate resolution, which he said "reflects not only lack of vision and sad error in appraising [the] world situation, but also the very low ebb of their regard for [the] President's judgment." Stassen said, however, that he felt certain that the Senate would support Eisenhower fully: "The majority will back your requests, but they are afraid of [the] President's decisions, unfortunately."

[5] On Eisenhower's correspondence with New York Governor Thomas E. Dewey see no. 92.

[6] William H. Burnham would visit the Eisenhowers on April 12. On Burnham, a friend and political adviser to Eisenhower, see nos. 40 and 102.

[7] James DeCamp Wise was president of the Columbia Associates (see Galambos, *Columbia University*). Eisenhower met with Wise the morning of April 9; on the same day he wrote the next document, to Major General William Joseph Donovan, chairman of Columbia University's Council on Development and Resources (for background on Donovan see *Eisenhower Papers*, vols. I–XI).

129   *Eisenhower Mss.*

To WILLIAM JOSEPH DONOVAN   *April 9, 1951*

Dear Bill:[1] Just a few minutes ago Jim Wise was in my office, a circumstance which reminds me of my long held intention of writing you a letter.[2] My first purpose is to express again my deep sense of obligation for the way you stepped in to help the rest of us in the job of assuring adequate income for Columbia and in spreading everywhere the good word of her accomplishments and potentialities. My second purpose was to express the hope that you would be more active in this job than ever before.

There is probably no doubt in your mind of the need that Columbia has for close association with those members of its family who are now in the business world and other civil practices. Grayson Kirk[3] will understand this as clearly as anybody else, and I assure you that you would be doing him a favor, as well as a great service for Columbia. I should like to feel that you are sticking closely with him in the job of keeping alive the teamwork that must exist if America is to get out of Columbia all the good that she can deliver.

Jumping quickly to another subject, I saw a paper this morning dealing with the idea of a European Youth Congress this summer. I am sure that you will be interested in the plan (if it gets far enough along to be called a plan) and will probably know a lot more about it than I do. Suspecting that I may be called upon either to express an opinion about it or possibly even to help out in some way of promoting it, I wonder whether, at your convenience, you would write me a letter giving me your ideas about it. If you have not heard of it at all, I am quite certain that you will later.[4]

Finally, this letter brings you a renewed assurance of my continuing regard and esteem; also an invitation to drop in and see me anytime you are in Europe. I can always get together a bit of lunch for you— maybe even one or two interesting guests. *Cordially*

[1] Donovan was Chairman of Columbia University's Council on Development and Resources (for background see the preceding document, n. 7).

[2] James DeCamp Wise was president of the Columbia Associates (see *ibid.*).

[3] Grayson Kirk, vice-president and provost of Columbia University, was serving as acting president in Eisenhower's absence (see no. 31, n. 1). For developments see no. 155.

[4] There is no further correspondence on this subject in EM. A Memorandum for Record dated May 22, 1951 (EM, Donovan Corr.), indicates that Eisenhower sent General Alfred M. Gruenther a copy of this letter.

130   *Eisenhower Mss.*

To WALTER BROADMAN KERR, JR.   *April 9, 1951*

Memorandum for Mr. Kerr:[1] While my memory is not of such excellence that I can give you specific answers to many of the questions included in the two documents you have submitted, I can possibly be of a little bit of help.[2]

I begin with a bit of background on my friendship with Jim Forrestal. I met him during the war when he was Assistant Secretary of the Navy. My first long talk with him was at the time of the Potsdam Conference in 1945, after he had become Secretary of the Navy. In our three or four contacts during that period, I was struck by one thing—he was the only prominent official that I met during the war who insisted, always, that the chief danger to the United States was Communism. He pointed out that the leaders of that doctrine had consistently announced their implacable hatred for free government as we understood it, and that this enmity would sooner or later bring us into a position of great danger, unless we, as a nation, were careful to guard against it.

I was brought to Washington at the end of 1945 to serve as Chief of Staff of the Army. My contacts with Mr. Forrestal were casual and infrequent, but, such as they were, they did serve to impress upon me that he was selfless, energetic, and an extraordinarily honest public servant.[3]

I began to meet him with some frequency during the inter-Service arguments prior to enactment of the Unification Law in 1947. He opposed unification; I was for it. An argument between him and me took place one day in the presence of the President; there ensued an exchange that seemed, later, to be the beginning of a closer association between us—possibly, it was a growth of mutual respect. In any event, this interchange in front of the President ended in my statement that, if and when unification came about, he, Mr. Forrestal, would certainly receive my vote as the first Secretary of Defense.[4]

After Mr. Forrestal became Secretary of Defense,[5] he fell into the habit of asking me to his office occasionally for casual conversations about his duties and the development of his organization. All of these conversations were devoid of argument and were, in fact, enjoyable for me. While he appeared to be keenly aware of the importance of the task he had assumed, he was confident as to the outcome and was accordingly cheerful, if not optimistic.

As a result of conversations through late 1947 and early 1948, he asked me, upon termination of my tour as Chief of Staff (which took place in early 1948)[6] to provide him with a written memorandum of observations concerning his task, and the organizational and procedural principles that should be observed. I gave him such a memorandum on the 12th of February, 1948. (Copy probably in his papers.)[7] Thereafter, from time to time during 1948 he sought my advice on various phases of his task, which I gave sometimes in written, sometimes in verbal form. We had telephone conversations and occasional unprearranged meetings. (After 2 May 1948, I was in New York City.)[8]

With respect to
"Questions for General Eisenhower"
(1 through 5)[9] In October 1948, Mr. Forrestal noted, in a conversation with me, that the Services had *not* been getting, during preceding years, the amount of money that they had been informally promised; namely, $15 billion a year for military purposes. On the contrary, he said, through one device or another, their appropriations had fallen far below this amount and that we were arriving at a point where, in view of the threatening international situation, we should take corrective steps promptly. He still believed that, if the Services could get *a full $15 billion a year for their own uses* (exclusive of all such things as

stockpiling, and so on), and could be assured of this amount for all succeeding years, we could build a very effective defense. Effectiveness of this amount was, he believed, dependent upon the finest kind of cooperative and objective work on the part of the Joint Chiefs of Staff in devising a balanced budget. Taking into consideration the human factors and realizing that each Service was going to advocate special projects of its own, he estimated that, until the whole National Defense organism got to functioning better, we would have to go somewhat above the $15 billion mark. He told me that the Staffs had tentatively agreed upon a 1950 budget of 16.9, but that, in asking me to come down intermittently as his adviser, he did *not* ask me to intervene directly into that particular budget.[10] What he wanted me to do was to help work out an agreed-upon war plan that would be planned as the basis for future budgets, each of which was to be as close to $15 billion as possible. My first task, after coming down to Washington for indefinite assignment, was to work on the FY 1951 budget and I came to Washington on 21 January 1949 for this purpose. I worked with the JCS until early July.[11] I am quite certain that Mr. Forrestal did not specifically relate the 14.4 billion amount to a war plan and the 16.9 to another. He was concerned in stopping the deterioration in our defenses and in establishing a stabilized budget that would reflect the critical nature of the world institution.

(6 through 8)[12] Mr. Forrestal gave a number of reasons for wanting me to return, at least temporarily, to duty with the Armed Services. He had become disturbed by mounting evidence that the Services themselves were never going to reach any kind of agreement as to a properly balanced budget within a limiting figure of reasonable size, and he hoped that I might do something to help diminish the bitterness of the arguments developed out of this situation. He said that, while he had the greatest respect, individually, for the principal military people with whom he came in contact, and especially for the members of the Joint Chiefs of Staff, yet it became clearer and clearer to him that the Secretary of Defense had to have available to him some disinterested separate professional advice—from an individual who owed no particular allegiance to any one Service and who was not responsible for the administrative welfare of any Service.[13] Mr. Forrestal had apparently always had a curious faith in the value of Committees and Boards. He established many (I served on one that he considered most important) and, initially, his concept of organizing a Department of Defense, was a loose Committee arrangement. One of the functions he had under consideration when I left Washington in January was the organization of a Military Committee, entirely outside of Chiefs of Staff. One group he thought of was myself, Towers[14] and Eaker.[15] Thus he thought he would get consolidated advice and counsel, unaffected by responsibility for daily service administration.

Finally he abandoned this idea. There were probably two or three reasons why he turned to me in this feeling of need that he had developed. First, he and I, by this time, had become good friends, and I had performed a number of special chores for him, largely because of my respect and liking for him. I had gone to several firms to help secure for temporary service in Washington, needed individuals from civil life, and had agreed to serve on one or two special boards that he believed to be necessary to assure proper coordination in the Defense Department.

Another reason was undoubtedly because I had always believed that the Secretary of Defense would need some kind of experienced and independent professional opinions. Finally—he told me—he had talked the matter over with the President, who had urged him to bring me back to temporary duty if I would consent to serve.[16] (As I recall, Admiral Leahy,[17] who had, up to that time, been the Presidential Chief of Staff, had suffered a decline in health and was no longer working actively; although I believe he still held his title as Presidential Chief of Staff.) In general, the Secretary was very anxious to have my help in revising the Defense Law of 1947,[18] and in assisting in the drawing up of a war plan that could be made the basis of future budgets.

Incidentally, he was passionately devoted to the idea of keeping the Defense Establishment completely outside of partisan politics. He often talked to me, during 1948 especially, of the need for placing both the State Department and the Defense Department in a status completely different from the traditional one and to make them, in actual fact, bipartisan.

So far as I know, the idea of my coming back to temporary duty originated exclusively with Secretary Forrestal.[19]

In his case, one of the reasons that he felt such an acute need for some help was his inborn honesty and his very great desire to serve the country well. He would listen carefully to presentations, even where he was certain that these were partisan and even prejudiced; his ability to see truth on both sides of bitter questions led him into a turmoil, out of which it was difficult to form a clear-cut decision in which he could personally have real confidence.[20]

I assume, of course, that you will talk to Mr. McNeil[21] and Mr. Leva[22] concerning these same queries. McNeil will be specially helpful with the budget questions.

With respect to
"General Questions"

(1)[23] My recollection is that it was sometime about the middle of February 1949 before Mr. Forrestal specifically spoke to me about the possibility of his resigning. However, he had said to me, before this time, that there had been a great deal of misinterpretation and misrepresentation concerning his great effort, during the fall of 1948, to abstain from partisan politics. He keenly felt the effect of this misrepresentation and would occasionally say that some of his detractors might make it impossible for him to retain his position.

(2)[24] Mr. Forrestal constantly emphasized his hope that, with his background of experience, he could get the Defense Department well established, coordinated, and operating before he should leave office. I know that he wanted to get through what he considered to be necessary amendments to the National Defense Act of 1947[25] (although he would frequently change his mind as to the need for revision in certain details), and he wanted to get adopted by the several Services a common defense plan that would thereafter be the basis for appropriations.

(3)[26] The answer to this one is obvious from what I have heretofore said.

(4)[27] The answer to this one is implied above.

(5)[28] I do not recall that Secretary Forrestal ever specifically told me about his conversations with the President that led up to his resignation. I do remember that, after he told me about his intention and its acceptance, in principle, he spoke once or twice to the President. The latter always referred to Mr. Forrestal in terms of highest esteem (a sentiment which he knew I shared) and told me in confidence one day that he intended to appoint Louis Johnson[29] as the successor. From about the 1st of March onward, Mr. Forrestal began to worry a great deal about the future of the Defense Establishment, after he should leave. Somewhere along about this time, Mr. Johnson came to the Department, and I began to hold frequent conversations with him as well as Mr. Forrestal. By this time, everybody realized that Jim was exceedingly tired, and all his friends were quite anxious that he should obtain a rest at the earliest possible moment. Jim himself did not talk so much about his relations with the President as about his worry concerning the future of our defense.

(6)[30] My own belief is that, during the final weeks of Mr. Forrestal's incumbency, he was not functioning at his outstanding efficiency and effectiveness. At that time, I thought, of course, that a good long rest of a month or something of that kind would cure him completely, because I retained my basic feelings of respect, esteem, and liking for him.

(7)[31] Mr. Forrestal never, by any hint, indicated that Mr. Johnson was responsible for his (Forrestal's) resignation. While he allowed himself once or twice to speak a bit bitterly about the baneful influence of politics in public service, yet I never heard him say anything whatsoever about Mr. Johnson as an individual.

(8)[32] I do not recall that his criticisms of others were ever put in terms of loyalty, although, with respect to two of the Service Secretaries, he frequently would imply that their concern for their own Services was greater than their concern for the nation as a whole.[33] He asked my help in preparing a paper for a meeting in which matters of this sort could be cleared up for once and all. I did once prepare a draft to explain to him that I thought this should be done in a personal meeting with the President and himself present, and even indicated the kind of statements that should be made. However, I have no inkling as to whether he ever attempted to use it.

(9)[34] In spite of a variety of problems and differences that prevented the Services from getting together completely, Mr. Forrestal always believed that the only basic difficulty between the three Services was in solving the struggle between the Navy and the Air Forces as to which would have the authority to take charge of strategic bombing functions for the United States. While, in the early days of the struggle, the Navy denied any such intention—and Mr. Forrestal believed this absolutely at that time—he later came to believe that the argument, no matter how presented, and no matter how it was dressed up, did, in fact, involve this basic issue. Consequently, to him, the approval of procurement of so-called intercontinental bombers (B–36's) meant a curtailment of money for active carriers and the planes to go with them. He believed that all other issues would fall into place, or at least were susceptible to settlement by conciliation, if this one could ever be solved. I think that he never became convinced, in his own mind, that there was any real solution for it, and he was likewise convinced that both Services became something less than completely frank in their arguments in support of their respective positions. For example, he believed that the Navy did not put all its cards on the table when it said that its need for super-carriers was based solely on *Naval* missions. On the other hand he thought that the Air Forces constantly underestimated the eventual cost of the B–36 and over-estimated its capabilities.

An officer who was closely associated with Mr. Forrestal[35] had this to say with respect to his attitude during the latter part of his service: "I accompanied him in his November 1948 trip to Europe. It was clear to me he was having great mental anguish while the trip was in progress. I was in his party when he went to Key West about November 18, 1948 to see the President. From then on his worry increased. President Truman did not see him alone on that occasion."

(10)[36] I have no information on this point at all.

(11) I have a number of various memoranda that I kept, but none that I think would add greatly to an understanding of Mr. Forrestal's life and service.[37] I have no objection whatsoever to testifying to my conviction that, through a great part of his service in Washington, he was one of the finest public servants I ever knew. I still believe that he was what I considered him then—a wholly devoted, selfless, and highly intelligent public servant.

[1] Kerr, who was foreign editor of the *New York Herald Tribune*, had been asked by William E. Robinson, executive vice-president and a director of the newspaper, to meet with Eisenhower to discuss a series of questions concerning the General's relationship with James V. Forrestal, the late Secretary of Defense. Robinson was eager to have Eisenhower's views because the *Herald Tribune*, in cooperation with Eugene Schulte Duffield, confidential secretary to Forrestal, and Walter Millis, of the paper's editorial staff, was planning to publish Forrestal's diary and papers in book and serial form (for background on Eisenhower's involvement in the publication of Forrestal's papers see Galambos, *Columbia University*, no. 1002; on Forrestal see *ibid.*, no. 425).

[2] On March 21 Kerr had met with Eisenhower in Paris, at which time he had submitted two sets of questions for the General's consideration, one, numbering eight questions, designed specifically for General Eisenhower, the other, numbering eleven questions, of a general nature. Both sets had been prepared by Duffield. There are several drafts of Eisenhower's reply in EM, all showing handwritten emendations by Eisenhower and by his C/S, General Alfred M. Gruenther.

[3] For additional background on Eisenhower's early relationship with Forrestal see Chandler and Galambos, *Occupation, 1945*; and Galambos, *Chief of Staff*. See also Eisenhower, *At Ease*, pp. 329–33.

[4] In regard to armed services unification see *Eisenhower Papers*, vols. VI–XI. The meeting to which Eisenhower refers was probably one called by President Truman on June 4, 1946 (see James V. Forrestal, *The Forrestal Diaries*, ed. Walter Millis [New York, 1951], pp. 166).

[5] Forrestal's appointment as Secretary of Defense was confirmed by the Senate on July 27, 1947.

[6] Eisenhower was relieved of duty as C/S, U.S. Army, on February 7, 1948 (see Galambos, *Chief of Staff*).

[7] This memorandum, marked personal and confidential and dated February 7, 1948, appears in *ibid.* as no. 2055; it is summarized in Forrestal, *Diaries*, pp. 369–70.

[8] Eisenhower had moved to New York City to take up his duties as president of Columbia University (see Galambos, *Columbia University*).

[9] The first five questions concerned (1) Forrestal's position in October 1948 regarding the 1949/50 military budget and military policy; (2) Eisenhower's part during October and November 1948 in developing an intermediate military budget for 1949/50 of $16.9 billion; (3) Forrestal's position on the relations between strategic planning and the President's $14.4 billion budget ceiling for 1949/50, as well as the intermediate budget of $16.9 billion; (4) Forrestal's understanding of the final disposition of the intermediate budget; and (5) Eisenhower's responsibility, in February 1949, regarding 1949/50 military appropriations and 1950/51 military budgeting (EM).

[10] See Galambos, *Columbia University*, nos. 189 and 223; and Forrestal, *Diaries*, pp. 498, 500, 502–6, 508–11, 535–38.

[11] In a letter of November 9, 1948, Forrestal told Truman that "the talents of Ike, in terms of identification of problems and the accommodation of differing views, would be highly useful" (Galambos, *Columbia University*, nos. 223 and 294, n. 2; Forrestal, *Diaries*, pp. 547–48).

[12] Questions 6–8 concerned (6) Eisenhower's assistance to Forrestal in revising the National Security Act of 1947; (7) Forrestal's assignment to Eisenhower, who was then acting chairman of the JCS; and (8) Eisenhower's understanding of whether his recall as an adviser to the Secretary of Defense originated with Forrestal (EM).

[13] See Galambos, *Columbia University*, nos. 183, 189, and 223, n. 3; and Forrestal, *Diaries*, pp. 500, 547–48.

[14] Admiral John Henry Towers (USN, ret.), former Chief of the Bureau of Aero-

nautics and, later, Commander of the Pacific Fleet (see Galambos, *Columbia University*, nos. 183, n. 3, and 303, n. 12).

[15] Lieutenant General Ira Clarence Eaker (USAF, ret.), former Deputy Commander, Army Air Forces, and Chief of the Air Staff. Since 1947 Eaker had been vice-president of the Hughes Tool Company (for further background see Chandler, *War Years*; and Galambos, *Chief of Staff*, nos. 979 and 1547).

[16] See Galambos, *Columbia University*, no. 294.

[17] William Daniel Leahy, Fleet Admiral of the U.S. Navy, served as Chief of Staff to President Truman from April 1945 until he resigned in March 1949 (for further background see *Eisenhower Papers*, vols. I-XI).

[18] Eisenhower may have meant to say the National Security Act of 1947. For background on the act and the amendments of 1949 see James E. Hewes, Jr., *From Root to McNamara: Army Organization and Administration, 1900-1963* (Washington, D.C., 1975), pp. 271-72. See also U.S., *Statutes at Large*, vol. 61, pt. 1, pp. 495-510, and *ibid.*, vol. 63, pt. 1, pp. 578-92; and Galambos, *Chief of Staff*, no. 1675, and *Columbia University*, esp. nos. 165, 183, 222, 288, 327, 348, and 369.

[19] See n. 11 above.

[20] Eisenhower gave Kerr permission to quote from this paragraph and from the final two sentences in this document (see memorandum, Cannon to Kerr, Apr. 11, 1951, EM). A passage from the paragraph above appears in Forrestal, *Diaries*, p. 548.

[21] Wilfred James McNeil, Assistant Secretary of Defense since 1949 (see Galambos, *Columbia University*, no. 295, n. 4; and Hewes, *From Root to McNamara*, p. 277).

[22] Marx Leva, special assistant and general counsel to the Secretary of Defense since 1947 (see Galambos, *Columbia University*, no. 288).

[23] The question was whether Eisenhower recollected, from conversations with Forrestal or letters from him, that the Secretary did not intend to resign during the first half of 1949. As early as the fall of 1948 Forrestal had written several friends that he expected to end his public career in January 1949 (see Forrestal, *Diaries*, p. 473).

[24] The question was whether in early 1949 Forrestal explained to Eisenhower his goals before leaving office (see *ibid.*, p. 547).

[25] See n. 18 above.

[26] The question was whether Eisenhower recalled what subjects held Forrestal's attention in late 1948 and early 1949.

[27] Here Kerr had asked whether Forrestal discussed with Eisenhower his relationship with Truman after the 1948 presidential election. For Millis and Duffield's view on this question see Forrestal, *Diaries*, pp. 5, 518-19, and 544-46.

[28] This question was whether Forrestal discussed his resignation with Eisenhower and whether he described a meeting with Truman concerning the resignation (see *ibid.*, pp. 544-49).

[29] Louis Arthur Johnson became Secretary of Defense on March 28, 1949 (see Galambos, *Columbia University*, esp. no. 401, n. 3).

[30] The question was whether Eisenhower believed that Forrestal, because of overwork, fatigue, and criticism, was unable to discharge his duties in early 1949 (see *ibid.*, nos. 315, n. 4, 401, and 425; see also Forrestal, *Diaries*, pp. 547, 554-55). Eisenhower's recollection of Forrestal's physical condition in the months shortly before his suicide in May 1949 is more vivid in his memoir *At Ease* (see pp. 330-33).

[31] Kerr asked, whether Forrestal ever told Eisenhower that he believed Louis Johnson had been responsible for his resignation (see Forrestal, *Diaries*, p. 549).

[32] The question was why did Forrestal want Truman to exact from the three Secretaries a pledge of loyalty and unity?

[33] The three Secretaries were Secretary of the Army Kenneth C. Royall, Secretary of the Navy John L. Sullivan, and Secretary of the Air Force W. Stuart Symington

(for background on these men and their roles in the interservice rivalries of that time see Galambos, *Columbia University*). Eisenhower is probably referring to Sullivan and Symington. For Forrestal's account of his differences with Sullivan and Symington see Forrestal, *Diaries*, pp. 298, 462-65, 514, 516. For Forrestal's attempt to exact a pledge from the Secretaries see *ibid.*, pp. 545-46; and Galambos, *Columbia University*, nos. 288, 313, and 315.

[34] Here the question was whether in 1949 Forrestal discussed with Eisenhower the renewed demand by the Air Force for seventy groups or the matter of the Air Force's reliance on the B-36 long-range bomber (on these issues see Galambos, *Columbia University*, nos. 336, 360, 378, and 418; and Forrestal, *Diaries*, pp. 374, 378, 401-3, 412-13, and esp. 414-19, 544).

[35] The officer was Lieutenant General Alfred M. Gruenther (see memorandum, Cannon to Gruenther, Apr. 9, 1951, EM; and Forrestal, *Diaries*, p. 519).

[36] The question read: "Forrestal's diary becomes sparse and highly impersonal after the election and after his trip to Europe in November, 1948. His correspondence files dry up similarly during January, 1949. Does your recollection suggest any reason for his changed attitude?"

[37] Kerr asked whether Eisenhower would be willing to contribute any notes or letters from Forrestal for inclusion in the published diary. For Eisenhower's further admiring remarks on the former Secretary of Defense see no. 614; and Dwight D. Eisenhower, *The Eisenhower Diaries*, ed. Robert H. Ferrell (New York, 1981), pp. 209-12. For developments see no. 307.

131   *Eisenhower Mss.*

To Lucius Du Bignon Clay   *April 16, 1951*
Personal and confidential

Dear Lucius:[1] I am grateful to you, both for your letter and for the trouble you took to telephone me on Sunday last.[2] I assure you that I am going to maintain silence in every language known to man; not only because I see no other attitude for a soldier in uniform to take, but more importantly because I share your belief that some extreme partisans will do their best to use the incident to impede our effort to strengthen Europe. The job is tough enough as it is.[3]

These countries, as you so well know, are torn to pieces by violent differences of opinion, and by ancient fears, prejudices, and superstitions. The job of welding the whole Western world into a unit in which each of the parts is willing to exert its full capabilities in support of a common cause is one that will be accomplished only through enlightened leadership and through example that will inspire and sustain confidence. Nevertheless, since it is not possible for America to devise (at least in my fairly fertile imagination) any reasonable alternative to the attainment of success in this venture, we have simply got to keep plugging away, all of us, until we are assured that collective security for the free world is an accomplished fact.

Because of my complete absorption in this task, I cannot even give sufficient time to the controversies at home to have a worthwhile comment concerning them. This is true, in spite of the fact that, on the outcome of some of those controversies, I think the future of our country can very well depend. Please assure our friend[4] that I am deeply appreciative of his thoughtfulness, and that I completely agree with him as to the advisability of sticking to my knitting.

My love to Marjorie[5] and, of course, my very warmest regard to yourself. *Cordially*

[1] For background on General Clay see no. 46.

[2] Clay had telephoned Eisenhower on Sunday, April 15, to discuss the relief of General MacArthur by President Truman. Clay's letter to Eisenhower, dated April 13 and marked "Personal and Confidential" (EM), concerned the same matter.

On Wednesday, April 11, 1951, President Truman had relieved General MacArthur of his commands as Supreme Commander, Allied Powers (SCAP); Commander in Chief, United Nations Command; Commander-in-Chief, Far East; and Commanding General, U.S. Army, Far East. Truman had concluded with "deep regret" that General MacArthur had been "unable to give his wholehearted support to the policies of the United States government and of the United Nations in matters pertaining to his official duties." MacArthur would be replaced by Lieutenant General Matthew B. Ridgway, CG of the Eighth Army in Korea since December 1950 (for background on Ridgway see *Eisenhower Papers*, vols. I–XI; on the controversy over MacArthur's command in the Far East see nos. 101, nn. 4, 5, and 128, n. 3. See also *New York Times*, Apr. 11–18, 1951).

[3] Clay had asked Eisenhower to keep silent on the subject of General MacArthur. "This we know," he wrote. "The Taft forces are definitely aligned with MacArthur who, because of his age, no longer seeks office but is determined to obtain vindication. Their *official* strategy (this is not hearsay) is to maneuver you into taking a position on the MacArthur issue, thus aligning you with the President and indirectly with his party and its inept conduct of government."

It was well known that Senator Robert A. Taft was hopeful of becoming the Republican candidate for the presidency in 1952. Taft understood the threat that Eisenhower's great popularity and his leadership of the NATO forces in Europe might pose to his quest for the nomination. Eisenhower, on the other hand, thought that the Republican isolationists could shake the very foundations of the NATO plan by attacking what they considered to be America's favoritism for Europe and European problems. MacArthur's rejection of Truman's foreign policy in the Far East was thus converted into a vehicle for partisan politics (see Barton J. Bernstein, "Election of 1952," in *History of American Presidential Elections, 1789–1968*, ed. Arthur M. Schlesinger, Jr., 4 vols. [New York, 1971], vol. IV, *1940–1968*, pp. 3215–25; Rovere and Schlesinger, *MacArthur Controversy*, pp. 230–31; James T. Patterson, *Mr. Republican: A Biography of Robert A. Taft* [Boston, 1972], pp. 484–89; and Manchester, *American Caesar*, pp. 632–33).

"Insist that your job is Europe," Clay wrote Eisenhower, and "you are in an unassailable position as Allied Commander in Chief to avoid being entangled in this mess." He reminded Eisenhower that it would require "careful thought" to escape involvement in U.S. Asiatic policy because "every effort will be made to use the MacArthur incident to hamper you, thus trying to arouse your anger and thus bringing about statements which can be interpreted as anti-MacArthur." For developments see no. 136.

[4] Clay said he had discussed this matter with "a mutual friend" and that the friend

was "as much opposed to isolationism as are you and I." The "mutual friend" was probably New York Governor Thomas E. Dewey. For developments see no. 196.
[5] Clay's wife, Marjorie McKeown Clay.

132   *Eisenhower Mss., Family File*

To John Sheldon Doud Eisenhower   *April 16, 1951*

Dear John: I have heard that your nomination as a permanent Captain has gone to the United States Senate. I am delighted—though it is, of course, agreed that, in my view, the nomination should have been for Colonel at the very least.[1]

I have just finished a week of inspection in the Allied Zones of Western Germany, and ended up by spending the weekend at Luxembourg.[2] Mrs. Mesta, our Minister there, had Mr. and Mrs. McCloy as her guests, also. This gave me a valuable opportunity to discuss the affairs of state with our High Commissioner in Germany.

Mamie is remaining at Luxembourg for the week, and I will run back and pick her up next weekend. It is a good thing for her to have this kind of a change, because, when she is here, she has nothing to do all day long but sit in her apartment and worry because our house is not available. I must say that such things move slowly in this country.[3]

Everywhere she goes, she carries pictures of her grandchildren.[4] I think that some of the stories she tells spring full-blown right out of her glowing imagination—nevertheless, I am not one to quarrel with her when she is talking about such a subject in such a tone.

We are, of course, counting on all of you coming over to visit us this summer. As I understand it, you figure you can be free to leave the United States about June 15th. If I were you, I would start in plenty of time to apply for passports, and get all your necessary innoculations and that sort of thing. While I cannot, as of this moment, state exactly the date that one of our airplanes will be making a trip back this way, still I know that I can arrange things so that our time can coincide fairly accurately with your first opportunity to come.[5]

Give our love to Barbie[6] and the children. *Devotedly*

[1] John Eisenhower's promotion from second lieutenant to the permanent rank of captain in the Regular Army was made official on May 14, 1951. At this time, John held the rank of captain in the AUS.
[2] For background on Eisenhower's trip to Germany and his visit with Perle Mesta in Luxembourg see no. 128, n. 1. On John J. McCloy, High Commissioner for Germany, see no. 12. Mrs. McCloy was the former Ellen Zinsser.
[3] The Eisenhowers were waiting for permanent housing near Paris (see no. 82, n. 5).

[4] The Eisenhower grandchildren were Dwight David II and Barbara Anne.
[5] John Eisenhower and his family would visit the senior Eisenhowers in June 1951 (see no. 183, n. 6). On April 23 Eisenhower would write again to John, enclosing a sum "to help defray whatever expenditures" he might incur during their forthcoming visit (EM).
[6] Barbara Jean, John's wife.

133   *Eisenhower Mss.*

To PHILIP YOUNG   *April 16, 1951*

Dear Phil:[1] Long before this, I should have answered your long and informative letter of April 2nd written from Florida.[2] I can plead nothing but preoccupation with a number of things; complicated by a week of flu, during which period I wasn't fit to do anything at all, much less writing a letter.

Of course, I am intensely interested in everything you are doing, but, as always, my primary Columbia concern—at least for the moment—is the Assembly and the related projects. I am tremendously excited by the impending "first conference." Unfortunately for me, you must go ahead and plan your schedule without the certainty that I can be there with you. While I have to say this with the deepest regret, I see no way, in view of constantly recurring crises and unpredictable development of problems, to count on being present for your conference even for the few days that would be necessary.[3]

Progress in my current job is slow, but, as long as progress can be detected, we are at least heading in the right direction. There is always hope that we can get the rails sufficiently well greased that speed will pick up. It seems odd to me that, while one never encounters any argument against the truth of the generalization that only in collective and unified action can the free world be assured of safety from the Communistic menace, yet numbers of nations can seem to find every kind of plausible excuse for failing to increase their efforts so as to assure the success of the collective effort. The world is certainly in a bewildered and confused state of mind.[4]

I am writing a note to Lew Douglas to tell him about my inability to come to New York in late May.[5] While, of course, if events should so shape themselves that I could drop in—on the spur of the moment, so to speak—you may be sure that I will do so; but, as of this writing, that appears to be a remote possibility.

Give my love to Faith,[6] and my warm regards to yourself and to your associates in the Assembly project. *Cordially*

[1] Young was executive director of the American Assembly conference program. The first conference was to be held May 21–25, 1951, at Columbia's Arden House (for background on Young and the American Assembly see no. 8, n. 6).

[2] Young had written to Eisenhower from St. Augustine, Florida, where he was recuperating from surgery (EM). His letter, which he described as a "progress report," concerned the plans and arrangements for the first American Assembly.

[3] Young had said: "Everyone is looking for you as they seem to think around the country that it is some mark of your continuing interest in the project. . . . So, if you don't have a major war on your hands, make your plans to be with us and get a little perspective on what you are trying to do!" On Eisenhower's reasons for not attending the first conference see no. 177, n. 4.

[4] Eisenhower frequently touched on this concern (see nos. 115 and 131).

[5] Lewis W. Douglas was chairman of the American Assembly's National Policy Board; Eisenhower's letter to him, dated April 16, 1951, is in EM.

[6] Mrs. Young.

134   *Eisenhower Mss.*

To CLARENCE FRANCIS   *April 16, 1951*

Dear Mr. Francis:[1] Thank you very much for your letter. It reached me while I was on a trip, and this is my first chance to answer it.[2]

When Sir Oswald Birley was in the United States, some months ago, I made a tentative engagement to sit for him. However, when I found that he would need eight sittings of more than an hour each, I had to cancel out, as I simply did not have that much time.[3]

If he should be ready to come to Paris, and could do the portrait at such irregular hours as I could give to him, I shall be glad to do as he suggests. Incidentally, within a day or so, my friend Lord Ismay[4] is to come over to visit me. He is a great friend of Sir Oswald's, and I shall tell him what I am putting in this letter. But I shall make no attempt to reach Sir Oswald because I understand that he will communicate with me after you write to him.[5]

I am glad that you are Chairman of the Civilian Committee appointed by Secretary Marshall. An investigation that is carried on concurrently with an operation and so serves as a spur for better performance, is far better than one necessarily initiated after the event, to discover reasons for failure.[6]

Please remember me to my friends in "General Foods," particularly to Marjorie Davies.[7] With warm personal regard,[8] *Cordially*

[1] Francis was chairman of the board of the General Foods Corporation (for background see no. 8).

[2] Francis's letter of April 4 (EM) had been received at SHAPE while Eisenhower

was inspecting troops in the British, French, and U.S. zones of Western Germany (see no. 128).

[3] Francis had said that his portrait had been painted recently by Captain Sir Oswald Hornby Joseph Birley, a New Zealand-born British artist, who had done portraits of King George V and Queen Mary. Francis noted that Birley was so anxious to do Eisenhower's portrait that "he would go anywhere in the world to paint it." Francis urged Eisenhower to comply: "I think," he said, "it would be considered very good public relations if you can spare the time." In 1949 Birley had been unable to arrange a schedule of sittings with Eisenhower (see McKinnon to Eisenhower, Jan. 14, 1949, EM).

[4] Lieutenant General Lord Ismay (for background see no. 5) would visit Eisenhower on April 17 (see Ismay to Eisenhower, Apr. 11, 1951, and Bowers to Ismay, Apr. 17, 1951, EM).

[5] On May 6 Birley would write to Eisenhower about a sittings schedule. It was finally agreed that sittings would begin on August 28 in Paris (all correspondence regarding these arrangements is in EM).

[6] Francis was chairman of the Citizens Advisory Committee on Military Training Installations. Secretary of Defense George C. Marshall had made the appointment (for developments see no. 206).

[7] Marjorie Merriweather Post Davies was a director of the General Foods Corporation (for background see Galambos, *Columbia University*, no. 414).

[8] Francis's reply of April 24 is in EM.

135   *Eisenhower Mss.*

To Sigfrid B. Unander   *April 17, 1951*
Personal and confidential

Dear Mr. Unander:[1] Fully appreciative of the public spirited purposes underlying your request to me of April 3rd, I must adhere to my feeling that, as an American soldier in uniform and on active service, I must abstain from claiming membership in a political party.[2]

It is true that, in the past, while temporarily released from active military duty in the American Army and serving as a University President, I have frequently expressed, publicly, my convictions and opinions respecting certain economic, social, and political questions, where I felt it appropriate for me to do so.[3] But under the circumstances of my present duties, in the performance of which my sole purpose is to serve the interests of our country as a whole, I must not only remain silent on all questions except those closely related to the military profession, but must certainly avoid participation in any kind of political argument.[4]

Permit me to extend to you, as a veteran of the ETO,[5] my very best wishes, and to express again my appreciation of the spirit that prompted your inquiry.[6] *Cordially*

[1] Unander, of Portland, Oregon, was chairman of Oregon's Republican State Central Committee.

[2] In a letter of April 3 Unander had asked Eisenhower to state his political party affiliation. "A number of your well-wishers," he said, "have expressed interest informally in placing your name on the ballot for the 1952 presidential primary in Oregon by petition of 1000 electors." Under these circumstances, Unander said, he would be required by law to take "certain formalities," and he hoped for Eisenhower's "assistance in clarifying matters." Unander pointed out that placing Eisenhower's name on the ballot did not require Eisenhower's consent. He also assured Eisenhower that if he wished, his party affiliation would be held confidential and "no information in this connection" would be "disseminated or 'leaked' to unauthorized persons" (EM). Unander had enclosed with his letter a copy of Oregon's Election Law #81–1107, 1950, and an Oregon Supreme Court decision regarding the law.

[3] See Galambos, *Columbia University*.

[4] In his role as Supreme Allied Commander heading NATO forces in Europe, Eisenhower repeatedly wrestled with this problem (see, for instance, his letters to Lucius Clay, no. 131; and to his brother Milton, no. 195. See also nos. 267, 551, 583, and 587).

[5] European Theater of Operations.

[6] Unander would write again on July 12, 1951, requesting once more Eisenhower's political party affiliation. In his reply of July 19 the General said, "I still hold firmly to my belief expressed in my letter of April 17th. I must remain, under the circumstances of my present duties, silent on all questions not closely related to the military profession." This and other similar correspondence from Unander is in EM. For developments see no. 358.

136   *Eisenhower Mss., Diaries*

DIARY   *April 17, 1951*

I have just returned from an inspection trip of allied units in Germany. The trip was really more one of a courtesy visit than an inspection—but I did contact service units at their daily training—ceremonies were forbidden.[1]

On Wednesday last, while visiting in the French zone, a reporter told me that MacArthur had been relieved, by order of the President, from his duties in Japan. I naturally refused to comment—and shall continue to do so.[2]

[1] For background on this trip see no. 128.

[2] Eisenhower had inspected French troops in Coblenz, Germany, on Wednesday, April 11, 1951 (see EM, Subject File, Aircraft, Trips. See also *New York Times*, Apr. 16, 1951). On the controversy between General MacArthur and President Truman see nos. 101, 128, and 131.

Immediately following his dismissal by Truman, MacArthur returned to the United States. He delivered a dramatic address at a joint meeting of Congress on

April 19, and on May 3 he began his testimony before a joint session of the Senate Armed Services and Foreign Relations committees. The inquiry, an investigation of his relief and the military situation in the Far East, would continue until August 17, 1951. By the time it was over, there was little doubt that Truman had had the support of his closest advisers in the decision to relieve MacArthur. A great deal has been written about the relief of General MacArthur and the events that followed (see the sources listed in no. 128, n. 3. See also U.S. Congress, Senate, Committee on Armed Services and Committee on Foreign Relations, *Military Situation in the Far East: Hearings*, 82d Cong., 1st sess., 1951; and Schnabel and Watson, *History of the Joint Chiefs of Staff*, vol. III, *The Joint Chiefs of Staff and the Korean War*, pt. 1, pp. 506–62).

137   *Eisenhower Mss.*

To ANDREW BROWNE CUNNINGHAM   *April 17, 1951*

Dear Andrew:[1] Your book arrived today, and, in spite of the fact that my desk is piled deep in papers due to my absence from Paris during the past week, I can scarcely keep myself from throwing everything overboard and retiring into a corner with your intriguing looking volume.[2] Thank you very much for sending it so promptly—I assure you that I am going to find in it many hours of interesting reading. Moreover, I pledge that, no matter what it says, I agree in advance. I can remember only one question on which you and I found ourselves on opposite sides; namely, the wisdom of Anvil[3] which the P.M.[4] finally renamed Dragon.[5] This christening he always claimed was more descriptive of the feeling he had of the operation.[6]

With warm regard and a cordial invitation to come over to see me any day that you can find the opportunity. *As ever*

[1] For background on Admiral of the Fleet Viscount Cunningham of Hyndhope see no. 96.

[2] Cunningham had written Eisenhower on March 31 (EM) that he was sending a copy of his newly published autobiography, *A Sailor's Odyssey* (New York, 1951).

[3] ANVIL was the code name for the Allied operation in the Mediterranean against southern France, August 15, 1944.

[4] British Prime Minister (PM) Winston S. Churchill.

[5] DRAGOON was the new code for ANVIL, selected by Churchill because, the story goes, he felt that he had been "dragooned" into the operation.

[6] Accounts of the controversy over ANVIL/DRAGOON may be found in Chandler, *War Years*, esp. nos. 1883 and 1884; Galambos, *Columbia University*, no. 114; and Forrest C. Pogue, *The Supreme Command*, U.S. Army in World War II, ed. Kent Roberts Greenfield (Washington, D.C., 1954), pp. 224–28. For Eisenhower's recollection of the disagreement see Eisenhower, *Crusade in Europe*, pp. 295, 281–84. Churchill discusses the operation in his memoir, *The Second World War*, vols. V, *Closing the Ring* (1952), pp. 511–14, and VI, *Triumph and Tragedy* (1953), pp. 57–71. Cunningham's views are in *A Sailor's Odyssey*, pp. 606, 608–9.

To William Thomas Faricy   *April 17, 1951*

Dear Bill:[1] Your nice note made a very pleasant punctuation mark in a busy day.[2]

My instant reaction is that Floyd Parks should immediately lose his amateur standing—a 73 at Columbia, including two birdies, is enough to force him to seek membership in PGA.[3]

Of course, I am glad that you got to have a chat with my brother. He is, by far, the brainiest of the Eisenhowers—and perhaps that is handing him faint praise.[4]

Please remember me kindly to Mrs. Faricy[5] and to your railway associates. With warmest regard to yourself, *Cordially*

P.S. A special Hello to Mr. Moorman.[6]

[1] Faricy, of Washington, D.C., was president of the Association of American Railroads.
[2] In his note of April 12 (EM) Faricy had said that he had played golf on April 11 at the Columbia Country Club in Chevy Chase, Maryland, with their mutual friend Major General Floyd Lavinius Parks, the Army's Chief of Information. Faricy had enclosed the scorecard, showing Parks's excellent performance, which Faricy said was due "to the prettiest work with a putter that it has been my privilege to witness" (for background on Parks see *Eisenhower Papers*, vols. I–XI).
[3] Professional Golfers' Association.
[4] On April 7 Faricy had called on Milton S. Eisenhower, president of Pennsylvania State College.
[5] Norma Hauser Faricy.
[6] Dan L. Moorman, general passenger agent for the Baltimore and Ohio Railroad, had also played golf with Faricy and Parks on April 11.

To Paul Gray Hoffman   *April 17, 1951*

Dear Paul:[1] Just today, I found quoted in my daily paper excerpts from a talk you had made. As usual, I find myself in emphatic agreement with what you had to say.[2] This reminds me to suggest that, possibly, the time is here when you should make another visit to this region. I would most certainly like to see you, and I urge that, if any reason at all should bring you across the Atlantic, you give me enough notice so that I can make sure of the time to have a long visit with you.[3]

Phil Young has told me about the cooperative effort between the Ford Foundation and the Columbia Business School in making a study of our current manpower situation. As of today, the importance of such a study cannot be over-estimated. I am certain that your effort to produce, through the Ford Foundation, explorations into the possibilities of bringing new light upon critical world problems, will be productive of real good. We have had enough of ritualistic and routine approaches to such matters. It is time that imagination, determination, and elbow grease were substituted for complacency, partisanship, and just sheer stupidity.[4]

Remember, there will be a warm welcome, always, for you here. With personal regard to you and to your nice family, *Cordially*

[1] Hoffman, former head of the Economic Cooperation Administration, was president of the Ford Foundation (for background see Galambos, *Columbia University*).

[2] Eisenhower was probably referring to an account of Hoffman's radio talk aired over the Mutual Broadcasting System from Washington, D.C., on April 15 (*New York Times*, Apr. 16, 1951). Hoffman was one of a series of weekly speakers who had been invited to discuss current problems facing the nation. According to the article, Hoffman had cited the political differences arising from the dismissal of General MacArthur as an example of the sort of "quarreling on the home front" that would "lessen morale on the fighting front" at a cost to be "reckoned in blood." He urged Americans to rise above partisanship (see no. 131), and he praised Congress for approving the deployment of U.S. troops in Europe—proof, he said, that "we are emerging from our historic isolationism and complacency" (see no. 128).

Hoffman also touched on the need for Congress to levy extra taxes to put the nation on a "pay-as-you-go basis" to "avert serious inflation." Inflation, he said, would be a "cheap victory for the Communists. . . ." He also endorsed the establishment of universal military service.

[3] Hoffman would visit Eisenhower in June 1951 (see no. 200).

[4] Columbia University's Graduate School of Business, in cooperation with the Ford Foundation, had established a National Manpower Council to study the nation's human resources and manpower needs (for background see no. 10). Philip Young, dean of the Business School, would serve as deputy chairman of the council; funding would be provided by a grant of $100,000 from the Ford Foundation. Columbia's existing Conservation of Human Resources Project would be expanded to accommodate the council's research (for background on the Human Resources Project see Galambos, *Columbia University*).

140   *Eisenhower Mss., Family File*

TO MILTON STOVER EISENHOWER   *April 17, 1951*

Dear Milton: I think the suggestion given to you by the official of C.I.O. is a most appropriate one. I regret that you cannot find it possible to come over here personally, but I should like the name of your friend so that, if he should come over, my staff can be on the look-out for him and arrange a meeting.[1]

Of course, it is not my personal business to sell any idea to civilians, either nationally or internationally. Nevertheless, once embarked on such a responsibility as this is, there is no escaping many collateral duties—if for no other reason than there seems to be no one else to undertake them.

My love to Helen[2] and the family, and, of course, all the best to you. *Cordially*

[1] In a letter of April 12 Eisenhower's brother Milton had passed on a suggestion made to him recently by a leading official of the Congress of Industrial Organizations (CIO). The suggestion had come from Frank Grasso, former president of the CIO Paperworkers Local 292 in New York City and currently an officer of the United Paperworkers of America. Grasso had proposed that Eisenhower might wish to employ the aid of outstanding labor leaders in the United States, Great Britain, and other countries as well to "help sell the whole idea of cooperation for the defense of Western Europe." Such an effort would be possible, Milton related, without direct involvement of Eisenhower himself or of his headquarters (EM).
[2] Milton's wife.

141   *Eisenhower Mss.*

To ALPHONSE PIERRE JUIN   *April 19, 1951*

Dear General Juin:[1] I agree with your reply to Mr. Jenkisson, the Paris Bureau Chief of LIFE Magazine, and I also agree with the observations you make in your letter to me. We have, of course, taken all necessary steps to see that classified material does not reach unauthorized sources, but "our collaborators" represent a more complicated problem.[2]

We find that our Office of Public Information is very useful in handling such matters as the LIFE queries that were directed to you. Here in my Headquarters, we receive many such inquiries. If I, my Chief of Staff, or my principal staff officers were not shielded from this sort of thing by specialists in the field of public information, we would be unable to accomplish any other work. I imagine you will be deluged with such queries from the press, and in particular the United States press, once you have established yourself at Fontainebleau.[3]

As a matter of interest, I have learned from General Lanham[4] that Mr. Jenkisson submitted these queries to you as the result of a direct order from his editor in the United States. He himself had protested the absurdity of the queries but was over-ruled. He told General Lanham that he did not expect an answer to these questions.[5] *Sincerely*

[1] General Juin was Commander in Chief, Allied Army Forces, Central Europe (see no. 16, n. 6).

[2] Juin, in his April 7 letter to Eisenhower (EM), had protested a request from John Jenkisson, chief of *Life* magazine's Paris bureau, for information to be used in a comprehensive article on the military defense of Europe. Juin had enclosed copies of Jenkisson's letter and of his reply (both letters, dated Mar. 21, 1951, and Apr. 7, 1951, respectively, are in EM, Juin Corr.). Juin had declined the request on the grounds that "General Eisenhower has the exclusive right to transmit such information to the press without creating difficulties." To Eisenhower, Juin explained that "subjects which should be carefully avoided in superficial conversation are often discussed without abiding by the necessary precautions that security involves." It would be wise, he said, if "our collaborators be imbued with the necessity of observing these rules, pertaining to confidential information of which the importance is all to [*sic*] obvious." In a handwritten notation to General Gruenther penned at the bottom of Juin's letter, Eisenhower had asked, "What are we to do about this?"

[3] Headquarters, Allied Army Forces, Central Europe.

[4] Brigadier General Charles Trueman Lanham (USMA 1924), who had been Chief of the Army's Information and Education Division from 1945 until 1948, was currently SHAPE Chief of Public Information (for background see Chandler, *War Years*, no. 2447; and Galambos, *Chief of Staff*, no. 581).

[5] See Lanham to Gruenther, April 18, 1951, EM, Juin Corr. As it turned out, *Life* magazine would publish two comprehensive articles on the military defense of Europe (see Charles J. V. Murphy, "The War We May Fight," *Life*, May 28, 1951, p. 76; and Andre Laguerre, "Optimist in Arms," *ibid.*, July 16, 1951, p. 108). For developments see no. 273.

142   *Eisenhower Mss.*

To WILLIAM AVERELL HARRIMAN   *April 20, 1951*
Confidential

Dear Averell: Thank you very much for your long letter.[1] Your communications contain exactly the things that I like to hear about.

Recently, I have been visiting some of the troop training areas.[2] I find the morale of the troops to be at a much higher level than it is among civilians—especially those politicians who are concerned chiefly with the "next election." Incidentally, the training standards are high; it is in numbers and material that we are weak.

Field Marshal Montgomery has been a fine team-mate.[3] He is one of the best trainers of troops that I know. He is thorough, painstaking, and, surprisingly enough, he is patient. Moreover, he makes no attempt to seize the limelight at the expense of his subordinates and assistants. I could say similar things about practically all my principal associates. (I think I told you that I plan, soon, to recommend Gruenther to Collins for promotion.[4] If any disability should overtake me, we should have at least one American of suitable rank and fairly well-known in Europe who could be regarded as a logical successor.)

Gruenther, of course, is tops, as is Larry Norstad.[5] Saunders, of the British Air Force, and Admiral Capponi, of the Italian Navy, are both exceedingly capable men;[6] and I have others, some of whom you possibly know, that are equally good.

There is a growing feeling among us that we should soon establish a combined college, possibly under some such name as the NATO Defense College. It would be small, but the student body, probably of about forty or fifty, should contain individuals from all participating nations, except, possibly, Portugal, Iceland, and Luxembourg. I think that, in both the instructional and student staffs, we would have representatives from the diplomatic world, as well as from the military and economic fields. The general purpose would be to build up common doctrine and basic convictions applicable to the defense of the North Atlantic community. There is no question in our minds as to the potential efficacy of such an institution. Because Paris is a great center of communications for travelers from many countries, I think that such an institution would have to be located close to this city. This would assure us the presence of experts as lecturers, and would be a central place for the concentration of the student body.[7]

There is nothing to do about the matter until we can prepare a plan, because the Standing Group and Council of Deputies will have to approve and support the idea, or it could not go forward.

We need a somewhat similar institution in the tactical field, but this we can develop—I think—under our own steam, with little or no outside help. It will probably be located in one of the occupational areas so as to use a troop unit as a demonstrating organization, and because a great deal of the instruction would be practical rather than merely theoretical.[8]

I have told you of my interest in the development of an effective information service for NATO. This is a question that I am sure Spofford has under consideration, and I do hope that he gets to going on it in a big way.[9]

In France, almost every proposal or worthwhile NATO discussion now finds itself stymied on the need for postponement *until after the election.*[10] Such matters as airbases,[11] extension of term of military service,[12] use of French conscripts outside Continental Europe, and a dozen others all must await eventual decision until the election is out of the way. This is bad enough if the election is held—as some hope—on June 10th. But many observers believe that the elections will not be held before October, because of the need for prior electoral reform. If local progress is to be largely stagnated until next October, it will be annoying, to say the least.

Pug Ismay came over from Britain to spend a night with me.[13] Our talk was general in nature and, of course, a lot of it involved reminiscences of World War II. However, our real purpose was to talk over relationships of the moment, and he seemed to think that, in Britain, there has been a considerable amelioration of the bitterness that swept that country with the first hint of the Fechteler appointment.[14] There is a general impression that the whole matter was handled without sufficient regard for public opinion—but I do not know that, in that particular instance, the British Government should be too much blamed, since I understand that the matter came to public attention accidentally, through a leak in Copenhagen. Everybody was apparently caught by surprise.

This brings up again the thought that we must constantly work at the job of producing and sustaining NATO solidarity; it will not develop among peoples unless their leaders take constant and positive action. An obstacle to such a growth is found in every crisis that is brought about by the Communists throughout the world, because of the human tendency always to "take sides" in a quarrel, no matter how little we may know about causes and consequences.

The first obvious truth is that there is an inescapable relationship between attainment of NATO objectives and the numerous aggressions and activities of the Communists in many fronts throughout the world. The Iranian incident is particularly disturbing. If all Western Europe countries have to forgo the oil now received from Iranian sources, the situation will be awkward; yet many people believe the entire trouble springs from British exploitation of nations.[15] The building up of Satellite forces on the borders of Yugoslavia causes uneasiness in this region; but many say, "Tito is just another Communist, to hell with him." I am glad to know that the American Government has been studying this situation, together with its own intentions and attitudes with respect to future eventualities.[16] Another question mark is Spain— some think her important to us; others deride such an idea.[17] The Moslem world grows restive—I firmly believe that, in this case, the Russians are getting far closer to the masses than we are; I sometimes have the uneasy feeling that in those countries our side deals primarily with the classes that have been exploiting their own people since time immemorial. The Soviet method is, through bribery, the use of agents, and the skillful use of propaganda, to appeal *directly to the massses*. But serious as is the attitude of a united Arab world, it is surprising how many people want to treat the Moslem nations with disdain, if not complete callousness.[18] The arguments over the wars, both in Indo China and in Korea, are not only important domestically, they have great weight in determining progress in NATO.

A recent example of one phase of this whole problem was presented in the French effort to decide whether or not to reinforce her troops in Indo China.[19] Militarily, the thing boils down to the hope of gaining a quick and definite tactical victory in that region and thereafter trusting the defense largely to native troops, bringing the Frenchmen back here to participate, directly, in the defense of Europe. If this much of a victory is not possible in Indo China, then reinforcement is obviously silly, but it is clear that there is a *close relationship* between the activities in the two regions. Therefore, the question transcended the strictly nationalistic limits of French responsibility and appeared important to us all. (In this particular case, when my opinion was requested locally, I refused to give it on the grounds that, for the moment at least, it had to be treated as a strictly French decision. It isn't.) But when I commented on this matter to some of my colleagues, the interesting fact was that they did not seem to discern the inescapable effects of this struggle upon NATO prospects and purposes. Such a failure, it seems to me, results direct from the habit of thinking of "West *versus* East" instead of "West *and* East."

So I repeat that a constant concern of leadership should be to see that differing national attitudes and policies toward Iran or Indo China, or Korea or India, or any other subject, do not become such bitter issues between NATO nations that we tend to fall apart. The Soviets will certainly not fail to give us enough opportunities to make this mistake!

Well, I see that I have gotten into a mere speculative observation at this point, so I stop for now.[20] *Cordially*

[1] Harriman's three-page letter of April 9 is in EM. He told Eisenhower that Congress, which had been pressing the Truman Administration to take more vigorous action to cope with the "state of emergency" occasioned by the American defeats in Korea (see no. 16, n. 5), had lost its sense of urgency and was now "trying to find ways to cut back on proposals." Harriman also told Eisenhower that General Douglas MacArthur's latest "series of 'ind[i]scretions' (to put it mildly)" were "causing new bewilderment—not to speak of what they are doing on your side of the Atlantic" (see nos. 101 and 128). Harriman hinted that President Truman would soon move to correct the situation: "Action will be taken by the time you get this letter."

[2] On Eisenhower's trip to Germany see no. 128, n. 1.

[3] For background on Bernard Law Montgomery's appointment as Deputy SACEUR see no. 74; see also Alun Chalfont, *Montgomery of Alamein* (New York, 1976), pp. 298–99.

[4] See nos. 230 and 231.

[5] For background on General Lauris Norstad, Eisenhower's air commander in Central Europe, see no. 77, n. 17.

[6] Air Chief Marshal Sir Hugh Saunders was Eisenhower's deputy for air; Ferrante Capponi was Assistant Chief of Staff for Personnel and Administration at SHAPE. For background see no. 77, nn. 5 and 8, respectively.

[7] Eisenhower would soon propose the creation of a NATO defense college along the lines indicated here. He would recommend that the students be senior officers (colonels or higher) or selected civil servants who might later be available for high NATO posts (DUSM-253-51, May 2, 1951, OS/D, 1951, Clas. Decimal File, CD 092.3 NATO; D-D [51] 160, June 19, 1951, NATO Files, microfilm). On June 25

the NAC deputies would agree to Eisenhower's proposal and would direct the immediate establishment of the defense college. The capital, operational, and maintenance costs were to come out of the SHAPE budget; pay, allowance, and subsistence costs were to be borne by the students' governments (D-D [51] 172, July 2, 1951, NATO Files, microfilm). The NATO Defense College would open on November 19, 1951, in a wing of the Ecole Militaire in Paris. The curriculum would feature lectures and round-table discussions on weekday mornings; during the afternoons the students would prepare written reports on North Atlantic defense problems (Ismay, *NATO*, p. 79; *New York Times*, Nov. 18, 20, 1951).

[8] Eisenhower would recommend "the establishment of a centralized agency for the dissemination of standard Land/Air warfare doctrines and procedures." He would advocate using the existing facilities at the School of Land/Air Warfare in Old Sarum, England. The instructors would come from Great Britain, France, and the United States (*U.S. Draft Report by the International Planning Team* to the Standing Group, [May 1951], CCS 092 Western Europe [3-12-48], Sec. 90).

[9] On the NATO Information Service see nos. 77, n. 3, and 111, n. 6. On Charles M. Spofford, the U.S. representative on the Council of Deputies, see no. 16, n. 16.

[10] For background on the political situation in France see no. 53. The election would not be held until June 17 (see no. 318).

[11] The United States was trying to obtain airfields for use by U.S. forces in Europe and Morocco (see nos. 98 and 115, n. 9). For developments see no. 223.

[12] For the length of the French military service term see no. 16, n. 5.

[13] On Lieutenant General Lord Hastings Ismay's visit see no. 134, n. 4.

[14] For background on the controversy over the proposed appointment of an American, Admiral William Fechteler, as SACLANT see no. 45, n. 8.

[15] For background on the situation in Iran see no. 149, n. 5. Secretary of State Dean Acheson would later attribute the crisis in part to "the unusual and persistent stupidity of the [Anglo-Iranian Oil] company and the British Government in their management of the affair" (Acheson, *Present at the Creation*, p. 501). Harriman would tell Eisenhower that the United States was "trying . . . to help the situation in Iran." Harriman noted that apart from U.S. foreign-and military-aid programs, "CIA is increasing its activities" (Harriman to Eisenhower, Apr. 26, 1951, EM). For developments see nos. 233, n. 6, and 259.

[16] In 1948 Yugoslavia's Communist government, led by Marshal Josip Broz Tito (see no. 150, n. 4), had broken away from the Soviet bloc to establish a more independent position in international affairs (Daniel Yergin, *Shattered Peace: The Origins of the Cold War and the National Security State* [Boston, 1977], pp. 380–82; Herbert Feis, *From Trust to Terror: The Onset of the Cold War, 1945–1950* [New York, 1970], pp. 313–15). In 1951 the United States was considering a program of military aid for the Yugoslavs, and on March 1 Harriman had written Eisenhower that the U.S. officials had reached "agreement to ship Tito secretly a part of the military equipment he asked for. . . . At Tito's request, all of this has been kept very quiet and only a few people in Washington know about it" (EM). A U.S. interdepartmental intelligence estimate of March 20 concluded that "the continuing military build up in the neighboring Satellite states (increase in armed forces, stockpiling, re-equipment, gasoline conservation, stepping up of war industry, etc.) . . . has given the Satellites the capability of launching a major invasion of Yugoslavia with little warning" (State, *Foreign Relations, 1951*, vol. IV, *Europe: Political and Economic Developments, Part II*, pp. 1755–58; and vol. III, *European Security and the German Question, Part I*, p. 128). In Harriman's April 9 letter he told Eisenhower that Tito was sending his C/S to explain to Secretary of Defense Marshall and the JCS "not only the Yugoslav capabilities and plans if attacked, but also what Tito is prepared to do in other eventualities. . . . All of this is being arranged outside

of the normal diplomatic channels, and is therefore particularly secret" (see also Harriman to Eisenhower, Apr. 26, 1951, EM; and Bradley to Marshall, Jan. 9, 1951, OS/D, 1951, Clas. Decimal File, CD 091.3 MDAP [Yugoslavia]). For developments see no. 332.

[17] For background on the issue of Spain's relations with NATO see nos. 16, n. 3, and 240, n. 5.

[18] Eisenhower was probably referring to events in Iran (see n. 15 above) and in Egypt, where nationalistic feelings and anti-British sentiment threatened to undermine Anglo-American strategy (see no. 408). Under current war plans (see no. 124), the Cairo-Suez area was to be an important staging position for the U.S. strategic bombing campaign; it was also important because it was near vital Middle Eastern oil fields (see Galambos, *Columbia University*, nos. 294 and 380). For developments see no. 573 in this volume.

[19] See nos. 88 and 89.

[20] Harriman would reply in a letter of April 26 (EM) that he had passed Eisenhower's letter on to President Truman. For developments see no. 167.

143 *Eisenhower Mss.*

To William Edward Robinson

April 20, 1951

Dear Bill: If a Congressional Committee should investigate me on the charge of procrastination, I would have no chance at all if it should pose the simple question, "How often have you put off your intention of writing to Bill?" Even now, I could find a hundred reasons for convincing myself that I am very, very busy, but none of them is so blankety blank important. Besides, only a few minutes ago, Helen Reid was in my office, which reminded me to get off a note to you before I do anything else.[1]

For the past week, Mamie has been in Luxembourg. I was delighted for her to visit with her friend Perle because, as of now, we have no place to stay except a rather boring apartment, and Mamie gets exceedingly fed up staying in it day after day. I am going to Luxembourg this afternoon, to bring her back tomorrow.[2]

I have been following the papers closely on the progress of the MacArthur incident. In some ways, it is another "Billy Mitchell" case. We have, in a way, the reverse of Voltaire's statement; in other words, "right or wrong, *was there* an inherent right to say it?"[3]

There seems to be an alarming amount of heat developing in some of the relationships among various NATO nations. Right now, every day's paper brings an account of some new case of friction between the United States and Britain. Frankly, in most of these instances, I have believed our Government to be completely and absolutely correct. Nevertheless, I must say that I regret the existence of the quarrel itself.[4]

I do hope that you and Cliff, Slats and Pete, Jack Budinger, Bob

Woodruff, Jay Gould, George Allen, and some of the others find a reason for coming over this way sometime during the summer. After all, if I were in Denver this summer, you would find an opportunity to come out there, and I believe it takes only about ten hours more to fly to Paris than it does to Denver. (I admit that I have heard that every scheduled plane is already booked solid, but, for people with such great influence as the gang I have just named, this would be a very minor difficulty. In fact, I would suggest you just turn it over to the great Allen.)[5]

My very best to all our friends, and, of course, my warm regard to you. *Cordially*

[1] For background on Robinson, executive vice-president of the *New York Herald Tribune*, see no. 39. In his letter of April 9 (EM) Robinson had said that *Herald Tribune* president Helen Rogers Reid was then "on the high seas" on her way to Europe (on Reid see no. 36). A copy of this document is in the Robinson Papers.

[2] For Mamie's visit with U.S. Minister to Luxembourg Perle Mesta see no. 128, n. 1. On the Eisenhowers' residence at the Trianon Palace Hotel in Versailles and their search for a house see no. 180.

[3] The MacArthur affair in many ways paralleled the controversial 1925 courtmartial of the late Colonel William "Billy" Mitchell. Mitchell, a former assistant chief of the Air Service, had been a staunch advocate of air power in the years immediately following World War I. Frequently reprimanded for his outspoken criticism of U.S. defense policy, Mitchell nonetheless continued to advocate the establishment of an autonomous air arm and increased appropriations for aircraft. On one occasion, Mitchell released strongly worded press statements accusing the Navy and War departments of incompetence and "criminal . . . almost treasonable negligence" in national defense. As a result of these unauthorized statements, President Calvin Coolidge preferred charges against the colonel, who was tried by courtmartial in 1925. Ironically, MacArthur (at one time a close friend of Mitchell's) had served as a member of the court that, amidst wide publicity, found the airman guilty on all counts and ordered his suspension from rank, command, and pay for a period of five years (see Burke Davis, *The Billy Mitchell Affair* [New York, 1967], pp. 218–329; Alfred F. Hurley, *Billy Mitchell: Crusader for Air Power* [Bloomington, Ind., 1975], pp. 100–107; Manchester, *American Caesar*, pp. 136–37; and *New York Times*, Apr. 12, 1951). On the MacArthur case, which also involved presidential action following the release of unauthorized statements, see nos. 101, 131, and 136.

The statement attributed to Voltaire is, "I disapprove of what you say, but I will defend to the death your right to say it."

[4] Two major issues, NATO command appointments and British recognition of Communist China, had created strained Anglo-American relations from almost the day Eisenhower assumed command of SHAPE. During February the proposed appointment of American Admiral William Fechteler to the important NATO post of SACLANT had produced such heated debate in the House of Commons that any appointment to the position (which was roughly equivalent to Eisenhower's own) was postponed until 1952 (see nos. 45 and 142). Soon after this incident, there was more friction over the appointment of a commander to the Mediterranean area (see nos. 390 and 507).

The issue of British and American relations with the Communist and Nationalist Chinese, a point of contention between the two allies since 1950, had been exacerbated by the MacArthur affair. MacArthur's threats to carry the Korean War across the Yalu River by either conventional or atomic means and his expressed desire to use Nationalist troops to open a second front in mainland China had evoked strong protests from the British (see no. 101; Donovan, *Tumultuous Years*, pp. 260, 299–302, 316–18; and *International Herald Tribune*, Paris ed., Apr. 14, 16, 1951). The U.S. government flatly rejected later British proposals that the Communist Chinese be allowed to participate in the negotiations for a Japanese peace treaty and ultimately to take control of the Nationalist-held island of Formosa.

[5] These were friends and golfing partners of the General's. Clifford Roberts, Ellis Slater, Robert Woodruff, William Alton "Pete" Jones, Frankfort Distillers Corporation executive vice-president Jay Gould, and John Michael Budinger, president and director of the Commercial National Bank & Trust Company of New York, were all members of the Augusta (Georgia) National Golf Club. On the General's farming partner George Allen and his airplane see Galambos, *Columbia University*, no. 92. Of this group, only Budinger would fail to visit Eisenhower in Europe during the coming summer (see appointment calendar and individual correspondence in EM).

144   *Eisenhower Mss.*

To WALTER BEDELL SMITH   *April 20, 1951*

Dear Beetle:[1] I suppose that the idea of writing you a letter has occurred to me a hundred times in the past few weeks; always, I seem to stumble in the carrying out of my intention. However, when C. D. Jackson stopped to see me the other day, and we began to talk about a lot of things of current interest to you as well as to me, and then reminisced awhile about the Algiers days, I could not wait longer to start a message to you.[2]

First of all, I sincerely hope that you continue to improve in health. Along this thought occurs another very important one, which is that maybe you would improve even more rapidly if you would take a few days away from Washington and come over to see me. Although Mamie and I are still living in a hotel apartment, we could have a nice time and, possibly, one that would be of benefit to both our jobs. I realize that you may have the fear that I would try to put a "touch" on you, but, if I do, I will try to make it of minor proportions in spite of the fact that we seem to have no one to pay our bills.[3]

Schow seems to be doing a splendid job for us, although our whole Intelligence problem is not an easy one to solve. We, of course, must depend upon London and Washington, and this introduces a lot of difficulties, particularly because of the fact that we have one or two other nations represented in our G–2 organization. Incidentally, one of our fine G–2 officers is an Italian named Pasquale.[4]

Many people bring to me tales of fine fishing opportunities. So far,

I have had no chance at all to investigate the truth of any of these rumors, so I cannot give you the facts. It occurs to me, though, that it would be a splendid Intelligence objective to prepare a full report on this type of thing. If you undertake the job personally, I will try to assist you.

All this may be just an idle dream, but I still think it would be a very splendid thing for you to come over here for a visit, even if it had to be a brief one.[5]

Give our love to Norry,[6] and, of course, warmest regard to yourself. *Cordially*

[1] Smith, who had been Eisenhower's chief of staff during World War II, was head of the Central Intelligence Agency (for background see Galambos, *Columbia University*, no. 950).

[2] Charles Douglas Jackson, vice-president and managing director of Time-Life International, had visited Eisenhower on April 19. Eisenhower is referring to the period (1942–43) when he was Allied C in C, North Africa Theater of Operations, and Jackson was Deputy Chief, Office of War Information, in North Africa and the Middle East (for further background on Jackson see Galambos, *Chief of Staff*, no. 1650).

[3] Smith, who had undergone surgery for a chronic peptic ulcer a year before (see Galambos, *Columbia University*, nos. 745, n. 6, and 776), would visit the Eisenhowers in September 1951 (see no. 360 in these volumes).

[4] For background on intelligence problems see no. 125. Colonel Robert Alwin Schow, Assistant Director of the CIA from 1949 to 1951, was deputy to the assistant chief of staff for intelligence (see Chandler, *War Years*, no. 1700; for developments see nos. 271 and 510 in these volumes). The personnel in SHAPE's Intelligence Division (G–2) numbered nearly fifty, most of them from the United States and the United Kingdom. Other members represented France, Italy, Belgium, the Netherlands, and Norway. The officer Eisenhower mentions was Brigadier General Vincenzo Pasquale.

[5] Smith would assure Eisenhower that the CIA would provide "everything of interest" to the American officers at SHAPE. He added that Eisenhower's G–2, General Airey, could not receive U.S. intelligence information until the British government granted him clearance. For developments see no. 162.

[6] Smith's wife, the former Mary Eleanor ("Nory") Cline.

145   *Eisenhower Mss.*

To HERBERT BAYARD SWOPE   *April 20, 1951*

Dear Herbert:[1] Many thanks for your nice letter. I regret to note your opinion that the controversial heat will mount a long ways before it reaches its peak.[2] If ever this poor old world, including our part of it, needed some unifying influence based upon common comprehension of essential values, common appreciation of the danger under which they exist, and common determination to join in their protection, this is the time. It is so easy to develop centrifugal force; every time one whirls a club about his head, he does so. On the other hand, centripetal force is produced with much greater difficulty and much less frequency, but how we need it!

When you see B.B.,[3] please give him my warm greetings and best regards. Before I left Washington, I had quite a talk with Charlie Wilson concerning the project Bernie had suggested to me. I have now issued an invitation to Charlie to come over here, because I want to talk to him about it further.[4]

With my very best to you, *Cordially*

[1] For background on Swope see no. 66.
[2] Swope had written to Eisenhower about President Truman's dismissal of General Douglas MacArthur. "All Hell has broken loose," Swope said, "but the present moment will be a summer breeze in comparison to what we will see in a month from now." He was worried about the international repercussions of the dismissal and about the "really bitter political battle coming." Swope thought, however, that Americans should stand behind the President. For background on the Truman-MacArthur conflict see nos. 101, 128, 131, and 136.
[3] Bernard M. Baruch (for background see no. 25, n. 4).
[4] Charles E. Wilson was Director of the Office of Defense Mobilization (for background see no. 45, n. 4). In a letter of April 16, 1951 (EM), Eisenhower had invited Wilson to visit him in Paris to discuss "prospects in the production field" that were of mutual interest (for background on Baruch's proposal see no. 100). Wilson would visit Eisenhower from April 28 until May 1, 1951 (see EM, Wilson Corr.).

In a reply of April 23 Swope said, "I agree with the opinion you expressed in your note of 20 April. . . . Both sides are characterized by a venom which is incredible. . . . I am so glad you are out of it" (EM).

146   *Eisenhower Mss.*

To EDWARD JOHN BERMINGHAM   *April 20, 1951*

Dear Ed:[1] I am grateful for the trouble you took in writing to me. Without any argument whatsoever, I agree with your observation about "capitalistic system."[2]

With respect to the observation I had previously made that my readiness to respond to the call of duty defeated my former hope of devoting my remaining years to constructive aims, I meant to imply something different, I think, than what you read into the sentence. I meant, first, that I had become very absorbed in the value of the service that Columbia could perform for the nation and felt that the work I could do there would be completely constructive. My present assignment definitely interfered—for what period of time, we cannot tell—with that program.[3]

Secondly, I meant to imply that any military task (except in unusual or exceptional circumstances) is largely negative in character. Its purpose is to protect or defend, not to create and develop. These were the thoughts I had in mind when I wrote that particular sentence.

Helen Reid was in today, and, within the past several weeks, numbers of old friends from the United States have dropped in for brief talks.[4] I find that there is little difficulty in explaining the purposes and need for NATO when there is opportunity for a calm, unimpassioned conversation. Because of this, I am quite astonished at the number of people who come over here who have apparently given almost no thought to these important—vitally important—affairs.

I shall be on the look-out for the Noe Xercisor. With it, possibly I can go back to some of my boyhood games, such as boxing, baseball, and the like. I doubt, however, that it can restore hair to a bald head.[5]

My love to Kay[6] and the other members of your nice family, and, of course, warm regard to yourself. *Cordially*

---

[1] For background on Bermingham see no. 23, n. 1.

[2] In a letter of April 14 (EM) Bermingham had pointed out that in Europe "capitalism is a system of rigid low wages" that is "handily used by the Communists to damn us and all our works." On the other hand, he defined capitalism in the United States as an "overall system of individual endeavor, profitable to management, labor, and ownership. . . ."

[3] Bermingham had said, "I like to believe that the extraordinary effort you are making and the example you are setting will in no manner defeat your hope."

[4] For background on Reid see no. 36, n. 1; for the names of Eisenhower's current visitors from the United States see the Chronology in vol. XIII.

[5] Bermingham said that he was sending Eisenhower a "Noe Xercisor," which he described as "simply a rubber band with a 27 pound pull and a couple of handles." He was certain that Eisenhower would enjoy the contrivance because, he said, "wherever you are you can always have it with you for a refreshing morning interlude" (see no. 265).

[6] Mrs. Bermingham (see no. 23, n. 12).

---

147   *Eisenhower Mss.*

To CLIFFORD ROBERTS   *April 23, 1951*

Dear Cliff:[1] Thanks for your letter and the check. I must say that I can't remember having been ahead on any sporting venture in years; maybe I have been neglecting my opportunities.[2]

Your letter gives a succinct review of the situation that prevails in the United States.[3]

Recently, I have been on a jaunt, and tomorrow I start a new trip, this time to Italy.[4] I am in pretty fair condition, but I have had so little opportunities for golf that I am going to be an easy mark for anyone, even with my habitual handicap of 18.

My very best to all the gang, and, again, thanks for the fine check. (I have endorsed it to John and Barbie[5] to help them to defray their vacation expenses this summer.) *As ever*

[1] Roberts was an old friend of Eisenhower's (see no. 7 for background).

[2] Eisenhower had won eighty-two dollars on the Masters Golf Tournament in a betting pool organized by Roberts and other friends at Augusta National Golf Club (for background see no. 113; and for correspondence regarding the bet see EM).

[3] Roberts's letter (Apr. 18, 1951, EM) concerned President Truman's dismissal of General MacArthur on April 11, 1951. "Harry Truman has succeeded in making a popular hero out of McArthur [*sic*]," wrote Roberts, "something that the General was never able to do for himself." Roberts worried that MacArthur had unknowingly become the "Standard Bearer" for those who were critical of U.S. foreign policy. On April 19 Roberts would write again: "I thought MacArthur's speech today, and its delivery, added to the *popular* hero position handed to him by Truman" (EM; *New York Times*, Apr. 20, 1951). On the controversy see nos. 101, 128, n. 3, 131, and 136, n. 2.

[4] Eisenhower had returned on April 16 from an inspection trip in Germany (see the Chronology in vol. XIII). On the General's trip to Italy see no. 153.

[5] Eisenhower's son and daughter-in-law, John S. D. and Barbara T. Eisenhower, who would visit the General and Mrs. Eisenhower in June (see no. 183, n. 6).

148

CCS 092 Western Europe
(3-12-48), Sec. 80

To Joint Chiefs of Staff
Cable ALO 121. Top Secret

April 23, 1951

SACEUR Paris France from P&O Div Personal from Eisenhower[01]

1. I concur with your view that it is essential to resolve the Mediterranean Command problem and that for Southern Europe as soon as possible.[2] Our precarious position in the Austro-Italy couverture, the uncertainty of Soviet intentions with respect to Yugoslavia, and the adverse psychological applications among Southern European-Mediterranean nation[s] from further delay are impelling reasons for early action.[3]

2. I accept, with minor modifications, the JCS position on command arrangements as proposed for me in JCS 86466[4] both because these arrangements provide for a simple and definite allocation of responsibilities between commanders concerned and also because they simplify my own command structure for my Southern Area. It seems clear to me that neither the British nor the compromise solutions proposed in JCS 88848 satisfy those requirements.[5]

3. Study of this problem convinces me that much of the difficulty inescapably arises from the necessary establishment of 2 Supreme Commanders in adjacent areas, portions of which cannot reasonably be separated one from the other. Specifically it is impossible to conceive of the defense of Western Europe including Italy without concern for naval problems involved in the Adriatic, the Ionian, the Tyrrhenian and the Ligurian Seas. The naval aspect of these four areas, as part of the Mediterranean Sea thus becomes of equal concern both to the Supreme Commander, Europe, and to the Supreme Commander of the Mediterranean or Mediterranean–Middle East Command. In time of emergency it would be impossible for any higher authority to coordinate the actions of the two Supreme Commanders in the many situations that might arise. With full realization of this problem, I first assumed, when the President of the US assured me that I would have operational command of all US forces in Europe and European waters, that the Mediterranean itself would have to be included in the area under my command. Subsequently, in deference to viewpoints presented to me in London and Wash,[6] I receded from this view and proposed an arrangement that I then thought, and still believe, will come closest to satisfying the conflict of responsibilities.

4. This solution involves placing the command of my Southern flank under a Naval Officer who, because of the many considerations involved, should be a US officer.[7] His hq will be ashore in Italy. Under him will be Army, Naval and Air Forces that are allocated to me. His Naval Force will include a striking force of which its important element will be US carriers and the supporting elements including such components as normally are included in a balanced fleet. This fleet will operate under its designated commander who will be afloat.

5. I have no objection whatsoever to the CINC of my Southern flank being assigned additional duties and responsibilities on behalf of the Supreme Comd,[8] Mediterranean or Mediterranean–Middle East, so long as three conditions are fulfilled, namely:

First, that his primary duty and responsibility are to me;

Second, that no additional responsibilities are assigned him on behalf of another Supreme Comd that will require, without my concurrence, his absence from the area under my comd;

Third, that the naval striking force under his comd is assigned primarily for the accomplishment of my missions, and its allocation to the other missions in the Mediterranean must be by agreement between the two Supreme Comd concerned. This will normally be arranged through the CINC of my Southern flank. Thus he may not only function as the CINC of Southern

Europe, but for particular and specific naval purposes may act as a subordinate to the Supreme Comd, Mediterranean–Middle East. He will serve as a definite connecting link between the two Supreme Comd. While I am thus anticipating that my CINC, Southern Europe will be required to wear 2 hats, he will be an officer of such rank and judgment that for him it should be a relatively simple problem.

6. I consider that the strategical situation with respect to Southern and Southeast Europe is such as to require a comd structure which is potentially capable of providing centralized direction and control over all forces which may be required for its security. Thus, I believe that provision must be made for the CINC of my Southern flank to conduct such consultative planning for the coordination of the forces of Greece (and perhaps Yugoslavia) with NATO Forces, to the extent authorized by higher authority. I am willing to concede that similar planning with respect to Turkey could be assigned as a responsibility of some other Supreme Commander subject of course, to close liaison which I anticipate would exist between that commander and the CINC of my Southern flank.[9]

7. I recognize that many complications that [sic] arise in an attempt to solve problems of this kind involving as they do national fears and prides, and political implications over and above the military problems themselves. We must therefore depend upon the cooperative attitude and good sense of the two commanders involved. Organization per se should seek to provide a means to facilitate such cooperation rather than prescribe limits within which the forces of each commander should be confined. The threat in the European-Mediterranean region may shift from time to time, and will therefore require rapid shifts in the concentration of force to meet the threat. We cannot accurately predict the character, location and timing of the attack, consequently we must depend upon the good will and cooperative spirit of the participating commanders, rather than upon specific instructions from higher authority in effecting the arrangements to meet the exigencies of the situation as it develops.

8. I have no objection to the establishment of a CINC for Air in the Mediterranean if the Standing Group determines that such a command is necessary in the light of forces available.[10] I must point out, however, that this CINC will have no authority over any of the Air Forces allocated to my comd except when such forces are, by agreement, temporarily detailed for service to the Supreme Commander, Mediterranean–Middle East. My own air responsibilities will constantly involve operations over the Western Mediterranean if, for no other reason than the fact that certain of our bases will be located in Northwest Africa. The defense of Italy will require similar

activity on the part of the Air Forces not under the comd of a CINC, Air Mediterranean. Thus in the case of air activity also it will be necessary for coordination to be arranged through the CINC of my Southern flank who will be in comd of the Air Force allocated to me in that area.

9. In conclusion, I consider that the comd arrangements which I have sponsored provide the best means for the discharge of the responsibilities that are to be assigned separately to the Supreme Commander, Europe, and Supreme Commander, Mediterranean–Middle East. It will most certainly provide best for the concentration of naval striking power in the area and facilitate coordinated action depending upon the character of any particular situation.

10. With respect to minor modifications of the subordinate comd structure for Southern Europe as visualized in JCS 86466, it is my intention that:

(A) The title of the Army Commander in Italy should be Commander, Allied Army Forces, Italy;

(B) That the Commander, Allied Air Forces, Southern Europe should be established concurrently with the other commanders in order to stimulate the generation and effective employment of National Air Forces in the area. He should be a US Officer;[11]

(C) The Allied Forces, Austria, and the Anglo-US Forces, Trieste, under their respective US and British Commanders should, on a covert basis, remain under peacetime comd as at present but they should be subordinated to the CINC, Southern Europe, for war planning and for actual operations in war.[12]

11. I feel strongly that these comd arrangements should be discussed with both the French and Italians, while in the formative stage.[13] I have not gone into details with them on my own arrangements but I have explained to all the basic ideas described in this msg.[14] Similarly, I have not yet submitted my detailed views for comd in Southern Europe, in hope that prior agreement with respect to the Mediterranean could be reached by you with the British. Should you consider the time to be appropriate for me to introduce my views formally to the Standing Group, I am ready to do so. Should you desire that I send a Senior Staff Officer to Wash for further discussion, this can be arranged.

12. I have no objection to your making known these views to the British, or, if you prefer, I am prepared to present them to the British myself.[15]

---

[1] This cable was circulated as enclosure B to JCS 1868/257, of April 27, 1951 (same file as document). It was designated as "NOFORN 34," meaning that the

information contained in it was not to be shown to foreigners. The message was probably routed through SHAPE's Plans, Policy and Operations Division.

[2] For background on the dispute over the Southern European and Mediterranean commands see no. 107. The British, unlike the Americans, wished to curtail the responsibilities to be exercised by Eisenhower's southern-flank commander and, at the same time, to increase the importance of a proposed Mediterranean command (under a British commander) (see Poole, *History of the Joint Chiefs of Staff*, vol. IV, *1950-1952*, p. 237). Eisenhower's views are given in no. 77.

[3] On couverture forces, the troops covering a mobilization, see nos. 77, n. 16, and 153, n. 1; on the situation in Yugoslavia see no. 142, n. 16.

[4] JCS 86466, a cable sent by the Joint Chiefs of Staff to Eisenhower on March 21, was reprinted as enclosure C to JCS 1868/257 (same file as document). In this message the JCS proposed the appointment of a supreme allied commander, Middle East (SACME), responsible to the British Chiefs of Staff. Subordinate to the SACME would be an Allied naval C in C, Middle East. A commander, Gibraltar-Alexandria Line of Communication Forces, would also be appointed, and this officer would be either subordinate to or identical with the Allied naval C in C, Middle East. Eisenhower's C in C, Allied Forces, Southern Europe would have as his principal subordinate commanders an Italian heading the Allied Army Forces; the American commander of the United States Sixth Fleet; and an Allied Air Forces commander whose nationality would be "held in abeyance pending force buildup." He would have responsibility for Greece, European Turkey and the Turkish Straits, and the Aegean Sea littoral in addition to his other responsibilities in and around the Mediterranean. SACME's command would include Asiatic Turkey and the remainder of the Middle Eastern area. Eisenhower would fulfill his requirements in North Africa on a unilateral basis through the two American naval and air commanders in Europe, Admiral Carney and General Norstad (see no. 77, nn. 15, 17). The JCS proposal also called for coordination between SHAPE and SACME "to be as appropriate with specific arrangements to assure SACEUR necessary support. . . ."

[5] JCS 88848 (Apr. 18, 1951, same file as document) was a personal message from the JCS to Eisenhower. In it was described a British command proposal that differed in some features from the earlier plan outlined in no. 107, n. 5. The new British proposal again called for a British supreme commander in the Mediterranean, but with an American naval C in C to command all naval forces, including the U.S. aircraft carrier task forces. Two British admirals, one in the Levant and one at Gibraltar, would serve in this command. These two officers would also report to the commanders of the Middle East and Atlantic commands, respectively. "Appropriate sub areas" would be established, including a French-commanded region in the Toulon-Algiers sector and an Italian-commanded region around Italy and including the Adriatic Sea. Greece and Turkey would be left as national commands, like Norway and Denmark (see no. 77; and n. 8 below).

In this same message, the JCS proposed a "compromise command structure" that envisioned a British supreme commander for the Mediterranean–Middle East, with an American (presumably Admiral Carney) as Mediterranean naval C in C. Carney would be subordinate both to Eisenhower and to the British supreme commander, and the British supreme commander would report to both the Standing Group and the BCOS. The remainder of the JCS proposal was similar to the British plan, except for the promise to Eisenhower that the American naval C in C, Mediterranean, would place under his "operational command naval forces of whatever nature required in execution of your mission." These forces would include "amphibious, gunfire support or carrier forces . . . consistent with assignment to you, by the President, of operational command of United States Naval Forces in Med[iterranean] to extent necessary for accomplishment of your mission."

[6] Washington, D.C.

[7] This would be Admiral Carney (see no. 77, n. 15).

[8] "Command" or, as used by Eisenhower here, "commander."

[9] Although Greece and Turkey had accepted NATO's September 1950 invitation to associate themselves informally with the North Atlantic nations for military planning purposes, no contact had yet been made with these two countries. Further steps had been held in abeyance pending a clarification of "the role and mission of SACEUR's Southern Command." Discussions concerning Greece and Turkey had continued in Washington, and on May 24 President Truman would approve an NSC policy statement calling for the admission of both countries as full members of NATO (Beebe to Marshall, May 1951, OS/D, 1951, Clas. Decimal File, CD 092.3 NATO; State, *Foreign Relations, 1951*, vol. III, *European Security and the German Question, Part I*, pp. 501–6, 511–15, 520–22, 524–25. See also JCS to Marshall, Oct. 19, 1950, OSD, 1950, Clas. Decimal File, CD 092.3 NATO; Harriman to Eisenhower, Mar. 1, 1951, EM; Kibler to Carney, Apr. 25, 1951, Carney to Eisenhower, May 19, 1951, and Carney to Kibler, May 21, 1951, all in EM, Carney Corr.; and Melvyn P. Leffler, "Strategy, Diplomacy, and the Cold War: The United States, Turkey and NATO, 1945–1952," *Journal of American History* 71, no. 4 [1985], 807–25). For developments see nos. 233, n. 5, and 423. On the relationship between NATO and Yugoslavia see no. 142, n. 16.

[10] Both the British plan and the JCS compromise had called for an air C in C for the entire Mediterranean area; this officer was to be the direct subordinate of the British Mediterranean (or Mediterranean–Middle East) supreme allied commander (JCS 88848, Apr. 18, 1951, same file as document).

[11] For the JCS proposals for an Italian army commander and for the Southern European Allied Air Forces commander see n. 4 above. On May 11 Eisenhower would ask the JCS to nominate an American general to be commander, Allied Air Forces, Southern Europe, as soon as the proposed command structure for Southern Europe had been approved (SH 20456, May 11, 1951, CCS 092 Western Europe [3-12-48], Sec. 81).

[12] For Eisenhower's plans to employ the forces in Austria and Trieste see no. 69.

[13] Eisenhower was probably trying to avoid a controversy such as the one that had arisen after the Malta conference (see nos. 81, n. 5, and 126. See also State, *Foreign Relations, 1951*, vol. III, *European Security and the German Question, Part I*, pp. 533–35, and vol. IV, *Europe: Political and Economic Developments, Part I*, pp. 369–72, 610.

[14] Message.

[15] Eisenhower's cable would slow the efforts to resolve these command problems. In their reply of April 25 the Joint Chiefs informed Eisenhower that his suggestions had already been made to the Standing Group, which had "tabled" the proposals. They told Eisenhower that they were going to ask the State Department to reopen the question of the Atlantic and Mediterranean commands before NATO's multinational Military Committee; they also recommended that Eisenhower submit his proposals "formally" (and independently) to the Standing Group (Poole, *History of the Joint Chiefs of Staff*, vol. IV, *1950-1952*, pp. 235–36; JCS to Eisenhower, JCS 89430, Apr. 25, 1951, CCS 092 Western Europe [3-12-48], Sec. 79). On May 6 Eisenhower would submit his proposals to the Standing Group. Three days later Secretary of State Acheson, who was fearful of political repercussions in the United Kingdom, disapproved the proposed reopening of the entire command question and urged the continuation of private, bilateral discussions with the British. The Defense Department agreed with this approach, and the negotiations continued. The Joint Chiefs informed Eisenhower on May 21 that his proposals would, for the most part, receive their support in the Standing Group. They also expressed their view that Carney should "have command of all NATO naval forces in [the]

Western Med[iterranean] except such inshore and coastal operations and forces as would appropriately be under nat[iona]l authorities" (JCS to SHAPE, JCS 91869, May 21, 1951, CCS 092 Western Europe [3-12-48], Sec. 82; Poole, *History of the Joint Chiefs of Staff*, vol. IV, *1950-1952*, pp. 236-37). For developments see nos. 198 and 236.

149   *Eisenhower Mss., Diaries*

DIARY   *April 23, 1951*

Had to stop. Since writing above[1] I've been very busy both in the office and travelling. Tomorrow I go to Italy for 2 days, to be followed almost at once by a trip to Holland, Belgium, Norway and Denmark![2]

Adm. Lemmonier (French) has joined us as a Naval Deputy.[3] While the need for such an assistant is not so obvious as in some of the other cases, yet his presence assures that France's maritime interests (which are, of course, considerable) will not be neglected by this hq.

He (Adm. L.) has given me a preliminary memo of his views. They conform almost exactly to the principles I urged upon the interested staffs last January. (Use naval power on flanks!!)

It is difficult to assess the mental attitude of Europe. Gruenther and I had lunch today with French C/S. They seem fatalistic, if not apathetic.[4]

More the same day,

Iran. Numbers of people (today an American Oil Man) have been saying that the position of the west—specifically Britain—is deteriorating rapidly in Iran. They say the situation is getting far worse than most realize.

Lord knows what we'd do without Iranian oil.

My talks with British friends indicate that that country is alive to the danger, but no one yet has told me the real trouble.[5] My American friend merely said that we'd better get busy and give the Iranians an acceptable contract, "or else."

---

[1] For the previous entry see no. 136.

[2] Eisenhower would inspect Atlantic Pact forces in northeastern Italy from April 24 until April 26 (see no. 153). On May 7 he would begin a four-day military visit to Belgian forces in Germany and Belgium and to Dutch forces in the Netherlands; he would return to Paris on May 10. On May 20 the General would depart Orly Airport for a four-day military visit to Denmark and Norway. He would spend one day, May 21, in Schleswig, Germany, where he would inspect Danish, Norwegian, and British forces in the British zone of Germany. For Eisenhower's itineraries to the Benelux countries and to Denmark and Norway see EM, Subject File, Trips, SHAPE no. 7.

[3] Vice-Admiral André Georges Lemonnier, France's Chief of Naval Operations,

had been appointed chief naval adviser to Eisenhower. Lemonnier had commanded the Free French naval forces under Charles de Gaulle during World War II. In addition to duty as Eisenhower's naval deputy, Lemonnier would soon be named first commandant of the newly established North Atlantic Treaty Defense College in Paris (see no. 142, n. 7; Chandler, *War Years*, no. 1131; Eisenhower to Lemonnier, Apr. 3, 1951, EM; and *New York Times*, Nov. 18, 20, 1951). We have been unable to locate Lemonnier's memo to Eisenhower.

Eisenhower had met with the French defense staffs in Paris on January 8, 1951 (for background see nos. 11 and 16; and Record of Conversation, Jan. 8, 1951, EM, Subject File, Trips, SHAPE no. 1).

[4] Eisenhower and his C/S, General Alfred M. Gruenther, had met for lunch with the French Chiefs of Staff, General Clément Blanc (army); General Pierre Fay (deputy for air); and Vice-Admiral Roger Lambert (navy).

[5] In recent weeks a longstanding dispute over royalty rates for the British oil concession in Iran had reached crisis level. The Iranian parliament had nationalized holdings of the British-owned Anglo-Iranian Oil Company. Since then, strikes and riots had plagued the Iranian oil industry. Among the several factions involved in the controversy were the Tudeh (Iran's outlawed Communist party) and a number of Moslem nationalistic societies. The Iranian government itself, headed by the young Shah Mohammed Reza Pahlavi, had been unable to take a strong stand against the political pressures exerted by the societies (*New York Times*, Mar. 18, 19, 20, 1951; Apr. 22, 29, 1951). Eisenhower would soon show even greater concern over the discontent in oil-rich Iran (see no. 233, n. 6).

150   *Eisenhower Mss.*

To Charles Peake   *April 23, 1951*

Dear Charles:[1] Thank you very much for the note you sent me by hand of Mr. Donnelly.[2] While it took almost four weeks to reach me, it was, nevertheless, most welcome. I always get a real lift out of messages from my old associates in SHAEF.

Ham Armstrong[3] will be with me for lunch tomorrow, and I have asked Mr. Donnelly to come back at the same time so that we can all have a little conference together. I am tremendously interested in Tito, his character, his strength, and his intentions, and I assure you that I shall always be glad to hear anything from you that may help give me better information on such points as this.[4]

I do hope that the first time you come through Paris, you will call my office and so give me the opportunity of seeing you once again. I would thoroughly enjoy a long talk with you.

Thanks again for the trouble you took in writing to me.[5] *Cordially*

[1] Sir Charles Peake had been British Ambassador at Belgrade, Yugoslavia, since 1946. During World War II he had served as political adviser to Eisenhower at SHAEF.

[2] Walter Joseph Donnelly, Minister and first U.S. civilian High Commissioner to

Austria, had met with Eisenhower the morning of April 23. At that time he had given Peake's letter of March 31 to the General. The letter, marked "Personal and Secret," is in EM.
[3] Hamilton Fish Armstrong was editor of the quarterly review *Foreign Affairs*, published by the Council on Foreign Relations (for background see Galambos, *Columbia University*).
[4] Marshal Josip Broz Tito was Prime Minister and Minister of National Defense of the Communist government of Yugoslavia. He had broken with Moscow in 1948 (see *Eisenhower Papers*, vols. I–XI).
[5] For further developments involving the situation in Yugoslavia see nos. 332, n. 2, and 343.

151   *Eisenhower Mss.*

To Frederick Augustus Irving   *April 23, 1951*

Dear Irving:[1] Thank you very much for your interesting letter informing me of Mr. McCormick's intention of establishing a fund to provide an award for outstanding excellence in West Point's Department of Military Psychology and Leadership. Quite naturally, I am delighted that the Department has achieved such a degree of success that the authorities and friends of the Academy have decided that excellent performance in the course entitles the Cadet to some unusual distinction.[2]

Of course, I am highly complimented by your suggestion that my name be attached to the award. Such a designation quite possibly overemphasizes the influence I have had in developing the course, since my own effort was largely confined to holding a series of discussions with General Taylor in the period immediately succeeding the close of World War II. The letter that I wrote on the 2nd of January 1946, a copy of which you sent to me, was a part of our verbal and written communication on the subject. In any event, my interest in the course is such that I assure you of my approval of your suggestion.[3]

In the matter of submitting to you any suggestions as to a suitable type of distinguishing gift, I am truly diffident. However, out of a bit of experience, I do give you the following which you are at liberty to use or discard, as you see fit. I have tried to confine my suggestions to those articles which would involve, I think, a modest cost, and I present them in a rough order of priority as representing my own idea of articles that combine attractiveness and usefulness.

> *Desk set*, either a simple stand with pen or pens, or, if desired, can be expanded to include ashtray, cigarette box, etc.
> *Clock*, small one either for office or for household use. (A special favorite of mine is a combination clock and barometer.)

Watch, any suitable type.

Silver cup or tray.

Medal, suitably engraved and encased in a plastic block. This plastic block is 6" × 6" × 1½"; thus, the medal stands on its edge in any desired location.

I most certainly claim no originality about these particular suggestions; I submit them more to jog your memory than to class them as recommendations.

I express again my very deep appreciation of your suggestion, and my assurances that I am flattered by the knowledge that you, Mr. McCormick, and the Head of the Department of Military Psychology and Leadership should all consider that the attachment of my name to the award will add to its value for the recipient.[4]

Please remember me kindly to Mrs. Irving,[5] and with warm regard to yourself, *Cordially*

[1] Major General Irving had been superintendent of the United States Military Academy since January 1951 (see Galambos, *Columbia University*, no. 517; and *New York Times*, Jan. 12, 30, 1951).

[2] On April 16 (EM) Irving had written to the General concerning the establishment of an annual award at West Point honoring the graduating cadet with the highest rank in military psychology and leadership courses. Charles Perry McCormick, president and chairman of the board of the Baltimore, Maryland, spice firm McCormick and Company, Inc., had offered to fund the award.

[3] McCormick and Colonel Samuel Edward Gee, head of the Department of Military Psychology and Leadership since 1949, had proposed calling the award the Eisenhower Award. Irving explained in his letter that this was an acknowledgment of Eisenhower's contribution to the founding of the department in 1946. He said he wanted to be sure that the General had no objections to the use of his name, "which we have all agreed would be most appropriate."

Major General Maxwell Davenport Taylor had been the superintendent of West Point from 1945 to 1949 and was now the Army's Assistant Chief of Staff for Operations. Eisenhower's letter to Taylor is Galambos, *Chief of Staff*, no. 613.

[4] The Eisenhower Award, an engraved silver tray, would be presented to cadet Richard L. Harris of Pittsburgh, Pennsylvania, on June 3, 1951, at West Point; neither Eisenhower nor McCormick would be able to attend the ceremony (see Irving to Eisenhower, May 8, 1951, and Canon to Irving, May 18, 1951, EM; and *New York Times*, June 4, 1951). Each year since 1951 the Military Academy's Department of Behavioral Sciences and Leadership has continued to present the award (Ronald C. Sims to Faith Townsend, Mar. 19, 1985, EP).

[5] The former Vivian Dowe.

Dear Monty:[1] I have been studying your memorandum on the subject of the Organization and Training Division. I note that you have given the Chief of Staff a copy, which insures that it will be examined promptly and carefully by the staff.[2] At this moment, I am about to start a couple of trips,[3] but as soon as we have the opportunity, I will be quite interested in discussing the matter further with you.

It is entirely possible that, in the end, I shall agree completely with your conclusion that the organization and the training functions should be separately organized.[4] Moreover, I certainly agree with what you say about the importance of organization and the general backwardness of the European region in this regard.

However, as is usual in such cases, not all the arguments are on one side. There is an inescapable relationship between organization and training that we must never fail to recognize. Organization is not an abstraction, nor is it something that lives in a vacuum, achieving perfection or failure according to the faithfulness of observation of certain academic rules. Organization in a military plant becomes effective only when all are properly trained and indoctrinated in the employment of that *particular* organization.

While I could go on for some time to show this direct relationship, it is enough to say that this kind of reasoning led to the American habit of thinking always of these two functions as a single package. Hence, we have had the Organization and Training Divisions of the General Staff.[5]

Here, however, we have a somewhat different problem because we do want to achieve a common type of organization—at least as nearly as possible. To do this, it appears that SHAPE will have to take the lead, although, of course, our functions will be advisory rather than executive. This, for the reason that it is clearly the responsibility of each nation to organize and equip forces before they are allocated to us either in the active or in the reserve formations.

You make the point that, in the matter of training, the details will fall upon the several Commanders in Chief. This is, of course, true so far as troops allocated in time of peace are concerned. But it is likewise true that forces allocated in time of peace will have been *organized* by other authority—in this case, by the national Chiefs of Staff.

I make these observations merely to question your statement that the organizing function for SHAPE will be far more important than the training function. Maybe you are right, but I think it is something we must go into a bit further.

You can see the kind of things I am thinking about, but we must make up our minds quickly—that is sure.[6] *As ever*

[1] Field Marshal Montgomery was Deputy SACEUR under Eisenhower (see no. 74).

[2] In an accompanying note, Montgomery said that he had written the paper to clear his own mind and that he would discuss the matter with Eisenhower's C/S, General Alfred M. Gruenther.

[3] See no. 149, n. 2.

[4] The two functions were presently combined in SHAPE's Organization and Training Division.

[5] Eisenhower had given a good deal of thought to the relationship between military organization and training when he was U.S. Army Chief of Staff. For his role in the reorganization of the War Department in 1946 see Chandler and Galambos, *Occupation, 1945*, no. 312; and Galambos, *Chief of Staff*, no. 847. See also Hewes, *From Root to McNamara*, pp. 148–49, 154–62.

[6] There is in EM no further correspondence between Eisenhower and Montgomery on this subject.

153   *Eisenhower Mss., Diaries*

DIARY   *April 27, 1951*

Have just completed an inspection trip to couverture forces[1] in North Italy. Spirit is high in that section—the morale of the troops I saw was surprisingly good. These units included, however, both Alpini[2] and Bersaglieri[3] formations—traditionally elite groupments in the Italian forces.[4]

Gen. Marros seems most capable.[5] He is the chairman of their J.C.S. The General in charge of the Air Force is also (to all appearances) a most efficient leader.[6] Gen. Castiglione, who is to be named by Marros to command the ground forces in our "southern flank" organization, seems thoughtful & almost scholarly.[7] I don't know whether he can produce the necessary "punch."

Cappa (Army C/S) is fairly old and I assume will soon retire. He is fat but appears energetic.[8]

The armament of the Italian forces is a bewildering assortment of obsolete and cast-off equipment from several nations—U.S., U.K. and Italy. Training ammunition is meager, even though I was told that Italy makes fine ammunition and would be happy to make its own *if* the U.S. would let it have the necessary specifications.[9]

I hope we can give Italy a few T 26 tanks, at least. Thus each armored formation could have a tiny core of fairly well armored and armed vehicles. A few Shermans are all they have in anything larger than the T 24 (lt) tank.[10]

In the U.S. the "Great Debate"—which is nothing more than a heterogeneous collection of personal partisan and private quarrels—still rages. For most it has now been simplified (over-simplified I mean) into a Truman-MacArthur struggle.[11] How tragic that, at this critical stage in world history, we should be torn apart by human selfishness. We should, by all means, continue to debate seriously the various means and methods open to us for waging effective war against communism. There is much room for instructive discussion and argument—but we have not a minute to waste, nor any right to weaken ourselves—in the wicked business of attempting to satisfy personal ambition.

So far as I know, every senior officer in this hq. would like to be somewhere else. Every man here is serving because of an overpowering sense of duty and of urgency in human affairs. It is too bad that they have to combat daily the pessimism and discouragement born of a realization that in London, Washington and Paris, unworthy men either guide our destinies or are fighting bitter battles in the hope of getting an opportunity to guide our destinies.

If ever we needed moral and intellectual integrity—now is that time. Thank God (and I mean it) for the few who still hold the respect of the masses. For my family and for America; the only real passions of my life; I shall continue to work as effectively and optimistically as I have the strength to do. But I desperately wish that there could be now established in places of influence in the free world, new, young, & virile civil and military leaders devoted only to their respective countries, to decency and to security.

[1] Troops covering a mobilization, in this case troops protecting the border of the Italian side of the Alps.

[2] The Alpini, or Alpine troops, were specially trained for service in the Alps (see no. 158, n. 3).

[3] Italian light infantry soldiers, originally sharpshooters of the Sardinian Army (see no. 158, n. 3).

[4] Eisenhower had left Paris on April 24 for an inspection of Atlantic Pact forces in northeastern Italy. Near Udine, on the twenty-fifth, he observed the Giulia Alpini Brigade on morning maneuvers. In the afternoon he reviewed the Mantova Infantry Division exercises, and in the evening he attended a regimental dinner in Udine with the 76th Napoli Infantry Regiment. On the twenty-sixth, at Beano and Pordenone, the General inspected the Ariete Armored Brigade and saw the plumed Bersaglieri in field exercises. On the same day, before he returned to Paris, Eisenhower inspected the 51st Italian Fighter Squadron and the U.S. Air Force technical experts who advised them (see Kevin McCann, *Man from Abilene* [Garden City, N.Y., 1952], pp. 219–26; *New York Times*, Apr. 24, 26, 1951; *International Herald Tribune*, Paris ed., Apr. 27, 1951; and *Life*, May 21, 1951).

[5] Lieutenant General Efisio Luigi Marras was chairman of the Italian Joint Chiefs of Staff and the Italian representative on the Military Committee, North Atlantic Council. During World War II Marras had served as the Italian military attaché in Berlin until September 1943, when he was arrested; he had escaped to Switzer-

land and returned to Italy at the close of the war to become Rome Artillery Commander and C/S of the Italian Fifth Army. For developments see no. 158.

[6] General Mario Aimone Cat, Italian Air Force Chief of Staff.

[7] General Maurizio Lazzaro de Castiglioni would be appointed commander of ground troops of the integrated European Army for Southern Europe. General de Castiglioni would command only the divisions that Italy had assigned to the North Atlantic alliance.

[8] General Ernesto Cappa, Italian Army Chief of Staff.

[9] Eisenhower had been aware of Italy's armament problems since January 1951, when he had met with government and military leaders in Rome (see "Memorandum of Conversation with Italian Prime Minister and Ministers" and "Memorandum of Conversation with Italian Defense Minister and Military Leaders," both Jan. 18, 1951, EM, Subject File, Trips, SHAPE). For background see no. 18, n. 1, and for developments see nos. 156, n. 3, 167, and 339.

[10] For background on the T–20 tank series and the Sherman, or M–4, tank series see Charles M. Baily, *Faint Praise: American Tanks and Tank Destroyers during World War II* (Hamden, Conn., 1983), pp. 32-33, 37, 86, 155-56.

[11] The Great Debate dealt with American involvement in the defense of Western Europe and the Far East (see nos. 23, 112, n. 4, and 128, n. 2). On the MacArthur controversy see nos. 101, 131, and 136.

154   *Eisenhower Mss.*

To PHILIP YOUNG   *April 27, 1951*
Cable AP 80441

Suggest you and Lewis Douglas consider possible advisability of postponing initial assembly conference until late September.[1] Current atmosphere could conceivably even though mistakenly lead many to suspect complete objectivity of the work, and the first requirement for ultimate success in this great undertaking is the full confidence of the public in its thoroughness, integrity and objectivity.[2] Please make no attempt to answer this cable because full responsibility belongs to you two and to University authorities. The only thing to be considered is the long term value to the public of these investigations, studies and conferences.[3] Warm regards to you both.

[1] For background on Columbia University's first American Assembly conference, scheduled to begin on May 21, see nos. 8 and 10. On the Assembly's executive director, Philip Young, and on its policy board chairman, Lewis Douglas, see nos. 87 and 65, respectively.

[2] Eisenhower, who would not attend the conference (see no. 133, n. 3), probably suggested this postponement because of the recent Senate vote on the assignment of U.S. troops to NATO (see no. 128, n. 2). In light of the sharp divisions the debate had produced, there was reason to fear that the topic for the first conference, U.S. relations with Western Europe, would arouse accusations concerning the Assembly's objectivity (see the following document and no. 112).

[3] For developments see no. 182, n. 2.

To Grayson Louis Kirk   *April 28, 1951*

Dear Grayson:[1] Long before this, I should have written to you, if for no other reason than to assure you of my appreciation for your very fine letter of April 9th.[2] But I have been truly busy, and find little time to fulfill all the promises that I make to myself—one of which is to keep in close touch with old friends and associates. (Another of my self-promises was to keep up my exercise, and, in the performance of this one, I have been even more of a failure than in carrying on my accustomed correspondence.)

I have written or cabled once or twice to Phil Young and to others connected with the American Assembly. Only yesterday, I sent Phil a cable suggesting that it might be advisable to postpone the first meeting until next September.[3] My reason was merely that I was afraid that no discussion or analysis of the American-European relationship could, at this moment, attain an objective status in the public mind, but would probably be considered another contribution to partisan warfare. Even if this danger might not be so important as I fear, there is the added thought that, unless the public did consider it as a skirmish in the current war, the results of the conference would possibly be lost or ignored. In any event, I made it clear that the whole matter was for decision by *Douglas,*[4] *Young,*[5] and the *University authorities.* I find it impossible to concentrate any thinking or study on University matters. Moreover, I have had to abandon my earlier intention of returning to the States for the first conference under the Assembly program.[6]

Of course, I am delighted that the other members of the Higgins Board of Control accepted you instantly as a full-fledged member. The will was a bit tricky on the point, but I was quite certain that the others on the Board were ready to understand the need for you representing Columbia.[7]

Naturally, I hope that the budget will not turn out to be as much of a financial disaster as we have feared. It will certainly be interesting to learn just to what extent enrollment does fall off for the coming academic year.[8]

I hope that you will convey my warm greetings to John Krout,[9] George Pegram,[10] Joe Campbell,[11] and other members of the informal committee that meets with you every Monday (at least, I most certainly hope it is meeting with you every Monday, because I found that group to be of immeasurable assistance to me).[12] Incidentally, my greetings include, also, Bill Donovan,[13] George Cooper,[14] Frank Hogan,[15] James Wise*,[16] and all the others that are so important to us at Morningside.

With cordial personal regard, *Sincerely*

*P.S. Also all members of "Trustees."[17]

[1] Kirk was acting president of Columbia University (see no. 184, n. 6).
[2] Kirk's letter is in EM.
[3] Eisenhower's cable to Philip Young, Executive Director of the American Assembly conference program, is the preceding document.
[4] Lewis W. Douglas, chairman of the American Assembly's National Policy Board.
[5] See n. 3 above.
[6] See no. 133.
[7] Kirk had replaced Eisenhower (at Eisenhower's request) as a member of the board of control of the Eugene Higgins Trust. The trust had allocated to Columbia, Harvard, Princeton, and Yale universities the income from a $34 million endowment managed by the U.S. Trust Company (for background see Galambos, *Columbia University*, nos. 328 and 1158). Kirk had reported to Eisenhower that Columbia would receive $250,000 from the fund in 1952 "as against $180,000 for the present year."
[8] Kirk had predicted that the university would have a deficit at year's end of about $500,000. He also told Eisenhower that he was concerned about the possibility of low student enrollment for the coming year and its effect on university income.
[9] John A. Krout was associate provost and dean of the faculties of political science, philosophy, and pure science (see no. 31, n. 1).
[10] George B. Pegram, who had retired as university vice-president for education, was a special adviser to the president (see no. 71, n. 4).
[11] Joseph Campbell was the university's treasurer and vice-president for business affairs (see Galambos, *Columbia University*, no. 514).
[12] During his tenure at Columbia, Eisenhower had met regularly on Monday mornings with what he termed his "staff" (see *ibid.*, vol. XI, Chronology).
[13] William J. Donovan was chairman of the university's Council on Development and Resources.
[14] George V. Cooper was chairman of the Columbia Club Reorganization Committee (see *ibid.*, no. 710).
[15] Frank Smithwick Hogan was president of Columbia's Alumni Federation (see *ibid.*).
[16] James D. Wise was president of the Columbia Associates.
[17] For background on the board of trustees see *ibid.*, esp. nos. 124 and 215.

156   *Eisenhower Mss.*

To Omar Nelson Bradley   *April 28, 1951*
Secret

Dear Brad: Your letter of the 12th was most welcome and informative. I shall make this reply very short because, from what I can read in the newspapers, you people in Washington must be really busy these days.[1] Moreover, I note by the papers that you are to be over here in early June, so I will save up for discussion at that time those items that would probably consume a lot of space in their telling.[2]

On a recent trip to Italy, I ran into the statement that the Italian forces are denied reasonable amount of ammunition for training—and for stockpiling—because of a refusal on the part of the United States to give to Italy the necessary designs, even where the type of ammunition has apparently long since ceased to be classed "Secret." I am told by the Italians that they can manufacture any type of ammunition from the small arms up to and including the 105 howitzer. (I believe they make an exception in the case of the rocket launcher, which apparently has such close tolerances that they are a little fearful of that one.) The Italian forces are armed with an amazing variety of weapons, many of which are cast-offs from other Services. They are now manufacturing the ammunition for their own makes of weapons, and for those provided by the British. But they cannot understand why they do not have the designs for the ammunition of such weapons that have been given to them by the United States; for example, the 3-inch tank gun, the 76-millimeter, etc., etc. I am writing to you about this because I have a suspicion that there may have been a clogging of red tape somewhere along the line.[3]

Recent exchanges with the United States Chiefs of Staff on the matter of organization on my southern flank have, from my viewpoint, been most satisfactory. It seems to me that there is no misunderstanding between us and we should be getting along with the matter very speedily.[4]

Give my very best to my friends on the JCS, and personal regard to yourself. *Sincerely*

[1] General Bradley was Chairman of the JCS. Eisenhower is referring to the controversy following President Truman's dismissal of General MacArthur (see no. 136, n. 2). In his letter of April 12, 1951 (EM), Bradley had told Eisenhower that "business has been particularly rushing here the last few days, largely because of the MacArthur situation."
[2] On Bradley's trip to Paris see no. 176, n. 1.
[3] On Eisenhower's trip to Italy see no. 153, esp. n. 9. Bradley would refer this matter to General J. Lawton Collins, Chief of Staff of the Army, who in turn would pass it to General Wade Hampton Haislip, Vice Chief of Staff of the Army. In a letter to Eisenhower of May 22 (EM) Bradley enclosed a memorandum on the subject from Haislip, which Bradley said indicated that the request from the Italians "has not been in the mill very long." For developments see nos. 167 and 339.
[4] For background on Eisenhower's problems with command positions in southern Europe see no. 148, n. 2.

157   *Eisenhower Mss.*

To Wilton Burton Persons   *April 28, 1951*

Dear Jerry:[1] A note from Tracy Voorhees tells me what a remarkable job you did in rallying support for the NATO concept, even though you had to use a hospital bed as your headquarters.[2] The only thing that makes all this work worthwhile is a conviction that we are doing something for the security and advantage of the United States. Consequently, there is little for me to say that can add to the approval of your own conscience of the work you have been, and are, doing. Nevertheless, I want you to know that it is a tremendous satisfaction to me to realize that someone of your ability, in spite of illness that would have made most people quit cold, is working away at the job of informing people of the exact issues involved in the effort to build up a collective security for the free world.

I heard, also, that Miles Reber[3] volunteered to help you out during a critical phase of your work. When you see him, I hope you will convey to him, also, an expression of the sentiments I have tried—probably unsuccessfully—to describe above.

With very best wishes for your speedy return to health, and with warm personal regard,[4] *Cordially*

[1] Major General Persons (USA, ret.) had been recalled to active duty in January 1951 to become special adviser to General Eisenhower. His responsibilities included direction of the four sections of SHAPE concerned with troop indoctrination, psychological warfare, legislative liaison, and public relations. Until his retirement in 1949 Persons had been Director of the the Office of Legislative Liaison for the Department of Defense. Following retirement, he became superintendent of the Staunton Military Academy in Virginia (for further background on Persons see *Eisenhower Papers*, vols. I–XI, esp. Galambos, *Columbia University*, no. 534).

[2] Tracy Stebbins Voorhees had been Under Secretary of the Army since August 1949 (for background see Galambos, *Chief of Staff*, no. 1904).

Persons had been hospitalized at the Walter Reed General Hospital in Washington, D.C., during the congressional debate over the "troops-to-Europe" issue (for background see no. 128, n. 2).

[3] Major General Miles Reber (USMA 1923) had been Director of the Office of Legislative Liaison for the Department of Defense since August 1950.

[4] Following his release from the hospital, Persons would convalesce in Florida before joining Eisenhower in June. In his reply to this letter Persons wrote, "Your note on my recent efforts to create a greater awareness on Capitol Hill of the NATO concept was quite a tonic to a man in Florida with a twinge of conscience for lying in the sun at a critical time such as this" (May 18, 1951, EM).

158 *Eisenhower Mss.*

To EFISIO LUIGI MARRAS *April 28, 1951*

Dear General Marras:[1] Although several times in conversation with you I expressed my satisfaction with the spirit and soldierly qualities of the officers and troops I saw on Wednesday and Thursday of this week, I should like to say again, in writing, that I am proud to be associated with them in the defense of Western civilization, its culture and freedom.[2]

In a lifetime of service, I have reviewed troops of many nations and have watched them demonstrate their skill in arms and their grasp of military principles. Seldom, however, have I encountered men who put so much heart and enthusiasm into tactical exercises. Specifically, the superb morale and discipline of the Alpini and Bersaglieri were striking. Troops such as they are a dynamic influence of immeasurable value. Moreover, if the spirit of all the units I saw this week can be developed in all other units of the Italian Armed Forces—land, sea, and air—Italy will take second place to none in its contribution to the security of the free world.[3]

I should add that I am greatly pleased by your assignment of Lieutenant General Maurizio Lazzaro de Castiglioni as Commander of the Couverture Forces. His lifetime record as a soldier—courageous in battle and wise in council—is assurance that he will be effective. Moreover, I formed the impression, during my inspection, that his subordinates, of all ranks, look up to him as an inspiring leader.[4]

Will you, on my behalf, once again extend to all those asssociated with you my thanks for a most pleasant and heartening tour of inspection. *Cordially*

[1] Marras was chairman of the Italian Joint Chiefs of Staff and the Italian representative on the NAC Military Committee (for background see no. 153, n. 5).

[2] On Wednesday, April 25, and Thursday, April 26, Eisenhower had inspected Atlantic Pact forces in northeastern Italy (see no. 153, n. 4).

[3] Summaries of the maneuvers and field exercises that Eisenhower had observed in Italy are in EM, Subject File, Trips, SHAPE no. 1.

[4] On April 30 (EM) Eisenhower would write to de Castiglioni, "I shall not soon forget the extraordinary demonstrations staged by the elite units of your Command and the soldierly qualities of the officers and men I saw." On the same day Eisenhower sent letters of appreciation (all drafted by Kevin McCann) to Lieutenant General Ernesto Cappa, Italian Army C/S; Brigadier General Camillo Costamagna, commander of the Julia Alpini Brigade; Colonel Bernadino Grimaldi di Crotone, commander of the Bersaglieri Regiment (EM, Subject File, Trips, SHAPE no. 1); and Brigadier General Cesare Gandini, commander of the Mantova Infantry Division (EM).

159   *Eisenhower Mss.*

To JOHN ALLEN KROUT   *April 30, 1951*

Dear John:[1] Your letter was on my desk this morning, and, I must say, I was delighted to have the week started off with your news that the Institute of War and Peace Studies is ready for launching.[2] I am in heartiest accord with all your proposals, and you may assure all those concerned of the fact. The names that you suggest for the Columbia group in administrative control and for the Advisory Board are perfectly satisfactory to me. In particular, if you can persuade all those you list to join the Board, you are assured the finest sort of counsel for the operation of the Institute.[3]

From your two paragraphs about him, I should say that Professor Fox is an ideal man to head the Institute. I have not read the study he published. However, his background, present position, and interests seem to fit him uniquely well for the job.[4] While my original hopes centered on either George Kennan or Ed Earle for Director, your proposal that they be named Associates—available for active participation in seminars—will add immeasurably to the effectiveness of the Institute.[5]

Although there is no chance, so far as I can see, that I shall be in the New York area during May, I hope you will not delay a single day in announcing the establishment of the Institute, its program and staff members. Now that you are assured the working funds for the first year, I think you have a clean-cut case of "the sooner, the better." Of course, I would be delighted if I could be there. But, as matters now stand, I have written off the possibility of a visit home within the foreseeable future.

This is an entirely new development. Back a month ago, I felt reasonably confident that there would be a period of a week to ten days toward the end of May when I could, without any jeopardy to my duties here, take off for New York City and the American Assembly. Since the middle of the month, however, my schedule of inspection trips, conferences, and meetings of all sorts has been building up at such a rate that my staff now tells me I am committed here in Paris or somewhere in Europe for every day up to and including May 30th.[6]

Last week, I cabled to Phil Young a suggestion that some way might be found to delay the first meeting of the American Assembly; the present domestic atmosphere, I feel, might make it possible for some—outside the University and Assembly scene—to interpret the Assembly discussions into a one-sided and partisan presentation.[7]

I know that you will understand my thought in that matter. The sole idea is to preserve as far as possible in the public mind the complete independence and intellectual integrity of the Assembly. Since we all hope it will be an enduring and productive element in American life, we should bend backwards—and even risk temporary setbacks—to guard it against any chance of a partisan tag or label—however unwarranted by the facts.

Nevertheless, I am still looking forward to a visit home when I can go over with my old associates all the University developments since my departure. I know that you and I will have plenty to talk about, and I hope one topic will be the activities of the War and Peace Institute.[8] *Sincerely*

[1] Krout was associate provost and dean of the faculties of political science, philosophy, and pure science at Columbia University (see no. 31, n. 1).

[2] Krout's letter of April 19 (EM) concerned final proposals for the inauguration of Columbia's Institute of War and Peace Studies. He asked Eisenhower to comment on the plans that had been formed in cooperation with Grayson L. Kirk, Schulyer Crawford Wallace, and Edwin N. Clark (on Kirk and Clark see nos. 31, n. 1, and 1, n. 2, respectively; Wallace [Ph.D. Columbia 1928] had been Director of Columbia's School of International Affairs since 1946 [see Galambos, *Columbia University*, no. 544]).

[3] Krout had included a list of those proposed for membership on the advisory board.

[4] William Thornton Rickert Fox (Ph.D. University of Chicago 1940), professor of international relations and a member of Columbia's Department of Public Law, was Krout's candidate for director of the institute. Fox had taught at Temple, Princeton, and Yale universities before going to Columbia in 1950. He would meet with Eisenhower in Paris on August 30. For his ideas on the purpose of the institute see Fox's "Memorandum on Institute of War and Peace Studies," [Aug. 1951], EM, Krout Corr. Fox's appointment as director of the institute would be announced in December 1951 (see *New York Times*, Dec. 10, 1951).

[5] George Frost Kennan, a distinguished diplomat and scholar, was currently affiliated with the Institute for Advanced Study in Princeton, New Jersey (see Galambos, *Columbia University*, nos. 1056 and 1116). Edward Meade Earle had been a professor of history at the Institute for Advanced Study since 1934 (see Galambos, *Chief of Staff* and *Columbia University*). Both men would become consultants to the Institute of War and Peace Studies (see *New York Times*, Dec. 10, 1951).

[6] The institute would be officially established in December 1951 (see *ibid.*). On the General's hectic schedule see no. 177, n. 4.

[7] This cable is no. 154. Young was Executive Director of the Assembly (see also no. 155; on Young see no. 8).

[8] For developments see nos. 342, n. 2, and 568. See also *New York Times*, October 12, 1956; March 22, 1957.

160   *Eisenhower Mss.*

To JOHN OLIVER STOVER, JR.   *May 2, 1951*

Dear John: So you are one of the Stovers whose ancestors once lived in the Shenandoah Valley in Virginia![1] That surely makes us kin of some kind, for my Mother, whose maiden name was Stover, came from a little village named Mt. Sidney, which is close to Ft. Defiance and not far from Staunton in "the Valley." She was born during the "War between the States."[2]

I understand that you are only eight years old, but maybe, someday, a few years from now, you can look up the records in that area and determine exactly what our blood relationship may be. I would certainly like to know![3]

In the meantime, I send to you and your parents the best wishes of one kinsman to another.[4] *Sincerely*

[1] In a letter of April 12 (EM) Betty F. Stover of Charlotte, North Carolina, had requested that the General write this note to her eight-year-old son John. She had been prompted to do so by an earlier note that Eisenhower had written during a visit to Colonial Williamsburg in 1946. On that occasion the General had complied with a request to write a greeting to some friends of the governor of Virginia who were related to Eisenhower's mother. One of those friends was the boy's grandfather, and because of that message, John Stover, Jr., had told his schoolmates that he was Eisenhower's cousin. But according to his mother, "To date no one has believed a word of it. . . ." For background on the Williamsburg visit see Galambos, *Chief of Staff*, nos. 687 and 753.
[2] The General's mother, Ida Elizabeth Stover Eisenhower, was born on May 1, 1862 (for background see no. 82; and the General's memoir *At Ease*, pp. 76–78).
[3] On the Eisenhower genealogy see Kornitzer, *The Great American Heritage*, pp. 1–8; and *The New York Genealogical and Biographical Record* 76, no. 9 (1945), in EM, Subject File, Genealogy.
[4] For similar correspondence with relatives see Galambos, *Columbia University*, no. 824; and EM, Eisenhower, Link, Matter, and Stover Corr.

161   *Eisenhower Mss.*

To Clifford Roberts   *May 2, 1951*

Dear Cliff:[1] The news that you had an ulcer really knocked me over; you have always been so careful, not to say abstemious, as to diet that you are one of the few persons in the world that I would never have suspected of running into that kind of difficulty. I suppose, of course, that every one of your friends who has ever heard the word "ulcer" has been busy giving you advice. Since I know nothing whatsoever about the subject, I ought to be one of those most prolific in this regard—however, I think I shall cross up custom and keep still. Possibly, I should tell you about my friend Bedell Smith who fooled around with the darn things for so many years (in the meantime, insisting that he knew more than the doctors did about it) that he ended up with two major operations and *no* stomach.[2]

My first reaction was to insist that you come over here and do your loafing. As you know, there are innumerable points of interest to visit, and, around Paris, there are three available golf clubs that I know of— although I have played only one.[3] The reason that I did not send you an immediate cable urging your favorable consideration of this idea is that I have a hazy recollection of a statement that ulcer patients always require a great deal of fine milk. I find that, here, milk of the quality to which we are accustomed is difficult to get. All milk is pasteurized, but the doctors tell me that herds are not tested for undulant fever. (I am guessing as to the correctness of that adjective.) Nevertheless, there is always the possibility that milk has nothing to do with modern thinking on this subject or, alternatively, your doctor may say that, as long as the milk is pasteurized, that is all that is necessary.[4] If either of these things should be true, I strongly suggest that you consider coming over here as quickly as it becomes too warm in Augusta for you to enjoy staying there. In any event, the club closes along about the 15th, so, when you have to go somewhere else, you may as well come here as go to Bermuda.[5]

As for the rest and relaxation angle, I can only say that, as long as a person is away from his office and daily work, one place would seem to be about like another. I do not assume that you are anxious to play golf every single day, but, even if you did, that could be arranged also. In any event, give the whole idea a sympathetic study—and be sure of a warm welcome if your doctor will allow you to come over here.[6]

Yesterday, I played golf with Ralph Reed and Ed Lane. It was my first time out for quite a while, but my partner and I took the two of them over the jumps. There were one or two points about the day that I hope to relate to you sometime.[7]

I understand that Slats is coming over here in July, and I hear that Fred Manning may come over sometime during the summer. If you would hurry up and come on, you could be my official golf representative to take visiting friends out into the country when I cannot go.[8]

Take care of yourself and, for goodness sake, keep us informed of how you are getting along. Mamie is feeling rather well and joins me in affectionate regard.[9] *Cordially*

[1] For background on Roberts see no. 64.

[2] In a letter of April 24 (EM) Roberts had told the General that he was suffering from a duodenal ulcer and was going to follow his doctor's orders to take a rest and maintain a strict diet. For background on Walter Bedell Smith, Eisenhower's former chief of staff and presently Director of the CIA, see no. 144, n. 1. On Smith's ulcer operations see Galambos, *Columbia University*, nos. 745 and 776.

[3] Eisenhower was to play at three French golf clubs during his assignment in Europe—the St. Germain, the Morfontaine, and the Fontainebleau; at this time he had played only the Morfontaine course (see appointment calendar; correspondence in EM, Clubs and Associations; and n. 7 below).

[4] On May 5 (EM) Roberts thanked Eisenhower for his invitation but declined because "it would be most difficult to obtain the things that I am supposed to eat." Soon, however, Roberts would change his mind (see n. 6 below).

[5] On April 26 (EM) Roberts had written that he would be leaving for the Augusta National Golf Club, Augusta, Georgia, on the following day and that he would remain there until the club closed, on about May 20. He also said that if it turned too warm in Augusta, he would complete his recovery in Bermuda. On Augusta National, where Roberts was chairman of the executive commmittee, see no. 113.

⁶ In a letter of May 10 (EM) Roberts would inform the General that he had made reservations to fly to Europe and would arrive in Paris on June 10.
⁷ Edward D. Lane, a vice-president and director of the Pond's Extract Company; Ralph Thomas Reed, president of the American Express Company; and SHAPE military assistant Brigadier General James Frederick Gault had played golf with Eisenhower at Morfontaine the previous morning (see appointment calendar). For background on Reed see Galambos, *Columbia University*, no. 913; on Gault see no. 96 in this volume.
⁸ On Eisenhower's friend Ellis ("Slats") Slater see no. 95. Fred M. Manning, Sr., another of the General's personal friends, had formerly run one of the largest oil-drilling concerns in the United States (see Galambos, *Columbia University*, no. 1057). Slater would visit Paris in August 1951 (see no. 95, n. 4, in this volume).
⁹ Mrs. Eisenhower had recently recovered from an attack of influenza, followed by a severe cold (see nos. 101 and 118).
The postscript to this letter has been deleted.

162   *Eisenhower Mss.*

To Walter Bedell Smith   *May 2, 1951*

*Dear Bedell:*¹ Thanks very much for your fine letter. I hasten to answer at once so as to assure you that nothing would please me more than to have you carry out the suggestion that "I believe I will write you from time to time and give you the confidential picture as we see it here." That will be most helpful.²

I was quite astonished at the enclosure to your letter. Mr. McDavid is a man that I first met in 1915, and I am quite sure that I have not seen him since sometime around 1920. He and his wife were great friends of ours in our very early married days. It is good to know that he has the desire to rush to the defense of an old friend, but I wonder how it ever occurred to him to use you as a message center in order to get a copy of the letter to me. Also, I wonder whether he knows how useless it is (even unwise) ever to answer the charges in a newspaper column. Anyway, my thanks for your kindness.³

As of now, I do not count on coming home, at the very earliest, before midsummer. For a long time, I had hoped very strongly to come back for a week in late May, but I have had to give up this plan, primarily because of the numerous trips, inspections, and engagements that crowd in on me here.⁴ (I doubt that it would be a good thing to come home now, anyway. There has been so much distortion of issues involved in the great "American argument" that it seems difficult to believe that calm presentation of fact and truth, or logical evaluation of the pros and cons of any situation, is either desired or would be useful.) For the moment, everything seems to be pitched on an emotional level.⁵

I really regret keenly that you, on your part, have been forced to give up the idea of a quick trip. Actually, this is a point that I covered twice with the President in conversations with him, and he faithfully promised to "order" you, if necessary, to come to see me when I should so request. Within a couple of weeks, we will have awfully nice weather here, and you and I could have some fine hours on one of these streams—particularly since you are well acquainted with some of them.[6]

My love to Norry,[7] and thanks again for your fine letter. *Cordially*

---

[1] For background on Smith, Director of the CIA, see no. 144.

[2] Smith had made this offer in his letter of April 25 (EM).

[3] Smith had enclosed a letter to Westbrook Pegler, the journalist, from Eisenhower's old friend Albert C. McDavid. See the following document for developments on McDavid's correspondence with Pegler, whom Smith had referred to as "our mutual friend, . . . (the SOB)."

[4] Eisenhower would not return to the United States until November. His schedule would soon include trips to Belgium, Germany, Holland, France, and Norway (see the Chronology, vol. XIII; and EM, Subject File, Trips).

[5] The "great 'American argument'" was the dispute over President Truman's dismissal of General MacArthur and over the related issue of Far Eastern defense policy (see no. 136).

[6] Eisenhower and Smith both enjoyed fishing (see Galambos, *Columbia University*, no. 564). Smith had suggested the Andelle River, northwest of Paris near Rouen, as a good place to fish (see also Smith to Eisenhower, Oct. 23, 1948, EM). Smith would visit the Eisenhowers in Paris in late September (see no. 360).

[7] Smith's wife (see no. 144).

163   *Eisenhower Mss.*

To ALBERT C. McDAVID   *May 2, 1951*

Dear Albert:[1] Bedell Smith forwarded to me a copy of the note you wrote to a columnist who had apparently criticized me severely. This is just to assure you how fine it makes me feel to realize that one of my old friends is ready and anxious to jump to my defense.[2]

Actually, I never make any reply of any kind to these attacks. Whatever a person does is bound to be misunderstood by some individuals, and each of them has a right to his own opinion. All of this would have some significance if I had any intention ever of getting into the political field. But, as it is, it just runs off my back.

So, while it is heartwarming to know that you were ready to express yourself so emphatically and promptly, I beg of you to ignore such future incidents and just be sure that I am trying to do one thing and one thing only—my duty as I see it.[3]

I just called Mamie on the phone to tell her about your note, and she asked to be included in my warm greetings and affectionate regards to you. *Cordially*

[1] McDavid, an attorney in San Antonio, Texas, had known the Eisenhowers since the General's graduation from West Point and his assignment to Fort Sam Houston in San Antonio in 1915 (see the preceding document).

[2] McDavid had defended Eisenhower in a letter of March 16 (EM) to journalist Westbrook Pegler, who had recently criticized the General in his column "As Pegler Sees It" (see *New York Journal American*, Mar. 13, 14, 1951). McDavid had sent a copy to Eisenhower by way of Bedell Smith (see the preceding document).

In his March 13 column Pegler had questioned Eisenhower's belief that "political estimates are the functions of Government, not of soldiers." The journalist said Eisenhower was a "yes-man" who was unqualified to be a military commander. On March 14 Pegler said that Eisenhower's "sole political assets" were "a military reputation that might crumble if attacked, and a grin of amiability." He again criticized the General for not challenging President Roosevelt's instructions during World War II (see nos. 78 and 101, n. 3).

In his March 16 letter to Pegler, McDavid explained that as a soldier Eisenhower could not be held responsible for President Roosevelt's foreign-policy decisions. "If ever there was an upright gentleman of honor, it is Ike. . . ," McDavid said. This was the second time that McDavid had defended the General in this manner (see McDavid to Sokolsky, Jan. 3, 1947, and Eisenhower to McDavid, Jan. 12, 1948, EM).

[3] Eisenhower had previously taken this position in regard to the press (see Galambos, *Columbia University*, no. 136). In several recent letters he had stressed his "duty" to remain nonpartisan and to fulfill his assignment as SACEUR (see nos. 131 and 135. On the General's public position concerning entering politics see nos. 195 and 232).

164   *Eisenhower Mss.*

To Philip Dunham Reed   *May 2, 1951*
Personal and confidential

Dear Phil:[1] For two or three days, I have been busily studying the paper that accompanied your letter to me of April 13.[2] As far as I have gone, I think it is a masterpiece. It expresses most accurately, and far more thoughtfully and analytically than I could, my own convictions and feelings about this great effort in which we are engaged. I have not had a chance yet to complete my study of the paper, and so have not reached final conclusions. But if it continues to develop the way it has done in the first 25 pages, I must say that I am delighted with the document that the C.E.D. has produced.[3] I hope to get a chance to drop Jim Brownlee a line, and will tell him the same thing.[4]

Charlie Wilson has just left here; he and I had some interesting, and, I hope, mutually profitable, conversations. He is certainly a most likeable person.[5]

With best regard,[6] *Cordially*

[1] Reed was chairman of the board of the General Electric Company and vice-chairman of the Committee for Economic Development (see no. 87, n. 6). For background on Reed see Chandler, *War Years*, no. 1501; and Galambos, *Columbia University*, nos. 721 and 1148. On the CED see *ibid.*, no. 732.

[2] With his letter of April 13 (EM) Reed had enclosed an advance copy of a policy statement entitled "Economic Aspects of North Atlantic Security," soon to be issued by the CED's Research and Policy Committee (copies in EM, Clubs and Associations). The Research and Policy Committee, of which Reed was a member, was made up of businessmen who referred specific questions to qualified scholars for their examination (see Committee for Economic Development, *Economic Aspects of North Atlantic Security* [New York, 1951]).

[3] Strongly supporting U.S. security efforts in Western Europe, the CED policy statement agreed with Eisenhower's recent remarks on the U.S. mission in the NATO alliance and on his own role as SACEUR (see, for example, *ibid.*, pp. 2, 4, 5; Senate Committee on Foreign Relations and Committee on Armed Services, *Assignment of Ground Forces of the United States to Duty in the European Area*, 1951, pp. 3–5, 9; and nos. 23 and 54).

According to the CED study, Western Europe had recovered a portion of its pre–World War II industrial capacity, but it could not prepare for possible Soviet aggression without U.S. aid in "free dollars" and "end-item" defense equipment. Military end items would enable European industry to concentrate on producing export items and consumer goods, which, in turn, would lower the current Western European trade deficit and greatly reduce the amount of "free-dollar" aid necessary (see Committee for Economic Development, *North Atlantic Security*, pp. 1, 24–26).

At this critical time, the CED group pointed out, it would be dangerous to expect these nations to bear the brunt of the NATO industrial/military mobilization. Only the United States and Great Britain had the means to supply the necessary economic aid; Continental countries could supply most of the needed manpower (*ibid.*, pp. 11–22; cf. nos. 6, n. 2, and 84).

Two particular aspects of the CED statement closely followed Eisenhower's thinking: the need for the United States to create an "upward-going spiral" in the morale of Western Europe; and the need to integrate Western European markets (Committee for Economic Development, *North Atlantic Security*, pp. 2–8, 31–33; Senate Committee on Foreign Relations and Committee on Armed Services, *Assignment of Ground Forces of the United States to Duty in the European Area*, 1951, pp. 4–7; Galambos, *Columbia University*, no. 1072; nos. 174, n. 4, 215, and 251 in this volume).

[4] James Forbis Brownlee was a partner in the New York investment firm of J. H. Whitney & Company and a member of the CED's Research and Policy Committee (for background see Galambos, *Columbia University*, no. 732). Eisenhower would write Brownlee on May 5 (not in EM) enclosing a copy of a May 3 cable to Meyer Kestnbaum, chairman of the Research and Policy Committee, requesting permission to distribute the report on a limited basis (Brownlee to Eisenhower, June 1, 1951, EM; Eisenhower to Kestnbaum, May 3, 1951, EM, Clubs and Associations). On May 4 the CED would cable its permission (Kestnbaum to Eisenhower, EM, Clubs and Associations).

[5] For background on Charles Edward Wilson, president of the General Electric

Company and Director of the Office of Defense Mobilization, see no. 54, n. 5; for Wilson's visit with Eisenhower see no. 145, n. 4.

[6] In his April 13 letter Reed had written that copies of the CED study were going to be made available to the participants in the first American Assembly conference, which would take place from May 21 to May 25. For background on the Assembly see nos. 65 and 87.

165   *Eisenhower Mss.*

To James Von Kanel Ladd   *May 2, 1951*

Dear Jimmy:[1] I was truly delighted to have your letter of the 15th. Not only am I always interested in keeping up correspondence with young Americans who are engaged in actual field operations, but it was grand to have news of you, personally.

I can well understand that you are getting ready for "rotation." I have not yet heard anything about the Korean campaign that makes it sound attractive for the participants. When you come back to the United States, if I should then have any vacancies in my staff, I shall put in a proper request for your assignment to the Department. However, the chances of this coming about are rather meager. We have been desperately trying to hold down the American section of my staff. Moreover, because of the character of the work, relatively senior individuals are normally picked. The one exception to this, of course, is on my personal staff, on which I have currently my full quota. (While I think of them as young men, I notice that they have been around so long that they are now wearing Lieutenant Colonel leaves on their shoulders.) In any event, it is possible that you would want nothing to do with that kind of job. The only other possibility would be in the Headquarters Command![2]

There is the likelihood that the Army will insist upon your going back to school upon your return from Korea. I know that John, who will complete his tour of instruction at West Point in another month, is scheduled to go to advanced course at Benning or Knox.[3]

Mamie is well, as are the other members of the Eisenhower family— at least, they were the last time we had news from home. I am hoping that John and his family, which now includes two young children, will be able to make a trip over here this summer for a short vacation.[4]

I hope that you will write to me again when you have both the time and the inclination. I am sure that your whole command will find Generals Ridgway and Van Fleet to be two of the best leaders that we can produce. They both served closely with me in World War II, and I had for them great admiration as well as personal liking. So far as I know, this applied also to their subordinates.[5]

With warm regard to you and yours,[6] *Cordially*

[1] Ladd (USMA 1946), son of long-time Eisenhower friend Brigadier General Jesse Amos Ladd (USA, ret.), was a captain in the 7th Infantry, on duty in Korea (for background on General Ladd see *Eisenhower Papers*, vols. I–IX).

[2] In his letter of April 15 (EM) Captain Ladd had expressed his dissatisfaction with the mission in Korea: "It is difficult to picture ourselves beating Communism by nibbling at the edges. . . . I guess the point of this letter is that if you ever need a young Captain . . . I am at your service anytime. . . ." For similar requests for positions with SHAPE see nos. 21, 29, n. 2, and 59, n. 2. The General was probably referring to his aides Lieutenant Colonel Paul Thomas Carroll and Lieutenant Colonel Robert Ludwig Schulz (see nos. 29, n. 3, and 1, respectively). Another Eisenhower aide was Charles Craig Cannon, a Regular Army major and AUS lieutenant colonel (see no. 29, n. 3).

[3] The General's son, Captain John S. D. Eisenhower, had been an instructor of English at West Point since the fall of 1948. Later this year he would attend the Army's Armored School, Advanced Officers' Course, at Fort Knox, Kentucky, before assignment to Korea (see John S. D. Eisenhower, *Strictly Personal* [New York, 1974], pp. 130–55; for background see no. 24).

[4] John Eisenhower, his wife Barbara Jean, and their two children, Barbara Anne and Dwight David II, would visit Paris during June and July (see nos. 132, 173, n. 2, and 298; appointment calendar; and correspondence in EM, Family File). For background on Barbara Jean and the General's grandchildren see no. 82, n. 2.

[5] Ladd had said that the recent removal of General Douglas MacArthur from his posts as CINCFE and SCAP had caused concern among the officers and men in Korea. MacArthur's replacement was General Matthew Bunker Ridgway (see no. 131, n. 2); General James Alward Van Fleet had been assigned as CG, Eighth Army (for background see *Eisenhower Papers*, vols. I–XI).

[6] Ladd would not receive an assignment with SHAPE (see SHAPE staff lists in EM, Subject File, Personnel).

166   *Eisenhower Mss.*

To Clifford Roberts   *May 3, 1951*

Dear Cliff: Just today, I discovered that I had not yet read carefully your three notes of April 23rd and 24th. To take up the most important question first, I should say that there is no *easy* way to quit cigarettes. However, it is not nearly so difficult as many people who have accomplished the feat try to make you believe. After all, smokers would never understand how great is the will power and self-control of the reformed addicts unless we did something to exaggerate the difficulty.[1]

Actually I think the whole thing is far more psychological than it is physical—if you can succeed in throwing out of your mind any feeling of self-pity or privation or hardship, I think that you will be amazed how quickly you can accustom yourself to a new regime. In my own case, I adopted the habit of feeling just a bit sorry for people who *had* this fault and so I attained a slight feeling of superiority. My ability to sneer, internally, I nursed to the utmost.[2]

* * * * *

Please keep writing to me—I want to know how you are getting along.[3] *Cordially*

[1] There are in EM no letters from Roberts dated April 23 and only one for April 24, to which Eisenhower had replied on May 2 (see no. 161). In a postscript to the April 24 message, in which he had informed the General of his recently diagnosed duodenal ulcer, Roberts had written, "How do you quit cigarets [*sic*]—easily?"
[2] The General had broken his own four-pack-per-day habit following an illness in 1949 (see his memoir *At Ease*, pp. 354–55; and Galambos, *Columbia University*, no. 422).
[3] Roberts would soon be in Europe for a visit with the General (see no. 161, n. 6). A portion of this letter dealing with family financial matters has been deleted.

---

167   *Eisenhower Mss.*

To WILLIAM AVERELL HARRIMAN   *May 4, 1951*
Confidential

Dear Averell: Since last I wrote you, I have been to Northern Italy where I spent a couple of days watching troop training.[1] The experience was encouraging; there was evidence of a morale and a physical fitness that was most satisfactory. In fact, some of the training exercises that I saw done by the Alpini and Bersaglieri I have never seen duplicated, in their daring and audacity, by any other units except by some of the American Rangers in World War II. There are, of course, many shortages in Italy, especially in professional leadership, training facilities, and necessary equipment. All these, however, can be overcome if what I saw was a fair sample of existing spirit and morale in Italian armed forces, and if the equipment can be produced or imported as needed.

In the case of Italy, I do not even worry too much about the limitations of the Treaty.[2] While I have no doubt that certain details of the Treaty will eventually prove burdensome or frustrating, I am, as of now, more concerned in developing quality than I am quantity in Italy.

This coming week, I shall make a similar trip in Holland and Belgium. Before the end of the month, I will do the same in Denmark and Norway.[3]

On the other side of the picture is a record of minor frustrations, most of them similar to the difficulties I described to you in my letter of April 2nd.[4] I do not want to burden you with repeating all those details, but I think you can readily understand that the apparent inability of governments to hit upon some acceptable plan for sharing the relatively inconsequential costs of our preliminary activities and of establishing required overhead, is inexcusable.[5] Certainly, such a record does not augur well for success in the cooperative solution of the vast substantive problems with which we are, and will be, faced.

One of my acute needs of the moment is the prompt establishment of a joint headquarters in the Fontainebleau area for Juin and Norstad.[6] After weeks of exploration and haggling, it becomes more and more apparent that we will have to carry out at least some construction. We have gotten exactly nowhere, and I cannot blame Norstad for displaying sharp impatience as he seeks to get down to his real work.

For a week, we have had a committee over here from the Deputies (at my invitation) to go over our budget.[7] I certainly do not want to appear arbitrary, and I know of no better way of creating confidence than to open up to all participating governments the record of everything we are doing. (Except, of course, when security would be clearly involved.) The committee examined and re-examined us for something like a week, and, so far as I know, had no criticism whatsoever to make on our estimates. But, while they are doing this, we have to face the fact that the minimum costs of establishing a headquarters for the Central Command will probably be three or four times what we originally hoped it would be.

The E.C.C. is meeting in Paris today, and I have a hunch that they will propose some expedient to Washington to get over this initial financial hump, so that we may all get down to work on more important problems.[8] Just what their proposal will be, I do not know—in fact, I am not even sure that they will submit one. But I must say that, if this particular point is not solved soon, I am going to adopt some drastic methods—it is silly to keep sweating, working, and worrying about collective security for a dozen nations if we can't even get collective action on properly starting the job.

All of us are naturally sympathetic with the great difficulties under which these governments operate, due to their financial shortages. But the costs with which we are now concerned are small, and the adopted method of meeting them does not need to establish a pattern for later burden sharing in greater matters.

Someone told me that Marie is soon to be here, and I believe that the Katz's are giving her a cocktail party shortly after she arrives.[9] Mamie will see her then, unless we happen to be out of town. While I never go to cocktail parties, I certainly hope to see her before long.

Our own house—which has been purchased by the French Government and which is now undergoing considerable repair—should be ready for occupancy by midsummer. I never imagined it would take so long, but you know how those things go.[10]

In the meantime, we seem to be making some slow progress on the establishment of our "Allied Village." This is a housing project, to be carried out by the French Government in an area very close to our headquarters, which should likewise be ready for occupancy about mid-July.[11]

It is possible that, in one of your letters, you have already given me a guess as to the date on which you will come to Europe this summer. I do not recall it at the moment, so please be sure to give me as much advance notice as you possibly can. Thus I won't plan to be absent at that moment.[12]

Please pay my respects to the President, and, of course, warmest regard to yourself.[13] *Cordially*

[1] Eisenhower's last letter to Harriman is no. 142. On his trip to Italy and his inspection of Italian Army units see nos. 153 and 158.

[2] For background on the Treaty of Peace with Italy (1947) see Galambos, *Chief of Staff*, nos. 1504, 1592, and 1825. Under the terms of the treaty Italy was to limit the size of its armed forces and its military production. The Italian Army was to comprise only 185,000 combat, service, and overhead personnel, and the total number of heavy and medium tanks was not to exceed 200 (U.S. Department of State, *Treaties and Other International Acts Series*, no. 1648-1649 [Washington, D.C., 1947], pp. 146, 149-50). In January 1951 President Truman had decided to "take diplomatic action as appropriate to assure that the Treaty limitations do not prevent Italy from meeting its joint defense obligations" (State, *Foreign Relations, 1951*, vol. IV, *Europe: Political and Economic Developments, Part I*, p. 620). The United States, Great Britain, and France, prodded by the U.S. Congress and the Italian government, would jointly announce in September that the treaty restrictions would be ignored because they had been "wholly overtaken by events" and had "no justification in present circumstances" (*ibid.*, pp. 717-18; see also pp. 589-91, 597-607).

[3] Eisenhower would be in Belgium, the Netherlands, and Germany (to inspect Belgian troops going through field maneuvers) from May 7 to May 10. From May 20 to May 25 he would visit Denmark and Norway in order to inspect military units in those countries (see *New York Times*, May 8, 9, 23, 1951; see also nos. 149, n. 2, 183, n. 3, and 196).

[4] No. 128.

[5] For background on the SHAPE budget problem see no. 111, n. 2. The NAC deputies had considered the issue in meetings held on April 9, 12, and 16, but no agreement had been reached (State, *Foreign Relations, 1951*, vol. III, *European Security and the German Question, Part I*, pp. 128-30; D-R [51] 28, Apr. 14, 1951, and D-R [51] 29, Apr. 19, 1951, in NATO Files, microfilm). At a subsequent meeting (Apr. 23) Charles Spofford, the chairman of the NAC deputies (see no. 16, n. 16), had noted that there had been no progress toward resolving the issues; he had scolded his fellow deputies for their failure to agree upon even an interim advance for SHAPE. On May 2 the deputies, although still unable to reach agreement on the size of an interim advance, agreed that all governments (not just those with military forces under Eisenhower's command) should be compelled to pay costs. On this same day a committee proposed a formula for sharing the costs of interim advances to SHAPE and its subordinate headquarters, and the NAC

deputies approved this formula on May 7 (State, *Foreign Relations, 1951,* vol. III, *European Security and the German Question, Part I,* pp. 128–30. D-R [51] 28, Apr. 14, 1951; D-R [51] 29, Apr. 19, 1951; D-R [51] 31, Apr. 25, 1951; D-D [51] 124, May 2, 1951; D-R [51] 35, May 10, 1951, all in NATO Files, microfilm). The NAC deputies would approve the SHAPE budget for the first half of 1951 on May 28 and that for the remainder of the year in October. In August the deputies would agree on a final plan to apportion SHAPE costs among the NATO member nations. The United States would pay 22.5 percent of the operating costs and 40 percent of the capital costs; the United Kingdom would pay 22.5 percent of both capital and operating costs; and France would contribute 22.5 percent of the operating costs and 17 percent of the capital costs. The other nations would contribute smaller amounts, with Canada and Italy paying the most (8 percent operating, 5.1 percent capital) and Iceland and Luxembourg paying the least (0.25 percent operating, 0.1 percent capital) (see D-D [51] 181 [Final], Aug. 29, 1951; D-D [51] 231, Sept. 13, 1951; and D-D [51] 276, Nov. 10, 1951, all in NATO Files, microfilm). Eisenhower's financial troubles would nevertheless continue: as the NAC deputies would note, the member governments had paid only 16 percent of their share as of November 10, 1951 (D-D [51] 276, Nov. 10, 1951, *ibid.*).

[6] For background on General Alphonse Juin, whom Eisenhower had designated as C in C, Allied Army Forces, Central Europe, and on General Norstad, who commanded the Allied Air Forces, Central Europe, see nos. 16, n. 6, and 77, n. 17. Norstad had assumed command on April 2. He would announce the structure of his command and the appointment of several of his principal subordinates on May 26 (*New York Times,* May 27, 1951).

[7] This was probably the SHAPE Budget Committee, established in April to advise the NAC deputies. On May 28 the committee would report that only three countries (the United States, Great Britain, and Norway) had contributed their share to the scheduled interim advances. The NAC deputy from the Netherlands would complain that SHAPE had not indicated how the money would be spent (D-D [51] 117, Apr. 25, 1951; D-R [51] 42, May 29, 1951, both in NATO Files, microfilm).

[8] The European Coordinating Committee (ECC) was formed in 1949 to help formulate a coordinated military supply program for Europe and to provide the relevant U.S. agencies (the State and Defense departments and the ECA) with firsthand impressions of the progress being made in Western Europe. Charles M. Spofford (see no. 16, n. 16) was Chairman of the ECC, whose members comprised most of the senior U.S. civilian and military representatives in Europe. Included on the committee were General Thomas T. Handy (see nos. 77, n. 21, and 286), Milton Katz (see no. 16, n. 7), General Cortlandt Schuyler (see no. 2, n. 1), William L. Batt (see no. 16, n. 16), and William R. Herod (see no. 81, n. 4). See also Senate Subcommittee on Foreign Relations, *United States Foreign-Aid Programs in Europe: Hearings,* 1951, pp. 24–25; and Kaplan, *Community of Interests,* pp. 23–24, 29, 140–41. We have been unable to locate any ECC proposal concerning SHAPE finances.

[9] Mrs. Harriman, the former Marie Norton Whitney, would visit Paris in May (see no. 173, n. 1). See n. 8 above for background on Milton Katz, American Special Representative in Europe under the Foreign Assistance Act.

[10] The Eisenhowers would not move into their house until August (see no. 314, n. 1).

[11] For background on the "SHAPE Village" housing project see nos. 68, n. 4, and 395, n. 2.

[12] Harriman would visit Europe in June (see nos. 191 and 218).

[13] In a handwritten postscript Eisenhower informed Harriman that "Monty [Field Marshal Montgomery] has just returned from Italy. His impressions are even more favorable than those expressed in [this letter]." In his reply (May 7, 1951, EM)

Harriman discussed the controversy generated by the removal of General Mac-
Arthur from his command (see nos. 128, n. 3, 131, n. 2, and 136, n. 2): "There
is no doubt MacArthur has stirred an emotion which is second to none in this
country's history. On the other hand, it seems to be cooling off and I am counting
on the great American reaction when they have been sold a goldbrick. If you think
the French are volatile people, come home and see what Americans are like!" For
developments see no. 173.

168   *Eisenhower Mss.*

To ARTHUR HAYS SULZBERGER   *May 7, 1951*

Dear Arthur:[1] Your letter of May 1st arrived on schedule, but I haven't
yet seen the communication from Professor Powell. It is possible that
someone in my office sidetracked it momentarily because I have been
so busy with conferences, arguments, briefings, and inspections. However, as soon as I get back to my headquarters (I am now in an airplane
heading for Cologne) I shall look the matter up.[2]

I can't tell you how disappointed I am to hear about your unfavorable reactions to the Army's I&E program. The fact is, of course, that
it is difficult to keep military leaders intensely interested in this kind
of thing. They respond to the compulsions of their profession by re-
gretting every minute they have to take away from strictly professional
training. They are quite apt to say, "Everything that is taught in the
I&E program should have been absorbed by the good citizen long
before he came into uniform. If he hasn't learned it by this time,
there is no use in my fooling with the matter." Of course, the basic
truth, of which we are likely to lose sight, is that maximum military
proficiency cannot be attained by any man unless he has a cause, in
which he believes implicitly, for which to fight or to work.[3] Occasionally, a man can be found who becomes a great fighter merely for
money. Massena, one of Napoleon's marshals, was this kind.[4] But,
speaking generally, only a burning patriotism, or belief in a fundamental cause will lead a soldier to maximum performance on the
battlefield. For this reason—if for no other—the I&E program ought
to be even more important to the military than other forms of training or instruction.[5]

If you go to Japan and Korea you will meet one of the finest men
the armed forces has produced—General Ridgeway. He is a man of
force, of magnetism, and of culture. Also, you will like General Van
Fleet. He, like Ridgeway, is a real fighting man.[6]

Please convey my warm greetings to your charming wife[7] and remember me to people like Doug Black, John Jackson[8]—in fact, any of
the trustees whom you may run into. *Sincerely*

[1] *New York Times* publisher Sulzberger was a life trustee of Columbia University and chairman of the university's Bicentennial Committee (see no. 114 for background).
[2] In his May 1 (EM) letter Sulzberger had said that Columbia law professor Richard Roy Belden Powell had recently written to Eisenhower concerning plans for the 1954 bicentennial ceremonies (see Powell to Eisenhower, Apr. 24, 1951, EM). For background on Powell, who was vice-chairman of the Bicentennial Program Committee, see Galambos, *Columbia University*, no. 495. On the proposed celebration see nos. 372, n. 2, and 703 in this volume; and for developments see no. 282.

Eisenhower was on a four-day military inspection tour of West Germany, Holland, and Belgium (see appointment calendar; and no. 167).
[3] Sulzberger had written that the *New York Times* education editor, Benjamin Fine, had recently toured the United States to study the Armed Forces Information and Education (I&E) Program and had been disappointed by his findings. According to Sulzberger, the program was being poorly managed and had "degenerated into training publicity experts." For background on the I&E program, which was founded to explain the mission of the armed forces to enlisted personnel, see Chandler and Galambos, *Occupation, 1945*, no. 387; and Galambos, *Columbia University*, nos. 1073 and 1130. On the Citizenship Education Project and its similar work in military education see no. 70 in this volume.

In July Fine would report that the Armed Forces Information School at Fort Slocum, New York, had been established to train I&E instructors properly and thus to meet many of the criticisms made about the I&E program (see *New York Times*, July 27, 1951).
[4] One of Napoleon's ablest commanders, Marshal of the Empire André Massena, duke of Rivoli and prince of Essling, was notorious for his avarice (see David G. Chandler, *The Campaigns of Napoleon* [New York, 1966], pp. xxxiv, 55, 366, 511).
[5] In testimony before the House Armed Services and Foreign Affairs committees during February Eisenhower had expressed sentiments similar to these. He said that the first duty of leadership was "to instruct, to give an understanding to the followers," and that in order to ensure that a soldier would fight, he must be made to believe in his nation and in "something more general in scope" (see House Committee on International Relations, *Selected Executive Session Hearings, 1943–50*, vol. VI, *Military Assistance Programs*, pt. 2, pp. 286, 288).
[6] For background on General Ridgway, newly appointed CINCFE and SCAP, Korea, see no. 131, n. 2; and on Eighth Army CG, General Van Fleet, see no. 165.
[7] Iphogene Ochs Sulzberger (for background see Galambos, *Columbia University*, no. 577).
[8] On Columbia trustees Douglas MacCrae Black, president of Doubleday & Company; and New York lawyer John Gillespie Jackson see *ibid.*, nos. 28 and 225, respectively.

169   *Eisenhower Mss.*

To Sergius Klotz   *May 7, 1951*

Dear Serge:[01] Thank you very much for the note you sent to me from the Ritz in London. It was brought to me by Mr. Herod the other day.[2]

I am sorry that we did not have greater opportunity for a real visit when you were in Paris. However, I must say that I did enjoy the brief conversation permitted us by the complexities of my schedule.

Incidentally, time seems to become an ever more precious commodity for me—my calendar for the next two months is already so jammed up that I hate even to look at it.[3]

With respect to the observations made in your note, I agree with them; all excepting those that refer to me personally. My feeling as of today is that there is considerable progress toward the attainment of Europe's basic objective of eventual security. This progress is not spectacular, nor is it even at a considerable rate. However, I believe that there is an increasing confidence that, through some form of practical unification of effort, Europe *can* defend itself. And I believe that there is gradually developing a real determination to do it. The road ahead is long and difficult, but all of us knew that from the beginning. So we keep plugging away.[4]

Please convey my greetings to your nice wife,[5] and cordial regard to yourself. *Sincerely*

[1] Klotz, an investment broker, had been associated with Reynolds and Company in New York since the beginning of May. Prior to this he had been a partner in the New York brokerage firm of Charles Slaughter and Company.

[2] Klotz's note, dated April 30, 1951 (EM), had been delivered to Eisenhower on May 5 by William Rogers Herod, Coordinator of the Defense Production Board of NATO (on Herod see no. 100, n. 5; and Herod to Eisenhower, May 7, 1951, EM). Klotz had described his impressions of general attitudes in Europe, based on his recent two-month visit there. He noted the "war weariness" of the European people, their fear of the Soviet Union, and their gratitude for American aid.

[3] Klotz and his wife had visited Eisenhower on April 18 (see Schulz to Klotz, Apr. 10, 1951, EM). The Klotzes had arrived in Paris on April 12, but because the General was on an inspection tour of Germany, they were only able to spend a short time together. In the next two months Eisenhower would visit Belgium, Germany, Holland, Denmark, Norway, and Normandy and Reims, France (see EM, Subject File, Trips; and the Chronology in these volumes).

[4] See n. 2 above. Klotz had said that Europeans had "utter confidence" in Eisenhower. He predicted, however, that because of the complexities of the situation, progress would be slow unless Eisenhower could "find workable means to personally exert the overall leadership Europe's public hopes for." From the beginning, one of Eisenhower's primary goals had been to enable Europe to defend itself. He knew that the NATO countries needed time to rebuild their defenses, however, and he had concluded that the United States should be prepared to support "this wall of security we have built up—so long as the wall is needed" (Senate Committee on Foreign Relations and Committee on Armed Services, *Assignment of Ground Forces of the United States to Duty in Europe*, 1951, p. 19). For background see also nos. 23, 112, and 164.

[5] Terry Klotz.

Dear George: No news that I have had in a long time has pleased me quite so much as that in your latest letter to the effect that you are getting truly interested in animal husbandry. If this is true (and I most certainly hope that your feeling is keen and lasting) it is exactly what makes fun out of farming.[1] With your interest in animal husbandry and mine in soil conservation, we can certainly—if we mix these with a judicious amount of golf and bridge, to say nothing of a bit of fishing and shooting—find plenty to occupy our time.[2]

It has been a long time since I have heard from Art Nevins. In a way, this is a very hopeful sign because a possible reason is that he is working so hard he simply hasn't time to write letters. In any event, I was keenly interested in the decision reached by Mr. Kirchner and Art after the two of them together had looked over the Gettysburg project. In my speculations for our need for a Guernsey bull, I had supposed that we might do a little cross breeding in the hope of raising the butter content of the milk. The changed program makes sense to me.[3]

If Art is as truly interested as he seems to be, you and I have a real asset in his services. Consequently, I do hope that we find some way of pulling into the venture the pasturage on your farm. Of course, it is possible that the agricultural advisors might find that the grass there is non-nutritious; however, it certainly looks like it would support quite a bit of live stock on summer feeding. My point simply is that I think that Art could manage a bigger operation than that represented in the one relatively small farm. We don't want him to get too deep in hard physical labor himself or he will get tired of the whole thing and quit on us.

One thing that occurred to me is that with him right there on the spot, he might eventually be able to pick up a fairly good bargain for himself; in which event, you and I could help finance him at nominal cost to him.[4]

All this is mere speculation, written in my airplane as I am leaving for an inspection trip to Belgium. So don't take too seriously any of my meditations and comments about the farm.[5]

One disappointment in your latest letter to me was your failure to mention any possibility of you and Mary making an early trip over this way. While it is true that Mamie and I are still living in a hotel, we could still have a lot of fun and interesting times if you two would come over for a month or so. Why don't we settle for the month of August right now? That would give you plenty of time to plan the trip and would get you out of Washington and New York during the very worst part of the year. Moreover, by that time we should certainly be well settled in our new home, and we could really have a pleasant time.[6]

Give my love to Mary and be sure to remember me to any of our mutual friends you may happen to encounter. I think instantly of Charlie White, Victor Emmanuel, and Clark Clifford, as well as the members of our "New York bridge gang."[7] *As ever*

[1] In a letter of April 30 (EM) Allen had said that following a recent trip to Gettysburg, Pennsylvania, he had become interested in the herd of milk cattle he and the General were establishing on their farms there. For background on Allen and his farming partnership with Eisenhower see nos. 33 and 73, n. 3.

[2] On Eisenhower's interest in and attempts at improving the soil fertility of his Gettysburg property see his memoir *At Ease*, p. 193; and Nevins, *Five-Star Farmer*, pp. 84, 86.

[3] Retired Brigadier General Arthur Nevins managed the Eisenhower farm (see nos. 33, n. 4, and 73, n. 4). The General's next letter to Nevins is no. 179. On Allen's recent visit to the farm he had been accompanied by New York clothing retailer Walter Kirschner, who had earlier presented the partnership with two young bulls (see no. 33, n. 2).

[4] Aside from the dairy and cattle venture, Nevins raised hay, corn, oats, barley, wheat, and sheep on the Eisenhower and Allen farms (see Nevins, *Five-Star Farmer*, pp. 99, 105, 108). Nevins would not purchase a farm in the Gettysburg area, but he would later rent a house north of the town. He would continue as manager of the Eisenhower property until 1967 (see *ibid.*, pp. 108, 142).

[5] For background on the tour of Belgium and the Netherlands see no. 167, n. 3.

[6] Allen would visit the Eisenhowers during June (see appointment calendar). On the difficulties the General and Mrs. Eisenhower encountered searching for a house see nos. 44, n. 2, and 60.

[7] For background on Clark McAdams Clifford, Special Counsel to President Truman since 1946; and Charles McElroy White, president of the Republic Steel Corporation of New Jersey, see Galambos, *Columbia University*, nos. 282 and 944, respectively. Victor Emanuel was president and chairman of the board of the Avco Manufacturing Corporation, producers of home appliances (see EM, Emanuel Corr.).

171   *Eisenhower Mss.*

To Harry Cecil Butcher   *May 7, 1951*

Dear Butch:[01] While I have had your letter of April 25 for some days, I don't think you will be greatly astonished to learn that up to this moment, May 7th, I have had no chance whatsoever to read the draft of the article that you sent with it. In fact, I have not read it even yet, for I am taking advantage of an airplane trip from Paris to Cologne to prepare this reply. However, I intend to read it before I land.[2] (Incidentally, I am reminded that it was six years ago today that Jodl and Beedle Smith signed the articles of surrender over in Rheims. At this moment, I am about 25 miles south of Rheims, heading eastward.)[3]

Of course I am delighted that Mickey and Pearlie have reached the point where they can buy their own house. Please give them both my warm greetings. I hope that they and their little one are in good health and are prospering.[4]

You are right in your surmise that I am in the middle of a very complicated situation, and that my problems are rendered all the more difficult by reason of the confusion of thinking applied to them. Nevertheless, I am always assisted by a few simple truths. The first of these is that the preservation of a free Europe is of great, if not vital, importance to the United States. The second truth is that the free world has such moral, intellectual and material strength that, if it will only organize these efficiently, and rapidly, the communistic world will not dare attack. The third is that anything that I can do to bring about this unification of effort is going to be done cheerfully and as well as I know how.

We are building a sort of "Wide Wing" some miles outside of Paris, and hope to move into it early in the summer.[5] I have a good staff, and I assure you I keep it busy.

With warm regard. *Cordially*

[1] For background on Butcher, a wartime aide of Eisenhower's, who now owned radio station KIST in Santa Barbara, California, see Galambos, *Columbia University*, no. 33.

[2] In his letter of April 24 (EM) Butcher had enclosed two articles, one suggesting Eisenhower's nomination by both parties, the second, written by Butcher, discussing Eisenhower's credentials and motivations as a potential presidential candidate (see *Los Angeles Times*, Apr. 24, 1951, and *Look*, June 5, 1951, pp. 67–71, copies in EM; see also no. 190).

[3] On May 7, 1945, Field Marshal Alfred G. Jodl and General Walter Bedell Smith had been present at the signing of the German surrender documents for World War II (see Walter Bedell Smith, *Eisenhower's Six Great Decisions* [New York, 1956], pp. 202–6; and Eisenhower, *Crusade in Europe*, pp. 425–26. On Jodl see Galambos, *Chief of Staff*, no. 1124; on Smith see no. 144 in this volume). On this same day Eisenhower began an inspection trip to Belgium, Germany, and Holland (see EM, Subject File, Trips, SHAPE no. 5).

[4] Mickey, Pearlie, and their "little one" are Michael James McKeogh, his wife Pearl Hargrave McKeogh, and their daughter Mary Ann. McKeogh, who had been Eisenhower's orderly during the war, had become the vice-president of KIST radio station (see McKeogh to Eisenhower, Mar. 29, 1951, EM; and Galambos, *Columbia University*, nos. 311 and 919. See also Michael J. McKeogh and Richard Lockridge, *Sgt. Mickey and General Ike* [New York, 1946]).

[5] The "Wide Wing" was probably the new SHAPE offices at Marly (see no. 281, n. 4).

To Hoyt Sanford Vandenberg   *May 11, 1951*
Cable SH 20460. Restricted. Routine

Personal for Gen. Vandenberg[1] from Gen. Eisenhower. I have your letter
of May 3[2] alerting us to the major problems developed in the recent
meetings in Washington of the four Air Chiefs[3] and I am having the
staff give urgent attention in determining what assistance we can give.
I also discussed the subject with Norstad[4] who was here today.

Another subject I discussed with Norstad is our need for a top flight
air planner in our Plans, Policy and Operations Division. Larry told
me that he has suggested to you Colonel W S Steele for that position.[5]
Steele is well and favorably known here, and he will make a material
contribution to our organization. I shall indeed be grateful if he can
be released for this assignment.

[1] General Vandenberg had been C/S of the U.S. Air Force since April 1948. For
further background see *Eisenhower Papers*, vols. I–XI.

[2] In his letter (EM) Vandenberg had outlined the steps that NATO's principal air
force leaders thought Eisenhower should take in order to provide SHAPE with
sufficient air support. In 1950 NATO had adopted as a strategic wartime goal the
establishment of a defense line east of the Rhine River in Germany and in the
Netherlands. This concept of operations, which became known as the "forward
strategy," required combat forces at the start of the war that were greater than
those called for in NATO's Medium Term Defense Plan (see nos. 15, n. 4, and
16). SHAPE planners also believed "that the farther forward combat operations
begin, the greater is the amount of air units required." They reasoned that it would
be more difficult to obtain air superiority over a battlefield east of the Rhine and
that more aircraft sorties would be necessary to offset SHAPE's inability to move
its air forces forward with the ground units (Beebe to Wright, June 5, 1951,
Records of the Assistant Secretary of Defense for International Security Affairs,
ONATA Subject File 1949–53. See also Bradley to Marshall, Jan. 26, 1951, CCS
092 Western Europe [3-12-48], Sec. 67; Roger Hilsman, "NATO: The Developing
Strategic Context," in *NATO and American Security*, ed. Klaus Knorr [Princeton,
1959], pp. 18–20; Stikker, *Men of Responsibility*, pp. 297–99; and State, *Foreign
Relations, 1951*, vol. III, *European Security and the German Question, Part I*, pp. 460–
61). In his letter Vandenberg had asked Eisenhower to give his personal attention
to the political and military problems involved in creating a larger combat-ready
air force for NATO, and he had asked that Eisenhower apply "unrelenting pressure" on the NATO member governments so that they would "increase production
now for airpower, materiel, and munitions for combat training and adequate war
reserves, and to provide now for the construction of vast facilities on the European
continent." Vandenberg also had warned Eisenhower that the necessary funds had
to be made available by the NATO nations "by the end of the summer" and that
this would "not be possible if prolonged legislative and military reviews of the
entire program are required."

[3] The air chiefs of staff of Great Britain, Canada, France, and the United States
had met in Washington to discuss the acceleration of NATO air force programs.
Their preliminary report, dated May 3, is not in EM. See Vandenberg to Eisen-

hower, May 3, 1951, and Slessor to Eisenhower, May 15, 1951, both in EM. For developments see no. 187, n. 2.
[4] For background on General Lauris ("Larry") Norstad, Eisenhower's air commander in Central Europe, see no. 77, n. 17.
[5] Air Force Colonel William Swinton Steele (USMA 1936) would later be assigned to the Office of the Special Assistant to the Chief of Staff at SHAPE. He was currently serving in the Office of the Secretary of the Air Force. During World War II he had been with the Seventh Air Force in the Pacific.

173   *Eisenhower Mss.*

To WILLIAM AVERELL HARRIMAN   *May 12, 1951*
Confidential

Dear Averell: Marie told Al,[1] last evening at a cocktail party, that you plan to come over here about June 21. I have been secretly hoping that you would come sometime a bit earlier in June because I may have a need for asking some VIP to pick up my family on his plane and bring them over for a visit.[2] I hate to contemplate ordinary ship travel because of the amount of time it would cut off of any leave that my son, John, could get. While as of this moment I am not certain as to the date that John can leave West Point, if there does develop any change in your plan so that you might be leaving the States anywhere from the 5th to the 12th of June, please let me know so that I may put upon you the burden of a personal favor. You understand that they cannot come by ordinary MATS[3] because regulations do not provide for travel by dependents on normal transport planes.

Recently we had a meeting here in Paris attended by Spofford, Katz, Batt, Herod, Handy and a few members of my staff.[4] A number of comments were made about the great delay normally experienced in obtaining answers or approval from Washington on most official requests and suggestions, particularly when these dealt with munitions. It seemed to be the general impression that the delay occurred in the Munitions Board, but whether or not this view is accurate, I have no means of knowing. Please do not look upon this as a complaint; I pass it to you as a piece of information on which you may do a little bit of quiet investigation.[5]

Of course, when a European country is behind schedule in meeting its defense programs, it eagerly seizes upon any excuse to exercise delay or inaction. Consequently, not long ago in Holland one of the Chiefs of Staff gave to me as an excuse for delay in mobilizing men the allegation that scheduled American delivery of equipment would make it impossible for him to train them if they were called to the colors.[6]

Quite naturally, I don't allow these people to get away with that kind of excuse. I tell them bluntly (though, of course, in the confidence of official conference) that merely because some American promise may have been a little bit too enthusiastically made does not excuse the European country from doing its best to meet its own security problems. Of course, alibis never did mean much to me in anything.

I notice that the papers say a great deal about soldiers necessarily clearing with higher authority in advance anything they may have to say on matters lying outside their own professional concerns.[7]

Of course, when I came over here I was warned by you, as well as all the others with whom I talked, that much of my effort would be devoted toward creating enthusiasm among peoples, as well as armies. In other words, it seemed to be expected, at that time, that I would be working in many fields that could not be classed strictly as military. The general result of the whole thing is, of course, that I will keep still, in every language known to man, for the simple reason that it would be a complete impossibility for anyone to clear, with twelve governments, anything that touched upon the interests, beliefs or prejudices of all of them.[8]

However, I shall, of course, keep working in the confidential rooms of governmental offices to advance the idea of common security and the necessity of mutual contributions in order to make it a success.

We have a virtual flood of visitors, most of them from America. However, they do not come for the purpose of idle gossip or merely for consuming the time of a busy staff and commander. I find that all of them are seriously concerned with European developments and attitudes, and many of them contribute to us a great deal in understanding and information. So I do my best to meet and talk to all of them, even though at times it is a very time-consuming process. An added value to this kind of thing is to give to many Americans a better comprehension of the basic problems involved in the development of common security and of the real reasons we have for establishing a cooperative enterprise in which America and Europe are both involved.[9]

One idea that I hear repeated in different forms by some of the American representatives is about as follows:

"Pressure directed toward a percentage of the Gross National Product spent by the members of NATO on defense is not having a good psychological effect. It has put the governments of nations in a 'comparative' mood, compounded with resentment and suspicion instead of inducing them to an all-out effort. It would appear better to urge them to do their utmost, that no less is acceptable. The U.S. could use quietly, as a guide only, the percentages for applying confidential pressure when necessary. It is impossible to put a nation's valuation of freedom and liberty on a percentage basis. Threats to withdraw aid if the percent of Gross National Product spent on defense is not increased, are bad for concerted effort and cause resentment against U.S.A. Leadership, not threats, are badly needed."[10] Every day is a business lunch of some kind. I have hit upon a good scheme avoiding excess weight and the ruination of digestion. My lunch is invariably and exclusively a fruit salad without dressing (I wish I had your build since I enjoy food so much), but I must admit that I cannot remember any other time in years when I have felt in better health—and this in spite of the fact that exercise periods are very few and far between. *Cordially*

[1] Harriman's wife was visiting Europe (see no. 167, n. 9). "Al" is Eisenhower's C/S, General Alfred M. Gruenther.

[2] Eisenhower was planning to have his mother-in-law and his son and his family visit France (see nos. 183, n. 6, and 224, n. 2). Harriman replied in a letter of May 18 (EM) that he would not leave Washington before June 20 and that he was "not the kind of a VIP that has a plane." He told Eisenhower that he would ask whether "a real VIP from the Pentagon" would be traveling to Europe at that time and could help Eisenhower.

[3] Military Air Transport Service.

[4] For background on Charles M. Spofford, Milton Katz, and William L. Batt see no. 16; on William R. Herod see no. 81, n. 4; and on General Thomas Handy see no. 77, n. 21.

[5] For background on the Defense Department's Munitions Board, which coordinated military production, procurement, and distribution plans, see Galambos, *Columbia University*, nos. 165, 327, and 369. In Harriman's May 18 reply he admitted that there had been delays in furnishing American supplies and equipment for Europe. The delays, he felt, could be attributed to the lack of an "overall production plan"; to problems involving patent rights; to military indecision as to the acceptability of proposed military products; and to "our own increased requirements, particularly the Korean war." He told Eisenhower that he was glad the General had mentioned the matter and that he would "get into it to see whether there was anything I could do to speed up decisions." Eisenhower would also mention this problem in a letter to Secretary of Defense George Marshall (see the following document).

[6] Eisenhower had inspected Dutch military forces in the Netherlands from May 7 to May 10 (see no. 167).

[7] Late in 1950 General Douglas MacArthur had made a number of policy statements that were critical of the Truman Administration's Korean War policies. In response, President Truman had ordered public officials and military leaders to clear all public statements on foreign or military policy with either the State Department or the Defense Department. On March 24 MacArthur apparently had violated this directive with his offer to negotiate a cease-fire settlement with the Chinese (James, *Years of MacArthur*, vol. III, *Triumph and Disaster*, pp. 540–42, 585–91; see also no. 101, n. 5).

[8] In his reply (May 18) Harriman urged Eisenhower to speak out publicly whenever he thought it would be useful. He added: "The trouble in the other situation was that the individual [MacArthur] was not in sympathy with his government's policies, and in addition did not conform his public statements to these policies." He also told Eisenhower that although he tried to "check with the President on whether he agrees that I should talk about a certain general subject" and although he also tried to conform the details of his speeches with the Pentagon and the State

Department, he had "never yet had a speech cleared, principally because I've never gotten it finished on time."

[9] On Eisenhower's visitors see no. 176. See also Gunther, *Eisenhower*, pp. 7–8.

[10] In April Robert D. Murphy, the American Ambassador to Belgium (see no. 16, n. 9), had scolded the Belgian government for its failure to contribute a sufficient amount toward the defense of Western Europe. At that time he had noted that while the United Kingdom, France, and the United States were allocating 10–19 percent of their national production for defense, the comparable figure for Belgium was only 5 percent. He had also warned the Belgians that the United States might reduce its assistance to countries that did not contribute enough of their own resources (*New York Times*, Apr. 17, 24, 1951; see also State, *Foreign Relations, 1951*, vol. IV, *Europe: Political and Economic Developments, Part I*, pp. 273–81, 285–88).

174   *Eisenhower Mss.*

To GEORGE CATLETT MARSHALL   *May 12, 1951*
Top secret

Dear General: I have just received your letter referring to the German situation and will reply very soon.[1]

I am back in my old routine of mixing up a vast amount of office work with frequent trips to troops and installations, and I must say that the whole procedure leaves one with the feeling that he has no control whatsoever over his own time.[2]

Here and there I uncover some complaints, either implied or direct, concerning American participation in the mutual defense. I need scarcely assure you that I never allow any complainant to assume that he has given me a satisfactory explanation of any failure on the part of his own country.

In the confines of a secret conference room, I never hesitate to give them a pretty stern reminder that no performance of their own that is less than their best can be considered satisfactory.[3]

However, I have at times the uneasy feeling that there may be some truth in a few of the allegations they make. This is especially true when it is confirmed by information received by the very fine group of American civilian representatives we have in Europe. These include Spofford, Katz, Batt, Herod, and several good Ambassadors. A number of these men think that there should be some person in the Munitions Board, or in a similar office, whose whole duty would be to expedite, follow and push through requests of every kind from this sector.[4]

The kind of thing reported to me, sometimes in terms of complaint and sometimes in terms of information, is almost limitless. For example, in Belgium and Holland it was brought to my attention that delays were being experienced in obtaining plans and specifications for manufacture of various items. This delay may be unavoidable, but it has two bad results:

(a) It provides an excuse for not fulfilling obligations on the part of nations involved.

(b) It creates a bad impression as to the efficiency and seriousness of U.S. effort.

Two specific instances given were:

(a) Belgium is anxious to obtain specifications for manufacture of 52 types of ammunition. It was regionally approved last December. Continued inquiries have been made by Military Defense Assistance personnel. Ambassador Murphy[5] took it up about a month ago when he was in Washington. Mr. Cabot[6] and General Burns[7] promised action. To date, no action.

(b) In March specifications were requested to permit manufacture of field telephones, since Bell and Automatic have large factories in Belgium. Here again, what appears to be an unreasonable delay, is taking place.

In Holland the same complaints were made, particularly in regard to manufacture of ammunition.[8]

Phillips was discussed in both countries. No one could see any reason why it should not be given contracts.[9]

Not long ago I made an inspection of troops in Italy. I was most favorably impressed by the élan and spirit of all the troops I saw. Some time after that, Montgomery went to Rome and was similarly favorably impressed by what he found among the higher ranking military leaders of the country. I attach hereto a copy of his report and of my later note to him. I give you these merely as an example that we are making progress—that things are not stagnated at dead-center. Incidentally, I believe that Italy offers the Western World a chance to develop a great defensive asset.[10]

Recently the Committee for Economic Development in America published a statement on the relationship between America and Western Europe that I consider to be admirable. If you have not seen a copy, I strongly suggest that you have some staff officer obtain a copy (I think it was issued under date of May 11) and have it briefed for you. It is very worth-while.[11]

Since the attached report of Montgomery's is labeled "Top Secret", I request that after you and any of your close associates have read it you have it destroyed. I would not want it to come to the attention of any international group because it might be considered as inviting comparison.

With best wishes. *Sincerely*

P.S. Before destroying, however, I would appreciate it if you could have it passed to Averell Harriman for his perusal.[12]

[1] Eisenhower's reply to Secretary of Defense Marshall's letter of May 7 is no. 186.

[2] For background on Eisenhower's recent visits with Belgian and Dutch forces see no. 167, n. 3.

[3] Eisenhower made the same observations in his letter to Averell Harriman (see the preceding document).

[4] On May 22 William T. Van Atten, the Munitions Board's vice-chairman for international programs, would comment on Eisenhower's implication that the Munitions Board needed a mechanism to expedite decisions or requests for foreign military aid. Van Atten pointed out that within the Munitions Board, the Office of International Programs provided guidance and support for NATO's Defense Production Board (see Galambos, *Columbia University*, no. 1095) and helped set production priorities within the United States for NATO-related matters (Van Atten to Burns, May 22, 1951, OS/D, 1951, Clas. Decimal File, CD 370.21 [SHAPE 1951]). Marshall would explain to Eisenhower (June 1, 1951, EM) that he had appointed Major General James Henry Burns as his assistant for international security affairs. Burns, who had retired from the Army in 1944, had served with the Munitions Assignment Board and the Lend-Lease Administration during World War II (see Chandler, *War Years*, no. 59). Burns, together with the director of the Office of Military Assistance, would have responsibility "for the expeditious and efficient implementation" of the foreign military aid program. Marshall also sent Eisenhower transcripts of presentations made by the Army, the Navy, and the Air Force (dated May 9, 10, and 11, 1951, EM) that Marshall said showed "that our foreign military assistance program is being attacked with vigor."

[5] See the preceding document, n. 10.

[6] For background on Thomas D. Cabot, Director of the Office of International Security Affairs, Department of State, see no. 30, n. 2; see also no. 111, n. 12.

[7] See n. 4 above.

[8] Eisenhower had already expressed his concern that the United States was not doing everything it could to increase European defense production (see nos. 16, n. 18, and 81, n. 4). With his May 31 reply Marshall enclosed a memorandum concerning the specifications desired by the Belgians. The delays had occurred as a result of "the time-consuming elements which are experienced by Washington in the assembly and screening of the drawings prior to the transmittal." After the drawings in question had been collected from "various outlying depots and arsenals," they were "screened for security reasons and to determine whether licensing arrangements with U.S. commercial firms are required." The Belgian requests had not been received in Washington until February, and in April the Belgians had requested that the plans be converted into a special type of print. One shipment of drawings and specifications had been made on May 11, and another would be sent one week later. The Belgian request for specifications for the field telephones had been approved on April 16, and the materials were being assembled for shipment. The Defense Department had received only one official request from the Netherlands (for 90 mm ammunition) and expected to send the specifications out later in May. Earlier, the Dutch had made an informal request for a different type of ammunition, and the necessary information had been transmitted on April 25.

[9] For background on Eisenhower's involvement with this issue see no. 16, n. 18. The U.S. Army Signal Corps had considered the Phillips Corporation branches in Belgium and the Netherlands as possible producers for three types of radio sets; in the end, however, it had decided to award these contracts to two French firms (Marshall to Eisenhower, June 1, 1951, enclosure no. 1, EM).

[10] On Eisenhower's trip to Italy see nos. 153, 158, and 167, n. 1. Field Marshal Montgomery's Top-Secret report, dated May 4, is in EM. On May 5 Eisenhower had sent the following letter (in EM) to the Deputy SACEUR:

I am particularly pleased at the impression made upon you in Rome by the Italian Armed Forces, because the impression I gained in North Italy in the Udine region corresponds exactly with yours. Since my return, I have repeatedly told my staff and others that I believe we can make out of Italy one of the great cornerstones of our defensive structure.

Chief of Naval Operations Forrest Sherman would agree with Montgomery's assessment of Italian capabilities. He noted that Italian Army officers "were experienced and strangely unbowed by the reverses experienced in World War II. They seemed to feel themselves the victims of circumstances—unfortunate allies, and unfortunate higher direction." Sherman also said that after inspecting the Italian Navy, he was left with the impression of "an exceedingly well disciplined and competent cadre capable of expansion, and loyal to the Navy—no matter what government it serves" (Sherman to Marshall, May 22, 1951, OS/D, 1951, Clas. Decimal File, CD 370.21 [SHAPE 1951]).

[11] For Eisenhower's comments on this report see no. 164.

[12] As requested, Marshall showed Montgomery's report to Harriman before he destroyed it. He also agreed with Eisenhower's favorable assessment of Italian capabilities: "It would appear that with proper integration and strategic guidance you may have something on your south flank which will prove to be of value" (Marshall to Eisenhower, June 1, 1951, EM).

175   *Eisenhower Mss.*

To Edward John Bermingham   *May 12, 1951*

Dear Ed:[1] I am most appreciative of your letter of May 4th. I have no trouble whatsoever in understanding Sewell Avery's impressions and concern regarding many of our universities.[2] In fact, it was because of an uneasiness of my own concerning the influences exerted by our universities which helped influence me to reach the decision to enter the educational world myself. I wanted to see whether I could do something about the matter. I announced at the time that if I encountered communists in a university and could not get rid of them the university would immediately get rid of me.

So alert—and I might say, so allergic—was I to the possibility of finding Columbia honeycombed with socialistic teachings that I made it my first business to acquaint myself well with operations in Teachers College, previously reported to me as practically a hotbed of this kind of indoctrination. I was happily able to disprove much of what I had heard.[3] Grave accusations had been made against Professor George Counts. In this specific case, I recall that I had not only read, with approval, things that he had previously written on such matters, but since then, he has become quite famous for publishing some of the most damaging evidence we have against governmental procedures in Russia.[4]

I then proposed to Teachers College that it undertake to develop programs for use in the secondary schools of America, designed specifically and directly for the improvement of citizenship in a free democracy. This suggestion was enthusiastically received and within a matter of months, Teachers College of Columbia University had developed such an effective program that one of our most important Foundations donated $1,500,000.00 to help install the system in numerous schools throughout the country. The program—which is intensely practical and avoids, as far as possible, the academic classroom lecture—has been adopted in many school systems, and is tremendously successful.[5]

The whole theory underlying the American Assembly is to determine, in the democratic method, the facts pertaining to the problems that today vitally affect the future of freedom. During the course of developing this program, Phil Young and I have engaged in many activities of an auxiliary, or supporting, nature. For example, we have established a chair, with the support of American businessmen, that has the name, if my memory serves me correctly, of the Chair in Competitive Enterprise. We have started an institute of Peace and War, which, as you know, has as one of its great functions, the job of investigating how a free democracy can organize itself to conduct a war effectively, without falling prey to the trend toward centralization of government.[6]

I merely remind you of all these things so that you can see that the type of thing that is bothering our friend Sewell Avery is exactly the kind of thing to which I gave my attention during the many months I spent at Columbia.[7]

With warm personal regard. *Sincerely*

[1] For background on Bermingham see no. 23, n. 1.

[2] In his May 4 letter (EM) Bermingham had said that he recently had spoken to Montgomery Ward chairman Sewell Lee Avery concerning support for Columbia University's American Assembly (on Avery see Galambos, *Columbia University*, nos. 810 and 1118; on the American Assembly see nos. 47 and 65 in this volume). According to Bermingham, Avery was reluctant to participate in any university-inspired project because of the "inertia" shown by American institutions of higher education in curbing their trend toward socialism. For an example of Eisenhower's views on the possibility of Communist influences at Columbia see Galambos, *Columbia University*, no. 70.

[3] On the controversy surrounding alleged Communist activities at Columbia's Teachers College see *ibid.*, nos. 54, 115, and 206; and Lawrence A. Cremin, David A. Shannon, and Mary Evelyn Townsend, *A History of Teachers College, Columbia University* (New York, 1954), pp. 171-72, 226. On Eisenhower's work to improve the college's image see Galambos, *Columbia University*, nos. 70 and 346.

[4] Teachers College professor of education George Sylvester Counts was a former president of the American Federation of Teachers and former chairman of the New York State Labor Party (see *ibid.*, no. 676; and Lawrence J. Dennis and William Edward Eaton, eds., *George S. Counts: Educator for a New Age* [Carbondale, Ill.,

1980], pp. 1-18). In 1929, following an extended visit to Russia, Counts had called for closer U.S. relations with the Soviet Union and for greater social planning in America. Counts wrote favorably of developments within Russia during the early 1930s, but by the following decade he had begun to criticize both Soviet education and the Soviet government severely (see, for example, George S. Counts, *A Ford Crosses Soviet Russia* [Boston, 1930], pp. 153-202; George S. Counts, et al., *Bolshevism, Fascism, and Capitalism: An Account of the Three Economic Systems* [New Haven, 1932], pp. 3-54; and George S. Counts and Nucia Lodge, *The Country of the Blind: The Soviet System of Mind Control* [Boston, 1949], pp. 41-76. On the distribution of *Country of the Blind* to the Columbia Associates and on Eisenhower's approval of the book see Galambos, *Columbia University*, no. 676, n. 2; and Eisenhower to James D. Wise, Feb. 4, 1950, in EM, Wise Corr.).

[5] On the Citizenship Education Project see Galambos, *Columbia University*, nos. 351, 492, 647, and 854; and Teachers College, *Improving Citizenship Education*, in EM, Russell Corr. On the program's adaptation for use in the American armed forces see Galambos, *Columbia University*, no. 1073; and no. 70 in this volume.

Between 1949 and 1952 the Carnegie Corporation of New York pledged grants amounting to over $1.4 million to Teachers College for programs in citizenship education (see Carnegie Corporation of New York, *Report of Officers, 1950* [New York, 1950], pp. 39, 50, and *Report of Officers, 1952* [New York, 1952], p. 49).

[6] For background on Philip Young, dean of the Columbia University Graduate School of Business and Executive Director of the American Assembly, see no. 8. The Samuel Bronfman Chair in Democratic Business Enterprise had been established in 1951 (see "The Samuel Bronfman Fellowship in Democratic Business Enterprise, 1952-53," in EM, Young Corr.). For background on the Institute of War and Peace Studies see Galambos, *Columbia University*, no. 1056.

[7] Bermingham would write to the General twice more during May. On May 17 (EM) he reported on an effort Senator Karl Earl Mundt, a Republican from South Dakota, had under way to establish a coalition of Southern Democrats and Northern Republicans for the 1952 presidential election. (On Bermingham's political activities see nos. 23, n. 1, and 55, n. 1; and Lyon, *Portrait of the Hero*, pp. 388-90, 413-14).

On May 22 (EM) Bermingham wrote that he had sent a copy of this document to Philip Young. He enclosed a copy of his letter (same date) to Young, which said that he (Bermingham) would continue his efforts "to have Montgomery Ward & Co., become sponsor of the American Assembly." On the first meeting of the American Assembly, which would be held later this month, see no. 182.

176 *Eisenhower Mss., Diaries*

DIARY *May 15, 1951*

Bradley, with a party, is coming to Europe on June 2. Collins & wife will be here before that. Each will stay 2-3 days.[1]

We are having a stream of American visitors. Publishers, industrialists, professors, etc. I give time to all—and am astonished at the lack of knowledge of basic facts on the part of many who are supposed to be educated.[2]

Today I intended to get out for exercise, golfing with a lot of war friends & with Mr. Hilton & Joe Binns (Waldorf-Astoria). Rain intervened! Possibly Saturday will be O.K.[3]

Just read an article by Bertrand Russell, philosopher. Very good indeed as a mode or code of living *today*.[4]

[1] JCS Chairman General Omar Nelson Bradley would fly to Paris on June 2 for Western defense talks with Eisenhower and French officials (on Bradley see no. 50, n. 5). He would be accompanied by his wife, the former Mary Elizabeth Quayle; Major General Wilton B. Persons; Clayton Fritchey, Director of the Defense Department's Office of Public Information; and several military aides (see *International Herald Tribune*, Paris ed., May 26, June 2, 4, 1951; appointment calendar; EM, Bradley Corr., esp. JCS 91220, CJCS to SACEUR, May 14, 1951). For background on Persons, who would join SHAPE as an assistant to Eisenhower, see no. 157, n. 1; and Wood to Gruenther, May 17, 1951, in EM, Persons Corr.

Army Chief of Staff Collins and his wife, Gladys Easterbrook Collins, would be in Paris from May 27 to May 29, on an inspection tour of U.S. installations in Europe. On General Collins see no. 52; for background on his European trip see no. 183.

[2] Aside from the many meetings with military and government officials incident to the establishment of the NATO field forces, Eisenhower frequently had appointments with important U.S. citizens traveling abroad. During April and May 1951 he met with more than thirty such persons, representing Harvard, Princeton, and Columbia universities, Gulf Oil, Firestone Rubber, the Morgan Bank, *Collier's*, the *New York Times*, and many other business, educational, and publishing institutions (see appointment calendar).

[3] The General may have made an error in dating this diary entry; according to his appointment calendar, the rain-canceled golfing date had been planned for May 16. For background on Conrad Nicholson Hilton, president of the Hilton and Roosevelt hotels, and on Joseph Patterson Binns, executive vice-president and general manager of New York's Waldorf-Astoria Hotel, see Galambos, *Columbia University*, nos. 549 and 704, respectively. The General would play golf at the Morfontaine course on Saturday, May 19, with a party including Binns and Hilton (see appointment calendar).

[4] British philosopher Bertrand Arthur William Russell (third earl Russell) had recently published two articles on the Soviet Union and the state of the free world. The first piece, concerning the purely political content of most Soviet humor, cautioned Americans not to allow their hatred of the Communists to become an obsession. According to Russell, a reaction of "equal and contrary hate" would gradually make America more and more as it was depicted in the Soviet press (see Bertrand Arthur Russell, "Soviet 'Humor' Offers a Moral for Us," *New York Times Magazine*, Apr. 1, 1951, p. 9).

Russell's second article, and probably the one to which Eisenhower refers here, outlined the dangers and duties then facing citizens of the free world. While accepting the possibility of "great upheavals and vast disasters . . . within the next ten years" as the result of Soviet aggression, Russell wrote that free people could not give in to feelings of despair, frivolity, or fanaticism; they should instead maintain hope ("No Funk, No Frivolity, No Fanaticism," *ibid.*, May 6, 1951, p. 1).

TO CLIFFORD ROBERTS *May 15, 1951*

Dear Cliff:[1] I am delighted to have your letter of the 10th and am already looking forward to your arrival here. While I am, of course, sort of in and out of the town, there will always be available good friends and companions for you.[2] Possibly we can even find someone who would accompany you to Paris' most famous night spots if your Doctor's orders will allow you to go.[3]

Personally, I think that the people at Columbia did the right thing in deciding to go ahead with the American Assembly conference in May. I cannot be there, of course—on this point, your judgment is impeccable. But, even had conditions at home been such that I could attend, I could scarcely have gotten away from here. My schedule grows more crowded every day.[4]

In any event, come a-running. We shall be looking for you. *Cordially*

[1] For background on Eisenhower's friend Roberts see nos. 7 and 38.

[2] In Roberts's letter of May 10 (EM), sent from Augusta National Golf Club, he had discussed his plans to visit Eisenhower. Roberts would arrive in Paris on June 10 and would play golf and dine with Eisenhower several times during his visit (see no. 217).

[3] Roberts was recovering from an ulcer (see nos. 161 and 166, n. 1). On May 25 (EM) Roberts wrote again to say that Clarence J. Schoo and Freeman F. Gosden, friends from Augusta National, would be in Paris at the same time (see Galambos, *Columbia University*, nos. 956 and 821, respectively).

[4] Eisenhower would not participate in the first American Assembly conference (see nos. 87, n. 4, and 102, n. 2). Many of the General's friends had recently advised against his return to the United States, hoping he could avoid testifying again before the Senate Committee on Foreign Relations or Committee on Armed Forces on the need for aid to Europe (see no. 23, n. 5). His friends also hoped that he could avoid involvement in the debate over the defense of the Far East and MacArthur's dismissal as CINCFE (see nos. 112 and 136, n. 2). Roberts warned (May 10): "If you are obliged to go to Washington you might as well be prepared to get into the over-all policy argument." Eisenhower, who would not be in the United States again until November, would not have to testify in the months ahead (see the Chronology in these volumes).

TO ALBERT COADY WEDEMEYER *May 15, 1951*

Dear Al:[1] Following the suggestion of your note, I will instantly notify my office staff to be on the look-out for Mr. Jerd Sullivan and to set up an appointment as soon as we get in touch with him. Thank you for thinking of me in this connection.[2]

Unfortunately, there is not the slightest chance that I can come to Bohemian Grove this summer—unless, of course, some wholly unforeseen and almost cataclysmic circumstance should bring it about.[3]

The other day, I read in the paper that you were retiring this summer. I cannot tell you what a shock this is to me. While I understand that you are going to associate yourself with a University—in which post, I assure you, you will find plenty of opportunity for constructive work and the kind of job that will demand your full attention and energy—yet I deeply regret your passing from the active list of the Army. We cannot afford to spare our best, and you have amply proved your right to this kind of classification.[4]

Incidentally, when we read this news in the paper, my Aide reminded me of my great affection for Sergeant Cargill and suggested that I submit an inquiry to the War Department concerning his future services. This, of course, assumes that he will stay in the Army and not follow you in retirement. I hope that this request was not put to you in such a way as to make you feel any embarrassment whatsoever.[5]

This note brings to you my very warmest regard and best wishes, both now and for the future.

If you come this way, be sure to plan for a stay in France to have a long visit with me. *As ever*

[1] Since August 1949 Lieutenant General Albert Coady Wedemeyer had been CG of the Sixth Army, stationed at the Presidio of San Francisco, California. On his long friendship with Eisenhower see *Eisenhower Papers*, vols. I–XI.

[2] In a letter of May 11 (EM) Wedemeyer had informed the General that a mutual acquaintance, Jermiah Francis Sullivan, Jr., president and director of the Crocker National Bank, was planning a trip to Europe in the near future. Wedemeyer had told Eisenhower, "Inasmuch as Mr. Sullivan would be an outstanding man under any circumstances . . . but also because of his business acumen, I thought you should see him." There are, however, no letters to Sullivan in EM, and his name does not appear on the General's appointment calendar during this period.

[3] In the same letter Wedemeyer had expressed the hope that Eisenhower would be able to attend the annual summer encampment of the Bohemian Club, near San Francisco (for background see Galambos, *Columbia University*, nos. 388, 873, and 991).

[4] Wedemeyer would retire from the Army on July 31 but would not take a position with a university. He would instead become vice-president and director of the Avco Manufacturing Corporation of New York and Delaware (see *New York Times*, May 8, June 30, 1951; *International Herald Tribune*, Paris ed., May 8, 1951; and Wedemeyer to Eisenhower, June 21, 1951, and Eisenhower to Wedemeyer, June 30, 1951, EM).

[5] For background on former member of the Eisenhower household staff Sergeant Cargill see Galambos, *Columbia University*, no. 809. He would not join Eisenhower in Europe (EM, Wedemeyer Corr., esp. Wedemeyer to Eisenhower, July 26, 1951).

Dear Art:[1] I am grateful to you for the trouble you took in writing to me such an interesting and informative letter. I cannot tell you how I should like to sit down and talk over with you all of the farm matters— and just to have the pleasure of a personal visit with you and Ann.[2]

Recently, I sent to you a couple of letters I had written to George Allen. There was no particular point to sending them except as they might serve to show you some of the few ideas I had with respect to the farm.[3]

Certainly you should not put up with any noticeable disrepair or unseemly appearance in the house. If part of it needs papering or painting or anything of that sort, you should get it done and charge it to the operations of the farm. As I think I explained in one of those letters to George, I feel that any permanent alterations to the house are matters between you and me, and, if authorized, are charges against me because the alterations would presumably constitute a permanent increase to the value of the property.[4]

In one of those letters, I probably also expressed the view that you could, in your capacity as a manager, handle more property than was represented in the one farm. At the very least, I think we ought to work out something that would use the pasturage on George's farm; and you could handle even more than that, I suppose, as long as we do not expect you to be a "farm laborer." I am sure of one thing: if you should find a conveniently located property that you and Ann would like to buy for yourselves, I am sure that George would agree with me that you could throw that into the pool with such financing as you might need taken care of by loans from George and me. Then, by your continuing to manage the properties of the combine, you could gradually discharge that indebtedness and so acquire full ownership of such property.[5] Because you live there, you would certainly be more nearly able to pick up a "bargain" than was represented in my hasty purchase of the Redding farm. I agree with you that he likes to drive a hard bargain.[6]

Of course, I am tremendously excited by the arrival of the Guernsey cows. They will certainly build up your butter fat content, and I have no doubt that the sale of their yearly calf crop—if we can preserve good blood lines—should add a fine little sum to the income. Likewise, we should make a good thing out of the Black Angus cattle if and when they arrive.[7]

From what you say, I rather suspect that the poultry end of the business does not appeal to you as being quite such a good proposition as the dairy business. So far as I am concerned—and I am sure George would agree—you can dispose of the chickens if you so desire. As I understand it, that would be merely a refunding of capital investment and would not be income. I assume that you and Ann, of course, would keep a few chickens to satisfy your own family requirements.[8]

There are a million things I would like to talk to you about. But it is hopeless for me to sit here in a Paris office in the shadow of the Arc de Triomphe and talk intelligently about doings on a Gettysburg farm. My heart is there, even if my alleged brain is struggling with "NATO" problems.[9]

My love to Ann, and, of course, warm regard to yourself. I thoroughly enjoy your letters and am sorry that the writing of one of them compels you to get down to good old longhand work. In any event, any news you can send is welcome.[10] *As ever*

P.S. Mamie had lunch with me today, and, when she heard I was writing to you, asked me to give you her love and to say that she had received Ann's letter.

[1] For background on Eisenhower's friend Nevins, who was manager of his Gettysburg farm, see no. 48, n. 4; and *Eisenhower Papers*, vols. I–XI.

[2] In his letters of May 6 and 13 (EM) Nevins had written concerning the operation of the farm. For background on Ann Stacy Nevins see no. 33, n. 4; and Galambos, *Columbia University*, no. 61.

[3] The two letters the General had written to his farming partner, George Allen, are nos. 48 and 170.

[4] In his May 6 letter Nevins had explained that he was reluctant to have extensive work done on the house because he believed the Eisenhowers would remodel when they settled there. In July Eisenhower would again urge Nevins to have the house repaired (see no. 270, n. 9. See also Nevins, *Five-Star Farmer*, pp. 83–155; and Galambos, *Columbia University*, nos. 1075 and 1080).

[5] For earlier discussions of this subject see nos. 48 and 170.

[6] Allen S. Redding had owned the Gettysburg farm Eisenhower bought in November 1950 (see Galambos, *Columbia University*, no. 1080; and Nevins, *Five-Star Farmer*, pp. 83–87, 93). Nevins had written that Redding had offered to sell him a 1941 army-surplus weapons carrier for hauling feed to the local mill for five hundred dollars. Nevins said that the vehicle "wasn't worth half that amount," adding that "Redding is honest . . . but he certainly tries to get all that the traffic will bear" (Nevins to Eisenhower, May 6, 1951, EM).

[7] The cows were a gift from Walter Kirschner (see nos. 33 and 185, n. 3). Nevins had also mentioned the possibility of acquiring some Black Angus cattle with the help of Eisenhower's friend Ed Clark (see no. 1, n. 2). Though these arrangements failed, Eisenhower later would develop his own Angus herd (see no. 270; and Nevins, *Five-Star Farmer*, pp. 97, 109, 125–29, 133–34).

[8] The chickens would later be sold (see no. 270, n. 3; and Nevins, *Five-Star Farmer*, pp. 90–93, 108, 115).

[9] For background see nos. 176, 186, and 191.

[10] For developments see nos. 249, n. 2, and 250, n. 2.

To George Edward Allen   *May 15, 1951*

Dear George:[1] You have not yet told me *when* you and Mary are planning to be here. Let me know at once so that Mamie and I can be sure to keep our calendar in the proper shape for the month or so you can stay.[2]

Over and beyond the recreational aspects of such a program (including, of course, the fact that my pocketbook is getting very flat since I have been separated from my bridge victims), you and I have many serious matters to talk over; for example, your weight. Again, our farming interests and investment programs will probably require a meeting of the Board of Directors. We have to discuss world trends and a number of international questions that need attention.[3]

In fact, the more I think about the way you and I have neglected many of these vital affairs, the more I am convinced that it will possibly take us *three* months to get the world back on an even keel. In any event, please give me promptly the approximate date of your arrival. I am quite content to have your date of departure on a sort of flexible arrangement, depending completely upon the demonstrated rate of improvement in your bridge game.[4]

As I told you once before, it will probably be some time before we can get into our own house, but this should not postpone your coming because I assure you that the Hotel in which we live is a quite comfortable one. I shall expect a cable answer from you as soon as you get this letter.[5]

With love to Mary, and, as always, warm regard to yourself.

Cordially

[1] For background on Allen, a lawyer, business executive, and friend of Eisenhower's, see no. 9, n. 2.
[2] Allen would visit Paris briefly beginning June 17. His wife, the former Mary Keane, would not accompany him (see appointment calendar; and Allen to Eisenhower, June 22, 1951, EM).
[3] Losing weight was the target of a bet between Eisenhower and Allen (see no. 48, n. 3. For developments see no. 493; and Schulz, Memorandum for Record, June 21, 1951, EM, Allen Corr.). On Allen's partnership with the General in the farm see no. 48, n. 5; for developments see nos. 179 and 185.
[4] Eisenhower valued Allen's opinions, describing him as a "shrewd and highly intelligent observer." The General said that he had never known "a more capable judge of national political trends" (see Eisenhower's *Mandate for Change, 1953–1956* [Garden City, N.Y., 1963], pp. 270–71).
[5] The Eisenhowers had lived in the Trianon Palace Hotel in Versailles since their arrival in France (see nos. 44, n. 2, and 82, n. 5). For Allen's reply see no. 192; and Allen to Eisenhower, May 19, 1951, EM.

To Douglas MacArthur   *May 15, 1951*
Personal

Dear General:[1] Sometimes I think that we shall never see the end of the persistent efforts of some sensation-seeking columnists to promote the falsehood that you and I are mortal enemies. Occasionally they go so far as to assert that this antagonism existed even before I first met you, when you were Chief of Staff.[2] I assume their purpose to be an increase of circulation.

Of course, I need not tell you that, through these years, I have truly valued your friendship. But I do want to express my appreciation of the fact that, during all the stresses and strains to which you have been subjected since the beginning of World War II, you have never, even accidentally, uttered a word that could give an atmosphere of plausibility to this curious lie.

The preoccupations of my job are such that it will probably be months before I can ever find opportunity to return, even briefly, to the United States. But I must say that I look forward, as I hope you do, to indulging again on some quiet evening in the kind of conversation on absorbing military subjects that we had at our most recent meeting—almost exactly five years ago today, in your home in Tokyo.[3]

Please convey my warm greetings to Jean,[4] and with best regard to yourself,[5] *As ever*

[1] General of the Army Douglas MacArthur, who had been dismissed by President Truman on April 11, 1951 (see nos. 101, n. 5, 128, n. 3, 131, and 136).
[2] MacArthur had become U.S. Army Chief of Staff in 1930; Eisenhower had been his personal military assistant from 1933 until 1935 and had accompanied MacArthur to the Philippines. See also no. 116, n. 12.
[3] On May 10, 1946, Eisenhower, then U.S. Army Chief of Staff, had visited MacArthur in Tokyo during a tour of Army installations in the Pacific (see Galambos, *Chief of Staff*, esp. nos. 882 and 896 and the Chronology in these volumes. See also MacArthur, *Reminiscences*, p. 315; and Lyon, *Portrait of the Hero*, pp. 372–73).
[4] MacArthur's wife, the former Jean Faircloth.
[5] In his reply of May 18 (EM) MacArthur assured Eisenhower that he paid "absolutely no attention to scuttlebut[t]s who would like to make sensational headlines." He added that his esteem for Eisenhower, "born of . . . many years of intimate association," was "well known and understood by everyone."

Eisenhower Mss.

May 16, 1951

Dear Phil: Please forgive me for failing to answer sooner your very fine letter of May 7th. I simply have not been able to take the time.[1]

I am quite enthusiastic about the plans you have made for the opening conference of the American Assembly. Having Senators Douglas and Taft on the same evening will be a ten strike—particularly if that meeting is as I assume it to be, a confidential one. I suppose that you have stuck to the idea that only the final session will be open to the public. (Now that I think of it, I believe that Lew Douglas told me, either by letter or telephone, that they were contemplating holding the opening meeting as a public one. If that should be the case, I believe I would ask Taft and Douglas to be at the second meeting, because I think that, otherwise, results would not be so good.)[2]

I don't know why I should be so free in submitting suggestions that just happen to flash into my mind. I know that you people are there on the job working at these things all the time. But I simply cannot control my binding interest in Columbia, and particularly in that great project that you and Lew are heading. All the luck in the world to you both.[3]

Give my love to Faith,[4] and, as always, warm regard to yourself.

Cordially

[1] Young's letter of the seventh (EM) had been written in reply to an April 27 cable from Eisenhower suggesting possible postponement of the first American Assembly meeting (see no. 154).

[2] As Young had explained, Eisenhower's suggestion for postponement was discussed with the director of Columbia's School of International Affairs, Schuyler C. Wallace, members of the Assembly's National Policy Board, and board chairman Lewis Douglas. This group "considered very carefully the advisability of an orderly retreat, but finally came to the conclusion that the situation called for attack" (on Wallace see no. 159; on Douglas see no. 65, n. 1). To emphasize the truly objective nature of the Assembly, it was decided to invite two senators who had taken opposing sides in the recent Great Debate over U.S. participation in the defense of Western Europe. Republican Robert Taft (a leader of the congressional faction against the assignment of U.S. troops to Europe) and Senator Paul Douglas (a Democrat and supporter of participation in the NATO alliance) both accepted invitations to attend the opening plenary session of the Assembly on May 21 (for background on Taft see no. 112, n. 6; on Douglas see no. 109, n. 7. See also L. Douglas to P. Douglas, n.d., EM, Young Corr. On the first plenary session, which would be closed to the public, and on the entire Assembly program see no. 201).

Eisenhower had spoken to Lewis Douglas concerning the Assembly by telephone on May 9, 10, and 11 (see telegrams, EM, Douglas Corr.; and appointment calendar). In a letter following this conversation (May 12, 1951, EM, Douglas Corr.) Douglas had told the General that the participation of Senators Douglas and Taft would provide "a major defense against the charge that the Assembly is an appendage to the Administration policy."

[3] For Eisenhower's development of the American Assembly idea see his memoir *At Ease*, p. 350.
[4] Young's wife, the former Faith Adams.

183

To Joseph Lawton Collins

May 16, 1951

Personal and confidential

Dear Joe:[1] I am truly delighted to hear that you are definitely planning on an early trip this way.[2] I cabled you this morning to find out whether you believe that you and Gladys might feel up to a small dinner on the night of the 25th. The 26th would be better from your point, I suppose, but on that night the hotel where I live is to be crowded with a local convention, possibly the Versailles Chamber of Commerce. Since it is always awkward for me to go downtown to have a dinner, this is the reason that I have suggested the 25th.[3] However, having had a great deal of experience in trotting around the world and being hauled off to dinners when I wanted to see nothing quite so much as my pillow, I want to make quite sure that you and Gladys understand that Mamie and I merely want to see you under such circumstances as would be pleasing to you. If you accept, we would, under no circumstances, have a large dinner—probably a total of ten people.[4]

We deeply regret that we are not yet in a house and, therefore, cannot ask you to stay with us. We should certainly like to have you. However, I doubt that our place will be ready before late June.[5] In the meantime, we expect Mamie's Mother to come over, and our youngsters and their children are planning to spend about a month with us before the school opens at Fort Knox in August. We will have to find hotel rooms for them for a little while. But Mamie is missing her family so much and is so deeply concerned about her Mother, that I must move heaven and earth to get them here as soon as I can.[6]

Please send us a cable if you think of anything you should like for us to arrange in advance, or if anything occurs in which I could help either personally or through the staff.[7]

My love to Gladys, and very best to you.[8] *Cordially*

[1] For background on Army Chief of Staff Collins see no. 176, n. 1.
[2] Collins, who was about to embark on an eight-day inspection tour of U.S. forces in Europe, would cable Eisenhower on the following day to thank him for the dinner invitation and to inform him that his wife, Gladys Easterbrook Collins, would be unable to make the trip. He also said that his own departure would

probably be delayed due to the Senate investigation of General Douglas MacArthur's removal as CINCFE (DA 91478, EM, Collins Corr.).

Chief of Staff Collins would testify in the MacArthur case, delaying his departure for Europe until May 27 (see *New York Times*, May 26, 27, 28, 1951; *International Herald Tribune*, Paris ed., May 26, 27, 1951; and Larsen to Gruenther, DA 91756, May 19, 1951, EM, Collins Corr.).

[3] In Eisenhower's cabled invitation he explained that he also would be arriving in Paris on the twenty-fifth, after completing an inspection trip to Norway (SH 20481, EM, Collins Corr.).

[4] Collins would attend two dinners with Eisenhower during his brief stay in Paris. The first engagement, the evening of May 27, was a small dinner with American members of the SHAPE staff and their wives; the second, on the following day, was a stag affair attended by American Special Representative to Europe Milton Katz (see no. 16, n. 7) and several European members of the SHAPE high command. During the day on May 28 Collins held discussions with American Ambassador to France David Bruce (see no. 88, n. 5) and French military officials. Following morning golf and lunch with Eisenhower on the twenty-ninth, the Chief of Staff departed for a tour of U.S. forces in Germany and Italy, returning to the United States on June 5 (see appointment calendar; *International Herald Tribune*, Paris ed., May 29, 1951; seating plan, dinner for General Collins, and Collins to Eisenhower, June 5, 1951, both in EM, Collins Corr.; and EM, Subject File, Aircraft, Trip Itinerary, no. 23).

[5] On the Eisenhowers' housing difficulties see nos. 18, n. 3, 104, and 170.

[6] The Eisenhowers' son John, his family, and Elivera Doud would arrive in Paris on June 13, traveling on the return flight of the SHAPE aircraft that had taken Collins and his party back to the United States (see correspondence in EM, Subject File, Trips [Family]; SHAPE; and Aircraft, Trip Itinerary, no. 23). On their arrival see nos. 222 and 224; for developments see no. 298. On John Eisenhower's plans to attend an officers' course at Fort Knox, Kentucky, later this year see no. 165. On Mrs. Doud see no. 118.

[7] On arrangements made by the SHAPE staff for Collins and his party see cables in EM, Collins Corr.

[8] The copy of this document in EM indicates that it was sent by embassy courier.

184   *Eisenhower Mss.*

To ARTHUR HAYS SULZBERGER   *May 16, 1951*
Personal and confidential

Dear Arthur:[1] Thanks for your note and the clippings. I must say that I've never been conscious, at Columbia, of any reluctance on the part of student or faculty member to speak his mind. Perhaps, though, such could have existed without my ever hearing of it.[2]

I truly hope that you will attend every session of the Conference at Arden House. Your analysis of procedures, methods, and personnel will be invaluable for the future. Moreover, your contributions to the current study will be enormous. How I wish I could attend with you![3]

Douglas Black is here for a rest. His doctor apparently put him on a strict program after an acute attack of some kind at one of these public dinners! (I've so often felt like collapsing at banquets and "cultural" dinners that I'm moved to suspect something deliberate in Doug's difficulty.)[4]

When he comes home, he may talk to you about some of our conversations and ideas of Columbia's future. I am fearful that many of the gains of the past 2 1/2 years will either be lost or, at best, not fully exploited. A lot of hard work is still necessary—not only on the part of those in charge of specific projects—but by the University leadership.[5]

That leadership may be or feel handicapped by reason of the uncertainties surrounding my University status. I am definitely becoming convinced of the existence of what I outlined to the Trustees, last February, as a possibility, namely that my retention as the nominal President is working against Columbia.

The whole subject is far too complex and conclusions necessarily represent such a nice balance between advantage and disadvantage that it is not one for a letter. I've always urged the Trustees to act only on their convictions as to the good of the University—but it may be that I shall have to lay before them specific proposals. I appreciate, and am grateful for, their constant concern for me—but that very concern might allow them to tolerate an unhealthy situation because of a belief that the cure would hurt my feelings.[6]

Of course, I don't want to be cast aside like a dead cigarette, but there are more ways of killing a cat than choking it to death with butter.

Out of my talks with Doug, some ideas may emerge. If so, I know that you will be one of the first he'll later want to hear about them![7]
Cordially

[1] For background on Sulzberger, publisher of the *New York Times* and a Columbia University trustee, see no. 168.

[2] With a letter of May 11 (EM) Sulzberger had enclosed clippings of a recent two-article series from the *New York Times* (May 10, 11, 1951) on the inhibition of freedom of thought and speech on American college campuses. The first piece in the series reported that a study of seventy-two major colleges had revealed a reluctance on the part of many academic community members to speak out on controversial issues, to participate in political activities of any type, or to discuss unpopular ideas. Continuing investigations of the supposed Communist affiliations of both individuals and organizations had made college students, administrators, and teachers wary of any associations or deeds that might earn them the " 'pink' or Communist label." The final installment of the series had explained reactions of some universities to the current atmosphere of repression, saying that in many instances there had developed a "counter-force" demanding that free inquiry and expression be protected. On the General's reaction to accusations of Communist influences at Columbia see no. 175; on recent congressional investigations of communistic activities within the United States see, for example, Galambos, *Columbia University*, nos. 502 and 744; and no. 84 in this volume.

[3] For background on the American Assembly conference see nos. 182, n. 2, and 201. On the donation of the Arden estate to Columbia see Galambos, *Columbia University*, nos. 605, 689, and 945.

[4] President of Doubleday & Company and a life trustee of Columbia, Black had seen the General the previous morning (see appointment calendar). For background on Black see no. 168.

[5] On the projects Eisenhower launched at Columbia, including administrative reorganization, the Institute of War and Peace Studies, and the American Assembly, see Galambos, *Columbia University*.

[6] In December 1950, following his appointment as SACEUR, Eisenhower had taken an indefinite leave of absence from his post as president of Columbia University. Vice-president Grayson Kirk, as acting president, had assumed the General's responsibilities (see *ibid.*, no. 1141).

[7] Eisenhower's status at Columbia would continue to be the topic of letters and discussions with university officials over the next several months. See, for example, Black to Eisenhower, June 15, 1951, in EM, Black Corr.; and nos. 229, 234, n. 2, and 370.

185   *Eisenhower Mss.*

To WALTER KIRSCHNER   *May 17, 1951*

Dear Mr. Kirschner:[1] Your mass shipment of dates created a sensation in our household. They are quite the largest and sweetest I ever saw and, because of the number of tins that came, it was obviously appropriate to share our good fortune with a few of our good friends and principal associates in Allied Headquarters. So the fame of the Desert Golds has spread widely through our particular community here in France.[2]

A recent letter from our friends the Nevins[es] told us of their excitement over the arrival of the Kirschner Guernseys. Of course, all of us concerned in the "Gettysburg Agricultural Operations of the Great Allen" are mightily set up by such an acquisition. Our gratitude to you is all the greater because of the personal interest and effort you have devoted to the job of making certain that your extraordinary gift exactly fitted the environment.[3]

I hear that we may get a few head of blooded beef cattle. If that is so, we *may* find some way of using the pasturage on George's farm, assuming that the County Agent reports that particular grass as nutritious. In any event, the whole business is tremendously interesting—I think George and I will find in it a way of satisfying the normal craving to do something *constructive* and *visible!*[4]

How I'd like to be there. Quite obviously, I never expect to make a cent out of it, but I'd give anything for the opportunity of devoting my time to making that farm a model of its kind for that region.[5] (Of course, I'd like to spend some time each winter in the Desert, and in Texas and Georgia.)[6]

Well, I haven't time to dream!

Thanks again—we are constantly in your debt for your kindly thoughtfulness in our behalf. *Most sincerely*

P.S. Our fond greetings to Mrs. Kirschner[7]

[1] For background on Kirschner, a business executive, see no. 33, n. 2.

[2] Kirschner, who was associated with the California Date Growers Association, had frequently made the General similar gifts since 1948 (see EM, Kirschner Corr., esp. Kirschner to Eisenhower, Dec. 9, 1948, and Mar. 31, 1951).

[3] Kirschner had visited the Eisenhower farm and had consulted with Arthur Nevins, Eisenhower's farm manager, several times to determine what type of cattle was best suited to the farm (see nos. 170, n. 3, 179, n. 7, and 192, n. 3; and Nevins to Eisenhower, May 6, 13, 1951, EM). "The Great Allen," George E. Allen, was Eisenhower's partner in the Gettysburg farming investment (see also no. 270, n. 4; and for developments see nos. 249, n. 2, and 315).

[4] Eisenhower was probably referring to the plans to add Black Angus cattle to the livestock of the farm (see no. 179, n. 7). The Adams County, Pennsylvania, agricultural agents gave Nevins "substantial help" (see Nevins, *Five-Star Farmer*, p. 96).

[5] The General would not see the farm this year but would speak with Nevins on his brief visit to the United States in early November (see no. 487, n. 2; and appointment calendar).

Nevins later wrote that great efforts were made to make the farm operations pay a profit. As there was little income during the early years, the business was conducted at a loss (see Nevins, *Five-Star Farmer*). Only later would a profit be realized on the farm (see Eisenhower's memoir *At Ease*, pp. 193–94).

[6] The General was probably referring to southern California, where Kirschner and George Allen had homes (see no. 33, n. 8). For background on Eisenhower's friends in Texas see Galambos, *Columbia University*, nos. 826, 989, and 1160; and no. 102 in this volume. On his friends in Georgia see no. 113 in this volume.

[7] The second Mrs. Kirschner, the former Madeline Yeo.

186   *Eisenhower Mss.*

To GEORGE CATLETT MARSHALL   *May 18, 1951*
Top secret

Dear General Marshall: In reply to your letter of 7 May, I share your view that agreement on the military aspects of the German rearmament program should be achieved between the Occupying Powers and Germany at an early date, even though all the necessary political arrangements may not have been completed.[1] It is, of course, obvious that any satisfactory political arrangement must envisage the Germans as willing partners in our integrated defense efforts.

With regard to the 16 April memorandum to you from the Joint

Chiefs of Staff, I concur in their view that the designation of the members of the Standing Group as military representatives of the Chiefs of Staff of the Occupying Powers, in a capacity distinct from that of members of the Standing Group is an appropriate method for dealing with the military aspects of the German proposal. Likewise, I concur in the general procedures proposed by the Joint Chiefs of Staff in paragraph 2 of their memorandum of 16 April.[2]

The military considerations implicit in such questions as unit size and level of integration are of evident concern to me, but, since such questions as these have become so inseparably linked to the political aspects of the problem, I feel that I should not voice an opinion at this time. Rather, I feel that I should look to the Joint Chiefs of Staff to develop the military point of view in the light of their extensive experience with all aspects of the problem.[3] It may be, however, that I shall have a few general comments which would be helpful before arriving at the final U.S. position on this problem. Accordingly, I should appreciate your forwarding informally to me the recommendations of the U.S. Joint Chiefs of Staff for my comment on a "U.S. Eyes Only" basis before the U.S. position is presented to the members of the Standing Group.[4] *Very sincerely*

[1] For background on the problem of German rearmament see nos. 12, n. 1, and 16; see also Galambos, *Columbia University*. At its December 1950 meeting in Brussels the North Atlantic Council had authorized discussions between the West German government and the Allied High Commission for Germany (composed of representatives of France, Great Britain, and the United States) on the subject of a proposed German contribution to Western defense. The discussions had started in January, and by May the Germans had outlined their proposals for what a Defense Department report described as "a program that would give a realistic and adequate contribution to Western European defenses" (Beebe to Burns, May 1951, OS/D, 1951, Clas. Decimal File, CD 092.3 NATO). The Germans proposed that a defense ministry, headed by civilians, be established to oversee a program of rearmament. German ground forces were to be organized into division-size units (including armored divisions) of ten thousand men each. The Germans also insisted that their armed forces should come into Eisenhower's NATO command on a basis substantially equal relative to the units of other nations (State, *Foreign Relations, 1951*, vol. III, *European Security and the German Question, Part I*, pp. 990, 1044–47. See also Acheson, *Present at the Creation*, p. 487; and Poole, *History of the Joint Chiefs of Staff*, vol. IV, *1950–1952*, pp. 256–58). In his letter of May 7 (EM) Marshall had advised Eisenhower of his concern that the "increasing complexity" of the "political aspects of a German contribution" might "delay practical military programming to an extent detrimental to United States policy objectives." He concluded, "I am therefore of the opinion that military agreement as to a logical and forceful German military program should be achieved between the Occupying Powers and Germany in a steadfast, orderly manner." U.S. Army Colonel Vernon Price Mock (USMA 1935) drafted this letter for Eisenhower. At SHAPE Mock was assigned to the Office of the Secretary of the Staff; his previous position had been with the Army's Plans and Operations Division in Washington.

[2] With his letter of May 7 Marshall had sent a memorandum from JCS chairman Omar Bradley (April 16, 1951, EM). Bradley's memorandum had been in re-

sponse to Marshall's request that the JCS recommend a procedure whereby the three Allied occupying powers could obtain military advice on the German rearmament proposals. The JCS thought that the Standing Group would be an appropriate forum to consider the German proposal because it met "in continuous session," possessed the "machinery necessary to facilitate consideration of problems given to it," and was "readily available." The JCS recommended, however, that the Standing Group members not act in their official NATO capacities. This recommendation was prompted by the fear that the Standing Group "would probably be required to make its reports to NATO," which the JCS felt was undesirable "from the standpoint of expeditious handling" (JCS 2124/42, Mar. 23, 1951, CCS 092 Germany [5-4-49], Sec. 7). The JCS also suggested a five-step procedure in considering the German proposals: (1) the American, French, and British chiefs of staff were to transmit the proposals, which would be combined into a "single package," to their respective representatives (the members of the Standing Group); (2) the three representatives would reach agreement on the proposal, if possible, and then (3) would report their findings back to their chiefs of staff; (4) any unresolved matters would be "duly set forth for resolution on the governmental level or, if necessary, in the North Atlantic Treaty Organization"; and (5) in the case of the United States, the JCS would forward the representatives' report, together with their recommendations, to Marshall for his decision (Bradley to Marshall, Apr. 16, 1951, EM, Marshall Corr.; another copy is in CCS 092 Germany [5-4-49], Sec. 7).

[3] In June the JCS, after some hesitation, endorsed the concept of German rearmament within the framework of the proposed European Army, an outgrowth of the Pleven Plan of 1950 (see Galambos, *Columbia University*, no. 1045). The European Army, which was currently the subject of a European conference being held in Paris, was to be a multinational force administered by a European defense minister and under Eisenhower's operational control. The French government had originally proposed the idea as a way to use German troops for Western European defense without creating a German national force or a German general staff. The American JCS, desiring the immediate formation of German military units, agreed to the creation of the European Army as long as division-size German units could be raised and assigned to any area at Eisenhower's discretion (Poole, *History of the Joint Chiefs of Staff*, vol. IV, *1950-1952*, pp. 256-60; State, *Foreign Relations, 1951*, vol. III, *European Security and the German Question, Part I*, pp. 789-96).

[4] We have been unable to locate any cable to Eisenhower containing the JCS recommendations. For developments see nos. 218 and 304, n. 4.

187

To JOHN COTESWORTH SLESSOR
Top secret

Eisenhower Mss.

May 19, 1951

Dear Jack:[1] Thank you very much indeed for your fine letter of the 15th and its enclosure.[2] I have been discussing this whole business with my staff, including Saunders.[3] At the very least, we are all cheered by the prospects of a strong British reinforcement that now seems to be in sight.

We are developing some ideas of our own which I hope may have some value. In the meantime, I am writing to Sherman on the carrier business[4]—Saunders will explain to you what will be the tenor of my presentation. *Cordially*

[1] For background on Marshal of the Royal Air Force Sir John Slessor see no. 62, n. 1.

[2] Slessor's letter of May 15 is in EM; the enclosure, a report entitled "Preliminary Report on Acceleration of NATO Air Force," dated May 3, was removed from Eisenhower's files in 1953. (For background on this report and on the shortage of available air power for NATO see no. 172.) Slessor told Eisenhower that the United Kingdom had already taken action to increase the size of its Royal Air Force above the figures promised in the Medium Term Defense Plan (DC 28; see also nos. 15 and 16, n. 3). Under the MTDP the British commitment had totaled 640 fighters, ground support aircraft, light bombers, and reconnaissance planes. Under the new British defense program (see no. 111, n. 9) the RAF would make 1,060 of these aircraft available by 1954. Furthermore, the British would also have a force of 152 medium bombers, 66 day fighters, and 22 night fighters, to be allocated to Eisenhower's command if the strategic situation warranted it. Slessor concluded by expressing to Eisenhower the hope that "it will be clear to you that the R.A.F. have, in fact, already gone some way towards the closing of the gap." For further developments see no. 209.

[3] For background on Sir Hugh Saunders, Eisenhower's air deputy, see no. 77, n. 5.

[4] We have been unable to locate Eisenhower's letter to Chief of Naval Operations Forrest Sherman (see no. 98, n. 1). On May 25 Sherman would reply: "Am unaware of reason for doubts mentioned in your letter of 18th. All our plans are predicated on making minimum essential provision for Pacific and then sending to Mediterranean all available large carriers. Additionally if anti-submarine requirements should permit we would expect initially to augment large carriers by embarking squadrons for air support in light and escort carriers just as we have done in Far East" (cable 251446Z, EM).

188   *Eisenhower Mss.*

To Herbert Bayard Swope   *May 20, 1951*

Dear Herbert:[1] I am quite amazed by your report that the snarls and vituperation continue in undiminished intensity. I would have supposed that, by this time, people would have had some new interests.[2]

Of course, your news about the series of yearly prizes is tremendously interesting. I am sure that the University family will cooperate effectively in carrying out the purposes of yourself and of the donor of the prizes.[3] *Cordially*

[1] For background on Eisenhower's friend Swope, a public relations consultant, see no. 66, n. 1.

[2] Eisenhower was referring to the controversy over the dismissal of General

MacArthur by President Truman (see nos. 104, n. 5, 128, n. 4, and 136). "The feeling is deep and bitter," Swope had said in his May 15 letter (EM). "There are no arguments; there are only snarls and vituperation." In his May 21 reply (EM) Swope added that he was glad Eisenhower was not currently planning on a trip to the United States, because "the political and military situation has not improved . . . it's jelled into a sort of sullenness that is not good" (see also Swope to Eisenhower, May 8, 1951, EM; and no. 145).

[3] In Swope's May 15 letter he had told the General that he was helping a friend establish yearly prizes at Columbia University "for those whose efforts yield the most for mankind." On May 21 Swope wrote that the annual amount of thirty-five thousand dollars was to be awarded through Columbia because of Eisenhower's affiliation there.

189   *Eisenhower Mss.*

To WILLIAM EDWARD ROBINSON   *May 26, 1951*

Dear Bill:[1] Thank you very much for your fine letter. Mamie and I had enthusiastic letters from John and Barbie about their weekend, and I need not tell you how appreciative both of us are to you. That sort of kindness and generosity toward our youngsters just practically makes us lyrical.[2]

Incidentally, John wrote me a long and involved description of his gambling experiences the day you had him out at Blind Brook. I think he is still laboring under a vague fear that he did not pay his full share of the losses—but, in his defense, you must remember that he never bet that much money in his whole life. In fact, he apparently did not know what a "nassau" actually was. In any event, I finally figured out that you got so much fun out of his seriousness and complete innocence of what he was engaging in, that I did *not* suggest to him that he still owed you money. (He told me, with a rather odd mixture of chagrin and pride, that he donated two points to his side. He added that if he had been given the handicap that he really deserved, he might have turned in one or two more.)[3]

Of course, you don't have to give us any advance notice whatsoever about your coming. Short of a catastrophe of unmanageable proportions, both of us will be on the job and waiting for your arrival, even if we have nothing more than one hour's notice, which will be exactly enough time for us to get to the airport.[4]

Give our love to Helen Reid; we certainly enjoyed her visit here.[5]

Also remember me to all the members of the "gang" as you run into them. Within a week or two, we shall be seeing Cliff Roberts and Barry Leithead, for whom we have already reserved some quarters.[6]

As ever

[1] Robinson was a newspaper executive and friend of Eisenhower's (see no. 39).
[2] In his letter of May 19 (EM) Robinson had said that he had entertained John S. D. Eisenhower and his wife Barbara, the General's son and daughter-in-law, in New York during the weekend of April 28.
[3] John Eisenhower had played golf at the Blind Brook Club on April 28 and 29. Robinson wrote that "John admitted to having a real yen for the game and seemed to get a great kick out of playing with your gang. He hit the ball very well indeed." A "nassau" is a golf match in which winning the first nine holes counts as one point, winning the second nine is one point, and winning eighteen holes is one point.
[4] On Robinson's visit in June see no. 217, n. 3.
[5] According to Robinson, Helen R. Reid had given him a "report" on the General after her visit to France in April. She said she had enjoyed Eisenhower's "positive and affirmative spirit of confidence" (see no. 146, n. 1).
[6] On Clifford Roberts and Barry T. Leithead's visit see nos. 193, n. 4, and 217, n. 2; for background on Roberts see no. 7.

190   *Eisenhower Mss.*

To Harry Cecil Butcher   *May 26, 1951*

Dear Butch:[1] I have just gone over the LOOK article. One thing is sure—as long as magazines are foolish enough to pay for articles about an individual who is trying to do nothing but his own work, I know that the victim would always prefer that the article be written by a friend.

As always, you are more than generous to me.[2] *Cordially*

[1] For background on Butcher see no. 171.
[2] In a letter of April 24 (EM) Butcher had sent Eisenhower a copy of the article he had submitted to *Look* magazine. In a letter of May 18 (EM) Butcher had reported to Eisenhower that his article had been published by *Look* and that it would appear on the newsstands on May 22 (see *Look*, June 5, 1951, 67–71).

The article concerned Butcher's own ambivalence over the possibility of Eisenhower becoming President. As his friend, Butcher did not want Eisenhower to be elected, but as a concerned citizen he believed the General was well qualified for the position. He praised Eisenhower's ability to act under pressure and to express himself. An important quality, Butcher had written, was Eisenhower's potential to motivate people. Physically "a commanding military figure," Eisenhower, Butcher concluded, would make a "great" President (for reactions to the article and a copy of the original draft see EM, Butcher Corr.; for developments see no. 515).

To William Averell Harriman   *May 26, 1951*

Dear Averell: Possibly, I shall have to answer your letter of May 18th in installments, but, without waiting a moment, I do want to say that we are delighted that you will be arriving here toward the end of June.[1] It makes no difference whatsoever about passage for John and his family.[2] I can always get them onto some plane coming this way, but I just thought it would be very nice for them if they could have the opportunity of traveling with you. Actually, my pilot wants to take one of our planes home for some important repairs, and, if he does, I shall have him bring back a whole bevy of SHAPE dependents. On that trip, he could easily pick up my own family.

There are some things connected with this job, particularly such abstractions as my understandings with Allied and American officials, that simply cannot be intelligently discussed in a letter. These will have to await your arrival. From the beginning, I realized that it would be highly necessary for me to keep the kind of touch with some individuals and offices at home that can be best done only by intermittent visits to Washington. However, there is no difficulty in realizing that circumstances of the past weeks have made completely impracticable the carrying out of such a scheme. Moreover, I believe it will be many months before there is any slightest thread of wisdom in my coming back there, even briefly.[3]

For the moment, this will have to do. I shall try to set aside an hour next week to do better. *Cordially*

[1] See no. 173, nn. 2, 5, and 8, for a discussion of Harriman's letter of May 18 (in EM). Harriman had told Eisenhower that he would visit Europe some time after June 20. See also nos. 218, n. 1, and 251, n. 1.
[2] Eisenhower was planning for his son's visit to France in June (see nos. 183 and 224, n. 2; see also Schulz to Davidson, AP 80523, May 12, 1951, EM, Subject File, Trips). In a letter of May 12 (no. 173) Eisenhower had asked Harriman about the possibility of having John Eisenhower and his family fly over to Europe with Harriman.
[3] Eisenhower would take up this subject again in his next letter to Harriman (see no. 198, n. 1).

192   *Eisenhower Mss.*

To George Edward Allen   *May 26, 1951*

Dear George:[1] I am somewhat disappointed to see you using the adjective "quick" in describing the trip you are planning to Europe. Moreover, Mamie is shocked to see no mention of Mary in connection with your travel plan. Will you please correct both these things instantly?[2]

Everything we hear about the farm makes us want, more and more, to get there as soon as we can. There are a thousand things connected both with the farm and my daily life that I should like to talk over with you.[3] In any event, you could look upon a good long trip over this way as a conditioning period. I guarantee to put you on the right kind of diet and exercises to reduce your girth to the point of requiring new clothes, and your handicap to the point that you will have to give me five strokes a side.[4] So hurry along, and bring Mary to join Mamie's canasta group. They badly need a fourth; besides, one of the big reasons for getting you over is that Mary will be here. *Cordially*

[1] For background on Eisenhower's friend Allen see no. 9, n. 2.

[2] Allen had written on May 19 (EM) that he hoped "to get over soon for a quick trip to see you" and that President Truman had told him he "certainly should do so." Allen would visit Eisenhower for a short stay in Paris beginning June 17 (see appointment calendar; and Allen to Eisenhower, June 22, 1951, EM). Allen's wife, the former Mary Keene (see no. 9, n. 2), would not accompany him on this trip.

[3] The most recent development at the Eisenhower farm was the addition of ten Guernsey heifers, a gift from Walter Kirschner (see nos. 33 and 170, n. 3). In his letter of May 14 (EM) Allen had commented that "Kirschner sent them across the country with a cowboy and it was quite an event in Gettysburg when they arrived." A calf had been born the day after the Guernseys' arrival, and on May 19 Allen said that the "new calf christened 'Mamie' is doing wonderfully" (see nos. 179, n. 7, and 185, n. 3).

[4] Eisenhower had been trying to get Allen to lose weight by making a series of bets with him (see nos. 48, n. 3, and 493; see also memorandum, Schulz to Allen, June 21, 1951, EM, Allen Corr.).

193   *Eisenhower Mss.*

To Ralph Thomas Reed   *May 29, 1951*

Dear Ralph:[1] Thank you for your note and for the news it contained. It is nice to know that Schooie and his wife are on their way over here. While I have to be out of town on June 6th, I will see him as soon as possible and try to work up a golf game with him. I have played once on the Saint Germain course which is considerably longer than the one at Morfontaine. Its fairways are in excellent condition and, moreover, it is situated only about fifteen minutes from Versailles, so it is a much handier place for me. But I still have an abiding affection for the course where you and I played.[2]

Mamie is completely thrilled with her fireplace fan. I am sure she has already written to Mrs. Reed about it, but I assure you that you can tell her she could have looked all over Europe but could not have found a present that meant more to Mamie.[3]

A telegram just came in saying that Bill Robinson will be over here about the end of the month. I am delighted, and it will be even better if he and Cliff can be here at the same time. I will see Phil Reed in a few days.[4]

When you see Bob Jones—or write to him—be sure to remember me to him most warmly. He is a man that I always think of with a combination of affection and admiration.[5]

With warm personal regard, *Cordially*

[1] For background on Reed, president of the American Express Company and a member of the Augusta National Golf Club, see no. 161, n. 7.

[2] Reed had written Eisenhower on May 24 (EM) and had mentioned another Augusta National member, Clarence J. Schoo. Schoo and his wife, the former Grace Harwood, would visit Paris beginning June 6. Eisenhower would be in Normandy that day for D-day ceremonies (see the Chronology in these volumes; and Eisenhower to Schoo, July 26, 1951, EM. See also no. 177, n. 2).

The St. Germain golf course was located at St. Germain-en-Laye, about six miles from Versailles (on this golf club and on the Morfontaine Golf Club, where Reed and the General had played in early May, see no. 161, n. 3).

[3] Mrs. Reed, the former Edna May Young, had probably purchased the fireplace fan for Mamie during the Reeds' visit earlier in the month (see Reed to Eisenhower, May 24, 1951, EM).

[4] Robinson would visit the General in late June (see no. 38; and EM, Robinson Corr.). In Reed's letter of May 24 he had said that Clifford Roberts had had a "check-up to find out whether he can go to Europe or not." Roberts was recovering from an ulcer but would be well enough to visit Eisenhower from June 10 through July (see nos. 7, n. 1, and 161, n. 2). Philip Reed, who would visit with Eisenhower on June 7, would play golf with the General and Schoo at the Morfontaine golf course on June 8 (see no. 164, n. 1). Robinson, Roberts, and Philip Reed were all members of Augusta National (on these visits and on Eisenhower's schedule see the Chronology in these volumes).

[5] Reed had told Eisenhower in his letter of May 24 that their friend Robert T. Jones, Jr., had seen a doctor in New York: "someone from whom he got some encouragement." Jones had a disease of the spinal cord that had required surgery in 1948 and 1950 (see *New York Times*, May 19, 1950; Dec. 19, 1971. See also Jones to Eisenhower, Nov. 30, 1948, and Mar. 20, 1950, EM). Eisenhower's friendship with Jones had begun with the General's introduction to Augusta National in 1948 (see Galambos, *Columbia University*, no. 36; and no. 113 in this volume).

(Decoration day in the U.S.)

Another decoration day[1] finds us still adding to the number of graves that will be decorated in future years. Men are stupid!

MacArthur seems to have retired into the Waldorf Towers, from which stronghold he issues statements and occasionally emerges to see a baseball game. The first he does through Whitney—who, I think, is one of the Old Chief's mistakes![2]

I cannot much blame MacA—I get the impression that he is in a state of "Watchful waiting." For what, I wouldn't know—but I do know that in his position I'd be after the bass of Wisconsin, the trout of Wyoming or vacationing on the beach!!![3] Recently, I wrote to him—had a nice reply.[4] While I'm determined to stay aloof from all the current snarling and fighting in the U.S. I'm most of all determined never to get into the "personality" kind of argument. In that respect the military men (especially including MacA) have been exemplary.[5]

Messages reaching me since the MacA fight began are even more consistent than previously that I _am_ going to get involved in *1952* politics. In the back of this book I've placed a couple of samples![6]

[1] Decoration Day was the former designation of the holiday Memorial Day. Although similar observances had taken place earlier in both North and South, the day was officially established in 1868 by order of the Union veterans' organization, the Grand Army of the Republic (GAR). Originally set aside as a day to decorate the graves and honor the memory of the Northern Civil War dead, with the passage of years it became a day to pay tribute to the American dead of all wars. In 1882 the GAR urged that its proper designation be Memorial Day (see Jane M. Hatch, ed. and comp., *The American Book of Days* [New York, 1978], pp. 501-4; and *New York Times*, May 24, 1964).

American casualties in Korea since the beginning of the war there in June 1950 reportedly would reach 68,352 on June 6, 1951. Of this figure, 11,503 American servicemen were known to be dead (see *New York Times*, June 7, 1951).

[2] Since his return from the Far East General Douglas MacArthur had been in the press almost daily, as controversy concerning his dismissal as CINCFE and speculations regarding his future plans grew (see nos. 131 and 136, n. 2). Through his principal aide, Major General Courtney Whitney, MacArthur had recently issued a number of statements defending his actions and policies in Korea and answering the testimony of many of the congressional witnesses (see, for example, *New York Times*, May 8, 18, 1951; and *International Herald Tribune*, Paris ed., May 11 and 26, 1951. See also Manchester, *American Caesar*, pp. 378-79, 657, 685; and Rovere and Schlesinger, *MacArthur Controversy*, pp. 23, 255-56, 258).

[3] Since 1944 MacArthur had been mentioned repeatedly as a potential presidential candidate. After his hero's welcome upon his return to the United States, many public speaking engagements, and embroilment in controversy with Truman over his dismissal, the former Far East commander was once again being discussed as a Republican presidential possibility. On MacArthur's political strategy during

this period see Manchester, *American Caesar*, pp. 656, 664, 681–84, 691; see also nos. 131, n. 3, and 136, n. 2.

[4] The General's letter to MacArthur is no. 181.

[5] See no. 136.

[6] Fearing that any involvement in the MacArthur affair would injure Eisenhower's potential as a 1952 presidential candidate, some of his friends had advised the General against either issuing any statements on the matter or returning to the United States before the debate had quieted down (see, for example, nos. 131, n. 3, 177, n. 4, and 188, n. 2). For Eisenhower's comments on the political pressure see the following document. These letters are not appended to the Eisenhower diaries.

195   *Eisenhower Mss., Family File*

To MILTON STOVER EISENHOWER   *May 30, 1951*

Dear Milton:[1] I can understand the dilemma in which you often find yourself in trying to answer the kind of question put to you by Mr. Tope. My own mail becomes more and more of a burden as more and more of my friends hint openly at what they usually call "my future duty to my country."[2]

While I can sympathize with individuals who feel the need of a flag-bearer in their fight to prevent a party's leadership falling into the hands of someone whose convictions they do not share, yet I think that, if these people would pause to reflect for even a moment, they would understand that, as long as I have to be on this job, I cannot say a word, even of an advisory character. The slightest word on my part that could be interpreted as any kind of a political move would be disastrous to the vital work I am trying to do; it would no longer be possible to keep discussion and consideration of the great task of common security on a plane of objectivity and impartiality. Lord knows it is hard enough to do that now, but you could well imagine what would happen if I should ever admit that I belong to the same political alignment as you do.[3]

Consequently, I think that all you can say, in reply to the questions put to you, is something to the effect that you know that so far as inclination and desire are concerned I have not changed my violently negative attitude by one iota. Next, you could say that the obvious requirements and limitations of my current and vitally important job compel complete silence as to such questions. Thirdly, you could say that it has been many months since you and I have had a chance to talk together and that, even then, we did not talk about questions of this kind.[4]

Knowing that you will destroy this letter at once, I do not mind telling you (for no repetition to anyone) that some of my friends have, in recent months, given me some anxious doubts as to the correctness of my confident assumption that I would never have any duty outside of uniform. (In fact, the hope of discussing some of these doubts with you was one of the reasons that I so earnestly requested you to come over here and stay with me awhile this summer.)[5] But I am clear as to one thing. I shall not, under any circumstances, even admit a party sympathy or affiliation as long as I am on this military assignment, and I have no intention of voluntarily abandoning this critical duty unless I reach a conviction that an even larger *duty* compels me to do so. I cannot believe that I shall ever feel such compulsion. I flatly stick to my resolution that I shall never *seek anything*.[6]

I realize that this is not a satisfactory letter, but the things that I would really like to talk to you about would require pages. To prepare such a message would require time that I do not possess. In this situation, I suggest the following: My very fine friend, Bill Robinson, is coming to see me at the end of next month and will return home about the 10th of July. I trust him implicitly, and I have great confidence in his judgment. So far as secrecy and security are concerned, he is 100%. I shall talk over these things with him (as I did in 1948). When he returns home, I shall ask him to get in touch with you either in New York or out at your home, at your convenience. He will be glad to do it.[7]

A letter from George Allen, just received, tells me that Helen continues to improve. I cannot tell you how completely delighted we are with such news.

Love to the whole family, and, as always, the very best to yourself.[8]

As ever

[1] For background on the General's brother Milton see no. 9, n. 1.

[2] In his letter of May 17 (EM) Milton had told his brother that he had met with a Mr. Tope, leader of the Michigan Young Republicans. This was probably John K. Tope (B.A. Maryville College 1933), a Detroit businessman who had been active with the Michigan Young Republicans and had been named chairman of the Young Republican National Federation in 1949. Tope argued that some Republicans were becoming apathetic because of the assumption that Senator Taft would be their nominee for President. Milton needed to know how to reply to those who, like Tope, asked him if the General would change his mind about becoming a presidential candidate (see nos. 94, 190, and 194. On Taft see no. 25, n. 3; and on Milton's meeting with Tope see Steve Neal, *The Eisenhowers: Reluctant Dynasty* [New York, 1978], p. 267).

[3] Milton had said that "the anti-Taft forces in the Republican party feel that they must begin to rally behind someone." (For further information on Eisenhower's position see nos. 135, 196, 483, and 490, n. 16.) Milton was a Republican (see Stephen E. Ambrose and Richard H. Immerman, *Milton S. Eisenhower: Educational Statesman* [Baltimore, 1983], p. 36).

[4] Milton would take the General's suggestions when he met in June with Hugh Doggett Scott, Jr., past chairman of the Republican National Committee, and

Harold E. Talbott (Ph.D. Yale 1910), past chairman of the Republican National Finance Committee (on Talbott see no. 196). Scott (LL.B. University of Virginia 1922) was a Pennsylvania congressman and lawyer. On the meeting see MSE to Eisenhower, June 18, 1951, EM; Neal, *Reluctant Dynasty*, pp. 268–69; and Kornitzer, *Great American Heritage*, p. 195.

[5] Milton had not seen his brother since February 1951 in Washington, D.C. The brothers would next see each other briefly in November (see nos. 119, 140, and 473; see also the Chronology in these volumes).

[6] In November Eisenhower would reject a possible Democratic presidential candidacy, and in January 1952 he would be pressured by his supporters into announcing his Republican party affiliation (see no. 196; Eisenhower's *Mandate for Change*, pp. 13–22; and Lyon, *Portrait of the Hero*, pp. 427–34). For developments see nos. 480, n. 3, 486, 587, and 592.

[7] William E. Robinson, a newspaper executive, had visited Eisenhower in June 1948 when the Republicans tried to persuade the General to become their presidential candidate. Robinson would see Milton in October after visiting Eisenhower in Paris (see nos. 39 and 217, n. 3; and Eisenhower, *Mandate for Change*, pp. 9–10, 26–27).

[8] Eisenhower was referring to George Allen's letter of May 19 (EM). Concerning the recent illness of Helen Eakin Eisenhower, Milton's wife, Allen had reported that she "is getting along just wonderfully" (see no. 9, n. 4). Eisenhower would keep a copy of this letter in a separate file, instead of placing it with his regular correspondence (see no. 196, n. 1).

196   *Eisenhower Mss.*

To LUCIUS DU BIGNON CLAY   *May 30, 1951*
Top secret

Dear Lucius:[1] Your two letters were handed to me just as I returned from a week long inspection trip in Scandinavia. This accounts for the delay in answering.[2]

I am somewhat confused by the realization that any of the individuals you mention should feel the need for any comment on my part.[3] This is all the more true because, only recently, I was visited by Winthrop Aldrich[4] who seems to be very close indeed to Our Friend. I gathered from him that they *both* hoped and prayed that, until future, and extraordinary, circumstances might compel a statement from me, I would keep still, both publicly and privately.[5]

As a first consideration, it is obvious that I cannot serve in this complex and critical military post if I should make a declaration of party affiliation or political interest. I realize that none of these individuals requests such a statement from me. Moreover, they all understand that, so far as desire and personal preference are concerned, my feelings are the same as they have always been, completely and flatly negative.[6]

These friends believe that, if the opposition suffers another national defeat, the risk of the two-party system disappearing will be intensified. Deeply concerned with such a disastrous possibility, they are not going to be satisfied with party leadership that does not inspire their confidence and respect and does not provide, in their opinion, the best chance of victory.[7]

As I have understood the reasoning of both Our Friend and A,[8] they have separately concluded that there could develop circumstances that would leave me no opportunity of remaining aloof from all these problems. They seem to visualize a situation that would obviously represent a higher call to duty than does even my present job.[9] But I am sure that none of them could imagine me in the role of assisting, even remotely, in bringing about such circumstances, since any such connection would give me the uneasy feeling of being dishonest, if not with others, then with myself.

Now, as to what others may or should do; I have always insisted upon the right of every free-born American to do what he pleases, as long as it is legal and ethical. Incidentally, entirely aside from any specific reason for their meeting, I think that some kind of understanding between Our Friend and A should be very valuable from the standpoint of advancing the policies in public affairs for which they both seem to be working.[10]

I like and admire all the individuals mentioned in your letter.[11] I am not going to make any comment of any character, publicly or privately, on what they may or may not do in advancing what they believe to be the best interests of our country. All of them realize that if I were, at this moment, and while I am on this job—in the absence of the extraordinary circumstances that they visualize as occurring at some future date—forced into such a position that I *had* to make a statement, I would simply have to adhere to what I have said previously on this subject. I am certain that my friends will be exceedingly careful to avoid putting me in a corner.

I know that you understand the sincerity of my views, and realize that I am not trying to duck any difficult question, or to be evasive or coy. All I am trying to do is to meet a situation as it now stands, and to perform to the best of my ability the duty imposed upon me by our nation. My present duty is to help develop the defensive power of twelve countries. If I ever have to do any other, I shall have to be *very clear* that I know it to be *duty*.[12]

Love to Marjorie[13]—best to you.[14] *Cordially*

[1] For background on Clay see no. 112. The General kept carbons of this document and his same-day letter to his brother Milton (no. 195) in his personal possession instead of filing them with regular correspondence (Good, Memorandum for Record, May 30, 1951, in EM, same file as document).

[2] Clay had written on May 18 (EM) and then, by another letter (not in EM), had

conveyed an important memorandum on political campaign strategy (see n. 3 below). Clay had expressed a wish for prompt answers to questions raised in the memorandum, and before writing this letter the General twice had promised a reply (AP 80579, May 26, 1951; Eisenhower to Clay, May 28, 1951, EM, Clay Corr.). Eisenhower had left Paris for Copenhagen and Oslo on May 20, returning on May 25 (see nos. 183, n. 3, and 198, n. 5).

³ Clay's messages had called on the General to approve small steps toward an Eisenhower presidential candidacy. The memorandum Clay enclosed had been received from New York Governor Thomas E. Dewey (Clay, who was in New York City, referred to him as "our friend up the river"), who had sent roughly coded comments and recommendations for Eisenhower's benefit. Dewey (referred to by Eisenhower as "our friend") posed the General certain specific questions. One of them concerned overtures Senator James Duff of Pennsylvania—Dewey called him "A" (see no. 94, n. 5)—had made to one of Dewey's close associates, New York lawyer and former Republican National Committee Chairman Herbert Brownell, Jr. ("B" [see Galambos, *Columbia University*, no. 638]). Duff had met with Brownell and said "that if the two states involved could work together, the appropriate result would be more easily achieved. . . ." Duff further had requested a meeting with Dewey himself. Dewey proposed that the two men meet "entirely upon our own responsibility, without the knowledge or approval of anyone and I would prayerfully hope, no publicity." He argued that neither he nor Duff should take any public leadership in the pro-Eisenhower movement. That role Dewey would leave to Harry Darby ("D" [see *ibid.*, no. 767]), a banker and Republican national committeeman from Kansas.

A second issue involved exploratory campaign traveling and its funding. Dewey mentioned the encouraging impressions Harold Elsner Talbott, New York businessman and former chairman of the Republican National Finance Committee, had collected in talking to Eisenhower about his political future before his departure for SHAPE. Dewey reported Talbott's opinions that Eisenhower "should announce something this year" and that the General's supporters, by way of loans, each under three thousand dollars, should raise a fund to finance "the trips that various people will be taking." Dewey strongly opposed the announcement idea as "fatal" but mildly favored the fund proposal. He concluded his memo by asking whether Eisenhower objected to the Duff meeting and for the General's views on the travel-fund plan.

"I hope you will let me know that it is satisfactory for me to proceed," Clay wrote on May 18. "It is time to move now—and this can be done without direct commitment from you. In my opinion we must move and I feel strongly that there will be no one else who can unite this nation." On Clay's close ties to the Republican moderates then working to secure Eisenhower's nomination see Lyon, *Portrait of the Hero*, pp. 428–29. On Dewey's support of an Eisenhower candidacy see Smith, *Dewey*, pp. 556–57, 577–79; and Marquis Childs, *Eisenhower, Captive Hero: A Critical Study of the General and the President* (New York, 1958), pp. 128–29. For another code name Dewey employed in his dealings with Eisenhower see no. 33, n. 7.

⁴ Winthrop Williams Aldrich, chairman of the board of the Chase National Bank and of the trustees for the American Heritage Foundation (see Galambos, *Columbia University*, no. 168), was among Dewey's (that is, "Our Friend's") financial supporters. Aldrich had met with Eisenhower the afternoon of May 29.

⁵ Dewey had reiterated the need for Eisenhower to remain silent on the MacArthur affair. "The banner headlines given to General Marshall's testimony that General MacArthur's program would handicap General Eisenhower in Europe was elicited and inspired by those who wish to create an embroilment," the governor had written. "This should be avoided at all costs by reason of total concentration on

the job at hand" (see *New York Times*, May 8–13, 15, 1951; and nos. 131, 136, and 145, n. 2).

[6] Eisenhower expressed similar sentiments in a letter of the same date to his brother Milton (see the preceding document). Though forbidden by regulations from actively seeking public office, Eisenhower faced increasing pressures to reveal his party affiliation and declare himself a candidate. His name appeared in most Gallup polls conducted on the 1952 election, newspapers speculated on his partisan leanings, and personal letters urging him to run—on either party ticket—arrived regularly at SHAPE headquarters (Army Regulations, 600–10, par. 18, cited in Parmet, *Eisenhower and the American Crusades*, p. 45; *U.S. News & World Report*, Apr. 27, 1951, 13–14, and June 8, 1951, 22–23; nos. 63, n. 2, and 135; correspondence in EM, Political Files).

[7] After nearly twenty years as the opposition in national affairs and after Dewey's defeat in the 1948 presidential election (see Galambos, *Columbia University*, no. 245), the Republican party stood badly divided between its Dewey-led liberal Eastern wing and the more conservative Midwestern element headed by Senator Robert A. Taft of Ohio. The Great Debate in Congress over sending U.S. troops to Europe (see nos. 128, n. 2, and 153, n. 11) further polarized these "internationalist" and "isolationist" factions. Eisenhower—a national hero of broad appeal, a strong advocate of collective security, and an outspoken opponent of tendencies toward larger, more intrusive government—had the firm support of Dewey and the internationalists. They saw the General as the only potential candidate who could win the 1952 election, revitalize the party, and carry out the foreign and domestic policies they supported (see Bernstein, "Election of 1952," pp. 3215–25; Eugene H. Roseboom, *A History of Presidential Elections* [New York, 1964], pp. 508–9; and Robert T. Elson, "Taft or Eisenhower: The Choice Narrows," *Life*, August 13, 1951, 86–101). Galambos, *Columbia University*, no. 1041, supplies background on Dewey's October 1950 personal endorsement of Eisenhower.

[8] The reference was to Governor Dewey and Senator Duff (see n. 4 above).

[9] Because Eisenhower opposed Taft's position on foreign-policy issues, the Ohio senator's possible nomination for the presidency prompted the General to write of "circumstances" and a "higher call to duty" that would force him to enter the campaign. In January, after returning from the NATO inspection tour (see no. 23, n. 2), Eisenhower had held a private meeting with Taft at the Pentagon. According to the General's memoirs, he had seen the meeting as an opportunity to end all of the rumors about his own presidential ambitions. Before Taft arrived, Eisenhower drafted a statement "of flat refusal to contemplate any political career at any time, including . . . a request that all Americans recognize its unequivocal character." This statement was to be issued only after Taft had assured the General that he would support the concept of collective security in Western Europe. When the Ohio senator failed to give such assurances, Eisenhower destroyed the statement, aiming to maintain "whatever political influence I might possess to keep us on the right track" (*At Ease*, pp. 371–72. See also *Mandate for Change*, pp. 13–14; Patterson, *Mr. Republican*, pp. 483–84; Lyon, *Portrait of the Hero*, pp. 417–18; and Ambrose, *Eisenhower*, vol. I, *Soldier, General of the Army, President-Elect*, pp. 498–99). Dewey and the General agreed fully on the dangers of a Taft presidency. In a May 10 address to the New York Republican State Committee, Dewey had blamed Taft's isolationist faction for "inviting the third World War by weakness and indecision" (see *New York Times*, May 11, 1951).

[10] Dewey and Duff would meet in the spring of 1951 (see Smith, *Dewey*, p. 577; and *Newsweek*, July 2, 1951, 14–15).

[11] See n. 4 above for these early Eisenhower supporters.

[12] In his reply of June 12 (EM) Clay said that he "understood fully" Eisenhower's message but that the General may have mistaken Dewey's intentions. The governor

"wants no declaration from you," Clay explained. "On the other hand, he did not want to take steps which you might disapprove." Reporting that Dewey planned to go ahead and talk to Duff, Clay said he believed "things will begin to evolve slowly, quietly, but surely" (EM).
[13] Clay's wife, Marjorie McKeown Clay.
[14] For developments in the Eisenhower presidential movement see no. 331, n. 4.

197   *Eisenhower Mss.*

To Jean de Lattre de Tassigny [1]   *May 31, 1951*
Cable AP 80615

My heartfelt sympathy is with you in your bereavement.[2] It is my hope that the tragic burden may be lightened in some degree by the pride you must feel as the father of a hero whose deeds will be a continuing inspiration to the youth in France.[3]

[1] For background on General de Lattre, Colonial High Commissioner in Indochina and Commander of French forces in the Far East, see no. 28.
[2] On the afternoon of the previous day de Lattre's only son, a twenty-three-year-old lieutenant of armored infantry, had been killed in action against Vietminh forces south of Hanoi (see Buttinger, *Vietnam*, vol. II, *Vietnam at War*, p. 755; O'Ballance, *Indo-China War*, p. 130; and *International Herald Tribune*, Paris ed., May 31, 1951). General de Lattre would accompany the body of his son Bernard to Paris for special memorial services on June 4. While the Eisenhowers apparently did not attend the ceremonies at Paris's Church of the Invalides, they did have a wreath placed upon the young lieutenant's coffin (see *International Herald Tribune*, Paris ed., June 4, 5, 1951; and de Lattres to Eisenhowers, July 3, 1951, original and translation in EM). On the French war in Vietnam see nos. 28 and 89.
[3] See no. 88, n. 2.

SHAPE and the Unity of Europe

JUNE 1951 TO OCTOBER 1951

3

The "rocky road to unification"

To WILLIAM AVERELL HARRIMAN   *June 1, 1951*
Top secret. Personal and confidential

Dear Averell: Lately, there has been much discussion about the possibility of my having to return to the United States to give testimony in connection with the European Defense Program. I personally think that, from every viewpoint, it would be a very grave error.[1]

In the first place, I have an international, as well as a national, role to play; if I should have to go to the United States to testify on *international* questions, it is easily possible that other countries in NATO could consider the incident as a precedent. If any of these governments should later request that I come to their capitals for the purpose of testifying on similar subjects, I could be quite red-faced in making my explanations.

There is, of course, the clear fact that I am, after all, an American officer and, as such, am responsive to orders of my government to testify on *any* appropriate subject. But the distinction between my obligations, loyalties, and responsibilities in the two roles might be difficult to describe clearly in some other government where there could already have been made the old charge of American arrogance or imperialism.

Another aspect of the proposition is that any honest testimony would have to present the discouraging as well as the encouraging features of this project. Those who oppose European rearmament would emphasize the discouraging aspects of my testimony, and I could easily be quoted as being exceedingly pessimistic. Yet the last thing that a leader may be is pessimistic if he is to achieve success.

All this is just thinking aloud; I know that you and others are fully aware of these various implications and possibilities. In spite of these facts, I know that, if Congress should want to make a point of it, I could scarcely refuse to come home because we obviously need continuing and active participation of the Congress.[2]

I think it would have been a wise move on my part, before I came over here, to have asked that a modest international fund be set up to be spent under my direction, in accordance with policies fixed by the Council of Deputies. A reasonable sum in such a packet would have greatly facilitated progress in the business of getting established. At this moment, I am greatly concerned because of the difficulty in getting Norstad's headquarters properly and promptly set up in conjunction with Juin.[3] This is our most important operational command, and it is extremely unfortunate that physical limitations are standing in the way of its early functioning. There is one building in Fontainebleau—now used as a French military school, the rehabilitation of which cost the government some 4 or 5 million dollars—that would be ideal for our purposes. But the French feel that, as the host country, they have already been compelled to indulge in a considerable amount of unilateral expenditure, and that they cannot go much further in this direction without having very serious budgetary difficulties. But if I had an international fund at this moment with which to establish a school building somewhere else, I think I could get this particular problem straightened out quickly.

We have sent word through the Standing Group that failure to approve our command arrangements on the southern flank is causing us acute embarrassment. Moreover, similar information has been conveyed, indirectly, to the British Government which we understand has objected to public announcement at this time. This is more irritating because of the fact that, so far as we know, not a single individual or government seriously questions my own authority to organize my own forces or the soundness of my particular plan. The difficulty seems to be that there is a hope that the postponement of public announcement may have some effect on the negotiations involving the over-all organization for the Mediterranean and the Middle East. My plan was drawn up in full consultation with French and Italian authorities, as well as British and American. The consequence is that failure to establish it promptly must mean to staffs in those countries that little interest is taken in my own personal convictions about such matters. I feel strongly about it, and patience is just about ceasing to be a virtue. I may have to make an issue of it. While I believe *our* military authorities are doing what they can—I think you could do us some good on this one through a direct needling of the British—maybe through the Secretary of State.[4]

My recent visit to Norway impressed me with the tightness of the economic situation in that region. While the case is probably an extreme one, it nevertheless provides a very fine example of the soundness of the conclusions reached by the CED in the recent study the Committee published on Western Europe.[5]

Right now, I understand there is a hot argument going on between the French and American Governments as to the amount of aid originally promised for 1951, as well as the budgetary commitments that the French Government had been originally prepared to make for the same period. Economic, political, and military questions are so inextricably inter-twined that it is almost silly to attempt even their practical segregation; each category under the authoritative influence of some particular Allied official or body.[6]

The French elections are now less than three weeks off.[7] I most sincerely hope they show better results than did the Italian elections. Actually, of course, there is no such proportion of vicious and unmanageable Communistic sentiment as is represented in 28% of the vote cast.[8] People are misled and misinformed. This fact is obvious after the most cursory examination of the problem, and should indicate to all concerned the very urgent necessity for *skillful* propaganda on the part of the Allies, of the highest quality and of adequate volume. (If it is really skillful, its governmental source, support, and connection will be carefully concealed.) Each nation could have one little "Voice of America" to keep its own specific policies and positions clearly before the world. All the rest of the program ought to be carried out so as to educate and inform through sources that are, at least on the surface, divorced from officialdom.[9]

My reports on the first conference of the American Assembly continue to be very favorable—in fact, glowing. If Lew Douglas and Phil Young both keep their health, I know that the project will grow into a highly respected, widely known, and very valuable national institution.[10]

Of course, Al[11] and I are looking forward with great anticipation to your forthcoming visit.[12] Not only are there a thousand things to talk about, but we may even be able to have a bit of fun together. Incidentally, Al and I have not played a game of bridge since I last saw you.

My continuing respects to the President, and warmest regard to yourself. *Cordially*

---

[1] Eisenhower, who did not want to become involved in the controversy surrounding the recall of General Douglas MacArthur, was reluctant to return to the United States (see no. 177, n. 4). Several newspaper stories had speculated on the possibility of Eisenhower's appearing before the Senate Foreign Relations Committee, which was looking into MacArthur's dismissal and its relationship to American foreign policy (*New York Times*, May 4, 5, 9, 15, 1951). On May 15 the General told *New York Times* correspondent Cyrus Sulzberger (see no. 114, n. 1) that he would resign his commission if he were forced to testify before Congress (Sulzberger, *Long Row of Candles*, p. 635). The pressures on Eisenhower to return home would continue; in July Secretary of Defense Marshall would tell him that there had been "constant requests" for Eisenhower to testify in Washington on aspects of the Mutual Security Program (Marshall to Eisenhower, July 21, 1951, JCS 96929, EM; see also no. 286, n. 2).

[2] Eisenhower would soon meet with several congressional committees that had come to Europe in order to determine the need for U.S. military and economic aid (see nos. 111 and 209, n. 2). In his reply to this letter (June 4, 1951, EM), Harriman wrote, "For your personal information, the President has told me that he thought it would be a good idea for you to come home occasionally so that you can get the feel of what's going on in this country and be in touch with people who are either directly or indirectly [*sic*] involved in decisions that affect your operations." In a postscript Harriman added, "Since dictating the above I have seen the President. He agrees with you as to your not returning to testify on the Foreign Aid program. He seems to have in mind your coming back some time after the hearings are over." Eisenhower would not return to the United States until November.

[3] On May 16 SHAPE had announced that it would establish headquarters for both the Allied Army Forces, Central Europe, and the Allied Air Forces, Central Europe, in Fontainebleau, approximately fifty miles southeast of Paris (*New York Times*, May 17, 1951; see also nos. 77 and 108). The air forces in the central sector were placed under the command of General Lauris Norstad, and French general Alphonse Juin was to command the ground units in that region. Juin, who was then French Resident General of Morocco (see no. 16, n. 6), would not assume command until September (*New York Times*, Sept. 22, 1951). Norstad would not finish building his permanent headquarters in Fontainebleau until July 1952. The headquarters would provide work and housing space for two thousand people in forty buildings. Construction costs would total $10 million (*ibid.*, July 20, 1952).

[4] Negotiations with the British concerning Eisenhower's Southern Command and Allied command arrangements in the Mediterranean and Middle East had been continuing since April (see no. 148, n. 2). On May 24 the British had once again proposed placing the entire Mediterranean under the overall command of a British officer. American Chief of Naval Operations Forrest Sherman had rejected the proposal, and Admiral Robert Carney, Eisenhower's designated southern flank commander, had urged Sherman to press for approval of Eisenhower's command arrangements pending settlement of the Mediterranean–Middle East command controversies. Army Chief of Staff Collins also advised that this should be done and cited Eisenhower's strong feelings about the matter (State, *Foreign Relations, 1951*, vol. III, *European Security and the German Question, Part I*, pp. 522–24, 526; Carney to Eisenhower, June 1, 1951, EM). For developments see no. 236.

[5] Eisenhower had made an inspection tour of Denmark and Norway from May 20 to May 25 (see correspondence and itineraries in EM, Subject File, Trips; and *New York Times*, May 21, 1951. On the report issued by the Committee for Economic Development see no. 164). The CED report had noted that the pursuit of European security would necessitate "continual compromise between greater armed strength on the one hand and economic well-being and advancement on the other. . . . The security of Western Europe must be understood as resting upon the condition of life of the people of that region, on their hope for a better future, and on the social and political unity of their countries—as well as on their armed might" (Committee for Economic Development, *North Atlantic Security*, p. 37. See also no. 16; and Halaby to Chairman, International Security Affairs Committee, Aug. 8, 1951, OS/D, 1951, Clas. Decimal File, CD 091.7 Europe).

[6] The governments of France and the United States were involved in a dispute over the nature and amount of U.S. aid that would be given to France for purposes of rearmament. The French were convinced that the United States had arbitrarily disregarded earlier agreements and had cut back the aid neeeded to finance imports and prevent French inflation. The United States had replied that the French had misinterpreted those agreements and that U.S. dollar aid was contingent upon the amount of French imports and on an anticipated French balance-of-payments deficit. The United States was also concerned that the French were contemplating the use of U.S. aid to help balance their national budget rather than to rearm. The disagreement would continue until the end of 1951 (see State, *Foreign Relations, 1951*, vol. III, *European Security and the German Question, Part I*, pp. 383–90, 392–93, 397–414, 430–62, 474–79; see also no. 467).

[7] Although the French national elections would take place June 17, a new government would not be formed until August (see no. 318). The Communists would receive 26.1 percent of the popular vote, a loss of 9 percent from the 28.5 percent they had received in the elections of 1946 (State, *Foreign Relations, 1951*, vol. IV, *Europe: Political and Economic Developments, Part I*, pp. 395–97).

[8] Local elections were held in northern Italy during May and June 1951, and the Italian Communists achieved only slight gains over the last major campaign (1948)

(see *ibid.*, pp. 616–17. See also Muriel Grindrod, *The Rebuilding of Italy: Politics and Economics, 1945–1955* [London, 1955] pp. 75–76; and Senate Subcommittee on Foreign Relations, *United States Foreign-Aid Programs in Europe: Hearings*, 1951, p. 165). The anti-Communist coalition of political parties won approximately 55 percent of the total vote of 15 million, while leftist parties received an estimated 35 percent (Brookings Institution, *Current Developments in United States Foreign Policy* 4, no. 10 [1951], 28).

[9] In 1947 the Central Intelligence Agency had initiated a program for covert psychological operations against Communist activities around the world (see Galambos, *Chief of Staff*, no. 1863). In 1948 the CIA had intervened in the Italian elections by providing money, advice, and support to anti-Communist politicians. The following year Eisenhower had become associated with the CIA-affiliated National Committee for a Free Europe, which sponsored such activities as Radio Free Europe and the Crusade for Freedom (see Galambos, *Columbia University*, nos. 428 and 739). In October 1951 Eisenhower would tell Cyrus Sulzberger (see n. 1 above) that he had urged Walter Bedell Smith, then Director of Central Intelligence (see no. 144), that "the CIA should have its men here and there working quietly in foreign countries fostering political movements and propaganda." According to Sulzberger, Eisenhower said that Smith's reply had been, "What the hell do you think I've been doing for the last year?" (Sulzberger, *Long Row of Candles*, p. 686. See also Steven L. Rearden, *The Formative Years, 1947–1950*, vol. I of *History of the Secretary of Defense*, ed. Alfred Goldberg, 1 vol. to date [Washington, D.C. 1984–], pp. 173–74; Ray S. Cline, *Secrets, Spies, and Scholars: Blueprint of the Essential CIA* [Washington, D.C., 1976], pp. 99–102; Stephen E. Ambrose with Richard H. Immerman, *Ike's Spies: Eisenhower and the Espionage Establishment* [Garden City, N.Y., 1981], pp. 167–68; and William M. Leary, ed., *The Central Intelligence Agency: History and Documents* [University, Ala., 1984], pp. 37–48). For background on the State Department's Voice of America radio broadcasts see Galambos, *Chief of Staff*, no. 1446, and *Columbia University*, no. 55.

[10] For information about the American Assembly conference see no. 201, n. 2. For background on Lewis Douglas see no. 47, n. 4; and on Philip Young, no. 8, n. 6.

[11] Eisenhower's chief of staff, Alfred M. Gruenther.

[12] On Harriman's visit see no. 191.

199   *Eisenhower Mss.*

To MILES CHRISTOPHER DEMPSEY   *June 2, 1951*

Dear Bimbo:[1] Monty has just shown me the letter that you wrote to General Bradley. I assure you of my very deep regret that anything should have been published by any American General that was unnecessarily embarrassing to any of my old friends. I have not read the book, and I suspect that the parts you have seen must have been removed from context—an old publishers' trick in order to promote argument and discussion.[2] Nevertheless, I most fully agree with you that there is no point in giving legitimate reason for building up dissension and mutual resentment among old friends. Of all times when we should be working in complete accord, this is the most important.[3]

This note brings to you my very best wishes, and a warm invitation to come over here to visit us for a day or two if ever you should get the chance. I understand that you have something to do with the administration of the horse-racing business in the United Kingdom, but possibly you also play golf.[4] This is the only outdoor sport in which any of us get a chance to indulge, and we might be able to arrange a game on the day you could be here. I can easily provide you a good set of clubs—you need nothing but golf shoes and slacks.[5]

For the immediate ensuing days, I am quite busy; but, beginning along about the 20th of June, the pressure will not be so great. Incidentally, I am to be in London on July 3rd and 4th—I might get a chance to see you.[6] *As ever*

[1] Dempsey, who had commanded the Second British Army during World War II, had been named C in C of the United Kingdom Land Forces in May (see *Times* [London], May 2, 10, 1951. For background see Galambos, *Chief of Staff*, no. 1833; and Eisenhower, *Crusade in Europe*, pp. 275, 289, 313).

[2] On May 31 Field Marshal Montgomery had written Eisenhower explaining that Dempsey was "extremely angry with Brad[ley] and has written to him. He sent me [the] enclosed copy of the letter and asked me to show it to you" (both letters are in EM, Dempsey Corr.). The May 25 letter from Dempsey to Bradley concerned an article on Bradley's recently published war memoir, *A Soldier's Story* (New York, 1951). The article quoted passages critical of Dempsey's performance during World War II (there is no copy of the article in EM). For background on Montgomery and Bradley see nos. 2, n. 4, and 50, n. 5, respectively. On Bradley's opinion of Dempsey see Bradley's *A Soldier's Story*, pp. 209–10, 380–83, 424; and his autobiography, *A General's Life*, pp. 254, 288).

[3] In Dempsey's May 25 letter he had told Bradley that he knew there was "a lot of money" to be made in the writing of a war memoir but that he felt Bradley was disappointing Eisenhower by damaging the collective security effort (for Eisenhower's view of Anglo-American relations and the need for unity see nos. 143, n. 4, 248, and 252, n. 5. On some of the conflicts between the United States and Britain during World War II see Eisenhower, *Crusade in Europe*, pp. 151, 284–86, 298–99, 356; and Bradley, *A Soldier's Story*, pp. x, 18, 58–59, 210, 352–54. For reactions to the book similar to Dempsey's see no. 203, n. 2).

[4] Since 1947 Dempsey had been chairman of the Racecourse Betting Control Board (see *Times* [London], June 9, 1951).

[5] In his reply of June 12 (EM) Dempsey mentioned a possible visit to Paris, as he was planning to see Montgomery in July. Eisenhower and Dempsey would meet July 21 (appointment calendar). In his letter Dempsey also suggested a foursome for golf the next time they were together (see nos. 161 and 193).

[6] Eisenhower would attend D-day ceremonies in Normandy on June 6 (see no. 208, n. 3), and during the rest of the month he would be busy with visits from Bradley, a group of congressmen, and friends. On July 3, 4, and 5 the General would be in London (on Eisenhower's schedule see nos. 209, 217, and 250; and the Chronology in these volumes. See also *New York Times*, June 10, 21, July 4, 1951).

Dinner last eve with Paul Hoffman, Henry Ford and Mr. Paul Helms (of California).[1] Paul has just published a book, "We Can Win the Peace."[2] He is determined I'll have to get into politics and he is *sad*—he knows how I feel about it & agrees with me. I'd like to see him in politics—I'd resign to work for him.[3]

[1] On June 3 Eisenhower had dinner with Paul Gray Hoffman, Henry Ford II, and Paul Hoy Helms. Hoffman, president of the Ford Foundation, was in Europe to address members of the International Chamber of Commerce in Lisbon (see no. 139; *New York Times*, June 4, 8, 14, 1951; and *International Herald Tribune*, Paris ed., June 4, 1951). Ford was president of the Ford Motor Company (see Galambos, *Columbia University*, nos. 113 and 419). Helms (A.B. Syracuse University 1912) was president of the Helms Bakeries of Los Angeles. He was also a member of the Fund for Adult Education, an organization established by the Ford Foundation (see Helms to Eisenhower, July 2, 1951, and May 9, 1952, EM).

According to Eisenhower's appointment calendar, the three had lunch on June 4, and on June 5 the General and Ford played golf. On June 7 Hoffman met with Eisenhower in his office.

[2] Hoffman's recently published book was entitled *Peace Can Be Won* (Garden City, N.Y., 1951). Hoffman had suggested a plan for the United States to "wage the peace" on economic, political, military, and psychological fronts. He believed the United States should lead in a cooperative effort to defend the free world. He saw Eisenhower's current work as an important part of Western defense. The General, Hoffman said, was someone with "the ability to inspire, the diplomacy to gain assent and the toughness to get things done which can do much to develop a European Army into both shield and buckler for the West" (*ibid.*, pp. 43, 70–72).

[3] On Hoffman's support for an Eisenhower run at the presidency see no. 411, n. 2; and Ambrose, *Eisenhower*, vol. I, *Soldier, General of the Army, President-Elect*, pp. 519, 522, 544–45. On his interest in the General's work at SHAPE see nos. 237 and 238. Hoffman would later become involved with the General's campaign (see Parmet, *Eisenhower and the American Crusades*, pp. 55, 107, 111–12).

Dear Mrs. McCormick:[1] Someone just sent to me the article you wrote about the American Assembly, published in the May 28th issue of the *Times*.[2] I cannot tell you how heart-warming it is for me to realize that thoughtful persons agree that the idea was a good one, and that execution, up to date at least, has been intelligent and aggressive.[3] I am delighted that you found the effort to be worthwhile—you have certainly accurately described its purposes and hopes.[4]

With very best wishes,[5] *Cordially*

[1] Winner of the 1937 Pulitzer Prize for Foreign Correspondence, McCormick was a member of the *New York Times* editorial board and author of the paper's thrice-weekly "Abroad" column.

[2] McCormick's article on her participation in Columbia University's first American Assembly conference discussed the value of the conference to the American people and praised Eisenhower for creating the program (see copy in EM, same file as document; and *New York Times*, May 28, 1951). For background on the Assembly plan see Eisenhower's memoir *At Ease*, p. 350; Galambos, *Columbia University*; and American Assembly, *American Assembly in Action*, pp. 1–3. On the first Assembly meeting see nn. 3 and 4 below.

[3] The American Assembly organized conferences of representatives from labor, business, government, and the professions, with the aim of throwing "impartial light on the major problems which confront America" (see American Assembly, *American Assembly in Action*, p. 1). In the first conference (May 21–25) eighty-five men and women had met at the Assembly's New York facility, Arden House (see Galambos, *Columbia University*, nos. 605, 844, and 1119; and American Assembly, *American Assembly in Action*, pp. 17–20), to discuss U.S. relations with Western Europe. Transcripts of the conference speeches and accounts of its conclusions, together with various study and discussion aids, were to be printed for dissemination to school and community groups across the nation. It was the hope of the Assembly administration that in this way "as large a number of American citizens as possible" could use the materials in discussions (see American Assembly, *United States–Western Europe Relationships as Viewed within the Present World-wide International Environment* [New York, 1951], pp. 1, 179; *New York Times*, May 21, 1951; and materials in EM, American Assembly, esp. "Memorandum to Editors about the American Assembly," Mar. 30, 1951).

[4] At the opening plenary session, the Assembly's National Policy Board chairman, Lewis Douglas, read a message from Eisenhower offering regrets for not being able to attend and expressing his support for the conference (see EM, Douglas Corr., esp. Eisenhower to Douglas, May 12, 1951, and PSW 556, Douglas to Eisenhower, May 19, 1951). Following Douglas's opening remarks, the Assembly was turned over to Senators Paul H. Douglas (see no. 109, n. 7) and Robert A. Taft (see no. 131, n. 3), who represented the "internationalist" and "isolationist" congressional factions in the recent Great Debate over America's role in the defense of Western Europe. They presented opposing views on the Assembly's theme. On May 22, following a second plenary session, the Assembly divided into three round tables. These groups met daily until the twenty-fifth; accounts of each group's proceedings were then combined into a single preliminary statement, which was read to the participants and members of the press by the Assembly's executive director, Philip Young (see no. 8, n. 6).

The final statement recognized that "Soviet imperialism" was a threat to the security of the United States and also an ideological threat to democratic institutions worldwide. The majority of conference participants had agreed upon the importance of defending Western Europe and had expressed confidence in the ability of the United States and its allies to "deter Soviet aggression or to meet it successfully whenever and wherever it emerges. . ." (see American Assembly, *United States–Western Europe Relationships*, pp. 179–218; *International Herald Tribune*, Paris ed., May 25, 1951; and *New York Times*, May 22, 26, 1951). For a personal account of the Assembly meetings see David E. Lilienthal, *The Journals of David E. Lilienthal*, 4 vols. (New York, 1964–69), vol. III, *The Venturesome Years, 1950–1955* (1966), pp. 169–70.

[5] At the close of the conference a message had been sent to Eisenhower commenting on the success of the first Assembly and assuring the General that "the participants, irrespective of their vocations . . . have without exception discussed the problems as American citizens and not as members of special groups. The controlling approach has been, 'What is best for America and for peace in the world' " (see American Assembly, *United States-Western Europe Relationships*, p. 202). For other comments on the Assembly meeting see nos. 202, 204, and 211.

202   *Eisenhower Mss.*

To Philip Young   *June 4, 1951*

Dear Phil: As I have already told you, I have had a number of most glowing reports upon the success of your first conference. You and Lew Douglas surely did the thing up brown.[1] In a letter today, I had one faint criticism, which I transmit to you exactly as I got it:

"The only criticism I had, and it is a minor one, is that there were possibly too many participants from the academic side at this first Assembly in proportion to the total number of participants. I appreciate that a terrific amount of work is involved preparing for such an Assembly, which burden must be carried almost entirely by the academic[s]; they are entitled, therefore, to see the results of their labor. I and a number of others, however, felt that the professors were somewhat inclined to take over the various discussion groups unless they were sat on which, fortunately, happened. The only controversies that occurred during the meetings always involved an academic man; I never witnessed a case of a dispute between labor and management, management and agriculture, journalism and labor, or between any of the other possible combinations. Perhaps this can be explained by the fact that an academic man is naturally articulate and thrives on argument."[2]

This criticism comes from one of our warmest supporters and the letter was filled, otherwise, with glowing accounts of the affair. For this reason, I pass this particular little criticism on to you for your consideration—nothing else.[3] *Cordially*

P.S. I've seen Arthur Sulzberger's comments to you.[4]

[1] Young was dean of Columbia University's Graduate School of Business and Executive Director of the American Assembly. For background on the first conference and on the Assembly's National Policy Board chairman, Lewis Douglas, see the preceding document.

[2] This paragraph was taken from a May 28 letter (EM) to Eisenhower from J. P. Morgan assistant vice-president Robert Whitney (see no. 50, n. 3). Of the eighty-one Assembly participants mentioned in the *New York Times*, eighteen represented college and university education or administration—more than from any other

group represented at the conference (see *New York Times*, May 21, 1951). Eisenhower's reply to Whitney, written on the same day as this document, is in EM, Whitney Corr.

[3] Young would reply on June 7 (EM) telling Eisenhower, "My own feeling would be that we did not have too much academic but too much Columbia academic." Of the eighteen participants from education, four had been members of the Columbia faculty, and one, Young himself, was from the university's administration. For Young's own evaluation and criticism of the first Assembly conference, which he termed "definitely successful," see his May 30 letter to Eisenhower in EM.

[4] *New York Times* publisher Arthur Hays Sulzberger had recently sent Eisenhower a copy of a letter he had written to Young concerning the Assembly meeting (see Sulzberger to Young, May 29, 1951, and Sulzberger to Eisenhower, May 30, 1951, both in EM, Sulzberger Corr.). On Sulzberger's criticisms and suggestions to Young see no. 204, n. 3; on Young's response see no. 220, n. 2.

203   *Eisenhower Mss.*

To Harold Roe Bull   *June 5, 1951*
Personal

Dear Pink:[1] While I am a bit pushed this morning with conferences and engagements with a variety of people, I am going to put off everything for a minute as I attempt to answer, however briefly, your letter of the 31st.[2]

In the first place, I have found that most people who attempt to put down their war reminiscences, consciously or unconsciously, fall into the habit of making themselves such important figures that sometimes I think these books become more an expression of how the authors would like to be remembered—rather than what they really thought and accomplished at the time.[3]

I have not read the articles and passages to which you refer in Bradley's book. I do, however, remember that Bradley called me on the night we captured the Remagen Bridge. He was not in any way perturbed at that time, and certainly gave no evidence of having been in any argument. He reported that you were at his headquarters and that you had merely asked him to be cautious that he did not interfere with any major plans of mine. On the telephone, he did not even tell me that he had already ordered any move of a major scale across the Bridge—not even that he had given a warning order. When I told him to rush ahead and reinforce with the $4\frac{1}{2}$ or 5 divisions that he thought he could get hold of, he said something to the effect that that was what he wanted to do, but the question had been raised as to possible interference with broader plans. I remarked to him that, since we had saved the divisions which we had allotted for the anticipated siege of

Cologne (already surrendered), he had those divisions available without any slightest change in other phases of plans.[4]

Your letter gives me my first intimation that Bradley had fought a battle throughout the war to avoid the "Montgomery pressures, aided and abetted by the SHAEF staff." I was the individual who accepted Bradley as one of my fine subordinates in Africa, had brought him along successfully through the posts of Deputy Corps Commander, Corps Commander, Army Commander, and Army Group Commander. During all that time, we conferred frequently and intimately—I never before thought that he had any resentment toward SHAEF or felt that he was put in the position of fighting anybody else.

Don't forget that it is always popular to represent oneself as being "against the furriners." Nevertheless, I can give you no possible hint as to the motivating causes for writing about doubts, fears, suspicions, and resentments that none of us—at the time—knew existed.[5]

At least, I can say this much: Not only was there never any complaint made to me throughout the war as to your abilities as G-3, but, on the contrary, commanders and staffs alike spoke of you only in terms of highest admiration and respect. (When you come down to it, this applied to Jock, also; as I write, my memory cannot bring back a single instance of the entire war when my planning or operational staff was alleged to be faulty or lacking in quality.)[6]

Yours is the third letter that has come to my attention that has been inspired by the same book. As you point out in your letter, it is completely out of character for Brad to engage in the business of beclouding or damaging the reputation of his friends. Of course, it is possible that the book was largely "ghosted" or that publishers, in their anxiety to promote dissension and criticism as a sales factor, egged on the author into statements that otherwise might never have been made.[7]

In any event, you can be perfectly certain that every associate of yours in SHAEF felt toward you only the highest in admiration, respect, and affection. There was never the slightest doubt as to your complete loyalty, your energy, and your professional qualifications. If someone is to rise up and say that the SHAEF personnel was not qualified to judge in such matters, the obvious answer is that, after all, we did accomplish what we were sent to Europe to do. Moreover, we did it far more expeditiously, with far less cost in life and treasure, than even the most optimistic dared hope for in the spring of '44. If SHAEF had been comprised only of a bunch of lunkheads, I doubt that this result could have come about.

I most clearly understand and deeply sympathize with your distress. The only thing that I can say is that, if, at any time, I can bear witness to your soldierly qualifications and to my complete and intense satisfaction with your services during the war, I shall be more than happy to do so. After all, I selected and retained in important wartime posts, *both* you and Bradley. If my judgment was right in one place, it must have been at least passable in the other.[8]

With warm personal regard, *Cordially*

[1] Bull was commandant of the National War College in Washington, D.C. (see Galambos, *Columbia University*, no. 1043).

[2] On this day Eisenhower met with nine people, the discussions lasting through lunch. In the afternoon the General played golf with Bradley and then attended a dinner for him (see appointment calendar; and EM, Subject File, Entertaining). For background on Bradley and his recent visit see nos. 50, n. 5, and 176, n. 1.

On May 31 (EM) Bull had written Eisenhower concerning Bradley's recently published war memoir *A Soldier's Story* and the excerpts from the book published in *Life* magazine on April 9, pp. 82–90; April 16, pp. 90–94; April 23, pp. 88–94; and April 30, pp. 56–58. Bull, who had been an assistant chief of staff with SHAEF during World War II, told Eisenhower that he was confused because Bradley depicted him "not only as your thoroughly stupid G–3 but also as one disloyal to American interests." He was surprised that "such damaging conclusions" could be drawn "from our loyal and honest efforts."

Bradley had written about an incident involving Bull on the night the Remagen Bridge was captured, March 7, 1945. Bull was depicted as unenthusiastic; to Bull "Remagen was nothing more than an unwelcome intruder in the neatly ordered SHAEF plan" (see Bradley's books, *A Soldier's Story*, pp. 510–18, and *A General's Life*, pp. 405–12; see also *Life*, Apr. 30, 1951, pp. 64, 66). As Bull explained to Eisenhower, his concern had not been to "interfere with an accomplished fact . . . but rather to learn through him [Bradley] how this new action would affect your over-all plans." Bull suggested several reasons for the misunderstanding and for the manner in which Bradley had singled him out to be the "SHAEF whipping boy."

[3] Eisenhower was agreeing with Bull's comment that the " 'holier than thou' tone of most war books is to be expected" (on Eisenhower's own experiences in writing a war memoir see Galambos, *Columbia University*, nos. 82, 83, and 114).

[4] Eisenhower's account of the evening the Remagen Bridge was captured is in *Crusade in Europe*, pp. 378–81, 392; see also Chandler, *War Years*, no. 2319; and Memorandum for Record, March 9, 1945, in EM, Bull Corr.

[5] In his letter Bull had mentioned Bradley's "well concealed" resentment. When Bull had visited Bradley recently to discuss the book, Bradley had expressed surprise that Bull felt the Remagen Bridge story to be damaging to his reputation. Bradley explained that the story was told "to emphasize the struggle he had throughout the war to fight off the Montgomery pressures, aided and abetted by the SHAEF staff in our alleged effort to support the 'British' plan" (on Bradley during the war see Chandler, *War Years*; on Anglo-American relations see no. 199 in this volume; and on Field Marshal Bernard L. Montgomery's relationship with Bradley see Bradley, *A Soldier's Story*, pp. 209–10, 299–300, 355, 487–89; Montgomery, *The Memoirs of Field-Marshal the Viscount Montgomery of Alamein, K.G.* [Cleveland and New York, 1958], pp. 272, 285–87; and Chalfont, *Montgomery of Alamein*, pp. 205, 226–27, 264–67, 322–23).

[6] Bull had become G–3 at SHAEF in 1944 (see Chandler, *War Years*, nos. 225 and 2271; and Chandler and Galambos, *Occupation, 1945*, no. 389). Jock was General John Francis Martin Whiteley, Bull's assistant G–3 at SHAEF. Bull had written

the General that Whiteley had actually been the person Bradley admitted he distrusted (on Whiteley see Galambos, *Chief of Staff*, no. 623, and *Columbia University*, nos. 213 and 568; and Bradley and Blair, *A General's Life*, pp. 362-63, 388-89).

[7] The three letters Eisenhower mentions were probably the ones he had received from Dempsey, Bradley, and Montgomery (see no. 199; and in EM, Bradley to Eisenhower, May 22, 1951, and Montgomery to Eisenhower, May 31, 1951). Bradley's war memoir had been "ghosted" by his aide Lieutenant Colonel Chester Bayard Hansen (see Galambos, *Columbia University*, no. 834; and Bradley and Blair, *A General's Life*, pp. 9, 138, 584, 638).

[8] On SHAEF personnel see Chandler, *War Years*, nos. 1701 and 2125; Chandler and Galambos, *Occupation, 1945*, nos. 151 and 177; and Eisenhower, *Crusade in Europe*, pp. 211, 220, 285-86, 433-35. On June 22 (EM) Bull wrote to thank Eisenhower for his reply.

204   *Eisenhower Mss.*

To Philip Young   *June 5, 1951*

Dear Phil: We shall be on the look-out for you when you, Faith, and the children reach the Continent. I truly hope that, by that time, we shall have a home of our own where we can spend a long evening or two together, talking over things that are of such tremendous interest to us both.[1]

Every mail brings me a new report on your first conference at the Assembly. Even those that contain criticisms—such as the one from Arthur Sulzberger—are basically nothing less than glowing in their general tenor. All this must be a great satisfaction to you and Lew Douglas.[2]

With respect to Arthur Sulzberger's feelings about publicity, he is, of course, such an expert in the field that every idea of his deserves the fullest consideration. Yet I am anxious that he does not miss the point that one of the ways in which we hope to differentiate the Assembly from other round table discussions is that its results would be promptly and widely disseminated. Just to produce another study and have it gather dust on a library shelf has no appeal for me. So, while I would go along with him in all his efforts to keep the thing dignified and serious, I would certainly not want to agree to anything that would tend to limit or narrow the field that should profit from the work.[3]

Incidentally, I am hopeful that, when your formal report goes out to some of the people who have been our supporters, they will be inspired to put us down for *annual* participation in their public service expenditures.[4]

I doubt that you can understand how deeply grateful I am to you for your brilliant work in bringing the Assembly along this far. You will always, of course, be one of the principal figures in its policy-making and in its operation. Nevertheless, I hope that, by this time, you have identified the person that you want to secure as your full-time Manager and Director. I wish you were two persons so that you could be both that Director and the Dean of the Business School. Since I suppose your first love will always be with the Business School, it will be the other job that will have to get along with a man of lesser ability—but, for God's sake, don't take any second-rater.[5]

My love to Faith and the children, and warm regard to yourself.
Cordially

P.S. I must confess I am somewhat astounded that no one used any of your recreation facilities. Much as I like to argue, I think I would have gone fishing on the lake, even if I had to go after Bob Kleberg finished his champagne supper.[6]

[1] In a letter of May 30 (EM) Young had informed the General that he, his wife Faith Adams Young, and their daughters Faith and Shirley would be sailing for Europe on June 13 (on Young see no. 202). For background on the Eisenhowers' long delay in finding a permanent home in France see nos. 180, n. 5, 183, n. 5, and 207, n. 3; on the Youngs' visit see no. 220, n. 4.

[2] For background on Columbia University's American Assembly see no. 201. On Arthur Sulzberger's letter to Young see no. 202; and n. 3 below.

[3] In his letter of May 29 (EM, Sulzberger Corr.) Sulzberger had congratulated Young on the Assembly's success and suggested several possible improvements for the next conference, including a decrease in the amount of publicity sought. According to Sulzberger, "the Assembly offers authority rather than spot news," and public sessions of the conference and daily press handouts on the proceedings had detracted from the seriousness of the gathering. In sending a copy of this letter to Eisenhower, Sulzberger had remarked that the Assembly "is not the place where headlines should be made and it is not the place in which to promote the development campaign of . . . Columbia University . . ." (see Sulzberger to Eisenhower, May 30, 1951, EM). On the Assembly see no. 201.

[4] On Eisenhower's efforts to obtain financial support for the Assembly see Galambos, *Columbia University*.

[5] While Young would continue as Executive Director of the Assembly until 1953, General Foods executive and Deputy Administrator of the Defense Production Administration Edwin T. Gibson would be named Associate Director of the Assembly in April 1952 (see no. 47; Gibson to Eisenhower, Mar. 31, 1952, EM; EM, Young Corr.; and *New York Times*, Apr. 14, 1952).

[6] For background on the recreational facilities see Galambos, *Columbia University*, nos. 844 and 1039; and no. 87 in this volume. Young had mentioned that Texas rancher Robert Justus Kleberg, Jr. (see *ibid.*, no. 623), had "felt an urge for champagne about 11 o'clock at night." For other letters criticizing the Assembly see EM, Young Corr., esp. Hamilton A. Long to Eisenhower, May 23, 1951. For developments see no. 220.

Lawrence Whiting (Chicago)[1] and Clare Francis both came to see me today.[2] The same story on the political side. One thing is certain. The average U.S. citizen is confused—if not fearful and afraid. Otherwise, there'd be no feeling that I should get into the political field.[3] The feeling is of course not so widespread as my informants would have me believe (a human generalizes quickly from a few incidents) but even its meager existence is disappointing![4]

[1] American Furniture Mart Building Company president Lawrence Harley Whiting had served on the staff of General John Joseph Pershing (see Galambos, *Columbia University*, no. 119) during World War I and had been in the War Department's Personnel Division from 1941 to 1945. Presently working as a writer on world military systems for the Defense Department, Whiting had been traveling in Europe since April, investigating the military/industrial capacities of the various nations. He had met with Eisenhower and General Gruenther this morning and reported on his recent visits to Germany, Austria, and Turkey (see appointment calendar; and "Whiting Survey and Report #1," in EM, Miscellaneous Corr., Whiting).

[2] Clarence Francis (see no. 8, n. 1) had seen the General during a separate appointment this morning (see appointment calendar). The General Foods executive, who was then serving as chairman of a Defense Department civilian committee on military training installations, discussed the possibility of visiting NATO training facilities with Eisenhower and other SHAPE personnel (for background see no. 134, n. 6. See also the following document; and Francis to Eisenhower, Apr. 4, 24, 1951, EM).

[3] For discussions of the foreign and domestic crises confronting the nation at this time and of public attitudes toward the Truman Administration see Donovan, *Tumultuous Years*; see also nos. 5, n. 2, 67, 75, and 131. On the burgeoning Eisenhower-for-President movement see Parmet, *Eisenhower and the American Crusades*, pp. 7-11, 16-19, 30-44; and nos. 195 and 196.

[4] For other SHAPE visitors concerned with Eisenhower's candidacy see, for example, nos. 308, 440, and 538. For developments see nos. 587 and 678; Lyon, *Portrait of the Hero*, pp. 417-18, 428-39; and Ambrose, *Eisenhower*, vol. I, *Soldier, General of the Army, President-Elect*, pp. 500-528.

206

Eisenhower Mss.

TO ANNA MARIE ROSENBERG

June 5, 1951

Dear Anna:[1] Clarence Francis came in today. He is a friend of mine from my New York days.[2] Right now, he is discussing some business with General Lanham, the man who used to be Head of I&E in the Army. We are trying to determine whether there is anything in connection with his Advisory Commission work that he would like to do or see here, either among American troops or those of our Allies. You may be sure that, if there is any way in which we can help him, it will be done instantly.[3]

Incidentally, I think it might be good for a lot of us to know something of the austerity of the ordinary European training camp. Recreational and entertainment features are exceedingly meager, often non-existent. There are no swimming pools, no tennis courts, no golf courses, but occasionally there is a vacant field on which soldiers can kick around a soccer football. Strangely enough, in one or two of these camps, I have found existing a most surprising esprit de corps.[4]

General Bradley is here for a few days. This morning, he is meeting with the French Chiefs of Staff.[5]

With warm personal regard,[6] *Cordially*

[1] Since 1950 Rosenberg had been the Assistant Secretary of Defense in charge of Manpower (for background see Galambos, *Columbia University*, no. 1083).

[2] In a letter of May 15 (EM) Rosenberg had written that a Citizens Advisory Committee on Military Training Installations, chaired by Clarence Francis, had been working with the Defense Department; she suggested that Eisenhower contact Francis to "consult with some of your people or visit [NATO] installations" (for background see no. 134, n. 6; on Francis's visit with Eisenhower see the preceding document).

[3] Brigadier General Charles T. Lanham, SHAPE Chief of Public Information, had been Chief of the Army's Information and Education Division from 1945 until 1948 (for background see no. 141, n. 4). On June 8 Lanham would inform Eisenhower that he had passed the General's views on the work of Francis's committee on to Rosenberg with a request that the information be conveyed to Francis (see Memorandum, Lanham to Eisenhower, EM, Rosenberg Corr.). There is no further correspondence in EM concerning Francis's committee.

[4] On the training of the European NATO forces see Paul J. Black, "Training Our Allied under MDAP," *Army Information Digest* 5, no. 12 (1950), 14–18; and George H. Olmsted, "Advancing Mutual Security," *ibid.* 7, no. 7 (1952), 11–16. For Eisenhower's comments on European morale see, for example, nos. 153, 158, 388, and 404.

[5] On Bradley's visit to SHAPE see no. 176, n. 1.

[6] Rosenberg would come to Europe in early August for manpower and personnel discussions with Eisenhower and for inspection tours of U.S. forces (see appointment calendar; and EM, Rosenberg Corr., esp. Rosenberg to Eisenhower, July 13, 1951).

207   *Eisenhower Mss.*

To KENNETH DALE WELLS   *June 6, 1951*

Dear Ken:[1] Your report on "Our Freedom in Action" is a good one. After going all through it, no doubt remains in my mind as to the excellence of the job you did with the school program. I congratulate you.[2]

As to the Black Angus, I think that we will be all set for the steaks and roasts by early fall. We hope to be in a house—now being prepared for us—by the first of July. Thereafter, we will get an adequate deep freeze, and by September *should* be able to take the packages. When that time comes, I will take up details with you and arrange transportation. It was wonderful of you to renew your suggestion.[3]

Mamie joins me in warm regard to you both and, with me, requests that when you run into any of your friends, who are ours also, you convey to them our best wishes. This includes, of course, Dr. and Mrs. Johnson, Mr. and Mrs. Hutton, and so on, and so on.[4] *Cordially*

[1] Wells (B.S. Northwestern 1930), an economist who had been associated with the Freedoms Foundation since 1949, had become president of the organization in March of this year.

[2] In a letter of May 25 (EM) Wells had enclosed for Eisenhower's review a case study in education titled "Our Freedoms in Action" (no copy in EM). Eisenhower had presided over the first Freedoms Foundation awards ceremony at Valley Forge, Pennsylvania, in November 1949; in February 1951 he had been awarded top prize for an address given in April 1950 to members of the Associated Press in New York City (for further background on Eisenhower's participation in Freedoms Foundation activities see Galambos, *Columbia University*, nos. 600 and 712; Eisenhower to Wells, May 25, 1951, and Wells to Eisenhower, Feb. 4, 1949, and Oct. 17, 1950, EM; and *New York Times*, Nov. 22, 1949).

[3] Wells had offered Eisenhower a gift of home-butchered beef from cattle kept at his farm in Valley Forge, Pennsylvania. In a postscript to his letter Wells had said, "Your black angus heifer is doing well in my pasture. I'll transform it into steaks and roasts, packaged for your freezer whenever you tire of continental cooking." The Eisenhowers were waiting at this time for renovations to be completed on their home in Marnes-la-Coquette, where they would move in August (see no. 314, n. 1). On November 2 (EM) Eisenhower would write Wells again, telling him that storage facilities were limited at home and that he needed time to "develop a plan." For developments see no. 496, n. 6.

[4] Mrs. Wells was the former Ruth Van Allen. The others were Robert Livingston Johnson and his wife, the former Anna Talcott Rathbone, and Edward F. and Dorothy Hutton. Johnson had been president of Temple University since 1941 (see Galambos, *Chief of Staff*, no. 703). Hutton, an investment banker, was a special partner with E. F. Hutton and Company and a director of the Chrysler and General Foods corporations. Both were associated with the Freedoms Foundation, Johnson as a director and Hutton as chairman of the board of trustees.

208   *Eisenhower Mss.*

To John Leslie Hall, Jr.   *June 6, 1951*

Dear Hall:[1] It would seem from this distance that the chances should be better than average for one of my senior staff officers finding a necessary chore in the United States sometime between next September and the following January. In fact, by that time, some of them will probably welcome any kind of an opportunity that they can even remotely class as a necessity. So I shall put your invitation on the calendar and, if you will remind me about the matter in late summer, possibly we can plan the matter definitely. If at all possible, I shall detail General Gruenther to carry out the assignment.[2]

Within a matter of an hour, I am to take off for Normandy where I am to participate in several ceremonies later in the day commemorating the landings in 1944. It would be most fitting if you could accompany me.[3]

Admiral Kirk was here a few days ago, but remained for a brief visit only.[4]

With warm personal regard,[5] *Sincerely*

[1] Vice-Admiral Hall was presently commandant of the Armed Forces Staff College in Norfolk, Virginia (for background see Chandler, *War Years*, nos. 716, 1092, 1191, and 1885).

[2] In a letter of May 29 (EM) Hall had requested that an officer from SHAPE address the next staff college class sometime between September 1, 1951, and January 23, 1952. The JCS had founded the college in 1946 to instruct officers of all services in joint operations, and Hall felt that it would be "appropriate and most enlightening" to have a SHAPE officer explain the "planning problems confronting the North Atlantic Treaty Organization" (for background on the college see Chandler and Galambos, *Occupation, 1945*, no. 307; and Galambos, *Chief of Staff*, nos. 682, 938, and 1136). Hall, who specifically mentioned SHAPE C/S Alfred Gruenther as the possible speaker, said "the Faculty and the Student Body would be most fortunate to hear him" (on Gruenther see no. 59, n. 4).

[3] During the late morning the General, members of his staff, and Mrs. Eisenhower would fly to Normandy to participate in ceremonies commemorating the seventh anniversary of the D-day invasion (see Chandler, *War Years*). Beginning in the town of Sainte-Mère-Eglise, where he placed a wreath on the Milestone Zero marker of the "Liberty Highway" and made impromptu remarks, the General and his party proceeded by automobile convoy to the American cemetery at St. Laurent, overlooking Omaha Beach. There Eisenhower inspected a model of the American memorial that was soon to be erected and visited the graves of Brigadier General Theodore Roosevelt, Jr., and Lieutenant General Lesley James McNair (see *ibid.*, nos. 1848 and 1857, respectively). Following photographs and the placing of a wreath by Mrs. Eisenhower, the party drove to Bayeux to participate in ceremonies at the British cemetery there (see itineraries and invitations in EM, Subject File, Trips, Normandy; *New York Times*, June 7, 1951; *International Herald Tribune*, Paris ed., June 6, 7, 1951; and *Washington Post*, June 7, 1951, copy in EM, Subject File, Trips). For background see Galambos, *Columbia University*, nos. 876, 959, and 1037; see also American Battle Monuments Commission, *Normandy American Cemetery and Memorial* (Washington, D.C., 1973).

In his only formal address of the day, Eisenhower told the Bayeux participants that "freedom is not won and forever possessed—it must be re-earned every day in every generation." Praising the efforts and sacrifices of the Allies during the war, he stressed that these nations were once again united to defend freedom and would not permit "those who seek the enslavement of men [to] separate us so that one by one we may be more easily incorporated into the regimented world" (see copies in EM, Subject File, Speeches; and Trips).

[4] For background on Admiral Alan G. Kirk, who had commanded the American Naval Task Force on D-day, see no. 22, n. 2.

[5] Hall would shortly leave his post as commandant to become commander of the Western Sea Frontier, and there is no indication in EM that Gruenther or any other member of the SHAPE senior staff addressed the Armed Forces College between the dates suggested (see *New York Times*, Aug. 2, 1951).

209   *Eisenhower Mss.*

To WILLIAM AVERELL HARRIMAN   *June 7, 1951*
Secret

Dear Averell: Attached hereto is a little squib that came to my notice today.[1] I realize that it would be miraculous if a columnist ever got anything reported accurately, but I am just a trifle amazed that anyone could think of me as "discouraged and disheartened," even a columnist. Moreover, well knowing the destructive influence of a long face around a headquarters such as this, I assure you I have no intention of abandoning the policy that I have followed for years with respect to members of my own staff. It is stated very simply, "Believe in what you are doing or go someplace else."

A large Congressional Committee is to be with us in a day or so.[2] We are arranging for them to meet with ECC,[3] ECA,[4] and all the other fancy-lettered organizations, including SHAPE. I think that Chuck Spofford[5] is actually taking the lead in designing the schedule for the Committee, but, quite naturally, we have a heavy share of its available time.

My staff and I shall most certainly strive to present a balanced and fair picture, attempting to avoid over-emphasis on either the optimistic or the pessimistic side. But I most certainly intend that there shall be no failure on the part of the Committee to understand that, in my conviction, there is no acceptable alternative for the United States to taking the lead in welding the Western nations into a strong security organization. As a consequence of this conviction, every effort of the United States must be to *lead* all these countries into maximum effort, until the security is an accomplished fact.

The difficulty, of course, is to determine the maximum military effort that should be encouraged, or indeed permitted, in any country.

Except in a very limited way, Norway, I believe, should be prevented from doing more, measured in terms of its total cost upon the country, than it is now doing. Standard of living is low, taxes are extremely high (in lower brackets, just about doubling our own, to say nothing of a 10% sales tax), manpower is very short, and the people are holding their own against inflation only by dint of extraordinary and courageous effort.[6]

On the other hand, there are nations that, I feel convinced, can do more. In telling this whole story to the Committee, it is going to be very difficult to be completely honest and still to prevent distortion.

The Air Chiefs of Staff are now meeting in Paris. For the moment, we have only the four representing America, Canada, Britain, and France. Later, they plan to invite all the others in, at least for a thorough orientation. I hope that the Air Chiefs find out how to increase materially the air strength that presently is in sight. Air strength will be extremely important during the next two or three years, during which period there simply will not be available the land forces that can make a satisfactory showing against aggression. Many factors favor the production of this additional air force by the four nations I have just named—in fact, I am not so sure that France should not emphasize ground force—but I am certain that other nations in NATO will have to depend largely upon the four just named for air protection.[7]

We are very busy, and this is probably the last letter I shall write to you before you leave Washington.[8] I wish you were here this evening. I am having both Phil Reed and Al Gruenther for dinner.[9] We'd like you for a fourth. *Cordially*

---

[1] An undated memorandum attached to this letter in EM summarized a newspaper column written by Marquis Childs (see Galambos, *Columbia University*, no. 109). Childs had described Eisenhower as being upset about delays, distractions, and inertia in Washington. According to Childs, Eisenhower feared that lack of progress at home would harm efforts to achieve European collective security.

[2] Eighteen members of the House Foreign Affairs, Armed Services, and Appropriations committees would arrive in Paris on June 9 and spend ten days studying Western European security problems and U.S. aid programs (see Memorandum for General Schuyler, June 5, 1951, and other materials in EM, Subject File, Congressional Visits, 1951. See also *New York Times*, June 9, 10, 1951; and *International Herald Tribune*, Paris ed., June 11, 1951). Eisenhower would meet with the group on June 9 and 18. A transcript of his meeting with the congressmen is in EM, Subject File, Congressional Visits, 1951. For developments see no. 218, n. 16.

[3] European Coordinating Committee (see no. 167, n. 8).

[4] Economic Cooperation Administration (see no. 45, n. 3).

[5] For background on Charles M. Spofford, chairman of both the North Atlantic Council deputies and the European Coordinating Committee, see no. 16, n. 16.

[6] The Norwegian economy was having difficulty coping with the Norwegian rearmament program. In April sales taxes had increased from 6.25 percent to 10 percent on all transactions, and controls on wages, prices, and investments had been instituted to prevent inflation. There was also a labor shortage, which prevented any rapid expansion of Norway's armed forces (Senate Subcommittee on Foreign Relations, *United States Foreign-Aid Programs in Europe: Hearings*, 1951, pp.

96-98, 101-2; Halaby to Chairman, International Security Affairs Committee, Aug. 8, 1951, OS/D, 1951, Clas. Decimal File, 091.7 Europe; State, *Foreign Relations, 1951*, vol. IV, *Europe: Political and Economic Developments, Part I*, pp. 763–64).

[7] At Eisenhower's request, the commanders of the four leading NATO air powers met in Paris on June 7 to plan for the air forces necessary to defend Europe by the target date of 1954 (for background see nos. 172, nn. 2, 3, and 187, n. 2). Their report, dated June 9, would become known as the Paris Plan. The report, based on the requirements stated for the medium-term plan contained in DC 28 (see no. 15, n. 4), outlined measures necessary to raise and support these forces. Included in the study were such topics as training, logistics, the allocation of tasks among the NATO nations, airfield construction, and the fixed installations necessary for establishing communications networks and supply systems. The Paris Plan called for a total of 9,300 active front-line aircraft, of which 1,400 were to be supplied by the United States (*New York Times*, June 12, 15, 1951; Davis to Bradley *et al.*, July 2, 1951, CCS 092 Western Europe [3-12-48], Sec. 85; Gruenther to Marshall, June 15, 1951, Gruenther to Standing Group, June 30, 1951, Burns to Lovett, July 3, 1951, and "United States Forces in Defense of Western Europe," approved June 27, 1951, all in OS/D, 1951, Clas. Numeric File, CD 091.7 Europe). In August, after soliciting comments from the NATO nations, Eisenhower would inform the Standing Group that those nations had professed themselves willing and able to provide a force of 7,293 front-line aircraft by December 1954. This figure, Eisenhower said, was a considerable advance over the 5,769 aircraft envisioned in DC 28 (the MTDP). Eisenhower recommended that a definite schedule to provide these aircraft be drawn up as soon as possible and that NATO begin moving toward the larger force outlined in the Paris Plan (JCS 2073/269, Dec. 28, 1951, CCS 092 Western Europe [3-12-48], Sec. 112).

[8] On Harriman's visit see nos. 191, 218, n. 1, and 251, n. 1.

[9] For background on Philip Reed see nos. 164, n. 1, and 193, n. 1.

210   *Eisenhower Mss.*

To Henry Junior Taylor   *June 7, 1951*

Dear Harry: Your cablegram about Lucius was welcome not only for the news it contained but because it reminded me that I wanted to write you a note.[1] You and Fay often come to our thoughts—we were talking about you just the other evening.[2]

As you can well imagine, my life seems to be, if possible, even more complicated than it has during the past few years. There are great problems to solve in the world, and I think that the dearest wish that any of us ought to have these days is for just a bit more wisdom, each day, to apply to his own share of the whole task of decision. I think it is some vague wish of this kind that helps to remind me, from time to time, how much value I would derive out of a long visit with you.[3]

Mamie joins me in warm greetings to you both. We hope that everything goes well with you and yours.[4] *Cordially*

[1] A writer and former war correspondent, Taylor had cabled Eisenhower on June 6 informing him of the election of their mutual friend Lucius Clay to the board of directors of the General Motors Corporation (see PSW 220, June 6, 1951, EM, same file as document; and *New York Times*, June 5, 1951. On Clay see no. 196; and on Taylor see n. 2 below).

[2] For background on Eisenhower's acquaintance with Taylor see Chandler, *War Years*, no. 2313; and Galambos, *Chief of Staff*, nos. 962 and 1421. Fay was Taylor's wife, the former Olivia Fay Kimbro.

[3] Taylor would visit the General in France on July 9 (see appointment calendar, and Taylor to Eisenhower, 1046, June 27, 1951, both in EM, same file as document).

[4] Eisenhower would send Clay his personal congratulations on this same day (EM, Clay Corr.).

211   *Eisenhower Mss.*

To Charles Vincent McAdam   *June 7, 1951*

Dear Charlie:[1] Thank you very much for your nice note. I shall send off a word of thanks to Mr. Storer immediately. In the meantime, I assure you of my gratitude to you for interesting him in the American Assembly project. You have been a grand friend, both to me and to this proposition which I think is going to mean so much to our country.[2]

I must say that I am astounded by the one hope expressed in your letter—that my game is "below 92." You would have been more reasonable had you said that you hoped it was "below 102." Do you think I have nothing to do except play golf, just as if I were the President of a Newspaper Syndicate?

In spite of the deficiencies of my game, I am counting on having a grand time with Cliff while he is here. Moreover, I am going to try to get him into a schedule that will be good for him physically and give him complete relaxation. I shall try to get him temporary membership in a couple of golf clubs, and fix it up so that he can always have a game, even if he has to play a twosome. I should be able to get out with him at least once a week; the rest of the time, maybe we can work up an occasional bridge game. I have reserved accommodations for him at a very quiet hotel.[3]

Later in the month, I believe that Bill Robinson is also coming. You should consider coming along with him. You know how welcome you would be. (I say this with additional emphasis because, although all of you may rob me on the golf course, I could always have my chance of getting even at the bridge table.)

In any event, thank you again for your great thoughtfulness and helpfulness, and with warm regard to you and yours.[4] *Cordially*

[1] President of the McNaught Syndicate, Inc., since 1930, McAdam was also a member of the Blind Brook and Augusta National golf clubs (see Galambos, *Columbia University*, no. 260; and no. 39, n. 5, in this volume).

[2] McAdam had become a golfing partner of Eisenhower's in New York in 1948, had followed the General's career at Columbia University, and had helped to raise funds for the American Assembly (see Galambos, *Columbia University*, nos. 631 and 1126. See also McAdam to Eisenhower, Dec. 2, 1948, EM; and EM, Subject File, Clubs and Associations, Blind Brook Club). McAdam had written Eisenhower on June 4 (EM) about a twenty-five-hundred-dollar donation to the American Assembly. The donation had been sent to McAdam from his "very dear friend" George Butler Storer, who had been president of the Storer Broadcasting Company since 1927. Storer and McAdam both had homes in Miami Beach, Florida, and belonged to several of the same clubs there.

The General wrote Storer this same day to express his appreciation (see Eisenhower to Storer, June 7, 1951, EM). Although not actively participating in the American Assembly program, Eisenhower told Storer that "its progress remains very close to my heart because I believe that it has very great potentiality for the good of our country. Reports I have received on the first conference . . . reinforce this conviction" (see nos. 201, 202, and 204).

[3] McAdam expressed hope that the General's golf game was "below 92" and his "putting a lot better" (on Eisenhower's golfing see nos. 143, n. 5, 161, and 193).

Cliff Roberts would visit the General from June 10 to July 21 (see no. 217, n. 2). Roberts would stay at the Coque-Hardy, "a quiet place outside the city" (see Roberts to Eisenhower, May 25, 1951, EM). The General's appointment calendar shows that he had dinner with Roberts, Clarence John Schoo, and Freeman F. Gosden at the Coque-Hardy on June 10. Schoo had been vice-president and a member of the executive committee of the Longview Fibre Company since 1929, and Gosden was a writer and producer of the "Amos 'n' Andy" show (see nos. 177 and 193. On Roberts see no. 7; on his health see no. 161, n. 2).

[4] William E. Robinson, executive vice-president and a director of the *New York Herald Tribune*, would visit the General in late June (see nos. 39, n. 1, 217, n. 3, and 265). McAdam would see Eisenhower in Washington in early November, and later that month he and his wife, the former Marguerite Wimby, would visit the General in Paris (see appointment calendar).

Eisenhower added a handwritten note to this letter saying, "Today I took Schooie and Phil Reed to a cleaning!" (on Reed see no. 164, n. 1). According to the General's appointment calendar, he was to play golf with Schoo and Reed on June 8, and this note was probably added after that game.

212   *Eisenhower Mss.*

To Robert Cutler   *June 7, 1951*

Dear Bobby:[1] As you may know, Jerry Persons' arrival in Paris was delayed by almost four months—hence, your personal letter of 19 February which you requested that he carry has just reached me.[2]

Most certainly I understand your dilemma—and with full sympathy, since often I have been confronted by similar decisions. The compelling reasons you cite as origin for your declination are more than sufficient.[3] In my letter and telegram, I merely sought to insure that you knew of my conviction that the job was deserving of the talents and calibre of a man such as yourself.[4] I'll say no more except to thank you for the obviously serious study you gave to the proposition.

With assurance of my continuing respect and admiration, *Cordially*

[1] Cutler was the president and director of the Old Colony Trust Company of Boston (see no. 30). *

[2] The arrival of Major General Wilton B. Persons, an assistant to Eisenhower at SHAPE, had been delayed because of illness (see nos. 157 and 176). In his letter to Eisenhower of February 19 (EM) Cutler had written that he had decided "*not* to accept Cabot's offer." Thomas D. Cabot, Director of the State Department's Office of International Security Affairs, had hoped to persuade Cutler to become his deputy director. For background on this matter see no. 30.

[3] Cutler explained that both business and private commitments would prevent him from accepting any new position. He also said that he was reluctant to accept a post in a new agency about whose policies he held a number of doubts.

[4] Eisenhower's letter is no. 30; the telegram, Eisenhower to Cutler, February 14, 1951, is in EM. Cutler would become Special Assistant for National Security Affairs in Eisenhower's first presidential administration (see Lyon, *Portrait of the Hero*, p. 502).

213   *Eisenhower Mss.*

To MARCELLUS HARTLEY DODGE   *June 7, 1951*
Personal and confidential

Dear Marcy:[1] It was fine to have your letter. As you know, I have always maintained that a large, modern university has very definite need for two men in high executive positions, so, discussing your suggestion in the abstract, I am very much in favor of what you apparently are trying to do.[2]

There is one possibility that I think you should consider every time you are faced with a need for accomplishing any organizational revision at Columbia, particularly in the highest echelons. This possibility is that it could be such a long time before I am released from my current job that Columbia would be forced, in justice to itself, to name a new Chief Executive. If my absence becomes prolonged unconscionably, the Trustees are going to have this problem squarely in their laps. If they do, I personally think they should try to name such an individual from among the present Columbia "family." They will want to be sure that they have not, in the meantime, created a situation that would cause needless embarrassment either to themselves or to any of the valuable members of the staff.

The possibility of having to replace me is not bringing up any new idea. Several times, I spoke about it in Trustee meetings. I repeat it here merely to indicate that some degree of flexibility should be preserved during these highly uncertain times.[3]

I shall, of course, be glad to discuss with Kirk anything that he wants to bring up concerning the University; as you request, I shall not initiate any conversation that has to do with the change of assignment for Krout.[4]

I scarcely need to assure you that Columbia is often and earnestly in my thoughts. I have had the most glowing reports on the first conference of the American Assembly; in fact, I have just finished writing a note to a man who I learned has donated $2,500 to its future support. I would regard it as a great privilege if I could come to Morningside Heights, if for only one day, to meet and talk with all the Trustees about Columbia's future.[5]

Last week, Doug Black was over here for a couple of days, and we discussed many things connected with the University.[6] I most certainly hope that I will always be able to have some kind of vicarious or tenuous connection with the University so that I can class myself as one of the "family."

Mamie joins me in warmest regards to you and yours.[7] *Cordially*

[1] Dodge, a New York businessman, was a member of Columbia University's board of trustees (see no. 6).

[2] On June 2 (EM) Dodge had written Eisenhower about promoting John A. Krout to the post of vice-president and provost at Columbia, to enable him to be of greater help to acting president Grayson L. Kirk (for background on Krout and Kirk see no. 31). This change was supported by Dodge, who added that on Eisenhower's return he would probably welcome the "extra help which this would give to the whole work."

[3] Eisenhower believed that his role as nominal president of Columbia was becoming detrimental to the university because it limited the acting president's ability to make needed changes (see no. 184). For developments see nos. 229, 325, and 370.

[4] Eisenhower's appointment calendar indicates that he met with Kirk on June 14.

[5] Eisenhower would not visit Columbia University again until June 1952 (see nos. 738 and 767). On the American Assembly's first conference see nos. 201, 202, and 204; on the twenty-five-hundred-dollar donation see no. 211.

[6] According to his appointment calendar, the General had seen Douglas M. Black on May 15, 19, and 27. Black was also a Columbia trustee (see nos. 168 and 184).

[7] Dodge was married to the former Ethel Geraldine Rockefeller.

To Mary Woodward Lasker   *June 8, 1951*

Dear Mrs. Lasker:[1] The article made interesting reading. Winston has had to learn much since he wrote it in 1939, but the interesting thing is that he did *not* miscalculate the probable reaction of his own people to bombing.[2]

It was nice to see you and Mr. Lasker again. My best wishes to you both—and my grateful thanks for sending the article.[3] *Sincerely*

[1] Lasker (A.B. Radcliffe 1923), a former art dealer, in 1942 had established the Albert and Mary Lasker Foundation with her husband, Albert Davis Lasker, a retired advertising executive (see Galambos, *Columbia University*, no. 225). This letter to the Laskers was handwritten by Eisenhower.

[2] On May 28 Mrs. Lasker had sent Eisenhower a copy of an article they had recently discussed (EM). The article, written by Winston Churchill and entitled "Let the Tyrant Criminals Bomb!" had appeared in the January 14, 1939, edition of *Collier's*, pp. 12-13, 36. Churchill had warned against allowing Germany to rearm, asserting that "Herr Hitler has now ordered the German air force to be doubled by 1942. . . ." Citing the Spanish Civil War as an example, Churchill expressed the opinion that air bombing was limited in its destructive capabilities and would cause those being bombed to fight with renewed strength. For Churchill's view, in retrospect, of World War II see his memoir *The Second World War*.

[3] According to the General's appointment calendar, he had met with the Laskers on May 17.

Diary   *June 11, 1951*

I am coming to believe that Europe's security problem is never going to be solved satisfactorily until there exists a U.S. of Europe— to include all countries now in Nato; West Germany & (I think) Sweden, Spain, & Jugoslavia, with Greece definitely in if Jugoslavia is. (If *necessary*, U.K. could be omitted)[1]

It seems scarcely necessary to enumerate the problems that arise out of or are exaggerated by the division of West Europe into so many sovereign nations.

Norway is short of manpower,[2] Italy way over. Italy has excess productive capacity in vehicles & planes—many others have none at all![3] France & Germany (the key powers of the region) are on opposite sides in many problems because of French hatred for the Boche as well as the fear of a restored western Germany.[4] Each nation watches its neighbor to see that the neighbor's contribution to the common security is at least equal to the first nation's ratio—and none is ever so convinced!

As Shape I have no ministries to take over ministerial functions in finance, construction, policy, etc etc. The weak, unarticulated mechanism that tries to serve as the NATO overhead is futile.[5]

I think that the real and bitter problems of today would instantly come within the limits of[6] capabilities in solving them if we had this single govt!

Moreover, I believe *inspired* leaders could put it across. But everyone is too cautious, too fearful, too lazy and too ambitious (personally).

So many advantages would flow from such a union that it [is] a tragedy for the whole human race that it is not done at once.

American help—which could soon be radically reduced both in amount and duration—would quickly render such an organization immune to attack! With this one problem solved—all lesser ones could soon disappear. I could write a *volume* on the subject.

Local govts would not necessarily be identical. It *would* be necessary that each adopt & observe a simple "bill of rights." Socialist Sweden would live alongside a capitalist Germany, but [with] the elimination of trade barriers & all economic & political restraint on free movements[7]

[1] Eisenhower's concern with the problems and possibilities of European unity had begun while he was Chief of Staff of the Army (see Galambos, *Chief of Staff*, no. 2023, and *Columbia University*, nos. 1009 and 1051). For background on the growing American support for European integration see Ernst H. Van Der Beugel, *From Marshall Aid to Atlantic Partnership: European Integration as a Concern of American Foreign Policy* (Amsterdam, 1966); Michael J. Hogan, "American Marshall Planners and the Search for a European Neocapitalism," *American Historical Review* 90, no. 1 (1985), 44–72; Max Beloff, *The United States and the Unity of Europe* (Washington, D.C., 1963); Hogan, *The Marshall Plan*; and State, *Foreign Relations, 1951*, vol. IV, *Europe: Political and Economic Developments, Part I*, pp. 1–138. Of the nations listed by Eisenhower, only the United Kingdom was a member of NATO; Greece, however, would soon join the Atlantic alliance (see nos. 148, n. 8, and 233, n. 5). For background on Yugoslavia see no. 142, n. 16; on Spain see no. 240, n. 5; and on West Germany see no. 186. Although not a member of NATO, neutralist Sweden had advocated greater European integration (see State, *Foreign Relations, 1951*, vol. IV, *Europe: Political and Economic Developments, Part I*, pp. 1–4, 872–73). Eisenhower had met with Dutch Foreign Minister Dirk Stikker, a noted internationalist, on June 9 (see no. 218, n. 2).

[2] For background on Norway's difficulties in creating an effective defense force see nos. 16 and 209, n. 6. See also Memorandum of Conversation with Norwegian Government and Defense Officials, January 13, 1951, EM, Subject File, Trips, SHAPE no. 1.

[3] For background on the situation in Italy see nos. 18, n. 1, 153, and 156. Italy had nearly two million unemployed workers and a large number of excess employees in its manufacturing plants (Senate Subcommittee on Foreign Relations, *United States Foreign-Aid Programs in Europe: Hearings*, 1951, pp. 179–81; see also Memorandum of Conversation, Sept. 26, 1951, OS/D, 1951, Clas. Decimal File, CD 092 Italy). In August Eisenhower would urge Italy to utilize its excess production capacity for the manufacture of munitions (see no. 339).

[4] For background on the questions of German rearmament and the proposed European Army see nos. 186 and 252. For Eisenhower's earlier involvement with the German problem see Galambos, *Columbia University*, nos. 1045, 1064, and 1129.

[5] Eisenhower was becoming increasingly critical of the support given him by the Council of Deputies (see, for example, nos. 77 and 167). On June 20 Douglas MacArthur II, Counselor of the American Embassy in France and Eisenhower's political adviser, would tell the State Department that Eisenhower felt that the Council of Deputies did not "have the organization, terms of reference, and level of representation which make for the most effective action" (State, *Foreign Relations, 1951*, vol. III, *European Security and the German Question, Part I*, pp. 188–90). For developments see no. 238.

[6] At this point in his handwritten diary entry Eisenhower deleted the word *prompt*.

[7] Eisenhower did not complete this sentence in his diary. He may have intended to end the sentence with the words "would be necessary." In his July 3 address to the English Speaking Union in London Eisenhower would call for greater European unity (see no. 252, n. 2). At that time Eisenhower said, "Free men, facing the spectre of political bondage, are crippled by artificial bonds that they themselves have forged, and they alone can loosen." A copy of this speech is in EM, Subject File, Trips, SHAPE no. 9.

216   *Eisenhower Mss.*

To Alfred Maximilian Gruenther   *June 11, 1951*
Confidential

Memorandum for Chief of Staff: Through Bishop Griffiths, the Cardinal has extended an invitation to me to address the Alfred E. Smith dinner on 18 October.[1] Apparently, the Cardinal attaches the most enormous importance to this dinner, and I was informed by the Bishop that Clay's return to address the meeting during the Berlin Airlift made a most profound impression upon the United States.[2] Unfortunately, the Cardinal has to have an answer soon, and I have promised to send an answer within a week.

Would you please talk to me about it.[3]

[1] Roman Catholic Bishop James Henry Griffiths, Chancellor of the Military Ordinariate, Army-Navy Diocese, had visited Eisenhower this afternoon. The meeting, which had been arranged through Francis Joseph Cardinal Spellman (for background see Galambos, *Chief of Staff*, no. 599), concerned the role of the Church in the fight against communism and the possibility of receiving Catholic encouragement in urging Allied women to join volunteer service corps (see Spellman to Eisenhower, Apr. 28, 1951, in EM, Spellman Corr.; and Weaver to Schulz, May 16, 1951, in EM, Griffiths Corr.). The Alfred Emanuel Smith Memorial Foundation, which had been founded in memory of the former New York governor and 1928 Democratic presidential candidate, was then building a new wing onto New York's St. Vincent's Hospital (see *New York Times*, Oct. 20, 1950). Spellman, president of the foundation, had also invited Eisenhower to address the group's

1948 fourth annual dinner (see Spellman to Eisenhower, July 8, 1948, and Eisenhower's declination, July 16, 1948, in EM, Spellman Corr.).

[2] In 1948 General Lucius Clay (see no. 46), then Commander in Chief, European Command, had addressed the Smith Foundation dinner on American efforts to break the Communist grip on Europe (see *New York Times*, Oct. 22, 1948; and Lucius D. Clay, *The Papers of General Lucius D. Clay, Germany, 1945-1949*, ed. by Jean Edward Smith, 2 vols. [Bloomington, Ind., 1974], vol. II, pp. 789, 896-97). For background on the Soviet blockade of Berlin and the resultant Allied airlift see Galambos, *Columbia University*, nos. 183, 303, and 375; and Clay, *Papers*, vol. II, pp. 607, 701-2, 707-8, 736, 847, 852, 878-79, 890-91, 1169-70).

[3] On Eisenhower's responses to the invitation and Gruenther's assistance with one of the replies see no. 245.

217   *Eisenhower Mss.*

To George Edward Allen   *June 11, 1951*

Dear George: Two notes from you, one dated the 4th and the other the 7th, remind me principally to tell you that your partner, Mr. Alvord, was here the other day. He informed me that his success as a lawyer is assured; apparently, it has become widely known that you are his partner.[1]

Cliff Roberts and Barry Leithead (the latter, Head of Cluett Peabody) are here for a few days. Actually, I hope to keep Cliff on rather indefinitely if the weather stays nice and he likes our golf courses. I am arranging for him to get cards because I personally have little time for golf, and I would like to have him play a few holes every day.[2]

I have word that Bob Woodruff is soon to come over, as are Bill Robinson, Jay Gould, and others of the old Augusta gang. Slats Slater will be here late in the summer.[3]

I still don't understand why you cannot ever take a nice long vacation, on the order of four or five weeks. If you and Mary would just say you are both worn out and have to go to Paris for a rest—especially in the night spots—everybody would understand thoroughly. Frankly, I'm getting a little tired of your weak excuses. Give my love to Mary.[4]

Devotedly

[1] Eisenhower's close friend Allen (see no. 9, n. 2) was counsel with the Washington, D.C., law firm of Alvord and Alvord. In his letter of June 4 (EM) Allen had informed the General that the firm's head, Ellworth Chapman Alvord (LL.B. Columbia 1921), was then on his way to Paris and would be coming to see Eisenhower. The two had met the afternoon of June 7.

[2] For background on Eisenhower's friend and investment counselor Clifford Roberts and on his reasons for vacationing in Europe see nos. 7, 161, 177, and 193. On Barry T. Leithead, president and director of Cluett, Peabody & Company, Inc., an American clothing manufacturer, see Galambos, *Columbia University*, no.

1068. Roberts would remain in France until July 21 (see Eisenhower to Frank Willard, July 21, 1951, EM).

[3] Eisenhower's friends Robert Woodruff (see no. 143) and Ellis Slater (see no. 161) would visit the General in early July and late August, respectively (see appointment calendar and individual correspondence in EM). The "Augusta gang," members of the Augusta National Golf Club, were: William Robinson, Jay Gould, Frank Willard, and former boxing champion James ("Gene") Tunney, who would come to France together on June 29 for a brief visit (see Robinson to Eisenhower, June 6, 1951, and Robinson to Schulz, PSWA 375, June 25, 1951, both in EM, Robinson Corr.).

[4] Allen would arrive in Paris on June 17, but he would not be accompanied by his wife Mary (see nos. 9, n. 2, and 180, n. 2).

218   *Eisenhower Mss.*

To WILLIAM AVERELL HARRIMAN   *June 12, 1951*
Top secret

Dear Averell: While I had thought I would not send you another letter prior to your arrival in Paris,[1] I have recently had a couple very interesting conversations that might be of some interest to you. One was with Foreign Minister Stikker of Holland, the other with Foreign Minister Van Zeeland of Belgium.[2]

The first of these conversations was held at my request, Mr. Stikker coming to my office from The Hague last Saturday morning.[3] The reason I wanted to talk to him was to urge him to take some kind of position of leadership in building up European morale, especially its determination to carry through to a success the plans of NATO.

Before asking him to come see me, I had heard that he was very keenly aware of the need for developing and sustaining this kind of morale—but felt that accomplishment would demand positive and inspired leadership from Great Britain.[4] My purpose was to convince him that *he* could proceed to build up an international team in Western Europe that could do the job.

We had a long talk, during the latter part of which Milton Katz was present.[5] There is no doubt that Mr. Stikker is anxious to see a growing fervor in Western Europe and a greater readiness on the part of all countries to contribute heavily and more urgently to the success of NATO. There is likewise no doubt that he feels that the British Government should be the natural leader in this effort and that he is deeply disappointed that that leadership is not forthcoming. This, he feels, in spite of the fact that he knows that Great Britain is already contributing, on the material side, an amount that our own ECA and other officials believe should *not* be exceeded at this time—in other words, that the United Kingdom is flat-out in support of NATO.[6] But, beyond this, he feels that Britain should provide an inspirational type of leadership which he said disappeared from the Labor Government with the departure of Cripps and the death of Bevin.[7] My effort was to convince him that, recognizing this gap in the kind of leadership he thinks Europe should have, he should get busy in building up a group of people who, by their combined influence, would provide an effective substitute. I shall be interested to watch his progress; I am quite sure of his deep-seated concern and, therefore, of his readiness to do what he believes he can. I hope that I gave him real self-confidence.[8]

Mr. Van Zeeland came to see me on his own initiative. But, though we talked about many subjects of his choosing, I seized the opportunity to give him the same kind of speech that I did Mr. Stikker. In response to Mr. Van Zeeland's specific questions, I gave him opinions that:

a. The NATO superior council (Foreign and Defense Ministers, in person) should meet at intervals not greater than three months.[9] Moreover, I said that this should be done even if there were no definitely prepared agenda; Parliaments in each of the free countries meet in spite of the fact that there is no carefully prepared agenda in advance. We need to keep together and to keep NATO matters high in our concern.

b. I would always be glad to accept a so-called "European Army" in my command, but that, since I had no administrative power or responsibilities, ample provision would have to be made for the performance of all ministerial functions—pay, supply, discipline, and so on.[10]

c. I should like to see instituted a system encouraging the production of military equipment in *all* NATO countries. I agreed to a suggestion of his that, if NATO authorities should prepare a list of military equipment to be exchanged among countries without custom duties, it would be helpful. I further concurred in his idea that these exchanges should include every kind of item necessary to an Army, even involving such types of things as food and clothing. He went into some detail as to methods of financing the balances left at the end of each year. He suggested long-term credits guaranteed by the twelve nations. So far as I can see, his idea made sense in that it not only would encourage production in each country, according to the particular capabilities of that country, but might be a helpful step in breaking down economic barriers, which now hold these countries so definitely apart. There were other features to this particular idea, all of which I feel sure will eventually be submitted by him to the highest council.[11]

d. I agree with him that the intricate policy and administrative machinery of NATO is not going to function successfully unless the Governments accord to it greater authority. Questions of *major* policy will necessarily be handled by the quarterly meetings of the highest council itself. But delegated *authority* must be exercised by the Deputies between quarterly meetings, and there must be a responsibility for submitting to the Council specific programs for approval.[12] Interestingly enough, I had a long talk with Paul Hoffman on this general subject, and he thinks that *my* responsibilities and authority must be vastly widened in scope if we are to have successful machinery.[13] Regardless of the answer along that line, I do think it is clear that we must have a better way of reaching policy and ministerial decisions than we now have. We must get over the practice of allowing details and minor problems to block our own purposes—we must begin to operate in such fashion that major progress, month by month, and day by day, is obvious to any observer.

In any event, Mr. Van Zeeland's enthusiasm and interest, to say nothing of his initiative, are refreshing.

Much of this becomes of immediate importance because of the current visit of the Congressional party. I have already appeared before it once, going to the trouble of explaining again the basic concepts of NATO, as I understand them.[14] Incidentally, I urged each member to look up the latest studies of the CED on the relationships between the United States and Europe, as well as the studies made by the Nelson Rockefeller Committee, on which my friend Harvey Firestone served.[15]

The Committee spent the entire afternoon, last Saturday, in my headquarters. The next day it spent with ECA and ECC. Thereafter, it went off to London, and I believe that the members are going to spend most of this week traveling about Europe, either as a unit or in small subcommittees. We expect them back here next Saturday, and I am to spend the entire day of next Monday with them.[16] While I have no doubt that those who are already of fixed convictions will remain of the same mind, I am quite sure that the facts, opinions, and convictions that they encounter on this side will be of real benefit to most.

This morning, John Foster Dulles came to see me. We talked for two hours. He gave me a most interesting account of developments about the world, especially as they affect the Japanese Peace Treaty and the reactions of certain other capitals to our efforts in this direction.[17] We did not get to talk much about the Mediterranean and Indian Ocean areas—an omission that could not be helped because of the lack of time.

I continue to get glowing individual reports on the conduct of the first conference at the American Assembly.[18] Needless to say, I am highly gratified, as I hope you are.

With warm personal regard,[19] *Cordially*

[1] For background on Harriman's visit to Europe see no. 191. Eisenhower would see him several times between June 21 and June 27 (see no. 251).

[2] On Dutch Foreign Minister Dirk Stikker and Belgian Minister of Foreign Affairs Paul van Zeeland see no. 16. Van Zeeland, who had been in his present post since 1949, had been his nation's prime minister from 1935 until 1937 and president of the League of Nations Assembly in 1936. He was a fervent supporter of both the NATO concept and European unity.

[3] Eisenhower had seen Stikker on June 9 (see no. 215, n. 1).

[4] While the United Kingdom supported the concept of European unity, the British were reluctant to associate themselves with the Continental nations in some of the specific proposals that were designed to achieve European integration. The British were fearful of jeopardizing their ties to the other British Commonwealth nations by joining in a European union, and they were also hesitant about committing their forces to the proposed European Army (see no. 186). The Dutch were disappointed in the British attitude (Stikker, *Men of Responsibility*, pp. 302-3. See also F. S. Northedge, *British Foreign Policy: The Process of Readjustment, 1945-1961* [London, 1962], pp. 132-55; Roger Eatwell, *The 1945-1951 Labour Governments* [London, 1979], pp. 138-39; Kenneth Harris, *Attlee* [New York, 1982], pp. 314-15, 506-7; and Hogan, *The Marshall Plan*, pp. 49, 75, 318).

[5] For background on Milton Katz, American Special Representative in Europe for the Marshall Plan, see no. 16, n. 7.

[6] For background on the British rearmament program see no. 111, n. 9. In July SHAPE Chief of Staff Gruenther would say, "The British economy is fully extended as of the present time and the U.K. is undertaking approximately as great a military production and financial effort as it is believed to be in the U.S. interest for them to attempt to program. . . . Considering the amount of effort of which the U.K. is capable without gravely damaging repercussions upon her economy, financial position and already austere standard of living, it appears that the effort currently being made by the United Kingdom compares well with that being undertaken by the United States" (SHAPE Briefings for Senate Foreign Relations Committee, July 1951, EM, Subject File, Congressional Visits, 1951. See also State, *Foreign Relations, 1951*, vol. IV, *Europe: Political and Economic Developments, Part I*, pp. 911-14; Senate Subcommittee on Foreign Relations, *United States Foreign-Aid Programs in Europe: Hearings*, 1951, pp. 110-11, 114-16; Nash to Lovett, Sept. 7, 1951, and other papers in OS/D, 1951, Clas. Decimal File, CD 091.3 MDAP [U.K.]; and nos. 248 and 578).

[7] Sir Richard Stafford Cripps had been a Member of Parliament from 1931 until 1950. A member of Britain's Labour party, he had served as Chancellor of the Exchequer from 1947 until his retirement in October 1950. During World War II he had been Minister of Aircraft Production. For background on British Secretary of State for Foreign Affairs Ernest Bevin, who had died on April 14, see Galambos, *Columbia University*, no. 261.

[8] Stikker would later write in his memoirs that his conversations with Eisenhower at this time led him to believe that Eisenhower's pressure on the Europeans to create an effective European Army was motivated by a desire to send U.S. forces back to the United States (Stikker, *Men of Responsibility*, pp. 303-4).

[9] For background on the North Atlantic Council see no. 2, n. 2. The NAC met annually, with special meetings called as the occasion arose. On May 3 the NATO

nations had decided to include defense and financial ministers, at each government's discretion, as members of the NAC. NATO's Defense Committee and Defense Financial and Economic Committee were thus incorporated into the NAC (Ismay, *NATO*, pp. 24-25, 41). Van Zeeland agreed with Eisenhower's proposal and told the General that he would instruct the Belgian representative on the Council of Deputies to put the matter on the agenda for their next meeting (Memorandum of Conversation, June 12, 1951, EM, Subject File, Conversations). For developments see nos. 363 and 375.

[10] For background on Eisenhower's involvement with the multinational European Army see no. 186, n. 5; for Eisenhower's feelings about the lack of civilian ministries to handle SHAPE's administrative and logistical needs see no. 215. Eisenhower told van Zeeland that he "thought it might be difficult to establish such a European Army until unified political, economic, and financial institutions had first been developed." Eisenhower also told van Zeeland of "his own conviction that eventually a united Europe in some form or other was the answer to many problems" (Memorandum of Conversation, June 12, 1951, EM, Subject File, Conversations).

[11] Van Zeeland said that excess European armament productive capacity should be used in order to accelerate the progress of rearmament. He proposed that NATO designate weapons acceptable for use and that the various NATO nations describe the items they needed so that if possible, shortages could be filled from within Europe. Van Zeeland said that U.S. plans to purchase a "limited number" of items from the Europeans were acceptable as an intermediate solution but that "from the psychological as well as [the] practical view," it was more desirable to "require the Europeans themselves to make maximum use of their total productive facilities" (*ibid.*).

[12] See no. 215, n. 5. Eisenhower told van Zeeland that his requests to NATO had to pass "through a series of committees which is time consuming and sometimes results in watering down of effective plans." Van Zeeland replied that he would work to have the Council of Deputies given "authority to act within agreed policy, including the authority to commit certain limited funds for necessary projects" (Memorandum of Conversation, June 12, 1951, EM, Subject File, Conversations).

[13] Eisenhower is probably referring to his June 7 meeting with Hoffman (see no. 200). For developments see no. 238.

[14] On Eisenhower's June 9 meeting with members of the House Foreign Affairs, Armed Services, and Appropriations committees see no. 209.

[15] For background on the CED report see no. 198, n. 5; in regard to industrialist Harvey Firestone see Galambos, *Columbia University*, no. 641. In November 1950 Firestone had been appointed to the International Development Advisory Board, a group appointed by President Truman to advise him on a national policy to aid underdeveloped areas (*Public Papers of the Presidents of the United States: Harry S. Truman, January 1 to December 31, 1950* [Washington, D.C., 1965], pp. 717-18, 723-24). The chairman of this committee was Nelson Aldrich Rockefeller (A.B. Dartmouth 1930), president of Rockefeller Center and the son of John D. Rockefeller, Jr. (for background see Galambos, *Columbia University*). During World War II Rockefeller had served as Coordinator of Inter-American Affairs and Assistant Secretary of State.

[16] A transcript of the remarks made during Eisenhower's June 18 meeting with the visiting congressmen is in EM, Subject File, Congressional Visits, 1951. Eisenhower would tell his visitors: "We have got to help our European Allies in every way that we can—morally, spiritually and materially. But we must eventually phase out our effort as they take over; otherwise, we are just going to have another dependent on our backs."

[17] For background on Dulles see Galambos, *Columbia University*, no. 12. In July

1949 he had been appointed interim U.S. senator from New York but had lost the following special election to a Democratic candidate. Dulles was currently serving as President Truman's special representative in the negotiations on a Japanese peace treaty. This afternoon, after meeting with Eisenhower, Dulles talked with *New York Times* correspondent Cyrus Sulzberger and told him that he wanted "negotiations as rapidly as possible to draft and sign a peace treaty permitting Tokyo to recreate a land army and employ it for defense against aggression in an overall system of Pacific Ocean collective security pacts." Dulles also told Sulzberger that Great Britain mistrusted "American wisdom and temperance in Asiatic questions of policy" and that the British were afraid that American "impulsiveness might precipitate a new Far Eastern crisis" (Sulzberger, *Long Row of Candles*, p. 640). For background on the Japanese peace treaty see Acheson, *Present at the Creation*, pp. 539–50; and Ronald W. Pruessen, *John Foster Dulles: The Road to Power* (New York, 1982), pp. 437–98.

[18] See no. 201.

[19] Eisenhower added a postscript to this letter: "Al [Gruenther] & I are *waiting* for you. DE"

219   *Eisenhower Mss.*

To Alfred Maximilian Gruenther   *June 13, 1951*

Memorandum for Chief of Staff: I agree with an idea the Field Marshal has just presented to me, to the effect that there should be developed a really big command exercise for next spring. It could be held, I suppose, either at SHAPE or at Fontainebleau.[1]

I am certain that the development of a proper CPX would require the services of a small special staff, possibly a total of 6 officers from three Services, approximately on the ratio of 3 Army, 2 Air, and 1 Navy. While such a group could call upon our staff or any other for all kinds of assistance and information, it would be directly responsible to a chief, either Festing or, if we so desire, we could put the Field Marshal in direct charge. I do not believe that our own general staff or the staffs at Fontainebleau could take on the job just as an additional chore.[2]

This exercise would, of course, take place before normal field maneuvers and would be in line with what the Field Marshal has to say in the attached document concerning the need for training of higher commanders.[3]

Please have the whole matter studied by your Plans and Training groups, and let me know what they think of it.[4]

[1] Eisenhower had met with Montgomery (see no. 17) that morning to review two reports that the Deputy SACEUR had recently submitted (see two notes, Montgomery to Eisenhower, both dated June 12, 1951, in EM, Montgomery Corr.). The second of these papers was primarily concerned with the development and

training of the NATO forces over the following year. Montgomery's suggestion of a command post exercise (CPX) at either SHAPE outside of Paris or NATO forces Central Command headquarters at Fontainebleau had probably arisen from a discussion of this report (see FM/47, "Visits to U.K., Belgium and Holland," June 12, 1951, in EM, Montgomery Corr.).

[2] From the SHAPE Organization and Training Division Gruenther would shortly select for CPX One an exercise planning staff responsible to Montgomery (see undated note, Gruenther to Eisenhower, on Montgomery to Eisenhower, June 15, 1951, in EM, Montgomery Corr.; memorandum, Cole to Schulz, Mar. 5, 1952, in EM, Subject File, Command Post Exercises; and *International Herald Tribune*, Paris ed., Apr. 8, 1952). Major General Francis Wogan Festing (U.K.), Assistant Chief of Staff of the Organization and Training Division, would leave SHAPE before the April 1952 exercise took place (see Festing to Eisenhower, Feb. 18, 1952, and Eisenhower to Festing, Apr. 25, 1952, both in EM).

[3] Beside this paragraph on the copy of this letter in EM is the handwritten notation "(FM/47)," referring to Montgomery's report on recent visits to Britain, Holland, and Belgium (see n. 1 above). In outlining the military manpower contributions to the NATO forces that these nations could be expected to make within the next year, the Field Marshal had stressed the urgent need for trained and experienced officers in establishing Western European security. Concerning the necessity of collective field training and maneuvers for the Central Command during 1951 and 1952, Montgomery had written, "Only in this way can the Commanders and Staffs be given experience and the machinery of Command be exercised. And only if this is done can we be satisfied that we will be ready by the winter of 1952/53" (see FM/47, p. 1). For Eisenhower's own comments on the need for experienced European officers see Senate Committee on Foreign Relations and Committee on Armed Services, *Assignment of Ground Forces of the United States to Duty in the European Area*, 1951, p. 7.

[4] For developments with CPX One see no. 228.

220   *Eisenhower Mss.*

To Philip Young   *June 13, 1951*

Dear Phil:[1] You may be sure that my confidence in your ability to work out conflicting views about The American Assembly is unlimited. And I fully appreciate the difficulties of your dual position in the development and educational fields. Outside Arthur Sulzberger's comment— and, as I recall it, his was much closer to a purely personal impression than a reflection of general opinion—there has not been one word of complaint in letters to me about education being the tail to the development kite or any conflict between the academic and promotional aspects of the Graduate School of Business or the University. Such complete silence is the highest testimony to your conduct of both the Graduate School and The Assembly.[2]

So far as the public relations problem is concerned, I am not in a position to advise or to judge. Undoubtedly, many decisions on that and other points had to be made on the basis of specific circumstances with which I am not acquainted. Moreover, you had absolutely no precedent on which to work. In any case, however, I have full confidence in your judgment.[3]

I must say that I am delighted to hear that Faith, you and the children are coming to Europe, and I know Mamie will be, too, when I pass the word to her. As of now—and it is improbable that there will be any change in our plans, we shall return to France sometime during the day of July 5. During the following two weeks it is unlikely we will take any sort of trip outside the Paris area. If you can be here then, I shall set aside whatever time is necessary for us to go over in detail the past, present and future of The Assembly. I am sure that you must be full of ideas.[4]

Both Mamie and I have been looking forward with pleasure to the London visit. It will be still more pleasant with Faith and you there. Until then, our best to all of you.[5] *Sincerely*

[1] This letter was drafted for Eisenhower by his aide Kevin McCann (see no. 70).
[2] For background on Arthur Sulzberger's letter to Young concerning the first American Assembly conference see no. 204. For other comments on the conference, some of which the General passed on to Young, see no. 202; EM, Young Corr.; and David E. Lilienthal to Eisenhower, June 8, 1951, in EM, Lilienthal Corr.
[3] On the publicity for the first Assembly conference and on Sulzberger's criticism of it see nos. 201 and 205, n. 1, respectively.
[4] In a letter of June 7 (EM) Young had informed Eisenhower that he, his wife Faith, and their two daughters (see no. 205, n. 1) would be arriving in Liverpool on the twenty-second. Young, who was traveling as a delegate to the conference of the English Speaking Union (which Eisenhower would address on July 3), wrote that he would adjust his own plans to suit the General's schedule. On the Union see Galambos, *Columbia University*, nos. 959 and 1037; on Eisenhower's address see no. 252 in this volume.
[5] Eisenhower would meet with Young and American Assembly National Policy Board chairman, Lewis Douglas, on July 9 (see no. 239, n. 6).

221   *Eisenhower Mss.*

To George Whitney   *June 14, 1951*

Dear George: Your letters are one of the brightest things in my office life—even when the sentiment they express seems to lean to the pessimistic side I am still so impressed by your clarity and conciseness of expression that I get a real feeling of satisfaction out of reading them.[1]

I gather that your resigned feeling in the MacArthur business is that now all the country need do is be patient in the belief that eventually "this, too, shall pass."[2]

Your statement about the acute shortages of machine tools is disturbing. Even though Charlie Wilson and others had talked to me about it before, they seemed, a few months ago, to have great hopes that ways would be found to overcome this deficiency. I assume that they are now getting more pessimistic. I remember that once, during World War II, General Knudsen[3] spoke to me to the general effect that one lack of preparation experienced in that war would never have to be repeated in the United States—a lack of a sufficient number of machine tools. I suspect that a reasonable expenditure in 1945 might have saved us very much in money and time right now.[4]

My feeling about the points you make on the economic condition is that, if the measures you enumerate are successful in preventing the recession from reaching unmanageable proportions the net result will be good. What a godsend it would be to us to have a couple years of stable prices! Certainly during a period when long-term contracts are the order of the day rather than the exception, we are desperately in need of such a condition. Entirely aside from the immediate effects of spiraling prices, there could be produced a situation where manufacturers could not possibly afford to make any commitments except on the objectionable (and inflation-producing) cost-plus system.[5]

Since you were here, I have had some long and interesting talks with Paul Hoffman and others. Particular individuals continue to talk to me in a disquieting way about the future—disquieting in the sense that they insist I cannot, even in my present position, remain permanently aloof from domestic struggles in which I certainly want no part. But their talk is even more alarming because they tell of the existence of a feeling at home that the country is deteriorating, first, in its support of freedom as a human right; secondly, in its comprehension of the vital factors in today's problems; and, thirdly, in its confidence that unified and unremitting effort could lift us out of all our troubles. As you express it, people are just plain scared.[6]

One feeling I have out of all this is an added reason for regret that you do not find it necessary to make a quick trip to Europe at least once every three months. I derive tremendous satisfaction out of talking to you. Most certainly, I deeply appreciate the trouble you take to write to me.[7]

My warm greetings to every member of your nice family. *Cordially*

[1] Whitney, chairman of J. P. Morgan & Company, had been sending Eisenhower periodic letters on the American business and political scenes since March of this year (see nos. 50 and 105).
[2] In letters to the General on June 11 and 12 (copies in EM, same file as document) Whitney had commented on the MacArthur dismissal controversy, writing that "this tempest has accomplished practically nothing" (June 11). For background on the dismissal and on the resultant congressional hearings see nos. 128, n. 3, and 136, respectively. On the twelfth, Whitney explained that since his return from a

visit with Eisenhower (see n. 6 below) he had been questioned in regard to the General's views on the MacArthur affair and had replied that they had not discussed the case. (For advice that Eisenhower remain silent on the firing see no. 131.) Although Eisenhower probably dictated this letter on the fourteenth, a handwritten notation on the copy in EM indicates that the General did not sign it until June 16.

³ Lieutenant General William S. Knudsen had been Director General of the Office of Production Management during World War II (see Chandler, *War Years*, no. 140).

⁴ Concerning the American defense effort, Whitney had written (June 11) that "the date when actual materiél will be flowing is getting further [*sic*] off rather than nearer . . . the old problem of tooling and the capacity of the tool industry . . . is undoubtedly going to be a bottleneck." Machine tools (power-driven devices for shaping, cutting, and forming metals) had been in increasing demand since the outbreak of the Korean War in 1950, and the MDAP and NATO requirements for military goods had placed additional strain upon the industry.

The manufacture of machine tools, described as a feast-or-famine enterprise, had contracted drastically since the close of World War II. From an average annual production valued at $772 million for the years 1940–1945, output within the industry had tumbled to slightly over $300 million by 1950; costs had increased nearly 100 percent (see U.S. Congress, Senate, Joint Committee on Defense Production, *Defense Production Act: Progress Report No. 13, Machine Tools*, 82d Cong., 2d sess., 1952, S. Rept. 1107, pp. 6–7; and Harless D. Wagoner, *The U.S. Machine Tool Industry from 1900 to 1950* [Cambridge, Mass., 1968], p. 344).

The Office of Defense Mobilization, established in December 1950, had not immediately recognized the difficulties involved in producing machine tools both to meet the Korean War emergency and to rearm Western Europe (see no. 45, n. 4). Price ceilings and restrictions placed on the allocation of raw materials hampered production and increased industry reluctance either to expand operations or to abandon unfilled civilian orders to meet defense needs (see Senate, Joint Committee on Defense Production, *Defense Production Act*, 1952, pp. 24–28). For developments see the following document.

⁵ About U.S. economic conditions Whitney had commented (June 11) that "it is clear that we are in a slight recession . . ." and that due to mismanagement and "bungling" by the Truman Administration, inventories were high and consumer demands low. According to Whitney, the defense effort had failed to rectify this situation, and he predicted layoffs unless manufacturers could "switch this around through holidays, etc."

⁶ In his letter of June 11 Whitney had said that "fear psychology" was on the rise within the United States: "fear of war, fear of labor troubles, [and] fear of almost anything," but that he was certain the 1952 elections would determine what course the nation would follow. On the continuing support for an Eisenhower presidential candidacy see nos. 135, 196, and 205; on Hoffman's visit see no. 200.

⁷ Whitney had been in Paris during May (see Whitney to Eisenhower, Apr. 11, 1951, with attached memo from DDE, same file as document; and Bernard Carter to Eisenhower, Apr. 17, 1951, in EM, Carter Corr.). For Whitney's continuing correspondence with the General see nos. 355 and 385.

John & Barbie with David and Anne—and Min—arrived yesterday. Weather, fine![1]

Mr. Foster of ECA was here today.[2] He paints a sorry picture of Washington—the mere fact of Presidential support almost certain to defeat any bill before Congress. Taft, Wherry, et al (and especially Kem & McCarthy) are disciples of hate—hate and curse anything that belongs to the administration.[3] Heaven knows there is plenty for which to criticize the adm legitimately & decently & _strongly_—but what they are doing is apt to make him (HST) an "underdog" and backfire on them![4] How we need some brains (on both sides) and some selflessness.

There seems to be a bad shortage of machine tools. When we get over this emergency I am going to take as one element of my personal ambitions, that of preaching machine tools as part of military preparation until some d—— administration will take the necessary measures. I've heard the same story time after time and it seems to me we _should_ learn.[5]

Also in stocking some materials! I thought I worked on this one in '46, '47, '48. But when this emergency lets up I'm _really_ going to town!![6]

---

[1] On the visit of Mrs. Eisenhower's mother and the Eisenhowers' son John and his family see no. 224.

[2] Eisenhower had had lunch this afternoon with ECA Administrator William Chapman Foster, who was then on a twelve-day tour of ECA missions (see *New York Times*, June 14, 1951). Foster's trip coincided with that of an eighteen-member congressional party investigating the economic and military needs of the NATO allies prior to holding hearings on Truman's recently proposed $8.5 billion foreign aid budget (see nos. 209 and 218). According to Foster, it was "the devout hope of the President" that the program be passed, and his purpose in coming to Europe was to gather information before testifying before Congress (see *International Herald Tribune*, Paris ed., June 14, 1951). For developments see nos. 238, 251, and 268.

[3] Difficulties between the Truman Administration and Congress had continued following resolution of the troops-to-Europe issue during April (see no. 128). Corruption in government agencies, divisions over the MacArthur dismissal, the ever-present question of European aid, loyalty investigations, and the Administration's inability to conclude the Korean War had fueled Republican congressional attacks on Truman policies (see nos. 75, n. 4, 84, n. 3, and 194; and Donovan, *Tumultuous Years*, pp. 332–73). Senators Taft (see no. 196, n. 7), Wherry (see no. 51, n. 12), McCarthy (see no. 84), and James Preston Kem (Republican, Missouri) were in the forefront of the anti-Administration factions on most major foreign and domestic issues. All were among the "Asia-firsters," who favored American military emphasis on the East over the defense of Western Europe; all had taken an anti-Truman stance in the MacArthur controversy, with McCarthy calling for the President's impeachment; and all now opposed both the recent foreign aid request (see n. 2 above) and Truman's desire to extend wage and price controls (see

Patterson, *Mr. Republican*, pp. 484–92; Donovan, *Tumultuous Years*, pp. 368–69; and *New York Times*, June 22, 28, 29, 30, July 1, 1951. See also Kem to Eisenhower, Dec. 2, 1950, and Eisenhower to Kem, Dec. 6, 1951, both in EM).

[4] Eisenhower was probably referring to the 1948 presidential election, in which Truman, despite most polls and predictions, had defeated New York Governor Thomas Dewey (see no. 196, n. 7). Truman had been viewed as an underdog throughout the race, and that perception may have helped him retain the presidency (see Roseboom, *Presidential Elections*, pp. 492–507; Richard S. Kirkendall, "Election of 1948," in *History of American Presidential Elections, 1789–1968*, ed. Arthur M. Schlesinger, Jr., 4 vols. [New York, 1971], vol. IV, *1940–1968*, pp. 3099–3145; and Galambos, *Columbia University*, nos. 34, 116, and 147).

[5] On the machine tool crisis see the preceding document. On the efforts to deal with this problem see U.S. Congress, Senate, Select Committee on Small Business, *Report of the Committee on the Impact of Machine-Tool Shortages on Small Manufacturers*, 82d Cong., 2d sess., 1952, S. Rept. 1988, pp. 14–16; and reports of the Director of Defense Mobilization, in EM, Wilson Corr.).

[6] For Eisenhower's views on industrial mobilization see *Eisenhower Papers*, vols. I–XI.

223

Eisenhower Mss.

To Jules Moch

June 14, 1951

Secret

Dear Mr. President:[1] I refer to the requirements for air bases in Metropolitan France for the North Atlantic Treaty Organization tactical air forces previously approved by the Standing Group and notified to the French and United States Governments by the Western European Regional Planning Group under date of 13 March 1951.[2]

I am informed that three United States Air Force fighter bomber wings and one troop carrier wing are scheduled for arrival in France in early July and August as part of the above-mentioned NATO tactical air forces.[3] However, I understand the locations of the permanent NATO air bases from which these units would operate still remains to be determined.

I have the honor accordingly to confirm the urgent requirement for temporary facilities necessary to receive these units at sites to be agreed between the appropriate authorities of the French and United States Governments.[4] *Sincerely*

[1] Eisenhower may have addressed Moch as "Mr. President" in deference to Moch's service as president of several organizations in France. For background on Moch, the French Minister of National Defense, see no. 11, n. 1.

[2] There had been a controversy over French NATO bases and the regional planning groups (see nos. 115 and 99, respectively). The Western European Regional Planning Group, after studying the American military operating requirements within

France, had invited the French and American governments to begin bilateral negotiations for proposed airfields. Both Eisenhower and the Standing Group had urged the two countries to act quickly (SGM 491–51, Apr. 5, 1951, OS/D, 1951, Clas. Decimal File, CD 092.2 General). Progress had been slow, however, and the French Foreign Office had informed the American Embassy in Paris that "it was essential that General Eisenhower (in his NATO capacity) bring this to the attention of M. Moch" (MacArthur, Memorandum for Record, June 15, 1951, EM, Moch Corr.; see also *New York Times*, May 29, June 8, July 2, 1951). Douglas MacArthur II, Eisenhower's political adviser, drafted this note for the General.

[3] In April President Truman and Secretary of Defense Marshall had approved a JCS proposal to augment U.S. forces by three fighter bomber wings (June–July 1951); one troop carrier wing (July 1951); one tactical reconnaissance wing (Oct. 1951); and one light bomber wing (Oct. 1951). These increases were contingent on securing adequate air bases from the host nations (Bradley to Marshall, Apr. 4, 1951, OS/D, 1951, Clas. Decimal File, CD 371 Europe).

[4] Delays in the French airfield construction program would continue despite SHAPE pressure to act. When the first U.S. air reinforcements for NATO arrived in Europe, they were sent to Germany. U.S. air units would not be sent to French bases until November, and the United States would not reach agreement with the French government concerning base construction until the following year (*New York Times*, July 30, Nov. 18, 1951; Feb. 14, Apr. 11, 26, June 21, 1952. See also Memorandum of Conversation, July 19, 1951, Records of the Assistant Secretary of Defense for International Security Affairs, ONATA Subject File 1949–53; CINCUSAFE to CS USAF, Oct. 11, 1951, EOPL 5732, and other papers in OS/D, 1951, Clas. Decimal File, CD 092.2 General; and JSPC 876/408, Dec. 19, 1951, CCS 092 Western Europe [3–12–48], Sec. 111).

224   *Eisenhower Mss.*

To Mabel Frances Doud Moore   *June 14, 1951*
and George Gordon Moore, Jr.

Dear Mike and Gordon:[1] Yesterday the family arrived about one hour late because of unusual delay in refueling at a field in Newfoundland. They were all in splendid spirits and health, although a bit tired and sleepy. Incidentally, I think that Miss Min looks fine; to me, she shows no effects of nervous strain or even of her bad bout with pneumonia some months ago. If, at 73, I am as mentally alert and physically spry as she is, I shall feel very fortunate indeed.[2]

I have no doubt that you were delighted with the news that George Horkan is to be the new Quartermaster General. I suppose I already told you both how very influential and helpful George was at the time of the integration business in the regular Army; I know that his satisfaction in the way that Gordon has so obviously made good in the Corps is very great. Of course, I don't think you should ever, by any remote chance, mention this particular point to him, but I am quite certain that you will find him the most human and efficient Quartermaster General that the Army has had in many years, and one who will take a great interest in Gordon's future. I have just written him a letter of warm felicitations.[3]

Strangely enough, I have not yet spoken to the two grandchildren. When I got home yesterday afternoon, they were in bed, asleep. Then Mamie and I had to go off to a reception which was so far out in the country that we were absent from home a full three hours. Consequently, when we returned, the children were again in bed, asleep. This morning, I waited around the house until 10 minutes after 8, hoping that they would awaken, but the change in hours is so great that they were still sleeping like logs. A few minutes ago, however, I had one word with David on the telephone. He said, "Hi, Ike, come to see me soon."[4]

Mamie has the two photographs of Mike and the family in our hotel living room. The group picture attracts a great deal of comment—it certainly is a lovely photograph of a family. I do not mean that the picture of Mike alone does not get many compliments, but the other seems to strike people as rather unique.[5]

Luckily, Paris has suddenly decided to put on two or three nice days—something that has been completely missing here all spring. If the weather stays like this, the family should certainly have a wonderful time.[6]

Very soon after this reaches you, Richard will be starting off for West Point. I am sure that he will make good, if he will merely keep his sense of humor. It is a fact that many boys get a bit discouraged in the early days, but, if he remembers that many thousands have gone through the same thing ahead of him, he shall have no trouble.[7]

Love to the entire family, *As ever*

[1] Mabel ("Mike") Moore was Mamie Eisenhower's sister (see no. 118, n. 2). Lieutenant Colonel George Gordon Moore, Jr., her husband, was assigned to the Quartermaster General's office in Washington, D.C. (see Galambos, *Columbia University*, nos. 430 and 702).

[2] Mamie Eisenhower's mother, Elivera Doud ("Min"), had arrived in Paris along with the Eisenhowers' son John and his family (see no. 183, n. 6; on Mrs. Doud's health see no. 40, n. 3). The family had traveled aboard Eisenhower's plane, *Columbine* (see EM, Subject File, Aircraft—SHAPE [*Columbine*]).

[3] Major General George Anthony Horkan would become Quartermaster General in October 1951 (see Galambos, *Columbia University*, no. 692). This same day Eisenhower wrote to congratulate Horkan on his new position (see no. 226).

[4] The Eisenhower grandchildren were Dwight David II and Barbara Anne (see no. 132). The reception, given for SHAPE personnel, was held at Field Marshal Montgomery's Château de Cournance in Milly (see Montgomery to Eisenhower, May 18, 1951, EM).

[5] The family included Richard Gill, Jr., and Michael Doud Gill, sons of Mabel Doud Moore and her first husband, Richard Gill, and daughters Ellen Doud Moore and Mamie Eisenhower Moore.

[6] During their visit the family would follow a busy schedule of entertaining and

traveling. Eisenhower himself would arrange a number of golf dates with John. For more information on their activities see EM, Subject File, Entertaining; Trips, SHAPE; Aircraft—SHAPE (*Columbine*), and EM, Family File. For developments see nos. 240 and 252.

[7] For Eisenhower's interest in Richard Gill, Jr.'s, appointment to West Point see Galambos, *Columbia University*, no. 441.

225

Eisenhower Mss.

To James Weldon Jones

June 14, 1951

Dear Weldon:[1] Your letter was welcome not only because of its news of you and Johnny,[2] but because it was such a poignant reminder of more peaceful and serene days. It is difficult for me to recapture now even a faint memory of the spirit in which I used to go gaily off to Caloocan, in the afternoon, to play a round of golf, or sit around the Manila hotel in the evenings to discuss the rise of "this upstart, Hitler."[3]

While at this moment I do not know of a job in this headquarters worthy of your talents, I am more than glad to have your offer of service. First of all, I have always found that, in this kind of headquarters, new requirements and needs are constantly popping up, and sometimes they exactly fit the qualifications of some friend of the past. It may be the same in your case—at least, your note will be on file in the office of my Chief of Staff, together with a statement of your qualifications as a public servant. Another reason for getting a lift out of your offer was the spirit of selflessness in which it was made. The world needs more of such.[4]

My love to Johnny, and, of course, warmest regards to yourself. *Cordially*

[1] Jones, an old friend of Eisenhower's, had been Assistant Director of the U.S. Bureau of the Budget, in charge of the Fiscal Division, since 1940.

[2] On April 30 (EM) Jones had written the General. "Johnny" was probably Jones's wife, the former Ruby Hackett (see Jones to Eisenhower, Feb. 24, Mar. 30, 1952, EM).

[3] For background on Jones and his service with the General in the Philippines see Galambos, *Chief of Staff*, nos. 547 and 937. Caloocan was a municipality north of Manila, on the Philippine island of Luzon.

[4] In his letter Jones had asked Eisenhower to consider him for a job at SHAPE if he could be of any use "in budget or economic matters [or] as an assistant who shares your views." Jones would, however, continue in his present job.

To George Anthony Horkan   *June 14, 1951*

Dear George:[1] For some time, rumors have been flying around here that you were to be the next Quartermaster General. Every time I had a breath of this sort of news, I was warned that I must keep very, very still or I might be the reason for something going awry. Now Mamie tells me that you have apparently received some official notification, and so I hasten to send you my felicitations and congratulations. (I am assuming you want the damn job; although I think that, right this minute, you are occupying about as nice a billet and doing about as good a job as one fellow could do in this Army.)[2]

I know that you and Mary[3] will thoroughly enjoy going back to your old haunts, and I can understand—in spite of all its drawbacks— why the job itself should appeal to you. Of course, your selection represents the official opinion that you should be at the head of your particular service; naturally, a real personal satisfaction is derived from that. My own feeling is that your friends have known this a long time. The real challenge of doing something constructive in a service to which you have given so much of your life will bring you many rewards; I am for you 100%.[4]

Mamie did not tell me when you expect to be leaving for the States, but I do hope we will get to see you and Mary before that time. I have given up on Buckshot.[5] She apparently is one of these "remote" types of gals that a fellow can see only by arranging an engagement through the State Department—a meeting complete with agenda, secretaries, and simultaneous interpretation.

Right now, Mamie is talking about taking her family up to Heidelberg for a day or two. Whether she will pull it off, I don't know, because John seems to be determined to stay around here to play golf. John and Barbie, the two grandchildren, and Miss Min all arrived yesterday, in blooming health and glad to be here.[6]

My love to that beautiful bride of yours, and, as always, warmest regard to yourself. *Cordially*

[1] Major General Horkan was Chief Quartermaster of the European command, stationed in Heidelberg, Germany (see no. 224, n. 2).
[2] In October Horkan would become Quartermaster General, following the retirement of Major General Herman Feldman (see Galambos, *Chief of Staff*, nos. 614 and 648; and in this volume, no. 485. See also *New York Times*, Sept. 14, Oct. 2, 1951).
[3] Horkan's wife, the former Mary Thompson.
[4] Horkan had joined the Quartermaster Corps in 1921 (see EM, Quartermaster General File).
[5] In his reply of June 21 (EM) Horkan told Eisenhower that he planned to leave Germany on July 24. "Buckshot" was probably Horkan's daughter, Katherine

Sanford (see Eisenhower to Horkan, Apr. 16, 1951, and Horkan to Eisenhower, Oct. 5, 1951, EM).

[6] John Eisenhower, the General's son, his family, and Mamie's mother, Elivera Doud ("Min"), were visiting the Eisenhowers (see no. 224).

227 *Eisenhower Mss.*

To WINTHROP WILLIAMS ALDRICH *June 18, 1951*

Dear Winthrop:[1] Only a few days ago, Grayson Kirk, now acting head of Columbia, passed through here at the beginning of a short European trip. I think he is due back here in three or four weeks.[2] But, in answer to your inquiry about Columbia's attitude toward a talk by Anthony Eden, I am writing at once to John Krout, Dean of Graduate Faculties at Columbia.[3] I am going to ask him to communicate directly with you, so I suspect that, within a matter of a day or so after receipt of this letter, you should have [a] preliminary report from him. If Anthony Eden is soon to leave for Canada, he should have this kind of arrangement made at the earliest possible date, and so I feel I must not wait for Kirk to come back here.[4]

It was nice having you here; I trust that it will not be too long before business of some kind brings you back and we can renew our golf battle. I have played twice within the last few days, but, preceding these two outings, I had a lapse of more than two weeks. The quality of my game suffered badly.[5]

Please remember me warmly to Harriet.[6] *Cordially*

[1] For background on Aldrich, chairman of the Chase Manhattan Bank, see no. 196, n. 4.

[2] Kirk, acting president of Columbia in Eisenhower's absence, had been on a business trip to Italy. He had met with Eisenhower the morning of June 14, but the General would be unable to schedule another visit before Kirk's departure for the United States (for background on Kirk see no. 31, n. 1; see also McCann to Kirk, June 8, 1951, and Kirk to Eisenhower, July 23, 1951, EM).

[3] On June 16 (EM) Aldrich had written the General about the possibility of asking Sir Robert Anthony Eden to speak at Columbia. As deputy leader of the Conservative party in Great Britain, Eden hoped that speaking engagements in the United States and Canada would be beneficial to him just prior to a British general election in the fall. In October Eden would become Foreign Secretary and Deputy Prime Minister (see *New York Times*, Oct. 28, 1951).

This same day Eisenhower wrote to Krout about this matter (see Eisenhower to Krout, June 18, 1951, EM; on Krout see no. 31, n. 1).

[4] Krout informed Eisenhower in a letter of July 6 (EM) that Eden's schedule made it difficult for him to speak at Columbia before the university's summer session ended. It would be January 1952 before Eden visited Columbia, where he received an honorary Doctor of Laws degree and delivered the 1952 Gabriel Silver Lecture

(see *New York Times*, July 7, 25, 1951; Jan. 12, 1952). On Eden's later visit to the General see no. 556, n. 2.

[5] Aldrich had met with Eisenhower on May 29 and had played golf with him on May 31 (see no. 196, n. 4).

[6] Aldrich's wife, the former Harriet Alexander.

228   *Eisenhower Mss.*

To BERNARD LAW MONTGOMERY   *June 18, 1951*

Dear Monty: The staff is working on a plan to get together a group for developing the SHAPE exercise next April.[1]

I haven't seen you lately to thank you again for a grand afternoon at your chateau. The occasion was obviously and understandably enjoyed by every guest.[2] *As ever*

[1] During a meeting with Eisenhower on June 13 Deputy SACEUR Montgomery had suggested that a command post exercise for top-ranking NATO officers be held in the spring of 1952 (see no. 219). Preparations for this exercise, which would be named CPX One, were handled by a four-man staff chosen from the SHAPE Organization and Training Division and chaired by Colonel George Sinclair Cole (U.K.) (see Gruenther to Eisenhower, n.d., and Montgomery to Eisenhower, June 15, 1951, in EM, Montgomery Corr.; and Cole to Schulz, Mar. 5, 1952, in EM, Subject File, Command Post Exercises). On the exercise itself, which would be held in Paris April 7–11, 1952, see *International Herald Tribune*, Paris ed., April 8, 9, 12, 1952; Eisenhower, *Mandate for Change*, p. 23; and materials in EM, Subject File, Command Post Exercises, esp. Supreme Headquarters Allied Powers Europe, *CPX One Administrative Instructions*.

[2] On the June 13 reception at Montgomery's chateau in Milly see no. 224, n. 4. A note at the bottom of the EM copy of this document indicates that the original was handwritten by Eisenhower.

229   *Eisenhower Mss.*

To ARTHUR HAYS SULZBERGER   *June 18, 1951*

Dear Arthur:[1] Please don't take the following as any studied analysis or recommendation—it represents only my quick reactions to your suggestion.

As I recall Columbia's charter, it definitely places certain responsibility and authority in the hands of the *President,* and no amount of reorganization or shifting of titles can change that inescapable fact. This means, to my mind, that we will not correct the existing situation by setting up a Chancellor to be the day-by-day executive carrying out policies approved by the Trustees. In other words, I think your suggestion is possibly just a bit turned around—because you must have a "President" on Morningside Heights.

I think some title could be devised for me that would allow me to retain a definite connection with the University. Possibly, this title could be Chancellor. Certain duties of a supervisory and general character, including that of heading up Columbia's liaison machinery with the outside world, could be prescribed by the Trustees for the Chancellor. The new President's duties would then be exactly as now, except that when the Chancellor could be actually on the job the President's duties would not include those specifically prescribed for the Chancellor by Trustee action.

All this may, of course, be completely haywire. It might be far simpler just to allow me to retain—if this is possible—my position as a Trustee. Certainly I am quite ready to accept any scheme that the Trustees may decide upon. I know that any error they will make with respect to me will be on the over-considerate side. But my real concern is that they try to be completely fair to Columbia.[2]

I don't believe that I am quite ready to state my own particular preference and ideas with respect to a successor if the time comes when the Trustees believe that one should be appointed. I suppose that, at that time, I would be expected to vote as would any Trustee, and, frankly, I do not know all the possibilities. I assume that Kirk has proved his capacity to serve as a satisfactory President. I think the Trustees would now be in a better position than I to judge on this point. I do know that he shares my feeling that we should keep fighting to place matters of real policy and University interest in front of the Trustees, rather than mere statistics of deaths, resignations, appointments, and transfers of small amounts of money. I think there are others in the University family who are likewise highly qualified men. I am assuming—at least for the moment—that the Trustees would far prefer to make a selection from among members of the Columbia family than to go outside in the search for a so-called "name" man.[3]

As you can see, my whole idea about this business is rather hazy and unformed; possibly it is even uninformed. I have had little opportunity to think about the matter objectively, and I merely repeat my feeling that Columbia cannot afford to go on too long in its present state. We have gotten a good start on Morningside in rebuilding internal morale and determination on a number of fronts, and in stirring up outside interest in some worthy and fairly unique developments. Momentum must not be lost. I would regard my entire $2\frac{1}{2}$ years' work as completely wasted unless these things are carried on with enthusiasm and effectiveness.[4]

This is not a very good answer to your letter. It is the best I can manage at this minute. *Cordially*

[1] For background on Sulzberger, publisher of the *New York Times* and a Columbia University trustee, see no. 114, n. 1.

[2] In a letter of June 14 (EM) Sulzberger had suggested creating the post of Columbia University chancellor to provide a "chief administrative officer of the University acting . . . under the President." The question of Eisenhower's status as absentee university president and its possible ill-effect upon Columbia had been raised by the General in earlier letters to Sulzberger and a fellow trustee and had been a topic of discussion when trustee Douglas Black visited Eisenhower in Paris during May (see nos. 184, 213, and 234). This suggestion of Sulzberger's was the result of later conversations with Black (see Sulzberger to Eisenhower, June 6 and 14, 1951, both in EM, same file as document).

[3] Grayson Louis Kirk was acting president of Columbia during Eisenhower's absence (see no. 155). On Eisenhower's efforts to make the board of trustees more effective see Galambos, *Columbia University*, nos. 552, 585, and 1130. For developments involving Kirk and the continuing question of Eisenhower's status see, in this volume, nos. 325 and 370, respectively.

[4] On the programs Eisenhower developed during his active service as Columbia's president see Galambos, *Columbia University*.

230   *Eisenhower Mss.*

To JOSEPH LAWTON COLLINS   *June 19, 1951*
Personal and confidential

Dear Joe: Further to the conversation that we had relative to Gruenther's promotion, I am now preparing, and sending along with this letter, a formal written recommendation to accomplish this object.[1] As I told you, I discussed the matter briefly with the President and with the Chairman of both the House and Senate Committees for the Armed Services. The reason that I mentioned it to both Chairmen was because of the possibility that a joint resolution might be necessary in order to create the necessary vacancy.[2]

With respect to this last point, I feel that American members of such staffs as this should not actually be charged against Army quotas. It has been my experience that, in all Allied groupments, the United States finds itself in the position of necessarily providing the lion's share of the personnel; and, because so much of the work applies to land bases, lines of communication, and logistics in general, to say nothing of strategic planning and operations, this personnel comes largely from the Army instead of the other Services. Consequently, I believe that our legislation should make some general proviso for making good this definite drain upon personnel resources, particularly in qualified staff and command officers.[3]

There are two reasons for Gruenther's promotion that, to my mind, are compelling. The first of these is that too much of the work here is devolving upon me individually. Much of this work falls upon me because I am a senior American, and because of the obvious importance to all of Europe of MDAP and of other American activities.[4] I need someone who will be accepted naturally and cheerfully as my personal representative, especially in these American matters. By the nature of things, my job is a complicated *Allied* one; my principal American assistant should be one who bears in his own right every proof we can provide that he is a responsible, respected, and authoritative American officer. Actually, Gruenther's duties in this field make him my *American Deputy*; these duties are fully as important as his function in serving as my Allied Chief of Staff.[5]

The other reason for this move is so that we may always be prepared for the eventuality of my possible disability. While I have no special reason for fearing any personal disaster, yet prudence demands that we, as Americans, be fully prepared for any unforeseen circumstance of this character.

The problem is to have someone available with appropriate rank, and who, we have reason to believe, would be fully acceptable to all the countries involved. Of course, you fill this bill personally, but it is equally clear that you are already involved in a job of tremendous importance; and it is easily possible that, because of your age, the President would want you to stay on even after the expiration of your current tour. Moreover, we should certainly have more than one string to the bow. (Incidentally, in this connection, I understood that Bradley has said that he would never want to be considered for this post.)[6]

I have thought over your feeling that we should make no mention of Gruenther's possible promotion until you are ready to accompany it by a promotion for Van Fleet. Certainly I am not going to argue against the desirability of promoting Van—he is not only one of my warm friends and classmates, but his fighting record in World War II and his performances since have been outstandingly brilliant. However, I must point out that you can find and provide out of the American Army today far more combat commanders than you can individuals to fill satisfactorily the kind of post that Gruenther has. So, while I should like, of course, to see them promoted together, I do not quite understand why either case cannot stand on its own merits.[7]

I have not talked over this particular matter with Secretary Pace— at least, so far as I can remember. But I have decided to wait no longer because, frankly, I want to get relieved of some of the things that are now so demanding upon my time. One of these, incidentally, is to meet and talk with a stream of important, semi-important, and self-important visitors from all nations that want to pay a call at this headquarters. Because our problem is so much one of selling and inspiring—of making people see this job from the American viewpoint—we consider it highly important to greet most of these people. I want Gruenther to share more of the load while he, in turn, puts more of his detailed staff work on the shoulders of someone else.[8]

I have written this long explanation on a personal and confidential basis; however, if you want to use it in conferring with any official who has definite responsibility in these matters, you are at liberty to do so. In the meantime, I know you will observe my request for complete secrecy. Not a soul in this headquarters, except for my own personal secretary, knows about this letter or has any faintest knowledge of my intention to write it. So, until this thing is an accomplished fact, I would very much like to keep it on the secret list.[9]

It was grand to have you over here for a few days; I hope that your future plans will include an occasional weekend, at least on a quarterly basis, in this region.

With warm personal regard, *Cordially*

[1] Eisenhower had probably discussed Gruenther's promotion with Collins during the Army Chief of Staff's May visit to SHAPE (see no. 183; on Gruenther see nos. 2, n. 3, and 219). The recommendation that Gruenther be promoted from lieutenant general to general, Regular Army (RA), is the following document.
[2] The chairmen of the House and Senate committees were, respectively, Congressman Carl Vinson (see no. 80, n. 2) and Senator Richard Brevard Russell, Democrat from Georgia (see Galambos, *Columbia University*, no. 1123). There are no records of the discussions in EM. According to the Officer Personnel Act of 1947 (and its subsequent 1948 amendment), there were to be no more than nine Army officers above the rank of lieutenant general; this quota included the officer serving as Chief of Staff but excluded Generals of the Army such as Eisenhower. It was probably this limit that made Eisenhower think a congressional joint resolution might be necessary (see U.S., *Statutes at Large*, vol. 61, pt. 1, pp. 886–87, and vol. 62, pt. 1, pp. 1069–70; and Galambos, *Columbia University*, nos. 16 and 100).
[3] Neither an alteration of the official quotas nor a special act of Congress would prove necessary to secure Gruenther's promotion. Not only was the number of full generals then carried on the Army's active list well below the allotted maximum of nine but the existence of a state of national emergency (proclaimed by Truman on December 16, 1950) permitted promotions in excess of the peacetime quotas established in 1947 (see U.S., *Statutes at Large*, vol. 61, pt. 1, pp. 886–87; *Public Papers of the Presidents: Truman, 1950*, pp. 741–47; and Galambos, *Columbia University*, no. 1129). Of fifty-three officers above the rank of colonel assigned to SHAPE between April 1951 and May 1952, sixteen (nearly one-third) were members of the U.S. military (see "SHAPE Personnel Roster," in EM, Subject File, SHAPE).
[4] Beside this sentence on the EM copy of this letter are two asterisks, indicating the handwritten notation at the bottom of the page: "Not my *official* responsibility—but demands much of my time." On MDAP see nos. 2, n. 2, and 286.
[5] On Gruenther's many duties with SHAPE see, for example, nos. 149, 284, and 855; and C. L. Sulzberger, "NATO's No. 2 Man—Gruenther," *New York Times Magazine*, December 30, 1951, pp. 9–35.
[6] Collins, who was fifty-five, would continue to serve as Chief of Staff until 1953,

when he would succeed Bradley (see no. 50, n. 5) as U.S. representative to the NATO Military Committee and Standing Group. On the selection of a successor for Eisenhower as SACEUR see no. 836; and Eisenhower to Ridgway, April 30, 1952, in EM.

[7] For background on Van Fleet, then serving as CG of the Eighth Army in Korea, see no. 165, n. 2. In a letter to Eisenhower on this same day (EM) Collins told the General that he had discussed both the Van Fleet and Gruenther promotions with the JCS and with Secretary of Defense Marshall (see no. 2) and had received their endorsements. Because Gruenther occupied a NATO position, Collins suggested that it would be appropriate for Eisenhower to write or wire Marshall directly in regard to the matter. There is in EM no correspondence with Marshall concerning the promotion, but on June 23 Eisenhower wired Collins that both a formal recommendation (the following document) and an informal explanation (this document) had been sent to him on the twenty-first (see AP 80755, EM).

On July 9 President Truman would send to Congress the nominations for promotion to general of Gruenther, Van Fleet, and Lieutenant General John Edwin Hull (see *New York Times*, July 10, 1951). The Senate would confirm these and other appointments, including the promotion to General of CIA Director and Eisenhower's friend Walter Bedell Smith (see no. 144, n. 1) on July 27 (*Congressional Record*, 82d Cong., 1st sess., 1951, 97, pts. 7–8: 9032–33; *New York Times*, July 28, 1951). In a small ceremony in Collins's office on July 30, Hull, Gruenther, and Smith received their fourth stars from the Chief of Staff (see Schulz to Davidson, AP 80946, July 20, 1951, in EM, Subject File, Cables, Outgoing; and Schulz to Cannon, DA 3811, July 30, 1951, in EM, Gruenther Corr.). On Hull, who would become Army Vice Chief of Staff on August 1, see *Eisenhower Papers*, I–XI.

[8] On the many visitors to SHAPE see, for example, nos. 183, 218, and 394. For background on Eisenhower's views concerning the SHAPE role in NATO see nos. 23, 111, and 215. In his formal recommendation Eisenhower noted that he had not spoken with Secretary of the Army Frank C. Pace, Jr. (see no. 116, n. 21), concerning the Gruenther promotion (see the following document).

[9] Eisenhower's personal secretary, Yeoman Helen E. Weaver (USN), typed this letter.

231   *Eisenhower Mss.*

To JOSEPH LAWTON COLLINS   *June 19, 1951*
Confidential

Dear General Collins: In accordance with an intention previously communicated to you verbally, I submit formal recommendation that Lieutenant General Alfred M. Gruenther, assigned as my Chief of Staff in Supreme Headquarters, Allied Powers Europe, be promoted to the grade of General.

The importance and difficulties of his position, and the character of the duties that I am compelled to assign him in order to prevent unwarranted drains on my own time are the basis for this recommendation. It would be helpful to me if the matter could be acted upon favorably at an early date.

I have previously discussed this matter with the President of the United States, but not with the Secretary of the Army.[1] *Cordially*

[1] See the preceding document.

232   *Eisenhower Mss.*

To Sɪᴅ Wɪʟʟɪᴀᴍs Rɪᴄʜᴀʀᴅsᴏɴ   *June 20, 1951*

Dear Sid:[1] It has been a long time since I have received a letter so interesting and intriguing as yours of June 14th. Everything in it was the kind of thing I like to hear you talk about.[2]

In the first place, I am delighted that you are cashing the check and handling the investment according to your own judgment and convictions. While I, of course, understand the explanation that accompanies your letter, my sole interest is to be in with you as a tiny partner in some of your ventures and to see how the thing works out. Needless to say, my family and I are more than appreciative of the care and time you expend in our behalf.[3]

I was quite amused to read of the political ambitions and finagling as you saw it exposed in Texas. Politics brings about amazing developments. But one thing about it seems constant—it excites all that is selfish and ambitious in man. I know you can understand why I never wanted any of it—but I must assure you that no Washington Queen[4] or anybody else has any right to speak for me. As a matter of fact, I have talked to you as intimately about these matters as I have to anyone else—possibly moreso.

You did not mention Amon in your letter, so I assume that he and his family are fine. In any event, give them and Perry Bass my very warm regards.[5]

Of course, both Mamie and I are delighted to know that you may be coming over here in late summer or early fall. By that time, we should certainly be in our house, and we will have a very nice time, I assure you. We can have many long evenings to talk over the affairs of the world—no matter how little we know about them. As a matter of fact, possibly our ignorance will make us better talkers. (It just occurs to me that you might resent being classed as ignorant as I am about such matters.)[6]

The pressures on me are of several kinds. One kind involves the obviously difficult and perplexing problems that are attached to this job. There are fresh ones every day—all of different types, but all are difficult. Another type of pressure is a continuation and intensification of the kind that have been plaguing me for the past several years, and of which I have so often talked to you. Many individuals are still insisting that I have a duty at home that must take eventual precedence over this job. Possibly the kind of activity that you have seen recently in Texas will eventually eliminate this kind of pressure completely. But I do notice that new polls have just been run by Mr. Gallup which don't give me a lot of immediate encouragement. However, I always console myself with the thought that a man crosses each bridge as he comes to it.[7]

The first paragraph of your letter made me laugh a bit. I did not realize that, in my former note, I had said that Aldrich was with you in England. I meant Texas, and my mind must have been wandering a bit as I put that one down. Forgive my stupidity, and write again as soon as you can.[8]

With warm personal regard, *As ever*

[1] Richardson was an old friend of Eisenhower's (see no. 34).

[2] Richardson's letter is in EM.

[3] Richardson had written Eisenhower about one of his current investments, 1,478 acres of Texas property for oil exploration. Reassuring the General, Richardson told him, "Don't worry about your money—I am using it to good advantage" (see nos. 474 and 558).

[4] This was probably Perle Mesta, American Minister to Luxembourg, who had had several speaking engagements in the United States in May (see *New York Times*, May 13, 1951).

[5] Amon G. Carter, Sr., was a friend of both Eisenhower and Richardson; Perry R. Bass was Richardson's nephew (see no. 35).

[6] Richardson would see the General in Washington, D.C., in November and would visit him in Paris in February 1952 (see no. 474; and appointment calendar. On the Eisenhower home see no. 82, n. 5).

[7] For background on Eisenhower's current concerns see nos. 174, 186, and 218; on the pressure to declare himself a presidential candidate see nos. 200, 205, and 221. In the recently published Gallup polls Eisenhower had been the most popular choice among Democratic and Republican voters as a potential presidential candidate (see *New York Times*, Apr. 16, 1951; and Gallup, *The Gallup Poll*, vol. II, *1949-1958*, pp. 989-90).

[8] The General was referring to his letter of May 29 (EM) and to Winthrop W. Aldrich, who had visited with Richardson in Forth Worth, Texas.

233   *Eisenhower Mss.*

To EDWARD EVERETT HAZLETT, JR.   *June 21, 1951*

Dear Swede: Recently, I have been wondering when I was to get another letter from you; a question that was finally answered by your letter dated June 1st.[1]

Trying to make some comment on each subject you raise—and,

God knows, my observations will not only have to be limited, but will possibly be better classified as hazy day-dreaming—I start out by saying that, if anyone thinks this whole task is "comfortably in hand," he had better acquaint himself a little more accurately with facts as they are. How can anyone in the world believe that numbers of nations could, within a short space of months, so organize, develop, and train themselves that they were even capable of putting out timely and necessary decisions in such a matter as mutual defense, to say nothing of accomplishing all the material, mental, and psychological jobs as are included? Time and effort and understanding, and renewed effort and tireless study, and still more effort, would comprise a fair recipe for the product we are trying to obtain.[2]

There are, of course, certain encouraging developments. I am quite sure that anyone acquainted with Europe would, as of now, sense a tremendous increase in morale, courage, and determination as compared to the level of these only six months to a year ago. On every front, there has been some improvement, even though progress is far less rapid than we could wish or even have the right, in certain instances, to expect.

The one indispensable thing to remember is that, if the free world cannot provide for its "collective" security, the alternative for every one of these nations, including our own, is an eventual fate that is worse than any kind of expense or effort we can now imagine. Consequently, American leadership must be exerted every minute of the day, every day, to make sure that we are securing from these combined countries their maximum of accomplishment. Where any nation fails— as some of them are, of course, partially failing now—we must take a certain portion of the responsibility by admitting that, in that particular instance, our leadership has been partially ineffective.

I assure you that, as I go around to various capitals and meet with members of the several governments, I never let up for one single instant on pounding home some serious facts. The first of these is that each country must provide the heart and soul of its own defense. If the heart is right, other nations can help; if not, that particular nation is doomed. Morale cannot be imported.[3]

Next, I insist that Europe must, as a whole, provide in the long run for its own defense. The United States can move in and, by its psychological, intellectual, and material leadership, help to produce arms, units, and the confidence that will allow Europe to solve its problem. In the long run, it is not possible—and most certainly not desirable— that Europe should be an occupied territory defended by legions brought in from abroad, somewhat in the fashion that Rome's territories vainly sought security many hundred years ago.[4]

To my mind, Turkey and Greece are nations that must be brought into our defensive structure very definitely and soon. Whether or not they should be militarily attached to my command, or should be divided—possibly with Greece under our particular umbrella and Turkey under another—are problems that are susceptible of several solutions. The main thing is that they, with us, should make common cause against a common enemy and make this job one of top priority in each country.[5]

As to Iran, I think the whole thing is tragic. A stream of visitors goes through my office, and some of the individuals concerned seem to consider themselves as authorities on the Iranian question. Numbers of them attach as much blame to Western stupidity as to Iranian fanaticism and Communist intrigue in bringing about all the trouble. Frankly, I have gotten to the point that I am concerned primarily, and almost solely, in some scheme or plan that will permit that oil to keep flowing to the westward. We cannot ignore the tremendous importance of 675,000 barrels of oil a day. The situation there has not yet gotten into as bad a position as China, but sometimes I think it stands today at the same place that China did only a very few years ago. Now we have completely lost the latter nation—no matter how we explain it, how much we prove our position to have been fair and just, we *failed*. I most certainly hope that this calamity is not repeated in the case of Iran.[6]

So far as all the MacArthur–Korean–administration–partisan politics affair is concerned, I have kept my mouth closed in every language of which I have ever heard. I have some very definite views about parts of the sorry mess, but I do not have a sufficiently clear picture of the whole development, starting with some of the machinations and incidents of World War II, to allow me to make up my mind on many of the important features of the affair. I guess that the most we can hope out of the thing is that soon the Communists will quit pushing the conflict (terminating it somewhat as they did the attacks on Greece), and that we succeed in developing a sufficient strength among the South Koreans to withdraw the vast bulk of our own forces.[7]

Wedemeyer's testimony left me in complete bewilderment as I attempted to follow his reasoning. Moreover, I am not quite sure what *you* mean when you talk about "punishing the aggressor." Unless you can get at Mao and the small group of advisers he has right around him, I do not believe we would be punishing the aggressor merely by bombing Canton, Shanghai, or any other place where we would most certainly be killing a number of our friends along with the people who are true followers of the Communists.[8]

I will not comment at all upon your observations concerning your dilemma in the next election if you have to vote for either of the two men you name. With respect to your statement, "Worse luck, you seem to be pretty well out of the present picture," I wish I could feel that way as definitely as you do. Not only has there been a very recent poll taken which continues to stir up trouble, but a whole bevy of visitors here, and correspondents in the States, keep plugging away at a contrary view and determination.[9]

I never heard of Clugston. Moreover, I am told that his book was written as a very sly piece of "smear" work. I can't be bothered, although he is one campaigner who is apparently in league with another fellow named Dewey Taft who publishes a queer little paper down in Wichita. This latter character insists that I am one of the great friends of Communism in our country, and the darling of Moscow. I wish to God he could see some of the propaganda spread around this country by the Communist Party. If I am not Moscow's number one public enemy today, then I am certainly running that number one man a close race.[10]

You are right in your idea that I had nothing to do with the appointment of Fechteler, but you are wrong that I went over backward in naming Monty as my Deputy. Monty not only has a very fine reputation in this region as a soldier, but *he is one*. Moreover, he is a very determined little fellow who knows exactly what he wants, is simple and direct in his approach, and minces no words with any soldier, politician, or plain citizen when he thinks that that particular individual (or the country he represents) is not fulfilling his complete obligations to NATO. He is one man who clearly recognizes the truth of the assertion that Europe cannot forever depend upon America for military and economic aid and assistance. He hammers away at the idea that this region must become self-sufficient.[11]

We shall be on the look-out for your friend Corydon Lyons. If he brings along his students, I think I shall be secretly a bit on the pleased side. Sometimes I get quite weary of talking to the old, the fearful, and the cautious. I like to meet young people with their fresh outlook and their fixed, even if sometimes too complacent, assumption that they can meet the problems of their own time.[12]

It was nice to hear that Bob Baughey had been to see you. Not long ago, I had a letter from him.[13]

I assure you that we are not enjoying Paris in the sense that we would prefer to be here instead of in the United States. I think that, if ever two people have had enough of foreign service, we are they. We look forward to coming home—not the least of our pleasures will be a visit with you and Ibby.[14] In the meantime, please keep writing.

Cordially

[1] On Hazlett (USNA 1915), a close friend of Eisenhower's since their high-school days, see *Eisenhower Papers*, vols. I–XI; and the General's memoir *At Ease*, pp. 104–6. See also *Ike's Letters to a Friend: 1941–1958*, ed. Robert W. Griffith (Lawrence, Kans., 1984).

[2] In what he had termed "a biased report from the home-front" Hazlett had commented (June 1, 1951, EM) on the public attitude toward Eisenhower's SHAPE

efforts. He said that "everyone seems to think you are doing a magnificent job over there. . . ," but he also wondered whether Americans were not being too complacent and expressed doubts that the NATO forces were prepared to meet a determined Russian onslaught.

[3] Since the time of his January exploratory trip to the NATO nations the General had repeatedly stressed thoughts similar to these (see, for example, nos. 11, 23, and 218). On some of his recent trips to the NATO capitals see nos. 149, 153, and 199.

[4] In both the United States and Europe, where industry had not yet recovered from the wartime devastation, defense production was proving to be a major stumbling block to Eisenhower's organizational efforts (see, for example, nos. 6, 100, n. 5, 156, and 221).

[5] Both Greece and Turkey had recently renewed their requests for membership in the North Atlantic alliance, and the question was then under study by both military and political components of NATO (see Ismay, *NATO*, pp. 39–40). For background see no. 148, n. 8; for developments see nos. 384, n. 1, and 494.

[6] Iran had been in a state of turmoil since World War II (see *Eisenhower Papers*, vols. I–IX). Recently Iran's Communist party and several anti-Western Moslem factions had gained power along with Prime Minister Mohammad Mossadeq. The May 2 nationalization of the immense British-owned Anglo-Iranian Oil Company (see no. 149) had produced threats of war and anti-British/U.S. riots and demonstrations (see Hassan Arfa, *Under Five Shahs* [New York, 1965], pp. 396–98; Donald N. Wilber, *Iran: Past and Present* [Princeton, 1976], pp. 142–44; and *New York Times* and *International Herald Tribune*, Paris ed., May and June 1951). For developments see no. 259.

[7] Hazlett said of the MacArthur dismissal investigation (see nos. 136, 145, and 196, n. 5), "On the whole . . . the effect has been good." On Eisenhower's relationship with MacArthur and his opinion of him see nos. 153 and 181; and his memoir *At Ease*, pp. 213–14, 223–26, 246–48. On the Communist unrest in Greece during Eisenhower's term as Chief of Staff see Galambos, *Chief of Staff*, esp. nos. 1482, 1711, and 1815.

[8] During the MacArthur hearings General Albert C. Wedemeyer (see no. 178) had defended many of the controversial actions of the former Far Eastern commander and had been highly critical of U.S. policy in China and Korea (see Senate Committee on Armed Services and Committee on Foreign Relations, *Military Situation in the Far East: Hearings*, 1951, pt. 3, pp. 2294–2567).

Recent proposals for a negotiated Korean cease-fire had entailed the redivision of the country at the thirty-eighth parallel. Hazlett had commented: "What do we gain by that? Certainly it involves no punishment of the aggressors—and it smacks strongly of appeasement." On the cease-fire proposals see *New York Times*, May 18, 19, 20, June 2, 10, 24, 1951. Eisenhower was probably referring to statements made by MacArthur before his removal as CINCFE in which he had threatened both conventional and atomic air attacks on mainland China (see nos. 101, n. 5, and 143, n. 4).

[9] Hazlett had voiced his displeasure with the prospect of choosing between Truman and Senator Robert Taft (see no. 196) in the 1952 election. Hazlett said of the Eisenhower-for-President movement that "with only a nod of your head the spark could quickly be fanned into a flame." On the political pressures being brought to bear on the General see, for example, nos. 190, 196, and 205, n. 3. Recent Gallup polls had given Eisenhower a wide margin over the other potential 1952 candidates (see no. 232).

[10] Kansas newspaperman and political writer William George Clugston had recently published a book on the General entitled *Eisenhower for President?* Hazlett had enclosed a clipping about the book with his June 1 letter. The volume was extremely

critical of both Eisenhower's character and his military career, hinting broadly that he was the puppet of conservative monied interests (see W. G. Clugston, *Eisenhower for President? or Who Will Get Us Out of the Messes We Are In?* [New York, 1951], pp. 11–43). Dewey M. Taft, the conservative editor and publisher of the *American Digest* (whom the General had mistakenly associated with the more liberal Clugston), said his paper "crusades for the American spirit of free enterprise and promotes an active campaign against communism" (see *Wichita Eagle*, July 30, 1950). Writing to Eisenhower's friend and former aide Harry Butcher (see no. 190), Dewey M. Taft had referred to the General as "the man who wears Stalin's medal . . . the man who used the American army to help the Kremlin war criminal place one-third of the human race behind the Iron Curtain" (see Taft to Butcher, May 23, 1951, and *American Digest* 13, no. 2 [May 1951], both in EM, Butcher File). For European Communist petitions and other materials aimed against Eisenhower and the work of NATO see EM, Subject File, Trips, SHAPE no. 1, Communistic Material.

[11] For background on the controversy between Britain and the United States over the proposed appointment of American Admiral William Fechteler to the important post of SACLANT see nos. 45 and 142. On Field Marshal Montgomery's work with SHAPE see nos. 17 and 219.

[12] Hazlett had written that his friend Dr. John Cor*iden* Lyons, of the University of North Carolina at Chapel Hill, would shortly be conducting a student tour of Europe and had requested a letter of introduction to Eisenhower. The General would meet with the educator and thirty students on August 24 (see appointment calendar; and correspondence in EM, Miscellaneous Corr., esp. Lyons to Eisenhower, Oct. 14, 1951).

[13] Fellow Kansan Air Force Reserve Colonel Robert Martin Baughey (Galambos, *Columbia University*, no. 527) had recently been appointed Chief of the USAF section of the Los Angeles Armed Forces Public Information Office. He had visited Hazlett in North Carolina during March (see Baughey to Eisenhower, Apr. 27, 1951 [incorrectly dated 1941]; and *Los Angeles Times*, Mar. 16, 1951, both in EM, Baughey Corr.).

[14] Hazlett's wife Elizabeth.

234   *Eisenhower Mss.*

To Douglas MacCrae Black   *June 21, 1951*

Dear Doug:[1] Your letter shows that you not only grasp my point very accurately, but that you have proceeded in what I would consider the very finest way.[2]

I quite agree with you that there is no sense "pushing" these things. What I did rather expect was that the Chairman might appoint a small committee to prepare, during the summer, a tentative plan that could be presented to the Trustees in the early fall for consideration. This would have placed the matter in the realm of serious consideration rather than mere speculation, and this kind of plan could even have been expanded to include tentative nominations, and so on. However, this omission may not have been particularly serious, since I have no doubt that most of the Trustees will be thinking earnestly about the matter from time to time before the next Trustees meeting can be held.[3]

The other day, I saw Ken McCormick briefly, and I know that he has had some talks with Kevin. As you can well appreciate, I instinctively shy off from any discussion of a project that has in view writing about me—so I am not certain what the outcome of their conversations has been.[4]

The last couple weeks have been particularly busy ones for me, complicated by the presence of a Congressional Committee and other important visitors. My golf is suffering terribly.[5]

Love to Maude, *Cordially*

[1] For background on Black, president of Doubleday & Company, Inc., and a member of the Columbia University board of trustees, see no. 168, n. 8.

[2] In his letter of June 15 (EM) Black had explained that he had recently spoken with trustee chairman Frederick Coykendall (see no. 114, n. 1) and with several other members of the Columbia board concerning Eisenhower's position as president of the university. Black, who had discussed the matter with Eisenhower during May, wrote, "I outlined to them as accurately as I could our conversations, pointing out that . . . you felt it essential that the University have a permanent and not an acting head" (for background see nos. 184, 213, and 229). Black had also "made it abundantly clear" that Eisenhower desired to remain closely affiliated with Columbia, even if it were not as the university's president.

[3] In his reply (June 28, 1951, EM) Black said it seemed better "to let this matter ride" while several of the trustees were on vacation. He would try to develop a concrete proposal by the end of the summer. For developments see nos. 370 and 373.

[4] Eisenhower had seen Doubleday's editor in chief, Kenneth Dale McCormick, on June 17 (see appointment calendar; for background see Galambos, *Columbia University*, no. 27). Over the next few months McCormick would work with the General's civilian aide Kevin McCann (see no. 53, n. 10) on a biography of Eisenhower. The book, entitled *Man from Abilene*, would serve as the the General's campaign biography (see McCormick to Eisenhower, Jan. 15, 1952, EM; and Lyon, *Portrait of the Hero*, p. 426).

[5] On the Eisenhowers' recent schedule see nos. 218 and 222; and the Chronology in these volumes.

235   *Eisenhower Mss.*

To Aksel Nielsen   *June 21, 1951*

Dear Aksel:[1] Both your letters were most interesting, particularly the one that gave me a clear picture of the Blackmer deal.[2] While I would not bother you to send me periodic reports—because I do not know enough of the details to develop any real opinion about them—it would be nice if you would send me word whenever there is any particularly important development.

While I am sorry that you could not acquire possession of the farmland southeast of the city on the basis that we had discussed, I am certainly glad that you did not go into it either on the basis of exorbitant price or, what would have been even worse, to go in with people that you did not trust.[3]

When I bought our little farm in Pennsylvania, a friend of mine wanted to send me several head of Black Angus purebreds. I think that he has now forgotten this—I certainly hope so. If I hear no more of this, I am going to get, at an early date, a very few white-faced heifers. Through them, I may try to raise enough cattle to consume pasturage that is otherwise unusable, and run the off chance finally of producing some calf that could turn into a champion. This is something about which I shall have a lot of fun talking to you one of these days. Right now, I am going to do nothing at all.[4]

Min has heard nothing from Denver, and I think she is wondering why Mrs. Cannon has not written to her. For this reason, I am taking out to her your letter of June 11th which will give her some idea of how things now are, even though it was written the day after she left.[5]

It would be difficult for me to tell you how really grateful I am for all your kindness, especially to her. I think she is enjoying herself, but, naturally, she does do some worrying. She has complete and implicit confidence of your wisdom in the handling of her affairs—in fact, I think she places more confidence in you (with me running a respectable, but nevertheless distant, second) than in any other person in the world, including any member of her own family. For the kindness, the thoughtfulness, and the generosity that have built up this kind of feeling in her, none of us will ever be able to thank you enough.[6]

Give our love to Helen and to Virginia and her nice family,[7] and, of course, warm regard to yourself. *Cordially*

---

[1] Nielsen was a Denver, Colorado, business executive and an old friend of the Eisenhowers' (see no. 34, n. 3).

[2] The two letters were probably those of April 24 (EM) and June 11 (no copy in EM). In the earlier letter Nielsen had said that preliminary papers had been signed concerning the sale of property in which he and Eisenhower had invested. This property, located in the Denver area, included the Blackmer house and barns, set on approximately thirty acres (see Nielsen to Eisenhower, Aug. 3, Sept. 4, Dec. 12, 1951, and Eisenhower to Nielsen, Sept. 10, 1951, EM).

[3] This property was probably discussed in the letter of June 11.

[4] Edwin N. Clark had wanted to give the General Black Angus cattle (on Clark see no. 1, n. 2; for background on the cattle at the General's Gettysburg farm see nos. 179, n. 7, and 192, n. 3). Nielsen had given Eisenhower several bulls (see Galambos, *Columbia University*, nos. 695 and 881; and nos. 275, n. 3, and 600, n. 2, in these volumes).

[5] Mamie's mother, Elivera ("Min") Doud, had arrived on June 13 for a visit with

the Eisenhowers (see no. 224, n. 2). She was concerned about the health of her husband, John S. Doud, who had stayed behind in Denver under the care of Mrs. Cannon (on Mrs. Cannon see no. 118, n. 10; for developments see no. 240, n. 1).
[6] Nielsen had been an adviser to the Douds and would continue to give Mrs. Doud financial and legal advice (see no. 275, n. 2).
[7] Nielsen's wife was the former Helen Maurer; Virginia Elaine Nielsen Muse was their daughter (see Galambos, *Columbia University*, no. 630).

236   *Eisenhower Mss.*

To FORREST PERCIVAL SHERMAN   *June 23, 1951*
Secret

Dear Forrest: I renew my expressions of gratitude to you for the great part you took in getting my annoying little "Southern problem" settled.[1] While we were waiting for this outcome, I did learn (I think quite accurately) that our Service Associates in Britain were not the ones holding up the announcement; it was apparently civilian members of the government. While I don't know exactly what their idea was, it is obvious that they were hoping to use some factor in the situation in order to obtain compliance with their wishes in the larger organizational problem of the Mediterranean.

In this connection, I have come to the conclusion that Carney must have no responsibilities and no command that is not a portion of my official responsibilities and delegated to him by me. If—as seems very probable—you find it necessary for the United States Navy to be represented in some different way in that area, I must ask you to see the virtue of naming some other individual. I have specific reference to those responsibilities assigned to Carney by the Joint Chiefs of Staff or the Navy Department relative to Spain, Yugoslavia, Greece, and Turkey, all of which predated his appointment as the Commander in Chief of my Southern flank. In a similar category would be any other responsibilities not charged to me.[2]

Of course, I expect Carney to be my connecting link with all other Allied interests in the Mediterranean, and I have no doubt that certain of his functions with respect to lines of communication in the Western Mediterranean will have to be carried out in close cooperation with some other Allied commander—possibly even under that other commander's over-all coordinating power for that particular activity. Such things as this are, of course, normal and are not the kind of thing of which I am speaking. But, on the other hand, I could not possibly consent to Carney's being given any over-all responsibility with respect to that whole region if the particular function or activity lay completely outside my official responsibility. I do not think I have to labor this point; I am sure you see the complete logic and need for the position I am trying to describe.[3]

Recently, I have had quite a stream of visitors from Washington, and I notice that there is practically universal recognition of the wisdom, patience, and leadership you bring to our complicated defense problems. You are earning your way—beyond all doubt. *Cordially*

[1] For background on the controversy over Eisenhower's southern flank command arrangements see nos. 148, n. 2, and 198, n. 4. The BCOS, at a June 8 meeting with JCS Chairman Omar Bradley, had agreed to accept Eisenhower's command arrangements for the Southern Command. The British made their agreement conditional on the understanding that future overall command of the Mediterranean was yet to be settled and that Eisenhower's Southern Command would not include Greece and Turkey. The Standing Group approved these arrangements on June 14. On June 18 SHAPE announced that Admiral Robert Carney had been appointed Commander in Chief, Allied Forces, Southern Europe (CINCSOUTH). Carney, whose headquarters was to be ashore in Italy, was also to act as Commander of the Allied Naval Forces, Southern Europe, with a separate staff. At this time SHAPE also announced that Italian General Maurizio de Castiglioni (see nos. 77, n. 15, and 153, n. 7) had been appointed to command the land forces in southern Europe. The Commander, Allied Air Forces, Southern Europe, was to be U.S. Air Force Major General David Myron Schlatter (see Galambos, *Columbia University*, no. 322, n. 6, for background). Eisenhower told Carney that his "primary mission" would be "the integrated defense of the Southern European area." Carney would also "be responsible in the Mediterranean for the protection of the sea communications for the southern flank of Allied Command, Europe" (Eisenhower to Carney, June 19, 1951, EM; see also State, *Foreign Relations, 1951*, vol. III, *European Security and the German Question, Part I*, pp. 526, 528–33; D-D [51] 159, June 19, 1951, NATO Files, microfilm; and Bradley to Eisenhower, June 14, 1951, and Eisenhower to Schlatter, June 19, 1951, both in EM).

[2] In April Eisenhower had asked that his CINCSOUTH be given authority to deal directly with Greece (and perhaps Yugoslavia) for planning purposes (see no. 148, n. 4). On May 21 the JCS had agreed, telling Eisenhower that "Carney, as Commander in Chief, Allied Forces, Southern Europe, should coordinate the planning of Greece, Turkey and also of Yugoslavia insofar as such planning pertains to NATO and defense of Western Europe" (JCS 1868/264, May 19, 1951, CCS 092 Western Europe [3-12-48], Sec. 81). Admiral Carney would continue to serve as the U.S. Navy commander in Europe and in the Mediterranean (CINC-NELM) after he assumed his CINCSOUTH NATO command.

[3] Sherman responded in a cable sent on July 3: "Believe that matters involved will be best resolved by my conferring with you personally as soon as possible." In his response (SH 20793, July 6, 1951), Eisenhower agreed to meet with Sherman in Europe and told him, "Gruenther is only other individual aware of contents of my letter to you. We will keep matter confidential." Both cables are in EM. For developments see nos. 304, n. 4, and 429, n. 1.

To PAUL GRAY HOFFMAN   *June 23, 1951*

Dear Paul: During your recent visit, you asked my view on the "International Federation of War Veterans' Organizations," and whether I believed this group could be helpful to the North Atlantic Treaty Organization in developing the security of Western Europe.[1]

Although neither I nor any member of my staff has had direct contact with this organization, I am told that it was formed to enlist the active support of the very influential war veterans' organizations in furtherance of the objectives of the free world. You doubtless recall that, following World War II, the Communists made serious efforts to infiltrate and obtain control of war veterans' organizations as a further means of supporting Kremlin policy. I hear it was in an effort to prevent this that certain individuals who oppose Communism decided to form the International Federation of War Veterans' Organizations. I am also told that, although the Communists have made some penetration in certain of the groups which are associated in this international organization, the control and leadership rest in the hands of the non-Communist elements. It is also my understanding that the American Legion has refused to be associated in any way with the International Federation of War Veterans' Organizations, possibly on the basis of the reports of penetration mentioned above.[2]

Although I see no way in which it can be directly useful to the North Atlantic Treaty Organization, I do believe that private organizations whose objective is to gain support for our efforts to build up free world strength can indirectly be very important.[3] In view of the somewhat indeterminate character of the information I've been able to gather, I'd venture to suggest that you have some investigator look up the plans and programs of the organization, as well as the ability, energy, and loyalty of its governing body. If these are all satisfactory, I'd vote for its support on about the basis you mentioned to me.[4] *Cordially*

---

[1] During a visit with Eisenhower earlier in the month (see no. 200 and the following document) Ford Foundation president Hoffman had given the General copies of two memorandums concerning a $100,000 grant request to the Ford Foundation made by the International Federation of War Veterans' Organizations. On one of these Hoffman had written, "General, In your opinion—will this organization be helpful—to you?" (see memorandum from Howard, International Federation of War Veterans' Organizations, Project NY 93, May 7, 1951; and memorandum with Hoffman addition, Gladieux to McDaniel, May 10, 1951, both in EM, same file as document).

[2] Formed in Paris during November 1950, the International Federation of War Veterans' Organizations (soon to be renamed the World Veterans Federation) represented more than ten million former World War II servicemen through its affiliations with veterans' groups from thirteen nations. Although the first official conference of the organization would not be held until July 1951, the federation's

leaders had previously publicized their endorsement of the U.N. actions in Korea and included among their goals the establishment of a "genuine peace [opposed to] the phoney peace of Soviet Russia and her satellites" (see *New York Times*, Dec. 2, 1950, July 19, Dec. 1, 1951; and Gilbert Harrison, "Getting Together at Belgrade," *New Republic*, January 7, 1952, 15–16). In spite of the reluctance of the American Legion to become associated with the federation, other veterans' organizations in the United States, including one group in which Eisenhower was a life member (Amvets), would become federation affiliates (see *New York Times*, Sept. 1, 1951; Newcomb to Schulz, Jan. 6, 1949, in EM, Miscellaneous Corr.; and correspondence in EM, Subject File, Clubs and Associations).

[3] Eisenhower had turned the question raised in Hoffman's letter over to SHAPE C/S Gruenther with instructions that the matter be investigated "as quickly and as rapidly as possible" (see memorandum, Eisenhower to Gruenther, June 18, 1951, in EM, same file as document). Brigadier General Anthony J. Drexel Biddle, Jr., Executive of the NATO National Military Representatives Committee, conducted the investigation, replying on June 20 that the federation merited Eisenhower's endorsement for its "aims to counter the activities of a similar [veterans'] organization to the east [i.e., a Communist group]." He warned the SHAPE commander, however, to confine his support to the organization's stated objectives, for fear of drawing fire from the American Legion (see Wood to Biddle, June 18, 1951, and memorandum, Biddle to Wood, June 20, 1951, both in EM, same file as document; for background on Biddle see Galambos, *Columbia University*, no. 554). At Gruenther's suggestion, the matter was also given to SHAPE's adviser on international affairs, Douglas MacArthur II (see no. 32, n. 3), who concurred in Biddle's analysis and drafted this reply for Eisenhower (see Gruenther to Wood, June 21, 1951, on Wood to Gruenther, June 18, 1951; and MacArthur to Wood, June 20, 1951, with attached draft, all in EM, same file as document).

[4] The Ford Foundation apparently rejected the federation's request (see *New York Times*, Sept. 26, 1951; Apr. 11, 1952). Eisenhower made only slight alterations in MacArthur's draft, aside from the last two sentences, which the General apparently added.

238   *Eisenhower Mss.*

To PAUL GRAY HOFFMAN   *June 25, 1951*
Personal and confidential

Dear Paul: Thank you very much indeed for your note, sent to me from London.[1] I not only profited from the succinct statement of your ideas, but I found that when Averell, Milton Katz, Chuck Spofford, Al Gruenther, and I met to discuss the subject of NATO reorganization, all of us used your memorandum as a place from which to start.[2]

Before giving you the general conclusions of the group, I want to mention a sort of instinctive reaction I have obtained from the study I have been able to give the matter. It is that we are so badly in need of reorganization in Washington that I feel rather reluctant to undertake a change on this side of the water until these affairs can be handled properly in our own capital. To do so—especially if there should be put out any information concerning a centralization of functions over here—the effect on the public mind would be the creation of a conviction that opportunity and responsibility alike now rest in the hands of one person; whereas the actual truth would be that, without a headquarters reorganization in Washington, we would have done little to remove frustration and unnecessary delay. On the other hand, assuming intelligent reorganization on both sides of the water, it is clear that progress would be speeded up and would be more effective. The particular thing, from our viewpoint, that is needed in Washington is the setting up of one responsible authority to be the executive in these affairs. He should be responsible to the President and a top flighter in every respect.[3]

In all of our discussion, we did *not* bring in the question of personality whatsoever; we tried to discuss the matter purely on the basis of efficiency in organization and function, without regard to the identity of the individuals that might be assigned to different posts therein. I think it was generally felt that any attempt, at this late date, to move me back into a civilian post could have repercussions of an almost unpredictable nature.

I do not need to repeat to you how sincerely I believe that the SHAPE effort must work or the results are going to be well nigh disastrous for the free nations. Consequently, I think it is particularly important in any talk about possible reorganization to avoid any damage to what we are *now doing*. Of course, I, as an individual, seek neither added responsibility nor additional authority—to my mind, it would be very bad if even the slightest thought of such a purpose would be held by any of the participating nations. Nothing matters except the job itself. In a somewhat different sense, this same observation applies to the American position of leadership. Certainly we don't want to give ammunition to the charge of "American imperialism."

There are two objects, our group felt, to be accomplished by reorganization in Europe. The first of these is to bring about a coordination and greater efficiency in American activity in this region, especially in directing all appropriate activities more effectively toward the purpose of building up collective security.[4] The second purpose is to produce efficiency in the *Allied* machinery set up in NATO. It is to this latter part of the problem that you have principally addressed yourself. The first part also attracted our immediate interest.

I think we agreed generally that an "ideal" solution would be something along the line you suggest, under the assumption that the top Allied man would be an American.[5] He should have American authority to make final recommendations to Washington concerning MDAP; and to utilize the ECA as well as the Production Board to make certain that MDAP programs did not work against the economic welfare of the several nations. Under this scheme, I, as SACEUR, would (in military affairs) be the principal adviser to the top man, including, particularly, recommendations as to the end item program.[6]

From this kind of thinking, you can see that, pending the establishment of such a completely reorganized machinery, it would seem advisable, starting now, to route MDAP and the affected parts of ECA recommendations so as to give SACEUR the final and controlling voice in recommendations to Washington on these particular points.[7]

There was no disposition in our group to minimize the consequences of the organizational defects that disturbed you so greatly. On the contrary, I believe most of us felt that your recommendations (without reference, of course, to any personalities involved) were sound and timely. One of our purposes in insisting upon getting our own house in order was because part of it at least could be done quickly, and that this would promote the over-all efficiency of a reorganized Allied machinery.

I most certainly enjoyed my few all too brief visits with you. Whenever you can come back this way, you must be sure to allot a good portion of your time to SHAPE.

My love to Dorothy,[8] and warmest regard to yourself.[9] *Cordially*

---

[1] Hoffman's letter of June 20 is in EM. He told Eisenhower that "if we are to get maximum results in the shortest possible space of time, you have got to be moved out of left field and into the pitcher's box." The two men had met on June 7 (see no. 218; see also State, *Foreign Relations, 1951*, vol. III, *European Security and the German Question, Part I*, pp. 190–92).

[2] Eisenhower had apparently met with Averell Harriman, Milton Katz, Charles Spofford, and Alfred Gruenther on June 23. In his undated memorandum (EM) Hoffman had maintained that "until a realistic posture of defense is attained, there is always a possibility that the Kremlin, in the rash hope for a quick victory, might start its armies marching toward the Atlantic." Citing the progress made by the "free nations," Hoffman said, "The foundation has been laid for startlingly rapid progress from now on provided the next logical step is taken: The establishment in NATO of a unified command." Hoffman concluded that Eisenhower should exercise this overall NATO command because he was "one of the few men living today—and quite possibly the only man—who is held in great respect and affection by people in and out of government, both in the United States and Europe."

[3] For background on Eisenhower's dissatisfaction with the support given NATO in Washington see nos. 173 and 174. On June 20 Douglas MacArthur II had informed the State Department that Eisenhower favored appointing a single "man of Cabinet stature" to direct all U.S. NATO-related activities and to solve "many questions which now are batted about among the different agencies in Washington for protracted periods of time" (State, *Foreign Relations, 1951*, vol. III, *European Security and the German Question, Part I*, pp. 188–90). In October 1951 Congress would establish a Mutual Security Agency, and President Truman would appoint W. Averell Harriman as the first Director of Mutual Security. Harriman would be given the power to direct, supervise, and coordinate programs of military, economic, and technical assistance (Mutual Security Agency, *First Report*, pp. 44–45; Kaplan, *Community of Interests*, pp. 158–62).

[4] For a summary of the organizational problems involved in the American Mutual

Defense Assistance Program in Europe see U.S. Department of Defense, "Activities in Europe Concerned with Materiel Support of NATO and MDAP," October 5, 1951, OS/D, 1951, Clas. Decimal File, CD 092.3 NATO.

[5] In March 1952 NATO would name British General Lionel Hastings Ismay as its first secretary-general (see nos. 5 and 734, n. 8). In this position Lord Ismay would oversee the civilian functions of NATO, including many of those previously exercised by the Council of Deputies (Ismay, *NATO*, pp. 55–56).

[6] "End items" delivered to Europe under MDAP were pieces of equipment ready for use, such as ships, tanks, and aircraft and their components (see Senate Subcommittee on Foreign Relations, *United States Foreign-Aid Programs in Europe: Hearings*, 1951, pp. 46, 50, 55; and U.S. Department of Defense, "Activities in Europe Concerned with Materiel Support of NATO and MDAP," Oct. 5, 1951, OS/D, 1951, Clas. Decimal File, CD 092.3 NATO).

[7] In August Secretary of State Dean Acheson would approve a policy statement calling for "full, though largely informal, participation by General Eisenhower and his U.S. Staff in all U.S. activities connected with NATO in Europe" (State, *Foreign Relations, 1951*, vol. III, *European Security and the German Question, Part I*, pp. 236–37).

[8] Hoffman's wife, the former Dorothy Brown.

[9] For developments see no. 268.

239   *Eisenhower Mss.*

To Lewis Williams Douglas   *June 25, 1951*

Dear Lew:[1] This note is just to bring to your attention a few thoughts that I want to make certain I do not forget.

Mr. Potofsky came to see me today and, after quite a talk on the international situation and the attitude of American and international labor toward various aspects of this situation, he gave me his comments on the American Assembly:[2]

a. He thought, in general, that the Assembly was a little bit too "Republican" in tone.

b. He definitely thought that the labor viewpoint was not sufficiently represented.

c. He felt that Philip Young should be relieved of other duties within the University and given the sole job of acting as the Executive, under the direction of the Policy Board, of the Assembly.

We discussed these points at some length, and I flatly told him that one of the reasons there was normally so little labor representation on boards and commissions of this kind was that, after all, the number of recognized and intelligent labor leaders was not unlimited and those who were qualified for this kind of work were in such demand that it was exceedingly difficult to get them to serve. I told him we had insisted upon a broad base representation and have done as best we could in this regard.[3]

With respect to the conservative or, what he called, Republican weighting of the Assembly, I told him that that was certainly something we never intended.[4] I most heartily agreed with him that I would like to see Philip Young take direct charge of the executive work.[5]

With warm regard, *Cordially*

P.S. Looking forward to seeing you within a few days.[6]

[1] On Douglas, Chairman of the National Policy Board of Columbia University's American Assembly, see no. 221, n. 5.

[2] Jacob S. Potofsky was president of the Amalgamated Clothing Workers of America, a former adviser to the Office of Manpower, Department of Labor, and a member of the National Policy Board of the American Assembly (for background see Galambos, *Columbia University*, no. 1083; on the first Assembly session see no. 201 in this volume). Potofsky would write to the General on June 29 (copy in EM, Miscellaneous Corr.) thanking him for their talk and expressing his appreciation of Eisenhower's views on "this idealogical [*sic*] war we are engaged in. The moral, spiritual and economic aspects [of which] are just as important as the military." For Eisenhower's views on the importance of labor and industry to the NATO effort see, for example, nos. 1 and 23. For more on Potofsky's visit with the General see the following document.

[3] Of eighty-one participants in the first Assembly only four, including board member Potofsky, were representatives of organized labor (see *New York Times*, May 21, 1951; and no. 201). On the selection of Assembly participants see nos. 25, 47, and 87.

[4] On other criticisms concerning bias at the Assembly see nos. 202 and 220.

[5] For similar opinions that Columbia Graduate School of Business dean and American Assembly Executive Director Philip Young should relinquish one of his posts see no. 204; and Lewis Douglas to Eisenhower, May 31, 1951, in EM, same file as document. Potofsky's meeting with Eisenhower had been arranged through Young earlier this month (see Young to Eisenhower, PSN72, June 6, 1951; and Cannon to Davidson, AP 80661, June 8, 1951, both in EM, Miscellaneous Corr., Potofsky).

[6] Douglas would meet with Eisenhower and Philip Young in Paris on July 9 (see no. 220, n. 5; and Schulz to Douglas, July 7, 1951, and undated wire, Douglas to Eisenhower, both in EM, same file as document).

240   *Eisenhower Mss., Diaries*

DIARY   *June 25, 1951*

On Sat. night, the 23rd, we received word that Pupah (John Sheldon Doud, Mamie's father) had died. He has been in precarious health for many years—when I met him in 1915 he had a blood pressure of 240 and weighed that many pounds—but, as always in such case, the finality of death came as a shock.[1] Min (Mamie's Mother) was visiting us at the time and so I sent her, Mamie, John and Dr. Snyder off to

Denver. They left here at midnight, Saturday. This morning we rec'd news that the party had arrived safely. . . .[2]

*   *   *   *   *

Mr. Potofsky came to see me.[3]

Opposes any thought of dealing with Spain—quite bitter about it.

Insists that for every advantage we would obtain we would lose so many friends as to suffer a *net* loss. There is a definite chance he is completely right—particularly if our efforts to deal with Spain place another early drain on our scarce items & raw materials. All these erstwhile enemies and near-enemies *want* the "world" and sometimes they are close to arrogant in saying what they will *not* give as quid pro quo.[4] Our lesson with Russia from 41–46 ought to be remembered!

[1] Mr. Doud had suffered a cerebral hemorrhage at his home in Denver on June 22 and had died the following day (see *New York Times*, June 24, 1951; *International Herald Tribune*, Paris ed., June 25, 1951; and appointment calendar). News of his death was telephoned to the Eisenhowers by family friend Cyril Croke (on Croke see no. 118, n. 4).

[2] This party, along with Robert Schulz (see no. 1, n. 4) and Mrs. Eisenhower's personal maid, Rose Wood (see no. 118, n. 6), had flown to the United States aboard the SHAPE commander's aircraft, the *Columbine*. Departing on the twenty-third, they arrived in Denver at noon on the twenty-fifth (see EM, Subject File, Aircraft, Trip Itinerary, no. 25). For background on the visit of the Eisenhowers' son John and Mrs. Doud to Paris see no. 224, n. 2; on SHAPE physician Snyder see no. 59, n. 4.

A portion of this document was deleted in the original diary in accordance with the General's instrument of gift to the Eisenhower Library.

[3] See the preceding document.

[4] The issue of U.S. relations with fascist Spain, an unresolved dilemma since the close of World War II, had recently been brought to public attention by both the press and members of Congress. Debarred from participation in the United Nations by a 1946 General Assembly resolution, Spain had been purposely neglected by the United States. The advent of the cold war and U.S. commitment to the defense of Western Europe had, however, prompted calls for a reassessment of this policy. The April 4 sense-of-the-Senate resolution ending the debate on the assignment of U.S. troops to Europe (see nos. 128 and 222) had strongly recommended the "utilization on a voluntary basis of the military and other resources" of Spain (*Congressional Record*, 82d Cong., 1st sess., 1951, 97, pt. 3: 3283).

Over the last year congressional pressures, the desire of the Navy to establish bases on the Iberian Peninsula, and the pro-Spanish sentiments of many American Catholics had gradually eroded the Truman Administration's resistance to normalizing relations with the Franco regime. During August 1950 Congress approved appropriations to Spain, and in December of the same year Stanton Griffis (LL.D. Union College 1944) was named U.S. Ambassador to Madrid (see Theodore J. Lowi, "Bases in Spain," in *American Civil-Military Decisions: A Book of Case Studies*, ed. Harold Stein [Birmingham, Ala., 1963], pp. 667–99; memorandum, Bradley to Baele, Dec. 13, 1950, CJCS, Bradley Files, 092.2 NATO; and memorandum, Vandenberg to Marshall, Aug. 27, 1951, Clas. Decimal File, OS/D, 1951, CD 092.3 NATO).

The question of possible Spanish participation in NATO had arisen frequently since Eisenhower had assumed his duties as SACEUR. During discussions with Portuguese officials in January the General had learned that the Lisbon government urgently desired Spain to take part in the defense of the Iberian Peninsula. Communications the General had received from some members of Congress also indicated support for Spanish inclusion in NATO (see Memorandum of Conversation with the Portuguese Foreign Minister, Jan. 17, 1951, in EM, Subject File, Trips, SHAPE no. 1; and nos. 80 and 84). For Eisenhower's thoughts on Allied relations with Spain see no. 16, n. 3.

On July 18 Secretary of State Acheson would announce that "for strategic reasons," the United States had initiated conversations with the Spanish government to determine what Spain might contribute to the defense of Western Europe. Acheson stressed that America's commitments to its NATO allies would receive clear priority over any future aid to Spain (see Lowi, "Bases in Spain," pp. 692–93; and *New York Times*, July 19, 1951). In his letter of June 29 (EM) Potofsky enclosed four newspaper clippings concerning the situation in Spain. For developments on the Spanish question see no. 865.

241   *Eisenhower Mss.*

To Gerald Pawle   *June 26, 1951*

Dear Pawle:[01] Thank you very much for your note.

Of course, the Committee on the Present Danger has as its fundamental purpose the combating of Communism, since the Communist ideology employing Russian power and Russian imperialism constitutes the great threat to our way of life. In actual practice, however, the Committee on the Present Danger does far more than to undertake mere counter-propaganda campaigns. It supports every constructive effort that it believes worthwhile and appropriate to its basic purpose. For example, it urgently supports universal military service in our country—likewise, it has been a great champion of collective security for the North Atlantic community. I believe I gave you a short printed page on its general objectives; so I suppose it is not necessary to labor this point.[2]

Because of Lord Kemsley's interest, I am writing at once to my friend Dr. Conant, President of the American Committee on the Present Danger. I shall ask him to send to you everything that is printed on the matter, together with any suggestions that he may have. With your permission, I shall send to him both your letter to me and the one you wrote to Jimmy Gault. This ought to help him understand the approach that Lord Kemsley believes would be most applicable in the United Kingdom.[3]

All success to you both. *Sincerely*

[1] Pawle, a former Royal Navy flag lieutenant commander, was a defense correspon-

dent for both the *London Sunday Times* and the British Kemsley Group newspapers. On June 13 he had met with the General and later attended a SHAPE luncheon for British Ambassador to France Oliver Charles Harvey (see appointment calendar).

[2] In a note of June 22 (EM) Pawle had thanked Eisenhower for his time and for having explained to him the activities of the Committee on the Present Danger. Founded in September 1950 as a nonpartisan citizens' group dedicated to the security of the free world, the Committee had been active in rallying public support for the U.S. defense of Western Europe, increased foreign aid to friendly governments, and a system of universal military training (see James Bryant Conant, *My Several Lives: Memoirs of a Social Inventor* [New York, 1970], pp. 469, 505–20, 524–32; and Galambos, *Columbia University*, nos. 1112 and 1125). For Eisenhower's role in the postwar debates over universal military training (UMT) and a proposal he originally preferred, universal military service, see no. 447.

[3] Pawle had told Eisenhower (June 22) that he had discussed the idea of forming a British counterpart to the Committee on the Present Danger with the chairman of the Kemsley Newspapers, Ltd., James Gomer Berry, first viscount Kemsley of Dropmore. This proposal, Pawle said, had made "an instant and deep impression" on Lord Kemsley. In a letter to SHAPE military assistant James Gault (see no. 96) Pawle had said that Kemsley desired to be put in touch with the American committee to determine "what methods they themselves have been adopting with success." Gault had sent the request on to Eisenhower (see memorandum, Gault to Eisenhower, with extract, June 25, 1951, in EM, same file as document). Eisenhower's letter to Harvard University president James Bryant Conant follows.

242   *Eisenhower Mss.*

To James Bryant Conant   *June 26, 1951*

Dear Jim: The other day, I attempted to describe to a British friend of mine the purpose of and the operational methods employed by the Committee on the Present Danger. My friend is a trusted member of the Kemsley organization of newspapers, and he immediately interested Lord Kemsley in studying a similar proposition for the United Kingdom.[1]

I think it would be a very useful thing if you would send to Gerald Pawle at Kemsley House, London, W.C.1, all the printed material that now exists on the Committee on the Present Danger. If this could be accompanied by copies of speeches that have been made by the various members and associates of the Committee, I think that also would be helpful. Finally, if it is not too much of an imposition on your time, I should think it would be wonderful if you could add a few suggestions in the terms of advice gleaned from your experience in this fine program.[2]

Of course, this letter brings to you my very warmest wishes for your continued good health and happiness. *Cordially*

[1] For background see the preceding document. Conant, president of Harvard University, was one of the founders and president of the Committee on the Present Danger (see Galambos, *Columbia University*, nos. 285, 575, and 1016).
[2] Conant would reply on July 7 (EM) that he had sent the requested materials to Pawle. There is no further correspondence on this subject in EM, but see memorandum, Gault to Eisenhower, June 25, 1951, with extract, in EM, Pawle Corr.).

243   *Eisenhower Mss.*

To Hugh Roy Cullen   *June 26, 1951*

Dear Roy:[1] Thank you very much for your letter. You have a knack of packing your communications brimful of interesting subjects.

As you have suggested in the past, I never comment, in my replies, on certain phases of your messages.[2]

Here I am working as hard as I ever have in my life. It is a long job and, as you can well imagine, it was quite a wrench for me to leave the things at Columbia University in which I was so interested when I was again assigned to duty in the military field. Except for my very earnest conviction that the future of our way of life demands successful establishment of collective security in the free world, nothing could have induced me to take on such an onerous task. Progress is, of course, frequently slower than we could wish, or even behind that which we would seem to have every right to expect. But at least to date there is progress, and this is the important thing.

As you know, I feel that every single person who can boast of American citizenship must do his utmost in these days of tension and bewilderment to help preserve and sustain our nation and our system. Every man must work in the field for which he is best fitted, and every man owes it to himself to try to understand the great issues of the day. This applies with particular force to the Communist threat which combines external pressure and aggression with internal subversion, bribery, and corruption. Their weapons are lies and deceit, and we have to make certain that the truth of the great American drama and system is kept constantly before the world. You have heard me so often talk along these lines that I am just being repetitive.

Please give my warm greetings to Lillie[3] and, of course, best regards to yourself. *Cordially*

[1] Cullen, president of the Quintana Petroleum Corporation of Houston, had become acquainted with Eisenhower through fund-raising and other activities of Columbia University (see Galambos, *Columbia University*, nos. 602 and 945; and no. 47 in this volume). A Texas Republican, the oil millionaire had become interested in an Eisenhower presidential candidacy and had frequently written to

the General concerning the U.S. political climate (see correspondence in EM, same file as document; and Edward W. Kilman and Theon Wright, *Hugh Roy Cullen: A Story of American Opportunity* [New York, 1954], esp. pp. 274–97).

[2] Due to Eisenhower's firm conviction at this time against taking any overt action regarding the upcoming presidential race, he had replied directly to none of the Texan's political comments. In a letter of March 27 (EM) Cullen had agreed with the General's decision to remain silent on these matters, writing that "up to now you have pleased the American people by refusing to discuss politics in any way. . . ."

[3] Lillie was Cullen's wife, the former Lillie Crantz (see Galambos, *Columbia University*, no. 634). On Cullen's continuing efforts to secure a political commitment from Eisenhower and on the eventual deterioration of relations between the two men see correspondence in EM, same file as document, esp. memorandums, Mulkey to McCann, May 23, 1952, and Cannon to McCann, May 26, 1952.

244

Eisenhower Mss.

To JOSEPH LAWTON COLLINS

June 27, 1951

Confidential

Dear Joe: Recently I have had some reports concerning great advances made in certain types of weapon development by Mr. Bührle of the Oerlikon Company in Switzerland.[1] I know that certain European countries have been very interested in these developments. It is rumored, for example, that the Spanish are trying to get a branch factory in their own country for the production of Oerlikon weapons.

Mr. Bührle has apparently produced very rapid fire 20 and 30 millimeter guns, their special purpose being defense against low-flying aircraft by using the principle of the revolving barrel and automatic fire. He has gotten up to some 1,600 to 1,800 rounds per minute, according to the information I have. Beyond this, he seems to have built very effective rockets using the shaped-charge principle.[2] One of these rockets is the 2.8 caliber. In guided missiles and control equipment, it appears that he has also made much progress.

Someone told me that the United States Navy has had a mission in Zurich studying these items. If this is true, there is unquestionably already in the Pentagon a lot of information on this subject. However, I do not know to what extent our Ordnance Department is familiar with these matters.

This note requires no answer. I just wanted you to know about the information that has been passed along to me.[3] *Cordially*

[1] Industrialist Emil Georg Bührle had been sole owner of Oerlikon Machine Tool Works since 1939. As General Manager of the Oerlikon Company in 1924, Bührle had begun development of the widely used 20 mm Oerlikon automatic cannon for

use by and against aircraft. The Oerlikon firm also manufactured high-precision machine tools and calculating machines (see John Quick, *Dictionary of Weapons and Military Terms* [New York, 1973], p. 33; and *New York Times*, Jan. 9, 1952).
[2] Shaped charges are designed to focus and concentrate explosive energy in one direction (see Willy Ley, *Rockets, Missiles, and Space Travel* [New York, 1958], pp. 185–88).
[3] Collins responded in a letter of July 19 (EM). He told Eisenhower that the Army was keeping in close contact with Bührle and Oerlikon. He added that the Air Force was developing a revolving-barrel, rapid-fire cannon for use in its aircraft and was then procuring a hollow-charge Oerlikon rocket. The Army, however, could not use the rapid-fire cannon for antiaircraft purposes because of the excessive heat it generated. The Army eventually employed a six-barreled 20 mm Gatling gun capable of firing 3,202 rounds per minute (Quick, *Dictionary of Weapons*, pp. 459, 493; see also *New York Times*, Jan. 4, 1952).

Eisenhower wrote the following note on the bottom of the file copy of this letter: "The above information was given to me on 26 June by John Olin, an explosives manufacturer from St. Louis, Missouri" (for background on John Merrill Olin see Galambos, *Columbia University*, no. 885).

245   *Eisenhower Mss.*

To Francis Joseph Spellman   *June 29, 1951*

Your Eminence: I am deeply touched by the consideration and compliment that is implicit in every word of your cordial letter and invitation. I sincerely wish that it were possible at this moment to tell you unequivocally that I shall plan to attend the Alfred E. Smith dinner on October 18th.[1]

The reasons that compel the observance of the strictest caution, not to say pessimism, in planning my future calendar, are so many as almost to defy much more than enumeration. Sheer preoccupation in work which includes, among other things, daily meetings with a stream of distinguished and important visitors; the strict observance of impartiality in my dealings with all of the twelve nations that make up NATO; complications that are almost certain to arise in connection with any current visit to the United States; a definite need to travel more frequently to the several countries of Western Europe; and similar types of activity have combined to force me to curtail drastically almost every kind of engagement that is outside of the official. I have even gone to the extent of eliminating a number of engagements that have been on my calendar for a year or more, for meetings in Western Europe. Of all these, the only future one that I am keeping is one that takes me to London on the 3rd and 4th of July for ceremonies commemorating the American dead of World War II.[2]

All this, of course, may disappear or become so greatly modified in the coming months that it would be possible for me to come home for a short period. Such a development would be little short of miraculous, and would be even moreso if it should come about soon enough that I could give you timely advice.

In spite of all the above, my regard for your work, to say nothing of my respect and affection for you personally, are such that I will be quite ready to consider the matter again in early September with a view to giving a decisive answer. Moreover, I am also ready to say that, if I can come home at all around mid-October, I will not only make my trip coincide with the time of your dinner, but will now assure you that I will accept no other invitation unless I can also accept yours. More than this, I do not feel I can say.[3]

With warm personal regard and great respect,[4] *Cordially*

[1] Earlier in the month Cardinal Spellman had extended an invitation to Eisenhower to speak at the annual dinner of the Alfred E. Smith Memorial Foundation (see no. 216). Following the General's declination, the Cardinal had urged him to reconsider and to accept the invitation on a strictly tentative basis (see Eisenhower to Spellman, June 14, 1951, and Spellman to Eisenhower, June 25, 1951, both in EM, same file as document).

[2] For Eisenhower's hectic schedule see the Chronology, in vol. XIII. On the visits to SHAPE of large congressional parties see, for example, nos. 209 and 256. In regard to Eisenhower's participation in the London memorial services see no. 252.

[3] In his reply Cardinal Spellman thanked Eisenhower for his consideration and assured him that even if he could make no definite commitment to the engagement "until the very night of the dinner," it would still be "most welcome news." A handwritten notation on Spellman's reply indicates that the General was at that time prescheduled to appear as guest of honor at the "Alamein Reunion" in London on October 19 (see notation, Cannon to Eisenhower, on Spellman to Eisenhower, July 28, 1951, in EM, same file as document). On the World War II battle of El Alamein see Chandler, *War Years*, nos. 539 and 569; on the 1951 reunion see no. 401.

Although Eisenhower would travel to the United States later this year, he would not do so until after the Smith Foundation dinner. U.S. Ambassador to Moscow Admiral Alan G. Kirk (see no. 22) would serve as guest speaker at the October 18 function (see Spellman to Eisenhower, Aug. 30, 1951, and Eisenhower to Spellman, Sept. 4, 1951, both in EM, same file as document; and *New York Times*, Oct. 19, 1951).

[4] Eisenhower had sought the assistance of his C/S in drafting this reply (see memorandum, Gruenther to Eisenhower, June 30, 1951, in EM, same file as document). The General would accept Spellman's invitation for the following year, addressing the Smith Foundation dinner as the Republican presidential nominee (see *New York Times*, Oct. 7, 1952).

To Robert Earll McConnell   *June 29, 1951*

Dear Mr. McConnell:[1] Recently, Cliff Roberts and I have been talking over some of the things that you discussed with him and Bill Robinson in New York, the early part of this month. In addition, I have read the report that you rendered on the German Bi-Zonal Fuel Economy in May 1948.[2]

I rather think you are right in your feeling that occasionally I over-state or over-simplify my raw material argument when I am engaged in showing the inescapable relationships between the United States and Western Europe. I think that when we consider all of these materials in the mass, the argument is more accurate than when confined to one such item as manganese. However, ordinarily I have only 5, 10, or 15 minutes in which to present a rather wide and comprehensive picture of a world situation, and the particular feature that we now have under discussion is only one part of that picture.[3]

Unless I am badly misinformed, it is true that, as of now, the United States produces less than 4% of the manganese it requires, and our requirements constantly go up and up because of our increasing production. It is easier to speak of this kind of figure than it is to discourse at any great length on cultural, historical, political, economic, and industrial relationships between two great areas of the world. Consequently, I usually content myself with the mere statement that if Europe should go Communistic it would obviously become increasingly difficult for us to keep some of the important raw material areas, such as India, out of the Communistic column. Therefore, it would grow, over the years, more and more difficult for us to get the needed quantities of manganese.

Now if we add up all of our needs in rubber, manganese, uranium, tin, oil, chrome, tungsten, and so on, and so on, we finally get to a place that would (assuming all the world except the United States to become Communistic) force us into a system of complete controls. In other words, we'd have a dictatorship of our own—and would have lost that for which we are struggling, freedom![4]

In any event, I am going to be more moderate and guarded in my future statements and, in the meantime, I am looking forward to a chance to discuss the whole matter with you at greater length.

With great appreciation of your interest, and with warm regard,
Cordially

---

[1] An alumnus of Columbia University, McConnell had been active in mining, industry, and defense production since his graduation in 1910 (for background see Galambos, *Columbia University*, no. 275).

[2] During a meeting in New York City on June 6, McConnell had discussed with

Roberts and Robinson certain of Eisenhower's recent statements concerning U.S. dependence on foreign-produced strategic raw materials. Disagreeing with the General's position (see n. 3 below), McConnell had supplied Roberts with two reports on defense and industrial resources, one of which urged an energy-source conversion of German industry from domestic coal to imported oil (see Memorandum of Conversation, McConnell with Roberts and Robinson, June 6, 1951; and Robert E. McConnell, "The German Bi-zonal Fuel Economy," both in EM, same file as document). On Roberts and Robinson, both of whom were then visiting the General, see nos. 193 and 260.

[3] Since assuming his post as SACEUR, Eisenhower had repeatedly stressed in speeches and correspondence that one reason the United States was compelled to defend Western Europe was to assure the nation's access to certain vital raw materials. Among these materials (supplied to the United States by or through its allies) were manganese and uranium, the former of which had previously been obtained in large quantities from the Soviet Union. McConnell had told Roberts and Robinson that he doubted the nation was in dire need of these materials, stating that in his opinion "there was more uranium in the United States than in Africa and Europe combined" (see Memorandum of Conversation, McConnell with Roberts and Robinson, June 6, 1951; and U.S. Department of the Interior, Bureau of Mines, *Minerals Yearbook, 1950* [Washington, D.C., 1953], pp. 757, 770. See also Senate Committee on Foreign Relations and Committee on Armed Services, *Assignment of Ground Forces of the United States to Duty in the European Area*, 1951, pp. 3–4; and nos. 26 and 51).

[4] Rapid expansion of U.S. defense production during 1950 had resulted in a 21 percent annual increase in manganese ore consumption. Of the total of 1,650,429 short tons of manganese consumed by the United States during 1950, 93 percent had been imported (see Interior, Bureau of Mines, *Minerals Yearbook, 1950*, pp. 757–72).

247   *Eisenhower Mss.*

To ROBERT TYRE JONES   *June 29, 1951*

Dear Bob:[1] Cliff has just read me a paragraph from a letter in which you told him that you were sending on to me, by Bob Woodruff, the latest set of golf clubs that you have personally used. I cannot tell you how touched I am by this news and how grateful I am for your thoughtfulness.[2]

It is true that I have great numbers of visitors, most of whom want to play one or two of the golf courses in this region. Ordinarily I cannot accompany them to the golf course, but it is nice to be able to provide them with the necessary tools. So far, I have put together $2\frac{3}{4}$ sets. With yours, I shall be able to equip an entire foursome because I have to get only one or two clubs to round out the works.[3]

I hope you realize how truly grateful I am for friends that can think of such nice things and carry them out so wonderfully.[4]

With warm personal regard, *Cordially*

[1] For background on Jones, a professional golfer and president of the Augusta National Golf Club, see no. 113, n. 4.
[2] On the visits to Paris of Eisenhower's fellow Augusta National members Clifford Roberts and Robert Woodruff see no. 217.
[3] For references to the General's frequent golfing visitors see, for example, nos. 143, n. 5, 217, and 227, n. 5.
[4] Eisenhower would write to Jones again on July 10 (EM) telling him that the clubs had arrived and that he had used them to shoot a one over par on the first nine holes of "one of our toughest . . . courses." For developments see no. 295.

248   *Eisenhower Mss.*

To Ralph Austin Bard   *June 29, 1951*
Personal

Dear Ralph:[1] I simply haven't the time at this minute to answer your long letter in the way it deserves.

I quite agree that there exists in Europe definite evidence to support the kind of conclusion that you express in a number of areas. However, we must not miss two other points that are also valid:

a. In each one of these fields, there can be unearthed a great deal of evidence of an opposing nature—that is, of an optimistic and encouraging type.

b. One of the reasons for the initiation of the NATO defense effort by the United States was its realization of the existence of a bewildered, defeated, neutralistic attitude among large sections of the European masses. Among other things, our country has undertaken the job of helping to lead them into a better frame of mind.[2]

I have often heard that our ECA program in one or two of the countries did not really succeed in getting down to the people. Recently, I talked to Mr. Katz about this, and he said that one point that has been missed is this—that except for the ECA program, factories could not have been kept open and there would simply have been *no jobs at all.* He gave me a lot of other information and conclusions that are too involved to try to recite here.[3]

In the case of Britain, I think your friend is somewhat wrong. All the American experts that I have contacted (and I assure you I have been quite assiduous in trying to dig out applicable information) agree that on the budgetary and financial side, Britain has gone flat out in the development of a military program. It is their conclusion that nothing more could be added under current conditions without definite danger of collapse. (Of course, the argument might be made that, if Britain were operating under a system of completely private enterprise, they might be in a healthier economic position and could, therefore, support a better program. The conclusions I give here are those based upon conditions as they now are.)

On the other hand, there is a definite feeling on the Continent that Britain has failed to produce any leadership in the spiritual or moral field. I think it is a general conclusion that Britain has been rather flat and colorless in the whole business.[4]

I am grateful to you for sending me your conclusions, and I hope that one of these days we will get another chance to talk them over at greater length.

Give Rawleigh[5] my warm greetings and, of course, best wishes to yourself. *Cordially*

[1] Bard (B.S. Princeton 1906), an investment consultant and former Under Secretary of the Navy, had visited Eisenhower with Chicago businessman Rawleigh Warner on May 4 (see appointment calendar; on Warner see Galambos, *Columbia University*, no. 1061).

[2] On June 20 Bard had written to the General (EM) concerning impressions gathered during his recent tour of Europe. As a result of World War II, Bard contended, the majority of the "lower strata of the population" in the devastated nations questioned whether Russian domination was not preferable to the horrors of another such war. Under these circumstances Bard doubted the dedication of the Allied countries to the NATO effort: "It would be appalling for us to be a party to a half-way job, not only because Western Europe would be destroyed, but our troops would be sacrificed." Since assuming the SACEUR post Eisenhower had repeatedly stressed the importance of America's role in improving the morale and self-confidence of the NATO allies (see no. 233, n. 3).

[3] Bard reported that through the mishandling of American economic assistance the Marshall Plan had failed in its efforts to eradicate communism in Western Europe. While the majority of corporations had benefited from the aid, the prosperity had not filtered down to the European workers, resulting in disaffection based upon the view that their lot was no better than that of their counterparts in the Communist satellite nations. For background on the ECA program see nos. 45, n. 3, and 288, n. 1; on Milton Katz, chairman of the NATO Defense Financial Economic Committee, see no. 16, n. 7.

[4] According to a British friend of Bard's, the efforts of Great Britain in the NATO defense would be only half-hearted as long as the nation was dominated by a "Socialist Government." This partial effort, according to Bard, would prove futile. Only a total commitment from all of the European allies would avert Russian domination of Western Europe. On British NATO contributions see, for example, nos. 218, n. 4, 563, n. 3, and 572, n. 2.

[5] On Rawleigh Warner see n. 1 above.

To Walter Kirschner

Dear Walter:[1] The pictures of the house and of the new cows, forwarded to me by Mr. J. B. Lim, are most intriguing. I am even more interested in the architectural sketches. Unfortunately, up to this moment, I have had no real time to study them; but as quickly as Mamie gets back, I intend to take out the whole works and go over it with her.[2]

At this moment, my first reaction was that the sketches seem to portray such a palatial home that I do not see how the Eisenhowers could produce it or support it—however, all this is a bridge that we shall cross when we get to it.[3]

In any event, our grateful thanks for your great interest and for your promptness in letting us have this visual portrayal of your ideas. I should write to George this afternoon, but I simply do not have the time. If you see him, won't you please give him my warm regard. (I am really more interested in sending my affectionate greetings to Mary; but she is such a poor correspondent that I have to stick to the masculine side of the family.) When George comes back this way about the first of August, I think that you and Mary and Mrs. Kirschner ought to be with him.[4] *Cordially*

[1] For background on Kirschner see no. 33, n. 2.

[2] Kirschner, who had become interested in the Eisenhower-Allen farming partnership through his association with George Allen, had made a gift of several head of Guernsey cattle to the two men in May (see no. 185). More recently he had sent architect J. B. Lim to visit the Gettysburg property to prepare designs for a proposed remodeling of the Eisenhower farmhouse and for the construction of a new residence for farm managers Arthur and Ann Nevins (see the following document). For background on the General's farming interests see nos. 48 and 179. Mrs. Eisenhower had flown to the United States earlier in the month to attend her father's funeral (see no. 240, n. 1).

[3] The construction of a new farmhouse for the Eisenhowers would be delayed until 1953 (see the General's memoir *At Ease*, pp. 358–60). The Nevinses would eventually move to a tenant house just outside of Gettysburg (see Nevins, *Five-Star Farmer*, p. 108).

[4] On Eisenhower's close friends George and Mary Allen see no. 9, n. 2; on Kirschner's wife Madeline see no. 185, n. 7. While Kirschner would come to Europe during July (see no. 315, n. 1), Allen would not be able to visit the General during this summer (see Eisenhower to Allen, Aug. 23 and 25, 1951, both in EM). For developments see the following document and nos. 270 and 315.

To ANN LOUISE STACY NEVINS
AND ARTHUR SEYMOUR NEVINS

Dear Ann and Art: For days, I have been hoping for a real opportunity to write you a long letter, but something always occurs to defeat my purpose.

Tomorrow I am expecting Mamie back from Denver where she attended Mr. Doud's funeral, and I am hoping that she has had a chance to talk to you on the phone. I should like very much to know how you are feeling about the farm these days, and I am particularly anxious to be assured that the two of you are not becoming mere drudges on the place—I want you to like it.[1]

Just yesterday, I got through the good offices of Mr. Kirschner and Mr. Lim a series of pictures of the farm and the cattle and an architectural drawing of proposed construction developments—that is, a future house for the two of you, and a rebuilding job on the existing structure. Incidentally, there were a number of pictures of interiors, and I must say that, if they were pictures of your house as it actually is, you have done a remarkable job in making it attractive on the inside.[2]

I have never worked harder in my life—even the hours that I get away from this office are normally involved in meeting with people who want to discuss NATO and its objectives, its organization, and its chances for success. Last evening, for example, I thought I was going to be entirely free; but, from 5 o'clock until 10:30, I had three prominent citizens on my neck—visitors from America—who wanted to know all about what we were doing and where we are going. Since it is exceedingly important that people understand this thing if we are to have any chance of successful accomplishment, I feel it necessary to give such persons whatever time is required.[3]

I have a number of letters from home urging me to come back for a short visit in the late fall. At this moment, I don't see how I can possibly do so, but I do assure you of one thing. It is that, if I come home, my real reason—no matter what may be given out publicly—will be the desire to see you two on the farm and to go over with you all the things that I would like to be able to discuss with you every day.[4]

With affectionate regard to you both, *Cordially*

[1] For background on the Nevinses and their management of Eisenhower's Gettysburg, Pennsylvania, farm see the preceding document and nos. 33, n. 2, and 170. On the death of Mrs. Eisenhower's father, John Sheldon Doud, see no. 240.
[2] The Nevinses were presently living in the original Eisenhower property farmhouse, a two-story brick structure that was then over one hundred years old (see Nevins, *Five-Star Farmer*, pp. 88–95). On Walter Kirschner and architect J. B. Lim see the preceding document.

[3] Eisenhower had spent the previous evening with Lieutenant General Ira Eaker (USAF, ret.), former Air Force Chief of Staff General Carl A. Spaatz (ret.), and General Jacob Louck Devers (USA, ret.) (see no. 130, n. 15; and Galambos, *Columbia University*, nos. 1074 and 363, respectively). The Generals were accompanied by their wives Ruth Huff Apperson Eaker and Ruth Harrison Spaatz and a "Mrs. LeMay," who was probably Helen Maitland LeMay, wife of Strategic Air Command CG Curtis Emerson LeMay (see appointment calendar).
[4] On Eisenhower's trip to the United States during November see nos. 457 and 468.

251   *Eisenhower Mss.*

To WILLIAM AVERELL HARRIMAN   *June 30, 1951*

Dear Averell: Now that you have come and gone, I do not feel that there is a great deal to be gained by writing a letter so quickly after your departure.[1] However, there is one point to which I do not believe we devoted much time. It is the bad consequences that would follow upon a financial and economic breakdown in European countries as a result of unjustifiable emphasis on their defense programs.[2]

This point comes up from time to time, and its importance clearly indicates the great need for striking a proper balance between runaway inflation and economic collapse on the one hand and dawdling and indifferent performance on the other. I am disturbed by the strictly statistical approach to the problem; this approach normally anticipates on the part of each nation a perfection in performance that humans are simply not capable of attaining. Tax systems are never adjusted perfectly to the twin considerations of ability to pay and maximum revenue. Decent distribution of the profits of industrial enterprise is always difficult, and probably nowhere has there been less lack of progress in this regard than in some of the European countries. Political parties will not, as a rule, forget partisanship in favor of the overall good and, as a result, the maximum in efficiency and in inspiring leadership is never fully realized.

I am *not* one of those who believes that American contributions should be increased to absorb unjustifiable deficiencies in the contributions of our Allies. To the contrary, no one works harder than I in the capitals of Europe to insist that nothing less than the best, on the part of the country concerned, can possibly be acceptable as a NATO objective. But, as a consequence of the conflicting considerations affecting the problem, I see the *time element* as the only factor that can supply the necessary flexibility to bring the whole tangled business into some kind of harmonious relationship.

Now I do not mean to belittle the importance of producing quickly the maximum amount of protection but, if we are to attain ultimate effort from these countries, and knowing that we push perilously close to the line of economic capacity, it is clear that we must, in our planning, contemplate a time factor that will provide, in this regard, a decent distribution of the load.

It is essential that, in the long-term view, the masses of Western Europe have complete conviction that the free governments of Western Europe will provide for them a better life than they can attain under Communist dictatorships. Each month, as we go ahead in attaining the maximum military preparation, there should be watchful regard for every kind of advance that will convince populations of this truth. It could be fatal if the workmen of Italy, France, and Germany came to believe that workmen in Poland, Czechoslovakia, Hungary, and so on were as well or even better off in their daily lives as they, themselves.

Yesterday I was visited by a World War II officer, now a French businessman.[3] He has been Mayor of the same village in France for twenty-six years. He knows every man in it, and he told me that this is the first year in which many of these old friends of his have voted Communist in *the sincere belief that conditions under any other kind of system would be better than they now are.* He said that in numerous instances full-time workmen in his village get only 9,000 francs a month. While, admittedly, living costs in his town are nothing like they are in Paris, just think of a person trying to maintain his family on such a wage.

Of course—as so many others think—I believe there is no real answer for the European problem until there is definitely established a United States of Europe.[4] As a consequence of the present tensions and emergencies, I believe that such a step should be taken by Europe's political leaders in a single plunge. The sooner the better! I get exceedingly weary of this talk about a step-by-step gradual, cautious approach. The United States and Britain could afford to do almost anything to support and make successful such a venture, because by this act, our entire objectives in this region could be almost instantaneously achieved.

In any event, the whole purpose of this letter is just to make sure that you occasionally remind your associates that European economic health and morale are both essential ingredients to the security of the region—and both must be maintained in satisfactory state as we proceed to the development of Armies, Navies, and Air Forces. If we are to bring "pressures" to bear on these countries (and, of course, we must), those pressures should be as much directed toward securing intelligent action to improve the economic lot of the people through efficient and effective tax laws, liberalizing trade restrictions and proper distribution of taxes as toward producing more military force.[5]

With warm personal regard, *Cordially*

[1] On Harriman's visit to Europe see nos. 191 and 218, n. 2.

[2] The economic strain associated with European rearmament had been a concern of Eisenhower's for some time (see nos. 198 and 209). On June 25 Thomas Cabot, Director of International Security Affairs, had warned Secretary of State Marshall that the effort to meet the MTDP goals would cause "serious economic problems" in Europe (State, *Foreign Relations, 1951*, vol. III, *European Security and the German Question, Part I*, p. 206). In July Eisenhower would tell a group of visiting senators, "You can't go in and pound the table and put every last cent you have got into guns when people are starving and children are crying at their mother's feet" (transcript of briefings, July 22, 1951, EM, Subject File, Congressional Visits, 1951; see also Acheson, *Present at the Creation*, p. 559).

[3] We have been unable to identify the individual Eisenhower mentions.

[4] For Eisenhower's views on European unity see no. 215.

[5] Harriman's reply, dated July 11, 1951, is in EM. He agreed that the United States "should not attempt to pressurize France and the other European countries to go beyond what is physically possible for them to do in their defense programs." He also said, "The idea is to put forward a program that can show that if people work hard and make certain sacrifices now, they can carry out the rearmament program and at the same time, in a couple of years, begin to get an improvement in the standard of living." See no. 259.

252   *Eisenhower Mss., Diaries*

DIARY   *July 2, 1951*

Tomorrow I go to London to keep 3 dates—made long before I took this job.

> a—Memorial Service at St. Paul's for 28,000 American dead of WW2 who lost their lives while serving in Britain.[1]
> b—Dinner of English Speaking Union.[2]
> c—" " with Winston Churchill—Pug Ismay—Cunningham—Portal. (Brookie is out of country).[3]

More & More political stuff these days. I'm saying "nuts"—because they urge me to "get into the fight"[4]

The German problem grows acute. The western allies are not too imaginative in coming forward with ideas that will safeguard west. Europe (allaying fears of Germany) and will at the same time get Germany wholeheartedly on our side in the struggle against Communism.[5] If I believed in taking time out to "regret" I could write several pages on some of the things Clay and I warned against in late 1945—and how we were told to mind our own business.[6] Chief of all our worries was that the world would come to be divided East vs West, and that our policies, then in vogue, would succeed in putting Germany in the other side—at least in making her ineffective on *our* side. As of this moment we ought to be showing Germany how definitely her national interests will be served by sticking and working with us!

[1] On the morning of Wednesday, July 4, Eisenhower would dedicate the American Roll of Honour at St. Paul's Cathedral. The solemn ceremony honoring the American dead of World War II was attended by Queen Elizabeth (consort) and other members of the royal family; Mrs. Eisenhower and her mother, Elivera Doud; Captain and Mrs. John S. D. Eisenhower; and a number of British and American leaders. On the longstanding arrangements for Eisenhower's participation see Galambos, *Columbia University*, nos. 745, 841, and 1037; see also *International Herald Tribune*, Paris ed., July 3, 5, 1951.

[2] On Tuesday evening, July 3, Eisenhower, accompanied by Mrs. Eisenhower, would be honored at a dinner given by the English Speaking Union in the great ballroom of Grosvenor House, Park Lane. Nearly one thousand dinner guests would hear Eisenhower deliver a major address in which he urged political unity and economic integration of the peoples of Western Europe. British Prime Minister Clement Richard Attlee, British Secretary of State for Foreign Affairs Herbert Stanley Morrison, and former Prime Minister Winston Churchill would be among the speakers to praise Eisenhower, whose own speech was widely covered by the press (see *New York Times*, July 4, 1951; and *International Herald Tribune*, Paris ed., July 4, 1951. See also Dwight D. Eisenhower, "The Challenge of Our Time: 'Hand of Aggressor Is Stayed by Strength Alone,' " *Vital Speeches of the Day*, 17, no. 20 [Aug. 1, 1951], 613. A copy of Eisenhower's speech is in EM, Subject File, Trips, SHAPE no. 9).

[3] General Lord Hastings L. Ismay would give a small reunion dinner in Eisenhower's honor the evening of July 4 (for background on Ismay see no. 5). The invited guests were former Prime Minister Winston Churchill and the British wartime chiefs of staff, Marshal of the Royal Air Force Lord Arthur Tedder; Admiral of the Fleet Viscount Andrew Browne Cunningham; Marshal of the Royal Air Force Viscount Charles Frederick Algernon Portal; and Field Marshal Alan Francis Brooke, the viscount Alanbrooke of Brookeborough (for background on these British leaders see *Eisenhower Papers*, vols. I–XI). Tedder and Brooke would not attend the dinner (see Ismay to Eisenhower, Apr. 18, 1951, and Ismay to Eisenhower [June 1951], EM).

[4] Political pressure on Eisenhower was increasing (see, for example, nos. 221 and 233).

[5] Eisenhower's concern was that the nations of Western Europe would allow their fear of Germany's militarism to block that country's political and economic recovery and its participation in the defense of Western Europe. On the problems of German rearmament and plans for a European army see nos. 186, 259, and 304. For background on Germany's complex problems see State, *Foreign Relations, 1951*, vol. III, *European Security and the German Question, Part II* (1981), pp. 1317–43; Laurence W. Martin, "The American Decision to Rearm Germany," in *American Civil-Military Decisions: A Book of Case Studies*, ed. Harold Stein (Birmingham, Ala., 1964), pp. 645–65; and Robert McGeehan, *The German Rearmament Question: American Diplomacy and European Defense after World War II* (Urbana, Ill., 1971).

[6] In 1945 Eisenhower was Military Governor of the U.S. Zone of Occupation in Germany, and Lieutenant General Lucius D. Clay was Deputy Military Governor and U.S. representative on the Coordinating Committee for Germany. Both Eisenhower and Clay, believing that German economic and political recovery would not progress under military rule alone, had worked to develop effective civilian authority in that occupied country. For further background see Eisenhower, *Crusade in Europe*, pp. 434–35, 442–43, 474; Lucius D. Clay, *Decision in Germany* (Garden City, N.Y., 1950), pp. 53, 82, 123; idem, *Papers*, pp. 111–18, 166, 212–17, 337–38, 479–80; and Chandler and Galambos, *Occupation, 1945*, esp. nos. 37 and 209.

To Anna B. Eisenhower   *July 2, 1951*

Dear Aunt Anna:[1] It was indeed nice of you to send Mamie and me the family news. I am distressed to know that Aunt Amanda is so ill—just as I am sorry that you had the misfortune to break your arm. I do hope that you are fully recovered and Amanda is much better.[2]

When we bought our farm near Gettysburg, it was in the hope that within a very few years we could go there permanently and, in the meantime, could spend weekends in fixing it up and getting it ready for a permanent home.

Since I have been ordered back to Europe, all these plans have been temporarily scrapped—I have no idea when I will again be able to resume that kind of planning and working.[3]

Of course, we have no right to complain. Our family, our friends, and our country have been good to us, and the least we can do is to try to accomplish whatever duty is given us, no matter where it is. All this does not prevent Mamie and me from getting quite homesick for the United States.

With affectionate greetings and very best wishes, *Devotedly, Your nephew*

[1] Anna Eisenhower was the wife of Abraham Lincoln Eisenhower, one of the General's uncles (see Galambos, *Chief of Staff*, no. 553).

[2] There is no copy of this letter in EM. Hanna Amanda Eisenhower Musser was a sister of the General's father (see Galambos, *Columbia University*, no. 351). In a letter of November 7, 1950 (EM), Anna Eisenhower had told the General that she was doing "as well as could be expected for 83 years" but that her left arm had been broken and was mending slowly. The letter had actually been written by Mrs. Ella Broyles, in whose house Anna Eisenhower was living. For developments see no. 367, n. 2.

[3] The Eisenhowers had bought their Gettysburg, Pennsylvania, farm in November 1950 (see Galambos, *Columbia University*, nos. 1075 and 1080; and Eisenhower, *At Ease*, pp. 358–61). On the current status of the farm see no. 179.

254   *Eisenhower Mss.*

To Fred M. Manning, Sr.   *July 3, 1951*

Dear Fred:[1] Thank you very much for your nice note, to say nothing of the great kindness you and Hazel showed toward my family when they were recently in Denver.[2]

The hunting and fishing permit from the LaBonte Ranch has been filed away with my choicest possessions. My great ambition will now be to get a chance to use it.[3]

So far as the beef is concerned, I should think that in less than a month I can write to you further on the subject, but certainly by that time we should have our deep freeze and refrigerating units in our house. On the other hand, we have been so frequently disappointed in successive postponements of the date of completion of repair and reconstruction, that I am not too sanguine. But you may be sure that I shall write as soon as everything is ready.[4]

Please give my love to Hazel, and warm regard to yourself. *Cordially*

[1] For background on Eisenhower's friend Manning see no. 161, n. 8.

[2] In a letter of June 28 (EM) Manning had explained that he and his wife Hazel, having just returned to Denver from a "long sojourn" in California, had been unable to assist with the funeral arrangements for John S. Doud, Mamie Eisenhower's father. After the funeral, however, the Mannings had visited with Doud's widow, Elivera Doud, and Mamie Eisenhower. Manning added that Mrs. Doud and Mrs. Eisenhower had looked "fine considering the sudden shock of Mr. Doud's passing" (see no. 240).

[3] The Mannings' LaBonte Ranch was in Douglas, Wyoming. Enclosed with the June 28 letter was a hunting and fishing permit for Eisenhower, which Manning said was "good for all the time that I own the property and as long as the fishing and hunting seasons last in Wyoming."

[4] Manning had sent Eisenhower a shipment of beef, but because the General did not have storage facilities in France, the beef was being kept at the Waldorf-Astoria Hotel in New York City (see Schulz to Manning, Jan. 16, 1951, and Eisenhower to Manning, Mar. 30, 1951, EM). On Eisenhower's problems with the house see no. 393.

Eisenhower would write Manning again on July 6 (EM) to thank him for sending a dozen golf balls by way of the family returning from the Doud funeral.

255   *Eisenhower Mss., France Corr.*

To Jules Moch   *July 5, 1951*

Reference: No. 893 E.M.C.F.A./3/A/S dated 23 June 1951[1]
Subject: Rear elements of the Allied Armies in France.
       Requirements in the matter of facilities.[2]
       I.—You have very kindly called my attention to the difficult problems which arise in connection with the organization of the rear elements of the Allied Armies in France, which problems the establishment of SHAPE should enable to be adequately defined and solved.

       II.—As a matter of fact, I consider that I am charged with coordinating the logistical plans of the forces placed at my disposal by the Allied nations.

As you suggest, I propose to inform the Governments of the nations concerned as to the logistical requirements, grouped by broad categories, which are necessary for the forces of the Allied Command in Europe, both for the combat and the communications zones.

I shall expect each Government to do its utmost to meet these requirements.

III.—An overall logistical plan should certainly be established. SHAPE is working to that end and is giving this problem a high priority. However, some further time will be required before the plan is ready for distribution.[3]

Pending the completion of the plan, I should be very grateful if you would continue your action to effect the bilateral agreements drawn up with the Atlantic Pact nations for the purpose of giving these nations all the logistical support desirable on the part of France, this being indispensable to our defense effort.[4] The requests which are now being presented to you by the Allied Governments, acting individually, are established within the scope of the short and medium term defense plans, which are the basis for the preparation of SHAPE's more complete calculations.

IV.—The question of methods and procedures for financing the logistical requirements of the forces of the Allied Command in Europe is not within my province. Such questions must be resolved in the higher Councils of the Atlantic Treaty Organization, but the method of financing facilities of current use should undoubtedly be similar to the method which you advocate in your letter under reference.[5]

I fully realize that your task will be much simpler when SHAPE's overall plan has been made available to you. I assure you that we are making every effort to expedite its completion.[6]

---

[1] We have been unable to locate any incoming letter from French Minister of National Defense Moch (for background see no. 11). A note on Eisenhower's copy of this document indicates that all files concerning this subject were sent to a staff officer. Eisenhower had seen Moch, together with the French engineer general, on June 30.

[2] Eisenhower was concerned about the construction of permanent facilities necessary to support NATO's military effort. Included among these facilities, which were commonly termed "infrastructure," were airfields, signal communications installations and cables, headquarters buildings, oil tanks and pipelines, and port facilities. In 1950 the members of the Western European Union had begun a $90 million infrastructure program that included thirty airfields. This "first slice" program was to be followed in 1951 by a second slice, comprising thirteen new airfields, eight airfield extensions, and fifty-three signals communications projects. The NAC deputies, however, could not agree on a cost-sharing formula for the second slice, and in June the U.S. government proposed that the European host countries pay most of the infrastructure costs except in cases of immediate military urgency. On June 26 Douglas MacArthur II, Eisenhower's political adviser, warned Washington that its proposals were likely to result in prolonged negotiations and

unacceptable delays. The following month Eisenhower met with Karl R. Bendetsen (Assistant Secretary of the Army since February 1950), whom Secretary of Defense Marshall had sent to Europe to try to settle the infrastructure costs problem. At that meeting Eisenhower agreed that the United States should finance completely the construction of air bases to be used by the U.S. Air Force exclusively. In return, Bendetsen assured Eisenhower that the U.S. negotiators would press for agreement on other second-slice infrastructure projects (Bendetsen to Lovett, two letters, July 19, 1951, and other papers in Records of the Assistant Secretary of Defense for International Security Affairs, ONATA Subject File 1949–53. See also State, *Foreign Relations, 1951*, vol. III, *European Security and the German Question, Part I*, pp. 207–10; James A. Huston, *One for All: NATO Strategy and Logistics through the Formative Period [1949–1969]* [Newark, Del., 1984], pp. 157–58; Ismay, *NATO*, pp. 114–15; and Kaplan, *Community of Interests*, p. 167).

[3] For background on SHAPE's defense planning see no. 124. In September Eisenhower would urge General Alphonse Juin, the commander of NATO's land forces in Central Europe, to formulate a series of war plans coordinated with NATO's logistical staff (see no. 364). Later in 1951 Eisenhower's headquarters would issue a tentative logistic annex (SHAPE/412/51) to its outline defense plan (see JCS to USLO SHAPE, JCS 91289, Jan. 7, 1952, CCS 092 Western Europe [3-12-48], Sec. 115). See also Huston, *One for All*, pp. 124–42.

[4] The most important infrastructure projects were undoubtedly the U.S. airfields to be built in metropolitan France. The United States was then in the midst of bilateral negotiations with the French government concerning these airfields (see no. 223); the two nations would not reach an agreement until early in 1952 (see *New York Times*, Feb. 14, 1952; and U.S. Department of State, *Foreign Relations of the United States, 1952–1954*, 16 vols. to date [Washington, D.C., 1981–], vol. I, *General: Economic and Political Matters, Part I* [1983], p. 478).

[5] After some delay in formulating a U.S. policy on infrastructure financing (see Bendetsen to Lovett, June 28, 1951, and Ernst to Lovett, July 26, 1951, OS/D, 1951, Clas. Decimal File, CD 092.3 NATO), the NATO nations at the Ottawa NAC meeting in September finally would agree to a cost-sharing formula for the twenty-one second-slice airfields (see no. 384). The costs of the land and utilities were to be borne by the host countries. The remaining construction costs were to be divided among the United States, France, Great Britain, Canada, the Netherlands, Belgium, and Luxembourg. The United States would agree to assume the largest portion of the costs (48 percent); France and Great Britain would pay 22 percent and 18 percent, respectively (see AC/4-D/21, Aug. 27, 1951, and AC/4-D/27, Oct. 5, 1951, NATO Files, microfilm).

[6] This letter was translated into French before it was sent to Moch; there is no reply in EM. For developments see no. 467; and State, *Foreign Relations, 1952–1954*, vol. V, *Western European Security, Part I* (1983), pp. 114–16, 192–93, 196–98, 366–67.

256   *Eisenhower Mss.*

To Richard Bowditch Wigglesworth   *July 6, 1951*

Dear Congressman Wigglesworth:[1] Thank you very much for your nice letter of June 29th. I assure you that it was a pleasure to have the

Congressional Committee here with us—it was a personal privilege to have the chance to talk to you.[2]

A recent letter from home indicates that I may have unwittingly given you a slightly erroneous impression of what I feel should be the evolving picture in this region, so far as it involves the character and scope of the American effort. You will recall that I firmly believe that we should be thinking in terms of *time*; that since we are attempting to raise confidence and instill determination, our wisest course would appear to strive for a very intensive but relatively short program of American assistance which should begin to pass its peak, especially in ground force content, within two and one-half or three years.

Readily admitting the obvious truth that no one can foresee actual development in this region, it nevertheless seems obvious that in the long term view Europe can be defended *only* from within. This applies with particular force to the provision of the ground elements, except for such specialized or small groupments that might always be necessary for the particular purposes of servicing and protecting American air and other installations. I would not want to be understood as meaning that we could merely keep a few units here a short time and then count upon their sudden and rapid displacement back to our home country. But I repeat that I do believe that our plan should call for reaching, within a reasonable space of time, the peak of our effort, immediately after which we would start phasing important units back home as equivalent and even greater strength was produced here through the operation of the training and preparatory system.[3]

If I have been unclear on what I meant, I am sorry.

This note brings to you my very best wishes and warm personal regard. Please remember us warmly to Mrs. Wigglesworth.[4] *Cordially*

[1] Richard Bowditch Wigglesworth (LL.B. Harvard 1916), a World War I veteran, had been a Republican congressman from Massachusetts since 1928.

[2] Wigglesworth had written on June 29 (EM) to thank the Eisenhowers for their hospitality during the recent congressional visit (on the visit see nos. 209, n. 2, and 218, n. 14). "The Western World," he had said, "is fortunate in having your broad military experience, driving personality and fine capacity for leadership."

[3] Eisenhower probably referred to Congressman Christian Archibald Herter's letter of July 3 (no copy in EM; see Gruenther to Herter, July 27, 1951, *ibid*. See also the transcript of Eisenhower's remarks to the congressional delegation (June 18, 1951, EM, Subject File, Congressional Visits, 1951). On the General's ideas concerning aid to Europe and Western European defense see no. 233; for developments involving congressional visits see no. 394.

[4] The former Florence Joyes Booth.

To Edward Mead Earle   *July 7, 1951*

Dear Ed:[1] Let me thank you for your thoughtfulness and for your services to SHAPE during your trip just now ending. I include among these services not only your contributions on specific problems which you have discussed with General Gruenther and with the staff, but also, and more especially, the ideas and observations you have imparted to me personally. Of particular value to us have been your interesting and thoughtful evaluations of trends in national spirit and attitudes, as developed from your personal contacts with various European groups that have a strong influence on the success of our effort here. While these appraisals are admittedly difficult, they are of central importance to our whole endeavor and we are indeed grateful for your help.[2]

Your excellent report on the seminar you held on "French Attitudes toward the Western Entente" has already paid off for us in better understanding of the tasks we face.[3]

It is not wholly hospitality that leads me to ask you to be sure to visit us again in Europe whenever you can. By the time you return we will be sure to have a new list of knotty but important problems upon which the Earle brand of wisdom and insight should be focused. In addition, it is always a great personal pleasure to see you.[4]

On behalf of the whole Headquarters I thank you for your contribution toward our success.

With warm personal regard, *Sincerely*

[1] Earle, who was a military historian, was a faculty member at the Institute for Advanced Study in Princeton, New Jersey, and was affiliated with Columbia University's Institute of War and Peace Studies. He had served as a consultant to SHAPE since May (see no. 159). General Alfred M. Gruenther, Eisenhower's C/S, drafted this letter.

[2] Earle had met with Eisenhower on May 31, June 7, and July 7 and 9 (see Earle to Eisenhower, May 2, 1951, EM; and appointment calendar).

[3] On the General's problems with the French see nos. 115, 142, and 251. For developments see nos. 304 and 459.

[4] Earle would write Eisenhower on July 10 (EM) concerning a conversation he had had the previous day (following a briefing for visiting senators) with his "friend and neighbor" Senator H. Alexander Smith of New Jersey (see no. 268, n. 3). A member of the Foreign Relations Committee, Smith (LL.B. Columbia 1904) said he supported the authorization of the $8.5 billion in aid to Europe but felt that Congress should appropriate only 4 billion at first and make supplementary appropriations based on the General's assessment of progress. Earle had warned Smith that any partial funding would pose a "grave threat to the whole program" of European rearmament and might "seriously undermine the faith of Europe." The General replied on July 11 (EM) that he had discussed the situation with General Gruenther. For developments see no. 377. On the impending visit to SHAPE of the Senate Foreign Relations Committee see no. 268, n. 3.

To Thomas John Watson, Sr.   *July 9, 1951*
Strictly personal

Dear Tom:[1] Thank you very much for your letter of July 2nd.[2]

Please do not worry as to any action that I personally shall initiate. I deliberately sought an opportunity to talk to Doug Black[3] and ask him, as opportunity offered, to talk to other Trustees so as to make sure that there would be no mistaking of my own position. I have come to the conclusion that there is no possible way of estimating the duration of my necessary absence from the Columbia post. At the same time, I am very much concerned that many projects, initiated at Columbia during the past two and one-half years may wither away and die, unless advantage is taken of the excellent start that has been made and these things pushed to fruition.[4]

It is a truism that "acting" executives are normally timid—a man has to be fairly sure of his position before he will take positive, constructive action if there is involved any risk or major difficulty. These are the things that I hope the Trustees will see.

By no means do I want my connection with Columbia completely severed—I want nothing else but that Columbia's Trustees will earnestly study the welfare of Columbia in the present circumstances and act accordingly. In doing so, it is necessary to remember that times are rarely, if ever, "normal." Always we face unusual circumstances. But I think it also true that present circumstances are just a bit further out of line than is usually the case. Therefore, there are no real precedents; the decision must be made upon a careful study of things as they are. Now, this is all I have meant in talking to Doug Black and in writing to Arthur, and it is all that I mean now.[5] I agree with you that this is something for the family only. By no means would any good purpose be served if there were any publicity to the fact that we had even discussed the matter; on the contrary, much harm could result. I, personally, shall never bring up the matter again. I discussed these things at one or two meetings of the Trustees, and since I am informed that it has later been discussed on the basis of my talks with Doug Black, I feel that there is nothing more for me to do. Frankly, I am far too busy to give much time to anything except the insistent and insatiable demands of this particular job.

I am delighted that you will be over in October. Mamie and I shall look forward to a reunion with you and Jeanette.[6] *Cordially*

---

[1] Thomas John Watson, Sr., was the chairman of the board of IBM and a trustee of Columbia University (see Galambos, *Columbia University*, no. 813).

[2] Watson's letter (EM) concerned various arrangements that had been proposed to

handle the problem of Eisenhower's absence from Columbia University (for background see no. 229).
[3] Douglas M. Black had visited the General in May (see no. 184).
[4] On the programs Eisenhower initiated see Eisenhower, *At Ease*, pp. 349–51, 363–64; concerning the duration of his position as SACEUR see Galambos, *Columbia University*, no. 1045.
[5] The General's recent letter to Arthur H. Sulzberger is no. 229 (on Sulzberger see no. 114, n. 1). See also no. 261.
[6] On September 21 (EM) Watson would write to say that he and his wife, the former Jeannette M. Kittridge, were postponing their visit until the spring. For developments see no. 373.

259   *Eisenhower Mss.*

To WILLIAM AVERELL HARRIMAN   *July 9, 1951*

Dear Averell: During a recent visit to Britain, I talked to a number of important individuals, including the Prime Minister and Winston Churchill.[1] Both of these were quite anxious that the United States stand firmly with them in the Persian struggle.[2] The Prime Minister especially hoped that the United States would not get nervous if the British found it necessary to take a very firm and tough position. When I talked to Winston he was considering the sending of a telegram to President Truman.[3]

It is, of course, entirely unnecessary for me to interject my own thinking in this matter; you and I have already agreed on the great importance of the Iranian oil to the Western World. All of us must look upon that area with the greatest concern, and all of us must certainly hope that we can weld the people of that region into a solidly supporting block. It will take statesmanship of high order and possibly some material effort. But the stakes are high.[4]

While in London I made two or three talks, and in one of them I most fervently urged the formation of the United States of Western Continental Europe. I scarcely need to enumerate to you the advantages that would flow from such a development. Our own lavish expenditures could quickly be reduced and the whole "German" problem would be solved. Again, this is a subject on which I do not need to elaborate.[5]

All my best to you, and please remember me respectfully to the President. *Cordially*

[1] For Eisenhower's trip to England and his meeting with Churchill and Prime Minister Clement Attlee see no. 252.
[2] For background on the Iranian oil crisis see no. 233. Following nationalization of

the Anglo-Iranian Oil Company, the British had taken a number of steps in an attempt to restore the status quo. From the International Court of Justice they had obtained a preliminary injunction reversing the Iranian action pending final resolution of the matter. (The Iranians later rejected this ruling.) They had also taken action to reduce oil production and to prevent the oil from being shipped abroad. Finally, the British began to make plans for military intervention and dispatched a naval force to the Persian Gulf. The United States urged both parties to settle the dispute without violence, and on July 8 President Truman offered to send Harriman to Teheran to help resolve matters. After some initial reluctance, Harriman's mission was accepted by both parties in the dispute, and he would arrive in Iran on July 15 (Acheson, *Present at the Creation*, pp. 506–8; Kenneth O. Morgan, *Labour in Power, 1945–1951* [Oxford, 1984], pp. 465–71; *Public Papers of the Presidents: Truman, 1951*, pp. 381–83; Brookings Institution, *Current Developments in United States Foreign Policy* 5, no. 1 [1951], 36–38; Poole, *History of the Joint Chiefs of Staff*, vol. IV, *1950–1952*, pp. 354–60; Patrick to Marshall, May 7, 1951, OS/D, 1951, Clas. Decimal File, CD 092.3 NATO).

[3] The telegram is not in EM. Eisenhower had seen Churchill on July 4, and at that time the former Prime Minister had read Eisenhower the text of his message to Truman. In a letter to Eisenhower sent the following day (July 5, 1951, EM) Churchill had urged Eisenhower to send "something home on the same lines in support from your angle." Prime Minister Attlee, whom Eisenhower had seen on July 3 (see no. 252, n. 2), was privately doubtful about the wisdom of using force to recover the British oil concessions (see Morgan, *Labour in Power*, pp. 469–71).

[4] In his reply (July 11, 1951, EM) Harriman told Eisenhower of his mission to Iran: "I haven't the least idea what I can accomplish, but as the President has asked me to go I will of course do so and hope for some break." He also told Eisenhower that should his efforts fail, the "loss of the oil in itself isn't so desperate as the possibility of the Communists taking over in the economic collapse following the shutdown of industry." For further developments see nos. 264 and 362.

[5] For Eisenhower's views on European unity and German rearmament see nos. 186 and 215. Eisenhower's July 3 London speech on European integration is discussed in no. 252, n. 2. In his July 11 reply Harriman said he felt that "if we can get the continental army going, a real rapprochement by the French and Germany, then there is a real basis for moving forward. The continent without Great Britain is not strong enough to face Germany, whereas if there is an understanding between Germany and France on security matters, there will be a basis for federation."

260   *Eisenhower Mss.*

To Freeman F. Gosden   *July 9, 1951*

Dear Freeman:[1] Many thanks for sending me the pictures of your new "Amos 'n' Andy" television cast. I should certainly like to see them in action.[2]

The last few days have been a curious combination of satisfaction and disappointment for me. The satisfaction has come about from the presence here of so many of my old friends, particularly Augusta friends. Cliff Roberts, Bill Robinson, Frank Willard, J. Gould and Bob Woodruff have all been in Paris for the past week. In fact, Cliff has been here about a month, and I hope he stays two more.[3]

The disappointing side of the matter has been that I have been so busy that I can see my friends only occasionally. Tomorrow I have a golf game slated with Bob, my son, and Cliff Roberts, but it will still be touch and go as to whether or not I can make the grade. Possibly by the time you can come back here I will be a little bit more the boss of my own activities. I certainly hope so.[4]

You will recall that I briefly met your partner one evening. Please convey to him my greetings, and as for yourself and your family, warmest regards and best wishes.[5] *Cordially*

[1] Gosden produced and wrote scripts for "Amos 'n' Andy," a longtime radio program and television show (see no. 211, n. 3).
[2] Enclosed with his letter of June 22 (EM) Gosden had sent a photo of several characters from the "Amos 'n' Andy" show, including "Amos," "Andy," and "Kingfish" (for background on the show see Galambos, *Columbia University*, no. 821).
[3] Clifford Roberts had been visiting the General since June 10 (see no. 177, n. 2). William E. Robinson had visited in late June, along with Frank A. Willard, Jay Gould, and Robert W. Woodruff, all members of the Augusta National Golf Club.
[4] The General had been in London from July 3 to July 5 and had since then carried a busy schedule (see no. 252; and the Chronology in these volumes). He would play golf with Woodruff on July 10 and with John Eisenhower and Roberts on July 11 (on John Eisenhower's visit see no. 224). Gosden had joined Eisenhower for dinner on June 10.
[5] The partner was probably Charles J. Correll, who had been associated with Gosden since 1925 (see Galambos, *Columbia University*, no. 821). Gosden was married to the former Jane Stoneham. For developments see no. 368.

261   *Eisenhower Mss.*

To FREDERICK COYKENDALL   *July 9, 1951*
Personal and confidential

Dear Mr. Coykendall:[1] It is true that I took advantage of Doug Black's presence in Paris to talk with him about matters that were of deep concern to me, respecting Columbia. Some of these things had already been discussed with the Trustees at the monthly meetings, but the principal one was that Columbia might begin to suffer through the lack of a properly designated chief executive actually on the job.[2]

It seems to me that my early hope, which was at least partially shared by the President of the United States, that I could personally complete my part of this European job in a very short time and turn over the work to another individual, is not materializing.[3] Therefore, it seemed only fair that I should keep the Trustees informed of developing circumstances—as they appear to me—and assure them again that any action they might desire to take in the circumstances would be cheerfully accepted by me. Beyond this I shall not go, except to point out that I would be most unhappy to have my connection with Columbia *completely* severed. For the past two and one-half years I worked very hard to get started a number of projects which I believe are not only of great value to our public, but also to Columbia. I most sincerely hope that they will be pushed, and it was my fear that an acting executive might be unwilling to operate with the necessary decision and courage that determined me to speak once more about these matters to the Trustees. Not having time to write the whole thing out in detail, I discussed them briefly with Doug Black so that the Trustees would be assured of my complete readiness to accept any decision that they might feel compelled to make. As I have just said, I shall do nothing more beyond this. The Trustees have had the welfare of Columbia at heart for many long years. I have no doubt that they will continue to formulate their decisions with Columbia's good as the sole and decisive factor.[4]

Thank you very much for the kindness and courtesy of your letter— needless to say, I am quite happy that you feel Columbia can still afford to wait awhile to see what happens to me.[5]

I have written Tom Watson in similar vein. It seems that he was also worried about the discussion of this matter, especially that it might get noised outside the members of the immediate Columbia family.[6]

My warm greetings to Mrs. Coykendall,[7] and with best wishes to yourself. *Cordially*

[1] Coykendall chaired the Columbia University trustees (see no. 114, n. 2).

[2] Douglas M. Black had visited the General in May (see no. 234, n. 2).

[3] On President Truman's appointment of Eisenhower as SACEUR see Galambos, *Columbia University*, nos. 1045 and 1129. At this point in the letter Eisenhower added a handwritten note: "Of course I still hope that the tour of duty will not be too prolonged!"

[4] On the General's regret at leaving Columbia see no. 3.

[5] Coykendall had written on June 27 (EM) that no action should be taken by the trustees without a direct request from Eisenhower: "It is our plan to carry on, as we are now doing so successfully, until such time as you can state a time for your return." For developments see no. 373.

On July 17 (EM) Eisenhower would write Coykendall thanking him for the flowers the trustees had sent for John Sheldon Doud's funeral (see no. 240).

[6] The letter to Watson is no. 258.

[7] The former Mary Beach Warrin.

DIARY[1]

On Sunday morning I was visited by Charlie White, President of Republic Steel.[2] His principal reason for looking me up was to say that he had just completed a close examination into the coal and steel industry in Britain. He is convinced that Britain is again going downhill economically and that the real reason is that they are not producing enough coal. He believes that labor is not performing efficiently and that management is not providing the incentives that will get labor to develop. He feels that since the Government has completely nationalized these industries, political leaders must participate in the problem and get busy, or slow disaster will overtake Britain. He feels that coal production must increase in Britain to the point where that country can again export coal.[3]

This whole conversation was so interesting that I asked Mr. White to meet with representatives from my Headquarters and possibly the ECA Headquarters. To this he enthusiastically agreed, because he thinks that with pressures exerted from the right directions, Britain can save herself.[4]

Mr. White then launched into a description of conditions, present and future, within the United States, as he sees them.

His first hypothesis is that in the next election there *must* be a Republican victory; that government has fallen so low in the minds of most Americans, that it can exert no leadership and has no prestige. This condition, he believes, influences adversely our position abroad. He thinks that the Republicans have been very stupid and have again and again allowed internal fights and personal struggles for nomination to be the cause of Republican defeat in general elections. He desperately hopes that such a fight may be avoided this time. At this point he brings in a prophecy concerning the business cycle in the United States. He says that in spite of the rearmament program, we are due for a recession, although probably not a full scale depression, in the United States. He is certain that this will occur as the rearmament program tapers off. In support of this he quotes figures concerning the annual output of passenger cars and refrigerators as being far in excess of the annual consumption rate in the United States. He says this observation applies to many other items. (While he gave approximate figures in several items, it seems unnecessary to repeat them here). As a result of this situation, he believes that the man elected President of the United States at this coming election cannot possibly be reelected in 1956. His next argument is that the Republicans must have two acceptable candidates to offer the public, one to win in 1952 and restore "sound business practices" to the United States, and the second to win the election in 1956.

He says that he speaks for no one except himself. He has worked out his plan by himself. This plan is that Mr. Taft[5] should be elected in 1952, that I should support him, and that I should accept the post of Secretary of Defense in the Cabinet. (He apparently does not know that it is against the law for a soldier to fill that particular post and that General Marshall is filling it now only by virtue of a special dispensation from Congress). The scheme would be for Mr. Taft to agree in advance that he would not seek reelection and that I should be promised this by the Republican leaders.

I told Charlie White that, of course, I was flattered that he should think of me in these terms, but so far as I was concerned (a) I now have a job of transcendent importance to the United States. Because it is a military post, I do not find it possible to participate in American partisan politics; (b) that I have always insisted that I would never be connected in any way with politics—even after I could finally lay aside my uniform, except in such exceptional circumstances where a duty was clearly indicated. In this case, I do not see any call to duty.

Mr. White left after repeating that the idea was solely his and not to be repeated to anyone else.[6]

---

[1] This diary entry was typed. In a marginal, handwritten note Eisenhower wrote: "Because of length—this dictated to Miss Tait—with *no* copies." Lois V. Tait was a civilian assigned to Eisenhower's office (see EM, Subject File, SHAPE).

[2] Charles McElroy White had been president of the Republic Steel Corporation since 1945 (see no. 170, n. 7).

[3] White had met with the General on July 8, 12, and 19 (see EM, White Corr.).

[4] There is no record in EM that White met with ECA officials. On the ECA see no. 45.

[5] On Senator Robert A. Taft and his relations with Eisenhower see no. 131, n. 3.

[6] At a later date Eisenhower added a handwritten note to the end of this diary entry: "Mr. White came back to lunch at my office on Thurs. July 12. He has become convinced that American Businessmen can do much to wake up European businessmen to the need for strong leadership in support of the common security. He is going to work at it." For developments see no. 357.

263   *Eisenhower Mss.*

TO ROBERT H. CROMWELL, SR.   *July 11, 1951*

Dear Bob:[1] Thank you for your nice letter. It is always good to hear from an old friend of the Philippine days—life seemed so less complicated then than it does now that I think most of us look back on those years with a feeling akin to nostalgia.[2]

So far as helping you in your current problem, I have been away from Washington so long that I do not know who is responsible for various kinds of allocations, priorities, and other decisions in which you apparently are interested. So even if I knew anything at all about the features of the particular business in which you are about to enter—which I don't—I would be helpless to make any reasonable suggestion as to how you should present the case to Washington. In these circumstances, you can well understand that I must simply keep my mouth closed.[3]

I confidently expect to be plugging away here for some time. If you are ever in the region, please give me a chance to see you.[4]

With warm personal regard, *Cordially*

[1] Cromwell, a manufacturer and exporter, had met Eisenhower when the General was stationed in the Philippines from 1935 to 1939 (see Chandler, *War Years*, no. 2428).

[2] Eisenhower had been promoted to lieutenant colonel during his tour in the Philippines and had become the senior U.S. military assistant to the Commonwealth government on defense affairs (see Eisenhower, *At Ease*, pp. 218–32, 246–48).

[3] Since 1949 import controls had negatively affected Cromwell's Philippine business (see Cromwell to Eisenhower, Dec. 19, 1949, and July 13, 1950, EM). In a letter of June 29 (EM) Cromwell had told the General that he had sold his business in the Philippines and had returned to the United States, where he planned to begin a staple and nail manufacturing company in California. The problem, Cromwell said, was that he needed an allocation from the "C.M.P., Washington, D.C." before he could purchase supplies and machinery. "What I would like for you to do," he requested, "is to write a letter of recomendation [*sic*] and introduction to someone in Washington whom you think could be of help."

Cromwell probably referred to the Controlled Materials Plan Divisions of the Production Controls Bureau, which during World War II developed and reviewed policies for the production and control of critical war-effort materials (see U.S. National Archives and Records Service, *Federal Records of World War II*, 2 vols. [Washington, D.C., 1950], vol. I, *Civilian Agencies*, pp. 385–86). Cromwell actually needed to contact the Iron and Steel Division of the National Production Authority, which was responsible for meeting the nation's large defense requirements while keeping businesses supplying civilian markets in operation (see U.S. Congress, Senate, Select Committee on Small Business, *Hearing on Impact on Small Business of Material Shortages*, 82d Cong., 1st sess., 1951, pp. 45–47).

[4] Cromwell would reply on November 7 (EM) that he had just bought the Western Saw Manufacturing Company, "the only one of its size on the Pacific Coast."

264   *Eisenhower Mss.*

To WINSTON SPENCER CHURCHILL   *July 11, 1951*

Dear Winston: It would be quite impossible for me to tell you how flattered I was by the nice things you had to say about my talk.[1] While

I have no great hope that the timorous leadership of Europe will, under the spell of Eisenhower eloquence, suddenly begin with head up and chest out to march sturdily forward along the rocky road to unification, yet the making of the talk did me the personal good of putting into public words something that I believe very deeply.

With respect to the Persian matter, I have already informed Washington with what seriousness I regard it and of my hope that our Government will find it possible to support some reasonable solution. I am, of course, particularly anxious that the technicians and the professional people now on the job should stay there, and an interim agreement should be reached that would allow the oil to keep flowing.[2]

Should you by any happy chance be traveling in this region, be sure to let me know so that we can arrange a long meeting. My evening with you and our old comrades of the wartime days was a high spot.

With warm personal regard, *Cordially*

[1] For background on Eisenhower's London speech see no. 252. Churchill had written, "As I am getting rather deaf I could not hear or follow your speech when you delivered it." Having obtained a copy ("with some difficulty"), Churchill told Eisenhower that it was "one of the greatest speeches delivered by any American in my life time,—which is a long one,—and that it carries with it on strong wings the hope of the salvation of the world from its present perils and confusions."
[2] For background on the Iranian oil crisis and Churchill's reaction to it see no. 259. For developments see no. 362.

265   *Eisenhower Mss.*

To WILLIAM EDWARD ROBINSON   *July 12, 1951*
Personal and confidential

Dear Bill:[1] This will be a kind of letter I have never written to any other person, and I can write it only because of your repeated assurance that you would not hesitate at any chore that I would seriously ask you to perform. This chore has to do with what I conceive to be your health and continued effectiveness, and these mean a lot to me because a man is rarely blessed with the kind of friend that I have found in you.[2]

The only other introductory remark I have to make is that, several times while you were here, I started to talk these matters over with you and then decided I could easily be guilty of effrontery or, at the very least, of sticking my nose into someone else's business. However, because of the very deep feeling I have in the matter, I will plunge into the middle of my thoughts without further apology.

I think that, when you were here, you showed signs of tension and worry and, moreover, did not seem to be in that admirable state of glowing health that I have become accustomed to associate with my picture of you. Possibly these two situations—if either exists—are related.[3]

In any event, I would advise (a) that you lose considerable weight, (b) that both your smoking and drinking be on a very moderate scale, (c) that you exercise regularly, and (d) that you eat wisely and get lots of sleep.

Now, of course, (a) and (d) are related. There are lots of good diets on the market, but the important point is that dieting is not the slightest bit difficult once you have *good humoredly* made up your mind to do it. My own invariable daily diet is:

Breakfast—One small jar of yogurt.
One cup of black coffee.

Lunch— Small fruit salad with no dressing of any kind.
One small jar of yogurt.
(Instead of yogurt, one small piece of Swiss cheese or any any other type except the very rich ones)

Dinner— Any *broiled* piece of meat, except pork.
Any green vegetable such as spinach, peas, string beans, but always cooked without any butter or sauce of any kind.
An apple, orange, or grapefruit for dessert.

In these diets, you can make any variant you want (except for the rather unique DuPont diet which allows a certain amount of fat meat). The secret is to do without any butter, sauces, sugar, creams, or anything of that kind, and never take more than one small piece of toast as a daily diet of bread. A small plain boiled potato is occasionally acceptable.[4]

As to (b), moderate smoking and very moderate drinking are probably not only of no damage to the nervous system or to physical health but, if the habit is absolutely moderate, they might even be helpful. As to cigarettes, I should say that moderate smoking is to keep your consumption under one pack per day. So put a pack in your pocket in the morning, refuse to take any off your desk or from a friend's pack any time during the day, and be sure there is one left in your own pack at night.[5] As to drinking, never drink at any time except just before dinner. At the end of a hard day, a couple of long weak highballs should be your ration. Never take a drink at noon and never drink a cocktail.

And (c), so far as exercise is concerned, your golf, of course, always helps. Its effect can be ruined both as to weight and health if you take a couple beers or highballs immediately after the game. (Wait until dinner time, and then only two weak ones.) Moreover, it is well to keep something in your office on which you can frequently exercise a little bit—even a few seconds at a time. One of the rubber bands often advertised for this purpose can be useful. For you, I should say a better instrument would be a niblick.[6] Keep it in your office and get up about six times a day to swing it—about ten or fifteen times at each session. On top of this, frequently raise your chest to the fullest extent, stretching up on the abdominal muscles; and, when you have occasion to walk, walk very rapidly, swinging the arms fairly high and with the chest raised. You may think you look ridiculous, but who in New York ever looks at what anybody else on the sidewalk is doing?

If at any time you feel that your diet may be lacking in some mineral or vitamin, these can always be supplied through the medium of pills or maybe even by yeast tablets.

There is, of course, no use of my talking in all this detail. What I am concerned about is your health and your ability to keep going for a long time at top speed. I know that people in your particular profession, with its odd hours and hectic demands, often make up excuses and alibis for themselves and for their failure to keep in tip-top condition. My contention is that all these unusual conditions simply emphasize the need for reasonable, sensible health programs.

Anglo-Saxon men usually find it difficult to exchange direct expressions of sentiment and affection. I am as subject to this inhibition as is any other person, but I am not exaggerating when I tell you that this letter is dictated only by sheer affection and esteem. I hope you will accept it in the same way, and I assure you that nothing could make me happier than to have you come back here in three or four months, weighing no more than 180 pounds (at the outside), shooting golf on a par basis, and looking like a 23 year old college lad.[7] (I will furnish MP's[8] to provide you protection against the lonely gals of the Champs-Elysees.)

Before sending this letter, I am going to show it to General Snyder who will, if he disagrees with any single thing that I said, add his own postscript. To assure his complete independence of opinion, I shall not even ask that he show me his comments.[9]

Of course, I sincerely trust that you do not explode in wrath or annoyance when you have read this far, so I refer to the old saw, "There are two fools in the world, he who gives advice and he who refuses to take it." In any event, fat or slim, in condition or out of condition, all the best to you.[10] *Cordially*

---

[1] For background on Robinson, a newspaper executive and friend of Eisenhower's, see no. 39.

[2] Robinson and the General had met in 1947 when Robinson had expressed an interest in publishing Eisenhower's war memoir (see Galambos, *Chief of Staff*, nos. 1811 and 1945). On their friendship see no. 39; and Ambrose, *Eisenhower*, vol. I, *Soldier, General of the Army, President-Elect*, pp. 476–77, 510.

[3] In late June Robinson had visited Eisenhower (see no. 217).

[4] The General was concerned about his own weight and had recently wagered with another friend, George E. Allen, that he could reduce effectively through diet and exercise (see no. 48).

[5] Eisenhower had himself quit smoking in 1949 (see no. 166).

[6] A niblick, or number nine iron, is a golf club with a metal head used for hitting the ball with maximum loft.

[7] In his reply of July 17 (EM) Robinson admitted that he had given "unstinting devotion" to his job but that he had been "careless, undisciplined and . . . unconsciously unfaithful" to his "unearned legacy of good health." He would reassure Eisenhower that his letter of advice was a "cherished treasure" and the "greatest manifestation of friendship" that he had ever known. Robinson added that his "crusade" for improved health had started July 16.

[8] Military police.

[9] General Howard M. Snyder, Sr., was the General's physician (see no. 59). Snyder would write Robinson on July 13 expressing his full approval of the advice from "Dr. IKE" (EM).

[10] On October 21 Robinson would write to say that he was down to one hundred eighty pounds (EM). For developments see nos. 323 and 382.

266   *Eisenhower Mss.*

To Crawford Hallock Greenewalt   *July 12, 1951*

Dear Mr. Greenewalt:[1] I am emboldened to write this letter by the record of E. I. du Pont de Nemours in the support of education and the vital interest shown by the corporation and its officers in public affairs. Because of this and of du Pont's long support of some of Columbia's scientific activities, I should like you to know of our most recent plans to establish an Engineering Center.[2]

About a year ago the University announced plans for a development to strengthen American engineering education and science at the highest professional level. Our Trustees believed then, as they do now, that there exists an unparalleled opportunity to be of service to the engineering profession and the nation.

Under the leadership of Dean John R. Dunning and his faculty, impressive strides have been taken to make the Center a reality. New faculty members have been added and several additional candidates are under consideration; land has been acquired and architects' plans are being prepared. It is estimated that upwards of $22,000,000 will be required to finance the program at its present stage.[3]

I cite this background for two reasons. Columbia plans shortly to launch a nationwide appeal for Engineering Center funds. We believe that the special significance given this undertaking by the new trend in world affairs, backed by Columbia's long record of service to American traditions and the democratic way of life, justify hope that our appeal will have support from many sources—individuals, corporations, and foundations—regardless of alumni ties.

Dean Dunning has discussed our plans with a number of prominent business leaders; the response has been most encouraging. I have suggested to him that he call on you at your convenience and tell you about this program. I earnestly hope it will be possible for you to see him.[4]

Obviously, preoccupation with my present job prevents me from writing you more than this simple letter. *Sincerely*

[1] Crawford Hallock Greenewalt (B.S. MIT 1922) had been the president of E. I. du Pont de Nemours and Company since 1948.
[2] Greenewalt had corresponded with the General in 1949 concerning his interest in contributing to the chemistry, chemical engineering, and mechanical engineering departments at Columbia University (see Eisenhower to Greenewalt, Jan. 4, 1949, EM; on du Pont contributions to universities see *New York Times*, Jan. 16, 1952, Jan. 8, 1954). In 1953 Columbia would give Greenewalt an honorary Doctor of Laws degree (see *New York Times*, June 3, 1953).
[3] Columbia had announced the plans for a new engineering center in 1950 (see Galambos, *Columbia University*, nos. 741 and 1122; see also *New York Times*, Nov. 5, 1951, May 21, 1953). Groundbreaking ceremonies for the first of the center's four buildings would be held in the spring of 1959 (see *New York Times*, Mar. 19, 30, Apr. 5, 1959; July 31, 1964).

John Ray Dunning had been the director of scientific research and dean of the School of Engineering at Columbia since 1950 (see no. 37, n. 6). Dunning and Eisenhower would discuss the engineering center when they met on July 12.
[4] Columbia would officially begin the fund-raising campaign for the engineering center with a dinner at the Waldorf-Astoria Hotel in New York City on November 7 (see *New York Times*, Nov. 8, 1951). For developments see nos. 327 and 328.

267   *Eisenhower Mss., Diaries*

DIARY   *July 13, 1951*

Mr. Paul Miller of Gannett Newspapers[1] thinks I'll soon have to say whether I'm a Republican or Democrat. I *think* he agrees now with my contention that a soldier *has* to keep his mouth shut on such matters.[2]

[1] Miller was the director and vice-president of the Gannett Company of New York, newspaper publishers; he had been the editor and publisher of the *Rochester Times-Union* since 1949.
[2] On July 13 Miller had visited with the General, who was feeling mounting pressure to declare his party affiliation (see nos. 135 and 195). For developments see no. 551.

To PAUL GRAY HOFFMAN   *July 13, 1951*

Dear Paul:[1] Thank you very much for your nice letter. I quite agree
with the observation in your first paragraph; namely, that in the minds
of the American people this whole business sort of centers in me. In
any event, I have told several of the Congressmen and Senators who
have come over this way that you have very specific comprehensive
ideas affecting organization of the American activities in Europe and
that they will probably be hearing something about them.[2]

The Senatorial Committee is now with us. While I had a very fine
initial meeting with them and Gruenther made his usual, lucid presentation, I hear that when they met with some of the other groups
here—Spofford, Katz, and so on—they were not too happy with what
they heard.[3]

I am delighted about the grant for the Free University of Berlin and
I am equally pleased that you are going to time the gift so as to give
West Berlin a chance to brag about something bigger and better than
a mere Communist Youth Rally in the East.[4]

I shall be looking forward to your arrival and we will have a big
"conference." I shall tell my office to keep me as free as possible on
the 2nd, 3rd, and 4th so that we can really get together. I wish I could
go with your party on your trip to the Near East and Pakistan. I have
never been in that area and I should like to go in such company.[5]
Cordially

[1] For background on Hoffman, president of the Ford Foundation, see no. 139.

[2] Hoffman had written on July 6 (EM) in response to a letter from Eisenhower
concerning NATO reorganization (see no. 238). Hoffman said that Americans
viewed the General as being in charge of all "activities contributing to the building
up of the defense of Europe." Eisenhower should, Hoffman explained, take on
additionally the position of chairman of the NATO Council of Deputies, because
no one "of lesser stature" could "get real action out of the officials who comprise
that body" (on the deputies see no. 2, n. 2).

[3] Members of the Senate Foreign Relations Committee had received their first
briefing at SHAPE on July 9. A transcription of General Alfred M. Gruenther's
remarks to the senators is in EM, Subject File, Congressional Visits, 1951; see
also *New York Times*, July 3, August 13, 1951. For background on Charles M.
Spofford, Chairman of NATO's Council of Deputies, and Milton Katz, American
Special Representative in Europe for the Marshall Plan, see no. 16.

[4] Hoffman had written that more than $1 million was being given in a grant to the
Free University of Berlin by the Ford Foundation. The official announcement
would be made on August 6, about the same time that a Communist Youth Rally
would take place in East Berlin (*New York Times*, Aug. 7, 1951).

[5] In his letter Hoffman had said that he would be in Paris in early August, after
which he would attend ceremonies at the Free University of Berlin and then travel
to the Near East, Pakistan, and India to look for "projects in these critical areas
which the Foundation could usefully finance" (on the visit see no. 308).

Eisenhower Mss.

To John Lawrence Hennessy *July 13, 1951*

Dear Jack:[1] Thanks very much for sending me the clipping from the Herald Tribune.[2] My little talk on the unity of Europe seemed to strike a sympathetic chord with lots of people. Of course, it is in no sense a new idea. The only thing that could be considered novel about my presentation was the fact that I insisted such unification is important to our common security and that the only way that the thing would ever be done would be by a sort of dynamic action rather than by gradualism.

All the best, *Cordially*

[1] Hennessy was the president and director of J. L. Hennessy Associates, Inc. The firm operated hotels and restaurants in New York City (see Galambos, *Columbia University*, no. 549).

[2] In a July 5 editorial entitled "The Unity of Europe," the *New York Herald Tribune* had praised Eisenhower's recent speech to the English Speaking Union in London (a copy of the editorial is in EM; for background see no. 252, n. 2). The General was described as a leader "who views his task in terms of its broadest possibilities and its loftiest implications." The editorial called Eisenhower a "master of the spoken word" who had demonstrated in his speech a "shrewd balance between the ideal and the necessity—between what ought to be done and what must be done. This is a supreme faculty of statesmanship." For other responses to the speech see nos. 264, n. 1, 279, n. 2, and 303. On the theme of European unity see nos. 215 and 251.

Eisenhower Mss.

To Arthur Seymour Nevins *July 13, 1951*

Dear Art:[1] At this moment, I have time for only a note but, within a few days, I shall certainly answer at length your fine letter of July 8th.[2]

First, I thank you for your illuminating account. Secondly, I want to say that I thought you already knew how much I agree with your paragraph which begins, "I continue to regard chickens as the dirtiest, nastiest, dumbest creatures on the earth." So far as I am concerned— and I thought I had put this in earlier letters—you can sell any chicken on the place any moment you choose, saving only those you want to keep for your own household purposes.[3] This I supposed was understood, and I am quite sure you will find George in agreement. So, from here on out, the decision as to chickens is entirely yours—if George agrees.[4]

You acted exactly right in the case of the blood tests and the cows. Neither George nor I can afford to have any untested cattle on the premises, and it is entirely possible that this particular development will merely give us a chance to improve our herd.[5]

With respect to the Angus cattle, I have gotten to the point where I hope Mr. Hammer forgets all about it.[6] There could be several ways of using up the Allen pasturage. We might buy "feeders" in the spring and sell every fall! Here again, I shall accept gladly whatever decision you and George reach. (In this connection, you know that I own a young white-faced bull, now in Colorado. While he has not shown championship characteristics as of now, he is of very fine stock, properly registered and so on. We could always bring him to Gettysburg if we wanted to do any actual breeding.)[7]

Give Ann my affectionate greetings and, of course, warm regard to yourself.[8] *Cordially*

P.S. I repeat that you should never want for little alterations around the house. Minor repairs and so on, as I see it, are absolutely chargeable to the farm operation. Permanent additions are, of course, chargeable to me.

I think Mr. Kirschner's interest is simply that of a wealthy, energetic friend of George's who is intrigued by our whole operation. In any event, I think he is pretty smart because he agrees with me about those damned chickens and the chicken houses.[9]

[1] For background on Nevins, an old friend of Eisenhower's and the manager of his Gettysburg farm, see no. 33, n. 4.

[2] In his letter of July 8 (EM) Nevins had discussed the condition of the farm, the crops, animals, and expenses.

[3] Nevins told Eisenhower that in a few months he would know whether the "egg business" was profitable. "If we keep the chickens," Nevins wrote, "I'll move them some distance away where the potent odors can be dissipated over open fields." In an earlier letter the General had given Nevins authority to sell the chickens if he wished (see no. 179).

[4] George E. Allen was the General's partner in the Gettysburg farm enterprise (see no. 9, n. 2).

[5] Nevins had written that Eisenhower's entire herd had been tested for brucellosis and that five infected Holsteins would be destroyed (see Nevins to Eisenhower, Oct. 14, 1951, EM).

[6] Armand Hammer, a petroleum magnate who owned a stock farm in New Jersey, had offered to provide Black Angus cattle for the Gettysburg farm. Nevins had written that a meeting in Gettysburg with Eisenhower's old friend Edwin N. Clark, Hammer, and Hammer's farm manager had been postponed. On July 13 the General had replied in a phone message (EM) that he was "rather indifferent about Angus cattle," adding that a declination to the offer could be made on the grounds that the farm was "not equipped to conduct this kind of operation." The plans for the Angus cattle would not develop further (see Nevins to Eisenhower, Oct. 14, 1951, EM; and nos. 179 and 235, n. 4).

[7] For background on Eisenhower's bull see no. 235.

[8] Mrs. Nevins, the former Ann Louise Stacy.

[9] The General had earlier urged Nevins to make the house more comfortable (see no. 179). Nevins had said that Walter Kirschner, a friend of Allen's, had sent an architect to evaluate the farmhouse and to draw up plans for remodeling. For background see nos. 249 and 250; for developments see no. 315.

Eisenhower added by hand: "Happy Birthday on the 19th." For developments on farm activities see no. 376.

271   *Eisenhower Mss., Schow Corr.*

To Joseph Lawton Collins[1]   *July 16, 1951*
Memorandum

Subject: Promotion of Three Colonels to Brigadier General

1. It is now slightly more than six months since I began the task of creating the command and staff organization necessary for the discharge of my responsibilities as Supreme Commander, Allied Powers Europe. By the nature of that organization and also in view of the fact that my Chief of Staff and I are United States Army Officers, I found it expedient to request the Department of the Army to furnish many of the key officers for my staff. Your response to this request has been most gratifying. The officers you made available to SHAPE have, almost without exception, been outstanding in their performance of duty.

2. Three of the United States Army colonels, who were especially selected because of their proven abilities, occupy positions of such great responsibility that, in my opinion, they should be promoted to the grade of brigadier general as soon as practicable. It is my understanding that contemporaries of these officers have been included on recent lists. The officers are:

   a. Colonel Robert A. Schow,[2] 012180, Deputy to the Assistant Chief of Staff for Intelligence, Major General Terence S. Airey,[3] British Army. As senior United States intelligence officer in SHAPE, his responsibilities to me and to the Chief of Staff are most important. He has already rendered outstanding service both in organizing the Intelligence Division and in establishing sound and workable intelligence procedures throughout the command. The deputies in my Organization and Training, my Plans, Policy and Operations, and my Logistics Divisions are already of brigadier rank. My intelligence deputy should likewise be a brigadier general. Colonel Schow has amply demonstrated his ability to discharge these responsibilities.

   b. Colonel Herbert M. Jones,[4] 012251, Adjutant General. He has shown a remarkable ability to deal with the multitudinous new and perplexing problems inherent in the operation of a headquarters which is faced with the task of reconciling the administrative procedures of nine different nations. He has done a superior job in setting up his division on an efficient basis. That division is the largest, in point of personnel, in the headquarters. His responsibilities are heavy and are increasing constantly as our volume of correspondence likewise increases. I consider that the Adjutant General, SHAPE, should be a brigadier general and that Colonel Jones has adequately demonstrated his capabilities for that rank and assignment.

c. Colonel Robert J. Wood,[5] 018064, Secretary of the General Staff. He has been one of the main sparkplugs of our staff organization throughout the difficult formative period. He has a genius for organization, and an ability to foresee difficulties and to keep things moving at the high tempo required in this headquarters. His keen mind and his broad background make him an ideal choice for this position. His responsibilities are such as to fully warrant his promotion to brigadier general.

3. I strongly urge that these three officers be promoted to the grade of brigadier general at an early date.

[1] For background on Army Chief of Staff Collins see no. 52, n. 1. Two additional copies of this memorandum, which had been drafted by Eisenhower's C/S, General Alfred M. Gruenther, are filed under Jones and Wood in EM, Miscellaneous Corr.
[2] For background on Schow, who would become a brigadier general (AUS) on September 5, 1951, see no. 144, n. 4.
[3] Before taking his present assignment at SHAPE, Major General Terence Sydney Airey had served as Allied commander and Military Governor of the British-U.S. Zone of Free Territory, Trieste. For further background on Airey see Galambos, *Chief of Staff*, esp. no. 1531.
[4] Colonel Herbert Maury Jones (USMA 1918) would become a brigadier general (AUS) on September 6, 1951. From 1946 to 1950 Jones had served as Chief, Management Staff Division, Office of The Adjutant General, Washington, D.C.
[5] Colonel Robert Jefferson Wood would become a brigadier general on July 2, 1952. For background on Wood see Galambos, *Chief of Staff*, no. 1636, n. 3; on his promotion see no. 322.

272   *Eisenhower Mss.*

To Dewey Short   *July 16, 1951*

Dear Dewey:[1] I am grateful for the thoughtfulness of your letter and read with interest, in the Kansas City Star clipping, the report of your findings on your trip. I made a mental bow in your direction when I saw, in the margin of the clipping, the complimentary sentiments with respect to me which the newspaper article itself omitted from the text. Your conclusion as to the importance of the effort for collective security in the free world was clearly and forcefully stated.[2]

Here at SHAPE, we have never had a more satisfying group of visitors than was the Congressional Committee of which you were a senior representative of the Republican Party. While the entire week was given over by the Committee to serious work, the cooperative attitude of its members was so noticeable as to make our own efforts a real pleasure.

With warm personal regard, *Cordially*

[1] Short, ranking Republican member of the House Committee on Armed Services, represented the Seventh Congressional District of Missouri (see Galambos, *Chief of Staff*, no. 1584).

[2] In a letter of July 10 (EM) Short had thanked Eisenhower for his courtesies during the recent visit to SHAPE of a congressional committee appointed to study the role of the United States in European defense (on the visit see no. 209, n. 2).

Short had enclosed a clipping from the June 20 edition of the *Kansas City Star*, which featured Short's account of the trip. Short noted that the printer had omitted a portion of one paragraph in the article; he had therefore typed in the margin the missing words: "—he has brought to Europe an emphasis on spiritual values and moral force. He has engendered good will." Short concluded that there were limits to America's capacity to aid European recovery. "Certainly," he was quoted in the article, "we must have collective security of all the free nations, but I must always think of America first."

273   *Eisenhower Mss.*

To Henry Robinson Luce   *July 16, 1951*

Dear Henry:[1] Thank you very much for your note. Most members of my staff, and I, have already read the LIFE article. We are particularly delighted with it because of its earnest attempt to place the various factors in their proper relationship, one to the other. The only point on which I am quite sure that my staff disagrees with the writer 100% is the extraordinary amount of credit Mr. Laguerre ascribes to me for any success so far achieved. However, that particular slant gave me a very fine opportunity to smile benignly upon my associates.[2]

Please convey my warm greetings to Mrs. Luce[3] and with warm regard to yourself, *Cordially*

[1] For background on Luce, founder, publisher, and editor in chief of *Time* and *Life* magazines, see Galambos, *Columbia University*, no. 381.

On July 10 Luce had written Eisenhower (EM) that the fifteen-page report on SHAPE had been published in the July 16 issue of *Life* (for background see no. 141, n. 2).

Luce had originally suggested the article in a letter of May 7 (EM). He had also suggested that the writer be his assistant, Andre Laguerre, who had been "outstanding" as head of the Time-Life Paris bureau for four years and who was now a special correspondent in Western Europe. Laguerre had met with the General on June 13 (see Laguerre to Eisenhower, June 30, 1951, EM). The *Life* article reviewed the progress of SHAPE during its first seven months. Although Laguerre dealt with the problems of Eisenhower's work, he also described "elements of hope" such as the teamwork of Eisenhower's "brilliant" staff and the General's determination to work toward greater European unity and self-sufficiency. Laguerre had concluded that "the heart of Europe is beating more strongly than at any time since World War II," and he credited this progress largely to Eisenhower's "energy, resolution, lucidity and almost boyish enthusiasm."

³ On Clare Boothe Luce see Galambos, *Columbia University*, no. 542.

To George Catlett Marshall   *July 17, 1951*
Cable ALO 206. Top secret

Eyes Only to Secretary of Defense Marshall
In response to messages from the President of the United States I request that after reading the message below you have it delivered on a TOP SECRET basis to President Truman:
Dear Mister President: I received your message from Averell Harriman and of course am ready to comply with any plan that you may decide to approve. My sincere thanks for your kind inquiry concerning my health sent through Ambassador Bruce. I am fully recovered from a slight illness.¹

In my opinion any attempt to conduct a meeting on clandestine basis would inevitably become known and the results would be obviously undesirable and even unpleasant. Among the several objections to my coming directly to Washington to report officially as an American officer to the President of the United States, only the one of timing seems to me to have any real importance. I believe it to be distinctly undesirable for me to come to the United States before enactment by the Congress of the military aid bill.² To do so would almost certainly involve me in hearings of indefinite length before Congressional committees. In this event I would probably be drawn into numerous argumentative subjects largely unrelated to my own responsibilities and concerning which I have little first hand knowledge. Complicating the matter is the fact that each House of Congress has sent over here large committees primarily because of my current inability to spare the time for prolonged appearances in Washington.[3] At least some of the members of these committees have stated that they made the trip at considerable inconvenience to themselves so as to obtain my personal testimony, in spite of my inability to appear in Washington at this time. If I should, at an early date, suddenly arrive in the capital city there would certainly be created some justifiable resentment among these particular people which might even cause some damage to the military aid bill.

If it is reasonable to assume that the Congress will complete the military aid bill within six or seven weeks, would it be satisfactory to you to plan on a meeting in Washington about the middle of September?[4] My own feeling would be that immediately after the completion of the legislative action on that bill I could without creating complications be summoned as an American officer to report to you and to the Secretary of Defense on any type of development here that you might wish to give as a reason for the meeting.

I realize from Mister Harriman's message that this suggestion might not suit your calendar and I therefore add as an alternative the thought that you might consider going on some appropriately planned maneuver with the Atlantic Fleet during the course of which you could anchor at some port to which I could easily be summoned. Examples would be Newfoundland, Iceland and the Azores, depending entirely upon your time and inclinations. I think that an important consideration, if this alternative has any merit at all, would be to select the point sufficiently far from Washington so as to make plausible my immediate return to Europe without venturing into the capital city.

I repeat that if none of these ideas would appear to you to form the basis of a reasonable plan I will be quite ready to adjust my engagements and activities so as to come to Washington at any time you may designate. I believe however that I have not exaggerated the possibilities of embarrassment if I should come during the period of Congressional consideration of the military aid bill.[5]

With my deep respects and best wishes

[1] Eisenhower had been ill on July 14, when W. Averell Harriman, foreign-policy adviser to President Truman, stopped briefly in Paris. Harriman, then on his way to Teheran to help settle the British-Persian oil dispute, had left the message that the President wished Eisenhower to return to the United States for a meeting, which the General mistook to mean a secret session (see Harriman to Eisenhower, July 11, 1951, EM; and nos. 149 and 259).

[2] For background on the pending military aid bill see no. 377.

[3] On such congressional visits see nos. 209 and 218.

[4] On July 19 the President wrote Marshall that he had read Eisenhower's message "with a lot of interest. His suggestions seem to me to be all right." Truman wondered, however, whether September might not be too far off for the proposed

meeting; he asked Harriman to suggest a date between August 10 and 15. "I wish you would think about the situation and when we get a chance to talk about it we will make a decision on it" (Marshall Papers).
[5] For developments see nos. 290 and 363. Eisenhower would not meet with Truman until November. There is a possibility that President Truman's request was prompted by the mounting discussion of Eisenhower as a potential candidate for the presidency (see nos. 457 and 480).

275   *Eisenhower Mss.*

To AKSEL NIELSEN   *July 18, 1951*

Dear Aksel:[1] With this note comes a long letter that I have dictated this morning after quite a conversation with Min last evening.[2]

This personal note is to say that I am delighted with the pictures of DD. From them, he looks to me to be a trifle long in the legs and there seems to be something a little bit different about his head than the picture I have in my mind of your best Herefords. However, on the whole, he looks fairly promising to me.

You will remember that it was always my plan that, if we should produce, in my name, one that might bring a pretty fair price as a range bull, I should propose the using of the proceeds for the special purpose of getting hold of the best cow we could—either out of your herd or, if necessary, purchasing one—and then getting that cow serviced by the finest bull that you know of in all Colorado. Of course, we might be investing a lot in a fairly wild gamble but, on the other hand, we would at least have the cow! Thereafter I would not own any animal individually—he would be yours and mine in partnership.

Now, of course, there might be a far better variation of the plan than I have outlined here, but you can see that what I am talking about is that you and I should see if we can't get together and produce a blue ribbon animal.[3]

I am sure that you know without saying how much I appreciate the time and trouble you are taking with respect to Mrs. Doud's affairs. I shall never forget it, and this goes for Mamie and our kids as well.

Give our love to Helen and, of course, to Virginia and her nice family.[4] *As ever*

[1] For background on Nielsen, an old friend of the Eisenhowers', see no. 34.
[2] Elivera Doud, Mamie's mother, had returned to France following her husband's funeral (see no. 240). Eisenhower had written Nielsen on July 7 (EM) that Mrs. Doud was "gradually regaining her equilibrium" and was beginning to consider ways to assist the family financially through Mr. Doud's estate. The General

concluded that "Min is very anxious indeed to do the right thing by members of her family." For developments see Nielsen to Eisenhower, Dec. 12, 1951, EM.
[3] With his letter of July 12 (EM) Nielsen had enclosed a picture of the General's bull, Denison Domino (see no. 235). For developments see no. 600.
[4] Mrs. Nielsen, the former Helen Maurer, and their daughter, Virginia Elaine Nielsen Muse.

276   *Eisenhower Mss.*

To Charles C. Auchincloss   *July 19, 1951*

Dear Charlie:[1] Thank you very much for your intriguing letter.[2] Any attempt at answering the subject matter must, of course, await the time when you and I can have a long meeting at the Links Club.[3] But I can thank you for sending me Walter Judd's article[4]—I admire him tremendously—and the Congressional Record containing Judd's statement about Wedemeyer.[5]

With warm personal regard, *Cordially*

[1] For background on Auchincloss, a New York City lawyer and stockbroker, see Galambos, *Columbia University*, no. 293.
[2] Writing on July 9 (EM), Auchincloss had urged Eisenhower to declare himself a candidate for the presidency as a Republican. "The Democrats have been in power too long," he said, "and think they own the Country including our private lives. . . . You are qualified in every way to render the very greatest service to all Americans regardless of what pressure group they may belong to. How the people would rally to your support!" Auchincloss went on to score the growing federal bureaucracy, "Palace Guard" politicians, American Far Eastern policy, "widespread crime" involving the RFC, and critics of large corporations. In a postscript Auchincloss added that no letter from Eisenhower would be given "the slightest publicity."
[3] Both Eisenhower and Auchincloss were members of The Links, a New York City golf club.
[4] Auchincloss enclosed a copy of an address Republican congressman Walter H. Judd (B.A. University of Nebraska 1920; M.D. 1923) of Minnesota (Fifth District) had delivered before the Executive Club of Chicago on February 2, 1951. Judd, a medical missionary and hospital superintendent in China during the 1930s and 1940s, had surveyed American foreign-policy mistakes since the end of World War II. He cited favorably Eisenhower's February 1 references to Europe's technical and industrial potential, and he mentioned the deterrents to Soviet expansion of European (including German) military might and the American ability, presumably by means of nuclear bombing, to destroy Russian factories, cities, and communications. Judd nonetheless argued that the security of Europe depended on a free Asia as an Eastern bulwark against the Soviets. Postwar American leaders, he said, "forgot that they couldn't get the security of Europe by effort in Europe alone" (Judd, "How Can We Be So Stupid? We Help Our Enemy and Deny Our Friends," *Vital Speeches of the Day* 17, no. 10 [1951], 293–300).

[5] Auchincloss also had enclosed a copy of Judd's remarks in the House of Representatives on June 28 praising Lieutenant General Albert C. Wedemeyer and decrying his retirement from the Army. "His only mistake," Judd declared, "was that he was right about the Communists in China and his superiors were wrong" (*Congressional Record*, 82d Cong., 1st sess., 1951, 97, pts. 13–14: A3983–86). For background on Wedemeyer, who left service July 31, see no. 178; on the Army's officer retirement policy see no. 321.

277   *Eisenhower Mss.*

To DeWitt Wallace   *July 21, 1951*

Dear Mr. Wallace:[1] As of this moment, I am so engrossed in perplexing problems, which seem daily to arise in locust-like swarms to plague me, that rarely do I get a chance to indulge my continuing and intense interest in the domestic scene. Your highly complimentary letter deserves, of course, a great deal of thought and, at the very least, a logical answer. Both of these are beyond my opportunities of the moment.[2]

You understand, of course, that I undertook this assignment out of a sense of duty as a soldier and because I believe that the free world has no acceptable alternative to the establishment of an adequate collective security system. To fail in the effort to which the NATO nations are now committed would incur vastly increased danger for the United States and such staggering costs that we could scarcely manage and expect to retain, over the years, a free economy. Because of these convictions of mine, you will quickly realize that, so long as I am on this job, I have no right to say anything that could tie me in with the political groupments and political struggles in America. The damage to this effort would be incalculable if our people should come to believe that it is being administered, not by a representative of the entire American complex, but by a political figure who could, after identifying himself as such, scarcely abstain from the many crosscurrents of politics that are constantly noticeable in our country.

This you may think is a very inadequate answer to your obviously sincere letter. Indeed, these ideas I am trying to express are little more than instant reaction rather than the product of deep thought, but I am certain you will see the essential soundness of the position.[3]

Won't you convey my greetings to Mrs. Wallace[4] and, of course, warmest regard to yourself. *Cordially*

[1] Wallace was founder and editor of the *Reader's Digest* (see Galambos, *Columbia University*, no. 448).
[2] Wallace's letter of June 26 (EM) was a strong appeal for Eisenhower to accept

the Republican nomination for the presidency. Wallace saw Eisenhower's lead in the presidential polls of both political parties as an "opportunity to unite the country and revitalize its purposes." Acknowledging that nomination and election would "involve great sacrifice" for Eisenhower and that some of the political activity "might be distasteful," Wallace nevertheless urged Eisenhower to allow his Republican friends to work in his behalf so that his nomination would be assured. "I do not believe," he said, "it is an exaggeration to say that the need for that to happen is as great as was the necessity to win World War II."
[3] Eisenhower apparently sent a copy of this letter to William H. Burnham, his political adviser, whose handwritten reply reads: "This is the very best philosophy yet. We can use it in many letters which I am sure are in the mail or about to be written over the next few months" (EM, Wallace Corr.). For background on Burnham see no. 40.
[4] The former Lila Bell Acheson.

278   *Eisenhower Mss.*

To Martin Withington Clement   *July 21, 1951*
Personal

Dear Clem:[1] I was vastly intrigued by your letter of the 12th. I quite agree with what you have to say about inflation, and I am more than amazed that everybody seems to want to duck the very obvious but highly unpopular methods of defeating inflation. We want nostrums and sugar-coated pills; but they will be no good against more and more planned economy and Socialistic trends.[2]

I read the Whaley-Eaton letter with tremendous interest. It seems to me that letter puts the problem right squarely up to us in simple and unmistakable terms. I wish everybody could read it.[3]

Of course, Mamie and I are looking forward to seeing you when you get here.[4] *As ever*

[1] Clement (B.S. Trinity College, Hartford, Conn. 1901) was chairman of the board of trustees of the Pennsylvania Railroad Company. His letter to Eisenhower of July 12 (EM) was marked "private."
[2] Clement told Eisenhower that he believed the overwhelming issue in the United States was inflation. "All cures for inflation are unpopular," he wrote, "but as you well know, . . . it means a drastic reduction in government spending, a broad base tax program to absorb the abnormal income generated by the defense program, rates of interest sufficiently high to prevent unsound expansion, and a sound money program that will make our money worth what we say it is worth."
[3] Clement had enclosed the July 7, 1951, issue of a newsletter published by the Whaley-Eaton Service (EM), which addressed the problem of inflation in the United States. According to the article, the U.S. economy would stabilize if the government used its own powers to control spending. On the problem of inflation at this time see Rockoff, *Drastic Measures*, pp. 177–99.
[4] Clement and his wife, the former Elizabeth S. Wallace, would visit the Eisenhowers in August (see Clement to Eisenhower, Aug. 6 and Sept. 21, 1951, EM).

TO HAROLD BOESCHENSTEIN   *July 21, 1951*

Dear Mr. Boeschenstein:[1] Thank you very much for your nice note. I am, of course, highly pleased that you liked my London talk and I was even more pleased to note your judgment that there is undoubtedly a growing understanding in the United States of the essentials and importance of this task.[2]

You cannot, of course, expect me to do any shouting with glee about the second paragraph of your letter. When problems pile up to the point that I feel almost round-shouldered, my dreams are of a quiet stream, not of another and even more strenuous duty.[3]

With best wishes and personal regard, *Cordially*

[1] Boeschenstein, of Toledo, Ohio, had been president of Owens-Corning Fiberglas Corporation since 1938.

[2] In a note of July 16 (EM) Boeschenstein had thanked Eisenhower for his hospitality on Tuesday, June 12, when the two had met at Eisenhower's headquarters in Paris. Boeschenstein praised Eisenhower's speech in London on July 4, saying that it "merits cheers for its eloquent forthrightness" (see no. 252).

[3] In the second paragraph of his letter, Boeschenstein had told Eisenhower that he had talked recently with a number of Eisenhower's friends, including Senator James H. Duff of Pennsylvania, former Republican National Finance Committee chairman Harold E. Talbott, and Kansas Republican National Committeeman and banker Harry Darby (see no. 196). "I believe deeply in what you stand for," Boeschenstein said, "and may as well tell you that—gratuitously—I have enlisted as a private in the movement to 'Draft Eisenhower.'"

280   *Eisenhower Mss.*

TO WALTER KIRSCHNER   *July 21, 1951*

Dear Mr. Kirschner:[1] Thank you for sending the clippings on to me. Frankly, I shudder every time I read the kind of thing reported in the stories you sent me. I am too busy to give any real thought to it.[2]

Art Nevins tells me that our situation with respect to Bangs disease is probably not so bad as we first figured.[3]

Cliff Roberts is leaving for home today and our children will leave at the end of this coming week. It will be a lonesome place.[4]

Our very best to your nice family and, of course, warm regard to yourself. *Cordially*

[1] For background on Kirschner see no. 33.

[2] Kirschner had sent Eisenhower four newspaper articles concerning the possible effect of an Eisenhower candidacy on the forthcoming presidential election (EM).
[3] Nevins was the manager of Eisenhower's Gettysburg farm. On the problems with diseased cattle see no. 270.
[4] In addition to Clifford Roberts, Eisenhower's son John and daughter-in-law Barbara were visiting the Eisenhowers (for background see nos. 193 and 222).

281   *Eisenhower Mss.*

To GEORGE CATLETT MARSHALL   *July 21, 1951*

Dear General:[1] Thank you very much for your nice letter about the reactions of the Congressmen who have visited us. Tomorrow we have our final meeting with the Senators and I hope that results will be as good as you feel they were in the first instance. However, my staff warns me that this hope will probably not be completely realized since we have one or two members of this group of eight who seem to be somewhat hostile. We shall do our best.[2]

As you know, I have always steadfastly pursued the policy that governmental officials bearing responsibilities for any activity in which I am involved are welcome in my headquarters, and every assistance is given to them to uncover any facts that they may desire. At times, of course, this policy imposes a sufficient burden on my associates— and me personally—to be more than a bit irksome, yet in the long run I know that no other policy could possibly maintain the feeling of confidence and mutual trust that is essential to success in this type of problem.

A veritable stream of American visitors passes through my office. Many of them are old friends, and nearly all are leaders in our educational, spiritual, industrial, or governmental activities. To save my own time, I have arranged a sort of briefing routine that each gets before he comes into my office. However, I insist on giving a few minutes to each because I believe that all of us have the responsibility of helping others to understand the issues involved. If we can give such an understanding to our visitors, they acquire an almost automatic interest in helping to pass it on when they get home.[3]

Sometimes this process seems like an attempt to empty the ocean with a teaspoon, but we still remain hopeful.

With personal regard, *Sincerely*

P.S. The Senators just left *apparently* in a very fine frame of mind.[4] I shall examine the possibility of dispatching Gruenther to you within the next few days.[5]

[1] Marshall was Secretary of Defense.

[2] In a letter of July 16 (EM) Marshall had commended Eisenhower for his work with the key House committee members who had visited SHAPE in mid-June (for background on the visit see no. 209). "These men," he wrote, "were very favorably impressed with what they saw and heard in the NATO countries they visited, and particularly with what they learned in your Headquarters. They have a very clear idea of the magnitude of the problems facing you and are very laudatory in their description of the way you are going about things."

At this time Eisenhower was hosting a group of U.S. senators, all members of the Foreign Relations Committee, who had been in Europe since July 8 surveying military and economic conditions (for background see no. 267).

[3] On Eisenhower's American visitors see EM, Subject File, Congressional Visits, 1951; and Senate Subcommittee on Foreign Relations, *United States Foreign-Aid Programs in Europe: Hearings*, 1951.

[4] This letter was written on Saturday, July 21, but Eisenhower did not sign it until the following day. According to his appointment calendar, the senators' final briefing had been held at Rocquencourt in Marly-le-Roi, France, some fifteen miles west of Paris, the location of Eisenhower's newly established headquarters. Since February 1951 SHAPE had operated from temporary headquarters in Paris. The move from Paris to Marly had taken place on July 21 and 22, thus making this senatorial briefing the first official event to be held at Marly (for background on Eisenhower's headquarters see nos. 45 and 60, n. 2; see also *International Herald Tribune*, Paris ed., July 20, 24, 25, 1951).

[5] On Gruenther's recall for congressional testimony see nos. 284 and 286.

282   *Eisenhower Mss.*

To Oliver Shewell Franks   *July 21, 1951*

Dear Mr. Ambassador:[1] This note is to tell you of an idea that has occurred to us at Columbia University and which, if ever translated into action, would affect members of The Royal Family. Bluntly, it is this:

In 1954, Columbia University will celebrate the 200th anniversary of the granting of its Charter by King George II.[2] We should, naturally, very much like to have The King and Queen come to an appropriate ceremony of celebration, a ceremony that could be arranged to suit almost any personal ideas or desires of Their Majesties.

We are, of course, completely innocent of any knowledge as to how such a request should be processed or, indeed, whether it might be deemed inappropriate by the British Government or Their Majesties for us to ask consideration of the proposal. However, our invitation is not only sincerely meant but gives some expression to our feeling that there is a very direct sentimental connection between the event we hope to celebrate and the reigning family at Great Britain.

The purpose of this letter, therefore, is to request that, in the event you are in sympathy with our idea, you conduct such informal conversations with the British Government as might be necessary in order to advise us as to how our invitation should be processed. I assure you of the very deep appreciation of the Trustees of Columbia University and of myself personally for your consideration and assistance.[3]

With my warm greetings to Lady Franks[4] and best wishes to yourself, *Cordially*

[1] Franks had been the British Ambassador to the United States since 1948.

[2] On the 1754 chartering of King's College, which later became Columbia University, see Horace Coon, *Columbia: Colossus on the Hudson* (New York, 1947), pp. 36–39; and Edward C. Elliott and Merritt M. Chambers, eds., *Charters and Basic Laws of Selected American Universities and Colleges* (New York, 1934), p. 150.

[3] In May Eisenhower had written Arthur H. Sulzberger, chairman of Columbia's Bicentennial Committee, about inviting King George VI and Queen Elizabeth (consort) to the 1954 celebration (see no. 168). In a letter of July 10 (EM) Eisenhower had explained to Sulzberger that because of the King's recent illness (see *New York Times*, June 13, 1951) and the suggestion that his daughter and son-in-law, Princess Elizabeth and Prince Philip, might substitute, an invitation should be sent to the British Embassy in Washington, D.C. On July 21 the General sent this letter to Sulzberger for his approval. Sulzberger replied on July 25 (EM) that Eisenhower's letter to Ambassador Franks had been "perfectly in order" and that he had forwarded it. The ambassador would write on July 27 that he would be glad to "get in touch with London to find out the lie of the land" (see EM, Sulzberger Corr.). For developments see no. 473, n. 4.

[4] The former Barbara Mary Tanner.

283   *Eisenhower Mss.*

To Clifford Roberts   *July 22, 1951*

Dear Cliff:[1] I hope to have this letter waiting for you at your office (and a copy at your hotel) when you arrive home. The reason is to ask you to avoid saying anything to Bill about having read the letter I wrote to him. I received from him an extraordinary answer—he has really taken me up, not only seriously, but in such a spirit as to make the whole business something of a crusade. So, while I don't mind your saying to him that you know that I wrote him a letter about his general health and welfare, I think it best not to admit that you actually read the letter unless, of course, he himself shows it to you.[2]

In any event, I have not the slightest doubt that Bill is starting instantly to put the whole program into effect.

This morning, Sunday, I had to come to the office to finish up our work with the group of traveling Senators.[3] The two grandchildren rode over with me and I asked them whether they had seen Cliff today.

They both said, "Yes"—I think the meaning they absorbed from my question was whether or not they knew you. In any event, David was as amusing as ever in his efforts to master the pronunciation of "Mister Roberts." Naturally we miss you. We truly hope you will be back before long.[4]

My very best to Barry and to Tom Silver and, of course, to all the members of the "Blind Brook gang."[5] *Cordially*

[1] For background on Roberts see no. 7, n. 1.

[2] Roberts had visited the General in Paris from June 10 to July 21 (see no. 217, n. 2). Apparently, Eisenhower had shown Roberts the letter he had written to William E. Robinson concerning ways to improve his health (no. 265). In his enthusiastic response of July 17 (EM) Robinson had written that he had begun his "new crusade" for better health with a "solemn promise that I shall not fail you—or me."

[3] Eisenhower and Gruenther had met at least twice with members of the Senate Foreign Relations Committee (see nos. 268, n. 3, and 281, n. 2).

[4] Eisenhower's son John was then in Paris along with his wife Barbara Jean and their children Dwight David II and Barbara Anne (see no. 224, n. 4). Roberts would visit again in late August (see no. 369, n. 3).

[5] On Barry T. Leithead see no. 217, n. 2. Tom Silver was no doubt Thomas Hammond Silver, president of the Lumber Mutual Casualty Insurance Company of New York since 1942. Both Leithead and Silver belonged to the Augusta National Golf Club. On the Blind Brook Club see no. 101, n. 8; on both clubs see EM, Subject File, Clubs and Associations.

284   *Eisenhower Mss.*

To George Catlett Marshall[01]   *July 23, 1951*
Cable. Top secret

Because of the conclusions the House combined committee apparently carried back to America from Europe, I am somewhat astonished that the members feel the need of a personal representative from me to present our story again.[2] Nevertheless, I shall of course make Gruenther available promptly. From my viewpoint the best time for him to leave would be this coming week-end, arriving in Washington sometime between Saturday evening, July 28 and Monday evening the 30. From your telegram I assume that this would be satisfactory to the committee since you did not imply any intention to close the hearings this week. I would appreciate your assistance in limiting the length of Gruenther's stay in Washington.[3]

If this plan meets your requirements won't you please confirm today so that we can make arrangements.

[1] Marshall had been Secretary of Defense since September 1950.

[2] In mid-June members of the House Foreign Affairs Committee, the Armed Services Committee, and the Appropriations Committee had visited Eisenhower in the course of a ten-day study of European defense developments (see no. 209). James Prioleau Richards, chairman of the Committee on Foreign Affairs, had requested that Lieutenant General Alfred M. Gruenther, Eisenhower's C/S, testify during committee hearings on the Mutual Security Program. Richards (LL.B. University of South Carolina 1921), a Democrat representing South Carolina's Fifth District, feared that without Gruenther's personal appearance the hearings might close in a "discouraging atmosphere" (Marshall to Eisenhower, JCS 96929, July 21, 1951, EM).

[3] Gruenther would leave Paris for Washington, D.C., on Friday, June 27, and testify on Tuesday, July 31 (see U.S. Congress, House, Committee on Foreign Affairs, *The Mutual Security Program: Hearings on H.R. 5020 and H.R. 5113*, 82d Cong., 1st sess., 1951, pp. 1505–52). For developments see no. 286.

285   *Eisenhower Mss., Family File*

To Edgar Newton Eisenhower   *July 23, 1951*

Dear Ed:[1] Of course, I know nothing whatsoever about the incident reported in the clipping that you forwarded to me recently. But I do know Joe Collins and I know that he would never be guilty of offering any promotion in return for violation of intellectual integrity.[2] About the only answer I can make, however, is one that I made to Arthur not long ago when he sent me an equally objectionable article from the same paper and by the same writer. My answer was, "Anyone who would believe anything he read in the Chicago Tribune would not be convinced by a denial."[3]

All the best. *As ever*

[1] For background on Eisenhower's brother Edgar see no. 24, n. 1.

[2] On July 10 Edgar had sent Eisenhower two clippings from Chicago newspapers (EM). One, an undated piece by Marquis Childs, was rife with speculation that Eisenhower would soon become the Republican nominee for the U.S. presidency. The second article, by Walter Trohan (A.B. University of Notre Dame 1926), had appeared in the June 30 *Chicago Daily Tribune*. According to Trohan, who was head of the *Tribune*'s Washington bureau, Lieutenant General Albert C. Wedemeyer had refused the offer of a promotion rather than change his testimony in the Senate investigation of General Douglas MacArthur's dismissal. Trohan alleged that it was Army Chief of Staff General Joseph Lawton Collins who had made the offer to Wedemeyer, who had been highly critical of the Truman Administration's policies on the Far East and had supported MacArthur's war plans for Korea. For background on these issues see no. 136; on Wedemeyer see nos. 178, n. 1, and 233, n. 8. See also Senate Committee on Armed Services and Committee on Foreign Relations, *Military Situation in the Far East: Hearings*, 1951, pt. 3, pp. 2409–

2567; Albert C. Wedemeyer, *Report to the President Submitted September 1947: Korea* (Washington, D.C., 1951); *idem, Wedemeyer Reports!* (New York, 1958); and *New York Times*, May 2, 8, 9, 13, June 12, 13, 14, 16, July 31, 1951.

[3] On June 28, 1951 (EM), Eisenhower's brother Arthur had sent him a Trohan article that had appeared in the *Chicago Daily Tribune* of June 27. In that piece Trohan had speculated that Eisenhower would run for President as a Republican unless Senator Robert A. Taft won the GOP nomination, in which case Eisenhower would run as a Democrat. In a letter of July 24 Edgar Eisenhower would send the General this same article (EM).

286

To George Catlett Marshall
Cable SH 20912. Confidential

Eisenhower Mss.

July 25, 1951

This is a NATO Message. Personal for General Marshall from Eisenhower: I am seriously concerned by the indication in DEF-97167 that a full explanation of the detailed planning involved in the preparation, review, and implementation of MDAP programs at country and regional levels may not yet have been put across to the committee. Inasmuch as I have not concerned myself with the details of these procedures, I do not consider that General Gruenther is the best prepared individual to present this phase of the matter to the committee.[1] At the same time, however, our experience with Congressional Groups visiting Europe has been that a full understanding on these matters is an indispensable preliminary to an effective presentation of the overall program in Europe. It is this overall program with which I am vitally concerned and with which Gruenther is fully prepared to deal. For this reason I suggest that strong consideration be given to having a responsible senior officer engaged in European MDAP activities deal with this subject prior to Gruenther's appearance before the committee. I understand that General Kibler[2] is in Washington at present and I suggest that he might be called upon to cover this matter if he has not already done so.

An alternative solution, and possibly a more effective one, particularly if the situation is as serious as reference radio leads me to believe, would be to call upon General Handy[3] as the Military representative on ECC to make the MDAP presentation prior to Gruenther's appearance.

If I have been misled as to the need for presenting additional material to the Congressional Committees on the detailed MDAP aspects, I hope you will disregard my suggestions herein. I do feel, however, that such additional details, if needed, can best be presented by someone charged specifically with this responsibility and that to have

Gruenther attempt to cover them might well detract from the overall value of his presentation.[4]

[1] Eisenhower was concerned because although a group of U.S. congressmen had recently been briefed at SHAPE, chairman James Prioleau Richards (Committee on Foreign Affairs) had nonetheless requested personal testimony on the Mutual Defense Assistance Program by Eisenhower's C/S, Lieutenant General Alfred M. Gruenther. For background on the congressional visits see nos. 2 and 284.

[2] Major General Abram Franklin Kibler, Director of the Joint American Military Advisory Group for Europe, had served as the U.S. Army representative to the U.N. Military Staff Committee from 1946 to 1948. Before taking his present assignment, he was chief U.S. delegate to the Military Committee of the Western Union. For further background see Galambos, *Chief of Staff*, no. 360.

[3] General Thomas Troy Handy was Commander in Chief, Europe, and the U.S. Military Representative for Mutual Defense Assistance in Europe. For further background see *Eisenhower Papers*, vols. I–XI.

[4] General Kibler would testify on Saturday, July 28, and would issue a statement that included a report on military activities in Europe by General Handy. General Gruenther would appear before the committee on Tuesday, July 31 (see no. 284). For their testimony see House Committee on Foreign Affairs, *The Mutual Security Program: Hearings*, 1951, pp. 1344–85.

287   *Eisenhower Mss.*

To Eric James Patrick Brind   *July 25, 1951*

Dear Admiral: Just to give you a written summary of our conversation reference organization in the Northern Command, I am sending you this note.[1]

We agreed that, while it was your exclusive responsibility to organize your own staff according to your best judgment, it was obviously important that you have, within your organization and directly and exclusively responsible to you, a senior ground officer of distinguished record. Such a man we agreed was important so as to assist or help in the performance of all the intricate staff work that involves ground movements and logistics, to represent properly the important ground function in dealings with all coordinate, associate, and superior staff echelons, and finally to represent you, when necessary, in dealing with staffs and commanders in the business of ground planning, training, and preparation.[2]

Because of a number of reasons, I personally favored a plan of transferring your present Chief of Staff to the position of your Naval Deputy and assigning a senior ground officer as your Chief of Staff. But I accepted your representations that such an arrangement would not only be highly embarrassing to you and to individuals already assigned to your staff, but would result in your separation from a Chief of Staff in whom you have the utmost and complete confidence.[3] Since it is an accepted truism that the relationship between a Commander and his Chief of Staff is an intensely personal thing, it is obvious that I would not presume to interfere in such a delicate and personal matter.

I accepted your own position in this matter the more readily because of your conviction that (a) the time would come within the reasonable future when the Governments of Norway and of Denmark would be glad to see you appoint a Deputy Commander for ground affairs, and (b) in the meantime, you would secure the services of a distinguished soldier as Deputy Chief of Staff, in which position he would have direct access to you for all matters involving the development of and planning for ground forces. The only matter you felt that you must clear with the Norwegian and Danish Governments was the nationality of this particular individual; this because of representations made to you by those Governments that it would be unfortunate locally for them to have too many senior British and American officers assigned permanently in that region.[4]

This record is made as an aide memoire, so, if there is anything in this that differs radically from your interpretation of our conversation, won't you please let me know about it promptly.[5] *Cordially*

[1] For background on Brind and SHAPE's Northern Command see nos. 90 and 99. Deputy SACEUR Montgomery had previously written to Eisenhower concerning these matters (Montgomery to Eisenhower, July 15, 1951, EM), and Eisenhower had met with Brind on this day.

[2] Brind's Northern Command did not have a single ground commander to lead all the northern land forces; the ground units were divided into separate Danish and Norwegian contingents (Ismay, *NATO*, p. 72). In June U.S. Army Chief of Staff Collins had informed Eisenhower that he was sending Major General James M. Gavin (see Galambos, *Columbia University*, no. 125) to serve as chief of staff in NATO's Southern Command. Collins wrote that Gavin "should be of help to Mick [Admiral Robert B. Carney, CINCSOUTH] in handling the Army side of his complex problem" (Collins to Eisenhower, June 19, 1951, EM; see also no. 236).

[3] Rear Admiral Hugh Dalrymple-Smith was then serving as Brind's C/S. Dalrymple-Smith had commanded HMS *Arethusa* during the Normandy landings of World War II. In April 1951 he had been recalled from retirement to assume his present position.

[4] In October Eisenhower would appoint Lieutenant General Sir E. C. Robert Mansergh as Deputy Commander in Chief, Allied Forces, Northern Europe. Mansergh, who had served with the British Army in Eritrea, Iran, Burma, and Singapore during World War II, was currently Commander of British forces in Hong Kong. He would later succeed Brind as C in C, Allied Forces, Northern Europe (CINCNORTH).

[5] There is no reply to this letter in EM.

President Truman greets General Eisenhower on his return from a tour
of the North Atlantic Treaty nations, Washington, D.C., January 1951. (U.S. Army)

SHAPE commanders meet in Paris in temporary quarters at the Hotel Astoria, Paris, June 19, 1951.
L to R: Admiral Sir Patrick Brind, General Lauris Norstad, Lieutenant General Augustin Guillaume, Field Marshal Bernard Law Montgomery, General Dwight D. Eisenhower, Air Vice Marshal Hugh Saunders, Admiral André Lemonnier, Admiral Robert Jaujard, Admiral Robert B. Carney. *Second Row, standing:* General Wilhelm Von Tangen Hansteen, General Maurizio De Castiglioni, General Alfred M. Gruenther, Major General Ebbe Gørtz, and Major General Robert K. Taylor. (Wide World)

Prime Minister Winston Churchill leaves SHAPE following a visit with
General Eisenhower, December 1951. (U.S. Army)

General Eisenhower chats with French Minister of National Defense Jules Moch, and General Alphonse Juin, Resident General in Morocco, January 1951, Paris. (U.S. Army)

General Eisenhower and his Chief of Staff General Alfred M.
Gruenther, December 1951, Paris. (U.S. Army)

General Eisenhower inspects the 2d Armored Cavalry Regiment in
Augsburg, Germany, April 1951. In the background are (*L to R*) General
Thomas T. Handy, EUCOM, and Lieutenant General Manton S. Eddy, CG, 7th
Army. (U.S. Army)

General Eisenhower meets with NATO Standing Group member Air Chief
Marshal Sir William Elliott, and General Omar Bradley, Chairman, U.S.
Army Joint Chiefs of Staff, November 7, 1951, the Pentagon. (U.S. Army)

General Eisenhower makes a point with members of the
parliaments of Belgium and Luxembourg, January 1952, Paris.

The Eisenhowers lived at Villa St. Pierre in the thirteenth-century village of Marnes-la-Coquette, France. (SHAPE)

The General turns tourist during a visit in Ankara, Turkey, March 3–5, 1952.

To Henry Parkman   *July 25, 1951*

Dear Mr. Parkman:[1] Chuck Spofford seems to be anxious that I talk to you about the importance of the work that he is doing over in London and asked me to do what I can to induce you to accept the position as his Deputy.[2]

As his request would imply, I am thoroughly imbued with the vital character of his task and, if you would care to hear my full exposition on this particular subject, I invite you out here to my new headquarters next Saturday morning at any hour convenient to you. I suggest 10 o'clock. Even if your mind has already been made up—which I hope it hasn't, if your proposed answer is in the negative—you might enjoy seeing our new headquarters, of which we are quite proud.[3]

With personal regard, *Sincerely*

[1] Henry Parkman (A.M. Harvard 1916), a Boston lawyer, had been with the Economic Cooperation Administration as chief of its special mission to France since June 1950 (on the ECA see no. 45).
[2] Charles M. Spofford was the U.S. representative and chairman of the North Atlantic Council of Deputies (on Spofford see no. 16, n. 16; on the NAC see no. 2, n. 2).
[3] In a letter to Spofford of June 19 (EM) the General had thanked him for his assistance with the visiting members of the House of Representatives: "Our work together . . . has brought us all that much closer in the pursuit of our common missions." On Spofford's efforts to encourage NATO nations in their rearmament see *New York Times,* January 5, April 22, May 27, 1951. On the congressional visit see nos. 209 and 218.

Parkman would not be one of the three assistant deputies who would join Spofford's office later in the year (*New York Times,* Nov. 26, 1951).

289   *Eisenhower Mss.*

To Roy Allison Roberts   *July 25, 1951*
Personal

Dear Roy:[1] Quite naturally I have been following very closely the accounts in my local newspapers about the Kansas floods. Then I was fortunate enough a week or so ago to pick up two or three copies of the *Star* in which, of course, I found many details that I would otherwise have missed.[2]

I was particularly interested to notice that the flood has been compared in its intensity and destructiveness with that of 1903, in which my family and my home town were intimately involved. We pumped water and shoveled mud out of our cellar for a long time after that one.[3]

That early experience gave me a real basis of understanding and personal sympathy for the thousands of people that have been compelled, this year, to undergo the terrors and sufferings of a major Kansas flood. I trust that things are rapidly returning to normal and I pray that the loss of life and the damage incurred were not so great as at first feared. I suppose the day will come when we shall be able to control these floods and prevent their destructive effects, but it seems that for the moment we still have to suffer.

When you see that brother of mine, convey my greetings to him.[4] With warm personal regard, *Faithfully*

[1] Roberts was president and general manager of the *Kansas City Star* of Kansas City, Missouri (see Galambos, *Columbia University*, nos. 160 and 767).

[2] Torrential rains had inundated more than 500,000 acres in Kansas and Missouri—the worst flooding in those states since 1903. On July 19 President Truman, who had viewed the flooded terrain on July 18 and declared parts of Kansas and Missouri disaster areas, had signed a bill providing $25 million in relief (see *New York Times*, July 12, 14, 16–20, 1951; and *Kansas City Star*, July 1, 2, 12–14, 17–20, 1951).

[3] On the 1903 Kansas flood see Eisenhower, *At Ease*, pp. 84–86; see also no. 296.

[4] The General's brother Arthur was executive vice-president of the Commerce Trust Company of Kansas City, Missouri (see no. 34).

290   *Eisenhower Mss.*

To Harry S. Truman   *July 26, 1951*

Dear Mr. President: Thank you for your thoughtful letter.[1] I understand exactly what you wish to arrange and I shall plan a trip to Washington for late September or thereabouts. While I'm sorry you were put to the trouble of explaining your idea a second time I'm very glad you did so—because I was not clear on the matter at first. You see, I was sick in bed when Averell went through here, so I didn't get his full explanation.

This note brings best wishes to you and yours.[2] *Respectfully*

[1] In a handwritten letter of July 20 (EM) Truman had replied to Eisenhower's cable of three days earlier (see no. 274). "I had never expected to try to hold a secret meeting with you," the President had said. "Reports had come to me that you were not getting the proper support and cooperation from other departments and that you were handicapped by having to talk to NATO governments on a low level. I wanted to meet the situation in a manner to make your job easier and more satisfactory to you. That is all I wanted to talk about." Truman said he could see

by Eisenhower's most recent message that "some progress has been made." The President did not want Eisenhower to "get mixed up in the MacArthur affair or be harassed by these nutty Congressional Committees. One man is enough for them to pick to pieces—and I'm accustomed to it. You come when you think conditions are right for a personal interview be it September or October." They would actually meet in November.

[2] For developments see no. 363.

291

To AMADO MARTELINO

Eisenhower Mss.

July 28, 1951

Dear Colonel Martelino:[1] I have your long letter of July 2nd, together with a copy of the affidavit made by the Honorable Jorge Vargas on the question of the claims of former Philippine Scouts for extra compensation for service rendered in 1936–1941. Today I had an appointment with Mr. Vargas to check my own memory of the circumstances surrounding the induction of the Philippine Scout officers into the Philippine Army during the period indicated. Unfortunately, my memory is not too sharp as to details, but I do have some recollection of the general understandings under which we worked.[2]

When General MacArthur and certain other officers from the United States, of whom I was one, came to the Philippines by arrangement between the President of the new Philippine Government and the President of the United States, we quickly found that our numbers were not sufficient to carry out the multitudinous tasks devolving upon a group engaged in building a new type of Army for the Philippines. In this situation, we arranged to have Philippine Scout officers detailed to the Philippine Government to assist in the development of a security system. The arrangement obviously could not damage the standing of the Philippine Scout officer in the United States Army, while it provided him an opportunity to be in on the ground floor in developing an Army for the Philippines, which island was to form an independent nation in 1946. In order to take full advantage of the professional training and experience of these Philippine Scout officers, it was determined to give them an assimilated rank in the new Philippine Army— a rank that was sometimes one or two grades higher than that held in the Philippine Scouts. As I recall the matter, there was no mention made, in the first instance, of any additional pay for the Philippine Scout officers; but this matter was brought up later by the Philippine Scout officers because of the fact that General MacArthur's assistants received, by agreement between the two Governments, an additional allowance of some ten pesos per day.

I have never known what was the attitude of the Philippine Govern-

443

ment itself on this subject. General MacArthur was, as I recall it, personally opposed to paying the Scout officers out of the funds previously and specifically appropriated for the support of the so-called "Military Mission," because that sum was estimated to cover only the ten-year expenses of the small mission originally organized. Since, in order to assimilate the Scout officers in the Philippine Army, they had at least nominally to be attached to the Military Mission, there appeared to be no other funds at that time from which to give the Scouts any additional funds, even if the Philippine Government should favor such an allowance. Moreover, I rather think it would have been necessary to have secured the approval of the American Government—at least I know that this was the fact in the case of General MacArthur and those officers who accompanied him to the Philippines in the fall of 1935. These particular American officers were detailed to duty in a foreign area, one which was to become independent within a stated number of years; whereas the Philippine Scout officers were engaged in helping develop an Army for their own nationalistic existence of the future.

Nevertheless, General MacArthur did not oppose, so far as I remember, the effort of the Philippine Scout officers to secure legal authorization of such an allowance. I believe that it was agreed at a meeting held in a private house one evening (possibly in 1936) that the whole matter would be deferred for the time being and the Philippine Scout officers would take their case directly to the Philippine Government in an attempt to secure this allowance from a separate appropriation.[3] I do not recall that any formal agreement was ever reached as between General MacArthur's office and the Philippine Scout officers—my own memory is that General MacArthur and his office merely agreed to keep hands off.

I realize that the contents of this letter can scarcely be very helpful in your efforts to secure the pay to which you feel you are entitled, but what I have put down represents about all I can recall of the specific subject to which you refer. On the other hand, my statements are not intended to constitute a contradiction to anything said in paragraphs 5, 6, and 7 of the affidavit made by Mr. Vargas.[4]

I note from your letter that some of my old friends of those days are still alive. But I am saddened to see that so many of them lost their lives during the war. Among these was, of course, your distinguished brother.[5] I tender you my sympathies in his death.

With best wishes,[6] *Sincerely*

[1] Martelino, of Manila, had served with the Philippine Scouts attached to the U.S. Military Mission in the Philippines under the command of General Douglas MacArthur.
[2] Martelino's letter (same file as document) concerned his claim, on behalf of officers and widows of the Philippine Scouts, that the Philippine government owed

them per diem compensation for their service in the Philippine Army. In support of his claim, Martelino had enclosed an affidavit (same file as document) written by Jorge B. Vargas, who from November 1935 until December 1941 had served as secretary to Manuel L. Quezon, President of the Philippines. Eisenhower had been assistant military adviser, later senior U.S. military assistant to the Commonwealth government on defense affairs, Philippine Islands, from September 1935 until December 1939.

[3] According to Martelino, Eisenhower had been present at a meeting in the home of General Vincente Lim when it was "agreed not to collect any per diem until the Philippine Assembly could appropriate additional funds for the expenses of the Military Mission."

[4] Paragraph 5 stated that Quezon's office considered that MacArthur's mission comprised all U.S. Army personnel detailed with the Commonwealth government. Paragraph 6 stated that there was no distinction made between American and Philippine Scout officers and that there was "no discrimination in the per diems and other allowances that they were to receive as members of the Military Mission. . . ." Paragraph 7 gave an account of the meeting at which Philippine Scout officers, "for patriotic reasons, agreed to defer collection of their per diems as members of the Military Mission until the Philippine government could appropriate money. . . ."

[5] Colonel Pastor Martelino had died during the Japanese occupation of the Philippines.

[6] In a letter of August 20 (same file as document) Martelino would thank Eisenhower for his reply, which he said would "go a long way in helping us secure the passage of a bill in Philippine Congress appropriating the money to pay our per diems."

292

To STERLING MORTON
Personal

Eisenhower Mss.

July 28, 1951

Dear Mr. Morton:[1] My sincere thanks for your letter; far from adding to my burdens, the kind of message you sent serves to help me clarify in my mind and get a clear appreciation of my problems.[2]

I hasten to agree with your conclusion that there is an inadequate understanding in Europe of the extent of American help. Moreover, there exists everywhere some of the apathy of which you speak. With respect to these things, my own reaction is that the stopping of the Communistic acquisition of new territories is so important that it is up to us to inspire better understanding and better cooperation in the areas that seem unusually important to our own welfare. None of these areas seems to be more necessary to our future than is Europe; in fact, it is difficult for me to see how we would ever stop the progressive disintegration of the entire European, African, Asian, and possibly even parts of South American areas if Europe should fall.[3]

This is the reason that I keep plugging away at a task that certainly has no personal appeal whatsoever—I simply believe that the job must be done in the interests of America's future.

Of course, I thank you sincerely for your expression of confidence; it is good to know that you have such convictions even though your survey of the European scene does not result in the optimism and enthusiasm that we all hope will soon replace the last vestiges of defeatism.[4]

When you see our good friend Ralph Bard, please convey to him my warm greetings. To you, my very best wishes—and again many thanks. *Sincerely*

[1] Morton (B.Litt. Princeton 1906) was chairman of the board and a director of the Morton Salt Company of Chicago.

[2] In a letter of July 23 (EM) Morton had said that he was writing because Ralph Bard, his former classmate, had reported that Eisenhower was "interested in hearing from people at home who were in ordinary walks of life" (on Bard see no. 248, n. 1).

[3] Morton told Eisenhower that he and his wife had recently returned from nine weeks in Europe: "We came back, to tell the truth, with a rather dim idea of European appreciation of our efforts and of European cooperation along either economic or military lines—in fact, we seemed to sense a disturbing degree of apathy as to what might happen."

[4] Morton had expressed confidence in Eisenhower's integrity and ability: "We know," he concluded, "that if anyone can solve the European riddle you can."

293   *Eisenhower Mss.*

To Bernard Law Montgomery   *July 28, 1951*

Dear Monty: Your note of the 27th adds nothing new to my thinking; from the very beginning, I have struggled to relieve Al from details and to allow him to confine his attention to the important matters that plague us daily.[1] Obviously, my thought was to establish for him a "Vice Chief of Staff." I hope that you have not failed to consider, though, some of the difficulties that arise when we attempt to develop such a plan! This business of nationalism penetrates even into the details of staff organization, and we certainly run smack up against it when we consider this one.[2]

Drop in and talk to me sometime when you get a chance. *As ever*

[1] Deputy SACEUR Montgomery's three-page letter, marked "*Private*," is in EM. Montgomery, claiming that "things were not quite right at our own Headquarters at SHAPE," had told Eisenhower that Gruenther was spending too much of his time on diplomatic and political tasks. According to Montgomery, staff work had suffered, and the resulting lack of supervision and coordination had "a good deal

to do with the trouble we are at present experiencing." Montgomery had written that the French officer responsible for staff supervision in Gruenther's absence was "quite unfit . . . and in any way he is useless." Montgomery had suggested that Eisenhower appoint an American lieutenant general as vice chief of staff. For Montgomery's later and very favorable evaluation of Gruenther's performance ("a Chief of Staff *par excellence*, most able, with a quick and clear brain, and very approachable") see Montgomery, *Memoirs*, p. 461. For Eisenhower's assessment of Gruenther's position and abilities see no. 230.

[2] In April Eisenhower had expressed concern over reports that some Europeans thought the United States was filling too many important NATO posts with Americans—a policy they resented (see no. 115). SHAPE would not create the post of vice chief of staff during Eisenhower's tenure as SACEUR.

294   *Eisenhower Mss.*

To Benjamin Franklin Caffey, Jr.   *July 28, 1951*

Dear Frank:[1] It was very nice to have your letter of the 22nd; I was particularly astonished to learn that you had reversed your field since the days of 1948.[2]

Here in Europe, there is even more bewilderment, confusion, and doubt than there is in America. The reasons are, of course, that, in addition to all the global problems that worry America, they have the aftermath here of the destruction caused by war and the defeatism caused by occupation.[3] It certainly looks like the poor old world needs a new Moses.

Give my love to Louise[4] and with warm regard to yourself. *Cordially*

[1] Brigadier General Caffey (USA, ret.) and Eisenhower had been friends since their tour of duty in the Philippines. Before his retirement Caffey had been the U.S. military attaché in Switzerland. For further background see Galambos, *Columbia University*, no. 182. Caffey's letter is in EM.

[2] Caffey had opposed an Eisenhower run for the presidency in 1948. In his reply to Eisenhower he wrote, "Yes, I have reversed my field. . . . For the sake of humanity in general and the United States in particular I most sincerely hope that you will be our next President" (Aug. 5, 1951, EM).

[3] This was one of Eisenhower's recurring concerns (see, for example, no. 292).

[4] Mrs. Caffey, the former Louise Battle.

To Robert Tyre Jones, Jr.   *July 28, 1951*

Dear Bob:[1] My constant prayer, these days, as I start my backswing is, "Oh, please let me swing slowly." The trouble is that sometimes I wonder whether I swing at all; whether I am not strictly a chopper.[2]

Recently when I have had a chance to go to the golf course, I try to go a few minutes ahead of my foursome and take the heavier clubs on the practice tee in the attempt to get adjusted to the new weight. After a few shots, I seem to get the hang of the business very well. But the second I move over to the first tee, old man tension overtakes me and I have trouble. What I need more than anything else is about two weeks down at Augusta National with you sitting there to lecture me.

Of course, I hope that you are feeling better every day. So many of our common friends have been over this way that you have frequently been the subject of conversation in my office, in my home, and at the golf course. But it would all have been so much better had you been here.[3] *Cordially*

[1] Jones, one of the greatest golf champions in the history of the sport, was president of the Augusta National Golf Club (see no. 113, n. 4).
[2] In early July Eisenhower had received a set of golf clubs from Jones (see no. 247). In a letter of July 20 (EM) Jones had suggested that because the clubs were slightly heavier than those Eisenhower was accustomed to, he "(1) grip the club lightly, and (2) swing slowly."
[3] Eisenhower had played golf several times this month with his son John and with friends from Augusta National (see nos. 211, 217, and 224, n. 6). On Jones's health see no. 193, n. 5.

To Emmett Schwedner Graham   *July 30, 1951*

Dear Emmett:[1] Many thanks for the pictures, to say nothing of your most interesting letter. Fortunately I have a small projector and will be able to take a good look at the tulip pictures this evening. I am not certain that I knew before the arrival of your letter that Res and Company had donated the tulip and jonquil bulbs to the Foundation. I shall look up my correspondence and, if I have not heretofore done so, shall send them a note of appreciation.[2]

I cannot tell you how intensely interested I was in the newspaper accounts of the Kansas floods. Only recently I wrote a personal letter to Roy Roberts to ask him about the progress of the flood and particularly its comparison with that of 1903. I was in the middle of that one and, while I note that the River reached a higher stage this time than it did in that year, still we really had our troubles down at our home. The cellar filled up completely and we had a terrible time pumping it out and cleaning up the mess that was left. I must say that my experiences then remain in my memories with sufficient sharpness to make me extraordinarily sympathetic toward the plight with those who had to suffer this time.[3]

Please remember me to all my Abilene friends, especially Mr. Harger and Charlie Case.[4] With personal regard to yourself, *Cordially*

[1] Graham served as secretary of the Eisenhower Foundation's executive committee (see Galambos, *Columbia University*, no. 278; on the foundation see no. 854).
[2] On July 21 (EM) Graham had written the General about the Eisenhower home in Abilene, Kansas, and had sent pictures showing the tulips and jonquils that had been donated by John Res of Res and Company, Holland. Eisenhower would write on August 8 to thank Res (EM).
[3] Kansas had experienced the "worst floods in history," Graham said, but there had been no damage to the Eisenhower home. Eisenhower's letter to Roberts is no. 289.
[4] Charles Moreau Harger, president of the Eisenhower Foundation, and Charles Augustine Case, a vice-president, were both friends from the General's childhood (on Harger see Galambos, *Columbia University*, no. 38; on Case see Eisenhower, *At Ease*, p. 105n).

297   *Eisenhower Mss.*

To George Edward Allen   *July 30, 1951*

Dear George:[1] I opened your letter in the great hope that it would say that you were on the way over here within a few days. I had to settle for the news that we have a new calf! I had one letter from Art about the Bangs disease among the cows. At that time, he thought that five were definitely infected. Whether or not there has been any addition to the casualty list, I do not know.[2]

Any progress at all on diminishing your belt line is good news—but you have to go more rapidly than one-half pound every two months or you are certainly going to lose a big bet.[3]

My love to Mary[4] and, of course, all the best to yourself. *Cordially*

[1] For background on Allen and his recent visit see no. 217, n. 4.
[2] In a letter of July 26 (EM) Allen had told Eisenhower of the birth of a Guernsey bull calf. Arthur S. Nevins, farm manager, had informed Eisenhower on July 8 (EM) of the loss of five Holsteins (see no. 270, n. 5).
[3] Allen had promised to lose a pound a week, adding that it would be "very easy

for a strong character like the great Allen" (on the wager see no. 48; for developments see no. 493).

[4] Allen's wife, the former Mary Keane.

To JOHN SHELDON DOUD EISENHOWER   *July 30, 1951*

Dear Johnny: Even though you've been gone but a few days, we miss all of you tremendously. It would have been nice if you could have remained here through your birthday—but, again, I have to send my congratulations through the mail!!![1]

Also I must thank you for the "Pitching Wedge." I was astounded and—in spite of a bit of chagrin because you'd deprived yourself of it—highly pleased to get it. I took it over to the house at Marne-la-Coquette yesterday and tried it out as a pitching club out of the rough![2] In practice it really worked! Many, many thanks! Hope you can find another!

Love to Barbie and the young'uns[3] and, again, congratulations to you! *Devotedly*

[1] The General's son, who with his family had been visiting Paris since June 13, had left on Eisenhower's plane, the *Columbine*, on July 27 (see no. 224). John would be in New York for his birthday on August 3 (see EM, Subject File, Aircraft— SHAPE [*Columbine*]).

[2] Eisenhower referred to a golf club with a broad, low-angled face, designed to send the ball in a high arc and with a backspin.

The Eisenhowers would move into their new home at Marnes-la-Coquette in August (see no. 18, n. 3; for developments see no. 314, n. 1).

[3] See no. 283, n. 4.

4

War Plans and Scarce Resources

To LE ROY MALLORY EDWARDS

Dear Mr. Edwards:[1] Interesting as I found your letter, I must say that everything in it paled to insignificance compared to its shocking news that Mrs. Joyce had died. I cannot tell you how saddened I am— Kenyon Joyce himself was always one of my favorite personalities in the Army and I was devoted to Helen. I shall write to him at once.[2]

Quite naturally, I wish I could join you and him on the Snake River. What a relief it would be to leave for a few weeks this atmosphere of worry and bewilderment, and work and struggle, and have no bigger fight than that involved in trying to net a twelve-inch rainbow.[3]

With personal regard, *Cordially*

[1] Described as "a great Eisenhower fan," Edwards, vice-president of both the Southern California Gas Company and the Pacific Lighting Corporation, had arranged through mutual friends to meet the General during May of this year (memorandum, Lawrence to Schulz, May 16, 1951, EM, same file as document).
[2] In his letter of July 26 (EM) Edwards had informed the General of the recent death of Helen Jones Joyce, wife of Eisenhower's friend and former commanding officer, Major General Kenyon Ashe Joyce (USA, ret.) (for background see *Eisenhower Papers*, vols. I–XI). Eisenhower's letter of condolence of this same date is in EM, Joyce File.
[3] Edwards's letter had been written during a fishing trip at Idaho's Flat Rock Club.

To LAWRENCE RAYFORD HAGY

Dear Mr. Hagy:[1] I am grateful for your letter and for the time you have so willingly given to explain to various groups the factors in the problem of collective security and the ideas which underlie this work. As we here see it, we are now engaged in a fight for the survival of our liberties and our way of life. It is easily possible that the future of the free world depends upon a successful outcome of this task.[2]

To win, it is necessary to have the cooperation of all. Therefore, anything I might say or do which diminished, in any way, whatever effectiveness I possess in my present position would be rendering a disservice to all—for all are involved in the present struggle. I am, of course, highly appreciative of your complimentary statements directed to me as an individual, but, as of today, I have little time for consideration of affairs other than those directly involved with my own responsibilities. I scarcely think it would be proper for me to turn my attention to the subject of your letter—even if I did have time to do so.[3]

Will you please convey to Frank Porter and Mr. Bullard my best wishes.[4] With warm regard, *Sincerely*

[1] Texas oil executive and former Mayor of Amarillo, Hagy had seen Eisenhower in Paris on June 6. He was accompanied by American Petroleum Institute president Frank Martin Porter and Edgar Fitch Bullard, president and a director of the Stanolind Oil & Gas Company (see Hagy to Eisenhower, July 25, 1951, EM).

[2] In his July 25 letter to the General, Hagy had said that since their June meeting he had had occasion to speak to several luncheon clubs concerning the NATO efforts and was of the opinion that the pact's "wonderful progress" was due largely to Eisenhower's "know-how, enthusiasm and personality."

[3] Like many of Eisenhower's friends and acquaintances, Hagy had urged the General to seek the presidency (see, for example, nos. 243 and 308). Hagy noted that the General had explained his acceptance of the Columbia University presidency as stemming from a desire to promulgate "some ideas about Democracy which would help this country." "By the same reasoning," Hagy wrote, "I think you should consider taking on the job as No. 1 man in our country."

[4] See n. 1 above. Hagy would reply on September 11 (EM), again urging the General to consider becoming a presidential candidate and assuring him of widespread popular support. Eisenhower's September 18, 1951, response is in EM.

301   *Eisenhower Mss.*

To Frank Alexander Willard   *August 1, 1951*

Dear Frank:[1] Thank you very much for sending on to me the material about Frank Barnett's plan. I am sending it on to the officials in Washington who have to do with this kind of enterprise. It is possible that Mr. Barnett will be hearing from them in the future. It certainly looks to me like there is a great deal of sense in the whole idea if the practical problems implicit in it can be solved.[2] *Cordially*

P.S. I hope you are shooting all birdies these days.[3]

[1] For background on Willard see no. 67.

[2] Frank Rockwell Barnett, an assistant professor of English and history at Indiana's Wabash College, was at this time seeking support for his proposal to establish military units of Iron Curtain refugees. As envisioned by Barnett, this "Free Slavic Legion" would consist of approximately five paratroop divisions, armed, equipped, supplied, and supported by the United States. These units, commanded at the staff level by Americans but with refugee line officers, would be attached to American NATO forces in West Germany and could be airlifted behind Russian lines in the event of war. Barnett argued that the contingents of the legion would be invaluable in establishing and aiding underground movements among their own peoples while carrying on a guerrilla war against the Soviets. A salient feature of the plan was

the provision that members of the legion would not be offered American citizenship in return for their service but would instead retain their own nationalities. In this way, Barnett felt, the United States could effectively export democratic revolution. The Free Slavic Legion plan called for American recognition of governments-in-exile for "all Soviet oppressed nationalities"; the adoption of full-scale psychological warfare, distinguishing and separating the majority of the Russian people from their Communist governments; and an end to all East-West negotiations based upon the assumption that the United States and the Soviet Union could "*co-exist peacefully* once we are strong" (Frank Rockwell Barnett, *Cold War, Atomic War,* or *Free Slavic Legion*, pamphlet in EM, same file as document).

Eisenhower had first written to Willard concerning the proposal on July 9 (EM), following the latter's return from a visit to Paris (see no. 217, n. 3). Turning the plan over to the SHAPE staff for further study, the General had written that he felt it might prove effective in the struggle against communism, "assuming that the various political and administrative problems inherent to such a proposal could be satisfactorily solved." For developments see nos. 392 and 444.

[3] In golf a birdie is a score of one stroke under par on a hole.

302   *Eisenhower Mss.*

To William Alexander Hewitt   *August 2, 1951*

Dear Mr. Hewitt: Any man who received such a letter as you and your seventeen friends recently sent me could not possibly escape feelings of high honor and gratification, mingled with an overwhelming sense of humility. In this case, the observation acquires additional emphasis because the letter comes from a group with whom I spent one of the most thoroughly stimulating, pleasant, and worthwhile afternoons in my career, and for whom I have the highest regard and affection.[1]

As I then told you, it was my firm belief that probably each one of you could do a better job of leadership in the world than most of us in the older generation have been doing. Since I have been in Europe, this has been more firmly borne in upon me. We need to replace the caution and hesitation so often associated with age by the thoughtful, gallant, and intelligent leadership of men and women of your generation if we are to preserve our own liberties and those of the free world.

It is highly encouraging to know that all of you are taking such an intense interest in the welfare of our country, even though I cannot agree with your convictions as to what I must personally do at this moment. I believe that, among the several vital questions affecting America's foreign affairs, success in the project of producing a collective security by cooperation between North America and the Western European Nations is of such importance to the United States that we must do nothing to risk that success unduly. Attainment is a matter of morale—of conviction and determination.

The support of all—not the support of a part of a population and enmity of other parts, based on political partisanship—is vital. The conclusion is that so long as I am assigned to this job I cannot, in justice to America's stupendous effort, become known *as a partisan of any kind*; I must be purely and simply an American public servant.[2]

I was deeply moved that you, collectively, should take the time to write me a letter so full of thought and of such unearned, but heart-warming, commendation. I shall value the document.

I am truly sorry that my complicated schedule prevented me from seeing you when you recently were in Paris. Will you kindly convey to each of those who signed the letter expressions of my deep appreciation and warmest regard.[3]

With every good wish for yourself, *Sincerely*

[1] A vice-president of the John Deere Plow Company, Hewitt and seventeen other San Francisco businessmen had written to Eisenhower on July 19 (EM) encouraging him to declare himself a 1952 Republican presidential candidate. Writing that it was their "sincere conviction that you are the person best qualified to serve as the next President," they said that their primary goal was to begin working toward the General's nomination. Eisenhower had met all eighteen of the letter's signers during July 1950 at a cocktail party given in his honor by Adolphus Andrews, Jr., assistant secretary of Pope & Talbot, Inc., of San Francisco (see Galambos, *Columbia University*, nos. 922 and 932; and Andrews to Eisenhower, Aug. 7, 1950, with enclosed guest list, and Eisenhower to Andrews, June 11, 1951, both in EM, Andrews Corr.).

[2] This had become the General's standard response to those urging him to declare his candidacy (see, for example, nos. 243 and 300, n. 2).

[3] Hewitt would eventually become president of the Eisenhower Volunteers for Northern California, an Eisenhower-for-President group founded by many of the same men who had attended the July 1950 cocktail party (see n. 1 above; and Hewitt to Eisenhower, Feb. 28, 1952, and Eisenhower to Hewitt, Mar. 20, 1952, both in EM, same file as document).

303   *Eisenhower Mss.*

To William Benton   *August 2, 1951*

Dear Bill:[01] Thank you for your note. By coincidence, it arrived just as I find on tomorrow's calendar an appointment with Paul Hoffman. I am certainly devoted to that man.[2]

Of course, I am glad that you found Mrs. McCormick's column worthy of inclusion in the Congressional Record. Incidentally, I am not quite certain where she got her impression that my London talk was so coolly received. The reverse was true, both at the time of the meeting and in my later correspondence and contacts.[3]

I know that you are working hard and I have heard that the Congress is so far behind in its normal legislative program that you probably won't get a vacation this summer. I imagine that the dispositions will be showing the strain after a bit.[4]

With best wishes and personal regard,[5] *Cordially*

[1] Senator Benton, a Democrat from Connecticut, was owner and chairman of the Muzak Corporation and former chairman and publisher of Encyclopaedia Britannica, Inc. (see Galambos, *Columbia University*, nos. 283 and 890).

[2] Benton's note is not in EM. For background on Hoffman, president of the Ford Foundation, see nos. 139 and 200 in this volume.

[3] *New York Times* columnist Anne O'Hare McCormick (see no. 201) had praised Eisenhower's July 3 address before the English Speaking Union (see no. 252) but had noted that its British reception was less than enthusiastic. According to McCormick, the concept of European political and economic integration that Eisenhower urged, while necessary to the ultimate success of NATO, ran against historic British sentiments of independence from the nations of continental Europe (see *New York Times*, July 7, 1951). Stating that the column was "one of the most important . . . which I have ever called to the attention of Congress" and agreeing with Eisenhower's argument, Benton had appended the article to the *Congressional Record* (82d Cong., 1st sess., 1951, 97, pt. 16: A4461–62). For Eisenhower's thinking on the need for European unity see nos. 251 and 259. On other responses to the General's address see nos. 264 and 279.

[4] Although the House of Representatives would take a two-week recess beginning later this month, the Senate's heavy legislative load would keep it in session until Congress adjourned on October 20 (see *New York Times*, Aug. 14, Oct. 21, 1951).

[5] Benton would reply on August 6 (EM) that he was "correcting Mrs. McCormick" on Eisenhower's behalf concerning British reaction to the address.

304   *Eisenhower Mss.*

To GEORGE CATLETT MARSHALL   *August 3, 1951*
Top secret

Dear General: From time to time, I have been sending to Averell Harriman informal reports, which frequently consist of nothing more than current observations on the European situation. I believe that he has normally shown these to the President.[1] While I realize that I may be bothering you unnecessarily by addressing this particular communication to you, it is nevertheless possible that you might like to be informed as to random phases of my reactions to existing factors in the European defense problem, whether or not you consider it advisable to present to the President such a rambling combination of fact, opinion, and assumption.

So many of our difficulties have their source in the existence of a badly divided Western Europe that on July 4th, I delivered myself of a fairly impassioned statement to this effect.[2] While, of course, I did not expect any immediate and drastic results, still I thought that the effort might have a bit of effect in promoting a clearer understanding of this particular difficulty and this, in turn, could be most helpful as we attack some of our problems of organization and administration. Certainly the occasion gave me the opportunity to state publicly, to Europe's several governments, that they could by no means assume that they are now performing at the maximum in developing security. Daily, of course, we run smack up against a myriad of difficulties that would not exist at all if this region were only reasonably unified.

One that is bothersome right now is a conclusion of the American MDAP group in Norway that the existing personnel programs of that country are so inadequate that we shall probably have to curtail American munition deliveries during the coming year. Manifestly, when this becomes generally known, the possible results could be serious for the European program, particularly in those countries where population morale is not yet as sturdy as it ought to be. Such an eventuality would be all the more disappointing because of the spirit of determination and courage in Norway. But manpower resources in that country are meager; it is quite possible that there is validity in their present conclusion that they cannot expand their training program. Obviously, we must not give equipment to anyone except where we know it will be used at maximum effectiveness in the common defense. But we must be sure that Norway is doing its utmost to train the men. I have tendered the good offices of my headquarters in the matter, and certainly we shall leave no stone unturned in an effort to produce an acceptable answer. It is easy to see that if Norway were merely a part of a Western European political unit, the problem would not exist.[3] In Italy there are almost 3,000,000 unemployed!

Such examples are multiplied every day. Because of the great efficiency, economy, and general progress that could result from a more effective union of these separate countries, I recently decided to intervene in the plan for developing a "European Army."[4] For a long time, I was firm in my refusal to get tied up in the project because it seemed, almost inherently, to include every kind of obstacle, difficulty, and fantastic notion that misguided humans could put together in one package.

I then felt that the attempt to develop a European Army might be more divisive than unifying in its effect on the Western European countries and this, of course, was an added reason for avoiding encouragement or personal participation. Moreover, it seemed to me that the plan was not above the suspicion that it may have been put forward in the certainty that it could not be achieved; thus a rebirth of any German military power would be avoided, but by such methods as to escape the onus of deliberate opposition.

Of course, the administrative difficulties are real and many; the risk still exists that the plan might create more antagonism than friendship, and we can never be certain that we shall not encounter double dealing. But, contingent upon unequivocal commitments from the new French Government, when formed, that it will support the program to the limit, and will address itself to problems of joint financing, etc., and quit blocking progress because of inconsequential military details, I am shifting my position. The reasons are:

a. I have come to believe that at least most of the governments involved are sincere in their efforts to develop a so-called European Army.

b. Some spectacular accomplishment is vitally necessary to us if we are to get this whole security program moving with the kind of rapidity that will generate confidence both here and in the North American Continent.

c. The plan offers the only immediate hope that I can see of developing, on a basis acceptable to other European countries, the German strength that is vital to us.

d. I am certain that there is going to be no real progress toward a greater unification of Europe except through the medium of specific programs of this kind. Consequently, believing that we have nothing much to lose except possibly patience, disposition, and effort, I shall, subject to the proviso stated, get behind this program with an auxiliary purpose of bringing about constantly increasing amalgamation of European resources and strength.

The French delay in organizing a new Government is bad.[5] Progress in our air-base program is stagnated and nothing decisive can be done at this moment.[6] The key position of France in any adequate security structure in this region is, of course, obvious. For this reason, I feel that her plans, and her ability to carry out plans, should be a matter of special concern to the United States. We should frequently sit down with her Government in combined diplomatic, economic, and military conferences to work out exactly what she is to do in order to perform to her own maximum in defending Western Europe and because of the effect that her example will have on other countries. Mr. Moch, who I understand is departing soon for the United States, may or may not be included in a new Government.[7] (He has told me he would not serve in a government headed by M. Peché.)[8] But I think that United States authorities might seize the opportunity presented by his Washington visit to have some very plain down-to-earth talks with him. Nothing that I am saying here should be taken to mean that any French official is backward in pledging to me his utmost cooperation. But it would manifestly be fatal to this whole development if we should accept lip service at the expense of solid achievement.

Throughout West Europe, there is needed greater understanding, greater fervor, greater faith. Our leadership must exert itself to create these. We must impart a sense of urgency to the solution of problems, and we must show every nation that it is serving its own interests when it places NATO matters in top priority. I have given some effort toward establishing a "framework of leadership," to be devoted to securing fervent European adherence to the essentials of the NATO concept. I want to get Stikker, Plevin, Lange, Spaack, Van Zeeland, DeGasperi, etc., each to surround himself with a group of young men, all dedicated to the task of educating populations in the basic factors of our problem.[9] So far, I've talked to three of these men, but cannot feel that I've had more than *meager* success.

Sherman's death was a blow to us.[10] He was understanding and cooperative—and, in his dealings with me, always presented a viewpoint bigger than a single service! You will miss him!

Encouraging signs in almost every category of moral, economic, and military progress continue to accumulate, but they are far from being what they could—and, therefore, should—be. In this connection, General Sarnoff is just starting home after spending four weeks or more in Europe. His impressions and convictions seem to me to be down to earth, comprehensive, and as accurate as one man's conclusions on such vast subjects could possibly be. I suggest you ask him in to lunch some day for a chat.[11]

There is no use enumerating our various problems, internal and external. The staff is getting really efficient (I'm still operating [with] a total of 225, which astounds everybody including the staff itself).[12] Our relations with cooperating and political agencies are good. Ulcers are no more prevalent than in most places. That reminds me that I wish Bedell Smith would come over for a month![13]

Mrs. Rosenberg has been here. She and I talked a couple of hours, after which she tackled the staff. Her approach to difficult questions is refreshing—and sound![14]

Please convey my greetings to Mrs. Marshall.[15] With personal regard,[16] *Sincerely*

[1] Eisenhower had last written to Harriman on July 9 (see no. 259).
[2] For Eisenhower's London address (July 3) on European integration see no. 252, n. 2; see also no. 264, n. 1.
[3] For background on Norway's economic difficulties and population shortage and their effect on NATO see no. 209, n. 6. On July 25 U.S. military officials in Oslo had recommended postponing shipments of equipment to Norway because it was felt that the Norwegians could not effectively use, store, or maintain the military supplies scheduled for delivery. On August 8 the State Department would object to this proposal, however, and the shipments would continue (State, *Foreign Relations, 1951*, vol. IV, *Europe: Political and Economic Developments, Part I*, p. 763, n. 4).
[4] For background on the French proposal for a European army and the related issue of German rearmament see nos. 186, 215, and 218. For military and political reasons, Eisenhower decided over the summer months to give the French plan his

strong support. John J. McCloy, U.S. High Commissioner for Germany, and Jean Monnet, an old French internationalist, apparently played a part in the General's decision. In June McCloy, then returning to the United States for consultations with Acheson, sent Eisenhower an undated memorandum commenting on the slow progress being made in rearming Germany. McCloy thought that if the European army would speed up that process, he "would be glad to support it but only on that condition and only on the condition that the scheme was an effective one from a military point of view" (Eisenhower had written in the margin, "This is most important and, of course, still very doubtful"). McCloy had urged the General to meet with Monnet, an economist who had been Deputy Secretary-General of the League of Nations between 1919 and 1923, had held a high position with the Free French during World War II, and since 1950 had headed the French delegation to the European conference responsible for developing the Schuman Plan. "He thinks on broad terms and he can put the case for the European Army as well as any," McCloy had informed Eisenhower. "I told him I would write you suggesting that you see him entirely informally and I believe it would be helpful if you would." McCloy had advised Monnet that he must convince all parties concerned, including the Germans, that the French proposal was not merely "a device to avoid and to delay German contribution" to European defense and also to persuade military officials that the scheme made military sense—which would mean "dropping off such excresancies as non-divisional units, etc." According to at least one writer, Eisenhower's ensuing discussion with Monnet won the General over to the European Defense Force (EDF) concept (McCloy to Eisenhower, n.d., EM, McCloy Corr.; McGeehan, *German Rearmament Question*, p. 129).

In late June, following talks between the Allied High Commission and the West German government, Secretary of State Acheson had proposed that the Western powers begin forming German military units immediately. These units would be placed under the command of General Juin, who led NATO's ground forces in central Europe. Acheson thought that creation of an appropriate civilian super-structure to administer and support the multinational force might proceed more quickly if military units had already been formed. Eisenhower, who generally favored these suggestions, insisted that they not delay European rearmament and that he have authority to deploy German units as he saw fit. He also suggested use of the term "European Defense Forces" in place of "European Army," since support and administrative structures as well as strictly military units were in-volved (and perhaps also because it would help to assuage French fears of a re-armed Germany). Eisenhower promised to cooperate in the attempt to establish the European Defense Force, but he also said that he would "avoid becoming involved in ministerial functions which more properly should be passed from national ministers direct to the new European Defense Organization at such time as that agency is prepared to receive and exercise them" (State, *Foreign Relations, 1951*, vol. III, *European Security and the German Question, Part I*, pp. 801–5, 820–21; Acheson, *Present at the Creation*, pp. 557–58).

On July 18 Eisenhower issued even stronger expressions of support for the EDF. After discussions with McCloy and David K. E. Bruce (U.S. Ambassador to France and American observer at the Conference for the Organization of a Euro-pean Defense Community [EDC]), Eisenhower had informed Acheson and Mar-shall of his strong feeling that "the US must exert constructive and vigorous leadership if a workable solution is to be found." The General also had been "convinced that a solution of the problem of Eur[opean] def[ense] is impossible until we have solved the Ger[man] problem" (State, *Foreign Relations, 1951*, vol. III, *European Security and the German Question, Part I*, pp. 838–39). On July 19 Marshall and Acheson had expressed their appreciation for Eisenhower's message and had also endorsed Eisenhower's proposal to send an observer from SHAPE to the EDC conference. On July 30 President Truman had approved the new policy of German rearmament within the context of an EDF under NATO, and on August 2 he had directed its implementation by all U.S. agencies (*ibid.*, 842–43, 847–52). For developments see nos. 442 and 540.

[5] From the time of the June 17 National Assembly elections and the subsequent resignation of Premier Henri Queuille and his cabinet (see no. 53), France had been in a state of political uncertainty due to its inability to establish a new government. The former Assembly's "Third Force" centrist coalition of Socialists, Radical Socialists, and members of the progressive Popular Republican Movement (MRP), which had controlled the parliament since 1946, failed to secure the necessary absolute majority of 314 seats and had ceased to be the deciding factor in the nation's politics. Repeated attempts by various party leaders to compromise and bring a new coalition into existence had proven futile (see *International Herald Tribune*, Paris ed., June 18, 19, July 11, 12, 14, 19, 27, 1951). The French Assembly would not confirm René Pleven's coalition government until August 11 (see no. 318, n. 1).

[6] For background on the question of NATO air bases in France see nos. 115 and 223; see also *New York Times*, July 18, August 24, September 2, 1951.

[7] Jules Moch, Defense Minister in the first Pleven and Queuille governments, would not serve in the new government. He was succeeded by Georges Bidault, former Premier and Minister of Foreign Affairs (see Galambos, *Chief of Staff*, no. 536). During World War II Bidault had led the French National Council of the Resistance.

[8] Maurice Pe*tsche* had been French Minister of Finance since 1949. Before World War II he had served as Under Secretary of State, Under Secretary of Finance, and Under Secretary of Fine Arts. He would serve the new government as Minister of State.

[9] For background on Dutch Foreign Minister Dirk Stikker and European leader Paul Henri Spaa*k* see no. 16. On French Deputy Prime Minister (and future Premier) René Plev*en* see nos. 11, n. 2, and 318. Halvard Manthey Lange had been the Minister of Foreign Affairs for Norway since 1946. A member of Norway's Labor party, he had been imprisoned by the Germans during World War II. For background on Belgian Foreign Affairs Minister Paul van Zeeland see no. 218, n. 2. Alcide De Gasperi had been Prime Minister of Italy since 1945; he had also assumed the post of Italian Foreign Minister in July 1951. De Gasperi, who had served in both the Austrian and Italian parliaments, was a staunch internationalist; he supported both European unity and the EDC.

[10] On July 22 Chief of Naval Operations Forrest P. Sherman, who had met with Eisenhower three days earlier, had died of heart failure while on a trip to Europe. He would be succeeded by Admiral William M. Fechteler in August. See nos. 429 and 490, n. 4.

[11] For background on David Sarnoff, chairman of the board of the Radio Corporation of America, see no. 100, n. 3. Sarnoff, who had met with Eisenhower on August 2, would call for a greater U.S. propaganda effort to oppose the Russians in Europe. He would also advocate "a Federated or United States of Europe" and continued U.S. aid while the Europeans rearmed (press release, Aug. 13, 1951, EM, Sarnoff Corr. See also Sarnoff to Eisenhower, Aug. 14, 17, and Eisenhower to Sarnoff, Aug. 23, 1951, EM; and *New York Times*, Aug. 14, 16, 19, 1951). Sarnoff, who in his letters addressed the General as "Dear Boss," would later meet with Marshall for two hours (Marshall to Eisenhower, Sept. 6, 1951, EM).

[12] See no. 115.

[13] CIA Director Walter Bedell Smith would visit Eisenhower in September (see no. 360, n. 4). Smith had suffered from an ulcer in World War II (Ambrose, *Supreme Commander*, p. 82).

[14] For background on Assistant Secretary of Defense Anna Rosenberg see no. 206, n. 1. On July 31 she had arrived in Paris, the first stop on an extended inspection trip. She had met with Eisenhower on August 1 (see Rosenberg to Eisenhower, July 13, 1951, and other papers in EM; and *New York Times*, Aug. 1, 5, 7, 8, 18, 1951).
[15] Marshall's wife, the former Katherine Boyce Tupper Brown (for background see *Eisenhower Papers*, vols. I–XI).
[16] Marshall replied (Sept. 6, 1951, EM) that JCS Chairman Bradley had read this August 3 letter to the JCS and that the President had also received a copy. Marshall would add that Truman had been "intensely interested" in Eisenhower's views. Marshall would soon resign his position (see no. 372).

305   *Eisenhower Mss.*

To CHARLTON OGBURN   *August 4, 1951*

Dear Mr. Ogburn:[1] My grateful thanks for the thoughtfulness of your letter. Certainly I share your conviction that it was only Washington's character and steadfastness, together with his wisdom and faith, that brought us safely through the perils and sufferings of the Revolutionary War. I believe that no other American in public life has ever been called upon to exhibit these great qualities to the same degree in order to achieve success.[2]

When you see our common friend, Neil Wickersham, please convey to him my warm greetings.[3] *Sincerely*

[1] Ogburn (LL.B. Mercer University 1905), senior partner in the New York law firm of Ogburn and Collins, had written to Eisenhower on July 24 (EM) congratulating him on his address before the English Speaking Union (see no. 303).
[2] Contained in Ogburn's letter was a long passage from an article the lawyer had written comparing Eisenhower's task in establishing the NATO defense forces with that of George Washington in 1775, when he had assumed command of the Continental armies. "The lack of any central government to . . . look [to] for authoritative instruction . . . the job of building up and welding the troops of an aggregation of separate states into a united military force [and] the disparity in numbers between such a force . . . and that of the potential enemy" were among the similarities Ogburn pointed out. He nevertheless concluded that Washington's task was more onerous, due to the Colonies' lack of material resources (see "Books for Lawyers," *American Bar Association Journal* 54, no. 5 [1951], 380–81; and Ogburn to Eisenhower, Aug. 28, 1951, with enclosures, EM). On Eisenhower's great respect for George Washington see, for example, Galambos, *Columbia University*, nos. 621 and 874; and no. 379 in this volume.
[3] For background on Cornelius Wendell Wickersham, a partner in the Wall Street law firm of Cadwalader, Wickersham and Taft, see *Eisenhower Papers*, vols. I–XI.

To GEORGE WHITNEY

Dear George:[1] When you get a chance, would you write down for me in as simple a package as possible, your own convictions about the need for "controls" in order to prevent displacement by the great munitions program in our economy. I read Henry Hazlitt on one side, and next I read articles that present an exactly opposite viewpoint. While my own instincts are for the minimum of "fiat" controls, I feel certain that under particular conditions of an emergency character these are sometimes necessary. At the same time, I feel they are useless except when supported by what we always call indirect controls which limit credit, raise taxes, and keep budgets balanced.[2]

It would seem to me, however, that indirect controls alone would not handle the problem when we have a scarce material that has to be apportioned or allocated, whether this be a raw material or a finished item.[3]

Finally, I have the feeling that if we have to apply "fiat" controls to one part of the economy, it has to be applied to the whole. I believe, of course, that all these things should be viewed only as emergency measures. Otherwise, we merely encourage the drift toward bureaucratic direction of our entire national life.

The reason that I put these particular things down here is in an effort to save your time in trying to give me a dissertation on the subject. I shall certainly be appreciative.[4]

Greetings to your nice family and, of course, best wishes to yourself.[5] *Cordially*

[1] For background on Whitney and his ongoing correspondence with Eisenhower concerning the U.S. economy see nos. 105 and 221.

[2] Heated debate over the need for wage and price controls both to meet defense production needs and to combat inflation had been taking place in the United States for several months. Congressional refusal to extend the controls instituted by President Truman in his December 1950 declaration of national emergency (see Galambos, *Columbia University*, no. 1129, n. 6) had resulted in the passage of an amended Defense Production Act for 1951–52 that substantially weakened presidential authority over wages and prices. The act restricted price rollbacks and permitted an increase in the prices of wholesale and retail goods to levels reflecting the "customary percentage margin of profits over costs of materials," calculated on pre–Korean War profit levels. This measure satisfied neither the Administration nor its detractors (see *New York Times*, July 1, 24, 28, 31, Aug. 1, 1951; and Donovan, *Tumultuous Years*, pp. 368–69). According to Truman, who had reluctantly signed the bill on July 31, the measure was "like a bulldozer, crashing aimlessly through existing pricing formulas"; he predicted cost-of-living increases for American workers and a disastrous wage-price spiral (see *New York Times*, Aug. 1, 1951). *Newsweek* business columnist Henry Hazlitt, on the other hand, maintained that the act was ill-conceived for continuing "the flagrant fraud of price and wage control," which he saw as a political invention handicapping industry and

aiding inflation (see Henry Hazlitt, "Business Tides," *Newsweek*, July 16, Aug. 6, 13, 1951).

[3] On Eisenhower's concerns over shortages in the machine tool industry and in U.S. raw materials production see nos. 221, 222, and 246.

[4] For Whitney's views on the role of economic and industrial controls see nos. 355 and 385.

[5] Eisenhower added a handwritten postscript, which on the copy in EM appears to be incomplete: "I realize that we 'talked' about these things—I want to get my lesson in simple. . . ."

307   *Eisenhower Mss.*

To WILLIAM EDWARD ROBINSON   *August 4, 1951*

Dear Bill:[1] Please have no concern about the items concerning me that are included in the Forrestal Diary. In the first place, we know that Forrestal wrote down the impressions and observations that frequently were only partial and certainly did not represent any complete story in any instance.[2]

With respect to the items you sent to me, I haven't the slightest concern. But I am, of course, pleased that you wanted my reaction. I shall certainly make no public announcement concerning them.[3] *Cordially*

[1] Robinson was executive vice-president of the *New York Herald Tribune*.

[2] The *Herald Tribune* had scheduled publication of the diary of James V. Forrestal, the late Secretary of Defense, in both book and serial form in the fall of 1951. (For background on Eisenhower's involvement in the publication plans see no. 130.) In a letter of July 30 (EM) Robinson had enclosed an excerpt from the Forrestal manuscript that he felt might upset Eisenhower. Robinson wrote the General that he would try to delete anything that may be "in any sense harmful to you. . . . Your importance to the country as a whole is of far greater concern than any possible benefit that might accrue from these Diaries. On the other hand," he said, "you may not consider the matter sufficiently important to warrant any action."

[3] The excerpt concerned the Eisenhower-for-President boom in 1947. Robinson finally made no change in the first diary entry (Oct. 6, 1947), regarding President Truman's reaction to "Eisenhower's presidential flirtation," but did in the second (Oct. 15, 1947). According to Forrestal, New York Governor Thomas E. Dewey had said, "Ike was obviously campaigning—'*He is going to at least one state fair a week.*'" The italicized sentence was deleted from the published book as well as from the serialized version (see Forrestal, *Diaries*, pp. 325–26; and *International Herald Tribune*, Paris ed., Oct. 9, 1951).

Paul Hoffman
John Cowles   came to see me.[1]
Paul Helms (California)

They recognize that I have an important *duty* in this post.

They believe that I have (rather, will have) a more important duty; to accept Republican nomination.[2]

They wanted to talk about the business of making it possible (at what they call the "proper" time) for the Republican party to place this duty upon me. They see of course that the requirements of the military post I now occupy are such that I must keep my mouth closed on all partisan matters.[3] The problem that they discuss at great length is the procedure of shifting from a military post to that of a receptive candidate for the Presidency next spring.[4]

I've told them—as I tell all—that I'll certainly always *try* to do my duty to the country, when I know what that duty is. As of now I have a duty; I cannot yet even describe the circumstances that would be conclusive in convincing me that my duty had changed to that of assuming a role in the political field. But I stick to one thing; if *I* have to help to prove that I have such a mission then the factor of duty becomes rather slim!![5]

[1] Hoffman (see no. 303), Helms (see no. 200), and John Cowles, chairman of the board of Cowles Magazines, president of the *Minneapolis Star and Tribune*, and a trustee of the Ford Foundation (see Galambos, *Columbia University*, no. 757), had visited the General on August 3 (see Cowles to Eisenhower, Sept. 29, 1951, EM).

[2] On the Democratic party's interest in Eisenhower as a potential presidential candidate see no. 313.

[3] A group of Eisenhower's friends and supporters had already begun laying the groundwork for a presidential campaign as a Republican candidate (see no. 196). For Eisenhower's continuing effort to keep military and political issues separated see, for example, no. 101.

[4] On the General's eventual decision to enter into politics see, for example, nos. 571, 582, and 784.

[5] For the General's responses to Cowles, Hoffman, and Helms concerning a possible candidacy see nos. 408, 411, and 899, respectively.

Dear Mr. Schmitt: Thank you very much for writing to tell me about Mr. Manning's condition, as well as something of his plans. Please inform him that I must regretfully say that the chances of my playing a game of golf at Cherry Hills this year are just about as slim as if I were living on another planet. But tell him also that there are one or two fairly attractive golf courses around Paris that I play just occasionally, and we could have a game here.[1] Incidentally, they are not too tough, but the fairways are narrow and the rough is terrific.

Tell Mr. Manning specially that I am hoping ever to hear good news about improvement in his health. Give my regards to all the members of his charming family, and, again, my thanks to you for your courtesy in writing.[2] *Sincerely*

[1] Schmitt, business manager for Eisenhower's friend Fred Manning, had written to the General on July 31 (EM) explaining that his employer was then in California undergoing treatment for emphysema (on Manning see no. 254). According to Schmitt, Manning hoped soon to be well enough to join Eisenhower for a game of golf either in Europe or at Denver's Cherry Hills Club (for background on the French courses played by the General see no. 161; on Cherry Hills see Galambos, *Columbia University*, nos. 545 and 938). Manning would not come to Europe this year (see appointment calendar and correspondence in EM).
[2] Schmitt would write Eisenhower again on August 9 (copy in EM, Manning Corr.) to say that Manning, greatly improved, looked forward to returning to his business ventures.

310   *Eisenhower Mss.*

To Paul Herbert Davis   *August 6, 1951*

Dear Paul:[1] The contents of your letter brought to me a feeling of astonishment; this for the reason that I had completely failed to sense that there is any lack of recognition of Bill Russell's fine work in the teaching profession. From the day I went to Columbia, I certainly left no stone unturned to show both him and others the importance I attached to the science of teaching and to the business of making the teacher's life attractive. You will recall that we got him made President of the Teachers College, instead of Dean, and that wherever I went to meet with Columbia graduates, I always made a special point of insisting that the teachers be invited. At those meetings I think, also, that I invariably paid a tribute to the Teachers College and to Bill Russell.[2]

As to the press conference, I don't see at the moment how your idea could be carried out without some awkwardness. He was in to see me the other day and I mentioned the idea briefly to him. He did not seem enthused, because he apparently had no better idea than I did how to stage such a thing and make it appear natural. I believe that he is to be back in Paris sometime after his vacation in the Pyrenees, and I shall talk to him about it again.[3]

Of course, it was nice to hear from you, and especially to know that you are doing so well in your new nitch. I am sure that you will find your association with Gordon Gray to be particularly stimulating. He is one of our fine people.[4]

Please convey my warm greetings to Mrs. Davis,[5] and with warm regard to you, *Cordially*

---

[1] Davis, a private consultant in institutional finance and public relations, had worked under Eisenhower at Columbia University as general secretary and vice-president in charge of development (see Galambos, *Columbia University*).

[2] In a letter of July 25 (EM) Davis had written that he was bothered by the "skimpy recognition" accorded Columbia Teachers College president William Russell (see no. 70 in this volume) and hoped that Eisenhower might help to correct the situation. For background on Russell's leadership of Teachers College and his work with Eisenhower see Galambos, *Columbia University*, esp. nos. 193, 529, and 811.

[3] Davis had suggested that Eisenhower, in his role as SACEUR, call a joint press conference with Russell to stress "the importance in the free world of our teachers" and to warn of the alarming "exodus of teachers" to higher-paying jobs. Russell, president of the World Organization of the Teaching Profession, had come to Europe to participate in the group's fifth delegate assembly; he had visited the General on August 1 (see *New York Times*, July 21, 26, 1951). Apparently no news conference took place. Davis replied to Eisenhower on September 7 (EM) that he had not intended to slight the General's previous work on Russell's behalf. He assured Eisenhower that he was "the one person in public life who on every occasion made a special effort to see that the teachers college group and teachers receive more adequate attention."

[4] In his letter of the twenty-fifth Davis had written that he was enjoying his work as a consultant and as such had advised Eisenhower's friend Gordon Gray, president of the University of North Carolina.

[5] Helen Brack Davis.

---

311   *Eisenhower Mss.*

To Edwin Palmer Hoyt   *August 7, 1951*

Dear Palmer:[1] I enclose a copy of the cablegram I just sent through my Washington office to Bing Crosby. You will note that I changed your wording a little bit, but I feel you will not mind—and certainly I did not tamper with the urgency of the case. I am personally delighted that you are to undertake, again, this particular chore. At this moment, I am just considering a letter from Lucius Clay who wants me to say a few words from my headquarters here in France on that same evening. I am quite prepared to do it, but I think I shall have to make a tape recording because, these days, I can never prophesy with certainty as to where I shall be on any particular date more than twenty-four hours ahead.[2]

Recently, I had a letter from Joe Dyer telling me about the forthcoming "Cherry Hillsdilly." How I wish I could be at the Club for the three days that affair is going on. That would be my idea of fun at one of my favorite spots.[3]

Please give my best to Aksel and any other of my friends that you may encounter in your ramblings about the city.[4] *Cordially*

[1] For background on Hoyt, the editor and publisher of the *Denver Post*, see Galambos, *Columbia University*, nos. 198 and 609.

[2] Hoyt, who was a regional chairman of the Crusade for Freedom (see nos. 86 and 112 in this volume), had written to Eisenhower on August 3 (EM) requesting that the General use his influence to secure the services of singer/actor Bing Crosby for the Crusade's 1951 Colorado "kick off." He assured Eisenhower that if he would "cable a congratulatory message to Crosby . . . Bing would undoubtedly forego other plans to come to Denver" for the program. The General's message and the singer's reply that he would be unable to accept the honor are both in EM (see Eisenhower to Davidson, AP 81112, Aug. 7, 1951, and Davidson to Schulz, DA 45128, Aug. 22, 1951, in EM, Crosby Corr. On Eisenhower's launching of the 1950 Crusade in Denver see Galambos, *Columbia University*, no. 962). The General's reply to national Crusade for Freedom chairman Clay is the following document.

[3] Joseph G. Dyer was a Denver businessman and chairman of the Cherry Hills Country Club's invitational golf tournament, the "Hillsdilly" (see Dyer to Eisenhower, July 5 and 30, 1951, and Eisenhower to Dyer, July 16, 1951, all in EM). On Eisenhower's interest in the Denver club see Galambos, *Columbia University*, nos. 938 and 960. For developments see no. 417 in this volume.

[4] Hoyt's letter of the third had also been signed by Eisenhower's friend Aksel Nielsen (see no. 235).

312   *Eisenhower Mss.*

To Lucius Du Bignon Clay   *August 7, 1951*

Dear Lucius: Of course, I am quite ready to help on your Labor Day business. In fact, I have just dispatched a cablegram to Bing Crosby to ask that great entertainer to help out in the Denver show on the same evening.[1]

Because of the uncertainties of my schedule, I think that possibly I had better do my little talk on a tape recording. In that way I can't go wrong, and my guess is that the hour of delivery of the talk here in Paris will be something like two in the morning. That's a little bit late for a man of my habits.[2]

Anyway, you had better send on the copy of the talk you want me to make (you know I always cut these things all to pieces) and also the details of exactly what I am to do.[3]

Give my love to Marjorie[4] and, of course, all the best to you. *As ever*

[1] Clay had written to Eisenhower on August 4 (EM) requesting that he make a brief statement for a radio broadcast launching the Crusade for Freedom's 1951 campaign (on the Crusade and Eisenhower's cable to singer Bing Crosby see the preceding document; for background on Eisenhower's earlier work with the propaganda organization see Galambos, *Columbia University*).

[2] At his SHAPE headquarters on August 24 Eisenhower would record a 141-word message for inclusion in the Crusade's Labor Day program (see appointment calendar; and n. 3 below).

[3] On August 13 (EM) Clay would thank Eisenhower for his agreement to participate, and later in the month a proposed statement, apparently drafted by Eisenhower's staff, would be sent to the Crusade's executive vice-chairman, Abbott McConnell Washburn (see Galambos, *Columbia University*, no. 948). This was the statement—in a greatly revised form—that the General would tape (see telegram, Levander to Washburn, Aug. 19, 1951, and Eisenhower to Clay, AP 81248, Aug. 22, 1951, both in EM, same file as document; and copy of final statement, in EM, Clubs and Associations, Crusade for Freedom). For developments in regard to the Labor Day program see nos. 330 and 331.

[4] Clay's wife (see no. 196).

313   *Eisenhower Mss.*

To Wright Francis Morrow   *August 8, 1951*

Dear Mr. Morrow:[1] Thank you very much for your thoughtful and interesting letter of August 2nd. I clearly recall the visit you and Governor Jester made to me at Columbia—I remember equally well the sadness I felt at the passing of what seemed to me on such short acquaintance to be a wonderful personality.[2]

Because of the impressions you formed in 1949 during your many contacts with the great and small of this particular region, it would be quite interesting to have your reactions should you make another such trip at any time in the near future. The rebuilding among these various peoples of faith, confidence, and determination is really the crux of the task that America has undertaken. Consequently, it would be instructive to have a comparison between your conclusions as of now and those formed in 1949.[3]

Of course, I am likewise interested in the observations you have to make on the domestic scene.[4] While my return to uniform limits my freedom in commenting upon such things, still I am grateful to you for providing me with some of the results of your own thinking.

This letter brings to you expressions of my continuing good wishes and personal regard.[5] *Sincerely*

[1] Morrow (LL.B. University of Texas 1916) was the senior member of the Houston law firm of Morrow, Boyd and Murrin and a Democratic National Committeeman.
[2] In his letter (EM) Morrow had recalled meeting with Eisenhower and late Governor of Texas Beauford Halbert Jester (see Galambos, *Columbia University*, no. 90) on June 17, 1948 (see *ibid.*, Chronology). Jester had been in the forefront of the movement to draft Eisenhower as the 1948 Democratic presidential candidate, and apparently Morrow had a similar plan in mind for 1952. Of their 1948 conversation Morrow wrote, "We had what . . . I regarded as a heart-to-heart talk . . . about the condition of our country and the need for leadership . . . and we found ourselves pretty well in agreement, particularly on fundamental American ideals" (for background see *ibid.*, nos. 90 and 106).
[3] During 1949 Morrow had spent four months in Europe as a special consultant to the President and the Secretary of State, investigating the impact of the Marshall Plan and the effectiveness of the U.S. Information Service. On the Marshall Plan see no. 248; for background on Eisenhower's concern over the rebuilding of confidence among the European Allies see, for example, nos. 233 and 248.
[4] Morrow had written that conditions were alarming and that the "task of preserving freedom and maintaining this country as a constitutional republic" was hampered at home by "a lack of conscience or . . . a cynical disdain of the things that really count in America." Again recalling their 1948 conversation, Morrow wrote that "the leader of this nation can be the greatest example for the rebuilding of the fiber and virility of the American citizen . . ." and was "the most important individual in the present scheme of things connected with world affairs."
[5] In his reply (Oct. 3, 1951, EM, same file as document) Morrow discussed the national political scene and enclosed a clipping from the *Houston Post* that quoted him as saying that Eisenhower would be a more logical presidential choice for the Democrats than he would for the Republicans. Eisenhower's October 10, 1951, response, which makes no mention of the clipping, is in EM. On the General's reactions to continuing Democratic interest in his candidacy see nos. 477 and 753.

314   *Eisenhower Mss., Family File*

To Barbara Jean Thompson Eisenhower   *August 9, 1951*
and John Sheldon Doud Eisenhower

Dear Barbie and Johnny: I have a hunch that Mamie has not been able to write to you since you left here; this for the reason that she has been working all day, every day, in an effort to get the house ready as quickly as possible. Every evening she comes home pretty well worn out.[1]

Since the two of you left, I have not had as much excuse for getting onto the golf course and, as a result, my game has suffered somewhat. Twice I have played a full eighteen holes since you left and made an

88 at Saint Germain and an 84 at Morfontaine. Yesterday we started some golf but a rainstorm overtook us and we had to quit.[2]

I know that the storm that recently broke out at West Point was as heart-breaking for you as it was for all the rest of us who have held the Academy so high in our affections and admiration. Of course, I realize that Johnny tried to tell me something about this when he was here, but it never crossed my mind that the situation was even a tenth as bad as it turned out to be. Moreover, there is a disturbing intimation that even yet the full story may not have been told.[3]

While I have been very greatly depressed by this whole development, still I think it is well to remember that a great institution with 150 years' traditions behind it is not going to be destroyed by this one disaster. The very fact that both cadets and official authorities were ready to tackle the problem head on and not try to duck the unpleasant notoriety and consequences gives assurance that the whole thing will be cleared up even if none of us will be able to forget it, so I think we must not get too pessimistic—but I do hope that from here on out there is rebirth in our veneration for the high moral standards that have characterized the institution in the past.

Of course, I realize that Academy football is probably shot for some years. My reaction to that is that I don't care—not so long as this situation is brought into the light of day and cured.[4]

The two of you are probably very deeply in work incident to the move to Fort Knox.[5] Mamie got a message yesterday saying, "Operation not necessary," which we assume to mean that you, John, did not have to have your impacted wisdom teeth removed by an operation. While I am delighted that you were spared the discomfort and inconvenience of such an experience, yet I do hope that the decision was not a bad one from the standpoint of your future health. You will recall that you suspected that impacted wisdom teeth might possibly be the cause of some headaches or other troubles that you occasionally experience.

Today is Thursday. On Saturday morning, Mamie and Min are going to accompany me to Germany where I will have three days of inspection work. They will stay at Garmisch and, after my inspections are completed, I will join them and do two or three days of golfing and fishing, coming back at the end of the week. We are really looking forward to the vacation even though the weather here has suddenly turned very cool and I have a little fear that we may be cold up in the foothills of the Alps. However, the change will be fine.[6]

The three of us send our love to the entire family—take care of yourselves. *Devotedly*

P.S. I think that, before you leave West Point, it might be well for you to give Cliff Roberts a ring on the phone and ask him to invest that extra thousand for you.[7]

[1] The Eisenhowers' long search for a suitable French home had ended in the spring with their selection of the Villa St. Pierre, ten miles west of Paris at Marnes-la-Coquette (see nos. 18, 132, and 180). Renovations at the Regency-style country house and the six acres surrounding it (formerly a residence to both Napoleon III and Louis Pasteur) were being carried out under Mrs. Eisenhower's close supervision and would be completed later in this month (on Mrs. Eisenhower's difficulties and on the property's improvements, which included a trout-stocked pond and a nine-hole putting course, see Brandon, *A Portrait of a First Lady*, pp. 267–68; and Hatch, *Red Carpet for Mamie*, pp. 230–33). Following a vacation in Bavaria (see n. 6 below), the Eisenhowers would officially occupy the house on August 22 (see *New York Times*, Aug. 23, 1951).

[2] On the recent visit to France of John and Barbara and their two children see no. 298. On the French golf courses played by the General see nos. 161 and 193.

[3] After two months of rumors, on August 4 it was reported that ninety West Point cadets faced dismissal from the academy for honor code violations. Many members of the football team were involved, and since the scandal surfaced shortly before the start of the 1951 season, it was then receiving wide publicity. A special academy board was appointed to investigate the charges that certain cadets had passed examination answers on to friends who were later to take the same tests. Following review by the board, the ninety accused cadets were permitted to submit "voluntary" resignations rather than receive dishonorable discharges or face courts-martial (see Stephen E. Ambrose, *Duty, Honor, Country: A History of West Point* [Baltimore, 1966], pp. 317–21; and *New York Times*, Aug. 4, 5, 6, 7, 8, 9, 10, 1951).

[4] The Army football team would win only two games during the upcoming season (see Ambrose, *Duty, Honor, Country*, p. 321). Of the West Point code of honor, which required absolute honesty from the cadets, General Eisenhower was quoted as saying that "the . . . system . . . seems to grow in importance with a graduate as the years recede until finally it becomes something which . . . occupies a position in his mind akin to the virtue of his mother or his sister" (*New York Times*, Aug. 4, 1951).

[5] Captain Eisenhower would shortly leave his teaching post to attend the Armored School, Advanced Officers' Course, at Fort Knox, Kentucky (see no. 165; and John Eisenhower, *Strictly Personal*, pp. 131, 133).

[6] On the morning of August 11 the General, Mrs. Eisenhower, Mrs. Doud, and several members of the SHAPE staff and their families would fly to the American Fürstenfeldbruck Air Base in West Germany to view a jet aircraft exhibition, followed by lunch at the base officers' club. The party would afterward travel by car to the Bavarian resort community of Garmisch-Partenkirchen, where Eisenhower would leave them for two days to conduct brief inspections. Traveling to Wiesbaden, Heidelberg, Sandhofen, and field areas on the thirteenth and fourteenth, the General and an aide reviewed elements of the 4th Infantry Division, the 547 Engineers, the Air National Guard, and the 2d Armored Division. Eisenhower would spend the succeeding six days, his first vacation since assuming the post of SACEUR, relaxing, fishing, and playing golf (see EM, Subject File, Trips; *International Herald Tribune*, Paris ed., Aug. 11, 14, 15, 17, 1951; and *New York Times*, Aug. 12, 13, 23, 1951).

[7] For background on Clifford Roberts, an investment adviser and friend of the Eisenhowers', see no. 246.

To WALTER KIRSCHNER

Dear Walter:[0] Your letter arrived a few minutes ago. I was startled to hear that you had been nursing a terrific fever since your return from Europe. I do hope that you are your old self again, and feeling fine.[1]

It takes no very careful reading of your engineer's letter to find out that he doesn't think much of the house at Gettysburg. I have no doubt that he is absolutely correct in all the comments he makes; as you know, I have never even seen the house at close range. Moreover, he makes the point that Mamie and I would always need a tenant's house; his suggestion that we build a house of our own at a different spot on the farm is, therefore, a logical one, always provided Mamie and I can produce the wherewithal to pay for it. This I figure will be quite a problem for us because, so far as I know, building costs are not only extraordinarily high but, seemingly, are going higher all the time.[2]

While I haven't talked to Mamie this morning, my own idea would be that we would want a brick house of fair size which would have modern facilities and utilities. When I say fair size, I am thinking—at least, at this instant—of a house in which the basement would probably contain an oil furnace, deep freeze, laundry and drying room, and certainly a storage room for trunks and baggage unless the house were so constructed that storage went into the attic. In addition—if the construction were such that a considerable amount of outside light came into the basement—I might try to include in it a small game room and studio where I could dabble with my paints.

When I try to imagine the general shape of a house for us, I haven't any very clear ideas, although it is possible that something in the shape of a *U* might be suitable. I think on the first floor we would require the normal kitchen, pantry, dining room, living room, and undoubtedly, in our case, a combination library and trophy room. Small powder rooms, I suppose, could be included; and possibly on the kitchen wing, there might be a place for Moaney and his wife to have their living quarters. On the second floor, Rosie would have to have a room and bath; for the family, assuming that we would have a glassed-in sleeping porch, I should think that three bedrooms and baths would be okay.

I realize that, from such a description, no one could possibly give me an estimate of cost because of the factors of size, thickness of wall, sturdiness of foundation, kind of floors and roofs, and so on, all make a tremendous difference. But if anyone could make a guess for me, I should say that in all these things a good sound "middle of the road course," which featured durability with a reasonable amount of attractiveness, would be the answer.[3]

With respect to your coming over here with George and Mary,[4] all you have to do is to say when you are starting. We will provide a warm welcome, and have a lot of fun and a lot of things to talk over.

Thanks again for your letter which I am sending to Mamie instantly. *Cordially*

P.S. Please send me a large, *un-retouched* photo of your head and shoulders. Some shadows on the face would be helpful to my tentative purpose of trying to paint you. Tell George to do the same. The one I did for him is awful![5]

[1] In his letter (Aug. 4, 1951, EM) Kirschner had written that since his return from Europe three weeks earlier he had been suffering from a viral infection and a 104° fever. Kirschner's name does not appear on Eisenhower's appointment calendar over this period, and it is unclear whether he visited the General while abroad. For background on Kirschner see no. 280.

[2] Enclosed with the letter of the fourth was a July 24 letter to Kirschner from Harry E. Holton, an engineer with Grayson-Robinson Stores, Inc. (copy in EM, same file as document). At Kirschner's request, Holton had conducted an examination of the farmhouse on Eisenhower's Gettysburg property, evaluating the condition of the structure and its potential for expansion and renovation (on the Gettysburg farm see nos. 48 and 73; on Kirschner's interest in constructing a new house for the General see nos. 249 and 250). According to Holton, the building was in such poor condition that "it would be wisdom to abandon the thought of remodelling . . . and think in terms of building a new home . . . ," keeping the existing structure as a tenant house for the Eisenhowers' farm managers Arthur and Ann Nevins (see no. 250). For a description of the original Gettysburg house see Nevins, *Five-Star Farmer*, pp. 88–93.

[3] On the eventual construction of a new home on the farm see Eisenhower's memoir *At Ease*, pp. 358–60. On Kirschner's continuing interest in the property, including the construction of a fish pond, see nos. 350 and 512; and correspondence in EM.

[4] On Eisenhower's close friends George and Mary Allen see no. 249.

[5] For background on the General's painting see nos. 102 and 117.

316   *Eisenhower Mss.*

To Grayson Louis Kirk   *August 10, 1951*

Dear Grayson:[1] The writing of this letter does not constitute even a suggestion concerning the subject on my mind at this moment. It is written merely to make certain that an article in this morning's paper, concerning termination by Poland of certain American cultural activities in Warsaw, did not escape your notice.[2] This *may* be important to Columbia because of our own effort through the Polish chair to keep alive knowledge of the ancient Polish culture.[3]

The point is this: If Poland interprets a cultural activity as a propaganda effort within its own country, then suspicion is aroused that they so regard the effort they make in helping to support a Polish chair in an American university. If they did so regard it, we would most certainly never have accepted the proposition in the first place, and we would most certainly terminate it at any second that we became convinced that such was their purpose or interpretation.

The actual decision to establish the chair in Polish culture was taken even before I came to Columbia. But any such venture requires, as I see it, a constant review in the light of any pertinent and changing circumstance. In this case, the attitude and purpose of the Polish Government would certainly be a "changing" circumstance if we were now forced to conclude that they had some propaganda purpose in the thing.[4]

Please give my best to all my friends at Columbia and, of course, warm regard to yourself. *Cordially*

[1] For background on Kirk, acting president of Columbia University in Eisenhower's absence, see no. 31.

[2] On August 8 the Communist government of Poland had ordered the cessation of all U.S. information activities within the nation, alleging that the U.S. Information Service had gone "far beyond the accepted scope of normal information work for an embassy" by issuing bulletins that "devoted a major part of their contents to propaganda." Housed in the U.S. Embassy in Warsaw, the information service had operated a library, motion picture theater, and radio bulletin program. In retaliation, the U.S. State Department had immediately ordered the Polish Research and Information Service in New York City to suspend all activities and close within twenty-four hours (see *International Herald Tribune*, Paris ed., Aug. 10, 1951; and *New York Times*, Aug. 10, 11, Oct. 17, 1951).

[3] Established in June 1948, Columbia's Adam Mickiewicz Chair of Polish Studies, partially funded by the Warsaw government, had been a matter of controversy from its inception (see Galambos, *Columbia University*, nos. 115, 131, 132, and 136).

[4] For developments see no. 346.

317   *Eisenhower Mss.*

To KENNETH ARTHUR NOEL ANDERSON   *August 10, 1951*

Dear Kenneth:[1] Jock Whiteley has just left my office after a long morning of business conversations and a luncheon. Interspersed with these were occasional recollections of old friends with whom we had served.[2]

Upon asking as to your current well-being, I was distressed to learn that your son had been lost in Korea.[3] I am dictating this just before departing on an inspection trip to Germany, but I did want you to know of our heartfelt sympathy for you and Lady Anderson.[4] It is my hope that the tragic burden may be lightened in some degree by the pride you must feel as the parents of a hero whose deeds will be a continuing inspiration to the youth of England.

With warm personal regard, *As ever*

[1] Lieutenant General Anderson (U.K.) was Governor and Commander in Chief of Gibraltar (for background see *Eisenhower Papers*, vols. I–XI).

[2] Eisenhower probably dictated this letter on August 9, the date of his appointment with Whiteley (see no. 203, n. 6) and his luncheon with several European and American officers (see appointment calendar).

[3] Anderson's only son, Lieutenant Michael Iain Anderson, of the Seaforth Highlanders, had been killed in combat, but the engagement had been against Malayan bandits during 1949 (see *Times* [London], Nov. 15, 1951).

[4] Anderson's wife was the former Kathleen Lorna Mary Gamble. On Eisenhower's inspection trip to Germany see no. 314, n. 6.

318   *Eisenhower Mss.*

To René Pleven   *August 14, 1951*

Pass following message from General Eisenhower to Prime Minister Pleven "My heartiest congratulations to you on having formed a Govt and ending long Governmental crisis. Now France can take its proper place.[1]

Upon return to Paris next week I hope to call on you to discuss various problems, including European Army."[2]

[1] For background on the French crisis see no. 304, n. 5. On August 8 Pleven had requested confirmation as Premier. A member of the Democratic Socialist Union of the Resistance, a splinter group of France's Socialists and Radical Socialists, Pleven had been able to draw support from both the centrist and independent elements of the Assembly, defeating opposition from Charles de Gaulle's Rally of the People of France (RPF) on the right and the large Communist party on the left. Pleven's cabinet had been accepted by the Assembly on August 11 in a vote of 390 to 222 (see *International Herald Tribune*, Paris ed., June 19, 23, Aug. 3, 4, 7, 8, 9, 10, 13, 1951). On Pleven's earlier service as French Premier see *ibid.*, February 8, 24, 27, March 1, 1951; and no. 53, n. 7. For developments see no. 586, n. 5.

[2] At this time Eisenhower was on an inspection tour and vacation in Germany (see no. 314, n. 6). He would have lunch with the new premier on August 24 (see appointment calendar). On Pleven's plan for the formation of an integrated European army see Galambos, *Columbia University*, nos. 1045, 1050, and 1064.

To Bernard Mannes Baruch   August 16, 1951

Dear Bernie: Your birthday gives me this opportunity to send my renewed best wishes and tell you again how delighted I am that we were
able to chat for those comparatively few minutes last month.[1] Already
I look forward to your next visit with real pleasure.

Anyway, Happy Birthday and may the years that follow be filled
with much-deserved happiness and contentment. Sincerely

P.S. Your fine letter of Aug. 8 just reached me down here in Bavaria.
You are exactly "on the beam" in what you are saying.[2]

[1] Baruch, who would turn eighty-one on August 19, had seen Eisenhower on July
7 and 18 (see New York Times, Aug. 20, 23, 1951). For background on Baruch see
no. 25, n. 4.

[2] In his letter of the eighth (EM) Baruch had commented on political speculation
concerning Eisenhower, writing that in conversations he always "drove home" the
point that the General was presently on the greatest mission of his life and that the
politicians who wished to make him a candidate should not distract him from a
NATO task that was "the salvation of all of us." For developments see no. 326. On
the General's Bavarian visit see no. 314, n. 6.

320   Eisenhower Mss.

To William Stuart Symington[1]   August 17, 1951
Confidential

Regarding subject of your confidential note please inform your
friend it is impossible for me to consider position mentioned. Assure
him of my appreciation of the compliment implicit in suggestion.[2]
Warm regard to yourself. Signed

[1] Symington, Chairman of the National Security Resources Board and former
Secretary of the Air Force, had recently been named Administrator of the Reconstruction Finance Corporation (for background see nos. 75, n. 4, 94, n. 3, and
130, n. 33).

[2] Symington had written (Aug. 10, 1951, EM) that Del E. Webb, New York
Yankees vice-president and representative of the sixteen major league baseball team
owners, had asked him to inquire whether Eisenhower would be interested in an
appointment as Commissioner of Baseball. Speculation regarding the identity of
the next commissioner had been widespread since the resignation of Albert Benjamin Chandler in July, with General Douglas MacArthur (see no. 194), Ohio
Governor Frank John Lausche, and both Eisenhower and his brother Milton
mentioned as possible candidates (see New York Times, June 7, Aug. 2, 3, 1951;

and no. 490). On September 20 the team owners would elect National League president Ford Christopher Frick to the post (*New York Times*, Sept. 21, 1951).

321   *Eisenhower Mss.*

To JOSEPH LAWTON COLLINS   *August 22, 1951*
Confidential

Dear Joe:[1] The other day, while talking to Handy,[2] I learned with feelings of astonishment—and even dismay—that the Department is planning to retire him early next year. The reason that he gave to me was that he has been five years in the grade of Major General.[3] Now while I am almost a fanatic in my support of any scheme that is designed to place younger men in the positions of highest responsibility,[4] yet in this case I must go into the opposition.

Of course, I am not familiar with the exact verbiage of our latest promotion law, but I do know what the intent was at the time of its proposal, and the instructions that Generals Paul and Dahlquist had.[5] If, through any fault of theirs, there was written into the law anything that requires a *3 or 4-star General* to retire because the date of his Major General's commission is five years old, then they certainly let me down badly.

While we all wanted the "five year in grade" provision in the law, this was to keep all lower grades from becoming jammed up with older men who might be jumped as the selective system picked out the best men for advancement.

The original intent was to retire Colonels at 58, Brigadiers at 60, Major Generals at 62, and all above the grade of Major General at 64. Congress did not fully accept this idea but did allow the Secretary of War the privilege of retaining a few men *after 62*; I believe up to a total of four on the list at any one time.[6] This particular provision I declined to use when I was Chief of Staff, except in the case of Eichelberger,[7] which exception was approved before I left there. However, that exception was not on the basis of five years in grade, but rendered necessary because he was 62 years of age.

In any event, here is my trouble. My deployment problem in the Center has been far from easy, and the clearest ray of hope I have had of getting it solved was a recent suggestion from Juin[8] to Handy that Handy take over the duties of Army Group Commander for the southern half of the whole front. This suggestion was made, of course, because of Handy's rank (as you know, the French are peculiarly sensitive on this question of rank), and because of the confidence and faith that the French have built up in Handy.[9] The whole thing is, as of yet, scarcely more than a brilliant possibility known, officially, *only* to Handy and Juin. Consequently, I am not in a position to commence bargaining on the matter. But I fear that any hint that Handy would not be the one to get the plan on the rails and to handle it in its early days would probably mean its defeat.

Of course, you are aware that when the President was outlining to me the European problem as he saw it, he pledged the greatest amount of personal support that was possible for him to give, together with over-all authority to me with respect to American forces in Europe.[10] When I explained to him that it would be awkward and needlessly burdensome for me to take too much administrative responsibility on my hands, he clearly understood that matters of normal administration were to be handled directly between United States administrative commanders here and the United States Departments concerned. However, he also stated, several times, that these commanders would always be men of whom I personally approved and that he would do his best to see that I would get the individuals that I desired.

Because of this, I at first thought that Handy must be mistaken when he gave me the information that he did. It seems natural that I should be consulted before any plans were considered that would change the identity of any of my senior commanders.

I cannot say with certainty, of course, that plans here will not develop on the best possible basis even with the contemplated relief of General Handy. Moreover, I am equally certain that no intentional slight to me or my position was intended; and don't get the idea that I am going "prima donna" on you. But the matter has far greater importance to the European defense plan than might appear if this were merely a routine change of personnel; consequently, I must tell you that, as of this moment, I feel it absolutely necessary that the scheme be held in abeyance. I realize, of course, that if the law is clear and definite and prohibits any administrative interpretation, there is little to be done (except that I still *think* I remember that the Secretary of the Army could make a legal exception, if such action appears necessary).[11]

In any event, won't you please look into the whole matter again, with the particular purpose of finding some way of avoiding what might easily become an upsetting of a very delicately balanced apple cart.

Tom was reticent in talking to me about the whole matter, and so I am not completely familiar with all details involved. I think he was fearful that I might interpret his explanation as a personal protest against his relief. Of course, he did not give any such implication whatsoever.

With personal regard, *Sincerely*

¹ Collins was Chief of Staff of the Army.
² General Thomas Troy Handy (for background see no. 286).
³ Handy (who was born in March 1892) had received permanent promotion to major general dating from March 1942 and temporary promotion to general dating from March 1945. By the terms of the 1947 Officer Personnel Act, permanent major generals in the Regular Army were forced to retire at age sixty-two (with exceptions for service chiefs, the Medical Corps, and West Point faculty). Each major general also could "be eliminated from the active list and retired on the fifth anniversary of the date of his appointment in that permanent grade" or after thirty-five years of active service, "whichever is later, unless he is permanently appointed in a grade above that of major general" before either of those dates. The law permitted the Secretary of War to make exceptions for up to ten general officers (otherwise ineligible for the active list or due for retirement) "who are either holding temporary appointments in any grade above major general or are serving in positions which carry rank above that of major general," retaining them on the active list until they reached age sixty-four (U.S., *Statutes at Large*, vol. 61, pt. 1, pp. 902, 904).
⁴ For Eisenhower's attention as Chief of Staff to the "involuntary retirement of officers whose records of performance after a maximum time in grade is not such as to justify selection for promotion to the next higher grade" see Galambos, *Chief of Staff*, no. 668. See also U.S. Congress, Senate, Committee on Armed Services, *Officer Personnel Act of 1947: Hearing on H.R. 3830*, 80th Cong., 1st sess., 1947, pp. 1–2.
⁵ Willard S. Paul, then a major general, had served as Director of Personnel and Administration during Eisenhower's tenure as Chief of Staff; John E. Dahlquist, then a brigadier general, had been Paul's deputy (see Galambos, *Chief of Staff*). For Eisenhower's and Dahlquist's testimonies on the bill see Senate Committee on Armed Services, *Officer Personnel Act of 1947: Hearing*, 1947; see also Galambos, *Chief of Staff*, no. 1596.
⁶ See n. 2 above.
⁷ Robert L. Eichelberger, a lieutenant general (born in March 1886), had commanded Allied and U.S. occupation forces in Japan in 1947–48 (Galambos, *Occupation, 1945*, no. 307).
⁸ General Alphonse Pierre Juin commanded the Allied Land Forces in central Europe (see no. 108).
⁹ Besides serving as CINCEUR, Handy recently had been U.S. Military Representative for Mutual Defense Assistance in Europe (see no. 286).
¹⁰ For Truman's mandate to Eisenhower as SACEUR see Galambos, *Columbia University*, no. 1136.
¹¹ For developments see no. 336.

322   *Eisenhower Mss.*

To Joseph Lawton Collins   *August 23, 1951*

*Dear Joe:*⁰¹ Your letter telling about Jones, Wood, and Schow just caught up with me.² Thanks a lot for your trouble—I quite understand the difficulty in the case of Wood. So long as I know that you share my very high opinion of him, my recommendation has really served its basic purpose.[3]

With warm personal regard, *Cordially*

[1] Collins was Chief of Staff of the Army.

[2] In a memorandum to Collins of July 16 (EM) Eisenhower had recommended colonels Herbert J. Jones, Robert J. Wood, and Robert A. Schow for promotion to brigadier general. For Eisenhower's evaluation of their performance of duty and the dates of their promotions see no. 271.

[3] In his letter of August 7 (EM) Collins had explained that Congress had moved to reduce the Army's budget ceiling of general officers from 500 to 496. He said that there were many vacant positions throughout the Army that should be filled by general officers but could not be because of the ceiling. As a result, only Schow and Jones were to be included on the list of recommendations. "I know Wood personally," Collins said, "and agree that he is an exceptionally able man. . . . We will keep him in mind for later lists, but unfortunately, for the present, it is not possible to promote him."

323   *Eisenhower Mss.*

To WILLIAM EDWARD ROBINSON   *August 23, 1951*

Dear Bill:[1] It was not until your letter of August 6th reached me that I realized that I must have failed to answer your very fine message of July 17th. Just yesterday, I returned from a combination vacation-business trip to Germany and hasten to say that you have my thanks for both communications. I am especially delighted to know that you have seen and spoken to Milton. He has a fine mind and is a splendid citizen.[2]

You can easily imagine how thrilled I was to know that you accepted my "preaching" letter in the spirit that it was meant. Far more than this, I am intensely gratified by your instant adoption of a health program—one that will keep you fit and fighting for many years to come. I venture the further prediction that you will gradually come to feel so much better, every day of the year, that you will constantly feel like jumping out of your skin.[3]

Cliff has returned here and I have just had the office calling him up to see whether he could not come out to lunch with me. Because I contracted a severe cold several days ago, I cannot play golf for the next few days, but I certainly do want to see and talk to him. I understand that Jerry Franklin is with him. If only you and Slats and Frank Willard and Jay Gould and Jack Buttinger and a few more of our old and good friends—including, of course, Bob Woodruff and the Georgia crowd—could be here at the same time, we would really have a fine reunion.[4]

Give my best to Helen[5] and, as always, cordial regard to yourself.
Sincerely

[1] For background on Robinson, a *New York Herald Tribune* executive and close friend of Eisenhower's, see no. 39.
[2] On Robinson's letter of July 17 (EM), a reply to several suggestions from the General regarding health and physical fitness, see no. 265, n. 7. In his letter of August 6 (EM) Robinson had written that during a recent long lunch with Eisenhower's brother Milton they had discussed the growing speculation concerning the General and the presidency. According to Robinson, Milton was receiving queries regarding his brother's intentions "from all corners," and while Milton was ready to deal with the questions, his concern over conditions in Washington led him to feel that there was "no hope of its correction except through a winning and fearless Republican leadership." For examples of recent proposals that General Eisenhower seek the presidency in 1952 see nos. 313 and 331. On Eisenhower's trip to Germany see no. 314.
[3] See nos. 265 and 283.
[4] Eisenhower, Robinson, and friends Clifford Roberts (see no. 368), Jerome Franklin (see no. 113), Ellis ("Slats") Slater (see no. 217), Frank Willard (see no. 301), Jay Gould (see no. 260), John Budinger (see no. 143), and Robert Woodruff (see no. 247) were all members of Georgia's Augusta National Golf Club.
[5] Helen Rogers Reid, owner of the *New York Herald Tribune* (see no. 146).

324   *Eisenhower Mss.*

To ROBERT WITHERS EWBANK   *August 23, 1951*
Secret

Dear Brigadier Ewbank:[1] I quite agree with the proposals of the British Chiefs of Staff as presented to me in your note of 20 August.[2] In view of the situation now existing, I think it would be a most unpropitious time for the publication of any document prepared by me on the occurrences and circumstances of World War II. Not only is Italy now one of the member nations of NATO, but all of us are convinced of the desirability of obtaining cooperative efforts of Western Germany.

Will you, therefore, please express to the Chiefs of Staff my conviction that the documents enumerated in your note should be circulated only on a confidential basis and only to officials bearing responsibilities in connection with the security of the United States and Great Britain. Please express to them also my appreciation of their tact and initiative in this matter. *Very sincerely*

[1] Brigadier General Ewbank, a Cambridge University graduate and career engineering officer, served as Secretary to the British Chiefs of Staff Committee, Ministry of Defense, from 1951 to 1953.
[2] In 1948 Eisenhower had agreed to British publication of his wartime reports on

operations in North Africa, Pantelleria, Sicily, and Italy (for background, see Galambos, *Chief of Staff*, nos. 1914 and 1993, and *Columbia University*, no. 20). Ewbank had written (EM) at the request of the BCOS to suggest that in view of the General's appointment as SACEUR and his command of Italian forces in particular, it might now be "inappropriate" to circulate those documents except confidentially within British service departments. "The position is a curious one," Ewbank wrote, "particularly as the Italian Government might have some ground for objection if you, as Supreme Commander and responsible to them as a member of the North Atlantic Treaty, were to publish reports of this kind reflecting on the morale and actions of their forces albeit in respect of a period when the North Atlantic Treaty did not exist."

325

Eisenhower Mss.

To GRAYSON LOUIS KIRK

August 23, 1951

Dear Kirk: Through two or three sources, I have received the good news that you have made the decision to remain at Columbia. As you can guess, I am delighted.[1]

You are well aware of the convictions I hold that your current authority should be unrestricted by the existence of a nominal but absent President—you have a big and responsible job and one that, from all reports I receive from Columbia, you are filling to everybody's satisfaction.[2]

With warm personal regard, *Cordially*

[1] Acting Columbia University president Kirk (see no. 31, n. 1) had apparently been offered the presidency of New Jersey's Rutgers University. Messages informing Eisenhower of Kirk's decision to remain at Columbia had come from University trustees Marcellus Dodge and Frederick Coykendall (see Dodge to Eisenhower, Aug. 16, 1951; Eisenhower to Dodge, Aug. 23, 1951; and Coykendall to Eisenhower, 162332, Aug. 16, 1951, all in EM. On Dodge and Coykendall see nos. 6, n. 1, and 114, n. 2, respectively).

[2] Kirk would reply (Aug. 28, 1951, EM) that the decision to stay on at Columbia had been "rather difficult" but that he had no regrets and was certain that he could be more useful continuing in his present post. For developments concerning the Columbia presidency see no. 991.

To Bernard Mannes Baruch   *August 23, 1951*
Personal and confidential

Dear Bernie: Since coming back from a combination business-vacation
trip in Germany, I have been told by Colonel Schulz of your message
to me concerning Arthur Godfrey. In the few contacts I have had with
him, I have been impressed by an apparent deep sincerity in his
expressed desire to do something useful in helping preserve the essentials of the American system. Beyond this, I always find him entertaining and amusing and therefore an interesting companion. So—on the
personal basis—he will always be welcome as a visitor at my headquarters.[1]

Another angle, however, is presented by the impression I have that,
when he returned home after his last trip, his support of the cooperative security effort was interpreted, as I understand it, to be more of a
personal endorsement of me than as a reasoned and strong presentation of the facts bearing upon this great problem. Since you, returning
to the States at the same time, issued your very splendid "Let the
General alone" statement, I feel that you are possibly in better position
than I to decide whether or not a return here by Arthur Godfrey would
be really helpful.[2]

In any event, I am sure that his intentions and purpose have always
been of the best. Consequently, if he should come back here, I shall,
of course, see him and at the very least discuss with him NATO affairs
on the same basis that I discuss them with other representatives of the
radio and press.

This basis is that of "no quotes and for background purposes only"
and is one that I have pursued for many years and, as a matter of
policy, could not possibly afford to break.

All this I am quite sure that he understands. In any event, it
represents about as definite an answer as I can possibly make. I hope
this answer seems logical and sufficient to you.[3]

With cordial personal regard, *Sincerely*

[1] Radio and television personality Arthur Godfrey (see no. 42) had visited Europe
with Baruch during July, seeing Eisenhower on two occasions (see no. 319, n. 1).
Baruch apparently felt that Godfrey's influence would increase public awareness of
the importance of NATO, and his message to Eisenhower may have been to
encourage a second SHAPE visit by the entertainer (see Margaret L. Coit, *Mr.
Baruch* [Boston, 1957], pp. 655–56; and n. 2 below). For background on the
General's trip to Germany see no. 314, n. 6; on aide Robert Schulz see no. 1,
n. 4.

[2] Upon his return to the United States, Godfrey had created a controversy by
urging his television and radio audiences to write to their congressmen to encourage
support for both Eisenhower's SHAPE efforts and the reinstitution of domestic

price controls. This editorial appeal had drawn heavy criticism from media and government officials and led the CBS network later to air a price-control forum—presenting the pros and cons—with Godfrey as host (see "CBS's Barefoot Boy," *Newsweek*, August 6, 1951, 55–56). For background on the price-control issue see nos. 222 and 306, n. 2.

While sailing home aboard the *Queen Mary*, Baruch had told reporters that "anyone seeking to divert Ike's attention to politics" was doing both Eisenhower and the nation a disservice by distracting him from his duties as SACEUR (see *New York Times*, Aug. 2, 3, 1951; and no. 319, n. 2).

[3] For more on Godfrey's visit and for developments see no. 333.

327   *Eisenhower Mss.*

To JOHN RAY DUNNING   *August 23, 1951*

Dear *John*:[1] I understand that Felix Wormser is to be in Paris in early September and has promised to drop in to see me. At that time, I will have certain things to talk over with him.[2]

I, of course, am delighted to sign the kind of draft that you sent me regarding a letter to Mr. Krumb, since it implies no real responsibility on my part for anything except an expression of appreciation for the services the individual has already rendered to Columbia.[3]

In the case of the letter to Mr. Beatty, I am reluctant to have him think that I, in my present post, can give sincere and detailed attention to Columbia's affairs since this, of course, is not the case. Consequently, it does not seem reasonable for me to be asking him for advice and counsel or in hinting so strongly that he contribute personally to the support of our plans. I think that you and others in the University are now in a better position to do this than I. However, as I said before, I shall talk these things over with Felix Wormser.[4] *Cordially*

[1] Dunning, dean of the Columbia University School of Engineering, had recently visited Eisenhower to discuss development plans for the university's proposed engineering center (see no. 266).

[2] A Columbia engineering graduate and vice-president of the St. Joseph Lead Company, Felix Edgar Wormser was then serving as general chairman of the Columbia Engineering Development Program (for background see Galambos, *Columbia University*, no. 783). He had written Eisenhower several times over the last few months concerning a grant from the Charles Hayden Foundation of Boston for a laboratory of extractive metallurgy and would visit the General in France on September 7 to discuss his development work (see Wormser to Eisenhower, June 25, 1951; Hayden to Wormser, June 28, 1951; Wormser to Eisenhower, Aug. 15, 1951; and other correspondence in EM, Wormser Corr.).

[3] With a letter to Eisenhower of August 6 (EM) Dunning had enclosed drafts of letters (copies in EM, same file as document) to School of Engineering alumni Alfred Chester Beatty (E.M. 1898), chairman of Britain's Consolidated African Trust, Ltd., and director of the American Metal Company, Ltd., and Henry

Krumb (see Galambos, *Columbia University*, nos. 741 and 1120). Both men had been instrumental in securing the Hayden grant for Columbia (see n. 2 above). The letter to Krumb, which Eisenhower did not alter, is the following document. On the Beatty message see n. 4 below.

[4] Earlier in the year Dunning had contacted Eisenhower concerning Beatty, mentioning him as a potential engineering center benefactor and requesting that the General arrange to meet with him. Following a luncheon meeting on May 30, during which Eisenhower had found Beatty interested in the expansion of Columbia engineering, Dunning had traveled to Dublin to meet with the alumnus. The draft of Dunning's suggested letter from Eisenhower to Beatty (EM, same file as document) discussed Beatty's plans for establishing a museum of engineering and a foreign-student scholarship fund at Columbia (see correspondence in *ibid.*, esp. Eisenhower to Beatty, Feb. 27, 1951, and Eisenhower to Dunning, May 30, 1951; and EM, Beatty Corr.). Eisenhower was concerned over his increasingly distant relationship with the university (see, for example, nos. 229 and 261).

328   *Eisenhower Mss.*

To Henry Krumb   *August 23, 1951*

Dear Mr. Krumb: Just a word of appreciation to you for all the work you did so effectively to produce the magnificent Hayden Foundation grant of $900,000 for our Engineering Center program.[1]

I was delighted to know of the honor which Columbia University was privileged to bestow upon you at the last commencement, and only regret that I could not be present to share with your many friends the delight which must have been theirs in seeing you so honored.[2]

There is no doubt in my mind, the deeper I get into the work here, that Columbia is on the right course in working hard to see the Engineering Center program realized, and from my point of view here in Europe, as I look at the world situation around me, all I can think of to say is that the sooner the Center plans are realized, the better.[3]

Our own country and the free people of the world need all that this great project can mean for security and for human welfare.

With kindest personal regards, and real appreciation, *Sincerely*

[1] See the preceding document for background on Krumb, the Hayden Foundation grant to Columbia University engineering, and the drafting of this letter by Columbia's dean of engineering, John R. Dunning. On the engineering center proposal, developed while Eisenhower was still active as president of the university, see no. 266.

[2] Columbia had awarded Krumb the honorary degree of Doctor of Science on June 7 (see *New York Times*, June 8, 1951).

[3] In his reply (Oct. 22, 1951, EM) Krumb thanked Eisenhower for his letter and said that the engineering center campaign was progressing more slowly than he had hoped. What the program needed, according to Krumb, was Eisenhower's "presence to stimulate and push it along."

To Gabriel N. Stilian   *August 23, 1951*

Dear Private Stilian: I shall attempt, in spite of a current pressure of business, to answer your letter, recently written to me from Fort Dix. I do so on a confidential and personal basis; I know that you will respect my earnest desire that this communication be shown to or read only by you and the particular associates that you mentioned in your letter.[1]

*   *   *   *   *

Rarely have I received a letter that has seemed to me to breathe the sincerity, the understanding, and the human qualities that I find in yours. I wish I had the wisdom to answer in such a way as to satisfy the hearts and minds of yourself and your comrades; as it is, I can do no more than to express to you, most sketchily, some of my convictions which in a sense are the product of a lifetime of study and pondering along lines somewhat similar to those that your particular group is pursuing.

With you, I believe that we must never fall prey to the depressing conviction that "kill or be killed" is the sole end of or the meaning to existence. No matter how clearly and specifically such a necessity may press upon us at any particular moment in the life of an individual or of a race, we must still regard this as a passing or emergency phase, and remember that true human objectives comprise something far richer and more constructive than mere survival of the strong. The theory of defense against aggressive threat must comprehend more than simple self-preservation; the security of spiritual and cultural values, including national and individual freedom, human rights and the history of our nation and our civilization, are included.[2]

One of the basic axioms of existence is that all things change; sometimes there is real comfort in remembering that "this, too, shall pass." What I mean to say here is that the tyranny and threat represented in the announced and implacable antagonism of Communism to our form of government and society *will not always be with us.* Sooner or later—no matter how bleak the situation may appear at any one moment—this threat to freedom and man's right to live in dignity will disappear. But in posing this threat, evil men have challenged the ability of living generations of free men to conduct their lives under governmental systems of their own choosing.

The Communists have clearly proved that in the international field they respect no law but force. The free world has no choice but to develop a volume of force that will prevent even the misguided Communists from putting their case to the test of arms. In other words, we are training and preparing now *not to fight a war but to preserve the peace.* This I believe with all my heart. I assure you that if I saw no end to the great ideological struggle through which we are now passing, other than global war with a destructiveness and suffering and anguish that would dwarf those experienced in any previous conflict, I would most certainly, both as a soldier and as a human being, pursue a far different course of action than I am now observing.[3]

I believe that the chances are favorable that we shall be successful in this effort to maintain the peace. Naturally I assume that there will be clear realization throughout the free world of the issues at stake and the urgency of the immediate situation. Moreover, I believe that we shall maintain the sturdy confidence in our own ability to meet this situation.

We must not forget that in total wealth, material strength, technical scientific achievement, productive capacity, and in rapid access to most of the raw materials of the world, we, the free nations, are vastly superior to the Communist bloc. But we are a whole congress of free nations, while the entire Communist bloc is subject to the orders of Moscow. To make our aggregate strength effective, and so be successful in our basic objective of organizing to preserve the peace, we must cooperate so effectively that we match the unity of the Communists, which they achieve through the threat of the slave camp and the whipping post. Our unity must be attained through common understanding of the essential factors in the problem, and common determination to meet the threat sanely and reasonably and with the single purpose of preserving our own security and peace.

It is well to remember that the Communist part of any nation, even in Russia itself, comprises only a small portion of the total population. In other words, Communists rule even in their domestic situations largely through organized threat. Consequently, in spite of the tyrannical methods they employ, they can never be wholly secure in the possession of their positions of power. The practice of their Godless doctrine of Communism carries within itself the seeds of its own destruction, because it suppresses the natural and decent aspirations of men. If we can be strong enough, if we can endure enough, we can wait for the inevitable explosive process to take effect. Thus there will arise, eventually, a situation that will allow us to devote less and less of our energies, our wealth, and our thinking to matters of self-preservation and protection, and more and more to those things which enrich human life spiritually, intellectually, and materially.

As for the role or function that I as an individual may have in helping sustain the integrity of the free nations while this process develops, I cannot say more than the simple truth that I hope always to be ready to do my duty, so far as I am able to see it. I am naturally highly complimented and deeply touched by your group's expressions of confidence and faith in me. But, as of this moment, I feel that any expression or act of mine that would tend to divide our country in support of the production of collective security, including that of the United States, or which would tend to make my headquarters less efficient in performing the strictly *non-partisan duties of an American soldier* would be completely out of character for me and certainly most unwise from the standpoint of the country. I hope this does not sound stuffy or egotistical; it represents my present thinking and convictions.[4]

I realize that this letter cannot be regarded by you and your comrades as a perfect or even a very satisfactory answer to the questions that are now so sorely troubling you. It is one of the characteristics of life that some crucial problem is always present with us that we alone can solve; in fact, the business of living seems to be the business of attempting to solve in decency, in fairness, and in justice the multitude of problems that constantly present themselves to us as individuals, as groups, and as nations.

This note brings to you and your comrades my very best wishes and the hope that, in something that I have tried here to suggest, you will find a small bit of optimism and of faith, as you push onward with your several careers.[5]

With best wishes to each of you, *Sincerely*

---

[1] Stilian, a private in the 47th Infantry, was then undergoing basic training at Fort Dix, New Jersey. In his undated letter to Eisenhower (EM) he had said that he and a few friends were "somewhat worried and depressed over the conditions existing today and . . . horrified over the trend of affairs to be expected in the future." These soldiers, according to Stilian, sought some guidance from Eisenhower.

[2] Stilian said he and his friends were willing to "kill or be killed" for the survival of their country, but they questioned whether it was absolutely necessary to produce a generation of "professional killers." Saying that they believed that the world situation was not yet hopeless, they were seeking the leadership of a " 'great man' of this generation to help guide us in our inter-relationship with the people of the world."

[3] For some of Eisenhower's thoughts on the weaknesses and dangers of communism see, for example, nos. 23, n. 4, 43, and 97, n. 3.

[4] A major theme of Stilian's letter involved support for Eisenhower as a 1952 presidential candidate. He said, "What this country needs is a man whose words and actions are completely moral and ethical [and] on a level of intelligent understanding and sympathy but with no trace of weakness." Stilian and his comrades believed Eisenhower could provide both guidance and harmony under world conditions that were "too gosh darn serious to fool around with."

[5] Stilian would reply on December 15 (EM) thanking Eisenhower for his letter and again encouraging him to seek the presidency. In a postscript he informed the General that he had recently been "graduated" from the Army through a medical discharge.

To Harold Edward Stassen

Dear Governor:[1] While in Germany, I received both your telegram dated the 15th and your note of the 7th. For both of them, I am grateful.[2]

Of course, when you reach here in December, I shall be looking forward to seeing you. I hope that you will find it possible to give my office a few days' advance notice so that I can reserve a period for a good meeting.[3]

With warm personal regard, *Sincerely*

[1] For background on Stassen, president of the University of Pennsylvania and former Governor of Minnesota, see nos. 63, n. 2, and 80, n. 1.

[2] On the seventh (EM) Stassen, who was serving as drive chairman of the 1951 Crusade for Freedom, had requested Eisenhower's help in launching the program. On the Crusade and on the General's agreement to make a tape-recorded message for its Labor Day opening see nos. 311, n. 2, and 312. For developments see the following document.

[3] In his telegram of August 15 (EM) Stassen had congratulated Eisenhower on the progress of SHAPE and informed him of his proposed visit to Paris. On the mid-December visit see no. 545, n. 1.

To Lucius Du Bignon Clay

Personal

Dear Lucius: Upon my return from Garmisch, where I had enjoyed about a week of golf and occasional fishing, I found your informative letter.[1]

I am glad to help in this year's Crusade. You know I believe sincerely that every avenue should be exploited if we are to win in the battle against Communism.[2] It would interest me to know the reactions you have obtained from the sending of the balloons over Czechoslovakia. This imaginative approach rather appeals to me, but I have no idea of its effectiveness.[3]

While in Bavaria, *F* was in Munich.[4] I was gratified by the fact that he did not feel it necessary to see me, which makes him one out of many. I understand from Bill Burnham who visited with him that he thoroughly understands the situation and my reactions to it. In fact, he is one of the few who have not attempted to dictate some type of a time schedule. He seems to comprehend, clearly, that until [this] venture is definitely on the road to accomplishment, I cannot give consideration to taking any other position or responsibility. It certainly would be easier for me if many of those who came here had a like understanding. *F* insisted to Bill that it was up to everybody to adapt their hopeful planning to the compulsions placed upon me by the requirements of this position.

John and family were over here for about a month—and when those grandchildren of mine left, there was a big void in the lives of both Mamie and myself. It is the longest time I have had with John in some years. He has turned into quite a student; is not bound by convention or ritual in his thinking, and has acquired a very broad base of general knowledge. We had great fun arguing and talking, although we didn't always agree.[5]

We are making progress here—but, as you can well imagine, each day brings forth one or more new problems for solution. So long as I can see a gradual improvement, such problems are simply part of the job of teaching, preaching, and implementing a cooperative security effort in peacetime.[6]

With thanks for your letters and with warmest regard to Marjorie[7] and yourself, *Sincerely*

[1] On Eisenhower's vacation in Garmisch-Partenkirchen, Bavaria, see no. 314, n. 6.

[2] Earlier in the month Eisenhower had agreed to make a pre-recorded message to help launch the 1951 Crusade for Freedom, an organization that Clay headed (see no. 312 and the preceding document). The tape, which the General recorded the morning of the twenty-fourth, would be aired over the CBS radio network on Labor Day as part of a fifteen-minute program using the "Freedom Bell" as its theme (see appointment calendar; and Clay to Eisenhower, Aug. 4, 1951, in EM). The broadcast included messages from five prominent figures, accompanied by recorded peals from historic free world bells. Eisenhower, Clay, Harold Stassen (see the preceding document, n. 2), West Berlin Mayor Ernst Reuter, and American Ambassador to Great Britian Walter Sherman Gifford each hailed the work of the Crusade broadcasting behind the Iron Curtain and urged support for its efforts to raise $3.5 million. Following the ringing of the Notre Dame Cathedral bell, Eisenhower called for the assistance of every American in bringing the truth to those Eastern Europeans who, "though . . . marched and countermarched in the lockstep of totalitarianism . . . yearn for a better day when freedom and the natural rights of man are theirs again to enjoy." The other bells included in the program were London's Big Ben, the Freedom Bell of West Berlin, the Chong-No Bell from Seoul, Korea, and the American Liberty Bell (see undated copy of message in EM, Clubs and Associations, Crusade for Freedom; EM, Clay Corr.; and *New York Times*, Sept. 4, 1951).

[3] On August 13 the Crusade for Freedom had begun a propaganda effort in Czechoslovakia, using hydrogen-filled balloons to carry leaflets across the West German border. More than 9 million messages of Western friendship and support, some bearing the frequencies and broadcast schedules of Radio Free Europe, were dropped in this manner by August 25 (see *New York Times*, Aug. 14, 17, 19, 27, 28, 1951). On an earlier suggestion to Eisenhower that the United States employ balloons in its propaganda efforts see Galambos, *Columbia University*, no. 785. For

the reactions of Czechoslovakia's government to both the balloons and Western radio broadcasts see *New York Times*, August 15, 17, 25, 1951.

[4] Clay, who was active in the growing Eisenhower-for-President movement, kept the General informed of political efforts on his behalf. In this correspondence, and in unsigned memorandums for Eisenhower written by New York Governor Thomas Dewey and forwarded through Clay, a letter-for-name substitution code was employed. Clay earlier had sent Eisenhower the first of these code keys with the names represented by the letters *A* through *D* (see no. 196, n. 3), and in June he sent an expanded key running through the letter *S* (see Clay to Eisenhower, June 27, 1951; memorandum, [Dewey to Clay], June 24, 1951; and undated code lists, all in EM). In this second key *F* represented University of Pennsylvania president Harold Stassen, who had recently begun to work with the unofficial Eisenhower-for-President committee (see no. 196; and memorandum [Dewey to Clay], June 24, 1951, EM). For background on Eisenhower's friend and political supporter William Burnham, who had recently joined the SHAPE staff as a civilian economic analyst, see no. 128, n. 6.

[5] On the visit to France of Eisenhower's son John and his family see nos. 132, n. 4, 252, n. 1, and 298, n. 1.

[6] On Eisenhower's recent SHAPE activities see, for example, nos. 304 and 321.

[7] Clay's wife (see no. 196, n. 13).

332   *Eisenhower Mss.*

To Joseph Lawton Collins   *August 25, 1951*
Secret

Dear Joe:[1] It was most encouraging to note in your letter of August 21st that Tito is becoming increasingly amenable to identifying himself more closely with the West.[2] Of course, I have no illusions as to his reasons; hence I agree with you that for every commitment that is asked of us we should obtain an appropriate quid pro quo. The contribution that Yugoslavia can make towards the security of my southern flank is brought into focus here every time we consider plans and forces required for the defense of Southern Europe, particularly Italy. I am *heartily in favor* of your visit.

I am sure that you are aware of the position which I have taken with the United States Joint Chiefs of Staff in regard to emphasizing my relationship with discussions and negotiations with European Nations in planning for the military support of Yugoslavia. I now have agreement from the Joint Chiefs of Staff and am directing Carney to proceed with planned conversations.[3]

Carney's discussions will necessarily take time since he will hold discussions with the United Kingdom and French and then have conversations with the Italians. Before any discussions with the Yugoslavs, I believe there will probably be a question of clearances with the

United Kingdom and French Governments. Under such circumstances, it is difficult now to predict when Carney will be in a position to hold conversations with the Yugoslavs.

It is possible that your visit might contribute markedly to future conversations between Carney and the Yugoslavs. However, in order that no misunderstanding occurs with respect to Carney's possible later visit, I believe that the United Kingdom, France, and Italy should be notified well in advance, particularly with regard to the purpose of your visit as differentiated from the task assigned Carney.

Your coming through Paris on your way to and from Yugoslavia would be mutually profitable. I am looking forward to seeing you again.[4] Warm regard, *As ever*

[1] U.S. Marine Corps Colonel George R. E. Shell prepared this letter to U.S. Army Chief of Staff Collins. Shell was a member of SHAPE's Plans, Policy and Operations Division.

[2] In his letter (EM) Collins had advised Eisenhower that he was contemplating a visit to Yugoslavia in order to determine the conditions under which military aid would be given to that country (for background see no. 142). Collins said that "the Joint Chiefs would not approve any large-scale program until some agreement was made with Tito that would initiate a check by American personnel on the use to which the Jugs would place our equipment and the ability of the Yugoslav Army to employ that equipment. . . . [T]he JCS also are concerned as to what quid pro quo we could obtain for whatever aid we gave." The American ambassador to Yugoslavia had informed Collins that Marshal Tito probably would want a personal meeting with Collins, even though Eisenhower's southern commander, Admiral Carney, "would be the officer who would ultimately have responsibility for the general area if war should come." Collins, who asked for Eisenhower's reaction, had assured him that "anything that we would do with reference to MDAP on the quid pro quo that we should endeavor to secure, should be in accordance with your over-all plans." For background on Collins's proposed visit see State, *Foreign Relations, 1951*, vol. IV, *Europe: Political and Economic Developments, Part II*, pp. 1836–37.

[3] In April Eisenhower had recommended that Carney be given authority to conduct planning for the coordination of NATO and Yugoslav forces in the event of war (see no. 148). The JCS had agreed in a message sent on May 21, 1951: "JCS feel that until such time as an arrangement is made for over-all planning in the area of Med–Middle East, Carney, as CINC, Allied Forces, Southern Europe, should be assigned responsibility for coordination of Greek, Turkish and also of Yugoslavian planning insofar as such planning relates to NATO and defense of west Eur[ope]" (JCS 91869, CCS 092 Western Europe [3-12-48], Sec. 82; see also Vandenberg to Secretary of Defense, Sept. 19, 1951, OS/D, 1951, Clas. Decimal File, CD 091.3 MDAP Yugoslavia). For developments see no. 378.

[4] Eisenhower would see Collins on October 4 and 5. Eisenhower would tell him that "no firm military agreements" involving NATO should be made with Yugoslavia until the requisite political arrangements had been made. He would agree, however, that it would be appropriate for Collins to discuss Yugoslavia's disposition of forces and to point out the importance of holding the Ljubljana Gap if the Russians should go to war (Collins to JCS, Nov. 2, 1951, EM, Collins Corr.). In November Collins would send Eisenhower copies of his report on his four-day visit

to Yugoslavia. The Yugoslavs, including Marshal Tito, assured Collins that they would hold the Ljubljana Gap area and would not withdraw their troops into the mountains in order to fight a guerrilla war. When Tito attempted to discuss the strategic deployment of NATO's forces, however, Collins told him that Eisenhower had not authorized any such talks. Collins concluded that "the defense plans of Yugoslavia can be integrated with those of NATO" and that "everything practicable should be done, both economically and militarily, to bind Yugoslavia to the West" (Collins to Eisenhower, Nov. 15, 1951, and Collins to JCS, Nov. 13, 1951, EM). In November the United States and Yugoslavia would sign a Mutual Defense Assistance Agreement (Poole, *History of the Joint Chiefs of Staff*, vol. IV, *1950–1952*, p. 316; State, *Foreign Relations, 1951*, vol. IV, *Europe: Political and Economic Developments, Part II*, pp. 1862–63).

333   *Eisenhower Mss.*

To Arthur Michael Godfrey   *August 25, 1951*
Personal

Dear Arthur: Thank you very much for your fine letter which was on my desk when I returned from a short trip, combining business and vacation, in Germany.[1]

The transcriptions to which you refer have not yet reached me, but I assume that they will be here before long. I am all ready to play them since only recently we have received at our home a new type of phonograph or record player which seems to be adaptable to the playing of almost any conceivable type of record.[2]

As to your coming back this way, you know that it is always a pleasure to see you. However, from your viewpoint, such a trip might provide very meager returns because there has been no spectacular development since you were here last. We are working on a number of things which we fervently hope will reach fruition during the late fall or winter, and I should personally think that you would get more out of your trip by deferring it for some time. But if you, for any reason, just want to make another trip to Europe, then be sure to drop in to see me if for nothing else but a chat.[3]

I was interested in what you had to say about reactions to your broadcasts that were based upon your findings here this summer. At the very least, you seem to have stirred up some thinking.[4]

With best wishes and personal regard, *Very sincerely*

[1] For background on Godfrey see no. 42; on Eisenhower's trip to Germany see no. 314, n. 6.
[2] Godfrey had written (Aug. 2, 1951, EM) that he was having recorded transcripts of several of his recent controversial radio and television programs sent to Eisenhower (see n. 4 below).

[3] Godfrey had recently traveled to Europe with Bernard Baruch (see no. 319, n. 1), seeing the General on July 7 and playing golf with him on the thirteenth. Baruch had suggested that the entertainer again visit SHAPE (see no. 326, n. 1).
[4] Of the controversy he created by asking his radio and television audiences to write to their congressmen in support of Eisenhower's efforts and the reinstitution of domestic price controls Godfrey said, "I raised a little hell . . . and over stepped my bounds no doubt, but I think I did accomplish a small part of what you wanted: people got excited, wrote to their folks in Washington . . . and got them off their collective and individual posteriors." For background on the broadcasts see no. 326, n. 2.

334   *Eisenhower Mss.*

To Roy Wilson Howard   *August 25, 1951*

Dear Roy:[1] It was good to see you again in Germany.[2] In line with our brief conversation there, I am enclosing a paraphrased extract from a talk I made to a visiting group in June. In one form or another, I have said this sort of thing over and over again to scores of people before and since. Not only are we in this struggle up to our necks—we are in it everywhere![3]

With warm personal regard and the best of wishes. *Sincerely*

[1] For background on Howard, editor and president of the *New York World-Telegraph and The Sun* and president of the Scripps-Howard Newspapers, see Galambos, *Columbia University*, nos. 646 and 1052.
[2] Howard, who was still traveling in Europe when Eisenhower dictated this letter, had seen the General at SHAPE on August 8 and must have visited him again while Eisenhower was in Germany later in the month (see no. 314, n. 6; and Howard to Eisenhower, July 9, 1951, Poster to Eisenhower, Aug. 30, 1951, and Howard to Eisenhower, Sept. 5, 1951, all in EM, same file as document).
[3] Enclosed with this letter was a two-page synopsis (EM) of remarks Eisenhower had made to a visiting congressional delegation on June 18. The brief warned of the repercussions of Communist actions in Korea and Indochina and the need for Western defense and industrial mobilization efforts. On the congressional visit and Eisenhower's talk see nos. 209, n. 2, 218, n. 14, and 256, n. 2.

335   *Eisenhower Mss.*

To Conrad Nicholson Hilton   *August 25, 1951*

Dear Mr. Hilton:[1] Thank you very much for your note and its enclosure. For some years, different organizations, societies, or individuals have seemed to find some interest in digging out that same page of my old Yearbook at West Point in an effort to quote it as an authority on my genealogical background. As you say, it is merely amusing—but one frequently wonders where the money comes from to pay for such trashy and obviously false purposes.[2]

With best wishes, *Cordially*

---

[1] For background on hotel executive Hilton see no. 176, n. 3.

[2] Hilton had sent the General (Aug. 15, 1951, EM) an anti-Semitic, anti-Eisenhower broadside with a heading that read "Ike Eisenhower (Swedish Jew)." The leaflet reproduced Eisenhower's picture from the 1915 *Howitzer*, the West Point yearbook, which had referred to him as "the terrible Swedish-Jew, as big as life and twice as natural." For background on the photostats and on the General's explanation of the *Howitzer* appellation see Galambos, *Columbia University*, no. 1084.

336   *Eisenhower Mss.*

To JOSEPH LAWTON COLLINS   *August 27, 1951*
Secret

Dear Joe: Today I received the letter that you dispatched from Ottawa.[1] I thank you very much for it and, of course, am delighted to have this explanation of the Tom Handy situation concerning which I wrote to you several days ago. I now thoroughly understand, also, the seeming oversight that had allowed me to remain in official ignorance of the important subject. If my letter expressed any impatience on this point, I hope that you likewise will understand and forget.

Your letter confirms a thing that Tom Handy gave me as fact about which, frankly, I thought he was mistaken. It is that Major Generals, in spite of temporary promotion to 3 or 4-star rank, are still subject to retirement after five years of service in grade, or, upon reaching the age of 60, whichever is later.[2] I feel that, unless this was deliberately written into the law by Congress and over G–1 objections, I should look up the stupid subordinate that was responsible for it and shoot him. What was actually intended was that promotion to 3 or 4-star grade would remove any compulsion for retirement—it was even my original intention to keep these very senior officers until 64.

In any event, my former letter to you lays out the reasons for my concern in this particular case. If the situation is as I believe it to be— that is, that General Juin's readiness to set up an Army group echelon with Handy in command is dictated by his confidence in a personality and by Handy's very high rank, then I think it would be unwise to plan on Handy's retirement before this whole thing can be carefully worked out.[3] On the other hand, it would be, of course, entirely unnecessary to insist on Tom's staying another two years; I am merely talking about this uncertain period in which we must get the whole series of command, deployment, and logistic problems straightened out, and in which are involved a thousand factors—some of which are factors of no greater significance than merely seniority of an individual.

Since I feel certain that the time factor in the solution of this particular problem is not too important, I think it can well await your arrival here on your way to Yugoslavia.[4] At that time, we should be able to get the whole thing worked out satisfactorily.

As I told you in a former letter, I am most heartily in favor of your trip to Yugoslavia.

With warm personal regard and the hope that you had a wonderful time in Alaska, *Cordially*

[1] U.S. Army Chief of Staff Collins had written on August 21 (EM) while flying to Ottawa on the first leg of a trip that would take him to Alaska. In this letter, which crossed Eisenhower's of August 22 (no. 321), Collins explained his embarrassment in finding that Handy "was so close to retirement," particularly because Collins "had not mentioned the subject to Tom himself when visiting him in Germany." Collins had reiterated the terms of the Officer Personnel Act as he understood them (see no. 321) and reminded Eisenhower that when he was Chief of Staff (1946–48), he had set a precedent of not employing a provision that allowed retention of a few officers to age sixty-four. "The Secretary and I carefully weighed the pros and cons as to whether or not we should hold on to Tom Handy to age 62. However, despite Tom's great abilities, present mental and physical vigor and his knowledge of the situation in Europe, we felt it inadvisable to vary from the sound policy which you had established." Collins suggested either Lieutenant General Manton S. Eddy or General Mark Clark as a replacement for Handy.
[2] For the terms of the act see no. 321, n. 3.
[3] Later, on September 8, Collins would write again after receiving Eisenhower's August 22 message. "If it appears that Juin's complicated command setup can be solved best by the retention of Handy as an Army Group Commander," Collins wrote, "I would certainly support a recommendation to the Secretary of the Army that an exception to the law be made in Tom's case." Handy would assume that command the following May (see no. 585, n. 3).
[4] For background on Collins's trip to Yugoslavia see no. 332. Collins would explain in his letter of September 8 that the Yugoslavs had shown "increased interest in my visiting their country and have been putting on a little pressure to have me go some time this month." Collins did not expect to leave until early October, however, by which time he would have learned more about the force levels the President would recommend in the fiscal year 1953 budget. For additional background on Marshal Tito's appeal for U.S. military assistance see no. 142, n. 16; for developments see no. 378. Eisenhower eventually would oppose Yugoslavia's entry into NATO (see no. 865).

To Virginia Morris Pollak   *August 27, 1951*

Dear Mrs. Pollak: Of course I remember the Baker Field incident, mentioned in your letter of the 9th. By the same token, it did not occur to me then that my chance remark about the bust would have any after effects.[1]

My own impression is that the bust was made at the instigation of a former staff officer of mine, General Edwin Clark of Westport, Connecticut. It is also my impression that he made the arrangements with the idea of presenting the completed item to West Point. Your letter gives me my first information that this has not been done.[2]

So far as I am concerned, I have no objection whatsoever to the bust going to West Point, subject to the following two provisos:

a. That General Clark be consulted and his approval obtained. This condition is because of my original understanding in the matter.

b. That the Superintendent or other appropriate officials at West Point desire to have the bust placed there.

In the event that you wish to pursue the matter under these conditions, General Clark's full address is as follows:

General Edwin N. Clark
32 East 57th Street
New York, New York

Quite naturally, I am highly complimented that you and Mr. Sands should interest yourselves in this project. My attitude with respect to any replicas is that, again, I have no objection provided General Clark agrees and that there can never arise any commercial aspects to the affair.[3]

With best wishes and personal regard, *Very sincerely*
P.S. Won't you please convey my greetings to Mr. Pollak.[4]

[1] Pollak, a New York City sculptor and art teacher, had written (EM) concerning a bust of Eisenhower by artist Jo Davidson. Recalling a meeting with the General at Columbia University's Baker Field (see Galambos, *Columbia University*, no. 714), during which they had discussed the likeness, Pollak informed Eisenhower of arrangements she had recently made to have the work purchased for donation to the West Point museum (see n. 3 below).

[2] A year earlier Clark (see no. 1) had attempted to purchase the two original castings of the Davidson bust, which was created from life during Eisenhower's term as Army Chief of Staff, but had found the cost too high (see memorandum, Schulz to Eisenhower, Feb. 20, 1950, in EM, Subject File, Busts).

[3] Pollak had explained that George E. Sands, director of the import firm of Hammel, Riglander & Company, Inc., had recently seen a replica of the Davidson sculpture at her home and had offered to purchase it for donation to the Military Academy. A "great admirer" of Eisenhower, Sands also wished to have reproductions of the work created "because of the inspiration he receives from [it]." Through

Clark, Sands would eventually purchase both original busts. One was donated to the West Point museum on May 29, 1953; the other was later given to the Royal Military Academy at Sandhurst, England (see Clark to Eisenhower, May 21, 1952, and Eisenhower to Clark, May 26, 1952, both in EM; and *New York Times*, May 30, 1953). There is nothing in EM to indicate that reproductions were produced.

[4] The artist's husband, Leo Lawrence Pollak (E.E. Columbia 1905).

338 *Eisenhower Mss.*

To Paul Gray Hoffman *August 28, 1951*
Personal

Dear Paul:[1] Thank you for your very interesting letter. I was particularly intrigued by your reactions to Nehru and your opinion of his qualifications and attitudes. I think that my own opinions coincide rather closely with yours, although it is extremely difficult for me to understand anyone that suspects the Western Powers have an aggressive or war-like motive. Because the processes of democracy are so open and aboveboard, because the whole world therefore knows about every move that we make, it is obviously impossible for us to mobilize the full strength of our nation or nations to make a surprise attack. Yet the true hope of success in a deliberately planned aggressive war lies in surprise.[2]

Of course, one might argue that our possession of the atomic bomb in numbers could give to us the opportunity of making such an attack. But I do not believe that any student of military history would claim that such an attack, even on an extensive scale, would necessarily bring a nation to its knees. Since in the case of Russia there would be a capacity on her part to react against our friends in Europe and in other spots where our interest would be rapidly jeopardized, it seems to me that expressed fears of our intentions are either the product of shallow thinking or are not completely sincere.[3]

I was delighted to read what you had to say about Liaquat Ali Khan and his wife.[4] I should very much like to visit them in their home country. My difficulty is that when I go to any new place there is apparently local feeling that I should be tendered a "reception." This always takes away the fun and particularly the intimacy of the visit. I have just about given up going to places other than those where I am simply a "repeater."

I am working very hard and, although I did steal a week's holiday in Germany, I do not foresee any similar opportunities for a long time to come. Consequently, when Mamie and I contemplate your invitation, it is with a feeling like that of the little kids outside the big plate glass window which is filled with candy. They can take a look and imagine how fine those chocolates would taste—that is all.[5]

Give our love to Dorothy[6] and, of course, warm regard to yourself. *Cordially*

P.S. When you see John Cowles or Paul Helms, or any of the other people on your Foundation that I have been privileged to meet, please remember me to them.[7] We were saddened the other day when Milton Katz and his family finally departed from our midst to go back to the United States.[8]

---

[1] For background on Ford Foundation president Hoffman see no. 139, n. 1.

[2] Hoffman had recently returned to the United States from a tour of India, Pakistan, and the Far East (see no. 268, n. 5; and *New York Times*, Aug. 10, 13, 18, 1951). Writing Eisenhower on August 23 (EM), he had described the situation in India as "confused and confusing." According to Hoffman, Indian Prime Minister Pandit Jawaharlal Nehru (see Galambos, *Columbia University*, nos. 512 and 779) was distrustful of the motives of the Western Powers and "genuinely concerned lest India once again become a subject nation due to the machinations of dollar diplomacy."

[3] On U.S. strategic planning for atomic warfare see *ibid.*, nos. 506, 575, 639, and 673.

[4] Writing of Pakistani Prime Minister Liaquat Ali Khan and his wife, Raana Begum Khan, Hoffman had told Eisenhower that they were true friends of the West and would soon make their nation "a strong, prosperous, modern democracy." Concerning the futures of both India and Pakistan, Hoffman had written that to remain free societies, they would have to experience "rapid development of a substantial property-owning middle class" through increased agricultural and industrial production. For developments see *New York Times*, October 25, November 2, 1951.

[5] Hoffman had expressed the hope that the Eisenhowers would be able to spend a few days with him "around the first of the year." On the Eisenhowers' German vacation see no. 314, n. 6.

[6] Hoffman's wife, the former Dorothy Brown.

[7] For background on Cowles and Helms, both of whom had traveled to the East with Hoffman, see nos. 308, n. 1, and 200, n. 1, respectively.

[8] Chairman of the NATO Defense Financial and Economic Committee and Special Representative of the ECA, Milton Katz (see no. 16, n. 7) had resigned his posts in June to join Hoffman as Associate Director of the Ford Foundation. He had departed Europe on July 23 (see *New York Times*, June 29, July 24, 1951).

339   *Eisenhower Mss.*

To Efisio Luigi Marras   *August 29, 1951*

Dear General Marras:[1] You will remember that, during the course of my visit to Northern Italy this spring, you brought to my attention the fact that there are Italian facilities available which might profitably be utilized in the manufacture of certain types of ammunition for your forces but that difficulties in obtaining designs and specifications from the United States were delaying initiation of manufacture of a number of these items.[2]

Following my return to Paris, I brought this matter to General Marshall's attention, and he has expedited the preparation of the necessary detailed papers.[3]

I am now happy to learn that specifications and other data covering some twenty-three types of ammunition and seven types of fuzes in which your Government has expressed an interest were forwarded to Rome last month, and I understand that similar information on a number of other ordnance items will be made available shortly.

I trust this action will assist in some measure in putting to work at least a portion of the facilities now lying idle which might contribute to our defense program. I regard it, however, as only a first step and will continue to give my support to all possible further efforts to increase the manufacture of badly needed military items of equipment throughout Europe.[4] *Sincerely*

[1] Lieutenant General Marras was Chairman of the Italian JCS and his country's representative to the NAC Military Committee (for background see no. 158).

[2] SHAPE staff member General Cortlandt van Rensselaer Schuyler (see no. 2) drafted this letter for Eisenhower. On Eisenhower's April inspection trip to Italy see nos. 153 and 158; on the manufacturing delays and difficulties that plagued NATO see nos. 167 and 174.

[3] See no. 156. There is no correspondence in EM with Secretary of Defense Marshall concerning this specific issue.

[4] In his reply (Sept. 7, 1951, EM) Marras thanked Eisenhower for his assistance and informed him that drawings and specifications for eleven types of ammunition and two types of fuses and detonators had been received. He also stated that he was hoping soon to receive similar information on forty-four types of arms and other ammunition to be produced in Italy.

340   *Eisenhower Mss.*

To Alfred Maximilian Gruenther[1]   *August 30, 1951*

Memorandum for Chief of Staff: Mr. Foley, Under Secretary of the Treasury, asked me several questions that I told him I would have looked up.[2] These are:

    a. Is the Red Cross doing for us everything that we think it should? This is probably a question for Tom Handy but, in any event, I would like to have an opinion on it.[3]

    b. While, in a war, the Coast Guard operates under the control of the Navy, it is required to do its own planning in time of peace.

The Coast Guard comes under Mr. Foley's supervision and he wants to know whether we ought to maintain liaison with it. For example, he suggested that we might want one of his officers in this headquarters.[4]

c. He has just inspected the hospital that has been started at Saint Lo through a combination of French and American donations. He states that this hospital was started on far too large a basis to be adapted to the local needs of the communities of that region. As a result, the thing was sort of abandoned in mid-stream, and now the Communists are using it as an example of the kind of thing that America does—start something with a big splash and hurrah, and then abandon it. He wonders whether some military need could not be satisfied by the utilization of this facility, possibly reserving a small section for private use at Saint Lo. He says that the American who knows most about it is Charley Dewey who lives at Longus, Sur la Mer.[5]

[1] On Gruenther see no. 230.

[2] Edward H. Foley, Jr. (LL.B. Fordham 1929), was Under Secretary of the United States Treasury and treasurer of the American National Red Cross. He had seen Eisenhower this same day.

[3] Gruenther would reply directly to Foley (Sept. 19, 1951, copy in EM, same file as document) that the Red Cross seemed to be "doing everything for SHAPE which could be expected from a national point of view." For suggestions of possible improvements, Gruenther referred Foley to General Thomas Handy (see no. 286), U.S. Commander in Chief, Europe, who supplied all logistical and administrative support to SHAPE.

[4] Since its establishment as a single branch of the American Armed Forces in 1915, the Coast Guard had operated in peacetime as a service of the Treasury Department. Gruenther told Foley on the nineteenth that the inclusion of a Coast Guard officer on the SHAPE staff had been discussed but that the number of American officers at the headquarters was already considered too high (see no. 230, n. 3). In the event of war, Gruenther assured Foley, "an appropriate number of US Coast Guard personnel . . . would bring to SHAPE part of the splendid tradition and background of the Coast Guard, and would . . . make a valuable contribution to the war effort."

[5] Gruenther would inform Foley that following an inspection of the St. Lô hospital, SHAPE staff officers had concluded that "it would be impracticable and uneconomical" to complete it "as a U.S. military facility." Charles Schuveldt Dewey (Ph.B. Yale 1904), who accompanied members of the SHAPE staff to the St. Lô site, had been Assistant Secretary of the Treasury from 1924 until 1927 and a Republican congressman from Illinois from 1941 to 1945. Dewey had recently been living in France at Longues-sur-Mer, Calvados (see memorandum, Schulz to Gruenther, Sept. 19, 1951; Memorandum for Record, Cannon to Eisenhower, Sept. 20, 1951; and Dewey to Eisenhower, Sept. 6, 1951, all in EM).

341   *Eisenhower Mss.*

To LUTHER GRAHAM McCONNELL   *August 30, 1951*

Dear Mr. McConnell: Thank you very much for sending me a copy of the official program of the 51st Amateur Championship.[1] You will note that my application for entry is missing from among the list you have; but you will understand that I am just a bit too busy to get in the practice this year that I really need in order to play in that kind of company. (Possibly a little bit of ability wouldn't be a bad thing either.)

Maybe sometime I could come down and, with the aid of a half-dozen strokes a side, give you a fair go—with stakes, a bottle of Coca Cola. *Cordially*

[1] McConnell (A.B. Columbia 1910) had written to Eisenhower on August 21 (EM) inviting him to participate in the fifty-first amateur championship of the United States Golf Association. The championship, held at the Saucon Valley Country Club, in McConnell's hometown of Bethlehem, Pennsylvania, would take place September 10–15 (see *New York Times*, Sept. 11, 12, 13, 14, 15, 16, 1951).

342   *Eisenhower Mss.*

To BERNARD MANNES BARUCH   *August 30, 1951*

Dear Bernie:[1] This morning I was visited by a Dr. William T. R. Fox who is going to head a new Institute at Columbia University called the "Institute of Peace and War." One of its great tasks will be to study the organizational requirements of a democracy at war—in other words, how does a democracy, featuring a system of free enterprise, so organize itself as to conduct a war effectively and so as to win it with the least cost in life and treasure?[2]

Since there is no greater living authority on this general subject than yourself, I have encouraged Dr. Fox to get in touch with you as he designs his course; I think it tragic that civilian institutions in our country have not long ago tackled this problem and, at least, put into one record the lessons to be derived from our experiences of the past. I know that you will be delighted, as I am, that we have at last got this kind of thing started at Columbia University.[3]

With warm personal regard, *Cordially*

[1] For background on Baruch see no. 25, n. 4.

[2] Work on establishing the Institute of War and Peace Studies, which Eisenhower had proposed during his active presidency of Columbia, continued in his absence (for background on the plan see Galambos, *Columbia University*). On the selection

of Fox as director of the research organization and on the goals and purpose of the institute see nos. 159, n. 4, and 31, n. 4, respectively.

[3] Baruch's extensive experience in economic and industrial mobilization dated back to World War I (see Coit, *Mr. Baruch*; and Robert D. Cuff, *The War Industries Board: Business-Government Relations during World War I* [Baltimore, 1973]). Baruch would reply (Sept. 4, 1951, EM) that he was "delighted" that Columbia had undertaken the type of study Eisenhower had described and that he would give Fox's request his prompt attention. For developments concerning the Institute of War and Peace Studies see no. 568.

343   *Eisenhower Mss.*

To HAMILTON FISH ARMSTRONG   *August 30, 1951*

Dear Ham:[1] I do not know whether I can send a staff officer along with Collins to Yugoslavia; but Collins is coming past here, and he and I are going to have a long conversation before he goes to Belgrade.[2] Anyway, thanks for your note. I quite agree with you that the talks must be based upon some common concept of Western European strategy that I cannot conceive of any military man omitting this from his "agenda."[3]

My warmest regards to my old friends in the "Council"—and, of course, special good wishes to yourself.[4] *Cordially*

[1] For background on Armstrong see no. 150, n. 3; and n. 4 below.

[2] In a letter of August 24 (EM) Armstrong had urged Eisenhower to assign a SHAPE staff officer to accompany Army Chief of Staff Collins on his proposed trip to Yugoslavia (see no. 332, n. 2). Armstrong thought that discussions concerning military aid to the Communist nation should be broadened to include a possible joint strategy; he assured the General that the impact "on the military relations between our two countries [of a SHAPE officer's visit] would be so good as to more than justify his expenditure of time and effort in flying out to Belgrade." During early October Collins would spend three days at SHAPE before departing on his month-long inspection tour. He apparently would not be accompanied by any of Eisenhower's staff (*New York Times*, Oct. 15, Nov. 2, 1951).

[3] On Collins's tour see no. 378, n. 3.

[4] Armstrong was editor of *Foreign Affairs*, the journal of the Council on Foreign Affairs. On Eisenhower's participation on the council see, for example, Galambos, *Columbia University*, no. 700.

To WILLOW SHARP   *August 31, 1951*

Dear Miss Sharp: It comes as something of a shock to me to realize that
you are going to leave Columbia; nevertheless, your reasons make
complete sense to me. I know of nothing more frustrating in life than
to be putting in time at any job that seems to demand less than the
occupant can give to it. Because of your competence as a secretary, it
never occurred to me that you would be used at less than your full
capacity—really good secretaries are always difficult to obtain.[1]

While my memory is not too clear as to the details of happenings
during my last hectic period in Columbia, I seem to recall that I gave
to you a general letter of a "To Whom It May Concern" type. It just
occurs to me that, in the event you apply to some firm for a position,
you might like for me to send to it a specific letter of recommendation.
Should this be the case, you have only to let me know—I would
consider it a very pleasant chore to meet such a request.

This letter brings from Mrs. Eisenhower and me our very best
wishes for your future, particularly the hope that whatever position
you secure will bring you both professional and personal satisfaction.[2]

As you know, Mr. McCann has left here and is now serving as
President of Defiance College. Miss Boyce has been with us for some
time, and Miss Nelson has recently joined our staff. Colonel Schulz,
Sergeant Dry, and Sergeant Moaney are all with me, operating with
their usual efficiency and cheerfulness.[3]

With very best wishes, *Sincerely*

[1] Sharp had written to Eisenhower on August 27 (EM) saying that she would soon
leave her position in Columbia's Office of the Vice-President and Provost because
she "felt like a 'fifth wheel.'" Sharp told the General that she would be pleased to
be of assistance to him when he resumed his duties as president of the University,
but "the indefiniteness of that time and the continued ennui of the present situation" made it impossible for her to remain in a job that was not challenging.

[2] On November 28 (EM) Sharp would inform Eisenhower that she had taken a
position as "relief secretary" with RCA and hoped soon to receive a regular
secretarial assignment. She had used both of the General's letters of recommendation (no copies in EM) in securing the post.

[3] For background on both Kevin C. McCann and Marguerite G. Nelson see no.
347. Former Columbia secretary Alice Boyce would continue to work for Eisenhower through both of his terms as President of the United States (see Eisenhower's
memoir *At Ease*, p. 346). On Robert L. Schulz and Leonard D. Dry see nos. 1 and
38, respectively. John Alton Moaney, Eisenhower's personal valet, had been a
member of the General's household staff for several years (see *Eisenhower Papers*,
vols. I–XI).

To Bert Andrews   *August 31, 1951*
Personal and confidential

Dear Bert:[1] Of course, I realize that your recent cable to me was inspired by the friendliest of motives. The news contained in it as to the double-barrelled purpose in Oregon is more than a bit astonishing; yet I fail to see why the mistakes of others should induce me to make a serious error of my own.[2]

I try to be reasonably free of the sin of taking myself too seriously; even though I thoroughly believe one should always take his *job* seriously. The job currently given to me is that of helping to develop collective security by cooperation among the western nations. This I consider to be of the utmost importance to America's future, a conviction that obviously is in accord with the interest of the United States Congress. The understanding and support of the American people, as a whole, are essential to success in this vast undertaking.

Now—for me to admit a partisan political loyalty, while I am on this job would, I believe, be properly resented by thinking Americans, because it would be the *job* that would suffer. If the two groups of which you speak in your cable honestly believe in the need for collective security through cooperation among the free nations (and they must believe something of this kind if they feel that I could represent their political convictions) it would seem to me that they would not desire at this time to damage my ability to serve here objectively and earnestly as an "American"—not as a partisan.

Possibly my thinking (if such it can be called) is all twisted; possibly my conclusions are the product of a personal desire to seek a quiet and peaceful life with my family—but to me the logic of the present situation (from the standpoint of America's present effort to develop security) points inexorably to the need of my maintaining silence so long as I continue to serve on this mission.[3]

With warm personal regard,[4]

---

[1] Andrews had been chief Washington correspondent of the *New York Herald Tribune* since 1941 (see Galambos, *Columbia University*, no. 87).

[2] In a cable of August 27, which arrived while Eisenhower was on a one-day inspection trip to Denmark, Andrews had informed the General that his name would be filed by both Republicans and Democrats in the Oregon presidential primary. In light of this development, Andrews said: "In all friendship think it time for you to say whether you are Republican or Democrat and whether you will run if nominated . . ." (see Andrews to Eisenhower, PSW 734, Aug. 27, 1951; and memorandum, Burnham to Eisenhower, Aug. 28, 1951, both in EM, same file as document). On the dual party movements to enter Eisenhower's name in the Oregon primary, the first to be held in 1952, see *New York Times*, August 12, 14, 28, 1951; and nos. 135 and 358.

[3] On the General's development of a standardized reply to such inquiries see no. 358, n. 3.

[4] On Democratic support in other states for an Eisenhower candidacy see nos. 313 and 753. For developments in Oregon see no. 358.

346

Eisenhower Mss.

To Grayson Louis Kirk

August 31, 1951

Dear Grayson:[1] Thank you for your note. I have seen none of the unfortunate publicity to which you refer. I believe that, if you and the Trustees should decide to terminate the present arrangement with Poland, you should make clear that Poland's recent action in closing the American cultural center has so strongly conveyed the implication that they regard such posts as propaganda mills that you do not feel Columbia can continue, even though you have had no evidence of any kind of an attempt to use the Columbia chair in this manner.[2]

I believe that, in the beginning, there was some hope that, through the establishment of this chair, great encouragement would be given to the dissidents in Poland—that the effort to keep alive respect for her traditional culture (including her frequently proved love of an independent existence)—would help to create trouble for the Communists in that region. The actual case has been that Poland has seemed progressively to come more and more under the heel of Russia. She has seemed to descend from the position of vassal state to practically an integrated part of the Russian complex. In any event—and no matter what the decision of the Trustees—it is one of those things that must be constantly watched.[3]

With warm regard. Please remember me to my friends around the campus. *Cordially*

[1] On Kirk see no. 325, n. 1.

[2] In his letter (Aug. 28, 1951, EM) Kirk had said that the action of the Polish government in closing the U.S. Information Office in Warsaw had forced Columbia to reexamine its policy concerning the Adam Mickiewicz Chair of Polish Studies (see no. 316, n. 3). Kirk said that Columbia had received an unusual amount of publicity since the Polish action because the chair was supported by an annual grant of $10,000 from Poland's Communist government; he wondered whether this financial arrangement should not now be terminated.

[3] At the close of 1953–54, when official Polish support for the chair ended, Columbia University would allow the position to lapse (see Ernest J. Simmons, "The Department of Slavic Languages," in *A History of the Faculty of Philosophy, Columbia University*, ed. Dwight C. Miner [New York, 1957], pp. 239–40).

To KEVIN COYLE MCCANN

Dear Kevin:[1] I still find myself—with undiminished frequency—automatically sending to you a request to come to my desk for a discussion of some abstruse or difficult subject. Each time I do so and have to face again the realization that you are not so handy any more, I form a tentative resolution to write you a letter. I don't need to tell you what always happens to the resolution.

Your preoccupations are of exactly the character, I think, that you had anticipated.[2] While you listed the subject of money as sort of a residual or merely auxiliary worry, I am quite sure that it is not only your principal one, but also one that will never be completely eliminated. Incidentally, I hope your new football coach turns out to be one that exactly fills your requirements—completely adequate to all your local needs, but not quite so good that some big college succeeds in taking him away from you before he is well settled in his new post. Since he is an ex-member of the 101st Airborne, please give him my very warm regards and wish him every success at Defiance College.

Little would be served by any attempt of mine to give you a list of current difficulties and problems in SHAPE. They are much of the same character as they have always been, with those involving me personally, constantly growing more pressing and insistent.[3]

A short time ago Miss Nelson, who was with us in Columbia, joined our staff. I did not know she was coming, so I was greatly surprised to see her one morning in the office. A day or so ago, I had a letter from Miss Sharp, who tells me that she is planning on leaving Columbia also.[4] However, I have always understood that she had no desire to come to Europe.

Mamie and I are in our new house at last. We have been there a week, and while we have had the usual irritations incident to moving into a brand new place, things have gone fairly well.[5]

All of us, of course, miss you and Ruth[6] very much. Your letter failed to give a list of her principal worries and problems these days, but I warrant that she is on the ball and meeting them with her usual efficiency and cheerfulness.

Your old friends here join me in warm greetings to you both. *As ever*

---

[1] McCann, Eisenhower's assistant at Columbia University and at SHAPE, had left Paris in June to assume the presidency of Defiance College in Defiance, Ohio (see *New York Times*, Apr. 8, 1951; on McCann see nos. 53 and 371).

[2] On August 25 (EM) McCann had written about the need for renovations at Defiance and his recent replacement of the football and basketball coach.

[3] On some of the General's difficulties with SHAPE see no. 304.

[4] Marguerite G. Nelson had worked in the General's office since August 1948.

Willow Sharp would find a new position in New York City in November (see no. 344).

[5] On the Eisenhowers' new home see no. 314, n. 1.

[6] Mrs. McCann, the former Ruth C. Potter.

348   *Eisenhower Mss.*

To Thomas Donald Campbell   *September 1, 1951*

Dear Tom:[01] It was indeed nice to have your letter and, of course, as always, I was interested in news about crops and farm prospects. I never lose an instinctive feeling for the land and for the things that grow in it.[2]

I was quite astonished to learn that the New Mexican land, which only five years ago was selling for $2.50 an acre, is now in the $10.00 and $12.00 bracket. I must say that, in view of the drought you are having, prices of that kind seem almost ridiculous.[3] It comes as much, I guess, from the cheapening of our money as from the other conditions you mention. When we stop to think of what we have done in our country with controls and subsidies, and just general tinkering with our money and all our economic processes, I sometimes wonder whether all of it has been necessary and whether the effects have been universally good. However, when I get to thinking along these lines, I get so entangled that I finally have to conclude that I had better just take things as I find them now, and not worry too much as to how we got here.

The international situation does not seem to improve so far as any effect we seem to be able to make on the Russian attitude.[4] Sometimes it would almost appear that they deliberately seek open conflict. On the other hand, I believe there is encouragement in what seems to be the increasing understanding of our own people as to the requirements of the situation and in the growing confidence and better morale throughout most of the free world. It does seem rather tragic though, that young people now growing up will never know the carefree existence and joyous student days that we used to feel was not only the heritage, but the logical right of every young boy and girl. I think that oldsters like you and I have had a lot of fun in life and have been treated pretty well. We haven't much to kick about, no matter what happens to us. But with the younger ones, the case seems to be different and I rather believe that among other things, we should all strive to turn the running of the world over to them as quickly as possible. They have to live with the situation we have created—so they ought to be given a decisive voice in its running.

In spite of all this kind of talk, I remain, as you know, an incurable optimist. I still look forward to the day when, with clear conscience and complete ease of mind, I can spend three-fourths of my time on the bank of some shady stream.[5]

This letter brings, of course, as always, my warm personal regard. *Cordially*

[1] Campbell was head of the Campbell Farming Corporation, wheat growers, near Hardin, Montana, and owner of a large cattle ranch near Albuquerque, New Mexico (for background see Galambos, *Columbia University*, no. 808).
[2] In a letter of August 23 (EM) Campbell had said that wet weather and hail had partially ruined his promising Montana wheat crop.
[3] Campbell had commented that "the only people engaged in agriculture who are complaining now are the stockmen, and they are getting 152 per cent of parity." Land values had increased accordingly, he reported, even though New Mexico was experiencing its worst drought in forty years.
[4] Campbell was convinced, he said, that "we will never have world peace until we have *a United Nations strong enough to remove the gangsters in Moscow who are determined to dominate the world* and who know that the only obstacle to such domination now is the good old United States."
[5] Eisenhower's reference to fishing side-stepped the following passage in Campbell's letter: "Your popularity continues to increase every day, and I am more convinced than ever that you will be the next President of the United States if you will accept the nomination. I hear this wish expressed everywhere I go, whether it be on the farm or ranch, in the oil fields, in the big cities or at the lunch counters in small towns. It now looks as if it were just as much your responsibility to accept the nomination as it was to assume your present assignment."

349   *Eisenhower Mss.*

To Marcellus Hartley Dodge   *September 1, 1951*

Dear Marcy:[01] I just had a telephone call from my house, where I am told there has arrived a box of shotgun shells from you. I am truly grateful, because I have been asked several times to drop in at a nearby farm for a bit of shooting, but I have not wanted to go because I did not have the equipment. The next time I am asked I will go out for an hour or two.

This note, of course, brings you my very best wishes. I frequently long to be back again at Morningside Heights with you and other fine friends I was privileged to work with on things that intrigued me mightily. Certainly, they were at least more constructive in their basic purpose than is the production of an army, or a navy, or an air force. But each of us must do what he is given to do—there is no use of complaining.[2]

My best to all my friends on the Hill. *Cordially*

[1] Dodge was a member and clerk of the Columbia University board of trustees (see no. 6, n. 1).
[2] For Eisenhower's special interests as president of Columbia University see Galambos, *Columbia University*; and Eisenhower, *At Ease*, pp. 345–51. Dodge's reply of September 7 is in EM.

350

Eisenhower Mss.

To WALTER KIRSCHNER

September 3, 1951

Dear Walter:[1] Your latest letter brings the news that perhaps, after all, the Gettysburg house can be satisfactorily remodeled. This, of course, pleases Mamie very much, as she has developed quite an affection for the particular spot on which that house stands.[2]

At the same time I find that you are proceeding with the idea of estimating a bit on a U-shaped house at another location. I hope that your engineer will not go to the expense and trouble of making detailed plans, but will content himself merely with an idea and a rough approximation of cost. (Perhaps you think I too often emphasize this question of cost, but you must remember that I am back on an Army officer's pay scale).[3]

In any event, we are gradually accumulating a number of farm problems to talk about so that when you, George and I again meet there will be no lack of conversational topics.[4]

Mamie joins me in affectionate regards to you both. *Sincerely*

[1] For background on Kirschner, a businessman and friend of Eisenhower's who was helping him make improvements on the Gettysburg farm, see no. 33, n. 2.
[2] In a letter of August 15 (EM) Kirschner had told Eisenhower that "the house can be remodeled with a lot of effort and expense." On August 27 (EM) Kirschner had written again, enclosing a letter from the engineer, Harry E. Holton, and plans for the additions (on Holton see no. 315, n. 2; the plans are not in EM). Holton had told Kirschner in a letter of August 25 (EM) that their original idea of expanding the house on ground level was not as practical as a "two story addition for the new three bedrooms and baths; and also a second bathroom upstairs and a trophy room." Plans for a den and kitchen addition increased the total new area to twenty-one hundred square feet. Holton further suggested the addition of wood siding, because it was less expensive than brick and would contrast well with the existing brick walls.
[3] Kirschner had said in his August 27 letter that he would select a plot for the "new Colonial home in a U shape." "After completing plans," Kirschner added, "we will . . . decide together on our future plan" (for background see no. 315; for developments see no. 512). On the General's salary see no. 35, n. 4.
[4] George E. Allen, an old friend of the General's (see no. 9, n. 2), would not visit him in Paris until February 1952.

To LEONARD V. FINDER

Dear Mr. Finder:[1] My thanks for your continued interest in sending me such informative letters. I read, with interest, your latest comments on the American scene.[2]

It appears to me that so long as I occupy this present position, which for the good of our country and the world requires the cooperation and support of all, I would be doing a disservice if any action of mine introduced the spirit of partisanship. Therefore, I have consistently refrained from making any comment on current political questions, and think it is the only proper policy for me to pursue.[3]

While I appreciate your kind offer of making a trip to Europe, there is so little to be added to my sincere feelings expressed above, that such a trip would be an unwarranted infringement upon your time.[4]

Of course, I hope that you completely understand my present position. *Sincerely*

[1] For background on Finder, who had recently become vice-president of the Universal Match Corporation of Saint Louis, Missouri, see Galambos, *Columbia University*, no. 7.

[2] Finder had written Eisenhower on August 25 (EM) concerning the current political situation in the United States. "So far," he had said, "there is nothing for the people to get excited about . . . they can scarcely be happy over the possibility of having to choose between Mr. Truman and Senator Taft. Ultimate victory by either would be a major calamity." Finder urged Eisenhower to "save America from so unhappy a choice" by declaring himself a presidential candidate soon.

[3] A more formal variation on this paragraph would become a set piece in Eisenhower's correspondence as pressure mounted for him to enter the political arena (see no. 358).

[4] Finder had proposed that he fly to France to "contribute toward clarifying the situation."

To JAMES ALOYSIUS FARLEY

Dear Jim:[1] I have just read your two talks, "Leadership" and "Reaching the Hearts and Minds of Men." I compliment you on them both; rarely have I read such down-to-earth, sensible and valuable discussions on one of the most important topics of our time.[2]

Finding myself in complete agreement with almost everything you say, I do want to take the opportunity of questioning one short sentence—"It is much more than mere tact." At this point you are talking about good manners, and I fairly chortled with glee to find you attaching so much importance to this item of leadership. You have done me and my staff a favor, because now I will have less occasion to bore them with my own wordy discussions on the subject and they can read your entertaining exposition instead of giving me the time that I would otherwise require. In spite of all this, your sentence, to my mind, belittles the importance of "tact" when that word is used in its true sense. Tact involves judgment and a nice sense of values, as well as a knowledge of most of the things you have put in your two little talks. Actually, I suspect we are, under different words, talking about the same thing.[3]

Again, my congratulations; and, of course, best wishes and warm regard. *Cordially*

[1] Farley, former Postmaster General of the United States, was chairman of the board of the Coca-Cola Export Corporation (see *Eisenhower Papers*, vols. I–XI).

[2] Farley's speech entitled "Reaching the Hearts and Minds of Men: The Path to Success" had been delivered at the Ithaca College Mid-Century Convocation, Ithaca, New York, on May 12, 1951 (*Vital Speeches of the Day* 17, no. 18 [July 1, 1951], 566–68). We have been unable to locate a copy of Farley's "Leadership" speech.

[3] Farley had said, "Now good manners is something more than knowing how to hold your soup spoon or how to dress when you go to a church wedding. It is much more than a capacity to say the pleasant but insincere thing. It is much more than mere tact. It is to feel and, above all, to show that you have a genuine concern in others. It means caring for people, respecting them, treating them as equals and sharing their fears and earthly concerns and their ideals" (*ibid.*, p. 567). Farley would thank Eisenhower for this letter in a reply of September 21 (EM). "And regarding 'tact,' " he said, "one of the subjects of our next conversation has already been selected. I agree, that we are probably talking about the same thing with different words."

353

To Edward Everett Hazlett, Jr.   *September 4, 1951*

Dear Swede:[1] It has been a long time since I last read one of the letters you receive periodically from "Whick."[2] Yet that interval is not so long that I fail to recall at once the primary emotion his writing always inspires in me—a feeling that here is one man who is able to put down in print a clear expression of the thoughts that flow through his brain as he contemplates the beauty of a sylvan scene, the capabilities of man for sacrifice, and the exceedingly disappointing result we seem always to get when we find men attempting to act as a group in the solution of common political and social problems. He finds ways and means of describing, with cameo-like sharpness, his disappointment that men respond far more easily to a selfish impulse than to a noble one; he is so convincing in this regard that his reader (this one at least) comes to feel that the conclusion as to relativity—wheat to chaff—is a gross overstatement.

Of course, I am intrigued by his explanation of his reasons for painting.[3] You may or may not know that I indulge in the same habit. But in my case there is no faintest semblance of talent, and certainly I paint for far less complicated or worthy reasons than does Mr. Whicker. Some years ago I found that I had to limit my hours devoted to serious and steady reading; my life is given over to such incessant contemplation of heavy and weighty problems—most of them made more difficult by the circumstance that they have no final and complete answer—that some kind of release or relief became necessary in order to keep me up to the bit and operating at reasonable efficiency during the hours when I deal in the affairs for which I bear some responsibility. So I took up painting. I did it without a lesson and I have persisted in it for more than three years with no more constructive help from the outside than an occasional piece of casual criticism from one of my artist friends. For me the real benefit is the fact that it gives me an excuse to be absolutely alone and interferes not at all with what I am pleased to call my "contemplative powers." In other words, I paint for fun, for recreation, for enjoyment. When the work is woefully bad, so that even I recognize its stupidity or banality, I merely turn it upside down and start again. After I do this often enough I burn that particular canvas. But once in awhile one comes out so that it is definitely better than I know how to do! That one I keep. Such a one may be a portrait, a picture of a tree, or merely a colored sketch of a couple of flowers. The point is that one with no talent, no ability to draw and no time to waste can get a lot of fun out of daubing with oils. Most of mine is done between the hours of 11 and 12 at night, but when the effort I am making seems worthwhile pursuing in daylight, then I have a fine early Sunday morning pastime.

All this to tell you how much I really envy your friend's ability to paint in a way that pleases himself and the time to do it.

I like his facility of expression—even his flow of words. His style reflects not only an appreciation of niceties and of nuances, but his unhurried and even wordy way of reaching his conclusions adds confidence, because it implies that he had time to think the matter through carefully. I am tempted to believe he is right in the suggestion that to attain sheer personal happiness one ought, through some judgment accepted by all, be relegated, inexorably, to a life in a woodland cottage.[4]

As to his conclusions about the American scene, I most thoroughly concur in his condemnation of public violators of the principles of decency and honor. Now, none of us is so strong that he is spared the painful embarrassment of looking back upon moments of weakness; none is so wise that he cannot recall times when his own ignorance bordered upon the stupid, even the moronic. Nevertheless, high standards must be upheld—he helps to do so! He beautifully expresses his respect for courage, integrity and honest effort.[5]

Some day I should like to spend a week with him, just sitting in his backyard and possibly talking about nothing more removed than the trees and the mountains that he loves so well.

My love to Ibby[6] and your nice family and, as always, my very best to you. *Cordially*

P.S. I see that you wrote your letter in longhand. Did the blankety-blank typewriter play out? The reason I ask is a bit more than mere concern for your convenience; I was told that the particular typewriter we got was the sturdiest and best in its field. If it wasn't, I would like to write a sarcastic letter to the producing firm.[7]

[1] On Hazlett, a boyhood friend of Eisenhower's, see no. 233, n. 1.

[2] Hazlett had written on August 22 (EM) and had enclosed a letter from his friend Harold W. Whicker (see the following document). Describing Whicker as a "he-man–ex-professional wrestler, English prof, outstanding painter and essayist, outdoorsman," Hazlett had said that he was also one of the few men he knew capable of "really deep thought and of putting his conclusions in words."

In his letter of July 29 (EM) Whicker had told Hazlett that he could not "subscribe to the sentimental notion that all persons have in them more good than bad. . . . Nature rigidly maintains her normal proportions in the relativity of wheat to chaff."

[3] Whicker said that in his painting he gave himself over "to the blessed mystery of the human hand, which is . . . an outer tendril of the human heart; and what I paint is my love of American earth and sea and sky" (on Eisenhower's interest in painting see no. 102, n. 4).

[4] Whicker had boasted that while his taxes on the cabin and property the previous year had been only $3.75 and his monthly grocery bill, "thanks to neighboring," was usually under $40.00, "day by day, I eat better and I live better than does the King of England, and damned if, since I'm an American, I am not more of an emperor."

[5] Whicker had written that "there is a vein of integrity in American life . . . presently overgrown with brambles, tares, moss, and fungus. These must be removed by the will and marching spirit of free men and women." "So long as we are Americans," Whicker concluded, "we can do anything that should be done."

[6] Hazlett's wife Elizabeth.

[7] For background on Hazlett's typewriter, a gift from Eisenhower, see Galambos, *Columbia University*, nos. 734 and 981; for developments see no. 490, n. 2, in this volume.

To Harold Wave Whicker   *September 4, 1951*

Dear Mr. Whicker:[1] Swede Hazlett gave me the privilege of reading your latest letter to him. You have a faculty of leading a person into many unaccustomed channels of thought and contemplation; the contemplation of standards in beauty, in human behavior and conduct, and in human purposes. I find particular delight in reading your paragraphs on painting. While I am myself a dauber in oils, my own purpose is nothing deeper than sheer enjoyment of the moment. I find it far more intriguing than working a cross-word puzzle and even though the result is nine times out of ten consigned to destruction, the occasional one that I keep represents some kind of personal triumph. I suppose this is because I never had a lesson in art, and I just barely scraped through my West Point course in mechanical drawing.[2]

Along with my appreciation of your approach to painting, I feel an even greater interest in your observations about the current American scene. I envy you your opportunities to think, and certainly I envy you your ability to express yourself.[3]

So I hope you won't mind knowing that Swede gave me a chance to read your intriguing letter.

With very best wishes, *Sincerely*

[1] Whicker, who lived on Guemes Island, Anacortes, Washington, was a writer, artist, and outdoorsman (see Galambos, *Chief of Staff*, no. 2002).

[2] Edward E. Hazlett had written to Eisenhower on August 22 (EM) and had included a recent letter he had received from Whicker (see the preceding document). In Whicker's letter of July 29 (EM) he had described his pleasure in painting, saying that the twenty-two oil paintings he had finished that year were the best he had ever done. The artistic quality of his works was not important, Whicker wrote, because "only God can paint a picture. The best any lesser artist can hope to accomplish is the enjoyment of what God paints."

[3] A recurring theme in Whicker's typewritten fourteen-page letter was his conviction that only Eisenhower could rescue America from the "political sewers" and restore national integrity and the democratic spirit. On September 28 (EM) Whicker would thank Eisenhower for this letter.

To George Whitney   *September 4, 1951*

Dear George: I found your letter of the 27th so completely intriguing that I called in my good friend Cliff Roberts (of the Reynolds Banking House) to consider it with me. In fact, I have taken the liberty of asking a few members of my staff to read it.[1]

So far as my own feeling about these matters is based upon study and thinking, I am ready to announce my complete concurrence with all that you have to say, except for a nagging feeling that you have not fully treated the question of the effect upon our economy of unusual governmental requirements.[2]

What we are really saying is that we have a greater fundamental faith in the workings of the law of supply and demand than we do in man-made edicts, which usually represent, in unbalanced fashion, the needs and the influences of different groupments, classes, or sections of a country. Certainly, no one could quarrel with such a generalization. Yet the problem remaining in my own mind could be stated somewhat as follows:

> Man's experience with the law of supply and demand began with very simple beginnings, and the results of the operation of that law made themselves apparent through the years under conditions that tended to balance man's desires and capacity for consumption against his capacity to produce. Prices reflected not only desire and the need to consume, but also the availability of items. Now, jumping a lot of obvious steps in a chain of reasoning, we come to a situation where a political authority, the Government, places upon the economy an extraordinary demand—it is extraordinary in the sense that it does not represent a requirement on the part of the individual at all. Moreover, the thing produced does nothing to satisfy any individual desire or need. Here is where I begin to experience bewilderment in attempting to understand how the law of supply and demand can control the whole matter *in time to avoid disaster.*

> You see that I am not going back to raise any arguments about other types of interferences with the operation of the fundamental economic law—for example, I ignore tariffs which certainly, from a philosophical point of view, were historically the forerunner of more direct types of subsidies and guaranteed price floors. It is simply the one great question of how to handle items that require, let us say, a quantity of tin, which under the stimulus of emergency demand and scarce supply reaches the price of $500.00 a picul.[3]

Of course, I should send along with such a letter my abject apologies for asking you to continue to give me lectures in the field of economics. My excuse is my terrific concern for America, including her difficulties and problems that arise out of our own mismanagement. Your comments on these matters are vastly intriguing and, to me, informative. Anyway, I shall be looking forward to your next letter—even if it takes you a number of weeks to find the opportunity of writing.[4]

With affectionate regard to your nice family and, of course, as always, to yourself, *Cordially*

[1] Eisenhower had asked New York City banker Whitney to write to him about the current economic controls in the United States (see no. 306). In a handwritten notation on Whitney's reply (EM) Eisenhower requested "several copies—give one to Cliff R." (on Roberts, a partner in the New York City investment firm Reynolds & Company, see no. 7; on Whitney see no. 50).

Whitney told Eisenhower that he abhorred controls, "not merely because they are socialistic, but because they do not work." He traced the history of controls back to the Hoover Administration's interference with the laws of demand and supply during the Great Depression of the 1930s. The way to control inflation, Whitney said, was "through the use of credit and taxes . . . to tighten money and impose taxes when there is an inflationary tendency and to ease money and reduce taxes when there is a depressive tendency, even to the point of causing deficit financing." He did not believe that governmental budgets needed to be balanced, because balancing "increases the powers of depression whereas deficit financing . . . becomes a corrective."

Whitney thought that the United States could have "financed and handled World War II without the creation of myriads of governmental agencies." "This," he said, "brings us down to the situation today where we have partial and sporadic controls which are breaking down in various places, partly because our governmental and legislative authorities are not prepared to stick to restrictions which are sufficiently unpopular." Whitney said that he would "abolish all controls and face the chaos that might ensue." He was influenced, he explained, by his convictions that (1) there were no real shortages in war production materiel, (2) the country was on the verge of another "inflationary spiral," and (3) politicians have a natural aversion in a presidential year to any kind of "let-up" in business. Whitney judged the political discussions on the amended Defense Production Act for 1951–52 "unilluminating" because nothing had been said about the "basic theory of controls" (see no. 306, n. 2). "When you once accept Federal interference with private economy," he concluded, "the damage is pretty thoroughly done." In a penned notation at the end of his four-page typewritten letter Whitney had written, "This is too d——d long."

[2] To this Whitney would reply (Sept. 17, 1951, EM) that in times of national emergency there is bound to be interference with the laws of demand and supply. He reminded Eisenhower, however, that he had stated in his earlier letter of August 27 that "regulation and cooperation have been and still are . . . the way in which emergencies can be most successfully met by a democracy. . . ."

[3] A picul, a measured weight used in China and Southeast Asia, equals 100 catties, or 133–43 pounds.

[4] Whitney's next letter is no. 385.

To Milton Stover Eisenhower
Secret

September 4, 1951

Dear Milton: The receipt of your note enclosing your file of correspondence with Jack Lesser reminds me once again that political speculation concerning me causes difficulties for my brothers, especially for you. Mr. Lesser's arguments and conclusions are not greatly different from those I receive from many other people—I must say that he seems to be very earnest and sincere.[1]

There is, of course, very little use for me to bore you with any repetition of my own feelings and instincts in the matter. The editorial you sent to me from the Washington Post represents fairly accurately what might be called the "minimum conditions" which could ever influence me in a positive direction in this regard. On the other hand, I realize that to a practical politician the conditions described in the editorial would be highly unusual, possibly even bordering on the miraculous. It is because I do believe that popular sentiment will have little effect in a convention of practical politicians, and that such miracles do not occur, that I am not spending my time worrying my head about bridges that are still a long ways ahead.[2] *As ever*

[1] Eisenhower's brother Milton had sent copies of his correspondence with Jack Lesser, of New Haven, Connecticut (Aug. 28, 1951, EM). Lesser, who greatly admired General Eisenhower, had written at length on his reasons for supporting an Eisenhower candidacy in the 1952 presidential election (July 31, Aug. 25, 1951, EM, same file as document). In an accompanying note Milton had told his brother that he thought the correspondence would be of some interest because "as you may suspect, I am receiving a great many letters, telephone calls, and personal visits which in one way or another affect you."

[2] Milton had also enclosed an editorial from the August 19, 1951, issue of the *Washington Post* entitled "If GOP Wants Ike, It Will Have to Draft Him." For developments see no. 381.

357 *Eisenhower Mss.*

To Charles McElroy White

September 5, 1951

Dear Charlie:[1] Whenever I learn through a letter that a friend of mine has been ill, I am delighted when the news reaches me after there has been a full recovery. So in your case my sympathy for your boredom and possible suffering in the hospital is accompanied by my happiness in knowing that you are your old self once again.[2]

Of course, it is good to know that you are doing such an effective job in carrying back to your associates in the business world the facts and convictions that you accumulated during your European trip.[3] To my mind, nothing is more important for America today than to have a clear understanding of all the complicated facts, statistics, trends and movements that affect our country's effort to promote true cooperation in the job of developing collective security. There is, of course, much room for individual difference of opinion concerning a myriad of important details connected with such a great undertaking; because of this very reason, it is highly important that basic facts be spread before all of us—basic facts in terms of objectives, major obstacles and the comparisons between our common assets and liabilities. The more these are discussed and studied, the more such outstanding individuals as yourself encourage such study and examination, the better off we will be.

With respect to your feeling that I should render the determining decisions in the allocation of various kinds of aid, you realize, of course, that Senator Taft was absolutely correct in his feeling that I could not take formal or official responsibility for such a thing, with the meager operational staff that I have assembled here. While I feel that people who have to make these decisions should consult SHAPE— and, in fact, they do—so that no lack of coordination can damage our progress, still the fixing of formal responsibility on an office such as mine would create a lot of administrative problems that would require a vast expansion in my corps of assistants.[4]

I have already had a note from Tom Girdler and am to have an appointment with him when he comes through Paris. I am most certainly looking forward to seeing him.[5]

It was grand to have you here. I hope that business will bring you back this way soon again. I particularly hope that your knowledge of the British coal situation may result in some increase in production in that badly stretched country.[6] *Cordially*

[1] White was president of the Republic Steel Corporation.

[2] In a letter of August 31 (EM) White had told Eisenhower that he had been hospitalized in Cleveland since his return from Europe. White had visited Eisenhower in mid-July (for background see no. 262).

[3] White reported that he had recently talked to a "good cross-section of American industry," the directors of the American Iron and Steel Institute. In October, he said, he would make an off-the-record talk to more than one hundred leading American editors in Cleveland, where he would give full credit to Eisenhower for his work on the "NATO job."

[4] White said that he had told Senator Robert A. Taft that he thought Eisenhower should have "final authority on the spending of Marshall Plan or other aid money which this country makes to Europe." Although Taft had agreed, White said, he was under the impression that Eisenhower preferred that such funds be handled by an agency that would respond to his wishes.

[5] Tom Mercer Girdler (M.E. Lehigh University 1901) was chairman of the boards

of the Republic Steel Corporation, of Cleveland, Ohio, and the Consolidated Vultee
Aircraft Corporation, of San Diego, California. Girdler would visit Eisenhower on
September 7; on September 15 Eisenhower would write to thank him for a gift of
bourbon (EM).
⁶ For White's views on the British coal situation see no. 262. In a handwritten
notation on White's letter Eisenhower had directed that it be sent to special
advisers William H. Burnham and General Wilton B. Persons and to Eisenhower's
C/S General Alfred M. Gruenther and his special assistant General Cortlandt van
Rensselaer Schuyler. "Then," Eisenhower wrote, "back to me."

358 *Eisenhower Mss.*

To MONROE MARK SWEETLAND *September 5, 1951*
Personal and confidential

Dear Mr. Sweetland:[1] It was kind of you to write and forward to me
detailed information in regard to the primary situation in your State.[2]

After much thought I decided some time ago that the only proper
course to be followed by an American officer in my position was to
refrain from making any comment on the American political scene.
Regardless of the sincerity of any statement I might make, various
interpretations would be made and much speculation would ensue
which I believe would be harmful to the success of the present task I
have been given—to help develop collective security by cooperation
among the Western Nations. This I consider to be of the utmost
importance to America's future, a conviction that is obviously in accord with the interest of the United States Congress. The understanding and support of the American people, *as a whole*, are essential to
success in this vast undertaking.

For me to admit, while in this post, or to imply or even to leave
open for interpretation by others a partisan political loyalty would
properly be resented by thinking Americans and would be doing a
disservice to our country, for it would interfere with the job to which
the country has assigned me. The successful outcome of this venture is
too vital to our welfare in the years ahead to permit any semblance of
partisan allegiance on the part of the U.S. Military Commander in
SHAPE.[3]

I realize that this may seem an unsatisfactory answer to your letter,
but, in the best interests of all, it appears to me the proper course to
pursue.

I appreciate the fine sentiments and understanding evidenced in the
final paragraph of your letter—I hope that you will understand sym-
pathetically my present position and decisions as outlined above.[4]
Sincerely

[1] Sweetland (A.B. Wittenberg College 1930) had been a member of the Democratic National Committee for Oregon since 1948.

[2] On August 31 (EM) Sweetland had written Eisenhower to inform him that a small group of Oregon Democrats had collected 1,150 signatures in order to place the General's name on the ballot for the Democratic primary on May 17, 1952 (for background see no. 345, n. 2). Blaming "political adventuring and publicity seeking" for the "extremely premature" action, Sweetland assured Eisenhower that Democratic party officials had not been consulted by the sponsors of the petitions. Sweetland pointed out that since Eisenhower's name would be presented in Oregon by Republican petitioners and President Truman's name also would be filed by Democratic petitioners, Eisenhower might wish to have the Democratic petition declared "inoperative." He suggested that Eisenhower submit a statement to the secretary of state of Oregon declaring that he was "not affiliated with, or enrolled in either political party, or specifically the Democratic Party." For background on the Oregon primary see nos. 135 and 386, n. 2.

[3] This paragraph would become Eisenhower's standard response to those who tried to persuade him to declare his party affiliation and his presidential candidacy (see, for example, no. 408; for developments see nos. 551 and 587).

[4] Sweetland had said, "You have a host of friends in Oregon . . . many of whom are also friends of the President and who have no desire to see a synthetic conflict whipped up in our state or anywhere which makes no contribution to the extremely important undertaking in which you are engaged, and which likewise makes more difficult the grave responsibilities of the President himself" (on developments in the Oregon primary see Warren to Eisenhower, May 18, 1952, and Eisenhower to Warren, May 19, 1952, EM; and *New York Times*, May 17–19, 1952).

359   *Eisenhower Mss.*

To HAROLD RUPERT LEOFRIC GEORGE ALEXANDER

September 5, 1951

Dear Alex:[1] While sitting for a portrait by Sir Oswald Birley,[2] our conversation turned to you and your well known ability as an amateur painter. In such fashion, I recalled that you and I had reached a mutual agreement to exchange one selection from each of our "collected works." Moreover, upon leaving the United States in February, I sent to you one of my laborious productions which your February twenty-third letter acknowledged.[3] I have received none from you—and am concerned that yours may be wandering through any of three or four postal systems in a vain attempt to catch up with my changing addresses. Have you sent one? If not, I'm preparing to sue!![4]

I certainly hope your records will help me out—but meanwhile this note gives me an opportunity to send warm personal greetings to you and Lady Alexander,[5] in which Mamie joins. *As ever*

[1] Viscount Alexander of Tunis had been Governor General of Canada since 1946

(for further background on Alexander see *Eisenhower Papers*, vols. I–XI). Eisenhower's aide Major Craig Cannon drafted this letter.
[2] For background on Birley see no. 134, n. 3.
[3] This letter is in EM.
[4] On September 10, 1951 (EM), Alexander would write to say that it was Eisenhower's own fault that he had not yet received a painting: "You have set such a high standard that anything I have already done could not possibly balance your work . . . in consequence I have been forced to get down to work and produce something which will be acceptable to you." On November 1 Eisenhower would write that Alexander's "truly attractive—to me, wonderful—landscape" had arrived. "The fine workmanship of your effort," Eisenhower said, "gives me a very red face when I remember the kind of thing I sent you" (EM).
[5] The former Margaret Diana Bingham.

360   *Eisenhower Mss.*

To Walter Bedell Smith   *September 6, 1951*
Secret

Dear Bedell:[1] As you know, General de Lattre is soon to be in the United States.[2] I know he is scheduled to see you, and I really believe you will find a meeting with him to be worthwhile. He realizes that his own little "hot" war in Indochina is only a part of a major and implacable struggle against Soviet despotism. He needs United States, or possibly I should say United Nations help, and I think is far more disposed to be cooperative than he may have been in the past. I told him that your office had resented some of his decisions in the Indochina area, but that, of course, I was not familiar with the details or the outcome. But I tried to point out that cooperation was a two-way street.[3]

Someone recently told me that you expect to come this way toward the end of the month. I have only one word to say about it, and this is, please arrange for a good long stay. I want to have long talks with you, and besides, you should take time out to go back over some of your old stamping grounds. By no means should you make it one of these split second affairs.[4]

My love to Norry,[5] and of course, as always, my very best to yourself. *As ever*

[1] Smith was Director of the Central Intelligence Agency.
[2] De Lattre was French High Commissioner in Indochina and C in C of French forces in the Far East. He had visited Eisenhower on Tuesday, September 4, and he would visit the United States later this month (see the following document, n. 2). For background on de Lattre and the war in Indochina see nos. 28 and 88; and *New York Times*, February 18, August 26, 1951.
[3] Eisenhower is probably referring to de Lattre's policies regarding U.S. operations

in Vietnam. Because he was suspicious about U.S. aims in Indochina, de Lattre had made it clear that he wished to be consulted on U.S. military, economic, and intelligence activities in Vietnam. De Lattre's attitude echoed French fears that calculated generosity in arms and economic aid by any foreign country would win over the Vietnamese people and Vietnam would be lost by the French Union (for background see State, *Foreign Relations, 1951*, vol. VI, *Asia and the Pacific, Part I*, pp. 418–84). For developments see the following document.
[4] Smith would visit Eisenhower on September 21 and 22. In a letter of October 9 (EM) Smith would thank the Eisenhowers for their hospitality.
[5] Smith's wife Mary Eleanor.

361   *Eisenhower Mss.*

To George Catlett Marshall   *September 6, 1951*
Secret

Dear General Marshall:[1] I have just had a long conversation with General de Lattre preliminary to his impending departure for the United States. I understand that he has quite a program already laid out for him in our country and will have an opportunity to see most of the individuals who have special responsibility in studying the Southeast Asia problems.[2]

General de Lattre, it seems to me, has mellowed quite a bit in late years. Certainly he understands that his own particular war in Indochina is a mere part or phase of the entire global conflict against a Communistic dictatorship. So I am sure that while he is hopeful of getting some help from the United Nations—or even directly from the United States—he does realize that his own requests must be weighed against other requirements that cover the globe. I have advised him to be perfectly frank and to listen patiently. I did not presume to go much beyond this for the simple reason that I do not know the priority of need from the viewpoint of the American Government.

In any event, I am quite sure that you will find conversation with him very interesting, even absorbing. For this reason I venture the suggestion that you might find it worthwhile to reserve a good hour or so at whatever time you may be scheduled to see him. (I am making the assumption that you are so scheduled.)[3]

With best wishes, *Sincerely*

[1] Secretary of Defense Marshall would soon retire (see no. 372).
[2] For background on de Lattre, French High Commissioner in Indochina and C in C of French forces in the Far East, see no. 28. De Lattre had been invited by the Joint Chiefs of Staff to meet with U.S. officials to discuss France's political and military involvement in Indochina. De Lattre, who would arrive in the United States on September 13, would meet with President Truman and Secretary of State

Dean Acheson, as well as a number of high officials of the Department of Defense and the Department of State. As Eisenhower had predicted, de Lattre would appeal to the U.S. government for financial aid to help support France's battle against the revolutionary Communist movement in Indochina. According to de Lattre, the war in Indochina was the same as the war in Korea and deserved the same priorities on the part of the United States.

[3] Marshall would meet with de Lattre on September 14 at the Pentagon (for de Lattre's visit see State, *Foreign Relations, 1951*, vol. VI, *Asia and the Pacific, Part I*, pp. 494–525; and *New York Times*, Sept. 14, 15, 16, 19, 1951). For developments see the following document.

362

Eisenhower Mss.

To WILLIAM AVERELL HARRIMAN
Secret

September 6, 1951

Dear Averell: General de Lattre is soon to come to the United States, and already there has been arranged for him a program that will bring him into contact with most of the people that he should appropriately see. However, I think it worthwhile to suggest to you that you make a special effort to see that nothing comes up to interfere with your opportunity of having a talk with him.[1]

He is, of course, primarily concerned in Indochina. But he does seem to appreciate thoroughly the fact that the struggle against Communistic dictatorship is a global one; that his own war is a particular phase and part of the whole. Consequently, it is not difficult to follow most of his arguments. Exactly what requests he will make upon our Government and/or the United Nations, I do not know. But he will, beyond all doubt, reflect clearly the French conviction that it is impossible longer for France to carry the full burden, or practically the full burden, of the Indochinese War and still to produce maximum defensive force in Europe and sustain economic stability. I have had numbers of talks with civil and military leaders on this particular subject. I am sure the French are sincere—my hunch is that they are also *reasonably* accurate. However, I know that the United States has so many difficult problems of its own, so many obligations to meet, that I cannot tell what priority this particular problem should assume in American calculations. I contented myself with advising General de Lattre to put his case frankly and fully in front of responsible officials. I told him also that he, on his part, should invite a free discussion and to study carefully whatever viewpoint the American authorities might bring to bear. I personally think that his greatest hope is that we can find some way of helping build up a native Indochinese army, one capable of defending the country with a minimum of French help. He seems quite worried as to what will happen in that corner of Asia if there is an actual "cease fire" in Korea.[2] While he indulges in a great deal of speculation on this particular point, my own feeling is that we should try to solve the problem on the basis of its present importance, significance and circumstances.

By the morning's paper I see that the Persians are really pouring it on the British once again. I hope that you don't have to go back to that corner of the world; but I must say that every new bit of evidence that seems to indicate the probability that Persian oil will no longer be available to the West gives me a sinking feeling in the middle.[3]

While you were away from Washington I wrote quite a lengthy letter to General Marshall.[4] From one of his assistants I later learned that it was considered important enough that it was circulated to a few officials about the City. As I recall, the letter contains nothing that I have not already told you, but if you think it worthwhile, I will send you a copy upon your request.

Please remember me kindly to Marie,[5] and, as always, warmest regards to yourself. Also, I should like you to pay my respects to the Chief.[6] *Cordially*

[1] For background on de Lattre's visit see nos. 360 and 361. In a letter of September 19 (EM) Harriman would tell Eisenhower that he had met with de Lattre and had discussed with him the increased materiel needs for the Indochina campaign. Harriman said that the French had asked for "a pretty big slug of stuff, both for the present fighting and for the equipping of the increased Indochinese native forces." Uncertain as to whether these requirements could be met, Harriman added that there were "more and more people who are beginning to understand Indochina is 'our' war" (see Ronald H. Spector, *Advice and Support: The Early Years, 1941-1960*, United States Army in Vietnam, ed. David F. Trask [Washington, D.C., 1983], pp. 141-48).

[2] The French feared that an armistice in Korea would allow Communist China to send troops to Indochina (State, *Foreign Relations, 1951*, vol. VI, *Asia and the Pacific, Part I*, pp. 500-501, 508).

[3] For background on the situation in Iran and Harriman's mission to Teheran see no. 259. Although Harriman had been unable to negotiate a settlement between the British and the Iranians, he had succeeded in getting both parties to exercise more restraint in their actions and to resume negotiations. The negotiators had again failed to reach agreement, however, and on August 22 the British had terminated the discussions and had threatened to discharge 76,000 Iranian oil workers. Harriman had returned to Washington on August 31. A few days later the Iranians announced that they would cancel the residence permits of the remaining British oil technicians unless the British moved to reopen the talks (Brookings Institution, *Current Developments in United States Foreign Policy* 5, nos. 1 [1951], 38-42, and 2 [1951], 34-37; *New York Times*, Sept. 1, 6, 1951). In his letter of September 19 Harriman would contend that ill-considered British pressure on the Iranians was hindering the growth of moderate political forces opposed to the ruling Mossadeq regime. He concluded, "There are still some cards which we can play before a debacle. It will require the closest kind of watching."

The United States would continue its attempts to resolve the conflict. These efforts were unsuccessful, although U.S. pressure was in large part responsible for the British government's abandonment of its plan to intervene militarily. Iran would expel British technicians in October, and the flow of oil would be curtailed sharply as a result. The dispute would not be resolved until after Shah Mohammed Reza Pahlavi (see Galambos, *Columbia University*, no. 544), with U.S. support, overthrew the Mossadeq government in August 1953 (see Rouhollah K. Ramazani, *Iran's Foreign Policy, 1941-1973: A Study of Foreign Policy in Modernizing Nations* [Charlottesville, Va., 1975], pp. 211-12, 225-31, 242-50; Acheson, *Present at the Creation*, pp. 509-11; Morgan, *Labour in Power*, pp. 470-71; Eisenhower, *Mandate for Change*, pp. 159-66; and Ambrose, *Eisenhower*, vol. II, *The President*, pp. 109-12, 129-30.

[4] This letter is no. 304.

[5] Harriman's wife (see no. 167, n. 9).

[6] The "Chief" was President Truman. In his brief note in reply (Sept. 14, 1951, EM) Harriman would remind Eisenhower that during their August 29 meeting in Paris the General had "mentioned the voting record of a certain Senator." With his letter Harriman would enclose a memorandum listing Senator Robert A. Taft's votes against the Mutual Security bill (see Tannenwald to Harriman, Sept. 14, 1951, EM, Harriman Corr.; see also nos. 198, 238, and 357, n. 4). This issue was important to Eisenhower and to Harriman, who would later become Director for Mutual Security.

363

To GEORGE CATLETT MARSHALL
Secret

Eisenhower Mss.

September 8, 1951

Dear General: One point in your letter of September 6 requires immediate answer. You are mistaken in thinking that the President did not reply to my message of July 17. He communicated directly to me by letter, to which I answered.[1]

I am hopeful that the Ottawa meeting[2] will be useful in encouraging governmental representatives in the several nations of NATO to exert whatever powers of leadership they may have in building up in their respective countries enthusiasm and support for the whole project. I have not been able to understand the failure of governments to meet more often on the problems of NATO.[3] Certainly, when I left the United States there seemed to be no lack of understanding of the great need for exerting leadership in the development of a common morale; to say, therefore, that there is no necessity for the governmental representatives to meet, seems to say to all the people of these countries that the whole matter is not so important after all. I most firmly believe that such conferences should be held, at a minimum, on a quarterly basis. Just the very fact of the meeting is of grave importance, sometimes even transcending agenda and visible results.

I am delighted that Bob Lovett seems to retain his strength in order to have the greatest of usefulness to you. He has always been, of course, one of my favorites.[4] *Sincerely*

[1] Marshall had written after returning from vacation to acknowledge Eisenhower's letter of August 3 (see no. 304). "I can understand your concern in not receiving a reply from the President to your message of 17 July," Marshall had remarked, referring to Eisenhower's suggestion of a September meeting with the President. "The situation at the moment is that the President is still thinking the matter over and while he has indicated a desire to talk to Acheson and me about it, has thus far not brought it up again." For the circumstances surrounding Eisenhower's July 17 cable to Truman see nos. 274 and 290.

[2] The NAC ministers planned to meet in Ottawa, Canada, September 15–20, 1951.

[3] Eisenhower repeatedly stressed the value of frequent NAC sessions (see, for example, nos. 218, n. 9, 365, n. 5, and 374). For developments see no. 384, n. 8.

[4] Robert A. Lovett had served as Deputy Secretary of Defense since October 1950. Marshall said that Lovett was leaving for a few days of rest. "He is a tower of strength to me. The Hill has been unusually demanding this year in the way of calling our top people as witnesses, and Lovett has absorbed most of it at terrific cost to his equanimity. How he takes it, and retains his sense of humor is beyond my understanding." Four days after Eisenhower wrote this letter, Marshall announced his own retirement; Lovett would succeed him (see nos. 372 and 380).

364   *Eisenhower Mss.*

To Alphonse Juin   *September 8, 1951*
Top secret

Dear General Juin:[01] It has now been some six months since SHAPE was established, and nearly three months since the principal subordinate headquarters was activated. Although some progress has been made, a very great deal remains yet to be done, and the time factor has become no less urgent. There is no doubt but that the establishment of the higher headquarters organization has instilled a degree of confidence in the peoples of Western Europe. But there is no room for complacency, always a potential danger to us. If Russia were to launch an attack now, we would not be ready to meet it. Therefore, we must progress to the point where we can handle any situation that may develop from the winter of 1952/53 onwards.[2]

In view of this, I feel it vital that we ensure that the very best use is made of the forces now available, and that we set and achieve a very high level of professional efficiency. These objectives will not be made unless we develop very close inter-service cooperation at Command level, and approach the defense of Western Europe as a joint problem. Of course this is not being done effectively, as yet. I am most anxious, therefore, that you do everything in your power to develop at all levels in your Command a common and joint approach to the problems which now confront us. This is of particular importance during the preparation of plans,[3] during the determination of force requirements,[4] and when dealing with the national authorities concerned.

The organization of combined planning at the headquarters of Northern Europe and Southern Europe is essential. It is equally important with regard to the three headquarters at Fontainebleau, since in the Central European Command there is no one Commander-in-Chief.[5]

The approach to every planning problem must be both realistic and practical. No operational plan can be of value unless there has been a thorough reconnaissance of the areas concerned. If a land operation is involved, the plan must be a joint Army and Air plan. Lastly, the logistical staff, to make an operational plan effective, must be brought into the planning from its very inception.

I wish you to keep me personally informed of any major difficulties you may encounter in all these matters. I have instructed my staff to ensure you are given every assistance, in our power to command, but I shall be glad to have your personal suggestions as to how we can help you most. In this respect, I have asked my deputies—Field Marshal Montgomery, Air Chief Marshal Saunders and Admiral Lemmonier[6]—to follow closely the development and coordination of all your plans, and to report to me accordingly. SHAPE's purpose is to be helpful—not critical.

I am sending a similar letter to Admiral Brind, Admiral Carney, and General Norstad and Admiral Jaujard.[7] *Sincerely*

[1] Juin would soon assume his position as C in C of the Allied Army Forces in Central Europe (see no. 198). At some point this letter was designated "SHAPE 460/51" and thus became an official SHAPE numbered document.

[2] The United States had determined that the NATO nations should be ready to withstand a Soviet attack by 1952 rather than 1954 as specified in NATO's Medium Term Defense Plan (see nos. 15, n. 4, and 16, n. 5).

[3] For background on SHAPE's efforts to develop war plans see nos. 124 and 172. In June U.S. Army Chief of Staff J. Lawton Collins had sent Eisenhower his thoughts on NATO's best course of action in the event of a Soviet invasion. Collins's "analysis of the terrain, coupled with the importance of protecting the Ruhr," had led him "to the conclusion that the key sector, if we are to hold east of the Rhine, lies between the Ruhr and Frankfurt." Collins, who was "thinking in terms of protecting the U.S. by winning the war east of the Rhine," suggested that U.S. and German units—"the best troops in Europe"—be assigned to this vital central sector. Trying to stop the Russians with French troops, according to Collins, could result in a quick Soviet conquest of the central area between the Ruhr and Frankfurt. The Soviet troops then "might well pin our forces between the Rhine and the Alps and go on about their business of overrunning western Europe" (Collins to Eisenhower, June 5, 1951, EM; see also Collins to Eisenhower,

Aug. 7, 1951, *ibid.*). Eisenhower would soon attempt to reconcile the differences between the NATO and U.S. war plans (see no. 405).

[4] In August SHAPE had sent to the Standing Group its requirements for the forces needed in 1954. The paper differed from the earlier MTDP in that it called for a "forward strategy" (see no. 172), with a "strong defensive zone between the Iron Curtain and the Rhine." The new requirements plan was also based on having a strong German military force and required "an earlier availability of forces relative to D-Day, decreasing the time of readiness of necessary forces for the first phase of a war from D + 90 to D + 30." Assuming the support of ten West German divisions (see no. 304), there was a "Gap" between SHAPE requirements and the projected national contributions of thirteen ground force divisions by D + 30 (Nash to Marshall, Aug. 25, 1951, OS/D, 1951, Clas. Decimal File, CD 091.7 Europe; see also JCS 2073/201, Sept. 7, 1951, CCS 092 Western Europe [3-12-48], Sec. 93). For developments see no. 405.

[5] General Juin commanded only the land forces in Eisenhower's central sector. U.S. Air Force General Lauris Norstad commanded the air forces, and French Admiral Robert Jaujard was Flag Officer, central Europe. Eisenhower himself retained overall command in the center (see nos. 108, 115, and 198).

[6] For background on Field Marshal Montgomery see no. 74; on British Air Chief Marshal Hugh Saunders see no. 77, n. 5; and on French Vice-Admiral André Georges Lemonnier see no. 149.

[7] On Admirals Brind and Carney see nos. 53 and 99; on Norstad and Jaujard, see n. 5 above.

365   *Eisenhower Mss.*

To PAUL VAN ZEELAND   *September 11, 1951*
Secret

Dear Mr. van Zeeland:[01] On the eve of the Ottawa meeting, I am taking the liberty of giving to you a few comments on the progress made in NATO. This I do on a purely personal and friendly basis since official communications from me would necessarily follow established channels.[2]

SHAPE has established a practical command framework, integrated the forces which have already been committed to the Allied Command, initiated necessary training programs, and coordinated such defense plans as could possibly be executed with the limited forces within sight at present. Prospects for our continuing progress over the next six months is now the subject that occupies all minds. Consequently, I have forwarded to the Standing Group a detailed report containing my views on the principal problems facing us.[3]

SHAPE is a military headquarters, but one whose successful functioning is entirely dependent upon political progress made within the North Atlantic Treaty Organization. It stands or falls upon the effectiveness of NATO leaders in uniting the people of the free world in a clear understanding of the perils facing us, and upon the degree of success achieved in uniting the potential power of the various participating countries. To produce such unity in NATO seems to me to be our first and transcendent purpose—so much so that it requires the highest priority in the thought and resources of every member nation.[4] There are many ways in which this understanding—this type of morale—can be created. One of them would be more frequent meetings of the North Atlantic Council.[5] For governments to meet only once a year conveys no sense of urgency. The decision to have a preliminary meeting at Ottawa, followed shortly thereafter by a session in Rome, is most heartening, and I hope it will set a pattern for the future.

For the good of all of us and for future generations everywhere, NATO must develop the vitality to overcome promptly all such problems as division of costs, requirements, and procedures. Even on a more immediate basis, any project that requires for its execution billions in wealth and the divergence of manpower and resources on a tremendous order deserves the joint and constant effort of all participating governments.[6]

I am always ready to refute the viewpoint of the pessimist who is ever present to remind us that alliances such as ours are historically irresolute and unstable. I have the utmost confidence that eventually we shall be able, as men of peace, to defend our rights and freedom against a clear and present danger. But postponement of solutions is not the answer and will not meet the present threat. The vitality and vigor of our NATO machinery is the first requisite to achievement of those purposes. We must stand together and labor together if we are to succeed. *Sincerely*

[1] Van Zeeland, Belgian Foreign Minister, would serve as chairman of the North Atlantic Council meeting at Ottawa from September 15 to September 20.

[2] Claiming that he was too busy to attend the Ottawa meeting, the first since the May 1951 NAC reorganization (see Ismay, *NATO*, pp. 41–43), Eisenhower apparently wrote this letter to help quiet unrest before the ministers convened. The Ottawa agenda as drafted by the Council of Deputies covered largely nonmilitary matters. The deputies nonetheless expected a progress report from the Military Committee, and after the Standing Group in Washington announced that it would be "premature to take up military questions" in Ottawa and that it would not appear there, a bitter debate on the proper role of the Standing Group, the balance between military and nonmilitary issues in NATO, and the alliance's character (the meeting would consider granting Greece and Turkey full NATO membership) had ensued at the August 29 meeting of the deputies. In a telephoned message to Washington on August 31 Eisenhower had declined to send General Gruenther to Ottawa to report on progress at SHAPE. "Possibly he does not wish to have SHAPE put in the position of bailing out the Standing Group," wrote the State Department deputy director for European affairs, "or it may be that he does not want Gruenther to appear when there is no agenda item to which he would speak." The place of military topics in the Ottawa discussions and the strength of military

representatives there remained on the General's mind. On September 7, after Eisenhower had heard a report that no high-ranking member of the Defense Department would be present at Ottawa, Gruenther had written to Harriman in Washington asking him to make discreet inquiries about the truth of the report. Harriman replied the same day that Eisenhower wrote van Zeeland, informing him that George C. Marshall and a full complement of civilian advisers planned to attend the conference—as, finally, did the Standing Group (State, *Foreign Relations, 1951*, vol. III, *European Security and the German Question, Part I*, pp. 258–60, 641–46, 691; Gruenther to Harriman, Sept. 7, 1951, and Harriman to Gruenther, Sept. 11, 1951, Gruenther Papers).

[3] We have not been able to locate this document, but Ismay reported that Eisenhower sent a message in support of the Military Committee's request for more NATO forces and equipment; the General "stated that he found the military effort to be 'so closely interlocked with economic, financial and social matters that it was often impracticable, and indeed quite unrealistic, to consider one of these fields without giving due attention to the others' " (Ismay, *NATO*, p. 43; see also *New York Times*, Sept. 16, 1951).

[4] For similar arguments see nos. 363 and 388.

[5] Eisenhower made other pleas for frequent NAC sessions (see nos. 218 and 375). For developments see no. 384, n. 1.

[6] On the principle of balanced collective forces see no. 532, n. 4.

366   *Eisenhower Mss.*

To Gordon Gray   *September 11, 1951*

Dear Gordon:[1] The creation by the United States of the Psychological Strategy Board is certainly another step toward achieving real progress in this relatively unfamiliar but most important field, and I am certain that you will find your duties as Director interesting and challenging.[2]

With regard to your query concerning the necessity for establishing some sort of a counterpart of the Board in Europe, I believe that until such time as your Board establishes its objectives, policies and procedures it would be premature to establish a Board in this theater, and that existing channels should be relied upon to provide you with the information you require. There is no doubt that the American representatives here, being closer to the scene of activity, are more sensitive to the European situation, and these reactions should be made available to your Board.

Subject to developments in Washington regarding the organization to be established for psychological warfare, I believe that your Board may find that a committee could be created here in Europe to give you the best possible advice concerning the success of the United States psychological effort. If your Board decides to establish such a committee, you will undoubtedly wish to determine its composition and terms of reference in light of the Washington organization. We, of course, would be glad to make comments and recommendations on any such drafts insofar as this headquarters is concerned.

As a long term project, and once the United States organization at home and abroad is crystallized, the personnel concerned could examine the possibility of establishing a means for coordinating psychological operations within the NATO.[3] All the best to you. *Sincerely*

[1] Gray, on leave from his position as president of the University of North Carolina, had become Director of the Psychological Strategy Board in July (for background see no. 32; and *New York Times*, June 21, July 19, 1951). This letter was drafted by General Cortlandt van Rensselaer Schuyler (see no. 2, n. 1).

[2] In April President Truman had established the Psychological Strategy Board for "the formulation and promulgation . . . of overall national psychological objectives, policies and programs, and for the coordination and evaluation of the national psychological effort" (see State, *Foreign Relations, 1951*, vol. I, *National Security Affairs; Foreign Economic Policy*, pp. 58-61, 178-80, 601).

[3] In his reply of September 14 (EM) Gray agreed that it would be premature to establish a psychological strategy board in the European theater. There is no indication in further correspondence that a European counterpart to the board was ever formed. For developments see no. 550; and *New York Times*, December 10, 1951.

367   *Eisenhower Mss., Family File*

To Arthur B. Eisenhower   *September 11, 1951*
Personal

Dear Arthur:[1] It has been a very long time since I have received a letter that I enjoyed so much as yours. I wish that I could use a pen for my reply—unfortunately, to do so would demand time that I simply cannot command just now—and, moreover, the result would be such that you could not possibly read it. My own office force maintains that one hour after I have scrawled a pencilled memorandum I cannot myself interpret its meaning.[2]

Naturally, we are sorry that Louise has been ill and that, because of her indisposition, you could not come over here to attend the TWA meeting this summer. However, any time that you can come you need send only sufficient advance notice so that we can meet you at the airfield or the railway station. The house, into which we have just moved, has a disappointingly small space for guest rooms. So, if it should happen that some other member of the family should already be here at the time of your coming, we could not put you up. But there is a nice hotel only a short distance from us, here in the country. It is one where we ourselves stayed for six months, so we know all of the people there very well indeed. But the normal outlook would be that we would be alone when you come, and so there would be no difficulty about putting you up.[3]

I am particularly delighted that you are not going to retire. While I am quite sure that the world needs young men in positions of responsibility (I certainly tried hard to get the President to name a younger man for this post), there are some types of jobs where judgment and experience are more valuable than the courage, fire and enthusiasm of youth. In any event, it seems to me that most of my friends who are 65 are far younger than the 65-year olds were some 40 years ago. Of course, we know this to be true if we look merely through our own eyes; because when we were 20 or 25 years old, 65 seemed to be the age of the everlasting hills! I am thinking, though, of how contemporary writers and historians then spoke of the 65-year old man, as compared to the way he is thought of now. I congratulate you on the prospect of continuing in harness.[4]

In my own case, it seems to me that what capacity I may have left for doing something for the country after I leave active military service, is in the way of counselling—from a completely unpartisan and disinterested viewpoint—concerning those matters in the international field and in the business of assuring national security in which I have had some experience and done some thinking. Because of this long-held belief, Mamie and I began some years ago to build plans whereby we could go into semi-retirement in some place from which I could, if requested, advise and confer with individuals who might bear responsibility in these matters. I still think that such would be a good and satisfying life. As you know, so far as personal desire is concerned, I have a violent antipathy for anything that might be called partisan politics. To me, the picture of a man seeking to satisfy personal ambition through the means of trumped up argument and by use of the devious routes and methods inherent in our current day politics is completely repulsive.[5]

I do not for one moment deprecate the necessity of hammering out needed public decisions on the anvil of debate and honest argument. This is the essence of free government. But when people descend to the practice of lying about particular individuals, of setting up straw men in order themselves to be the heroes to destroy them, and when we see the complete disregard for principle, truth, and the general good that are so frequently the characteristics of our political arguments, I do not see how anyone could contemplate with satisfaction the possibility of entering such a field.

There has been lately a great hue and cry about morals in government and in public life. Much as we need such a spiritual rebirth, yet one cannot escape the feeling that, except in individual cases, the people saying these things are doing it more for political advantage than they are with any intention of doing anything about the matter by their own example and efforts. As it is, we seem to approve, today, of the practice of maligning individuals and destroying reputations by charges that are false and unfounded, but so cleverly brought forward that the instigator is untouchable either by reason of legal immunity or because his attack is insinuation and implication rather than open allegation. On the other hand, we have clearcut cases of crookedness that supports gamblers, drug peddlers, and every other kind of violator; we have instances where men who have clearly proved themselves unworthy of their positions of trust in government are sustained and supported because of their close association with other powerful figures. All this, of course, requires stern action before we are going to regain our own self-respect. In spite of the fact that on some particular issues I find myself differing sharply from Herbert Hoover, I do have a very comfortable feeling that on this subject he is not only completely honest, but may be able to start a campaign that will be effective. Incidentally, I like, respect and admire Mr. Hoover very much—I truly believe that the only issue on which I find myself at variance with him is in his belief that America today can retire into its own shell and be safe in a role of "watchful waiting."[6]

The task I have here is not only complicated, it is extremely difficult. It requires constant study and effort and my days are, of course, studded with frequent disappointments because of some failure somewhere in the military, political or economic machinery that must support us. Nevertheless, I am sure we are making progress. The idea of developing among the free nations of the world some security through cooperation is gradually reaching the minds of people in such fashion as to be convincing.

It is possible that people are troubled by the suspicion that the United Nations, because it includes recalcitrant and vindictive nations as well as friendly ones, is incapable of keeping the peace.

Because of this, and realizing that peace cannot be unilaterally sustained, we have the reason for the birth of NATO. In any event, we here, Americans and others, firmly believe that the success of NATO is vital to the freedom of our children and grandchildren. If I did not believe this one simple fact—regardless of my disagreement with many things that have been done in the international field since 1945—I would resign as an officer of the Army so that Mamie and I could come home! I've already put many years into foreign service—I want to live in the U.S.—and, after all, I haven't *too* many years left to me.[7]

Love to Louise, best to you—*As ever*

---

[1] Arthur Eisenhower, the General's brother, was executive vice-president of the Commerce Trust Company of Kansas City, Missouri (see no. 34, n. 1).

[2] Arthur had written a nine-page letter to Eisenhower on September 6 (EM), remarking that it was the first "long hand" letter he had written in years. He told the General that their Aunt Amanda had recently died and described the "disas-

trous" floods that were "much worse than the one in 1903" (on Hannah Amanda Musser see no. 253, n. 2; on the recent Missouri and Kansas flooding see no. 289).

[3] The Arthur Eisenhowers would miss the International Air Transport Association (IATA) conference held in London beginning September 11 because Arthur's wife, the former Louise Sondra Grieb, was ill. Arthur was a director of the Transcontinental and Western Air Company (hence the General's reference to "TWA"). On the General's new home see no. 314, n. 2; and on the Trianon Palace Hotel of Versailles see no. 44, n. 2.

[4] On November 11 Arthur would be sixty-five, but he said he felt "too young to retire." The board of directors, he wrote, "passed a resolution inviting me to stay on with no time limit."

[5] Concerning the General's problem of "constant nagging on the presidency," Arthur said he hoped Eisenhower could "keep away from political entanglements until you have finished your task in Europe—Then retire to your farm" (on the Gettysburg farm see no. 350).

[6] On former President Herbert C. Hoover and his isolationist beliefs see no. 58, n. 3. For the General's position regarding a political career see no. 358.

[7] On Eisenhower's current difficulties as SACEUR see nos. 362 and 365.

368   *Eisenhower Mss.*

To Freeman F. Gosden   *September 12, 1951*

Dear Freeman:[1] For some reason or other, the three films of "Amos 'n' Andy" did not reach us until just this past week. Last evening we saw two of them, and Mamie and I, as well as a number of dinner guests, found them most amusing. It seems that in the film version of the show Andy and the Kingfish dominate the action, whereas I think that Amos has always been the great favorite of the listening public. Nevertheless, they were very enjoyable. The two we saw were the one about Andy's secretary and the one about the 1877 nickel. I think the choice of the small audience was the former, but we liked them both.[2]

Because of the delay in receipt, it is possible that the Columbia Broadcasting Company has gotten a little bit nervous about our failure to return the films promptly. We shall have them on the way back very shortly.

Again, our thanks, and our very best both to you and your charming bride.[3] Also, remember us to Mr. Correll.[4] *Cordially*

P.S. Cliff left here only the night before last, at the completion of his second visit to us.[5] I miss him very much, as you can well imagine.

[1] For background on Gosden, writer and producer of the "Amos 'n' Andy" show, see no. 177, n. 3.
[2] On July 24 (EM) Gosden had written the General to say that he was "air expressing" to him three "Amos 'n' Andy" television shows. "Show the 'Rare

Coin' film first," Gosden had suggested, "then, if you can stand the punishment, some other night take a look at the others" (for background on the show see no. 260, n. 2).

[3] Gosden's wife, the former Jane Stoneham.

[4] Gosden's partner, Charles J. Correll (see no. 260, n. 5).

[5] Clifford Roberts had returned to Paris for a visit in late August. He had dined with the General on August 25 and September 1, played golf with him on September 3, and visited Marnes-la-Coquette on September 9 (see no. 323). For developments see the following document.

369   *Eisenhower Mss.*

TO CLIFFORD ROBERTS   *September 14, 1951*

Dear Cliff:[1] Your letter of September 11 brings to me a bit of inspiration. I hope that without delay you will ask Mr. Black to give me thumbnail sketches of the financial situation of Great Britain, France, Norway, Belgium and Italy. If convenient, I should like this extended also to include West Germany and Denmark.[2]

Please assure him that I am not looking for great studies that may impose upon his staff an unconscionable burden—what I am really trying to find out is whether the view of the World Bank is substantially identical with that of the ECA officials I have talked to in the past. I must say this whole matter of economic liability in these countries, while something with which I have nothing to do officially, is one that is bearing down on me more than almost anything else at the moment.[3]

It is difficult, indeed, for me to tell you how much your visit here meant to me. You seem to be a very great safety valve, possibly because I not only have great respect for your judgment, but because I trust you so implicitly. I do hope that you will seize every possible excuse to repeat your visits in this direction. (Please remember that in spite of the free lecture that we all got on the way back from Norway, you are still one of my favorite partners either in a golf game or a bridge foursome.)[4]

Thanks again for your thoughtfulness in sending me the suggestion. *As ever*

P.S. Not an evening goes by that Mamie, Min[5] and I don't find some reason for recalling with some pleasant memory, various incidents of your stay here.

[1] For background on Roberts, a business executive and an old friend of Eisenhower's, see no. 7, n. 1.

[2] Roberts had written the General on September 11 (EM) about the International

Bank for Reconstruction and Development (World Bank). He had enclosed an editorial concerning the bank's successes during 1951 in moving physical capital and investment funds from the advanced industrial countries to the less developed countries (see *New York Herald Tribune,* Sept. 11, 1951). Roberts had suggested that Eisenhower might wish to request data on the economic, financial, and fiscal conditions in the NATO countries from World Bank officials. He specifically named World Bank president Eugene Robert Black as one who would be helpful. Black (University of Georgia 1917) had been vice-president of the Chase National Bank before joining the World Bank in 1947 (see memorandum, Schuyler to Gruenther, Sept. 25, 1951, in EM, Black Corr.). For background on the World Bank see National Archives and Records Service, *United States Government Organization Manual, 1952–53* (Washington, D.C., 1952), pp. 532–34.

[3] On the ECA see no. 45, n. 3. The "economic liability" that Eisenhower mentions was probably the debts the European nations had contracted as they sought to rebuild their economies; their immediate economic needs impinged on their efforts to rearm in support of NATO. For developments see no. 402.

[4] On his second visit to Paris Roberts had accompanied Eisenhower to a ceremony at Sola, Norway, on September 10 (see no. 375, n. 3). A September 8 note from General Alfred M. Gruenther to Colonel Robert L. Schulz had requested playing cards and a score pad for the trip (see EM, Subject File, Trips, SHAPE; Aircraft—SHAPE [*Columbine*]). The "free lecture" was probably given by General Gruenther, who also went on the Norway trip (see Roberts to Gruenther, Sept. 18, 1951, Gruenther Papers). On Roberts's visit see no. 368, n. 5; on his golf game see no. 392.

[5] On Mrs. Eisenhower's mother, Elivera Doud, see no. 275, n. 2.

370   *Eisenhower Mss.*

To Arthur Hays Sulzberger   *September 14, 1951*

Dear Arthur:[1] Thank you for remembering to include me on the list of those who will receive copies of your New York Times history. I shall keep it by my bedside, where I will get an occasional chance to read it.[2]

I am just in the midst of trying to write a note to Mr. Coykendall to explain that any suggestions I have made concerning my relations with Columbia have been inspired only by a great concern for that institution; for its present and for its future. If I could only have a sufficiently accurate crystal ball to predict my own obligations and tenure in this particular post, the answer would become clear. As it is, I can only hope that everybody will understand that I am trying to forget myself in a situation that could become embarrassing if the Trustees would allow their consideration and friendship for me to overweigh their judgment with respect to Columbia's good. Aside from this, I have no thoughts to offer—in fact, I simply do not have time to think of any matter these days that is not directly connected with this job.[3]

With warm personal regard, *As ever*

[1] Sulzberger, a Columbia University trustee, was the publisher of the *New York Times* (see no. 114).

[2] On September 10 (EM) Sulzberger had written that the centennial of the *New York Times* would be celebrated on September 18 and that he would send Eisenhower a newly published history of the newspaper by Meyer Berger, *The Story of the New York Times, 1851–1951* (New York, 1951), and a hundred-page publication called *One Hundred Years of Famous Pages from the New York Times, 1851–1951* (New York, 1951). In a letter of October 29 (EM) Eisenhower thanked Sulzberger for the gifts, although he would see him for lunch on October 30. On the centennial celebration see *New York Times*, September 16, 18, 1951.

[3] The General's letter to Frederick Coykendall is no. 373; see also no. 374. For background on Eisenhower's feelings concerning the Columbia presidency see no. 261; for developments see no. 398.

371   *Eisenhower Mss.*

To KEVIN COYLE McCANN   *September 14, 1951*

Dear Kevin:[1] Although I am sure that you entertain no doubts as to the high esteem in which I have held you since first meeting you in 1945, yet it occurs to me that I should carry in my files, for the benefit of any who may later browse through them, a brief summary of my opinions on this point. The duplicate of this letter will make such a record, no matter how inadequately it may express the true depth of my regard.[2]

Your departure from this headquarters weighs heavily upon me as a great personal loss, but I fully recognize that a man of your ability and potential has his own furrow to plough. I am most deeply grateful to have had you at my side during the past six years. Throughout our association—in the Department of the Army, at Columbia University, at SHAPE Headquarters—your loyalty, enthusiasm and wide range of knowledge have been a mainstay; more than this, your unswerving dedication to the highest ideals has been an inspiration.[3]

My heartfelt wishes are with you as you take up your responsibilities at Defiance College. However proud its past record, you and Mrs. McCann[4] have much to add to it. I know that neither of you will ever lose that crusading spirit and youthful enthusiasm which are invariably felt by all around you. As to your success, your own qualities give perfect guarantee. You have found that touchstone—known to few— by which to identify and show to others the true meaning and purposes of knowledge.

With lasting personal regard

[1] For background on McCann, who had been one of Eisenhower's assistants at SHAPE, see no. 53.
[2] When Eisenhower was Chief of Staff, McCann served as his public relations adviser and speech writer (see Galambos, *Chief of Staff*, nos. 1314 and 1551).
[3] McCann had become president of Defiance College in Defiance, Ohio, in August (see no. 347). For developments see no. 426.
[4] The former Ruth C. Potter.

372   *Eisenhower Mss.*

To George Catlett Marshall   *September 15, 1951*

Dear General:[1] When I received, the other evening, the cabled information concerning your impending retirement, with its complimentary references to myself, my mind flashed back over the hundred incidents of our personal association since I joined you in the War Department in December, 1941.[2] I am sure that throughout all that time you have never been in doubt as to the depth and sincerity of my respect and esteem; I hope that you are equally aware of the amount of inspiration I have drawn from your unselfish devotion to our country, with never an indication of desire on your part to count the personal cost. I most fervently hope that you and Mrs. Marshall[3] will have many more years together, all of them made happier by the knowledge that throughout a long career you have been concerned only with service, never with personal gain.

With best wishes and lasting regard, *Most sincerely*

[1] Marshall had been Secretary of Defense since September 1950 (for background see Galambos, *Columbia University*, no. 982).
[2] In a cable of September 12 Marshall had informed Eisenhower of his resignation, effective that day (EM). "I cannot leave this office," Marshall said, "without expressing to you my tremendous appreciation for the job you have done and are doing in Europe. . . . You are rendering a great service to this country and to the World in a manner that wins the approbation of everybody without exception." On September 24 Marshall thanked Eisenhower for this letter, saying, "It is difficult for me to express the feeling of appreciation I have for your appraisement of my service. We have been over many difficult roads together in our search for peace, and I hope and pray that the goal will soon be reached" (EM).
[3] Marshall's wife, the former Katherine Boyce Tupper Brown.

To Frederick Coykendall   *September 15, 1951*

Dear Mr. Coykendall:[1] Thank you for your letter of the tenth. During the course of the past few months, a number of individual Trustees have dropped into my office, and in each case I have naturally taken up with my visitor my concern about the situation at Columbia.[2]

When I came to Morningside Heights in May 1948, the University had then undergone a considerable period where the Chief Executive was an "acting" one. In such a situation it is always difficult, regardless of the abilities of senior administrative officers, to initiate and sustain the kind of competent, positive executive action that is vital, particularly in complicated organizations. Such an arrangement is normally unfair to the acting head.[3]

It was because of a fear that this kind of a situation might again develop that I have several times expressed to individual Trustees my sincere hope that the Trustees, as a whole, will make all decisions regarding the University's administrative needs with the single purpose of doing their best for Columbia. I have been anxious that none of them should have any possible embarrassment because of personal friendship or consideration for me.

It was in this kind of conversation that there have been mentioned the possibilities concerning a new title, as well as many other related subjects.

On July 9 I wrote to you trying to explain all of this, and I assure you that since that time I have given the matter no thought whatsoever. This does not mean, of course, that I have ceased in any way to have great concern for the welfare of Columbia. To the contrary, it is because of this continuing concern that I am trying to be completely objective.[4]

The fact is that I am not in position—which, last fall, I had hoped I would be by this time—to predict a possible date for my return to Morningside Heights. By no means do I want to be the cause of any difficulty. I am a bit disturbed to find that my intention, which was inspired solely by a desire to be helpful and tactful, has seemingly become a cause of confusion. I must admit that an immediate necessity for moving bag and baggage out of Number 60 would be quite an embarrassing chore for me. So I accept, without reservation, your suggestion that everything remain in the status quo until such time as I can return to New York to explore personally the whole situation in company with the Trustees.[5]

I should be very glad to have you read this letter to the Trustees, if you think it would be helpful.

With best wishes, *Sincerely*

[1] For background on Coykendall, chairman of the Columbia University board of trustees, see no. 114.

[2] Coykendall had written on September 10 (EM) that the trustees were disturbed by a reported conversation Eisenhower had had with Douglas M. Black and General William J. Donovan in which he had "expressed a desire" to have his title changed to chancellor and his "responsibilities very much reduced." Both Black and Donovan had visited the General in May (see no. 374; on Donovan see no. 128, n. 7).

[3] For background on Columbia's previous president, Nicholas Murray Butler, see Galambos, *Chief of Staff.*

[4] The General's July 9 letter to Coykendall is no. 261 (for background see no. 229).

[5] In his letter Coykendall had said that a change in Eisenhower's title at Columbia would involve "the occupancy of President's House and many other details of administration." Coykendall requested that the General let him know whether he wished the trustees to go ahead with the title change or whether he would rather have the matter wait until he knew definitely when he would be returning to Columbia.

Coykendall replied (Sept. 21, 1951, EM) that the trustees were going to "maintain the status quo . . . giving to Grayson Kirk all the assistance and facilities that he may require to properly function as the head administrative officer of the University" (on Kirk see no. 31). "Please be at ease about the whole thing," Coykendall concluded, "and know that we now are at ease also." For developments see no. 398.

374   *Eisenhower Mss.*

To Douglas MacCrae Black   *September 15, 1951*

Dear Doug:[1] I find that the conversations that I had with you, Al Redpath, and possibly one or two others have, instead of tending to clarify the situation at Columbia, caused a little difficulty and misunderstanding.[2] Because of this I have told the Chairman that I withdraw every possible suggestion I have made and I concur in his idea that we should allow everything to remain in status quo until I can come back, at least for a day or so, and talk over the whole affair with all the Trustees present.

As you know I have wanted to be only tactful and, I thought, self effacing. I was very much afraid the Trustees out of their friendship for me would permit a situation to develop that would be inimical to the best interests of the University.

Quite clearly I could not at this moment spare the time to come back and to pack up No. 60 and get out bag and baggage.

From my viewpoint nothing could be more unfortunate than to have any kind of rumors flying around the campus and around the city that there was developing some kind of argument involving my relationship to the University. Any hint of this kind of thing would start all sorts of speculation and gossip which would be reflected in an increase in my personal correspondence with the necessity for answering an entirely new set and kind of question. Please don't let this occur.

Actually I know, of course, that everybody is acting out of a very nice feeling of friendship for me, but since it has become clear that there is more than one viewpoint brought to bear, I agree with the Chairman that we must let the whole thing lie as it now is—even though it may cause some inescapable embarrassment for those who are trying to carry forward the affairs of the University.[3]

It seems a very long time since you were here. I hope that you can find some excuse for coming soon again.[4]

Would you please call Al Redpath on the phone and read this to him? I should like you to do the same in the case of Arthur Sulzberger, because I believe that in some correspondence I have also mentioned this subject to him. Beyond this I have told the Chairman that if he wanted to read to the entire body of the Trustees the letter I wrote him, he was at liberty to do so. However, I do sincerely hope that all of the Trustees will keep the fact that this subject was ever discussed at all entirely confidential among themselves.[5]

With love to Maude and the best to yourself,[6] *Sincerely*

[1] Black was a Columbia University trustee (see no. 168).
[2] Albert Gordon Redpath (LL.B. Columbia University Law School 1922), a partner in the New York City firm of Auchincloss, Parker and Redpath, was also a Columbia trustee. He had visited the General on June 14, and Black had visited in May (see no. 234).
[3] For background on the mutual decision by Eisenhower and the Columbia trustees to maintain the "status quo" see the General's recent letters to the chairman of the trustees, Frederick Coykendall, nos. 261 and 373.
[4] Black would visit Paris again in January 1952.
[5] Eisenhower had already written twice to Arthur H. Sulzberger concerning the Columbia presidency (see nos. 229 and 370).
[6] Black's wife, the former Maude Bergen. Black's reply of September 24 is in EM.

375   *Eisenhower Mss.*

To William Averell Harriman   *September 17, 1951*

Dear Averell:[01] I assume that I have told you in the past something of my convictions as to the need for holding more frequent meetings of the NATO Council.[2] I do not see how the United States can hope to exert the leadership that is necessary in NATO unless such meetings are held at least on a quarterly basis.

In the business of creating the over-all strength that is needed, the material side requires money. But the intellectual and spiritual side requires very little money; of principal importance are imagination, faith and energy. All are agreed that morale is the key to this whole problem; success depends upon a unification that is built upon a common scale of values, a common appreciation of the risks to those values, and a common determination to meet the risks cooperatively. Unless we achieve such unity, all of our expenditures on the material side will be in vain. Consequently, we should make a continuing effort in the spiritual field that will match our great expenditures for munitions and for economic support.

The peoples of the several NATO countries will never believe that the whole project is one to which they should give first priority if governmental officials meet as infrequently as once a year. By word and by example, we must exert every possible effort in this direction.

Today I am on my way to Germany to witness the British maneuvers. This trip will be followed, at intervals, by similar ones to the French Zone and to the American Zone.[3] (Already we are preparing a plan for next year's maneuvers that will contemplate a single, combined exercise of all forces available.)

It is possible that I may cancel one of these impending trips, in view of the tentative arrangements I have made for the meeting with the Chief.[4] I am making tentative plans that will allow me a full day in Washington, and another day to give me a chance to see, for a few minutes, members of my family. Thereafter, I plan to take off immediately for SHAPE. Thus, I could do the whole trip in an over-all absence of about five days. I was informed that, from that end, the exact date made little difference. But I shall nevertheless submit, for approval, whatever little plan I finally propose.

I am distressed to hear that you were laid up with a cold.[5] I hope that you are well now and that additionally you got the few days you were seeking for a bit of rest.[6] Give my love to Marie[7] and, of course, my respects to the Chief.[8]

As always, my very best to you. *Sincerely*

---

[1] For background on Harriman see nos. 16 and 46.

[2] For Eisenhower's earlier pleas that the NAC meet more frequently see nos. 218 and 363. For developments see no. 384.

[3] Eisenhower's heavy travel schedule for September had included a flight to Sola Airfield, Norway, on the tenth for presentation of five U.S. fighter jets to Norway under the Mutual Defense Assistance Program. On the day the General wrote this letter he began a three-day visit to the British zone of Germany to observe autumn maneuvers of the British Army of the Rhine, exercise COUNTERTHRUST. On September 28 and 29 he would travel to the French zone of Germany to witness similar military exercises, JUPITER and CIRRUS (EM, Subject File, Trips, SHAPE nos. 12, 13, 14; *International Herald Tribune*, Paris ed., Sept. 10, 11, 18, 19, 20, 1951).

[4] In July, replying to a message from Truman, Eisenhower had recommended that he visit Washington in September, following congressional hearings on military aid

legislation (see nos. 274 and 363). Eisenhower would travel to Washington for a meeting with the President in early November.

⁵ In a letter of September 7 (EM) Harriman had reported being ill with a cold. His purpose in writing had been to discuss the case of Ambassador at Large Philip Caryl Jessup, Truman's choice to serve on the U.S. delegation to the United Nations. Threatening to defeat the nomination, Senator Joseph R. McCarthy had condemned Jessup's "affinity for Communist causes." In the spring of 1950 Eisenhower had come to the Ambassador's aid during a similar McCarthy attack (see Galambos, *Columbia University*, no. 733), and Harriman hoped that Eisenhower would do so again. Nonetheless, Harriman described his handwritten note as entirely personal and requested no reply. There is no further correspondence on this matter in EM. On Jessup's hearings see *New York Times*, September 14, 28, October 19, 20, 1951.

⁶ On September 18 the NAC, then meeting in Ottawa, agreed to form a Temporary Council Committee (TCC) to examine the military and financial problems confronting the alliance (see no. 384). On September 26 President Truman would name Harriman as the U.S. representative on the committee (State, *Foreign Relations, 1951*, vol. III, *European Security and the German Question, Part I*, pp. 677–78).

⁷ Harriman's wife, the former Marie Norton Whitney.

⁸ When Harriman passed Eisenhower's letter along to Truman on September 24, the President immediately wrote that he agreed about having more meetings of the NAC. "You are also right about the necessity of our fight for peace," Truman said. "There are many things I want to talk to you about. I am sure you and I understand each other. You are doing a grand job" (Truman to Eisenhower, Sept. 24, 1951, EM, Truman Corr.).

376

Eisenhower Mss.

To Ann Louise Stacy Nevins and Arthur Seymour Nevins

September 17, 1951

*Dear Anne and Art:*⁰¹ My days are so full that I have gotten to the point where I must simply trust my friends to understand that my failure to write to them is no indication that they are, for a minute, absent from my thoughts and affections. Almost every day, for the past three weeks, I have told Mamie that "today I am going to write to Anne and Art." I do not have to tell you what has happened to those resolutions. This minute, I am on the Columbine, with a small staff, going to Germany to witness the maneuvers of the British Forces. This is Monday morning, and I shall return to my headquarters, the Lord willing, on Wednesday.²

Of course, I get a great kick out of each piece of news about the farm. Recently, Jerry Brandon allowed me to read a letter that Art had written to him. On top of that, I had a long letter from Walter Kirschner, who seems to have more ideas than a dog does fleas. I am very much afraid that he is planning more in the way of developments on the farm than I could afford. But just the same, I get a lot of fun reading about them.

More and more, Mamie and I project ourselves forward into that setting. Ever since we acquired title to that place we have been thinking ever more specifically and frequently of life in a secluded place, on a productive piece of ground. I simply cannot tell you how often we talk about you, and the idea of all of us living together in the Gettysburg district.[3]

I note that one week you sold 193 dozens of eggs. I think that, in a letter I wrote you some months ago, I urged the selling of those chickens on the grounds that you had enough to do without fooling with the vagaries of a whole flock of laying chickens. I still have youthful memories that made a chicken seem to me to be, except when properly cooked and on the the dinner table, an exasperating sort of beast. Either you must have a somewhat different reaction, or the farm must be making a lot of money out of the darn things—otherwise, you would get rid of them.[4]

From several people, I have heard that George Allen has gone into a television show. I must say, the idea sounds crazy to me. It must serve to tie him down still more. I do not see, to save me, how he can use a bigger income than he now has. So far, he has not written me a word about this venture, so there may be something to it that I don't understand. Nevertheless, the picture of George appearing each week as interlocutor on a show, in order to advertise some product, rather defeats me. Please tell him that I have the terms of our current bet well recorded with Colonel Schulz, and he is not going to be able to plead his new job as an excuse to get out of it. The only thing he can do is get down to weight—and he had better start now![5]

Mamie's mother hasn't been too well since Mr. Doud died. As a result, she stays pretty close to home and Mamie has been so concerned that she sticks closely by her mother's side. However, I think that Mamie herself looks very well. You may have heard that we are now in our new house—have been there for three weeks—and are gradually getting settled. It is a beautiful residence from the outside, and includes in its grounds a small pond in which I have a few trout. Inside, the space is surprisingly small, except for entertaining. There are two large salons and a very large dining room. Sleeping room is very meager.[6]

We have been wondering whether or not you two might find it possible to make a trip over this way. I don't know how long you would feel it practicable or advisable for you to be absent from the farm, but if you could make necessary arrangements, you would certainly be justified in charging the expense of additional help against the farm's operation. You are most certainly entitled to a yearly vacation.

If you should decide to come this way, you might be able to make a deal with the Transport Service, or maybe even come over here with my plane at some time when it makes a trip to the States; possibly you could return to the United States by transport. We could always put you up (providing, of course, that at the moment we were alone, or had only Mamie's mother with us). Certainly, we would be delighted to have you. Jessie Sayler was here a week or so ago and stayed a couple of days with us. She came over commercially but caught a transport going home. I understand that, normally, the west bound transports are lightly loaded.[7]

When you see George and Mary, give them my best; likewise Walter Kirschner, and any other friends that you may encounter. To you two and to your youngsters we, of course, as always, send our most affectionate regard. I have forgotten whether Anne said that Mary Anne is already in Britain, or is about to go there. In any event, on our next trip over there we shall try to call her on the phone, although I doubt that we shall have time to go down to Oxford. Usually, when we go to the United Kingdom, our time is scheduled to the last minute.[8]

Take care of yourselves. *As ever*

[1] For background on Ann and Arthur Nevins, who managed Eisenhower's Gettysburg farm, see no. 48.

[2] On the General's three-day visit to Germany see no. 375, n. 3.

[3] Jerry D. Brandon, an old friend of Eisenhower's, had played golf with him on September 11 and 12 (Galambos, *Columbia University*, no. 884). The General was probably referring to a letter to Brandon from Arthur Kimmins Atkinson, president of the Wabash Railroad Company since 1947 (no copy in EM).

Kirschner had written on September 16 and had enclosed a September 12 letter from Harry E. Holton (both in EM) concerning the construction of a fish pond at the farm (on Kirschner see no. 33, n. 2; for background on Holton and the farm see no. 315).

[4] Eisenhower had told Nevins in several letters that he could sell the chickens unless he felt that the profit on their eggs made it worthwhile to keep them (see, for example, no. 270, n. 3; for developments see no. 770).

[5] George E. Allen had become the coproducer of a television interview show, "Man of the Week" (see *New York Times*, Feb. 10, 1952). On Allen and the wager he had with the General see no. 297, n. 3.

[6] Elivera Doud had been staying with the Eisenhowers since her husband's death (see no. 240). On the General's new home see no. 314, n. 1.

[7] The Nevinses would see the Eisenhowers briefly in early November (see no. 487, n. 2). Jessie Dale Dixon Sayler was the wife of Major General Henry Benton Sayler (see Galambos, *Columbia University*, no. 92).

[8] For background on George Edward and Mary Keane Allen see no. 9, n. 2. Mary Ann, the Nevinses' daughter, had received her Ph.D. from Columbia in the spring and had become a Fulbright scholar of English literature at Cambridge University (see Nevins, *Five-Star Farmer*, pp. 80–81).

To JAMES PRIOLEAU RICHARDS[1]   *September 19, 1951*
Cable AP 81507

Personal from Eisenhower: This message is in response to your request for my views concerning the adequacy of military and economic aid in Senate and House bills in the light of recent security developments and prospects of West European military buildup.[2]

When the Committees of the Senate and the House of Representatives were here in connection with the Mutual Security Program of FY 52, I expressed to them my hope that all these problems could be solved with the aim of the overall good of the US and the importance to us of establishing collective security against the Communistic threat by true cooperation among all NATO countries.[3] In furtherance of this general idea, I told these committees of my views as to the moral, economic and military importance of American aid for countries in the area with which I am concerned. I indicated then that the proposed program of military aid was, in my judgment, a sound one from the standpoint of the rapid build-up of European military forces and of gain in terms of US security; also, that an essential component in this overall effort was the related program of economic aid for the support of national economies upon which the military build-up depended. Military and economic developments here since that time have merely emphasized the obvious conclusion that economic and military strength are inseparable.

It should be understood that no recommendation of mine is intended to urge upon the interested committees any expenditure that is beyond the U.S. capability to support during the critical years during which the current tensions may logically be expected to persist. Within these limits I believe that it is to our interest to accomplish the total build-up quickly and in a limited period of time, rather than risk the dangers and costs of dragging it out. The U.S. role is to provide the initial impetus to the program through assistance in the equipping of forces, with maintenance, replacement and other future outlays shouldered by the European nations at the earliest practicable time. I am keenly aware of the heavy burden being borne by the U.S. during this rearmament period, and of our necessary expenditures in the Far East where a critical phase of the global struggle against Communism is in progress. We here clearly appreciate the necessity of careful Congressional judgment in balancing the scale of aid against U.S. capacity. Nevertheless, any serious cuts in the end item program[4] or of materials required for increased industrial production in Europe will delay completion of our build-up program and, in my judgment, increase therefore the total cost. I have pressed, and will continue to press our

European Allies to accelerate and expand, rather than retard and curtail their military effort. It is of great importance to our country's announced aims that nothing be done during the coming months to halt the growth of the military forces of the European countries. As an essential corollary, we must guard with greatest care against the threat of inflation and downward spiralling in the European strength and morale. Therefore, just as I stress the need for the maintenance of American solvency, I urge the importance of adequate provision for the support of the industrial foundation required to carry out successfully the increase of forces now scheduled during FY 52.

You specifically asked for my views concerning the effect here of the amount of military and economic aid contained in the Senate and House bills. It is clear that reductions in military and items deliveries, while not extensive, will delay, proportionately, the development of new European military units. As to economic aid, my own conclusions can do no more than reflect the opinions of qualified American experts in this field. I cannot escape the depressing fear that cuts of the size contemplated will seriously unbalance the build-up program. These reductions have already given rise to proposals for cut-backs and postponing of defense production and of military outlays in Europe. This, if continued, would be a serious development for us. In short, my attitude toward and my interest in the economic side is measured exclusively by its inescapable effect upon the overall defense program. Therefore, I recommend that when final consideration is given to fixing the amount of military and economic aid from the U.S. under the FY 52 program, everything practicable be done to set the amount at a level which will adequately support the military build-up program as presented to the committee during their visit to Europe. With the complexity of this whole situation, it is obviously impossible to calculate the exact financial and economic requirements of Europe at this military headquarters. Consequently I cannot respond in specific terms to the question of the degree of damage that will result in the military program from reductions on the economic side. Nevertheless, the relationship is so clear that, at the very least, a considerable degree of flexibility should be permitted in the administration of the funds provided.[5]

[1] Richards was Chairman of the House Foreign Affairs Committee (for background see no. 284).
[2] Richards's cable of September 18 is in EM.
[3] For background on the congressional visit see no. 209.
[4] On "end items" see no. 238.
[5] Richards had requested Eisenhower's views for guidance at a conference among members of the U.S. Senate and House on an amendment to the Mutual Security Act of 1951 (H.R. 5113). Eisenhower's aides Colonels Paul T. Carroll and Andrew Jackson Goodpaster assisted in drafting this reply. On September 21 Eisenhower

would cable Richards again (EM), saying that he had understood that Richards was reluctant to use the cable of September 19 in view of its "personal" designation. "Please feel free," Eisenhower said, "to use this cable in any way you see fit, including its release to the press if you so desire." Richards apparently did not release Eisenhower's message to the press but did enter it into the *Congressional Record* on October 5, 1951 (*Congressional Record*, 82d Cong., 1st sess., 1951, 97, pt. 10: 12711–13). For more on the report of the conference committee see U.S. Congress, House, Committee on Foreign Affairs, *Mutual Security Act of 1951: Conference Report*, 82d Cong., 1st sess., 1951, H. Rept. 1090. President Truman would sign the Mutual Security Act of 1951 on October 10. The act authorized $5 billion in military aid to NATO countries. For problems in delivering that aid see nos. 461, 462, and 698.

378   *Eisenhower Mss.*

To OMAR NELSON BRADLEY   *September 20, 1951*
Secret. Personal

Dear Brad:[1] I was very glad to receive your letter of 7 September with respect to the problems involved in proceeding with necessary planning for aid in the event Yugoslavia is attacked.[2] At this point I want to make it clear that I understand your cooperation and those of the other members of the Joint Chiefs of Staff in the arrangements that they have made to accommodate their earlier plans to the changing situation incident to Admiral Carney now holding the position as my Commander-in-Chief of Southern Europe.[3] I appreciate your actions and your consideration of my views.

It is quite obvious that the objective must be to obtain firm commitments on the part of all concerned including Tito, to accomplish necessary preparatory measures, and to develop detailed plans so that we will have full coordination of effort when required. It must be made equally obvious that in the accomplishment of military arrangements essential to security, the United States refrain from adopting procedures which might weaken the existing cohesion we now have among the members of NATO.

It is clear that, due to circumstances, we must solve the Yugoslavian problem in separate stages and in an orderly manner. These seem to us here to be as follows:

First: A clear understanding should be evolved with the British as to the objective, the method and timing of subsequent stages. This should be accomplished in Washington on a politico-military level. In view of my interest and that of Admiral Carney, we should be kept fully informed possibly by according to a representative of Admiral Carney as my direct agent observer status at these meetings.

Second: Bilateral approaches should be made to the French and Italians on a political level in consonance with the agreement reached with the British.

Third: Preliminary military conversations with the British, French, and Italians should then be initiated under my direction with Admiral Carney acting for me within limits imposed by earlier political agreements. These would lead to agreed allied military requirements which would be in consonance with existing outline plans.

Fourth: The matter should be introduced into NATO to obtain political agreement that *contingent* military plans be developed under my direction by Admiral Carney.

Fifth: Approach should be made to Tito on a political level by either the United States or some other mutually acceptable agent of NATO to develop a basis of future military conversations.[4]

Sixth: Direct contact should then be made with Tito by Admiral Carney on purely military aspects, involved in coordination of effort in event of hostilities.

I realize that covert planning between the United States, British, French, and Italians[5] to render military support to Yugoslavia is probably necessary but could prove embarrassing if its progress should become generally known. Hence, the subject should be injected into appropriate NATO channels at the earliest point that it is politically feasible.

I hope the foregoing will be of assistance to you in the development of a sound approach to a very important matter which is of concern to us all.[6] *Sincerely*

[1] General Bradley was currently serving as Chairman of the JCS (see no. 304, n. 16).

[2] For background on Eisenhower's efforts to bring Yugoslavia into NATO's defensive framework see no. 332, n. 3. In his letter of September 7 (CJCS, Bradley Files, 091 Yugoslavia) Bradley had written that the British government had been pressing Washington to narrow the scope of Admiral Carney's discussions concerning aid to Yugoslavia. The British had also tried to prevent discussion of the subject by NATO's Standing Group. After talking the matter over with the State Department, Bradley had proposed that three preliminary steps be taken before actual talks with the Yugoslavs could start. First, the problem should be discussed by the British and Americans "on a politico-military level" in Washington. Second, after these discussions had produced "more specific instructions," Carney was to confer with the British Chiefs of Staff. Third, Carney should complete "bilateral talks with the British, French, and Italians" before making the Yugoslavian problem "a NATO matter" (see State, *Foreign Relations, 1951*, vol. IV, *Europe: Political and Economic Developments, Part II*, pp. 1845–46; and Gruenther to JCS, ALO 310, Sept. 7, 1951, EM, Bradley Corr.). Navy Captain George W. Anderson drafted this letter for Eisenhower.

[3] The JCS had urged Secretary of State Acheson to expedite the negotiations with the British and the Yugoslavs. The JCS also asked that Eisenhower be allowed to begin planning with the Yugoslavs "whether or not the U.S.-U.K. governmental

consideration proposed by the British is carried out" (Vandenberg to Secretary of Defense, Sept. 19, 1951, OS/D, 1951, Clas. Decimal File, CD 091.3 MDAP [Yugoslavia]. See also State, *Foreign Relations, 1951*, vol. IV, *Europe: Political and Economic Developments, Part II*, pp. 1845–46, n. 2; and SM 2275-51, Sept. 19, 1951, and DUSM 579-51, Nov. 1, 1951, both in CJCS, Bradley Files, 091 Yugoslavia).

[4] U.S. Army Chief of Staff J. Lawton Collins would meet with Marshal Tito in October (see no. 332; and transcript of interview, Oct. 14, 1951, EM, Collins Corr.). Eisenhower had already met with Colonel General Koca Popovic, Chief of Staff of the Yugoslav Army, for preliminary discussions concerning U.S. aid and the coordination of war plans (see Memorandum of Conversation, July 10, 1951, in EM, Subject File, Conversations). At this meeting, held at Ambassador David K. E. Bruce's residence in Paris, Eisenhower had asked Popovic whether "on the basis of the assumption that the Yugoslavs would receive all the equipment they required for their standing army and for an adequate number of reserves" Yugoslavia would be prepared to enter into "some form of coordination of planning with the Western powers." Eisenhower had added that it was "important to maintain touch with one another on a continuing basis so that each would be aware of what the other was doing, since when a soldier is dependent upon a flank he wants to know about it and be able to count on it." Popovic had replied that his "own personal view was that such contacts and exchanges should be developed at the appropriate time, and that the appropriate time was prior to the actual outbreak of hostilities." Eisenhower also asked Popovic whether the Yugoslavs would be willing to "fight shoulder-to-shoulder against the Soviet system with the Western capitalistic system—the latter being a system in which General Eisenhower believed profoundly." Popovic answered that "the imperialist nature of Soviet 'Communism'" had forced Yugoslavia out of the Soviet bloc and that "the doctrinaire position" would not "in any way impede the Yugoslav Army in resisting aggression alongside the soldiers of Western Europe."

[5] On September 19 the JCS had warned that Italy should not be brought into the discussions with Yugoslavia until "a much later date since she is a poor security risk" (Vandenberg to Secretary of Defense, Sept. 19, 1951, OS/D, 1951, Clas. Decimal File, CD 091.3 MDAP [Yugoslavia]).

[6] After considering Eisenhower's letter, the JCS would advise Bradley that there was "little prospect of NATO political agreement in the immediate future on Yugoslavian planning." The JCS urged that Bradley meet with Eisenhower and secure his agreement to bilateral talks held with the British and French in order "to move forward on planning for the short range" (Lalor to Bradley, Oct. 5, 1951, CJCS, Bradley Files, 091 Yugoslavia). Bradley would meet with Eisenhower on October 8 and 9 and would report back that Eisenhower "believes, and I concur, that [the] first step must be politico-military bilateral talks between US with British, French and Italians." These talks, Bradley felt, should be held as soon as possible and "should result in an agreed governmental position between these four powers" (Bradley to JCS, ALO 378, Oct. 9, 1951, *ibid.*). The American, British, and French governments would eventually agree to conduct military discussions outside NATO auspices, and in December 1952 U.S. General Thomas T. Handy would visit Yugoslavia for the purpose of conducting joint operational planning (Poole, *History of the Joint Chiefs of Staff*, vol. IV, *1950–1952*, p. 316n). Before this visit, however, Deputy SACEUR Montgomery had already made informal arrangements with Tito to have three Yugoslavian divisions "deployed in the Ljubljana Gap to defend the approaches to the Venezia-Guilia corridor" (JSPC 876/414, Dec. 29, 1951, CCS 092 Western Europe [3-12-48], Sec. 113).

Eisenhower Mss.

To DOUGLAS SOUTHALL FREEMAN *September 20, 1951*

Dear Dr. Freeman:[1] Of course, it was a long time since 1946 but, giving my answer in the absolute confidence that you suggest, your recollection of our conversation in my office in the winter of that year coincides exactly with my own.[2]

It was fine to hear from you again. It must be fascinating to be doing research on Washington's 1781 Campaign. His quick perception of his opportunity and his undertaking of a maneuver that must have seemed quite appalling to some of his assistants can be considered as nothing less than remarkable. After the many disappointments he had been forced to bear through so many campaigns, it was wonderful that he could have the great climax of Yorktown. What a man he was.[3]

With warm personal regard, *Cordially*

[1] Freeman was a historian and Pulitzer Prize-winning author (see Galambos, *Columbia University*, no. 980).

[2] On September 13 (EM) Freeman had written that he wanted to "present again . . . the issue I put before you in the winter of 1946." Freeman had wanted to verify that his memory was correct regarding their 1946 conversation, in which Eisenhower had said: "Of course no individual could decline a call to service if recognized leaders of the nation, regardless of party, told him a situation had arisen in which he was the only man who could save the country from ruin." Freeman believed that in order to draft the General as a presidential candidate, "leading men of both parties and of no party affiliation at all" would need to convince Eisenhower that America's welfare depended on his candidacy and that he was needed to "lead the nation out of the present disgraceful morass." For a similar letter Freeman had written in 1950 see Galambos, *Columbia University*, no. 980. On the 1946 meeting see Galambos, *Chief of Staff*, no. 1152.

[3] Freeman was working on the fifth volume of his biography of George Washington, entitled *Victory with the Help of France*. In November Freeman would send the General a copy of volumes 3 and 4, *Planter and Patriot* and *Leader of the Revolution*.

Eisenhower Mss.

To ROBERT ABERCROMBIE LOVETT *September 20, 1951*

Dear Bob:[1] My thanks for your note. Long before this I should have sent you a message to express my delight at your appointment to the position vacated by General Marshall. I have felt so close to you for so long a time, particularly in our approach to the security and foreign problems of our country, that I have the feeling that you realize without my saying so what tremendous confidence I have in your leadership.

Of course, I shall, from time to time, write you informally as to developments here. The frequency of my letters depends as much upon the availability of time as upon the occurrence of things worthy of reporting. Consequently, you will find some of my messages rather routine and uninteresting, but possibly some of the others can make up for this defect.[2]

All the best and, of course, warm personal regard. *Cordially*

[1] Lovett, former Under Secretary of State, was the newly appointed Secretary of Defense. Before taking the assignment he had served since October 1950 as Deputy Secretary of Defense (for background on Lovett see Galambos, *Columbia University*, no. 1018. On Marshall's retirement and Lovett's appointment see no. 372; and *New York Times*, Sept. 13, 23, 29, 1951).

[2] Lovett had told Eisenhower (Sept. 15, 1951, EM) that his letters to Marshall had been "extremely helpful to us all" and that he hoped Eisenhower would keep him advised in the same way. Eisenhower would soon do so (see no. 388).

381   *Eisenhower Mss., Family File*

To Milton Stover Eisenhower   *September 20, 1951*

Dear Milton:[1] For me, by far the most interesting statement in your letter was the last sentence, "Helen and I are at Fred Waring's for three days." My brief acquaintanceship with him has given me a very high opinion of him and, beyond this, I hear that he not only is an expert in Pennsylvania cooking but that he likewise has a private golf course. I wish I could have been with you for those three days.[2]

As for all the rest of the things that are worrying you, I went through it all a long time ago. I refuse to fret any more. My advice to you is to develop a good laugh when such questions are put to you, and merely make some facetious remark of the character, "If you ever find anyone who can speak authoritatively for that brother of mine, I should like very much to meet him." This or anything else of a like character would serve.[3]

Only this morning I went through a very long grilling, although my visitor pretended that he was "asking me no questions, but was merely presenting a picture of American public opinion."[4]

As I have told you before, I am completely of the conviction that the establishment of collective security by cooperation among the free nations is a *must* for the future of our type of civilization. Success in the venture will not take place except with strong support within the United States. I am one of the principal figures engaged in this task and am, in this region, the recognized representative of our country. If I should announce an affiliation or partisan leaning that would tend to divide our country's attitude toward this effort, such action could scarcely be regarded as anything less than calamitous; so I just keep still.

Please quit worrying and don't forget your sense of humor.[5] Better still, pick up Helen and Ruth, hop into a TWA plane, and be over here in eighteen hours. We could have a good time.[6]

Please give my love to Helen and the family and, of course, as always, all the best to yourself. *As ever*

[1] On the General's brother Milton see no. 9, n. 1.

[2] In a four-page handwritten letter of September 17 (EM) Milton had mentioned his visit with the Warings. Fred M. Waring, a popular musical conductor and producer of the Fred Waring television show, owned the Shawnee Inn and the Shawnee Country Club in Shawnee-on-Delaware, Pennsylvania.

[3] Milton was being pressured to reveal Eisenhower's political affiliation and to state whether the General would soon become a presidential candidate. He was concerned that he would be misquoted or that he would say the wrong thing: "I am becoming very worried about the political situation . . . my fear is that I am being used in a way that will be embarrassing to you." Milton wanted Eisenhower to know that he was "trying to keep out of everything." "If you have any advice for me," he concluded, "I hope you'll send it quickly because I'm in a very unhappy frame of mind about the whole thing" (for background see nos. 195 and 356).

[4] On the morning of September 20 Eisenhower's visitors had included Bernard S. ("Bunny") Carter (see no. 385, n. 6) and William Rothwell Plewman, assistant editor in chief of the *Toronto Star*.

[5] On the General's efforts to remain nonpartisan see no. 358. For developments see no. 410.

[6] Ruth E. Eisenhower was Milton and Helen E. Eisenhower's daughter. Milton would see the General in November (see no. 457).

382   *Eisenhower Mss.*

To WILLIAM EDWARD ROBINSON   *September 20, 1951*

Dear Bill:[1] We shall be looking forward to the arrival of Albert Bradley and Bernie Gimbel. I like them both.[2]

By far, the best news in your completely interesting letter was the item about the improvement in your own health and condition. I just cannot tell you how pleased I am.[3]

When Bert Andrews sent me the particular question he did, I don't suppose he really hoped for a specific answer—he knows that anyone making a statement of that kind would feel a compulsion to call in the entire press.[4]

Tell Cliff I am delighted that his physical examination came off so perfectly. Now that he has found out how good Paris and the Saint

Germain golf course are for his well-being, I hope he will make great use of them both.[5]

I am just back from maneuvers and have an accumulation of work to dig through. Possibly, however, I can write you a more intelligent-sounding letter within a few days. In the meantime, keep me on your correspondence list for any news that comes to your attention.[6] *As ever*

[1] Robinson was a friend of Eisenhower's and an executive with the *New York Herald Tribune* (see no. 39, n. 1).

[2] In a letter of September 14 (EM) Robinson had said that Albert Bradley (Ph.D. University of Michigan 1917) would soon visit Eisenhower. Robinson suggested that Bradley, who was executive vice-president of General Motors Corporation, might "shed some valuable light on certain regional economic situations from a new perspective" (see no. 434). Bernard F. Gimbel (B.S. University of Pennsylvania 1907), president of Gimbel Brothers since 1927, would also visit Eisenhower this month (on Gimbel see Galambos, *Columbia University*, no. 714). Gimbel would have lunch with the General on September 25, and Bradley would visit him on October 2.

[3] Robinson had given Eisenhower a "proud report": "Bristling with unbearable righteousness I am delighted to tell you that I am within two pounds of that 180 target" (for background see no. 265; for subsequent events see no. 447).

[4] On the cable from Andrews see no. 345, n. 2.

[5] "Cliff got a 100% clean bill of health from the doctors," Robinson wrote. "His second trip to Paris unquestionably clinched the recovery" (see no. 193, n. 4).

[6] The General had just returned from a trip to Germany (see no. 375).

383   *Eisenhower Mss.*

To Fred G. Gurley   *September 22, 1951*
Personal

Dear Fred:[1] I am grateful for your handwritten letter of the 17th. Anyone would certainly be proud to have the kind of friends who come rushing forward, with flags flying, whenever any unjustified attack is launched against the object of their friendship.[2]

So far as the Senator's insinuations are concerned, I have gotten accustomed to attacks that are made by people whom I have never met, and certainly have never harmed. So, normally, I pay no slightest attention to them. Of all charges that have been levelled against me— and continue to be in spite of the fact that I have steadfastly stood by the assertion that I desire no part of a political career—the most curious one is that I am or have been a part of the so-called "New Deal." My promotions in 1941-2-3-4 have been cited as evidence. The fact is that I never even met Mr. Roosevelt until a few days before I went to Britain to command in 1942; more than this, to the best of my knowledge, I had no close acquaintanceship prior to that time with any prominent "New Dealer." Every opinion and conviction I have ever expressed about governmental affairs has been *against* planned economy, the "hand out" state, and the trend toward centralization of economic and political power in the hands of Washington bureaucrats. But it seems useless to point out these facts because the character of the current attacks demonstrates that the people who launch them have no concern for facts or truth. They simply want to promote their own interests through the attempt to destroy others.[3]

Of course, I have from time to time been forced to give some thought to matters of the kind raised in your letter. I refer specifically to those parts that deal with the possibility of a future duty for me in the political field.[4]

In this connection, and considering the requirements of my present post, I have reached conclusions somewhat as follows: Successful development of collective security through cooperation among the free nations is, in view of the current Communistic military, subversive and political threats, mandatory if we are to survive as a nation featuring political freedom for the individual and a competitive, free enterprise. One of the most important factors in achieving success in this great task is the confidence that all Americans may have in the individuals designated to help carry forward the work. I happen to be one of those individuals. Consequently, as long as I am actually assigned to this job, I do not see how I can announce or indicate any partisan leanings or allegiance. To do so could not fail to arouse suspicion as to my devotion to the task, and would cast some doubt on the disinterestedness of my recommendations with respect to this work, in which our country is investing so much money. This task of developing security is one in which all Americans are involved—not merely Republicans *or* Democrats. Beyond this, you realize, of course, that I don't want a political job—but even some who are friendly find this hard to believe—to say nothing of enemies, who do *not want* to believe it! In any event, I know that I'm working long and hard—and to do so had to abandon activities in which I had personally become deeply interested, and had to give up once more the home Mamie and I have so long wanted to establish for ourselves.

You and I have gone over these things in private conversation; you know my convictions, not only as to the deportment that I feel I must myself observe, but you know my general views with respect to such matters as the economy of the country, the importance of our national solvency, the need for national strength and a strong attitude in conducting our foreign affairs, with the purpose of promoting our own enlightened self-interest.

I trust that you can make sense out of all this. I know that you will at least understand that it represents my honest feelings. I am not wise enough at this moment to foresee the entire future. Of course, it is possible that unusual or spectacular circumstances could convince me that I have been making errors in my own reasoning. Certainly I agree with you that there is little likelihood that I will be greatly bothered by the politicians unless I myself make some move. In this conviction, I have found a great deal of comfort. But I hope that it is clear to you that I can never simultaneously move toward political activity and remain on duty in uniform.

Since your letter did not say anything about your daughter, I assume that she is improving. Certainly Mamie and I pray so. A recent note from Streeter Flynn seemed also to imply that she was on the mend. In any event, both of us send to you and Ruth our profound wishes that she may soon fully recover and relieve your minds and hearts of this terrible anxiety.[5]

With lasting personal regard, *Cordially*

[1] Gurley was president and chairman of the executive committee of the Atchison, Topeka and Santa Fe Railway System (see no. 122, n. 1).

[2] In his letter of September 17 (EM) Gurley had enclosed a copy of a letter he had sent to William Ezra Jenner, U.S. senator from Indiana, and a clipping of an editorial that had appeared in the September 13 *David Lawrence Letter*, a nationally syndicated news column on domestic affairs in the United States. According to the editorial, Eisenhower was "slipping" as a possible nominee for either party and should not expect a draft by one or both parties; instead, the General should "show more interest in a Republican nomination if he is to get it." On this point, Gurley recommended that if Eisenhower wanted the Republican nomination, he should declare no later than March 1952. He then should "get away some place where reporters can't get to you . . . and meet a small group of political advisers who can help you on the treatment of questions that are implicit in the situation." Gurley suggested that such a place might be his Phantom Ranch on the Colorado River at Grand Canyon. "It can be reached only by mule back ride of $2\frac{1}{2}$ hours," he said. "Meals and rooms are for free. Also the mule."

[3] In his letter to Jenner of September 17 (EM) Gurley had called the senator to task for "casting aspersions" on Eisenhower in a speech before the Executives' Club in Chicago on September 14. Citing Eisenhower's swift rise from lieutenant colonel to five-star general, Jenner had said, "I never saw the New Deal pass out such favors to anyone unless he was one of its own." To this Gurley wrote Jenner, "I am one of the many Republicans who resent such off-color remarks and reflections by insinuation. Your all too obvious purpose was to influence Republicans against Eisenhower. I think he is a fine citizen, and, frankly, I would be quite pleased if the Republicans nominated him in 1952" (see *Chicago Tribune*, Sept. 15, 1951). On Eisenhower's promotions during World War II see Chandler, *War Years*.

[4] Gurley had urged Eisenhower to announce his candidacy for the Republican nomination, because he did not think that the General would be drafted by the Republicans. "I would certainly hope you do not get around to believing it to be your duty to run as a Democratic nominee, although I think you would be elected," Gurley said. "You would carry back into office with you a lot of people who in my opinion should not be returned to office and they would bother you to beat hell afterwards."

[5] Margaret Gurley Dow had been so ill that the Gurleys had canceled their plans to visit the Eisenhowers (see Gurley to Eisenhower, Sept. 6, 1951, EM). Streeter

Blanton Flynn, an attorney with the Oklahoma City firm of Rainey, Flynn, Green and Anderson, had written to Eisenhower about Margaret's illness (see Flynn to Eisenhower, Sept. 14, 1951, EM, Miscellaneous Corr.).

384   *Eisenhower Mss.*

To Harry S. Truman   *September 22, 1951*

Dear Mr. President: The news thus far from the Ottawa meeting is very reassuring to us here. While we shall have to wait for more complete information as to what was actually accomplished, it appears certain, in any case, that a good foundation was laid for concrete action at the meeting scheduled for November.[1]

Today I have been thinking of the trip home and, from a study of my calendar, it would be easier for me to visit Washington at the end of October rather than in the early part of the month when several maneuvers are scheduled. As you know, I have planned to make the trip a very brief one and it would appear possible to do this only after Congress has adjourned.[2]

In spite of all this, I could come earlier without serious dislocation if you so desire, since the only commitment here not entirely under my own control is at London on October 19th.[3]

The suggestions of this letter are based solely on my understanding that the exact time of my return was not considered a critical factor by you. Naturally, I stand ready to meet whatever desire you may have.[4]

With best wishes to you and yours, *Respectfully*

[1] The North Atlantic Council had held its seventh conference in Ottawa, Canada, September 15–20, 1951, and had made several important decisions. The NAC unanimously approved a resolution that the NATO nations invite Greece and Turkey to full membership in the alliance (see no. 423). The ministers established a twelve-member Temporary Council Committee "to survey urgently the requirements of external security, and particularly of fulfilling a militarily acceptable NATO plan for the defense of Western Europe, and the realistic political-economic capabilities of the member countries." The NAC invited Eisenhower to attend its Rome meeting in order to report on NATO military preparedness, including the issue of German partnership in European defense. Addressing one weakness that Eisenhower had pointed out (see nos. 218 and 363), the NAC also resolved to meet more frequently and at more regular intervals "in order to develop more effective unity of action, and in accordance with its duties as the institution for forming the policy and directing the operations of the Treaty Organization" (State, *Foreign Relations, 1951*, vol. III, *European Security and the German Question, Part I*, p. 692). For background on the Ottawa meeting see *ibid.*, pp. 240–63, 272–80, 646–92, and *passim*; Ismay, *NATO*, pp. 43–44; and Acheson, *Present at the Creation*, pp. 569–71. See also nos. 399 and 424. For Eisenhower's thoughts on the Rome meeting, finally rescheduled for November, see no. 494.

[2] On the planned Truman-Eisenhower meeting, which the President had first proposed in July, see nos. 274, 290, and 363; and n. 4 below.

[3] Eisenhower had accepted an invitation to speak that day in London, where British Eighth Army veterans would commemorate the ninth anniversary of the battle of El Alamein (see no. 401).

[4] On about September 25, responding to this letter, Truman cabled to suggest either October 31 or November 1 as an acceptable date (Truman to Harriman, c. Sept. 25, 1951, EM, Truman Corr.). Eisenhower would return to the United States in early November and would meet with the President on November 5 (see nos. 457 and 468).

385   *Eisenhower Mss.*

To George Whitney   *September 22, 1951*

Dear George:[1] Your latest letter reflects again the validity of the old adage that all things involving human society and human effort tend to find their solutions in a "gray zone." The only real blacks and whites are found in the fields of moral standards, abstractions, and exact sciences. As quickly as we begin to consider anything involved in a human society and its activities to satisfy its own needs and desires, we find that we are compelled to adjust, to accommodate, and to compromise. This, of course, is only natural since man himself is made up of all combinations of qualities, some of which are admirable while others belong to the villain who, in one degree or another, lurks within each of us.[2]

These observations—trite as they are—explain why you had to write your second letter in order that I could get clear in my mind the full meaning of your letter of late August.[3] The principles outlined in the first letter, while appealing as such, needed the modifications incident to application before they made unassailable sense. Now I am certain that there is little in your convictions with which I could possibly quarrel. On the contrary, I think that your explanations have served to provide me with a basis for developing a sort of doctrine out of what has been, heretofore, little more than instinctive reaction. I particularly agree with your expressed impatience with governmental officials (and others) who refuse to face facts because of the fear of unpleasant consequences.[4] If ever there was a time when we need individuals who have the ability to reduce complicated appearing problems to their barest essentials and to show us what those essentials inevitably mean to our future and to our way of life, now is that time. I truly am deeply obligated to you for your efforts to educate me.[5]

Bunny Carter dropped in to see me yesterday morning.[6] We had a nice chat and are planning to play a bit of golf very soon. This I cannot do at the moment because some peculiar affliction has taken up its dwelling place in my left wrist. It is weak and sore and, so far as I can determine, for no reason. I hope, though, that it is a passing complaint that will not keep me too long from a bit of exercise.

Even so, I cannot complain about my health. Ever since I stopped smoking about three years ago, my only complaint, aside from an occasional cold, has been the difficulty of reminding my appetite to have some consideration for my girth.[7]

With us, this is a very busy season. We have maneuvers at this period of the year because crops have been harvested and little damage is done to the countryside by the movement of troops and vehicles. I always try to visit each important unit engaged in such activity; even though it is no longer my job to supervise training techniques and methods, I find it important to let soldiers know that the so-called VIPs are tremendously interested in their progress and welfare.[8]

My greetings to all members of your nice family and, as always, warm regard to yourself. *Cordially*

[1] For background on Whitney and his continuing correspondence with Eisenhower see nos. 306, n. 1, and 355, n. 1.

[2] In his letter of September 17 (EM) Whitney had said, "I am afraid that I tend to be over-categorical on subjects which should not be treated that way and which must be subject to some give and take."

[3] For a summary of Whitney's August 27 letter concerning the economic controls imposed by government on U.S. business see no. 355.

[4] Whitney had said, "My impatience with all the twaddle that is talked and the aversion of those in public authority to face facts is my excuse for being so flat-footed." On others in authority he wrote, "Certain industrialists apparently think they are sent from God. . . ."

[5] Whitney would continue to correspond with Eisenhower on economic subjects (see no. 443).

[6] Bernard Shirley Carter (A.B. Harvard 1915) had been president of the Paris banking firm of Morgan and Cie since 1946; he was also a director of J. P. Morgan & Company, New York. According to Eisenhower's appointment calendar, Carter had visited the General the morning of September 20, bringing with him a message from George Whitney. Eisenhower and Carter had played golf a number of times at Morfontaine, located in Thiers, a small town in south central France.

[7] On Eisenhower's problems with smoking see no. 166, n. 2; on his diet see no. 265, n. 4.

[8] For Eisenhower's trips see no. 375, n. 3.

To Edward John Bermingham   *September 24, 1951*
Personal and confidential

Dear Ed:[1] I am deeply grateful for your thought-provoking letter on the course of action suggested by Senator Mundt.[2] Your letter was so persuasive—so logical in its presentation of a particular viewpoint—that I feel I should give you again an analysis of my own position.

The first consideration is NATO—and SHAPE, which comes under it. Since my appointment last December, I have been laboring to bring into existence a solid and viable military structure which could offer a reasonable guarantee of peace and assurance of America's security in this area of the world. While we have some results to show, I look upon my efforts up to this time as largely preparatory for what will be accomplished, we hope in the very near future.

This period will see the fruition not only of my own work over the past ten months, but of all the NATO efforts throughout the $2\frac{1}{2}$-year existence of that organization. Moreover, it will represent a critical period in the realization of net results sought through the tremendous financial support rendered to this area by the United States during the past six years.

Within NATO, we are now done with principles and are down on the hard rock of financial commitments, munitions productions, and troop allocations for the long as well as the short-term. Our governments appear to be ready to solve the German problem—inherently explosive but of transcendental importance to Western strength—military, political, or economic.[3] We see Europe on the verge of concrete action to bring its national economies into closer harmony and efficiency.

With weak governments the rule on the continent, and the possibility of having new governments in both Britain and France, continued momentum during this period will depend entirely upon American leadership. Our country is the keystone of the entire structure, and our unity before the world must be unassailable.

I don't want to overestimate my own contribution in these matters but I feel that whatever influence I can exert is increased by the fact that I represent no faction, group, or party in the United States or in any other country for that matter. I can speak confidently at SHAPE for that large segment of the public in Western Europe, Britain, and the United States who fear the menace of Communism and are determined, as a unit, to do something about it. Until we are definitely past the shoals, I could not jeopardize this position of non-partisanship, even by so much as a sneeze.[4]

I regret to hear that my silence on specific issues may at times be embarrassing to some at home.[5] However, I do not see how I could be blamed for anything more than preoccupation with the responsibilities assigned to me here. As you well know, they are considerable. Though inclined toward optimism, I make no pretense of reading the Kremlin mind, and am acutely aware of the precarious imbalance of power that exists in North Europe at the moment.

This should not be read with any interpretation that I might succumb to the flattering thought that I am an indispensable man in Europe.[6] In the first place, I don't believe there is such a thing. In the second place, I want to live in America. I have had more than my share of foreign duty. Consequently, I want to get the job done—just as quickly and effectively as possible.

With warm regard, *Cordially*

[1] Bermingham, a retired investment executive and Eisenhower's longtime friend, had become increasingly active as a political adviser (see no. 23, n. 1).

[2] Writing to Eisenhower on September 9, Bermingham had enclosed a letter of August 30 from South Dakota Republican Senator Karl Mundt (both letters in EM) in which Mundt proposed that Eisenhower authorize a statement declaring his Republican party affiliation in time to enter the May 1952 Oregon primary. Oregon law permitted a candidate's name to appear without his consent but required petitions signed only by members of his party (see no. 135, n. 2). By late July Mark O. Hatfield, Republican state legislator and college professor, had gathered the necessary number of pro-Eisenhower signatures and only awaited proof of Eisenhower's party membership to file on the General's behalf. Meanwhile rival Republicans and liberal Democrats collected signatures to place Eisenhower in the Democratic primary. Mundt believed that the Oregon situation offered a perfect opportunity for Eisenhower to clarify his party loyalty without announcing his candidacy. "The developments in Oregon can be changed from a liability to a definite dividend," Mundt had written, "unless Ike is going to remain aloof so long that the parade passes by and gets beyond reach before he determines which horse to ride . . . " (see no. 358; and Paul T. David, Malcolm Moos, and Ralph M. Goldman, eds., *Presidential Nominating Politics in 1952*, 5 vols. [Baltimore, 1954], vol. V, *The West*, pp. 193–94, 205).

Bermingham argued in favor of Mundt's proposal: by stating his party affiliation Eisenhower would "unloose the energies and activities of your friends all over America who want to get the delegate machinery moving in your behalf." Bermingham pointed out that the Taft forces had for some time organized a sizable block of delegates pledged to them, and many of Eisenhower's friends were reluctant to commit themselves until "some expression comes from you either to the effect that you are a Republican, that you are not a Democrat, or that you would not be available for the Democratic nomination."

[3] See no. 389. For developments see no. 442.

[4] See no. 365.

[5] Bermingham had said that many of Eisenhower's friends were seriously worried "lest the next six weeks or two months may produce developments in the direction of lining up so many delegates pledged to Bob Taft that he will be nominated by default."

[6] Bermingham saw Eisenhower's mission in Europe as being in "the process of completion." He stressed, however, that the idea of Eisenhower's indispensability

in Europe "—preached by many—can stem only from personal motives, and is just plain rot." For developments in Oregon see no. 450, n. 2.

387 *Eisenhower Mss., Diaries*

DIARY *September 25, 1951*

For the first time in years I've seen a "political poll" (as usual, conducted by Gallup) that puts me well down the list in the order of preference among Republicans.[1] It is comforting—maybe the pressure will ease up. I *hear* that the Democrats still rate me high—but that causes me no concern. I could never imagine feeling any compelling duty in connection with a Democratic movement of any kind.[2]

[1] Eisenhower may have referred to the National Republican Round-up Committee survey, which ranked him third behind Taft and MacArthur as a GOP presidential candidate (*New York Times*, Sept. 10, 1951). The most recent Gallup poll on Eisenhower, conducted July 7–13 and dated August 1, 1951, had asked respondents whether they thought Eisenhower would accept the Republican presidential nomination in 1952. About four in ten believed that he would, and the same proportion believed that he would not; among Republicans polled, half believed that Eisenhower would accept a draft (Gallup, *The Gallup Poll*, vol. II, *1949–1958*, pp. 999–1000). On Eisenhower's earlier standing as a potential candidate see no. 232, n. 7.

[2] A Gallup poll of June 18 had surveyed support for possible Democratic presidential candidates, including Eisenhower, and shown the General to be the most popular choice (Gallup, *The Gallup Poll*, vol. II, *1949–1958*, pp. 990–91). On the Democratic party's interest in the General see no. 345; and *New York Times*, August 26, 1951. For developments see no. 452.

388 *Eisenhower Mss.*

TO ROBERT ABERCROMBIE LOVETT *September 25, 1951*

Dear Bob:[1] I hope that you will never expect, in my letters, any exposition conforming to the dictates of unity, coherence, and emphasis. In fact, because the kind of letter that I have usually written to General Marshall or to Averell Harriman has been little more than representative of my current thinking on a number of different and sometimes unrelated subjects, I suspect that the two of them have often wondered whether I could have the slightest concern for such things as orderliness and logic.

This morning the first thing that comes to me is something that is never long absent from my mind. It is the need in NATO for the continuous, energetic exertion of American leadership. Frequently, all of us become so involved in the material side of our problems—in the importance of equipping and financing—that we sometimes lose sight of the fundamental importance of morale.

For some years, both through so-called economic and later through a combination of economic and military aid, we have been attempting to restore the morale of Europe. We do not need to argue the importance, to the future security and prosperity of the United States, of a secure and economically sound Europe. The case can be proved through industrial and economic facts alone—it is merely underlined by appeal to the cultural and social ties between us. But it is clear that the task of making Europe both secure and economically sound must, *in the long run, devolve upon Europeans*; the United States cannot build a Roman wall around all parts of the world in which American interests might be both deep and lasting. Since the heart of any defense is determination, faith, and confidence, it is logical that we should exert every bit of our influence toward the restoration of morale in this region.

Unfortunately—I almost said tragically—we have at times over-emphasized the material as opposed to the direct appeal in furthering this restoration. Morale is not created merely by good living conditions, by better housing and better health, no matter how necessary these may be. It is the product of many things! Of understanding, of belief in comrades, of pride and self-respect, of traditions, loves, hates, and even prejudices. It seems silly if we do not match our great material expenditures by inspirational efforts that cost nothing and which, in many cases, can be more efficacious than mere financial help.

Every responsible official in government has so many preoccupations that no one problem can be permitted to absorb the individual's entire attention, to the detriment of all others. Nevertheless, in the business of providing for our nation's security in today's world, we now have our Number One priority task. Congress is voting some 60 billion dollars in direct defense expenditures and another 7 or 8 billion dollars for foreign purposes that are very definitely and closely related to the same thing.[2] Such vast outlays are well nigh incomprehensible to such a simple person as I, but I do know that they mean great national sacrifices and, therefore, they throw upon governmental officials an incalculable weight of responsibility. Since, in the present state of the world, security is obtainable only through collective action, the solidity and efficiency of the NATO union are objectives that demand the best we can give them in leadership.

From this line of reasoning, I come to the conclusion, for example, that America should seek frequent meetings of the NATO governmental ministers. These meetings offer one means by which our ideas and our leadership can be exerted among other nations. Personally, I think that meetings should be held no less frequently than once every quarter.[3] In this way, we shall help populations understand how important NATO is to all of us.

Moreover, I believe that the United States should seek other ways and means of developing among the peoples of the free world wider understanding of the issues at stake. This understanding should comprehend a clear insight into the basic prerequisite to the attainment of our objectives. That prerequisite is unity. The free world, as compared to the Iron Curtain countries, is incomparably richer in its total of material resources, productivity, scientific advancement, and industrial know-how. But we do not concentrate and unify our strength. In the Iron Curtain countries, the needed unity is produced by force, by the practices of the police state. We cannot employ such methods; we must produce unification by means that are completely consonant with the principles of free government.

In striving to produce this unity through leadership, it is necessary, of course, to avoid numerous pitfalls. One of these is the danger of expecting conformity as to detail. Individuals and nations should agree upon basic principles, purposes, and methods and, under inspired leadership, should find it possible to carry these forward into the broad problems of burden-sharing both in preparation and in operations. But it would be a terrific mistake to demand conformity in all political, economic, and military details. We would soon fall apart!

Having warned you at the beginning that you would probably be reading some rather aimless observations, I do not think it necessary to apologize for this screed. If it merely emphasizes again the need of getting speakers, writers, teachers, preachers—people in government and out of government, in all the NATO countries—to spread the basic truths about NATO, then it does what I wanted it to do. We must come to realize that there is no other yardstick by which acceptable contributions to NATO can be measured except the single one of *each nation doing its best.*

We encounter, of course, the age-old problem of inducing the individual to sacrifice in order to promote the common good of the community or nation. I applaud and have been a part of the struggle of individuals and of organized groups to advance standards of living. It has been the desire of men for more conveniences for themselves and their families, and for greater comfort in living, that has brought about the extraordinary scientific and other advances from which we all profit. The desire for lower taxes, shorter work hours, and greater pay are human, reasonable, and understandable! But when they come into direct conflict with the ability of the nation to protect the system under which lower taxes, shorter hours, and higher standards can be attained, leadership should aim at creating the necessary understanding of the peril. Europe would have no problem if every single man here would demand for himself the right to work 50 hours a week instead of 40, and insist upon maximum instead of minimum taxes. If this same spirit were general throughout the free world, the great problem of making us all safe against Communism would be solved within a year!

From sad experience, we have learned that perfection in this kind of thing is too much to expect from humankind. Mutual suspicions between individuals, between classes, or between nations prevent the complete spontaneity of cooperation that is needed. But, even so, we should not fail to recognize the direction in which our spiritual and moral leadership should exert itself. We must appeal not only to governments but to entire populations—we must strive to reach the heart and mind of every single individual. There must be recalled to each his own conceptions of the dignity of man and of the value he places upon freedom; this must be accompanied by the reminder that freedom is something that must be earned every day that one lives! He must realize that only individual sacrifice can preserve individual liberty.

When there arise those occasions in civilization's history in which complete priority must be given to problems of national survival, we must realize that, until these are adequately solved, other things must wait if they demand the expenditure of time and money in their accomplishment!

Of course, I am talking in a fashion that can be labelled naive. But it is still true that, though all of us may realize that complete attainment of this kind of spontaneous cooperation is not possible—human beings are fallible—yet this only points up an even greater necessity for leadership; we must achieve the maximum in these directions, particularly in Europe. All of us should be everlastingly at the job of urging European governments to do this (I personally practice what I preach on this point) because each of these nations can do its best to support the NATO concept only if it has a spiritual revival; if its morale compares to its own glorious moments of history!

Throw this away—but I simply had to say that NATO needs an eloquent and inspired Moses as much as it needs planes, tanks, guns, and ships. He must be civilian and he must be legion—he must speak to each of the countries, every day of every year—he must be the product of American leadership.[4] *Cordially*

[1] Eisenhower wrote Lovett for the first time since congratulating him upon succeeding Marshall as Secretary of Defense (see no. 380).

[2] On September 13 the Senate had unanimously passed a defense budget bill of $59.5 billion for fiscal year 1952, the largest single military appropriation measure in the nation's history. On October 9 Congress finally would reach agreement on

legislation authorizing $7.4 billion in weapons and material aid to countries engaged in the fight against communism. (President Truman had asked for a total of $8.5 billion for the Mutual Security program; in the final appropriation bill the amount of aid for Western Europe would be $4.8 billion.) See *New York Times*, September 14, October 6, 9, 21, 1951.

[3] At the Ottawa meeting, concluded on September 20, the North Atlantic Council had agreed to meet more frequently, though as yet it had not specified how often (see nos. 384 and 399).

[4] Responding on October 2 (EM), Lovett thanked Eisenhower for his "interesting letter" and agreed on "the necessity for greater effort on matters of the mind and the spirit if we are to get the necessary degree of unity and trust in NATO. I think your point is persuasively made not only by your letter," Lovett went on to say, "but more particularly by the concrete results you have obtained through your leadership and evident faith that the job can be done." He pledged himself to give more attention to the matters that Eisenhower had raised and to press for more frequent meetings of the NATO ministers. Lovett also expressed a wish to talk over matters in person at the Rome session of the NAC, which had been scheduled for November to avoid conflict with the British elections.

389   *Eisenhower Mss.*

To ALFRED MAXIMILIAN GRUENTHER   *September 26, 1951*

Memorandum for Chief of Staff: The advance plans for the development of a European Army with its delicate included problem of organizing a politically satisfactory battle unit of professional efficiency brings up again the desirability of examining the whole question of tactical organization.[1] As you know, I have felt that the typical American division is far too expensive in personnel and, if this is even partially true, it will have most serious consequences in Europe where so many of the smaller countries are planning to organize in the exact pattern of America's units.[2]

The possibility that a combined study might develop an organization which, from the professional viewpoint, we would consider a great improvement over existing types and, at the same time, would be completely acceptable to Western European political circles, is one that should be explored exhaustively. A proper study would, of course, not only have to take into consideration all such factors as scientific and technical development,[3] but would have to consider also the geographical situation, resources in manpower, strategic concepts, and general tactical doctrine.

For my part, I believe that our greatest opportunity in land defense will involve exploitation of the armored vehicle. While we will, of course, attempt to hold certain specified areas on a somewhat static basis and make of them firm bases of operations, our best chance in front and to the flanks of such localities will involve speedy, bold and skillful use of armor. Attacking forces will be, necessarily, somewhat canalized by road nets. Our aim will certainly be to attack the flanks and rear of such columns, creating maximum confusion and paralysis.

For this kind of operation, decentralization to unit commanders, with each allowed a high degree of initiative, will be common practice. This means that the *armored* division should, in general, be self-contained for operations of two to three, or even four, days in length.[4] It should have fast, easily maintained vehicles of low silhouette. Each division should be relatively small, so that it can be easily committed to action and taken out of action. The mass of vehicles should develop a terrific fire power but, in the interests of mobility, should not be too heavy.

If this kind of battle is to be fully profitable, there are many details that must be so studied and practiced in time of peace within the armored division so that their accomplishment in time of war will be almost routine. When an armored unit penetrates to the flank or rear of the enemy, liaison with our own air forces will be of prime necessity. Mutual identification must be instantaneous. Each armored division will have opportunities for destroying communications, including wire lines, and so on. The exact timing of such destruction could in itself be important. For example, if the leader of such an armored unit found himself suddenly upon the communications of a hostile unit, it is probable that he would postpone the destruction of wire and other lines until he was sure that orders to deal with the situation as then known to the enemy had already been issued. Destruction, following immediately upon the issuance of such orders, would produce the maximum of confusion in the enemy ranks and would present maximum opportunity to our own forces. The marking of roads and headquarters by secret methods, the development of simple and easily changeable codes in radio work, the location of indigenous supplies and the exploitation of the country's resources in order to minimize dependence upon supply lines; all these and dozens of other practices will have to be studied and developed to the full if maximum advantage is to be derived from this kind of mobile warfare.

In the so-called infantry groupment or battle unit, we have another problem. In such formations, the element that most quickly shows fatigue and exhaustion, and must frequently be relieved from the battle line, is the infantry. Consequently, other elements in a typical unit should be held to a minimum—when infantry is relieved from the line for rest and recuperation and refitting, we should take out the *minimum* amount of those troops who have in no wise come close to the point of exhaustion. If we follow this principle, we will necessarily make the corps a more significant unit in the chain of administration, supply, repair, maintenance, and evacuation. I believe this to be a sound development because, nowadays, the corps headquarters and corps troops can remain in action long past the point where exhaustion has begun in the infantry of the lower units. In this connection, the ideas and suggestions brought forward by the SHAPE staff at a recent meeting seem to me to be sound and logical.

[1] Political issues, especially fear of German resurgence, influenced discussion of the proper size of ground units within a European defense force. Fear of a German military revival translated into a desire for relatively small German units. In February 1951 U.S. military officials envisioned German infantry units totaling about 440,000 troops organized into thirty regimental combat teams and appropriate combat- and service-support elements. These German personnel figures, which reflected in part the need to create German forces as quickly as possible, were "well under the size of comparable NATO forces." At this time former Wehrmacht generals favored building the new German army around twelve infantry divisions, each composed of 15,000 troops in peacetime and 18,000 in wartime. By early July French leaders had offered as a compromise plan German divisions of only 10,000 men. On October 15 the Defense Department noted that "American tables of organization and equipment modified to fit local circumstances and missions" had been applied to combat units in Belgium and the Netherlands. According to a later report, the size of the national units within the EDF "was fixed on the advice of SHAPE according to a formula which approximated divisional strength for the national units advocated by the Germans." In early November European leaders, meeting in Paris, announced plans for an EDF of 1,290,000 men by late 1953 organized into forty-three national contingents, each to consist of 12,000 combat and 18,000 support troops (SM 536-51, Feb. 28, 1951, CCS 092 Germany [5-4-49], Sec. 7; "Activities in Europe Concerned with Materiel Support of NATO and MDAP," Oct. 5, 1951, OS/D, 1951, Clas. Decimal File, CD 092.3 NATO; State, *Foreign Relations, 1952-1954*, vol. V, *Western European Security, Part I*, pp. 233-34, 601-2; *New York Times*, July 2, Nov. 8, 1951).

[2] After 1943, following principles that Chief of Staff Lesley J. NcNair had championed since the 1930s, the U.S. Army employed "triangular" divisions numbering between 10,000 and 15,000 men and designed to contain mainly the forces and equipment necessary to an attack. Divisions consisted of three infantry regiments and three artillery battalions, along with engineer, signal, ordnance, quartermaster, medical, police, mechanized reconnaissance, and headquarters personnel. Service and support units were largely allocated to a pool at the corps or army level. Though manpower shortages left postwar U.S. infantry divisions at skeletal strength, their tables of organization and equipment again included tank and antiaircraft units that the remodeling of 1943 had placed in the corps or army. Eisenhower thus called for a return to a leaner, offensive-oriented division of McNair's design.

Later in the decade, to achieve "flexible response" and in anticipation of tactical nuclear warfare, the U.S. Army would experiment with increasingly self-sufficient units below the corps level, divisions consisting not of regiments but of five "battle groups" (see Weigley, *History of the United States Army*, pp. 461-66, 502-3, 536-37; and Daun van Ee, "From the New Look to Flexible Response," in *Against All Enemies: Interpretations of American Military History from Colonial Times to the Present*, ed. Kenneth J. Hagan and William R. Roberts [Westport, Conn., 1986], pp. 330-32).

[3] Eisenhower developed these thoughts while discussing new antitank weapons and lightly armored cross-country vehicles in no. 422.

[4] According to the 1943 plan, U.S. armored divisions were supposed to contain

roughly equal tank, infantry, and artillery components. In practice, however, World War II infantry divisions laid first claim to infantry replacements, and armored divisions generally fought in battalion-size units, supporting infantry (Weigley, *History of the United States Army*, pp. 466–69). Where armored divisions fought as such, their value lay in exploiting breakthroughs in the opposing lines—an advantage highly dependent on fuel supplies.

390 *Eisenhower Mss.*

To ROBERT BOSTWICK CARNEY *September 27, 1951*
Top secret

Dear Carney: Thank you very much for your letter of September 21st with regard to your conversations with Admiral Edelsten.[1]

I regret to learn that Admiral Edelsten was not informed of your directives from me because the staff had taken special measures in that regard in the light of the prolonged delay and controversy in establishing your command.[2] Specifically a message was sent on 17 June to the Ministries of Defense, London, Paris and Rome, requesting that appropriate national commanders be informed of the pertinent provisions of the decisions that had been made and that they be instructed to cooperate in every way possible to facilitate the functioning of your command. Formal procedures have been established to keep the Ministries of Defense involved thoroughly informed of all matters of importance and it should be incumbent upon them to keep such commanders in chief as Admiral Edelsten fully advised. I am going to suggest to the British NMR[3] here that this matter be clarified with Admiral Edelsten.

I am also informed that a copy of the document received from Standing Group (SG 80/4) outlining the principles and arrangements for command in the Middle East and involving the Western Mediterranean was sent to you by my staff on 22 September.[4] While this represents a large measure of compromise and agreement on the part of the US, UK and French governments, final approval may still be a long way off because it is contingent on parliamentary action by the NATO nations in ratifying the request for Greece and Turkey to become members of NATO.[5] In the meantime agreements must be worked out at governmental levels with other interested parties on the details of the military command structure.

If the command arrangements, as now conceived by Standing Group, are accepted there would be under you a French Naval Commander in the Western Mediterranean with area responsibilities.[6]

There would probably have to be an Italian Admiral with similar responsibilities for an area around Italy. You would have to work out with Admiral Edelsten a mutually acceptable arrangement for the division of functional responsibilities. As General Gruenther informed you by personal message there is a special feature which remains to be resolved with the French involving the exact status and terms of reference of the French Admiral who will have the area command in the Western Mediterranean. I have no fixed conviction as to the solution to be adopted so long as we can avoid further controversy and that your personal attention is not distracted from the paramount job of coordinating land, sea and air forces for the defense of our southern flank.

I greatly appreciate your invitation to join you in the Mediterranean on the 15th of October to visit the 6th Fleet. As of now, I am certainly counting on being there. If you don't work me too hard, I look forward to two days of relaxation on one of your splendid ships.[7]

With warm personal regard, *Cordially*

[1] Carney had reported on a three-day visit that British Admiral Sir John Hereward Edelsten, C in C, Mediterranean Fleet, had paid him after sending papers that "represented an element of British naval thinking concerning the organization of the Mediterranean." Because those papers generally conflicted with Eisenhower's directives to CINCSOUTH—Carney mentioned in particular "that part outlining my maritime responsibilities and that part concerning my provisional geographical areas of responsibility"—he had refused official comment, though he and Edelsten did "cover the waterfront privately in our usual atmosphere of complete cordiality and warm personal friendship." Carney further stated that at first there had been disagreement with the British over who would command the four-nation naval exercises planned for February 28–March 6. "We later agreed that CINCSOUTH should set the stage and exercise over-all control and supervision of the exercise, consistent with my directive from you" (EM). Complicating command arrangements in the Mediterranean, as the British themselves admitted, was "the special position of the British Naval Force which had for so long wielded control of the Mediterranean" (Ismay, *NATO*, p. 73; see also Poole, *History of the Joint Chiefs of Staff*, vol. IV, *1950–1952*, pp. 238–41).

[2] For background on the establishment of CINCSOUTH see nos. 107, n. 2, 111, 148, 198, n. 4, and 236; and State, *Foreign Relations, 1951*, vol. III, *European Security and the German Question, Part I*, pp. 522–26, 528–35.

[3] National Military Representative.

[4] In this paper, dated August 22, 1951, the Standing Group had recommended creating an Allied Middle East theater to be commanded by a British officer, with a northern sector under Turkish command and a southern sector under the British. A Middle East Chiefs of Staff Committee would comprise American, British, French, Turkish, and Commonwealth officers. That committee would be served by a Middle East Standing Group drawn from American, British, and French members of the NATO Standing Group; they would serve in a dual capacity in both groups in order to provide "coordination and unity of higher strategic direction" (State, *Foreign Relations, 1951*, vol. III, *European Security and the German Question, Part I*, pp. 573–74).

[5] On the admission of Greece and Turkey to NATO see no. 423, n. 5.
[6] On the establishment of a French naval command in the western Mediterranean see no. 423, n. 5.
[7] Eisenhower would visit Carney's headquarters to observe naval exercises October 15–18.

391   *Eisenhower Mss.*

To Martin Withington Clement   *September 27, 1951*

Dear Clem:[1] Thank you very much for your letter. As usual, it was typical of all your communications—chock-full of news and interesting speculation.[2]

The problems of NATO show no signs of becoming less complicated or difficult. While we make progress every day, the inescapable fact is always with us that in such a project as this new problems and new obstacles seem to raise their heads as quickly as their predecessors are knocked over.[3]

At home, it seems to us that dispatches and articles show an increasing awareness of the true nature of the global struggle and of the measures that America must take to meet it. One thing is certain—no tactical defeat or set-back must ever deter us from steadfast pursuit of the one basic objective that all true Americans must adopt; this objective is the determination to preserve a free form of life and protect it from every threat that may arise, external and internal. In this struggle, we here are trying to do our part, as you know.

My warm greetings to any of our common friends when you encounter them, including Harold particularly.[4] Mamie and I send our biding affection to you both.[5] *Cordially*

[1] Clement was chairman of the board of the Pennsylvania Railroad Company (see no. 278).

[2] Clement's letter of September 21 (EM) included a memo dated September 10, 1951, in which he summarized his meeting with Eisenhower in Paris on July 31, 1951, and concluded that "Eisenhower is available to the Republicans if they want him."

[3] For Eisenhower's continuing concern regarding NATO and its goals see, for example, no. 388, n. 4.

[4] Harold E. Stassen, former Governor of Minnesota and a declared Republican candidate for the presidency, had promised to support Eisenhower if he chose to run (for background see no. 408, n. 4). Eisenhower understood that "Stassen is for him—first, last, always—and will be working for him," Clement had written in his memo.

[5] Clement's wife was the former Elizabeth S. Wallace.

To Clifford Roberts

Dear Cliff:[1] The news about your two rounds under 80 was not particularly astonishing but, of course, it is gratifying to know you are back on top of your game. Unfortunately I could not test out for myself your theory that I may have been swaying a bit. I have a bad wrist, which you will remember started ailing while you were here.[2]

I think I first noticed the soreness when I was in Germany but, shortly after you left, it became so bad that I had to ask Dr. Snyder for help.[3] Now I get it baked every morning and have to bind it up every night, and I don't know when it will be before I can take a full golf swing again. Otherwise I feel splendidly and, since I cannot recall any kind of even minor accident to my wrist joint, Howard is very puzzled as to what has occurred. Anyway, the whole thing is inconsequential except that, while it has kept me off the golf course, we have had three or four of the nicest days that I have seen this year.

Concerning Mr. Barnett's scheme, Frank Willard sent me some material in July on the Free Slavic Legion, and we forwarded it to the appropriate officials in Washington after study by the staff here. I understand that Mr. Barnett has already been asked by Washington to submit a detailed memorandum for consideration by the officials in the Defense Department.[4]

There have been quite a number of plans similar to that one advanced by Barnett. However, I think it is always possible that he has a better idea than any other that has been advanced. Already there is legal authority for enlisting in our forces certain displaced groups; but, of course, Mr. Barnett will find out about all these things in Washington.[5]

Charlie Yates and Mr. Danforth came back here after the ceremony in Saint Andrews. They were accompanied by Mr. Jones and the three of them played golf with Spyros Skouras. I, of course, could not go out because of my bum wrist. But I thoroughly enjoyed their visit. Both of them have winning personalities, and they seem to be extraordinarily good friends.[6]

I shall be going up to Germany again for maneuvers at the end of this week. This time it will be merely over the week end.[7]

Give my best to all our old friends. *Cordially*

---

[1] On Roberts, a business executive and officer of the Augusta National Golf Club, see no. 7, n. 1.

[2] There is no correspondence in EM, Roberts Corr., concerning the "two rounds under 80" that the General mentions here. In expressing pleasure at Roberts's return to the top of his game Eisenhower probably referred to his friend's recent difficulties with a stomach ulcer (see nos. 161, n. 2, and 193, n. 4).

[3] For background on Eisenhower's personal physician and head of the SHAPE medical staff, Major General Howard Snyder, see no. 59, n. 4.

[4] Frank Willard, a mutual friend of both Roberts and the General, had written to Eisenhower several times in the last three months concerning the Free Slavic Legion proposal of college professor Frank Barnett (see correspondence in EM, Willard Corr.; and no. 301, n. 1). The plan, which centered on the establishment of a large paratroop force of Iron Curtain refugees, had been referred by Eisenhower to Allen Dulles, CIA Deputy Director (see Galambos, *Columbia University*). Following an interview with Dulles on August 17, during which a letter from Eisenhower, "apparently favorably disposed toward the plan," had been discussed, Barnett was instructed to prepare a memorandum on the proposal for review by Gordon Gray (see no. 32, n. 2), Director of the Psychological Strategy Board (see supplemental Memorandum to proposal outlined in the pamphlet entitled *Cold War, Atomic War or Free Slavic Legion?* Barnett to Gray, n.d.; Barnett to Willard, Aug. 22, 1951; Willard to Eisenhower, Aug. 23, 1951; and Barnett to Gray, Aug. 29, 1951, all in EM, Willard Corr. On the Psychological Strategy Board see no. 366).

[5] In testimony before a subcommittee of the Senate on February 2 of this year Eisenhower had given his endorsement to plans then under consideration for increased alien enlistment in the U.S. Armed Forces and for the establishment of a foreign legion under U.S. auspices (see U.S. Congress, Senate, Preparedness Subcommittee of the Committee on Armed Services, *Universal Military Training and Service Act of 1951, Hearings on S. 1*, 82d Cong., 1st sess., 1951, pp. 1200–1201; and Joe C. Lambert, "These Aliens Also Serve," *Army Information Digest* 6, no. 11 [1951], 39–42). During August, Barnett's plan had received the support of Republican congressman Charles J. Kersten of Wisconsin and other congressmen, and the entire text of the pamphlet *Cold War, Atomic War or Free Slavic Legion?* was placed in the *Congressional Record*. Kersten also successfully proposed an amendment to the Mutual Security Act of 1951 that specifically allowed the expenditure of $100 million of the 1952 defense budget to aid the enlistment of escapees and refugees from Soviet-dominated countries "into elements of the military forces supporting the North Atlantic Treaty Organization or for other purposes when it is determined . . . that such assistance will contribute to the defense of the North Atlantic area . . ." (*Congressional Record*, 82d Cong., 1st sess., 1951, 97, pt. 16: 10226–63, A5214–16; and U.S., *Statutes at Large*, vol. 65, pp. 373–74). For developments with the Free Slavic Legion proposal see no. 444.

[6] Augusta National members William H. Danforth and Charles R. Yates, accompanied by golf course architect Robert Trent Jones, had visited the General on September 20. The three had come to Europe to witness the September 19 "playing in" ceremony of American golf great Francis D. Ouimet as the first non-British captain of Scotland's Royal and Ancient Golf Club of St. Andrews (see *New York Times*, Sept. 16, 20, 1951; and Eisenhower to Ouimet, Sept. 27, 1951, EM). For background on Twentieth Century-Fox Film Corporation president Spyros Panagiotes Skouras see Galambos, *Columbia University*.

[7] On the German maneuvers see no. 397, n. 6.

To Barbara Jean Thompson Eisenhower   *September 27, 1951*
and John Sheldon Doud Eisenhower

Dear Barbie and Johnny:[1] The other day I heard Mamie reproaching herself because of her failure to write to the two of you. I am not sure that she has, even yet, sent you any direct message. But if I just ramble on a little while, I probably won't duplicate too much of anything that she may have told you, even if she has sent you a letter within the past day or so.

We have been in our new house about four weeks. It takes Americans a long time to settle a house in France because everything is so strange to us. For example, there is frequently no water pressure at all on our second floor, and even though all electric cables were replaced before we moved into the house, I notice that we occasionally have trouble with lack of electric current. The grounds are beautiful and Moaney's garden has really produced.[2] We have had sweet corn, two kinds of beans, peas, radishes, tomatoes, turnips, and beets for some weeks, and in great quantity. Our corn did better than almost any other we have ever planted; we have sent a lot of it to the neighbors.

The fish pond was likewise doing splendidly for awhile but, by this time, I have thrown enough trout back into the water after catching them—others have frequently been snagged a little bit when striking at a fly and missing it—until it has become extremely difficult to hook one on an artificial fly. I may be reduced to fishing with liver or worms! Recently we put into the pond a few pike, which are supposed to eat the goldfish; I am told by the experts that they won't bother the trout.[3]

This is maneuver season for the troops in Germany. Last week I spent three days in the British sector where I saw, also, detachments of Danes, Belgians, Norwegians, and Dutch. For this coming visit, I think Mamie and Min will go with me as far as Luxembourg where they will spend the weekend with Perle Mesta, while I am out inspecting.[4]

One trip that I am looking forward to making is scheduled for mid-October. I plan to go to the Mediterranean and, for two or three days, will be on a United States Naval ship. If the weather is good, I will really have a good lazy time and possibly some sunlight.[5]

Of course, I am delighted that John is keeping up his golf. I hope that Barbie gets a chance to do the same. In my own case, I, as usual, as the summer wore on, got my short game working in good order. Because of that, I would frequently score quite well, having some 83s, 84s, and occasionally an 81 or 82. But several weeks ago my long game collapsed when I developed a soreness in my left wrist. As of this moment, I cannot play at all. *Devotedly*

[1] On John S. D. Eisenhower, the General's son, and his wife, the former Barbara Jean Thompson, see no. 132.

[2] John A. Moaney was a member of Eisenhower's household staff (see no. 344, n. 3).

[3] The Eisenhowers had moved into their newly renovated home, the Villa St. Pierre at Marnes-la-Coquette, in late August (see no. 314, n. 1).

[4] The General had been in Germany September 17–19 (see no. 375, n. 3). Mamie and her mother, Elivera Doud, would visit Perle Mesta the weekend of September 28 while Eisenhower continued his inspections (see EM, Subject File, Aircraft— SHAPE [*Columbine*]. On Mesta, American Minister to Luxembourg, see no. 128, n. 1; and on Elivera Doud see no. 275, n. 2).

[5] On the trip to the Mediterranean see no. 401, n. 4.

394   *Eisenhower Mss.*

To Jack Kirkham McFall   *September 27, 1951*

Dear Mr. McFall:[1] I was pleased to read your evalution of the visits to Europe made by the two Congressional Committee groups. Whatever success we achieved in the various presentations at SHAPE was due in good part to the fine cooperation we received from other U.S. agencies in Europe.[2]

We will be happy, naturally, to see members of Congressional Committees who find time to come to Europe this Autumn. I appreciate the efforts of you and your colleagues to give us as much advance information as possible.[3]

With best wishes, *Sincerely*

[1] McFall (LL.B. National University 1933) was Assistant Secretary of State for Congressional Relations. Colonel Paul T. Carroll drafted Eisenhower's letter to McFall.

[2] In a letter of September 21 McFall had told Eisenhower of the "splendid results" of his "inspiring briefings" during the visits of two congressional committee groups to NATO headquarters the past summer (for background see no. 281).

[3] McFall had said that members of the Senate Appropriations Committee and the Senate Armed Services Committee might visit Eisenhower before the end of the year.

395   *Eisenhower Mss.*

To René Pleven   *September 27, 1951*

Dear M. Pleven:[1] Two weeks ago, I had the pleasure of visiting SHAPE Village with M. Claudius Petit, Minister of Reconstruction, and I was particularly gratified to observe the splendid progress which has been made on the project. All of the Allied officers of my staff are anxiously looking forward to the completion of the Village.[2]

In this connection, I understand that General Carpentier, in a letter dated 1 September to the Minister of Finance, pointed out that it is estimated that an additional 1.1 billion francs are required to complete SHAPE Village, and that the cost of the proposed village at Fontainebleau for the Allied officers in that headquarters is approximately 2.5 billion francs.[3] Mr. Paul Porter and Mr. Henry Labouisse of the ECA have advised me that the ECA will agree to the use of up to 3.6 billion from the 95% counterpart funds for the purpose of completing the financing of these two villages and that, as soon as the ECA Mission to France receives a request from your Minister of Finance in this connection, ECA concurrence will be immediately forthcoming.[4]

In view of the extreme shortage of family housing in the vicinity of these two Headquarters, I place great importance upon the completion of SHAPE Village and the construction of a similar village at Fontainebleau. Such an accomplishment would not only facilitate the functioning of these two Allied Headquarters but would also assist in relieving pressure of demand for French housing in these areas.

I would be grateful for any assistance that you can render in the early solution of this problem.[5] *Sincerely*

[1] For background on French Premier Pleven see no. 318. General Cortlandt van Rensselaer Schuyler drafted this letter.

[2] On September 14 Eisenhower and Eugène Pierre ("Claudius") Petit, Minister of Reconstruction for France since 1948, had inspected SHAPE Village, a newly built community in Hennemont Park, several miles west of St.-Germain-en-Laye, where some 250 officers and noncommissioned officers assigned to SHAPE would soon live. It was hoped that the village, purchased from the French government, would provide SHAPE personnel with economical living conditions in an atmosphere of comradeship. For further background see *New York Times*, June 28, 1951.

[3] As Deputy Chief of Staff for Administration (see no. 77), General Marcel Maurice Carpentier had apparently written to René Mayer, French Minister of Finance, concerning the funding for SHAPE Village (see Eisenhower to Mayer, Nov. 2, 1951, EM). Carpentier had met with Eisenhower on September 26.

[4] See no. 68. Paul Robert Porter (A.B. University of Kansas 1928), an assistant administrator for the ECA, had recently been named American Special Representative in Europe. Also working for the ECA in France, Henry Richardson Labouisse, Jr. (LL.B. Harvard 1929), was Chief of the special mission to France (on the ECA see Galambos, *Columbia University*, no. 343). The funds were granted as Eisenhower had requested (Eisenhower to Mayer, Nov. 2, 1951, EM; see also State, *Foreign Relations, 1951*, vol. IV, *Europe: Political and Economic Developments, Part I*, p. 429).

[5] SHAPE Village would officially open on October 31 (see *New York Times*, Oct. 31, 1951).

To Lucius Du Bignon Clay   *September 27, 1951*
Personal and confidential

Dear Lucius: With the arrival of your most recent letter, I initially encountered some difficulty with the alphabetic key—the multitude of other preoccupations crossing my desk gave me the problem of distinguishing between I and the previously unidentified "I."

In some ways, I suppose it would be unnecessary to use such a system in our communications. After all, I am participating in nothing at the moment except those things which are directly related to this job. My general views are well known to you and to my friends, and my attitude concerning present and possible future duty should be clear. However, I realize that, if any single letter should go astray and should be read by outsiders, misinterpretations could be made. So I suppose the avoidance of proper names is wise and logical.[1]

Of course, it would be a great thing for me to talk to you personally. I know that you are terrifically busy and are intrigued by the many affairs of your own Company. But you and I think so much alike on so many problems connected with public service, and you are so detached from partisan affairs in the United States, that I think it would do me good just to have a long talk with you one of these days. (I suppose that, if such an opportunity should arise, we would find ourselves following the traditional practices of old soldiers and would do more reminiscing about old campaigns and service incidents than we would discuss affairs and problems of the present and future.)[2]

There is certainly no need to detail for you the character of our current progress and obstacles. As usual in such complicated projects, new problems arise as fast as we solve a current one; but we do our best and, certainly, we believe that day by day the free world is learning a little bit more about producing collective security by cooperation.[3]

In any event, my thanks to you for your continued interest and for informing me as to developments.

My very warm greetings to Our Friend and to any others of our common friends that you may encounter.[4] Love to Marjorie[5] and, of course, as always, warmest regard to yourself. *Cordially*

[1] Since May of this year Clay and New York Governor Thomas Dewey had employed a letter-for-name substitution code in their correspondence with Eisenhower (see nos. 196, n. 3, and 331, n. 4). The code keys, which identified both the members of an unofficial Eisenhower-for-President committee and others who would figure prominently in the 1952 election, had included no designation for the letter *I*, a symbol Clay had used in a September 24 message to Eisenhower (EM; see lists in EM, same file as document). On Clay's letter of the twenty-fourth and for developments see no. 409.

[2] Clay was at the center of a group of friends and supporters then working to

secure Eisenhower the 1952 Republican presidential nomination. He would prove instrumental in convincing the NATO commander to declare his candidacy (see, for example, nos. 551, n. 2, 587, and 678). For the possibility of Clay traveling to Europe in his role as chairman of the board of the Continental Can Company see no. 409, n. 9.

[3] On recent events involving the NATO defense effort see nos. 365, n. 3, 388, and 389.

[4] "Our Friend" and "Our Friend up the River" were code names used for Thomas Dewey in the Clay-Eisenhower political correspondence. On Dewey's role in the Eisenhower-for-President movement see no. 196, n. 8.

[5] On Clay's wife Marjorie see no. 112, n. 7.

397   *Eisenhower Mss.*

To Robert Winship Woodruff   *September 27, 1951*

Dear Bob:[1] Everybody who has been dropping into my office after recently passing through New York has brought me news of you and your illness. I think it is only lately that I began to realize that you had quite a tough time; I had been given the impression at first that you were merely a bit indisposed after going home from Europe and would recover within just a few days.[2]

My latest information is that you and Nell[3] have gone to the ranch. Now my only worry is that you won't have sense enough to stay there as long as you should. I think Nell ought to get a ball bat and begin to use a bit of persuasion mixed with a judicious amount of force.

But, beyond considerations of health, I should think that right now Wyoming should be really attractive. I assume the rainbow are still hitting, and there must be good sage hen and prairie chicken and grouse shooting. In any event, I wish Mamie and I could be there with you two, even if we had nothing to do but sit by a roaring fire and look out at the snowdrifts.[4]

We continue to have quite a stream of visitors, but recently I have not been able to take them out for even late afternoon golf because of a slightly injured wrist. Just what I did to it I don't know, but it is bad enough so that I cannot swing a golf club. Otherwise I feel splendid and, so far as Mamie is concerned, she looks to me to be in good shape indeed. She is finally getting the new house running very well.

Did I tell you I had put a few trout in the pond in back of my house? For a while, I could go out with either dry or wet fly and pick one out whenever I wanted to, but now they have gotten wary—I haven't caught one for a week.[5]

The fall weather is beginning to close in on us and, because harvests have been gathered, maneuver season is with us in Germany. Last week I spent three days in the British sector; this week I am going to do the same in the French. The American comes next, and then I go to the Mediterranean for three or four days.[6]

Only yesterday I got a letter from Bill Robinson who tells me that, after Cliff went home following his second tour over here, his doctors gave him a clear bill of health.[7] Apparently his ulcer is gone forever. Soon he will be going down to Augusta for the opening party and I only hope he can stick close enough to his diet to avoid getting into trouble once more.

This is sort of a rambling, aimless letter, but at least it brings to you from both Mamie and me our very best wishes and affectionate regards. *Cordially*

[1] Woodruff was chairman of the executive committee and director of the Coca-Cola Company (see no. 113).

[2] Woodruff had contracted a form of hepatitis while visiting Europe in July (see no. 489; on his visit see no. 217).

[3] Woodruff's wife, the former Nell Hodgson.

[4] Woodruff was recuperating at his TE Ranch in Cody, Wyoming.

[5] On the Eisenhowers' recently renovated house see no. 314.

[6] Eisenhower had visited Germany September 17–19 and would observe maneuvers there again on September 28 and 29 and October 9 and 10 (see no. 375). The General would travel to Italy and the Mediterranean on October 15 (see no. 401).

[7] On William E. Robinson's letter of September 14 (EM) see no. 382. Woodruff, Robinson, and Roberts were all members of the Augusta National Golf Club.

398

To PHILIP YOUNG

September 27, 1951

Dear Phil:[1] Thank you very much for your informative letter and for sending me the minutes of your luncheon meeting. I found both of them very interesting.[2]

Of course, I shall be glad to sign a few letters, provided they are not direct appeals for money. As you know, I have never participated directly in that business, but I am always ready to give a boost in any direction I think appropriate. As you point out, the time is fast approaching when I can no longer pretend to be too close to Columbia's affairs. For this reason, I have only recently declined to participate by radio broadcast in planned meetings and that sort of thing. I am simply too preoccupied with the affairs of this job to pretend that I am fully abreast of Columbia's development.

However, I share your very clear conviction that in certain directions we should strike quickly, while the iron is hot. In the development program, I do not see why some capital cannot be made out of my enforced absence. Letters and other approaches to prospective donors could point out that Columbia's President would be personally present to participate in the program under consideration, except that he is necessarily absent in the performance of vital governmental business. This observation, if skillfully used, might possibly have some value.[3]

When next your Policy Committee meets, please say that I read the minutes of their last meeting and found them to be of great interest; and I sent to them my warm greetings and my general approval of what I read of the sentiments they expressed.[4]

Love to Faith[5] and, of course, personal regard to yourself. *Cordially*

[1] Young was Executive Director of the American Assembly (see no. 8, n. 6).
[2] On September 21 (EM) Young had written concerning the next American Assembly conference and had enclosed a copy of the minutes from the meeting of the National Policy Board of the Assembly (on the meeting see n. 4 below; for background on the first American Assembly conference see no. 201).
[3] Eisenhower apparently had agreed to sign a series of letters written on behalf of the American Assembly. Young said that he was anxious to "capitalize as rapidly as possible on the popularity of the Assembly" and that the letters would "help us a great deal on the money-raising side of the business." The development program for Columbia had totaled over $5 million the previous year, Young wrote, "the second or third largest in the history of Columbia since 1918" (for developments see no. 497, n. 2).
[4] The minutes that Young had included with his letter had been taken at the luncheon meeting of the National Policy Board of the Assembly held at the Columbia University Club on August 30 (EM). At that meeting the board had decided that the topic for the next conference would be "Inflation—Its Causes, Consequences, and Cures." On the second conference see no. 519; and Young to Eisenhower, Oct. 9, 1951, EM.
[5] Young's wife, the former Faith Adams.

399   *Eisenhower Mss.*

To Paul van Zeeland   *September 27, 1951*

Dear Mr. van Zeeland: Thank you for your kind letter of September 15th.[1] I am glad to know that you found my letter of September 11th useful during the recent meetings of the North Atlantic Council in Ottawa.[2]

Thank you also for enclosing a copy of your introductory remarks at the Ottawa conference. It is a great satisfaction to me that you emphasized at the very outset of the conference those important points which we discussed during our conversations last May.[3]

Permit me to extend to you my most sincere congratulations for the progress which, due largely to your leadership, resulted from the Ottawa conference.[4] The conference represented tangible progress in the solution of some of our present problems of the defense of Europe and highlighted the even more pressing problems which must be solved in Rome.[5]

I am looking forward to seeing you at the Rome meeting of the North Atlantic Council and hope that we shall be able to make further and substantial progress on the solution of those problems which you have pursued so vigorously during your year of Chairmanship of the Council.[6] *Sincerely*

[1] Van Zeeland, Belgian Foreign Minister and Chairman of the North Atlantic Council, had presided at the Ottawa meetings, which had adjourned on September 20. On van Zeeland's letter (EM) Eisenhower wrote a note to Gruenther saying that the NAC chairman's enclosed talk (see n. 3) emphasized "the things we talked over with him last summer. Possibly I should write a note of congratulations." In drafting this letter to van Zeeland, Eisenhower had the aid of Major General Cortlandt van Rensselaer Schuyler. The director of North Atlantic Treaty affairs, Office of the Secretary of Defense, would write Schuyler on September 28 that it was "still too early to comment very fully on the developments in Washington following the Ottawa conference" (R. E. Beebe to Schuyler, Sept. 28, 1951, OS/D, 1951, Clas. Decimal File, CD 092.3 NATO).

[2] Van Zeeland had reported that he had received Eisenhower's letter (sent through Belgian Defense Minister Édouard De Greef) and "found in it, on the eve of the Ottawa Conference, an encouragement for which I thank you."

[3] In his letter to Eisenhower, van Zeeland had written that while serving as NAC Chairman he had been "able to understand at the same time the scope of problems which confront us and our capabilities to solve them. Like you I believe that unity in thought, action and execution is indispensable to implement in time plans which would be useless if they remain in the status of projects. Our resources are immense," van Zeeland continued. "They run the risk of being useless if we do not put them to work with feeling which should be pushed to the point of anguish of absolute urgency and priority." Van Zeeland credited these ideas to Eisenhower and said he would put them in his opening speech—in which, van Zeeland had written, Eisenhower would find "the echo of the conversations which we had during the month of May" (on that visit see no. 218). According to a State Department cable, van Zeeland's opening address had "stressed necessity of making decisions promptly and getting on with job using best tools available rather than putting off decisions until perfect job could be done" (State, *Foreign Relations, 1951*, vol. III, *European Security and the German Question, Part I*, p. 654. See also *New York Times*, Sept. 15, 1951).

[4] See no. 384, n. 1. Van Zeeland mentioned "a coincidence in our preoccupations for which I congratulate myself. I have once more asked for frequent meetings of the Council of the Pact where the responsible Ministers must give new vigor through constant stimulus to the activities of NATO," he wrote. "I have also emphasized the obvious necessity to give the supreme organisms of the Pact an authority corresponding to their responsibilities."

[5] On the General's preparations for the Rome meeting of the NAC, to be held November 24-28, see no. 502, n. 2.

[6] "I am convinced that the cause we defend is one of the future of Western civilization and that it can triumph because the size of the threat is not greater than the devotion and vigilance of a few men, of whom you are the symbol," van Zeeland had concluded. "I am happy as Chairman of the Council of the Atlantic

Pact to serve with you [in] such a noble cause." Lester Pearson of Canada, who would succeed van Zeeland as NAC Chairman, would preside at the Rome conference (see no. 407, n. 1).

400   *Eisenhower Mss.*

To Ralph Austin Bard   *October 1, 1951*
Personal and confidential

Dear Ralph:[1] This is a rather tardy reply to your last letter, but a series of inspection trips has kept me away from the desk quite often of late.[2]

We are hammering away at this project of developing collective security by cooperation, trying to keep things moving forward all the time. I am so close to things that it is rather difficult at times to resist impatience, but I suppose we are making headway as fast as anyone could reasonably expect.

Within NATO, we are now grappling with the thorny problems of financial commitments, munitions production, and troop allocations. The German problem, with all its complications, is also with us. Difficult as these questions are, I believe they can be settled with reasonable dispatch, provided American leadership in the spiritual and intellectual sphere is as powerful as it has been unique in the material sphere.[3]

I don't want to overestimate my own contribution, but I feel that whatever influence I can exert in these vital affairs is increased by the fact that I represent no faction, group, or party in the United States— or in any other country, for that matter. I can speak confidently at SHAPE for that large segment of the populations in the free world that is keenly aware of the menace of Communism and is determined, as a unit, to do something about it. Until all of us are definitely past the shoals, I could not jeopardize this position of non-partisanship without doing *serious disservice to our own country*; to whose future this cooperative effort is of utmost importance.[4]

I know that you are already fully aware of the high sense of distinction I feel in the commendatory opinions expressed or implied in the communications I receive from time to time from thoughtful and loyal Americans, such as yourself. If I knew all the answers required in meeting our country's problems of the next five years, or the next twenty-four hours, I would be happy and honored to communicate them to you and to other fine friends who are kind enough to overemphasize my possibilities for future service. Aside from my immediate family interests, my only ambition is to serve my country well and to see others serve her even better. If I should at this moment try to discuss in more specific fashion the points referred to in your letter, I would not, from my viewpoint, be honest either with others or with myself. At all times, and under all circumstances, I shall certainly pray for strength to do my duty—I can do no more and, as Lee said, I would not wish to do less.[5]

I hope this does not sound stuffy and, because I know that you will read this note with the eyes of friendship, I am quite ready to trust to your understanding to find in it nothing but a simple statement of fact and purpose. *Cordially*

[1] For background on Bard see no. 248.

[2] During September Eisenhower had taken a brief inspection trip to Norway and on two separate occasions had attended military exercises in the British and French occupation zones of Germany (see no. 375).

[3] For background on these and other difficulties being confronted in the establishment of the Western European defense see, for example, nos. 218 and 388.

[4] Bard had written (Sept. 19, 1951, EM) that while he and many other Republicans frequently spoke of an Eisenhower presidential candidacy, they were "very much up in the air . . . as to what is going on" because of the General's silence concerning his party affiliation. Little would be accomplished on Eisenhower's behalf until the situation was clarified, Bard said, so there was "no use talking much more about your possible candidacy unless it is clearly understood that you are a Republican, and available to our party." Eisenhower's reply is typical of many that he had written recently (see, for example, nos. 358 and 478). For developments see no. 582.

[5] The words of Robert E. Lee—"Duty then is the sublimest word in our language. Do your duty in all things. You cannot do more. You should never wish to do less"—are inscribed beneath the Confederate general's bust in the New York University Hall of Fame (see Robert Underwood Johnson, *Your Hall of Fame* [New York, 1935], p. 175). On the General's high estimation of Lee see Galambos, *Columbia University*, nos. 645 and 743. On Eisenhower's service as an elector to the Hall of Fame see EM, Subject File, Clubs and Associations.

401
Eisenhower Mss.

To DAVID RANDOLPH CALHOUN, JR. *October 1, 1951*

Dear Dave:[1] It was indeed nice of you to write me such an interesting letter right after you got back from Saint Louis.[2] I know Ralph Talbott very well (at least, I have met and talked to him a few times). Unfortunately, October 15th marks the beginning of two rather protracted trips for me.[3] The first takes me into the Mediterranean for three days; and the second, beginning the 19th, takes me into the United Kingdom for a week. However, I will tell Bob Schulz to be on the look-out for him and, if he reaches here a day or two before the 15th, I can see him then; or I might possibly be able to see him on the day of the 18th.[4]

I share your feeling about the international situation. It would be wonderful to wake up some morning and read a few encouraging items in the newspaper. Suspicions, pessimism, and discouragement are far too prevalent in the thinking of the free world; we have got to substitute for these some faith, optimism, and determination if we are to free ourselves from the Communistic threat and to do it without unconscionably piling up of debt at home. Bankruptcy and loss of freedom due to our own stupidity would, in the long run, be almost as bad as would be loss of freedom to the aggressor.[5]

Please convey our very warm greetings to your charming bride and, of course, our very best to you. *Cordially*

[1] For background on Calhoun, president of the Union Trust Company of Saint Louis, see no. 94.

[2] Eisenhower probably meant to say "back *to* Saint Louis," to which Calhoun and his wife Lucy (see no. 94) recently had returned after a trip to Europe that had included a visit with the Eisenhowers (see Calhoun to Eisenhower, Mar. 12 and Sept. 26, 1951, both in EM).

[3] In his letter of September 26 Calhoun had written that *Harold* Talbott would be arriving in Paris on or about October 15 and wished to meet with Eisenhower. A former chairman of the Republican National Finance Committee and what Calhoun described as "an ardent Eisenhower supporter," Talbott was already working with General Lucius Clay's unofficial Eisenhower-for-President committee (see Smith, *Dewey*, p. 579; Ambrose, *Eisenhower*, vol. I, *Soldier, General of the Army, President-Elect*, p. 517; Lyon, *Portrait of the Hero*, pp. 428–33; and no. 196). Clay would write to Eisenhower on October 3 (EM) urging the meeting with Talbott: "He will give you a very factual report of the situation as he sees it [and] he will not in any way attempt to ask you questions" (on the many questions concerning Eisenhower's party affiliation see, for example, no. 329 and the preceding document). Eisenhower's confusion about Talbott's first name probably resulted from Eisenhower's friendship with Brigadier General (USA, ret.) Ralph Talbott, Jr. (USMA 1905).

[4] Eisenhower would fly to Naples on October 15 to meet with SACMED/CINC-SOUTH Admiral Robert Carney (see no. 107) and to embark with him aboard the cruiser *Des Moines* to observe three days of battle maneuvers with the U.S. Sixth Fleet. Other members of the General's party, including Mrs. Eisenhower, her mother Mrs. Doud, and Eisenhower aide Robert Schulz, would fly with the SHAPE staff only as far as Rome, where they would spend two days shopping, sightseeing, and attending an audience with Pope Pius XII (see Trip Itinerary, no. 40, EM, Subject File, Aircraft; and MacArthur to Schulz, Oct. 13, 1951, and Eisenhower to Looram, Oct. 18, 1951, both in EM, Subject File, Trips, SHAPE no. 15).

Heavy seas and high winds encountered during the fleet's cruise would cause the cancellation of many of the proposed battle maneuvers on this, the first occasion on which the SHAPE headquarters flag had flown at sea. Despite the difficulties, Eisenhower was optimistic during a press conference held aboard the aircraft carrier *Franklin D. Roosevelt* off the coast of southern France on October 17. After requesting that "no political questions" be asked, the General expressed his confidence in the ability of the nations of the West to achieve a military balance with Russia and to cooperate with one another in winning the war of ideas against communism. Concerning the future foreign policy of the free world, he urged recognition of the "legitimate aspirations" for independence of the Middle East's Moslem countries and called U.N. inspection of Soviet atomic bomb facilities "the minimum we should demand" (see *International Herald Tribune*, Paris ed., Oct. 16, 17, 18, 19, 1951).

The morning of the eighteenth Eisenhower flew by helicopter to the French port of Nice, where he and the SHAPE staff members who had accompanied him on the maneuver were met by the SACEUR's aircraft, *Columbine* (see no. 224), and flown to Paris. Other members of the General's party, including Mrs. Eisenhower, had returned to Paris aboard the *Columbine* the previous day (see Trip Itineraries, nos. 40 and 41, both in EM, Subject File, Aircraft; *International Herald Tribune*, Paris ed., Oct. 19, 1951; and correspondence and schedules in EM, Subject File, Trips, SHAPE no. 15).

The morning of October 19 the General, Mrs. Eisenhower, and several members of the SHAPE staff flew to London, where Eisenhower addressed a dinner commemorating the ninth anniversary of the Battle of El Alamein (for background see Chandler, *War Years*, nos. 539 and 569). The dinner at London's Empress Hall was attended by seven thousand veterans, who also heard remarks by Winston Churchill and the El Alamein commander, Field Marshal Montgomery. In his brief speech Eisenhower praised the courage and determination of the British who had fought in North Africa during World War II and stressed that only through cooperation had victory been attained. He then called for a continuing spirit of cooperation among the nations of the West "to meet the plaguing terrible problems of peace" (see copy in EM, Subject File, Speeches, "El Alamein Reunion," Oct. 19, 1951; and *International Herald Tribune*, Paris ed., Oct. 20, 22, 1951).

The Eisenhowers would spend the following day in London calling on friends, and the afternoon of the twenty-first they would fly to Scotland to spend a week vacationing at their apartment in Culzean Castle (see Trip Itinerary, no. 42, EM, Subject File, Trips, SHAPE no. 16; on the Culzean apartment see *Eisenhower Papers*, vols. I–XI). The General would meet with Talbott immediately following his return from this trip (see no. 452).

[5] Calhoun had said that the international and domestic situations were worsening and that Eisenhower was the only person who as President could improve these conditions. If the General did decide to seek the nomination, Calhoun wrote, "I would do everything in my power, regardless of how large or small the assignment might be, to promote your candidacy."

402   *Eisenhower Mss.*

To Richard Owen Davidson   *October 1, 1951*

To SHAPE liaison for Davidson[1] *from Schulz.* Send the following day letter to Mister Eugene Black, Federal Reserve Building, New York City, at Government expense: "I am informed by Cliff Roberts that you have found it possible to be here on the week end of October six.[2] Assuming that you will let us know the exact time of your arrival I shall have someone meet you at the airport and we will work out whatever schedule seems appropriate. I hope that you and I can have a good personal talk sometime on Sunday and that on Monday morning you can meet with appropriate divisions of the staff at SHAPE. From there on we can arrange for anything additional that may seem advisable although as I informed Cliff I must go to Germany on the morning of the ninth. I am grateful for your readiness to contribute so generously of your time."

Phone the following to Clifford Roberts or Mary Finley in New York: "I have cabled a direct invitation to Mister Eugene Black. I had already read several times your letter of the nineteenth but had overlooked the emphasis you placed upon a direct cable to Mister Black. Sorry."

Send the following day letter to Honorable William Pawley; Mayflower Hotel, Washington DC at DDE Expense: "I have just heard that your son had succumbed to polio while in Mexico.[3] If this tragic rumor is true I send to you my very sincere sympathy and my assurances of all the support that affectionate friendship can render."

---

[1] Lieutenant Colonel Davidson served as SHAPE liaison officer at the Pentagon.

[2] Eisenhower's old friend Clifford Roberts had urged the General to invite World Bank president Eugene R. Black to SHAPE for informal talks about the economic condition of NATO countries (see no. 369). A few days after dispatching this message, Eisenhower explained the postponement to Roberts (no. 416).

[3] For background on former Ambassador William D. Pawley see no. 41, n. 1. There is no further correspondence in EM related to Pawley's son (see *New York Times*, Sept. 27, 1951). Eisenhower's next letter to Pawley (no. 506) would concern Pawley's appointment as a Defense Department troubleshooter.

---

403   *Eisenhower Mss.*

To Hastings Lionel Ismay   *October 2, 1951*

Dear Pug: Your letter of the 26th did not reach me until after Bedell had started his return trip to the United States. But I do hope that he had an opportunity during his few hours in London to see you or to give you a telephone call.[1]

I have just seen some advance copies of a few extracts from Winston's forthcoming book.[2] I notice that he is still rather bitter about the decision not to commit additional forces to the Rhodes, Leros, and Cos adventure in late '43. On questions of broad—and I mean really broad—strategy, I think there is no judgment in the world I respect more than I do Winston's. He clearly perceived that Germany had to be smashed, as a first task, by the Allies before great forces were concentrated for the Japanese war; he had a perfect sense of the value of the Mediterranean in the whole European war, a sense that was needed to balance the convictions of those who wanted to be too hasty in settling the whole affair by land battle. Above all, his uncanny judgments in the political-military field were of inestimable value throughout the conflict.

In spite of all my admiration for his judgment in these affairs (to say nothing of my personal affection for a character in whom I found so much to admire and like), I still cannot agree with him in many of his ideas about the tactical uses of troops and, sometimes, with his calculations as to great results that would have resulted from minor adventures. Secondary and supporting attacks are one thing; but yielding to the constant temptations that always present themselves so glitteringly in war for dispersion and more dispersion has brought about more disappointment and disaster than almost any other sin.[3]

In any event, I come always to the conclusion that books (and this most definitely includes my own) do very little to change opinions already formed.[4]

I cannot tell you how deeply I share your distress and that of your fellow citizens because of the illness of The King.[5] Recently I wrote a short note to Sir Alan Lascelles to express this sentiment, and then later discovered that Sir Alan himself had only recently lost his only son.[6] The world seems so crowded with both collective and personal grief and disappointment that it sometimes becomes difficult to keep the proper level of optimism. However, my underlying faith in the populations of the free worlds always come[s] to my rescue when I get to feeling too badly—while my possession of wonderful friends makes me feel extraordinarily rich even in a time such as this.

Mamie joins me in warm greetings and best wishes to you and yours. *As ever*

---

[1] For background on Walter Bedell Smith and his recent visit to SHAPE see no. 360. During World War II Ismay had worked closely with Eisenhower and Smith. Ismay served as head of the Secretarial Staff of the British War Cabinet and as C/S to Winston Churchill in his role as Minister of Defence (see Chandler, *War Years*). For further background see no. 5, n. 1. In a postscript to his September 26 letter to Eisenhower (EM) Ismay had written, "If Bedell is coming here please tell him to call me, however rushed he is!"

[2] *Closing the Ring*, the fifth volume of Churchill's history *The Second World War*, would be published in November (see *New York Times*, Nov. 23, 1951; and *New York Times Book Review*, Nov. 25, 1951). On the publication of earlier volumes in the series see Galambos, *Columbia University*, nos. 114, 366, and 1109.

[3] Churchill devoted an entire chapter of his latest work to Allied rejection of a proposal he had made during the summer of 1943 to capture three small Aegean islands that Churchill believed would have opened the way to south-central Europe. According to Churchill, the capture of Cos, Rhodes, and Leros would have put "command of the Aegean by air and by sea . . . within [Allied] reach." Because Eisenhower had been ultimately responsible for the decision not to support the proposal, Churchill had stated that the General and his Staff "seemed unaware of what lay at our finger-tips . . ." (see Churchill, *The Second World War*, vol. V,

Closing the Ring, pp. 203–25. See also Chandler, *War Years*, esp. nos. 1327, 1328, and 1329; and Eisenhower, *Crusade in Europe*, pp. 190–91. On correspondence between Eisenhower and the British statesman concerning the issue see Galambos, *Columbia University*, no. 114). In a reply to Eisenhower of October 11 (EM) Ismay wrote that in the original draft of the book "the wretched topic [of the Mediterranean islands] appeared so often that it was downright boring" and that Churchill had been persuaded to reduce coverage of the topic.

[4] On the writing of Eisenhower's war memoir, *Crusade in Europe*, see Galambos, *Columbia University*.

[5] George VI had undergone surgery for lung cancer on September 23, but the exact nature of the King's illness had not yet been released to the public (see *New York Times*, Sept. 3, 24, Oct. 1, 1951). For developments see no. 606, n. 3.

[6] Sir Alan Francis Lascelles had been private secretary to George VI since 1943 (for background see Chandler and Galambos, *Occupation, 1945*, no. 290). On September 25 (EM, Lascelles Corr.) Eisenhower had written to express his concern for the King's health, and on the twenty-seventh (EM) he had sent his condolences upon hearing of the death of the secretary's son. John Frederick Lascelles, a major of the Grenadier Guards, had died in Scotland on September 11 at the age of twenty-nine (see *Times* [London], Sept. 12, 14, Nov. 2, 1951).

404   *Eisenhower Mss.*

To Brian Gwynne Horrocks   *October 2, 1951*
Personal and confidential

Dear Horrocks:[1] This morning someone showed me your article entitled "Strengthen NATO Now." I most emphatically agree with your approach and your general conclusions. In the middle of the article, there are a few paragraphs that are especially appropriate. They are the three that begin, "Everything, therefore, depends upon the speed. . . ." I earnestly preach this doctrine to all the political leaders I meet in Europe.[2]

The only thing that I find lacking in your article is a reference to the essential factor of morale. You state the remainder of the problem very clearly, and certainly your outline of ground requirements is reasonable and fair.

One of the basic obstacles to progress has been, as you know, the pessimism, neutralism, and defeatism that engulfed this section of the world following upon its liberation in 1945.

These same negative characteristics were likewise discernible in other sections of the world. Enormous progress has been made in restoring the morale of Europe, but even greater progress is mandatory. In spite of difficulties, in spite of past disaster and everything else, the free world *can* do this job *if we just want, badly enough, to do so.* I think that every time a soldier, statesman, or politician opens his mouth on this subject, he should never forget this particular truth—that with the necessary morale, we can produce the necessary force.[3]

The next time you are over this way, be sure to drop in to see me; in the meantime, I just wanted to tell you how accurately I thought you had portrayed the problem. *Cordially*

[1] On Lieutenant General Sir Brian Horrocks, who had retired in 1949 as Commander of the British Army of the Rhine, see Chandler, *War Years*, no. 1202.

[2] In his article, written following a "tour in NATO military circles," Horrocks had called for rapid and increased effort from North Atlantic Treaty nations in providing the manpower necessary to European defense (see copy in EM, same file as document, n.d.). Primary, in Horrocks's view, was the need for trained contingents of reserves that could be immediately called up in division-size units in the event of war. Following the sentence that Eisenhower here quoted, the British general had called upon member nations to increase both the numbers of available reservists and their training periods. As Horrocks explained, an emphasis on citizen-soldiers was imperative because "no democratic country can afford to maintain in peace-time, sufficiently large active armies to ensure complete security." For Eisenhower's postwar positions on universal military service and universal military training in the United States see no. 447.

[3] Eisenhower had repeatedly stressed the importance of improved European morale to the defense of the West (see, for example, nos. 23, n. 7, 233, and 248).

405

CCS 092 Western Europe
(3-12-48), Sec. 96

To Joint Chiefs of Staff
Cable ALO 368. Top secret

October 3, 1951

Personal for Joint Chiefs of Staff[0]

1. Due to my frequent absences from the office incident to attending maneuvers in Germany,[1] the staff found opportunity only this week to present to me the provisions of the US Joint Chiefs of Staff joint emergency war plan "IRONBARK."[2]

2. Paragraph 31 of that plan,[3] and sub para 41 of the implementing directive thereto[4] evidences such serious differences of understanding between me and the Joint Chiefs of Staff that clarifying action is required as a matter of urgency.[5]

3. I thoroughly recognize the need for the Joint Chiefs of Staff to prepare emergency war plans on a worldwide basis. However, with respect to my area of responsibility, the fact that the US has taken the lead in establishing a unified allied command structure, and has, with other nations, agreed to place its forces under that command, makes it mandatory that US emergency plans recognize clearly my authority as the Supreme Allied Commander Europe.

4. If each of the ten allied nations now contributing forces to SHAPE should find it necessary to issue plans and orders governing both the initial operations of their national forces in event of emergency, and also making provision for subsequent contingent operations, there would, in fact, be nothing but chaos. Moreover, there would be neither logical function nor need for the Supreme Allied Commander Europe and his subordinate allied commanders.

5. I am quite ready to take into consideration and integrate into my plans, insofar as may be possible, the ideas and desires of any national Chiefs of Staff ground based upon the possible development of dire emergency. I understand fully the concern of the US Joint Chiefs of Staff for the ultimate safety of American forces under conditions of calamity. But if such conditions should develop, my responsibilities would be all the greater and unilateral national action with respect to forces under my command would be a complete breaking of faith. I consider, therefore, that it must be made absolutely clear that the directive of the President, placing all US forces in Europe under my operational command for the accomplishment of my mission,[6] has no qualifications or limitations other than the responsibility to ensure the evacuation of US civilians in the event of an emergency.

6. My staff and I are quite ready to meet the US planners and go into these matters in the utmost detail, and with full concern for the convictions and opinions that the Joint Chiefs of Staff may desire me to consider. In the meantime, I consider it a matter of urgency that:

A. The implementing directive for IRONBARK be modified clearly to indicate that the commanders of US forces in Europe, i.e., CINCEUR,[7] CINCNELM,[8] CINCUSAFE,[9] CGUSFA[10] will be subject to my orders and my directives in preparations for, and in the conduct of, operations in the event of emergency.

B. All Joint Chiefs of Staff plans and directives applicable to forces under my command or involving contemplated operations within my area of responsibility clearly recognize my overriding authority and the allied command structure I have established.

C. The US commanders in Europe be directed to coordinate their plans in support of JCS plans with me.[11]

[1] For background on Eisenhower's inspection trips to Germany see no. 375, n. 3. This message was marked "not releasable to foreign nationals" and received the designation "NOFORN 245."

[2] A copy of joint outline emergency war plan IRONBARK, which had been given to U.S. field commanders on May 14, 1951, may be found in CCS 381 USSR (3-2-46), B.P., Pt. 5. This plan, a successor to war plan OFFTACKLE (see no. 124, n. 2), outlined a course of action for the first two years of a war beginning on January 1, 1951, and based upon forces available on that date. IRONBARK assumed that the Soviet Union possessed thirty-five atomic bombs (fifty by mid-1951) and that both

sides would use these weapons. The United States and its allies would conduct a strategic offensive in western Eurasia and a strategic defensive in the Far East; at the outbreak of war the U.S. forces in Korea would be withdrawn and redeployed. IRONBARK contained a statement, originally written by Eisenhower in 1949 (see Galambos, *Columbia University*, no. 380), that the security of the United States required holding Western Europe or returning to the Continent as soon as possible after a Soviet attack. IRONBARK also followed OFFTACKLE in its recognition that the forces available to the United States and its allies were not capable of preventing the Soviet Union from overrunning Western Europe during 1951 (see JCS 2073/217, Oct. 4, 1951, EM, same file as document).

[3] This section of IRONBARK described the operations of U.S. and Allied forces in western Eurasia during the first three years of war. Since the Soviet troops would greatly outnumber the NATO armies, those operations would be "essentially defensive and delaying in nature." Western troops in Germany would first "be withdrawn to the line of the Rhine in accordance with approved emergency war plans of the respective commanders in chief of the occupation forces." Any further withdrawal "in the face of Soviet pressure" would be directed by Eisenhower. The U.S. commander was also to provide plans "for the extrication of his forces by withdrawal through western or southern French ports to the United Kingdom or to northwest Africa." IRONBARK also made provision for evacuating U.S. and Allied forces from Austria, Trieste, Iran, Turkey, and Greece.

[4] The JCS had approved directives implementing IRONBARK on August 6, 1951. Subparagraph 4*l* established the position that IRONBARK was intended to guide U.S. commanders in Europe until Eisenhower could formulate his own emergency war plan and have it approved by NATO (JCS 2073/217, Oct. 4, 1951, CCS 092 Western Europe [3-12-48], Sec. 96; JCS 83356, Oct. 5, 1951, *ibid.*, Sec. 97).

[5] The differences referred to by Eisenhower involved the reluctance of SHAPE and NATO leaders to contemplate any withdrawals from Germany in the event of war. The JCS, however, had decided that regardless of the "political implications that face SACEUR, the Joint Chiefs of Staff are vested with a statutory responsibility for the safety of U.S. forces throughout the world." Therefore, the JCS reasoned, it was "mandatory that the U.S. emergency war plan be based upon national considerations alone" (JCS 2073/217, Oct. 4, 1951, *ibid.*, Sec. 96). Meeting with Army Chief of Staff J. Lawton Collins in France on October 4 and 5, Eisenhower would point out that SHAPE plans then being prepared "would involve no details of possible forced withdrawal from the Rhine defenses." Eisenhower would also state that "he could not and would not prepare for any contingencies other than for the defense of the Rhine, as, in his judgment, it would not be practicable to predict in advance how the situation might develop." Collins replied that "in the event of a complete disaster it would be imperative for the Americans to withdraw along their lines of communication." Eisenhower agreed and, according to Collins, "stated tentatively, but with nothing definite, that under such conditions he would no doubt endeavor to hold as much as possible of the British and French forces together with the Americans" (Collins to JCS, Nov. 2, 1951, *ibid.*, Sec. 102). The differing concepts of operations held by NATO and the U.S. planners would continue to cause problems (see no. 553).

[6] See Galambos, *Columbia University*, no. 1136.

[7] Commander in Chief, Europe, General Thomas T. Handy.

[8] Commander in Chief, United States Naval Forces, Eastern Atlantic and Mediterranean, Admiral Robert B. Carney.

[9] Commander in Chief, United States Air Forces, Europe, General Lauris Norstad.

[10] Commanding General, United States Forces, Austria, General Stafford L. Irwin.

[11] The JCS would soon take steps to meet some of Eisenhower's objections. After

discussing the matter with Eisenhower, Collins would direct Handy to consult with SACEUR before putting IRONBARK into effect (Collins to JCS, Nov. 2, 1951, CCS 092 Western Europe [3-12-48], Sec. 102). In a cable to Eisenhower sent on October 4 the JCS would reassure him that his "authority as SACEUR" was "recognized by JCS." The Joint Chiefs maintained, however, that "there must be an overall United States emergency war plan based on United States nat[iona]l considerations alone available for implementation when and if situation so requires." Their intention was to make sure that the U.S. plan was "in consonance with your NATO plan within area of your responsibility." The Joint Chiefs promised to review IRONBARK as soon as Eisenhower's plan had been completed and sent to them by the Standing Group. They would also direct U.S. commanders in Europe "to coordinate their plans in support of JCS plans with you on a NOFORN basis" (JCS 83356, *ibid.*, Sec. 97). For developments see no. 553.

Partisan Pressures and European Duties

OCTOBER 1951 TO JANUARY 1952

5

National Rivalries

406

To Marcellus Hartley Dodge[1]   *October 3, 1951*
Cable AP 81648

Responding to the message telephoned to me through Colonel Schulz I consider that General Donovan possesses all the qualifications for an outstanding Trustee of Columbia.[2] *Signed*

[1] For background on Dodge, a member and clerk of the Columbia University board of trustees, see no. 6, n. 1.

[2] In a telephone conversation of October 2 with Eisenhower's aide Robert Schulz (see no. 29, n. 3) Dodge had asked the General to comment on the appointment of William J. Donovan to the Columbia board. Donovan would fill the position recently vacated by the rector of Trinity Parish, the Reverend Dr. Frederic Sydney Fleming (S.T.B. Western Theological Seminary 1911) (see memorandum, Schulz to Eisenhower, Oct. 3, 1951, in EM, same file as document). Writing directly to Eisenhower on October 2 (EM), Dodge explained that Fleming had also resigned his Trinity post. While tradition dictated that the trustee position be filled by the parish rector, Dodge believed that Donovan would be such an asset that he should be appointed to the board (on Donovan's recent work with Columbia see no. 129). Dodge urged Eisenhower to send a letter of recommendation to Albert Putnam (see no. 114, n. 2), chairman of the trustee committee on nominations. For developments see no. 428.

407

To Lester Bowles Pearson   *October 3, 1951*

Dear Mr. Pearson:[1] As Chairman of the NATO Council, Mr. Van Zeeland wrote me from Ottawa extending the Council's invitation to attend its next meeting. I have replied to him that I would be most happy to attend, and, since the Chairmanship has passed to you, I am also writing to inform you of my acceptance. I would, of course, be prepared to report to the Council on the problems we face at SHAPE and to make myself available for that part of the meeting which relates to our activities.[2]

Knowing of your constant efforts to strengthen NATO and to further our security aims, I am personally delighted that you will be at the helm during the critical period ahead. At the Ottawa meeting certain vital problems were discussed, and it is our hope at SHAPE that, under your leadership, the Council will find the solutions essential to continued progress toward attainment of our security objectives.[3]

I have heard that you may be in Paris early in November for the opening of the U.N. General Assembly. If your schedule permits, I hope you will be able to have lunch with me. It would be a great pleasure to see you.[4]

With best wishes, *Sincerely*

[1] Pearson, Canadian Secretary of State for External Affairs, had been named Chairman of the North Atlantic Council during a recent meeting of the group in Ottawa (see Ismay, *NATO*, p. 66; and *New York Times*, Sept. 22, 1951). For background on the NAC see no. 2, n. 2.

[2] On former NAC Chairman *v*an Zeeland and Eisenhower's acceptance of his invitation see no. 399. On the General's attendance at the upcoming NAC meeting in Rome see no. 494, n. 8.

[3] For background on the proceedings in Ottawa see no. 384, n. 1.

[4] Pearson replied (Oct. 20, 1951, EM) that he would be in Paris during early November and hoped to accept Eisenhower's invitation. The two would meet on November 14.

408

Eisenhower Mss.

To JOHN COWLES
Personal and confidential

October 3, 1951

Dear John:[1] As you know, my days are crowded and I live in an atmosphere of urgency, if not of tension. Consequently, and because my own notes of our conversations, necessarily dictated at high speed, are not very complete, I am at a bit of a loss to understand some of the points you make in your letter. For example, I am not quite sure of the "time-table" reference because I think I have always qualified any predictions as to the timing of significant accomplishments in SHAPE by saying that any one of a number of circumstances could change my calculations in a flash. In spite of this, I follow your general line of reasoning and reporting.[2]

Of course, all your letters are interesting, but I have difficulty—very great difficulty—in fitting myself into any mental picture involving the future of our domestic politics. Frankly, I simply do not have the time to give real consideration to the domestic scene. On an objective basis, I, of course, try to keep abreast of general events, trends, and developments. But it is almost impossible for me to go further than this.

I have steadfastly refused to comment on the growing partisan struggle, and I have most certainly refused to take part, in any way, in the individual contests that always precede our political battles. I have even refused to comment on one case where there apparently is developing the ridiculous and perfectly absurd situation of my name being entered in the primaries of *both* parties.[3]

Incidentally, the Governor has several times told me exactly the same things he has told you. I think it's fine for him to push ahead as he is doing; I can follow his reasoning.[4]

As I have often emphasized to you, I try my best to do my duty. My current duty is right here and you know how fully occupied I am. With regard to this point, and the requirement it places on me to abstain from expressing a party adherence, I am quoting here a paragraph that I include in most of the letters I send to individuals who demand from me specific statements:

"The job I am on requires the support of the vast body of Americans. For me to admit, while in this post, or to imply a partisan political loyalty would properly be resented by thinking Americans and would be doing a disservice to our country, for *it would interfere with the job to which the country has assigned me*. The successful outcome of this venture is too vital to our welfare in the years ahead to permit any semblance of partisan allegiance on the part of the United States Military Commander in SHAPE."

This paragraph, I think, states my current feeling about as accurately as it can be done. As long as I am here, I don't see how I can say anything else.[5]

You see that I am writing to you very frankly because I trust so implicitly in your friendship and sympathetic understanding.

I have just received a cable from Paul Hoffman saying that, in a month or so, he will be back this way and I am reserving time for a meeting with him. I do not know on what errand he is coming, but I expect to gain from him an even fuller report concerning your around-the-world trip than was given in your article in *Look*. Incidentally, the theme of your article was perfect. I wish, not only that you would repeat and repeat the same idea insistently and constantly, but that others would follow your lead to establish peace as the real warp and woof of all our propaganda and informational activity. Frankly, if I did not believe I were struggling to preserve the peace, I would have far less concern in this job and would feel toward it a far lesser sense of dedication. So I urge you to keep everlastingly at the job of hammering home not only the idea of preserving peace, but the fact that we should *say so*.[6]

If anything, the world situation has worsened since you were here. In Korea, the prospects of an armistice grow dim, and we are supporting a war there on a basis that makes difficult the job of building up defensive strength elsewhere—at least, to do so and, at the same time, to avoid the terrible danger of uncontrolled inflation.[7] In Iran, all of us (not just the British) have taken a bad set-back.[8] The Egyptians seem ready to lead the Moslem world in still greater expressions of impatience with and of their dislike for the West.[9] In Germany, it appears that the psychological initiative may have been snatched by the

Communists with their offer to unify the country, and there is no telling what the developments will be in that area. A united Germany is far more popular, even west of the Elbe, than a re-armed Germany.[10]

All this is a poor answer to such a fine letter as yours. But, with your fine understanding, you will know I've done my best. *Cordially*

[1] For background on Cowles, a publishing executive and trustee of the Ford Foundation, see no. 338.

[2] Writing to the General on September 29 (EM), Cowles had reported on his recent meetings with certain Republicans then working to secure Eisenhower the 1952 presidential nomination. In regard to a conversation with Harry Darby (see no. 196) and Roy Roberts (see no. 289), Cowles said he had told the two "what you had indicated to me might be your time table, and both of them thought it was o.k." This "time table" was most likely what Cowles assumed would be Eisenhower's schedule for announcing his party affiliation, declaring his candidacy, and eventually returning to the United States to begin an active campaign. On Cowles's August meeting with the General, during which they had discussed Eisenhower's political future, see no. 308. For developments with the growing Eisenhower-for-President movement see, for example, nos. 486 and 537.

[3] On the possible double entry of Eisenhower's name in the Oregon presidential primary see no. 386.

[4] Concerning former Governor of Minnesota Harold Stassen (see no. 330), who at this time was already seeking the Republican nomination, Cowles had written that Stassen "asked me to tell you that he would support you unconditionally if and when you became an open candidate and that he could deliver almost all of whatever delegates he might have to you." On Stassen's role as both an actual candidate and a "stalking horse" for an Eisenhower candidacy see Parmet, *Eisenhower and the American Crusades*, pp. 39, 53, 98–99; and the following document.

[5] For background on Eisenhower's use of this reply to political inquiries see no. 358.

[6] Following the August 3 meeting with Eisenhower (see n. 2 above), Ford Foundation president Paul Hoffman, Cowles, and Paul Helms had departed on a trip to the Far East on foundation business (see nos. 308 and 338). Cowles's article, tear sheets of which he had enclosed with his letter of the twenty-ninth, would appear in the October 9 issue of *Look* magazine, a publication of which he was chairman of the board (copy in EM, same file as document). The article, "Let's Launch an American Peace Offensive," called for a shift in American foreign policy from emphasis on military defenses against communism to a reliance on growing worldwide prosperity as a pathway to peace. Cowles maintained that if the United States would continually put forward plans for universal disarmament and effective international control of atomic weaponry, Soviet rejection of the proposals would prove "that it is Russia which is the aggressor and war monger." In its relations with the nations of Asia and the Far East, Cowles urged the United States to avoid imposing Western theories of free enterprise and social justice on other nations and to call for an end to European colonialism and exploitation.

[7] On the Korean stalemate and talk of an armistice see no. 362.

[8] For background on the crisis in Iran see nos. 142 and 259.

[9] Acts of terrorism, strikes, demonstrations, and a series of assassinations of government officials had flared within Egypt since the close of World War II. Central to the cause of the unrest were British military control of the Suez Canal and joint Anglo-Egyptian rule of the Sudan. The election of a new Egyptian parliament in January 1950 had marked the beginning of a nationalistic social and economic reform campaign under the Wadf party, with the issue of Anglo-Egyptian relations

as its cornerstone. On October 8 the Egyption government would unilaterally abrogate the 1936 Suez Treaty and the Sudan Condominium Agreement of 1899 (see Panayiotis J. Vatikiotis, *The History of Egypt*, 2d ed. [Baltimore, 1980], pp. 366–68; and *New York Times*, Sept. 22, Oct. 2, 9, 1951).

[10] On September 15 East German Premier Otto Grotewohl had called for "free all-German elections of a constitutional convention" to reunify the nation. Seen by the NATO countries as a ruse to forestall the rearmament of West Germany, this move was strongly opposed by the Allies. Although promptly rejected by West German Chancellor Adenauer (for background see no. 12), the Grotewohl proposal gained the support of Protestant church officials and West German nationalist groups. In Grotewohl's speech proposing the elections, he denounced his West German counterparts as puppets, saying "the real master in Bonn is a foreign general—Eisenhower." He accused the Allies of valuing West Germany only as a base for military operations against the East (see *New York Times*, Sept. 16, 17, 19, 20, 22, 25, Oct. 1, 3, 1951. For background on the German rearmament issue see nos. 389 and 442).

409 *Eisenhower Mss.*

To Lucius Du Bignon Clay   *October 3, 1951*
Personal and confidential

Dear Lucius: I shall do my best to make a decent answer to your letter of the 29th although I am badly pushed as to time, due to the presence here simultaneously of several groups of VIPs. Moreover, in your letter, you make mention several times of "I" and, as I told you in a recent note, I cannot interpret that particular symbol.[1]

My first remark is that I would, by no means, ever want you to think that I am insensible to the very great compliment you and others pay me when you express the belief that I could serve the country well in an exalted political post. In your case, my sense of humility and pride is all the greater because you've known me such a long time and have worked intimately with me. So please never forget, and allow none of the others to forget, that I am more than honored by their attitude. In replying to everyone who expresses such opinions to me, I try to be completely honest. But I never seem to have all the rights and privileges, with respect to free speech and acting, that apply to the normal citizen—right now, because of the nature of this job I have, less than ever before.[2]

As you might suspect, I have a fairly steady stream of correspondence dealing with this general question. I have found it necessary to state my present position, with the limitations it places upon my actions, as accurately and as definitely as I know how. This I have usually done in a paragraph about as follows:

"The job I am on requires the support of the vast body of Americans. Those Americans have the right to believe that their agent is serving all of them and is not seeking to advance the fortunes of any one group as compared to another. For me to admit, *while in this post*, or to imply a partisan political loyalty would properly be resented by thinking Americans and would be doing a disservice to our country, for it would interfere with the job to which the country has assigned me. The successful outcome of this venture is too vital to our welfare in the years ahead to permit any semblance of partisan allegiance on the part of the United States Military Commander in SHAPE."[3]

Since this is an honest expression of my convictions, I naturally cannot indicate or imply a choice in the "leadership" that Our Friend wants to see established. My sole attitude is that I am ready to do my duty in whatever direction I believe my duty to exist. It should be perfectly clear to us all that any move on my part that could be interpreted as a voluntary entry into the political field would be disastrous to this job and, therefore, damaging to our country.[4]

It has been asserted to me, time and again, that the character of the Washington leadership is more important to this job than is the identity of the commander on the spot. This is probably true; yet the fact is that I am *now* on a job assigned to me as a duty. This makes it impossible for me to be in the position (no matter how remotely or indirectly) of seeking another post. The suspicion would be aroused that I would only be trying to satisfy personal ambition. As you know, any ambitions I have do *not* move in that direction.[5]

Having said all this, I do not mind commenting upon the special items of news in your letter. First, with respect to your reference concerning "F" and what he told one of your friends, he has several times stated to me, in effect, "I shall be your loyal and sincere lieutenant any time that it becomes completely clear that you are available. In the meantime, since there would develop a vacuum in many areas unless there was someone in a position actively to challenge the doctrine of the reactionary isolationists, I expect to push ahead on my own so as to prevent the entire organization from falling into their hands. In this effort, *I must not be a stalking horse*—that is, I must honestly do it in my own right. Nevertheless, when and if the necessary condition respecting your own case may be established, at that moment I shall not only become your lieutenant but shall deliver to you, so far as it is possible, all the strength that has been pledged to me." A letter received today from a friend of mine states that "F" has just reiterated this purpose.[6]

I know "D" only through others. I have never talked to him alone, but my friends in Kansas have always spoken of him as a man of ability and character. It seems to me that someone said there might develop a Kansas Committee of "J," "D," and "K." If that happened, I suppose the fears of Our Friend would subside.[7]

You need not worry that I shall ever disregard Our Friend. In spite of the things that one occasionally hears from those who have not particularly liked him, I have implicit confidence in his sincerity and in his good faith.[8]

All the best, and warm personal regard. Thanks for your letters.

As ever

P.S. In your job, is there any *obvious* reason for you to make a European trip this fall or winter?[9]

---

[1] Clay employed a letter-for-name substitution code established earlier in the year for use in their political correspondence (see nos. 196, n. 3, 331, n. 4, and 396; and Clay to Eisenhower, Sept. 24 and 29, 1951, both in EM). In recent letters to Eisenhower, Clay twice had written of someone designated as "I," which appeared on none of the code lists he had supplied the General. Clay's meeting with "I" in Kansas City offered a clue that it may have been former Governor of Kansas Harry Hines Woodring (see Galambos, *Chief of Staff*, no. 1273), a Democratic supporter of an Eisenhower candidacy, but there is no explanation of the symbol in Clay's subsequent correspondence in EM.

[2] In his letters of September 24 and 29 Clay had reported on recent developments within the unofficial Eisenhower-for-President committee (see no. 196). Formed under the silent direction of New York Governor Thomas Dewey and utilizing much of the nationwide political organization developed for Dewey's 1948 presidential bid, the Eisenhower group was at this time hampered by old internal dissensions and by the lack of public support from their candidate. To solidify efforts on the General's behalf, Dewey was now working to coordinate and strengthen the group (see Smith, *Dewey*, pp. 577–80; and Parmet, *Eisenhower and the American Crusades*, pp. 37–38).

[3] For Eisenhower's recent use of this paragraph see, for example, no. 358.

[4] "Our Friend" and "Our Friend up the river" were code names used to identify Dewey in the Clay-Eisenhower correspondence. In his letter of the twenty-fourth, Clay had stated that Dewey was "shocked by the lack of progress" the Eisenhower group had made and believed a change in its leadership was necessary. Kansas banker Harry Darby (see the preceding document) had served as the group's director since its establishment in May, but following a Washington, D.C., meeting with fellow committee members Duff (see no. 279, n. 3) and Senator Frank Carlson (Republican, Kansas), Dewey had determined that Carlson should assume the role of chairman. On the twenty-ninth, however, Clay reported that objections raised by committee members (including the mysterious "I") during a meeting in Kansas City had blocked Darby's replacement.

[5] The debate over military versus political duty would continue for the next several months in the General's correspondence with Clay (see, for example, nos. 551 and 678). Certain that Eisenhower was the only Republican candidate who could win the election, Clay wrote on the twenty-ninth that a Truman-Taft race would result in an incumbent victory and "at a minimum four more years of the very bad government we have today, and it could even mean the downfall in this country of the two-party system."

[6] "F" was former Governor of Minnesota Harold Stassen, who was then contending with Taft for the Republican nomination. According to Clay (Sept. 29), Stassen had recently told Wisconsin Republican party chairman Thomas Emmet Coleman (Ph.B. University of Chicago 1914) that there was "a vacuum . . . created by the lack of purposeful opposition" to the isolation-oriented Taft and that he, Stassen, would campaign only as a true candidate and not as an Eisenhower "stalking

horse." Clay wrote that he was untroubled by this information, saying that Stassen had "no real chance" and would not offer his pledged delegates to anyone other than Eisenhower (for background on the General's relationship with Stassen see, for example, no. 330). Eisenhower's reply to the letter he mentions is the preceding document.

[7] On Kansas newspaperman Roy Roberts ("J") see the preceding document; on Darby ("D") and Carlson ("K") see n. 4 above. Leadership of the Eisenhower committee would remain in Darby's hands until November, when Massachusetts Senator Henry Cabot Lodge would be named as the first official manager of the group (see nos. 499, n. 1, and 538; and Smith, *Dewey*, p. 579. For background on Lodge's career see no. 961). In a visit with the General at SHAPE headquarters on September 4 Lodge had discussed the upcoming presidential race and encouraged Eisenhower to become an active Republican candidate. Writing later of what he termed their "significant" conversation, the General said Lodge had reviewed political events of the previous twenty years, emphasizing the dangers of Democratic, partisan dominance of the federal government, the drift toward federal-government paternalism, and the potential disasters of continued Democratic deficit spending. Lodge assured Eisenhower that he was the only electable Republican candidate who could reverse these dangerous trends while avoiding the "fatal errors of isolationism" associated with Taft. To a direct request from Senator Lodge that Eisenhower authorize entry of his name in the upcoming presidential primaries, Eisenhower replied in a new way. In agreeing to "think the matter over," Eisenhower wrote, he had reached a "turning point," after which "I began to look anew—perhaps subconsciously—at myself and politics" (Eisenhower, *Mandate for Change*, pp. 16–18). For further background on Lodge's role in the Eisenhower-for-President campaign see Henry Cabot Lodge, *The Storm Has Many Eyes: A Personal Narrative* (New York, 1973).

[8] The fear of reopening "too many old [political] sores" had prevented Dewey from seeking the 1952 nomination and had also prompted his silent direction of the Eisenhower group (see Smith, *Dewey*, p. 577).

[9] Clay would reply on October 16 (EM) that as president of the Continental Can Company, which had interests in France and Belgium, he had "a valid reason to visit Europe" and was at the General's command. Correspondence in EM indicates that while Clay did make plans for a European trip during the next month, the two would meet in Washington, D.C., in early November, when Eisenhower returned to the United States for a brief visit (see Cannon to Crittenberger, AP 81882, Oct. 25, 1951, with handwritten notes, in EM, same file as document. On Eisenhower's trip to the United States see nos. 457 and 468). In a handwritten second postscript to this letter Eisenhower said, "Wouldn't it be nice if we could just forget all this kind of thing?" For developments see the following document.

410   *Eisenhower Mss., Diaries*

DIARY   *October 4, 1951*

The temptation grows to issue a short, definite statement saying No (in almost arbitrary language) to all the arguments that seek to convince me that I should accept (if offered) the Republican nomination for the Presidency. Some go so far as to say I should so state publicly, now—others even that I should start seeking and scheming for the nomination. All this last is rot—I will never seek any nomination. But as to the first the difficulty arises in the mere attempt to be honest. If I _wanted_ to be P. I'd resign today & start travelling the U.S. about Jan. 1. But the personal belief that I could do a good job would have to be so strong as to make me feel justified in leaving this onerous and strenuous post of duty. That is impossible. The only way I could leave this duty is to believe that a great section of the U.S. want me to undertake a higher one. This could be a real draft—something that all agree _cannot_ happen. In this I take real comfort—because it will at least eliminate the necessity of my making any personal decision as to my own suitability. [I scarcely mean that—because no one is really suitable; I think I mean that I will never have to decide whether or not I'd make a _relatively_ good P.]. In the meantime I can give my best to this task and _hope_ that my silence will help politicians to consider the relative suitability of those that do want the nomination!!¹

Of course, because of the remote, very remote, possibility that persons may, in spite of my silence, succeed in producing a grass roots draft I have to think more about the subject than is involved merely in a negative attitude. When people like Paul Hoffman, Govs. Dewey & Stassen, Sens. Duff, Carlson, Lodge and etc. great friends like Clay, Clark, Roberts etc. etc. and others like Craig (Am. Legion Commander of last year) all begin to assert that I have a _duty_—it is not easy to just say NO.² I hear that a petition is circulating in Abilene to get a 90% demand from my home town. I don't know what the whole state would say but I do know that ex-Governor Woodring (Demo) and ex-Sen. Darby (Rep) both believe I should run.³ No more of this—I'll just have to rock along. But I'm growing concerned about one thing— the degree to which all this might hurt the job of establishing a collective, cooperative security for the free world. So far I can see no effect (the Congressional Conferees apparently gave sympathetic consideration to my views re the reducing of E.C.A. money) but when I do become _convinced_ that the constant newspaper and other speculation is hurting our national effort—then I'm going to do something.⁴ My replies (written or verbal) to everyone always include a para substantially as follows:

"The job I am on requires the support of the vast body of Americans. These Americans have the right to believe that their agent is serving _all_ of them and is not seeking to advance the fortune of any group as compared to another. For me to admit while in this post, or to imply, a partisan political loyalty would properly be resented by thinking Americans and would be doing a disservice to our country, for it would interfere with accomplishment of the job assigned to me. The successful outcome of this venture is too vital to our nation's welfare to permit any semblance of partisan allegiance by me."⁵

[1] The political pressures on Eisenhower had recently intensified. He was pressed to declare his candidacy both publicly and privately or, short of that, to state his party affiliation. Visitors to SHAPE and known supporters of an Eisenhower candidacy were questioned in the press regarding the General's intentions, and in correspondence friends and acquaintances continued their expressions of support and offers of assistance to the General in securing the nomination (see, for example, *New York Times*, Sept. 10, Oct. 15, 1951; and no. 383). In spite of Eisenhower's repeated assertions that any partisan personal connections might harm the NATO effort, the movement had grown and would continue to expand with the approach of the presidential primaries (see no. 386 and the preceding document; for background on the primaries see no. 345). On an earlier statement issued by Eisenhower disavowing interest in the presidency in 1948 see his memoir *Mandate for Change*, p. 7; and Galambos, *Chief of Staff*, no. 1998.

[2] For background on the efforts of Thomas Dewey, Harold Stassen, James Duff, Frank Carlson, Henry Cabot Lodge, and Lucius Clay see the preceding document. On Eisenhower's friends Paul Hoffman and Edwin Clark see the following document and no. 1, respectively. Roberts could have been either Kansas newspaperman Roy Roberts (see the preceding document) or Clifford Roberts of the New York investment firm of Reynolds & Company (see no. 7), both friends and political supporters of the General. George North Craig (LL.B. Indiana University 1932), national chairman of the American Legion from 1949 until 1950, had written to Eisenhower during the summer encouraging him to seek the Republican nomination (see no. 421).

[3] On Harry Woodring and Harry Darby see the preceding document.

[4] Eisenhower's cabled appeal to Congress asking that no reduction be made in the aid distributed through the Economic Cooperation Administration is no. 377. After receiving this message from Eisenhower, the Senate would double its authorization for European military and economic aid, with the House passing the compromise measure on October 5 (see *New York Times*, Oct. 6, 1951; and no. 434).

[5] For one of the many times Eisenhower used this paragraph see no. 358.

411   *Eisenhower Mss.*

To Paul Gray Hoffman   *October 4, 1951*

Dear Paul:[1] To reply to the first paragraph of your letter, and referring also to the first paragraph of the note you wrote to William Lowe, you have certainly failed to make clear to me why I should have a very special obligation with respect of a particular duty and you should have none. While Anglo-Saxons have never been particularly apt and skillful in starting mutual admiration societies, I should like to point out that I have frequently and for a long time stated that, if *you* would only get into this particular ring, you can be sure of at least one man in the front row cheering you on—I would even carry the water bottle.[2]

Now for the more serious part of your communication; that is, the copy of your talk. I compliment you on it most highly. For the time and occasion of its delivery, it well-nigh attained perfection. There is nothing in its chain of reasoning with which I could quarrel, and its language and construction seem to me to be ideally suited to the audience you were addressing. For more general use, I wish that the text could be streamlined, almost sloganized, and put out in such fashion that he who runs could read and understand.[3]

I personally believe that a case could also be made for the assertion that a free society is a *peaceful* society. But I admit that a man could develop some plausibility in an opposite argument for the reason that I think we must subscribe to the truism that the causes of war are found in each of us. I think you were very wise not to get into too much philosophical speculation that would have consumed hours in making minor points. But I do think it important to remember that people want *peace*.[4]

So much do I like your talk that I hate to appear professorial in suggesting one item of criticism. On page 5 of the copy you sent to me, you speak of the America of the Founding Fathers as if it existed simultaneously with the France of Napoleon. You will recall that, whether you speak of the Signers of the Declaration or the Framers of our Constitution, our Founding Fathers performed their great work long before the first appearance of Napoleon. They antedated the outbreak of the French Revolution. Please don't accuse me of being a flyspecker, but let us not forget that there are critics who search meticulously through any document to which they are opposed in the effort to find any slightest kind of factual error. Success in such a search is instantly magnified into the claim that the entire document is equally invalid or false.[5]

Quite naturally, I am looking forward with great pleasure to your forthcoming visit. I shall certainly plan to have the maximum amount of time with you and your friends.[6]

My love to Dorothy[7] and, of course, warm regard to yourself. In these sentiments, Mamie is my equal partner. *Cordially*

[1] For background on Ford Foundation president Hoffman see no. 139.

[2] Writing to Eisenhower on September 26, Hoffman had enclosed a copy of a letter of the same date that he had written to William Hyslop Lowe, Jr., the managing editor of *Look* magazine (copies in EM, same file as document). Both letters referred to a recent *Look* article by Lowe entitled "Why Not Paul Hoffman?" which put the foundation executive forward as a dark horse presidential candidate. Hoffman had thanked Lowe but explained that "I couldn't run if I would and wouldn't run if I could. . . ." To Eisenhower he had said that "the article may serve one useful purpose; namely, add somewhat to the value of my support of your candidacy." Replying on October 29 (EM), Hoffman explained to the General that the obligation to seek the presidency was Eisenhower's rather than his own because "almost *all* of the people and a *few* of the politicians want you while *some* of the people and *none* of the politicians want me." For background on Lowe see Galambos, *Columbia University*, no. 910.

[3] Hoffman had also enclosed with his first letter a copy of the acceptance speech

(copy in EM) he would give when he received the Freedom House Award on October 7 (see *New York Times*, Oct. 8, 1951). For background on Freedom House and on Eisenhower's receipt of the award in 1946 see Chandler and Galambos, *Occupation, 1945*, no. 185.

[4] In his address Hoffman criticized recent American trends toward the suppression of unpopular ideas, saying that he disagreed "with the Daily Worker's tagging of every opponent as a Fascist. I also disagree intensely with those who make reckless charges of Communist sympathies. But I would not for a moment suppress these irresponsible critics." Stressing freedoms of speech, thought, and expression as the essentials of a free society, Hoffman urged his audience to "remember too that a free society is a just society [and] one reason why we must encourage criticism is that we must encourage people to point out such injustices as remain in America and to fight for their elimination." For background on the continuing congressional loyalty investigations see, for example, no. 222, n. 3.

[5] In the section of the address to which Eisenhower referred, Hoffman said that the assumption that the American system received legitimacy only from its material supremacy "unconsciously mocks the America of the Founding Fathers when, in the material sense, we were relatively small and weak alongside the France of Napoleon. . . ." The American War of Independence in fact ended six years before the outbreak of the French Revolution in 1789, and Napoleon's rise to power through a coup d'état in 1799 followed ratification of the U.S. Constitution by eleven years. Hoffman evidently did not alter the passage, writing in his letter of the twenty-ninth that "up to now no one has picked me up on my having bracketed the Founding Fathers with Napoleon."

[6] Hoffman had written (Sept. 26) that he and Henry Luce (see no. 273) planned to travel to Europe during the fall and hoped to visit Eisenhower. Apparently Luce would not make the trip; Hoffman would see the General alone on November 12 (see cables in EM, same file as document). For developments see no. 486, n. 7.

[7] Hoffman's wife (see no. 338, n. 6).

412   *Eisenhower Mss.*

To Samuel Goldwyn   *October 4, 1951*

Dear Sam:[1] Thank you very much for taking the trouble to make it possible for me to have an early viewing of the new picture you have produced.[2] As soon as my office hears from your local representatives, we will make the necessary arrangements.

The more I live, the more I am convinced that it is the simple truths—the seemingly obvious truths—that need constant telling and re-telling. The development of such pride in American ideals that the citizen will rise devotedly to their defense is an absolute necessity if the freedom under which we have flourished is to survive. This involves civic responsibility, morality, selflessness—qualities so difficult to instill permanently in human nature that constant effort is required, not only through the home and church, but through every medium in our society. Millions will see a great picture and, from what you have told me of your theme, they will be inspired to better citizenship in the process.[3] I wish you the best of luck.

With warm personal regard,[4] *Cordially*

[1] For background on movie producer Goldwyn see Galambos, *Columbia University*, no. 826.

[2] Goldwyn had written Eisenhower (Sept. 28, 1951, EM) that he had recently completed a film entitled *I Want You*, which made him prouder than anything he had done since *The Best Years of Our Lives* (1946). Goldwyn was having a print of the film made available to Eisenhower in Paris. For the General's praise of *The Best Years of Our Lives* see Galambos, *Chief of Staff*, no. 1196.

[3] According to Goldwyn (Sept. 28), *I Want You* concerned the effects of the Korean War on American families. He called it "an eloquent sermon on basic American ideals and a powerful statement of how to preserve them in today's world." Well received initially, the film failed to attain either the popularity or the critical acclaim of Goldwyn's earlier work (see *New York Times*, Oct. 7, Dec. 24, 1951).

[4] Aide Paul T. Carroll drafted this letter for the General (see no. 377, n. 4; see also notes in EM, same file as document).

413   *Eisenhower Mss.*

To ROBERT EARLL McCONNELL   *October 4, 1951*

Dear Mr. McConnell:[1] Your letter evidences, I think, some slight misunderstanding as to my attitude toward the patents in atomic fission which, I have believed, belong to some Columbia professors and a few others. What follows outlines what I, with a background comprising mainly only a few short conversations and hasty reading of an occasional memorandum, have thought to be the facts. Your letter leads me to believe that I may be wrong in important particulars—in which case your letter should prevent me from making additional mistakes.[2]

Many months ago, John Dunning told me that a group of professors, holding certain patents, was preparing to enter negotiations with the Government, with a view of using income deriving from this ownership to support future scientific research. Since patents in this field are, of course, of great concern to the Government, official permission was obviously necessary before normal contacts could be sought with commercial interests who might want to use these patents. He explained that long discussions and negotiations would necessarily precede the making of final arrangements, so he and his colleagues were seeking some non-profit agency to take over the entire affair as an agent—both to carry on all negotiations and to set up a plan through which funds derived would be devoted to public service.

Now it appears that the patents have never actually been granted— something I suppose never registered with me. So far as my memory serves me, I thought that the only point in doubt was whether the Government, because of security reasons, would feel it proper to grant the necessary permission for the normal use of the patents by commercial institutions. It was understood that, should the Government feel their security might be adversely affected, everything was to be dropped, instantly.[3]

The professors were hopeful that whatever non-profit body was set up to administer the income from these patents would include on its governing body one or two of the interested professors. I believe it was also suggested that these men might rotate among themselves; and that possibly the others might be used as scientific consultants at agreed rates of remuneration.

Another point made to me was that, if such an arrangement were established through amicable agreement among all concerned, then Columbia University, as the home institution of several of the professors who were engaged in this project, would be one of the major beneficiaries of the contributions made for research and educational purposes. The reason for discussing the matter with me, therefore, was because of my official position as the President of Columbia.[4]

The project never became sufficiently advanced in my mind for me to say more than that—provided the plan should be completely approved by all concerned, including governmental officials and the Trustees of Columbia University, as a wise, ethical, and sound proposal—I would not object to serving in some unpaid, Trustee capacity in company with other individuals who would similarly serve.

Since the time of those indeterminate discussions, I have been called back into governmental duty. Moreover, my memory is quite vague as to important details, not only of fact, but of proposal. Consequently, grateful as I am for your continuing efforts in favor of Columbia and its hope of developing even greater usefulness for our country, I must be completely disregarded in any negotiations about the matter. I cannot even express a worthwhile opinion about it; for the University, this responsibility rests with the Columbia Trustees and the executive officers, including, of course, the Acting President, Grayson Kirk.[5]

I am sorry to give an indefinite answer to your letter, but the fact is that I am unable to do better. I know that you would not expect me, in the absence of a complete and clear understanding of all issues, values, and principles involved, to commit myself to any program; particularly where it appears that further negotiations with the Government may have to be the basis for any approach to private industry.[6]

I am sending a copy of this letter to John Dunning, another to Grayson Kirk. Incidentally, I assume that you know I am on a leave status from Columbia University—without authority, responsibility, or pay. Consequently, any ideas I might have as to the advisability of the suggestions made to you could be, in any case, nothing but personal.[7]

With warm regard to yourself and, of course, my thanks for your continuing interest in Columbia, *Most sincerely*

[1] For background on McConnell, chairman of the board of trustees of the Robert Earll McConnell Foundation and a Columbia University alumnus, see no. 246.

[2] McConnell had written to Eisenhower on September 28 (EM) concerning the possibility of Columbia's acquiring royalty rights to certain atomic energy patents applied for earlier by its physicists. Because these patents were related to atomic fission, they were at this time held on a royalty-free basis under the control of the Atomic Energy Commission, and any claim relating to them would entail involvement in a legal action. Approached by Columbia physicist and dean of the university's school of engineering, John Dunning (see no. 266, n. 3), regarding the matter, McConnell had told Eisenhower that he could understand why the Columbia trustees would be reluctant to "participate in a claim of this character against the government." But he saw no reason why the McConnell Foundation could not prosecute the case on behalf of the university. On the assignment of fission patent rights under the Atomic Energy Act of 1946 see U.S., *Statutes at Large*, vol. 60, pt. 1, pp. 768–70. For Eisenhower's earlier correspondence on this subject see Galambos, *Columbia University*, no. 446.

[3] Under the Atomic Energy Act of 1946, previously granted patents for the production and use of fissionable materials had been revoked, with a promise of just compensation after appeal to the Patent Compensation Board of the Atomic Energy Commission (see U.S., *Statutes at Large*, vol. 60, pt. 1, pp. 768–70; and Richard G. Hewlett and Oscar E. Anderson, *The New World, 1939–1946*, vol. I of *A History of the United States Atomic Energy Commission*, [University Park, Pa., 1962], pp. 495–98, 527, 528).

[4] On the atomic research carried out at Columbia during World War II see Ronald W. Clark, *The Birth of the Bomb* (London, 1961), pp. 14, 17, 30, 162; and Hewlett and Anderson, *The New World*, pp. 13–15, 40, 53–54, 68.

[5] For background on Kirk see no. 31, n. 1.

[6] Before passage of the Atomic Energy Act of 1954 the Patent Compensation Board granted only two cash awards. The first settlement, of $7,500, went to Westinghouse Corporation physicist Cyril E. McClellan, and the second, of $300,000, went to G. M. Giannini & Co. and several Italian inventors. Although the latter case would involve former Columbia faculty member Enrico Fermi, the claim was not one with which either Eisenhower or McConnell was concerned. The only atomic patents the university claimed would continue to be held on a nonexclusive, royalty-free basis (see U.S. Congress, Joint Committee on Atomic Energy, *Selected Materials on Atomic Energy Patents*, 86th Cong., 1st sess., 1959, vol. 1, pp. 6, 33, 66–97, 108). On the McClellan and Giannini awards see *New York Times*, March 9, 1952, and November 8, 1953, respectively.

[7] There is no further correspondence on this matter in EM.

414   *Eisenhower Mss.*

To Francis Wogan Festing   *October 4, 1951*

Memorandum for General Festing:[01] Thanks very much for your comments on the recent maneuvers. They agree with my observations so far as I was able to observe the same activities that you did. I trust that you will find it possible to witness all of the American maneuvers.[2]

I am sending your paper to the Chief of Staff,[3] although I assume you have probably given him a duplicate.

[1] For background on British Major General Festing, Assistant Chief of Staff, SHAPE Organization and Training Division, see no. 219, n. 2.
[2] Festing's comments on the recent British and French maneuvers in Germany are not in EM. For background see no. 375, n. 3. On other NATO maneuvers soon to take place see nos. 401, n. 4, and 416, n. 1.
[3] On SHAPE Chief of Staff Gruenther see no. 230.

415   *Eisenhower Mss., Diaries*

DIARY   *October 5, 1951*

Letters from John Cowles & Lucius Clay are purely political.[1] I'm amused to note that even good friends finally fall prey to the idea that anyone would want to be President. Not me!

[1] For the letters Eisenhower mentions see nos. 408, n. 2, and 409.

416   *Eisenhower Mss.*

To CLIFFORD ROBERTS   *October 5, 1951*

Dear Cliff: We got into just a bit of a snafu about the Black business, first, because after we had arranged for seeing him this week, I got so swamped with Bradley, Collins, Harriman, and a few other people who are going through here on an emergency basis that I had to ask Mr. Black to come the following week; and, secondly, because I failed to sense the urgency of your "direct invitation" suggestion.[1]

However, all seems straightened out now. My last message from him indicates that the week end of the 13th and 14th is quite acceptable to him. We shall keep in close touch with his plane schedule so that my staff and I can get maximum benefit from his visit.

I was unable to play golf with Albert Bradley. My wrist simply will not get well in spite of the fact that Howard bakes it every morning.[2] I don't believe he has the slightest explanation of the trouble, although I think he is a bit suspicious of my assertion that I have not had any accident of any kind to which my wrist suffered an unusual strain.

Thanks for the clipping from the Wall Street Journal. Mr. Grimes wrote a lot of sense, although I think that, even so, he minimizes the struggle I would have with myself—assuming that developments of the future came about something as he pictures as possible—before I could ever fall in with the idea that I was so necessary that I had to give up Augusta National, Blind Brook, Cherry Hills, and my favorite fishing places for four years.[3] I suppose that, possibly, a whole bevy of my intimate friends could convince me, but they would surely know they had been in an argument. Enough of such speculation and talking of nightmares!

Give my best to all the gang. *As ever*

P.S. Min has not been so well, but I think Mamie is looking splendidly.

[1] On Roberts's suggestion that Eisenhower invite World Bank president Eugene Black to SHAPE see no. 369, n. 2; for the final arrangements see no. 402. Army Chief of Staff Collins and his wife Gladys (see no. 183) had been guests of the Eisenhowers' from October 3 until this afternoon (see cables in EM, Collins Corr.). Traveling on a special mission to Europe, the Middle East, and the Far East, Collins first observed the large-scale NATO field maneuvers then taking place in West Germany (see "Cable Message to: SACEUR," Sept. 28, 1951, EM, Collins Corr.; and *International Herald Tribune*, Paris ed., Oct. 6, 8, 11, 1951). On the Chief of Staff's mission, which included discussions with Yugoslav leaders concerning European defense, see nos. 332 and 336, n. 4.

W. Averell Harriman, American member of the special NATO Temporary Council Committee formed in Ottawa (see no. 384, n. 1), would arrive in France on October 7 for meetings with the SHAPE staff (see *International Herald Tribune*, Paris ed., Oct. 8, 9, 10, 1951). For developments see no. 424, n. 1.

Omar Bradley, U.S. representative to the NATO Standing Group and Chairman of the JCS, would visit SHAPE on October 8 en route to Greece and Turkey for exploratory talks following the NATO decision to recommend them for full membership in the alliance (see no. 423; and *International Herald Tribune*, Paris ed., Oct. 9, 1951. For background see no. 233).

[2] On the visit of General Motors executive Albert Bradley to SHAPE see no. 382, n. 2. The General was being treated for difficulties with his left wrist by his physician, Dr. Howard M. Snyder, Sr.

[3] In a recent article concerning Eisenhower and the presidency *Wall Street Journal* editor William Henry Grimes had said that the General would probably not seek the nomination unless he felt convinced that his task in Europe was on the road to accomplishment. Echoing closely Eisenhower's own often expressed sentiments, Grimes also stated that Eisenhower could make no comment regarding his future intentions at this time: "Should he plunge into political turmoil by announcing his availability for the Presidency, his effectiveness [as SACEUR] would be injured, perhaps mortally injured" (see *Wall Street Journal*, Oct. 2, 1951, no copy in EM). Eisenhower had repeatedly been making statements similar to Grimes's (see, for example, no. 358).

To JOSEPH G. DYER   *October 5, 1951*

Dear Joe: All reports I have are to the effect that you did a masterly job in making the Hillsdilly a success.[1] I know something about organizing mass events, and I can almost hear the sigh of relief you must have let out when the thing was all over. Nevertheless, I am sure that the success of the project gave you a sense of great satisfaction and, of course, you must have felt well repaid for all the trouble you took.

I don't think I know the Mr. Brown that helped to win the first prize, but, in any event, I congratulate him. I hope that next year I can think of some little special memento to send along to the individual that does something unusual on the General Ike hole.[2] For example, possibly chipping in from off the green. That would be something that John Culbreath ought to win.[3]

I just wrote a note to Rip Arnold but, when you see Mr. Gordon and the others of my friends around the Club, please give them my best, and remind them how much I wish I could drop in for a day or two of golf with all of you.[4] *Cordially*

[1] For background on Dyer and his organization of the Hillsdilly, an invitational golf tournament of Denver's Cherry Hills Country Club, see no. 311, n. 3. Held on August 29 and 30, the Hillsdilly had been attended by 205 club members and their guests.

[2] Art Brown of Denver and partner LeRoy Sipes had won the tournament with a two-day net score of 127 strokes (see *Denver Post*, Aug. 30, 31, 1951). Dyer had written to Eisenhower on July 30 (EM) explaining that five of the Cherry Hills holes had been renamed for the Hillsdilly, with number 18 dubbed the Ike Eisenhower. The flags from these renamed five were to be presented to "those players making some kind of history on a specific hole during the course of the Tournament."

[3] John A. Culbreath, one of the General's many friends in the Denver area, was general agent for the Manhattan Life Insurance Company.

[4] Ralph ("Rip") Arnold was the Cherry Hills golf pro (see Galambos, *Columbia University*, no. 545). Gordon was probably D. G. Gordon, of Denver's Gordon Construction Company.

418   *Eisenhower Mss., Family File*

To EARL DEWEY EISENHOWER   *October 5, 1951*

Dear Earl:[1] It has certainly been a long time since I heard from you; possibly it has been equally long since I wrote to you. Yet you and your nice family are often in my thoughts, and I get to wondering particularly whether you ever got rid of the one radio station that you felt was becoming something of a burden. When you get a chance, you might tell me about it.[2]

This job is a most complicated and difficult one. Trying to work for an organization that is made up of twelve equal partners (but where one of them is disproportionately large in resources with respect to the others) can bring many irritations, sometimes even frustrations. Nevertheless, we have a good staff made up of citizens from a number of countries but which is, after all, about 50% American. We certainly make progress and, generally speaking, I think my gang retains a remarkable degree of optimism in the face of many problems that sometimes appear well-nigh unsolvable.

Of course, the thing that keeps us going is the knowledge that, unless America is successful in her effort to produce a collective security by cooperation among the nations of the North Atlantic, the United States will eventually be forced into an indefensible position. By this I mean that, if the other countries of the free world fall, one by one, under the domination of Russia, we will finally get to the point where we have no friends with whom to trade; and, after that, it would be only a short distance to economic disaster for us and consequent regimentation of some kind. The worst of it is that, if we abandon the rest of the free world, Russia might not even have to fight to get into a dominant position—or at least she would probably not have to fight until after her position had become so strong that, by bribery, subversion, corruption, and propaganda, she might take over, one by one, the countries bordering upon her own frontiers and continue to expand this process until it was too late to do much about it. It is to prevent both this and war that we are working here; so you see why we never allow ourselves to grow too discouraged even when the going is tough.[3]

Not long ago I had a short note from Milton, and the fact that he did not mention Helen's health makes me think that she must be coming along splendidly. I most certainly hope so. I have had both direct and indirect word from Edgar and, very recently, a long letter from Arthur. In all cases, situations seem to be about normal.[4]

Please give my very best to Dr. Sickman and his nice wife;[5] to Helen and the children,[6] our deep affection; and, of course, always warmest regard to yourself. *Devotedly*

---

[1] Eisenhower's younger brother Earl was an electrical engineer with the West Penn Power Company in Charleroi, Pennsylvania (for background see *Eisenhower Papers*, vols. I–XI).

[2] In a message of birthday greetings to the General on October 10 (EM) Earl would explain that he and his partners had sold 51 percent of their interests in an East Liverpool, Ohio, radio station but that the Federal Communications Commission (FCC) had not yet approved the transfer. The partners' Charleroi station, Earl

wrote, was doing well, and he expected it to pay dividends during the next year. On the younger Eisenhower's interests in these stations see Galambos, *Chief of Staff*, no. 1490, and *Columbia University*, nos. 37 and 43.

[3] For recent NATO developments see nos. 384 and 399.

[4] For background on Milton Eisenhower and his wife Helen, who had been seriously ill, see no. 195. On Eisenhower brothers Edgar and Arthur see nos. 285 and 367, respectively.

[5] Dr. Sickman was one of the younger Eisenhower's radio station partners; during 1947 he and his wife had attended the Army-Navy football game with Earl and the General (see Earl Eisenhower to Dwight Eisenhower, May 10, 1947, and Earl Eisenhower to Cannon, Oct. 14, 1947, both in EM, same file as document).

[6] The General meant to say *Kathryn*. For background on Earl's wife, the former Kathryn McIntyre, see Galambos, *Columbia University*, no. 43; on their children, Earl Dewey, Jr., and Kathryn Snyder Eisenhower, see Galambos, *Chief of Staff*, no. 1067.

419

Eisenhower Mss.

To Thomas Blazina

October 5, 1951

Dear Mr. Blazina:[1] I cannot tell you how delighted I am to hear the good news about your son. He is living up to all your high expectations, which is completely understandable in view of the splendid stock from which he sprang.[2]

If my brother Edgar really got a chance to tell you about our early life in Kansas, I wager he made a good story out of it. Actually, while luxuries and soft living were unknown, probably no group of boys ever had a better time in their work, their athletics, and their opportunities for healthful living and advancement—to say nothing of the priceless gift of wonderful parents.[3]

To you and yours, my very best—it is always nice to hear from you. *Sincerely*

[1] A former sergeant in the 7th Illinois Infantry (National Guard), Blazina had served with Eisenhower on the Mexican border during 1916 (for background on this, one of the General's first military assignments, see his memoir *At Ease*, pp. 118–25).

[2] In a letter to Eisenhower of September 26 Blazina had written of the recent promotion of his son, Thomas David Blazina (USMA 1946), to the rank of captain. A jet fighter and test pilot, the younger Blazina was an instructor in thermodynamics in the West Point Department of Mechanics. For earlier correspondence between Eisenhower and Blazina concerning his son's progress in the military see EM.

[3] Blazina had also written of a visit with the General's brother Edgar (see no. 24) in Tacoma, Washington, saying that they had had "a wonderful chat of yours and his early life and hardships." For Eisenhower's reminiscences of his early family life see *At Ease*, pp. 29–108.

To WINSTON SPENCER CHURCHILL

Dear Winston: Herewith the answers to the questions on the French Army, which occurred to you after recent talks in Paris.[1] I believe them to be reasonably accurate; I know they are gladly given.

Strengths vary greatly in French divisional formations on the Continent.[2] The average strength of divisions within metropolitan France is reported to be around 60% of war establishment, which is set at 19,085 for the Infantry Division; 18,164 for the Armored. The four divisions in French occupied Germany, which have been placed under SHAPE command, average 94% of war strength. Despite differences in strength, however, the pattern of induction and the level of experience at various critical experiences are about the same for all French formations in Europe.

As you know, France has eighteen months of National Service. Increments are brought in twice annually, in mid-April and mid-October. For the divisions in Germany, these semi-annual increments amount to roughly 28% of actual unit strength. Periods of maximum effectiveness would occur obviously just before these normal induction periods. It appears that at any given time a French division in Germany would have 28% of its men on the first six months of their service; 28% with more than six months of service but less than a year; and 28% more with over a year's service but less than eighteen months. The remainder—perhaps 15 or 16%—would consist of career officers and non-commissioned officers, and specialists and non-commissioned officers who extended for terms of service beyond their normal eighteen months of compulsory duty. Because of the drain of the Indo-China War upon the regular establishment, divisions within France have a far weaker professional cadre. I am told it would average only 8 or 9% of unit strength.[3]

On the personal side, I anticipate the Alamein dinner with great pleasure. It will be good to see you.[4]

With personal regard and best wishes, *Cordially*

[1] Eisenhower and Churchill had met over lunch at the British Embassy on September 11. Returning from a vacation in Venice, the leader of His Majesty's opposition had come to Paris for informal meetings with French officials (see *International Herald Tribune*, Paris ed., Sept. 12, 1951; and Eisenhower to Churchill, Sept. 15, 1951, EM). For developments with Churchill see no. 451.

[2] In a letter of September 30 (EM) Churchill had requested that Eisenhower supply him with information concerning the size, character, and make-up of French divisions "at various critical periods in the Service year." The General had turned the request over to his aide Paul Carroll (see no. 394), who drafted this reply. On the French contribution to the NATO effort see also nos. 16 and 304.

³ For background on the impact of the Indochina war on the French military see, for example, nos. 361 and 552.
⁴ On the El Alamein reunion dinner, scheduled for October 19, see no. 401, n. 4.

421   *Eisenhower Mss.*

To George North Craig   *October 6, 1951*
Personal and confidential

*Dear Commander Craig:*¹ Your thoughtful and interesting letter written on July 16th reached me only the other day, when Mr. and Mrs. Pulliam finally arrived at my office. Needless to say, I have read it very carefully because of my regard for your public-spirited attitude and my respect for your judgment in domestic trends and in our nation's international position. Additionally, your reflections have a special value because of the unique opportunities you have had for travel and study in all nooks and crannies of our great country.²

I know you must feel somewhat saddened by your own conclusion that the morale and spirit of the American people are not what should be expected in the greatest country in the world, and that our people, by and large, have lost faith in many individuals to whom they are entitled to look for leadership.³

Quite naturally, I am intensely complimented by your conviction that I might be able to help restore better standards in this regard. However, I am quite sure you will understand that, because of the critical character of the position to which I am assigned, I cannot comment in this regard. In an attempt to reply honestly and accurately to other letters, I have used a paragraph about as follows:

"The job I am on requires the support of the vast body of Americans. For me to admit, while in this post, or to imply a partisan political loyalty would properly be resented by thinking Americans and would be doing a disservice to our country, for *it would interfere with the job to which the country has assigned me.* The successful outcome of this venture is too vital to our welfare in the years ahead to permit any semblance of partisan allegiance on the part of the United States Military Commander in SHAPE."

I think this paragraph explains my situation about as accurately as it is possible to state it.⁴

Should you have any occasion to come into this region, you may be quite certain of a warm welcome. It would be most interesting to discuss with you some of the problems of the day, including those with which we here are faced.⁵

A few months back, your successor in office, Commander Cocke of

Georgia, was in to visit me.[6] We had a nice chat. He seemed to me to be a very fine type of young, virile, and public-spirited American. I assume that you had much to do with his selection.

With warm personal regard, *Cordially*

[1] For background on Craig, former National Commander of the American Legion and an Eisenhower political supporter, see no. 410.

[2] Craig's July 16 appeal to Eisenhower (EM) to seek the presidency had been delivered to the General during an October 2 meeting with Eugene Collins Pulliam and his wife Nina G. Mason. Pulliam and Mason, both journalists and Indiana newspaper and radio executives, would return to the United States as staunch advocates of an Eisenhower candidacy (see Pulliam to Darby, Oct. 11, 1951, and other materials in EM, Pulliam Corr.). For developments see no. 644.

[3] Craig had written that as American Legion National Commander, he had spoken with people in every state and everywhere had found "a lack of confidence in our national leadership that virtually borders upon fear." Eisenhower's election as President, according to Craig, would be "the greatest one thing that could raise the spirit and morale of the American people from the low ebb to which it has subsided."

[4] For background on Eisenhower's repeated use of this paragraph see no. 358.

[5] Craig apparently would not visit the General in Europe.

[6] The current National Commander of the American Legion, Erle Cocke, Jr., had seen Eisenhower on March 23 of this year.

422   *Eisenhower Mss.*

To MARK WAYNE CLARK   *October 8, 1951*
Personal

Dear Wayne: I think that the report given to you about my remark is meaningless for the reason that, whatever my statement was, it seems to be completely removed from context and it could possibly have been nothing more than some exclamation of impatience.[1]

What I have been trying to hammer home to many Service people coming over here is that it behooves the United States to streamline, simplify, and improve our equipment and organizational programs. [Nothing makes me feel better than to know you are devoted to this same idea and are working hard at it.][2]

In this region the matter takes on special emphasis because of the American commitments, made a couple years ago, to assist in arming Europe, largely by production and shipment of end items.[3] Most of the countries to whom this promise was made now say that without this promise they could not have undertaken, on their own, restoration of military strength.

Each of these nations, I find, confidently counting on receiving

United States equipment, has reached the conclusion that with American equipment they *must* adopt American organization. I personally think we have made some serious mistakes in the organization of our division. (There is no point in arguing here that particular item. However, I might remark by way of a bit of digression, that I believe we can save immeasurably by abandoning some of our old thinking about the self-sufficiency of a division as a battle unit and reassigning to the corps level some of the administrative, supply, and evacuation functions heretofore performed by the division. In the armored division, if it should be equipped and armed for the purposes for which I believe it best suited, this process could not go as far as in the infantry division, because I think the armored division would have to be ready to operate for fairly extended periods at considerable distances from railhead and bases.)[4]

Nevertheless, you can see that whatever extravagance or luxury is contained in American formations, either through over-organization, gadgeteering, lavish design, or distribution of equipment, are reflected in the units of those nations that, we hope, will soon be arming at a speedy pace.

Let me give you a specific example. Many "scientific" soldiers have been over here, who entertain me with wonderful stories about the growing efficiency of antitank weapons. I am told that the battlefield will be fairly crowded with light, inconspicuous, recoilless weapons that can hurl projectiles 2,000 or 3,000 yards with remarkable accuracy and with great destructiveness against armored plate, even of a very heavy variety.[5] Now, if this story is not wholly exaggeration, it appears that we ought to be doing some imaginative and forward-looking kind of thinking. If a piece of armor plate—and the expensive tank it is *supposed* to protect—is going to be about as valuable as a piece of warm butter, we'd ought to be ahead of potential enemies in taking advantage of this knowledge.

But we continue to demand more and more heavy tanks to fight other heavy tanks.[6] No one seems bold enough to suggest that maybe the day of the thick armored plate is passing on land just as it has largely passed at sea. I think that no one would deny the need for cross-country vehicles of great speed, reliability, and low silhouette. Moreover, they should have real gun power. But *possibly* we are getting to the point where we should use up steel in the making of their protective armor only to provide defense against fragments and, say, shells up to the 40 millimeter variety, or something of that sort. What I am getting at is that mere *improvement* in existing gadgets does not win wars; you yourself have been one of the first to preach that we also need military thinking that keeps up with scientific advances.

I find that all European armies that we have agreed to equip want to consider, as hand or shoulder armament, only the Garand rifle.[7]

Yet it seems possible that in the case of the men who do not give the majority of their attention to the use and care of the rifle, it would be better to have a cheaper, simpler arm. When I try to talk to foreign officers on the subject, they merely look at me and in great amazement say, "But this is the American rifle!" They imply that if we offer them anything except the weapon that America habitually issues, we are treating them as second-class troops. (This is the kind of thing that I was talking to your friend about.)[2]

No one has a right to quote me in terms of short, detached sentences when talking about such matters as doctrine and policy. I well know that there are many sides to some of these questions. Whenever I am quoted as expressing an indifference toward the combat soldier of the American Army, someone is asking for a fight in which he had better be fully prepared to undergo a grueling struggle. I want the best there is for the American soldier, but I contend that the best in killing weapons is not necessarily the most luxurious or the most costly. I also want the best organization, and the best organization is certainly not always the biggest. (We get to the point that we feel we do not amount to anything unless we have deputies, executives, chiefs of Staffs, and many assistants for each.)

I am talking to you personally, just exactly as we used to talk in the days when we were so long assigned together. Nothing would give me greater pleasure than if you would come over here for a visit. I should like to have you go into the various countries with which we work and I should most certainly value some long talks with you.

In any event, don't ever allow anybody to interpret any remark of mine as throwing off on the field soldier of the United States Army. When I talk about some of the technicians and so-called experts, it is something else again.

With warm personal regard, *As ever*

[1] Clark, who as Chief of Army Field Forces was responsible for manpower training and new weapons development, had written on October 2 after reading a report that quoted Eisenhower on the problem of complex and expensive equipment: "We need someone in the Department with absolute authority to tell those people (Field Forces) what they can and can't have," the General had reportedly said. "They demand too much." Clark wanted Eisenhower to know that he was "keenly aware of the implications of our spending for new equipment" and was "trying seriously to do something about it" (EM).

[2] During the summer of 1951 Clark had sent Eisenhower and Gruenther a progress report and copies of a tentative training manual on "the problem of battlefield illumination." Clark's command had experimented with tank-mounted searchlights and investigated "all types of pyrotechnics," Clark had written, the purpose being "to provide a coordinated system of . . . devices and a doctrine for their employment." After discussing Clark's draft circular with Marshal Alphonse Juin, C in C of NATO land forces in central Europe, and with SHAPE operations and training officers, Gruenther sent Clark a list of comments that included praise for searchlights "as a training aid during the first periods of instruction of new units

in night operations." "Finally," Gruenther had observed dryly, "it is believed this circular should make fuller mention of the problems posed when the using forces do not possess air parity in the area where use of search light illumination is planned" (Clark to Gruenther, July 6, 1951, and Gruenther to Clark, Aug. 27, 1951, Gruenther Papers. See also Henry J. Richter, "Battle without Darkness," *Army Information Digest* 9, no. 5 [1954], 10–20).

[3] A total of $10 billion in end items that included tanks, minesweepers, aircraft, rockets, machine guns, ambulances, quartermaster equipment, and walkie-talkies had been planned for delivery to the European Allies in fiscal year 1952 (Kaplan, *Community of Interests*, pp. 155–56. See also nos. 461 and, for background on the MDAP, 2, n. 1, and 238.

[4] On U.S. divisional organization of infantry and armored forces since 1943 see no. 389.

[5] The 106-mm M-40 recoilless rifle was an improvement upon the M-20 gun introduced late in World War II. By early 1953 U.S. Army officials would describe the BAT (Battalion Antitank) weapons system, made up of a 106-mm recoilless rifle and its equipment, as capable of stopping "any known enemy armor" (U.S. Department of Defense, *Semiannual Report of the Secretary of Defense, and the Semiannual Reports of the Secretary of the Army, Secretary of the Navy, Secretary of the Air Force, January 1 to June 30, 1953* [Washington, D.C., 1953], p. 126).

[6] In 1951 the Army had in operation the Walker Bulldog light tank and was conducting tests on two others, the T 42 medium and the T 43 heavy tank. With its heavy armament, the T 43 appeared "capable of defeating any other known tank in existence today," according to a report by Chief of Staff J. Lawton Collins. "There are those who feel that only by matching heavy tank for heavy tank can we hope to win on the battlefield" against the 40,000 estimated enemy tanks, he had written further. "However, others equally competent believe that we may be able to achieve the same results at considerable savings by equipping our highly mobile medium tanks with radically improved guns and ammunition" (Collins, "New Approaches to World Peace," *Army Information Digest* 6, no. 1 [1951], 7; Defense, *Semiannual Report of the Secretary of Defense, January 1 to June 30, 1951*, p. 86). On the development of one form of improved ammunition, the shaped charge, see no. 244, n. 2. In 1953 the Secretary of the Army would report that the new M-48 (Patton) tank, with its improved fire control system, was "capable of more first round hits than any other tank" (Defense, *Semiannual Report of the Secretary of Defense, January 1 to June 30, 1953*, p. 126).

[7] The M-1 rifle, the mainstay of U.S. forces in World War II, would be superceded in the early 1960s by the 7.62-mm M-14, designed for use by all NATO countries.

[8] The "friend" was probably one of Clark's staff officers. Clark had mentioned reading a short report that one of his officers apparently had made after observing the French assault-crossing exercise JUPITER September 28–29 (Clark to Gruenther, Sept. 12, 1951, Gruenther Papers; Clark to Eisenhower, Oct. 2, 1951, EM).

To ALPHONSE PIERRE JUIN,   *October 9, 1951*
WILLIAM JOSEPH SLIM, AND
OMAR NELSON BRADLEY
Memorandum. Top secret

Responding to your request,[1] I present my general view regarding the possibility of including Turkey as a part of my command.[2]

From the standpoint of the reputation of the Turks as excellent fighting men,[3] any commander would be delighted to have them in his organization. Moreover, Turkish demonstrated determination to oppose Communistic aggression clearly makes her a valuable addition to the NAT Organization. Beyond this, Turkish strength[4] is of great significance to the accomplishment of the task presently assigned to me, which is the defense of Western Europe, from Norway to Italy. The southern flank of this front will, of course, be directly affected by developments in Eastern Europe and Turkey, which region not only dominates the land routes to the Middle East, but safeguards the eastern approaches to the Mediterranean. But in considering the question of military organization and command, we are forced to consider the hard facts of geography and distance.

Despite the important contribution Turkey can make to the defense of my southern flank, I consider it militarily impracticable to watch over the interests and development of the Turkish armed forces from SHAPE, and to control operations from this headquarters.[5] I, therefore, believe that it would be in the best interests of NATO and of Turkey itself if Turkey should be included in the Middle East Command.[6] On the other hand, it is obviously essential that close liaison be established between Middle East Command and SHAPE. I shall always stand ready to give such assistance to the Middle East Command as the exigencies of the situation require.

[1] On October 1 Bradley had formally notified Eisenhower of the recent NATO decision to conduct preliminary discussions with Greece and Turkey on military matters (see below) and had relayed word of his plans to visit Athens and Ankara for that purpose October 10–15. En route Bradley wished to hold Standing Group conferences at SHAPE headquarters October 8–10 "in order to make certain that the US, UK, and French are in initial agreement." He requested Eisenhower to attend the meetings along with key members of his staff. Bradley also expected to discuss with Eisenhower "the relationships of Greece and Turkey to your Command." As a result, Eisenhower (with General Gruenther's assistance) prepared this memo for JCS Chairman Bradley and the two Allied officers—General Alphonse Pierre Juin, C in C, Allied Land Forces, Central Europe, and Sir William Joseph Slim, Chief of the British Imperial Staff—who would accompany Bradley to the Greek and Turkish capitals (JCS 82920, Oct. 1, 1951, EM). For Marshall's report to Truman on the Turkish and Greek situations see State, *Foreign Relations, 1951*, vol. III, *European Security and the German Question, Part I*, pp. 597–99, 680–83.

[2] At the NAC meeting in Ottawa September 15–20, 1951, the delegates had recommended that Greece and Turkey be admitted to full membership in the treaty alliance; NATO governments would sign the necessary protocol October 17. (For background see no. 148; Poole, *History of the Joint Chiefs of Staff*, vol. IV, *1950–1952*, pp. 269–70; State, *Foreign Relations, 1951*, vol. III, *European Security and the German Question, Part I*, esp. pp. 466–73, 501–6; and *ibid.*, vol. V, *The Near East and Africa*, pp. 1117, 1149, 1150).

[3] The Turks' reputation for ferocity in Korea was well established. In the summer, for example, the Turkish Brigade had received the U.S. presidential unit citation for "gallantry and extraordinary heroism" during a January bayonet attack on enemy positions (*New York Times*, July 7, 1951. See also *ibid.*, Aug. 9, 1951; and for reports of Turkish casualties, which in 1951 reached 38 percent of the Turkish U.N. contingent, *ibid.*, Dec. 9, 1951).

[4] Eisenhower was probably well versed on the limits as well as the strengths of Turkey's defenses. U.S. intelligence authorities rated the Turkish Army, at about 280,000 men, as a "compact, modern force" with a "theoretical mobilization potential of 1,500,000 men, although it could not equip or provide logistic support for this number." In addition to weaknesses in its supply system (which U.S. military aid helped to offset), the Turkish military lacked technically trained noncommissioned officers, an effective air force, and the industrial base required for contemporary warfare (State, *Foreign Relations, 1951*, vol. V, *The Near East and Africa*, pp. 1123–24).

[5] The addition of Greece and Turkey to the NATO alliance further complicated Eisenhower's problems with the command structure in southern Europe and the Mediterranean. The proposed appointment of an American naval officer as SACLANT in February 1951 had injured British pride and provoked a politico-diplomatic controversy within the alliance. Eisenhower thus had both military and political reasons for recommending that Greek and Turkish forces serve under a proposed supreme allied commander, Middle East, who would report to the British Chiefs of Staff. The issue of the southern Europe–Mediterranean organization of forces would remain unresolved for many months. Meanwhile, Bradley in his letter of October 1 had called for a Standing Group conference in Paris mainly to discuss "the French demand for an important naval command in the Western Mediterranean." Late in the afternoon of October 9, based on conferences held that morning, Eisenhower's headquarters notified the U.S. State and Defense departments that British, French, and American representatives had reached agreement on a French naval command under CINCSOUTH in the western Mediterranean (SHAPE to JCS, ALO 384, Oct. 9, 1951, CCS 092 Western Europe [3-12-48], Sec. 98). For background see nos. 148, 236, and 390; Ismay, *NATO*, p. 73; Poole, *History of the Joint Chiefs of Staff*, vol. IV, *1950–1952*, pp. 270–71; and Lawrence S. Kaplan and Robert W. Clawson, "NATO and the Mediterranean Powers in Historical Perspective," in *NATO and the Mediterranean*, ed. Lawrence S. Kaplan, Robert W. Clawson, and Raimondo Luraghi (Wilmington, Del., 1985), pp. 8–9. For developments see nos. 579, 651, 694, and 709.

[6] See no. 390, n. 3.

The NATO meeting at Ottawa set up a new committee—appropriately nicknamed the "wise men" because the purpose is to solve the problems that the existing civil machinery has failed to solve.[1] The several nations have promised to provide given amounts of military force on a specified time schedule. This so called "plan" does not contemplate a scale of effort that will meet the "requirements" for the defense of Europe as estimated by a combination of several military bodies. Yet already we've found that these schedules will *not* be met— the effort is too big, say the politicians if we are to avoid economic collapse. Since economic collapse in Europe would spell defeat of the NATO concept, it would appear we have a case of the immovable object and the irresistible force!

The big factor omitted from this kind of talk is morale. Civilian leaders talk about the state of morale in a given country as if it were a sort of uncontrollable event or phenomenon, like a thunder storm or a cold winter. The soldier leader looks on morale as one of the great factors (the greatest) in all his problems, but also as one about which he can and must *do* something.

The "wise men" must learn this lesson. Materialistic factors are important, but much more is involved here. Each should start, in his own country, a crusade to explain the purpose of NATO—the protection of a free way of life! The threats to freedom should be identified. The obstacles to providing defense against those threats should be clearly defined. The hopelessness of alternative solutions should be impressed upon us, proved by the facts of the case. The self interest of each nation in the success of the whole should be demonstrated. On this basis of understanding of facts, on this sense of values we should develop the highest possible head of steam (morale).[2] The job is just that—because—in total assets:

Raw materials,
Men,
Intellectual capacity of peoples
Productiveness
Scientific skill
Appeal of a cause

we are immeasurably stronger than the Iron Curtain Countries.[3]

I hope the wise men will see *this*. Certainly I'm going now to try to *make* them see it. (I'm scheduled for half an hour talk before them.)[4]

---

[1] On October 9 the Temporary Council Committee, which the North Atlantic Council had established in Ottawa (see no. 384, n. 1), formed a three-man Executive Bureau, soon dubbed the "Three Wise Men," which would carry out the

bulk of the TCC's task of reconciling NATO military needs with the economic capacities of the member nations. The "wise men" included chairman W. Averell Harriman and two vice-chairmen, French economist and former Deputy Secretary-General of the League of Nations, Jean Monnet, and British Chancellor of the Exchequer, Hugh Todd Naylor Gaitskell (see State, *Foreign Relations, 1951*, vol. III, *European Security and the German Question, Part I*, pp. 314–16; and *International Herald Tribune*, Paris ed., Oct. 10, 1951). With general elections about to take place in Britain, Gaitskell was represented on the three-man Executive Bureau by the chairman of Britain's Economic Planning Board, Sir Edwin Noel Plowden. Plowden would remain as vice-chairman after a Conservative parliamentary victory forced Gaitskell from office later in the month (see State, *Foreign Relations, 1951*, vol. III, *European Security and the German Question, Part I*, pp. 292–93; and *International Herald Tribune*, Paris ed., Oct. 29, 1951. On the British elections see no. 451, n. 1).

Beginning meetings at once, the TCC set about determining how much each nation could realistically contribute to its own defense and to the defense of its allies and how an overall program that satisfied NATO military planners might go into effect by 1954. Detailed questionnaires went to each of the NATO governments, requesting information on the numbers of regular and reserve troops to be raised and trained within the next three years; the types and amounts of defense production that could be expected; estimated finished and raw materials that could be made available for the defense of other nations; and the economic impact of these efforts for each nation. The TCC set a target date of December 1, 1951, when it expected to report its recommendations to the NAC, and in the interim held committee hearings on technical and special problems. One such committee, under General Joseph T. McNarney (see Galambos, *Columbia University*, no. 983), studied screening and costing and consulted directly with military officials of the member nations. Once the various programs had been studied and evaluated by the TCC committees, specific proposals were presented to each nation's government (see State, *Foreign Relations, 1951*, vol. III, *European Security and the German Question, Part I*, pp. 279–80, 288–89, 291–92, 308–14; Ismay, *NATO*, pp. 44–45; and *International Herald Tribune*, Paris ed., Oct. 9, 10, 12, 13, 1951). For developments see nos. 542 and 643, n. 1.

[2] The issue of rebuilding European morale and placing it on an "upward-going spiral" had been a major concern of Eisenhower's since he had assumed the post of SACEUR (see, for example, nos. 23, n. 7, and 164, n. 3).

[3] After viewing NATO troop maneuvers near Frankfurt, West Germany, on the preceding day, Eisenhower had told reporters that the Western Allies "have got the power and the machinery to develop all the strength we need" to halt Soviet aggression (see *International Herald Tribune*, Paris ed., Oct. 10, 1951, and no. 416, n. 1). TCC chairman Harriman would later cite resources, population, intellect, production, and scientific advancement as the assets that would enable the West to ensure peace (see *International Herald Tribune*, Paris ed., Oct. 13, 1951).

[4] Eisenhower and SHAPE C/S Gruenther were scheduled to meet this morning with all twelve of the TCC representatives (see *ibid.*, Oct. 10, 1951).

425

To Richard Gill, Jr.

Dear Richard: Thank you for your birthday card. I am just a bit astonished that a plebe could find time to think of such things as anniversaries.[1]

Of course, I am delighted to hear, mostly through your Mother, that you like the place and are getting along so well.[2] Incidentally, since I have always been on the perverse side, I really had more fun as a plebe (and knew it at the time) than I did later as an upper classman. I rather enjoyed getting upper classmen to brace me[3] and then letting them know, through some way or another, that I really enjoyed the experience. That always seemed to set them wild.

Best of luck and good wishes. *As ever*

[1] For background on Eisenhower's nephew Gill, who had entered West Point this year, see no. 224, n. 5. On the General's upcoming sixty-first birthday see no. 431, n. 2.
[2] Gill's mother was "Mike" Moore, Mrs. Eisenhower's sister. For background see no. 118, n. 2.
[3] Bracing was a form of Military Academy hazing in which a cadet was forced to stand for long periods in an exaggerated posture of attention, sometimes with his shoulder blades pressed against a wall. For Eisenhower's reminiscences of his days as a cadet see his memoir *At Ease*, pp. 4–26.

426

To Kevin Coyle McCann

Dear Kevin:[1] After reading your plan on a pre-induction course, I am convinced that you have brought forth a very useful idea. There is no question but that the physical training will be of considerable value both from the Service viewpoint and that of the individual. But I think the mental preparation might prove of even greater value. At the very least, it would rid the prospective soldier of that fear of the unknown which is liable to afflict anyone facing a radically new environment.[2]

I hope things are going well with you. We think often of you and Mrs. McCann.[3]

With warm personal regard, *Sincerely*

[1] For background on Eisenhower's former assistant McCann, now president of Ohio's Defiance College, see no. 371. Aide Paul T. Carroll drafted this letter.
[2] In a letter of September 28 to Eisenhower aide Robert Schulz (see no. 1, n. 4), McCann had requested that copies of correspondence he enclosed be brought to

the General's attention. These letters—a letter from McCann to Army Chief of Information General Floyd L. Parks (see no. 138, n. 2) and Parks's reply—concerned a premilitary induction course that McCann proposed to establish for Defiance students. The program would consist of two parts: "a one-hour compulsory class for all draft-eligible boys," to supply them with "a good working knowledge of what the Armed Forces are all about," and "as tough an obstacle course as there is in the country," to put "the boys . . . in perfect shape for any physical training program in the Services" (see memorandum, Schulz to Eisenhower, Oct. 6, 1951, and copies of letters, McCann to Parks, Sept. 17, 1951, and Parks to McCann, Sept. 24, 1951, all in EM, same file as document).
[3] The former Ruth C. Potter.

427

Eisenhower Mss.

To Dale Dixon Hull

October 11, 1951

Dear Dale:[1] I cannot tell you how nice it was to have such a long, newsy, and interesting letter from you. Immediately, though, I must tell you that you would be making a great mistake to depend too much on the "portrait" I shall attempt to paint when Diane's picture arrives.[2] Occasionally, I am lucky enough to get a fair likeness; at other times, I have complete failures. If it comes out at all, I shall send it along although, of course, it may be two or three months before I can find a chance to work on it seriously. I suppose the photograph you sent will soon be along, but it has not yet arrived.

Mamie and I are indeed proud of the way you have struck out for yourself and of the success you have already attained in your new work. I know that one of these days, when she grows old enough to understand, little Diane will be equally proud of her mother.[3]

When Jessie was here, she and Mamie had quite a visit. As usual, I was up to my neck in work and saw far too little of her. For a little while, we expected your Father to show up here likewise, but I guess he had too much to do in the States.[4] Perhaps one of these days you can become such a successful broker that your Company will find it necessary to send you to Europe. If you will just hurry up with this sort of thing, maybe Mamie and I will still be here—but we certainly are not going to prolong our absence from the United States a single day more than is necessary to get this job on the rails.

Your Mother will tell you that we now have a very nice house, particularly the downstairs. Nevertheless, it is far from being the kind of home that we really want. Our picture is not only of a simple and comfortable house tucked back in the rural regions of the United States, but it is also of one that is *our own*.[5]

Both of us send our love to you and Diane. Take good care of my godchild and, of course, take equally good care of yourself.

Affectionately

P.S. I am glad you sent a lock of Diane's hair. If I have any luck with the portrait, it will come in very handy.

[1] Hull was the daughter of Eisenhower's friend and West Point classmate Major General Henry Benton Sayler (ret.) and his wife Jessie (see no. 376, n. 7).

[2] In her letter of September 27 (EM) Hull had written that a photograph of her daughter, Diane Dale Hull, was then on the way to Eisenhower for his use in painting the girl's portrait. The General, who was the four-year-old girl's godfather, would send Hull the likeness at Christmas time (see no. 469, n. 4). On Eisenhower's painting see, for example, no. 353.

[3] Hull had written of her recent relocation to Savannah, Georgia, where she was in training as an account executive with the investment firm of Merrill Lynch, Pierce, Fenner & Beane. Presently working as manager of the non-sales section of her office, Hull told Eisenhower that she would shortly be taking the New York Stock Exchange examination to become a registered representative (for developments see no. 469, n. 5).

[4] Mrs. Sayler had visited the Eisenhowers during September (see no. 376, n. 7).

[5] On the Eisenhowers' French residence see no. 314, n. 1; on their farm in Gettysburg, Pennsylvania, the only home they ever actually owned—although they had not yet had the opportunity to live in it—see no. 350.

428   *Eisenhower Mss.*

To Albert William Putnam   *October 11, 1951*

Dear Bert:[1] Recently, in response to his request, I sent a cable to Marcy Dodge expressing, very briefly, my opinion as to General Donovan's suitability as a Trustee. Unfortunately, I overlooked a sentence in his request which suggested that I drop you a note on the subject and send Mr. Coykendall a copy. If action has not already been taken, you can use the following comments for whatever they may be worth.[2]

I think that General Donovan has all the qualifications to make a very splendid Trustee for Columbia. Moreover, even assuming that the Trustees should desire to maintain the tradition of having on the Board the Rector of Trinity Church, I would consider it unnecessary to hold, indefinitely, a vacancy for that ex officio selection because of my understanding that a new Rector may not be selected for a good many months.[3]

You understand, of course, that I am giving this opinion from a long way off. If I were there to participate in the discussions, someone might present considerations from which I would draw a contrary conclusion. However, subject to this one observation, I would certainly vote for the immediate election of General Donovan as a Life Trustee of Columbia.[4]

This note brings, also, my warm greetings to you and to the other members of your Committee—in fact, to any Trustee of Columbia that you may soon encounter. *Cordially*

[1] For background on Putnam, chairman of the committee on nominations of Columbia's board of trustees, see Galambos, *Columbia University*, no. 860; and no. 114, n. 2, in these volumes.

[2] On the suggestion of Marcellus Dodge that Eisenhower recommend William J. Donovan for this vacancy on the Columbia board of trustees see no. 406. For background on trustee chairman Frederick Coykendall see no. 373; see also Eisenhower to Coykendall, Oct. 11, 1951, EM.

[3] The vacancy for which Donovan was being recommended had been created by the resignation of life trustee Reverend Dr. Frederic S. Fleming, who for reasons of health was leaving both this post and his assignment as rector of New York's Trinity Parish (see no. 406). Putnam replied on October 19 (EM) that he could see no reason for keeping the position open until a new rector had been chosen and that he would pass the General's letter on to the other members of his committee.

[4] Tradition would triumph: Donovan would not fill this vacancy; instead, the board would announce on March 12, 1952, the appointment of the Reverend Dr. John Heuss, Jr. (A.B. Bard 1929), new rector of Trinity Church, to the post of life trustee (see *New York Times*, Mar. 13, 1952).

429   *Eisenhower Mss.*

To WILLIAM MORROW FECHTELER   *October 12, 1951*
Personal. Eyes only

Dear Admiral:[1] I am genuinely regretful that it has taken so long for me to get around to answering your letter of 29 September.[2] For the past two weeks we have been under very heavy pressure here at SHAPE trying to keep abreast of our own problems, to witness the Autumn maneuvers of our troops in Germany, and to assist our many distinguished visitors in the difficult undertakings that are upon their shoulders, i.e., Collins, Bradley, and Harriman.[3]

I hope that you received my message suggesting that you visit me on 29 October, if that date is convenient to you.[4] If it is not, and you prefer to defer the trip until November, do not hesitate to advise me and I will endeavor to select another time that may be mutually satisfactory. I will be delighted to see you.

In the light of your letter, and of recent developments in the higher councils of NATO, I have reviewed my earlier correspondence with Forrest relative to Carney's responsibilities as an Allied and as a

United States Commander-in-Chief. I greatly appreciate your concern and efforts to accommodate the United States Naval command arrangements to my needs and my desires, and I wish to assure you that my convictions are limited. I remain very open minded as to the exact command structure that you and the Joint Chiefs of Staff may determine to be most suitable for the efficient conduct of your affairs.

My convictions with respect to Carney's command responsibilities are that:[5]

First: He must be free to concentrate on those matters which are really germane to his allied command of my southern flank.

Second: His primary attention must be to the coordination of ground, naval, and air forces within his allied command areas, and to the solution of the many politico-military problems associated therewith, rather than preoccupation with purely naval affairs.

Third: His strategic responsibilities as a United States Commander-in-Chief should be limited generally to his allied responsibilities.

Fourth: He should have the necessary authority to discharge in full his responsibilities as a United States Commander within his own area.

If these principles are accepted, it would appear logical that Carney should be completely divorced from any responsibilities in Northern or Central Europe. Likewise, he should be free of direct responsibilities for the Middle East, although he might well retain a residual task to render logistic support of your Naval Forces in the Persian Gulf if that is desirable from the Naval standpoint. On the other hand, it would probably be proper for him to retain authority over the Naval facilities in Morocco in view of their vital importance to his own operations. Alignment of United States Naval responsibilities for Greece, Turkey, and the Eastern Mediterranean should conform to the pattern of Allied command arrangements which are evolving from the deliberations of our governments, modified slightly perhaps in order best to cover the exits from the Black Sea.[6]

Within this broad framework, I should rely on your good judgment to determine the command structure most suited to meet the Navy's needs. If you should conclude that the most acceptable arrangement would involve the establishment of a Naval Commander in London, with duties such as you outline, my only concerns would be, first, to insure that Carney have overriding authority for his own area and for the forces under his command; and second, that he continue to be recognized unqualifiedly as the senior United States Naval officer in Europe.

I will be very happy to discuss these matters with you during your visit, and I am certain that a thoroughly acceptable arrangement can be evolved.[7]

With warm personal regard—*Sincerely*

[1] Fechteler had been Chief of Naval Operations since August 1951 (see no. 304, n. 10).

[2] Fechteler had written the General to reopen discussion of Admiral Carney's responsibilities in Europe, an issue that Eisenhower, Forrest P. Sherman (Fechteler's predecessor as CNO), and the JCS had broached earlier (see nos. 107 and 236). Fechteler believed that it was especially important to review that issue in light of Greek and Turkish partnership in the NATO alliance. At Naples Carney served as CINCSOUTH in the NATO command structure; as Allied Naval Commander, Southern Europe; and as CINCNELM, with jurisdiction from just east of the Azores to a point east of India and from the North Pole to the Equator. Fechteler argued that Carney should now relinquish the post of CINCNELM. Originally, Fechteler wrote, Eisenhower had acquiesced in Carney's filling both U.S. and multinational roles.

> Subsequently, as things developed, it became apparent to you that this arrangement was not satisfactory, for reasons which I fully understand, and steps were initiated to effect the eventual separation of matters from Carney's cognizance which were outside NATO affairs. I am now planning to finalize the arrangement whereby there will be a unilateral U.S. Naval Commander in the European area located in London who will be responsible for certain matters both operational and administrative, in connection with over-all U.S. Naval affairs, general logistic support of naval forces, liaison with the British Admiralty, and responsibilities assigned by the Joint Chiefs of Staff not connected with strictly NATO matters.

Fechteler reported that he was working out details of this plan, guided, he wrote, "by what will best suit your needs and requirements" (EM). For Carney's reaction see no. 507. For further developments see nos. 526 and 527.

[3] For background on the maneuvers see no. 397, n. 6; on Collins, Bradley, and Harriman see no. 416, n. 1.

[4] Fechteler would visit SHAPE headquarters on October 29.

[5] Eisenhower here followed the suggestions he had made in April to the JCS (see no. 148; for their reiteration in December see no. 526).

[6] On plans to create a British-led Mediterranean command see nos. 390 and 423, n. 5.

[7] Fechteler, acknowledging Eisenhower's letter and confirming his plans to visit Paris in late October, would express confidence that "this matter can be solved to the complete satisfaction of all concerned" (Fechteler to Eisenhower, Oct. 16, 1951, EM).

430

Eisenhower Mss.

TO FRANCKE PALMER PICKARD AND SAMUEL PICKARD, SR.

October 12, 1951

Dear Francke and Sam: A few days ago, someone told me that you were in the Paris area and I asked the individual, whoever it was, to suggest that you come out to SHAPE for a short visit. Thereafter, I ran off to Germany for several days; so it is possible that you may have made the effort and I was absent. In any event, the note I have just received, dated the 9th, implies that you are on your way back to the States.[1] I am truly sorry that I missed the opportunity to say "Hello."

I assure you that, if future good fortune ever gives me the opportunity to come to Florida, I accept your invitation—as of this red-hot minute! I know of no more fun than to get on a good Florida stream and hook a nice bigmouth bass. That's my idea of a glorious vacation.[2]

Of course, I never fail to experience a deep sense of distinction and pride (although, in all honesty, seriously mixed with profound humility) when a message from one of my old friends expresses or implies real confidence in me or my abilities. But I think my feeling must be that, if one who has known me so long really thinks I have some good and useful qualities, then maybe I am not quite so stupid as I frequently think I am when I fail to solve the problems that daily confront me.

From this, you can understand that I am trying to say "Thank you" for some of your nice personal allusions.[3]

If ever again you get over this way, please let Mamie and me know. We should certainly like to see you. *As ever*

[1] Samuel Pickard, Sr. (B.S. Kansas Agricultural College 1922), an old friend of the Eisenhowers', was a former vice-president of the Columbia Broadcasting System. In a note from their Paris hotel (EM) Pickard and his wife Francke had sent the General greetings and invited him to visit them in the United States when he had the opportunity. Eisenhower had gone to Germany briefly in both late September and early October to witness NATO field maneuvers (see nos. 397 and 424, n. 3, respectively).

[2] Pickard had told Eisenhower that he had recently completed work on a resort at Crystal River—"Florida's finest fishing and hunting territory"—and requested that the General and his brothers stay there as his guests (see brochure, "Paradise Point Villas," in EM, same file as document). On the General's love of fishing see no. 299.

[3] Pickard had written that "no sincere friend and admirer could possibly wish you the cruel torture of being a party candidate . . . " but that if a coalition acclaimed Eisenhower a candidate, "then it should become a great pleasure and privilege to use your rich experience and good practical sense to put our great abused country back on the track again." On recent developments with the Eisenhower-for-President movement see no. 409. On the General's popularity with both Democrats and Republicans see no. 387.

Eisenhower Mss.

To Kate Murphy Hughes and Everett Strait Hughes

October 12, 1951

Dear Kate and Everett:[1] Thanks so much for your birthday wishes and for the amusing account of your experiences as proxy-grandparents—which Mamie also has read with sympathetic understanding.[2]

As you say, we will never be completely settled, although we are much happier with our current house after almost six months in a hotel room. The perennial Canasta games with Grace, Alice, and Min, combined with an occasional expedition to the shops or a visit from old friends, keep Mamie busy.[3] For me, the maneuver season and a constant stream of official visitors more than take care of my twenty-four hours.[4] We would love to be in a position to ask you to visit us on the farm at Gettysburg but, since our fondest wish is for the moment impossible, how about your recuperating from that arduous summer with a visit over here?[5]

With warm personal regard, in which Mamie and Min are my equal partners, *Sincerely*

[1] Major General (USA, ret.) and Mrs. Hughes were close friends of the Eisenhowers' (for background see *Eisenhower Papers*, vols. I–XI).

[2] Eisenhower would be sixty-one on October 14, an occasion celebrated with a surprise birthday party at the home of General and Mrs. Gruenther (see Gruenther to Roberts, Oct. 16, 1951, copy in EM, Roberts Corr.). In an October 4 message of birthday greetings to Eisenhower (EM) Hughes had said that he and his wife had recently "learned the meaning of the word adolescence" while spending a few months with their four grandchildren.

[3] The canasta partners mentioned here were Mrs. Eisenhower's mother (see no. 376, n. 6); Alice Snyder, the wife of Eisenhower's physician (see no. 24, n. 3); and Mrs. Gruenther, the former Grace Elizabeth Crum (see Galambos, *Columbia University*, no. 95). On the Eisenhowers' move to their French home see no. 314, n. 1.

[4] For background on the NATO military maneuvers see nos. 397, n. 6, and 424, n. 3.

[5] On the Eisenhower farm in Gettysburg, Pennsylvania, see no. 376.

Eisenhower Mss.

To Edward John Bermingham

October 12, 1951

Dear Ed: The subject matter of your son Johnnie's "Analysis" was not so interesting to me as the character of the document itself. I don't care whom the experts select for designation as the next President of the United States. But I am highly interested in young men who show such a splendid power of reading and grasping a complicated study and then reducing it either to its essential and worthwhile points or to the dust and ashes that sometimes represent a logical fate.[1]

Please thank him for allowing me to have a copy of the paper.

This note brings from both of us our very warm regards to you and yours. *Cordially*

[1] On October 3 Bermingham (see no. 386), a supporter of an Eisenhower presidential candidacy, had sent the General a five-page memorandum (Bermingham Mss.) analyzing the Republican party's potential for victory in the 1952 election. Written by Bermingham's son, John R. Bermingham, the memorandum examined the work of "two political analysts" who emphasized that the Republican party needed a conservative candidate to bring out Republican voters. The younger Bermingham had not agreed with most of the paper's conclusions, writing that no matter what the party's approach might be, it needed to be appealing to Americans in many regions of the nation and to both urban and rural voters. To achieve a lasting victory, according to Bermingham, the Republican candidate "must appeal to all Americans, and convince . . . them that their longings for housing, medicine, food and happiness can only be satisfied through liberty and integrity" (see "Memorandum on 'A Critical Study of the Problems Facing the Republican Party and Its Candidate in 1952,' " EM, same file as document).

433   *Eisenhower Mss.*

To John Monteith Gates   *October 12, 1951*

Dear Mr. Gates:[1] Thank you very much for your note of October 9th, and particularly for sending me a copy of the letter you received from Madame de Vandenay Tharand.[2] I agree, of course, with her sentiments concerning the beauty and appeal of Steuben Glass—in fact, this minute, I have an aide out searching to see if there is such a thing as Steuben Glass salt and pepper shakers. I am trying to find a birthday present for my wife.[3]

But I am distressed to find that Madame Tharand finds in the American system of production nothing except evidence of regimentation and universal conformity to dreary and boring standards. She apparently does not have the imagination to understand that it is this kind of production that has brought to many millions the opportunity to enjoy the pleasures of nature and the great outdoors, athletics, museums, and a vast array of recreational, educational, and cultural facilities. She apparently does not know that Steuben Glass is produced by a particular division of a great company that has done much to raise the material and—in my opinion—the cultural and esthetic standards of millions through the mass production of items at high efficiency and low cost.[4]

She protests against the stultification of the individual through repetitive work. It never crosses her mind that it is the individualistic character of our society that has provided the incentive for the designs of highly productive machinery. She fails to see that, through a civilization based upon mass production, that same worker has gained more opportunity, whether measured in real wages, in time, or in the opportunities that are created and preserved around him, to indulge his own esthetic sense, than has any sector of French labor. I will agree with her argument that the French jack-of-all-trades may get more fun out of his actual working hours than does the American who must engage in repetitive motions and who has little opportunity to indulge his imagination and inventiveness with respect to his work. But, during his working hours, the American is not worrying whether or not he can meet his family's bills for food, utilities, and shelter, or whether he can afford to [give] each of his children even the rudiments of an education. My feeling is that the world might be a great deal better off if some of the worshipers of spurious individualism could appreciate *the beauty of accomplishment, particularly when that accomplishment brings to a whole population opportunities to have and to enjoy beauty.* Moreover, I wish they could visualize a whole economic, political, and social system based upon true individualism—the opportunity to work for one's own family and self and carve out a career, unhampered by caste, socialistic doctrine and sheer narrow-mindedness.

In spite of my feeling of disappointment that she could not share these particular convictions of mine, I must say that her obvious enthusiasm for Steuben Glass has been expressed in very convincing and wonderful fashion. So, on that, I agree with her!

With warm personal regard, *Sincerely*

[1] Gates (B.Arch. Columbia 1929) had been the vice-president and director of design of New York's Steuben Glass Company since 1933.

[2] Gates's note to Eisenhower and the copy of Madame Tharand's letter are not in EM.

[3] Gates would cable Eisenhower on October 26 (EM) to inform him that Steuben salt and pepper cellars were not obtainable in France and to offer to have the items shipped to the General air express if he so desired. After receiving three sets of cellars and spoons and thanking Gates for his consideration, Eisenhower would return the tableware when he discovered that Mrs. Eisenhower was interested in shakers only (see EM, same file as document). On Mrs. Eisenhower's upcoming fifty-fifth birthday see no. 487.

[4] Steuben Glass, with headquarters in New York City, was a wholly owned subsidiary of the Corning Glass Works of Corning, New York.

To ALBERT BRADLEY   *October 12, 1951*

Dear Albert:[1] Thank you very much for bringing to my attention the point concerning the cost of American coal in France, which came up in your talk with Premier René Pleven.[2]

My staff has informed me that the Economic Cooperation Administration is continually seeking ways and means to alleviate the coal shortage in Europe and that they are also looking into the specific proposal of Mr. Pleven. As one step toward stabilizing the price of coal, a recent agreement has been reached among shippers whereby United States rates for ocean transport of coal from the United States to Europe will not be exceeded. I understand that this will be of some help.[3]

I know that the Economic Cooperation Administration and other appropriate agencies are giving every consideration to Mr. Pleven's suggestion, with a view toward effecting a more favorable price situation.[4]

With warm regard, *Sincerely*

P.S.: I'm still unable to swing a golf club![5]

[1] For background on Bradley, vice-president of the General Motors Corporation, see no. 382, n. 2. This document is misfiled in EM under Major Correspondents; all other correspondence with Bradley is in EM, Miscellaneous Corr., Bradley.

[2] In his October 5 letter (EM) Bradley had recounted a recent conversation with French Premier René Pleven (see no. 318) concerning the European coal shortage. According to Bradley, Pleven believed that high ocean freight costs for U.S. coal had caused an artificial increase in the quotation price of coal shipped to France from Poland, inflating its cost to the U.S. level. Pleven suggested that the landed cost of American coal could be reduced to the French domestically produced rate through an offsetting decrease in U.S. finished-goods aid to France. He believed that if the coal price were sufficiently reduced, not only could France expand its own finished-goods production but pressures for higher prices and wages within French coal-consuming industries would also be lessened.

[3] Eisenhower had turned the matter over to General Gruenther, suggesting that Assistant Chief of Staff Schuyler (see no. 2, n. 1) investigate the situation (see note, Eisenhower to Gruenther, on Bradley to Eisenhower, Oct. 5, 1951, EM). In a memorandum of October 10 (EM) Gruenther informed the General that within the past year the ocean freight rate for coal from Hampton Roads to Rotterdam had fluctuated between $4.50 and $16.00 per ton; he also mentioned a recent ECA agreement "with all shippers that the United States rate of $10.50 per ton will not be exceeded" (see no. 45).

[4] For developments see no. 468, n. 2.

[5] Eisenhower's sore wrist had prevented him from playing golf with Bradley during his visit to France (see no. 416, n. 2).

To Arthur Hendrick Vandenberg, Jr.   *October 12, 1951*

Dear Mr. Vandenberg:[1] When I came to Europe last winter, I left most of my personal files behind me. The only one of your father's letters that is in my European files was written on September 8th of 1949. It expressed his satisfaction concerning a talk I had just made at Saint Louis and expressed the hope that I would be placed in a position of leadership to bring about needed changes in the United States. Since you did not mention that particular period of his correspondence, I assume that you have a copy of that letter.[2]

In late 1947 and early 1948, he several times expressed to me a very definite hope that I would participate as a leader in the political affairs of our country. Whether or not he ever did this in writing, I cannot now recall. Unfortunately, my memory is clear on only one incident of this kind—it was when he called me on the phone following upon a dinner given by Mr. and Mrs. Gross at the F Street Club. He was so disturbed about a distorted report that had appeared publicly concerning statements I was alleged to have made at that dinner, that he talked at some length—he even suggested that he should publish an affidavit giving the truth of the occurrence. I assured him of my lack of concern in the matter, and his reaction to my rather light-hearted treatment of the occurrence was to tell me that, in his opinion, I had a very definite opportunity and responsibility to exert leadership in the highest political places, and that he was concerned that no false impressions of this kind should gain circulation and credence.

I have a hazy recollection, also, that he sent me a message of similar import through a young newspaperman named Milton Hill. I cannot recall whether the message was a verbal one or whether it had been reduced to writing. I should say, also, that I would have to have Mr. Hill's corroboration of the occurrence itself before I would be too positive that he was the messenger in that particular case.[3] In any event, these were merely two incidents out of a total of possibly five or six.

While I realize that this kind of information will probably do you no good whatsoever, since you are apparently writing your book around your father's written documents, I give it to you as indicative of the kind of thinking he then expressed to me. I regret that I can do no better, and I doubt that my New York or Washington files would contain any written record because whenever, in those days, I received messages from good friends that stated or implied that the message was to be considered "Confidential," I usually destroyed them immediately. Since any written note from him would probably have been a handwritten sentence or two, it would be natural to assume that any record of such a note—if written—had disappeared.[4]

With respect to the overgenerous and highly complimentary re-marks you addressed to me personally, I can only say that the reading of such expressions from a thoughtful American quite naturally arouses in me a feeling of intense pride that is accompanied by an equal sense of humility.[5] The obvious requirements of the position to which I am assigned preclude any comment of my own, of any nature, on the American political scene.

So far as the possibility of your coming to Europe is concerned, I assure you that, if you are in this region, it will be a pleasure to talk to you.[6]

Again, I express my regrets for the unsatisfactory character of this letter and assure you that, if you should like a copy of the one now in my files, I shall have one made and sent to you at once. In this event, I would appreciate your keeping the source confidential because, after all, the letter does make complimentary references to myself. If neces-sary, I would send on the original for your inspection, but it happens that I received the note while in my home and, no secretary being present, scrawled my answer on it in pen to be typed the next day—so it is a rather sorry looking document.[7]

With personal regard and good wishes, *Sincerely*

[1] Vandenberg had served as an aide to his father, Michigan Republican Senator Arthur Hendrick Vandenberg, Sr. (see Galambos, *Columbia University*, no. 537; and no. 25, n. 4, in this volume), who had died in office in April (*New York Times*, Apr. 19–21, 1951; Eisenhower to Vandenberg, Jr., AP 80403, Apr. 19, 1951, EM).

[2] Vandenberg, who was collecting and editing his father's papers for publication, had written Eisenhower (Oct. 9, 1951, EM) requesting a copy of a letter the senator apparently had sent in 1948 expressing support for an Eisenhower presiden-tial candidacy. On September 8, 1949, Vandenberg had written to compliment Eisenhower on a Labor Day address before the American Bar Association (Gal-ambos, *Columbia University*, no. 542, n. 2).

[3] On December 5, 1947, Eisenhower, then Army Chief of Staff, had been a guest at a dinner given by Mr. and Mrs. John Messick Gross at the F Street Club in Washington, D.C. Senators Taft and Vandenberg and several Pennsylvania politi-cians also had attended the affair (see Galambos, *Chief of Staff*, no. 1926; and invitation in EM, Subject File, Invitations). On the following Monday newspapers reported that during the dinner Eisenhower had spoken in favor of confiscatory tax measures. Outraged, Senator Vandenberg had offered both to set the record straight for Eisenhower and to expose Taft as the person who had passed the purported remarks to the press. Milt Dean Hill, Chief of the Washington bureau of Federated Publications, Inc., later told the younger Vandenberg that he had carried this written message from Senator Vandenberg to the General (see no. 464, n. 2; for background on Hill see Galambos, *Columbia University*, no. 466).

[4] Eisenhower sent inquiries concerning the Vandenberg message to the Department of the Army, but no copy was found (Schulz to McDuff, SH 21464, Oct. 12, 1951; McDuff to Schulz, DA 84141; Oct. 15, 1951; and other correspondence in EM, same file as document).

[5] "I am one of your many admirers," Vandenberg had written Eisenhower, "who will support your candidacy for President whether you are an avowed candidate or not—even whether you are an announced Republican or not."

643

⁶ Vandenberg had said that he would gladly interview the General for the forthcoming book but reluctantly had decided that it would be "a disservice to you—and hence to the country—to try to join the parade of visitors to Paris."

⁷ Eisenhower later would send copies of Senator Vandenberg's September 8, 1949, letter and his own reply (both in EM; see no. 464).

436   *Eisenhower Mss.*

To Charles Harrison Corlett   *October 12, 1951*

Dear Pete:[1] I get a great lift out of receiving from an old and valued friend such a generous offer as yours.[2] My feeling is that, if those who have known me a long time think I have something on the ball, maybe I'm not so stupid as I sometimes fear.

My current job is, I think, of vital importance to the United States. Even if my responsibilities were limited to assisting in seeing that the United States got full value received out of the tremendous sums it is pouring into Europe for security purposes, my duties here would still be so important as to preclude voluntary contemplation of possibilities such as you suggest. My attention and my energies are fully consumed in the attempt to meet the requirements of this post.[3]

Thank you for telling me about your young friend, Edwin L. Mechem. There is no kind of news that is more welcome at my desk than to hear about some up and coming young American that is giving his complete attention to public affairs. I have met two or three of them lately and, from the experience, I derive a lot of satisfaction.[4]

My thanks for your note—and, of course, warm regard. *As ever*

[1] Major General Corlett (USA, ret.) had written to Eisenhower on October 2 (EM) saying that he had recently taken over as head of the New Mexico Bureau of Revenue. For background on Corlett, who had been nicknamed "Cowboy Pete" during World War II, see *Eisenhower Papers*, vols. I–IX.

[2] Corlett had told Eisenhower that he sincerely hoped he would become an active Republican presidential candidate, because he was "the man destined to get this country straightened out." Corlett wanted to do all he could to support Eisenhower's candidacy.

[3] This paragraph was a variation on the General's standard reply (see no. 358).

[4] Edwin Leard Mechem (LL.B. University of Arkansas 1939), whom Corlett called "a very outstanding individual," was the newly elected Republican governor of New Mexico.

To WILLIAM WALLACE CHAPIN   *October 13, 1951*
Personal and confidential

Dear Mr. Chapin:[1] Thank you for your letter with its enclosures. It was pleasant to hear of the success of the last Carnegie meeting.[2] I miss my association with the Trustees, which I always found stimulating. At the meeting in December, won't you kindly convey to them my warm greetings?

Incidentally, I'm afraid your memory has played you false as to one particular point in which your article quotes me. I could never have said that my father was a lone Republican in his community! To the contrary, as of 1900, I think I knew no adults except Republicans (my two heroes were members of the GAR). What I must have said was that, in my boyish understanding, I thought that anyone other than a Republican deserved to be run out of the state![3]

No man, no matter how keenly aware of his own deficiencies, could possibly escape a feeling of intense pride in the high compliment paid me in your letter, as well as in your published convictions as to my possible future use.

Now as to my current responsibilities and freedom of action. The task to which I am currently assigned—obtaining the maximum of cooperation between the United States and Western Europe in the development of collective security against a clear and powerful threat— requires the support of all thinking Americans if our freedoms are to survive. Any statement I might make as to my own future would not only bring forth much discussion and speculation; it would tend to encourage partisanship consideration of this project. This could not fail to react adversely on a project in which our country is investing, at home and abroad, staggering sums of money and vast portions of her resources. Certainly any partisan activity involving me would reduce my effectiveness as an American Commander in Europe.

As a result of all this, I've concluded that I have no recourse, as long as I'm assigned to this post, except to maintain silence on all subjects even remotely connected with political partisanship.[4]

I regret that I cannot be more specific in answering your letter, which I well realize was written out of your own deep concern for our country. But I feel sure that you will understand that my current duty compels me to follow this course.[5]

With warm personal regard, *Sincerely*

[1] Chapin was publisher of the San Francisco *Argonaut* (for background see Galambos, *Chief of Staff*, no. 1867, n.1).

[2] In a letter of October 5 (EM) Chapin had said that Eisenhower's participation had been missed during a recent meeting of the trustees of the Carnegie Endow-

ment for International Peace. On the General's service as a trustee see *ibid.*, no. 63.

[3] Both in his letter of the fifth and in an *Argonaut* article of the same date, Chapin had recounted a 1947 conversation with Eisenhower concerning his political affiliation. Chapin claimed that when asked if he were a Democrat, Eisenhower had replied, "I am a Republican and my father was practically the only Republican in the State of Kansas. He was asked to get out of the state for that reason" (see *Argonaut*, Oct. 5, 1951, EM, same file as document. On Kansas as a traditional Republican stronghold see Paul T. David, *Party Strength in the United States: 1872–1970* [Charlottesville, Va., 1972], pp. 35, 43, 144–47. On the staunchly Republican Civil War veterans' organization, the Grand Army of the Republic, see no. 194, n. 1; and Mary R. Dearing, *Veterans in Politics: The Story of the G.A.R.* [Baton Rouge, 1952]). For a similar response by Eisenhower to an earlier letter from Chapin see Galambos, *Columbia University*, no. 164.

[4] This was currently Eisenhower's standard reply (see, for example, no. 358).

[5] Chapin would reply (Nov. 30, 1951, EM) that he still felt that Eisenhower would decide to run for President in "the very near future . . . and you certainly will be successful."

438   *Eisenhower Mss.*

To MARCELLUS HARTLEY DODGE   *October 13, 1951*

Dear Marcy:[1] Thank you very much for sending me the Certificate of Appreciation from Columbia.[2]

Today I received a very interesting, and somewhat disturbing, note from a man named Mr. Meehan from Ridgefield Park, New Jersey. Since he seems genuinely interested in starting a local "American Assembly" in his region, I should like to see him get some help in clearing up the difficulties that he explains in the attached letter. Would you take the trouble to confer with Philip Young about it and, possibly, one of you could invite Mr. Meehan to come to see you. I am sure it would not take a great deal of effort to straighten out this particular misunderstanding.[3]

Of course, I apologize for shoving this off onto you when Mr. Meehan addressed his request to me. The fact is that the press of duties here is such that I simply cannot give proper attention to the matter, and it could conceivably be of considerable importance to Columbia.[4]

With warm personal regard, *Cordially*

[1] For background on Dodge, a member and clerk of the Columbia University board of trustees, see no. 6, n. 1.

[2] With a letter of October 4 Dodge had sent Eisenhower a certificate of appreciation (both in EM, same file as document) acknowledging his support of the university's engineering center. For background on the ongoing Columbia engineering campaign see no. 327.

active presidency of Columbia, see nos. 201 and 398. In a letter to the General of October 5 (EM) Horace M. Meehan, district clerk of the Ridgefield Park, New Jersey, board of education and vice-president of the community's Rotary Club, explained that he had invited Russell Meixell to address a Rotary luncheon on the American Assembly and another university program, the Citizenship Education Project (see no. 70). Meixell, an employee of a Wall Street brokerage firm, Clark Dodge and Company, had earlier spoken with the Assembly's executive director, Philip Young, and had obtained information on starting local chapters of the Assembly. But following the luncheon presentation, which Meehan told Eisenhower was "excellent," a member of the audience had accused Columbia of harboring Communists and warned that the Rotary should be "careful of dealing with a school whose faculty is 'sprinkled with pinks.'" Meehan had appealed to Eisenhower for assistance, saying that "some method must be devised to prevent this interest [in the American Assembly] from being killed by the tactics used at our meeting." Replying on October 13 (EM) that he had turned the matter over to Dodge, the General said that the primary purpose of both of these Columbia programs was to present a true picture of the American system of government and to "encourage devotion to that system because of its superiority over all others that man has devised."

⁴ Dodge forwarded Eisenhower's letter to Young, whose staff assisted Meehan and Meixell in establishing their own Ridgefield Park American Assembly (see Chamberlin to Young, "Criticism of Columbia at a meeting of the Ridgefield Park, New Jersey, Rotary Club," Nov. 15, 1951, and Young to Eisenhower, Nov. 15, 1951, both in EM, Young Corr.).

439   *Eisenhower Mss., Diaries*

DIARY   *October 15, 1951*

The authorities in Washington are slowly but necessarily coming to the point where they tell *some* of the truth about America's production program.¹ I begged officials (when they were asking me to come over to this job) to know exactly *what* we were doing. I suppose they thought I was merely hopeful of ducking what we all know was a thorny assignment—at least they merely looked annoyed when I asked whether we were <u>certain</u> we knew the depth of the responsibilities we were assuming and knew that we could discharge them! Oh hell—*now* we cry, delay, delay, delay!

¹ On the previous day Charles E. Wilson (see no. 45, n. 4), Director of the Office of Defense Mobilization, and Manly Fleischman (LL.B. University of Buffalo 1933), head of the Defense Production Administration, had reported to Congress on the production outlook for the first quarter of 1952. Appearing before a special joint session of the House and Senate committees on banking and currency and select committees on small business, Wilson and Fleischman had testified that the mobilization efforts then under way would necessarily create shortages for private industry. Wilson had stated that the present delivery rate of $5 billion in military

goods per quarter would need to be doubled during 1952 to reach the hoped-for delivery peak of $50 billion per year by early 1953. This increase in defense production would place severe strain on the distribution of certain controlled materials (particularly copper, steel, and aluminum), severely limiting the supplies available to private industry and forcing a decrease in the manufacture of many civilian items. Fleischman warned that the United States was then "at the stage in the mobilization effort that necessarily involves economic dislocation, some localized unemployment, loss of profit and general difficulties for civilian industry." In spite of these strains, both officials had expressed the belief that prospects for civilian production would improve by July 1952 as a result of materials substitution, expansion of domestic raw materials production, and endeavors by small businesses (see U.S. Congress, *Joint Hearings before the Committees on Banking and Currency and the Select Committees on Small Business on Production and Allocations*, 82d Cong., 1st sess., 1951; and *New York Times*, Oct. 13, 1951). For background on Eisenhower's concern for the state of U.S. production see, for example, no. 221, n. 4. On the difficulties involved in meeting U.S. defense commitments in Europe see, for example, no. 461, n. 3.

440 *Eisenhower Mss.*

TO AKSEL NIELSEN *October 15, 1951*
Personal and confidential

Dear Aksel:[01] It is difficult indeed for me to attempt an answer to your message of October 10th. I have many times explained to the Senator, but never, that I can remember, to the Governor, my attitude toward the old proposal of my ever getting tagged for duty in the political field.[2] In fact, a number of my friends, including yourself, are well informed along this line. I have never made any real secret of it so far as my intimate friends are concerned, because the thing seems to simmer down to the existence or non-existence of a simple and clear duty. Anything short of a conviction to this effect would have no effect on me whatsoever.

As of the present, the requirements of my current job have, of course, imposed upon me very strict limitations which I have usually expressed to correspondents in a paragraph somewhat as follows:

"For me to admit, while in this post, or to imply or even to leave open for interpretation by others a partisan political loyalty would properly be resented by thinking Americans and would be doing a disservice to our country, for it would interfere with the job to which the country has assigned me. The support of the vast bulk of American opinion, regardless of party, is necessary if this work is to be accomplished. Since the successful outcome of this venture is vital to America's welfare in the years ahead, there cannot be permitted any semblance of partisan allegiance on the part of the United States Military Commander in SHAPE."[3]

It seems to me that these reasons are perfectly clear and compelling as long as I'm here.

Nevertheless, I have never hesitated to see and talk with any American traveling in this region and who has taken the trouble to come to see me. Both the gentlemen concerned are friends of mine and, if they are over here, of course I would be delighted to talk to them. I think it is only wise, however, to face the possibility that if I would get pushed into the position that I *now* have to make a public statement concerning these matters, the only thing I could do would be to make a negative statement of complete repudiation. This would be necessary for the reason that anything else could easily ruin an effort into which America has poured millions of dollars and is pouring more.[4]

Of course, among the things that my old friends know are such items as my oppositions to a number of governmental practices and theories now in vogue; and my sentimental, family, and intellectual ties with the middle-of-the-road section of political doctrine. In fact, I have stated this last publicly. Since all these facts are known by my friends, I am not exactly sure what further is wanted from me—because, as I said before, if there is any situation that requires me to speak publicly at this time, I can say only one thing. But I repeat that things of this kind never keep me from seeing friends if they want to come—my frequent opportunities to visit with them is one of the things that makes bearable this renewed tour of foreign duty.[5] *Cordially*

---

[1] For background on Eisenhower's old friend Nielsen see no. 34, n. 3.

[2] In his letter (Oct. 10, 1951, EM) Nielsen had said that he had recently seen Colorado Governor Daniel I. J. Thornton, who was "given . . . the job of lining up the Governors ready to go to work" for an Eisenhower presidential candidacy. Thornton had told him that he and Pennsylvania Senator James H. Duff wished to speak with Eisenhower but wondered how the General might feel about their coming to Europe at this time. Nielsen had said, "I can certainly get Dan to do it or not do it—whatever you like." For background on Thornton see Galambos, *Columbia University*, no. 992; on Duff and his work for an Eisenhower candidacy see no. 483 in this volume.

[3] Eisenhower used this paragraph as his standard reply (see, for example, no. 358).

[4] For background on the Mutual Security Act of 1951, which President Truman had signed on October 10, see no. 377, n. 5.

[5] For background on Eisenhower's political philosophy see, for example, Galambos, *Columbia University*, nos. 491 and 666; and no. 222 in these volumes. Apparently, neither Duff nor Thornton visited the General in Europe during the remainder of 1951.

Just back from a trip to the Med. Sea—where I visited the 6th Fleet for 3 days.[1] The more I look at present day armaments, of *all kinds*, including the most advanced (so-called), the more I'm convinced that we should institute a basic study at home to examine into the economics of Nat'l security.[2]

On a panel designated for the purpose I'd ask the following to serve:[3]

> 6 Leading manufacturing industrialists (working executives, not figure heads).
> 6 Bankers.
> 6 Lawyers.
> 6 Doctors & public health.
> 6 Red Cross—and professors in Social Science.
> 6 Labor Leaders.
> 6 (Working) shop superintendents & foremen.
> 6 Public Utility execs. R-R- Telephones, etc.
> 6 Labor Reps from same industries.
> 6 Experts from each fighting service.
> 6 Governmental Reps.

(My plan would be to have at least 2 of each group of 6 meeting continuously)

I think we should go clear back to methods of damaging the enemy in any possible war of the foreseeable future.

Then let us examine ways & means of inflicting that damage. The most economical & efficient methods should be evolved. We might find out just where in the world the several kinds of tactical orgs. would be most efficient & thus we might begin to get a dim idea of real efficiency in peace time organization.[4] I personally think we are pursuing certain programs merely because they *sound* efficient; we are afraid *not* to do them. Yet they are expensive and are driving us (along with a lot of political expenditures) straight toward inflation of an uncontrollable character. Wouldn't the monster in the Kremlin rejoice to see us admit insolvency!!!

Our heavy tank program, hydrogen bomb, B–36, very heavy carrier, and similar programs should all be dissected from the standpoint of comparative

> purposes,
> special & unique capabilities
> inescapable need
> duplicatory effort
> luxury.[5]

In the same way the whole organization

the Army

Navy (incl. Marines)

Air

should be ruthlessly pulled apart & examined in order to get down to the _country's requirements_.

We should re-examine our whole philosophy of defense in its foreign & domestic aspects & do what is intelligent for democracies to do. Industrial mobilization _could save_ our nation (if properly planned for) when our whole peacetime military strength _might_ cost us ten times as much & largely fail in a pinch. (In 1941 our peacetime Navy took a terrible blow on the first day of the war—but the Navy built after the war started did a great job in both oceans; particularly against Japan where it really, with Air Force help, won the war! And this does not ignore the work of the great divisions that won & held the bases from which air attacks were made.[6]

If we don't have the objective, industry—government—professional examination that will show us where & how to proceed in this armament business we will go broke and still have _inefficient_ defenses. We can have security without paying the price of national bankruptcy, if we will put brains in the balance. We cannot afford prejudice, preconceived notions, fallacies, duplications, luxuries, fancied political advantages, etc., etc. Our country is at stake. Many will give her lip service; few will give her self-sacrifice, sweat and _brains_!![7]

[1] Eisenhower had spent October 15, 16, and 17 observing U.S. naval battle maneuvers between Naples and Sardinia (see no. 401, n. 4).

[2] Fearing that extravagant and unnecessary spending would fuel inflation and result in eventual national bankruptcy, Eisenhower had for several years advocated a defense program funded at a consistent rate year after year. In 1949, while serving as a defense consultant to the JCS, the General and then Secretary of Defense Forrestal had agreed that an annual allocation of $15 billion would be sufficient to provide adequate national security, a belief that Eisenhower still held (see nos. 130, n. 9, and 614, n. 8; and Galambos, _Columbia University_, nos. 367 and 404). On October 18 President Truman signed the largest peacetime armed services appropriation bill to date. Of the $56.9 billion allocated for military use in fiscal year 1952, approximately $27 billion was earmarked for equipment development and procurement (see _New York Times_, Sept. 14, Oct. 19, 1951).

[3] Eisenhower had earlier made proposals for this type of national advisory council to aid the United States with long-range planning (see, for example, no. 25, n. 4). Later this month Eisenhower's future rival for the Republican presidential nomination, Senator Robert Taft, called for the establishment of "a joint civilian-military commission to determine . . . how large an expenditure is necessary to assure the peace and security of the United States" (see _New York Times_, Oct. 26, 1951).

[4] On the tactical organization of U.S. and NATO ground troops see no. 389.

[5] On developments in armor and antitank weapons see no. 422; for background on the super aircraft carrier and the B–36 bomber see Galambos, _Columbia University_, nos. 222 and 336; and on the interservice difficulties see _ibid._, no. 639.

Recent atomic tests at Eniwetok Atoll in the Central Pacific having proven the feasibility of detonating a tritium-deuterium, or hydrogen, bomb, Truman had requested an additional $500 million from Congress to bring the weapon into existence (see *ibid.*, no. 673; and *New York Times*, May 26, June 14, Aug. 1, Sept. 19, 1951).

[6] For background on Eisenhower's interest in industrial mobilization see, for example, nos. 342, n. 3, and 439.

[7] On Eisenhower's continuing concern with these issues see no. 614; and his memoir *Mandate for Change*, pp. 126–33.

442

TO JOHN JAY McCLOY

Eisenhower Mss.

October 18, 1951

Dear Jack: When last we talked,[1] you mentioned that you thought it might be useful if I had a quiet meeting with Schumacher[2] and perhaps one or two of his principal aides. I would, of course, be very glad to do this if you think it would be helpful. I assume that you could so arrange such a visit as to create no unfavorable reactions among non-Socialist sections of Western Germany.

As you know, the first elements of the 43rd Infantry Division are due to arrive in Bremerhaven about October 20.[3] I plan to make a brief visit to this Division after it is installed. It occurred to me that such a visit might also provide a suitable occasion for me to see Schumacher quietly at your house in Frankfurt if you still feel this desirable.

I will be proceeding to England and Scotland tomorrow for a few days' visit, but could possibly arrange to get up to Germany for a day's visit to the 43rd Division sometime during the first two weeks of November.[4] I realize that the timing of my visit might be a factor insofar as seeing Schumacher is concerned, and would appreciate your present view as to the desirability of my making a trip during the period mentioned above.

If I were to come, I would plan to leave Paris early in the morning, visit the troop area, and then proceed to Frankfurt in the afternoon. I could see Schumacher in the late afternoon or could stay over for an after-dinner talk if you deemed necessary.[5] I would, in the latter case, return to Paris first thing the following morning. I would bring Doug MacArthur along, as I have him following developments in the German situation with both your people and David Bruce. *Sincerely*

[1] Eisenhower and German High Commissioner McCloy had probably spoken on the issue of German rearmament while Eisenhower reviewed troops at Rhein Main on October 9 and 10. This letter drew upon a draft prepared by Douglas Mac-

Arthur II. To MacArthur's draft the General added the final sentence in the first paragraph and details of his willingness to delay his return trip to Paris.

[2] Dr. Kurt Schumacher, leader of the West German Social Democratic Party (SPD), had become a prominent critic of the Christian Democrats' policy of cooperation with the Western Allies and of Chancellor Konrad Adenauer's eagerness to rearm Germany. Though strongly anti-Communist, Schumacher argued that rearmament would lessen the likelihood of German reunification; nevertheless, he opposed Germany's being militarily inferior to other European countries, especially France (see James L. Richardson, *Germany and the Atlantic Alliance: The Interaction of Strategy and Politics* [Cambridge, Mass., 1966], pp. 21–22; and McGeehan, *German Rearmament Question*, pp. 73–74). On October 9 Schumacher had called for a four-power conference to discuss German reunification (*International Herald Tribune*, Paris ed., Oct. 10, 1951). In a cover note to the draft (Oct. 18, 1951, EM), MacArthur had spelled out the approach that he recommended Eisenhower take in any discussion with Schumacher: the General should make it clear that NATO intended to defend West Germany, not to make it a battleground; that defense of West Germany hinged on that country's participation in the effort; that French fears of German domination of the European Defense Force mirrored Schumacher's that the French would do the same; and that the EDF held out the best hope, if not the only hope, that Germany could contribute on an equal basis toward the defense of Europe. "You might also restate to him the point you have made so often that you fully agree that you wish no second-class group of soldiers under your command and that you whole-heartedly agree that the German units in the European Defense Force and NATO Command Structure must be on a full and equal footing with other participants."

[3] Lead elements of the 43d Infantry Division would land at Bremerhaven on schedule, on October 20 (*New York Times*, Oct. 21, 1951).

[4] Eisenhower would meet with the British General Staff on October 20 and 21 and would then proceed to Culzean Castle in Scotland for further meetings and some rest. He would return to Paris on October 28.

[5] On Thanksgiving Day, November 22, Eisenhower would inspect the 43d Division near Munich (see no. 502). He would return to Paris early that afternoon, apparently without seeing either McCloy or Schumacher.

443   *Eisenhower Mss.*

To George Whitney   *October 18, 1951*

Dear George:[1] Thank you very much for sending along to me the copy of C. E. Wilson's talk.[2] I am off for the United Kingdom for a few days and shall carry it along with me to read.

Not long ago I read a talk of his in which he attempted to prove that the General Motors contracts are not inflationary in any way. I must say that it seemed to me that, here and there, his argument had gaps in it; but I am bound to say that I am delighted to realize that he is making this matter of general inflation one of vital concern in his thinking and, it is to be presumed, in his future actions.[3]

I am in my office for only a few minutes between trips to the

Mediterranean and to the United Kingdom.[4] One of these days, possibly I shall get a chance to write you a longer letter.

With warm personal regard, *Cordially*

[1] For background on Whitney, who frequently advised Eisenhower on economic developments in the United States, see no. 385.

[2] With a letter of October 11 (EM) Whitney had enclosed a transcription of a talk recently given by General Motors president Charles Erwin Wilson (on Wilson see Galambos, *Columbia University*, no. 648. For Eisenhower's reaction to his talk, entitled "The Camel's Nose Is Under the Tent," see no. 448).

[3] In "Sound Principles for Determining Fair Wages" (copy in EM, Wilson Corr.), given on October 3, 1951, before the Men's Association of the Grosse Pointe, Michigan, Memorial Church, Wilson had maintained that the General Motors–United Auto Workers (UAW) wage formula was not inflationary. By linking wage increases to the Bureau of Labor Statistics Consumer Price Index and by adding an additional 2.5 percent annual incentive raise to this, General Motors enabled its employees to maintain their purchasing power at a constant rate from year to year, Wilson said. He claimed that the Cost of Living Adjustment, or COLA, would enable workers to improve their conditions without a drastic effect upon the economy.

[4] On Eisenhower's mid-October trips see nos. 401, 441, and 442.

444

Eisenhower Mss.

To FRANK ALEXANDER WILLARD

October 18, 1951

Dear Frank:[1] Thanks very much for your letter giving the latest information on Mr. Barnett's proposal for a Free Slavic Legion.[2]

During General Collins' visit here about a week ago, I had an opportunity to discuss the matter briefly with him. In essence, his view is that such a force should not be set up unilaterally by the United States since it would be most difficult for the United States to remove all legal, political, fiscal and military obstacles and to establish a sound plan which would be acceptable to our allies. He feels that if such a force is to be organized, it should be done under the aegis of some European organization.[3]

I also had an opportunity to discuss the Barnett proposal with Bedell Smith during his visit here. He pointed out that the concept for a Free Slavic Legion is similar to several schemes that have been presented to him and to others in Washington, and that while the question was under continuing study, he was not prepared to recommend any positive action at this time.[4]

Naturally, I am interested in making full utilization of all available manpower for the defense of Western Europe. Nevertheless, I do not feel that this is an appropriate time for SHAPE to take any specific action to sponsor Mr. Barnett's proposal or any similar scheme. The overall problem is so fraught with political complications that any premature action on our part could easily result in more harm than good, particularly at this time when important negotiations are in progress concerning the German contribution. In fact, I would estimate that in veiw of overriding political considerations, it would not be practical to initiate such a program for at least the next six or eight months.[5]

I am glad that you have advised Mr. Barnett not to be impatient about getting on with this proposal.[6] I am having the staff here study the entire question of utilization of anti-Communist persons and groups, and, since this question is continuously under examination in Washington, I feel that we have made a reasonable start.

With warm personal regard, *Sincerely*

[1] For background on Willard see no. 67, n. 1.
[2] College professor Frank Barnett had suggested that the United States raise and equip a paratroop force of Iron Curtain refugees (see nos. 301, n. 2, and 392, nn. 4 and 5). Fearing that national jealousies and suspicions about British and French imperialistic motives would make the formation of the legion impossible, Barnett had written that "only America is strong enough and rich enough to lead a crusade for freedom with dignity, justice and genuine altruism" (see supplemental memorandum to a proposal outlined in pamphlet entitled *Cold War, Atomic War or Free Slavic Legion?* in EM, same file as document). According to Willard's October 3 letter to Eisenhower (EM), Barnett had discussed the proposal with Army Chief of Staff Collins before the latter's departure for Europe. At that time Collins had explained that while he realized the "resistance potential" of the proposed force, he believed that the United States Army had no authority to recruit a foreign legion and that the task might better be the responsibility of the NATO forces.
[3] On Collins's visit to SHAPE see no. 416, n. 1.
[4] In regard to CIA Director Smith's visit to SHAPE see no. 360, n. 4.
[5] The continuing debate over West German rearmament and military participation in the defense of Western Europe is discussed in nos. 252, n. 5, and 710, n. 6.
[6] In his letter of the third Willard had said that he had advised Barnett against taking his campaign for the legion to the press and radio. Eisenhower aide Paul Carroll wrote this reply.

445

Eisenhower Mss.

To EDWARD JOHN BERMINGHAM   *October 18, 1951*
Personal and confidential

Dear Ed: Disregarding the personal allusions, I agree with a very great deal of what the Senator said to you in his letter dated October 5th— namely, that the success of NATO is largely going to be determined in Washington.[1] However, the point that affects me and my duty to our country is that I am now *assigned to a military post* that demands of its occupant complete devotion to the interests of the entire country. This means that he must so conduct himself and his job so that Americans are not tempted to divide themselves into partisan groups with respect to *the job.* This is a compelling reason for silence; I repeat that I appreciate very fully the force of the Senator's reasoning. *Cordially*

[1] Through Bermingham, Eisenhower's friend and political supporter, Republican Senator Karl Mundt of South Dakota had recently encouraged the General to become more actively involved in the 1952 presidential race (for background on the two men and on their activities see no. 386). In his October 9 letter to Eisenhower Bermingham had enclosed a copy of Mundt's letter (both in EM, same file as document). The senator expressed his regret at Eisenhower's continuing reluctance to reveal his party affiliation. While he acknowledged that the General was extremely busy with his important NATO tasks, Mundt said: "The final outcome [of the NATO efforts] will rest almost entirely with the kind of national leadership we have in the White House during the next four years." He expressed the hope that this fact would be impressed upon Eisenhower before it was too late for him to declare his candidacy.

446   *Eisenhower Mss.*

To Walter Bedell Smith   *October 19, 1951*
Secret

Dear Bedell: On 10 October, I received your message through Mr. Robert H. Thayer of the American Embassy in Paris, concerning your current ideas and planning for emigre work in Europe.[1]

On 11 October, Paul Reynaud came to my office for a brief visit. I used this occasion to mention to him that, although I have a great interest in the development of indigenous European groups, I feel that the political complexities of the question are such that I do not wish to sponsor the French Committee of National Emigre Councils or any other such organization at this time. I also mentioned to him my feeling that any such organization, if it is to succeed, must have a broader base than those which have been utilized in the past and that it must be established on an international European basis, as you mentioned in the message which you forwarded to me through Mr. Thayer. Mr. Douglas MacArthur, of my staff, is informing Mr. Thayer of the results of my meeting with Reynaud.[2]

I hope that you will continue to keep me advised of any further developments along this line, and I also hope that you can see your way clear to visit with us again in the near future.[3]

Am dashing this off just before leaving for England, but I want you to know how much I appreciated your birthday message.[4]

Give my love to Norry[5] and, of course, warm regard to yourself.

As ever

[1] Robert Helyer Thayer, Assistant U.S. Ambassador to France, had delivered a personal message to Eisenhower from CIA Director Smith concerning possible SHAPE support for anti-Communist propaganda activities on the part of Iron Curtain émigrés. Explaining that the agency had supported similar efforts of the Crusade for Freedom and Radio Free Europe in the United States, Smith wrote that it was now "thought to be desirable for us to shift our focus in emigre work from New York to Europe. . . . If properly sustained and used," according to Smith, "the psychological and operational contribution of these groups to all overt and covert propaganda activities throughout Eastern and Western Europe can be immense" (see Thayer to Eisenhower, Oct. 10, 1951, EM, same file as document).

[2] Smith had suggested that Eisenhower speak with French National Assemblyman Paul Reynaud, who was then believed to be about to launch a French committee of national émigré councils. Interested in working with this group if it freed itself "of the many dissensions and international conflicts" that afflicted it, Smith encouraged Eisenhower's involvement. "With the tacit support of the United States government and, eventually, of the NATO Powers . . . ," he said, the council could "be made the rallying point of all emigres." For background on MacArthur, SHAPE adviser on international affairs, see no. 32.

[3] There is no further correspondence in EM concerning this matter. On Smith's recent visit to France see no. 360. Eisenhower aide Craig Cannon drafted this letter.

[4] On Eisenhower's trip to England see no. 442; on his birthday see no. 431.

[5] Nory was the nickname of Smith's wife Mary (see no. 360).

447   *Eisenhower Mss.*

To WILLIAM EDWARD ROBINSON   *October 19, 1951*

Dear Bill: It has been a long time since I have had a first-hand report on the state of your health and weight.[1] I trust that both are in perfect shape. Recently I have seen a few notices concerning the next Herald Tribune forum.[2] It looks to me like you are going to have a very fine affair. I wish I could be there to listen to the discussions.

I have been doing a great deal of traveling lately and, up until the last two or three days, had very good weather for it. Ordinarily, I would have preferred to be here at my headquarters during the good weather periods—of which we have few enough—so as to get an occasional hour of golf; but I have been plagued by a very sore wrist for the past four or five weeks and, seemingly, there is nothing that cures it completely. It is of no bother whatsoever except when I try to exercise it, but it completely defeats any golfing effort. Travel has done something to prevent me from feeling sorry for myself.[3]

A curious allegation seems to be gaining some credence in the

United States to the effect that I was one of those responsible for the dissipation of American military strength immediately following the cessation of hostilities in 1945. The opposite is, of course, true. The record will show that, even before the end of hostilities, I recommended a system of universal military service for the United States and unification of her forces. By instructions of the President, and against my personal wishes, I took over the job of Chief of Staff in December 1945. My very first task was to appear before a very impatient Congress in a joint, informal, session at the Congressional Library to tell the members that the War Department refused, under conditions then existing, to discharge the two-year men. This struggle was so resented that a whole convention of women descended on me in Washington, and the press of that period carried pictures of me cornered in a room down in the Capitol, trying to explain to a group of women why their husbands would have to continue to do their military duty until others could be trained and put in their places. I tried to get every important military figure at home and abroad to make statements supporting Universal Military Training. I even went to Tokyo for this purpose.[4]

All this shows just how soon people forget the actual events of history and succumb to the effects of unwanted and baseless statement.

I hear that Cliff has been in San Francisco, but I imagine that it is about time he is returning to New York. In any event, my very best to him when you see him. This includes, of course, Pete Jones, Slats, and all the rest.[5]

As always, warm regard,[6] *Cordially*

[1] On Eisenhower's concern over his old friend's health see no. 265.

[2] The twentieth annual *New York Herald Tribune* Forum, a three-day series of presentations and panel discussions by prominent Americans, would begin on October 23 at New York's Waldorf-Astoria Hotel. The topic for this year would be "Balancing Moral and Scientific Responsibility" (see *International Herald Tribune*, Paris ed., Oct. 19, 22, 24, 25, 26, 1951). On Eisenhower's participation in the 1949 forum, largely at the urging of Robinson, the *Tribune*'s director and executive vice-president, see Galambos, *Columbia University*, nos. 177 and 555.

[3] On the General's recent trips see nos. 441 and 442. On his difficulties with his wrist see no. 392.

[4] After succeeding General Marshall as Army Chief of Staff, Eisenhower had faced myriad problems stemming from the conversion of U.S. forces from a wartime to a peacetime footing. On the postwar debate over reduction and reorganization of the armed services see Chandler and Galambos, *Occupation, 1945*, no. 340; and Galambos, *Chief of Staff*, no. 590. For background on the General's January 15, 1946, address to Congress and his later inspection tour of Japan, see Galambos, *Chief of Staff*, nos. 645 and 893.

Eisenhower had first advocated universal military service, or UMS (requiring of every male a multiyear term of active duty with the Army, Navy, Marine Corps, or Air Force), then the politically more feasible plan of universal military training, or UMT, usually meaning a brief period of indoctrination followed by lengthy reserve service (see Galambos, *Chief of Staff*, no. 1244, and *Columbia University*, nos. 912 and 1042). A week after Eisenhower's letter to Robinson the National Security Training Commission, which Congress had established in June, submitted its report entitled "Univeral Military Training: Foundation of Enduring National Strength." The report expressed beliefs that the General long had shared. Citing the possibility of sudden attack, the moral wrong of sending untrained men into battle, and the need for long-term military policies, commission members argued for a national training corps made up of inductees—not technically in military service—who would spend six months in one of the programs the service branches had devised to meet their peculiar needs (82d Cong., 2d sess., 1951, H. Doc. 315). For developments see nos. 697 and 702.

[5] Clifford Roberts (see no. 416), William ("Pete") Jones (see no. 143), and Ellis ("Slats") Slater (see no. 323) were mutual friends of Robinson's and Eisenhower's.

[6] Next to the complimentary closing Eisenhower wrote "& d—— hurriedly."

448   *Eisenhower Mss.*

To CHARLES ERWIN WILSON   *October 20, 1951*

Dear Charlie:[01] Finally I found opportunity to read the three talks that you were kind enough to send to me. Since it is only natural that I should make some distinction among them, based upon what seemed to me to be the power and soundness of their arguments, I must say that my favorite is "The Camel's Nose is Under the Tent."[2] It would be difficult for me to exaggerate the sense of satisfaction I have in the head-on fight you are making against the dangerous theory that bureaucratic control can solve our country's industrial, economic and financial problems.

In your text you quoted, on page 3A, some very fine editorial comment from the Detroit News.[3] With that editorial I find myself in almost perfect agreement, but I am compelled to say that I seriously object to the introduction of one superfluous word. About the middle of the page begins a paragraph with the phrase, "Those outside the military establishment. . . . ." My quarrel is with the word "outside." May I feebly protest that I have publicly, privately, and for months—with the support of many others in the U.S. Army—advanced the same type of conclusion that is so succinctly presented in that quotation. So, I wish the editor could realize that merely because an individual tries, in uniform, to serve his country, his thinking is not necessarily distorted to the extent that he believes in arms and arms alone as the basis of peace abroad and freedom at home. Any person who doesn't clearly understand that national security and national solvency are mutually dependent, and that permanent maintenance of a crushing weight of military power would eventually produce dictatorship, should not be entrusted with any kind of responsibility in our country.

I likewise derived great satisfaction from reading your talk on industrial preparedness.[4] While I am not qualified to express an opinion about the various advantages and disadvantages of the dual plant system, I am quite certain that if we will only put our industrial brains to the task of devising an efficient plan for emergency mobilization, we will save billions if ever we again face the tragedy of war. I hope that you and General Motors will keep pegging away on this vital problem. I was first assigned to duty in connection with it in 1930. In those days, it was difficult to get anyone in an important governmental or industrial position to give even a brief moment to discussion of the matter. Bernard Baruch was an exception. He was always ready to give generously of his time for this purpose; a circumstance that is one of the reasons I have, ever since those days, sustained a very warm feeling toward him.[5]

Forgive the length of this letter. But to my congratulations I wanted to add my fervent hope that you will continue your efforts to bring home to the American people the salient facts of our current existence. Especially I applaud your purpose of demonstrating that we can and must produce national security without falling into national bankruptcy.

With personal regard, *Cordially*

[1] For background on Wilson see no. 443, n. 3.

[2] Wilson had enclosed with his October 8 letter (EM) copies of three talks. On one of them, "Sound Principles for Determining Fair Wages," see no. 443, n. 3. The other two were "The Camel's Nose Is Under the Tent" and "Preparedness as a Continuing Policy" (see EM, same file as document). Wilson made the "Camel's Nose" address (based on an Arabian fable in which over the course of a cold night a camel, after receiving permission to warm its nose, finally takes over the master's tent). On October 10, before the Dallas, Texas, chapter of the Society for the Advancement of Management, the General Motors president compared the encroachments of the federal government on free enterprise to Aesop's camel (see copies in EM, same file as document). According to Wilson, the system of governmental controls that had been instituted for World War II and the Korean War comprised the first steps toward displacement of the economic liberties of competitive industry. Citing restrictions in the steel industry and wage and price controls aimed at curbing inflation, Wilson asserted: "One of the great evils of such government controls is that they rapidly create powerful vested interests and habits of mind" that lead eventually to a "fully regimented and planned economy. . . ." For background on the Truman Administration's system of controls see no. 306. On Eisenhower's own concerns with governmental interference in a free society see Galambos, *Columbia University*, nos. 419 and 445.

[3] Wilson had quoted a passage cautioning against the multiple dangers that would derive from continued excessive U.S. military spending. Stating that those "outside the military establishment" would not long tolerate a program that produced "preponderant power," the editorial warned that uncontrolled defense expansion might encourage a Soviet first strike out of fear and would likely lead to national

bankruptcy, political demoralization, and the development of an entrenched and aggressive U.S. militarism. For Eisenhower's own fears concerning excessive military spending see no. 441, n. 2.

[4] In Cincinnati on October 4 Wilson had addressed the American Ordnance Association on "Preparedness as a Continuing Policy." In the speech Wilson proposed as a permanent national defense policy the establishment of dual-purpose manufacturing facilities that could be utilized as total-war production plants, combined civilian and defense plants, and civilian production facilities. He urged the federal government to work closely with industry to develop these double-function plants as a part of the nation's ongoing defense effort.

[5] On Eisenhower's great interest in industrial mobilization, including his friendship with Bernard Baruch, see, for example, no. 342, n. 3. On the General's service under the Deputy Secretary of War from 1929 to 1932 see his memoir *At Ease*, pp. 210-13.

449   *Eisenhower Mss.*

To Alfred Maximilian Gruenther   *October 22, 1951*

Dear Al: I understand that a courier plane is due here on Tuesday—so you should have this by Wednesday, at the latest.[1]

On Saturday, I had a long talk with Field Marshal Slim.[2] He was anxious to talk about two matters, each of which gives me some concern.

The first of these concerns a replacement for General Airey.[3] As you know, we have been considering the naming of an American to this position, and this solution, because of the trouble Airey has had in obtaining access to American intelligence, was first favored by Slim.[4] At this point, however, enters the second subject which he wanted to talk to me about. This involves persistent rumors and reports reaching Slim (and apparently Whitely also) that our headquarters is, in fact, nothing but an American institution.[5]

I pressed hard to get at the botton of this rumor. I tried to find its basis because, so far as this charge is concerned, I not only have a clear conscience and a pure heart, but I also have a keen memory of how earnestly you and I have worked to avoid the growth of any such idea.

I first explained to Slim the difficulties we have had in finding qualified officers from any nation except our own, and reminded him that he himself had protested against giving us any great number of highly qualified British officers. It then developed that the sarcastic remarks he had heard were not founded so much on the ratio of American to other officers occupying key positions in our organization as they were on the feeling that we have organized, and are maintaining, a "shadow," or "inner" cabinet of Americans that, in fact, has all the influence in the headquarters.

This brought the whole business squarely into the light, since it is obvious that our efforts to keep away from the allied staff all those matters that are of interest only to America have apparently been misinterpreted. I explained to Slim what we were up against in the volume and variety of American questions, including those brought to us by MDAP, ECA, Congressional committees, visitations by editors, businessmen, etc., etc. I pointed out also the extent to which governmental officials in Washington look to you and me as responsible agents in every type of American activity carried on in Europe. This explanation—it apparently had not before occurred to him—seemed to satisfy Slim completely. I took advantage of the opportunity to request that when and if these reports were ever repeated to him that he put his informant through a real course of cross examination to try to find out exactly what the individual had in mind. I asked Jock to do the same.

In light of these misapprehensions and in spite of the logic of our current arrangements, it seemed apparent both to Slim and to me that we should attempt to find a British officer to replace Airey, if it were possible. To do otherwise would merely add fuel to the senseless impression already developing about us. He promptly offered Strong, but with a very clear proviso.[6] This proviso is that *we can make arrangements for Strong, as an individual, to have access to all kinds of American intelligence* (this does *not* include information on American atomic developments) that come into our office.[7] Since Strong has, for many years, been a participant in all our most secret joint intelligence efforts, I am sure there will be no objection to this. But I promised Slim that we would check in advance.

It may be that the gaining of this assurance should wait until I go back to the U.S. for the brief visit that I am planning.[8] On the other hand, I felt that you might start the ball rolling at once. Strong is so well known to our people, including Bedell,[9] that I cannot see how there could be any objection to the arrangement. In fact, if there is, I think I would be disposed to make an issue of it.[10] Slim was quite emphatic that he would not request that any other British officer, anywhere, be made a party to this intelligence arrangement.

From Slim's viewpoint, it is a matter of not putting Strong into an impossible situation, while from mine it is the perfectly obvious consideration that my principal G-2 should have before him every bit of available information before he advises me in his particular field.

I questioned Slim as to the effect of such a move upon Strong. He stated that he thought it would be to Strong's advantage to have the post, and he thought also that Strong would like to join us. On this last point you could make discreet inquiries if the scheme, up to this point, seems reasonable. In any event, you are well aware of the extraordinary confidence I have in Strong's ability, integrity and reliability as an intelligence officer.

Now, to refer again to the first subject. I believe that you should have a meeting of your whole staff, at least to include everybody above the grade of major or equivalent. In that meeting you could state that rumors appear to be afloat which imply a complete lack of understanding of the compelling reasons for organizing an informal group under Schuyler to help you and me in some of our American work.[11] I would then describe something of the character of our strictly American responsibilities and, with respect to these, I would make two principal points. The first is that if these questions were thrown indiscriminately to the General Staff for consideration, they would not only place additional and unwarranted burdens upon that Staff, but would involve problems concerning which the Staff could know nothing. My second point would be that these questions frequently affect materially the rearmament and military programs of the several cooperating nations, and it is to everybody's interest to keep them under study by a group of young and able officers who are acceptable to our Congressional committees. In other words, by having an American staff, it is solely for the good of the NATO organization. (Give them the example of a Congressional committee.)

After all, there are relatively few American officers engaged in this kind of thing. Schuyler, Burnham, Goodpaster, and one or two others are the principal ones; and I believe that a clear exposition to the staff would settle this thing once and for all.

There is no need to answer this letter; I shall talk to you about the whole business next Sunday. However, if I am to depart early next week for the States you should be doing a bit of thinking on these matters. Incidentally, this brings up the thought that some of our smart American boys should be putting into a single *short* memorandum, the series of subjects concerning which I should talk to our Washington friends on the day or two that I expect to be in that city.[12] *As ever*

[1] Eisenhower wrote from Culzean Castle, in Scotland, where he had arrived for a stay scheduled for October 21–28.

[2] While in London on October 20 the General had met with the British Imperial General Staff, of which William Joseph Slim had served as Chief since October 1948 (see no. 107).

[3] Major General Terence S. Airey, SHAPE Assistant Chief of Staff for Intelligence (see no. 271), had been promoted to lieutenant general and assigned command of British forces in Hong Kong.

[4] In the spring Eisenhower had described as intolerable SHAPE's difficulties in obtaining U.S. intelligence updates (see nos. 125 and 144; and n. 7 below).

[5] Eisenhower's meeting with British military leaders had taken place at the home of John Francis Martin ("Jock") Whiteley, who late in World War II had served as SHAEF Assistant G-3 (see no. 203).

[6] Lieutenant General Kenneth W. D. Strong, wartime SHAEF intelligence officer and afterward a director of British Foreign Office and defense intelligence bureaus, served as Deputy Chief of the Imperial General Staff (see Chandler, *War Years*, nos. 831 and 1473; and Galambos, *Columbia University*, nos. 480 and 568).

[7] Eisenhower's efforts to arrange the sharing of U.S. intelligence with his international staff had included letters to JCS Chairman Omar N. Bradley and CIA Director Walter Bedell Smith (see nos. 125 and 144); and a memorandum of July 25 requesting attention to the problem, SHAPE/261/51, ID-3500, CCS 092 Western Europe [3-12-48], Sec. 93). By the summer of 1951 considerable progress had been made. By means of daily briefings and weekly summaries, the U.S. Joint Intelligence Committee (JIC) routinely furnished the NATO Standing Group and major NATO commands information on the current deployment of Soviet and Soviet-satellite ground, sea, and air forces. By that time the JIC had also formed an ad hoc committee under Army Colonel Benjamin B. Talley and charged it with maintaining "cognizance of NATO matters" and providing "inter-service cooperation in furnishing Joint Intelligence Committee guidance and support" to the U.S. member of the Standing Group Intelligence Committee. The Secretary of Defense had designated the Army assistant chief of staff, G-2, as the "executive agent" for the JIC and ordered him "to furnish SHAPE with processed intelligence and such raw information as affects the immediate world situation" (JIC 558/53, [Sept. 19, 1951], CCS 092 Western Europe [3-12-48], Sec. 94).

Late that summer and in the early fall U.S. officials had made further efforts to improve working relations with NATO. On August 14 the JIC agreed to inform U.S. nonmilitary intelligence agencies of the procedures by which it supplied NATO with information and in September prepared a memorandum for the CIA director on that subject. Responding to SHAPE/261/51 on September 11, the JIC asserted that the United States regularly furnished virtually all that SHAPE requested. The JIC pledged "every practicable effort" in preparing intelligence for SHAPE, noting, however, that "the amount of work required to transpose existing intelligence into SHAPE standardized form" still posed a problem. Opening an intelligence conference held at SHAPE headquarters on September 24, the chairman of the U.S. delegation emphasized that the information the United States supplied to NATO, which possibly some NATO officers had judged overly fearful of Soviet strength, was based on the same intelligence estimate the JIC presented to the U.S. Joint Chiefs of Staff. "We may appear at times to be determined in our defense of this estimate," read a draft of the chairman's remarks, "but if we are determined in its defense, then it is because we have based our own entire defense program upon it" (JIC 558/46/D, Sept. 12, 1951, CCS 092 Western Europe [3-12-48], Sec. 93). For developments see nos. 482 and 510; for continuing U.S. restrictions on nuclear secrets see no. 837.

[8] Eisenhower would make a brief trip to the United States in early November (see nos. 457 and 468; and n. 12 below).

[9] Walter Bedell Smith, Director of the CIA (see no. 144).

[10] On Airey's eventual replacement with U.S. Brigadier General Robert A. Schow, Airey's deputy, whom Eisenhower would see during the respite in Scotland, see no. 722.

[11] Eisenhower apparently had directed Chief of Staff Gruenther to assign Major General Cortlandt van Rensselaer Schuyler (see no. 2), William H. Burnham (see the next document), and Colonel Andrew J. Goodpaster, Jr., to handle staff work relating specifically to U.S. issues. An Illinois native, Goodpaster (USMA 1939; Ph.D. Princeton 1950) had commanded a combat engineering battalion during World War II, served on the War Department strategic and policy staff between 1944 and 1947, and then undertaken graduate studies in international relations. He had accompanied Eisenhower to Paris as a special staff assistant.

We have located no such memorandum. For speculation on President Truman's underlying political purpose in summoning Eisenhower see no. 486.

450

Eisenhower Mss.

To WILLIAM H. BURNHAM[1]

October 25, 1951

I seem to be accumulating a lot of friend[s] whose names mean nothing to me. At times my memory could be at fault—but not 100%.[2]

[1] For background on Burnham, a friend of Eisenhower's and a political adviser who at this time was employed by SHAPE as a civilian economic analyst, see no. 40.

[2] Eisenhower wrote these sentences in longhand at the bottom of a message from Burnham of this same date. Eisenhower's note accompanied a copy of a three-page report from New York businessman and political organizer Robert Raymond Barry (EM, same file as document). Barry had written the report for Pennsylvania congressman Hugh Scott, Jr. (see no. 195, n. 4), on October 19 and had later sent it to SHAPE headquarters. Barry had reported on his efforts to organize the Republican forces of Washington state, Oregon, California, and Alaska in support of an Eisenhower presidential candidacy. Apparently assigned this task by Scott, who was actively seeking the General's nomination, Barry reported that attempts to establish Eisenhower-for-President committees had been successful in most areas, with "representative[s] of varying Republican backgrounds . . . quite capable of organizing other groups at the county and local level." Judging from evidence in EM, of the twenty-seven persons that Barry indicated were then working toward an Eisenhower candidacy, the General had had only slight contact with five up to this point in time. For developments involving Barry see no. 499.

451

Eisenhower Mss.

To WINSTON SPENCER CHURCHILL

October 26, 1951

Dear Winston:[0] The world pauses to contemplate your country's decision that you should once more direct her destinies in a moment of immeasurable significance to all of us. For my part I assure you of my complete confidence in your devotion to the cause of peace and my conviction that under your inspired guidance Britain's traditional dedication to the freedom, dignity and worth of the individual will be equal to any test that threatening dictatorships can impose. My hopes and prayers for a secure, peaceful, and prosperous advancement of free government among men are with you as you approach your new responsibilities and opportunities.[1] Mamie joins me in affectionate best wishes and congratulations[2] to you and Mrs. Churchill.[3]

[1] Eisenhower's wartime friend had been the opposition party leader since the fall of his government in July 1945 (see Chandler and Galambos, *Occupation, 1945*, no. 152). Churchill and the Conservative party had been returned to power after general elections on October 25 (see *International Herald Tribune*, Paris ed., Oct. 24, 25, 26, 27, 1951), defeating the Labor government of Clement Attlee and gaining a slim majority of twenty-five seats in the House of Commons. Churchill assumed the duties of Prime Minister this same day (see Lewis Broad, *Winston Churchill*, 2 vols. [New York, 1958–63], vol. II, *The Years of Achievement* [1963], pp. 541–43). On Attlee see no. 252, n. 2.

[2] Eisenhower added "and congratulations" in a handwritten addition to the original draft of this letter.

[3] Churchill's wife, the former Clementine Hozier. The General and Mrs. Eisenhower were vacationing in Scotland at this time (see no. 401, n. 4).

452   *Eisenhower Mss., Diaries*

DIARY   *October 29, 1951*

Today I was visited by several individuals who brought up the political struggle in the United States. Chief among these were Mr. Weir, Head of the National Steel Company; and Mr. Harold Talbott who, as I understand it, has been associated with Republican politics for some years.[1]

In general, the argument of both men was the same. It is about as follows:

    a. In the absence of some serious opposition, Mr. Taft is going to capture the Republican nomination for President *before* the convention itself meets. In other words, when the convention convenes, there will be so many delegates pledged to him that opposition will be useless.

    b. That Mr. Taft can get in an election the solid vote of the oldline Republicans, but no others. Specifically, Mr. Talbott said he could get no votes from anybody under 30 years of age. The further statement was made that in our country today are 40% Democrats, 31% Republicans, and 28% Independents. This last figure was completely astonishing to me and I doubt its accuracy.[2]

    c. The proof is clear, according to these gentlemen, that Taft cannot be elected President of the United States.[3] Fundamentally, they believe that Taft's lack of appeal is the belief in the United States that he represents a reactionary type of thinking, and especially that he represents a reactionary wing of the Republican Party.

    d. Mr. Truman, they believe, would beat Mr. Taft very easily.

Mr. Weir said that any other Democrat could likewise beat Mr. Taft.

e. Four years more of Democratic, uninterrupted, government in our country will put us so far on the road to socialism that there will be no return to a free enterprise.[4] They firmly believe that we would follow the example of Britain until we became fully socialized, which means, of course, fully regimented.

f. That the only way to halt this chain of events and to give the United States a breathing space is for me to make a proper move within a reasonable time (although neither man stated the exact time) to allow all elements of Republican Party, other than the supporters of Taft, to nominate me as President. They think that I would be easily elected because of what they call my appeal among Independents and also among certain sections of the Democratic Party.

These representations happen to coincide with four letters that I received today from people at home (one of them completely unknown to me), outlining the same argument.[5] The whole business is merely repetitive and, except for the utter seriousness with which it is presented, it grows very monotonous. It is certainly burdensome.

In reply, I said to these men as I have said before:

a. I do not want to be President of the United States, and I want no other political office or political connection of any kind.

b. I am now on a job in which success is of the most tremendous importance to the future of the United States.

c. One of the great factors in producing success in this job is support from the bulk of the American population. Consequently, I have no right to announce any partisan leanings of any kind, because to do so would jeopardize the great project on which the United States is spending so much money and on which her future so clearly depends.

d. I entered upon this post only from a sense of duty—I certainly had to sacrifice much in the way of personal convenience, advantage, and congenial constructive work when I left New York. I will never leave this post for any other kind of governmental task except in response to a clear call to duty. I will not be a participant in any movement that attempts to secure for me a nomination because I believe that the Presidency is something that should never be sought, just as I believe, of course, that it could never be refused. What future circumstances could convince me that I had a duty to enter the political arena, I am not prepared to say. I simply do not know what they could be. I merely admit that, as of now, I would consider the nomination of which they speak, if accomplished without any direct or indirect assistance or connivance on my part, to place upon me a transcendent duty.

e. Because of these convictions, if ever I should decide that I have a political duty to perform, it would be incumbent upon me instantly to submit my resignation to the President.

It is difficult indeed to maintain the attitude I tried to explain to my visitors. It would be much easier to simply have done with the whole business by arbitrarily declining to give it any thought whatsoever. Possibly I shall do this yet. As of now, I see nothing to do but to keep my mouth shut.

[1] According to Eisenhower's appointment calendar, the General spent this day in meetings and lunch with members of the SHAPE command and in two official photo sessions. Harold Talbott, who was already active in the Eisenhower-for-President movement (see no. 401, n. 3), and steel executive Ernest Tener Weir had separate appointments with Eisenhower during the late afternoon.

[2] According to polls and surveys conducted during 1952, the nation was 47 percent Democratic, 27 percent Republican, 22 percent Independent, and 4 percent unaffiliated (see William H. Flanigan and Nancy H. Zingale, *Political Behavior of the American Electorate*, 3d ed. [Boston, 1975], pp. 52–53).

[3] Taft had declared his candidacy on October 16, stating at a Washington, D.C., press conference that he would "conduct the only kind of campaign which will elect a Republican to office." In outlining his platform, he criticized the Truman Administration's political corruption, tendencies toward socialism, and handling of the Korean War (see *International Herald Tribune*, Paris ed., Oct. 17, 1951). For background on Taft's recent political career, including his opposition to the U.S. troop build-up in Europe, see, for example, nos. 112, 222, n. 3, and 409. Although undeclared, the other possible Republican candidates at this time were Eisenhower, Harold Stassen (see no. 409, n. 3), and California Governor Earl Warren (see Galambos, *Columbia University*, no. 937).

[4] For Eisenhower's concern over the Truman Administration's drift toward economic controls see, for example, no. 440.

[5] On the many political inquiries the General was receiving daily see nos. 437 and 445.

453

Eisenhower Mss., Diaries

DIARY

October 30, 1951

Mr. Colby Chester came in this morning to repeat the same argument.[1] He also brought to me a letter from a Texas mother.[2]

[1] For background on Colby Mitchell Chester, chairman of the New York chapter of the American Red Cross, see Galambos, *Columbia University*, no. 616. The "same argument" no doubt refers to the issue of Eisenhower's entry into politics.

[2] Mrs. J. J. Hults, of Corpus Christi, Texas, had written Chester on August 9

(copy in EM, same file as document) to lament the loss of traditional American values since the inception of the New Deal. Mrs. Hults wrote that Americans certainly "would rather earn what they individually prove themselves worth and live as their initiative permits instead of earning what some Labor Boss says they should earn and liveing [sic] better because the Labor Unions, Govt. financing and Govt. subsidizing has removed their initiative." Replying to Chester on October 30 (EM), Eisenhower wrote that Hults "has stated . . . the principal problems of our day: or perhaps . . . the principal item of worry with which each of us lives." On Eisenhower's own concerns over the paternalism and centralization of American government see no. 440 and the preceding document.

---

454   *Eisenhower Mss.*

To Harold Raynsford Stark   *October 31, 1951*

Dear Betty:[1] Many thanks for your birthday greetings.[2] As always, I appreciate your thoughtfulness in writing and the good wishes you send.

It seems strange for me to have a headquarters in Europe without you in London! It's not as much fun to run back there as it used to be.[3]

With warm regard,[4] *Cordially*

[1] For background on former CNO "Betty" Stark (USN, ret.) see Galambos, *Columbia University*, no. 1153.
[2] The Admiral's message (n.d., EM) had come on a postcard mailed from Lake Carey, Tunkhannock, Pennsylvania, where the Starks had a summer cottage.
[3] For background on Eisenhower's relationship with Stark during World War II see Chandler, *War Years*.
[4] In a handwritten postscript to this staff-drafted reply Eisenhower said, "I'm just reminded that your own birthday falls on the 9th of this coming month. My felicitations and best wishes—as always. D.E."

---

455   *Eisenhower Mss.*

To William Edward Robinson   *October 31, 1951*

Dear Bill: I know you will forgive me for sending again nothing but an excuse for writing a real letter. I simply haven't the time to do it because I am paying up, in terms of piled up work, for the short vacation Mamie and I have just taken in Scotland.[1]

I have just dispatched a short note to Cliff who will let you in on a piece of very secret information I sent him.[2]

When I get a chance, I shall, of course, write a decent letter to you. In the meantime, I assure you that I am overwhelmed by the overgenerous estimate the Herald Tribune makes of my qualifications and capabilities.[3] Helen Reid and her staff have always been far too complimentary to me—possibly a result of your direct influence.[4] In any event, it was a good antidote for a particularly critical item that came to my desk at almost the same moment. *As ever*

[1] On the vacation see no. 442. For background on Robinson, *New York Herald Tribune* executive vice-president and director, see no. 39.

[2] Writing to their mutual friend Clifford Roberts (see no. 447) on October 30 (EM), Eisenhower had said, "For your secret information, I may be in the States very briefly indeed the early part of next week." In a handwritten addition to this paragraph, the General told Robinson that "Cliff's letter may be lacking a date. I'd plan P.M. of Mon. 6." For developments with the trip see the following document.

[3] In a front-page editorial on October 25 entitled "The Times and the Man" the *Herald Tribune* had endorsed Eisenhower as its choice for the 1952 Republican presidential nomination. Saying that he was "Republican by temper and disposition . . . by every avowal of faith and solemn declaration of purpose," the newspaper had pledged to work toward the General's nomination (see *International Herald Tribune*, Paris ed., Oct. 25, 1951; see also the following document).

[4] For background on Eisenhower's friendship with *Herald Tribune* president Helen Reid, who on October 24 had closed the *Herald Tribune* Forum with the announcement that the paper would commit itself to an Eisenhower presidential candidacy the following day, see no. 323.

456

To WILLIAM EDWARD ROBINSON
Confidential

Eisenhower Mss.

October 31, 1951

Dear Bill: As I promised in a note of yesterday, I am going to try to write a more comprehensive answer to your recent letters than I have so far been able to do.[1] Because of the spottiness of the time available to me, it may require the next two or three days to finish this—but certainly I shall never finish it without starting.

First of all, let me tell you that the copy of the letter addressed to "Dear Willma," dated October 19th, contains the evaluation of a man that is a far worthier human than I can ever hope to be.[2] You have somewhat idealized your own mental picture of a friend; this is one of the privileges of friendship, possibly one of its bases for existence. In any event, it makes me exceedingly proud.

I am, of course, glad that you have been consulting with Milton from time to time about the developing American scene, particularly as it appears to concern me. I think he is not only a very wise and understanding person, but he has been very close to me for many years and I flatter myself that, in many respects, we think exactly alike. Certainly I know that he would approve of the attitude I consistently pursue these days.[3] He would possibly state the matter in slightly different words but he would agree with the following paragraph which I now put in almost every letter I write, when I am compelled to touch upon the possibility of a future political career:

> "For me to admit, while in this post, a partisan political loyalty would properly be resented by thinking Americans and would be doing a disservice to our country. Such action on my part would encourage partisan thinking, in our country, toward a job in which the whole nation has already invested tremendous sums. The successful outcome of this venture is too vital to our welfare in the years ahead to permit any semblance of partisan allegiance on the part of the United States Military Commander in SHAPE."

It should be clear that any deviation from this kind of statement would destroy me and any value I have to our country. Consequently, entirely aside from the matter of conscience and of conviction, no other attitude is possible as long as I am occupying this responsible post.[4]

With regard to the editorial in the Herald Tribune, my instant reaction is that I am highly complimented, and I mean highly. So far as its effect upon my own correspondence and stream of visitors is concerned, I doubt that this will be noticeable.[5] This is for the reason that already my days are crowded with appointments and my correspondence is so heavy, that every spare moment is devoted to it. As explained in your later editorial—one that came out this morning—the purpose seems to have been to give encouragement to a great underlying sentiment that might be called a truly grass roots, but definitely inarticulate, one. It was intended as something of a counter to the scheme of merely picking off organizational delegates.[6]

Incidentally, this morning's editorial says that the reaction noticed in the editorial rooms of the Herald Tribune, as judged by the letters from subscribers, reflects an opposition sentiment about equal to that of an approving kind.[7] This may be some evidence that gradually other influences and personalities are capturing the fancy of the public; it is possible that the pressure that I have felt over the past three or four months may gradually diminish instead of increase. If this should come about, it would, of course, be a complete answer to the question because, as we both know, I am never going to get tangled up in any kind of political activity unless forced to do so as the result of a genuine and deep conviction expressed by a very large segment of our people.

As I write this, I realize that there is very little that I can say in a letter either to you or to Milton that you do not already know. (Incidentally, I think I shall send a copy of this to Milton.) The only virtue in writing this way is to let you know that there has been no fundamental change in my thinking over the last several years because you both have known that I have always been ready to respond instantly to anything I saw as a clear duty. On the other hand, you both have known my complete lack of desire or ambition for any kind of political career. Both of you have emphatically agreed that, so long as I am compelled to be in uniform, it would be completely out of character and inappropriate for me to comment on the political scene. It happens that I am now assigned to the most delicate military task of my career; the need for singleness of purpose in serving the national interests is probably greater than ever before. Since it is clear that success in the task of establishing collective security by cooperative effort among the free nations is vital to the future of America, there must be nothing done that weakens the universality of American public support, so far as this can be achieved. Certainly we must prevent the tendency to consider this great project as a partisan, rather than a national, program.

It would, of course, always be a great satisfaction to me to talk to either or both of you. But I should say that there is no present crisis that would justify me in suggesting that either one of you should make a hurried trip in this direction.[8] The circumstances of this assignment require that I pursue the course that I have been pursuing for many months. If ever the time comes that I sense a crisis, then will be the time it will be necessary for me to see you both.

Regardless of any future personal possibilities, I am delighted that you, with the support of Pete and Cliff, are undertaking the study and analysis of some of our major questions of the day. You are really establishing a junior "American Assembly." All of us will unquestionably profit a lot from the results.[9]

Very confidentially, I shall probably be leaving here for a very brief visit to the United States this coming Friday evening. As of now, I hope to be able to go to Fort Knox to spend Saturday night and Sunday morning with our youngsters, after which I go to Washington for a day and a half of conferences respecting a number of vital problems affecting this job.[10] From there, I shall start immediately back to Europe, but (I have hinted of this to Cliff, but no one else knows about it) may stop a few hours in New York City in order that Mamie can go in and do a few things in the house that she wants to do. I personally may not even leave the airfield. In any event, if this comes about, I shall let you know so that a few of you, if available, could come out to the airport where we could have a chin. All this, of course, is still very much in the stage of mere possibility. *As ever*

---

[1] See the preceding document. Although dated October 31, Eisenhower's earlier note probably had been dictated on the thirtieth.

[2] With a letter to the General of October 21 (EM) Robinson had enclosed a copy of an October 19 letter (copy in EM, same file as document) he had written to his daughter Willma. Concerned with Eisenhower's political intentions and continuing reticence regarding the 1952 campaign, Robinson had outlined his own thinking on the General's qualifications for the presidency and on his need for silence until NATO was on a firm footing. Robinson told Willma that Eisenhower's candidacy was both "essential and inevitable" and that "a series of unforeseen events in the last ten years have added a priceless experience to the natural endowments of character and mind of this great American, who stands so well prepared in these critical times to give the nation the kind of leadership it so desperately needs." This letter apparently formed the basis for an October 25 *New York Herald Tribune* editorial endorsing Eisenhower for the 1952 Republican nomination (see the preceding document, n. 3) and for remarks made by Helen Reid at the closing of the 1951 *Herald Tribune* Forum (*New York Times*, Oct. 25, 1951; *International Herald Tribune*, Paris ed., Oct. 26, 1951. On the forum see no. 447).

[3] In his letter of the twenty-first Robinson had said that he had consulted with Eisenhower's brother Milton as the *Herald Tribune* moved toward public endorsement of the General. See also the following document.

[4] On Eisenhower's repeated use of this inset paragraph in responding to political inquiries see no. 358.

[5] See the preceding document, n. 3. Writing to Eisenhower on October 26 (EM), Robinson had said that he hoped the endorsing editorial did not cause the General "too much displeasure or irritation. . . . I can tell you that everyone here was always sensitive to the problems involved in your current work. That was why we stressed the point that we wanted no commitments or promises from you and, indeed, had none."

[6] On October 31 the *Herald Tribune* published an editorial explaining that the newspaper's endorsement had grown from the belief that an "under-surface feeling" for the General's nomination existed and that "those who shared this feeling should stand up and be counted" (*International Herald Tribune*, Paris ed., Oct. 31, 1951).

[7] The *Herald Tribune* of October 31 reported that it had received about as many letters opposing its position as supporting it and expressed gladness because "the very vigor of opposition is itself a tribute to the power of General Eisenhower's character and of what he stands for" and because "the real issues which the Republican party must face and decide provided it is to be victorious a year hence are not meanwhile going to go by bad compromises and default as they have so often done in the past."

[8] In his letter of the twenty-first Robinson had assured Eisenhower that he was "ready and eager" to fly to France "at a moment's notice" to consult with the General.

[9] To aid Eisenhower should he determine to run for the presidency, and to produce a series of articles for *Herald Tribune* syndication, Robinson had begun a project to examine "the various domestic issues which will come into daily discussion during the nomination and election campaigns" (Robinson to Eisenhower, Oct. 21, 1951, EM). Financed by Eisenhower's friends Clifford Roberts (see the preceding document) and Pete Jones (see no. 447), the study would survey the major issues of "Taxes, Labor Legislation, Agricultural Aid, Federal Aid to Education and Medicine, Housing, etc." On Columbia University's American Assembly see no. 438.

[10] On Eisenhower's brief trip to the United States, which would include a visit with his son John and his family at Fort Knox, Kentucky, see the following document.

To MILTON STOVER EISENHOWER   *October 31, 1951*
Confidential

Dear Milton: Last week Mamie and I foolishly took a week's vacation
in Scotland where, for those few days, we had a delightful and restful
time.[1] Nevertheless, I must call it foolish for the simple reason that,
since returning, I have not been able to approach catching up with the
volume of accumulated work. So far, I have been in my office ten
hours today; I am about to go home, with my accumulated papers
only slightly less voluminous than they were this morning.

At odd times during the past two days, I have succeeded in getting
off a fairly comprehensive and intelligent letter to Bill Robinson. In
that letter, I discussed some of the subjects that I wanted to discuss
with you, so I am enclosing herewith a copy. I know that you will
understand my reasons.[2]

If all goes well, I shall leave here late Friday evening for a quick
trip to the United States. I hope to spend Saturday afternoon and early
Sunday at Fort Knox with John and Barbie. Monday and Tuesday
morning I shall be in Washington; and, on Tuesday afternoon, will
take off for France. (All this, of course, is subject to change without
notice.)[3]

As of now, I have an engagement with General Clay for Monday
evening at my apartment in the Statler. I suspect that at that meeting
he wants to talk over some of the things that you and I have been
occasionally writing about.[4] If you could plan to be there, it would be
a great satisfaction to me. One of my assistants could call you on
Monday morning in plenty of time to let you know whether there has
been any enforced change in my program.[5]

If you find it inconvenient to come down, I shall, of course, understand; the favor I am asking is only to be granted in case it is absolutely convenient to you and your family. As of now, Mamie is counting on being with me, so if Helen could come along down, the two of
them would have a great get-together.

All this is confidential and no news of my impending visit will be
let out until it is announced at the White House. The basic reason for
the trip is pure business—I have to have a conference with officials in
Washington.[6]

With all the best to the entire family, *As ever*

P.S. If I fail to meet you, I shall write you a long letter after I
return here because there have been a few small developments of which
I think you are unaware.

[1] On the Eisenhowers' trip to Culzean Castle in Scotland see no. 442.
[2] See the two preceding documents.

[3] General and Mrs. Eisenhower, her mother Elivera Doud, and several SHAPE officials would leave Paris aboard the *Columbine* late the evening of Friday, November 2 (on Mrs. Doud see no. 40, n. 3). Before departing Orly airfield, Eisenhower met with W. Averell Harriman, newly appointed Director of the Mutual Security Agency. Because there had been a good deal of speculation regarding the political implications of Eisenhower's trip, he told reporters that the scheduled conferences with President Truman would be " 'strictly on the military aspects' of defense problems" (*New York Times*, Nov. 3, 1951. On Harriman see no. 424, n. 1). On November 3 reporters again confronted the General with questions during a brief stop in New York and on his arrival at Fort Knox, Kentucky, where the Eisenhowers would visit their son John and his family (*New York Times*, Nov. 4, 1951).

Soon after their arrival in Washington, D.C., on Sunday, November 4, the Eisenhowers called on Mrs. Eisenhower's sister and her family, the G. Gordon Moores. Later the General met with elder statesman Bernard M. Baruch at the Statler Hotel, where the Eisenhowers stayed (telegram, Baruch to Eisenhower, Nov. 2, 1951, EM. On Baruch see no. 25, n. 4; and on Mrs. Moore see no. 118, n. 2).

On Monday, November 5, Eisenhower visited a dentist at Walter Reed General Hospital before attending a luncheon meeting with President Truman (see no. 480, n. 2; and *New York Times*, Nov. 5, 1951). Later, at the Statler, the Eisenhowers saw Chief Justice Frederick Moore Vinson, Charles V. McAdam, Kevin C. McCann, the George E. Allens, the Arthur S. Nevinses, and Sid W. Richardson (*New York Times*, Nov. 6, 1951).

Eisenhower left Washington, D.C., following a meeting with NATO representatives and a press conference (see no. 486, n. 6). At La Guardia airport in New York Eisenhower met for several hours with his brother Milton, Philip Young, Clifford Roberts, William E. Robinson, Douglas M. Black, and Willis D. Crittenberger (see nos. 472, n. 2, and 489). The General faced reporters again on his arrival in France, where he reported that everything in his talks in the United States had been "strictly business" (see *New York Times*, Nov. 7, 8, 1951. See also EM, Subject File, Aircraft—SHAPE; and Trips, SHAPE no. 17. On Eisenhower's exasperation with the press see no. 474).

[4] Eisenhower would see General Lucius Clay in Washington, D.C., at breakfast on November 5 (telegram, Cannon to Clay, Oct. 25, 1951, EM). For developments as a result of the meeting with Clay see no. 561.

[5] Milton had written on October 13 (EM) that he and his wife Helen wished the General a happy birthday and that they hoped he would resolve to do whatever he wanted to after completing his NATO assignment. On October 20 Milton had written again, saying that he was sorry for the pressure on Eisenhower to declare himself a presidential candidate: "I know you would like to keep out of all this. . . . But that deep-seated sense of duty which was drilled into you must be causing you to suffer much anguish" (EM). Milton would make the trip to New York as his brother wished (see n. 3 above).

[6] The General's trip to the United States would not be announced until the day of his departure, November 2 (Memorandum for Record, n.d., EM, Subject File, Trips, SHAPE no. 17).

To Aksel Nielsen
Confidential

Dear Aksel:[1] I know you will forgive me for failing to give you a decent answer to the fine letters you have recently written me when I tell you that I am simply pushed beyond endurance.[2]

Much as I am complimented by Dan Thornton's confidence and readiness to support, I think he understands thoroughly how impossible it is for me to say anything definite while I am in this post. I have already given to you, in my letter of 15 October, the general tone of the answers I make to similar queries.[3] Of course, you are aware of the fact that, if ever any of these possibilities develop into what I consider to be a clear and unmistakable duty, then I shall shuck my uniform and go to work.

I still think you ought to come over here one of these days. You know how much I should like to come out to Denver but, even now as I am contemplating a week-end dash to the United States, I am making dates this minute for next Wednesday in my office here—so you can see how little time I have to indulge myself. I do hope to get in a few hours at Fort Knox to see the kids.[4] Something concerning this will be announced from Washington later. *As ever*

[1] Nielsen was a Denver, Colorado, business executive and a friend of the General's (see no. 34, n. 3).
[2] Nielsen's letters are in EM.
[3] Daniel I. J. Thornton, Governor of Colorado, was an Eisenhower supporter who wished to visit him in France (for background on Thornton see the General's letter of October 15, no. 440, n. 2; for developments see no. 600). For the General's current standard reply to political inquiries see no. 358, n. 3.
[4] Eisenhower's trip to the United States would include a visit with his son John and his family at Fort Knox, Kentucky (see no. 457, n. 3).

To Vincent Auriol

Dear President Auriol:[1] Only today I saw some extracts from the speech you made on the twentieth of October. May I express to you my very deep appreciation of the strong stand you took against subversive influences and in favor of America's purposes in cooperating with Europe. The problems facing SHAPE will be more easily solved because of your warm advocacy.[2]

Needless to say, I am highly complimented by the personal allusions contained in your talk. Thank you very much indeed.[3]

With assurances of my respectful regard, *Sincerely*

[1] For background on French President Auriol see no. 11, n. 4.

[2] In a memorandum of October 27 (EM) Eisenhower's adviser on international affairs, Douglas MacArthur II, had summarized Auriol's speech in honor of the hundredth birthday anniversary of Marshal Ferdinand Foch, French hero of World War I (on MacArthur see no. 32, n. 3; on the speech see *International Herald Tribune*, Oct. 22, 1951). According to MacArthur, Auriol had condemned anti-American propaganda, handbills, and posters "directed against a great and noble friendly people . . . who twice aided us in our struggle for liberation."

[3] Auriol had described Eisenhower as a great allied commander in chief, an "illustrious General who in the second World War led the armies of the free nations to victory."

460   *Eisenhower Mss.*

To Leonard V. Finder   *October 31, 1951*

Dear Leonard:[1] Having just returned from a brief vacation in Scotland, I found your letter on my desk this morning.[2] I am, of course, always grateful for the abundant news your letters contain and for the time you expend in writing.[3]

The Collier's article was as flattering as you could possibly make it—and your conclusions are most interesting! With one or two, at least, I disagree![4]

With warm regard, *Sincerely*

[1] Finder was a St. Louis, Missouri, businessman and a friend of the General's (see no. 351).

[2] On the Eisenhowers' vacation in Scotland see no. 442.

[3] On October 12 (EM) Finder had written a detailed letter on the U.S. political scene, characterizing Americans as being in a "state of low morale" and in need of the "tonic of fresh leadership."

[4] Finder had written again on October 23 (EM) to tell the General that he was sending a copy of his forthcoming article in *Collier's* magazine. "It might help the American people to understand your position," Finder said, "including the limitations placed upon you by your present office." Finder's piece described the General as "the outstanding political phenomenon of our times." Finder concluded that Eisenhower would accept the presidential nomination as his future responsibility—if the American people clearly made him their choice (Leonard V. Finder, "Why Ike *Will* Run," *Collier's*, November 3, 1951, 15-17). Finder would disagree that the article was flattering, describing it in his reply of November 17 (EM) as a "factual and accurate estimate of a distinguished American."

To Omar Nelson Bradley   *October 31, 1951*
Cable ALO 454. Top secret

Personal for General Bradley from General Eisenhower. No other distribution desired. Dear Brad,[1] As you are undoubtedly aware, I have recently had an exchange of telegrams with Secretary Lovett on the subject of MDAP deliveries, following which he dispatched General Olmsted to Paris to discuss further details of the matter with me and with my staff.[2]

After a review of the production and delivery schedules which Olmsted brought with him, it is apparent that unless some improvements in these schedules can be effected the NATO forces in being, as well as those to be built up during the coming year, will not achieve a state of combat effectiveness such as we had envisaged. A number of long-lead time items, including tanks, aircraft and communications equipment will continue in critical supply for some months ahead.[3] These items, as you know, are the backbone of our combat effectiveness.

As I understand the JCS policy regarding allocation of equipment, there are only 3 categories of activities which take priority over MDAP: (1) Korea; (2) Other operational requirements when specifically determined by the JCS; and, (3) Minimum US requirements for national security.[4]

I am in full accord with these general priorities. However, I am concerned over the manner in which the services may be interpreting the policy thus established. For example, according to the Army's projected allocations shown to me by General Olmsted, only about 100 of the 3600 odd medium tanks expected to be available for distribution during the first half of next year are destined for MDAP Europe, whereas approximately 1900 are allocated to meet US ZI[5] requirements. Yet, during the period in question there will be available to my command, either actually in being or deployable before D plus 30, at least 6 armored and 24 infantry divisions (exclusive of US and UK forces) already adequately trained, but the greater part of which, however, will still be equipped with only small training allowances of tanks. A somewhat similar situation is discernable with respect to other important major items in short supply.

These indications, to my mind, point to a situation whereby the JCS policy is probably being interpreted too rigidly resulting in the completing of many of our ZI requirements while our Allied Forces already trained and deployable to meet and stem the initial enemy attack in Europe continue on a training allowance basis. I am sure this situation is contrary to JCS intent.

It is apparent that at least part of the trouble arises from the fact that heretofore the allocations agencies of the JCS have not had available to them data as to which particular NATO units are fully trained and deployable and what specific major items are still in short supply for those units.[6] I am having this information compiled as a matter of urgency, from a combination of JAMAG and SHAPE sources, and it should be available to you within a week or 10 days.

In the meantime, since within the next few days I am to discuss a number of matters, including MDAP, with the President in Washington,[7] I would appreciate your help in looking into the JCS aspects of this problem to the end that we may between us, facilitate periodic prompt transmission to your allocations agencies of our urgent MDAP requirements for combat-ready units, and may insure treatment of these requirements in the priority they deserve as matters of special importance in the security of the United States. *Sincerely*

[1] Major General Cortlandt van Rensselaer Schuyler drafted this cable to JCS Chairman Bradley.

[2] Brigadier General George H. Olmsted (USMA 1922) served as Director of the Defense Department's Office of Military Assistance; earlier in the year he had been Chief of the MDAP mission to Yugoslavia. While visiting SHAPE, Olmsted also conferred with Colonel George A. Lincoln, special assistant to the Secretary of Defense and defense adviser to W. Averell Harriman, and other U.S. staff members assigned to the NATO Temporary Council Committee. Eisenhower and his staff earlier had met with another set of defense officials studying MDAP (see U.S., Department of Defense, "Activities in Europe Concerned with Materiel Support of NATO and MDAP," Oct. 5, 1951, in OS/D, 1951, Clas. Decimal File, CD 092.3 NATO).

[3] By the end of June 1951, besides aircraft and ships delivered under their own power, U.S. shipments under MDAP included 4,480 tanks and other combat vehicles, 2,930 artillery pieces, 18,837 general-purpose vehicles, 400,000 small arms and machine guns, and various quartermaster supplies. More than half the total of 1.6 million measurement tons had gone to Western Europe. Yet of $5.22 billion appropriated for fiscal year 1951, the United States actually shipped only about $1.2 billion worth of equipment (Huston, *One for All*, p. 50; see also Kaplan, *Community of Interests*, p. 156).

On October 27 Lincoln, with the concurrence of General McNarney of the Temporary Council Committee's screening and costing staff and U.S. representatives at SHAPE, had cabled Secretary of Defense Lovett that "initial appraisal of information on MDAP deliveries provided by General Olmsted is gravely disturbing" in terms of both TCC and SHAPE programs for speeding up the achievement of combat strength. Lincoln believed that the individual country reports to the TCC, beginning November 5, would disclose serious problems of U.S. end-item deliveries. By the time the United States made its own report it would be essential to make specific clarifying statements. He argued that the statements "should show US willingness to relate priorities and allocations to the developing military capabilities in NATO countries on basis of recommendations principally from SHAPE on (1) priorities of units related to strategic plan of the command, (2) realistic programs and commitments of European NATO countries to bring units receiving equipment to combat readiness, (3) similar realistic programs and commitments which generate requirements for training equipment preliminary to raising to combat readiness." The Lincoln report noted "slippage in production" and blamed the Korean War and increased U.S. mobilization for the high demand on U.S. military production. "US programming for MDAP," Lincoln wrote, "seems to have been on a basis keyed primarily to European national commitments of forces for mid-1954; rather than the SHAPE and TCC concept of the most rapid practicable build up of balanced effective combat forces . . ." (Lincoln to Lovett *et al.*, Oct. 27, 1951, EM).

All these problems would become more complicated in the event that the Allies rearmed Germany, Lincoln had pointed out. At about this time a separate memorandum for Bradley also discussed this subject. Although the Germans could produce the equipment required for arming ten of their own divisions, the study concluded, political considerations would probably preclude German production of tanks and artillery, which U.S. stocks could fill only by late 1954 based on optimistic estimates. "Total known NATO requirements for U.S. military assistance cannot be realized through currently approved production programs," the memorandum had stated. "The amount of equipment furnished the Germans will ultimately depend on the supply priority established for the Germans within NATO" (*ibid.*; J. E. Hull to Bradley, Oct. 23, 1951, CJCS, Bradley Files, 092.2 North Atlantic Treaty [Oct. 1951]).

The gap between promised U.S. military assistance to NATO countries and actual deliveries would continue to exist. The Army was able to disburse only $2.89 billion of the $8.3 billion available through December 1952. The Army's share of MDAP shipments, three quarters of the total, would amount to about 5 million measurement tons, compared with 25 million tons sent to Korea by that time (Huston, *One for All*, p. 50. For another view of the same issue, demonstrating that the FY 1950 and 1951 MDA programs should have brought approximately twenty-eight divisions up to full strength, see G. C. Stewart to Olmsted, Nov. 7, 1951, OS/D, 1951, Clas. Decimal File, 091.3 MDAP [General]).

[4] Eisenhower overlooked one claim on U.S. military equipment: in December 1950 the JCS had placed a priority on MDAP shipments to the French in Indochina second only to support of U.S. forces fighting in Korea (Frank C. Nash to Lovett, Sept. 20, 1951, OS/D, 1951, Clas. Decimal File 091.3 MDAP [Indochina]; Kaplan, *Community of Interests*, pp. 117–18).

[5] Zone of the Interior, or the continental United States.

[6] Lincoln described the present U.S. system of "block priorities" as no longer applicable. "We now have, in SHAPE," he had written, "an agency capable of developing the judgments and presenting recommendations which permit the most effective and economical use of our limited resources on basis of applying them where they best contribute within the SHAPE command" (Lincoln to Lovett *et al.*, Oct. 27, 1951, EM).

[7] Eisenhower would meet with President Truman the afternoon of November 5. On the General's brief U.S. visit see nos. 457 and 468.

462

Eisenhower Mss.

To ROBERT ABERCROMBIE LOVETT
Cable ALO 455. Top secret

October 31, 1951

Personal for Secretary Lovett from General Eisenhower. No other distribution desired. Dear Bob: Your cable of 21 October and General Olmsted's visit have been most helpful.[1] We now have a far fuller understanding of the many complicating factors which are involved in the problem of MDAP equipment deliveries. I have discussed these matters with Averell, and share his concern with regard to the impact that the delay resulting from presently planned delivery schedules will have on our overall NATO objectives, our position in the TCC, and the SHAPE concept for developing balanced and effective combat forces here in Europe at the most rapid rate that is practicable.[2]

As a result of his discussions here, Olmsted is entirely familiar with our views. He understands fully, I believe, our particular concern that certain essential training equipment is not yet forthcoming and also that a number of our Allied units, long after they are fully trained and ready for deployment to meet the initial onslaught of an aggressor, will, under present schedules, because of serious shortages of tanks, aircraft, communications equipment and certain other major items, in point of fact have only a limited combat effectiveness.[3] In this latter respect, the problem seems to be largely one of a too-rigid application by service agencies of broadly stated JCS policy guidance. I am cabling Bradley on this matter today, and hope he will have no difficulty in straightening it out. At the same time we are taking urgent steps at this end to insure that JCS allocations agencies will henceforth have better detailed information as to those serious shortages which are in fact significantly limiting the effectiveness of our otherwise battleworthy units.

These steps, together with the closer liaison with your MDAP staff which we have now established, offer promise of alleviating at least the more pressing of our MDAP troubles. I would wish, of course, that we could anticipate an early and substantial increase in overall military production, but I understand fully the obstacles to the achievement of this desirable goal. Again, my sincere thanks for your prompt and energetic efforts in our behalf. *Sincerely*

[1] On Olmsted see the preceding document. In his cable Secretary of Defense Lovett had acknowledged an earlier message from SHAPE discussing "the possibility of serious delays developing in the rate of future deliveries of military equipment under Foreign Aid Programs" (Lovett to Eisenhower, Oct. 21, 1951, DEF 84727, EM, Lovett Corr.).

[2] W. Averell Harriman, Chairman of the TCC, then meeting in Paris, had recently been named Director of the U.S. Mutual Security Program. In his October 21 cable Lovett had outlined the gravity of the situation: the United States, while fighting a war in Korea, had begun to build up its own forces and those of NATO and other allies "to a military strength capable of coping with Soviet imperialism, all within the framework of a limited mobilization effort which seeks to avoid so far as possible such drastic dislocations of the US economy as might, and probably would, curtail the Foreign Aid Program as the first area offering politically attractive cuts." Lovett further discussed problems of retooling, lengthy and costly work stoppages, and "the tendency on the part of some of our producers and suppliers

to string out their present contracts against the fear that after the present enormous budget Congress will cut down appropriations in a presidential election year." Lovett explained that he supported the policy of limited mobilization, but he admitted that "there will be definite limitations on the extent to which we can take on new commitments or will be able to accelerate the meeting of commitments already undertaken." On MDAP deliveries in particular Lovett wrote, "I have endeavored to keep myself informed of any reports that delays in the delivery of promised equipment have retarded the pace of mobilization effort of the NATO countries. . . . To date I have received none, although it is altogether possible there have been some that have not been brought to my attention" (*ibid.*).

[3] Olmsted had collaborated on a long message that Colonel George A. Lincoln and other U.S. military and mutual aid officials had sent Lovett four days earlier (see the preceding document).

463

To William H. Burnham

Dear Bill:[1] So that it may not slip my mind, I am attempting now— some twenty days in advance of your final relief from this office—to make an official record of my appreciation for your services.[2]

In the tangled, complicated situation that presented itself to us almost a year ago when we came to Europe, one of the most difficult factors was that involving the economic and financial situation of the various countries of Europe. In taking the lead, for me, in presenting an appropriate picture of each country in simple and readily under-standable form, you have been outstandingly valuable to me and to all the rest of my staff. In dozens of ways, you have made yourself unob-trusively but almost indispensably valuable in the handling of ques-tions that seemed to have no obvious home in the established sections of the staff.

This record, together with the facts that you came to this headquar-ters voluntarily and at a very considerable financial sacrifice to your-self, comprise some of the reasons for my official gratitude. Add to all this the satisfaction of having near me a warm and personal friend, and you can understand something of the regret I feel in the realization that the time has come for you to leave. To this I would never agree except for the fact that your months of work have established practices and procedures that should now keep us fairly well abreast of the information available in the civilian sections of the American organi-zations in Europe, and your own voluntary offer to return if at any time we should again find ourselves in a position of acute need for your special qualities.[3]

The members of my personal and official staff, as well as I, will miss you. All of us wish you Godspeed and good luck. *Cordially*

[1] For background on Eisenhower's friend Burnham see no. 40.

[2] For several months Burnham had been working at SHAPE as an economic analyst and adviser on U.S. issues (see nos. 331, n. 4, and 449, n. 11).

[3] After meeting with the General in March and April, Burnham had offered to examine the administration of European aid and to compile economic profiles on European nations for Eisenhower (see memorandums, Burnham to Eisenhower, May 29 and June 22, 1951, EM. On Burnham's decision to join SHAPE see Galambos, *Columbia University*, no. 1159; and on his visits to Eisenhower see in these volumes nos. 102 and 128, n. 6). In a letter of October 29 (EM) Burnham, who had taken leave from his position as a partner in F. S. Smithers and Company, a New York investment firm, had told Eisenhower that working for him had been a "distinguished honor." For developments in Eisenhower's relationship with Burnham see no. 626.

464   *Eisenhower Mss.*

To Arthur Hendrick Vandenberg, Jr.   *November 2, 1951*

Dear Mr. Vandenberg:[1] Insofar as my knowledge goes, I think that Milton Hill's memorandum to you gives a fairly accurate account of the incident to which he refers. However, I was never informed as to who gave out the distorted report of my conversation at the F Street Club. Senator Vandenberg offered to tell me and I asked him not to, saying that I was not interested.[2]

As to the message that Mr. Hill has reconstructed, I can only say that his language conforms rather accurately to the Senator's, although I am still unable to say whether it came in written or verbal form. Moreover, either on the telephone or in the original message, the Senator also offered to make his public statement, if I should so desire, regardless of my own silence regarding the matter.

Copies of his letter of September 8, 1949, and of my reply are enclosed.[3] I appreciate your suggestion that sources of information be kept confidential, because I most certainly do not want to get into the position of having to argue about something now that I refused to argue about at the time of its occurrence. This you can well understand.[4]

With personal regard, *Sincerely*

[1] Vandenberg, son of the longtime Michigan Republican senator, was editing his late father's papers for publication (see no. 435).

[2] Writing on October 29 (EM), Vandenberg had thanked Eisenhower for his cooperation and shed further light on a four-year-old incident at the F Street Club in Washington, D.C. (see no. 435), involving Eisenhower and Senators Taft and Vandenberg. The junior Vandenberg enclosed a report he had received from the Washington bureau chief for Federated Publications, Inc., Milt Dean Hill, in which Hill testified that after the F Street dinner Taft gave three Washington

correspondents a sheet of typewritten remarks that Eisenhower allegedly had made; one of them was a pledge to impose a "100 percent tax on profits if I were president" (see EM, Vandenberg Corr.). Hill had corroborated Senator Vandenberg's offer to correct the story publicly and to name Taft as the person responsible for the canard, which Eisenhower typically ignored (see, for example, no. 163). "There are aspects of the incident which probably will not seem in good taste to use in my book but I am inclined to believe that a reference to the meeting and my father's desire to correct the false public report of your remarks at the meeting, would be an interesting and useful episode in the political phase of the story I am attempting to tell. If you have any comments on Milt's recollections of the event, I will be most happy to have them."

[3] On the letter see Galambos, *Columbia University*, no. 542; and Arthur H. Vandenberg, *The Private Papers of Senator Vandenberg*, ed. Arthur H. Vandenberg, Jr. (Boston, 1952), pp. 473–76.

[4] Vandenberg would include the story (see *ibid.*, pp. 423–24).

465

To Cornelis Staf

Dear Mr. Minister:[01] I understand from Mr. Harriman, Chairman of the NATO Temporary Council Committee, that according to present plans the Executive Bureau of the Temporary Council Committee will meet during the next fortnight with appropriate government representatives of the Netherlands with the objective of reviewing with them the Dutch defense effort.[2] I assume that you or one of your principal assistants will be among your country's representatives.

The review, as I understand it, is to be a most important step in TCC work toward the overall improvement of our defense effort. It will aim at highlighting, for further study and analysis those problems in the defense effort the solution of which would provide greater military effectiveness at minimum cost.

I feel that this operation is a very important one to our common purpose since it seems certain to result in concerted action programs for increased military effectiveness and security. Indicative of this importance, the North Atlantic Council, in setting up the Temporary Council Committee, stated its desire that all possible help be given by NATO agencies. For these reasons I and my staff have, in every way possible, been assisting the work of the TCC and its agencies. Many of the problems upon which their study may be most valuable are exactly the problems with which SHAPE has been concerned over the past ten months, and with which we have gained a considerable degree of familiarity through conversations with your military authorities.

In this connection, I am hoping that the joint reviews with the TCC will help us materially toward a solution of the problem of providing equipment for the Dutch divisions for maneuvers in 1952, which was the subject of your letter to me of October 29th.[3]

As your representatives prepare for the review of these problems with the Executive Bureau, I want you to know that I and my staff stand ready to assist and support you in any way possible before, during or after the meeting. We are most grateful for the high degree of cooperation which you have afforded us in our joint effort to build up defensive strength, and we have so informed Mr. Harriman's committee. We will welcome the opportunity to help your representatives to the limit of our abilities.[4]

Please accept my warm personal regards and be assured that I am looking forward to our continued close collaboration in the furtherance of our joint NATO defense effort.[5] *Sincerely*

[1] Staf had succeeded Hendrik s'Jacob (see no. 14) as Netherlands Defense Minister in March. He had previously served as Director General of Agriculture and Chairman of the Agricultural Organization for Applied Scientific Research. On this day Eisenhower sent a similar message to several other NATO defense ministers (see letters to Joseph Bech of Luxembourg, Georges Bidault of France, Édouard De Greef of Belgium, Jens Hauge of Norway, Randolfo Pacciardi of Italy, and Harold Petersen of Denmark, all in EM).

[2] For background on the TCC and Harriman's role in it see nos. 384, n. 1, 416, n. 1, and 424, n. 1. On this day Eisenhower met with Harriman at Paris's Orly Airport shortly before the General's flight to the United States (see *New York Times*, Nov. 3, 1951).

[3] Staf's letter, with enclosures, is in OS/D, 1951, Clas. Decimal File, CD 091.3 MDAP (Netherlands). He had informed Eisenhower that the Dutch government would face internal political difficulties if it attempted to form additional divisions without the necessary American-supplied equipment. Staf was willing to begin training these new units with only half of the required equipment, but he stated that the Dutch divisions would have to receive all of the scheduled items before they could participate in the September 1952 maneuvers. For background on the Dutch rearmament effort see no. 15; for developments see no. 677.

[4] The TCC's Executive Bureau would meet with representatives of each NATO country from November 5 through November 16. These informal conferences considered such problems as military policy, infrastructure (see no. 255, n. 2), defense production, and economic matters. Harriman later would inform Washington that there had "been a high degree of cooperation and mutuality of approach throughout" (State, *Foreign Relations, 1951*, vol. III, *European Security and the German Question, Part I*, pp. 346–47, 360).

[5] We have been unable to locate any reply to this letter, but see Pacciardi to Eisenhower, November 8, 1951, and Bidault to Eisenhower, November 10, 1951, both in EM. For further developments regarding the TCC see no. 542.

To Ellis Dwinnell Slater

Eisenhower Mss.

November 2, 1951

Dear Slats:[1] Thank you for sending me copies of letters you have recently received. I am particularly delighted with the lucidity of the explanation you gave to your friend "Biggie."[2] Sometimes I wonder why so few people take the trouble to inform themselves accurately on the fundamentals of our great domestic and foreign problems. After all, during the past many months, we have been pouring billions of dollars, at home and abroad, into the security effort. It seems to me that each of us should be interested enough in the purpose of such expenditures to find out such things as their basic necessity, their objectives, and our chances of success. I am delighted to see that you are helping in spreading some facts about such matters.

It never bothers me to find that others disagree with my own conclusions, provided always that on both sides we have taken the trouble to dig out a factual basis on which to present our arguments. I get tired of demagoguery and obvious prejudice—never of honest differences of opinion. In fact, except for this kind of difference of opinion, democracy would be a pale and inefficient thing at the best.

You can well imagine how much I would like to join you and the others at the twenty-year celebration. I think one of the greatest of the disappointments I suffered when I realized that again I had to come back to military duty was when I faced up to the knowledge that I would be denied the opportunity of meeting with my friends at Blind Brook, Augusta National, and so on.[3] Maybe someday I can pick up those threads again.

There is just a faint chance that I may see you even before you get this letter. If not, you will at least know that I wanted to arrange a brief meeting as I come through New York with you, Cliff, Bill, and some of the others.[4]

In the meantime, all the best. *Cordially*

---

[1] For background on Slater, a business executive and friend of Eisenhower's, see no. 59.

[2] Slater had written on October 26, enclosing copies of his recent letters to Russell Bangs Stearns (A.B. University of Michigan 1916), president and director of the National Food Products Corporation since 1938, and Walter F. ("Biggie") Wylie (EM, Slater Corr.). On October 17 Slater had written to Wylie, his brother-in-law, who lived in Glencoe, Illinois, that Stalin "looks with envy on everything Western Europe has to offer" and that collective security provided the only means of stopping Soviet aggression. "Our natural resources . . . and our American way of life brought this country to a place of leadership in the world," Slater had said, "and leadership requires the assumption of responsibility. Our responsibility today is to see that the Stalin crowd are stopped dead in their tracks."

[3] The Augusta National Golf Club would celebrate its twentieth anniversary on November 17 (see no. 500). On the Blind Brook Club and the General's friends there see Galambos, *Columbia University*, no. 834.
[4] On Eisenhower's trip to the United States see no. 457. The General would see Clifford Roberts and William E. Robinson briefly in New York (see nos. 470 and 471).

467 *Eisenhower Mss.*

To René Pleven *November 2, 1951*

Dear Mr. Pleven:[1] I am extremely sorry that I will not be able to call upon you before leaving on my trip to the United States.[2] However, before departing, I wanted to assure you of my realization of the difficulties you face with respect to the French-dollar problem. Mr. Guillaume Guindey of the French Treasury discussed this matter with me yesterday.[3]

During our conversation, it occurred to me that this problem could be alleviated to a considerable extent if the legal and contractual arrangements for the infrastructure program can be quickly cleared away. This program entails the direct expenditure of substantial US funds in France. Moreover, the arrival of additional US forces, which is dependent upon completion of the numerous facilities required, will provide another source of dollar revenue. Hence, anything you can do to expedite the infrastructure program will not only contribute to NATO objectives but will, I am sure, assist in solving the French dollar problem.[4]

It seems to me that this possibility may have real value in terms of the difficult French financial situation.

With warmest personal regards, *Sincerely*

[1] Pleven was French Prime Minister. General Gruenther drafted this letter for Eisenhower.
[2] Eisenhower left France this evening for a brief visit to the United States that included a meeting with President Truman (see no. 457).
[3] On Thursday, November 1, Eisenhower had lunched with Guindey, French Inspector of Finance, who along with other French officials faced a serious fiscal year deficit. According to a U.S. report, at the end of 1951 Western Europe generally suffered the economic consequences of a sudden defense build-up, but the "most serious trouble remained in France." The French were paying more for imports (having imported $100 million worth of coal); meanwhile, a drop in exports, the diverting of resources to defense production, a manpower drain into the armed forces, and the monetary impact of defense spending all combined to place severe upward pressure on wages and prices. The French government complained that U.S. assistance to Europe neglected civilian economic needs; at the same time,

France appealed for funds to help finance the costly Indochina war (Mutual Security Agency, *First Report*, p. 9). For background on accounting procedures under the Marshall Plan and Mutual Defense Assistance Program see no. 68, n. 5; on the shift from U.S. economic to military aid see Ismay, *NATO*, pp. 136–37. For the impact of the Indochina conflict on French strength in NATO see nos. 539, n. 7, and 552; and *New York Times*, November 11, 14, 1951.

[4] At its September meeting in Ottawa the NAC had established a system of cost sharing (thereafter including the United States) to finance the second annual increment, or "slice," of fixed installations ("infrastructure") necessary for NATO military deployment and operations. The alliance necessarily would construct a large number of these facilities in France (see nos. 255 and 384, n. 1; Ismay, *NATO*, pp. 114–24; and *International Herald Tribune*, Paris ed., Sept. 22, 1951).

468   *Eisenhower Mss.*

To ALFRED MAXIMILIAN GRUENTHER   *November 5, 1951*
Cable. Top secret. Personal

In mixed groups meeting with President[1] much interest was evidenced in coal question.[2] Please check with Harriman for data reference cost[3] of coal on dock in United States as against selling cost to consumer in France and inform Lovett by wire including any pertinent facts you might have. Point was discussed at length in connection with filling French shortage. Foster[4] stated limitation on coal is both financial and physical. He feels Germans and British could produce more. Wilson[5] indicated plan to furnish British with steel ingots to save coal. New subject. Priorities and allocations problem well received but reaction of Army a bit disappointing.[6] Discussion with Pace and Collins[7] later in Collins office indicates we have a real problem in tank field due to production failing to meet requirements. Our tank figures accurate, so much so that instead of getting 100 in first half of 1952 we were told we get none.[8] It will be a cold winter. New subject. Plan to leave here noon tomorrow stopping at La Guardia leaving there before 1700 for Paris.

[1] Eisenhower, who had traveled to the United States for a brief visit, met with President Truman and other Administration officials the afternoon of November 5 (see no. 457). This cable carried a *No Foreigners* restriction.

[2] Earlier in October French Premier René Pleven had expressed the view that unnecessarily high U.S. shipping costs had driven up the European price for coal and thus worsened French inflation (for background see nos. 434, n. 2, and 467, n. 3; and State, *Foreign Relations, 1951*, vol. IV, *Europe: Political and Economic Developments, Part I*, pp. 139–46).

[3] "Data reference cost" means data with reference to the cost, that is, cost data.

[4] William C. Foster, Deputy Secretary of Defense and former Administrator for Economic Cooperation (see no. 222, n. 2).

Charles E. Wilson, Director of the Office of Defense Mobilization (see no. 45, n. 4).

The reference here is to the problems plaguing U.S. military aid to the European NATO countries, including the conflict between needs in Europe and those in Korea (see nos. 461 and 462).

Frank Pace, Jr., Secretary of the Army, and General J. Lawton Collins, Army Chief of Staff.

According to a recent report on the availability of U.S. tanks for German rearmament, about 400 M-24's would be available by late 1952, and another 800 would be available in early 1953. The M-26 would make its appearance by late 1952, with about 950 ready for shipment in early 1953. "There are available, and suitable for training, 900 M18 (76mm) tank destroyers and 1000 M4A3 (105mm) tanks," the paper had stated. "These latter would require 9–12 months for rebuild prior to delivery. The M4A3 (76mm) and M4A3 (75mm) will probably not be available for German use inasmuch as they are committed to active Army demands" (Hull to Bradley, Oct. 23, 1951, CJCS, Bradley Files, 092.2 North Atlantic Treaty [Oct. 1951]).

In his talks with Truman Eisenhower expressed great concern over the low rate of MDAP deliveries, prompting the President to direct all participants "to improve the system of allocations so that General Eisenhower got his equipment on the same parity band as U.S. Divisions subject, however, to the over-riding priority given to Korea." Truman "felt that those who would have to fight first should get the equipment first." At a cabinet meeting in December, after the President learned of $10 billion remaining in unexpended, although obligated, funds for Western Europe rearmament, he accused the three services of "contracting for MDAP but taking the end items for themselves, if it suited them." He again ordered concerned officials, including Secretary of State Acheson and Secretary of Defense Lovett, to pay "special attention" to U.S. obligations under MDAP and MSA to the defense of Western Europe. Truman reminded them of the pledges he had made during Eisenhower's visit (Lovett memorandum, Dec. 21, 1951, OS/D, 1951, Clas. Decimal File, 091.3 MDAP [General]; memorandum, July 17, 1951, Records of the Assistant Secretary of Defense for International Security Affairs, ONATA Subject File 1949–53).

469   *Eisenhower Mss.*

To Dale Dixon Hull   *November 8, 1951*

Dear Dale:[1] Thank you for your letter of the 2nd. I saw my godchild at the Washington Airport but, because I was just about to take off, I had no real chance to visit with her.[2] However, our picture was taken together by a whole gang of photographers, and it is faintly possible that you will see it in one of the newspapers. If not, it should still be possible for your dad to find a few copies by appealing to the Army's Pictorial Section in General Parks' office.[3]

I have finished the little painting and shall send it home at the earliest opportunity. If you are expecting an artist's production, you will, of course, be badly disappointed; but, on the other hand, if you are expecting nothing more than what an old soldier would do, maybe you will like it a little bit.[4]

Your parents told me about your success in passing the big examination—Mamie joins me in our warmest congratulations and in our hopes for your future.[5] *Cordially*

[1] Hull was the former Dale Dixon Sayler, who had been married to Major John Bowler Hull (for background see no. 427).

[2] Hull's four-year-old daughter Diane was Eisenhower's godchild. The November 2 letter is not in EM. On the General's visit to the United States see no. 457.

[3] General Henry B. and Jessie D. Sayler were Hull's parents (see no. 376). Major General Floyd L. Parks was Chief of the Army's Information Department (see no. 426).

[4] Eisenhower was working on a portrait of Diane D. Hull, which he would send at Christmas (see Eisenhower to Hull, Dec. 18, 1951, EM). On the General's enjoyment of painting see no. 353.

[5] Hull had taken the New York Stock Exchange exam in order to become an account executive with the stock brokerage firm of Merrill Lynch, Pierce, Fenner and Beane in Savannah, Georgia (see Hull to Eisenhower, Sept. 27, 1951, EM).

470

Eisenhower Mss.

To William Edward Robinson

November 8, 1951

Dear Bill:[1] I am not certain that I made much sense when I was talking to you and Cliff the other day.[2] I had just come through a rather strenuous experience and I suppose that my temper had not completely returned to normal.[3] In any event, I hope that I was clear enough so that you could understand what seems to me to be the logic of my position.

Incidentally, I occasionally receive requests from prominent publishers asking me to recommend to my brother Milton that he talk to them about the general political philosophy in which the Eisenhower brothers believe (at least four of us).[4] I assume that you would approve of his doing this. However, I send it to you as a query because I certainly don't want to appear to you to be false to my first loyalty.

You said something the other day about the amount of time that would be consumed if I should attempt to explain myself constantly to correspondents who write to me on serious public questions. You more or less hinted that friends should not need explanations and, therefore, I should not spend myself too much on this kind of thing. This suggested to me that, on those occasions when I do write a long letter dealing with any question of some concern to the public—NATO or otherwise—I might make a few copies for mailing simultaneously to intimate friends. Occasionally I find it is a good thing to attempt to write a fairly long letter about bothersome questions, because the effort of organizing the idea so that a friend can understand it helps to clarify it in my own mind.

Quite naturally, such an idea as this would not include anything that was confidential on a personal basis. My first thought was primarily of you, Cliff, and Milton; but it could be expanded at times to include others.[5]

I cannot tell you how appreciative I was of the trouble you took to come out to LaGuardia. For me it was old home week to see you and Cliff and Milton, all at the same time. Your visit must have done much to calm me down because that night I had the first full night's sleep that I enjoyed since leaving Europe. *As ever*

[1] Robinson was executive vice-president of the *New York Herald Tribune*.

[2] In New York City on November 6, while Mamie Eisenhower visited the Columbia University president's house at Morningside Heights to pick up some items left in storage, the General remained on the *Columbine* at La Guardia Airport for a three-hour meeting with political advisers Robinson, Clifford Roberts, Milton Eisenhower, Philip Young (see no. 8), and Douglas M. Black (see no. 168) to discuss a possible Eisenhower presidential campaign. The meeting marked another step forward in the movement to "draft" Eisenhower. On the formation of a political advisory group and the naming of a campaign manager later in the month see the following document and no. 486; Robinson to Eisenhower, November 15, 1951, EM; *New York Times*, November 7, 1951; and Ambrose, *Eisenhower*, vol. I, *Soldier, General of the Army, President-Elect*, pp. 517–18.

[3] Eisenhower's day had included a breakfast session with old friend and spokesman Lucius D. Clay, an afternoon meeting with President Truman, and merciless questioning by Washington reporters. Immediately following the meeting with Truman, rumors circulated that the President had urged Eisenhower to run as a Democrat to succeed him (see no. 480); in fielding reporters' questions the General made a reply he later sought to correct (see no. 486).

[4] Eisenhower and his brothers Arthur, Edgar, and Milton often agreed politically; Earl Eisenhower did not always do so (see Kornitzer, *The Great American Heritage*, pp. 107–15, 276–300). On Arthur H. Sulzberger's support for a plan by which Milton would disclose the General's recent voting preferences see no. 473. Robinson later described Milton as "better fitted" than any of the other Eisenhower brothers to deal with political queries (Nov. 15, 1951, EM).

[5] See n. 2 above.

471

Eisenhower Mss.

To Clifford Roberts

November 8, 1951

Dear Cliff:[1] When I returned to my office, I found your two notes of October 31. I agree with your observation that things are moving much faster than we had anticipated—certainly much faster than I ever thought was even possible. Also, I agree that the kind of little personal advisory group that we several times discussed seems to be growing into more and more of a necessity to me. I find that my time and my mind are both too jammed up with so many different types of subjects for me to think through any complicated item. I wonder whether you would do me the favor of suggesting the names of a group that could and would be helpful in this regard, and suggesting also your ideas of how and when they should meet. Quite naturally, some would always necessarily be absent, but the body as a whole would certainly represent cross-section thinking among my friends.[2]

Incidentally, as I see it, this whole group would be completely independent of whatever political group might organize itself around the idea of forcing me into the political picture—at this instant, at least, I am thinking more of a personal group that would take a hard-headed look at the propriety, decency, and desirability of any proposition that might affect me personally.[3]

It would be difficult for me to tell you how deeply touched I was by your thoughtfulness in arranging to get Milton up to New York on Tuesday. While it was completely typical of the kindliness that has always distinguished your friendship, still it was such a pleasant surprise that I cannot help making special mention of it. Incidentally, I shall write Barry Leithead instantly to tell him of my gratitude.[4]

By the time this note reaches the States, you will probably be in Augusta. Consequently, I realize that any renewal of an invitation to come over here will be delivered to you under circumstances that will probably inspire a hearty laugh, because I certainly have nothing to offer to compete with that heavenly spot.[5] But at least you know how much Mamie and I consider you practically as one of the family—as a result, we may be more demanding than we should.

Please give my very best to Ed Dudley, Mrs. Harris, Bowman, Eddie, and Cadillac. Also, if Cemetery is still on the caddie list, tell him that I am looking forward to the time I can again go around the Augusta National with him as my chief supervisor.[6] *Cordially*

P.S. Just this minute, I have picked up your memorandum enclosing the clippings concerning the anticipated "buyer's market." This note is just to say that not only do I trust your judgment in all these matters, but to make sure of your understanding that, if you consider it better to avoid pre-Christmas purchasing for my youngsters, I could always give them, this year, a check that they could put temporarily into a savings account and which they could later invest when you told them to do so. In other words, while I want to make certain that the year does not expire without making my legal sized gift to them, I do not want to appear to be overriding your judgment as to the time of actual investment.[7]

P.P.S. Thanks for the cigarette boxes. They came just this minute!

[1] Roberts, a New York investment banker, was a close friend of Eisenhower's.

[2] Both letters of October 31 from Roberts are in EM. The first, typewritten, reported on a query that golfer "Bobby" Jones had made to Roberts on the wisdom of joining the Eisenhower-for-President movement. In his reply, in which he described Eisenhower supporters as "decent folks," Roberts assured Jones that Eisenhower was beyond the point of further embarrassment as a public figure and said that the General could not possibly take offense at Jones's thinking he would make a good President.

A second letter, this one handwritten, concerned the formation of a personal advisory group to consider U.S. political and economic developments as they related to Eisenhower's political future. Roberts urged the General to confine the group to intimate associates, "none of whom would be politicians or seekers of political honors," and asked for a list of friends who might be invited to participate. Eisenhower had earlier agreed that Milton Eisenhower and William E. Robinson should belong to such a group.

[3] For Eisenhower's additional reply to the suggestion about an advisory group see the preceding document and no. 503.

[4] Roberts and Barry T. Leithead had arranged for Milton Eisenhower to visit the General at La Guardia Airport on November 6 shortly before his return flight to Paris (see the preceding document, n. 2).

[5] Eisenhower sent this letter to Augusta National Golf Club, Augusta, Georgia, where Roberts was staying. Roberts would visit Eisenhower in Paris in December 1951 (see no. 528).

[6] Ed Dudley was a golf professional at Augusta National Golf Club; Helen N. Harris was the club's office manager (for background on Dudley and Harris see Galambos, *Columbia University*). Bowman Milligan had been the steward at Augusta since the club's opening in 1932. Eddie Motta was a waiter, and Cadillac, a chauffeur. Willie Frank ("Cemetery") Parteet was a favorite caddy of Eisenhower's (see letter from Maureen Juwig, Executive Secretary, August National Golf Club, Augusta, Georgia, Dec. 16, 1985, EP).

[7] Roberts frequently advised Eisenhower on investment opportunities.

472   *Eisenhower Mss.*

To Barry T. Leithead   *November 8, 1951*

Dear Barry:[1] I am sure that you must have some idea of the depth of my appreciation of your kindness in sending my brother to New York the other day to see me.[2]

Whenever some of the Communist papers or the McCormick press[3] make some particularly vicious accusations concerning my stupidity, wickedness, or just plain uselessness, I have the comforting reflection that no man was ever blessed with warmer and better friends than I have been. I am sorry that I did not get to see you to thank you in person.

Cliff, Bill,[4] and my brother—and, a little later, two or three other friends—all came to visit me in my airplane which sat on the field at

LaGuardia for about two or three hours. We had a big time, but no bridge game.

With my very best to you and yours, *Cordially*

[1] For background on Leithead see no. 217, n. 2.

[2] Leithead apparently had helped arrange transportation on November 6 for Eisenhower's brother Milton from Pennsylvania State College, Pennsylvania, to La Guardia Airport in New York City, where the Eisenhowers had stopped briefly on their return flight to Paris (on Eisenhower's trip see no. 457; see also *New York Times*, Nov. 7, 1951).

[3] The reference is to Robert Rutherford McCormick, conservative editor and publisher of the *Chicago Tribune*.

[4] Clifford Roberts and William E. Robinson (see no. 470 and the preceding document). On the meeting at La Guardia see no. 470, n. 2, and the preceding document, n. 4.

473

Eisenhower Mss.

To Arthur Hays Sulzberger

November 8, 1951

Dear Arthur:[1] The pounding I have been taking recently has somewhat addled my memory; won't you please give me a sentence telling me what the little proposition was that I promised to think over when you left here? We talked about a number of subjects, and the exact one that I was going to think over with respect to Milton is not, at this instant, clear in my memory.[2] And even if I should think of it by the time you receive this note, it won't hurt anything to have your confirmation.

Don't forget to remember me kindly to Dr. Sulzberger.[3] *Cordially*

P.S. Attached is a note just received from the British Ambassador in Washington and a copy of my reply. I forward these to you because I think that, when the time comes for final decision on our request, the written evidence of the long consideration given it may turn out to be important.[4]

[1] For background on Sulzberger, publisher of the *New York Times*, see no. 114.

[2] Sulzberger had visited the General on October 30 (see no. 370, n. 2). On November 14 in a handwritten letter (EM) Sulzberger reminded Eisenhower that he then had broached "the difficulty which exists in bridging the gap from your present post to that of a candidate." Sulzberger had noted that if the Republicans nominated Taft, the *New York Times* would feel compelled, for Eisenhower's sake and that of the Mutual Security Program, to support President Truman.

I then added that if you could only identify yourself in some way with the Republican group that it might serve as the necessary bridge. During the course of this you told me that you had voted for Dewey & for Dulles & I suggested that I might "leak" about this. It would have been a cinch when I got off the steamer the other day. But you said no & I'm glad you did because while we are going to give you every support we can if you are nominated, I personally have no desire to appear in the role of a "King maker." The idea appealed to you though—the idea of letting it be known how you had voted. It seemed to me that you thought it consistent with your present responsibilities & certainly I do. And then you suggested that possibly your brother Milton could talk about you & say that he knew that you had voted for the two Ds. My reply was to cheer you on this course & ask if we could not send a good man to see Milton & ask him about you. It would be perfectly natural to do so & one of the questions would be if you had voted for Democrats or Republicans at Columbia. Your reply to me was not to do so until I had given you the opportunity of thinking it over.

Cyrus L. Sulzberger II, Sulzberger's nephew, personally delivered this message to Eisenhower, along with a speech Arthur Hays Sulzberger was about to make and on which he hoped to have Eisenhower's comments. For developments see no. 567.
[3] Eisenhower referred to Sulzberger's wife, Iphigene B. Ochs Sulzberger, who had received an honorary Doctor of Laws degree at Columbia University in June (*New York Times*, June 8, 1951).
[4] As chairman of Columbia's Bicentennial Committee, Sulzberger had written Eisenhower about inviting the British royal family to ceremonies scheduled for 1954 (for background see no. 282, n. 3). British Ambassador Oliver S. Franks had reported to the General on October 30 that the invitation had not been forgotten but that the King's illness had made it difficult to give a definite answer (see EM, Sulzberger Corr.). For developments see no. 809.

474   *Eisenhower Mss.*

To Sid Williams Richardson   *November 8, 1951*

Dear Sid:[1] It was a great treat to see you in Washington.[2] Pursuing for a moment your suggestion that I might have the opportunity at an early date of increasing my investment in one of your ventures, I find that, while I do not have left a great deal of uninvested capital, I still have a reasonable sum in my brother's bank in Kansas City.[3] If and when you tell me to send you another check, I shall do so in the name of my wife, my son, and my daughter-in-law. To each of these, I can give $3,000, right after January 1st, without paying gift taxes; and I should like to make my next investments in their names. (You mentioned $8,100 as one amount that soon might be advisable for me to put up. I find, on examination of my books, that I can put up a total of $12,000 without great difficulty.)[4]

In accordance with your suggestion, I am enclosing a letter to Billy Graham. I would appreciate it if you would forward it to him.[5]

Before I got out of the States, I was really close to exhaustion. That last Monday evening when I was talking to you, I was practically fit to be committed to an institution. In a fairly strenuous decade, I have never before had to face such a concentrated effort by newsmen and photographers as I did during those three days. In any event, I slept the clock almost completely around on my way home, and did it again last night. Consequently, I feel more or less normal once more.[6]

We are still looking forward to your coming over here. In the quiet of our home, we can have much more satisfactory talks than we could in the confusion, bordering on hysteria, of Washington.[7]

Give my very best to Amon[8] and his family; and, of course, warm regard to yourself. *As ever*

[1] For background on Richardson see no. 34, n. 2.

[2] Eisenhower had met with Richardson the evening of November 5, during the General's visit to the United States (see no. 457, n. 3).

[3] Arthur B. Eisenhower was a director of the Commerce Trust Company of Kansas City, Missouri (see no. 34, n. 1).

[4] In recent months Richardson had been advising Eisenhower on investment opportunities (see no. 35).

[5] This letter to the evangelist is the following document.

[6] For background on Eisenhower's encounters with the press during his visit to the United States see no. 457, n. 3.

[7] Richardson would visit Eisenhower in February 1952.

[8] Publisher and longtime Eisenhower friend Amon Carter, Sr. (see no. 35, n. 5).

475

Eisenhower Mss.

To WILLIAM FRANKLIN GRAHAM

November 8, 1951

Personal and confidential

Dear Mr. Graham:[01] Sid Richardson allowed me recently to read a letter which you had written to him. Certain of your observations struck me with such force that I wanted to express to you not only my congratulations on what you are doing, but my hope that you will continue to press and fight for the old-fashioned virtues of integrity, decency, and straightforwardness in public life. I thank the Almighty that such inspired persons as yourself are ready and willing to give full time and energy to this great purpose.[2]

Of course, I am flattered by the overgenerous personal allusions your letter made to me. Nevertheless, I cannot agree with what you say about an early declaration from me.[3] In various public statements, I have tried to make my own position clear. In general, it is about as follows:

For me to admit, while in this post, a partisan political loyalty would properly be resented by thinking Americans and would be doing a disservice to our country. Such action on my part would encourage partisan thinking, in our country, toward a job in which the whole nation has already invested tremendous sums. The successful outcome of this venture is too vital to our welfare in the years ahead to permit any semblance of partisan allegiance on the part of the United States Military Commander in SHAPE.[4]

It seems to me the logic of this position is unassailable, a conviction which I hope you will share after reading it.

I have marked this letter "Personal and Confidential" because, feeling as I do, I obviously do not desire to be quoted on public questions. On the other hand, I have no objection whatsoever to having it known that I applaud your efforts to support high moral standards and to remind us of the priceless privileges of freedom in our political, economic, and religious life.[5] *Sincerely*

[1] "Billy" Graham (Th.B. Florida Bible Seminary 1940) was an American evangelist who had developed a wide following through his "Hour of Decision" radio and television programs.

[2] Richardson had sent Eisenhower a letter from Graham dated October 20, 1951 (EM) (see the preceding document). Graham was convinced that "unless America has a moral and spiritual reform and revival within the next two or three years, we cannot possibly survive the severe tests that lie ahead. Church leaders across America are not going to sit idly by in 1952 as they have done in the past."

[3] Graham had said that he admired Senator Robert A. Taft but did not believe that he could be elected: "There is only one man on the horizon with courage, honesty, integrity and spiritual insight who has captured the imagination of the American people as no man in recent generations—and that man is General Eisenhower." Graham said that he believed it was Eisenhower's duty to "offer himself to the American people."

[4] The General had been using variations on this paragraph for some time now (see no. 358).

[5] In his reply of December 3 (EM) Graham said that he prayed daily for Eisenhower as he made the greatest decision of his life. Graham would visit Eisenhower in Paris on March 25, 1952.

476   *Eisenhower Mss.*

To Paul Herbert Davis   *November 9, 1951*

Dear Paul:[1] Thank you very much for your letter of the 30th.[2] I cannot tell you how much I appreciate the trouble you took to place pertinent facts before Pendleton Dudley concerning my tenure at Columbia. While you give me far too much credit, yet I never knew anyone to become very angry when his friends tended to over estimate, rather than underestimate, his qualities and contributions. More than this, I think your report to Mr. Dudley was very shrewdly calculated to cover every point of which I could possibly conceive.[3]

With warm personal regard, *Cordially*

[1] For background on Davis, who had worked with Eisenhower at Columbia University, see no. 310, n. 1.

[2] Davis had written on October 30 (EM) that the General's friends in New York were concerned about the "negative whispers" of people who questioned the success of his Columbia administration.

[3] Eisenhower's friends had "enlisted the services" of Pendleton Dudley, a public relations executive who had been a senior partner in the firm of Dudley, Anderson, and Yutzy since 1949. Davis said that Dudley had requested some information from him and that he had supplied background on the General's improvement of Columbia's finances; his good relations with the students, faculty, and alumni; his introduction of the Citizenship Education Project and the American Assembly; and his decentralization of the administration (on the American Assembly see no. 201; on the General's contribution to these various programs see also Galambos, *Columbia University*). Davis had concluded by saying that the comments were "highly favorable" on the job Eisenhower was doing in Europe "not only with the military but in vitalizing a spirit of confidence, unity and strength."

477

DIARY

Eisenhower Mss., Diaries

November 9, 1951

Senator Benton visited me to show that I have no true spiritual and intellectual affinity with the Republicans.[1] His arguments have been made to me before—but he had a hard time when I asked him about some of the Democratic stalwarts, McKellar, et al.[2] He merely insisted that there are more ignorant, venal, repulsive individuals in positions of influence in the Republican party than in the Democratic.

Tom Campbell came in the afternoon.[3] He doesn't care what party I'm in—prefers Republican liberals—but says U.S. *demands* me in politics.

[1] Senator William Benton (see no. 303), a Connecticut Democrat, had visited Eisenhower at 10:00 A.M. on this same day. Later in the day Benton wrote: "Our visit this morning cheered me on a lot of counts—and not the least of which is the fact that you seemed to be in such fine fettle. I don't need to remind you that I am high up on the list of your many admirers" (EM).

[2] Senator Kenneth Douglas McKellar was a Tennessee Democrat.

[3] For background on Campbell see no. 348.

To CHARLES MCELROY WHITE   *November 9, 1951*

Dear Charlie:[1] Your note of November 2nd was brought to me at Fort Knox but this is, almost literally, the first moment I have had to attempt an answer.[2]

I am, of course, happy that the Senator agrees that, in attempting to make it possible for Europe to defend itself, we are serving our country's enlightened self-interest. At least this is the interpretation I put upon the information you sent to me. Certainly I believe that America's security demands that Western Europe be kept outside the Iron Curtain, or I would not be here.[3]

With respect to any additional assurance or further action, I see no reason for bothering anyone to pursue the point. The job on which I am working cannot possibly be considered a partisan one, and certainly I have made it clear that I am not personally seeking political office.[4]

Jim Black is due in sometime this evening; I am not sure as to the hour, but will probably see him by tomorrow morning at the latest.[5]

With personal regard, *Sincerely*

[1] White had been president of the Republic Steel Corporation since 1945.
[2] White's note (EM) had been delivered to Eisenhower at Fort Knox, Kentucky, during his recent visit to the United States (on the trip see no. 457).
[3] White had enclosed a letter Senator Robert A. Taft had written to him concerning NATO's role in the defense of Western Europe (Oct. 30, 1951, EM, White Corr.). Taft had told White that the United States should "push vigorously the completion of the arming of Western Europe by the supplying of arms and equipment." Taft said that he approved the maintenance of six divisions abroad, but "the Europeans must provide the bulk of the army and ultimately all of it" and American forces should be "withdrawn within a reasonable time."
[4] White had offered to ask Senator Taft to write to Eisenhower and "commit" himself on the issue of Western European defense. On this issue Taft and Eisenhower had taken different positions (see no. 23).
[5] James Cunard Black, manager of the Republic Steel Corporation in Washington, D.C. (see Galambos, *Columbia University*, no. 944), would see the General on November 22 and play golf with him on November 24 and 29.

To JOHN WESLEY SNYDER   *November 10, 1951*
Personal and confidential

Dear John:[01] When I was in Washington, I hoped, for the sake of old friendship, to get a chance to talk to you.[2] Moreover, I wanted to ask you a question that has been bothering me a bit in the field of international finance. Because I didn't get to do so, I am going to try to put the point down in this letter.

You will probably get a chuckle to receive a communication from me that touches on such a question. Your reaction will be that it is a subject that is as foreign to my experience and knowledge as anything could possibly be. I cheerfully admit that I know nothing about its ramifications. It deals with *amortization* payments on the French dollar debt.[3]

Ever since I have come over here, one of the problems I have had is to attempt to achieve maximum speed in the growth of military strength but without straining the economy of any country to the point that collapse would result. From the beginning, the French financial and economic position has never seemed too strong and, with the drains placed upon the country by the necessity for waging the Indo Chinese war against the Communists, France has had a difficult path to pick between uncontrolled inflation on one side and military weakness on the other. I am informed that the cost of the Indo Chinese war in dollars alone is more than one billion per year. This, of course, is a very significant sum to France.[4]

An item that came to my notice during my necessarily sketchy examination of this subject was the currently large size of her payments on amortization as compared to later payments of decreased size. (I am definitely not talking about interest payments in any way.) Now this particular item is probably not exciting in itself. But in seeking for ways to advance early progress in the military build-up, and without adding to the danger of insolvency, it would seem that every little bit should help. My question merely is whether it would be wise and advisable to do whatever was proper in shifting some of the weight of amortization payments from the early years to the later years in the life of these several loans. So far as such things can be foreseen, it would appear that defense costs should, within a few years, be based upon maintenance rather than upon build-up. Consequently, decreased costs in the armament field should provide additional ways in which to meet amortization costs.

If there is any virtue in this idea, only you can tell. It is not even necessary to answer this personal and confidential letter. I just wanted to make certain that you would not overlook something, in which America's interests might be best served, by an examination of the kind I suggest. Most certainly, I do not believe that a mere increase in loans or an increased scale of American expenditures is either logical or wise. Of course, no Frenchman has mentioned this matter to me by any slightest hint or insinuation. If the idea has any virtue, please adopt it as your own—if it hasn't, please throw this thing in the waste basket and say no more about it.

The writing of this message gives me the chance of sending best wishes to you and your nice family. *Cordially*

[1] Snyder had been Secretary of the Treasury since 1946. This letter was apparently never sent (see typewritten "hold for possible use in the future" note, same file as document).
[2] Eisenhower had recently returned to Paris from a brief trip to the United States (see no. 457).
[3] For background on the financial crises in France see no. 467, n. 3.
[4] On the French war in Indochina see no. 361.

480   *Eisenhower Mss.*

To ARTHUR HAYS SULZBERGER   *November 10, 1951*
Personal and confidential

Dear Arthur:[1] I don't normally mark a letter to you "Personal and Confidential" but, since this one involves a recent story in your paper and the type of story upon which I consistently refuse to comment, I have to give my note this classification.

I refer to the report of Arthur Krock that the President, during my recent visit to the United States, made a proposition to me in the political field.[2] The story is completely without foundation. In fact, the President said nothing to me that could be so interpreted even by the most tortured and distorted type of reporting. I have no doubt that Mr. Krock thought he had an accurate source—if so, he was wrong.

I think we shall have to ask our electrical industry to develop for each of us pocket-size, automatic, and unstoppable recording machines.

Of course, there is probably nothing hurt by the story except possibly the President's feelings. But it is the kind of thing that is very startling to read, particularly when a man reads it about himself. *Cordially*

[1] On *New York Times* publisher Sulzberger see no. 114. Eisenhower filed this letter "for possible use in the future" (see typewritten note, same file as document).
[2] In the *New York Times* of November 9 Arthur Krock, a noted political correspondent, had written that during Eisenhower's meeting with Truman on November 5 the President had offered his support should Eisenhower seek the 1952 Democratic presidential nomination. Krock said he based his report on information from a person of "eminent" public position (Supreme Court Justice William O. Douglas). For further discussion of the article see Arthur Krock, *Memoirs: Sixty Years on the Firing Line* (New York, 1968), pp. 267-69. For developments see nos. 567 and 592.

This morning Congressman Javitts (my dist. in N.Y.) tells me that I must *lead, instruct* and exhort on basic issues in America.[1] Because we traditionally think of Pres. as our *only* real leader there is much talk of me for Presidency. (He is one working in this direction.) But what the U.S. *really* wants of me, he says, is to give the country my convictions, opinions and information—particularly in field of foreign affairs.

[1] Jacob Koppel Java*it*s, a Republican representing New York City, had met with Eisenhower at 9:00 A.M. as a member of a House Subcommittee on Foreign Affairs special study mission in Germany (then in Europe under chairman Clement John Zablocki, a Democrat from Wisconsin, to study democratization in West Germany) and again, this time alone, at 11:30 A.M. (see papers in EM, Javits Corr., esp. "Preliminary Report by Honorable Jacob K. Javits on Study Mission in West Germany of Zablocki Subcommittee, November 9-23, 1951").

Dear Slim:[1] While I was in Washington, I took up with the Joint Chiefs of Staff the question of the intelligence provided to my headquarters.[2] I found that all were very understanding and I am certainly hopeful that we will have no more trouble from that end.[3]

With regard to Airey's replacement, we are still doing a little scratching of heads.[4] One of the new elements that came into my thinking was an assertion made to me by the Field Marshal,[5] that the French think that my headquarters is becoming too wholly *British*. Since my experience in Allied command goes back now more than nine years, I suppose I should become accustomed to this type of allegation and criticism!

Of course, I am still embarrassed by my seeming rudeness at Jock Whiteley's house when I walked off to take an afternoon nap.[6] This was especially embarrassing because of the fact that I had expressed to Jock several times a hope that you and I could spend an afternoon and evening together. Frankly, I was looking forward to an "after dinner" period when you and I could sit around with a drink and have a really long talk.

My life is far from easy these days. We have a constant stream of visiting firemen, each of whom wants to know all the answers to his specific questions applying to SHAPE.

Please remember me kindly to your Lady[7] and, of course, my very warmest regard to you. *Cordially*

[1] Slim had served as Chief of the British Imperial General Staff since October 1948 (see no. 107, n. 5). His letter to Eisenhower, dated November 8, 1951, is in EM.

[2] On Eisenhower's brief trip to the United States see nos. 457 and 468. We have been unable to obtain a declassified copy of the letter that Eisenhower wrote Slim from Washington.

[3] For background on the problems involving U.S.-SHAPE intelligence sharing see no. 449. In Slim's letter of November 8 he had told Eisenhower that he "had hoped to be able to let you know straight away the position with regard to the intelligence which we are giving to SHAPE, but unfortunately," he said, he had not yet "got all the facts." On November 29 Eisenhower would acknowledge receiving a report that General Slim had made of the intelligence-sharing issue from the British perspective (see no. 510).

[4] Major General Terence S. Airey, SHAPE Assistant Chief of Staff for Intelligence, had been reassigned (see no. 449, n. 3). On his replacement with U.S. Brigadier General Robert A. Schow, Airey's deputy, whom Eisenhower had seen during his October 21–28 vacation in Scotland, see no. 722.

[5] Alphonse Pierre Juin, commander of NATO land forces in central Europe.

[6] While in London on October 20 the General had met (before an evening engagement) with the British General Staff at the home of John Francis Martin Whiteley, who late in World War II had served as SHAEF Assistant G-3 (see no. 203, n. 6).

[7] Aileen Robertson Slim.

483   *Eisenhower Mss.*

To Cornelius Wendell Wickersham   *November 12, 1951*

Dear Neil:[1] Thank you very much for your thoughtful letter of October 29th. I am most deeply appreciative of your kindness in giving me your analysis of the national scene—I am immeasurably complimented by your conviction that I could be really useful to our country in a position of high political leadership.[2] I would be less than human if I did not feel a sense of high distinction and pride, no matter what the depth of my humility.

Undoubtedly, you are fairly well aware of my negative personal attitude toward possible political activity. However, because every public statement is always subject to particular interpretations and misinterpretations by the people who report it through the press or radio, it might be a good idea for me, even at the risk of boring you with repetitive statements, to outline as succinctly as possible my present thinking on this matter.

There has been no change whatsoever so far as personal desire or ambition is concerned. I am not seeking any political position of any kind. There would seem to be no real reason for restating this except that it seems difficult for the public to accept such a statement as truthful. Among the reasons affecting me are the facts that my wife and I have had little opportunity during the past thirty-five years really to enjoy the advantages of home life. We have always seemed to be on the move and, possibly more than the average couple of our age, we earnestly hope to settle down into a home of at least semi-quiet and serenity.

Another angle has been a distinct, though possibly unwarranted, hope that through the years ahead I could be of some usefulness to our country in the role of completely unpartisan counsellor or at least as a chore boy—not precisely an elder statesman, but simply a person using such influence as he might have in helping to keep alive respect for and observance of the basic tenets of Americanism. It was in pursuance of such a hope that I agreed to go to Columbia. I have always felt that, if I should be fortunate enough to have another fifteen years of reasonably healthful existence, my total contribution to my country over the years would be greater if I could succeed in avoiding any kind of partisan connection than if I became identified with one or the other of our two great parties.

As I think you know, I believe I am possessed of at least an average sense of duty, the kind of inner compulsion that is absorbed by any loyal soldier through some forty years of service. I am now assigned to a duty, one that I deem to be of tremendous importance to the future of our country. In fact, if I did not believe that a reasonable measure of success in the effort to produce collective security by cooperation among free nations was serving the enlightened self-interest of the United States, I would most certainly never have given up the position I had in New York City to come over here in this assignment.

The effect on America's security program of my taking any partisan stand, as of today, would in my opinion be most destructive. Because of this belief, almost every letter I write in response to inquiries as to my position contains a paragraph somewhat as follows:

"For me to admit, while in this post, a partisan political loyalty would properly be resented by thinking Americans and would be doing a disservice to our country. Such action on my part would encourage partisan thinking, in our country, toward a job in which the whole nation has already invested tremendous sums. The successful outcome of this venture is too vital to our welfare in the years ahead to permit any semblance of partisan allegiance on the part of the United States Military Commander in SHAPE."[3]

Feeling as I do about this matter, it is quite clear that if ever I am to have anything at all to do with politics, it must be on the basis of response to a clear call to a duty that obviously takes priority in our nation over the one to which I am now assigned. Anything else would be a violation of my own sense of duty and a forfeiture of the good opinion of many thousands of people.

A number of persons—some of them in the political world—though fully aware of my personal feelings and opinions (including my dislike of the whole prospect), are still hoping to bring about my nomination. As I have stated above, this I consider to be their business; I have no intention either of repudiating their effort or, on the other hand, of making any public statement, while I am on duty in uniform, that would affect my usefulness on this job. For example, Senator Duff is one of those who has been openly stating his intention of organizing like-minded people so as to place before me a definite call to political responsibility. I have real admiration, esteem, and liking for Senator Duff, and respect him as a true public servant and patriot.[4] Neverthe-less, I cannot participate in any current effort of his along this line. But, on the other hand, I hope to say or do nothing that could be interpreted as placing my own personal desire or opinions above what-ever mass opinion may be uncovered in support of his position. This is not coyness, evasion, or fear. It is the logic of my special situation.

I most certainly hope that this letter makes sense to you and that you understand my position. It is because of my respect for your sound judgment, common sense, and complete devotion to our country that I am attempting to write so fully.

If you see any great defects in the line of reasoning I have herewith so haltingly attempted to present, I should be glad to have it. I know that you will realize fully that I am fervently trying to be forthright.

Please remember me kindly to your nice family and, of course, with warm regard to yourself,[5] *Cordially*

[1] Wickersham was a partner in the New York City law firm of Cadwalader, Wickersham and Taft (see *Eisenhower Papers*, vols. I–XI).

[2] Wickersham had said in his letter (EM) that the enthusiasm for Eisenhower as a presidential candidate was "very widespread and very great." Counseling the General to wait until February to announce his candidacy, Wickersham promised his support because "the country needs you, Ike. There is no one who can lead us so well."

[3] Eisenhower had used this paragraph many times in his recent correspondence (see, for example, no. 358).

[4] On Senator James H. Duff see no. 1, n. 2; on the Eisenhower-for-President committee see no. 409. A notation at the end of this letter directed that a copy be sent to Duff "without salutation & address block."

[5] Although he said he understood the General's reasons for not declaring himself a candidate, Wickersham replied on November 26 (EM) that there was no one to compare to Eisenhower in "leadership and all the other qualities that our difficul-ties and problems require." He advised Eisenhower not to make a decision until the spring.

To Joseph Howard McConnell   *November 12, 1951*

Dear Mr. McConnell:[1] Thank you very much for your cordial note of October 30th. I should have answered before this but, as you know, I have recently had to make a trip to the United States and this has set me back in the handling of my personal correspondence.[2]

I am delighted, of course, that you found an improving morale in Europe.[3] If this improvement is as real as I think it is, it is certainly the product of many factors and not of the efforts or presence of any one individual. This I say in spite of the glow of pleasure I get from the credit you give me in this regard. In any event, I hope that some day, before I am too old to swing a golf club, I can be relieved of this job and rejoin the crowd at Blind Brook that I like so much. *Cordially*

[1] McConnell (LL.B. University of Virginia 1931) had been president of the National Broadcasting Company since 1949.

[2] McConnell's letter is in EM. On Eisenhower's trip see no. 457.

[3] McConnell, who had visited Europe in September, had lunched with Eisenhower on September 24. He wrote that he had been pleased to talk with the people of France, "whose whole spirit has changed . . . from one of insecurity and almost despair to one of optimism and a will to do the things that are necessary." McConnell credited Eisenhower with the success of the NATO experiment and praised him for his accomplishment.

To George Anthony Horkan   *November 12, 1951*

Dear George:[1] I cannot tell you how appreciative I am of your understanding of the situation I was in while in Washington. I was so busy that I did not initiate a single telephone call while there, and saw only such friends as happened to drop in on us at our rooms in the Statler. I would most certainly have given a lot to see you and Mary—likewise Bo and his nice family. I understand that Buckshot is still in Germany.[2]

Undoubtedly you are finding life in Washington as full of irritations, useless work and frustrations, as most of us do when we have to serve in the Pentagon or in some of the other Army buildings. However, I know that both you and Mary are renewing contacts with many fine old friends and, to some extent, I hope that this makes up for any annoyances that you encounter.[3]

Mamie joins me in affectionate regards to the entire Horkan tribe. *Cordially*

¹ Horkan was Quartermaster General of the Army (see no. 226).

² In his letter of November 7 (EM) Horkan had expressed his regret at not seeing Eisenhower during his recent visit to the United States (see no. 457). Mary was Horkan's wife, "Bo" was the Horkans' son, George Anthony Horkan, Jr., and "Buckshot" was probably their daughter Katherine (for background on the Horkans see no. 226; and Galambos, *Columbia University*, nos. 642 and 692).

³ In September the Horkans had returned to Washington, D.C., from Heidelberg, Germany, where General Horkan had served as Chief Quartermaster of the European command.

486   *Eisenhower Mss.*

To James Henderson Duff   *November 13, 1951*
Personal and confidential

*Dear Senator Duff:*¹ Yesterday I was visited by Paul Hoffman and Mr. Maurice Moore, Chairman of the Board of Time, Incorporated.² Paul Hoffman has been my warm and respected friend for a long time and I have known Mr. Moore fairly well. Some months ago, he became a member of our Board of Trustees at Columbia. I trust both of them implicitly.

These men presented to me, during a long conversation, beliefs that were couched in emphatic language and which agree in essential detail with the convictions you have expressed to me at various times over the past months. In response to their opinions as to what I should do, I described to them my attitude and reactions, in terms identical with what I told you in a handwritten note dated about the middle of last month.³ They were, I think, impressed by the logic of my particular position, but they felt that there was possibly created a dilemma that needed a lot of thinking through. I then told them that, because of my trust in your judgment and purposes, I had already given to you the statement referred to above. I suggested, therefore, that they talk to you immediately upon returning home, and I promised that I would write you this note in order that the three of you, when you came together, could know that so far as I was personally concerned none of you would be violating my confidence if you talked freely to each other concerning the things I have told you. For you both expressed great admiration, and it is my understanding that they hope to be guided by your judgment.

There are, as you know, a number of my very good friends who have often talked to me about the possibility of my coming to feel a duty to take an active part in politics. To only a very few have I ever attempted to give a comprehensive statement on the matter. Of these, you and the gentlemen named in this letter are included—as is, of course, Ed Clark because of the fact that he was the messenger that carried my note to you.[4] My brother Milton, General Lucius Clay, and Bill Robinson (whom I think you know) are others.[5] Aside from these, I can think of none to whom I have directly communicated *all* the information that was in the note I sent to you. It is possible, of course, that others who may have been present at some of the conversations you and I have held during the past months have absorbed very accurate interpretations.

I hope that my final press conference in New York straightened out the mess that began to develop because of the extraordinarily intense inquisition through which I was going and during which I apparently dropped one inaccurate remark concerning an indirect communication from you. (Incidentally, I have no memory whatsoever of having made the statement, but one of my aides said that I did. It must have been one of those subconscious things.)[6]

I trust that the visit of my two friends to you will not be embarrassing. In any event, they will be able to tell their own story.[7]

With warm personal regard, *Cordially*

---

[1] On Duff, a Republican senator from Pennsylvania, see no. 196, n. 3.

[2] Hoffman was a close friend of Eisenhower's (see no. 411). Maurice Thompson Moore (LL.B. Columbia 1920), a New York City lawyer, had been a member of the Cravath, Swaine, and Moore firm since 1926.

[3] The note is not in EM.

[4] Eisenhower would soon establish a personal advisory group for politics (for background see no. 471). General Edwin N. Clark, an old friend and trusted messenger for Eisenhower, played a low-profile, "sphinx-like" role in the early activities of Eisenhower's political friends (see no. 492). For developments concerning the personal advisory group see no. 503.

[5] Milton Eisenhower, Clay, and Robinson had been laying the groundwork for an Eisenhower presidential candidacy (see nos. 470, n. 2, and 409).

[6] After Eisenhower's press conference in Washington, D.C., on November 5, the *New York Times* had quoted the General as saying that he would gladly speak with Senator James H. Duff of Pennsylvania, an Eisenhower-for-President principal, but that Duff had made no effort to see him. The following day, in New York City, Eisenhower told reporters that he had talked with Duff and that "quite naturally" there had been "one or two subjects of some slight interest" to discuss. "There were, of course, a few observations made along the line that I hope you will allow me to class as privileged," Eisenhower had said, stressing that neither Duff nor anyone else had authority to speak for him and that at the time he was interested only in his NATO assignment. The General pledged that should "duty" compel him to say anything on the subject of politics, he would speak out positively and definitely (*New York Times*, Nov. 6, 7, 1951).

[7] There is no reply from Duff in EM regarding the Hoffman-Moore proposals about Eisenhower's political candidacy. On November 19, however, Duff would send Eisenhower a detailed "Memo of Political Situation as of November 19" (EM).

Dear Ann and Art:[1] When we finally got the nose of our plane pointed
out across the Atlantic, Mamie and I agreed that one real disappointment of our trip was the wholly inadequate opportunity we had to talk
to you both there at the Statler.[2] Before arriving there we had talked
with such great anticipation of the subjects we were going to cover, and
then we found that the pressures were such that we felt we had scarcely
talked to you at all. I cannot tell you how sorry we both are.

Nevertheless I am sure that you got my main point, which is that I
want you two to be happy and contented on the farm—I particularly
want you to feel that you are getting a fair and just deal all around.
At any moment that this is not the case I hope that you would have
sufficient confidence to let me know at once. I am quite certain that
George[3] will always agree to any scheme or plan that you and I would
suggest to him, so there would never be any trouble on that score.

When I finally got a chance to look at the pictures of the farm I was
astonished that Ann had been so insistent upon apologizing for their
imperfections. I got a tremendous kick out of them, particularly the
Guernsey calves.[4] They look almost like deer in the fields.

Mamie and I had as one of the subjects we wanted to talk to you
about the possibility of the two of you making a trip over here to see
us. While wintertime is frequently rather dismal in Europe, still
weather alone need not be decisive in determining whether or not we
would have a good time. At periodic intervals one of our airplanes has
to go back to the United States and normally the two of you could be
picked up and brought along. I understand that on the west-bound
journey there is usually space available on the service transports,
which are very comfortable. If none of this would work I would vote
that the farm should bear at least half of the transportation expenses
for the two of you. In any event I do hope that you will seriously think
of making such a trip, and I feel that Mary Ann's presence on this
side of the Atlantic will constitute such an attraction for you that there
is a good chance you will take this suggestion seriously.[5]

Tomorrow night I am having a party to celebrate Mamie's birthday.
This year I am unable to gather together so many of her lifelong
friends because, except for the Snyders and the Gruenthers, there is no
one present here who has helped her celebrate so often in the past.
However, I am getting the Aides, the plane crew and two or three of
the older Army couples, and all together think I will have about thirty-
five people. (This makes it a buffet affair because Mamie's dining
room table takes a maximum of twenty-two.) The purpose of telling

you is, of course, to remind you how happy we would be if the two of you could be with us.[6]

Mamie joins me in all the best to you both. *Cordially*

[1] For background on the Nevinses, who managed Eisenhower's Gettysburg farm, see no. 48.

[2] The General and Mrs. Eisenhower had seen the Nevinses while staying at the Statler Hotel in Washington, D.C. (see no. 457; and EM, Subject File, Trips).

[3] On George E. Allen see no. 9.

[4] The farm currently had thirty-three head of cattle, which was about all that the barn could accommodate: "one Guernsey bull calf and 2 heifers and 6 Holstein heifers, in addition to 24 cows" (Nevins to Eisenhower, Nov. 26, 1951, EM; for background see no. 179).

[5] Over the Christmas holidays the Nevinses would visit the Eisenhowers in France for ten days (see no. 511; and Nevins, *Five-Star Farmer*, pp. 98–99). Mary Ann Nevins, the couple's daughter, was living in England (see no. 376).

[6] Alice and Howard M. Snyder, Jr., along with Grace and Alfred M. Gruenther, would help celebrate Mamie's birthday on November 14 (on the wives see nos. 24 and 431, respectively; on Snyder and Gruenther see no. 59).

On November 26 (EM) Nevins would write to say how much he and his wife had enjoyed their trip to Washington, D.C.

488   *Eisenhower Mss.*

To Lois Mattox Miller

November 13, 1951

Dear Miss Miller:[1] I am touched by the extraordinary tribute you have paid me; this in spite of the fact that I know it to be so largely undeserved. My appreciation is all the deeper because I know that you were motivated solely by a selfless and patriotic concern for our national good.[2]

No one can know the future, but the demands of the present press hard upon all of us. For my part, I am so intent on the job at hand, so fully engaged with our many problems, that I have had no time for other considerations. I feel strongly that until we see daylight here, with solid assurance of an ever-growing defense structure, my immediate duty lies in Europe.

I trust you will understand and forgive this preoccupation as it stems solely from my desire to serve our country.[3]

With appreciation and good wishes, *Sincerely*

[1] Miller was an editor for the *Reader's Digest* (see Galambos, *Chief of Staff*, no. 931).

[2] On October 30 (EM) Miller had written urging Eisenhower to become a Republican presidential candidate. Although recognizing the importance of NATO, Miller maintained that Eisenhower's accomplishments "could so easily be un-done by the

wrong person as President of the United States." With the General as President, she said, Americans would know that the "responsibility to our friends abroad would be in the best informed, most sympathetic hands." Miller said that she believed the United States needed to be "armed with unity, truth, and intelligent leadership" to "continue the fight for freedom over the tough years ahead."
[3] On developments in the presidential campaign see no. 592.

489   *Eisenhower Mss.*

To ROBERT WINSHIP WOODRUFF   *November 13, 1951*

Dear Bob:[1] It worries me a bit to find that you have not yet shaken this queer disease that you picked up in France. Please tell Nell for me that, if she finds herself unable to make you follow the doctor's orders, a ball bat applied in a suitable spot is quite frequently effective in quieting any tendencies to "be up and about." For the sake of your own health and your friends' peace of mind, please do exactly what the doctor says.[2]

I am delighted that Jim Farley liked the letter I wrote to him. His two little talks were chock-full of common sense and practical wisdom. Ralph Hayes' comment must have given Jim a real laugh![3]

During my hectic visit to the United States, I had a chance to see, very briefly, Cliff, my brother Milton, Bill Robinson, and Doug Black. They all came to my plane at LaGuardia. Wish you could have joined us—I'd far rather have talked about Ichauway than about "political duties."[4]

Mamie sends love to you and Nell—and, of course, I always go along with my "boss." *As ever*

[1] On Woodruff, chief executive of the Coca-Cola Company and one of Eisenhower's golfing partners, see no. 113.
[2] Writing from his Wyoming ranch on November 1 (EM), Woodruff had mentioned his slow recovery from infectious hepatitis (see no. 397). Woodruff's wife was the former Nell Hodgson.
[3] Eisenhower had complimented James A. Farley on two talks, "Leadership" and "Reaching the Hearts and Minds of Men," in a letter of September 3 (see no. 352). Ralph Hayes (A.B. Western Reserve University 1915), director of Coca-Cola International and executive director of New York Community Trust, had apparently seen this letter and had commented to Farley in a note: "According to my calculations this letter of September 3 from supreme Headquarters will have the effect of leaving you 67% paralyzed in the 1952 campaign" (see Hayes to Farley, Oct. 3, 1951, EM, Woodruff Corr.).
[4] On the General's visit see no. 457; on his meeting with Clifford Roberts, William E. Robinson, and Douglas M. Black see no. 472 (for background on Black see no. 168). Ichauway was Woodruff's plantation in Newton, Georgia (see Galambos, *Columbia University*, no. 656).

To Edward Everett Hazlett, Jr.   *November 14, 1951*

Dear Swede:[1] Thank goodness, you relieved my mind about the durability and efficiency of the Royal—until I received your reassuring letter, I had the unhappy feeling that Schulz may have been taken for a ride in the purchase he made.[2]

One of the infrequent chuckles that I have had in recent days was inspired by your sentence that "I see so much in the papers about Eisenhower these days that I sometimes wonder if I really know the man they are writing about." If *you* think that, what do you suppose I feel? I find in the Communist press that I am a bloody Fascist, a war monger, and a tool of American Imperialists. The cartoons that accompany these accounts picture a big-paunched, heavy-jawed Germanic type of brutal soldier. At the same time, I find somewhat similar cartoons in sections of our Isolationist press, but in which the labels assert that I am a great friend of Joe Stalin's or of all the Internationalist do-gooders in the world. In one paper, I am a New Dealer; in the next, I am such a Reactionary that the CIO finds it necessary to condemn me as an economic anachronism. In the eyes of one columnist, I am too fearful and frightened ever to attempt to fill a political office; another columnist asserts that I am, with Machiavellian cunning, pulling every possible string to become President of the United States.

All this is ordinary fare for anyone who tries to pursue a steady and honest course down the only path available when he is dealing in complex activities pertaining to large organizations of humans—a path straight down the middle of the road. Sometime in September of 1949, I think it was, I made a talk before the National Bar Association, then meeting in Saint Louis. I pointed out that anyone who chose the middle of the road was going constantly to be subject to attack from both extremes. He is hated by the bureaucrats and the national planners, and he is distrusted by those who think that Calvin Coolidge was a pink.[3] All of which would be rather terrifying to the victim if it were anything new or unique; actually, it is nothing but a mere repetition of what has been happening for hundreds, even thousands, of years.

You and I have had earlier correspondence concerning our common admiration for Forrest Sherman. So you must know how bitterly I regret his death.[4] To my mind, there was no real second to him and, as I recall, I wrote you one letter stoutly defending his selection as Chief of Naval Operations when I thought you had expressed some doubt about the matter. I do remember, though, that you wrote me a later letter to say that I had misunderstood the statements in which I thought I had found the criticisms.[5]

With respect to the top Service jobs in Washington, I believe that our people have, as yet, a lot to learn. For the Joint Chiefs of Staff to coordinate and balance the great military organisms that our country needs in these days of tension requires, in each member, selflessness, energy, study, and the broadest kind of viewpoint and comprehension. Each of these men must cease regarding himself as the advocate or special pleader for any particular service; he must think strictly and solely in terms of the United States. Character rather than intellect, and moral courage rather than mere professional skill, are the dominant qualifications required. Each individual will have to give only a modicum of his time to the establishment of policy affecting his own Service, because his great problem will be how to work with two others in devising and recommending to the civilian authorities a properly balanced force together with the programs and methods that should be applied to the problem of building global security for ourselves.

If you were choosing the Chief of Naval Operations by application of the standards I have just alluded to, I do not know where your choice would fall.[6] I am not well acquainted with some of the men now coming to the front in the Navy, but there is one whom you did *not* mention and who, on short acquaintance, has impressed me greatly. He is the Vice Chief of Naval Operations, named Duncan.[7] He is quiet, almost self-effacing, but he seems to me to have a value that far exceeds the noise that he makes. Just as I always felt that there was no one in uniform who loomed above Sherman in value to our country, so I have some suspicion that Duncan may finally make a similar impression upon me. (Not, of course, that this is important but, after all, our correspondence is a personal thing, and so I find no need to apologize for my personal views.) I believe Fechteler will do a good job—just possibly an outstanding one, because he seems to have a disposition that is neither easily upset nor particularly upsetting to others.[8] He is one of those people who does not make the mistake of confusing strength and bad manners.

Carney, of course, is a very skillful and able person.[9] I think at times that he may be tempted to argue points rather legalistically and, because of this tendency, may give unwarranted importance to minor detail. I think this is subconscious but it does, on occasion, give his presentations an atmosphere of contentiousness.[10] However, he is saved from any really bad effects because of his general popularity with his associates—all of us like him. He is most courteous and hospitable.

Incidentally, when I was in the Mediterranean recently, I renewed friendship with Admiral Gardner, I suppose of the Class of '17 or '18.[11] I like him very much and have a great respect for his easy-going but effective methods.

Your letter brought me my first news that there had been any public intimation that even one, much less two, Eisenhowers were considered for the job of Baseball Commissioner. Over the past several years, informal suggestions of this character have been made to me, but my refusals to consider the matter have been both prompt and emphatic. This has not meant that I was insensible to the compliment implicit in the suggestion, but it has meant that it is not the kind of work in which I felt it best for me to engage. I had no idea that the job had ever been suggested to Milton, but I am quite sure that, if it was, his reaction was somewhat the same.[12]

I feel impelled to pause for just a moment to make an observation concerning the topsy-turvy happenings that we accept, today, almost as commonplaces. If, some forty-five years ago, anyone had suggested to two barefoot boys of the Dickinson County region that they would each one day casually—without even a second thought—dismiss an opportunity to take over an honorable and decent job paying $75,000 a year, the entire countryside would have, at that moment, broken into a very hearty laugh, not to mention a few snorts of derision.[13] But that's the way it goes! I am not so terribly much richer in money than I was in those days (even though we had nothing then) but I guess that, in certain respects, my sense of values has changed considerably. And, after all, anyone with a $75,000 salary must have a great deal of anguish when he figures out his income tax!

The West Point scandal made me heartsick.[14] The only grain of comfort I get out of the whole business was that apparently the authorities, when aroused to the knowledge that something incompatible with the honor system was going on, met the problem head on and without equivocation.

One single observation about Korea-Iran-Egypt-Germany—and all the other spots on the earth in which we now sometimes find ourselves embarrassed. They are all part and parcel of the same great struggle—the struggle of freemen to govern themselves effectively and efficiently; to protect themselves from any threat without, and to prevent their system from collapsing under them, due to the strains placed upon it by their defensive effort. It is another phase of a struggle that has been going on for some three thousand years; the unique feature about it now is that it is much more than ever before a single worldwide conflict with power polarized in the two centers of Washington and Moscow.[15]

There is no point in my commenting further upon the political questions that you mention and with which I am so often personally confronted. Your own analysis remains accurate so far as I can foresee the future.[16]

When I am attempting to answer letters from inquiring friends on the point, I normally include in the explanation of my own attitude a paragraph about as follows:

"For me to admit, while in this post, a partisan political loyalty would properly be resented by thinking Americans and would be doing a disservice to our country. Such action on my part would encourage partisan thinking, in our country, toward a job in which the whole nation has already invested tremendous sums. The successful outcome of this venture is too vital to our welfare in the years ahead to permit any semblance of partisan allegiance on the part of the United States Military Commander in SHAPE."

I believe that a bit of reflection will establish that there is no other possible course for me as long as I am in uniform. A man cannot desert a duty, but it would seem that he could lay down one in order to pick up a heavier and more responsible burden. So far as personal desire or ambition is concerned, there will *never* be any change for me. I could not be more negative.[17]

I am glad you told me about the word "exegete." I am now going to look it up in the dictionary before I go home.[18]

My love to your nice family. *Cordially*

[1] For background on Eisenhower's friend Hazlett see no. 233, n. 1.

[2] In the spring of 1950 Eisenhower had sent Hazlett a new Royal portable typewriter that Eisenhower's aide Robert L. Schulz had purchased (see Galambos, *Columbia University*, nos. 734 and 981; and no. 353 in these volumes).

[3] A copy of Eisenhower's speech of September 5, 1949, is in EM, Subject File, Speeches; see also *New York Times*, September 6, 1949. For further background see Galambos, *Columbia University*, nos. 532 and 566.

Republican Calvin Coolidge, known for his steadfast conservatism, was the thirtieth President of the United States (1923–29).

[4] Chief of Naval Operations Admiral Forrest P. Sherman had died suddenly on July 22, 1951 (see no. 304, n. 10). "Too bad about Forry Sherman!" Hazlett had written. "He went in under a cloud of dubiousness but soon had everyone eating out of his hand" (Nov. 2, 1951, EM).

[5] See Galambos, *Columbia University*, nos. 598, 620, and 716. On Sherman's death see no. 304 in these volumes.

[6] Hazlett had listed his own candidates for the CNO assignment and mentioned the qualities he thought valuable in men named to high military posts. For developments see no. 669.

[7] During World War II Vice-Admiral Donald Bradley Duncan (USNA 1917) had been Assistant Chief of Staff for Planning. Since then he had served as Deputy Chief of Naval Operations for Air, Commander of the Second Task Fleet, and Deputy Chief of Naval Operations for the operations section. In August Duncan had assumed the post of Vice Chief of Naval Operations (*New York Times*, Aug. 2, 1951).

[8] On the appointment of Admiral William M. Fechteler as Sherman's successor see no. 304, n. 10.

[9] Admiral Robert B. Carney (see no. 53, n. 4) commanded NATO's southern flank and U.S. naval forces in the eastern Atlantic and the Mediterranean. Hazlett had said that he thought Carney would have made an "excellent" successor to Sherman.

[10] On Carney's current problems with NATO and NATO-U.S. command arrangements see nos. 390, 527, and 651.

[11] Vice-Admiral Matthias Bennett Gardner (USNA 1918), Commander of the U.S. Sixth Fleet (Mediterranean) since March 1951. Prior to that Gardner had commanded the Second Fleet (Atlantic) since August 1950 (for further background see Galambos, *Columbia University*, no. 296).

[12] Hazlett had said that he was "intrigued by the fact that TWO Eisenhowers were in the limelight for the Commissioner of Baseball job" (see no. 320, n. 2).

[13] The next baseball commissioner would earn an annual salary of $65,000 (*New York Times*, Sept. 21, 1951). For Eisenhower's account of his boyhood in Dickinson County, Kansas, see *At Ease*, pp. 64–102.

[14] On recent honor code violations at the U.S. Military Academy see no. 314. Hazlett believed that the academy administration should share the blame for the scandal.

[15] "Korea—Iran—Egypt!" Hazlett had written. "I can see no sure-fire answer to any of the questions they raise. A first class bunch of headaches!"

[16] Hazlett had said that he had been asked "almost daily" about Eisenhower's political plans. "Invariably," he said, "I answer that I know you don't want it but that you will, as always, answer a call to duty as your conscience hears it."

[17] See no. 358.

[18] Explaining why he favored proctored academic examinations (see n. 14 above), Hazlett wrote that recently his nineteen-year-old daughter had been asked during an unsupervised quiz to "exegete" a quotation. Hazlett pointed out that a professor or proctor might have defined the word for her.

491   *Eisenhower Mss.*

To Winston Spencer Churchill   *November 14, 1951*

Dear Prime Minister:[1] I well know that you are deeply immersed in great problems. I do not wish, therefore, unnecessarily to add to your correspondence, but there is a matter which I consider merits your attention.

During the past months, we have had many visits to this headquarters of representative groups of United States Senators and Congressmen. Their time here has been profitably spent because they have returned to the United States with a knowledge of how we are trying to build up the defense of Western Europe and an understanding of the means we require to accomplish it. Even of greater importance, they have gone home with a more realistic grasp of the dangers facing the free world today.[2]

These visits, and the good which has arisen from them, prompt me to tell you that I would be very pleased to receive here representative groups of Members of Parliament from London. I would personally ensure that they were carefully briefed on all SHAPE activities.

There seems to be evidence in some countries that they might be won over to cutting down the defense program of the West. I should like to help assure that these attacks, if made, are not occasioned by lack of knowledge.

If you agree with my suggestion, my staff will be at your disposal to make the necessary arrangements for any such visit or visits as you may deem desirable. We can easily handle groups up to twenty-five. As partners I need not tell you how much I would welcome such visitors to SHAPE.[3]

I hope you are in the best of health for the great burden you have once again undertaken.

With warm personal regard, *As ever*

[1] Churchill had been reelected British Prime Minister in October (see no. 451). According to a notation at the end of this letter, it was "hand carried by General Jock Whiteley" (see no. 482).
[2] On the visits from U.S. congressmen earlier in the year see no. 281. For Eisenhower's efforts to dispel the notion that SHAPE was "nothing but an American institution" see no. 449.
[3] In a message of November 16 (EM) Churchill thanked Eisenhower for his letter and promised to consider his invitation. Several members of Parliament would visit the SHAPE offices in December (see no. 543).

492   *Eisenhower Mss.*

To Edwin Norman Clark   *November 15, 1951*
Personal and confidential

Dear Ed:[1] This is a letter that must be classed as something of a protest against some of the things that seem to be happening to me. It may be based upon totally erroneous information or impression as to fact. If so, please ignore the whole thing—but, if I am even partially correct, it is high time we were taking a good look at what we are doing. Let me emphasize that this letter is completely personal and confidential between you and me—*its contents are not to be shared with anyone.*

In the two or three days just past, a few incidents have confused me almost to the point of irritation. For example: A couple of days ago, Bob[2] showed me a text prepared by an American columnist (whether or not it was ever used I do not know) which contained a fairly exact account of telephone calls that he and I carried out with others while in the United States.[3] The information was of such a character that it could scarcely have come from anyone except yourself or someone very close to you. Admittedly, I inadvertently made an inaccurate statement to a reporter alleging a complete lack of even indirect communication with Senator Duff during recent days.[4] This statement was made under a situation of great confusion and I have no memory even of the question. However, a staff officer near me at the time confirms the allegation. Possibly, as you later explained to me, there was immediate necessity for someone attempting to correct the error, but I must observe that there is little point in trying to prove that I was deliberately beclouding the issue or evading the truth. But this, in itself, is not so important as the uneasy feeling that you may have forgotten our basic agreement.

You and I have several times completely agreed that your role in any development that might come about would be a sphinx-like one so that you could constantly act as a trusted messenger. It seems to me to be terribly important that there remain to me one old friend who can trot back and forth to my headquarters without arousing undue notice. The importance of this point would not be so great if I *wanted* a political office; if I were openly and directly dealing with a group organized to promote such a purpose. But since my own current duty, to say nothing of personal preference, prevents me from any such participation, I am barred even from communicating, in ordinary fashion, with these friends. This is all the more true because of the unsatisfactory nature of trans-Atlantic telephone calls. They take hours to complete and are unsatisfactory, also, because of the danger of interception. Attempts to use codes are almost worse.[5] This is the situation that I feel you must keep in mind all the time.

So concerned was I about this point that, when I happened to be talking to General Clay yesterday, I asked him to call you when convenient to say that I hoped you would not be talking in such a way, even inadvertently, as to ruin your usefulness in this regard. It is clear that, if ever you should become known as an active participant in a political move, it would be very bad.[6]

I repeat that I do *not* know that you have made any indiscreet remarks of any kind, but enough disturbing things have occurred to make it necessary to point out the seriousness of the situation, from my viewpoint. Actually, I started to put through a telephone call to you last evening to talk about this point; and today (at 2 p.m.), we are still trying to complete the call.

The part of this letter that followed the above is now without meaning because of what I gathered from Bob as a result of his telephone conversation with you just now.[7] In fact, a great deal of my annoyance started from the fact that he had in a previous conversation completely misunderstood you; again showing the futility of a trans-Atlantic telephone call except on the simplest and most forthright of matters.

In fact, there seems to be little use even in sending you the first part of the letter I have written, but I shall do so because of my anxiety that you carefully preserve the position that you have so far filled so successfully.

Please destroy this instantly. *As ever*

[1] For background on Clark see nos. 1, n. 2, and 486, n. 4.

[2] Colonel Robert L. Schulz, Eisenhower's aide.

[3] While on a brief visit to the United States (see no. 457), Eisenhower had met with the leaders of the movement to nominate him as the next Republican presidential candidate (see no. 470, n. 2).

[4] On that exchange see no. 486, n. 6; and *International Herald Tribune*, Paris ed., November 9, 10, 12, 13, 1951.

[5] On Eisenhower's problems with code names see no. 396, n. 1.

[6] Clark would visit SHAPE headquarters in early December, and Eisenhower would repeat his warnings about the importance of being discreet (see no. 537, n. 1).

[7] See transcription of telephone conversation, Schulz to Clark, November 15, 1951, EM, Clark Corr.

493   *Eisenhower Mss.*

To George Edward Allen   *November 15, 1951*

Dear George:[1] I am delighted to have your letter telling me that your diet is proving effective and that you will be down to 195 by the first of the year. Actually, of course, the bet was made for Christmas day, but I am delighted to extend the time one week to conform to your schedule. However, you do not have to be down to 195—only 199.[2]

Now, as to the terms of the bet. You bet me $200 that you would be down to the 199 *and* (here is the point where we do not seem to agree) you bet me $200 that I would *not* be down to 172 on the same date. [Now, as I understand it, since you are going to be down to the weight you agreed, you have no objection to the bet being even bigger!] On the other hand, when we were in the Statler the other day, you asserted with tears in your eyes and a tremble in your voice that a single $200 bet involved two parts—that one would be down to weight and the other would not.

I propose that you answer this letter at once because I always feel sorry for fat men and I will let you off the hook to the extent of giving you the privilege of *stating right now exactly what the bet is*. If it is not a "do and don't" bet, I don't have to worry because I know *you will not* be down, so I couldn't lose no matter what happened.

If I have to insult you any more to get you to abandon desserts, potatoes, gravies, pork, butter, and all other fats and starches, I don't know how I could do it! Would you like to suggest we make the bet 500 bucks, do *and* don't??? I accept![3]

Love to Mary.[4] *As ever*

P.S. Of course, I expect an immediate answer to this letter because, if I have to get on my spinach diet, I want to get busy at once.

[1] For background on Allen see no. 48.

[2] This letter is not in EM; however, Allen would write again on this same day (EM) enclosing a copy of the Mayo Clinic diet through which he had lost six pounds. He offered Eisenhower the chance to "compromise" the bet at $150 so that he would not "rush this diet too much," although there was "no question" of his getting down to 199 pounds (for background on the wager see no. 297, n. 3).

[3] Allen had seen the General during his recent stay at the Statler Hotel in Washington, D.C. (on the trip see no. 457, n. 3). On November 20 (EM) Eisenhower would write to Allen again, defying him to revise the bet upward: "I am not interested in a compromise—I am interested in your waistline." The General added that he was hoping to learn what size bet would make Allen "get on a diet and stay on it for ten weeks straight." On Allen's response of December 4 (EM) see no. 529.

[4] Allen's wife, the former Mary Keane.

494   *Eisenhower Mss., Diaries*

DIARY   *November 16, 1951*

Paul Hoffman and "Tex" Moore (Chairman of the Board, Time, Inc) came to see me 4 or 5 days ago. The purpose was (as always) to convince me I must get into the political business.[1] I replied (as always) that any word of mine on this subject before I was relieved from current responsibilities would be flatly negative. Since such a relief doesn't seem logical (except in response to some command situation) I again urged that the progressive Republicans get behind some one else and work. To my mind Lodge, Hoffman, Driscoll or, possibly, Gov. Petersen of Nebraska could be built up if the necessary work could be done.[2] I'd be delighted to see any of them occupy the President's chair. The trouble is that the *practical* politician just dismisses such an idea with—"It can't be done," and yet we can sell Crazy Crystals,[3] Hauser's Book,[4] and Pepsi-Cola!

(Incidentally my real choice for Pres.—by virtue of character, understanding, administrative ability and personality is my youngest brother—Milton!)

Today Mr. Bradford, Vice-Pres. of United Press came in with the same story.[5]

Gen. Bradley called this a.m.[6] He was accompanied by Vice-Adm Davis.[7] They wanted to discuss the Rome meeting of NATO.[8] They fear that the question of incorporating Greece & Turkey into a NATO military command may be brought up & wanted to discuss possibilities with me. The real complication arises out of the insistence of both countries that they must be in SHAPE—they will not, initially at least, agree to their incorporation into a Mid-East command, to be headed by a British Supremo. Last month I told Bradley that the Mid-East command was certain to be a "can of worms." Many returning travellers have told me that the Greeks & Turks have a curious belief that under this hq they'd be safe—in a Mid-East Command they'd be in a dangerous situation. I am afraid there was not much skill used in making the approach to the Greeks & Turks; they are seemingly determined to oppose the simple and easy solution to the organizational question. The Oct. meetings between standing group and those 2 nations got nowhere![9]

[1] For background on Eisenhower's November 12 meeting with Hoffman and Moore see no. 486. In a letter of November 15 (EM) Hoffman had written that he and Moore had concluded that "only one move made sense, namely, the initiation of a draft Eisenhower movement of such intensity that the question of the extent of support for you in the Republican Party ranks could be quickly determined." In reply Eisenhower would send Hoffman a copy of a letter presenting "a somewhat different viewpoint—that of the rock-bottom political worker" (Nov. 23, 1951, EM). The letter, from which all identifying marks had been removed, questioned Eisenhower's political strength: "There is no doubt in my mind," the writer said, "that [Eisenhower's] backers are sincere, but I would like to remind you that those backers are on a level far above the average ordinary political captain, and it is the average ordinary political worker who decides the final issue." The writer was convinced, he said, that Eisenhower could best serve the American people by remaining in Europe "as an insurance policy against Russian aggression." Americans felt "safe with him at the helm there" (EM, Hoffman Corr.).
[2] On Henry Cabot Lodge, Jr., see no. 408, n. 7. Alfred E. Driscoll was Governor of New Jersey, and Frederick Valdemar Erastus Peterson was Governor of Nebraska. Both had held their posts since 1947.
[3] "Crazy Crystals" were mineral water crystals processed in Mineral Wells, Texas, where for sixty years people had come to "take the waters" in hopes of curing a number of ailments—including insanity (see letter from John Leslie Shone, Austin, Texas, Mar. 17, 1986; *Dallas Morning News*, Sept. 11, 1982; and *Fort Worth Star-Telegram*, Aug. 23, 1981, from files at Barker Texas History Center, University of Texas at Austin, all in EP).
[4] On Gayelord Hauser's *Look Younger, Live Longer* (New York, 1950), see Noel F. Busch, "You Can Live to be a Hundred, He Says," *Saturday Evening Post*, August 11, 1951, p. 30. Hauser, an internationally known author and lecturer, promoted his own line of health foods, including brewer's yeast, powdered skim milk, yogurt, wheat germ, and blackstrap molasses.
[5] A. L. Bradford had been vice-president and general manager of the European office of United Press since March 1948. Earlier he had been Director of Foreign Services for United Press.
[6] General Omar N. Bradley, Chairman of the Joint Chiefs of Staff.
[7] Vice-Admiral Arthur Cayley Davis (USNA 1915), USN, Director of the Joint Staff.
[8] The NAC would hold its eighth session in Rome from November 24 to November 28 (see no. 502).
[9] On the invitation to Greece and Turkey to join NATO as full members see no. 423. For developments see no. 709.

495

To RALPH THOMAS REED

Dear Ralph:[1] Your branch at SHAPE opened on schedule, and from all accounts I have heard the service it offers is excellent.[2] We are deeply appreciative of the trouble you have taken to provide convenient banking facilities for our people. I well remember our talk on the Queen Mary five years ago and I, too, am gratified to know that our joint brainchild has grown to such proportions throughout overseas stations.[3]

You make me homesick talking about Cliff, Bill and the gang.[4] I haven't been having much fun, although I enjoyed a round of golf yesterday—my first in about two months.

Again, my thanks for your great help to us here, and warm personal regard from Mamie and me to both Edna[5] and yourself. *Sincerely*

[1] Reed was president of the American Express Company (see no. 161). Aide Colonel Paul T. Carroll drafted this letter for Eisenhower.

[2] The American Express Company had opened a branch office at SHAPE headquarters, Rocquencourt, on November 5.

[3] In a letter of November 1 (EM) Reed had recalled his meeting with Eisenhower in September 1946 aboard the *Queen Mary*, bound for Europe (on the trip see Galambos, *Chief of Staff*, no. 1120, n. 4). On that occasion Eisenhower and Reed apparently had discussed establishing a network of American Express Company offices especially designed to serve American armed forces personnel throughout the world. Reed had enclosed for Eisenhower's information a list of American Express facilities in Germany, Britain, France, and Okinawa.

[4] Clifford Roberts and William E. Robinson (see nos. 7 and 39, respectively).

[5] Mrs. Reed.

496

To KENNETH DALE WELLS

Dear Ken:[1] Thank you for your welcome letter, with its comments on the usefulness of the symbol as a psychological weapon. My view is that anything which has a unifying factor or advances the cause of freedom constitutes progress.[2]

The choice of a particular symbol for freedom is certainly worth careful study. It would have to fulfill certain requirements, among which instant recognition and universality of understanding are important. Another is simplicity, and, for this reason, I *think* I'd argue that normally one hand should suffice for the making of the sign. Another factor is the avoiding of self-consciousness. Why it was, I don't know, but the V sign seemed to meet this test remarkably well.[3]

In World War II, the V sign was used in three ways—visually with the fingers, on the radio in Morse, and chalked on walls by members of resistance movements. Each method had great psychological and beneficial morale effects. The timing of this symbol at a low point in World War II, together with its presentation and use by Mr. Winston Churchill, resulted in immediate and widespread use.[4]

These are merely thoughts that have probably occurred to you.[5]

With warm personal regard, *Cordially*

P.S. I'll soon send you word on the beef![6]

[1] For background on Wells, president of the Freedoms Foundation, see no. 207.

[2] In a letter of October 29 (EM) Wells had said that he had been investigating the possibility of promoting a manual sign or symbol for freedom that would be "universal in its application, dramatic in its use, and indelible on the memory."

[3] Wells favored the universal symbol for freedom used by deaf mutes, and he urged Eisenhower to "put it to work." "I believe," he said, "it would spread like the prairie fires that our forebears faced on their farms on the great plain states." Wells had enclosed a drawing of the symbol for freedom (not in EM), as well as a "Paper and Pencil Conversation between Kenneth D. Wells and James Michael (Deaf Mute) on October 15, in Pittsburgh" (EM). According to Michael, the symbol was made in the following manner: "Both hands shake away means open for all. Cross the wrists before your breast and clench your fists, then quickly pull them apart, with both hands toward the hearer with palms and fingers widespread."

[4] See Harlan W. Morton, "Will Beethoven Stop Hitler?" *Etude*, September 1941, p. 586; and *Life*, July 28, 1941, pp. 26-27, and November 24, 1941, pp. 10-13.

[5] Wells would write again on April 22, 1952 (EM), to tell Eisenhower that he was convinced that the "Thumbs Up" sign was "just what the occasion demands."

[6] This is Eisenhower's reply to a postscript Wells had written: "The beef is fattening!" Eisenhower had promised to send Wells a plan for the delivery and storage of a gift of home-butchered beef that Wells had given him (for background see no. 207, n. 3). As it turned out, the Waldorf-Astoria Hotel in New York City would agree to store the beef for Eisenhower in February 1952 (see Eisenhower to Wells, Feb. 29, 1952, EM).

497   *Eisenhower Mss.*

To Philip Young   *November 20, 1951*

Dear Phil:[1] I signed several of the letters you sent me.[2] In the case of Mr. Drury, your letter implied a knowledge that I simply do not possess.[3] In the cases of Pete Jones and Charlie McAdam, these two men are such warm personal friends that I hesitate to write a letter for fear they would sense or feel an obligation on the personal side rather than to an idea.[4]

To cover these three cases, I am attaching a special note to you which you may use, if you so desire, in communicating with these three men yourself. The purpose of the note is to express a continuing interest in the American Assembly and my great hope that you will succeed in getting it quickly on a permanent five-year basis so that we may plan intelligently and effectively for its maximum service to the public.[5] *Cordially*

P.S. I am returning to you directly the drafts in the cases of the three men just named.[6]

[1] For background on Young and his work for the American Assembly see no. 8, n. 6. Eisenhower had seen Young in New York on his recent visit to the United States (see Young to Eisenhower, Nov. 13, 1951, EM).

[2] Young had written in September asking Eisenhower to sign letters to help with fund-raising for the second American Assembly conference (see no. 398).

[3] Theodore F. Drury was vice-president of the State Street Investment Corporation of Boston (on Drury and his interest in the American Assembly see EM, Drury Corr.).

[4] On W. Alton ("Pete") Jones and Charles V. McAdam see nos. 48, n. 5, and 211, respectively. McAdam would have dinner with the General on November 22 and would play golf with him on November 24.

[5] In the attached note to Young, also dated November 20 (EM), Eisenhower stressed the importance of putting the American Assembly "on a permanent five-year basis" to improve conference planning and to encourage continued support (for developments see no. 612).

[6] There are no copies of these drafts in EM.

498   *Eisenhower Mss.*

To James Bradshaw Mintener   *November 20, 1951*
Personal and confidential

Dear Brad:[1] Thank you very much for your letter.[2] As you know, I have, at no time, attempted to stand in the way of American citizens doing what they thought best in the domestic scene, even when their plans might involve me and my future. On the other hand, I have steadfastly refused to take any step, either positive or negative in character, that would or could give color to an allegation that I have any kind of ambition other than that of doing as good a job as I can on the task now assigned me.

This policy has literally been forced upon me. Every day I am besieged and importuned by people who have definite ideas as to what I should do now or at some date (usually specified by my visitor) in the future. To protect myself against involvements, the only thing I can do is just to stick to my knitting. Consequently, I have no recourse except to allow you to answer your own questions according to your own best judgment. As you know, I want nothing, but I do hope that I shall always do my duty. Nothing more.

I realize that you may consider this unsatisfactory but, in good conscience, I can say no more.[3] *Cordially*

[1] For background on Pillsbury Mills vice-president and general counsel Mintener see Galambos, *Chief of Staff*, no. 1974.

[2] Mintener had written on November 11 (EM) that he had begun a "Minnesotans for Eisenhower" organization. Local political candidates, he said, were going to start "Eisenhower Clubs" in order to use the General's popularity to their own advantage. "I thought it best," he wrote, "to get the thing in our hands. . . . The response has been tremendous." Mintener had asked for Eisenhower's approval of his efforts in Minnesota and other Northwestern states to explore the depth of sentiment for the General as a presidential candidate. He also asked whether the General would permit an Eisenhower slate of delegates on the ballot in the Minnesota presidential primary the coming March 18. "The only purpose," he explained, "would be to stop Taft."

[3] Mintener's reply of December 3 is in EM.

499   *Eisenhower Mss.*

To Lucius Du Bignon Clay   *November 20, 1951*
Personal

Dear Lucius: Thank you very much for your letter. You have a trick of reporting objectively and clearly.[1]

Today a man named Mr. Robert R. Barry visited me. He is full of ideas and information; in fact, he has a great deal more information than I could absorb if for no other reason than that I do not have time to give to the matter. Because I had to get back to work, I finally told him that he might carry the whole business to you some day. He seems to be both honest and public-spirited and a man of some thoughtfulness and ability. This will let you know that, if he does come to see you, I have at least talked to him. I took exactly the same attitude that I maintain with everybody. I told him that I would participate in nothing; that the decisions taken at home were taken by the people who were directly responsible for them, not by me. I think he understands this thoroughly.[2]

With cordial regard, *As ever*

[1] In a letter of November 15 (EM) Clay had written that Senator James H. Duff of Pennsylvania had leaked word to the press that Senator Henry Cabot Lodge of Massachusetts would head the Eisenhower-for-President drive. Clay said that although the official announcement had been scheduled for Saturday, November 17,

"the move is all to the good, and a really effective organization is certain to develop quickly." Of Lodge, Clay wrote, "The new manager is capable, sincere, and willing to give the job his full time. . . . At the moment, the professional background which is essential to success has been created and the building of an effective organization will follow apace" (see *New York Times*, Nov. 15, 1951; and *International Herald Tribune*, Paris ed., Nov. 16, 19, 1951. On Lodge see no. 409; Ambrose, *Eisenhower*, vol. I, *Soldier, General of the Army, President-Elect*, p. 517; and Parmet, *Eisenhower and the American Crusades*, pp. 37–41). For developments see no. 538.

[2] Robert R. Barry, who had been organizing Republicans on the General's behalf in the Western states (see no. 450), had been assistant to the president of the Yale and Towne Manufacturing Company from 1945 until 1950 and had been active in the political campaigns of Thomas E. Dewey and Wendell L. Willkie. Clay later would see Barry and suggest that he meet with Lodge (see no. 544).

500   *Eisenhower Mss.*

To Edward John Bermingham   *November 23, 1951*
Personal and confidential

Dear Ed:[1] Your note made me homesick. I began to think of how wonderful it would be to join you and the other members of Augusta National at the celebration of the Club's Twentieth Anniversary, and I got downright sorry for myself that I could not be with you. It's a good thing that I have to work like a dog every day; thus I have less chance to miss the counsel and companionship of my friends.[2]

As you know, every day brings through my office individuals who have some new angle or observation concerning the great political pot in the United States. They usually bring also some observation as to my possible connection with it. The latest one was an idea that, one of these days, the collection of money might be in the picture and, consequently, I ought to know who would be heading such a project in order that I could be confident the affair would not degenerate into something unworthy or undignified. I replied that it was not my business or intention to indicate a preference among individuals who are organizing *themselves*—that function belongs to the people doing it. Moreover, I had never given any particular thought to this possibility and couldn't believe that it would ever be necessary for me to do so; yet my own feeling was that if such a thing ever developed I would rather see you heading it than anyone else. I hope this casual statement will never come up to embarrass you but I am sure you know that I was expressing my deepest convictions.[3]

With all the best to you and yours, *Cordially*

[1] For background on Bermingham see no. 23.

[2] In his letter of November 15 (EM) Bermingham had said that he was leaving the

next day for the Augusta National Golf Club's twentieth-anniversary celebration (see no. 466, n. 3).
³ On the recent efforts of Eisenhower's friends to increase support for the General as a presidential candidate see no. 503, n. 4. For developments see no. 548.

501   *Eisenhower Mss.*

To Seth Gordon Persons   *November 23, 1951*

Dear Governor Persons:[1] My most sincere thanks for your thoughtful present; I am truly delighted to have a sample of the official identification of the Blue and Gray Colonels. For me, there is a peculiarly acute feeling of kinship with both sides in our War between the States because both my father and my mother were born during the years of that conflict, one in the South and the other in the North.[2]

It is impossible for me to write to anyone closely related to Jerry Persons without making mention of the fact that his services to our country continue to grow in value with each passing year.[3] In his field, he is almost unique, and the worth of his assistance to me is beyond all calculation.

Again, my thanks for your thoughtfulness, and with personal regard, *Most sincerely*

[1] Persons had been Governor of Alabama since January 1951.
[2] On October 18 (EM) Persons had written Eisenhower explaining that in Montgomery the annual Blue and Grey football game was held "to cement relations between the South and the North." Persons was sending the General, through his brother, a Confederate tie of the Blue and Grey "Colonels" team.
    Eisenhower's mother, Ida E. S. Eisenhower, was born in Virginia; his father, David J. Eisenhower, was born in Pennsylvania (see no. 160; and Eisenhower's *At Ease*, pp. 57–61).
[3] Wilton B. ("Jerry") Persons, the governor's brother, was a special adviser to the General at SHAPE (see no. 157, n. 1).

502   *Eisenhower Mss., Diaries*

Diary   *November 24, 1951*

Jean Monnet came to see me.[1] He cannot go to the Rome meeting[2] & is anxious that I stress the need for European amalgamation—political as well as the earlier steps involved in Schuman Plan[3] and European Army.[4] Since I believe implicitly in the idea I shall do so, even if some of the politicos present resent my intrusion into their field. America has spent billions in ECA, and is spending more billions in MDAP, and much of it will be sheer waste unless Europe coalesces. Denmark, Holland, Belgium, Luxembourg, France, Italy and western Germany should form *one* Federated State. To help this America could *afford* to spend a lot, because we'd *get* something successful, strong, sturdy![5]

But the politicos throw up their hands in fright & hopelessness; I doubt that even America could get many of them to fight courageously for this vitally *essential* development! (I made a speech last July 3, in London on subject.)[6] Day before yesterday I completed a trip to welcome the Canadian Brigade & the 28th and 43d U.S. Divisions to Europe.[7] The men of all units seem to me exceptional: possibly my advancing age makes *all* young men look intelligent, spirited, strong.

Today 9 Congressmen came to see me. Subject: "Expenditures in the Executive Departments."[8] I'm to be questioned about centralized procurement agencies; on the basis of past experience, not on my present job. I have enough to do; I grow weary having to give attention to some one else's task. The Committee could learn more by hiring an organization of Efficiency Engineers & staying right in Washington than it can by globe trotting for a solid year.

[1] For background on French economist Jean Monnet and his efforts on behalf of Western European defense see nos. 304, n. 4, and 424, n. 1. Monnet had met with Eisenhower this same morning.

[2] On Sunday, November 25, Eisenhower and his party would leave Paris for Rome, where the NAC would hold its eighth session November 24–28. Among those traveling with the General were Mrs. Eisenhower, the W. Averell Harrimans, and General Howard M. Snyder. The Rome conference considered preliminary reports of the TCC (see no. 384, n. 1) on work initiated at Ottawa in September in preparation for final decisions to be made in Lisbon in February 1952 (see no. 539; and Ismay, *NATO*, pp. 45–48).

[3] The Schuman Plan, named for French Foreign Minister Robert Schuman (and in part attributable to Monnet), called for coordinating Franco-German coal and steel production as the first step toward European economic federation (see Galambos, *Columbia University*, no. 1009; State, *Foreign Relations, 1950*, vol. III, *Western Europe*, pp. 728–38 and *passim*; and Hogan, *The Marshall Plan*).

[4] On the European Army see nos. 186 and 304, n. 4; see also n. 5 below.

[5] On November 26 Eisenhower would address members of the NAC in language that reflected his discussion with Monnet. The General stressed the advantages of a unified Western Europe—economic, military, and political. "Under such conditions," he said, "we would have Mr. Monnet's true concept of a single balanced force for the whole." Eisenhower urged creation of the European Defense Force, which would incorporate German strength in such a way that the Germans would pose no threat. "German help," said Eisenhower, "will be tremendously important as it is freely given; and it can be so given, I believe, through a European Defense Force. It would stand alongside the Schuman Plan—which must be successful—

and the two would constitute great steps toward the goal of complete European unity!" (Eisenhower's speech is in EM, Subject File, Speeches; see also *New York Times*, Nov. 27, 1951.)

[6] On Eisenhower's July 3 speech in London see no. 252, n. 2.

[7] On Wednesday, November 21, Eisenhower had traveled to Rotterdam, The Netherlands, to welcome the 27th Canadian Brigade Group to Europe, and that afternoon he had flown to Bremerhaven, West Germany, to greet elements of the U.S. 28th Infantry Division. The General and his party had then flown to Neubiberg, West Germany, and traveled by car to Munich, where they stayed overnight at the Green Forest Inn. On November 22 (Thanksgiving Day) Eisenhower had visited informally with the U.S. 43d Infantry Division and other U.S. Seventh Army units in the Munich area. He had returned to Paris that afternoon (see EM, Subject File, Trips, SHAPE no. 18).

[8] Congressman Herbert Covington Bonner (Democrat, North Carolina) and the subcommittee he chaired traveled throughout the Far East and Europe in the fall of 1951 while conducting this study (see U.S. Congress, House, Committee on Expenditures in the Executive Departments, *Federal Supply Management (Overseas Survey), Conferences Held by Subcommittee, Oct. 10–Nov. 28, 1951*, 82d Cong., 1st sess., 1952, pp. 1263–1343). The General would host a buffet luncheon for the committee this afternoon.

503

Eisenhower Mss.

To Clifford Roberts   *November 24, 1951*
Personal and confidential

Dear Cliff: Your note of the 15th gives the names of people that I, of course, trust implicitly.[1] General Clay would be a fine addition to the list, first, because he is a devoted friend of mine and, secondly, because he is always in touch with the group of politically-minded people who are organizing themselves into a "pressure group."[2] Dave Calhoun and McCollum would give some geographical distribution, as would Aksel Nielsen of Denver.[3] Because you are well acquainted with so many people that I trust and like, it occurs to me that you might want, from time to time, to add someone else—if so, you could act on your own initiative.

Incidentally, the only qualifications that we are thinking about are those of personal friendship, reliability, and keen judgment. It is far from necessary—it is possibly even undesirable—that all should think alike politically, especially about me and the possibility that I might get into the political business.[4]

I think I would get a great deal of satisfaction out of knowing that a few of the people you have mentioned would meet together periodically, talk over the important factors of the American scene and even some of the more or less inconsequential details, such as specific slants in public thinking and so on. Wherever the group saw that I was affected by any of these things, or believed that there was any new significance for me in the developing picture, one of you would write to me concerning the consensus of their thinking. (You might consider inviting Phil Young to join the group.)[5]

Of course, I assume that the whole business is to be confidential.[6] While I hate to put any chore on you, I think, also, that you would have to do it as your idea and merely on the basis of helping out a friend who hasn't time to think of a lot of these things himself, and in response to my referring the occasional questions to you for your conclusions. It should be quite clear to each that there is no intention of starting any organization of any kind whatsoever. Moreover, there is no intention of seeking support for any movement, idea, or person. The sole reason is to help keep me informed and advised. It would be terrible if any of my friends got the idea that we were seeking to organize them for any particular purpose over and above that of mere "thinking." Of course, if any word of it ever got out, no one else would believe that we could have such a simple and wholly logical idea; someone would try to crowd a nefarious purpose into the thing.[7]

I see by the paper that the market has been falling off—a circumstance that seems to vindicate your judgment completely.[8]

I am getting ready to go to Rome for the NATO meeting but I shall be back here, if all goes well, about Wednesday morning, the 28th.[9] *As ever*

---

[1] Eisenhower had asked Roberts to send him the names of people who might form a personal political advisory group (see no. 471). In his letter of November 15 (EM) Roberts had suggested Lewis B. Maytag (see no. 113), Robert T. ("Bobby") Jones, Jr. (see no. 113), W. Alton ("Pete") Jones (see no. 48), Philip D. Reed (see no. 164), William E. Robinson (see no. 455), Ellis D. Slater (see no. 59), Barry T. Leithead (see no. 217), Douglas M. Black (see no. 168), Milton Eisenhower, and Burton Francis Peek, a lawyer, chairman of the board of the John Deere Company of Moline, Illinois, and a member of the Augusta National Golf Club.

[2] On Clay see no. 409.

[3] David R. Calhoun, Jr., was a St. Louis, Missouri, banking executive (see no. 94); Leonard F. McCollum, a Houston, Texas, business executive (see no. 519); and Aksel Nielsen, a Denver, Colorado, business executive (see no. 34).

[4] "None are politicians," Roberts had written of this group, "but all qualify on the basis of (1) Unselfish devotion to you, and (2) Civic Mindedness. . . . Moreover, everyone of them are unusually conscientious people."

[5] On Philip Young, Executive Director of the American Assembly, see no. 8.

[6] Roberts's candidates were "entirely free of ambitions of the sort that would prevent them from giving you their unbiased judgement," he assured the General. "They would want no public recognition hence the existence of the committee would never need to be known."

[7] In a handwritten postscript at the end of this letter Eisenhower had written, "If any of this is unclear—please remember the state of pressure in which I live."

[8] See no. 471.

[9] On Eisenhower's attendance at the NAC meeting in Rome see no. 502.

To William Edward Robinson   *November 24, 1951*

Dear Bill:[1] It was fine to have your letter. It is amazing how difficult everything becomes for any individual the second that his name is mentioned in connection with politics. The paragraph in your letter telling about the various individuals that called you to tell about the Lodge selection is typical.[2]

It is strange what one sometimes gets into regardless of his own feelings and personal desire. Every passing day confirms and hardens my dislike of all political activity as a personal participant. It is not merely a matter of contemplating the giving up of friends, recreation, and activity of my own choice; it is the apparent change that takes place in most individuals the second that they begin to work in the machinery of politics. Thousands of people have said to me, "Of course, you are absolutely right in principle, but that isn't the way politics works." Beyond this, there is discernible very little desire to serve the public; often, the inspiration seems merely to gain opportunity to exploit the public.

I know that the obvious answer is, "Well, someone has got to combat these trends; we have to get back on a higher plane or we are lost." True enough, but, when you think of the years that will be necessary to make a sizeable dent in this particular problem, it seems that we should at least look for a chap who is in his 40s rather than one who has already entered his 60s.[3]

I desperately try to keep my own personal likes and dislikes from influencing any decision where the all-important item of duty is involved. In this, I am probably no more successful than the average man who tries to be honest with himself and others. But one thing is certain—feeling as I do—if ever I get into this business, I am going to start swinging from the hips and I am going to keep swinging until completely counted out. One great thing of doing a job where you feel it is not of your own choice, one doesn't have to placate or appease anybody.

Well, enough of this. The real purpose of this note is to say, "Come a-running for Christmas; we will be delighted to have you." If you can bring Cliff with you, Al and I will challenge you to a head-on bridge game two hours a day for the time you can stay.[4] While we would hope thus to accumulate some New York money, the fact is that, when we played Averell Harriman and Frank Pace the other evening on this basis, they took us for thirty-eight bucks each.[5] Both of us are still squealing, and they are still bragging. *Cordially*

[1] For background on Robinson see no. 39.
[2] In a letter of November 15 (EM) Robinson had reported on the reaction among

Eisenhower's top supporters to the selection of Henry Cabot Lodge, Jr., as campaign manager. Robinson said that he thought Lodge might be acceptable to Eisenhower as the final choice for campaign manager "if for no other reason than he would not indulge in the cheap or unscrupulous practices which so often occur in the pursuit of delegates . . . the important thing is the unanimous agreement on one man of character and integrity" (for background see no. 499). Robinson also said that he could not understand how he had come to be so involved in the controversy over Lodge. "I think you realize," he wrote, "that I've never represented myself as having any special information or influence. . . . Sometimes I've bent over backward so much that I must have assumed the posture of a burlesque comedian."

[3] Eisenhower had celebrated his sixty-first birthday on October 14.

[4] Robinson and Clifford Roberts would visit the Eisenhowers from December 23 until December 27 (see Roberts to Eisenhower, Dec. 5, 1951, EM). Eisenhower and his C/S, Alfred M. Gruenther, were avid bridge players. For developments see no. 546.

[5] Special Assistant to the President W. Averell Harriman and Secretary of the Army Frank C. Pace, Jr., apparently had accepted a bridge challenge from Eisenhower and Gruenther on Sunday, November 25 (see Gruenther to Pace, Nov. 21, 1951, AP 82136, EM; for background on Pace see no. 116).

505

Eisenhower Mss.

To GEORGE WHITNEY

November 24, 1951

Dear George:[1] The item that disturbs me most in your letter of November 15 is the one about the possibility of the Federal Government taking over the complete Federal Reserve System. Meager as is my knowledge concerning the operation of financial organizations and of the direct and indirect influences of these institutions upon our national economy, I react instantly to any suggestion that the Federal Government should increase its powers over any of the sensitive portions of our whole national life. You and I talked last summer, a bit wistfully, perhaps, of the possibility that some day the United States would begin to take the necessary steps to lead us back to a gold or similar standard. This suggested step would seem to be in the exact opposite direction.[2]

This minute I am getting ready to leave for Rome, where I will be for a couple of days attending the meetings of the NATO ministers.[3] I will have to make two or three talks, some of which will be, frankly, efforts at exhortation. The job of trying to impart courage to fearful men, forthrightness to those who have never met an issue squarely in their lives, really constitutes a drain upon a man's reserves of energy. I would rather take a good beating than to have to do this kind of thing. But, it is surprising how many people in this world seem to require a moral pat on the back before they will set their teeth and tackle a job that presents anything of difficulty or of risk.

Again, let me assure you how much I appreciate your letters. I am sorry that I do not have the time to attempt the kind of answer they deserve.

Please remember me warmly to Mrs. Whitney and, of course, my very best to Bob and his nice family—and also to Mr. Alexander.[4]

Cordially

[1] For background on banker George Whitney see no. 51, n. 3.

[2] Whitney had said that he was concerned over the possibility that the U.S. government would take over the Federal Reserve System and, "thereby, do away with the present checks and balances on credit." He pointed out that it was difficult for industrialists to understand the "tragedy that would result from the Government having full control of credit" (EM). On the Federal Reserve Board and congressional talk of reforming it see no. 64, n. 3; and *New York Times*, August 10, 19, November 3, 1951. On Whitney's opinion of governmental intervention in business see no. 560, n. 3.

[3] See no. 502.

[4] Mrs. Whitney was the former Martha Beatrix Bacon, and Robert B. Whitney was the Whitneys' son (see no. 50, n. 3). Eisenhower was probably referring to Henry Clay Alexander (LL.B. Yale 1925), president and director of J. P. Morgan & Company.

506   *Eisenhower Mss.*

To WILLIAM DOUGLAS PAWLEY   *November 24, 1951*

Dear Bill:[1] Your letter of the 16th reached me only yesterday. My comments on the suggestions made in Bob's letter are very clear and positive. The ramified activities of the Defense Department reach into so many nooks and crannies of American and international life that there will never be any lack of opportunity for a devoted, intelligent public servant in that Department to find plenty to occupy his entire attention. It seems to me that Bob will certainly have real need for a trouble shooter and handy man.[2]

You said nothing in your letter about the results of your trip to India. I hope they were at least favorable.[3]

I am sorry I did not get to see you at Washington. If you could have seen the "death watch" that was maintained on my door day and night, every hour of the twenty-four, you would have understood something of my difficulties. If I stay here until after next July, conditions will certainly be different and I can possibly come down to your Virginia farm for a couple of hours of bass fishing.[4]

Naturally, I was touched by your generous offer of personal support and assistance; if a man had to get into all the complexities and intricacies of political life, he would certainly need the kind of friend that you have been.[5] *Cordially*

[1] Pawley, former U.S. Ambassador to Brazil, was a special assistant to the Secretary of State (see no. 41).

[2] Pawley had asked Eisenhower to comment on the content of an enclosed letter from Secretary of Defense Robert A. Lovett, who had offered Pawley duty with the Department of Defense as " 'trouble shooter' on whom we could dump any particular nasty problem that did not normally fall into appropriate staff channels, or to whom we could look for assistance and guidance and *action* on a complicated matter involving delicate negotiations" (Sept. 26, 1951, EM). Pawley told Eisenhower that he had "considered dropping out of government work altogether" but had now agreed to return to Washington, D.C., and report to Lovett on December 5.

[3] In June 1951 Pawley had been in New Dehli, India, on a special mission for the Department of State.

[4] On Eisenhower's recent trip to the United States see no. 457. Eisenhower was referring to Belvoir Farm, the Pawley home in The Plains, Virginia.

[5] "I would like for you to know now," Pawley had written, "that you have a very strong, loyal friend and supporter, who believes in you and what you stand for—and that support carries with it no strings."

507

Eisenhower Mss.

To ROBERT BOSTWICK CARNEY

November 24, 1951

Dear Carney: Your letter[1] just arrived as I am in the midst of last-minute preparations for my trip to Rome.[2] I shall try to answer it next week.

My first hasty reading gives me a convincing picture of your stand with respect to the Mediterranean and your desire to be a commander of United States Naval Forces as well as their operational leader.[3] As you know, I have always felt that the London thing is a different problem.[4] However, my first rule has always been to support any subordinate who has definite views on a particular item within his own scope of interest—my instant reaction is always to stick by this simple formula. I say this merely to show you that, even if in some particular point I may feel it necessary to disagree with you, it will certainly be against instinct.[5] *Cordially*

[1] Carney had written three days before, having delayed "only because of the seriousness of the matter concerned" and his "desire to treat it with the utmost objectivity." He wrote on the thorny matter of U.S. Navy command arrangements in Europe, a topic that Eisenhower and the Chief of Naval Operations, Admiral

William M. Fechteler, had discussed in October and that Carney had addressed earlier in November (see no. 429; and Carney to Eisenhower, Nov. 8, 21, 1951, EM, Fechteler Corr. See also Gruenther to Eisenhower, Nov. 5, 1951, ALO 462, EM, Gruenther Corr.).

[2] Eisenhower referred to the Rome meeting of the North Atlantic Council, November 26–28 (see no. 502).

[3] Carney argued strenuously that he should retain the CINCNELM, and he was uncertain where Eisenhower stood on the issue. Carney believed that he should continue as CINCNELM precisely because of his NATO duties as CINCSOUTH. U.S. naval units supplied the only fully trained and battle-ready components of his NATO command. Their operational control would not suffice: "*Command* is essential if I am to be fully effective in the Mediterranean picture," he wrote the General. He cited Air Force General Lauris Norstad as a parallel case of a high-ranking officer serving under SACEUR while retaining important U.S. service responsibilities. "Shorn of the *command* of U.S. naval forces and activities in Europe, my personal effectiveness is certain to be lessened." "I firmly believe," Carney concluded, "that the status quo should be maintained for the present and I am equally firm in my conviction that this can be done without in any way detracting from my performance as your southern flank commander" (Carney to Eisenhower, Nov. 21, 1951, EM, Fechteler Corr.).

"Carney must look to the mountains and not to the sea," Eisenhower had said. According to Fechteler, Eisenhower shuddered every time Carney mentioned London (Carney to Eisenhower, Nov. 8, 1951, *ibid.*).

[4] CINCNELM's London headquarters had largely (though not completely) moved with Carney to Naples after he assumed the title of CINCSOUTH. Carney opposed dismantling remnants of his London office, which in Eisenhower's view diverted his attention from the Mediterranean; yet both U.S. and British naval concerns called for more effective London representation than Carney could provide from Naples (see no. 429).

[5] For Eisenhower's support of Carney, mingled with doubts that Carney's areas of concern need extend as far from the Mediterranean as his CINCNELM duties carried him, see nos. 526 and 527.

508   *Eisenhower Mss.*

To Fred M. Manning, Sr.   *November 28, 1951*

Dear Fred:[1] No news could be more welcome to me than that you are improving in health. Mamie and I envy you and Hazel the opportunity to relax in the Palm Springs sunshine. It would be wonderful to join you for a few days.[2]

Yesterday we returned from Rome where I had to attend several of the NATO meetings. The trip was something of a strain on me as I had to make three rather difficult speeches in a single day. However, after I got my work done and Mamie had completed a day of sightseeing, we were fortunate enough to have one of the most beautiful days I have seen in Southern Europe on which to make our trip back to France. The crests of the Alps were literally shining in the sunlight and the Ligurian Sea[3] could not have been more blue—a sight that one would never want to forget.

Incidentally, I think that Rome has a just claim to the title of "most interesting city" for the average traveler. Some of its structures go far back beyond the birth of Christ, and alongside them are often located some of the most modern buildings. History is everywhere; to travel through the streets with a native Roman is like reading the most interesting, illustrated, account of our Western civilization.

Both of us send our very best to the two of you; please remember us kindly to your nice children when you write to them. *Cordially*

[1] Manning was an oil executive (see no. 161, n. 8).

[2] In a letter of November 20 (EM) Manning had said that he and his wife Hazel were staying in Palm Springs, California, where the climate was beneficial to his improving health (on Manning's illness see no. 309).

[3] The Ligurian Sea, a branch of the Mediterranean, borders Italy on the west. On Eisenhower's trip see no. 502.

509   *Eisenhower Mss.*

To WILLIAM LINDSAY WHITE   *November 28, 1951*
Personal and confidential

Dear Mr. White:[1] I find that your long telegram of November 5th, addressed to me in Washington, was not, because of the inability of an inadequate staff to cope with a flood of incoming mail and telegrams, brought to the attention of a responsible member of my staff until several days ago, at a period when I was absent from my headquarters. While acknowledgment of its receipt was sent off to you at once, I, of course, am anxious for you to understand that such a thoughtful and obviously sincere message as yours, coming from a distinguished citizen of my own State, would never have been treated in what must seem to you to be a discourteous fashion if the circumstances had been such that I could have given the matter personal attention.[2]

While there is little of substance that I can add to what I have already publicly said concerning the possibility of my participation in the domestic political struggles, I hope that additional explanation will do something to convince you of the complete sincerity and honesty of my position; a position forced upon me by compelling circumstances over which I have no control.

It is a matter of deep concern, even distress, to me that you should entertain for a moment the idea that I am disrespectful of the responsibilities resting upon a delegate to national political conventions.[3] In view of the fact that I have consistently and publicly stressed the need for each of us to fulfill the obligations of citizenship, to include participation in the procedural details of the political party of the individual's choice, I do not consider that this suspicion is justified. I do not feel that any fair-minded citizen can find justifiable grounds for accusing me of coyness, evasion of responsibility, or of disregard for the fateful decisions that in our country must periodically be made by the membership of political conventions.

The simple fact is that I am serving in the uniform of my country, assigned to a critical duty by an administration elected by the people of our nation. In view of the oath of office of an American Army officer and of my passionate belief in our form of government, which includes acknowledgment of the superiority of civil over military authority, I would most certainly have been guilty of serious dereliction had I tried to find excuse or reason for evading the responsibilities placed upon me at the moment I was assigned to this post. Exactly what your convictions are with respect to the need for the free nations of the world to develop, through cooperation, the military strength necessary to their own security, I do not know. The prospect is that, if we were indifferent to this problem, nation after nation would succumb to the pressures of Communistic propaganda, subversion, bribery, and economic and military threats. Eventually we would find ourselves isolated and deprived of many raw materials essential to our economic life. So, the conclusion is that, unless we are successful in this effort, there is no acceptable alternative for the United States.

Because of this, I do not have in my present position all of the rights that belong to the ordinary citizen; service in uniform denies opportunity to exercise certain political rights. Because of my convictions in these matters, I have almost inevitably, in written replies to thoughtful suggestions and inquiries concerning a possible political career for me, included a paragraph somewhat as follows:

"For me to admit, while in this post, a partisan political loyalty would properly be resented by thinking Americans and would be doing a disservice to our country. Such action on my part would encourage partisan thinking, in our country, toward a job in which the whole nation has already invested tremendous sums. The successful outcome of this venture is too vital to our welfare in the years ahead to permit any semblance of partisan allegiance on the part of the United States Military Commander in SHAPE."[4]

Because of my very great respect for your judgment, your sincerity, and your devotion to the welfare of our country, I do hope that you will sense the honesty of my argument even in the event that you cannot subscribe to its complete validity. In any event, I do not see how it would be possible for me to lay down the duties and responsibilities of this post except in response to a call to duty which would, almost by common consent, be recognized as a greater responsibility than the one I am now carrying.[5]

You referred in your message to numbers of individuals who have been attempting to organize citizens in the United States with a view to confronting me with such a type of duty—the decision of a political convention. So far as I know, all of these people—and they include men with whom I have been warm and devoted friends for many years—completely and thoroughly understand my attitude and agree with me that to do other than I am now doing would constitute a serious dereliction of duty. In the practical sense, any partisan statement, made at this time, would lose for me thousands of friends who now believe in my disinterestedness and in my assertion that, *as a matter of personal desire*, I want nothing whatsoever in the way of further acclaim, award, or office. These same friends know that, as a consequence of this kind of thinking, I have no intention of doing anything, either positive or negative, respecting their current efforts.[6] So, they have avoided forcing me into an untenable position.[7]

I, of course, admit that, in my great preoccupation to preserve the unpartisan attitude of this great defense effort, an effort in which I must point out that America has from the first been the leader, I may have unwittingly misinterpreted my own attitude to people who feel entitled to some explanation as to my future decisions, under a variety of hypothetical circumstances. This, you will understand, cannot always be avoided, and I must simply trust my friends to believe I'm doing my best. I am quite sure that people like Senator Duff, Roy Roberts, Senator Lodge, DeWitt Wallace, and many, many others would agree to these statements without major difference.[8]

I am asking you to keep this letter Personal and Confidential because my purpose is merely to clarify my position with you.

My attention was recently called to an editorial you wrote in your paper concerning my qualifications for the highest office in the land.[9] As to this, I can only say that, like any other loyal American, the knowledge that any thoughtful citizen considers me qualified for such a post fills me with feelings of the most intense pride, accompanied by equal feelings of humility. Coming from you, they have special value.[10]
Most sincerely

[1] White (A.B. Harvard 1924) was editor and publisher of the *Emporia* (Kans.) *Gazette*. The son of another distinguished Kansas editor, William Allen White, he was also an author and a former foreign correspondent.
[2] White's telegram (EM) had been addressed to Eisenhower care of the Department of Defense. A handwritten notation indicates that it had been redirected to the Statler Hotel in Washington, D.C., where Eisenhower had stayed earlier this month (see no. 457). On November 16 Eisenhower's aide Lieutenant Colonel C. Craig

Cannon had acknowledged White's message in a short note from Paris that said, in part, that since his return to Paris the General had been exceedingly busy. According to Cannon, Eisenhower had asked him to acknowledge White's message, which was greatly appreciated but called for no further comment (EM).

[3] White had said that he felt it a "deeply serious and responsible duty to choose a candidate for President of the United States" and that an offer of support for the Republican nomination is "something which should be met with candor and respect by any citizen." He thought that Eisenhower should no longer wrap his attitude in "mystery," and he concluded that "Republicans from the crossroads, with no importance beyond that, feel that they are offering you support which should not be the subject of baffling tactics."

[4] See no. 358.

[5] According to White, Republican leaders had convinced him that Eisenhower would accept a call to "higher duty," but, he wrote, "every statement you make challenges this conclusion and makes me doubtful. . . ." He pointed out that Senator Robert A. Taft's announced candidacy had created a new situation that in professional political terms meant that "you can't beat somebody with nobody." White favored Eisenhower's nomination, he said, but if Eisenhower would not accept, who could challenge Taft? "He is honest, able and candid. He deserves the highest consideration. . . ." For Eisenhower's views on Taft's candidacy see no. 452.

[6] White had asked Eisenhower to consider the effect upon the leadership of such men as Senators James H. Duff (Republican, Pennsylvania) and Leverett Saltonstall (Republican, Massachusetts), Governor Thomas E. Dewey, and Roy A. Roberts (for background see no. 289) if he continued to repudiate assurances that they had given others regarding an Eisenhower candidacy.

[7] This last sentence appears as a handwritten addition by Eisenhower on the copy of this letter in EM.

[8] On Lodge see no. 499; on Wallace see no. 277.

[9] See "Mud Creek to the Elbe," *Emporia Gazette*, October 26, 1951.

[10] A memo in EM, White Corr., indicates that an extract from this letter was sent to General Edwin N. Clark by Eisenhower's aide Colonel Robert L. Schulz on December 5, 1951.

510   *Eisenhower Mss.*

To WILLIAM JOSEPH SLIM   *November 29, 1951*
Top secret

Dear Slim: I must say that you made a most thorough investigation of intelligence service to SHAPE, and for that I am naturally grateful and deeply appreciative.[1] At the same time, I regret that the matter took so much of your valuable time. While Airey[2] did take up all of these various subjects during the visit of the Chairman of the J.I.C.,[3] I have not personally been overly concerned about them.

This is not to say that I do not appreciate their importance but I have felt, like you, that they were mere creakings in the machinery that time and experience would soon eliminate.[4] If there ever was a command that had no cause to complain about cooperation, it is ours right here at SHAPE!

I am perfectly happy over the various actions you have taken in this matter and truly grateful for the time and personal attention you have given us.

With warm regard, *Cordially*

[1] For background on SHAPE's problems in gaining access to U.S. intelligence see no. 125. Slim's report is not in EM.

[2] Major General Terence S. Airey, a British officer recently reassigned (see no. 449), had served as SHAPE Assistant Chief of Staff for Intelligence.

[3] Eisenhower apparently referred to Colonel Louis B. Ely, Army member and ranking officer of the Joint Intelligence Committee, JCS.

[4] Following the JIC chairman's visit, a U.S. delegation of three staff officers (Colonel Benjamin B. Talley, USA; Colonel Edward H. Porter, USAF; and Lieutenant Colonel W. G. Muller, USMC) would attend an intelligence conference conducted at SHAPE on September 24 to discuss the release of classified U.S. military information to NATO headquarters. On January 22, 1952, based on the Talley group's recommendations, the JIC approved several changes to or clarifications of JIC 558/69, the document that established U.S.-SHAPE lines of communication. In the future, JIC representatives would visit SHAPE "as frequently as considered necessary and desirable" (Talley *et al.* had suggested regular visits about every three months); all communications between JIC and the SHAPE Intelligence Division would follow normal staff channels except in cases of "extreme urgency and warning of attack"; and certain categories of intelligence would proceed directly to the SHAPE director of intelligence rather than through the U.S. liaison officer. The JIC further adopted a procedure whereby SHAPE, instead of U.S. officers in Washington, marked classified documents "COSMIC" (the designation for the most sensitive NATO items). The United States eliminated other restrictions on the dissemination of classified information, and the Secretariat, State-Defense Military Information Control Committee, arranged a briefing of U.S. officers at SHAPE—a meeting to cover State-Defense policy on the release of U.S. intelligence to foreigners (on the problem of guarding atomic secrets while formulating war plans on an international staff see no. 837). The briefing would "include advice to U.S. officers [at SHAPE] to allay their curiosity in intelligence matters with a higher security classification than that to which they have access" (JIC 558/85, Jan. 9, 1952, CCS 092 Western Europe [3-12-48], Sec. 116).

Easing restrictions on the routing of U.S. intelligence and lowering slightly the "need to know" threshold required for access did not immediately lay to rest the problem of SHAPE's ability to acquire important information. On January 28 General Gruenther wrote a memorandum noting that some intelligence of "major interest" failed to reach NATO because of an earlier joint U.S.-British agreement requiring both countries to consent to the release of information identifiable by source. Gruenther complained that the British had cited this protocol, worked out by Major General James H. Burns (see no. 174) and General Sir Gerald Walter Robert Templer, Director of British Military Intelligence from 1946 to 1948, in denying SHAPE information the two countries shared. The JCS doubted that the Burns-Templer agreement actually curtailed the flow of essential information to SHAPE and in March declined to modify it—although the Chiefs sent to the British the substance of a statement that the United States never had considered the Burns-Templer arrangement "an obstacle in releasing intelligence which otherwise would be provided SHAPE" (JCS to U.S. Liaison Officer, SHAPE, JCS

900784, Feb. 11, 1952, CCS 092 Western Europe [3-12-48], Sec. 124; Gruenther to JCS, ALO 718, Feb. 14, 1952, *ibid.*, Sec. 125; JCS to U.S. Liaison Officer, SHAPE, JCS 903408, Mar. 12, 1952, *ibid.*, Sec. 130).

In the meantime, the Secretariat, State-Defense Military Information Control Committee, would request release to SHAPE of U.S. information on such subjects as Soviet seaborne logistics and amphibious warfare capabilities (JIC 558/87/D, Jan. 16, 1952, CCS 092 Western Europe [3-12-48], Sec. 117). In April, as SHAPE conducted a study of enemy atomic capabilities against central Europe, the U.S. member of the Standing Group would obtain data on the locations of fields from which the Soviets might launch aircraft loaded with atomic bombs (JIC 558/109, Apr. 17, 1952, *ibid.*, Sec. 136).

511   *Eisenhower Mss.*

To Mabel Frances Doud Moore   *November 30, 1951*

Dear Mike:[1] The Columbine is to be in Washington this coming week end and will be returning to Europe sometime about the middle of the week. We have asked the Nevinses to come over on the ship if they can possibly get away. We not only want to see them as old friends but, of course, want to talk over with them the affairs of the farm.[2]

We would be delighted if you could come along on the same trip. The capacity of our house cannot be stretched to take any more for the present than yourself, but Mamie and I figured that all the children are probably in school anyway and could not leave.

While I would rather suspect that you might have to go back to the States on a commercial liner or airplane if you wanted to be home by Christmas time, still that would probably not be too expensive. The Nevinses, of course, will probably be able to get westward passage on an Army transport since they are retired officers. If you can possibly make it, please let Colonel Davidson know at once. He will send me a cable.[3]

With love to all the family. *Devotedly*

[1] Mabel ("Mike") Moore was Mamie Eisenhower's sister (see no. 118, n. 2).
[2] Eisenhower's plane, the *Columbine*, would depart from Washington, D.C., with the Nevinses aboard on December 5 (see EM, Subject File, Aircraft-SHAPE [*Columbine*]; on the Nevinses' visit see no. 487, n. 5). For current developments on the General's Gettysburg farm, which the Nevinses managed, see the following document, n. 1.
[3] Moore would be unable to accept Eisenhower's invitation (see no. 564). Richard O. Davidson was SHAPE liaison officer at the Defense Department (see no. 402, n. 1).

To WALTER KIRSCHNER   *November 30, 1951*

Dear Walter:[1] Your note from Florida, photographs of the architects'
model, and the floor plans of the farm have just been handed to me.
My first impression is that the home is an absolutely magnificent
dream but, as I have said before, I am doubtful that such a fabulous
place is more than just that—a dream. But its contemplation is a lot
of fun.[2]

Mamie has asked me three questions:

(a) Are there trees growing on the selected site?

(b) Can an attractive covered porch be provided on the front—
where she can sit and rock on summer evenings?

(c) Is there a basement, including at least one room well away from
furnaces and hot water pipes where she could keep fruits, etc.,
that demand a cool place?[3]

Mamie joins in affectionate regards to you both.[4] *Cordially*

[1] Kirschner, George E. Allen's friend, had become interested in helping to improve
the Gettysburg farm (see no. 33). Craig Cannon and another staff officer helped
Eisenhower in drafting this letter.

[2] On October 29 (EM) Kirschner had promised to send Eisenhower a complete set
of plans and a model of the proposed new home (see EM, Kirschner Corr.). The
plans are not in EM. For background see no. 350.

[3] Mamie's questions would be answered by Kirschner in a letter of January 25,
1952 (EM). He explained that there were trees on the site selected for the house
and suggested that more could be transplanted. A covered porch could easily be
added, Kirschner wrote, as well as storage space, a playroom for the grandchildren, and an art studio in the basement.

[4] Mrs. Kirschner was the former Madeline Yeo.

6

A "transcending" call to duty

To James Lawrence Walsh   *December 1, 1951*

Dear Colonel Walsh:[1] It was good to hear from you again and especially to know that you have continued to devote some attention to the project that I described to you last January. Particularly, I remember with real pleasure our visit to Mrs. Crozier; it was a pleasant hour sandwiched between a lot of high-pressure engagements.[2]

The project for which I am anxious to secure adequate support for successful operation is known as the American Assembly, sponsored by Columbia University. Basically, its purpose is to secure study and analysis of America's great problems of today through competent academic research, supplemented by conferences participated in by an entire cross-section of America to include both the industrialists and the laboring man, as well as all other types and groups. An added feature of the plan is to help initiate similar studies in every locality in America—so that the net result will be not only a better understanding of Americanism but a more fervent support of its essentials.

In order that donors may comply easily with the requirements of tax laws, it is usual for them to make gifts or bequests directly to Columbia University with a statement that it is for the support of the American Assembly. Both the Trustees and I, as President, have agreed that such a statement of preference on the part of the donor is binding upon us.

As you know, I am President of the University, currently on leave of absence. The Acting President is Grayson Kirk; the Chairman of the Trustees is Mr. Frederick Coykendall; and the Clerk of the Trustees is Mr. M. Hartley Dodge.[3]

The American Assembly is directed by our Dean of the Business School, Philip Young, son of Owen D. Young. I am sending a copy of this letter to Dean Young so that, if there is any further information that could be helpful to you at this moment, he will send it to you at once.[4]

In spite of all the preoccupations of this task, I never lose interest in these programs and projects that I so firmly believe will be of great importance to the people of our country. So it is especially heartening to have such an understanding letter as yours.

With warm personal regard, *Cordially*

---

[1] James Lawrence Walsh was the president of the American Ordnance Association (see Galambos, *Chief of Staff*, no. 1834).
[2] On November 5 (EM) Walsh had written Eisenhower reminding him of their meeting on January 2, 1951, with "a very gracious lady at her home on Massachusetts Avenue in Washington, D.C." Mrs. Crozier, the former Mary Hoyt Williams, was the wife of William Crozier, who had been the Chief of Ordnance during World War I.

Walsh said that before making a donation, he would like to know more about the "foundation" that he and Eisenhower had discussed that day.

[3] On Kirk, Coykendall, and Dodge see nos. 31, n. 1, 114, n. 2, and 6, n. 1, respectively. On the American Assembly see no. 398.

[4] On February 12, 1952 (EM), Walsh replied, explaining that Philip Young had sent him a progress report on the American Assembly and a booklet on its aims (see also Young to Walsh, Dec. 28, 1951, EM). Walsh said that he was "most enthusiastic" about the project. On Philip Young see no. 8, n. 6; on Owen D. Young see Galambos, *Columbia University*, no. 801.

514   *Eisenhower Mss.*

TO JOHN HAWK   *December 1, 1951*

Dear John:[1] You asked for a picture of me in full dress, but it has been so many years since I wore a full dress uniform that I have no picture taken in that regalia. Moreover, I have with me here in Europe only the field type of uniform; consequently, I am sending you a copy of a picture in plain summer uniform. I hope you will not be too much disappointed.

Of course, all of us hope that, by the time you have grown up to military age, our country will have less need for great military forces than is now the case. Nevertheless, I am happy to know that you have planned a military career for yourself and, in it, I wish you all sorts of good luck.[2] *Sincerely*

[1] John Hawk was a young boy from Long Beach, California, who was planning a career in the Army.

[2] In his recent handwritten letter (n.d., EM) Hawk had told Eisenhower that "it sure would be nice" to have a picture of him in full dress uniform. A postscript said he "allready [*sic*] wrote to General Matthew Ridgeway in Tokyo, Japan" (on Ridgway see no. 31).

515   *Eisenhower Mss.*

TO HARRY CECIL BUTCHER   *December 3, 1951*

Dear Butch:[1] The "out of favor" angle was a new one to me. Moreover, your classifying yourself as the "bearer of bad news" was another one that had never occurred to me. I realize that everybody who possesses any kind of patronage power—promotions, reductions, and assignments—has to be very careful when listening to the opinions of a close subordinate. When those opinions deal with the qualifications and general abilities of the boss, they are normally completely valueless. However, I must point out that anyone who has been possessed of two such Chiefs of Staff as Bedell Smith and Al Gruenther does not need to worry too much about the banal effect of "Yes" men.[2]

Incidentally, whenever I read one of the articles written about me, I am astonished how much better imagination seems to provide material for a story than does just the sheer drudgery of investigation.

With all the best to you and yours, and to Mickey and Pearlie and their youngster.[3] *Cordially*

[1] For background on Butcher, the General's naval aide in World War II, see no. 171.

[2] In his letter (Nov. 24, 1951, EM) Butcher had said that he had heard from Virgil M. Pinkley (A.B. University of Southern California 1929), who was publisher and editor of the *Los Angeles Mirror* (on Pinkley see Chandler and Galambos, *Occupation, 1945*, no. 86). Pinkley, after visiting Eisenhower on October 31, apparently had related to Butcher that the General's opinion of him was favorable. Butcher said this news was gratifying, especially after reading in an article by John Gunther that he was "out of favor" with Eisenhower (see John Gunther, "Inside Ike," *Look*, December 4, 1951, pp. 30–35. On Gunther see Galambos, *Columbia University*, no. 53; and no. 649 in these volumes. See also Gunther's book, *Eisenhower: The Man and the Symbol*, in which Butcher is quoted extensively. "I am quite certain," Butcher wrote, "I was out of favor with you . . . during the war, probably because of my argumentive attitude and because I was frequently the bearer of bad news"). For background on Walter B. Smith see no. 144; on Alfred M. Gruenther see no. 2, n. 3. See also Chandler, *War Years*.

[3] On Michael J. and Pearl H. McKeogh and their daughter Mary Ann see no. 171.

516   *Eisenhower Mss.*

TO WINTHROP WILLIAMS ALDRICH   *December 3, 1951*

Dear Winthrop:[1] Thank you very much for your note. It has been months since I saw you and, consequently, nice to have news of you and yours. I particularly envy you your opportunity of making a trip to Texas.[2] I know some fine ranches in that country, and this time of year is exactly the best one during which to visit them. If I could have a couple of weeks on San Jose Island, for example, I think I could come back here with renewed energy and dedication.[3]

To my mind, Mr. Harte's findings were astonishing, almost astounding. Whatever may happen in the future, I do know one thing—I am presently so preoccupied in the duties pertaining to this job that I simply have no time to think very seriously about anything else.[4]

Mamie sends her love to you and yours, along with which come[s], of course, my very warmest regard. *Cordially*

[1] For background on Aldrich, chairman of the board of the Chase Manhattan Bank, see no. 196, n. 4.

[2] Aldrich had visited Eisenhower on May 29 and 31. On November 26 (EM) he had written the General about his recent trip to Texas, where he had investigated the amount of political support Eisenhower had. Although many Texans seemed to favor Senator Taft, Aldrich's impression was that Eisenhower could "carry the state" as a Republican candidate (on Taft see no. 452, n. 3).

[3] On the General's previous visit to San José Island, off the Texas coast in the Gulf of Mexico, see Galambos, *Columbia University*, no. 607.

[4] During his visit to Texas Aldrich had spoken with newspaper publisher Houston Harte (B.J. University of Missouri 1915), a member of Harte, Hanks and Company and vice-president of the Texas Publishers Association. Harte's newspapers had already announced their support for Eisenhower as a candidate, and Harte had sent a questionnaire to other Texas newspapers to poll their support. On November 23 Harte sent Aldrich a copy of the questionnaire and the incomplete results (copy of both in EM, Aldrich Corr.). Of the thirty newspapers that had responded so far, approximately two-thirds favored Eisenhower. Aldrich had described the results as "important and encouraging."

517 *Eisenhower Mss.*

To William Samuel Paley

December 3, 1951

Dear Bill:[1] I have already seen Prescott Bush. We had a very nice chat about ten days ago.[2] I liked him very much.

My thanks for your complimentary references to my work. Sometimes I must admit that I can use a moral pat on the back, particularly when someone has depressed me with what he believes to be incontrovertible proof that the economies of each of these countries is about to go into a transcontinental nosedive.

Likewise, I was happy to have your impressions of the University affairs and of the American Assembly.[3]

When next you see George Allen, ask him how his waistline is coming and remind him that the time draws near when he must be down to 199 pounds or send me a check for four hundred bucks and, in addition, ten dollars for each pound he is out of line. Do anything else you can think of to make him stop eating like an Aberdeen Angus being fattened for market.[4]

Mamie and I send our best to you and your bride. *Cordially*

[1] For background on Columbia Broadcasting System executive Paley see Galambos, *Columbia University*, no. 717.

[2] Paley had written on November 9 (EM), mentioning Prescott Sheldon Bush's

hopes of visiting Eisenhower. Bush (M.A. Yale 1917), a partner of Brown Brothers Harriman and Company and a director of CBS, had seen the General on November 20.

[3] Paley had praised Eisenhower's "truly remarkable performance," saying that he had raised "the hopes and aspirations of the people of Western Europe" in a short period of time. Paley also had noted that Columbia University seemed to be doing well under Grayson L. Kirk's direction and that the American Assembly had gotten a "good start" (on Kirk see no. 31, n. 1; on the American Assembly see no. 398).

[4] Paley had lunched with George E. Allen several times recently (on Allen's bet with Eisenhower see no. 493). For developments see no. 777.

518   *Eisenhower Mss.*

To Edward D. Nicholson   *December 3, 1951*
Personal and confidential

Dear Eddie:[1] Thank you for sending me the editorial from The Denver Post dated November 25th.[2] I must say that, if Palmer Hoyt was responsible for its writing, he was not only generous in his attitude but he showed that, during the years of our friendship, he has quite obviously gained a clear impression of the motives that I hope will always animate my actions.[3] I am complimented that his convictions should reflect such confidence in my devotion to duty and my integrity of intention.

Needless to say, this year we have sadly missed the opportunities we had while at Columbia to visit Denver at intervals. It is not merely a question of going to the Cherry Hills Country Club—I like everything about that city.[4] For us, it is too bad that Mamie's health forbids long periods in that altitude and that I seem to keep so busy that we cannot come back with greater frequency. Please give my very best to all my old friends that you encounter.

In spite of the fact that I have marked this letter Personal and Confidential, I do not mind if you show it to Palmer, provided my assumption is correct that he authorized the editorial. Except for him, it is to have no circulation because, sure as you're a foot high, any remark of mine on the political situation, no matter how innocent, is subject to a thousand interpretations and misinterpretations. But Hoyt will not make any mistakes in that respect.

With warm personal regard, *Cordially*

[1] Nicholson was the manager of regional affairs for United Air Lines in Denver, Colorado.

[2] An editorial entitled "A Hypothesis about Eisenhower" (*Denver Post*, Nov. 25, 1951, copy in EM) said that it was a mistake to try to make Eisenhower fit "the

749

rigid mold of the conventional politician." The editorial concluded that if Eisenhower believed that the long-term goals of SHAPE required his leadership at home, he would then become a presidential candidate: "Under any less compulsion he will not."
[3] On Edwin P. Hoyt see no. 311.
[4] On the Cherry Hills Country Club see no. 417.

519   *Eisenhower Mss.*

To Leonard Franklin McCollum   *December 3, 1951*

Dear Mc:[1] Thank you very much for your interesting letter about the American Assembly. From all that I can learn, it is going forward as well as we could possibly expect—this is true in spite of the fact that I would have personally liked to have seen an early, additional, conference on America's relationships with Europe. I realize that one item in any study of inflationary tendencies at home will involve the money that America has devoted to the rehabilitation of economic and military strength of Europe. However, I would have very much liked to have seen the American Assembly carry forward with a very definite and specific examination of the economies, finances, and political conditions in each of the several European countries with which we are associated. Thus, we could gradually have formed conclusions as to the actual requirements of our cooperative purposes and our combined success in meeting those requirements.[2]

Every day, travelers from the United States bring me new questions concerning this whole great project. Some of these questions are searching, even profound, in character. Others display a complete ignorance as to basic relationships among the free countries, the purposes of NATO, and the inevitable results on the United States of success or failure. I am sure that we have got to promote study of these questions at all levels; I should like to see a small American Assembly in every town and village of the United States, earnestly studying the things that are going to mean so much to us and to our children. I make no claim that my own conclusions and convictions on all these matters are correct. But I do know that I earnestly attempt to get down to facts in making my conclusions, and I frequently wish that I had the help of an American Assembly that could remain constantly in session to which I could refer some of my own questions and problems in the certainty that a cross-section of America, when informed as to the facts, will decide correctly.[3]

Mamie joins me in all the best to you and yours. We envy you your opportunity to see your daughter, and to all of you we send "Merry Christmas and Happy New Year."[4] *Cordially*

[1] McCollum was president of the Continental Oil Company and a supporter of the American Assembly (see Galambos, *Columbia University*, no. 826).

[2] On November 21 McCollum had written Eisenhower concerning the American Assembly and had enclosed a copy of the minutes from the National Policy Board meeting held on November 1 (both in EM). Attributing a large part of the Assembly's success to the "firm foundation" the General had established, McCollum commended Philip Young and Lewis W. Douglas for their work in the organization. For background on Young see no. 8, n. 6; on Douglas, no. 47, n. 4. On planning for the second American Assembly see no. 398.

[3] For developments see no. 612.

[4] McCollum had mentioned that he and his wife, the former Margaret Wilson, would soon be flying to Montevideo, Uruguay, to visit their married daughter, Olive Glennell Brown.

520 *Eisenhower Mss.*

To Julius Earl Schaefer *December 3, 1951*
Personal and confidential

Dear Earl:[1] While I had never before read one of Paul Harvey's broadcasts, I found most interesting the two copies that you sent to me. By accident, I read first the one dated November 11th and I found myself saying, "Amen," at the end of almost every sentence. Of course, when he took a passing shot at foreign relations, he seemed to think (and here I am doing a bit of guessing) that all we had to do was drop everything abroad and that this alone would allow us to live in peace and security. Such an idea is, of course, worse than naive; it reflects a complete ignorance of the world today. On the other hand, his insistence that the only thing that is going to save the world is a return, on the part of the American people, to the philosophy of work and to the purpose of directing our own affairs rings a bell with me.[2]

Then I picked up the copy of his November 4th broadcast, and my opinion of Paul Harvey fell into a bottomless chasm.[3] Why anyone should believe that another American should be so callous, so indifferent to his duty, and, in short, such a deceitful sort of person as he makes me out to be in his broadcast, I shall never know. My only conclusion is that a man must be reflecting his own type of thinking. He dopes out what someone else would do on the basis of his own reactions to a temptation or a given set of circumstances.

Actually, there was not one single word of politics spoken at the meeting that this man attempts so ignorantly to describe. If I were so contemptuous of the responsibilities resting upon me in this assignment that I would regard those responsibilities nothing more than an opportunity for my own political advancement, then I ought to be shot. Moreover, and here possibly is the key to the whole thing, I simply do *not want* a political office. This I have told you before, so it is no news—but at least there has been no change.

I realize you didn't expect me to answer at such length, but I gathered from your note that this man is one of your favorite news commentators and I wanted to point out that, while he may be entertaining on the air, you are wrong if you look upon his efforts as "news." At least, in the one case, it was not only sheer fiction, it was the product of a distorted imagination.[4] *Sincerely*

[1] Schaefer was a Wichita, Kansas, executive with the Boeing Airplane Company (see Galambos, *Columbia University*, no. 759).

[2] On November 16 Schaefer had written that because he doubted Eisenhower had opportunities to hear Paul Harvey's Sunday night broadcasts, he was enclosing copies of Harvey's commentaries of November 4 and 11 (EM). On November 11 Harvey, a news analyst and commentator with the American Broadcasting Company (ABC) since 1944, had discussed the poor state of the national economy, concluding that only if people "really go to work" would American self-government "last intact through all the earthly time there is." The "passing shot at foreign relations" to which Eisenhower objected was Harvey's statement that the United States had "given away eleven billion dollars trying to buy friends abroad, though a hired soldier, never in history, won a war" (copy in EM).

[3] In his November 4 broadcast Harvey had described a possible scenario for Eisenhower's meeting with Truman, scheduled to take place on November 5 (on the meeting see no. 480). Harvey had predicted that Truman would offer the General the Democratic nomination for the presidency.

[4] Schaefer would reply on December 15 that he usually enjoyed Harvey's broadcasts and found him to be a responsible journalist. Schaefer agreed, however, that the commentary of November 4 had been "quite imaginative" (EM). For developments see no. 617.

521   *Eisenhower Mss.*

TO HARRY AMOS BULLIS   *December 3, 1951*
Personal and confidential

Dear Harry:[1] Within recent days, I have had three interesting notes from you.[2] I am grateful that you continue to keep me informed as to elements of the current scene, as you view them. I have so little time to give attention to anything other than the pressing daily requirements of this job that I am peculiarly dependent upon my friends to tell me about things that do not appear in the headlines of the newspapers.

I sometimes wonder whether many people in the United States understand the extreme delicacy and the extraordinary significance of the effort that the United States is making to get the free nations to produce collective security through cooperation. The success of the whole effort is so important to our country that nothing must be allowed to interfere with its progress. For example, while I believe that the people of Europe would approve of my responding to anything that they might consider a more important duty than the one I am now performing, they would certainly be resentful of my becoming "just another candidate" and with no apparent duty involved in the picture whatsoever. As long as I have to serve in uniform, I can be governed by no other policy than that of giving my complete attention to the duties assigned to me.

All this is understood thoroughly by many good friends who are now engaged in the attempt to lay before me another kind of duty. They realize that for me to participate, even directly or by implication, in their effort would not only be a great disservice to our country in the tremendous effort it is making in the international field but would do much to destroy such reputation I have had for a disinterested and loyal public servant.[3]

With warm personal regard,[4] *Cordially*

[1] Bullis was chairman of the board of General Mills, Inc., in Minneapolis, Minnesota (for background see Galambos, *Columbia University*, no. 893).
[2] In his first note, dated November 21, Bullis had enthusiastically called for an Eisenhower presidential candidacy. A second message of the same date concerned the American Assembly at Columbia University. On November 26 Bullis had again expressed his hope that Eisenhower soon would launch a political campaign (all in EM).
[3] For a similar reply to the same question see no. 509.
[4] Bullis's reply of December 18 is in EM.

522 *Eisenhower Mss.*

To Martin Withington Clement *December 4, 1951*
Personal

Dear Clem:[1] I cannot tell you how much I appreciate the trouble you took to write out for me the essentials of a loyal American's creed. I value it highly, not only because it rather accurately outlines the doctrine that you and I have agreed constitutes our guiding philosophy, but because you have taken the trouble to state each point in a direct and utterly simple manner.[2]

Incidentally, it is possible that you may have secured a copy of a little book put out by The Reader's Digest called, "The 30th Anniversary, Reader's Digest." It is a selection of articles previously published by that magazine. In the book is a short piece I wrote many months ago, entitled, "An Open Letter to America's Students."[3] I call attention to this little article, not through any pride of authorship, but because it so closely follows the line of reasoning that resulted in your memorandum.

Of particular interest to me was your statement, "Everybody loves prosperity and the country is prosperous." I believe that some people have questioned the accuracy of the term *"prosperous."* Some seem to believe that everything now has the appearance of prosperity, but doubt that it is *real*. Because some stock a man owns may gain a few points, or because he may be able to sell real estate for more dollars than he paid for it, he cannot be certain that he is prospering. He may be nothing but the victim of inflation. These things were true of Germany in the late 1920s and we know what happened; utter and complete collapse! Everybody is working and wages are high, but a lot of people maintain that, unless there is a sound, recognizable consumer need stretching on into the future which will profitably absorb the products of that labor, it is time to take a look—to determine whether we are having real prosperity or whether we just think so.

However, all would agree with you that, as of this moment, the mass of people *believe* we are prosperous and, therefore, your conclusions as to the difficulty of making any political change are indeed correct.[4]

A clearcut and thoughtful analysis of our situation would be valuable, particularly if couched in such terms that all of us could understand it. It may be that anyone attempting to call attention to the danger signs would be more than repudiated—he might be scorned and hated as a prophet of doom. But we need to know more about the meaning of important factors in our financial-economic world. Among other things, they include expenditures so high as to be frightening; taxes so high as to approach the point of destroying initiative; enormous portions of our labor and materials flowing into the negative and sterile organizations known as armies, navies, and air forces; a corresponding lack of many things that people want and need; a constant spiral of rising commodity prices and the costs of everything that go into the production of commodities; a lack of assurance that tremendous allocations of public funds are fully required or wisely spent; and the increasing tendency to depend upon government instead of self![5]

Love to your family—all the best to you. *Cordially*

---

[1] For background on Eisenhower's friend Clement see no. 278.

[2] Writing Eisenhower on November 23 (EM), Clement had included an outline of the General's beliefs entitled "Points for Eisenhower." "First of all," Clement wrote, Eisenhower is "for God and Country." The list continued by describing the General's aversion to bureaucracy, inflation, and excessive governmental regulation. His goal, Clement said, was a "free world, with local autonomy; free states,

with representative forms of government, allied together for united defense" (copy in EM).

[3] Eisenhower's article had first appeared in October 1948 (see Galambos, *Columbia University*, no. 351; see also *The Thirtieth Anniversary Reader's Digest Reader* [Garden City, N.Y., 1951], pp. 11–15).

[4] Clement had commented on the "peculiar" condition of the United States: "Everybody loves prosperity and the country is prosperous. You are never able to defeat a party in power in prosperous times; yet people are uncertain and disturbed; some are afraid and wonder where we are going—and that runs from labor leaders to business leaders." For Eisenhower's own concern for the U.S. economy see no. 441. On Germany's economy after World War I see Fritz K. Ringer, ed., *The German Inflation of 1923* (New York, 1969).

[5] For developments see no. 590.

523   *Eisenhower Mss., Family File*

To EDGAR NEWTON EISENHOWER   *December 6, 1951*
Secret. Personal

Dear Ed: My clock tells me that I have about half an hour to myself, an event that in this headquarters, these days, is little short of miraculous. I hope to employ it in answering your recent letter and, if I get down half the thoughts that are now running through my head, this will be long—I hope not boring.[1]

With a great deal of what you say, I am in complete agreement, especially that part of your letter that deals with the purposes and methods of political parties. The core of a political party is, of course, the skeleton organization that holds it together, and this organization is composed of professionals; men whose party must win if they are to wield any power and influence and who, therefore, become cold-blooded—or, as they would say, extremely practical—in their methods of attaining victory.[2]

Where I think I depart somewhat from your conclusions is in your statement that the people as a whole are just as partisan as are the politicians. Now, I hasten to admit that the so-called "pressure groups" have been developed through appeals to the narrow and selfish interests of the members. Even so, the organizers of these groups have *normally* had to assert and insist that what they were advocating was also for the good of the country as a whole.[3] While I would not quarrel with the statement that people are partisan in the sense that they sometimes fail to look beyond their own private and immediate gain to the ultimate good of their nation and themselves, still people reacting in this way are responding to one of the recognized factors in human nature.

I know that when I read about a man who admires the armed services, and who finds among the individuals of those services a high average of brains, loyalty, and devotion to duty, then I automatically conclude that that particular individual is a very wise and discerning person. I venture that you do the same when anyone talks that way about lawyers.[4] Now, possibly you and I would not be tempted particularly if someone offered lawyers or soldiers a few more dollars a year, but let us remember that when we react favorably to group flattery and personal blandishment, we are responding to the same element in human nature that helps to develop pressure groups.

I am often struck by the regularity with which people, as they grow older, become much more ready to live by principle than by immediate advantage—how much they begin to substitute philosophy for emotion and impulse. This is particularly true if, with advancing years, the individual accumulates a fair share of this world's goods and, as a result, a degree of confidence in his ability to take care of his own future.

Now, if we look back to the time when you and I were kids working in the Belle Springs, trying to get together a few dollars to apply to the expenses of a college education,[5] I wonder what would have been our decision had we been selected as the judges in a debate in which one side held that we were entitled to an additional dollar a day; and the other side held that, if we got that dollar a day, there would be in the offing the threat of inflation, a dangerous trend in the industrial relations of the country, or even, let us say, a more or less direct threat to some provision of the Constitution. What I am getting at here is not that I disagree with your observations, but that I feel you have neglected to consider how you would put these choices before an electorate whose average opportunities in education have not taken them further than we had progressed in 1909 or 1910.

I believe that leaders in the political, educational, and religious world must do more to inform all of us as to the simple facts of our system and of our existence as a free nation. There should be incessant repetition in the essentials of our system and in the various kinds of dangers that can threaten them, from both internal and external sources. Let me take a specific example:

> Most of us think of the United States as a completely self-sufficient industrial and political giant that can go its own way in the world without any thought at all to what the rest of the world may do. We speak with great pride of the accomplishments of our free system, including its necessary basis of a free economy, and assume that this system can continue indefinitely regardless of external relations. Although science is doing much to make use of substitutes of various kinds for critical materials, yet the fact remains that *we must annually import great quantities of raw materials*

or our whole industrial system will begin to dry up and great political changes would necessarily ensue. There is a whole list of critical materials in this category. So, we are instantly struck with the fact that we must not only keep open communications to the countries where these materials are produced, but we must make sure that, in those areas, *there are governments and populations that desire to trade with us.* If those areas should be occupied by enemies of ours, the conditions requisite to trade would not exist. It would do no good merely to offer more money to get the goods. Witness the cessation of our manganese imports from Russia.[6]

Now, such simple facts as these ought to be understood by everybody, but they are not; and one of my chief quarrels with the so-called political leader is that he normally makes no attempt to help us understand these things. As you say, many are interested merely in obtaining power; like so many other individuals, they are far more interested in immediate gain than in the eventual good of the nation and themselves.

It is this kind of thing that disturbs me mightily as I survey the national scene. I have frequently expressed to you my feeling concerning any possible political role for myself—I don't think anyone could have a greater personal antipathy than I toward such an eventuality. But what bothers me is that, if I criticize (and I mean criticize even in my own mind) what is now being done or not being done by our governmental officials, I am forced to ask myself, "What am *I* doing about it, or what do I *intend* doing about it?" Certainly I share with you your constantly expressed regard for the Constitution.[7] I still believe it outlines the greatest form of government that was ever devised. *But the framers of the Constitution had to assume that citizens would shoulder their responsibilities as such*; they could not for one moment assume that a citizen, completely dissatisfied with the political situation of any moment, would remain silent and inactive regardless of the depth of his resentment and criticism.

Through this kind of thinking, I arrive at the conclusion that each of us must strive to do his *duty*. Certainly in my case, there is no duty involved that would dictate my seeking service in any kind of political position. Most appeals made to me are based upon the theory that I have duties to the nation outside the military—but the point I am trying to make is that, for me, there can be no political duty, even as the product of the most distorted reasoning, at least before there is something substantial in the way of a public mandate, something far more compelling and more official than "Gallup Polls" and the like.

My personal ambition has remained unchanged for a number of years. It includes a hope that I may withdraw into a more reasonable tempo of daily duties and pressures than I have been confronting during this entire decade. I would like to go to a farm and, operating from there, I should like occasionally to meet with people whose opinions I respect, to exchange with them views and ideas as to how greater interest can be aroused in the essentials of Americanism and what the individual might do to further such efforts. I should like to remain completely unpartisan and devoted solely to the good of our country.

To live this kind of a life with Mamie (with occasional visits from our children) would, to my mind, constitute about the last word in contentment. Of course, I would want to intersperse my duties with a bit of golf, trout fishing, and bird shooting. More than this, I could not want—except, of course, that I would want all my brothers and their families to come to the farm annually for a reunion, or maybe I would at long last even have time to go to theirs.[8]

My love to your Lucy.[9] *As ever*

[1] Eisenhower's brother Edgar had written on November 28 (EM) of his concern about the mounting pressure on Eisenhower to declare himself a candidate for the presidency (for background on Edgar see no. 24, n. 1).

[2] Edgar had expressed doubt that either political party was interested in the people of the United States; party leaders, he said, do not "give a damn about you personally, or about your own ideas of domestic or foreign policy—what they are thinking is that you are popular with the people as a whole, and if you will declare yourself as a candidate on either ticket, that ticket has a better chance of winning. . . ."

[3] "The people of this country are not intellectually honest," Edgar had written. "Each person's thinking is governed largely by some selfish interest. . . ."

[4] Edgar was senior partner of Eisenhower, Hunter, and Ramsdell, a Tacoma, Washington, law firm.

[5] See Eisenhower's memoir *At Ease*, pp. 102–4.

[6] Since 1948, when the United States had banned export of material that might aid Russia's war potential, Russia had reduced its shipments of manganese to the United States. By the spring of 1951, however, the United States had found new sources for the valuable raw material and was importing manganese from India, the Union of South Africa, and Brazil (see no. 246; and *New York Times*, Jan. 19, Apr. 29, 1951).

[7] "We have torn the Constitution to shreds," Edgar had written, "and anyone trying to make an effort to put it back together again will find some pieces missing. . . ." He blamed the Congress, the executive branch of government, and the courts for the nation's problems (see also no. 824).

[8] Since the end of World War II the Eisenhower brothers had held annual reunions (see Galambos, *Chief of Staff*, nos. 660 and 1017, and *Columbia University*, no. 454). In a reply of December 11, 1951 (EM), Edgar would tell his brother, "Basically, there is no difference between you and me, but I think that you express your thoughts so much better than I do. . . . I am against your running, but dammit, if you do accept such importunities as are made to you, I will support you wholeheartedly."

[9] Edgar Eisenhower's wife, the former Lucille Dawson.

To Harold Kennan Daniels   *December 6, 1951*

Dear Mr. Daniels:[1] These days afford me little time for correspondence, but I couldn't read a letter like yours without some attempt at reply.

Naturally, I am flattered by the kindness of your personal references to myself. But confidence such as you have expressed would be impossible unless I insisted on giving my full attention to the job to which I've been assigned; that of serving as the American Commander of a collective security force.[2]

The world-wide threat of Communism has been and still is of serious consequence to America and its future. Since the war, it has been a constant worry, accounting for tremendous outlays in the foreign field and in the Armed Services. More than this, in Korea it has cost the lives of thousands of young Americans and many of our Allies.

The United States has, therefore, led other free nations in joining together the key nations of the Atlantic community. I am honored to have a part in this enterprise because I feel that it is the only way in which we can build a lasting security for ourselves and for other lands vital to our welfare. How long the job will take, nor how long I may be considered necessary to it, I cannot even hazard a guess. But realizing its significance to our people, I continue to give it my undivided effort. To do otherwise—more specifically, to do anything that would tend to encourage in the United States partisan thinking toward this task—would be a disservice to the country.[3]

I appreciate your taking the time to write and hope you will view with sympathy my position, and my determination to get the job done. With best wishes, *Sincerely*

[1] Daniels was the labor-relations director for the pharmaceutical manufacturer Parke, Davis and Company, in Detroit, Michigan.

[2] On November 26 Daniels had written to report wide support for an Eisenhower presidential candidacy and to praise the General for "those attributes which inspire universal affection and confidence" (EM). Daniels commended Eisenhower for attempting to complete his assignment as SACEUR but worried that delay might jeopardize Eisenhower's political future.

[3] This was the General's stock answer at this time to questions about his future in politics; however, compare this reply with the preceding document.

525

525   *Eisenhower Mss.*

To Arthur Hays Sulzberger[1]   *December 7, 1951*
Cable AP 82295

Fully endorse procedure proposed in your letter of December 3.[2]
Warm regards

[1] For background on the *New York Times* publisher and Columbia University trustee
see no. 114.

[2] In his letter (EM) Sulzberger, chairman of the trustees' Honors Commmittee,
had requested Eisenhower's approval of a plan to stage a luncheon for General
Douglas MacArthur; on that occasion the university would award him the hood
and diploma he had been unable to accept four years earlier, when the university
had granted him and Eisenhower honorary Doctor of Laws degrees. Upon the
former commander's return from the Far East in the spring of 1951—at the height
of the relief-from-command controversy—Sulzberger had rejected a proposal to
fete MacArthur (see nos. 101 and 136). Sulzberger now reminded Eisenhower that
the degree had recognized MacArthur's military leadership in World War II and
stipulated that the luncheon would receive no advance publicity, would include no
speeches, and would not be open to the public. In a handwritten note at the bottom
of the letter, Sulzberger commented that the ticklish issue proved "the wisdom of
not giving degrees in absentia." There is no further correspondence in EM regarding this matter. For background on the honorary degrees see Galambos, *Chief of
Staff*, no. 1331.

526   *Eisenhower Mss.*

To William Morrow Fechteler   *December 7, 1951*
Secret. Personal

My dear Admiral:[1] You will recall that during your visit to SHAPE we
discussed some of your tentative ideas as to possible changes in U.S.
Naval command arrangements in Europe so that they would harmo-
nize with the NATO structure.[2] At the time I felt that we reached clear
understanding of the principles on which you could proceed satisfactorily in meeting our different needs and desires with respect to Carney's command responsibilities. Roughly, those principles were:
    First: Carney must be free to concentrate on those matters which
are germane to his allied command of my southern flank.
    Second: His primary attention must be directed toward the coor-
dination of ground, naval and air forces within his allied command
area, and the solution of the many politico-military problems associated therewith, rather than preoccupation with purely naval affairs.
    Third: His strategic responsibilities as a U.S. commander should

be defined generally by his allied responsibilities. His position as the highest U.S. Naval authority in Europe should be carefully sustained.

Fourth: He should have the necessary authority to discharge in full his responsibilities as commander within his own area.

Under these general guides, I thought it possible for you to make whatever changes you considered mandatory for U.S. Naval command requirements without any diminution of the prestige and authority which I feel that Carney must retain.

Since I talked to you, Carney has discussed the subject with me.[3] He has very strong convictions that it is neither timely nor desirable to separate him from his U.S. Naval command. He considers that he should continue personally to retain the title of Commander-in-Chief over U.S. Naval Forces in view of the transcending importance of *command* and the prestige associated with it in the military scheme. He does not consider operational control adequate to meet the needs of his position. He stresses the importance of *command* in order to obtain fully effective naval support for his NATO headquarters.

Another point made by Carney is that the present is a peculiarly awkward period in which to make any changes in Naval command. In this I agree. There is still uncertainty as to the exact form of NATO command that will evolve for the Atlantic and for Greece and Turkey. Hence, I propose that you maintain the status quo until those decisions are made.[4]

I am sympathetic to Carney's desire to retain command over U.S. Naval Forces within his NATO area. While it is my natural instinct as a Commander wholeheartedly to back up my subordinates, I have told Carney that I've never understood why his U.S. Naval domain needs to extend substantially beyond that area. I have emphasized that he should continue to be recognized unqualifiedly as the senior U.S. Naval Officer in Europe, but I do not feel that such recognition is necessarily contingent upon the retention of a U.S. title as Commander-in-Chief in addition to that of an Allied Commander-in-Chief. My own situation is a good example.[5]

I must leave to your judgment to determine how you later resolve these conflicting considerations, especially as I note that both you and Carney hold to the importance of having only one U.S. Naval Commander-in-Chief in Europe.

I am sending Carney a copy of this letter in order that there may be a common understanding of my position.[6] He is better equipped to express, in naval terminology, the views he has stated to me. Therefore, I am going to suggest that he communicate directly to you such recommendations he may have, within the framework of the principles I have set forth, to assist you in making your decision. *Sincerely*

[1] For background on Admiral Fechteler, Chief of Naval Operations, see no. 45, n. 8. Eisenhower's letter, dispatched by courier, arrived in Washington on December 13, 1951 (EM).

[2] Fechteler had visited SHAPE headquarters on October 29 (see no. 429).

[3] For Admiral Robert Bostwick Carney's protests against giving up his CINC-NELM responsibilities see no. 507.

[4] In his November 21 letter Carney had mentioned that the SACLANT vacancy (due to controversy over American and British responsibilities in the North Atlantic) made it "impossible to draft terms of reference for the London headquarters." He also noted the possibility that CINCNELM headquarters might in the future "be placed somewhere other than in Naples"; until then, he insisted, "the present arrangement should stand" (Carney to Eisenhower, Nov. 21, 1951, EM; see also no. 507). On the command-structure problems that Greek and Turkish membership in NATO presented see no. 423.

[5] While Eisenhower served as SACEUR, General Thomas Troy Handy filled the role of U.S. Commander in Chief, Europe. On Handy's possible retirement see no. 321; for developments in the U.S. command structure in Europe see no. 836.

[6] See the following document. For developments see no. 694.

527   *Eisenhower Mss.*

To ROBERT BOSTWICK CARNEY   *December 7, 1951*
Secret. Personal

My dear Carney:[1] I hope that you will understand that the press of affairs incident to the Rome Meeting of the North Atlantic Council and the activities of the Harriman Committee[2] has precluded an earlier consideration of the command problem which I am sure is very much on your mind.

Attached is a copy of a letter which I have just sent to Admiral Fechteler.[3] I have endeavored to set forth to him those principles to which I adhere. I have avoided becoming involved in the details of *how* he solves what is essentially a problem of U.S. naval administration and command relations, albeit a knotty one.

You will note that I have concurred with you as to the wisdom of not making any change at the moment. I have proposed that he await decisions that have yet to be made in regard to the NATO command structure for the Atlantic and for Greece and Turkey.[4]

While I support fully the need for you to have essential authority over the U.S. Naval Forces within your NATO command area, I do not perceive any advantage for an extension of that authority to Northern or Central Europe, London or the Persian Gulf. Indeed, there seem to me to be practical disadvantages. Similarly, while I wholeheartedly endorse the necessity for unqualified recognition of your status as the senior U.S. naval officer in Europe, the maintenance of your prestige and the importance of the effective U.S. naval support to your NATO command, I do not hold that these are contingent on the retention of a specific title on your part. My own command status over U.S. Forces is a good example. So, I'm not taking a definite stand on those points.

I suggest that you communicate directly to Admiral Fechteler any further recommendations you may have to assist him in the evolution of a mutually acceptable solution and a decision which must be his in his capacity as Chief of Naval Operations.[5] *Cordially*

[1] For background on Carney see no. 53, n. 4.
[2] See no. 539.
[3] See the preceding document.
[4] For background on these issues see the preceding document and no. 423.
[5] For developments see no. 694.

528

Eisenhower Mss.

To Clifford Roberts
Personal and confidential

December 8, 1951

Dear Cliff:[1] Of course, you are right about what you must say as you invite individuals to join a group to advise me. Since their generous readiness to help me would be the uniting link among the several members, it is necessary that each should know that I personally want him in the group.[2]

There has apparently arisen a crisis in the whole effort that is being made at home to drag me into the political field. This crisis involves a growing conviction on the part of "political engineers" that I must, as of now, make a positive announcement of political intent. Otherwise, I am told, the whole effort is hopeless.[3]

As you know, I simply am not going to do any such thing. To my mind, it would be a dereliction in duty—almost a violation of my oath of office. This brings into a head-on collision the convictions of the practical politician as to what are the conditions prerequisite to nomination and my determination to do my present duty—and to go into anything else only if confronted with a greater duty! I have sensed that this sort of thing was building up. It has always worried me to realize that too many people did not believe me when I told them I do *not want* a political career and, moreover, that I would do nothing of any kind to get a nomination. I have promised only that I would not repudiate their efforts. I, of course, do not want to be in the position, even through negative action, of allowing friends to say I had let them down. But they have no right to say such a thing as long as I do not refuse a definite call that would be recognized universally as a summons to duty. (Some of these political enthusiasts are trying to make it appear that I have a duty to *seek* a nomination. This is ridiculous, as I know you will agree.)

To comply with the advice and urgent insistence that I have just received would have the most damaging effects on this job. Not that I could not be replaced; I am not egotistical enough to pose as an indispensable man in any job. But for me voluntarily to participate in an active or semi-active way in the pursuit of a political nomination would not only create confusion in twelve governments—to each of which I have preached incessantly the paramount importance of NATO—but it would almost instantly divide, along partisan lines, American support of this project. This would be fatal.

It is understood that, whenever I mark a letter to you Personal and Confidential, there is still no objection to your discussing it with any particular member of the group that we have already named. But since mail normally has to pass a rather devious route in a man's office, I think it is well to label letters in this fashion even though I know that your personal treatment of such communications is completely discreet in any case.

The last word I had from home indicated that maybe you would come over with Bill Robinson for a few days at Christmas.[4] I hope you will allow nothing to interfere with such a wonderful intention. The Nevinses are here right now, and we are hoping they will stay throughout the holidays.[5] If they do, we might succeed in collecting up enough people so that the gatherings would look like 60 Morningside. In any event, we could certainly stir up some bridge games. Since you and Bill are not sightseers, we could just get you some accommodations at the Trianon.[6] *As ever*

P.S. I have just received your second note saying you'd come. Wonderful! I cabled you saying December 22nd meeting okay.[7]

---

[1] Roberts was Eisenhower's friend and adviser (see no. 7).

[2] On planning for Eisenhower's political advisory group and its early membership see no. 503. In a letter of December 3 (EM) Roberts had assured Eisenhower that he would begin organizing the circle at once. "It will all be done by telephone and I will explore the possibilities of holding a meeting before Christmas," he reported. "It seems to me the first meeting should be held as quickly as possible." Roberts had asked the General to reconsider as "impractical" his suggestion that Roberts assume responsibility for forming the group—as if it were his idea. "In my opinion," Roberts wrote, "this would not work, because I would be in the position of asking pretty serious minded people to furnish unasked advice which they of course would balk at doing. Further, each one would very greatly prefer to know he had been chosen by you. I think the best idea is to recite just what happened, which as I recall it, involved a conversation you and I had in Paris. I asked you what you

would do in the event a proposal was made to you by a group to whom you could not give anything other than a direct reply. You told me your reaction would be to at once get 'The Gang' together, tell them the pros and cons and particularly the stumbling blocks and ask their advise [sic]." Having discussed this idea further, Roberts recounted, a group had formed (1) to gather information and develop opinions—in Eisenhower's words, to "talk over the important factors of the American scene and even some of the inconsequential details such as the specific trend in public thinking and so on"; (2) to prepare to advise Eisenhower, if requested, "with respect to a major decision"—not overlooking his "negative thoughts" on the subject; and (3) to "cause a proper effort to be made to scrutinize material being distributed concerning you. It is to be made abundantly clear that no one is asked to do anything beyond the three items listed," Roberts concluded. "Further, I am inclined to think the group can function without public notice."

³ See no. 533.

⁴ On earlier plans for such a visit see no. 504.

⁵ For background on the Arthur Nevinses' visit see no. 487.

⁶ As Columbia University president, Eisenhower had lived at 60 Morningside Drive, often the scene of bridge games with these several friends and supporters (Galambos, *Columbia University*, no. 898). Eisenhower's office would arrange accommodations for Roberts and Robinson at the Trianon Hotel in Paris.

⁷ In a letter of December 5 (also in EM) Roberts accepted Eisenhower's invitation and announced plans to leave for Paris December 23. He also noted that he had discussed the " 'my gang' idea" with Milton Eisenhower and Robinson, both of whom approved of it. He had mentioned it to no one else so that the General might abandon the plan if after further thought he wished to do so. "What I want to say specifically is that you should not feel wedded to the idea just because I have kept it alive." Though Roberts had set the first meeting of the advisory group for December 22, he pledged to call no one unless he received "a go-ahead cable" before the twelfth. In a cable of December 11 (EM) Roberts acknowledged Eisenhower's December 8 message. For further developments see no. 596.

529 $\qquad$ *Eisenhower Mss.*

To George Edward Allen $\qquad$ *December 8, 1951*

*Dear George:*¹ Of all the abject, cowardly surrenders to an appetite that I ever heard, the worst is the one you made in your letter of December 4th. Only a fat man could think more of gravy than he does of his tailor's problems—to say nothing of $275.50.²

As to the disposition of the amount, here are your *instructions*. Send a draft to my daughter Barbie. You tell her that this is a present from yourself, sent because of your abysmal failure to keep an agreement with me. Now, of course, if you want to make yourself a bit virtuous, you can tell her that you failed deliberately in order that she would have a little sum of her own to spend on new clothes or a new coat or something of that kind the instant that the new baby appears on the scene. I shouldn't give you such a good out, but, after all, in some way or other, you are going to make yourself appear a hero—or a martyr—so you might as well make some character with Barbie.[3]

Now, as to next year's bet—and this is my official proposal:

(a) To make the bet effective on September 30th instead of the end of the year, because this will get you out of the agony of going through Thanksgiving and Christmas on any reasonable diet—that, I know you will never do.

(b) We each bet $500, do or don't. My weight will be established at the lowest my doctor will allow, which is 172. Yours will be 199, which is at least 25 pounds more than you should be for your height and age. But if I could ever get you down to that weight, maybe then I can make a bet that will bring you down to some reasonable limit.

(c) For every pound by which either fails to attain the agreed upon weight, he forfeits another $25.

(d) Either one not attaining the agreed upon weight will, in any case, subscribe $500 to a recognized charity designated by the other. This item is inserted so that any cowardly attempt to compromise bets next year will nevertheless contain an additional penalty and will benefit some worthy purpose.

If you would like to increase the size of any part of the above bet, please notify me. (From experience in the past, you can start now figuring up your alibis for next September 30th; I expect you to fail, as usual. Eventually, however, I will get the bet up to such size that you will either comply or I'll get you jailed for debt.) In any event, you'd better give up that sausage instantly; it will take you longer than a mere nine months to get down to the approximate size of a hippopotamus. *As ever*[4]

---

[1] For background on Allen and his bet with the General see no. 493.

[2] In his letter of December 4 (EM) Allen had accepted Eisenhower's suggestion that he pay $275.50 to end their present wager. Allen said he was happy to have the issue settled because he could now "eat some crepe suzettes, chocolate milkshakes, and some other things for a few days" before starting on a new diet. For the coming year Allen proposed a $500 "do-and-don't" bet.

[3] Allen would write to Barbara Eisenhower, the General's daughter-in-law, on December 13 (EM). He explained the wager, claiming that he could have won the bet if he had wanted to, but he "didn't feel in the mood." He wrote that he hoped she would enjoy whatever she purchased as much as he was enjoying fattening foods since the bet for 1951 had ended.

The Eisenhowers' third grandchild would be born in late December (see no. 594). Barbara Eisenhower's December 23 reply to Allen is in EM.

[4] For developments on the new wager see no. 549. In a handwritten postscript at the end of this letter Eisenhower had asked, "*When* are you and Mary coming over?" Mrs. Allen was the former Mary Keane.

To Robert Anthony Eden

Dear Anthony:[1] My telephoned message to you the other day was occasioned by what seemed to me to be a serious misunderstanding in Europe of Britain's position in respect of the European Army idea. Sometimes I wonder whether all of you, on that side of the Channel, realize how hungrily many Europeans look to Britain for political guidance. They read with real concern every British pronouncement, or even opinion, when such pronouncement or opinion affects continental Europe.

As of now, many Europeans believe that the British Government really opposes a unity of European nations or the formation of a united defense force. I have frequently told some of these people that I personally believe it would merely complicate matters if Great Britain should, at present, attempt to participate directly in the formation of a European defense force or in joining a European political union. I have pointed out the great benefit to all of us of Great Britain's continuing to carry out her world-wide responsibilities. Nevertheless, the apparent emphasis in some British statements on the negative attitude toward participation has obscured the approval of these ideas so far as the Western Continental countries are themselves concerned.[2]

Consequently, I am venturing the hope that—and here I assume that my interpretation of your attitude is correct—authoritative statements would emphasize Britain's approval of these projects, its readiness to use its good offices where desired and appropriate to further them, and its readiness to associate on a cooperative basis with European organisms so as to advance the development of collective security.

It seems to me, of course, that your position at this moment is indeed sound. This is something that I tried to make clear in my talk to the English Speaking Union on July 3rd, but it is equally clear that many influential Europeans interpret your position as being antagonistic and it is only to this point that I am addressing myself.[3]

I just cabled to Winston asking him whether the two of you could not come to lunch with us here at SHAPE on either the 17th or 18th. I could also invite your Ambassador and one or two others to luncheon. I should like for the key members of the staff to meet you both; this kind of an informal visit with you would be a real inspiration for a very hard working and capable group of people.[4]

With warm personal regard, *Cordially*

[1] Eden was Deputy Prime Minister and Foreign Secretary of Great Britain (see no. 227).

[2] For an earlier statement about this view of the British position on European unification see no. 248.

[3] In Eisenhower's London speech of July 3 he had described Great Britain and America as "joined together in purpose and growing determination" to achieve an economically sound Europe, united in strength (see *New York Times*, July 4, 1951; see also no. 252).

[4] There is no copy of this cable in EM, but on December 12 Churchill cabled his acceptance for December 18 (EM). For developments see nos. 552 and 556.

531   *Eisenhower Mss.*

TO ROBERT BOSTWICK CARNEY   *December 10, 1951*
Confidential

My dear Carney: This will acknowledge your letter of the 30th of November enclosing the translation of Defense Minister Pacciardi's letter to you of 26 November.[1]

I agree with the positions which you intend to take on the points which the Minister has raised in his letter.[2] At this point, it is premature for you to make any commitment or changes on your own command or staff structure contingent upon the accession of Greece and Turkey to NATO. Similarly, it does not appear necessary at the moment for you to decide on whether or not you will require a Deputy CINCSOUTH or what his nationality or service should be. If the Minister has reference to the appointment of a British Army Officer, General Mansergh, as Deputy CINCNORTH, you could point out that the situation in that command is somewhat different as Admiral Brind has a naval officer as his Chief of Staff, whereas you have General Gavin.[3]

With very best regards, *Sincerely*

[1] For background on the issues raised by Admiral Carney, who commanded NATO's southern forces, see nos. 390 and 423, n. 5. Carney had enclosed Italian Defense Minister Randolfo Pacciardi's memorandum on what Pacciardi described as "major problems": (1) the Italian expectation of obtaining a native commander of all land forces in southern Europe following the admission of Greece and Turkey to NATO; (2) the matter of "proper and proportioned assigning of vacancies in the Atlantic Commands," to solve which Pacciardi recommended the appointment of an Italian deputy commander of CINCSOUTH; (3) the distribution of responsibilities between NATO commands and national authorities in peacetime—an issue of "great importance for Italy, because the forces are dislocated on national territory and on this territory the anticipated operations would take place" (in this paragraph the translator noted uncertainty of meaning); and (4) shortages of American-supplied " 'end-items' (and especially those of great importance)," which hampered the Italian military build-up (both Carney's letter and the translation of Pacciardi's note are in EM). Captain George W. Anderson drafted Eisenhower's reply.

Carney's relations with the Italians and with the British would again cause him concern a few days after Eisenhower sent him this message. On December 5 he had attended a meeting Field Marshal Montgomery had called with the Italian General Staff in Rome. Carney complained that he was not apprised beforehand of the meeting's purpose or agenda; he was "astonished" to read in Montgomery's report that the outbreak of war would bring "intense confusion in Northern Italy" and that "no progress" had been made "during the last six months" in dealing with the problem of effective command and control of Italian army and air force units. Carney strongly disagreed with Montgomery's assessment. In a letter to Montgomery Carney said that had Montgomery directed questions to him "as the responsible commander," he would gladly have acquainted the Deputy SACEUR with his "appraisal of progress and remaining deficiencies." "I would be most grateful," Carney went on, "if, in the future, I could be given timely information concerning conferences which I am invited to attend" (Carney to Eisenhower and Carney to Montgomery, both Dec. 16, 1951, EM).

[2] Carney reported that he had declined as premature any comment on retaining an Italian officer as Commander, Allied Land Forces, Southern Europe (COMLANDSOUTH), or on Pacciardi's suggestion about a deputy CINCSOUTH. The obscure paragraph on distributing peacetime responsibilities between NATO and the Italian government Carney regarded as perhaps implying "a desire to have the Italian General Staff more fully cut in on HAFSE [Headquarters, Allied Forces, Southern Europe] planning—not a bad idea, in many respects, because it can be made a two-way street which would afford us better access to the Italian staff." Carney said he would study the Italian request for speedier supply and remedy the problem through proper channels.

[3] For background on Admiral Eric Brind and Generals Robert Mansergh and James Gavin see no. 287; for subsequent developments see no. 651.

532   *Eisenhower Mss.*

To WILLIAM MORROW FECHTELER   *December 10, 1951*
Top secret

Dear Admiral: I received your letter of the 24th of November[1] upon my return to SHAPE from the meeting of the North Atlantic Council in Rome.[2]

In our appearances before the Military Committee, both Gruenther and I emphasized the importance of naval forces to the defense of Europe. In his presentation before the Council itself, Gruenther stressed particularly the part which I visualize carrier task forces would play in the early critical stages of a war. As you know, I count heavily upon them.[3]

I have heard that during the course of the deliberations of the McNarney and Harriman Committees[4] there has been some question as to the correctness of the estimates of naval force requirements and the balance of the contributions to be made.

This has been generally along three lines:

The first has involved the principle of balanced collective forces and as to whether some of the nations should continue to maintain certain types of naval forces at the expense of what might be considered to be more useful contributions. Examples are Norwegian submarines, Danish destroyers, Dutch and French light carriers, cruisers, and submarines. I believe that this issue has been satisfactorily resolved.[5] Obviously, if these nations do not maintain such units, and there are strong domestic political and inter-service considerations involved in each case, the United States or the United Kingdom would have to take over the D-day commitment. I doubt if this is practicable.

The second question has been concerned with the requirement for carriers.[6] I believe that there is genuine doubt in some quarters as to their potential effectiveness. Perhaps this stems from experiences over here during early phases of the last war when carriers were used in inadequate numbers. In part, it may be incidental to a lack of familiarity with modern United States carriers or to a pessimistic reaction to the optimism and confidence of the United States Navy. In any event, it is disturbing to me to learn that the McNarney group only develops a buildup of 9 fleet carriers for all of NATO by D + 30 days even through 1954. You will recall that our SHAPE requirement envisaged 8 on each flank. The McNarney group figure is disappointingly low, especially as I understand that the ships themselves are available if only the planes and crews can be provided. The carriers are needed as an important element of our deterrent force, in the early days of an emergency, and during these critical years when we are endeavoring to build up our ground and air forces. We certainly need their atomic capabilities.[7] I earnestly hope that you can do something to increase the availability and readiness of the carriers. The present planning figure of having only 14 of the 16 we need and these by D + 180 is most unacceptable. I will have the SHAPE staff comment on this feature in our review of the reports.

The third facet of the naval problem is the continuing deficiency of escorts and minesweepers.[8] This appears to be serious particularly should an enemy submarine and mining threat materialize to the proportions of which they are capable in the early weeks of a war. Undoubtedly the shortages will have a grave impact on both SACEUR and Atlantic operations. I believe that this matter should receive most careful consideration by the Standing Group with a view best to alleviating deficiencies within the capabilities of the nations involved and also towards the adoption of selected offensive operations with both conventional and atomic weapons to limit and localize the threat until post D-day forces can be developed.

I will continue to emphasize the importance of naval forces and will insure that SHAPE comments on naval needs are brought into proper focus.[9] *Sincerely*

[1] Chief of Naval Operations Fechteler had written to voice concern "that due to the delay in the appointment of SACLANT [Supreme Allied Commander, Atlantic] proper emphasis may not have been accorded to the importance of naval forces" in recent meetings of the NATO Temporary Council Committee. Fechteler also deplored "any attempt to approach the question of requirements for naval forces on the basis of a comparison between Russian naval forces and NATO naval forces." That view ignored the value of NATO naval units in supporting ground action. "I want you to know," he concluded, "that regardless of any language which may be contained in Standing Group documents and irrespective of any command arrangements that may be evolved you will continue to have the full support of the U.S. Navy for any operations that may be required" (EM). Captain George W. Anderson assisted Eisenhower in drafting this letter.

[2] For background on the Rome meeting see no. 502.

[3] For Eisenhower's ideas on the role of aircraft carriers in the event of war in Europe see no. 98; see also Gruenther to Bradley, August 30, 1951, CCS 092 Western Europe (3-12-48), Sec. 93.

[4] W. Averell Harriman chaired a Temporary Council Committee of NATO country representatives formed at the September NAC meeting in Ottawa to examine the conflicting needs of European economic recovery and defense spending. General Joseph F. McNarney chaired the TCC Screening and Costing Committee (see nos. 539, n. 6, and 424, n. 1, respectively).

[5] According to the NATO principle of balanced collective forces, certain nations would focus their rearmament efforts on ground forces, while others (especially the United States) would furnish the men and materiel for high-seas fleets and strategic air units. NATO forces thus would achieve an overall balance—with complimentary land, air, and ground units—while each national contingent would vary in service strength and self-sufficiency (see Eisenhower, *At Ease*, pp. 373–74). In January Eisenhower had criticized the Netherlands for building up their naval forces at the expense of ground strength (see no. 15). In September the Dutch had reported to NATO that their navy possessed one light carrier and nine light cruisers, and three additional light cruisers were under construction (C-7-D/10, Sept. 15, 1951, NATO Files, microfilm). Lurking beneath this specific question was of course the more general problem of national versus NATO-wide development, an issue that surfaced regularly and provided Eisenhower with some of his most trying negotiations.

[6] The question of aircraft carriers for Eisenhower's NATO command had been discussed with the TCC during the previous month. The TCC had been concerned about the inability of SHAPE to plan for employment of naval vessels before a SACLANT had been named. The TCC had also noted that U.S. carriers could be withdrawn from Eisenhower's command if the situation warranted such a move. Informed of these concerns, Secretary of the Navy Dan A. Kimball (see no. 614, n. 19) responded that "all U.S. Naval forces deployed in the Mediterranean are specifically assigned to the operational command of SACEUR as required for the performance of his missions and U.S. naval forces deployed in the Atlantic operating under SACLANT, will by his terms of reference, be operating in support of SACEUR" (Lincoln to Beebe, Nov. 11, 1951, and Kimball to Lovett, Nov. 19, 1951, OS/D, 1951, Clas. Decimal File, CD 092.3 NATO). These concerns would nevertheless continue to arise throughout Eisenhower's term of service as SACEUR (see JCS 2073/349, Apr. 29, 1952, CCS 092 Western Europe [3-12-48], Sec. 140). On December 13 the JCS would report to the Secretary of Defense that a total of eight U.S. fleet carriers had been earmarked for Eisenhower's command in the event of war. The last three carriers would arrive on station 210 days after the outbreak of war (D + 210) (see Vandenberg to Lovett, Dec. 13, 1951, OS/D, 1951, Clas. Decimal File, CD 091.7 Europe).

[7] In February 1951 the U.S. Sixth Fleet (Mediterranean) had received the first naval aircraft capable of carrying nuclear weapons, the AJ-1 Savage. Although by design these large planes could operate from the decks of aircraft carriers, the navy usually based them ashore (Floyd D. Kennedy, Jr., "The Creation of the Cold War Navy, 1953–1962," in *In Peace and War: Interpretation of American Naval History, 1775–1978*, ed. Kenneth J. Hagan [Westport, Conn., 1978], p. 306).

[8] In May the JCS had reported that the NATO forces were short 11 fleet destroyers and first-rate escorts; 145 ocean and coastal escort vessels; and 291 minesweepers (Sherman to Marshall, May 28, 1951, OS/D, 1951, Clas. Decimal File, CD 092.3 NATO). Early in 1952 the JCS would again note that "serious shortages still exist, particularly in destroyers, escorts and minesweepers "(JCS 2073/278, Jan. 8, 1952, CCS 092 Western Europe [3-12-48], Sec. 116).

[9] Fechteler, replying on January 8, 1952, would write that in his opinion the recommendations of the Harriman and McNarney committees did not reflect the "current full capabilities" of the U.S. Navy and that his staff soon would submit recommendations to the JCS "to correct this defect." Fechteler expected also to recommend measures "to increase the state of readiness of critical ships" then in the reserve fleets. "If these recommendations are implemented, NATO force requirements can be met at a much earlier phase date than now indicated" (EM). For subsequent developments see no. 651, n. 1.

533

Eisenhower Mss., Diaries

DIARY

December 11, 1951

A day or so ago I received a comforting letter from Cabot Lodge, who has been selected by a number of Republican politicians, of the progressive wing, as their leader in the effort to nominate me for the Presidency. He says that the project is hopeless without my active *pre-convention* cooperation! That settles the whole matter! As to the path of duty in the possible case of an honest Republican draft I could have (do have) honest doubts. But there is no slightest doubt in my mind as to the impropriety—almost the illegality—of any pre-convention activity as long as I'm on this job. So—since I cannot in good conscience quit here, my reaction is "Hurrah." I've just prepared a letter to Cabot saying that he and his friends must stop the whole thing, now.[1]

The Rome meetings were, in many ways, highly valuable and, certainly, interesting. Because there was no startling development to hand to the press the reports have been of a pessimistic & cynical tenor! In spite of difficulties (and Lord knows they are big) there is no cause to despair![2]

[1] For background on Henry Cabot Lodge, Jr.'s selection as leader of the Eisenhower-for-President campaign see nos. 499 and 504. On Eisenhower's correspondence with Lodge regarding an announcement of his candidacy see no. 538.

[2] On the November 1951 meeting of the North Atlantic Council in Rome see nos.

502 and 539. See also *New York Times*, November 25-28, 1951; and *International Herald Tribune*, Paris ed., November 24, 27, 28, 1951.

534   *Eisenhower Mss.*

To Elizabeth Rankin   *December 11, 1951*
Personal

Dear Mrs. Rankin:[1] Thank you for your recent letter. It was most thoughtful of you to send me your views and you may be assured that they are of interest to me.

I am somewhat distressed that you question the appropriateness of my use of the quotation from Luke although I fully understand your interpretation of it.[2] I believe that I can safely say that our ultimate aims and hopes are identical—we both seek a lasting peace.

I agree with you that complete disarmament of all nations and complete adherence to Christian principles by all would bring peace. However, the free nations of the world now stand confronted with a militant Communist ideology which admits of no God and which is a proven enemy of our Christian faith. The Communists rely on armed strength and have proved that they are unwilling to cooperate with the other nations in effective disarmament. As long as we are faced with such threat, our best hopes for peace lie in the timely provision of military and economic strength sufficient to convince an aggressor that he cannot gain through war.

Like you, I hope for the day when people everywhere will be able to live in peace—free from fear of war—and I sincerely believe that the course we are now following is the one best suited to accomplish our aim.[3]

With thanks for your interest, and with good wishes, *Sincerely*

[1] Elizabeth Rankin lived in Glasgow, Scotland.
[2] On November 27 (EM) Rankin had written that she objected to Eisenhower's use of a biblical quotation in his speech to the North Atlantic Council in Rome on November 26. In an analogy to the power of the NATO nations, Eisenhower had said, "When a strong man armed keepeth his palace, his goods are in peace" (Luke 11:21). Mrs. Rankin argued that the verse meant "the exact opposite" of what Eisenhower thought it meant. She cited the following verse from Luke 11:22: "But when a man stronger than he shall come upon him and overcome him, he taketh from him all his armour wherein he trusted, and divideth his spoils." The message, she said, was that "when a strong man puts his trust in arms his goods are only in peace until a stronger man comes along." On Eisenhower's appearance before the NAC see no. 502, n. 5; a copy of his speech is in EM, Subject File, Speeches.
[3] Disarmament was necessary to avert war, Rankin had said, and it was her hope that Eisenhower would use his "great influence to lead the world in better ways."

535

To Herbert Bayard Swope

Dear Herbert:[01] Thank you very much for your note and its enclosure.[2] Of course, I do not know the name of your friend who wrote to Jack McCloy, but his observations on the propaganda value in Germany of the "unity" theme are completely accurate. I think that almost everybody realizes this, but too few put it into practice. I have had many talks about it with individuals very highly placed in many governments, including ours. But it seems astonishing how few people recognize the sales value of pushing projects in which the customer is interested. When talking to soldiers in wartime, any discussion will be fairly successful if it is somehow related to the subject of, "When do we go home?"

As for the latter part of the man's letter to Jack, I don't know what he means by his statement that there is too much military around! I think most of them are serving only because they are required to do so—not because they are seeking a particular post.[3] *Sincerely*

[1] For background on Swope see no. 66, n. 1.

[2] Swope's note and the enclosure are not in EM. On High Commissioner for Germany John Jay McCloy see no. 12, n. 1.

[3] Swope would reply that "too much military" did not include Eisenhower: "I don't think you are thought of as a military mind" (Dec. 17, 1951, EM).

536

To William H. Burnham
Personal and confidential

Dear Bill:[1] Your two fine letters have reached me in the last couple days.[2] Since they are mostly interesting information, I shall not attempt any lengthy comment. However, there is one point on which I should like to reassure you.

When Ed Clark was last here, I heard some rumors from home to the general effect that he was taking an attitude of "speaking" for me. I called him in and was very emphatic on this point. Not only does *no one* speak for me but I specifically told him that it was, in his case, exceedingly dangerous for him even to try to interpret my ideas and beliefs because any such attempt would, sooner or later, make him unsuitable as a messenger—and he has no other function that I know of.[3]

All of this may soon become very innocuous because, if anybody believes that I am going to participate in any pre-convention activity, we had better have a quick and unmistakable understanding. I shall do no such thing.[4] *Cordially*

[1] Burnham, a longtime adviser to Eisenhower, had left SHAPE to return to the United States and the investment banking business. He would, however, continue to keep Eisenhower informed on political developments at home (see no. 463).

[2] Burnham's letters of December 4 and 7 are in EM.

[3] For background on Eisenhower's irritation with Edwin N. Clark for speculating on Eisenhower's presidential candidacy see nos. 486 and 492. Eisenhower had met with Clark on December 3 and again on December 6.

[4] See no. 538.

537   *Eisenhower Mss.*

To Lucius Du Bignon Clay   *December 12, 1951*
Personal and confidential

Dear Lucius: Thank you very much for your nice letter of the 7th.[1] It is disturbing to learn of deep personal antipathies existing between people who apparently see eye to eye in their ideas of the policies affecting the public good. So far as I am concerned, I deeply deplore the existence of this kind of thing where the parties involved are friends of mine. But I certainly can make no move in such matters.

Only a few days ago, Ed Clark was in my office. I had already heard rumors to the general effect that some people believe he is taking on himself a responsibility as some kind of a "spokesman" for me. I made certain that he understood my complete repudiation of any such impression. Actually, of course, no one has the authority to speak *for me*—and, least of all, one whose usefulness as a messenger would cease as soon as he sought any other role. I assure you I made these sentiments unmistakably clear.[2]

I get very jumpy about any individual who, on the basis of past association, arrogates to himself an unwarranted degree of authority in interpreting another's viewpoints and intentions. Two people that I was sure would never offend in this regard were Bill Burnham and Ed Clark. Actually, as I remember it, I asked you on the telephone to warn Ed about this, even before he came over here to Europe a week or so ago.[3]

The pressure seems to grow (even among my friends who I thought understood my position completely) to induce me to undertake some kind of pre-convention political activity. To everyone who has brought up this suggestion, and who would listen to me, I have explained the impossibility of my doing so. This is particularly true since I was assigned to this job as the American Military Commander of SHAPE. If the "pros" conclude that my refusal makes the whole project an impossible one, I will be free of a lot of extra-curricular anxiety and worry.[4]

I agree with what you say about the inherent dangers of direct communication with political personalities, but I have had to send off one to establish, emphatically, my attitude on this one point. In justice to my own conscience and convictions, I could do no less, and I felt it was also necessary in justice to any of these friendly "pros" who may have been unaware of my earnestness in declining to participate in pre-convention activity.[5]

I realize that this is a very poor excuse of a letter, but I have got so much on my desk that I simply cannot give the time, at this moment, to write as I should like.[6] Soon I shall make another attempt; possibly I can induce you to come see me right after the first of the year.[7]

Love to Marjorie.[8] *As ever*

[1] In a "personal and confidential" letter of December 7 (EM) Clay had written of developments in the Eisenhower-for-President movement, which he described as hampered by personal bickering. Clay complained that the Lodge group, apparently at the request of Senator James H. Duff of Pennsylvania, John Hay ("Jock") Whitney, and Edwin N. Clark, had excluded him from its meetings. Clay wrote that he and Burnham considered Clark "unreliable, in fact, dangerous." The Pennsylvania senator reportedly was "full of ego and determined to be the 'anointed' "; despite his valuable "fighting qualities," Duff, according to Clay, could not even deliver the vote in his home state—where Governor John Sydney Fine apparently stood ready to declare for Eisenhower but for his dislike of Duff and Dewey. Meanwhile Dewey had grown irritated with Duff, to whom Clay urged Eisenhower not to send "further messages." Clay described Stassen as an "enigma" and warned the General to be "careful in talking to him. He can be very valuable, but no one, I repeat no one, of your group trusts him fully."

Clay further reported on a "mix-up" over the job of campaign finance manager: "Talbot is very much upset as he has been dumped rather unceremoniously. Aldrich too was unhappy over Whitney's entry into this picture. As I understand it, this decision is being changed again and Cabot is still looking for a mid-westerner. Talbot and Aldrich should not be out front but neither should they be hurt as they are essential behind the scenes." As a possible vice-presidential candidate, Clay recommended New Jersey Governor Alfred E. Driscoll, who had promised to swing his state delegation toward the General (equally promising reports had come from the Maryland governor). "I believe Lodge is moving ahead reasonably well," Clay had concluded. Lodge was "not a strong man, and hence tends to be dominated by Duff. However, he is intelligent and a good, practical politician. If he will listen to the more experienced party workers, he can do an even better job." For background on Clay see no. 499; on Duff, no. 486; and on Clark, no. 492. Whitney was senior partner of J. H. Whitney and Company, a New York financial firm. For further background on the rivalries developing among Eisenhower's supporters see Ambrose, *Eisenhower*, vol. I, *Soldier, General of the Army, President-Elect*, pp. 519–20.

[2] See no. 492.

[3] On Burnham see the preceding document.

[4] See no. 509.
[5] See the following document.
[6] For Clay's anxious response to this letter see no. 561.
[7] Eisenhower would see Clay in London on February 16, 1952, when they attended the funeral of King George VI.
[8] Mrs. Clay.

538   *Eisenhower Mss.*

To Henry Cabot Lodge, Jr.   *December 12, 1951*
Personal and confidential

Dear Cabot:[1] Your letter of the 3rd reached me just a few days ago. I am grateful for such a forthright exposition of your views and have considered the whole matter at some length before attempting to reply. In this letter, I give you certain conclusions reached as a result of your presentations. Of course, I mean to be friendly and sympathetic but, in view of the revolutionary change you state to be necessary in my attitude and actions, I must be completely frank, particularly in emphasizing again the limitations that propriety, ethics, and custom impose upon me.[2]

The reason that a very frank and full analysis of the situation is now necessary is the change brought about by your emphatic conclusion that mere assurance that I would not repudiate the efforts of my friends is no longer sufficient.

I accept, without reservation, your observations and comments on the political scene at home; you fully convince me of the impracticability of nominating an individual who, for any reason, must remain inactive in the political field prior to the National Conventions. From my viewpoint, this is an entirely new factor in the problem; and, since my current responsibilities make pre-convention activity impossible for me, the program in which you and your close political associates are now engaged should, logically, be abandoned. To this, I assume you agree. Under no circumstances should friends, whom I admire and respect, continue to work on a project involving me when they have become convinced that my personal convictions condemn their efforts, in advance, to futility and defeat.

There is nothing revolutionary or radical in what I am now saying. I have always insisted over the past few years that it would be difficult for me to envision circumstances that could possibly draw me into a pre-convention role. Since the day of my assignment to the critical military post I now occupy, this instinctive conclusion has, for me at least, been transformed into obvious and incontrovertible fact.

Most of those who have urged me to enter the political world have agreed as to the importance of preventing a Communistic domination of Europe. They have also expressed agreement with the conclusion that partisan activity by the American Commander of NATO would dangerously divide American support of the job of producing collective security for the free world. Therefore, they have engaged themselves in an undertaking to place before me a summons to duty as their standard bearer, a duty which would, by common consent in our country, take priority over the one I am now performing.

With these things understood, I have, out of regard for the opinions of people I respect, agreed to one thing and to one thing only; namely, to avoid repudiation of the efforts of these friends and their associates. Never have I agreed to any personal pre-convention activity of a political nature. But there is a vast difference between responding to a duty imposed by a National Convention and the seeking of a nomination.[3]

I realize that you and your group may feel that some explanation is due the public to account for abandonment of your current effort. This, I suppose, would require a recitation of the essentials of the current situation; namely, that (a) your group has come to the conclusion that the nomination of any individual without his active participation is an impossibility, and (b) since this kind of action is impossible for me in my position as a military commander in NATO, there is no other course open to your group.

If there is anything in this letter that is contrary to your understanding of the situation as it has existed and has now developed, I regret it most sincerely.

I could not close such a letter without expressing to you and, through you, to all of those who have been associated with you, the very great sense of pride I have in the knowledge that such a distinguished group of Americans should consider me worthy of occupying what is, of course, the greatest position an American citizen could possibly achieve. In fact, it was the character of the men who urged me to do so that caused me to give any consideration whatsoever to possible political responsibilities; I have never had any personal aspirations to such office. As you know, my personal inclination has been the reverse. So far as my abilities allow, I hope to continue to serve our country as long as I live. But realization of such a hope certainly does not require occupation of a political office.

My warm greetings to you and your associates.[4] I hope that you will convey to each of them, not only an expression of the convictions I have tried to outline, but also my gratitude and cordial good wishes.

With personal regard, *Sincerely*

[1] Since November 17 Lodge had managed the Eisenhower-for-President campaign (see no. 499, n. 1).

² Enclosing a report on the headquarters organization, Lodge had written on December 3 (EM) to inform Eisenhower of "an extremely important meeting" in San Francisco in mid-January—a gathering of Republican National Committee members, state chairmen, vice-chairmen, the state-level GOP women's leadership, and Young Republican leaders from eleven Western states. "I can't emphasize too strongly my hope that you will be able to attend this meeting," he had written. "There is no doubt whatever of your tremendous popularity here in the United States, but, as you know, the winning of the convention does not depend on public opinion alone. There has been so much talk about your plans that it is becoming vital that you appear and speak in various parts of the United States. People want to know what you think from your own lips and no amount of speaking by Senator Duff or myself or by anyone else can possibly take the place of you." "The talk of the draft is no good any more," Lodge argued. "Even people of a patient and conservative turn of mind ask: 'When will he get into it?' " Failure to do so was promoting Senator Taft, who was being praised "for his willingness to 'get out and discuss the issue.' " Lodge wrote that he had hoped to let the last day for withdrawing from the New Hampshire primary pass "and then simply make my own announcement that this automatically put you in the race"; in a telephone conversation earlier that day William Burnham (see no. 536) had reminded Lodge that the General would rather not announce until the spring. "But the situation has developed in such a way as to make it impossible to wait that long."

³ Lodge had said, "You have tremendous political strength and you have tremendous strength among political leaders from whom will come the delegates. They understand your situation, but they are unable to make it plain to the rank and file of people who will be the delegates" and who "cannot understand why—assuming you do regard it as a duty to be a candidate—you do not get out into the open."

⁴ For the tensions evident among some Republican party leaders who played a part in Lodge's Eisenhower-for-President movement see the preceding document. See also Ambrose, *Eisenhower*, vol. I, *Soldier, General of the Army, President-Elect*, pp. 518–22; Lyon, *Portrait of the Hero*, pp. 427–32; and Neal, *Reluctant Dynasty*, pp. 270–71. For developments see no. 545.

539 *Eisenhower Mss.*

To Robert Abercrombie Lovett *December 13, 1951*
Personal

Dear Bob: I have read many stories about the Rome meeting,¹ most of them written in lugubrious terms.²

Reporters have asserted that the United States is badly in arrears in her munitions equipment; that the European Army is a fantastic conception; that the Ministers listened to but repudiated my personal appeals at Rome for united effort; that Europe is broke; that Germany is lost to us; that Britain will not cooperate with the continent; and that next year America will desert the whole concept of developing collective security. Some of the reports are fair and accurate, but others add up to the personal opinion of their authors that NATO is the misbegotten offspring of wishful thinking in America and narrow-minded selfishness in Europe. This offspring, it appears, will never fulfill any useful purpose, but will actually endanger and impoverish all those who put any trust in either his abilities or intentions.

In spite of all this, my own reactions to the meeting were generally good!

But the fashion of the moment seems to demand, in discussions of difficult problems, a high degree of sophistication, if not sheer cynicism. It is little short of amusing to find that many people apparently consider these characteristics to be marks of a superior mind. Actually, of course, they are the opposites of faith and of belief in humanity, the two qualities that have been most responsible for man's progress through the ages. I have come to believe that the cynic is the most damaging witness to his own littleness and cowardice.

Humans are so constructed as to make [it] impossible for any one of us to agree in toto and invariably with the opinions or actions of any other. As a consequence of the inborn ego of the human, it follows that everyone else in the world is to some degree wrong! Therefore, a critic of another is always at least partially *right*! I think it is this obvious truth that gives such appeal to the products of the voluble and caustic critic. When his strictures coincide with our own natural fears and hesitations, they become doubly credible.

We must be constantly on guard against the influence of self-anointed authorities who would have to give up great projects merely because difficulties are monumental.[3]

This perhaps sounds odd coming from one who honestly seeks criticism. Long ago I learned to do so because in this way only can ideas be constantly tested, advanced, and adjusted to meet the changes that constantly take place in human affairs and projects. But I resent so-called criticism that is actually no more than an appeal to cowardice, laziness, and selfishness. I grow almost bitter when I see such appeals circulated in this region, where the ravages of war have created an extraordinarily fine climate for the persistence of these ignoble characteristics. What Europe needs more than anything else is someone to make her understand how much she *can* do if she really wants to do it rather than someone who is constantly preaching futility and defeatism.

Every day some new aspect of this kind comes to my attention. But today there was a hopeful incident when Eugene Black[4] talked to me at some length about plans and possibilities of increasing Europe's coal production. These particular plans and possibilities hinge upon an early approval of the Schuman Plan. At this moment, it appears that the Plan is certain to be approved by the French Parliament.[5]

The danger is that mass morale, which obviously had been growing over the past many months, may suffer a setback. To present properly to the populations of Europe such matters as the European Defense Force, the Schuman Plan, the findings of the Harriman Committee,[6] the deterioration in the French, British, and Danish financial and economic positions (a situation somewhat paralleled in other countries), and the problem in Indo China,[7] we need inspired, courageous, and articulate political leaders; people who will tell the truth, propose reasonable answers to major questions, and rest their political fortunes on the result. There are plenty of Communists and other selfish groups ready to depress the spirit of the population and so render even more difficult the accomplishment of our common purposes.

As of now, the most discussed question among governmental circles in Europe is the European Defense Force. It is, of course, not difficult to marshal against the idea an array of arguments that can be made to sound almost conclusive. However, I think it is well, always, in such matters to go clear back to fundamental factors before being too sure that surface reasons or appearances are as valid as we sometimes think.

Stated, implicitly and explicitly, in official expressions of American intentions in Europe is the expectation that Europe will do its collective best in cooperating with the United States in producing economic and military strength in this region, and that some German strength will be incorporated in our composite defense organization. One of the late laws applying to mutual aid announces an American purpose of furthering both economic and political integration in Western Europe.[8] This statement reflects an instinctive understanding that the economic and military strength of Western Europe cannot be fully developed as long as the region is just a hodge-podge of sovereign political territories.

For awhile it appeared that we were making real progress toward an intermediate goal—the quick approval of the Schuman Plan and the authorization of a European Army. With regard to the latter, the technical and professional meetings conducted over the past few months have been working on a better and far more realistic basis than formerly. Day by day, a workable, even if tentative, plan for the organization of a European Defense Force seemed closer to completion.

The growing economic crisis in Europe was, of course, bound to create additional difficulties in such a development, particularly when the establishment of any contractual relationship between Germany and the occupying powers would throw great additional expenses on France and Britain. In fact, this one consideration may be at the bottom of what appears to be, at this moment, a considerable confusion in the European Army project.

Britain has been considered, by all of us, as a warm advocate of European union. Of course, she has always maintained her inability, in view of world-wide responsibilities, of becoming one of the participating parts in such a union. Consequently, if we were to consider the development of a European Defense Force as one of the effective steps in producing political union, it followed that Britain should *not* be an active participant in a European Defense Force. Again, however, I had understood that she would be an ardent supporter of the idea.[9]

This may still be a fairly accurate reflection of the British position but, if it is, there is a woeful misunderstanding in many continental circles. There has grown up a feeling that Britain is bitterly opposed both to continental union and to the establishment of a European Defense Force. I must say that there has been little done in the way of public pronouncement to dispel this misunderstanding—if such it is.

This misunderstanding is far more serious than may appear at first glance. Particularly in Northern Europe, Britain's prestige and influence are still very great. The Dutch, Danes, Norwegians, and Belgians have a high respect for British political maturity and look in that direction for political guidance. They have an equal respect for the British system of military organization and, I assume, have an instinctive feeling that their fortunes are largely tied up with those of Great Britain.

As a consequence, any belief that Britain opposes an important political move has a very serious effect on continental thinking. So, if the British attitude is really what I think it is, then too many British speakers have emphasized the negative aspects of their non-participation instead of the positive aspects of their moral support and intellectual approval.

These matters have been the subject of some conversations and correspondence, including, I know, some communications from Washington to London.[10] The whole point is, as I see it, that there is no possibility of obtaining German strength in the NATO formation and, at the same time, avoiding placing Germany in a position unacceptable to her people except through one of two methods:

The first of these would be to accept Germany at once as a full NATO member, which would mean that she automatically became again a full sovereign power subject to no kind of outside control. This, of course, Western Europe will not for a moment accept.

The second method is to organize some kind of a European Defense Force. It is difficult, but it can be done. All of us ought to get behind it energetically, but, in doing so, there is one great caution to observe. We must not admit (and it is not true) that Western Europe cannot establish a military equilibrium within its own territorial limits without German aid. But the consequences of so doing, entirely aside from considerations of continuing expense and instability of equilibrium, would be the tendency to force Germany, eventually, into the arms of the Soviets. Then we would have a problem!

The Harriman Committee will complete its work Saturday or Sunday.[11] The very fact that twelve nations have cooperated in this exercise is in itself a great advance in the operation of NATO. But, beyond this, I am very hopeful that, although each of the twelve representatives will have to make reservations because of his inability to commit his own country, the report itself will be of such validity in each country that it will have a definitely beneficial effect.

After the favorable French action yesterday, I am hopeful that the Schuman Plan will be rapidly approved by all parties, and that this will tend to break the log jam and release a great amount of enthusiasm and energy in support of the developments that must go forward in this region.

Tomorrow I am having our friend Spaak[12] from Belgium to lunch and, on the 18th, Winston and Anthony[13] are coming out for a chat with us at SHAPE. I hope to get in some good licks for the things that we must get done.

This is a weird sort of letter; it mainly reflects my constant hope that a few inspired people will "take the stump" in this region. *Sincerely*

[1] For background on the November 24–28 meeting of the North Atlantic Council and the proposals Eisenhower made there for a European military build-up and a European army with twelve German divisions see no. 502. Secretary of Defense Lovett had attended the meeting, his first such NATO conference, and Secretary of State Acheson wrote that Lovett had been "most effective in all the discussions in which he participated" (State, *Foreign Relations, 1951*, vol. III, *European Security and the German Question, Part I*, p. 751).

[2] The *New York Times* noted that Eisenhower's recommended build-up, or "Operation Stiffener," faced "formidable opposition" in the parliaments of the six nations involved. In France both the Communists and the Gaullists already had come out against it (*New York Times*, Nov. 29, 1951). Formal council discussions, Acheson reported to Truman the next day, "did not reflect the confusion and strain presently in Europe over the establishment of a European defense force." He noted a general feeling that the project was "not going well" (State, *Foreign Relations, 1951*, vol. III, *European Security and the German Question, Part I*, p. 749). "While the military men— who nowadays agree much more easily than their civilian colleagues—have drawn up a plan acceptable to them for a European Defense Force," C. L. Sulzberger wrote shortly afterward, "there is no such accord among the participating Governments for a common budget to support it or a unified political body to direct it"; he rated chances of achieving the necessary compromises in Germany and France "very doubtful" (*New York Times*, Dec. 2, 1951). Sulzberger would meet with Eisenhower on December 11, two days after another *Times* reporter wrote that due to serious doubts about finances, the European Army project had "suffered a major setback in Rome" (*ibid.*, Dec. 8, 1951).

[3] At the Rome meeting Eisenhower had said that "when your self-preservation demands the accomplishment of a job there is nothing that is impossible. The impossible then merely becomes a difficulty, something to be solved and something to be done" (EM, Subject File, Speeches).

[4] Eugene R. Black, president of the World Bank, had met with Eisenhower in early October (see nos. 369 and 416).

[5] On December 9 the French National Assembly had opened debate on the Euro-

pean Coal and Steel Treaty, based on French Foreign Minister Robert Schuman's plan for pooling those resources in Western Europe. France, West Germany, Italy, Belgium, the Netherlands, and Luxembourg had signed the document in April. On December 13 the Assembly passed the bill of ratification, 377 to 233 (Brookings Institution, *Current Developments in United States Foreign Policy* 5, no. 5 [1951], 23–24).

[6] W. Averell Harriman chaired a Temporary Council Committee of NATO country representatives formed at the September NAC meeting in Ottawa to examine the conflicting needs of European economic recovery and defense spending (see no. 424). The committee had issued an interim report in Rome. Its final report, written in Paris and forwarded to member governments on December 18, would make specific proposals for "force targets and military standards, which are to be considered as firm goals for the coming year and as provisional goals and guidance for the years thereafter" (Ismay, *NATO*, p. 46; see also no. 542).

[7] French appeals for U.S. aid in bearing the burdens of both the Indochina war and European defense had continued in the fall of 1951, but Congress and popular opinion had placed practical limits on such aid. At a conference with Secretary of State Acheson in Washington on September 11 Schuman noted that the French were spending 1 billion francs a day to fight the war and by July 1952 would be 150 billion francs in debt. "Without going into details," read a memorandum of the meeting, "it was clear that it would be impossible for France to carry out the proposed effort in Indochina and to fulfill its obligations with respect to the defense of Europe" (State, *Foreign Relations, 1951*, vol. III, *European Security and the German Question, Part I*, p. 1249; on French General de Lattre's visit to Washington later that month see nos. 361 and 362). On November 1 Ambassador Bruce reported that French authorities, "in face of serious balance of payments crisis and increasing demands for Indochina, are convinced that size of their own defense program in Europe will have to be reduced . . ." (State, *Foreign Relations, 1951*, vol. III, *European Security and the German Question, Part I*, p. 908; see also pp. 403–4, 719–20, 1289). In mid-November Army Chief of Staff General J. Lawton Collins wrote that "there appears to be no possibility of removing any sizable number of French forces now in Indo-China. It is well known that a large part of the finest regular forces of France are now employed there" (Collins to JCS, Nov. 13, 1951, in State, *Foreign Relations, 1951*, vol. VI, *Asia and the Pacific, Part I*, p. 545). Eisenhower would comment further on this subject in no. 552, and by the time Lovett replied on January 3 the Secretary of Defense had seen reports in French newspapers stressing budgetary problems "and the allegedly hopeless situation in Indo-China." Picked up by U.S. papers, Lovett would write, those reports injected "a considerable amount of new uncertainties . . . into the picture here and on the Hill" (EM).

[8] The Mutual Security Act of October 1951 aimed to maintain the economic stability of the North Atlantic countries of the area so that they might meet their responsibilities for defense "and to further encourage the economic unification and the political federation of Europe" (U.S., *Statutes at Large*, vol. 65, p. 373).

[9] Eisenhower labored to convince continental Europeans that Britain supported collective defense despite its unwillingness to become part of a European defense force; he repeatedly requested strong British statements of such support (see nos. 218, 530, and 543). For Churchill's December 19 public statement on this issue see no. 552; for a discussion of the British position see Hogan, *The Marshall Plan*, pp. 398–400; for developments see nos. 556 and 569.

[10] For a principal document in the correspondence Eisenhower referred to see Acheson's "Memorandum on German Rearmament and Problems of the Defense of Europe (July 12, 1951)," State, *Foreign Relations, 1951*, vol. III, *European Security and the German Question, Part I*, pp. 827–32; for official British reaction see *ibid.*, pp. 1229–31, 1270–71.

[11] See n. 6 above.

[12] For background on Paul Henri Spaak see no. 16.

[13] Prime Minister Winston Churchill and Foreign Secretary and Deputy Prime Minister Sir Robert Anthony Eden. For developments see nos. 552 and 556.

540

Eisenhower Mss.

To Bernard Law Montgomery

December 13, 1951

Top secret

Dear Monty: Herewith I give you my comments on your DSAC 2990. I begin with your heading, "Solid Facts."[1]

2. No comment, except to observe that the only other possibility would be through making Germany a full-fledged member of NATO, after which she would be authorized to produce a national army of her own.[2] As of now, this is certainly unacceptable to France and some others.

3. To this sentence, I would add, "Except at greatly increased cost and with a much lower degree of confidence."[3]

4. No comment.[4]

5. I do not like to use important words which may mean one thing to one person and something else entirely to another. I refer to the word "fused."[5] I think your thought in paragraph 5 would better be stated somewhat as follows: "Since a completely amalgamated army, in which nationalistic differences were completely ignored, cannot be organized except by an integrated political authority, it is obvious that, for the time being at least, some compromise form of organization between a national army at one extreme and a completely monolithic concept at the other must be devised. This compromise must be acceptable to German aspirations for a respectable position in the family of nations and to the western European determination that Germany shall not again be a threat to the peace of Western Europe. The purpose of the organizational efforts now in progress is to design such a compromise."

6. I would omit.[6]

7. I would add to this sentence, "The British position should be so clearly defined that there is no possibility of misunderstanding in the minds of our continental friends."[7]

8. Exactly right.[8]

9. Since this is really taken care of under paragraph 7 above, I would omit it.[9]

10. Again, I would omit.[10] *As ever*

[1] Montgomery had written Eisenhower a memorandum after speaking with him on December 12 on the European army (which Montgomery described as "approaching a difficult moment") and Great Britain's relationship to it. He wrote "to clear my own mind," he explained, "and as a basis for discussion" with Churchill, Eden, and other British political and military leaders, who were to visit SHAPE on December 18 (see no. 552). Montgomery had placed his thoughts under four headings: "Solid Facts," "Factors which cannot be disregarded," "The Position of Britain," and a "Final Suggestion re Britain." Montgomery sent the document to the General in a handwritten note dated December 13, calling attention to paragraphs 8 and 9 as "the important ones" (EM). Eisenhower's comments adopted the paragraph numbering in Montgomery's message.

[2] "If the European Army conception does not materialise," Montgomery had stated, "there will be no German contribution to Western Defence."

[3] Montgomery had written: "We cannot make the West secure against possible aggression without a strong German contribution." For background see nos. 442 and 539.

[4] "If the European Army conception breaks down, the Lisbon Conference may well be stultified," Montgomery argued. Eisenhower hoped the Europeans would reach an agreement on the EDF before the NATO conference scheduled for February 20–25, 1952, in Lisbon (see no. 569, n. 2).

[5] Referring to his experience in European defense planning since October 1948, Montgomery gave as his "very definite opinion that the nations of Western Europe have not yet reached the stage when their armies can be 'fused' into one." He further cited "immense political decisions to be agreed upon before the nations can have a common army, a common budget, a common supranational authority to take vital decisions and give orders to Governments about their armed forces." Montgomery warned that if political association were not defined first, proceeding with an integrated European army would lead to "an awful mess." Eisenhower viewed a European army as a stepping stone toward political unification; he expected the various nations composing the EDF to bear the burden of administering and supplying their contingents (see, for example, nos. 215, 304, 539, and 556).

[6] Montgomery had written that "the question as to whether the armies of Europe should be integrated or fused is entirely a matter for detailed consideration by the nations concerned," and Europeans ought to remember "that once you destroy national esprit and morale, you will be unlikely to win your battles."

[7] "In my view the British stand, far from being blameworthy, is right," Montgomery had written. On Eisenhower's efforts to convince continental Europeans of British support for collective defense see nos. 218, 530, 539, and 543.

[8] "I suggest we should ask Britain to promise moral support for the European Army conception, together with technical and professional assistance, and cooperation in working out the political and military and financial implications: and they should ask that this task be treated as urgent?" See no. 552; for developments see no. 569.

[9] Montgomery had written that at present it was "impracticable" for Britain to join a European army.

[10] Montgomery's "final suggestion re Britain" was to prompt Churchill to pledge full British moral support for a European army.

To Bernhard, Prince Consort   *December 13, 1951*
of the Netherlands
Secret

Dear Bernhard: We have been examining the possibility of training a few senior Dutch officers as you and I discussed last Sunday at my house.[1] Apparently, the prospects look very well, and we have instructed General Williams of General Handy's staff in Heidelberg to deal directly with the Dutch staff when this matter finally gets on an official basis.[2] I think that the Dutch Military Representative here at my headquarters will carry the necessary message to the Dutch Chiefs of Staff.

This morning, I had to send word to you that I can't possibly make our date on the 20th. Events just simply crowd me too much. I regret it exceedingly, but it is apparently not in the cards that I am to have a shoot with you this year.[3]

We found out that the United States admits the old paintings without customs duty and, early next week, my plane, which will then be on the way home, will stop at the usual airfield in your country to pick up the paintings. Somebody in the staff will keep you notified of the details. I believe it is necessary for the American Consul or similar official to certify that the paintings are in fact "old."[4]

With all the best, and won't you please convey my warm and respectful greetings to The Queen.[5] *As ever*

[1] Bernhard, a friend of Eisenhower's since World War II days, had been the General's guest at lunch on Sunday, December 2 (for background on the Prince see Chandler, *War Years*; and Galambos, *Columbia University*).

[2] Major General Paul Langdon Williams was assigned to the staff of General Thomas T. Handy, Commander in Chief, Europe (for background on Williams see Galambos, *Columbia University*, no. 5; on Handy see in these volumes no. 286, n. 3).

[3] Bernhard had invited Eisenhower to a pheasant shoot on December 20 (Bernhard to Eisenhower, Dec. 5, 1951, EM).

[4] Bernhard had asked Eisenhower whether he might send some old paintings to Walter Bedell Smith in the United States by way of Eisenhower's office. In a handwritten note on Eisenhower's letter to Bernhard, Colonel Robert L. Schulz had noted that the paintings would be picked up on Sunday, December 16. The "usual airfield" was probably the Soesterberg military aerodrome near Soestdijk Palace (see memorandum, BJF to Schulz, n.d.; and Bernhard to Eisenhower, Oct. 8 and Nov. 17, 1951, all in EM, same file as document).

[5] Juliana, Queen of the Netherlands.

To William Averell Harriman   *December 14, 1951*
Confidential

Dear Averell:[1] I am happy to know that your entire Committee is now meeting to put its work into final form. Responding to your request for my personal comment on the Committee's draft "Plan of Action," I can offer only broad comments since we here at SHAPE have had no opportunity for exhaustive study.[2]

My first comment is that the results of the work of the Temporary Council Committee and of its Screening and Costing Staff represent a truly monumental piece of work. The participants in that task will certainly deserve a real tribute from the whole NATO community if they are able to complete their difficult work as effectively as they have advanced it thus far. I am impressed not only by the spirit of cooperation that must have animated the members of the Committee in achieving the kind of agreement that is represented but also by the objective manner in which they have tackled this most difficult problem.

I have the feeling that we are really seeing for the first time the dimensions, in terms of an integrated military, economic, and financial effort, of our build-up task.[3] It will be a real milestone in NATO development to have carried out with this degree of success the difficult task of reconciling rapid build-up of security forces with practical limitations in the economic field, and to have done this through joint and cooperative action.

The general approach indicated in the plan—of building balanced, combat-effective forces at the maximum rate which the availability of resources will permit—is clearly one which gives strong support to the fulfillment of the NATO mission entrusted to me and, accordingly, I heartily welcome it.

I think your Committee has reached something both practical and effective in your handling of the programs proposed for each of the next three years. I assume this same method of operation would be continued until the full requirements necessary for the planned strategy were provided for. In my opinion, the forces envisaged are such as to provide a sound basis for actions utilizing the resources which will become available during the coming year. I am ready to assist in every way I can in the attainment in the greatest possible measure of the "maximum practicable" goals you have shown.

The standards for manning, training, equipping, and providing cadres are directly related to this build-up of defensive forces. Those proposed as interim standards for 1952 seem well designed as general guides which will contribute during the coming year to the maximum practicable build-up of effective forces. In this field also SHAPE will be in a position to advise and assist in making the best practicable application of this guidance to the particular forces and particular circumstances of each country.

From my own standpoint, and in the interest of saving time, I would welcome the immediate and urgent initiation by the countries of the actions recommended in 1952 for the achievement of the build-up program. It is understood, of course, that Parliaments will have to determine the eventual levels, but the Temporary Council Committee has already achieved a great deal by cooperative action in preparing a program for the consideration of the NATO nations. If our joint effort follows the broad lines the TCC is suggesting, and if it reaches the levels recommended, it is clear to me that there should be full value received in return, in terms of a more rapid development of defensive capability and creation of a real deterrent to aggression in Western Europe.[4] *Cordially*

---

[1] Harriman chaired the Executive Bureau of the Temporary Council Committee, which the North Atlantic Council had established at its Ottawa meeting in September to examine the conflicting goals of military production and peacetime economic growth. Colonel Andrew J. Goodpaster drafted this document for Eisenhower.

[2] For a summary of the TCC's interim report see State, *Foreign Relations, 1951*, vol. III, *European Security and the German Question, Part I*, pp. 389–92; and Poole, *History of the Joint Chiefs of Staff*, vol. IV, *1950-1952*, pp. 275–79. The proposed "plan of action" incorporated the Screening and Costing Staff mobilization proposals (see below) and recommended that by 1954 NATO countries increase their budgetary expenditures by about $3.5 billion above the FY 1952 levels. After including estimated North American end item aid, the TCC calculated that financial deficits for the three-year period would run $6.1 billion, "with inconsequential deficit in fiscal 52, 2.4 in fiscal 53, and 3.6 in fiscal 54." The TCC draft report also proposed that NATO set firm priorities for the European rearmament program and that U.S. aid be furnished in accordance with those priorities (Lincoln to Bradley, Dec. 10, 1951, CCS 092 Western Europe [3-12-48], Sec. 110).

[3] Eisenhower praised the TCC despite its conclusion that the NATO build-up in Europe ought to proceed at a slower rate than the NATO Military Committee and SHAPE had recommended earlier (see no. 364, n. 4). In Military Committee 26/1 NATO's military authorities (including Eisenhower) had set as the 1954 objective 642 warships, some 9,200 aircraft, and 46 divisions prepared to fight on mobilization day, or M-day, when war broke out; MC 26/1 called for 31 more army divisions ready three days afterward and another 21 available in thirty days, on M + 30—for a total of 98 divisions in the field a month after mobilization (Eisenhower's August 1951 proposal had called for 97 divisions). By 1954 the TCC instead called for M-day forces of 402 combatant ships, nearly 10,000 warplanes (counting reserves), and $41^2/_3$ divisions, with 12 more divisions available three days later and another 33 (or a total of $86^2/_3$) divisions at SHAPE's command on M + 30. The TCC estimated 1952 and 1954 production shortfalls at $11.6 billion; thus the TCC further differed from MC 26/1 in recognizing that due to equipment shortages, financial considerations, or both, Eisenhower's requirements for 1954 might not be met until 1955 or even 1956 (Poole, *History of the Joint Chiefs of Staff*, vol. IV, *1950-1952*, pp. 275–76).

Nonetheless, the TCC, "(in accordance with Eisenhower desire for maximum effective force at earliest possible date)," established "firm" targets for 1952: 25

combat-ready divisions, six more than in 1951, with a total of $54\frac{2}{3}$ in readiness on M + 30. The committee set "provisional" goals for 1953 ($36\frac{2}{3}$ divisions combat-ready, $69\frac{1}{3}$ on M + 30) and described its objectives for 1954 and beyond as "goals to be used for planning purposes to guide those early actions required to make possible the achievement of the targets" (State, *Foreign Relations, 1951*, vol. III, *European Security and the German Question, Part I*, p. 389; Poole, *History of the Joint Chiefs of Staff*, vol. IV, *1950–1952*, p. 276; Lincoln to Bradley, Dec. 10, 1951, CCS 092 Western Europe [3-12-48], Sec. 110; JSPC 876/417, Jan. 5, 1952, and JSPC 876/434, Jan. 25, 1952, *ibid.*, Secs. 115, 119. See also no. 553 and, for developments, no. 643, n. 1).

[4] The following day, testifying before Harriman and the TCC, Eisenhower would recall his wartime work in setting up a unified command and describe NATO's present task as similar. He commended the labors of the TCC and repeated his strong support of the European army concept (TCC-D/25, Dec. 15, 1951, NATO Files, microfilm). "General Eisenhower's degree of acceptance of the TCC and SCS reports are indicated in his letter to the Chairman of the TCC and in my message reporting his statements before the TCC," Harriman's military adviser would later write the Secretary of Defense (Lincoln to Lovett, Dec. 21, 1951, OS/D, 1951, Clas. Decimal File, CD 092.3 NATO).

543   *Eisenhower Mss.*

To Winston Spencer Churchill   *December 14, 1951*

Dear Prime Minister: Yesterday we had a number of members of Parliament here at SHAPE for a briefing. They were addressed by my Chief of Staff, by Field Marshal Montgomery, and by Air Chief Marshal Saunders. After they had been through this ordeal, I appeared before them to make certain that they could not possibly complain of a lack of oratorical effort on the part of their friends in the Armed Services.[1]

They were very interested in discussing the European Defense Force. Their questions on this general subject were directed largely to two or three special points in my explanation. These particular points were my belief that, in the long run, security and stability in Western Europe and, therefore, in the free world will be most difficult to assure except with a political unification of Western Continental Europe, including West Germany.

The next point that they discussed at length was my assertion that the European Army, primarily designed in order to secure German strength in the Western coalition under conditions acceptable to both Germany and West Europe should be used also as a stepping stone toward developing political union. Because of my belief that Great Britain cannot join the political union in Western Europe, it should not be an active participant in the European Army.

Additionally, they were interested in my statement that the European Army project will never succeed except with the active, enthusiastic, and incessant moral support of Great Britain. The prestige and standing of Great Britain in Europe are very real things. There is great respect for Britain's political maturity and her approval in any complicated political problem is eagerly sought. In my opinion, it is scarcely too much to say that, as of this moment, Britain's attitude is one of the key factors in this whole situation.[2]

Needless to say, I am eagerly looking forward to a long talk with you on the 18th. We informed your office, through the British Embassy, that we would design our schedule according to your personal preferences. My own thought is that if you would say a word to my assembled staff immediately after you entered the headquarters—not over two minutes unless you should desire to say more—we could then proceed to my office for a chat. Just before lunch, I would have a few of my senior staff officers step in to have a glass of sherry with us and then we would have not over three individuals, outside your own party, for lunch.

Following lunch, we would take you directly to Orly Airfield. The trip from out here at Versailles requires less time than from the heart of the city. If you have any special wishes concerning the visit, please send them either through your Embassy or to me directly.[3]

Remember me kindly to Mrs. Churchill[4] and, as always, my warm regard to you. *Cordially*

[1] On December 12 Eisenhower had lunched with several members of the British Parliament and then assisted in briefing them concerning Western European defense (for background see no. 491). On Chief of Staff Alfred M. Gruenther, Bernard L. Montgomery, and Hugh W. L. Saunders see nos. 2, nn. 3 and 4, and 77, n. 5, respectively.

[2] The General was concerned that many European governments perceived Great Britain as being opposed to a united European defense force (see nos. 530 and 540).

[3] On Churchill's visit to SHAPE on December 18 see no. 556; for developments see nos. 563 and 569. Churchill would write on December 19 (EM) to thank Eisenhower for the visit.

[4] The former Clementine Hozier.

544   *Eisenhower Mss.*

To ROBERT RAYMOND BARRY   *December 14, 1951*

Dear Mr. Barry:[1] Just a note to tell you that I, too, enjoyed our talk here and am grateful for your friendly and continuing interest. As I told you during your visit, I have no knowledge of the various things brought up again in your last letter and, therefore, I can assume no responsibility whatsoever for them. The responsibilities of my present position not only make any other attitude inappropriate, but, even if I should try to do anything else, I have no time to do so.[2]

With warm personal regard and good wishes, *Sincerely*

[1] For background on Barry, who was actively supporting Eisenhower's candidacy, see no. 499.

[2] In an eight-page typewritten letter of December 8 (EM) Barry had complained to Eisenhower that he had been rebuffed by Senator Henry Cabot Lodge, Jr., manager of the Eisenhower-for-President campaign in the United States. Barry had acted on General Lucius Clay's suggestion that he talk with Lodge. But, Barry wrote, "Lodge's disregard of elementary politics in refusing to see me . . . is certainly evidence of a lack of ordinary horse sense, and provocative in view of my several months of work at my own expense plus my trip to see you and General Clay's directive—not withstanding my trip to Boston for that purpose." Barry went on to tell Eisenhower that he thought his campaign was "shrouded and controlled by Yankee scepticism and abruptness in combination with Dewey team Machiavellian tactics and slickness." Eisenhower would ask aide Paul T. Carroll to draft a reply to Barry disclaiming "all knowledge and responsibility" regarding the events described in Barry's letter.

545   *Eisenhower Mss., Diaries*

DIARY   *December 15, 1951*

Gov. Stassen came to see me.[1] He is trying to get the Rep. nomination, but calculates his chances as very low. But he feels that by trying he keeps the party from surrendering to the reactionaries. He is still asserting that *if* I will enter the race before "it becomes too late" he will immediately announce as my lieut. The nice thing about his visit was that he asked me nothing—he, as he said, merely reported developments, and re-stated his position, frequently given to me during the many months since 1948. In any event, I said nothing except that "Do as you please. I'm busy at my duties. I shall never, in advance of a convention indicate a political intention."[2]

*   *   *   *   *

From every side, in Europe, I get complaints reference Britain's attitude toward a European Army.[3]

[1] Stassen, former Governor of Minnesota and now president of the University of Pennsylvania, was a contender for the Republican presidential nomination. He and Mrs. Stassen had dined with the Eisenhowers the evening of December 12; Stassen himself had met with Eisenhower the following afternoon. For background on Stassen see no. 409, n. 6. See also *New York Times*, December 23, 1951; and *International Herald Tribune*, Paris ed., December 13, 14, 1951.

[2] For more on Stassen and his preconvention activity see Parmet, *Eisenhower and the American Crusades*, pp. 53–55; for developements see no. 555.

[3] Great Britain's seeming opposition to the formation of a European defense force troubled Eisenhower (see, for example, no. 530).

546   *Eisenhower Mss.*

To WILLIAM EDWARD ROBINSON   *December 18, 1951*

Dear Bill: Thank you for your letter of the 11th. I shall not attempt any long reply as of this moment because, within a few days, you will be starting for this side with Cliff. I cannot tell you how eagerly we are all looking forward to seeing you both.[1]

I cannot fail to remark, however, that you are absolutely right about the "disaster screams" that are reaching me these days. Of course, I am relatively unmoved because, if the predictions made in them should come about, it would mean far more of relief and happiness to Mamie and me than it would disaster. Beyond this, I don't see how people win fights by getting scared.[2]

At the same moment I got the cable from you and Cliff this afternoon, I had a letter from George saying that he and Sid were planning a visit over this way, although there was no indication of the time.[3] Of course, I have asked them both many times, so I assume that they are planning on some time after the first of the year. In any event, upon receipt of your cable, I suggested to them about the middle of February which would seem to dovetail fairly well with your ideas.

I'll be seeing you soon—I hope. *Cordially*

[1] Eisenhower's close friends Robinson and Clifford Roberts planned to visit the General and Mrs. Eisenhower on December 23 (see no. 504, n. 4).

[2] Robinson had written that "the cries of political urgency you are getting from this side are exaggerated, as well as insensitive and inconsiderate." "I've heard them all," he assured Eisenhower, "and perhaps I'm stupid, but I am relatively unmoved" (EM). For the General's own response to mounting political pressures see nos. 509, 533, and 538.

[3] "Dependable friend of yours tells us prominent Texan and genial resident of Washington plan visit you last of this month," Robinson and Roberts cabled Eisenhower on the eighteenth (EM). "The friend advises you to diplomatically cause them delay their trip and we support this. Advise pending time we see you." George E. Allen and Sid W. Richardson would visit Eisenhower in February 1952. For Eisenhower's replies see nos. 549 and 558.

To Robert Justus Kleberg, Jr.   *December 18, 1951*
Personal and confidential

Dear Bob:[1] It is nothing but understatement to say that I was touched by your letter. I cannot tell you how complimented I am that anyone so seriously interested in the welfare of America as yourself should believe me fitted for the high office you suggest.[2]

I think that it will be perfectly obvious to you why I do not feel able, while on duty in uniform, to comment on the American political scene—at least so far as any possibility of personal participation is concerned.

The project I am now working on is one in which America has invested billions of dollars. If I should take any partisan stand whatsoever, while I am engaged in that project, it would tend to inspire partisan thinking in our country toward the whole affair. This would be fatal.

With this out of the way, I must say that I agree that the critical problem of our times is the preservation of personal freedom under a free enterprise system. This whole political and economic order is being challenged from every angle. Some of the attacks are launched through ignorance, some even through an idea that human welfare is thus served. Other attacks are inspired by tyrannical intent—these, of course, come largely from Communistic adherence.[3]

Right this minute, we are facing a dreary Christmas in Europe, with the fog blanketing the entire countryside. I don't possess much of this world's goods, but I would give a good portion of it to be able, with Mamie, to sit down with you on your beautiful ranch and just loaf for about two solid weeks. Not that I have been asked, but I would even be presumptuous to come without awaiting the faintest kind of suggestion.

Mamie and I send our best wishes to you and yours for a fine Holiday Season and a prosperous New Year. With warm personal regard, *Cordially*

[1] Kleberg was the president of King Ranch, Inc., in Kingsville, Texas (see Galambos, *Columbia University*, no. 623).
[2] In a letter of November 28 (EM) Kleberg had urged the General to become a presidential candidate, arguing that as President, Eisenhower would be in a better position to strengthen Western European defenses.
[3] Eisenhower's stenographer may have mistranscribed the word *adherents*. Kleberg had suggested that if Eisenhower decided to become a presidential candidate, he should make "personal freedom under a free enterprise system" the sole issue of his campaign. That "world-wide" issue, Kleberg said, has become "a contest between the two ideologies of who is master, the citizen or the state."

Dear Ed:[1] Since yesterday morning I have received two letters from you.[2] Both were intensely interesting.

First of all, I most enthusiastically agree with what you say about Fred Gurley, Bob Jones, and McCollum.[3] Along with them, you can list also a few of my good friends in the Augusta National Club. When a man has such friends as I am fortunate enough to claim, he certainly can never look upon himself except as a very lucky individual, regardless of his cares, worries, and preoccupations.

Beyond this, I agree with your general evaluation of the developments described in your note of the 8th. I have done, as you well know, a great deal of soul searching in the effort to determine whether or not I have any duty other than the obvious one I am now attempting to carry out. While I admit that eventualities could create a personal duty taking precedence over the one I am now performing, I cannot, to save me, see how any reasonable man could urge upon me any course except the one I am now pursuing. The future will have to take care of itself; I have plenty to do in the present.[4]

Your invitation to Enon Farm brings up many lovely memories.[5] I most earnestly wish that Mamie and I could be with you there this Holiday Season. Possibly this wish is all the more intense because of the character of our weather here for the past few days. We have had dense fogs that make travel on the roads, even at very slow rates, a very dangerous business. The main highway toward Paris has been littered with wrecks.

Our love to Kay[6] and, of course, as always, warm regards to yourself. *Cordially*

[1] On Bermingham see no. 23, n. 1.
[2] Bermingham had written on December 8 and 13 (both in EM). In his second letter he had quoted an American corporation representative in Europe to whom French General Alphonse Juin had spoken freely of Eisenhower's possible departure from NATO. According to Juin, Eisenhower "was the only man living who could handle his present position and that under no circumstances should he be tempted to accept any other offer that might be made him, no matter how appealing it might be." The American listener had almost wondered whether Juin was a Democrat. Bermingham had concluded that Juin "must eventually be persuaded that the ultimate and complete success of yours and his endeavors lies with your directing it from the White House." See also below.
[3] "Of your many devoted friends," Bermingham had written in his earlier letter, "you can paste gold stars beside the names of Fred Gurley, Bob Jones, and 'Mc' McCollum" (see nos. 122, n. 1, 471, and 519).
[4] Bermingham had written extensively of presidential politics: his effort "to fabricate the nucleus of an organization which could be properly and constructively

used by the professionals"; the Eisenhower forces Lodge headed; Taft's own campaign; Eisenhower's possible support in the South; large pro-Democratic voting patterns that only Eisenhower could reverse; and the issue of timing an Eisenhower announcement of candidacy. Bermingham described Taft followers as "a hard hitting outfit of professional politicians, only honest when it suits their interests"; as for the Eisenhower supporters, he said that "the Dewey, Duff, Lodge combination is their dish." "The confusion, lack of intelligent planning and the crosscurrents are disheartening," wrote Bermingham of the professionals who had begun organizing on Eisenhower's behalf. "Perhaps it can't be otherwise, and nothing will be grooved until you decide in which direction you will move. Then, should it come about that you answer the call, you can fire everybody and start fresh" (in Bermingham's December 13 message he toned down references to the pro-Eisenhower professionals but emphasized that "the spotlight must be switched away from them").

In his letter of December 8 Bermingham had enclosed a copy of a letter he had received from South Dakota Senator Karl E. Mundt, begging Bermingham not to give anyone in the South the impression that Eisenhower supported Truman's civil-rights or fair-employment policies. Then traveling in Louisiana and Texas, Mundt said he had "found many who are convinced Ike as a GOP candidate can carry the total South and win *provided* he handles the Civil rights issue via State Action instead of by totalitarian Federalized coercion." "Through the proper channel," Bermingham assured Eisenhower, "the Honorable Senator Lodge has been told to keep severely away from controversial questions and to say nothing, imply nothing that could be interpreted as even an indication of your thinking."

Although "run of the mill" Republican politicians wanted to nominate Taft, wrote Bermingham, a "secret analysis" of voting trends conducted at Columbia University proved "that a Joe Doak running Democrat will soundly trounce anyone other than yourself." He believed that the people, not the politicians, would decide this election, and he hoped that the General would continue his "unhurried course."
[5] "Enon Farm has never been quite so beautiful," Bermingham had written of his home in Midway, Alabama; he invited the Eisenhowers to visit there before the quail season ended in February (see also Galambos, *Columbia University*, no. 656).
[6] Bermingham's wife.

549   *Eisenhower Mss.*

To George Edward Allen   *December 18, 1951*

Dear George: Just a few minutes ago, I received your letter telling about mailing Barbie the check you failed to earn for her. While I am perfectly ready to talk over with you the terms of any reasonable bet for next year's weight contest, I assure you that, if you put if off, my terms will grow tougher and the amounts bigger.[1]

You talked vaguely about the possibility that you and Sid might be coming over here some of these days. At the same time, you were talking about spending the Holidays in California.

Because January is going to be a particularly tough month for me (preparing for the Lisbon meeting—and that meeting itself will be held probably during the first week of February), I suggest that, if convenient to you both, you start your trip to get here about the middle of February. If this doesn't suit you both, let me know; but, of course, when, you, Mary, and the inimitable Sid are here, Mamie and I want to be around as much as we can.[2]

Never have I been more preoccupied than I am these days. It seems that I never catch up, and daily topics for conferences, communications, and study range all the way from the economy of Greece to the politics of Norway. It is truly a complex job and my chores are often wearing as well as perplexing. However, there is no acceptable alternative for the United States to the establishment of a collective security among the countries whose welfare directly affects our own. So we must succeed—therefore, we will.

Give my very best wishes to Sid and my love to Mary.[3] To all three of you, best wishes for a happy Holiday Season and a bright New Year. Let me know as soon as you can whether the date I suggest is suitable to the three of you. Of course, Mamie is my partner in all the good wishes that come with this letter. *As ever*

[1] On December 13 (EM) Allen had written Eisenhower that he had settled their weight-loss bet of 1951 by sending a check to the General's daughter-in-law, Barbara Eisenhower (see Allen to Barbara Eisenhower, Dec. 13, 1951, EM). Although he had promised to begin dieting in January, Allen wanted to discuss the details of their new wager in person. During a visit with Eisenhower in February the terms of the new bet would be set: Eisenhower's goal would be 172 pounds, and Allen's would be 199, to be achieved by December 15, 1952. Compromising the bet would cost five-hundred dollars. For background on the wager see no. 529; and EM, Allen Corr. On Allen's visit see n. 2 below.

[2] Allen had said that Sid W. Richardson would spend Christmas with him in California and they would discuss visiting Eisenhower then (on Richardson see no. 34, n. 2). Richardson and Allen would see the General on February 16, 18, and 22, 1952. On the NATO meeting in Lisbon, Portugal, see no. 643, n. 1.

[3] Allen's wife.

550

Eisenhower Mss.

To Gordon Gray

December 19, 1951

Dear Gordon:[1] As of now, it would be extremely awkward to let Buck Lanham come back to the United States.[2] However, I never like to stand in the way of a deserving officer and, if this assignment would mean a promotion to him, I should like to inform him to that effect. As a matter of personal preference, I think that he feels he would not want to give up what both he and I believe to be an important post in a critically important program; nevertheless, if the job meant some advancement for him, I would personally urge him to take it in spite of the gap that would be created here.[3]

This note brings to you my best wishes for a very fine Christmas and New Year. *Cordially*

[1] Gray, Director of the Psychological Strategy Board (see no. 366), planned to leave government service for the presidency of the University of North Carolina in January 1952. Dr. Raymond Bernard Allen (Ph.D. University of Minnesota 1934), president of the University of Washington in Seattle since 1946, had been named to replace him (*New York Times*, Nov. 23, 1951).

[2] In a letter of December 11 (EM) Gray had discussed his staffing difficulties and the hope that he might place Brigadier General Charles Trueman ("Buck") Lanham, Chief of Public Information at SHAPE since February (see no. 141), in a "key spot" when he left the board. Before formally requesting Lanham's transfer, Gray wanted to ensure that the change would be agreeable to Eisenhower.

[3] Lanham preferred to remain in his present position "as a small part of this critical enterprise which shall ultimately determine the fate of all of us" (Lanham to Gruenther, Dec. 18, 1951, EM, Gray Corr.). In a handwritten endorsement to Lanham's note, Gruenther recommended informing Gray that Lanham was unavailable unless the position included a promotion. Gray could offer none (Gray to Eisenhower, Jan. 14, 1952, *ibid.*).

551   *Eisenhower Mss.*

To Lucius Du Bignon Clay   *December 19, 1951*
Personal and confidential

Dear Lucius:[1] Thank you very much indeed for your longhand note and for the memorandum that accompanied it.[2] I must say that, while I have very little time to devote to the kind of exhaustive thinking that was responsible for the production of the memorandum, I instinctively find myself largely in agreement with it. Certainly it represents a far clearer analysis of my own personal position—a position that cannot be escaped even if I should fervently desire—than is evidenced by some individuals who nevertheless insist upon the depth of their friendship for me and of their own disinterestedness.

Time and time again, I have tried to make clear that the American Military Commander of the Allied Forces in Europe cannot possibly allow his own actions or words to inspire partisan argument in America concerning the merits or demerits of this whole project. To my mind, this would be close to disloyalty.[3]

Of course, Our Friend[4] discusses a possibility that, by January 15th, some more positive assurance must be given as to my political allegiance, or increasing confusion will result. Even to contemplate such a thing makes me extremely uneasy, although I have in the past admitted to Our Friend and to others (of whom A[5] is one) that my family ties, my own meager voting record, and my own convictions align me fairly closely with what I call the progressive branch of the Republican Party. This, of course, I have done on a personal and confidential basis and only because it came out as a natural development of discussions of principle and policy in our country. But to be a party to engineering a statement, the purpose of which would be to help clarify a partisan political situation, would, in my present post, indeed be a tough thing and cause me a lot of anxious thought.[6] As you well know, my attitude has been, "I shall do my duty as I see it— at this moment, there can be no doubt as to where my duty lies and of the limitations my current duty places upon my own rights and privileges as a citizen."[7]

Bill Draper was in to see me yesterday.[8] We had a long talk about you and, incidentally, about Governor Dewey. When you see the latter, please extend to him and to Mrs. Dewey warm greetings from Mamie and me, and our best wishes for the Holiday Season and the New Year. These wishes go double from both of us to you and Marjorie[9]—we earnestly wish that we could see you and talk to you. *As ever*

[1] Clay was Eisenhower's old friend and close political adviser.

[2] On December 13 Clay, then flying to Florida after a meeting with New York Governor Thomas E. Dewey in Albany, had written a hurried, penciled cover letter to a political memorandum (sent by separate cover) that the Governor meant for Eisenhower (both in EM). In it Dewey regretted, as earlier Clay himself had (see no. 537, n. 1), the failure of campaign manager Henry Cabot Lodge, Jr., to invite Clay to recent political strategy meetings. "Please forget it," Clay wrote in his message. "Clark has somehow poisoned Duff and Lodge. That is not important— and an attempt to solve it might be damaging." Clay also reported plans William E. Robinson and Clifford Roberts had made for an upcoming "meeting of your very special friends (no politicians)," among whom there might be "someone in whom you have confidence who could sit with the politicians in their strategy meetings and interpret you—without specific authorization."

Dewey's long memorandum analyzed the political situation and offered his own plan for bringing about Eisenhower's Republican party nomination. Dewey downplayed the number of Senator Robert A. Taft's pledged delegates (see no. 567, n. 2). "I have tried to point out," Dewey wrote, "that 'commitments' in December can and usually do weaken or evaporate in the June heat." Harold Stassen's bid for the nomination did not concern Dewey, who reported that Stassen "knows he cannot win, even in a deadlock" (see also no. 545). Dewey recommended that the General choose primary contests carefully. He approved Eisenhower's entry in the New Hampshire primary but doubted the political value of an uncontested victory; he believed some opposition could be "artificially stimulated." Dewey strongly opposed Eisenhower's entry in the Wisconsin primary—preferring to leave it to Stassen "with our enthusiastic blessings"—and also recommended avoiding Oregon. "Once people talk you into entering these primaries they then start crying bloody murder for you to come out and save the bacon when the going gets rough."

Dewey's "program of action" for Eisenhower embraced (a and b) a discreet announcement by January 15 of Eisenhower's party affiliation (see n. 6 below); (c) Eisenhower's declaration, within two weeks of January 15, that he had accomplished his task at NATO and that the work was ready for others to carry on; (d) farewell speeches in Europe emphasizing Eisenhower's strong views on military and economic unity there ("Such speeches," Dewey wrote, "will be inoffensive to those of our point of view and will please the isolationist group which is in opposition"); (e) Eisenhower's resignation of all military titles and salaries (not absolutely necessary, according to Dewey, but "an exceedingly dramatic and impressive move"); and (f) a number of Eisenhower speeches full of "fight and vigor," some of them on controversial subjects, all of which would satisfy the "professionals." Dewey stressed that Eisenhower need not make a public statement of candidacy before mid-January (for some of the pressure to announce his political allegiance see no. 538). "Everyone is hysterically insisting upon an announcement," he wrote. "I insist with equal vigor that the one thing the American people want most is the one thing they can not get" (see also Smith, *Dewey*, pp. 580-81).

[3] Eisenhower spelled out this view in no. 561, n. 4.

[4] Governor Dewey.

[5] Pennsylvania Senator James H. Duff. On the letter-for-name code system used by Eisenhower and Clay see no. 331, n. 5.

[6] New Hampshire law required petitioners placing a name on the primary ballot to swear to the party allegiance of their candidate. By Dewey's plan (see n. 2 above), New Hampshire Governor Sherman Adams would inquire of one of Eisenhower's brothers, presumably Milton (see no. 473, n. 2), as to the General's party affiliation; Milton would reply that the General was indeed a Republican, and Eisenhower himself would publicly attest to the fact.

[7] See no. 400, n. 4.

[8] Long Island Transit Authority Chairman William H. Draper, Jr. (see no. 588, n. 1).

[9] Clay's wife.

552

Eisenhower Mss.

To ROBERT ABERCROMBIE LOVETT

December 19, 1951

Personal and confidential

Dear Bob: Some of my earlier letters from SHAPE dealt with the influence of the Indochinese war on the development of security forces in Europe, especially the French contingent.[1] I shall not bother you with a repetition of facts with which you are already familiar. My only purpose in mentioning the thing again is to urge that a real examination be made of the Indochina problem, particularly as it may affect America. I like to see our country foresighted in its study and handling of difficult situations.

Occasionally, new evidence becomes available that seems to indicate a gradual build-up of Chinese Communist forces in Southeast Asia.[2] Obviously, if Communist China should extend its aggressive operations to include, soon, a Southeast Asia front, it will at some point become impossible for the free world to allow them to continue with the fiction that only Chinese "volunteers" are participating. If American interest should become acutely involved, we would have a de facto war on our hands, no matter what we might call it in official communiques.

Prospects such as these indicate the great necessity for advance thinking about such things. Possibly a timely diplomatic warning would have some effect, but certainly a study of the available forces, our own capabilities, local aspirations, the terrain, and possibilities of impeding or deterring operations by blocking of communication routes and so on, would all be indicated.

I know that all of this has been done to some degree. But we can never forget that the global struggle is an indivisible whole, and changes, to some degree, every day. The cold war everywhere, our effort to create strength in Europe, our fighting in Asia—all these are bound together and it *might* easily be that America's interest would be best advanced by some method of assisting the French to bring their particular war in Indochina to an early end. More munitions for that region—or anything else—might prove to be best for *us*.[3]

Mr. Churchill was over here the other day and we had a long talk about many things of common interest.[4] While here, he issued a very fine statement about the European Defense Force and European unity.[5] Already it has had some effect—one of the Italian officials came to see me this morning to say that the whole atmosphere among the negotiators was better because of what Mr. Churchill had said.[6] This man believed that this feeling would be reinforced if you, personally, could make some public statement to the same effect. I think that you and I have talked over the subject often enough so that you know my convictions about it. In substance, my basic belief is that *we must unite Western Europe, including Western Germany*, or there is no logical basis for a long-term, enduring peace for the Western world. (Unless, of course, Russia should completely and unexpectedly collapse.) It seems to me that it takes no great study to realize that this is true—consequently, the production of a European Army should be really only an included and far simpler problem than the one we must eventually solve. So if you, as well as Dean Acheson and Bradley—to name three—could find opportunities for stating publicly that you *heartily support the principle* of the European Army and hope that, by this means, we will bring German strength into the Western defenses and take another step toward European unity, you would be doing a great service for NATO.[7] This would, of course, be in conformity with Congressional intent, expressed in the 1951 Mutual Aid law.

Since writing the above, I have had a conference with a group of Frenchmen and was amazed to find that they believe that you and I do not see eye to eye on certain important subjects! The way they expressed it was, "The Pentagon and you do not seem to be in agreement on some matters."[8] I pressed them hard to find out what could give rise to such a curious impression and found that most of the Pentagon opinions of which they were speaking had been uttered some time back; most of them long before I came to Europe.

The particular subject under discussion was the European Army. The group included two newspaper people, the Minister of State (Army), two members of Parliament, and a businessman. Unanimously, they felt that the "Pentagon" was against the European Army idea. I told them that, on the contrary, long before I came over here I had encountered this subject among the staffs in Washington and that the only objection expressed to me was the size of the unit the French, at that time, wanted adopted.

In any event, this incident underlines the desirability of some public statement of the kind that I suggest above. It also draws attention to the anxiety with which the European populations watch the statements of public figures in America.

I really started this note to say Merry Christmas and Happy New Year; but, as usual, I could not avoid telling you about some of the things that were on my mind for the moment.[9] *Cordially*

---

[1] See nos. 89, 142, 361, and 362; see also the General's December 13, 1951, letter to Secretary of Defense Lovett, no. 539.

[2] Visiting the United States in September, French General de Lattre had estimated that the Chinese Communists then were forming five or six divisions within the Vietminh forces, providing them many technical and strategic advisers, and training Vietminh officers in Chinese military schools. De Lattre further estimated that between 80,000 and 150,000 Chinese "volunteers" had gathered in southern China and could invade Indochina in a matter of two or three weeks over newly built roads. In Paris for a meeting of the High Council of the French Union in late November 1951, de Lattre repeated his estimates and warnings. On the same day Eisenhower wrote Lovett, the National Security Council met to discuss the possibility of Chinese intervention in the Indochina conflict; according to a State Department letter to Ambassador Bruce in Paris, the "volume and character of intelligence reports foreshadowing massive" Chinese attacks in late December or early January raised the question what action the French planned to take in the United Nations in that event (State, *Foreign Relations, 1951*, vol. VI, *Asia and the Pacific, Part I*, pp. 509, 556, 562–64).

[3] On December 14 the American Embassy in Paris had relayed an urgent French request for materiel—specifically trucks, automatic weapons, and radio equipment—to replace that lost since mid-November as fighting in Indochina intensified (*ibid.*, p. 562).

[4] After arriving in Paris on December 17 for talks with French Ministers Pleven and Schuman, Churchill had traveled to SHAPE the following day for morning meetings and lunch with Eisenhower and his senior staff. Accompanying the Prime Minister were Sir Norman Brooke, Secretary of the British cabinet; Sir Oliver Charles Harvey, British Ambassador to France; and Sir Roger Makins, Economic Secretary. Sir Anthony Eden joined them in time for lunch with Eisenhower, Gruenther, and Air Marshal Sir Hugh Saunders (*New York Times*, Dec. 19, 1951).

[5] For background on this visit and the issue of British support for European unity and the European Defense Community see no. 530. The evening of December 18 (following Churchill's discussions with W. Averell Harriman), Churchill, Eden,

Pleven, and Schuman had issued a communiqué disclosing their "complete accord" on all problems the current international situation raised in the Far East, the Near East, and Europe. The conferees agreed that in light of "the dangers that threaten Europe, everything that reinforces European unity should be received with favor and encouraged." Churchill and Eden welcomed French adoption of the Schuman Plan and reaffirmed the intention of the British government "to establish close relations with the High Authority as soon as it will be set up." They said the British would maintain armed forces on the Continent "as long as will be necessary to fulfill the obligations toward the common powers" and welcomed an accord among the six countries soon to participate in the Paris conference on European defense (see no. 557). Both the British and the French government were "convinced that such an accord constitutes the true means of integrating democratic Germany in a purely defensive organization for European security." Churchill and Eden pledged to associate "as closely as possible with the European defense community at all stages of its political and military development. The British forces under the direction of the Supreme Allied Commander in Europe," they declared, "will be linked to the forces of the European Defensive Community for training, supply and operation on land, sea, and air. They will remain side by side in the spirit of true comradeship" (*New York Times*, Dec. 19, 1951).

[6] Eisenhower referred to Ivan Matteo Lombardo, with whom he had met that morning. Lombardo, former Italian Minister of Foreign Commerce, was head of the Italian delegation to the Conference for the Organization of a European Defense Community.

[7] Lovett, in his reply of January 3, said that he and Bradley planned to use Churchill's forthcoming visit to the United States "as a peg on which to hang some encouragement." He believed that an end-of-conference communiqué would gain wider publicity than a single statement (EM). For the Truman-Churchill joint announcement, which declared that "the defense of the free world will be strengthened and solidified by the creation of a European defense community," see *New York Times*, January 10, 1951.

[8] Lovett replied that he was baffled by these remarks. He supposed that they originated in one of then Defense Minister Jules Moch's visits to the United States in the fall of 1950, "at which time the discussion was entirely on the small size of the units the French were prepared to accept as Germany's contributions. With that problem apparently disposed of, I imagine the only other area of difference in point of view might be the one associated with allocations"—an issue that in Lovett's opinion was resolved (Lovett to Eisenhower, Jan. 3, 1951, EM). On the size of units within the proposed EDF see no. 389.

[9] Eisenhower added a handwritten postscript to this letter: "Excuse errors in grammar—etc.—am in a terrible jam—as usual! DE."

553

To JOSEPH LAWTON COLLINS
Top secret

Eisenhower Mss.

December 20, 1951

Dear Joe:[1] The detailed study of our force structure incident to the development of the SHAPE Emergency Defense Plan has occasioned a reexamination of the composition of the U.S. Seventh Army in the light of its mission.[2] Tom Handy has participated fully in this undertaking, and his views on the subject are reflected in my remarks that follow.

As you know, during the emergency period we are placing great reliance upon the U.S. Seventh Army to effect major delay and destruction on any Soviet attack east of the Rhine and to defend a sector on the west bank of the river from the Hunnsbruck to the French border.[3] The nature of this mission is such as to require, east of the Rhine, the interdiction of two major Soviet avenues of advance through the U.S. Zone: the Eisenach-Mainz axis, and the Nurenberg[4]-Karlsruhe axis. The separated nature of these axes requires that operations on each be under separate field commands. The present missions of V and VII Corps are calculated to provide for this arrangement.

For the delaying operations east of the Rhine there will be required highly mobile corps armored cavalry units. The recent phasing out of the Constabulary and the conversion of its three regiments to V and VII Corps troops fulfill this requirement. It also eliminates the idea in the minds of some that EUCOM has had six divisions; the sixth being a "Constabulary division equivalent."[5]

You can see that defense of the west bank of the Rhine in the U.S. Sector entails the integrity of an army front which logically breaks down into two corps sectors. Each of these sectors is vulnerable to major Soviet armored exploitation, and each should be backed up by an armored division in corps reserve. This balanced structure is not now possible due to the fact that VII Corps on the south has no armored division.[6]

I consider this problem to be of major importance to the success of a Rhine defense by the end of 1952. Accordingly, I have discussed with Handy the implications of a request on my part for an additional U.S. armored division to be allocated during calendar year 1952. The salient points which present themselves are these:

   a. EUCOM combat and service support structure is adequate to accommodate the division.
   b. Arrival of the unit would make available the French 5th Armored Division to the French Alsatian sector from the outset of hostilities, thereby overcoming a deficiency in armor there.
   c. Depending upon whether an additional French division is deployed in the northern portion of the U.S. Zone, it may be possible to provide the bulk of the housing from available facilities; in any case, I understand that a separate budget for housing has been submitted to you by EUCOM.
   d. Decision on deployment of the division must be made at least six months in advance so as to permit the housing to be prepared for occupancy.

On balance, these considerations support the provision of an additional division.

I note that in its position before the Military Committee in MC 26/1,[7] the U.S. plans to commit an additional armored division to Europe in 1953, thereby increasing its five divisions to six. For the reasons I have outlined above, however, I consider that the additional division should be deployed to my command during the course of 1952. It is to this end that I request you to take such steps as you deem appropriate to obtain U.S. Governmental approval of the augmentation of EUCOM by an additional armored division early in 1952.[8]
Cordially

[1] General Collins was Chief of Staff of the U.S. Army.
[2] For background on SHAPE's efforts to develop emergency war plans see nos. 124, n. 3, and 405. Eisenhower's headquarters had recently completed a plan based on forces available, or expected to be available, on January 1, 1952. This plan, designated as SHAPE EDP 1-52, assigned to the central-sector land forces commander (General Juin) the task of preparing (and being prepared to implement) "alternative courses of action to maintain forces intact west of the Ijssel and Rhine Rivers." Although both the JCS and the BCOS also believed that contingency plans for withdrawal should be made, Eisenhower, believing that the unfavorable political repercussions would outweigh any possible military benefits, had forbidden within his command any planning or discussion of possible withdrawals from the Rhine (JSPC 876/414, Dec. 29, 1951, CCS 092 Western Europe [3-12-48], Sec. 113. See also JCS 2073/258, Dec. 8, 1951; SHAPE to JCS, ALO 566, Dec. 21, 1951; Fechteler to JCS [Jan. 5, 1952]; and Dunn to Bolte *et al.*, Jan. 7, 1952, in *ibid.*, Secs. 110–15).
Eisenhower solved this problem by operating, in effect, under two different concepts of emergency action: the forward strategy, reflected in SHAPE EDP 1-52, of engaging the Soviets east of the Rhine; and the more pessimistic U.S. plan, which he had coordinated "on a NOFORN basis" with General Handy (CINCEUR), contemplating a retreat from central Europe to Great Britain or to the Pyrenees and the Iberian Peninsula (Poole, *History of the Joint Chiefs of Staff*, vol. IV, *1950-1952*, p. 308). General Schuyler drafted this letter for Eisenhower.
[3] For background on NATO's official "forward strategy" see no. 172, n. 2. The U.S. Seventh Army, commanded by Lieutenant General Manton S. Eddy (see no. 836, n. 7), had been reactivated on November 24, 1950. This unit, which comprised five divisions and three armored cavalry regiments, constituted the major U.S. ground force in Europe (Vandenberg to Lovett, Dec. 13, 1951, OS/D, 1951, Clas. Decimal File, CD 091.7 Europe; Neil W. Mold, "Seventh Army Deploys for Defense," *Army Information Digest* 7, no. 10 [1952], 3–5). The mountainous Hunsrück region of the Rhineland was situated between the Moselle and the Nahe rivers, south of Koblenz.
[4] That is, Nuremberg.
[5] The United States Constabulary consisted of three armored cavalry regiments and served as an occupation force in Germany (see Galambos, *Chief of Staff*, no. 528; and Mold, "Seventh Army," pp. 3–4). In May Eisenhower and Collins had told *New York Times* reporter Cyrus Sulzberger that the Constabulary was equivalent to an additional U.S. division in Germany (see Sulzberger, *Long Row of Candles*, p. 637; and *New York Times*, Dec. 9, 1951).
[6] Only one armored division, the 2d Armored, had been assigned to Eisenhower's

NATO command. In May Collins had requested an additional armored division for SHAPE, but no action had been taken. U.S. war planners had earmarked the 1st Armored Division, then in the United States, for service in Europe at the outbreak of war; a third armored division, not yet activated, was scheduled for shipment five months after the outbreak of hostilities (JCS 2147/33, June 1, 1951, CCS 381 [2-8-43], Sec. 20; Vandenberg to Lovett, Dec. 13, 1951, OS/D, 1951, Clas. Decimal File, CD 091.7 Europe).

[7] MC 26/1 was a revised version of a paper approved by the Standing Group (SG 20/37), which in turn had taken into consideration Eisenhower's own revised statement of requirements necessary to carry out the MTDP (see no. 364, n. 4). MC 26/1 specified that 46 divisions, 642 major combatant vessels, and 9,212 airplanes were to be available at the beginning of a war that might start in 1954. Thirty days after the beginning of mobilization NATO's ground forces were to increase to 98 divisions (Eisenhower's August proposal had called for 97 divisions) (see JCS 2073/198, Aug. 29, 1951; JCS 2073/201, Sept. 7, 1951; JCS 2073/235, Oct. 31, 1951; JCS 2073/252, Nov. 15, 1951; JSPC 876/417, Jan. 5, 1952; and JSPC 876/482, May 1, 1952, all in CCS 092 Western Europe [3-12-48], Secs. 92–141. See also Poole, *History of the Joint Chiefs of Staff*, vol. IV, *1950–1952*, p. 276). These force requirements were later revised by the NAC's Temporary Council Committee (see nos. 542 and 643, n. 1).

[8] Collins would not reply until February 1952. He would tell Eisenhower that a recent budget cut and force reduction had resulted in abandonment of the Army's plan to call up an additional armored division from the National Guard. Collins had then concluded that the 1st Armored Division should not be sent to Europe until after the Korean War ended. Collins would tell Eisenhower that since it took at least six months to train and ship a division, there was "little possibility of dispatching the 1st Armored during calendar year 1952." The Chief of Staff would add that the political repercussions involved in sending an additional division "might well result in a disapproval which could have quite serious effects on the military situation as a whole in Europe" (Collins to Eisenhower, Feb. 11, 1952, EM). Collins would, however, ask the JCS to approve shipment of the additional division to Eisenhower "at an early date following the cessation of hostilities in Korea" (JCS 2147/60, Feb. 6, 1952, CCS 381 [2-8-43], Sec. 21). Although the Joint Chiefs would approve Collins's proposal, JCS Chairman Omar Bradley and Secretary of Defense Robert Lovett would later persuade them to reverse themselves and withdraw the request from consideration so that they "would not force the issue prematurely and before the Chiefs actually think it should be sent anyway" (Bradley to Cabell, Mar. 18, 1952, CJCS, Bradley Files, 092.2 North Atlantic Treaty. See also Lalor to Bolte, Mar. 19, 1952; Vandenberg to Lovett, Apr. 16, 1952; and note to the holders of JCS 2147/60, Apr. 17, 1952, all in CCS 381 [2-8-43], Sec. 21).

554   *Eisenhower Mss.*

To DOUGLAS ELTON FAIRBANKS, JR.   *December 20, 1951*
Personal and confidential

Dear Douglas:[1] At last I've filched a bit of time to attempt a reply that may, in some partial degree, reflect the earnestness that such a letter as yours deserves. I was very much moved by the sincerity and depth of your thinking. But more than this, many of the views expressed were so close to my own that they could have been written only with sympathetic and complete understanding of my position.[2]

Many people write to tell me that I must leave now, or in January, or February, or announce some partisan domestic position—with absolutely no regard for the almost certain effect of such action on the program on which I am now working; a program instituted by America and one in which our country's future is heavily involved. One writer even said I should come home now because our enterprise here was failing!

Such black pessimism is difficult to understand—we have made a great deal of headway in the past ten months. Forces have been increased, commands organized, training instituted, and a tremendous amount of work is under way to construct the bases, lines of communication, and other facilities essential to an effective military defense. Governments have supported NATO loyally, although many have held only a precarious balance of power while pushing through difficult defense legislation. I am sure that the morale of the people is incomparably higher than it was when this project was born at Brussels a year ago.

There is great satisfaction in what appears to be a constantly increasing public support of a political concept—the Federation of Europe. As you know, the French Assembly ratified the Schuman Plan about a week ago. This outcome was predicted, but never by a margin of 144 votes.[3] The Schuman Plan will constitute, as it develops, real progress toward unity in Europe. Currently, we are devoting attention to the European Defense Force, another great step toward ultimate unification. In this military project, there are serious complications, of course, but I believe that public opinion is swinging in favor of the concept. Once you bring Frenchmen and Germans together in the same army, the struggle for security and *unity* is more than half won.

In short, I feel, in all sincerity, that the populations of Europe are gradually coming around to the belief that they *can do those things which their own self-interest demands.* If American leadership can bring about this restoration of faith and confidence, this part of the cold war will have been won.

There is little in your letter with which I would have cause to differ. The only exception would be in the unlimited confidence you seem to have in my capacity to serve in other fields. I agree with you that, if a mandate for service, such as nomination by a national party, were tendered, it would be difficult for any responsible citizen to do other than to answer such a call. On the other hand, with our system of state primaries, advance commitments and internal bartering, it would seem highly improbable that such a nomination might eventuate for one who did not actively seek public office. Many believe that such an eventuality is absolutely impossible.

It seems surprising to some that I have no regret or dismay over the improbability of such a mandate. However, I know you will understand that I have never wanted political office. Neither do I want to stay in Europe indefinitely. I have had my share of foreign service and I want to live in America. I feel there is much I can do to serve American ideals in a civilian capacity—even in retirement. But above all such personal feelings and desires is the clear conviction that, possibly as never before, our country needs dedicated men—among these I include you. We need individuals whose first ambition is to perform their indicated duty—whatever it may be. I can only pray to see my duty; thereafter, for the strength to deny any other enticement in the effort to perform it.

Of course, I hope that I am not sounding egotistical or pontifical. But if I have any value to our country, I have always believed that, over the years, I could be of more usefulness in a completely nonpartisan role than would be possible if I ever became indelibly identified with either party. I still believe this—and it will take real evidence— solid, mass, evidence—to convince me otherwise.

It was good of you to write me such a thoughtful letter, and I can do no more than offer a frank explanation of the situation as I see it. I am marking this letter "Personal and Confidential" as I have found that I can't say anything to more than one person without causing a vast amount of wild speculation.[4]

Mamie and I send warm personal regard and all the best wishes of the Holiday Season to you and Mrs. Fairbanks.[5] *Sincerely*

---

[1] Fairbanks was a well-known actor and producer (see Galambos, *Columbia University*, no. 794).

[2] On December 6 (EM) Fairbanks had written to express his sympathy for Eisenhower on his "multi-horned dilemma." Fairbanks recognized the vital importance of the General's work in Europe and understood Eisenhower's aversion to a political career; he nonetheless hoped that Eisenhower would offer Americans his leadership and integrity: "There are wider and deeper considerations . . . than the hoped-for life of any one of us."

[3] On French approval of the Schuman Plan see no. 539.

[4] For similar recent letters see nos. 521 and 524.

[5] The former Mary Lee Epling.

With reference to the Stassen visit, I intended to summarize the account he gave to me.[1] He has done that himself in the form of a note which I have just received.[2] It is contained in my correspondence files under his name.

[1] For background on Harold E. Stassen's visit with Eisenhower see nos. 537 and 545.

[2] Eisenhower referred to an eighteen-page handwritten letter dated December 15 (EM) which Stassen had composed on Hotel Crillon (Paris) stationery. In it Stassen commended the General for a "near miracle" in "developing the morale and the defense of Western Europe," then wrote that he would keep his personal visit with Eisenhower confidential but would report that Eisenhower was not a "seeker" after the Republican nomination and would not challenge Senator Robert A. Taft for it. Only a draft, Stassen understood, would answer the question whether Eisenhower would respond to such an appeal. Stassen judged Taft to be the leading Republican candidate, gauged the Ohioan's chances of defeating Truman as poor, and believed in any event that especially in matters of foreign policy Taft would make a poor President.

For these reasons, Stassen wrote, he would present himself as a candidate for the Republican nomination—campaigning, he said, on his own feet for his own beliefs, not as a standard bearer or a "stalking horse" for anyone else. Stassen calculated that one of three things could happen as a result of his entering the race: he might find Taft's lead insurmountable; he might bring about a preconvention stalemate that would produce an Eisenhower draft (in that event, Stassen wrote, "I am confident that you will be elected and will be a superb president and I will be very happy with this result"); or Stassen might upset Taft in key states and take the nomination himself.

Stassen wrote that his campaign would stress the issues of "inflation and sound money, integrity and honesty in government, mutual respect between economic, social, and racial groups in our country, and an effective affirmative dynamic foreign policy." Returning to the United States on December 22, Stassen announced his candidacy five days later in Philadelphia (*New York Times*, Dec. 28, 1951).

Two or three days ago, the Prime Minister of Great Britain made a visit to SHAPE. He was accompanied by the British Ambassador to France and by Anthony Eden, the Foreign Secretary.[1]

Our talk largely centered around the concept of a European Army. General Gruenther has made a rather extensive summary of the conversation, but it is easy to see that the plans presently under discussion on the Continent do not conform with the ideas Mr. Churchill has had in mind. Consequently, he is very lukewarm—it is better to say he is instinctively opposed—toward them. However, since we here agree with him that the attempt to make Great Britain a participant in the European Army project would only slow the matter up, it is clear that his personal opinions have no real significance except as they affect the warmth of his political and moral support.[2]

It is quite true that Europe really needs the morale and support of Great Britain; several of the Continental countries have become accustomed to look to Britain for this kind of leadership. We had a very warm discussion on the whole matter and, while I most certainly did not convince him, I am sure that he realizes he must do something in the way of giving us the kind of support we ask. He is quite ready to admit that, in the long run, a politically unified Western Europe is essential to the welfare and security of the free world. He is likewise ready to admit that we should try to make the formation of a European Army one of the stepping stones toward such a political union. But he balks at the idea of attempting to set up a single ministry to deal with the administrative and other ministerial problems of a European Army and will go no further, in his own convictions, than to propose and support some kind of a coalition force. In other words, he wants to go back to exactly the thing we had in World War II and merely multiply the number of participating nations (and most certainly multiplying the difficulties).

Frankly, I believe that, subconsciously, my great friend is trying to re-live the days of his greatest glory. He has taken upon his own shoulders, as he did in World War II, the dual position of Prime Minister and of Defense Minister.[3] He is struggling hard to bring about a recognition of specially close ties between America and Britain, and is soon to depart for the United States in furtherance of this purpose.[4] I am back in Europe in a status that is not too greatly different, in his mind, from that which I held with respect to him in World War II. To my mind, he simply will not think in terms of today, but rather only those of the war years. (Yet it is a curious fact that, in spite of his insistence that men must wear their own national uniforms, wave their own national flags, sing their own national hymns, and serve under their own national officers, it is still true that in the late summer of 1942 he offered to put British soldiers in American uniforms in order to facilitate their entry into North Africa.[5] For that one moment, he saw a special need and, therefore, acted in accordance with that need.)

My regretful opinion is that the Prime Minister no longer absorbs new ideas; exhortation and appeals to the emotions and sentiment still have some effect on him—exposition does not.

[1] For background and the communiqué Churchill, Eden, Schuman, and Pleven issued after their Paris discussions see no. 552.

[2] According to the *New York Times*, close observers of British diplomacy expressed doubts that the Churchill announcement represented much more than a "holding operation" and noted that the British Prime Minister could make no formal policy commitment without cabinet approval. Nonetheless, the *Times* reported that the communiqué might "help overcome the Belgian and Dutch hesitancy to accept the present plan." The British-French talks also supposedly reassured the French, who reportedly grew alarmed whenever they heard of British-U.S. bilateral conversations (*New York Times*, Dec. 19, 1951; see also nos. 218 and 578).

[3] On December 25 Churchill, who in October had received the King's commission to form a new government, would write Eisenhower (EM). Churchill would explain that he intended to name as British Defense Minister Field Marshal Viscount Harold R. L. G. Alexander, who had served as Allied C in C in the Mediterranean late in World War II and who in 1951 was Governor General of Canada. Although Alexander had already accepted the offer, Churchill explained that he would not make the appointment public until later. Buckingham Palace would announce Alexander's replacement at Ottawa on January 24, his elevation to the rank of earl three days later, and his appointment as Defense Minister on January 28. Alexander would assume office in late February (*New York Times*, Jan. 25, 28, 29, Mar. 1, 1952).

[4] On Churchill's trip to the United States and Canada see no. 569.

[5] Planning the invasion of North Africa in 1942, Allied leaders had faced a shortage of properly trained and equipped American forces. They wanted, nevertheless, to minimize Vichy French opposition to the landings by coloring them so far as possible as wholly American operations (see Chandler, *War Years*, vol. I, esp. nos. 505 and 541). Eisenhower had written of Churchill's remarkable offer in *Crusade for Europe*, p. 88.

557

To René Pleven
Secret. Personal

Eisenhower Mss.

December 24, 1951

Dear Mr. President:[1] Mrs. Eisenhower and I are profoundly touched by your kindness in sending us such beautiful Christmas flowers. The plant is an extraordinary one—in fact, in our experience, it is unique.

This new evidence of your friendship emboldens me to present to you a suggestion concerning something that has been very deeply in my mind. It involves the various steps that might now be taken in Europe, without increased financial cost, to create from this side of the water a feeling of closer partnership and understanding among all the several nations of NATO and so strengthen that organization in its crusade for security and peace. For some time I have had the conviction that three such steps would be the full consummation of the Schuman Plan,[2] the speedy and decisive approval of the Pleven Plan for forming a European Army,[3] and the issuance and acceptance of an invitation to the European Continental Powers of NATO to meet in an official constitutional convention to consider ways and means for promoting a closer union among these Powers. These three steps are, of course, interrelated and, as we know, some people even hold that step number two cannot possibly be accomplished without establishing some kind of binding political ties among these particular European Powers. Taken together, I feel certain that these three steps would be interpreted in my own country as evidence of a clear determination in Europe to bring about the objectives of the Mutual Security Pact[4] under terms of maximum economy, efficiency, and rapidity.

As you know, the American Congress expressed the hope in the last Mutual Aid Bill[5] that the nations of Europe would find ways and means to draw closer together both politically and economically.

The meeting of the Ministers in Paris on December 27th to consider further steps in devising the European Army would take place, it seems to me, under circumstances of added significance and complete earnestness if there were previously issued from a responsible source such a dramatic and inspiring call to action.[6] Another reason that, to my mind, would underline the timeliness of such an invitation is that we are in the midst of celebrating the anniversary of the Prince of Peace. Its terms would, I assume, want to emphasize the peaceful purposes of the European union and the hope that in this joining of friendly hands would come about progress toward higher levels of security, culture, and individual and collective prosperity. Thus, to identify the invitation with the Christmas spirit would strike a very responsive chord among all those devout millions who so earnestly long for the abolition of the wickedness of war. Even those who disassociate themselves from religious conviction could find little reason for objecting to the basic purpose.

As of this moment, you seem to me to be the one person in Europe who, by reason of nationality and political, intellectual, and moral leadership, is outstandingly qualified to take such an action. If the idea has any merit, it must belong to you alone. Because of this obvious truth, I am sending this suggestion to you on a "Secret" basis to be used or not, as you see fit. Although the American Ambassador, who I understand has spoken to you in similar vein,[7] knows that I intended to write this note, no other person except my Chief of Staff[8] and my confidential secretary[9] is aware of its existence. Consequently, if you should decide to do anything of this character, you can be completely certain that no one can allege that I, a citizen of a foreign country, have laid before you a suggestion or recommendation that might be considered exclusively as a matter of internal policy and decision.[10]

I repeat that only my confidence in your personal friendship, so amply proven, gives me the temerity to write in this vein to one who is so much more experienced in these matters than I could possibly be.

My only excuse is my devotion to NATO's peaceful purposes and the fact that no outsider will learn of my proposal.

With assurances of my continued devotion and esteem—no matter what action you may decide to take—and renewed thanks from Mrs. Eisenhower and myself for your kindly thoughtfulness, *Most sincerely yours*

[1] For background on French Premier Pleven see no. 11, n. 2. Pleven's formal title was President du Conseil.

[2] On the Schuman Plan see no. 502, n. 3.

[3] On the Pleven Plan see Galambos, *Columbia University*, no. 1045; and in this volume, no. 186, n. 3.

[4] Eisenhower referred to the North Atlantic Treaty (see Ismay, *NATO*, pp. 12–16).

[5] See no. 539, n. 8.

[6] The foreign ministers of France, West Germany, Italy, Belgium, the Netherlands, and Luxembourg would meet in Paris from December 27 to December 30 to discuss formation of an integrated European army that would include West German units (*New York Times*, Dec. 28–31, 1951; *International Herald Tribune*, Paris ed., Dec. 27, 28, 29, 31, 1951; State, *Foreign Relations, 1951*, vol. III, *European Security and the German Question, Part I*, pp. 980–89).

[7] David K. E. Bruce had discussed this proposal with Eisenhower at lunch on Sunday, December 23, at the American Embassy in Paris (Eisenhower to Bruce, Dec. 24, 1951, EM).

[8] General Alfred M. Gruenther.

[9] Yeoman Helen E. Weaver (USN).

[10] There is no reply from Pleven regarding Eisenhower's proposal in EM. For developments see no. 607.

558   *Eisenhower Mss.*

To Sid Williams Richardson   *December 26, 1951*
Secret. Personal

Dear Sid:[1] While my own convictions about the possibility of a political career have undergone no change, I have to admit that the persistence of the pressures against me sometimes make me unsure that I could— if ever I come back to the United States—remain completely aloof. For this reason, I have been going over all of my own personal and business affairs in the United States to make sure that nothing I am doing could ever occasion even a lifted eyebrow on the part of the most extreme critic.

This brought up the question of my fairly modest investment in one of your ventures.[2] It is something from which I have derived very considerable satisfaction, not only because of my normally human instinct to "take a chance," but because it gave me some business relation—even if a rather insignificant one—with a friend of long standing. Moreover, because I know the whole thing to be a perfectly legal and ethical venture, I have had, as a personal feeling, no other feeling than that of satisfaction.

However, the one risk now arises that the thing *might* become fantastically successful, in which case I might have some future explaining to do.

When I was in Washington, you told me that the particular venture for which you were looking had not yet arisen, so I am proceeding on the assumption that you have not yet invested my modest capital in any venture and, therefore, I could withdraw easily. Consequently, I request that you send back to the Commerce Trust Company, Kansas City, Missouri, for deposit to my credit the twenty thousand dollars that I sent from that Bank for investment.

In the event that you have already invested any or all of this money and, as of this moment, it would stand to take a loss, won't you please sell it out for whatever can be obtained for the equity and transmit to me only the remainder. In no case am I to have any profit.

Assuming that I shall still be a free individual and (relatively) private citizen after the summer has come and gone, I hope that you will allow me to *re*-invest with you on the same basis that I did last year. But I am so much of the conviction that a public official should, under no circumstances, be involved in anything that might even *look* unreasonably profitable, that I am guarding against the very remote possibility that circumstances might compel me to have some connection with a political responsibility.

I know you will understand this letter as it is meant. Unless you were a warm and understanding friend, I would have great difficulty in writing. As it is, I feel that no further explanation is necessary.

George has written to me that you and he may be able to make a trip over in this direction and I have suggested to him a period right after the first week in February.[3] If that particular time is not convenient to both of you, he is to let me know. In any event, I assure you of a real welcome.

I understand from George that you are now out in California. I shall send this to your Fort Worth address with the request that it be forwarded to you immediately.

Manifestly, I have to ask that this letter be regarded as extremely secret because, otherwise, it would be interpreted as a statement of my intention to get into politics. I assure you that I have no such intention! You well know that my long held view is that, if ever such a misfortune overtakes me, it is because I am forced into it.

Mamie joins me in wishes for a fine and happy New Year to you. Give my regards to George and Mary[4] if you are with them now. *Cordially*

P.S. I should like to hear from you as quickly as possible so that I may know you received this letter.[5]

[1] For background on Richardson see no. 34, n. 2.
[2] On Richardson's investment advice see no. 474.
[3] George E. Allen and Richardson would visit Eisenhower in February 1952 (see no. 549, n. 2).
[4] Mr. and Mrs. George E. Allen.
[5] Eisenhower sent this letter air-mail, registered, return receipt requested, for delivery to addressee only. Arrangements were made through the American Embassy in Paris to include it in a pouch of December 27 destined for Washington, D.C. (see Memorandum for Record, Dec. 27, 1951, EM, Richardson Corr.). The message reached Richardson in Los Angeles, California, on January 4, 1952 (telegram, Perry R. Bass to Robert L. Schulz, Jan. 5, 1952, EM, Richardson Corr.).

559   *Eisenhower Mss.*

To James Stack   *December 27, 1951*

Dear Jim:[1] I was interested in your attitude toward the "public political meeting."[2] My own idea is that you are privileged to do and say whatever you want—in fact, you can become a tremendous partisan in favor of any of those seeking the Presidency (of whom I am *not* one) and I will understand and approve of your action.

As for myself, I am assigned to a duty. I shall try to perform it to the best of my ability. As you know, both law and regulations impose very strict limits upon the direct or indirect political activity of any regular Army officer serving on active duty. So my sole answer to all inquiries is that I am just trying to do my duty.

Not very long ago, Louis Marx was over here and he tells me you are continuing to do splendidly in the toy business.[3] I am delighted to know it.

Please give my warm greetings to Elsa and the children[4] and, of course, Mamie and I wish for you the happiest of New Years. *Cordially*

[1] Stack, a former aide of Eisenhower's, had established a toy distributing company in Tacoma, Washington (see Galambos, *Columbia University*, no. 427).
[2] On December 10 (EM) Stack had written to report on a dinner meeting he had attended that evening with Senator James H. Duff (see no. 486) and other supporters of an Eisenhower presidential candidacy. "In reply to questions launched at Senator Duff he said that he knew you were a Republican because you told him so," said Stack. "He said that he knew you would run because he was in touch with you. He added if he were not certain he would not waste his time running around the country." Stack's only comment had been that if this information were

correct, Duff could count on him to join the campaign, but that first he would have to see a statement from the General. Stack refused to attend public meetings for Eisenhower until he became a candidate—"IF," he wrote his one-time commander, "you should so specifically and personally indicate" (see also *Tacoma News-Tribune*, Dec. 11, 1951, copy in EM; and no. 538).

[3] Louis Marx had visited the General on September 25. For background on Marx see Galambos, *Columbia University*, no. 493. Stack's company distributed toys manufactured by Louis Marx & Company.

[4] Elsa was Mrs. Stack; the Stack children were Carol Lee and Linda.

560   *Eisenhower Mss.*

To GEORGE WHITNEY   *December 27, 1951*
Personal and confidential

Dear George:[1] Thank you for your note of the 20th. I shall read Ben Fairless' talk this evening.[2]

I note a lot of discussion these days as to whether or not there will be a business recession soon.[3] In fact, one man who is always urging me to get into politics uses as a curious reason his conviction that within the next two years there is going to be such a serious depression that only someone who has almost the complete confidence of the nation will be able to hold us together and keep us from doing something foolish. For this reason, he says that I should be the one to take it on the chin. I merely quote this to you as a reason of a different type; I think all the others have been used on me also.

This reminds me that, of all the arguments directed against me, one of the strangest is that I am a part of the "Roosevelt conspiracy," and have owed to that membership all the promotions I have ever received. No one has ever taken the trouble to look up the easily proven fact that I never met Mr. Roosevelt or any of his intimates until I had been designated to go overseas to command. In the few times after that when I met the man, he never mentioned a word of domestic politics to me. There seems to be an inability on the part of prejudiced partisans to understand that someone could be interested in doing nothing more than his simple duty.[4]

When I get to feeling irritated and frustratated by such thoughts, I always come back to the basic one that no man can be considered anything but fortunate who has such friends as I do. I am, as the New Year approaches, more grateful for them than I have ever been before—and among them I am certainly bold enough, and very proud, to number you.

With the happiest of New Years to you and yours, *Cordially*

[1] For background on Whitney see no. 50, n. 3.

[2] Whitney had sent Eisenhower a copy of a statement (not in EM) that Benjamin Franklin Fairless, president of the United States Steel Corporation, had made concerning a possible steelworkers' strike (see *New York Times*, Dec. 22, 1951; and Whitney to Eisenhower, Dec. 20, 1951, EM).

[3] Whitney had written that "the politicians and some of the industrialists are talking boom times next year." Eisenhower would soon hear more from Whitney on the subject of the U.S. economy (see no. 609, n. 2).

[4] Eisenhower probably referred to the attacks of columnist Westbrook Pegler and Senator William E. Jenner. For background see nos. 163, n. 2, and 383. See also the following document.

561   *Eisenhower Mss.*

To Lucius Du Bignon Clay   *December 27, 1951*
Personal

Dear Lucius: Your letter[1] has just come to my desk and it disturbs me so much that I am putting everything else aside to answer immediately.[2] I hasten to admit of the possibility that I may have given some impression in our Washington conversation that I have now forgotten;[3] these days, I sometimes wonder at myself when I find I am still outside a mental ward. However, in the absence of information as to the specific point in which I have apparently diverged from the understanding of our conversation, I can address myself only to generality.

Only yesterday I was asked to name the personality in the United States who was best acquainted with me and my methods, who had a good knowledge of Europe and the European problem, and who also had a wide acquaintanceship with people of substance at home. Without hesitation, I gave your name. This came about in connection with the discussion as to who was best qualified to act as an intermediary between me and the "pros," since direct communication between us could obviously be embarrassing. So I hope that whatever I have done to embarrass you is not serious and can be overlooked.

Frankly, my current decision not to come home until the transfer could be on a permanent basis was partially formed as a result of my experiences in Washington the last time I was there. My life was almost unendurable. However, I do not recall that the possibility of a future trip was the real crux of our conversation—I really thought it was the question of providing, for the public, some greater assurance of personal intention than could heretofore be given by people who were anxious to avoid any violation of confidence.

Of course, you understand that the preoccupations of my current job are very great. As you know, I think that the effort to produce collective security must succeed—otherwise, I see nothing but a bleak future for our country. Not only does this task absorb every bit of my energy and my brain capacity, but an added consideration for my aloofness from the current American scene is found in the following paragraph from Army Regulations:

"AR 600-10. 18. Election to, and performance of duties of, public office.—a. Members of the Regular Army, while on active duty, may accept nomination for public office, provided such nomination is tendered without direct *or indirect* activity or solicitation on their part. They may then file such evidence of their candidacy as required by local law."[4]

In view of all this, I hope you find it possible to forgive any seeming slight of which I have been guilty. I assure you that it was unintentional and I still hope that one of these days you are going to find it possible to make a business trip in this direction.[5]

With love to Marjorie[6] and, of course, best New Year's greetings to you both from Mamie and me. *As ever*

---

[1] In his letter, dated December 21 and marked personal (EM), Clay had replied to Eisenhower's of nine days earlier (see no. 537) and expressed confusion. "Frankly, I do not understand your letter of 12 December," he began. "It does not seem entirely consistent with our conversation in Washington. There, I did understand, that if a group could prove it was a duty, on their advice you would return home. The question of activity on your part other than return home was not raised. I also read the implication in your letter that perhaps I have taken on too much authority or, at least, suggested to others an authority I do not have. This is possible as I have on several occasions taken the liberty of 'interpreting your reactions' to a particular set of circumstances." I have two motives," Clay emphasized, "a sincere belief that you are essential to the future well-being of our country, and a sincere friendship which wants nothing now or ever." Clay wished neither to destroy that friendship nor "to be listed with Clark and Burnham" (on Eisenhower's problems with Edwin N. Clark and William H. Burnham see no. 537). Clay pledged "as an individual" to do all he could for Eisenhower but planned to withdraw "from any further activities with the 'pros' and thus avoid any possible arrogation of unwarranted degree of authority."

[2] When Clay's message reached Eisenhower, two of his closest friends and political advisers, Clifford Roberts and William E. Robinson, were in Paris for the Christmas holidays. Robinson hand-carried this reply to Clay in New York City.

[3] On Eisenhower's early November parleys while on a brief visit to the United States see no. 470.

[4] U.S. Department of the Army, *Army Regulations*, No. 600–10 (Washington, D.C., Nov. 10, 1950), pp. 6–7.

[5] On January 2 (EM) Clay asked the General to forget his letter of December 21, apologizing for the apparent misunderstanding. "For this I am truly sorry," he wrote, "as I know how beset you are, and I would not add to your burdens." For developments see no. 620.

[6] Clay's wife.

Dear Earl:[01] Of course, I receive from time to time criticism of the type voiced in the extract of the letter included in yours of the 15th.[2] I have no doubt that the writer is as completely patriotic and efficient as you say. Nevertheless, he shows obvious signs of ignorance, to use no stronger word!

He has not bothered to read the law of the land and the regulations of the Army concerning the limitations placed upon an officer in uniform.[3] Moreover, how could I ever have been a part of the "Roosevelt-Truman socialism game?" I never held political office and, in the war, my single job was to bring victory in Europe as quickly as possible, with minimum loss in lives. Your friend talks about flinging armies around Europe as if he would enjoy incurring American casualties. Frankly, I don't.

As for anyone giving me orders as to where to stop my armies, no one gave me such orders. If he will look up the history of the particular period, he will see that, when we started our final drive, we were three hundred miles from Berlin and back of a great River, the Elbe, while the Russians were less than thirty miles away from the city and with no obstacle between. Yet he thinks I should have gone all out for Berlin and, because of this, possibly turned all of Austria over to the Soviets. He apparently does not know that, long before the date of this final attack, the present division of Germany had already been fixed.[4]

He knows nothing at all about General Patton's plans, orders, and actions. General Patton was not only my great and intimate friend for twenty-five years, he was, in his attacks, acting under my orders, and those orders demanded the maximum speed and advance possible with the amount of supplies that we could deliver during such rapid movement.[5]

What your friend means by his expression, "General MacArthur didn't," I haven't the slightest idea. I saw in the papers that the General was very justifiably resentful of the fact that he could not, under his orders, attack the airfields north of the Yalu. Those fields have never yet been attacked. Yet, in obeying his orders, *General MacArthur was absolutely right* because, when the day comes that American soldiers can in war successfully defy the entire civil government, then the American system will have come to an end. If your friend is not bright enough to see this, then I should say that there is some remarkably *obscure* reason for the success he has achieved.[6]

He talks about foreign policy as if it were something that soldiers in uniform were called upon to formulate and execute. From my viewpoint, foreign policy is, or should be, based primarily upon one consideration. That consideration is the need for the United States to obtain certain raw materials to sustain its economy and, when possible, to preserve profitable foreign markets for our surpluses. Out of this need grows the necessity for making certain that those areas of the world in which essential raw materials are produced are not only accessible to us, but their populations and governments are willing to trade with us on a friendly basis. To my mind, this simple need, with all the short and long term arrangements necessary to assure its fulfillment, are the things that should concern us in the international field.

I am not at all interested in the invectives he chooses to use. He is obviously the victim of his own prejudices—otherwise, he would at least *inquire* before he arrives at such positive judgments.

Have no fear that you have "disturbed my equilibrium"—I am so used to this type of snarling that I am hardened to it.[7] But I just want you, as my friend, to know that I don't have a guilty conscience and that I have, after all, tried to do my duty as I see it.

Curiously enough, in spite of the fact that I came out of retirement, took a tremendous loss in income, gave up congenial and constructive work in which I was intensely interested, and am keeping *silent* on a job that is anything but a pleasant one, I am accused of every kind of nefarious plot and purpose.[8]

I most certainly applaud your friend's teachings in the line of self-dependence and against governmental paternalism. In this I go along with him one hundred percent; a fact that can easily be established by a glance at almost every public utterance I have ever made.[9]

What has actually been happening over the last forty years or so is an acceleration in the progress of the "social revolution." In general, the revolution was inevitable as educational averages rose from their unsatisfactory levels of a hundred years ago, and many of its results have been good—others very bad. Like all great movements of this kind, it has produced paradoxes and instances of extreme error. History cannot be turned back, but we can get busy and, by teaching and by work, prove to people—and I mean on a very widespread scale— that initiative is preserved by personal incentive, that the struggle to excel produces progress. The needed correctives are not going to be produced merely by putting such and such a person in the White House or by electing some particular individual to the United States Senate. Everybody who understands what is going on has got to jump into the business of teaching and preaching both by word and by example.

One more word. Your friend addresses all his criticisms to the possibility that I might become a political figure. The final point in which *I agree with him is his objection to me in that role.*[10] I have never sought a political office, and I certainly have not tried to put myself in a favorable light before anybody in an effort to be considered for such. I am simply trying to do my duty today; I shall try to do it tomorrow. Incidentally, I think that that single word "duty" could well be talked about just a little bit more if we are so anxious to preserve our form of government and economy.

With warm personal regard, and Happy New Year to you and yours. *Cordially*

[1] For background on Schaefer see no. 520.

[2] In his letter (EM) Schaefer had excerpted at great length from one he had received criticizing Eisenhower as a military leader as well as a potential presidential candidate. Schaefer's friend accused Eisenhower of playing "at least the military part of the Roosevelt-Truman socialism game for more than 10 years" and in the spring of 1945 of having halted the Allied armies in Europe, "presumably on orders of the infamous Roosevelt, to let the Russians occupy Vienna and Berlin." For Eisenhower's account of Allied decisions during the last months of the war see nos. 680 and 805; and *Crusade in Europe*, pp. 396–403.

[3] For the regulation against seeking political office while on active military duty see the preceding document.

[4] Eisenhower disclaimed any role in the Allied conferences at Teheran and Yalta (see nos. 805 and 946).

[5] "Of course, it can be said in extenuation of Eisenhower that a soldier—even a General must obey his Commander-in-Chief," Schaefer's correspondent had written, "but I cannot envision that principle being carried to the point of betraying his Country. General Patton, in all probability, would not have done it; General McArthur [*sic*] didn't do it." On Eisenhower's long friendship with General George S. Patton, Jr., see *Eisenhower Papers*, vols. I–XI; and Eisenhower, *At Ease*, pp. 169–78, 269–71. See also Pogue, *Supreme Command*, pp. 441–47; Martin Blumenson, *Patton: The Man behind the Legend, 1885–1945* (New York, 1985); and Patton's memoir, *War as I Knew It* (Boston, 1947).

[6] See above. For background on the controversy surrounding Truman's dismissal of MacArthur see no. 131.

[7] Schaefer sent these extracts, he said, "at the risk of disturbing your equilibrium a bit"; he acknowledged that his friend, though sincere, was a person of "deep seated prejudices." Schaefer added that "faced with such as this," he could well understand why someone of Eisenhower's "capacity and capability would have no interest in public office."

[8] "General Eisenhower is furthering Truman's unconstitutional, socialistic stupidities in Europe," claimed the unnamed critic. "If silence gives consent, then the General must favor our money being scattered all over the world and our soldiers embroiled in every quarrel on the globe."

[9] Schaefer's friend had declared that he could not possibly vote for Eisenhower as a Republican "unless he publicly repudiates the foreign and domestic policies of the socialist Presidents he has so ably served." Schaefer noted that his friend's son, a veteran of Pacific combat in World War II, had gone so far as to refuse the GI bill "on the basis that he didn't fight for his country for money or benefits—he fought to preserve his freedom of choice and opportunity."

[10] "I would gag over the thought of any General being President," this business executive had said.

Eisenhower Mss.

To Herbert Bayard Swope

December 28, 1951

Dear Herbert:[1] Of course, I am a rather ignorant lout, but I would have to be much more stupid than I am if I failed to realize that I've "got a tough job, My Dear Young Man."[2]

Curiously enough, while I agree with you that Britain isn't helping matters very much by her attitude, the fact is that the logic of her *actions* seems to me to be unassailable.[3] But, with a complete reversal of form, our friend Winston seems to have developed the habit of emphasizing in a cooperative venture the negative features of Britain's limitations instead of the positive portions of the work it is prepared to do. The last time he was over here, you would have much enjoyed our conversations on this particular point—especially if you could have been behind a door and been sort of a Banquo.[4] Incidentally, our old friend is getting very deaf and, of course, even he is not immune to the deteriorations due to the passing years.[5]

With my very best wishes for the coming year, *Cordially*

[1] For background on Swope see no. 66.
[2] Eisenhower was quoting one of the last lines of Swope's letter of December 17 (EM), in which Swope sympathized with the General on his problems at SHAPE.
[3] Swope had written that he believed Great Britain was slowing NATO efforts at strengthening Western European defense. For background on Eisenhower's involvement with this issue see nos. 530 and 540.
[4] In William Shakespeare's *Macbeth*, Banquo is a Scottish nobleman whose ghost appears to Macbeth.
[5] On British Prime Minister Winston Churchill's recent visit to SHAPE see no. 556; on his health see Lord Charles Moran, *Churchill: Taken from the Diaries of Lord Moran* (Boston, 1966), pp. 361, 372–73, 395–96. For developments see no. 810.

Eisenhower Mss.

To Mabel Frances Doud Moore

December 28, 1951

Dear Mike:[1] You, Gordon,[2] and the children[3] sent me so many nice Christmas presents that I must answer you in a community letter.

I start off with the pepper grinder, something I have wanted for a very long time. Ellen made a perfect selection in cards because the men that play with me are always nagging me to get out a "new" deck. They don't like the dog-ears that I so frequently dig out. Little Mamie, of course, knew that matches are always necessary; while the things for the pantry and kitchen were particularly welcome. You know how I love to put in a Sunday afternoon in the kitchen after everyone else has cleared out, and fool around with a pot and a frying pan. On top of this, the paints were in use within an hour of the time that "Santa Claus" handed them to me. All in all, your things truly made my Christmas a lot happier and more interesting. Thank you all very much indeed.

Poor Mamie is swamped in the most terrific stack of Christmas mail you ever saw—but I know she will get around to writing to you when she can. Both of us send love and, of course, best wishes for the happiest of New Years. *Cordially*

[1] Mrs. Moore was Mamie Eisenhower's sister (for background see no. 118, n. 2).
[2] For background on Lieutenant Colonel George Gordon Moore, Jr., Mrs. Moore's husband, see no. 224.
[3] Ellen Doud Moore and Mamie Eisenhower Moore.

565   *Eisenhower Mss., Family File*

To John Sheldon Doud Eisenhower and   *December 28, 1951*
Barbara Jean Thompson Eisenhower

Dear Barbie and John: This morning I sent you a cable to tell you how truly thrilled Mamie was with your telephone call. It was a nice thought and I am grateful to you both for thinking of it.[1]

I had a talk with Cliff about the possibility of establishing an account in a New York bank for you so that you could have a permanent address to which could be sent dividends from stocks and so on, for deposit to your credit. It would be easy enough and would involve no cost, because Cliff would be glad to do it as a favor for you, except for the fact that part of the account is owned by minors. He tells me that there would have to be some kind of a trust appointment made for the children and so, apparently, that scheme won't work.[2]

In the old days, I used to merely give the Adjutant General of the Army as my permanent address, but that is not so efficient these days because of the size to which the Army has grown. Consequently, I guess there is nothing to do except for you people to take care of it yourselves and merely deposit your stocks in the safe deposit box when you can get back to it. This means, of course, that you will have to keep very detailed books in order that you make certain that you do not, unknowingly, miss a dividend through a misdirection in the mail. When Mamie and I can once get back to the United States and establish a permanent home, maybe we can help out. In the meantime, I can't think of anything worthwhile to suggest.

George tells me he sent a check on to Barbie that I won from him in a bet.[3] I am needling him into making a really big bet for next year so that, *if he tries to compromise it, we will sting him properly.* Actually, all I am trying to do is to get his waistline down to proportions that could be called reasonably healthful—so far, I have not been able to do anything with him.

I know you will cable us as soon as the new baby arrives.[4] Mamie and I will not be able to rid ourselves of a bit of worry until we know that everything is again okay.

Take care of yourselves. *Devotedly*

P.S. My goodness, I forgot the real reason for starting this note to you—to thank you very much for the book you sent me. I am reading parts of it already and find it tremendously interesting. You were very thoughtful, to say nothing of being skillful in picking out the nice present. *Love*

[1] Eisenhower's cable is in EM.

[2] The General's friend Clifford Roberts (see no. 7), who advised him on investments, had been visiting the Eisenhowers at Marnes-la-Coquette (see no. 546, n. 1). For more on investment gifts see no. 471.

[3] George Allen's letter is in EM. For background on Allen and his weight bets with Eisenhower see no. 529.

[4] Susan Elaine Eisenhower would be born on December 31 (see no. 594, n. 6).

566 Eisenhower Mss.

TO LEE ALVIN DUBRIDGE December 28, 1951

Dear Dr. DuBridge:[1] Your letter of the 21st means a great deal to me. It did not occur to me that the members of your distinguished group would feel that they had gained anything from their visit with me; rather, I regarded myself as the sole beneficiary of such a meeting. In any event, the conversation was stimulating to me—not to say vastly encouraging.[2]

Sometimes I think that, in my passionate search for peace, I get a bit warped, possibly impatient, when I see so many people pursuing their accustomed and complacent ways without any attempt to contribute thought and time to the grave issues of the day. These can, of course, be stated in many ways, but certainly to be classed close to the top is the question of peace or war.

So you can see what it means to me in the way of inspiration when I am confronted with solid evidence that a group of our eminent scholars and scientists are unselfishly devoting their earnest attention to America's problems and helping her, directly and indirectly, to preserve the peace.[3] *Sincerely*

[1] DuBridge (Ph.D. University of Wisconsin 1926), a physicist, had been president of the California Institute of Technology in Pasadena since 1946.

[2] In his message (Dec. 21, 1951, EM) DuBridge had thanked Eisenhower for the informative and enjoyable visit he and three other scientists had made to SHAPE headquarters the week of December 3 (*New York Times*, Dec. 5, 7, 1951). Accompanying DuBridge were the following: Dr. J. Robert Oppenheimer (Ph.D. Göttingen University 1927), a physicist who had helped develop the atomic bomb, was director of the Institute for Advanced Study at Princeton, and served as the chairman of the general advisory committee of the Atomic Energy Commission; Dr. Charles Christian Lauritsen (Ph.D. California Institute of Technology 1929), a professor of physics at the California Institute of Technology since 1935; and Professor Walter Gordon Whitman (M.S. MIT 1920), head of the Department of Chemical Engineering at the Massachusetts Institute of Technology since 1934. DuBridge's group had traveled to Europe to gather information for the California Institute of Technology's Project Vista, an investigation of the "application of firepower to the ground battlefield" for the armed services (see *New York Times*, June 5, July 18, 1952).

DuBridge had written that the four regarded the General's job as one of the most important in the world; after the visit, he said further, they realized that it was being accomplished "in a most inspiring, stimulating and effective way." Now reporting to various scientific groups concerning the trip, DuBridge informed Eisenhower that he had many "warm friends" among American scientists.

[3] Thinking along these same lines, the General had earlier helped establish the Institute of War and Peace Studies at Columbia University (for background see no. 31; for developments see no. 568).

567

To Arthur Hays Sulzberger
Personal

Dear Arthur:[1] Thank you very much for sending on to me the results obtained by your "investigators."[2] I have not failed to give a great deal of thought to your suggestion about Milton. The real reason I have not written to him is that I do not want to burden an already busy man, one devoted to me, with chores and vexing questions that I suppose belong to me alone.[3]

In all the political arguments that center around my own appropriate role in the near future, I have earnestly tried to keep personal desire from influencing me in the slightest. As you well know, my own ambitions involve the hope of a quiet, stable family life for Mamie and me and a chance, on a basis relatively free of strain and pressure, to contribute something useful and constructive to the system that provided to my brothers and me unlimited opportunity.

While I have never, for a single instant, considered myself as an "above average" College President, or as any particular value to Columbia, it is equally true that I felt that Columbia and the type of activity in which I was there engaged was good *for me*. Consequently, I had always hoped that I would not be retained on this job too long because of my great desire to return to Columbia and pick up where I left off. As time has gone by, I have, as again you know, worried somewhat about Columbia's position in this whole business.[4]

I think the only point I am trying to make is that my own feelings and instinct have always been so definitely turned away from any thought of political office that it is quite possible that I fail to think clearly and objectively about such matters. Nevertheless, I feel that, if the personal pot cooks up to the boiling point, it is only I who should have to tackle the business of grabbing the hot handles. So, as of this moment, I'm not planning on trying to divert the pressure of inquiry and advice toward my brother.[5]

All the best in 1952 to you and Iphigene.[6] *Cordially*

[1] For background on *New York Times* publisher Sulzberger see no. 114.

[2] On December 13 (EM) Sulzberger had sent Eisenhower letters from three *Times* staff members from whom he had requested estimates of Senator Robert A. Taft's political strength. According to Turner Catledge (B.S. Mississippi State College 1922), executive managing editor of the *New York Times*, Taft seemed to have the support of most of the convention delegates "because no one else is in the field." Should Eisenhower run, however, Catledge doubted that "Taft will ever get off the floor." James Barrett Reston (B.S. University of Illinois 1932), a Pulitzer Prize-winning reporter for the Washington, D.C., bureau of the *New York Times*, had replied that the decline of the Truman Administration had strengthened Taft's position and had reduced Republican fears that the senator could not win. Republicans, he said, were hoping to create "a band-wagon psychology" for Taft "while Eisenhower hesitates, and this is the reason for all the confident predictions about winning the first ballot." Journalist Arthur Krock (see no. 32) had seen Taft's strength as "entirely potential" because no delegate had yet been elected: "The claims you may read that Taft already has 600 are moonshine." On the other hand, Krock had pointed out that Taft's people were well organized, that his favorable mail from all ages was heavy, and that he had great strength in the South. "Taft has thought all along," Krock had concluded, "that Eisenhower would run against him and make it known before the Convention. But he hopes very much this will not be made sufficiently clear for many months." All three letters are in EM, Sulzberger Corr. Sulzberger had also sent Eisenhower a copy of Krock's column of that day (*New York Times*, Dec. 13, 1951).

[3] Sulzberger had suggested that it would be "rather nice for you to let us talk with Milton" (see no. 473).

[4] On Eisenhower's concerns over remaining president of Columbia University see no. 373.

[5] For developments see no. 602.

[6] Sulzberger's wife, Iphigene B. Ochs Sulzberger.

To John Allen Krout   *December 29, 1951*

Dear John:[1] Thanks for your note. I am delighted to know that Dr. Fox is off to such a good start. I am convinced that the Institute of Peace and War can be made into one of our finest services to the public and, of course, it is good news to know that twenty-two outstanding men have already accepted positions on the Policy Committee.[2]

Please remember me warmly to my friends about the campus, and to you my very best for the entire 1952. *Cordially*

[1] For background on Krout, associate provost and dean at Columbia University, see no. 31.

[2] In a letter of December 18 (EM) Krout had told the General that the Institute of War and Peace Studies had received some good publicity recently and that twenty-two out of thirty people who had been invited had accepted positions on the institute's Public Policy Committee. Krout had also written that the director of the institute, William T. R. Fox, had met with Bernard M. Baruch (for background see nos. 159 and 342).

To Winston Spencer Churchill   *December 29, 1951*
Cable SH 22028. Secret

Dear Winston: This is a message of bon voyage and good wishes for a pleasant trip.[1] Here in Paris I am meeting tonight with the delegates to the European Army Conference.[2] Among other things I intend to assure them that you and I have always been in complete agreement as to the proper place of the United Kingdom in the venture of producing a European Army and eventually an economically or politically unified Western Europe.[3] Nevertheless I hope that your unqualified moral support and readiness to help will in some way or other get out of the small print of the news columns and find its way into the headlines.[4] That will help us a lot particularly in BENELUX.[5]

My warm greetings to all my friends that may be accompanying you and to all of you a very Happy New Years Day which of course you will be spending at sea.[6] *With warm and respectful regards*

[1] Churchill would sail from England on December 31, 1951, and arrive in New York on January 5, 1952. On the sixth and in the days following, he met with President Truman and high officials from the State and Defense departments. Churchill left for Ottawa on January 10 for several days of talks with Canadian

officials, returned to Washington on the fifteenth, and departed New York on the twenty-second. He arrived home six days later (*New York Times*, Jan. 6–29, 1952).

[2] The Paris Conference for the Organization of a European Defense Community had convened on December 27 (see no. 557; on Eisenhower's informal appearance the evening of the twenty-ninth see no. 572). At a luncheon meeting the day before writing Churchill, Eisenhower had met Italian Prime Minister De Gasperi, Secretary-General of the Foreign Ministry Vittorio Zoppi, and Italian Ambassador to France Pietro Quaroni to discuss the foreign ministers' progress. The General had stressed the importance of reaching an agreement before the NATO conference scheduled for February 20–25 in Lisbon. Appreciating that need, De Gasperi nonetheless had noted the slowness of the Benelux countries and urged the United States to "encourage and press" them while also obtaining British help in that regard (State, *Foreign Relations, 1951*, vol. III, *European Security and the German Question, Part I*, p. 983).

[3] For background see no. 304. Eisenhower would begin the new year as he had closed the old one: pressing for European unity. The General reiterated the need for a strong British stand in a letter to Foreign Secretary Eden, as Eden sailed for the United States (see no. 574); he summarized his views and the situation in an early 1952 letter to the President (no. 578).

[4] The British Prime Minister's preliminary discussions with President Truman on January 6 would produce newspaper speculation that Churchill had agreed to persuade the Dutch and Belgians to join the European defense force. Two days later Truman and Churchill announced their intention to give "emphatic support" to the EDF (while keeping Britain and the United States out of a European army) and to Eisenhower's plans for strengthening Western European defenses. In their January 10 communiqué Truman and Churchill repeated their resolve to develop a European army that would include German units; Churchill made further such remarks in Ottawa on January 14. Finally, addressing a joint session of Congress on January 17, Churchill clearly stated his belief that Europe was making "real and rapid progress" toward unity and that both Great Britain and the United States ought to do their utmost "to help and speed it." "As a forerunner of united Europe," the Prime Minister said, "there is the European Army, which could never achieve its necessary strength without the inclusion of Germany." He observed that European "fusion" did not remove the need for NATO, and he concluded this passage of his address by saying, "We stand together under General Eisenhower to defend the common cause from violent aggression" (*New York Times*, January 7, 9, 15, 18, 1952. See also "The President Exchanges Views with Prime Minister Churchill," *U.S. Department of State Bulletin* 26, no. 656 [January 21, 1952], 83–84; "Mutual Assistance Programs Discussed by U.S. and U.K.," *ibid.* 26, no. 657 [January 28, 1952], 115–16; and "Close Anglo-American Unity Urged for Defense of Global Freedoms," *ibid.*, 116–20).

[5] Eisenhower often had noted the weight of British influence in northern Europe (see nos. 218, 530, and 539; see also no. 578).

[6] For developments see no. 574.

To Henry Cabot Lodge, Jr.   *December 29, 1951*
Personal and confidential

Dear Cabot: Thank you very much for your note of December 22nd
which assures me that you clearly understand the position I shall
maintain with respect to the effort you and your friends are making.[1]
It should be quite clear—at least in my view—that I have no right
whatsoever to say or do anything that could possibly tend to divide
along partisan lines American thinking toward the job of producing
collective security. Consequently, I shall abstain from any action or
word of this kind as long as I am on this job.

It is entirely possible that I may have inadvertently given General
Clay a contrary impression from that which I expressed to you.[2] I
know one thing: my confidence in General Clay is such, his accuracy
in interpretation is so great, and his personal loyalty to me is so
complete, that nothing he could ever say about me could be contrary
to his belief as to what I would want him to say. If an error was made,
therefore, it was mine, and I assure you that Clay retains my complete
confidence and friendship. This I cannot overstate.[3] *Sincerely*

[1] In response to Eisenhower's cautionary letter of December 12 (see no. 538),
Lodge had said that the General had helped to clear the air. "It is gratifying to
know that you will not oppose our efforts, which have assumed great proportions,
to obtain the Republican nomination for you," Lodge wrote. "Although some
public word or intimation may well be eventually desirable, particularly for technical reasons, I have always fully understood the grave difficulties involved in
having you participate actively in a political contest at this time. I well recognize
that it would be both inadvisable and unfair to have you assume such a role just as
you are completing so successfully the vast and formidable task of welding our
allies into an effective instrument to prevent communist aggression" (EM, Lodge
Corr.).

[2] "Indeed I would not have felt impelled to write at all," Lodge had said, "had I
not derived the impression from talking with General Clay that your position was
quite different from what I had all long understood it to be—an understanding
which your letter of December 12 now clearly confirms." In a telephone conversation with General Wilton B. Persons (see no. 157) on December 20 Lodge had
explained that Clay had led him to believe that Eisenhower intended to return to
the United States "within a month." Lodge had thought that in that case the
General might come back ten days earlier and attend the San Francisco meeting
(Memorandum for Record, Dec. 20, 1951, EM, Lodge Corr.; Lodge, *The Storm
Has Many Eyes*, pp. 91–92). For Clay's interpretation of his November 5 meeting
with Eisenhower see no. 561, n. 1.

[3] On the friction that had developed between Clay and the group of Republicans
that Lodge headed see no. 537; for a recent expression of the General's feelings for
Clay see no. 561.

To Harry S. Truman

Dear Mr. President: Your letter of December 18 was delayed in transit, not reaching me until the 28th.[1] At that moment I was intensively engaged in an effort to spur our European friends into developing an acceptable plan for a European Army as well as, eventually, some form of European political Union.[2] All this explains the time required for my answer to reach you. I am deeply touched by the confidence in me you express, even more by that implied in the writing of such a letter by the President of the United States.[3] It breathes your anxious concern for our country's future.

Part of my answer must almost paraphrase your own language where you say, "If I do what I want to do . . ." There has never been any change in my personal desires and aspirations, publicly and privately expressed, over the past six years or so. I'd like to live a semi-retired life with my family, given over mainly to the study of, and a bit of writing on, present day trends and problems with a little dirt farming thrown in on the side. But just as you have decided that circumstances may not permit you to do exactly as you please, so I've found that fervent desire may sometimes have to give way to a conviction of duty. For example—I'm again on military duty and in a foreign country![4]

Now, I do not feel that I have any duty to seek a political nomination, in spite of the fact that many have urged to the contrary.[5] Because of this belief I shall not do so. Moreover, to engage in this kind of activity while on my present military assignment would encourage partisan thinking in our country toward a project of the utmost importance to the nation as a whole. (Incidentally it would be in direct violation of Army Regulations.)[6] So I shall keep still in all this struggle for personal position in a political party. Of course, a number of people know of my belief that any group of American citizens has a right to fight, politically, for any set of principles in which its members believe and to attempt to draft a leader to head the fight!

Because of these beliefs and because particularly of my determination to remain silent you know, far better than I, that the possibility that I will ever be drawn into political activity is so remote as to be negligible. This policy of complete abstention will be meticulously observed by me unless and until extraordinary circumstances would place a mandate upon me that, by common consent, would be deemed a duty of transcendent importance.[7]

This answer[8] is as full and frank as I am able to devise and I would be very regretful if you thought it otherwise.[9] But when one attempts to discuss such important abstractions as a sense of duty applied to unforeseen circumstances of the future neither brevity nor arbitrary pronouncement seems wholly applicable.

This note brings to you and yours, from Mamie and me, our best wishes for a happy and prosperous 1952. To you personally, my continued esteem and regard. *Respectfully*

[1] "The columnists, the slick magazines, and all the political people, who like to speculate are saying many things about what is to happen in 1952," Truman had said in his brief, handwritten message (EM), which Eisenhower noted receiving in his appointment calendar for December 28. "As I told you in 1948 and at our luncheon in 1951, do what you think best for the country. My own position is in the balance," the President had written of the new year. "I wish you would let me know what you intend to do. It will be between us and no one else." Truman had held off-the-record meetings with Eisenhower on December 12, 1947, and January 28, 1948 (Harry S. Truman Library, President's Appointment Books, Index. See also Ambrose, *Eisenhower*, vol. I, *Soldier, General of the Army, President-Elect*, pp. 459–60; and Robert J. Donovan, *Conflict and Crisis: The Presidency of Harry S Truman, 1945–1948* [New York, 1977], p. 338). For the rumors that flew after Eisenhower's conference with the President on November 5, 1951, and on the continuing discussion of Eisenhower's political plans see nos. 470 and 480; and the growing tide of letters in 1951 noted below.

[2] During Christmas week Eisenhower had written French and British leaders urging them to support the European army concept (see nos. 557 and 569). The General's schedule also included serious discussions with two of his closest political advisers and the drafting of important letters on his possible candidacy (see nos. 546, 561, and 570).

[3] "If I do what I want to do, I'll go back to Missouri and *maybe* run for the Senate," Truman had remarked. "If you decide to finish the European job, (and I don't know who else can) I must keep the isolationists out of the White House."

[4] For Eisenhower's personal misgivings upon accepting NATO service see Galambos, *Columbia University*, no. 1045.

[5] See no. 538.

[6] The General had spelled out this proscription in a recent letter (see no. 561).

[7] On January 7 the General would issue a statement to this effect (see no. 583, n. 2).

[8] Eisenhower replied to the President's longhand letter with one of his own, keeping a typescript (same file as document) from which he later quoted in *Mandate for Change* (see p. 19).

[9] For developments see no. 619.

572   *Eisenhower Mss.*

To ROBERT ABERCROMBIE LOVETT   *January 2, 1952*
Cable ALO 580. Confidential

Paris negotiations on European army made some progress but from our viewpoint not yet enough to be classed as satisfactory.[1] Part of the difficulty is unquestionably a Benelux belief that Britain is no more than lukewarm in its support of the project. Actually the position announced by Britain is in my opinion exactly appropriate to the situation and I have so stated to the 6 Foreign Ministers.[2] That position is to give maximum moral, political and military support to the enterprise and to the further project of European political and economic union but to abstain from actual participation. However in certain areas of the continent it is feared that Britain's nonparticipation also means disapproval. I am hopeful that during the Prime Minister's visit to America he will find several occasions to repeat his enthusiastic approval of the project and his intention to explore the concrete ways in which his Government may be of assistance.[3] I have told him that it was my personal belief that such approval on his part would be warmly accepted by majority opinion in our country and I felt certain that every step toward a closer union of the European countries would be applauded by most of our people.

Mister Eden is aware of my feelings in this matter and I believe that his view coincides almost exactly with mine.[4] On Saturday evening I met with delegates to the Paris Conference[5] and I stressed the need for speedy and specific accomplishment in this matter even if it should mean an early reconvening of the same representatives. Of course I realize that this is not strictly my responsibility but it is high time that we put our eyes upon the main business of cooperation and union and refuse to be diverted from basic purposes by technical questions of budget, command, organization and official lines of responsibilities.

If you agree with me and decide to mention these matters to Mister Churchill or Mister Eden I suggest that you do it as your personal idea since I have several times urged my views upon them.[6]

My present frame of mind is still normal enough that I can wish for you and yours the finest of New Years. Possibly 1952 will see all of our troubles disappear and we can live happily ever after.

[1] The Conference for the Organization of a European Defense Community (see no. 557) had adjourned Sunday, December 30, after making what Ambassador Bruce called "considerable progress." The ministers had agreed to a federal structure for the European Defense Force (consisting of an executive, council of ministers, assembly, and court) and, in principle, to eventual federation among the six countries. They discussed financing of the federation but failed to settle on the issue of a common budget, thus delaying decisions on military procurement. The ministers also fell short of an agreement on the EDF command structure and operational control of those forces not under SHAPE command (see State, *Foreign Relations, 1951*, vol. III, *European Security and the German Question, Part I*, pp. 985–89).

[2] The General had previously corresponded with Secretary of Defense Lovett about this matter (see no. 552 for the British-French December 18 communiqué, which urged Continental economic and military unity and pledged British support of the venture).

[3] Churchill would make several such statements (see no. 569).

[4] Eisenhower wrote British Foreign Minister Anthony Eden the same day he sent this message to Lovett (see no. 574).

[5] The General's schedule for December 29 had included meetings with several Italian leaders (whom Eisenhower the day before had invited to visit SHAPE) and Belgian Defense Minister De Greef; in the evening Eisenhower and General Gruenther had attended a cocktail party for the European ministers held at French Foreign Minister Robert Schuman's home, where, according to a report Douglas MacArthur II made to the Secretary of State, Eisenhower "gave the min[ister]s a good and inspirational pep talk stressing urgency and vital importance to Eur[ope] and NATO to reach agreement on EDC prior to Lisbon." Eisenhower congratulated the ministers on their progress, declined to comment on the possibility of Atlantic union, and repeated that the EDF was "essential" if there was to be adequate defense of Western Europe (State, *Foreign Relations, 1951*, vol. III, *European Security and the German Question, Part I*, pp. 984–85).

[6] Eisenhower's messages to the British included nos. 530, 543, and 569.

573   *Eisenhower Mss.*

To Douglas MacArthur II[01]   *January 2, 1952*
Confidential

Aside from the intensive study of NATO and included programs to insure its success, it seems to me that two other major problems in the world now demand the closest kind of study and cooperation between the United States and Britain, together with certain other nations in specific cases.

   a. The development of a common set of principles to govern Western relationships with Asiatic [and] Moslem populations. France and Britain are the two countries having major political ties with these areas, but America, from the standpoint of its sources of raw materials, is equally and vitally involved. We also are dependent upon certain of these countries for military bases, notably Morocco, Libya, and the Philippines. It seems to me that we must develop a set of principles to be observed by all three nations in their relationships with these great areas—principles that will take into account both the legitimate aspirations of these people and the practicalities of earning a living in the modern world.[2] We should develop a program that would at least eliminate differences in essentials in our several approaches to all these people and a program which would be appealing vis-a-vis the Russians, who are in effect offering nothing but political and social revolution.[3]

   b. These three countries might well expand this idea to include relationships with other important areas of the world.

   c. The second problem that I have in mind involves interests of these three countries together with those of Australia and New Zealand in Asiatic areas of the Philippines, Indochina, Malaya,

Burma and Indonesia. We should be exploring *in advance* the degree to which our interests and our thinking are identical, and so avoid piece-meal presentation of our programs before the world.[4]

Some day when you have some time, drop in and we will talk about these things.[5] I hope they don't sound visionary.

[1] Douglas MacArthur II was SHAPE adviser on international affairs (see no. 32, n. 3).

[2] For background on Western relations with developing Moslem nations in the Middle East and Asia see nos. 142, 233, 401, n. 4, and 408.

[3] For background on Eisenhower's concern over the Soviet Union's propaganda techniques see no. 142.

[4] See State, *Foreign Relations 1951*, vol. VI, *Asia and the Pacific, Part I* and *Part II*; and nos. 15 and 360.

[5] MacArthur met with the General on January 3; there is no reply to this memorandum in EM.

574   *Eisenhower Mss.*

To ROBERT ANTHONY EDEN   *January 2, 1952*
Cable SH 22030. Confidential

I am grateful for the Prime Ministers cable.[1] He knows of course that I was delighted with the press statement he made at the end of his Paris visit.[2] The trouble if any is that apparently some of the BENELUX people thought that the tone was influenced mainly by his consideration for his hosts. I met with the 6 Foreign Ministers on Saturday night and emphatically stated my agreement with the position of the British government.[3] Mister Schuman took occasion to reinforce my statements in this regard. It seemed to be opinion of ministers that if their people could be certain that I was correct about the British position then there should be no real trouble on that score. As you probably know the ministers took a long step in approving a practical approach to the business of political and economic federation and this also I hope will get several enthusiastic boosts from the British.[4]

Please tell the Prime Minister I am delighted with the news he sent me through Monty.[5] Also convey to him my warm greetings and of course I extend to the entire party my hope that you are having a good voyage and some semblance of a rest.

[1] For background see no. 569. Churchill had responded to Eisenhower's bon voyage message by assuring the General that they both had "always been in

complete agreement about the proper place of the United Kingdom with [respect to] the European Army. . . . I understand your difficulties so much and will do my utmost to help you" (DEF 284, Dec. 30, 1951, EM).

[2] For the communiqué Churchill, British Foreign Minister Eden, French Foreign Minister Schuman, and French Prime Minister Pleven issued after their Paris discussions of December 17–18 see no. 552.

[3] See no. 572.

[4] Eden would reply on January 4, thanking Eisenhower for his cable and assuring him that the British ministers would indeed bear in mind all he had said and the difficulties he was "battling so bravely. You can be sure that we shall take every opportunity to make it plain that the Paris communique is truly our policy and that we mean to give effect to it" (BMR/30/52, EM).

[5] Churchill had sent Eisenhower a letter (Dec. 25, 1951, EM) by way of Field Marshal Montgomery informing the General that he would soon appoint Field Marshal Harold Alexander as British Minister of Defense (see no. 556; and Anthony Seldon, *Churchill's Indian Summer: The Conservative Government, 1951-55* [London, 1981], pp. 296-97).

575   *Eisenhower Mss.*

To William Joseph Donovan   *January 3, 1952*

Dear Bill:[1] Thank you very much for your letter of the 28th.[2] It is direct and to the point.

You know so well what my convictions are about all this political activity that there would seem to be little profit in my repeating them. Fundamentally, it boils down to a desire to do my duty as I see it. I am currently assigned to a duty that a great number of people, at least in our country, believe to be vitally important to our welfare. How there can be any possibility of announcing my intention to leave this task except, and only, if called to a higher duty, I cannot quite see.[3] It is this conviction that seems to differentiate my thinking from that of the individuals who believe I should make preconvention statements, thus directly or indirectly encouraging partisan thinking toward the European project—a project that is certainly important to the American people as a whole, not merely to any single political party.

I try to be reasonable, objective, and practical—but I also try to be respectful of my own conscience.

I truly appreciate the thoughtfulness of your letter. For my part, I can report that I honestly believe we are making progress toward a European union. I attended a meeting the other night of six Foreign Ministers and was quite astonished at their announcement of their intentions to take concrete steps in this regard.[4]

With best wishes for 1952, *Cordially*

P.S. Just this minute my attention was called to an item in the *Stars and Stripes* saying that you had lost your little granddaughter through a tragic accident. If this report is true, I send you assurances of my deepest sympathy and of my earnest hope that you and her parents will be able to bear your burden of grief with the certainty that the mercy of the Almighty will be yours for the asking.[5]

[1] For background on Major General Donovan see no. 128.

[2] In his letter Donovan had summed up Senator James H. Duff's remarks to him at the December 22 opening of the Eisenhower headquarters in Washington, D.C.: a great majority of the American people were for Eisenhower, but the movement was seriously weakened by the General's refusal to commit himself openly (for background on Duff see no. 1; for more on his campaign activities see no. 486). Donovan had added that he was sending separately his own team's report on the situation (Donovan's letter and ten-page report are in EM).

[3] See no. 538.

[4] See the preceding document and no. 572.

[5] General Donovan's acknowledgment of Eisenhower's condolences is in EM.

576

Eisenhower Mss.

To George Arthur Sloan

January 3, 1952

Personal and confidential

Dear George:[1] I am grateful for the report contained in your letter of the 21st.[2] An item in the report that attracted my attention particularly was that concerning the possibility of a serious economic setback—possibly even a rather prolonged depression.[3] I have heard this matter discussed pro and con by a number of individuals, and I am astonished at the way in which convictions seem to divide almost fifty-fifty.

Curiously enough, I think that we need a certain moral and intellectual preparation against the possibility of such a development. When people are out of work, bewildered, and see their families enduring privation, they instinctively turn to the greatest temporal force of which they know—the government—for relief. In doing so, it is easy enough to forget that all powers of government must always be carefully and intelligently limited or it is certain to become the master of the people who have set it up. In other words, catastrophes of the kind we are now describing become the occasion for weaving into governmental organization, procedures, and functions a net in which is caught an increasing portion of the individual political and economic liberty which is the basic characteristic of our system.

These things could be thought about in advance—they could be studied and the intellectual climate so developed that, in time of emergency, the individual would get all the help he needed but without permanent damage to the essentials of representative government.[4]

The other day Cliff Roberts told me that you are now associated in some way with the firm in which he is a partner. I suppose that your recent trip around the country was in connection with this new activity.[5] In any event, whatever the cause for your travels, you are certainly gathering up impressions, ideas, and information which you could never do if you were pinned down in New York City.

All of us here have been working at top speed, particularly in the effort to produce concrete steps in the development of a European Army and of some form of Continental European political and economic union. Without this latter, I do not believe there is any permanent and assured peace for the Western world as long as the Communistic menace exists in its present form and with its present intentions. As a consequence of such preoccupation, I have little time to give to reflection and contemplation on the American scene. For this reason, interesting condensed reports such as you have written are of peculiar value to me. The one kind of message from America that upsets me is the one that urges me to assert a partisan political loyalty in spite of the fact that I am assigned to activity in a project the success of which is of utmost importance to our entire nation.[6] I simply cannot follow the logic of the people—many of them real friends—who seem to think that I am completely and entirely privileged to consider myself a private citizen and to act accordingly. It seems to me that an individual can leave an important duty only when called to a higher one—he can scarcely, in advance, merely "resign."

I truly appreciate the trouble you took to write me such an interesting letter. This note brings to you and Mrs. Sloan[7] very best wishes from Mamie and me for a fine and prosperous 1952. Write again when you have time.[8] *Cordially*

[1] A director of the United States Steel Corporation and the Goodyear Tire & Rubber Company, Sloan (see Galambos, *Columbia University*, no. 723) had visited the General in Paris in October 1951.

[2] On that date (letter in EM) Sloan had reported on his talks with Malcolm Muir, president of *Newsweek* magazine, and with editors of the *New York Times*. Sloan had praised Eisenhower's "sound economic views" (see, for example, no. 522) and his work at SHAPE. Sloan also had written of his recent visit to New Orleans, where he found growing Eisenhower sentiment among Mississippi, Alabama, and Louisiana businessmen and civic leaders. He found "without exception that they are counting on DE as the Republican candidate. There was unanimous feeling among them that only he could carry five or six southern states." "These men are anti-New Deal Democrats who stand ready to go all-out for DE," Sloan noted. "Their names and many others are catalogued in my little book. In fact Bob Woodruff and I will be ready at the appropriate time with a host of influential names in and from the South" (on Woodruff see no. 113).

[3] Sloan's discussions in New Orleans had included one with a local leader who "expressed a somewhat new thought as to why DE was by far the best bet for the

Republican Party, and nation," Sloan wrote. "He felt that the tide is turning so definitely against the present administration that the gentleman from Ohio can win today and may conceivably win in November. But there is the danger, he said, that we may be confronted with a serious economic setback during the next few years. If that should happen with Ohio in the White House he would not have sufficient hold on the people to lead them through and out of it." Sloan's friend believed the result would be a Republican defeat after four years and perhaps a "prolonged depression," whereas "with DE at the helm the people would look to him for leadership and would follow his leadership."

[4] Eisenhower probably had in mind the American Assembly, which had held its first meeting the previous May (see no. 201). In May 1952 the American Assembly would address the problem of inflation in the United States (see no. 612).

[5] Eisenhower's close friend Clifford Roberts was a partner with Reynolds & Company, a New York City investment firm. Sloan's recent assignments had also taken him to Philadelphia and San Francisco (see Sloan to Eisenhower, Jan. 8, 11, 1952, EM).

[6] For Eisenhower's late efforts in support of creating a European army within a unified Europe see no. 578; on the pressure to declare himself a presidential candidate or at least to privately state his political plans see nos. 570 and 571.

[7] The former Florence Lincoln Rockefeller.

[8] For developments see no. 634.

577   *Eisenhower Mss.*

To John Jay McCloy   *January 4, 1952*
Confidential

Dear Jack: I have read with great interest your telegram No. 294 of January 3 to Paris,[1] in which you set forth your reaction to developments with respect to the European Defense Force. I am dropping you this brief line to let you know that I concur wholeheartedly with the views expressed therein.[2] It is a succinct and clear statement of the situation.

Within my orbit of travel, I am doing my utmost with the various European personalities with whom I come in contact to move them forward toward rapid agreement on a satisfactory basis of organization and control. Last week I was asked to meet privately with the Ministers who were attending the Paris conference. I think we made some progress. I was particularly impressed by Mr. Adenauer, not only by what he said when I met with the group, but also by the accounts I have seen of the clarity and soundness of his presentation to the conference.[3] When you see him, would you convey to him greetings for me? *Cordially*

[1] McCloy, U.S. High Commissioner for Germany, had sent this top-secret telegram to the Department of State; "eyes only" copies went to Eisenhower and Ambassa-

dor Bruce in Paris and to U.S. Ambassador to Italy James C. Dunn (see State, *Foreign Relations, 1952-1954*, vol. V, *Western European Security, Part I*, pp. 576-78). Douglas MacArthur II assisted Eisenhower in drafting this letter.

[2] McCloy noted "clear-cut" German support for an EDF, with France and Italy "closely allied"; he also described as unfortunate the absence of strong U.S. representation in Brussels and at The Hague. McCloy urged Acheson to hold serious discussions with the Dutch and Belgian ministers in Washington, pointing out to them "that we have an historic, even momentous opportunity which cannot be allowed to escape." The Benelux countries, McCloy argued, should realize that (1) a European army would bring stronger, not weaker, U.S. interest in regional security; (2) in light of the aims of the 1951 Mutual Security Act, U.S. aid would likely go preferentially to countries taking part in European integration; and (3) U.S. public opinion would surely look disapprovingly on resistance to a community designed to bury "the long-time antagonisms of Europe" (*ibid.*, p. 577).

[3] For a summary of Eisenhower's remarks that evening and for the progress the European ministers had made at the six-power meetings see no. 572. Konrad Adenauer had served as Mayor of Cologne from 1917 until 1933, when the Nazi government had dismissed him from office; after World War II he had helped to found Germany's Christian Democratic Union, and in September 1949 he had been elected the first Chancellor of the new Federal Republic of Germany. In March 1951 Adenauer had additionally become Foreign Minister.

578   *Eisenhower Mss.*

To Harry S. Truman   *January 4, 1952*

Dear Mr. President: It occurs to me that an informal account of recent development in SHAPE might be of some usefulness to you in connection with the forthcoming visit to Washington of the Prime Minister of Great Britain.[1]

You are, of course, fairly familiar with the strictly military accomplishments of Europe during the past year.[2] The facts that most of their economies have become rather badly strained and that these governments have not, so far as I know, materially increased their expenditures for purely civil purposes would indicate that they are now financing about as great a military effort as can be expected under the circumstances.[3]

Because of by and large acceptance of this rough conclusion, our urgent attention has been directed toward those things in which significant accomplishment is possible in Europe without great expenditure of money. These possibilities are very real. They include:

Rapid implementation of the Schuman Plan[4]—already well underway.

Six-nation agreement to a broad plan for developing rapidly a European Defense Force as the only way in which German strength can be included in our security arrangements without re-creating Germany as a military menace to the Western world.

Concrete and practical steps toward the sine qua non of permanent Western security in the face of the Russian threat, namely, the political and economic union of Western Continental Europe. (I call this a sine qua non of permanent security because, without it, there cannot be long-term economic health in this region; and, without economic strength, adequate military force cannot be maintained.)

All three of these questions partake much more of the political and economic than they do of the military. You may, therefore, wonder why I, individually and with my staff, should be so involved in them. It is because that only through the accomplishment of a program of this kind can the long-term security of Western Europe be assured. Such security is the business of SHAPE.

There would seem to be no need for commenting on the Schuman Plan other than to note that, when in full operation, and especially if paralleled by an effective European Defense Force, it will exercise great and direct influence toward achievement of the third and essential objective—political union.

The conception of a European Defense Force has come a long way forward during the past year.[5] You will recall that a year ago governments were haggling about such details as the allowable size of strictly nationalistic units within the framework of a European Army.[6] At the insistence of Americans, these questions have been largely relegated to the professionals to whom they belong, while Ministers have finally begun to attack basic political problems such as policies applying to budgets, methods of military control, and the degree of authority to be delegated a central international or super-national agency.

It has probably been reported to you that a surprising amount of progress has recently been achieved in these questions. However, there seems to have developed some fairly serious cleavages in opinion—with the three larger countries of Germany, France, and Italy on one side, and Belgium, Luxembourg, and Holland on the other. Parenthetically, I should say that I believe the Luxembourg Minister[7] to be very able and ready to go along with any reasonable plan, but he is almost compelled to stand shoulder to shoulder with Belgium.

The large countries contend that:

There must be a common budget from the beginning, and other detailed arrangements made to avoid discrimination against any member, including Germany.

There must be a partial surrender of sovereignty to responsible central executives, who will in some respects exercise supra-national functions.

Belgium and Holland do not yet accept these ideas. It happens that

I agree in general with the large nation position and do not believe that what Belgium and Holland propose is workable. But the point is that Belgium and Holland seem to be somewhat influenced by what they *believe* to be the attitude of Great Britain, and we run the risk that these differences may seriously delay any worthwhile development.[8]

I have always held that Great Britain should not be an active *participant* in the European Defense Force, but that it should give to the whole plan, on the Continent, an enthusiastic and earnest support, including political and military cooperation.[9]

My reason here is very simple. I do not see how, in the reasonably near future, the United Kingdom could amalgamate politically with Europe. Since the European Army should constitute not only an immediate means of obtaining German strength but also a definite step toward political union, we must *not* seek British participation. This is the official British position stated only recently by the Prime Minister.[10]

I have told all the Foreign Ministers that I agree with the British opinion in this regard. Nevertheless, it remains clear that the smaller countries (which have traditionally looked to Britain as their protector and political mentor) still feel that they must not commit themselves too deeply toward military or other unification of Europe because of their fear that their relationships with Britain would suffer. I have had a number of communications with Mr. Churchill and with Mr. Eden on this point and they made a statement in Paris that would seemingly settle this point in the desired direction.[11] But I repeat that this uneasiness continues to influence the Belgians and the Dutch, a fact that crops up in almost every conversation with one of their top officials.

We here have heard that the Prime Minister is soon to address a Joint Session of the Congress.[12] That body expressed the hope, in its last Mutual Aid Bill, that Europe would quickly achieve an economic and political unity.[13] Mr. Churchill has, in the past, enthusiastically supported the idea of such a union of Western Europe. Consequently, it would seem that Mr. Churchill would please the Congress very much if he would repeat his support of this concept with all the fervor and oratorical effect that have characterized his great moments. If, along with this, he would voice his earnest hope for the early establishment of an effective European Army (if for no other reasons than as a long step toward political union), such a statement could not fail to have a profound effect in Europe. We need the publicity that attends a major speech rather than the routine treatment given by the press to a routine communique.

There are a thousand angles to each of the subjects that I have mentioned in this rough report. I shall not consume more of your time in their description, but I really believe that if some hint or advice from you could lead the Prime Minister into making a ringing statement that would minimize British non-participation and *emphasize British moral, political, and military support* for the European Army, you would be most helpful to us in what we are trying to do here. If the thought appeals to you, I earnestly request that you use it as your own and do not suggest that it comes from me. The reason for this is that I have several times made approaches of a similar kind to Mr. Churchill, so yours would have maximum force if you act independently of any recommendation from me.

It is my understanding that our own Government firmly supports these ideas of union and does not fail to make such support a matter of public knowledge.

I know that David Bruce emphatically agrees with what I have set out here. However, if you should like to seek the advice of the Secretary of State, the Secretary of Defense, and Mr. Harriman on the subject matter of this letter, I have no objection to your showing it to them. Incidentally, I sent a message in similar vein to the Secretary of Defense.[14]

With warm personal regards, *Respectfully*

[1] On Churchill's North American visit see no. 569. According to a note at the end of this letter, Eisenhower's message arrived in Washington by an overnight flight and reached the President shortly after noon on January 5.

[2] For many months Eisenhower had reported to the President through Harriman (see esp. nos. 45, 115, 218, and 259). For an overview of NATO's achievements and difficulties to date see Ismay, *NATO*, pp. 39–48.

[3] Six months earlier Eisenhower had made equally guarded assessments of the European economy and its effect on NATO (see no. 251).

[4] On French Foreign Minister Robert Schuman's plan for pooling Western European coal and steel production see no. 502, n. 3.

[5] For Eisenhower's support of an EDF during the past year see, for example, nos. 115, 304, and 539.

[6] For background see no. 186. In October 1950 French leaders had spoken publicly of German units of eight hundred to twelve hundred men each, while American estimates of adequately sized German combat units had ranged between five thousand and six thousand troops; in December the French, agreeing to larger German "combat teams," nonetheless maintained that these units ought to belong to larger ones employing non-German troops at a ratio of five to one (see McGeehan, *German Rearmament Question*, pp. 81–85).

[7] Joseph Bech, Luxembourg's Minister for Foreign Affairs, Foreign Trade, and the Armed Forces, had led the European resource-pooling efforts since 1926; after World War II he became a vocal proponent of the United Nations and European collective security.

[8] On the weight of British influence in northern Europe see nos. 115, 530, and 539.

[9] For another succinct statement of Eisenhower's position see no. 530.

[10] See no. 552.

[11] Eisenhower's messages to the British included nos. 530, 543, and 569; for the communiqué Churchill, Eden, Schuman, and Pleven issued after their Paris discussions see no. 552, n. 5.

[12] For the substance of Churchill's remarks and the publicity that surrounded his U.S. visit see no. 569, n. 4.

[13] See no. 539, n. 8.

[14] See no 572. David K. E. Bruce was U.S. Ambassador to France.

579   *CCS 092 Western Europe (3-12-48), Sec. 118*

To Omar Nelson Bradley   *January 5, 1952*
Cable ALO 600. Top secret

Personal for General Bradley:[1] 1. The problem of evolving a militarily sound and politically acceptable command arrangement incident to the accession of Greece and Turkey to NATO[2] prompts me to emphasize several important points:

> First: Extension of command involves acceptance of grave responsibility on the part of commanders concerned.
>
> Second: Any command structure that may be adopted must be considered subject to evolution or change in the light of new factors either in peace or in war.
>
> Third: The separation of the land sectors requires concentration of attention on the part of two or more army commanders. Each land sector must have supporting tactical air.
>
> Fourth: Ideally, best advantage may be taken of the mobility and flexibility of Naval and Air Forces by having one each over-all Air and Naval commander for the whole area. This is of special importance when our resources are limited.
>
> Fifth: The current shortage of qualified staff officers indicates need for restraint in imposing requirements for new headquarters.
>
> Sixth: Each allied commander must have a basic task of supporting adjacent allied commanders.

2. I desire to assure you that I, and my subordinate commanders, stand ready to implement any command arrangements that the governments adopt. We will make any structure function and will overcome those disadvantages which appear to be attached to any of the solutions proposed.

3. On balance I am inclined to favor, as in initial arrangement, a structure which extends the command of the present CINCSOUTH to the eastward and set up along the following lines:[3]

A. The Theater Commander in Chief would have an allied staff. He would hold no other command position either of a component force or over forces of his own nation.[4] He would have a senior deputy who would be a ground officer.

B. Subordinate to him would be two or more land commanders. The Theater Commander in Chief would have an over-all Air Commander and an over-all Naval Commander. Each of the Air and Naval Commanders would be allied, with an allied staff, and would exercise no national command.

C. The Allied Air and Naval commands would each be organized on a functional and/or geographical basis with due regard being accorded to the objective of having forces largely of one nationality under the direct command of an allied commander of the same nationality.

D. All of the nations would assign to or earmark for the command all forces normally in the area "for operational command as required for the accomplishment of the mission." Their normal administration would remain with their properly designated national authorities.

4. I recognize that there is inherent in the solution set forth in paragraph 3 above the disadvantage of extending CINCSOUTH's responsibilities at a time when we are all still concerned over the importance of devoting attention to the security of the Italian frontier.[5] On the other hand, I believe that this factor is not of an overriding nature and can be satisfactorily compensated. I must stress, however, that the command should be considered temporary and may be changed in the light of further developments.

[1] Eisenhower's NOFORN cable, enclosure B to JCS 1868/345 (Jan. 24, 1951), was in reply to JCS 90949 of January 3 (enclosure D, *ibid.*). In that earlier message JCS Chairman Bradley had sent the General a Joint Strategic Plans Group memorandum outlining, in advance of Churchill's visit to the United States, the "expected question of integration of mil[itary] forces of Greece and Turkey into NATO." Anticipating a split between the British and the Greeks and Turks (see below), the planning group "clearly realized" that giving support to either position would have "far reaching political effects throughout western and Arab worlds" and adjudged itself "not fully qualified to analyze" the issue (see also the following document).

[2] For background see no. 423; Ismay, *NATO*, p. 73; and Poole, *History of the Joint Chiefs of Staff*, vol. IV, *1950-1952*, pp. 310-11.

[3] On the earlier Standing Group plan of establishing a separate, British-led Middle East theater in the eastern Mediterranean see no. 390. Eisenhower's proposal to include Greek and Turkish forces in Carney's CINCSOUTH command reflected the strong sentiment within both those countries against service under British officers. Acutely aware of Britain's history as an imperial power, Greece and Turkey defined "equal" NATO membership as involving placement within Eisenhower's command (see State, *Foreign Relations, 1951*, vol. III, *European Security and the German Question, Part I*, pp. 598, 608-9, 613-15; and *New York Times*, Jan. 8, 1952). For developments see nos. 645, 651, 692, and 694.

[4] For earlier discussion of Carney's dual responsibilities as NATO CINCSOUTH and U.S. CINCNELM see nos. 429, 526, and 527.
[5] Eisenhower's reference was to the so-called couverture forces in northern Italy (see nos. 77, 148, and 153).

580   *CCS 092 Western Europe (3–12–48), Sec. 118*

To OMAR NELSON BRADLEY   *January 5, 1952*
Cable ALO 601. Top secret

Personal for General Bradley:[0] 1. I have couched my reply ALO 600 to you in a manner such that you should be free literally to quote my views in the course of your discussions.[1]

2. You will note that I have refrained from suggesting the nationality of the commanders involved. My thought is that the land sector commanders would be Italian, Greek and Turkish.

3. The nationality of the Land Deputy to the Commander in Chief might be British, French or US. However, I am tentatively inclined to favor a US officer.

4. I believe the Allied Air Commander should be a US Air Force Officer. The other nations would, of course, provide appropriate subordinate commanders.

5. The Allied Naval Commander should be British. I would hope that both the US and the British Navies, in the interest of the common good, could see their way clear to compromising what have heretofore been strongly held views. French and Italian Admirals would each have a Naval command substantially in accordance with recent announcements but within the new over-all Naval command.[2] The Greeks and Turks should have similar commands.

6. In JCS 90949[3] I have noted the emphasis that has been placed on the position of the Greeks and the Turks that their forces not be placed under the command of a British officer.[4] I question the propriety of their position and the weight that is accorded to it. If such feelings are so dominant it raises serious doubt as to the true strength of the structure we are building.

7. I hope that you can stimulate the conviction that NATO command arrangements do not involve placing the forces of one nation under the command of another nation but rather that they fit into an allied command structure responsive to all the nations. In no way are we furthering the political influence of any nation or service. This may help to clear the air and break the deadlock.

8. Many of the nations are extremely sensitive to any United States–United Kingdom agreements on matters of importance and general

concern which are reached without their active participation. I hope that there will be no "leaks" as to the extent of your discussions and that any announcements made clearly indicate that NATO command arrangements are not matters for bilateral negotiation but must be worked out by established NATO agencies.

[1] JCS Chairman Bradley and the NATO Standing Group were deliberating on the command structure to follow upon full Greek and Turkish membership in the alliance (see the preceding document; and Poole, *History of the Joint Chiefs of Staff*, vol. IV, *1950–1952*, pp. 310–11).

[2] On the British hope of remaining a naval power in the Mediterranean and on the creation of a French NATO command in that region see no. 390; and Ismay, *NATO*, p. 73.

[3] See the preceding document, n. 1.

[4] See the preceding document, n. 2.

581   *Eisenhower Mss.*

To Drew Pearson   *January 7, 1952*
Personal and confidential

Dear Mr. Pearson:[1] Many thanks for your letter and for your thoughtfulness in having Mr. Bennett deliver the Christmas cards from your radio listeners.[2] I am particularly grateful for your appreciation of our efforts to further NATO purposes in Europe.

Moreover, I am deeply gratified by your description of the response to your recent poll as proof of the interest Americans are taking in national affairs and, therefore, in the preservation of our democratic way of life, dependent as it is upon active participation of the individual in the processes of government. I would be less than human not to be moved by the compliment implied by fellow Americans who, at your suggestion, have addressed their letters to me, and by their further courtesy in sending me holiday greetings. I wish I could find time to thank each one for the sentiments thus expressed.[3]

Any American would like to feel himself in some small degree worthy of the confidence of so many of his countrymen. I earnestly hope that I may perform my duty in my current assignment of developing security against Communist aggression in such fashion that the project may command the support of the vast body of Americans, regardless of partisan political allegiance. *Sincerely*

[1] For background on Pearson see no. 78.

[2] Eisenhower had met with John Gordon Bennett (see no. 72) on January 3. On December 31 Pearson had written Eisenhower that he was sending with Bennett

about sixteen thousand Christmas cards from his radio listeners and readers of his column, "The Washington Merry-Go-Round." "Each card is an expression of the hope that you will make yourself available for selection as the Republican Presidential candidate" (EM). Pearson had invited his listeners and readers to send penny post cards to the candidates they favored; on the basis of the response, he predicted that in the next year's election "a lot of people may cross party lines" (*Washington Post*, Dec. 3, 1951). As of December 31, the straw poll gave Eisenhower 49 percent, Taft 36 percent, California Governor Earl Warren 8 percent, and MacArthur 7 percent of the Republican vote (EM). Pearson and Bennett would continue to tender support and advice to Eisenhower through March 1952 (EM; see also no. 610).

[3] In the past Eisenhower had responded more cooly to personal grass-roots appeals than was the case in early 1952 (see, for example, Galambos, *Columbia University*, nos. 64, n. 4, and 106, n. 2).

582   *Eisenhower Mss.*

To Ralph Austin Bard   *January 7, 1952*

Dear Ralph:[1] Thank you very much for your letter of 20 December. Needless to say, I am happy to have your observations about our work here. I am reassured to know that you feel that the American people have confidence and faith in me and I am grateful for your having mentioned it in your letter.[2]

However, I am concerned to learn that you are hearing a great deal of talk about a lack of interest in our program on the part of Western Europeans.[3] Undoubtedly, there are many people here who, for one or more of the reasons you outline in your letter, are not wholeheartedly behind our security effort. In addition, of course, the Communists are doing everything in their power to turn public opinion against NATO.

Actually, one of the biggest jobs we faced at the beginning of our program was to bolster the morale and the will to fight of our European allies. It has been no easy task to restore the confidence of people who have just emerged from the physical and moral devastation of a modern war. No one can blame Western Europe for a lack of enthusiasm for another liberation—they have experienced one such liberation! Consequently, the primary aim of our program is the build-up of military forces adequate to prevent this area from being overrun. Therefore, an evaluation of information reported to me from a wide variety of sources—plus my own personal observations—convinces me that the NATO concept and the United States military and economic assistance programs in Western Europe are receiving the genuine support of a substantial majority of the people in this area.

In all humility, I feel able to report prodigious changes in the last year—I am not *entirely* satisfied with progress made to date but I *am* encouraged by the positive signs of improvement which are evidenced.[4] In terms of organized military forces, in terms of economic strength supporting the military effort, and in terms of resurgent morale, Europe has made tremendous forward strides during the past twelve months. Although the European defense force is not yet a reality, there has been real progress toward its formation, particularly in light of the magnitude of the issues involved.

I would like to point out one factor which may not have been given adequate consideration by those who advocate a change of policy in this area. In simple terms: What can we substitute for our present program here which would produce comparable security for the United States? Each of the nations participating in NATO is doing so for one reason and for one reason only—that of *enlightened* self-interest. Personally, I can see no acceptable alternative to a policy designed to prevent Communist domination of the immense human and economic resources of Western Europe.

I am confident that United States economic and military assistance to this area and active participation in NATO are our best guarantee against losing European allies. I feel that the yardstick which our fellow citizens should apply to our program here is the net effect of that program on our own security.[5] So long as we are able to note moral and military progress on the scale of the accomplishments of the past twelve months, without bankrupting our allies and exposing ourselves to a vastly increased threat, I believe that SHAPE as an implement of NATO is making a vital contribution to our own defense.

Please be assured that I shall keep my countrymen as fully informed as possible on our program in Europe.[6] I would not hesitate to speak out should it ever become apparent to me that our European allies are not living up to their obligations under NATO, or should I come to believe in the necessity for a change of policy on the part of the United States. I am happy to report that I could not honestly make either statement at this time.

Again, my thanks for your letter. With every good wish and with warm personal regard, *Sincerely*

P.S. Today I finally made a "statement" that was confined mainly to affirming that such voting record as I had been able to accumulate was Republican.[7]

---

[1] For background on Bard see no. 248. Lieutenant Colonel C. Craig Cannon and Chief Warrant Officer Sigmund W. Musinski drafted this letter.

[2] Bard's message (in EM) had come at the request of "a number of important people here in Chicago" who wanted to assure Eisenhower "that the great mass of people in this country have an abiding faith in you, which they do not have from the standpoint of foreign relations, in the present administration, or the State Department, and they look to you for guidance and an honest appraisal of the situation in Western Europe and the Atlantic Pact program."

[3] "We hear from all directions during the past few weeks of a serious lack of interest on the part of the populations of Western Europe in the Administration's program, the common army, and the Atlantic Pact set-up," Bard had written. "Of course, you know the answer and I do not, but every important business man, who has been to Europe this summer, that I have talked to, has the same report to make;—that most of Western Europe—primarily, France, Italy, Germany, and perhaps a few of the others, as far as the great bulk of their population is concerned, do not care for our program for the protection of Western Europe—1st, because its accomplishment may in the preliminary stages provoke a war; 2nd, because they do not think the Russians will march anyway, having been too successful in accomplishing their objectives through infiltration; 3dly, that the Russians will not march because they do not dare turn loose their army in Western Europe for fear of fraternization and disintegration—and 4th, and most important, because they can visualize their countries over run by an attacking Russian army and then again over run and torn to pieces by an Allied Army driving the Russians back through their countries. They have clearly seen the devastation in Korea due to our attempts to save the South Koreans, and it has not impressed them favorably."

[4] See nos. 572 and 578.

[5] Bard had enclosed a newspaper report on a foreign-policy speech financier Joseph Patrick Kennedy (A.B. Harvard 1912), former U.S. Ambassador to Great Britain, had given in Chicago on December 17. Kennedy had pronounced U.S. foreign policy "a total failure": without firing a shot the Soviets had impoverished most of Western Europe, saddled Americans with heavy military and foreign-aid expenditures, deprived the United States of many friends, and by means of the Korean conflict brought tragedy or death to 100,000 American homes (see *Chicago Tribune*, Dec. 18, 1951, copy in EM).

[6] "The real point I want to make," Bard had written, "is that if what we hear over here is true, even to some considerable extent, that [*sic*] you would be doing your country the greatest possible service in so advising us publicly at this time. If you could honestly take this position, coming to the conclusion that for the good of the United States a radical change should be made in our approach to the Western European situation, I am confident that the whole country would be tremendously aroused by this example of selfless patriotism and demand that you show them the way during the next four years" (for background see no. 400; for developments see no. 621).

[7] Eisenhower wrote this postscript in longhand. On his announcement of party affiliation see the following document, n. 2.